# Management Accounting

# Brief Contents

**Management Accounting**
Canadian Sixth Edition

by Don R. Hansen, Maryanne M. Mowen,
David W. Senkow, and Raili M. Pollanen

**Editorial Director and Publisher:**
Evelyn Veitch

**Acquisitions Editor:**
Veronica Visentin

**Senior Developmental Editor:**
Elke Price

**Marketing Manager:**
Bram Sepers

**Managing Production Editor:**
Susan Calvert

**Senior Production Coordinator:**
Hedy Sellers

**Copy Editor/Proofreader:**
Matthew Kudelka

**Creative Director:**
Angela Cluer

**Interior Design:**
Peggy Rhodes

**Cover Design:**
Rocket Design

**Cover Image:**
EyeWire Collection/Getty Images

**Compositor:**
Gerry Dunn

**Indexer:**
Andrew Little

**Printer:**
Transcontinental Printing Inc.

**National Library of Canada Cataloguing in Publication Data**

Management accounting / Don R. Hansen...[et al.].— 6th Canadian ed.

Includes bibliographical references and index.
ISBN 0-17-622464-5

1. Managerial accounting.   I. Hansen, Don R.

HF5657.4.M35 2003     658.15'11
C2003-900967-X

CANADIAN SIXTH EDITION

# Management Accounting

**Don R. Hansen**
Oklahoma State University

**Maryanne M. Mowen**
Oklahoma State University

**David W. Senkow**
University of Regina

**Raili M. Pollanen**
Carleton University

THOMSON

NELSON

Australia   Canada   Mexico   Singapore   Spain   United Kingdom   United States

# Contents

# PART 3

## Planning and Control 563

# Preface

The Canadian Sixth Edition of *Management Accounting* introduces students to the fundamentals of management accounting. Although it is assumed that students have been introduced to the basics of financial accounting, extensive knowledge of financial accounting is not needed. The emphasis is on the use of accounting information. Thus, the text should be of value to students with a variety of backgrounds. Although written to serve undergraduate students, the text has also been used successfully at the graduate level. There is sufficient variety in the assignment material to accommodate both undergraduate and graduate students.

Many business students who are required to take a course in management accounting are not accounting majors. It is often difficult for these students to appreciate the value of the concepts being taught. The Canadian Sixth Edition overcomes this attitude by using introductory chapter scenarios based on real-world settings and by presenting realistic examples illustrating the concepts within the chapters. Seeing that effective management requires a sound understanding of how to use accounting information should enhance the interest of both accounting and nonaccounting majors.

The Canadian Sixth Edition emphasizes a systems-based approach and the need to custom tailor management accounting and control systems to fit organizations and their unique circumstances. The evolution in systems design has been from functional-based to activity-based systems, and recently to strategic-based systems. The coverage on the use of strategic-based systems and activity-based systems as strategic management tools has been substantially extended, while still maintaining a strong coverage of traditional functional-based systems.

## Strategic-Based Management

Effective strategic-based management is essential for organizations operating in an increasingly dynamic environment in order to ensure that organizational strategy and objectives are achieved in a cost-effective manner. Strategic-based management accounting and control systems provide tools that are necessary for strategic-based management, as they link an organization's mission and strategy with operational objectives and use both financial and nonfinancial measures from various stakeholders' perspectives. The coverage of the balanced scorecard, a widely used strategic evaluation tool, has been extended. In addition, new coverage on the design criteria for and the use of performance measures for performance evaluation, reward, and accountability purposes has been added.

## Activity-Based Management

The use of activity-based management practices is widely established, particularly in companies operating in continuous improvement environments. Activity-based management accounting and control systems provide tools for activity-based management. They assign responsibility to processes and emphasize both financial and process perspectives. Such notions require the treatment of activity-based concepts within an integrated, comprehensive framework. The Canadian Sixth Edition provides such a framework with extensive coverage on such topics as activity-based costing, kaizen costing, target costing, activity-based budgeting, process value analysis, life cycle cost management, and quality management. The business process analysis necessary for activity-based management can provide a foundation for the subsequent development of strategic-based management tools.

## Functional-Based Management

In order to provide a balanced coverage, the Canadian Sixth Edition also continues to provide extensive coverage of traditional topics. A widespread use of costing models relying on production functions and control models focusing on functional organizational units still exists in many organizations. Covering functional-based models is essential not only because they are used but also because significant differences between the strategic-based, activity-based, and functional-based approaches can be highlighted. Such comparisons help students understand when it is appropriate to use these approaches.

The understanding that comes from the integrated approach of this text should help future managers initiate change when it is merited. Furthermore, the realization that management accounting is not a static discipline may itself contribute to additional innovative developments. Take a few minutes to review the table of contents. You will find a balanced, integrative presentation of strategic-based, activity-based, and functional-based concepts and techniques.

## Major Revisions to the Canadian Sixth Edition

Highlights of the major revisions to the Canadian Sixth Edition are as follows:

**All Chapters**: The Canadian Sixth Edition features many new and modified exercises and problems, including multiple-choice exercises. Several chapter opening scenarios are new or updated. The text has been streamlined to improve readability and terminology has been updated to reflect current usage.

**Chapter 1**: Brief sections on e-business and supply chain management have been added.

**Chapter 4**: The chapter has been revised to provide greater focus on activity-based costing. A section covering ABC supplier costing has been added, and JIT material has been moved to another chapter.

**Chapter 5**: The order of presentation has been changed, with the coverage of journal entries moved to an appendix.

**Chapter 13**: The explanations of the cash budget, the budgeted balance sheet, and participative budgeting have been strengthened. In addition, a comprehensive master budget review problem has been added.

**Chapter 14**: A more thorough discussion on the responsibility for and the interpretation of variances has been included.

**Chapter 16**: The sections dealing with responsibility accounting and decentralization have been revised. A discussion of residual income has been added and the examples updated accordingly. A section covering special issues in multinational companies has also been added.

**Chapter 17**: The chapter has been significantly rewritten and restructured with emphasis on strategic performance management. New Learning Objectives 1 and 5 dealing with control environment and managerial evaluation and reward systems have been added. Furthermore, the scope of Learning Objectives 2 and 4 has been extended to relate process value analysis to strategic performance management and to cover the design criteria and features of strategic performance management systems. Overall, a substantial amount of new material, including eight new exhibits, has been added. New and extended coverage is provided, for example, in the areas of value chain analysis and supply chain management, strategic-based responsibility systems, criteria for performance measures, nonfinancial performance measures, and the balanced scorecard. Material related to activity performance measurement has been condensed and integrated into other topics or placed in an appendix.

## Chapter Organization and Structure

Each chapter is carefully structured to help students focus on important concepts and retain them. Components found in each chapter include:

**Learning Objectives.** Each chapter begins with a set of learning objectives to guide students in their study of the chapter. These objectives outline the organizational flow of the chapter and serve as points of comprehension and evaluation. Learning objectives are tied to specific sections of topic coverage within the chapter.

**Scenario.** An interesting real-world scenario opens each chapter. The scenario ties directly to concepts covered in the chapter and helps students relate chapter topics to actual business situations. "Questions to Think About," critical-thinking questions that appear at the end of each scenario, are designed to pique students' interest in the chapter and stimulate class discussion.

**Summary of Learning Objectives.** Each chapter concludes with a comprehensive summary of the learning objectives. Students can review and test their knowledge of key concepts and evaluate their ability to complete chapter objectives.

**Key Terms.** Throughout each chapter, key terms are highlighted for quick identification. A list of key terms, with page references, is presented at the end of each chapter for additional reinforcement. All key terms are defined in a comprehensive glossary at the end of the text.

**Review Problems.** Each chapter contains at least one review problem with the accompanying solution. The review problems demonstrate the application of major concepts and procedures covered in the chapter.

**Questions for Writing and Discussion.** Approximately 15 to 25 short-answer questions appear at the end of each chapter to test students' knowledge of chapter concepts. Many questions call for students to use critical thinking and communication skills, and they can be used to stimulate class participation and discussion.

**Exercises.** Exercises usually emphasize one or two chapter concepts and can be completed fairly quickly (30 minutes maximum). Most exercises require a basic application and computation, as well as ask students to interpret and explain their results.

**Problems.** Each chapter contains many end-of-chapter problems, with varying degrees of length and difficulty. Problems generally take longer to complete than exercises and probe for a deeper level of understanding. Problems usually have more than one issue and present challenging situations, complex computations, and interpretations.

**Managerial Decision Cases**. Most chapters contain at least two cases. Cases have greater depth and complexity than problems. They are designed to help students integrate multiple concepts and further develop their analytical skills. Several cases deal with ethical behaviour.

**Research Assignments**. Research assignments appear in all chapters, allowing students to develop their research and communication skills beyond the classroom. Many research assignments, labelled "Cybercases," require students to research information on the Internet.

## Additional Features of the Canadian Sixth Edition

**Ethics**. The Canadian Sixth Edition continues to emphasize the study of ethical conduct for management accountants. The role of ethics is discussed in Chapter 1. Examples of ethical conduct relative to management accounting issues are provided in other chapters as well. Chapter 1 has several substantive problems on ethics, and subsequent chapters have at least one problem or case involving an ethical dilemma. These problems allow the instructor to introduce value judgments into management accounting decision-making.

**Real-World Emphasis**. The Canadian Sixth Edition incorporates many real-world applications of management accounting concepts, making the study of these concepts more familiar and interesting to students. Opening scenarios introduce chapter topics within the context of realistic business examples.

**Increased Coverage of Service Industry**. Service businesses are experiencing unprecedented growth in today's economy. Managers of service businesses often use same management accounting methods as manufacturers, but they must adapt them to their own unique service-oriented environments. To address this need, we have increased the coverage of service industry applications in the Canadian Sixth Edition.

## Ancillaries

**Instructor's Resource CD-ROM (0-17-640567-4).** Key instructor ancillaries (solutions manual, instructor's manual, test bank, computerized test bank, and PowerPoint slides) are provided on CD-ROM, giving instructors the ultimate tool for customizing lectures and presentations.

**Check Figures**. Key figures for solutions to selected problems and cases are provided as an aid to students as they prepare their answers.

**Study Guide (0-17-640569-0).** The study guide provides a detailed review of each chapter and allows students to check their understanding of the material through quizzes and exercises. Specifically, students are provided with a key terms test, a chapter quiz, and practice exercises. Answers are provided for all assignment material. Learning organizers help students compare and contrast key concepts and aid in visual learning.

**Instructor's Manual (0-17-641465-7).** The instructor's manual contains a complete set of lecture notes for each chapter and a listing of all exercises and problems with estimated difficulty and time required for solution.

**Solutions Manual (0-17-640570-4)** Prepared by David W. Senkow at the University of Regina, the solutions manual contains the solutions for all end-of-chapter questions, exercises, problems, and cases. Solutions have been error-checked to ensure their accuracy and reliability.

**Students' Solutions Manual (0-17-640571-2).** The students' solutions manual contains the solutions to all of the odd-numbered questions.

**Test Bank (0-17-640572-0).** Extensively revised for the Canadian Sixth Edition, the test bank offers multiple-choice problems, short problems, and essay problems. Designed to make exam preparation as convenient as possible for the instructor, each test bank chapter contains enough questions and problems to permit the preparation of several exams without repetition of material. The test bank is available in computerized format, allowing instructors to design and edit their own tests.

Spreadsheet

**Spreadsheet Templates.** Spreadsheet templates using Microsoft Excel® provide outlined formats of solutions for selected end-of-chapter exercises and problems. These exercises and problems are identified with a margin symbol. The templates allow students to develop spreadsheet and "what-if" analysis skills. The spreadsheet templates are available in the Student Resources on the Hansen Web site (**www.hansen6e.nelson.com**).

**PowerPoint Slides (0-17-640568-2).** PowerPoint slides are available for use by students as an aid to note taking, and by instructors for enhancing their lectures. Selected transparencies of key concepts and exhibits from the text are available in PowerPoint presentation software.

**Web Site (www.hansen6e.nelson.com ).** A Web site designed specifically for *Management Accounting*, Canadian Sixth Edition, includes on-line and downloadable instructor and student resources.

**Cases in Management Accounting (0-324-02011-2).** These forty cases require students to think critically and strategically as well as apply technical accounting analysis to familiar scenarios and settings. The cases are also integrative in that they involve aspects of manufacturing and service operations, organizational design, and data analysis. The casebook includes Excel spreadsheet applications and Microsoft Access cost accounting/management databases. Case topics include process value analysis, the DuPont method, activity-based costing (ABC), activity-based management (ABM), break-even analysis, budgeting, performance measurement (including the Balanced Scorecard approach), and transfer pricing. Photos that accompany the case provide the student with a contextual perspective that facilitates learning.

**Adams California Car Company: An Active Learning Costing Case Set   ISBN 0-324-18450-6** (developed by Steve Adams, California State University–Chico). This case involves students in the hands-on simulation of a production process using model cars to learn cost management principles. The cases in this simulation are built around important, "Real-World" business decisions. Students will become more effective decision makers in today's society as they develop problem solving, interpersonal, and computer skills. The Lego Mega Bloks™ Set is included and additional sets may be purchased. California Car company received the 1997 AAA/IMA James Bulloch award for Innovations in Management Accounting.

# Acknowledgments

We would like to express our appreciation to all who have provided helpful comments and suggestions. The reviewers of the prior editions helped make it a successful product. Many valuable comments from instructors and students have helped us make significant improvements in the Canadian Sixth Edition. In particular, we would like to thank the following individuals, who provided formal comments. Their input was deeply appreciated.

## For the Canadian Sixth Edition:

Lynn de Grace, Concordia University

Mariann Glynn, Ryerson University

Yu Li, University of Toronto

David McConomy, Queen's University

Sheila McGillis, Laurentian University

Jeanbih (Jean) Pi, University of Manitoba

Johan de Rooy, University of British Columbia

Linda Thibeault, Nipissing University

We would like to thank our verifier—Glenys Sylvestre, CA, University of Regina, who served as the error-checker for the text. Her careful editing helped us produce a text and ancillary package of higher quality and accuracy.

We also want to express our gratitude to the Society of Management Accountants of Canada and the Institute of Management Accountants for their permission to use adapted problems from past CMA examinations. Extracts from Management Accounting 1 (MA1), published by the Certified General Accountants Association of Canada (© CGA-Canada, 1991, 1992, 1993, 1995), are reprinted by permission.

Finally, we offer special thanks to all the Nelson staff. They have been most helpful and have carried out their tasks with impressive expertise and professionalism. We especially wish to thank Veronica Visentin, Elke Price, Susan Calvert, and Evelyn Veitch for their exceptionally insightful comments and dedicated work.

David W. Senkow
Raili M. Pollanen

# About the Authors

**David W. Senkow** is Associate Professor of Accounting in the Faculty of Administration, University of Regina. He received his Ph.D. from the University of Minnesota in 1992. His research interests include the effects of regulation of information and institutional structures on economic decision behaviour. He has published in *The Accounting Review*, *The Economic Journal*, *Auditing: A Journal of Practice & Theory*, and *Research in Accounting Regulation*. Dr. Senkow has served the accounting profession through committees of CMA-Canada (Saskatchewan) and the Institute of Chartered Accountants of Saskatchewan and on the board of the Accounting Education Foundation of Saskatchewan. He has served as a vice-president of the Canadian Academic Accounting Association. His outside interests include music, walking, watching a variety of sports, and drag racing his 1967 Mustang.

**Raili M. Pollanen** is Assistant Professor of Accounting and Accounting Coordinator at the Sprott School of Business, Carleton University. Previously, she was with the Faculty of Administration, University of Regina, where she also held a Saskatchewan Accounting Education Foundation Faculty Fellowship. She received her Ph.D. from Lancaster University in 1997, and she is also a CMA. Dr. Pollanen's research interests focus on performance measurement and control systems, and her recent research has been funded by research grants from the Canadian Institute of Chartered Accountants and the Association of Public Service Financial Administrators. She has published in *Accounting, Organizations and Society*, *Issues in Accounting Education*, *FMI Journal*, *Perspectives on Performance*, and several conference proceedings. Her nonacademic interests include fitness, reading, and travel.

**Don R. Hansen** is Professor of Accounting at Oklahoma State University. He received his Ph.D. from the University of Arizona in 1977. He has an undergraduate degree in mathematics from Brigham Young University. His research interests include activity-based costing and mathematical modelling. He has published articles in both accounting and engineering journals, including *The Accounting Review*, *The Journal of Management Accounting Research*, *Accounting Horizons*, and *IIE Transactions*. Dr. Hansen has served on the editorial board of *The Accounting Review*. His outside interests include family, church activities, reading, movies, watching sports, and studying Spanish.

**Maryanne M. Mowen** is Associate Professor of Accounting at Oklahoma State University. She received her Ph.D. from Arizona State University in 1979. Dr. Mowen brings an interdisciplinary perspective to teaching and writing in cost and management accounting, with degrees in history and economics. In addition, she does scholarly research in behavioural decision theory. She has published articles in journals such as *Decision Science*, *The Journal of Economics and Psychology*, and *The Journal of Management Accounting Research*. Dr. Mowen's interests outside the classroom include reading, playing golf, travelling, and working crossword puzzles.

# Management Accounting

# Introduction: The Role, History, and Direction of Management Accounting

## Learning Objectives

**After studying Chapter 1, you should be able to:**

1. Explain the need for management accounting information.

2. Explain the differences between management accounting and financial accounting.

3. Provide a brief historical description of management accounting.

4. Identify and explain recent developments affecting management accounting.

5. Describe the role of management accountants in an organization.

6. Explain the importance of ethical behaviour for managers and management accountants.

7. Identify the different professional accounting designations available for management accountants.

# Scenario

Consider the following comments made by individuals from several different organizations:

A. **Manager of a For-Profit Water-Testing Facility**: "I have just received a request to bid on the lab work for a large water-bottling company. The competition for this job is intense. Given the specifications described in the written request and the level of competition we are facing, I need an accurate assessment of cost for each lab test that will be performed. Once I have the unit cost for each type of lab test, I can obtain the total cost based on the expected volume of tests. With this cost information, I can then calculate the minimum bid that will provide a reasonable dollar return." (Product costing and pricing decision)

B. **Local Operator**: "I am confident that replacing the tooling in our machines and redesigning the grinding process will improve quality and decrease the time required to perform the operation. However, I would like to know if the number of defective units really drops and by how much. I also need to know if cycle time actually decreases because of the changes. Furthermore, do these changes reduce the cost of performing the work we do? I also need to know the cost of resources used before and after the proposed changes to see if cost improvement is really taking place." (Continuous improvement)

C. **Bank Manager**: "This is incredible! The no-equity loans were supposed to be our most profitable new product. Yet costs exceeded expectations by $150,000. What happened? Did we spend too much time with each client? Was there less demand for the product than expected? Were processing costs greater than budgeted? Did more loans go into default than expected? I need information that reveals what happened so that corrective action can be taken." (Operational control)

D. **Chief Executive Officer of an Airline**: "Our profits are being squeezed by the intense competition we are facing. My marketing vice-president argues that we can improve our financial position by reducing our airfares. She claims that if we reduce fares by 20 percent and simultaneously increase advertising expenditures by $500,000, we can increase the number of passengers by 20 percent. I need to decide whether the price decrease coupled with an increase in advertising costs and passenger volume will be profitable." (Cost–volume–profit decision)

E. **Hospital Administrator**: "I am very pleased with the performance of the laboratory. This latest performance report reveals that costs have been reduced while the number of tests run has increased. I am told that the activity-based management approach used in the lab has resulted in the elimination of significant waste and improved turnaround time. I want to meet with the assistant administrator of that area to discuss if these procedures can be used in other parts of the hospital." (Managerial control)

F. **Manager of a Manufacturing Facility**: "We must soon decide whether the acquisition of the computer-aided manufacturing equipment is in our best interest or not. This is a critical decision involving enormous amounts of capital, and it carries with it some long-term implications regarding the type of labour we employ. To help us in that decision, our controller has estimated the cost of capital and the increase in after-tax cash flow that would be expected over the life of the equipment." (Capital investment decision and strategic planning)

### Questions to Think About

1. Who are the users of management accounting information?

2. How is management accounting information used?

3. Should a management accounting system provide both financial and nonfinancial information?

4. What organizations need a management accounting information system?

## Management Accounting Information System

**Objective 1**

Explain the need for management accounting information.

**management accounting information system**

An information system that produces outputs using inputs as well as the processes needed to satisfy specific management objectives.

The **management accounting information system** is an information system that produces outputs using inputs and processes needed to satisfy specific management objectives. Processes are the heart of a management accounting information system and are used to transform the inputs into outputs that satisfy the system's objectives. Processes are described by activities such as collecting, measuring, storing, analyzing, reporting, and managing information. Outputs include special reports, product costs, customer costs, budgets, performance reports, and even personal communication. The operational model of a management accounting information system is illustrated in Exhibit 1–1.

The management accounting information system is not bound by any formal criteria that define the nature of the inputs or processes—or even the output. The criteria are flexible and based on management objectives. The management accounting system has three broad objectives:

1. to provide information for costing of services, products, and other objects of interest to management;
2. to provide information for planning, controlling, evaluation, and continuous improvement; and
3. to provide information for decision making.

Management accounting information can help managers identify opportunities, identify and solve problems, and evaluate performance. Accounting information is needed and used in all phases of management: planning, controlling, and decision making. Furthermore, the need for management accounting information is present in all organizations: manufacturing, merchandising, and service.

EXHIBIT    1-1

Operational Model:
Management Accounting
Information System

| | Collecting | Special Reports |
| | Measuring | Product Costs |
| | Storing | Customer Costs |
| | Analyzing | Budgets |
| Economic Events | Reporting | Performance Reports |
| | Managing | Personal Communication |

Inputs → Processes → Outputs → Users → (back to Inputs)

## Information Needs of Managers and Other Users

We can use the opening scenarios to illustrate each of the management accounting system objectives. Scenario A (the manager of a for-profit water-testing facility), for example, shows the importance of determining the cost of products (illustrating objective 1). Scenario B emphasizes the importance of tracking costs and nonfinancial measures of performance over time. Thus Scenario A emphasizes the importance of accuracy in product costing, while Scenario B underscores the importance of tracking efficiency measures—both financial and nonfinancial (illustrating objective 2). Trends in these measures can suggest ways of improving a company's operations. For example, Milliken & Company, a leading textile manufacturer, began to use trend charts to track the change time for its dye nozzles. These charts provided the incentive for engineering and production personnel to reduce change time from 22 minutes to 8.2 minutes—a dramatic improvement.[1] Accuracy in cost assignments and the use of nonfinancial information by both managers and nonmanagers have emerged as fundamental requirements for many organizations. These and other related issues have led to the development of an improved management accounting information system known as an **activity-based cost management information system**.

Scenarios B, C, E, and F illustrate planning, control, evaluation, and continuous improvement (objective 2). Managers, executives, and workers need an information system that will identify problems, such as the possibility of cost overruns (Scenario C), or benefits, such as the ability of a manager in a subunit to innovate and increase efficiency (Scenario E). Once problems are known, actions can be taken to identify and implement solutions. Scenario B also illustrates that both financial and nonfinancial information are needed so that workers can evaluate and monitor the effects of decisions that are intended to improve operational and unit performance. Informing workers about operational and financial performance allows workers to assess the effectiveness of their efforts to improve their work. Workers and managers should be committed to continuously improving the activities they perform. **Continuous improvement** means searching for ways to increase the overall efficiency and productivity of activities by reducing waste, increasing quality, and reducing costs. Thus, information is needed to help identify opportunities for improvement and to evaluate the progress made in implementing actions designed to create improvement.

The third objective, providing information for decision making, is intertwined with the first two. For example, information about the costs of products, customers, processes, and other objects of interest to management can be the basis

**activity-based cost management information system**

An improved management accounting information system based on the principles of activity-based management and activity-based costing.

**continuous improvement**

The process of searching for ways to increase the overall efficiency and productivity of activities by reducing waste, increasing quality, and reducing costs.

---

1. James Don Edwards, "How Milliken Stays on Top," *Journal of Accountancy* (April 1989): pp. 63-74 (see especially pp. 72-74).

**strategic decision making**

Choosing among alternative strategies with the goal of selecting the strategy or strategies that provide a company with reasonable assurance for long-term growth and survival.

**employee empowerment**

The authorization of operational personnel to plan, control, and make decisions without explicit authorization from middle and higher-level management.

for identifying problems and alternative solutions. We can make similar observations about information pertaining to planning, control, and evaluation. Examples include using product cost to prepare a bid (Scenario A), helping a manager decide whether to reduce prices and increase advertising to improve profitability (Scenario D), or helping a manager decide whether to automate (Scenario F). This last scenario also underscores the importance of **strategic decision making**, which is defined as the process of choosing among alternative strategies with the goal of selecting one or more strategies that provide a company with a reasonable assurance of long-term growth and survival.

## The Management Process

The management process is defined by the following activities: (1) planning, (2) controlling, and (3) decision making. The management process describes the functions carried out by managers and empowered workers. Empowering workers to participate in the management process means giving them a greater say in how the plant operates. Thus, **employee empowerment** is simply authorizing operational personnel to plan, control, and make decisions without explicit authorization from middle- and higher-level management.

Employee empowerment is justified by the belief that the employees closest to the work can provide valuable input in terms of ideas, plans, and problem solving. Workers are allowed to shut down production to identify and correct problems, and their input is sought and used to improve production processes. Two examples illustrate the power of this concept. First, empowered workers at Duffy Tool and Stamping saved $14,300 per year by redesigning a press operation.[2] In one department, completed parts (made by a press) came down a chute and fell into a parts tub. When the tub became full, press operators had to stop operation while the stock operator removed the full tub and replaced it with an empty one. Empowered workers redesigned the operation so that each press had a chute with two branches—each leading to a tub. Now completed parts are routed into one branch of the chute. When the tub associated with the active branch becomes full, the completed parts are routed to the other branch and its tub while the full tub is being removed and replaced with an empty tub. This new design avoids machine downtime and produces significant savings. Second, GR Spring and Stamping implemented an employee empowerment program. Within a four-year period, the number of ideas implemented increased from 0.67 per employee to 11.22 per employee.[3] Increased involvement in managing the company through employee empowerment is a key element in enhancing continuous improvement efforts.

### Planning

The detailed formulation of action to achieve a particular end is the management activity called planning. **Planning**, therefore, requires setting objectives and identifying methods of achieving those objectives. For example, a company may have the objective of increasing its short-term and long-term profitability by improving the overall quality of its products. By improving product quality, the company should be able to reduce scrap and rework, decrease the number of customer complaints, reduce the amount of warranty work, reduce the resources currently assigned to inspection, and so on, thus increasing profitability. But how is this to be accomplished? Management must develop some specific methods that, when

**planning**

Setting objectives and identifying methods of achieving those objectives.

---

2. George F. Hanks, "Excellence Teams in Action," *Management Accounting* (February 1995): p. 35.

3. Joseph F. Castellano, Donald Klien, and Harper Roehm, "Minicompanies: The Next Generation of Employee Empowerment," *Management Accounting* (March 1998): pp. 22-30.

implemented, will lead to the achievement of the desired objective. A plant manager, for example, may initiate a supplier evaluation program that has the objective of identifying and selecting suppliers who are willing and able to supply defect-free parts. Empowered workers, on the other hand, may be able to identify production causes of defects and create new methods for producing a product that will reduce scrap and rework and the need for inspection. The new methods should be clearly specified and detailed.

### Controlling

Planning is only half the battle. Once a plan is created, it must be implemented and its implementation monitored by managers and workers to ensure that the plan is being carried out as intended. The managerial activity of monitoring a plan's implementation and taking corrective action as needed is referred to as **controlling**. Control is usually achieved with the use of feedback. **Feedback** is information that can be used to evaluate or correct the steps being taken to implement a plan. Based on the feedback, a manager (or empowered worker) may decide to let the implementation continue as is, take corrective action of some type to put the actions back in harmony with the original plan, or do some midstream replanning.

Feedback is a critical facet of the control function. It is here that management accounting once again plays a vital role. Feedback can be financial or nonfinancial in nature. For example, the chute redesign at Duffy Tool and Stamping saved more than $14,000 per year (financial feedback). But the redesign also eliminated machine downtime and increased the number of units produced per hour (nonfinancial feedback). Both measures convey important information. Often financial and nonfinancial feedback take the form of formal reports that compare the actual data with planned data or benchmarks (internal or external). These reports are referred to as **performance reports**.

### Decision Making

The process of choosing among competing alternatives is **decision making**. This pervasive managerial function is intertwined with planning and control. A manager cannot plan without making decisions. Managers must choose among competing objectives and methods for carrying out the chosen objectives. Only one of numerous competing plans can be chosen. Similar comments can be made concerning the control function.

Decisions can be improved if information about the alternatives is gathered and made available to managers. One of the major roles of the management accounting information system is to supply information that facilitates decision making. For example, the manager in Scenario A was faced with the prospect of submitting a bid on laboratory tests for a water-bottling company. A large number of possible bids could be submitted, but the manager must choose one and only one to submit to the prospective customer. The manager requested information concerning the expected production costs of the laboratory tests. This cost information, along with the manager's knowledge of competitive conditions, should improve his or her ability to select a bid price. Imagine having to submit a bid without some idea of the production costs.

## Organization Type

The use of accounting information by managers is not limited to manufacturing organizations. Regardless of the organizational form, managers must be proficient in using accounting information. The basic concepts taught in this text apply to a variety of settings. The six scenarios at the beginning of this chapter involved manufacturing, health care, transportation, profit, and not-for-profit organiza-

**controlling**

The managerial activity of monitoring a plan's implementation and taking corrective action as needed.

**feedback**

Information that can be used to evaluate or correct the steps being taken to implement a plan.

**performance reports**

Reports that compare the actual data with planned data.

**decision making**

The process of choosing among competing alternatives.

tions. Hospital administrators, presidents of corporations, dentists, educational administrators, and city managers can all improve their managerial skills by being well-grounded in the basic concepts and use of accounting information.

## Conceptual Framework of Management Accounting

We can gain a better understanding of the link between management accounting information and management processes by referring to a conceptual framework. Management accounting is a discipline with both theoretical and practical roots. Its theoretical foundations are found in such disciplines as economics, finance, organization theory, management, and psychology. Its practical applications are found in all organizations where decisions are based on financial and other quantitative information. From routine decision making (for example, how many units to produce on a production run) to strategic decisions (for example, how best to redesign the organizational structure to meet the new global competitive pressures of producing a wider variety of products at a lower cost), effective decisions depend on a thorough understanding of management accounting concepts and techniques. The following sections set out the conceptual framework that will be followed in the text.

### Cost Accumulation and Product Costing

Decision making in all organizations must consider costs, and systems of cost accumulation and cost assignment are found in all types of organizations. A basic understanding of the capabilities and limitations of cost accounting systems is crucial for good decision making. This material is covered in Part 1, Cost Accumulation and Product Costing. Economics provides the theoretical foundation of cost accumulation and cost allocation. In a simple economy, with few exceptions, most costs can easily be traced to the primary product. Today, the bulk of costs are often not directly traceable to the wide variety of products or services an organization offers. Indirect or overhead costs have increasingly become a major component of total costs in many organizations, and the largest single cost component in some organizations. The challenge of relating costs to products or services (and other cost objects) can be met only by understanding the economics of overhead. Management accounting attempts to apply economic concepts of cost in practical settings, where costs must be accumulated and allocated to (1) products and services, (2) departments (subunits of the organization), or (3) activities.

### Managerial Decision Making

Management accounting concepts and techniques are useful for decision making, which involves making choices between competing alternatives. This area is the domain of decision theory, and an understanding of the basic concepts of decision theory is important to making good choices. This material is covered in Part 2, Managerial Decision Making.

In Part 2, the emphasis is on operating decisions. We will come to understand that accounting information produced for one economic purpose may not necessarily be useful for another purpose; the nature of the decision determines the relevance of the information. The application of decision theory also requires a number of logical steps:

1. identify the objective or problem that requires a decision,
2. determine the set of feasible alternative courses of action,
3. measure or estimate the effects of these alternative courses of action,
4. assess the possible outcomes, and
5. make the choice that best satisfies the objective for the decision and all of the objectives of the organization.

By necessity, decision making affects future outcomes, and questions of uncertainty about the future are important and require particular attention.

We make two basic assumptions in Part 2. First we will assume that decision makers make rational choices in the traditional economic sense. That is, if alternative A is more profitable (or less expensive) than alternative B, other things being equal, A should be accepted and B rejected. The validity of the assumption of rational choice will be examined briefly in Part 2, but a fuller discussion of it lies outside the scope of this text. The second assumption we make is that what is good for a subunit of the organization is good for the organization as a whole. The effects of relaxing the second assumption are dealt with in Part 3.

### Planning and Control Systems

A major reason many organizations, particularly large ones, run as well as they do is the existence of a planning and control system. In Part 3, we explore the requirements for effective planning and control. For a single decision maker, the theoretical foundation of planning and control is embedded in the concept of feedback and corrective action, as discussed earlier. Where there are multiple decision makers, additional problems arise. Different managers may have different objectives, resulting in conflict. Domains of accountability (that is, responsibility for actions, outputs, or outcomes) are often blurred, and the information available to one manager may not be shared with other managers within an organization; that is, there is information asymmetry. These factors contribute to problems for planning and control.

Information asymmetry often also exists between managers and owners. A manager is delegated specific activities to perform with specific objectives and makes decisions on behalf of the owner. The success of this manager's decisions may be due to good effort or to good fortune, but information asymmetry prevents direct observation of the cause. Monitoring of managerial performance and the use of incentives to encourage a harmony of objectives or goal congruence are some of the issues that we will consider in Part 3.

Modern organizations rely on delegation of authority and on accountability for actions or results or both. As with other systems, we can achieve a fuller understanding of planning and control systems by studying their structure and process. For example, the responsibilities of various positions within the organization (structure) are identified, in general terms, in a typical organization chart. A more specific understanding of the way the organization works, however, might be obtained by examining how people actually make decisions and how products and documents flow within the organization (process). In terms of structure, organizations usually assign responsibilities for cost, revenue, profit, or investment performance. In terms of process, managers usually formulate plans and budgets, compile actual performance records, track differences between budgeted and actual performance, examine the reasons for these differences, and take corrective actions if required. In this sense, a manager of a subunit is primarily concerned with the performance of his or her own subunit. Suboptimization results from actions that are best from the subunit's (or its manager's) point of view but may not be best from the organization's point of view. It raises a number of planning and control issues. Some of these will be dealt with in Part 3.

# Management Accounting and Financial Accounting

**Objective 2**

Explain the differences between management accounting and financial accounting.

**financial accounting information system**

An accounting information subsystem which is concerned mainly with producing outputs for external users and which uses well-specified economic events as inputs and processes that meet certain rules and conventions.

**Accounting Standards Board**

Establishes financial accounting standards, including the nature of inputs and the rules and conventions governing financial accounting processes.

The accounting information system within an organization has two major subsystems: a management accounting system and a financial accounting system. The accounting information system is, itself, a subsystem of a organization's overall management information system. The two accounting subsystems differ in their objectives, the nature of their inputs, and the type of processes used to transform inputs into outputs. The **financial accounting information system** is primarily concerned with producing outputs for external users. It uses well-specified economic events as inputs and processes that meet certain rules and conventions. For financial accounting, the nature of the inputs and the rules and conventions governing processes are defined by the financial accounting standards established by the **Accounting Standards Board** of the Canadian Institute of Chartered Accountants.[4] The overall objective is to prepare external reports (financial statements) for investors, creditors, government agencies, and other outside users. This information is used for such things as investment decisions, stewardship evaluation, monitoring activity, and regulatory measures.

The management accounting system produces information for internal users, such as managers, executives, and workers. Thus, management accounting could be properly called internal accounting, and financial accounting could be called external accounting. Specifically, management accounting identifies, collects, measures, classifies, and reports information that is useful to internal users in planning, controlling, and decision making.

We can identify several differences when comparing management accounting to financial accounting. Some of the more important differences follow and are summarized in Exhibit 1–2.

- *Targeted Users* As mentioned, management accounting focuses on providing information for internal users, whereas financial accounting focuses on providing information for external users.
- *Restrictions on Inputs and Processes* Management accounting is not subject to the requirements of generally accepted accounting principles. The Accounting Standards Board sets the accounting policies that must be followed for financial reporting. The inputs and processes of financial

**EXHIBIT    1-2**

Comparision of Management and Financial Accounting

| Management Accounting | Financial Accounting |
|---|---|
| 1. Internally focused | 1. Externally focused |
| 2. No mandatory rules | 2. Must follow externally imposed rules |
| 3. Financial and nonfinancial information; subjective information possible | 3. Objective financial information |
| 4. Emphasis on the future | 4. Historical orientation |
| 5. Internal evaluation and decisions based on very detailed information | 5. Information about the firm as a whole |
| 6. Broad, multidisciplinary | 6. More self-contained |

---

4. The *Canada Business Corporations Act* specifically refers to the *CICA Handbook*, and provincial securities commissions require compliance with it. Although provincial securities commissions (for example, the Ontario Securities Commission [OSC] and the Quebec Securities Commission [QSC], etc.) play a less predominate role in standard setting than does the Securities and Exchange Commission [SEC] in the United States, they do influence the direction of standard setting. The OSC specifically has become more directly involved in standard setting.

*Management Accounting Guidelines*

A document published by CMA Canada to help management accountants fulfil their responsibilities; however, management accountants are under no obligation to follow any set of standards except as they relate to external reporting.

accounting are well-defined and, in fact, restricted. Only certain kinds of economic events qualify as inputs, and processes must follow generally accepted methods. Unlike financial accounting, management accounting has no official body that prescribes the format, content, and rules for selecting inputs and processes and preparing accounting reports. Managers are free to choose whatever information they want—provided that it can be justified on a cost–benefit basis. CMA Canada issues **Management Accounting Guidelines** to assist management accountants in fulfilling their responsibilities, but management accountants are under no obligation to follow any set of standards except as related to external reporting.

- *Type of Information* The restrictions imposed by financial accounting tend to produce objective and verifiable financial information. For management accounting, information may be financial or nonfinancial and may be much more subjective in nature.
- *Time Orientation* Financial accounting has a historical orientation. It records and reports events that have already happened. Although management accounting too records and reports events that have already occurred, it also exhibits a very strong emphasis on providing information about future events. Management, for example, may want to know not only what it cost to produce a product in the past, but also what it will cost to produce a product in the future. Knowing what it will cost helps in planning purchases of material and making pricing decisions, among other things. This future orientation is demanded because of the need to support the managerial functions of planning and decision making.
- *Degree of Aggregation* Management accounting provides measures and internal reports used to evaluate the performance of entities, product lines, departments, and managers. Essentially, very detailed information is needed and provided. Financial accounting, on the other hand, focuses on overall organization performance, providing a more aggregated viewpoint.
- *Breadth* Management accounting is much broader than financial accounting. It includes aspects of managerial economics, industrial engineering, and management science, as well as numerous other areas.

It should be emphasized, however, that both the management accounting information system and the financial accounting information system are part of the total accounting information system. Unfortunately, all too often the content of the management accounting system is driven by the needs of the financial accounting system. The reports of both management and financial accounting are frequently derived from the same database, which usually was originally established to support the reporting requirements of financial accounting. Many organizations need to redesign this database in order to satisfy more fully the needs of the internal users. For example, a company's overall profitability is of interest to investors, but managers need to know the profitability of individual products. The accounting system should therefore be designed to provide both total profits and profits for individual products. The key point here is flexibility—the accounting system should be able to supply different information for different purposes.

## A Brief Historical Perspective on Management Accounting

**Objective 3**

Provide a brief historical description of management accounting.

Most of the product-costing and management accounting procedures used in the twentieth century were developed between 1880 and 1925. [5] Interestingly, many of the early developments (until about 1914) concerned managerial product costing—tracing a company's profitability to individual products and using this information for strategic decision making. By 1925, however, most of this emphasis had been abandoned in favour of inventory costing—assigning manufacturing costs to products so that the cost of inventories could be reported to external users of a company's financial statements.

Financial reporting became the driving force for the design of cost accounting systems. Managers and companies were willing to accept aggregated average cost information about individual products. Apparently, more detailed and accurate cost information about individual products was not needed. As long as a company had relatively homogeneous products that consumed resources at about the same rate, the average cost information supplied by a financially driven costing system was good enough. Furthermore, for some companies, even as product diversity increased, the need to have more accurate information was offset by the high cost of the processing required to provide the information. For many companies, the cost of a more detailed costing system apparently exceeded its benefits.

Some effort to improve the managerial usefulness of conventional cost systems took place in the 1950s and 1960s. Users discussed the shortcomings of information supplied by a system designed to prepare financial reports. Efforts to improve the system, however, essentially centred on making the financial accounting information more useful to users rather than on producing an entirely new set of information and procedures apart from the external reporting system.

In the 1980s and 1990s, many recognized that some management accounting practices were no longer serving managerial needs. Some even claimed that existing management accounting systems were obsolete and virtually useless. More accurate product costing and more useful and detailed input were needed to allow managers to improve quality and productivity and reduce costs. In response to the perceived failure of the traditional management accounting system, efforts were made to develop a new management accounting system—one that satisfied the demands of the current economic environment.

## Recent Developments Affecting Management Accounting

**Objective 4**

Identify and explain recent developments affecting management accounting.

The economic environment has required the development of innovative and relevant management accounting practices. Consequently, activity-based management accounting systems have been developed and implemented in many organizations. Additionally, the focus of management accounting systems has been broadened to enable managers to better serve the needs of customers and manage the company's value chain. Furthermore, to secure and maintain a competitive advantage, managers must emphasize time, quality, and efficiency, and accounting information must be produced to support these three fundamental organizational goals. More recently, the emergence of e-business requires management accounting systems to provide information that enables managers to deal with this new environment.

---

5.  A more complete discussion of the history and origins of management accounting can be found in H. Thomas Johnson and Robert Kaplan, *Relevance Lost: The Rise and Fall of Management Accounting* (Boston: Harvard Business School Press, 1987).

## Activity-Based Management

**activity-based management**
A systemwide, integrated approach that focuses management's attention on activities with the objective of improving customer value and the profit achieved by providing this value. It includes driver analysis, activity analysis, and performance evaluation, and draws on activity-based costing as a major source of information.

The demand for more accurate and relevant management accounting information has led to the development of activity-based management. **Activity-based management** is an integrated systemwide approach that focuses management's attention on activities with the objective of improving customer value and the resulting profit. Activity-based management emphasizes activity-based costing (ABC) and process value analysis. Activity-based costing improves the accuracy of assigning costs by tracing costs first to activities and then to the products or customers that consume these activities. Process value analysis, on the other hand, emphasizes activity analysis—trying to determine why activities are performed and how well they are performed. The objective is to find ways to perform necessary activities more efficiently and to eliminate those that do not create customer value.

## Customer Orientation

**customer value**
The difference between what a customer receives (customer realization) and what the customer gives up (customer sacrifice).

**total product**
The complete range of tangible and intangible benefits that a customer receives from a purchased product.

**postpurchase costs**
The costs of using, maintaining, and disposing of a product.

**strategic cost management**
The use of cost data to develop and identify superior strategies that will produce a competitive advantage.

The objective of activity-based management is increasing customer value by managing activities. Customer value is a key focus because companies can establish a competitive advantage by creating better customer value for the same or lower cost than that of competitors, or by creating equivalent value for a lower cost than that of competitors. **Customer value** is the difference between what a customer receives (customer realization) and what the customer gives up (customer sacrifice). What is received is called the total product. The **total product** is the complete range of tangible and intangible benefits that a customer receives from a purchased product. Thus, customer realization includes basic and special product features, service, quality, instructions for use, reputation, brand name, and any other factors deemed important by customers. Customer sacrifice includes the cost of purchasing the product, the time and effort spent acquiring and learning to use the product, and **postpurchase costs**, which are defined as the costs of using, maintaining, and disposing of the product. Increasing customer value means increasing customer realization or decreasing customer sacrifice, or both.

### Strategic Positioning

Increasing customer value to create a sustainable competitive advantage is achieved through judicious selection of strategies. Cost information plays a critical role in this process and does so through a process called *strategic cost management*. **Strategic cost management** is the use of cost data to develop and identify superior strategies that will produce a sustainable competitive advantage. Generally, companies choose a strategic position corresponding to one of two general strategies: (1) cost leadership or (2) superior products through differentiation.[6]

The objective of the cost leadership strategy is to provide the same or better value to customers at a *lower* cost than competitors do. Thus, a low-cost strategy has the objective of increasing customer value by reducing customer sacrifice. For example, reducing the cost of making a product by improving a process would allow the company to reduce the product's selling price, thus reducing customer sacrifice.

A differentiation strategy, on the other hand, strives to increase customer value by increasing realization. Providing something to customers that is not provided by competitors creates a competitive advantage. For example, a retailer of computers could offer on-site repair service, a feature not offered by other rivals in the local market. Of course, for a differentiation strategy to be viable, the value added to the customer by the differentiation must exceed the company's cost of

---

6. The Japanese have also shown that an organization can pursue a strategy that combines the two: a differentiation with a cost advantage.

providing the differentiation. Also, different strategies usually require different cost information, implying that the cost systems may differ according to the strategy adopted by an organization.

### *Value-Chain Framework*

A focus on customer value means that the management accounting system should produce information about both realization and sacrifice. Collecting information about customer sacrifice means gathering information outside the company. But there are even deeper implications. Successful pursuit of cost leadership and/or differentiation strategies requires an understanding of a company's *internal* and *industrial* value chains.

Effective management of the internal **value chain** is fundamental to increasing customer value, especially if a company employs a cost leadership strategy. The **internal value chain** is the set of activities required to design, develop, produce, market, and deliver products and services to customers. Thus, emphasizing customer value forces managers to determine which activities in the value chain are important to customers. A management accounting system should track information about a wide variety of activities that span the internal value chain. Consider, for example, the delivery segment. Timely delivery of a product or service is part of the total product, and thus of value to the customer. Customer value can be increased by increasing the speed of delivery and response. Federal Express exploited this part of the value chain and successfully developed a service that was not being offered by the postal service. Today, many customers believe that a delivery delayed is a delivery denied. This seems to indicate that a good management accounting system ought to develop and measure indicators of customer satisfaction.

The industrial value chain is also critical for strategic cost management. The **industrial value chain** is the linked set of value-creating activities from basic raw materials to the disposal of the final product by end-use customers. Exhibit 1–3 illustrates a possible value chain for the apple industry. A given company operating within the industry may not—and likely will not—span the entire value chain. The exhibit illustrates that different companies participate in different segments of the chain. Company A's activities go from planting and cultivating through apple sauce production to distribution of the apple sauce to supermarkets. Company B's activities are limited to planting and cultivating through distribution of apples and Company C is involved only in apple sauce production and distribution.

Understanding the industrial value chain is critical to understanding a company's strategically important activities. Breaking down a company's value chain into its strategically important activities is basic to successful implementation of cost leadership and differentiation strategies. Fundamental to a value-chain framework is the recognition of existing complex linkages and interrelationships among activities both within and external to the company. Thus, there are two types of linkages: *internal* and *external*. **Internal linkages** are relationships among activities that are performed within an organization's portion of the industrial value chain (the internal value chain). **External linkages** are activity relationships between the company and its suppliers and customers. Thus, we can talk about *supplier linkages* and *customer linkages*. Using these linkages to bring about a win–win outcome for the company, its suppliers, and its customers is the key to successful strategic cost management. It is also a feature of what is now called *supply chain management*. **Supply chain management** is the management of material flows beginning with suppliers and their upstream suppliers, moving to the transformation of materials into finished goods to customers and their downstream customers. Understanding the industrial value chain and going beyond immediate suppliers and customers may reveal hidden benefits. The objective, of

---

**value chain**

The set of activities required to design, develop, produce, market, and deliver products and services to customers; *or,* an interrelated set of activities that increases the usefulness or value of products or services to customers.

**internal value chain**

The set of activities required to design, develop, produce, market, distribute, and service a product (the product could be a service).

**industrial value chain**

The linked set of value-creating activities, from basic raw materials to end-use customers.

**internal linkages**

The relationships among activities that are performed within an organization's portion of the industrial value chain (the internal value chain).

**external linkages**

The relationship of a firm's activities within its segment of the value chain with those activities of its suppliers and customers.

**supply chain management**

The management of material flows beginning with suppliers and their upstream suppliers, moving through the transformation of materials into finished goods, to customers and their downstream customers.

EXHIBIT   1-3

Value Chain: Apple
Industry

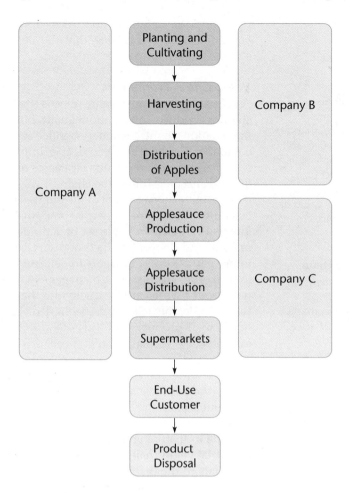

course, is for a company to manage these linkages better than its competitors, thus creating a competitive advantage.

It is important to note that companies have internal customers as well. For example, the procurement process acquires and delivers parts and materials to producing departments. Providing high-quality parts on a timely basis to managers of producing departments is just as vital for the procurement department as it is for the company as a whole to provide high-quality goods to external customers. The emphasis on managing the internal value chain and servicing internal customers has revealed the importance of a cross-functional perspective.

## Cross-Functional Perspective

Managing the value chain means that a management accountant must understand many functions of the business, from manufacturing to marketing to distribution to customer service. We see this, for example, in the varying definitions of product cost. Activity-based management accounting has moved beyond the traditional manufacturing cost definition of product cost to more inclusive definitions. These contemporary approaches to product costing may include initial design and engineering costs, as well as manufacturing costs and the costs of distribution, sales, and service. An individual well-schooled in the various definitions of product cost, who understands the shifting definitions of cost from the short run to the long run, can be invaluable in determining what information is relevant in decision making. For example, strategic decisions may require a product cost definition that assigns the costs of all value-chain activities, whereas a short-run decision that is concerned with whether a special order should be accepted or rejected may require a product cost that assigns only marginal or incremental costs.

Why try to relate management accounting to marketing, management, engineering, finance, and other business functions? When a value-chain approach is taken and customer value is emphasized, we see that these disciplines are interrelated; a decision affecting one affects the others. For example, many manufacturing companies engage in frequent trade loading, the practice of encouraging (often by offering huge discounts) wholesalers and retailers to buy more product than they can quickly resell. As a result, inventories become bloated, and the wholesalers and retailers stop purchasing for a time. This looks like a marketing problem, but it is not—at least not entirely. When selling stops, so does production. Thus in the past, trade-loading companies experienced wild swings in production. Sometimes the factories were producing around the clock to meet demand for the heavily discounted product; other times the factories were idle and workers were laid off. In effect, the sales ended up costing the companies millions of dollars of added production cost. A cross-functional perspective lets us see the forest, not just one or two of the trees. This broader vision allows managers to increase quality, reduce the time required to serve customers (both internal and external), and improve efficiency.

## Global Perspective

The current global trend in business, the formation of the European Union, and the rising fortunes of Japan and the Asian Pacific Rim countries (until the late 1990s) have placed tremendous pressures on North American businesses. These pressures have also opened up new opportunities for increased economy and efficiency. No doubt the revamping of the tax structure in Canada that resulted in the elimination of the manufacturing tax and the introduction of the Goods and Services Tax in 1991, the Free Trade Agreement (FTA) with the United States, and the North American Free Trade Agreement (NAFTA) between Canada, the United States, and Mexico are all reactions to increased global competition. Even prior to these reactions, Canada's role in the international economy was substantial, as evidenced by its representation among the G8 countries. Many large and medium-sized corporations in Canada have foreign operations in the United States and elsewhere or are themselves divisions of foreign-based multinational corporations. Competition can spring up overnight from unsuspected sources. Because of intense global competitive pressures, the cost of making bad decisions based on low-quality information has increased significantly. Thus, increasing global competition has created a demand for improved management accounting information.

## Environmental Perspective

An increased awareness of the environmental pressures facing society has highlighted the need for accountability for the environmental costs of doing business. Environmental factors are increasingly becoming an integral part of the decision-making process and of the management control system. Reasons for this development include trends involving environmental regulation, potential substantial fines that may result if environmental factors are ignored, or a genuine concern for the environment by management.

The emphasis on environmental issues poses a threat to companies that are thought to be unconcerned with the environment. That was certainly the case with calls in Europe for boycotting Canadian lumber and with logging blockades by environmentalists concerned with the effects of MacMillan Bloedel's clear-cut foresting practices. (A new management was brought in that made the company more responsive to sustainable development.) At the same time, it also provides an opportunity for environmentally minded Canadian entrepreneurs to respond to environmental challenges around the world. [7]

## Total Quality Management

**total quality management**

An approach to quality in which manufacturers strive to create an environment that will enable workers to manufacture perfect (zero-defect) products.

Continuous improvement is fundamental for establishing a state of manufacturing excellence. Manufacturing excellence is a key to survival in today's world-class competitive environment. Producing products with little waste that actually perform according to specifications are the twin objectives of world-class organizations. A philosophy of **total quality management**, in which manufacturers strive to create an environment that will enable workers to manufacture perfect (zero-defect) products, has replaced the "acceptable quality" attitudes of the past. This emphasis on total quality has also created a demand for a management accounting system that provides financial and nonfinancial information about quality. Service industries are also dedicated to improving quality. Service organizations present special problems because quality may differ from employee to employee. As a result, service organizations are emphasizing consistency through the development of systems that support employee efforts.

Measuring and reporting information about quality costs are key features of a management accounting system for both manufacturing and service industries. In both cases, the management accounting system should be able to provide both operational and financial information about quality, including such information as the number of defects, quality cost reports, quality cost trend reports, and quality cost performance reports.

## Time as a Competitive Element

Time is a crucial element in all phases of the value chain.[8] World-class organizations reduce time to market by compressing their design, implementation, and production cycles. These organizations deliver products or services quickly by eliminating nonvalue-added time—time that is of no value to the customer (for example, the time a product spends on the loading dock). Interestingly, decreasing nonvalue-added time appears to go hand in hand with increasing quality.

What about the relationship between time and product life cycles? The rate of technological innovation has increased for many industries, and the life of a particular product can be quite short. Managers must be able to respond quickly and decisively to changing market conditions. Information that allows them to accomplish this must be available. For example, Hewlett-Packard has found that it is better to be 50 percent over budget in new product development than to be six months late. This correlation between cost and time is the kind of information that should be available from a management accounting information system.

---

7. Discussion of these issues can be found in Nabil Elias, "Environmental Issues in Accounting," 16th annual Congress of the European Accounting Association, Turku, Finland, April 1993; Deloitte Touche Tohamatsu International Institute for Sustainable Development and Sustainability, *Coming Clean*, Deloitte Touche Tohamatsu International, 1993; *Accounting for the Environment*, Management Accounting Issues Paper #1, Society of Management Accountants of Canada, 1992; Leonard Eckel and Kathryn Fisher, "Being Accountable for the Environment," *CMA Magazine* (December/January 1992): p. 10; Daniel Ruch and Janice John Roper, "The Greening of Corporate Canada," *CMA Magazine* (December/January 1992): pp. 15-18.

8. An excellent analysis of time as a competitive element is contained in A. Faye Borthick and Harold P. Roth, "Accounting for Time: Reengineering Business Processes to Improve Responsiveness," *Journal of Cost Management* (Fall 1993): pp. 4-14.

## Efficiency

While quality and time are important, improving these dimensions without corresponding improvements in profit performance may be futile, if not fatal. Improving efficiency is also a vital concern. Both financial and nonfinancial measures of efficiency are needed. Trends in costs over time and measures of productivity changes can provide important measures of the efficacy of continuous improvement decisions. For these efficiency measures to be of value, costs must be properly defined, measured, and assigned; and the overall financial effect of productivity changes should be calculated.

## E-business

**electronic business (e-business)**

Business transactions and information exchanges executed using information and communication technology.

**electronic commerce (e-commerce)**

Buying and selling products using information and communication technology.

**Electronic business (e-business)** is any business transaction or information exchange that is executed using information and communication technology. **Electronic commerce (e-commerce)** is buying and selling products using information and communication technology. E-business is expected to grow significantly over the coming years. It provides opportunities for a company to expand sales throughout the world and may lower costs significantly relative to paper-based transactions. It also facilitates value-chain (supply) management. Management accountants need to understand the benefits and risks of e-business as well as its opportunities. They also play a vital role in providing relevant cost information concerning e-business. For example, managers may need to know the cost per electronic transaction versus the cost per paper transaction.

## The Role of the Management Accountant

**Objective 5**

Describe the role of management accountants in an organization.

Today's business press writes about world-class companies. These are companies at the cutting edge of customer support. They know their market and their product. They strive to continually improve product design, manufacture, and delivery. These companies can compete with the best of the best in a global environment. Management accountants must also be world-class. They must be intelligent, well-prepared, and up to date with new developments. They also must be familiar with the customs and practices of the countries in which their organizations operate.

The role of management accountants in an organization is one of support. They assist those individuals who are responsible for carrying out an organization's basic objectives. Positions that have direct responsibility for the basic objectives of an organization are referred to as **line positions**. Positions that are supportive in nature and have only indirect responsibility for an organization's basic objectives are called **staff positions**.

**line positions**

Positions that have direct responsibility for the basic objectives of an organization.

**staff positions**

Positions that are supportive in nature and have only indirect responsibility for an organization's basic objectives.

For example, assume that the basic mission of an organization is to produce and sell laser printers. The vice-presidents of manufacturing and marketing, the factory manager, and the assemblers are all line positions. The vice-presidents of finance and human resources, the cost accountant, and the purchasing manager are all staff positions.

The partial organization chart shown in Exhibit 1–4 illustrates the organizational positions for production and finance. Because one of the basic objectives of the organization is to produce, those directly involved in production hold line positions. Although management accountants, such as controllers and cost accounting managers, may wield considerable influence in the organization, they have no authority over the managers in the production area. The managers in line positions are the ones who set policy and make the decisions that impact production. However, by supplying and interpreting accounting information, management accountants can have significant input into policies and decisions.

The **controller**, the chief accounting officer, supervises all accounting departments. Because of the critical role that management accounting plays in the operation of an organization, the controller is often viewed as a member of the top management team and is encouraged to participate in planning, controlling, and decision-making activities. As the chief accounting officer, the controller has responsibility for both internal and external accounting requirements. This charge may include direct responsibility for internal auditing, cost accounting, financial accounting (including reports to securities commissions and financial statements), systems accounting (including analysis, design, and internal controls), and taxes. The duties and organization of the controller's office vary from company to company. For example, in some companies the internal audit department may report directly to the financial vice-president; similarly, the systems department may report directly to the financial vice-president or some other vice-president. A possible organization of a controller's office is shown in Exhibit 1–4.

The **treasurer** is responsible for the finance function. Specifically, the treasurer raises capital and manages cash and investments. The treasurer may also be in charge of credit and collection and insurance. As shown in Exhibit 1–4, the treasurer reports to the financial vice-president.

**controller**

The chief accounting officer, who supervises all accounting departments and activities.

**treasurer**

The person responsible for the finance function. Specifically, the treasurer raises capital and manages cash and investments.

**EXHIBIT    1-4**

Partial Organization Chart, Manufacturing Company

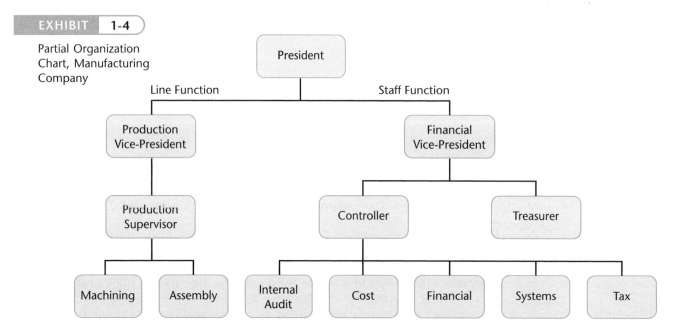

## Management Accounting and Ethical Conduct

**Objective 6**

Explain the importance of ethical behaviour for managers and management accountants.

Virtually all management accounting practices were developed to assist managers in maximizing profits. Traditionally, the economic performance of the organization has been the overriding concern. Yet managers and management accountants should not become so focused on profits that they develop a belief that the *only* goal of a business is maximizing its net worth. The objective of profit maximization should be constrained by the requirement that profits be achieved through legal and ethical means. While this assumption has always been implicit in management accounting, it should be made explicit. To help achieve this objective, many of the problems in this text force explicit consideration of ethical issues.

## Ethical Behaviour

**ethical behaviour**

Choosing actions that are "right" and "proper" and "just." Our behaviour can be right or wrong, it can be proper or improper, and the decisions we make can be fair or unfair.

**Ethical behaviour** involves choosing actions that are right, proper, and just. Our behaviour can be right or wrong; it can be proper or improper; and the decisions we make can be just or unjust. People often differ in their views of the meaning of the ethical terms cited; however, there seems to be a common principle underlying all ethical systems. This principle is expressed by the belief that each member of a group bears some responsibility for the well-being of other members. Willingness to sacrifice one's self-interest for the well-being of the group is the heart of ethical action.

This notion of sacrificing one's self-interest for the well-being of others produces some core values—values that describe what is meant by right and wrong in more concrete terms. James W. Brackner, writing for the "Ethics" column in *Management Accounting*, made the following observation:

> For moral or ethical education to have meaning, there must be agreement on the values that are considered "right." Ten of these values are identified and described by Michael Josephson in "Teaching Ethical Decision Making and Principled Reasoning." The study of history, philosophy, and religion reveals a strong consensus as to certain universal and timeless values essential to the ethical life.
>
> These ten core values yield a series of principles that delineate right and wrong in general terms. Therefore, they provide a guide to behaviour.[9]

The ten core values referred to in the quotation follow:

1. Honesty
2. Integrity
3. Promise keeping
4. Fidelity
5. Fairness
6. Caring for others
7. Respect for others
8. Responsible citizenship
9. Pursuit of excellence
10. Accountability

Although it may seem contradictory, sacrificing one's self-interest for the collective good not only may be right and bring a sense of individual worth but also may be good business sense. Companies with a strong code of ethics can create strong customer and employee loyalty. While liars and cheats may win on occasion, their victories are often short-term ones. Companies in business for the long term find that it pays to treat all of their constituents honestly and loyally.

## Standards of Ethical Conduct for Management Accountants

Organizations commonly establish standards of conduct for their managers and employees. Professional associations also establish ethical standards. For example, CMA Canada in each province has formulated a code of ethics for its

---

9. James W. Brackner , "Consensus Values Should Be Taught," *Management Accounting* (August 1992): p. 19. For a more complete discussion of the ten core values, see also Michael Josephson, "Teaching Ethical Decision Making and Principled Reasoning," *Ethics Easier Said Than Done* (Los Angles, Ca.: The Josephson Institute, Winter 1988): pp. 29-30.

members. Although the details vary from one province to another, the standards of competence, confidentiality, integrity, and objectivity are typical of those used in codes of professional ethics.[10]

To illustrate an ethical perspective, suppose a manager's bonus is linked to reported profits, with the bonus increasing as profits increase. Thus, the manager has an incentive to find ways to increase profits, including unethical approaches. For example, a manager could increase profits by delaying promotions of deserving employees or by using cheaper parts to produce a product. In either case, if the motive is simply to increase the bonus, the behaviour could be labelled unethical. Neither action is in the best interest of the company or its employees. Yet where should the blame be assigned? After all, the reward system strongly encourages the manager to increase profits. Is the reward system at fault or is the manager who chooses to increase profits? Or both?

In reality, both are probably at fault. It is important to design the evaluation and reward system so that incentives to pursue undesirable behaviour are minimized. Yet designing a perfect reward system is not a realistic expectation. Managers also have an obligation to avoid abusing the system. Manipulating income to increase a bonus can be interpreted as a violation of this standard. Basically, the prospect of an increased bonus should not influence a manager to engage in unethical actions.

## Professional Designations

**Objective 7**

Identify the different professional accounting designations available for management accountants.

Three different Canadian professional designations are available to management accountants. They are issued by the provincial arms of national accounting organizations: Certified Management Accountant (CMA—issued by CMA Canada), Chartered Accountant (CA—issued by the Institute of Chartered Accountants), and Certified General Accountant (CGA—issued by the Certified General Accountants Association). Each designation offers particular advantages to a management accountant. In each case, an applicant must meet specific educational and experience requirements and pass a qualifying examination to become certified. Thus, all three certifications offer evidence that the holder has achieved a minimum level of professional competence. Furthermore, all three designations either require or encourage the holders to engage in continuing professional education. Because certification reveals a commitment to professional competency, most organizations encourage their management accountants to hold a professional designation.

### The CMA

**Certified Management Accountant (CMA)**

An accountant who holds the CMA designation after satisfying the entrance examination, the professional program, and experience requirements. CMAs are found primarily in private- and public-sector organizations.

One of the main purposes of the **Certified Management Accountant (CMA)** designation [11] was to establish management accounting as a recognized professional discipline, separate from the profession of public accounting. A management accountant with the CMA designation has satisfied education, examination, and experience requirements. See www.cma-canada.org for the specific requirements

---

10. Examples of provincial codes of ethics can be found at the following websites: for Manitoba [http://www.cma-canada.org/manitoba/pdf/rev%5feb%5F2000%5Ffinal.pdf]; for Ontario [http://www.cma-canada.org/Ontario/70_consulting_40.asp]; and for Prince Edward Island [http://www.cma-canada.org/pei/pdf/code%5Fof%5Fethics.pdf]

11. There is also a separate CMA designation in the United States. The Certificate in Management Accounting is sponsored by the Institute of Management Accountants (IMA).

**Chartered Accountant (CA)**

An accountant who holds the CA designation after satisfying the examination and public practice requirements. CAs are found in both public practice and private and public sector organizations.

**Certified General Accountant (CGA)**

An accountant who holds the CGA designation after satisfying the examination and practice requirements. CGAs are found both in public practice and in private- and public-sector organizations.

to obtain the CMA designation and other information about the CMA profession in Canada.

## The CA

Although the **Chartered Accountant (CA)** designation's primary orientation is external reporting and auditing, not management accounting, many management accountants are CAs. CAs occupy positions in management, management accounting, and other branches of accounting in business, not-for-profit, and government organizations. See www.cica.ca for the specific requirements to obtain the CA designation and other information about the CA profession in Canada.

## The CGA

The **Certified General Accountant (CGA)** designation offers several areas of specialization including management accounting. CGAs work in management and accounting positions in business, not-for-profit, and government organizations. See www.cga-canada.org for the specific requirements to obtain the CGA designation and other information about the CGA profession in Canada.

## Summary of Learning Objectives

**1. Explain the need for management accounting information.**

Managers, workers, and executives use management accounting information to identify problems, solve problems, and evaluate performance. Essentially, management accounting information helps managers carry out their roles of planning, controlling, and decision making. Planning is the detailed formulation of action to achieve a particular end. Controlling is the monitoring of a plan's implementation. Decision making is choosing among competing alternatives.

**2. Explain the differences between management accounting and financial accounting.**

Management accounting differs from financial accounting in several ways. Management accounting information is intended for internal users, whereas financial accounting information is directed toward external users. Management accounting is not bound by the externally imposed rules of financial reporting. Furthermore, it tends to be more subjective and uses both financial and nonfinancial measures, whereas financial accounting provides objective financial information. Finally, management accounting provides more detail than financial accounting, and it tends to be broader and multidisciplinary.

**3. Provide a brief historical description of management accounting.**

Most of the product-costing and internal accounting procedures used in the 20th century were developed between 1880 and 1925. By 1925, management accounting procedures emphasized inventory costing, stemming from the emphasis on external reporting. In the 1950s and 1960s, some effort was made to improve the managerial usefulness of traditional cost systems. In recent years, significant efforts have been made to radically change the nature and practice of management accounting, largely in response to some dramatic changes in the competitive environment.

**4. Identify and explain recent developments affecting management accounting.**

Management accounting must provide information that allows managers to focus on customer value, total quality management, and time-based competition. To this end, information about value-chain activities and customer sacrifice (such as postpurchase costs) must be collected and made available. Activity-based management is a major innovative response to the demand for more accurate and relevant management accounting information. Additionally, managers must decide on the strategic position of the organization. One of two positions is usually emphasized—either cost leadership or product differentiation. Which position is chosen can affect the nature of the management accounting information system.

### 5. Describe the role of management accountants in an organization.

Management accountants are responsible for identifying, collecting, measuring, analyzing, preparing, interpreting, and communicating information used by management to achieve the basic objectives of the organization. Management accountants need to be sensitive to the information needs of managers. Management accountants serve as staff members of the organization and are responsible for providing information; they are usually intimately involved in the management process as valued members of the management team.

### 6. Explain the importance of ethical behaviour for managers and management accountants.

Management accounting aids managers in their efforts to improve the economic performance of the organization. Unfortunately, some managers have overemphasized the economic dimension and have engaged in unethical and illegal actions. Many of these actions have relied on the management accounting system to bring about and even support that unethical behaviour. To emphasize the importance of the ever-present constraint of ethical behaviour on profit-maximizing behaviour, this text presents ethical issues in many of the problems appearing at the end of each chapter.

### 7. Identify the different professional accounting designations available for management accountants.

There are three certifications available in Canada: the CMA, the CA, and the CGA. The CMA is a certification designed especially for management accountants. The CA is primarily intended for those practising public accounting but is held by many leading management accountants. Holders of the CGA designation include both public and management accountants.

## Key Terms

Accounting Standards Board 9
Activity-based cost management
   information system 4
Activity-based management 12
Certified General Accountant
   (CGA) 21
Certified Management Accountant
   (CMA) 20
Chartered Accountant (CA) 21
Continuous improvement 4
Controller 18
Controlling 6
Customer value 12
Decision making 6

Electronic business (e-business) 17
Electronic commerce (e-commerce) 17
Employee empowerment 5
Ethical behaviour 19
External linkages 13
Feedback 6
Financial accounting information
   system 9
Industrial value chain 13
Internal linkages 13
Internal value chain 13
Line positions 17
*Management Accounting Guidelines* 10

Management accounting
   information system 3
Performance reports 6
Planning 5
Postpurchase costs 12
Staff positions 17
Strategic cost management 12
Strategic decision making 5
Supply chain management 13
Total product 12
Total quality management 16
Treasurer 18
Value chain 13

## Questions for Writing and Discussion

1. What is a management accounting information system?

2. Describe the inputs, processes, and outputs of a management accounting information system.

3. What are the three objectives of a management accounting information system?

4. What types of organizations need management accounting information systems?

5. Management accounting concepts apply only to manufacturing operations. Do you agree with this statement? Explain.

6. Who are the users of management accounting information?

7. What is management accounting information used for?

8. Should a management accounting system provide both financial and nonfinancial information? Explain.

9. What is meant by continuous improvement?

10. Describe what is meant by employee empowerment.

11. Explain why operational (nonmanagement) workers need management accounting information.

12. Describe the connection between planning, feedback, and controlling.

13. What role do performance reports play with respect to the control function?

14. How do management accounting and financial accounting differ?

15. Explain the role of financial reporting in the development of management accounting. Why has this role changed in recent years?

16. What is activity-based management? Why is it important?

17. Explain the meaning of customer value. How is focusing on customer value changing management accounting?

18. What is the internal value chain? Why is it important?

19. What is the industrial value chain? Why is it important?

20. Explain why today's management accountant must have a cross-functional perspective.

21. What is supply chain management? Explain its relationship to the industrial value chain.

22. What is e-business? Explain why it is important for a management accountant to understand e-business.

23. Discuss the relationship of time-based competition and management accounting information.

24. What is the difference between a staff position and a line position?

25. The controller should be a member of the top management staff. Do you agree or disagree? Explain.

26. What is the role of the controller in an organization? Describe some of the activities over which he or she has control.

27. What is ethical behaviour? Is it possible to teach ethical behaviour in a management accounting course?

28. Companies with higher ethical standards will experience a higher level of economic performance than companies with lower or poor ethical standards. Do you agree? Why or why not?

29. What are the three accounting designations in Canada? Can a holder of any of these designations practise management accounting?

# Exercises

**1–1**

Management
Accounting
Information System

LO1

Spreadsheet

The items that follow are associated with a management accounting information system.

a. Surveying customers to assess postpurchase costs
b. Incurrence of postpurchase costs
c. Costing out products
d. Assigning the cost of labour to a product
e. Report showing the cost of a product
f. Measuring the cost of quality
g. Repairing a defective part
h. Providing information for planning and control
i. Designing a product
j. Measuring the cost of design
k. A budget that shows how much should be spent on design activity
l. Using output information to make a decision
m. Usage of materials
n. A report comparing the actual costs of quality with the expected costs of quality

**Required:**
Classify the items into one of the following categories:
1. Inputs
2. Processes
3. Outputs
4. System objectives

**1–2**

Management
Accounting versus
Financial Accounting

LO2

The actions that follow are associated with a company's accounting information system.

a. Preparing financial reports that comply with generally accepted accounting principles.
b. Preparing a report that details profit by product.
c. Voluntarily reporting environmental costs to potential and existing investors.
d. Preparing a budget for direct materials purchases.
e. Reporting on the trends in defect rates to the plant manager.
f. Disclosing off-balance sheet financing in the company's annual report.
g. Researching to determine how to report an uninsured facility destroyed by flood.
h. Determining the cost of producing a new product.
i. Amortizing an asset using its historical cost.
j. Assessing the cost of making versus buying a component.
k. Preparing a budget that shows how much should be spent on design activity.
l. Reporting the value of land to investors using its historical cost.
m. Determining how to consolidate the financial reports of two subsidiaries.
n. Preparing a report that compares the actual costs of quality with the expected costs of quality.

**Required:**
Classify the above actions as belonging to either management accounting or financial accounting.

**1–3**

Choose the best answer for each of the following.

1. Most of the product costing and management accounting procedures used in the twentieth century were developed
   a. between 1929 and 1940.
   b. between 1880 and 1925.
   c. between 1950 and 1970.
   d. by the Accounting Standards Board in 1905.

2. After 1925, the driving force for the design of cost accounting systems was
   a. the stock market crash of 1929.
   b. the need for strategic planning.
   c. financial reporting.
   d. the need for sound cost information for internal decision making.
   e. None of the above.

3. In the 1980s and 1990s, many recognized that
   a. the efforts in the 1950s and 1960s to improve the managerial usefulness of conventional cost systems were entirely successful.
   b. the cost of more detailed cost systems exceeded their benefits.
   c. the traditional management accounting system was often no longer serving managerial needs.
   d. more accurate product costing was needed.
   e. All of the above are true.
   f. Only c and d are true.

**1–4**

Choose the best answer for each of the following:

1. Management accounting is best characterized by which of the following statements?
   a. It produces (principally) objective and verifiable financial information.
   b. It has a historical orientation.
   c. It focuses on overall company performance, providing an aggregated viewpoint.
   d. It is subject to generally accepted accounting principles.
   e. None of the above.

2. The current focus of management accounting can best be described as
   a. a system that achieves relevance by making financial accounting information more useful to internal users.
   b. having emphasis on activity-based costing and process value analysis.
   c. lacking a customer orientation.
   d. having emphasis on assigning manufacturing costs to products so that inventory cost can be reported to external users.
   e. All of the above.

3. Which of the following is not part of the current focus of management accounting?
   a. It emphasizes the use of cost information for strategic decision making.
   b. It measures and reports quality costs as well as nonfinancial measures of quality such as defect rates.
   c. It emphasizes the use of aggregated average cost information for individual products.
   d. It tries to determine why activities are performed and how well they are performed.
   e. None of the above.

**1–5**

*Current Focus of Management Accounting*

**LO4**

Match the following items:

1. Continuous reduction in cost
2. Linked set of value-creating activities
3. Using cost data to identify superior strategies
4. Selling over the Internet
5. A product's total tangible and intangible benefits
6. Suppliers and customers
7. Flow of materials from upstream to downstream
8. Internal value chain
9. Zero defects
10. Realization of less sacrifice
11. Activity-based costing and process value analysis

a. Strategic cost management
b. Total quality management
c. Internal linkages
d. Activity-based management
e. Customer value
f. E-business
g. Industrial value chain
h. External linkages
i. Total product
j. Supply chain management
k. Efficiency

**1–6**

*Line versus Staff*

**LO5**

The job responsibilities of two employees of Barney Manufacturing follow.

*Joan Dennison, Cost Accounting Manager.* Joan is responsible for measuring and collecting costs associated with the manufacture of the garden hose product line. She is also responsible for preparing periodic reports comparing the actual costs with planned costs. These reports are provided to the production line managers and the plant manager. Joan helps explain and interpret the reports.

*Steven Swasey, Production Manager.* Steven is responsible for the manufacture of the high-quality garden hose. He supervises the line workers, helps develop the production schedule, and is responsible for seeing that production quotas are met. He is also held accountable for controlling manufacturing costs.

**Required:**
Identify Joan and Steven as line or staff and explain your reasons.

**1–7**

*Ethical Behaviour*

**LO6**

Consider the following scenario:

*Manager:* "If I can reduce my costs by $40,000 during this last quarter, my division will show a profit that is 10 percent above the planned level, and I will receive a $10,000 bonus. However, given the projections for the fourth quarter, that does not look promising. I really need that $10,000. I know one way I can qualify. All I have to do is lay off my three most expensive salespeople. After all, most of the orders are in for the fourth quarter, and I can always hire new sales personnel at the beginning of the next year."

**Required:**
What is the right choice for the manager to make? Why did the ethical dilemma arise? Is there any way to redesign the accounting reporting system to discourage the type of behaviour that this manager is contemplating?

**1–8**

*Ethical Issues*

**LO6**

Assess and comment on each of the following statements that have appeared in newspaper editorials:

a. Business students come from all segments of society. If they have not been taught ethics by their families and by their elementary and secondary schools, there is little effect a business school can have.
b. Sacrificing self-interest for the collective good won't happen unless a majority of Canadians also accept this premise.
c. Competent executives manage people and resources for the good of society. Monetary benefits and titles are simply the byproducts of doing a good job.
d. Unethical organizations and individuals, like high rollers in Las Vegas, are eventually wiped out financially.

# Problems

**1–9**

*Employee Empowerment*

LO1

Duffy Tool and Stamping has formed "excellence teams" made up of production line employees. These teams have been given the charge to improve production processes and enhance employee safety. The teams follow a very structured problem-solving methodology and have managed to make numerous improvements in production as well as safety. During a six-year period, pretax profits increased each year. Duffy's management largely credits the excellence teams for the cost reductions and increased profits.

Another company, Grand Rapids Spring and Wire Products, has formed minicompanies within its factory. The objective of minicompanies is to have each employee assume ownership of his or her work. Each minicompany has its own suppliers and customers (all within the factory). Furthermore, each minicompany is assigned its own support people: accountants, engineers, marketing people, and so on. The individuals within the minicompany are given responsibility for developing and maintaining good relations with their suppliers and customers, identifying problems, and developing and implementing solutions to those problems. The focus of each minicompany is on quality, cost, delivery, safety, and morale. The company has successfully created a quality culture, achieved a reputation for being a competitive, world-class manufacturer, and has become "a learning organization."

**Required:**
1. What are the objectives of excellence teams and minicompanies? Did the companies achieve these objectives?
2. Do you think that employee empowerment is a good idea? Explain your answer. If yes, do you see any disadvantages? Explain.
3. What role, if any, does management accounting information have in employee empowerment?
4. What do you suppose is meant by the phrase "quality culture"? What is meant by "a learning organization?"

**1–10**

*The Managerial Process*

LO1

Each of the following scenarios requires the use of accounting information to carry out one or more of the following managerial activities: planning, control (including performance evaluation), or decision making. Identify the managerial activity or activities that are applicable for each scenario, and indicate the role of accounting information in the activity.

*A. Water-bottling Company Manager:* "A water-testing facility approached me recently and offered us its entire range of tests. It provided a price list revealing the amount it would charge us for each test. I need to know what it costs our company to perform the individual tests in-house to assess the feasibility of accepting the offer and perhaps suggest some price adjustments on some of the tests."

*B. Operating Manager:* "This report indicates that we have 30 percent more defects than originally targeted. An investigation into the cause has revealed the problem. We were using a lower-quality material than expected, and the waste has been higher than normal. By using material of the quality originally specified, we can reduce the defects to the planned level."

*C. Divisional Manager:* "Our market share has increased because of higher-quality products. Current projections indicate that we should sell 25 percent more units than last year. I want a projection of the effect this increase in sales will have on profits. I also want to know our expected cash receipts and cash expenditures on a month-by-month basis. I have a feeling that some short-term borrowing may be necessary."

*D. Plant Manager:* "Foreign competitors are producing goods with lower costs and delivering them more rapidly than we can to customers in our markets. We need to decrease the cycle time and increase the efficiency of our manufacturing process. There are two proposals that should help us accomplish these goals, both of which involve investing in computer-aided manufacturing. I need to know the future cash flows associated with each system and the effect each system has on unit costs and cycle time."

*E. Marketing Manager:* "At the last board meeting, we established an objective of earning a 25 percent return on sales. I need to know how many units of our product we need to sell to meet this objective. Once I have the estimated sales in units, we need to outline a promotional campaign that will take us where we want to be. However, in order to compute the targeted sales in units, I need to know the expected unit price and a lot of cost information."

*F. Manager (Health Minister):* "Perhaps the Victoria Hospital should be closed since health care costs are mounting and we cannot support all the health facilities in the province. While other hospitals in the city have had a tough time breaking even, Victoria's deficit has been larger than most. I want to know what costs can be avoided if Victoria shuts down. I want some assessment of the impact on the other health services we offer and on other hospitals."

## 1–11

**Customer Value; Strategic Positioning**

**LO4**

Nadira Persaud has decided to purchase a personal computer. She has narrowed the choices to two: Drantex and Confiar. Both brands have the same processing speed, 6.4 gigabytes of hard-disk capacity, a 3.5-inch disk drive, and a CD-ROM drive, and each comes with the same basic software support package. Both come from mail-order companies with good reputations. The selling price for each is identical. After some review, Nadira discovers that the cost of operating and maintaining a Drantex computer over a three-year period is estimated to be $300. For the Confiar machine, the operating and maintenance cost is $600. The sales agent for Drantex emphasized the lower operating and maintenance costs. The agent for Confiar, however, emphasized the service reputation of the product and the faster delivery time (a Confiar can be purchased and delivered one week sooner than a Drantex). Based on all the information, Nadira has decided to buy Confiar.

**Required:**
1. What is the total product purchased by Nadira?
2. How does the strategic positioning differ for the two companies?
3. When asked why she decided to buy the Confiar machine, Nadira responds, "I think that Confiar offers more value than Drantex." What are the possible sources of this greater value? What implications does this have for the management accounting information system?
4. Suppose that Nadira's decision was prompted mostly by the desire to receive the computer quickly. Informed that it was losing sales because of the longer time it was taking to produce and deliver its products, the management of the company producing the Drantex PC decided to improve delivery performance by improving its internal processes. These improvements decreased the number of defective units and the time required to produce its product.

Consequently, delivery time and costs both decreased, and the company was able to lower its prices for the Drantex. Explain how these actions translate into strengthening the competitive position of the Drantex PC relative to the Confiar PC. Also discuss the implications for the management accounting information system.

**1–12**

Ethical Issues

LO6

The Alert Company is a closely held investment service group that has been very successful over the past five years, consistently providing most members of the top management group with bonuses equivalent to 50 percent of their salaries (commonly called "50 percent bonuses"). In addition, both the chief financial officer and the chief executive officer have received 100 percent bonuses. Alert expects this trend to continue.

Recently, Alert's top management group, which holds 35 percent of the outstanding shares of common stock, has learned that a major corporation is interested in acquiring Alert. Alert's management is concerned that this corporation may make an attractive offer to the other shareholders and that management would be unable to prevent the takeover. If the acquisition occurs, this executive group is uncertain about continued employment in the new corporate structure. As a consequence, the management group is considering changes to several accounting policies and practices that, although not in accordance with generally accepted accounting principles, would make the company a less attractive acquisition. Management has told Roger Deerling, Alert's controller, to implement some of these changes. Roger has also been informed that Alert's management does not intend to disclose these changes immediately to anyone outside the top management group.

**Required:**
Using the standards of ethical conduct for management accountants, evaluate the changes that Alert's management is considering and discuss the specific steps that Roger should take to resolve the situation. (US CMA adapted)

**1–13**

Ethical Issues

LO6

Webson Manufacturing Company produces component parts for the airline industry and has recently undergone a major computer system conversion. Michael Darwin, the controller, has established a troubleshooting team to alleviate accounting problems that have occurred since the conversion. Michael has chosen Maureen Hughes, assistant controller, to head the team that will include Bob Randolph, cost accountant; Cynthia Wells, financial analyst; Marjorie Park, general accounting supervisor; and George Crandall, financial accountant.

The team has been meeting weekly for the last month. Maureen insists on being part of all the team conversations in order to gather information, make the final decision on any ideas or actions that the team develops, and prepare a weekly report for Michael. She has also used this team as a forum to discuss issues and disputes about him and other members of Webson's top management team. At last week's meeting, Maureen told the team that she thought a competitor might purchase Webson's common stock because she had overheard Michael talking about this on the telephone. As a result, most of Webson's employees now informally discuss the sale of Webson's common stock and how it will affect their jobs.

**Required:**
Is Maureen Hughes's discussion with the team about the prospective sale of Webson unethical? Discuss, citing specific standards of ethical conduct for management accountants to support your position. (US CMA adapted)

**1–14**

Not-for-Profit
Organization

LO5

The Board of Directors of the Royal Montreal Orchestra was grappling with potential budget cuts and their impact on the orchestra's devoted fans. At a special meeting of the Board, one of the directors commented that no one on the Board had extensive management accounting training and recommended that they bring in a management accounting consultant.

Another member of the Board stated the following:

*Keep those accountants out. First, this is a cultural organization, and accountants don't understand what we are grappling with: they only understand the numbers. Second, it is important to keep our organization dominated by our strategy, and accountants do not understand strategy. Third, we are not here to make a profit, and the training of accountants has to do with profit and how to measure it. We would probably have had to shut down many years ago if accountants were involved in our difficult decision-making process.*

*I suggest that we keep our orchestra at last year's size. We cannot afford to have a substandard orchestra. If we cut salaries this year, we risk losing our best talents. Let's keep our expenditure side untouched, and hope that our revenue side will catch up.*

**Required:**

1. Comment on the role of management accountants in cultural and not-for-profit organizations. Do you agree with the Board member's statement regarding management accountants?

2. Comment on the Board member's statement regarding budgeted expenditures and revenues. Do you agree with her point of view?

# Cost Accumulation and Product Costing

Part 1 deals with cost accumulation and product costing. Systems of cost accumulation and product costing are concerned with the determination of costs for different purposes. The costs accumulated and recorded by a management accounting cost system form the foundation for inventory valuation and income measurement, for decision making, and for planning and control.

**Part 1** primarily addresses the product costing ideas of cost assignment and cost measurement using the key cost concepts of traceability and activity cost behaviour. The difficulty of product costing when costs are indirect and common, with low traceability to products, is carefully considered. How managers use cost information will affect the choices made when developing a product costing system. These uses—costs for decision making and for planning and control—are the background for the cost assignment and cost measurement alternatives examined in Part 1.

**Chapter 2** introduces basic cost and management accounting concepts and terminology. Cost assignment is based on an attempt to trace the cost to its most logical cause or driver. The degree to which costs can be identified with particular activities, departments, processes, or products is a central concern. Some costs are more difficult to trace to activities, departments, processes, or products; these are considered indirect and common costs. The problem of assigning indirect and common costs—the overhead cost allocation problem—is briefly discussed in Chapter 2, and discussed further in later chapters in Part 1. A solid understanding of Chapter 2 is essential for the topics that follow.

**Chapter 3** introduces activity cost behaviour— the basis for many costing decisions and the core of decision making and of planning and control. Activity cost behaviour is concerned with how costs change with activity levels. A cost behaviour model based on the concepts of fixed and variable costs is examined. Chapter 3 covers several methods for estimating the activity cost behaviour model.

**Chapter 4** is a comprehensive discussion of activity based costing—a discussion embracing both functional-based and activity-based approaches. Cases where costs are not easily traceable to products or services are given particular attention. For example, costs not directly traceable to a particular product can be assigned in many different ways if there is no predominant cause and effect relationship between cost and product. Some methods of cost assignment are more useful than others; some methods can be misleading. When common costs are fixed and insensitive to changes in volume, as is the case in many high-tech environments, any cost allocation may be arbitrary.

Many companies with multiple products and joint facilities have adopted activity-based costing (ABC) systems. Chapter 4 provides a full discussion of ABC and its application to the service sector. The chapter also examines when activity-based costing is more applicable.

**Chapters 5 and 6** deal with specific cost systems: job costing and process costing. The main theme of these two chapters is how costing systems differ depending on the way the production activity is organized. These chapters also illustrate some of the mechanics of product costing.

**Chapter 7** examines other cost allocation questions and several approaches for cost allocation. Chapter 7 completes the discussion of product costing.

## *The Cost Allocation Problem*

Consider the following examples:

- During a severe recession a heavy-equipment manufacturer found that its costs (per unit) were much higher than during an earlier boom period. Why? It became clear that some costs were insensitive to volume changes and were fixed costs. Fixed costs were spread over fewer units during the recession, which resulted in a substantially higher per unit cost. Yet prices had to be lower in order to attract sales during the recession. Conversely, the fixed costs were spread over a larger volume of products during boom periods, and the fixed cost per unit was much lower. Yet prices could be set much higher since the company could not cope with the demand during the boom.

- A company found that it could not compete on price for a particular product against smaller, less efficient manufacturers. Why? The cost accounting department was producing cost figures based on an allocation method that apparently overcharged indirect and common costs to this particular product and undercharged other products not produced by their competition.

- A company installed a product deletion program for unprofitable products. As unprofitable products were deleted, some profitable products gradually showed lower profits and eventually losses. Why did this happen? Common costs were allocated among products to determine product profitability; the elimination of apparently unprofitable products did not eliminate the allocated common costs. These common costs now had to be spread over fewer products, making the remaining products less profitable.

In the above examples, the product costing system was not providing the information managers needed. Allocation challenges due to indirect and common costs, coupled with the increase in fixed costs in modern business organizations, require a careful approach to cost accumulation and allocation. Chapters 2 and 4 emphasize the *why*, *when*, and *how* of cost allocation. Chapters 5 to 7 focus on the *how* of allocation in common cost accounting systems.

# Basic Management Accounting Concepts

## Learning Objectives

After studying Chapter 2, you should be able to:

1. Explain the cost assignment process.

2. Define tangible and intangible products, and explain why there are different product cost definitions.

3. Prepare income statements for manufacturing and service organizations.

4. Outline the differences between functional-based and activity-based management accounting systems.

# Scenario

Kaylin Johnson, manager of Perry Electronics Division, scheduled a visit with the division's controller, Randy McManus, to address some issues discussed in the most recent executive meeting. The following conversation was recorded.[1]

**Kaylin**: "Randy, you've been my controller for ten years. You, more than anyone, should be able to respond to some of the concerns expressed at our last executive meeting. Specifically, we have engineers, production managers, and marketing managers who are no longer comfortable with our cost accounting system. Our continuous improvement and total quality management programs have been underway for two years, and yet we have no clear picture of the effect

they are having on our financial performance. Customer demand pushes us to create new technology with increased capabilities. Our traditional product costing and cost accounting methods seem at a loss to provide the financial information we need. How do I know if the changes we are making in our processes are beneficial?"

**Randy**: "There is no question that there is substance to your concerns. Our current cost accounting system does not have the capability to trace costs to activities and processes. Our costing approach overemphasizes direct labour and its use to trace costs to cost objects. I am afraid that our system simply cannot provide very accurate or useful cost information to support continuous improvement or total quality management."

**Kaylin**: "Does this lack of accuracy extend to product costing? I look at

our reports and I see product costs reported to the fourth decimal place, which seems to imply great accuracy. I have managers who are saying that these costs are almost useless—that they really do not reflect the differences in product attributes such as colours, capabilities, packaging, and service."

**Randy**: "Well, I am pretty comfortable that in the aggregate our product costs are accurate. What we report on our balance sheet and income statements is pretty much on target. However, I'm not as confident that our cost assignment procedures allow us to make strong statements about individual product profitability. Many of the costs are assigned using assumed relationships and may not reflect a cause-and-effect relationship."

**Kaylin**: "If what you're saying is correct, how can we rely on the individual costs for decision making? For example, can we use them to help us price our products and determine the right product mix? Can these costs be used to help us improve product designs? And how do we know if the quality improvements we are making are really reducing product costs as they are claiming? I am also interested in tracking process costs over time to see if the continuous improvement initiatives are really working. There must be some way we can trace the effects of these actions to products and processes—preferably before we commit to them."

**Randy**: "Well, the points you make are good. First, we shouldn't mistake precision for accuracy. Reporting a number to the fourth decimal place doesn't mean that the costs have been assigned correctly. And if these costs are not assigned correctly, relying on them for pricing and design decisions could be disastrous. We don't know the real costs of the product differences you mentioned, nor do we know the real cost effects of our quality and continuous improvement initiatives."

**Kaylin**: "Well, Randy, something must be done. Can we improve the accuracy of our product costing? We must know how much each product is costing. It is also vital to have accurate cost information about our improvement activities. It seems to me that we need to learn more about costs and then make decisions that bear directly on the costs. Understanding the nature of costs is fundamental to good management, and I need your help. After all, if we are going to pursue continuous improvement, we must know where we are and what we can do to make things better."

**Questions to Think About**
1. What is meant by product-costing accuracy?
2. How will increasing the accuracy of product costing improve decision making?
3. Why does Randy feel that the division's product costs are not very accurate?
4. Is assigning costs accurately as important for services as it is for tangible products?

## Cost Assignment: Direct Tracing, Driver Tracing, and Allocation

**Objective 1**

Explain the cost assignment process.

To study management accounting, it is necessary to understand the meaning of *cost* and the associated cost terminology. Assigning costs to products, services, and other objects of managerial interest is one of the principal objectives of a management accounting information system. Increasing the accuracy of assignments produces higher-quality information, which can then be used to make better decisions. For example, Lord Corporation, a producer of products that reduce vibration and noise, found that more accurate cost assignments produced better pricing decisions and significant increases in profits.[2] However, before discussing the cost assignment process, we first need to define what we mean by "cost" and more fully describe its managerial importance.

### Cost

**cost**

The cash or cash equivalent value sacrificed for goods and services that are expected to bring a current or future benefit to the organization.

**Cost** is the cash or cash-equivalent value sacrificed for goods and services that are expected to bring a current or future benefit to the organization. We say *cash equivalent* because noncash resources can be exchanged for the desired goods or services. For example, it may be possible to exchange equipment for materials used in production. In effect, we can think of cost as a dollar measure of the resources used to achieve a given benefit. In striving to produce a current or future benefit,

---

1. Many of the issues described in the scenario were confronted by two subsidiaries of United Technologies: Carrier and Otis Elevator. Their experience is described in greater detail under the service category at www.abctech.com/successes.

2. Alan W. Rupp, "ABC: A Pilot Approach," *Management Accounting* (January 1995): pp. 50-55.

managers should make every effort to minimize the cost required to achieve this benefit. Reducing the cost required to achieve a given benefit means that an operation is becoming more efficient. Costs, however, must not only be reduced but should be managed strategically. For example, managers should have the objective of providing the same (or greater) customer value for a lower cost than their competitors. In this way, the company's strategic position is improved, and a competitive advantage created.

Managers should also understand what is meant by *opportunity cost*. **Opportunity cost** is the benefit given up or sacrificed when one alternative is chosen over another. For example, a company may invest $100,000 in inventory for a year instead of investing the capital in a productive investment that would yield a 12 percent rate of return. The opportunity cost of the capital tied up in inventory is $12,000 ($0.12 \times \$100,000$) and is part of the cost of carrying the inventory.

Costs are incurred to produce future benefits. In a profit-making company, future benefits usually mean revenues. As costs are used up in the production of revenues, they are said to expire. Expired costs are called **expenses**. In each period, expenses are deducted from revenues in the income statement to determine the period's profit. For a company to remain in business, revenues must consistently exceed expenses; moreover, the income earned must be large enough to satisfy the owners of the company. Thus, cost and price are related in the sense that price must exceed cost such that sufficient income is earned.

Furthermore, lowering price increases customer value by lowering customer sacrifice, and the ability to lower price is connected to the ability to lower costs. Hence, managers need to know cost and trends in cost. Usually, however, knowing cost really means knowing what something or some object costs. Assigning costs to determine the cost of this object is therefore critical in providing this information to managers.

## Cost Objects

Management accounting systems are structured to measure and assign costs to entities, called cost objects. A **cost object** is any item—such as a product, a customer, a department, a project, an activity, and so on—for which costs are measured and assigned. For example, if we want to determine what it costs to produce a bicycle, then the cost object is the bicycle. If we want to determine the cost of operating a maintenance department within a plant, then the cost object is the maintenance department. If the objective is to determine the cost of developing a new toy, then the cost object is the new toy development project.

In recent years, activities have emerged as important cost objects. An **activity** is a basic unit of work performed within an organization. It can also be defined as an aggregation of actions within an organization useful to managers for purposes of planning, controlling, and decision making.

Activities not only act as cost objects but also play a prominent role in assigning costs to other cost objects. Examples of activities include setting up equipment for production, moving materials and goods, purchasing parts, billing customers, paying bills, maintaining equipment, expediting orders, designing products, and inspecting products. Notice that an activity is described by an action verb (for example, paying and designing) joined with an object (for example, bills and products) that receives the action. Notice also that the action verb and the object reveal very specific goals.

## Accuracy of Assignments

Assigning costs *accurately* to cost objects is crucial. Our notion of accuracy is not evaluated based on knowledge of some underlying "true" cost. Rather, it is a rel-

---

**opportunity cost**
The benefit sacrificed or forgone when one alternative is chosen over another.

**expenses**
Expired costs.

**cost object**
Any item, such as products, departments, projects, activities, and so on, for which costs are measured and assigned.

**activity**
A basic unit of work performed within an organization. It can also be defined as an aggregation of actions within an organization useful to managers for purposes of planning, controlling, and decision making.

ative concept and has to do with the reasonableness and logic of the cost assignment methods used. The objective is to measure and assign as well as possible the cost of the resources consumed by a cost object.

Some cost assignment methods are clearly more accurate than others. For example, suppose you want to determine the cost of lunch for Elaine Day, a student who frequents Hideaway, an off-campus pizza parlour. One cost assignment approach is to count the number of customers Hideaway has between noon and 1:00 p.m. and then divide the total receipts earned during this period by this number of customers. Suppose that this comes out to $6.179 per lunchtime customer (note the three-decimal precision). Thus, based on this approach we would conclude that Elaine spends $6.179 per day for lunch. Another approach is to go with Elaine and *observe* how much she spends. Suppose that she has a slice of pizza and a medium drink each day, costing $3.49. It is not difficult to see which cost assignment is more accurate. The $6.179 cost assignment is distorted (despite its three-decimal precision) by the consumption patterns of other customers (cost objects). As it turns out, most lunchtime clients order the luncheon special for $6.99 (a mini-pizza, salad, and medium drink).

Distorted cost assignments can produce erroneous decisions and bad evaluations. For example, if a plant manager is trying to decide whether to continue producing power internally or to buy it from a local utility company, then an accurate assessment of how much it is costing to produce the power is fundamental to the analysis. An overstatement of the cost of power production could suggest to the manager that the internal power department should be shut down in favour of external purchase, whereas a more accurate cost assignment might suggest the opposite. It is easy to see that bad cost assignments can prove to be costly. As the pizza example suggests, establishing a cause-and-effect relationship between the cost to be assigned and the cost object is the key to creating a reasonably accurate cost assignment.

### *Traceability*

**indirect costs**

Costs that cannot be traced to a cost object.

**direct costs**

Costs that can be easily and accurately traced to a cost object.

**traceability**

The ability to assign a cost directly to a cost object in an economically feasible way using a causal relationship.

The relationship of costs to cost objects can be exploited to help increase the accuracy of cost assignments. Costs are directly or indirectly associated with cost objects. **Indirect costs** are costs that cannot be easily and accurately traced to a cost object. **Direct costs** are those costs that can be easily and accurately traced to a cost object.[3] "Easily traced" means that the costs can be assigned in an economically feasible way, and "accurately traced" means that the costs are assigned using a *cause-and-effect relationship*. Thus, **traceability** is simply the ability to assign a cost to a cost object in an economically feasible way by means of a cause-and-effect relationship. The more costs that can be traced to the object, the greater the accuracy of the cost assignments. Establishing traceability is a key element in building accurate cost assignments.

It is possible for a particular cost item to be classified as both a direct cost and an indirect cost. Management accounting systems typically deal with many cost objects. It all depends on which cost object is the point of reference. For example, if a manufacturing plant is the cost object, then the cost of heating and cooling the manufacturing plant is a direct cost; however, if a product produced in the manufacturing plant is the cost object, then this utility cost is an indirect cost.

### *Methods of Tracing*

**tracing**

Assigning costs to a cost object using an observable measure of the cost object's resource consumption.

Traceability means that costs can be assigned easily and accurately, whereas **tracing** is the actual assignment of costs to a cost object using an *observable*

---

3. This definition of direct costs is based on the glossary of terms prepared by Computer Aided Manufacturing-International, Inc. (CAM-I). See Norm Raffish and Peter B.B. Turney, "Glossary of Activity-Based Management," *Journal of Cost Management* (Fall 1991): pp. 53-63.

**direct tracing**

The process of identifying costs that are specifically or physically associated with a cost object.

measure of the resources consumed by the cost object. Tracing costs to cost objects can occur in one of two ways: (1) direct tracing, or (2) driver tracing.

**Direct tracing** is the process of identifying and assigning costs that are specifically or physically associated with a cost object to that cost object. This is most often accomplished by *physical observation*. The pizza example illustrates the concept. The cost object is Elaine Day's lunch. By observing that she has a slice of pizza and a medium drink, we can assign the cost of $3.49. The cost is directly traceable to her. As a second example, let the cost object be a product: bicycles. The product uses both materials and labour. It is easy to observe how many wheels and other parts are used by the product and how many hours of labour it takes to produce each bicycle. Both material and labour usage are physically observable; therefore, their costs can be directly charged to a bicycle. In both examples, the cost objects are the exclusive consumers of the resources in question. Ideally, all costs should be charged to cost objects using direct tracing. Unfortunately, it is often the case that cost objects are not the exclusive consumers of resources. In such cases, we appeal to driver tracing to assign costs.

**driver tracing**

The use of drivers to assign costs to cost objects.

**drivers**

Factors that cause changes in resource usage, activity usage, costs, and revenues.

**Driver tracing** is the use of drivers to assign costs to cost objects. In a cost assignment context, **drivers** are observable causal factors that measure a cost object's resource consumption. Therefore, drivers are factors that cause changes in resource usage and thus have a cause-and-effect relationship with the costs associated with a cost object. For example, assume that Elaine Day and Martin Small go to lunch together. Elaine and Martin agree to share the cost of the lunch. They order a large pizza (divided into ten slices) for $11 and a pitcher of root beer (containing five glasses) for $2.50; Elaine also orders a small salad for $1.25. How much cost should be assigned to each person? Note that the two share the pizza and root beer, whereas the salad is a "resource" exclusive to Elaine. The cost of the salad is assigned by direct tracing ($1.25 to Elaine and $0 to Martin). To assign the costs of the pizza and root beer, drivers are chosen: slices of pizza and glasses of root beer, respectively. A rate is calculated per unit of resource (as measured by the drivers): $1.10 per slice of pizza ($11/10) and $0.50 per glass of root beer ($2.50/5). Next, usage of the driver is observed for each person (cost object). Assume that Martin eats six slices of pizza and drinks three glasses of root beer, with Elaine consuming the remainder. The cost per person is then calculated as follows:

|                            | Elaine  | Martin  |
| -------------------------- | ------- | ------- |
| Salad (direct tracing)     | $1.25   | $0.00   |
| Pizza (driver tracing)     |         |         |
| 4 slices @ $1.10           | 4.40    | —       |
| 6 slices @ $1.10           | —       | 6.60    |
| Root Beer (driver tracing) |         |         |
| 2 glasses @ $0.50          | 1.00    | —       |
| 3 glasses @ $0.50          | —       | 1.50    |
| Totals                     | $6.65   | $8.10   |

It is also important to understand that this simple pizza example of a shared resource directly extends into more complex management settings. The activity of inspecting products may be the "pizza" shared by precision surgical instruments produced in a plant. The cost of inspection can be assigned to individual instruments (the cost objects) using the number of inspection hours ("slices of pizza") consumed by each type of instrument. Consider as a second example the cost of a heart monitor used by cardiac patients (the cost object). The heart monitor is the "pizza," and monitoring hours used could be the "slices of pizza" chosen to assign the costs to cardiac patients. Thus, the tracing principles used in the pizza example relate directly to costing in realistic management environments.

Driver tracing is usually less precise than direct tracing. However, if the cause-and-effect relationship is sound, then a high degree of accuracy can be expected. Consider, for example, the driver: number of pizza slices. Suppose that the slices are not exactly equal in size and that Elaine chose to eat four of the smaller slices. Thus, her cost for pizza is really less than $4.40. Even so, if the difference in the size of the slices is not great, then we can still say that the cost is sufficiently accurate. Nonetheless, this illustrates the importance of how we select, specify, and measure drivers. We explore these issues in greater depth in Chapters 3 and 4. For now, it is sufficient to understand their role in cost assignment and that they can produce somewhat less accurate assignments than direct tracing. Of more immediate concern is the situation where cost objects are not exclusive consumers of resources and where no cause-and-effect relationship can be defined (or where defining a causal relationship would be cost-prohibitive).

### Assigning Indirect Costs

**allocation**

Assignment of indirect costs to cost objects.

Indirect costs are those costs that cannot be assigned to cost objects using either direct tracing or driver tracing. This occurs when no causal relationship exists between the cost and the cost object or when tracing is not economically feasible. Assignment of indirect costs to cost objects is called **allocation**. Since no causal relationship exists, allocating indirect costs is based on *convenience* or some *assumed* linkage. For example, consider the cost of heating and lighting a manufacturing plant in which five products are manufactured. Suppose that this utility cost is to be assigned to the five products. Clearly, it is difficult to see any causal relationship. A convenient way to allocate this cost is simply to assign it in proportion to the direct labour hours used by each product. Arbitrarily assigning indirect costs to cost objects reduces the overall accuracy of the cost assignments. Accordingly, the best costing policy may be to assign only direct (traceable) costs to cost objects. However, allocations of indirect costs may serve other purposes besides accuracy. For example, allocating indirect costs to products (a cost object) may be required to satisfy external reporting conventions. Nonetheless, most managerial uses of cost assignments are better served by accuracy; thus, at the very least, costs that are traced should be reported separately from costs that are allocated.

### Cost Assignment Summarized

We have seen three methods of assigning costs to cost objects: direct tracing, driver tracing, and allocation. These methods are illustrated in Exhibit 2–1. Of the three methods, direct tracing is the most accurate; it relies on physically observ-

**EXHIBIT** 2-1

Cost Assignment Methods

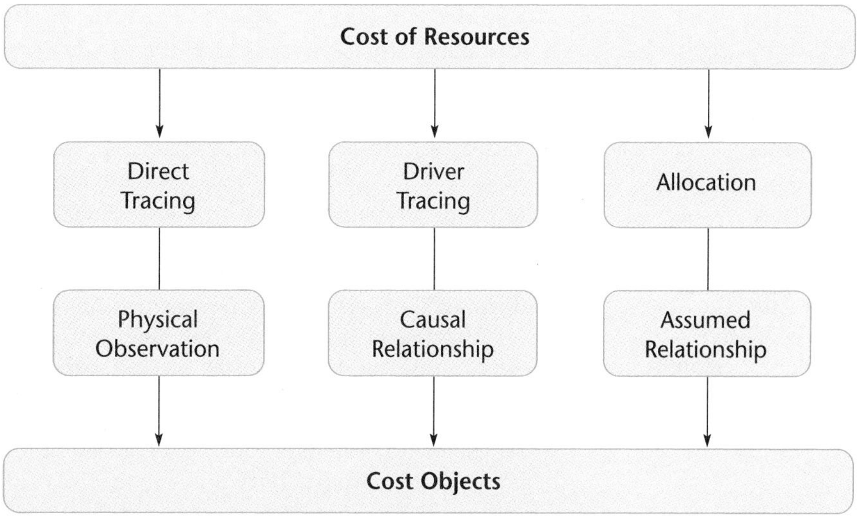

able, exclusive causal relationships. Direct tracing is followed by driver tracing in terms of cost assignment accuracy. Driver tracing relies on causal factors, called drivers, to assign costs to cost objects. The accuracy of driver tracing depends on the quality of the causal relationship described by the driver. Identifying drivers and assessing the quality of the causal relationship are much more costly than either direct tracing or allocation. In fact, one advantage of allocation is its simplicity and low cost of implementation. However, allocation is the least accurate cost assignment method: its use should therefore be minimized, and it should be avoided where possible. In many (maybe most) cases, the benefits of increased accuracy outweigh the additional measurement cost associated with driver tracing. This cost–benefit issue is discussed more fully later in the chapter. What it really entails is choosing among competing management accounting information systems.

## Product and Service Costs

### Objective 2

Define tangible and intangible products, and explain why there are different product cost definitions.

**tangible products**
Goods that are produced by converting raw materials through the use of labour and capital inputs such as plant, land, and machinery.

**services**
Tasks or activities performed for a customer using an organization's products or facilities.

**intangibility**
Buyers of services cannot see, feel, hear, or taste a service before it is bought.

**perishability**
Services cannot be stored for future use by the consumer.

**inseparability**
Producers of services and buyers of services must usually be in direct contact for an exchange to take place.

**heterogeneity**
There is a greater chance of variation in the performance of services than in the production of products.

The output of organizations represents one of the most important cost objects. There are two types of output: *tangible products* and *services*. **Tangible products** are goods produced by converting raw materials through the use of labour and capital inputs, such as plant, land, and machinery. Televisions, hamburgers, automobiles, computers, clothes, and furniture are examples of tangible products. **Services** are tasks or activities performed for a customer or an activity performed by a customer using an organization's products or facilities. Services are also produced using materials, labour, and capital inputs. Insurance coverage, medical care, dental care, funeral care, and accounting are examples of service activities performed for customers. Car rental, video rental, and skiing are examples of services where the customer uses an organization's products or facilities. Services differ from tangible products on four important dimensions: intangibility, perishability, inseparability, and heterogeneity.

- **Intangibility** means that buyers of services cannot see, feel, hear, or taste a service before it is bought. Thus, services are *intangible products*.
- **Perishability** means that services cannot be stored for future use by a consumer but must be consumed when performed. (There are also a few unusual cases where tangible goods cannot be stored.) Although services cannot be stored, some services, like plastic surgery, have long-term effects and need not be repeated for a given customer. Other services have short-term effects and generate repeat customers. Examples of repetitive services are janitorial services and dry cleaning.
- **Inseparability** means that producers of services and buyers of services must usually be in direct contact for an exchange to take place. In effect, services are often inseparable from their producers. For example, an eye examination requires both the patient and the optometrist to be present. However, producers of tangible products need not have direct contact with the buyers of their goods. Thus, buyers of automobiles never need to have contact with the engineers and assembly line workers who produce their automobiles.
- **Heterogeneity** means that there is a greater chance of variation in the performance of services than in the production of products. Service workers can be affected by the specific job they undertake, the mix of other individuals with whom they work, their education and experience, and personal factors such as home life.

These factors make providing a consistent level of service more difficult. The measurement of productivity and quality in a service company must be ongoing and sensitive to these factors. These differences affect the types of information managers need for planning, control, and decision making. Exhibit 2–2 illustrates the features associated with services, some of their derived properties, and how they interface with the management accounting system. Notice that accurate cost assignments, quality, and productivity are concerns shared by producers of services and producers of tangible products.

Organizations that produce tangible products are called *manufacturing* organizations. Those that produce intangible products are called *service* organizations. Managers of both types of organizations need to know how much individual products cost. Accurate product costs are vital for profitability analysis and for strategic decisions concerning product design, pricing, and product mix. Individual product cost can refer to either a tangible or an intangible product. Thus, when we discuss product costs, we are referring to both intangible and tangible products.

## Different Costs for Different Purposes

**product cost**
A cost assignment method that satisfies a well-specified managerial objective.

**Product cost** is a cost assignment that supports a well-specified managerial objective. Thus, what "product cost" means depends on the managerial objective being served. The product cost definition illustrates a fundamental cost management principle: "different costs for different purposes." We will look at three examples to illustrate this idea.

1. As a first example, suppose that management is interested in strategic profitability analysis. To support this objective, management needs information about all the revenues and costs associated with a product. In this case, a *value-chain product cost* is appropriate, because it accounts for all the costs necessary to assess strategic profitability. A company's *internal value chain* is the set of all activities required to design, develop, produce, market, distribute, and support a product. The internal value chain is illustrated in Exhibit 2–3. A value-chain product cost is obtained by first assigning costs to the set of activities that define the value chain and then assigning the cost of these activities to products.

EXHIBIT 2-2

Interface of Services with Management Accounting

| Feature | Derived Properties | Impact on Management Accounting |
|---|---|---|
| Intangibility | Services cannot be stored | No inventories |
| | No patent protection | Strong ethical code* |
| | Cannot display or communicate services | |
| | Prices difficult to set | Demand for more accurate cost assignment* |
| Perishability | Service benefits expire quickly | No inventories |
| | Services may be repeated often for one customer | Need for standards and consistent high quality* |
| Inseparability | Customer directly involved with production of service | Costs often accounted for by customer type* |
| | Centralized mass production of services difficult | Demand for measurement and control of quality to maintain consistency* |
| Heterogeneity | Wide variation in service product possible | Productivity and quality measurement and control must be ongoing* |
| | | Total quality management critical* |

* Many of these effects are also true of tangible products.

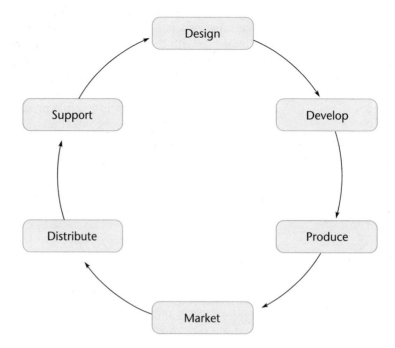

2. As a second example, suppose that the managerial objective is short-run or tactical profitability analysis. In this case, the costs of designing and developing may not be relevant—especially for existing products. A decision, for example, to accept or reject an order for an existing product would depend on the price offered by the potential customer and the costs of producing, marketing, distributing, and supporting the special order. Thus, only the operating activities within the value chain would be important. The assignment of the costs of these activities to the product defines an *operating product cost*.

3. As a third example, suppose that the managerial objective is external financial reporting. In this case, *traditional product costs* are needed. The rules and conventions that govern external financial reporting mandate that only production costs can be used in calculating product costs.

Exhibit 2–4 summarizes the three product cost examples. Other objectives may use still other product cost definitions.

## Product Costs and External Financial Reporting

One of the central objectives of a cost management system is the calculation of product costs for external financial reporting. For product-costing purposes, externally imposed conventions dictate that costs be classified in terms of the special purposes, or functions, they serve. Costs are subdivided into two major functional categories: production and nonproduction. **Production costs** are those costs associated with the manufacture of goods or the provision of services. **Nonproduction costs** are those costs associated with the functions of designing, developing, marketing, distribution, customer service, and general administration. The costs of marketing, distribution, and customer service are often placed into one general category called *selling costs*. The costs of designing, developing, and general administration are placed into a second general category called *administrative costs*.

For tangible goods, production and nonproduction costs are often referred to as *manufacturing costs* and *nonmanufacturing costs*, respectively. Production costs can be further classified as *direct materials*, *direct labour*, and *overhead*. Only these three cost elements are assigned to products for external financial reporting.

**production costs**

Costs associated with the manufacture of goods or the provision of services.

**nonproduction costs**

Costs associated with the functions of selling and administration.

## Direct Materials

**direct materials**
Materials that are traceable to the goods or services being produced.

**Direct materials** are those materials that are directly traceable to the goods or services being produced. The cost of these materials can be directly charged to products because we can use physical observation to measure the quantity consumed by each product. Materials that become part of a tangible product or those that are used in providing a service are usually classified as direct materials. Steel in an automobile, wood in furniture, alcohol in cologne, denim in jeans, braces for correcting teeth, surgical gauze for an operation, a casket for a funeral service, and food on an airline are all examples of direct materials.

## Direct Labour

**direct labour**
Labour that is traceable to the goods or services being produced.

**Direct labour** is the labour that is directly traceable to the goods or services being produced. As with direct materials, we can use physical observation to measure the quantity of labour used in a product or service. Employees who convert raw materials into a product or who provide a service to customers are classified as direct labour. Workers on an assembly line at General Motors, a chef in a restaurant, a surgical nurse attending an open-heart operation, and a pilot for Air Canada are all examples of direct labour.

## Overhead

**overhead**
All production costs other than direct materials and direct labour.

All production costs other than direct materials and direct labour are lumped into one category called **overhead**. In a manufacturing company, overhead is also known as *factory burden* or *manufacturing overhead*. The overhead cost category contains a wide variety of items. Many inputs other than direct labour and direct materials are needed to produce products. Examples include amortization on buildings and equipment, maintenance, supplies, supervision, material handling, power, property taxes, landscaping of factory grounds, and plant security.

**supplies**
Those materials necessary for production that do not become part of the finished product or that are not used in providing a service.

**Supplies** are generally those materials necessary for production that do not become part of the finished product or that are not used in providing a service. Dishwasher detergent in a fast-food restaurant and oil for production equipment are examples of supplies.

Direct materials that form an insignificant part of the final product are usually lumped into the overhead category as a special kind of indirect material. This approach is justified on the basis of cost and convenience. The cost of the tracing is greater than the benefit of increased accuracy. The glue used in furniture or toys is an example.

The cost of overtime for direct labourers is usually assigned to overhead as well. The rationale for doing so is that typically no particular production run can

**EXHIBIT   2-4**

Product Cost Definition

| Product Cost Definition | Value-Chain Product Costs | Operating Product Costs | Traditional Product Costs |
|---|---|---|---|
| | Research and Development | | |
| | Production | Production | Production |
| | Marketing | Marketing | |
| | Customer Service | Customer Service | |
| Managerial Objectives Served | Pricing Decisions Product-Mix Decisions Strategic Profitability Analysis | Strategic Design Decisions Tactical Profitability Analysis | External Financial Reporting |

be identified as the cause of the overtime. Accordingly, overtime cost is common to all production runs and is therefore an indirect manufacturing cost. Note that only the overtime cost is treated this way. If workers are paid an $8 regular rate and a $4 overtime premium, then only the $4 overtime premium is assigned to overhead. The $8 regular rate is still regarded as a direct labour cost. In certain cases, however, overtime is associated with a particular production run—for example, when a special order is taken while production is at 100 percent capacity. In such cases, it is appropriate to treat overtime premiums as a direct labour cost.

### Selling and Administrative Costs

**noninventoriable (period) costs**

Costs that are expensed in the period in which they are incurred.

There are two broad categories of nonproduction costs: selling costs and administrative costs. For external financial reporting, selling and administrative costs are *noninventoriable* or *period costs*. **Noninventoriable (period) costs** are expensed in the period in which they are incurred. Thus, none of these costs can be assigned to products or appear as part of the reported values of inventories on the balance sheet.

In a manufacturing organization, the level of these costs can be significant (often greater than 25 percent of sales revenue), and controlling them may bring greater cost savings than the same effort exercised in controlling production costs. For service organizations, the relative importance of selling and administrative costs depends on the nature of the service produced. Physicians and dentists, for example, do very little marketing and thus have very low selling costs. On the other hand, a grocery chain experimenting with alternative shopping and delivery technologies may incur substantial marketing costs.

**marketing (selling) costs**

The costs necessary to market and distribute a product or service.

**Marketing (selling) costs** are the costs necessary to market, distribute, and support a product or service. They are often referred to as *order-getting* and *order-filling costs*. Examples of selling costs include salaries and commissions of sales personnel, advertising, warehousing, shipping, and customer service. The first two items are examples of order-getting costs; the last three are order-filling costs.

**administrative costs**

All costs associated with the general administration of the organization that cannot be reasonably assigned to either marketing or production.

**Administrative costs** are all costs associated with research, development, and the general administration of the organization that cannot be reasonably assigned to either marketing or production. General administration has the responsibility of ensuring that the various activities of the organization are properly integrated so that the overall mission of the organization is realized. The president of the company, for example, is concerned with the efficiency of selling, production, and research and development as their respective roles are carried out. Proper integration of these functions is essential to maximize the overall profits of a company. Examples of general administrative costs are top executive salaries, legal fees, printing the annual report, and general accounting. Research and development costs are the costs associated with designing and developing new products.

### Prime and Conversion Costs

**prime cost**

The sum of direct materials cost and direct labour cost.

The production and nonproduction classifications give rise to some related cost concepts. The functional delineation between nonmanufacturing and manufacturing costs is essentially the basis for the concepts of noninventoriable costs and inventoriable costs—at least for the purposes of external reporting. Combinations of different production costs also produce the concepts of conversion costs and prime costs. **Prime cost** is the sum of direct materials cost and direct labour cost. **Conversion cost** is the sum of direct labour cost and overhead cost. For a manufacturing company, conversion cost can be interpreted as the cost of converting raw materials into a final product.

**conversion cost**

The sum of direct labour cost and overhead cost.

# External Financial Statements

**Objective 3**

Prepare income statements for manufacturing and service organizations.

For external reporting, costs are usually classified according to function. In preparing an income statement, production costs and selling and administrative costs are segregated from each other. They are segregated because production costs are viewed as product costs, and selling and administrative costs are viewed as period costs. Thus, production costs attached to the products sold are recognized as an expense (cost of sales) on the income statement. Production costs that are attached to products that are not sold are reported as inventory on the balance sheet. Selling and administrative expenses are viewed as costs of the period and must be deducted each and every period as expenses; therefore, they appear only on the income statement.

## Income Statement: Manufacturing Organization

**absorption costing**

A product-costing method that assigns all manufacturing costs to a product: direct materials, direct labour, variable overhead, and fixed overhead.

The income statement based on a functional classification for a manufacturing organization is displayed in Exhibit 2–5. This income statement follows the traditional format taught in an introductory financial accounting course. We usually refer to income computed following a functional classification as **absorption-costing** (full-costing) income, because all manufacturing costs are fully assigned to the product.

Under the absorption-costing approach, we segregate expenses according to function and then deduct expenses from revenues to arrive at income before taxes. As we can see in Exhibit 2–5, there are two major functional categories of expense: *cost of goods sold* and *operating expenses*. These categories correspond, respectively, to a company's manufacturing and nonmanufacturing expenses. **Cost of goods sold** is the cost of direct materials, direct labour, and overhead attached to the units sold. To compute the cost of goods sold, we must first determine the cost of goods manufactured.

**cost of goods sold**

The cost of direct materials, direct labour, and overhead attached to the units sold.

### Cost of Goods Manufactured

**cost of goods manufactured**

The total cost of goods completed during the current period.

The **cost of goods manufactured** represents the total cost of goods completed during the current period. The only costs assigned to goods completed are the manufacturing costs of direct materials, direct labour, and overhead. The details of this cost assignment are given in a supporting schedule, called the *statement of cost of goods manufactured*. An example of this supporting schedule for the income statement in Exhibit 2–5 is shown in Exhibit 2–6.

**EXHIBIT 2-5**

Income Statement for a Manufacturing Organization

| Income Statement: Manufacturing Organization For the Year Ended December 31, 2004 | | | |
|---|---|---|---|
| Sales | | | $2,800,000 |
| Less cost of goods sold: | | | |
| Beginning finished goods inventory | | $ 500,000 | |
| Add: Cost of goods manufactured | | 1,200,000 | |
| Goods available for sale | | $1,700,000 | |
| Less: Ending finished goods inventory | | 300,000 | 1,400,000 |
| Gross margin | | | $1,400,000 |
| Less operating expenses: | | | |
| Selling expenses | | $ 600,000 | |
| Administrative expenses | | 300,000 | 900,000 |
| Income before taxes | | | $ 500,000 |

**Statement of Cost of Goods Manufactured
For the Year Ended December 31, 2004**

| | | |
|---|---:|---:|
| Direct materials: | | |
|   Beginning inventory | $200,000 | |
|   Add: Purchases | 450,000 | |
|   Materials available | $650,000 | |
|   Less: Ending inventory | 50,000 | |
| Direct materials used | | $ 600,000 |
| Direct labour | | 350,000 |
| Manufacturing overhead: | | |
|   Indirect labour | $122,500 | |
|   Amortization | 177,500 | |
|   Rent | 50,000 | |
|   Utilities | 37,500 | |
|   Property taxes | 12,500 | |
|   Maintenance | 50,000 | 450,000 |
|     Total manufacturing costs added | | $1,400,000 |
| Add: Beginning work in process | | 200,000 |
|     Total manufacturing costs | | $1,600,000 |
| Less: Ending work in process | | 400,000 |
|     Cost of goods manufactured | | $1,200,000 |

Notice in Exhibit 2–6 that the total manufacturing costs added during the period are combined with the manufacturing costs found in beginning work in process, yielding total manufacturing costs to account for. The costs found in ending work in process are then deducted from total manufacturing costs to arrive at the cost of goods manufactured. If the cost of goods manufactured is for a single product, then we can compute the average unit cost by dividing the cost of goods manufactured by the units produced. For example, assume that the statement in Exhibit 2–6 was prepared for the production of bottles of perfume and that 480,000 bottles were completed during the period. The average unit cost is $2.50 per bottle ($1,200,000/480,000).

**Work in process** consists of all partly completed units found in production at a given point in time. Beginning work in process consists of the partly completed units on hand at the beginning of a period. Ending work in process consists of those on hand at the period's end. In the statement of cost of goods manufactured, the cost of these partly completed units is reported as the cost of beginning work in process and the cost of ending work in process. The cost of beginning work in process represents the manufacturing costs carried over from the prior period; the cost of ending work in process represents the manufacturing costs that will be carried over to the next period. In both cases, additional manufacturing costs must be incurred to complete the units in work in process.

**work in process**

All partly completed units found in production at a given point in time.

## Income Statement: Service Organization

An income statement for a service organization is shown in Exhibit 2–7. In a service organization, the cost of services sold is computed differently from the cost of goods sold in a manufacturing company. As the income statement reveals, there are no beginning or ending finished goods inventories. Unlike a manufacturing company, the service organization has no finished goods inventories—it is impossible to store services. Thus, in a direct comparison with manufacturing companies, cost of services sold would always correspond to cost of goods manufactured. Furthermore, as we see in Exhibit 2–7, the cost of services sold during

EXHIBIT 2-7

Income Statement for a
Service Organization

**Income Statement: Service Organization**
**For the Year Ended December 31, 2004**

| | | | |
|---|---|---:|---:|
| Sales | | | $300,000 |
| Less expenses: | | | |
| Cost of services sold: | | | |
| Beginning work in process | | $ 5,000 | |
| Service costs added: | | | |
| Direct materials | $ 40,000 | | |
| Direct labour | 80,000 | | |
| Overhead | 100,000 | 220,000 | |
| Total | | $225,000 | |
| Less: Ending work in process | | 10,000 | 215,000 |
| Gross margin | | | $ 85,000 |
| Less operating expenses: | | | |
| Selling expenses | | $ 8,000 | |
| Administrative expenses | | 22,000 | 30,000 |
| Income before taxes | | | $ 55,000 |

a period (equivalent to cost of goods manufactured) can be computed following the same format shown in Exhibit 2–6. Exhibit 2–7 reveals that it is possible to have work in process for services. For example, an architect may have drawings in process and an orthodontist may have numerous patients in various stages of process for braces.

# Types of Management Accounting Systems: A Brief Overview

**Objective** 4

Outline the differences between functional-based and activity-based management accounting systems.

**functional-based management (FBM) accounting system**

An accounting information system that emphasizes the use of functional organizational units to assign and manage costs.

**activity-based management (ABM) accounting system**

An accounting system that emphasizes the use of activities for assigning and managing costs.

**process**

A series of activities (operations) that are linked to perform a specific objective.

Management accounting systems can be broadly classified as *functional-based* and *activity-based*. Both functional-based and activity-based approaches are found in practice. **Functional-based management (FBM) accounting systems** were used throughout the 1900s and are still widely used in both the manufacturing and the service sectors. **Activity-based management (ABM) accounting systems** are much newer (developed within the final two decades of the 20th century). Activity-based cost management systems are also extensively used, and their use is increasing—particularly among organizations faced with product and customer diversity, more product complexity, shorter product life cycles, increased quality requirements, and intense competitive pressures.

## FBM versus ABM Accounting Systems

The general models for functional-based and activity-based management accounting systems are displayed in Exhibits 2–8 and 2–9. Notice that both models have two dimensions. The vertical dimension of the models describes how costs are assigned to cost objects like products and customers, whereas the horizontal dimension is concerned with how the systems try to improve operational efficiency and control costs. The central element or heart of the FBM model is functions; the corresponding element of the ABM model is activities. Functions are usually grouped into organizational units, such as departments or plants (for example, engineering, quality control, and assembly are functions organized as departments). Activities with a common objective are grouped together to form **processes**. For example, purchasing goods, receiving goods, and paying for goods received are major activities that define the procurement process. Comparing each dimension provides significant insight into how the two management accounting models differ.

Functional Based
Management Model

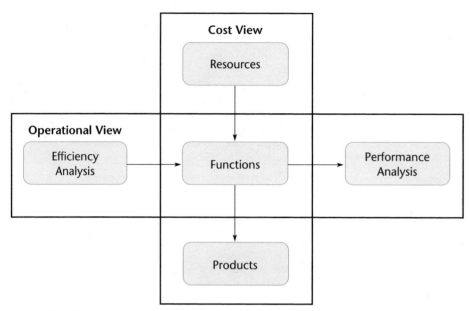

### FBM Cost View

In an FBM accounting system, resource costs are assigned to functional units and then to products. In assigning costs, both direct tracing and driver tracing are used, although in an FBM system, driver tracing uses only **production drivers** (also called **unit-level drivers**)—measures of consumption that are highly correlated with production output. Thus units of product or drivers that are highly correlated with units produced—such as direct labour hours, direct materials, and machine hours—are the only activity drivers assumed to be of importance. Because FBM systems use only drivers related to the production function to assign costs, this cost assignment approach is referred to as production- or **functional-based costing (FBC)**.

The production or unit-level drivers on which FBC relies are often not the only drivers that explain cause-and-effect relationships. Drivers other than production drivers that explain cause-and-effect relationships are referred to as **nonunit-level drivers**. For example, production drivers like units produced or direct labour hours may have nothing to do with the cost of purchasing raw materials. In reality, the number of purchase orders might be the appropriate measure of consumption by each product. Yet in an FBC system, purchasing costs would be assigned using a measure like units produced or direct labour hours. Cost assignments made in these cases must be classified as allocation (recall that allocation is cost assignment based on *assumed* linkages or convenience). Furthermore, if nonunit-level costs—such as purchasing—are significant, functional-based costing can be described as allocation-intensive.

The product-costing objective of a functional-based costing system is typically satisfied by assigning production costs to inventories and cost of goods sold for purposes of external financial reporting. More comprehensive product cost definitions, such as the value-chain and operating cost definitions illustrated in Exhibit 2–4, are not available for management use. However, production-based costing systems often furnish useful variants of the traditional product cost definition. For example, prime costs and variable manufacturing costs per unit may be reported (variable costs are discussed in Chapter 3).

### ABM Cost View

In **activity-based costing (ABC)**, costs are traced to activities and then to products. As with functional-based costing, both direct tracing and driver tracing are used; however, the role of driver tracing is significantly expanded by identifying and

**production drivers**

Drivers that are highly correlated with production output (volume).

**unit-level drivers**

*See* production drivers.

**functional-based costing (FBC)**

An approach for assigning costs of shared resources to products and other cost objects using only production or unit-level drivers.

**nonunit-level drivers**

Factors, other than the number of units produced, that measure the consumption of activities by cost objects.

**activity-based costing (ABC)**

A cost assignment approach that first uses direct and driver tracing to assign costs to activities and then uses drivers to assign costs to cost objects.

EXHIBIT 2-9

Activity-Based
Management Model

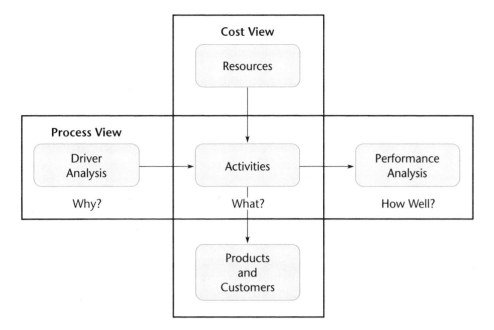

using nonunit-level drivers. Thus activity-based cost assignments emphasize tracing over allocation; in fact, it could be called tracing-intensive.

The use of both unit-level and nonunit-level activity drivers increases both the accuracy of cost assignments and the overall quality and relevance of cost information. For example, consider the activity "moving raw materials and partly finished goods from one point to another within a factory." The number of moves required for a product is a much better measure of the product's demand for the material-handling activity than the number of units produced. In fact, the number of units produced may have nothing to do with measuring products' demands for material handling. (A batch of 10 units could require as much material-handling activity as a batch of 100 units.)

Activity-based product costing tends to be flexible. Cost information is produced to support a variety of managerial objectives, including the financial reporting objective. More comprehensive product-costing definitions are emphasized for better planning, control, and decision making. For example, a more flexible accounting system, with its wealth of information on costs, activities, and drivers, could act as an early warning system of ethical problems. Metropolitan Life Insurance Company in the United States was dismayed to learn that some of its agents were selling policies as retirement plans. This practice is illegal, and cost the company more than $20 million in fines as well as $50 million in refunds to policyholders.[4] Comprehensive data on sales, individual agents, types of policies, and policyholders could have alerted Metropolitan Life to a potential problem. Thus, the maxim "different costs for different purposes" takes on real meaning.

### FBM's Operational Efficiency View
Another objective of management accounting is providing information for planning and control. The FBM accounting approach to control assigns costs to organizational units and then holds the organizational unit manager responsible for controlling the assigned costs. Performance is measured by comparing actual outcomes with standard or budgeted outcomes. The emphasis is on financial measures of performance (nonfinancial measures are usually ignored). Managers are rewarded based on their ability to control costs. Thus, the functional-based

---

4. Chris Roush, "Fields of Green—and Disaster Areas," *Business Week* (January 9, 1995): p. 94.

approach traces costs to individuals who are responsible for incurring costs. The reward system is used to motivate these individuals to manage costs by increasing the operating efficiency of their organizational units. This approach assumes that maximizing the performance of the overall organization is achieved by maximizing the performance of individual organizational subunits (referred to as responsibility centres).

### ABM's Operational Efficiency View

Activity-based control subsystems also differ significantly from functional-based systems. The functional-based emphasis is on managing costs. The emerging consensus, however, is that management of activities, not costs, is the key to successful control. Activity-based management focuses on the management of activities with the objective of improving the value received by the customer and the profit received by providing this value. It includes driver analysis, activity analysis, and performance evaluation and draws on activity-based costing as a major source of information.[5] The process view is concerned with identifying factors that cause an activity's cost (explaining *why* costs are incurred), assessing *what* work is done (identifying activities), and evaluating the work performed and the results achieved (looking at *how well* the activity is performed). Thus, activity-based control requires detailed information on activities.

This approach focuses on accountability for activities rather than costs and emphasizes the maximization of systemwide performance instead of individual performance. Activities cut across functional and departmental lines, are systemwide in focus, and require a global approach to control. Essentially, this form of control admits that maximizing the efficiency of individual subunits does not necessarily lead to maximum efficiency for the system as a whole. Another significant difference should also be mentioned. In an activity-based management accounting information system, both financial and nonfinancial measures of performance are important. Exhibit 2–10 compares the characteristics of the functional-based and activity-based cost management systems.

EXHIBIT　2-10

Comparison of Functional-Based and Activity-Based Cost Management Systems

| Functional-Based | Activity-Based |
|---|---|
| 1. Unit-level drivers | 1. Unit- and nonunit-level drivers |
| 2. Allocation-intensive | 2. Tracing-intensive |
| 3. Narrow, rigid product costing | 3. Broad, flexible product costing |
| 4. Focus on managing costs | 4. Focus on managing activities |
| 5. Sparse activity information | 5. Detailed activity information |
| 6. Maximization of individual unit performance | 6. Systemwide performance maximization |
| 7. Use of financial measures of performance | 7. Use of both financial and nonfinancial measures of performance |

## Choice of a Management Accounting System

Activity-based management accounting offers significant benefits, including improved product-costing accuracy, improved decision making, enhanced strategic planning, and better ability to manage activities. Furthermore, the activity-based system is particularly suited for supporting the goal of continuous improvement—an objective that is critical for organizations competing on a

---

5. This definition of activity-based management and the illustrative model in Exhibit 2-9 are based on Norm Raffish and Peter B.B. Turney, "Glossary of Activity-Based Management," *Journal of Cost Management* (Fall 1991): pp. 53-63. Many other terms throughout the text relating to activity-based management are also drawn from this source.

global basis. These benefits, however, are not obtained without costs. An activity-based management accounting system is more complex, and it requires a significant increase in measurement activity—and measurement can be costly. However, with the advances in information technology, the costs of measurement have declined, making activity-based systems more attractive. Simultaneously, the cost of making bad decisions has increased (because of more intense competition resulting from the emergence of a worldwide economy, deregulation of services, and so on). The need to improve the quality of decision making has increased the appeal of activity-based approaches.

For many companies, the benefits of replacing an FBM system with an ABM system outweigh the costs. As a result, the use of activity-based costing and activity-based management is spreading, and interest in activity-based management accounting is high. Companies like J. M. Schneider, Inc., Volkswagen Canada, Royal Bank of Canada, Hughes Aircraft, Caterpillar, Xerox, National Semiconductor, Tektronix, Dayton Extruded Plastics, Armistead Insurance, and Zytec have adopted activity-based costing and management systems.[6] Furthermore, this is only a very small listing of companies that are using activity-based systems.

---

6. *Activity-Based Management*, Management Accounting Issues Paper 10, The Society of Management Accountants of Canada, 1995, Hamilton, Ontario; Peter B.B. Turney, "Activity-Based Management," *Management Accounting* (January 1992): pp. 20-25; Jack Hedicke and David Feil, "Hughes Aircraft," *Management Accounting* (February 1991): pp. 29-33; and Lou F. Jones, "Product Costing at Caterpillar," *Management Accounting* (February 1991): pp. 34-42.

## Summary of Learning Objectives

### 1. Explain the cost assignment process.

Costs are assigned to cost objects such as products, projects, plants, and customers. There are three methods of cost assignment: direct tracing, driver tracing, and allocation. Direct and driver tracing offer more accuracy because they are based on cause-and-effect relationships. Direct tracing relies on physical observation to assign costs. Driver tracing relies on the use of causal factors called drivers to assign costs. Allocation relies on assumed relationships and convenience to assign costs. Allocation is essentially an arbitrary assignment and should be avoided as much as possible.

### 2. Define tangible and intangible products, and explain why there are different product cost definitions.

There are two types of output: tangible products and services. Tangible products are goods that are produced by converting raw materials through the use of labour and capital inputs such as plant, land, and machinery. Services are tasks or activities performed for a customer or an activity performed by a customer using an organization's products or facilities. Product cost is defined as cost assigned to a product that satisfies a particular managerial objective. Since managerial objectives can differ, product cost definitions can differ—each depending on the managerial objective being served.

### 3. Prepare income statements for manufacturing and service organizations.

If expenses are grouped according to function and then deducted from revenues, we have absorption-costing income statements. Absorption-costing income statements are generally used for external financial reporting. For manufacturing companies, the major functional classifications are manufacturing and nonmanufacturing; for service organizations, the categories are production and nonproduction. For manufacturing companies, the cost of goods manufactured must be calculated. No such requirement exists for a service organization.

**4.  Outline the differences between functional-based and activity-based management accounting systems.**

A functional-based management accounting system uses only unit-level drivers, tends to be more allocation-intensive, uses narrow product cost definitions, focuses on managing costs, provides little activity information, emphasizes individual organizational unit performance, and uses financial measures of performance. An activity-based management accounting system uses both unit-level and nonunit-level drivers, is tracing-intensive, allows flexible product-costing definitions, focuses on managing activities, provides detailed activity information, emphasizes systemwide performance, and uses both financial and nonfinancial measures of performance.

## Key Terms

Absorption costing  45
Activity  36
Activity-based costing (ABC)  48
Activity-based management (ABM)
 accounting system  47
Administrative costs  44
Allocation  39
Conversion cost  44
Cost  35
Cost object  36
Cost of goods manufactured  45
Cost of goods sold  45
Direct costs  37
Direct labour  43
Direct materials  43

Direct tracing  38
Drivers  38
Driver tracing  38
Expenses  36
Functional-based costing (FBC)  48
Functional-based management (FBM)
 accounting system  47
Heterogeneity  40
Indirect costs  37
Inseparability  40
Intangibility  40
Marketing (selling) costs  44
Noninventoriable (period) costs  44
Nonproduction costs  42
Nonunit-level drivers  48

Opportunity cost  36
Overhead  43
Perishability  40
Prime cost  44
Process  47
Product cost  41
Production costs  42
Production drivers  48
Services  40
Supplies  43
Tangible products  40
Traceability  37
Tracing  37
Unit-level drivers  48
Work in process  46

## Review Problems

### I.  MANUFACTURING, COST CLASSIFICATION, AND INCOME STATEMENT

Pop's Burger Heaven produces and sells quarter-pound hamburgers. Each burger sells for $1.50. During December, Pop's sold 10,000 burgers (the average amount sold each month). The restaurant employs cooks, servers, and one supervisor (the owner, John Peterson). All cooks and servers are part-time employees. Pop's maintains a pool of part-time employees so that the number of employees scheduled can be adjusted to the changes in demand. Demand varies on a weekly as well as a monthly basis.

A janitor is hired to clean the building on a weekly basis. The building is leased from a local real estate company. The building has no seating capabilities. All orders are filled on a drive-through basis. The supervisor schedules work, opens the building, counts the cash, advertises, and is responsible for hiring and firing. The following costs were incurred during December:

| Hamburger meat | $1,600 | Utilities | $500 |
|---|---|---|---|
| Lettuce | 300 | Amortization | |
| Tomatoes | 250 | Cooking equipment | 200 |
| Buns | 300 | Cash register | 50 |
| Other ingredients | 20 | Advertising | 100 |
| Cooks' wages | 2,550 | Rent | 800 |
| Servers' wages | 2,032 | Janitorial supplies | 50 |
| Supervisor's salary | 2,000 | Janitor's wages | 120 |

### Required:

1. Classify the costs for Pop's December operations in one of the following categories: direct materials, direct labour, overhead, or selling and administrative.
2. Prepare an absorption-costing income statement for the month of December.

### Solution

1. Classification:
   Direct materials: Hamburger meat, lettuce, tomatoes, and buns
   Direct labour: Cooks' wages
   Overhead: Utilities, amortization on the cooking equipment, rent, janitor's wages, janitorial supplies, and other ingredients
   Selling and administrative: Servers' wages, supervisor's salary, amortization on the cash register, and advertising

### Explanation of Classification:

Cooks are direct labourers because they make the hamburgers. "Other ingredients" are overhead because of cost and convenience, even though technically they are direct materials. Because the primary purpose of the building is production (cooking hamburgers), all of the rent and building-related costs are classified as indirect production costs. (An argument could be made that the building also supports the selling and administrative functions and, consequently, a portion of the rent and building-related costs should be classified as selling and administrative costs.) Servers are responsible for taking and filling orders and are, therefore, classified as sales personnel. The cash register is used to support the sales function. The supervisor is responsible for overseeing the business as a whole and for coordinating the sales and production functions, so salary is an administrative cost.

2. Income Statement

| | | |
|---|---|---|
| Sales ($1.50 × 10,000) | | $15,000 |
| Less cost of goods sold: | | |
| Direct materials | $2,450 | |
| Direct labour | 2,550 | |
| Overhead | 1,690 | 6,690 |
| Gross profit | | $8,310 |
| Less operating expenses: | | |
| Selling expenses | $2,182 | |
| Administrative expenses | 2,000 | 4,182 |
| Net income | | $4,128 |

## II.  SERVICES, COST SYSTEMS, AND INCOME STATEMENT

Celestial Funeral Home offers a full range of services. Based on past experience, Celestial uses the following formula to describe its total overhead costs: $Y = \$100,000 + \$25X$, where $Y$ = total overhead costs and $X$ = number of funerals. Overhead costs are assigned by dividing the total overhead by the number of funerals. For a given funeral, the cost of direct materials ranges from $750 to $5,000, depending on the family's selection of a casket. The average is $2,000. Direct labour averages $500 per funeral. During 2004, Celestial conducted 1,000 funerals. The average price charged for each funeral is $3,500. Celestial incurs annual selling expenses of $25,000 and administrative expenses of $75,000.

**Required:**
1. Does Celestial sell a tangible or an intangible product? Explain.
2. Does Celestial use a functional-based or an activity-based management accounting system? Explain.
3. What is the total overhead cost incurred by Celestial for the year?
4. What is the overhead cost per funeral for the year?
5. Calculate the unit product cost for the year.
6. Prepare an income statement for Celestial.

**Solution**
1. Funerals are intangible products. They are services: as such, they cannot be stored and are connected to the producer (inseparability).
2. The use of a unit-level driver (number of funerals) to assign overhead costs (and, apparently, direct materials and direct labour) suggests a functional-based system.
3. $Y = \$100,000 + \$25(1,000)$
   $Y = \$125,000$
4. $\$125,000/1,000 = \$125$
5. **Unit product cost:**

| | |
|---|---:|
| Direct materials | $2,000 |
| Direct labour | 500 |
| Overhead | 125 |
| | $2,625 |

6. **Income Statement:**

| | | |
|---|---:|---:|
| Sales | | $3,500,000 |
| Less cost of goods sold: | | |
| Direct materials | $2,000,000 | |
| Direct labour | 500,000 | |
| Overhead | 125,000 | 2,625,000 |
| Gross profit | | $875,000 |
| Less operating expenses | | |
| Selling expenses | $25,000 | |
| Administrative expense | 75,000 | 100,000 |
| Net income | | $775,000 |

# Questions for Writing and Discussion

1. What is meant by "product-costing accuracy"?
2. What is a cost object? Give some examples.
3. What is an activity? Give some examples of activities within a manufacturing company.
4. What is a direct cost? an indirect cost?
5. What does traceability mean? What is tracing?
6. What is allocation?
7. What are drivers? Give an example of a driver.
8. Explain the difference between direct tracing and driver tracing.
9. Explain how driver tracing works.
10. What is a tangible product?
11. What is a service?
12. Explain how services differ from tangible products.
13. Give three examples of product cost definitions. Why do we need different product cost definitions?

14. Identify the three cost elements that determine the cost of making a product (for external reporting).

15. How do the income statements of a manufacturing company and a service organization differ?

16. Describe some of the major differences between a functional-based cost management system and an activity-based cost management system.

17. When would a company choose an activity-based cost management system over a functional-based system? What forces are moving organizations to implement activity-based cost management systems?

# Exercises

**2–1**

Direct Tracing and Driver Tracing

LO1

Harry Whipple, owner of an inkjet printer, has agreed to allow Mary and Natalie, two friends who are pursuing master's degrees in English, to print several papers for their graduate English courses. However, he has imposed two conditions. First, they must supply their own paper. Second, they must pay Harry a fair amount for the usage of the ink cartridge. Cartridges for the printer cost $80 and usually provide a printing capacity of 4,000 normal pages before replacement (normal means a page without graphs). Paper is bought in reams of 500 units at $4 per ream. Mary's printing requirements are for 500 pages, while Natalie's are for 1,000 pages.

**Required:**
1. Calculate the cost per page for the papers produced by Mary. Repeat for Natalie.
2. In computing the cost per page, which cost was assigned through direct tracing? through driver tracing?
3. Suppose that Natalie uses a lot of graphs in her writing, whereas Mary uses hardly any. Explain how this difference could affect the accuracy of the ink cost assigned to Natalie. What recommendation would you make for improving the cost assignment? Explain.

**2–2**

Direct Tracing and Driver Tracing

LO1

Merril Machining produces machine parts. On one very specialized machine, two parts are produced on an ongoing basis: Part #627A and Part #1725C. The production equipment is able to perform both drilling and shaping operations. Part #627A requires 250 grams of steel, and Part #1725C requires 350 grams of steel. The two parts are produced in batches of 10,000, and each part requires 10 batches per year. For each batch, the production equipment must be configured so that the correct diameters, number of grooves, and other features of each part are correctly produced. The cost of steel for the year was $1,800,000. The cost for configuring (setting up) the equipment for batch production is $800,000 per year.

**Required:**
1. Calculate the cost per part (for steel and setup costs).
2. In computing the cost per part, which cost was assigned through direct tracing? Through driver tracing?
3. Suppose that the setup time for Part #627A is 30 hours per batch and that of Part #1725C is 20 hours. Explain how this could affect the accuracy of the setup cost assigned to the two parts. What recommendation would you make to improve the cost assignment? Explain and calculate the cost per part based on your recommendation.

**2–3**

*Driver Tracing*

LO1

Listed below are costs that are to be assigned to certain cost objects. For each case, identify possible drivers that could be used for the cost assignment. Example: *Cost:* setting up equipment; *Cost Object:* Products; *Driver:* Number of setups used by each product

| | Cost | Cost Object |
|---|---|---|
| a. | Processing cheques in a bank | Customer accounts |
| b. | Unloading shipments of raw materials | Products |
| c. | Shipping goods | Customers |
| d. | Ordering supplies | Departments |
| e. | Reworking products | Products |
| f. | Moving materials | Products |
| g. | Nursing care | Patients |
| h. | Processing insurance claims | Claims |
| i. | Special product testing | Products |
| j. | Physical therapy in a hospital | Patients |

**2–4**

*Cost Assignment Methods*

LO1

Hummer Company uses manufacturing cells to produce its products (a cell is a manufacturing unit dedicated to the production of subassemblies or products). One manufacturing cell produces small motors for lawn mowers. Suppose that the small-motor manufacturing cell is the cost object. Assume that all or a portion of the following costs must be assigned to the cell:

a. Salary of cell supervisor
b. Power to heat and cool the plant in which the cell is located
c. Materials used to produce the motors
d. Maintenance for the cell's equipment (provided by the maintenance department)
e. Labour used to produce motors
f. Cafeteria that services the plant's employees
g. Amortization on the plant
h. Amortization on equipment used to produce the motors
i. Ordering costs for materials used in production
j. Engineering support (provided by the engineering department)
k. Cost of maintaining the plant and grounds
l. Cost of the plant's personnel office
m. Property tax on the plant and land

**Required:**
Identify which cost assignment method would likely be used to assign the costs of each activity to the small-motor manufacturing cell: direct tracing, driver tracing, or allocation. When driver tracing is selected, identify a potential activity driver that could be used for the tracing.

**2–5**

*Value-Chain Activity*

LO2

The following activities are performed within a manufacturing company. Classify each activity according to its value-chain activity category (for example, activity: grinding parts; value-chain activity category: producing).

a. Advertising products
b. Repairing goods under warranty
c. Designing a new process
d. Assembling parts
e. Shipping goods to a wholesaler
f. Inspecting incoming raw materials and parts
g. Storing finished goods in a warehouse
h. Creating a new computer chip

i.  Answering product-use questions using a customer "hot line"
j.  Moving partly finished goods from one department to another
k.  Building a prototype of a new product
l.  Creating plans for a new model of an automobile
m.  Conducting a sales campaign by phone
n.  Picking goods from a warehouse
o.  Setting up equipment

**2–6**

*Product Cost Definitions*

**LO2**

Three possible product cost definitions were introduced: value-chain, operating, and traditional. Identify which of the three best fits the following situations (justify your choice):

a.  Setting the price for a new product
b.  Valuation of finished goods inventories for external reporting
c.  Choosing among different products in order to maintain a product mix that will provide the company with a long-term sustainable competitive advantage
d.  Choosing among competing product designs
e.  Calculating cost of goods sold for external reporting
f.  Deciding whether to increase the price of an existing product
g.  Deciding whether to accept or reject a special order, where the price offered is lower than the normal selling price
h.  Determining which of several potential new products should be developed, produced, and sold

**2–7**

*Cost of Goods Manufactured and Sold*

**LO3**

Spreadsheet

Lawton Company manufactures sleeping bags. At the beginning of September, the following information was supplied by their accountant:

| | |
|---|---|
| Raw materials inventory | $37,000 |
| Work-in-process inventory | 18,000 |
| Finished goods inventory | 20,200 |

During September, direct labour cost was $40,500, raw materials purchases were $61,500, and the total overhead cost was $105,750. The inventories at the end of September were as follows:

| | |
|---|---|
| Raw materials inventory | $16,800 |
| Work-in-process inventory | 29,500 |
| Finished goods inventory | 19,100 |

**Required:**
1.  Prepare a statement of cost of goods manufactured for September.
2.  Prepare a statement of cost of goods sold for September.

**2–8**

*Preparation of Income Statement: Manufacturing Organization*

**LO3**

Bohanan manufactures a stuffed bear called Smokee. Last year 100,000 bears were made and sold for $30 each. The actual unit cost for a stuffed bear follows:

| | |
|---|---|
| Direct materials | $ 4.00 |
| Direct labour | 6.00 |
| Overhead | 13.00 |
| Total unit cost | $23.00 |

The only selling expenses were a commission of $2 per unit sold and advertising totalling $50,000. Administrative expenses equalled $150,000. There were no beginning or ending work in process or finished goods inventories.

**Required:**
1.  Prepare an income statement for external users. Did you need to prepare a supporting statement of cost of goods manufactured? Explain.

2. Suppose 100,000 bears were produced (and 100,000 sold) but that the company had a beginning finished goods inventory of 5,000 bears produced in the previous year at a cost of $20 per unit. The company follows a first-in, first-out policy for its inventory (meaning that the units produced first are sold first for purposes of cost flow). What effect does this have on the income statement? Show the new statement.

**2–9**

Functional-Based versus Activity-Based Management Accounting Systems

LO4

Iquitos Manufacturing produces two different models of cameras. One model has an automatic focus; the other requires the user to focus manually. The two products are produced in batches (an equal number of batches is used for each product). Each time a batch is produced, the equipment must be configured (set up) for the specifications of the camera model being produced. The machine configuration required for the automatic-focus model is more complex and consumes more of the setup activity resources than that for the manual-focus camera. Total setup costs are $100,000 per year. Total setup hours are 10,000, with 7,000 hours needed for the automatic model and 3,000 hours needed for the manual model.

The manual model is more labour-intensive, requiring much more assembly time and less machine time. Total direct labour hours used for both products are 100,000, with 70,000 hours used for the manual model and 30,000 hours used for the automatic model. Iquitos produces 40,000 units of the manual model and 60,000 units of the automatic model each year. The company currently assigns only manufacturing costs to the two products. Overhead costs are assigned to the two products in proportion to the direct labour hours used by each product. All other costs are viewed as period costs.

Iquitos budgets costs for all departments within the plant—both support departments (like maintenance and purchasing) and production departments (like machining and assembly). Departmental managers are evaluated and rewarded on their ability to control costs. Individual managerial performance is assessed by comparing actual costs with budgeted costs.

**Required:**

1. Is Iquitos using a functional-based or an activity-based management accounting system? Explain.
2. Setup costs are overhead costs. What is the setup cost assigned per unit for each model using Iquitos's current method of assigning overhead costs to products? Would you classify this cost assignment as direct tracing, driver tracing, or allocation? Explain.
3. Can you suggest a better way of assigning setup costs? Provide calculations, and explain why you think the method is better. Is this method compatible with functional-based costing or with activity-based costing? Explain.

**2–10**

Cost of Goods Manufactured and Sold

LO3

Spreadsheet

Hayward Company, a manufacturing company, has supplied the following information from its accounting records for 2004 (in thousands):

| | |
|---|---|
| Direct labour cost | $10,500 |
| Purchases of raw materials | 15,000 |
| Supplies used | 675 |
| Factory insurance | 350 |
| Commissions paid | 2,500 |
| Factory supervision | 2,225 |
| Advertising | 800 |
| Material handling | 3,745 |
| Work-in-process inventory, December 31, 2003 | 12,500 |
| Work-in-process inventory, December 31, 2004 | 14,250 |
| Materials inventory, December 31, 2003 | 3,475 |

| Materials inventory, December 31, 2004 | 9,500 |
| Finished goods inventory, December 31, 2003 | 6,685 |
| Finished goods inventory, December 31, 2004 | 4,250 |

**Required:**
1. Prepare a statement of cost of goods manufactured.
2. Prepare a statement of cost of goods sold.

**2–11**

*Income Statement; Cost Concepts; Service Company*

**LO2, LO3**

Lance Peckam owns and operates three Confiable Muffler outlets in Red Deer, Alberta. Confiable Muffler specializes in replacing mufflers; the replacement mufflers have a lifetime guarantee. Confiable is a franchise popular throughout western Canada. In April, purchases of materials equalled $200,000, the beginning inventory of material was $26,300, and the ending inventory of material was $14,250. Payments to direct labour during the month totalled $53,000. Overhead incurred was $120,000. The Red Deer outlets also spent $15,000 on advertising during the month. A franchise fee of $3,000 per outlet is paid every month. Revenues for April were $500,000.

**Required:**
1. What was the cost of materials used for muffler-changing services during April?
2. What was the prime cost for April?
3. What was the conversion cost for April?
4. What was the total service cost for April?
5. Prepare an income statement for the month of April.
6. Confiable purchases all its mufflers from Remington Company, a muffler manufacturer. Discuss the differences between the products offered by Remington and Confiable.

**2–12**

*Cost Assignment; Product Cost Definitions*

**LO1, LO2**

Halverson Company produces chemicals used in the mining industry. Each plant is dedicated to producing a single industrial chemical. One of its plants produces an electrolyte used in the copper industry's solvent extraction process. During the most recent year, the electrolyte plant produced and sold 2,000,000 kilograms of electrolyte. No inventories of the chemical are carried. The chemical sells for $2 per kilogram. Annual manufacturing costs for the electrolyte plant totalled $2,800,000. The plant is also responsible for packaging and shipping its products. Distribution and packaging costs for the electrolyte plant were $200,000. Research and development costs are incurred centrally and assigned to each plant in proportion to its sales revenues. The revenues of the electrolyte plant were 25 percent of the company's total revenues. For the year just completed, the company reported $1.2 million for research and development. The company also reported $320,000 in sales commissions. Commissions are also assigned to plants in proportion to their sales.

**Required:**
1. Compute the unit product cost that must be used for external financial reporting purposes (cost per kilogram of electrolyte). How would the other costs be treated for external financial reporting?
2. Compute the unit operating product cost. What purpose might this cost serve?
3. Compute the unit value-chain product cost. Why would management want to know this product cost?
4. Classify the cost assignments for the value-chain product cost as direct tracing, driver tracing, or allocation. For any cost classified as allocation, is it possible to change that assignment to direct tracing or driver tracing? Explain.

**2–13**

Various Topics;
Multiple Choice

LOI, L02, L03, L04

Choose the *best* answer for each of the following questions:

1. An example of driver tracing is
   a. assigning the cost of raw materials to a product.
   b. assigning the cost of grounds maintenance to products using direct labour hours.
   c. assigning the cost of assembly labour to products.
   d. assigning the cost of inspection to products using inspection hours.
   e. Only b and d.

2. Services differ from tangible products in that
   a. services cannot be stored for future use.
   b. producers and buyers of services must be in direct contact for an exchange.
   c. there is less variation in the performance of services.
   d. buyers cannot see, feel, hear, or taste a tangible product before it is bought.
   e. Only a and b.

3. Kolaser Company has the following production data for the month of July:

   | | |
   |---|---|
   | Direct labour | $250,000 |
   | Actual overhead | 350,000 |
   | Direct materials used | 400,000 |
   | Warehousing | 40,000 |

   Kolaser's conversion cost for July is
   a. $600,000.
   b. $640,000.
   c. $650,000.
   d. $750,000.

4. Refer to the data in Question 3. Kolaser's prime cost for July is
   a. $600,000.
   b. $640,000.
   c. $650,000.
   d. $750,000.

5. Activity-based management differs from functional-based management on which of the following dimensions?
   a. It is more tracing intensive.
   b. It provides detailed activity information.
   c. It uses both unit- and nonunit-level drivers.
   d. It focuses on managing activities.
   e. All of the above.

**2–14**

Various Topics;
Matching

LO1, LO2, LO3, LO4

Match the following items (by definition or example):

| | | | |
|---|---|---|---|
| 1. | Direct costs | a. | Customers |
| 2. | Drivers | b. | Attending college instead of working |
| 3. | Tracing | c. | Measures of a cost object's resource usage |
| 4. | Intangibility | d. | Variation in performance of services |
| 5. | Overhead cost | e. | Producers and buyers in direct contact |
| 6. | Heterogeneity | f. | Uses only unit-level drivers |
| 7. | Perishability | g. | Assigning costs using causal relationships |
| 8. | Absorption-costing income | h. | Uses unit- and nonunit-level drivers to assign costs |
| 9. | Functional-based costing | i. | Partially finished goods |
| 10. | Activity-based costing | j. | Direct materials plus direct labour |
| 11. | Inseparability | k. | Inability to store services |

| | | | |
|---|---|---|---|
| 12. | Prime cost | l. | Cannot see, hear, taste, or feel before buying |
| 13. | Opportunity cost | m. | Costs traceable to a cost object |
| 14. | Work in process | n. | Functional, full-costing income |
| 15. | Cost object | o. | Production costs not directly traceable |

## Problems

**2–15**

*Direct Tracing and Driver Tracing*

**LO1, LO2**

Shellbrook General Hospital has two types of patients: normal care and intensive care. On a daily basis, both types of patients consume resources necessary for their care. For example, they occupy beds; receive nursing care; use care supplies (lotion, gauze, tissues, etc.); have bedding, towels, and clothes laundered; eat meals, and so on. Bill Simons, the hospital administrator, wants to calculate the cost per patient day for each type of patient.

To illustrate how daily care costs can be assigned to each type of patient, information has been gathered for nursing care. There are always four nurses on duty. There are three shifts, each lasting 8 hours. Nurses work 40 hours per week and are paid an average of $40,000 per year, including benefits. Full-time nurses work 50 weeks per year. The hospital employs only one part-time nurse, who is paid $20,000 for the hours worked during the year (only the amount needed to ensure that the four-nurse coverage policy is satisfied). Assume that a year is exactly 52 weeks. During the year, normal care patients accounted for 8,000 patient days and intensive care patients accounted for 2,000 patient days. Intensive care patients use half of the nursing care hours.

**Required:**
1. Calculate the nursing cost per patient day for each patient type, using patient days to assign the cost.
2. Calculate the nursing cost per patient day for each patient type, using nursing hours used to assign the cost. Is this cost assignment more accurate than the one using patient days? Explain your reasoning.
3. Suppose that one nurse each shift is dedicated to the intensive care unit and that the other three nurses provide additional help as needed. What additional information would you like to have in order to assign nursing costs so that a cost per patient day can be calculated for each patient type? Which of the three assignment methods are you using?

**2–16**

*Cost identification*

**LO2**

Following are a list of cost items described in the chapter and a list of brief settings that describe the items. Match the items with the settings. There may be more than one cost classification associated with each setting; however, select the setting that seems to fit the item best.

Cost items:
 a. Opportunity cost
 ⊁ b. Period cost
 c. Product cost
 d. Direct labour cost
 e. Selling cost
 f. Conversion cost

　　　g. Prime cost
　　　h. Direct materials cost
　　　i. Overhead cost
　　　j. Administrative cost

Settings:

c b　1. Marcus Armstrong, manager of Timmins Optical, estimated that the cost of plastic, the wages of the technician producing the lenses, and overhead totalled $30 per pair of single-vision lenses.

a　2. Linda was having a hard time deciding whether to return to school. She was concerned about the good salary she would have to give up for the next four years.

e j　3. Randy Harris is the finished goods warehouse manager for a medium-sized manufacturing company. He is paid a salary of $90,000 per year. As he studied the financial statement prepared by the local CA firm, he wondered how his salary was treated.

j　4. Jamie Young is in charge of the legal department at company headquarters. Her salary is $95,000 per year. She reports to the chief executive officer.

i　5. All factory costs that are not classified as direct materials or direct labour.

d　6. A new product required machining, assembly, and painting. The design engineer asked the accounting department to estimate the labour cost for each of the three operations. The engineer supplied the estimated labour hours for each operation.

h　7. After obtaining the estimate of direct labour cost, the design engineer estimated the cost of the materials that would be used for the new product.

g　8. The design engineer totalled the costs of materials and direct labour for the new product.

i　9. The design engineer also estimated the cost of converting the raw materials into their final form.

f　10. The auditor pointed out that the amortization on the corporate jet had been incorrectly assigned to finished goods inventory (the jet was primarily used to fly the CEO and other staff to various company sites). Accordingly, the amortization charge was reallocated to the income statement.

**2–17**

Functional-Based
versus Activity-Based
Management
Accounting Systems

LO4

The following actions are associated with either functional-based management accounting or activity-based management accounting.

　　a. Budgeted costs for the maintenance department are compared with the actual costs of the maintenance department.
　　b. The maintenance department manager receives a bonus for "beating" the budget.
　　c. The costs of resources are traced to activities and then to products.
　　d. The purchasing department is evaluated on a departmental basis.
　　e. Activities are identified and listed.
　　f. Activities are categorized as adding value or not adding value to the organization.
　　g. A standard for a product's material usage cost is set and compared with the product's actual material usage cost.
　　h. The cost of performing an activity is tracked over time.
　　i. The distance between moves is identified as the cause of material-handling cost.

j. A purchasing agent is rewarded for buying parts below the standard price set by the company.

k. The cost of the material-handling activity is reduced dramatically by redesigning the plant layout.

l. An investigation is undertaken to find out why the actual labour cost for the production of 1,000 units is greater than the labour standard allowed.

m. The percentage of defective units is calculated and tracked over time.

n. Engineering has been given the charge to find a way to reduce setup time by 75 percent.

o. The manager of the receiving department lays off two receiving clerks so that the fourth-quarter budget can be met.

**Required:**

Classify these actions as belonging to either a functional-based management accounting system or an activity-based management accounting system. Explain your classification.

**2–18**

Income Statement Cost of Services Provided; Service Attributes

LO2, LO3

Spreadsheet

Berry Company is an architectural firm. The firm is located in Windsor, Ontario, and employs ten professionals and five staff. The firm does design work for small and medium-sized construction businesses. The following data are provided for the year ended July 31, 2004:

| | |
|---|---|
| Designs processed | 2,000 |
| Designs in process, August 1, 2003 | $ 60,000 |
| Designs in process, July 31, 2004 | 100,000 |
| →Cost of services sold | 890,000 |
| Beginning direct materials inventory | 20,000 |
| Purchases, direct materials | 40,000 |
| Direct labour | 800,000 |
| Overhead | 100,000 |
| Administrative | 50,000 |
| Selling | 60,000 |

**Required:**

1. Prepare a statement of cost of services sold.
2. Refer to the statement prepared in Requirement 1. What is the dominant cost? Will this always be true of service organizations? If not, provide an example of an exception.
3. Assume that the average fee for a design is $700. Prepare an income statement for Berry Company.
4. Discuss three differences between services and tangible products. How do these differences affect the computations in Requirement 1?

**2–19**

Income Statement; Cost of Goods Manufactured

LO3

W. W. Phillips Company produced 4,000 leather recliners during 2004. These recliners sell for $400 each. Phillips had 500 recliners in finished goods inventory at the beginning of the year. At the end of the year, there were 700 recliners in finished goods inventory. Phillips's accounting records provide the following information:

| | |
|---|---|
| Purchases of raw materials | $320,000 |
| Raw materials inventory, January 1, 2004 | 46,800 |
| Raw materials inventory, December 31, 2004 | 66,800 |
| Direct labour | 200,000 |
| Indirect labour | 40,000 |
| Rent, factory building | 42,000 |
| Amortization, factory equipment | 60,000 |

| | |
|---|---:|
| Utilities, factory | 11,956 |
| Salary, sales supervisor | 90,000 |
| Commissions, salespersons | 180,000 |
| General administration | 300,000 |
| Work-in-process inventory, January 1, 2004 | 13,040 |
| Work-in-process inventory, December 31, 2004 | 14,996 |
| Finished goods inventory, January 1, 2004 | 80,000 |
| Finished goods inventory, December 31, 2004 | 114,100 |

**Required:**
1. Prepare a statement of cost of goods manufactured.
2. Compute the average cost of producing one recliner in 2004.
3. Prepare an income statement for external users.

**2–20**

Cost Identification and
Analysis; Income
Statement

LO2, LO3

Melissa Southern has decided to open a printing shop. She has secured two contracts. One is a five-year contract to print a popular regional magazine. The contract calls for 5,000 copies each month. The second contract is a three-year agreement to print tourist brochures for the province. The provincial tourism office requires 10,000 brochures per month.

Melissa has rented a building for $1,400 per month. Her printing equipment was purchased for $40,000 and has a life expectancy of 20,000 hours with no salvage value. Amortization is calculated for a period based on the hours of usage. Melissa has scheduled the delivery of the products so that two production runs are needed. In the first run, the equipment is prepared for the magazine printing. In the second run, the equipment is reconfigured for brochure printing. It takes twice as long to configure the equipment for the magazine setup as it does for the brochure setup. The total setup costs per month are $600.

Insurance costs for the building and equipment are $140 per month. Power to operate the printing equipment is strongly related to machine usage. The printing equipment causes virtually all of the power costs. Power costs will run $350 per month. Printing materials will cost $0.40 per copy for the magazine and $0.08 per copy for the brochure. Melissa will hire workers to run the presses as needed (part-time workers are easy to hire). She must pay $10 per hour. Each worker can produce 20 copies of the magazine per printing hour or 100 copies of the brochure. Distribution costs are $500 per month. Melissa will receive a salary of $1,500 per month. She is responsible for personnel, accounting, sales, and production—in effect, she is responsible for coordinating and managing all aspects of the business.

**Required:**
1. What are the total monthly manufacturing costs?
2. What are the total monthly prime costs? total monthly prime costs for the regional magazine? for the brochure? Did you use direct tracing, driver tracing, or allocation to assign costs to each product?
3. What are the total monthly conversion costs? Suppose that Melissa wants to determine monthly conversion costs for each product. Assign monthly conversion costs to each product using direct tracing and driver tracing whenever possible. For those costs that cannot be assigned using a tracing approach, you may assign them using direct labour hours.
4. If Melissa receives $1.80 per copy of the magazine and $0.45 per brochure, how much will her income be for the first month of operations? (Prepare an income statement.)

**2–21**

LO3

On January 30, 2004, the manufacturing facility of a medium-sized company was severely damaged by an accidental fire. As a result, the company's direct materials, work-in-process, and finished goods inventories were destroyed. The company did have access to certain incomplete accounting records, which revealed the following:

1. Beginning inventories, January 1, 2004:

   Direct materials    $32,000
   Work-in-process    68,000
   Finished goods    30,000

2. Key ratios for the month of January 2004:

   Gross profit = 20% of sales
   Prime costs = 70% of manufacturing costs
   Factory overhead = 40% of conversion costs

3. Ending work-in-process is always 10% of the monthly manufacturing costs. All costs are incurred uniformly in the manufacturing process.

4. Actual operations data for the month of January 2004:

   Sales    $900,000
   Direct materials purchases    320,000
   Direct labour incurred    360,000

**Required:**

1. From the above data, reconstruct a statement of cost of goods manufactured.

2. Calculate the total cost of inventory lost, identifying each category where possible (i.e., direct materials, work-in-process, and finished goods), at January 30, 2004. (CMA Canada adapted)

**2–22**

LO3

In January 2004, Sayers Manufacturing incurred the following costs in manufacturing Detecto, its only product:

| | |
|---|---|
| Direct materials purchased | $900,000 |
| Direct labour incurred | 710,000 |
| Benefits | 75,000 |
| Overtime premium | 50,000 |
| Supervisory salaries | 125,000 |
| Utility expenses | 92,500 |
| Amortization (equipment) | 22,800 |
| Supplies (factory) | 10,000 |
| Factory rent | 31,300 |

An analysis of the accounting records showed the following balances in the inventory accounts at the beginning and end of January:

| | January 1 | January 31 |
|---|---|---|
| Direct materials | $ 80,000 | $ 90,000 |
| Work in process | 110,000 | 74,600 |
| Finished goods | 95,000 | 108,000 |

Sayers treats overtime premium and benefits as indirect costs.

**Required:**
1. Determine the cost of goods manufactured for January 2004.
2. What was the cost of goods sold for January 2004? (CMA Canada adapted)

## Managerial Decision Cases

⚹ 2–23

Cost Classification;
Income Statement;
Unit-Based Cost
Behaviour; Service
Organization

LO2, LO3

Gateway Construction Company is a family-operated business that was founded in 1950 by Samuel Gateway. In the beginning, the company consisted of Gateway and three employees laying gas, water, and sewage pipelines as subcontractors. Currently, the company employs 25 to 30 people; Jack Gateway, Samuel's son, directs it. The company's main business specialty continues to be laying pipeline. Most of Gateway's work comes from contracts with city and municipal agencies. All of the company's work is located in Saskatchewan. The company's sales volume averages $3 million, and profits vary between 0 and 10 percent of sales.

Sales and profits have been somewhat below average for the past three years due to a recession and intense competition. Because of this competition, Jack Gateway is constantly reviewing the prices that other companies bid for jobs; when a bid is lost, he makes every attempt to analyze the reasons for the differences between his bid and that of his competitors. He uses this information to increase the competitiveness of future bids.

Jack has become convinced that Gateway's current accounting system is deficient. Currently, all expenses are simply deducted from revenues to arrive at net income. No effort is made to distinguish among the costs of laying pipe, obtaining contracts, and administering the company.

With these thoughts in mind, Jack began a careful review of the income statement for the previous year (see below). First, he noted that jobs were priced on the basis of equipment hours, with an average price of $165 per equipment hour. However, when it came to classifying and assigning costs, he decided that he needed some help. One thing that really puzzled him was how to classify his own salary of $114,000. About half of his time was spent in bidding and securing contracts, and the other half was spent in general administrative matters.

**Gateway Construction**
**Income Statement**
**For the Year Ended December 31, 2004**

| | | |
|---|---:|---:|
| Sales (18,200 equipment hours at $165) | | $3,003,000 |
| Less expenses: | | |
| Utilities | $ 24,000 | |
| Machine operators | 218,000 | |
| Rent (office building) | 24,000 | |
| Accounting fees | 20,000 | |
| Other direct labour | 265,700 | |
| Administrative salaries | 114,000 | |
| Supervisor salaries | 70,000 | |
| Pipe | 1,401,340 | |
| Tires and fuel | 418,600 | |
| Amortization, equipment | 198,000 | |
| Salaries of mechanics | 50,000 | |
| Advertising | 15,000 | |
| Total expenses | | 2,818,640 |
| Net income | | $ 184,360 |

**Required:**

1. Classify the costs in the income statement as (1) costs of laying pipe (production costs); (2) costs of securing contracts (selling costs); or (3) costs of general administration. For production costs, identify direct materials, direct labour,

and overhead costs. The company never has significant work in process: most jobs are started and completed within a day.

2. Using the functional classification developed in Requirement 1, prepare an income statement. What is the average cost per equipment hour for laying pipe?

3. Assume that a significant cost driver is equipment hours. Identify the costs that would likely be traced to jobs using this driver. Explain why you think that these costs are traceable using equipment hours. What is the cost per equipment hour for these traceable costs?

**2–24**

Cost Information and Ethical Behaviour; Service Organization

**LO1**

Jean Erickson, manager and owner of an advertising company in Winnipeg, Manitoba, had arranged a meeting with Leroy Gee, the chief accountant for a large local competitor. The two were lifelong friends. They had grown up together in a small town and attended the same university. Leroy was a competent, successful accountant but was currently experiencing some personal financial difficulties. The problems were created by some investments that had turned sour, leaving him with a $15,000 personal loan to pay off—just at the time that his oldest son was scheduled to enter university.

Jean, on the other hand, was struggling to establish a successful advertising business. She had recently acquired the rights to open a branch office of a large regional advertising agency headquartered in Edmonton, Alberta. During her first two years, she had managed to build a small, profitable practice; however, her chance to gain a significant foothold in the Winnipeg advertising community hinged on her successfully winning a bid to represent the province of Manitoba in a major campaign aimed at attracting new industry and tourism. The meeting she had scheduled with Leroy concerned the bid she planned to submit.

**Jean**: "Leroy, I'm at a critical point in my business venture. If I can win the bid for the province's advertising dollars, I'll be set. Winning the bid will bring $600,000 to $700,000 in revenues into the company. On top of that, I estimate that the publicity will bring in another $200,000 to $300,000 in new business."

**Leroy**: "I understand. My boss is anxious to win that business as well. It would mean a huge increase in profits for my company. It's a competitive business, though. As new as you are, I doubt that you'll have much chance of winning."

**Jean**: "You may be wrong. You're forgetting two very important considerations. First, I have the backing of all the resources and talent of a regional agency. Second, I have some political connections. Last year, I was hired to run the publicity side of the premier's campaign. He was impressed with my work and would like me to have this business. I am confident that the proposals I submit will be very competitive. My only concern is to submit a bid that beats your company. If I come in with a lower bid and with good proposals, the premier can see to it that I get the work."

**Leroy**: "Sounds promising. If you do win, however, there will be a lot of upset people. After all, they are going to claim that the business should have been given to local advertisers, not to some out-of-province company. Given the size of your office, you'll have to get support from Edmonton. You could take a lot of heat."

**Jean**: "True. But I am the owner of the branch office. That fact alone should blunt most of the criticism. Who can argue that I'm not a local? Listen, with your help, I think I can win this bid. Furthermore, if I do win it, you can reap some direct benefits. With that kind of business, I can afford to hire an accountant, and I'll make it worthwhile for you to transfer jobs. I can offer you an up-front bonus of $15,000. On top of that, I'll increase your annual salary by 20 percent. That should solve most of your financial difficulties. After all, we have been friends since day one—and what are friends for?"

**Leroy:** "Jean, my wife would be ecstatic if I were able to improve our financial position as quickly as this opportunity affords. I certainly hope that you win the bid. What kind of help can I provide?"

**Jean:** "Simple. To win, all I have to do is beat the bid submitted by your company. Before I submit my bid, I would like you to review it. With the financial skills you have, it should be easy for you to spot any excessive costs that I may have included. Or perhaps I will have included the wrong kind of costs. By cutting excessive costs and eliminating costs that may not be directly related to the project, I should be able to make my bid competitive enough to meet or beat your company's bid."

**Required:**

1. What would you do if you were Leroy? Fully explain the reasons for your choice.
2. What is the likely outcome if Leroy agrees to review the bid? Is there much risk to him personally if he reviews the bid? Should the degree of risk have any bearing on his decision?
3. Assume that Leroy is a CMA. Apply the standards of ethical conduct for management accountants to the proposal given to Leroy. What standards would be violated if he agrees to review the bid?

## Research Assignments

**2–25**

Cybercase

LO1, LO3, LO4

Obtain copies of financial statements for a manufacturing company and a service organization from the Internet. Write a memo discussing the differences and similarities of the two statements.

**2–26**

Research Assignment

LO1, LO3, LO4

Interview an accountant who works for either a manufacturing company or a service organization (preferably one who works in cost accounting). Ask that person the following questions, and write up his or her responses:

a. What product or products does your organization produce?
b. What costs are assigned to the product or products produced?
c. For a particular product, what direct materials are used?
d. What percentage of total manufacturing costs is direct labour? materials? overhead?
e. How is overhead assigned to the products?
f. Do you use or plan to use an activity-based management accounting system? Why or why not?

# Activity Cost Behaviour

**After studying Chapter 3, you should be able to:**

1. Define and describe cost behaviour for fixed, variable, and mixed costs.

2. Explain the role of the resource usage model in understanding cost behaviour.

3. Separate mixed costs into their fixed and variable components using the high–low method, the scatterplot method, and the method of least squares.

4. Evaluate the reliability of a cost equation.

5. Discuss the role of multiple regression in assessing cost behaviour.

6. Describe the use of managerial judgment in determining cost behaviour.

# Scenario

"I have just been told that our quality costs make up about 20 percent of divisional sales revenues. I was also told that quality costs are incurred because poor quality exists or may exist. Twenty percent seems high to me. All this time I thought that we were spending money to create better quality, not because we had poor quality. Rick, what am I missing here?" asked Patricia Fernandez, manager of a small-appliance division. "What do we need to do to increase our efficiency?"

Rick Anderson, divisional controller, pondered the questions a moment and then responded.

Rick: "Patricia, based on some recent seminars that I have attended, I now realize that managing costs and increasing efficiency have a lot to do with managing the activities that we perform inside the division. But to manage activities, we really need to understand how the costs of activities change as activity output changes. Consider our rework activity. When our inspection activity detects a bad appliance, we tear it apart and redo the work so that the product functions as it should. Some costs, such as the amortization on the equipment used, do not change as the number of reworked products increases. Other costs, like materials and power, do increase with the number of units reworked. And some costs will change only with fairly large changes in activity output."

Patricia: "This is interesting, but how will understanding this cost behaviour help me increase my division's efficiency?"

Rick : "Simple. If it is really true that the cost of the rework activity is a function of the number of units reworked, then you can manage costs by focusing on what drives rework costs: reworked units. If we can find ways to reduce the number of defective units, then the cost of the rework activity should decrease, increasing our overall efficiency. And it would be interesting—in fact, essential—to know how the cost of resources used changes as the activity output changes. For example, we may need to spend more in preventing bad units to reduce rework. If the increase in prevention costs is less than the reduction in rework costs, then we would want to increase our prevention activity."

**Questions to Think About**
1. Suppose that the division reduces the demand for rework activity. Will resource spending be reduced by the same proportion for this activity? Is there a difference between resource spending and resource usage?

2. Suppose that I know the total cost of rework activity and the total number of units reworked. Given this information, can I determine how much of this total cost is variable? How much is fixed? Is knowing fixed- and variable-cost behaviour important?

3. What role does management play in determining cost behaviour?

4. Can you think of reasons other than those suggested by the scenario that make it important for managers to understand cost behaviour?

## The Basics of Cost Behaviour

**Objective 1**

Define and describe cost behaviour for fixed, variable, and mixed costs.

In Chapter 2, we looked at the way costs can be used to determine the cost of goods sold and the value of ending inventory. These costs are important for preparing external financial reports—namely, the income statement and the balance sheet. The costs that are reported on these statements are organized by function. That is, all of the company's costs are put into one of three categories: production or manufacturing (in the cost of goods sold account), marketing expenses, and administrative expenses. This organization is fine for external reporting: in fact, it is required. However, the functional groupings are not helpful at all for budgeting, control, and decision making. For these purposes, we need to understand cost behaviour.

Suppose that a new company is expanding rapidly. Last year, the company made and sold 10,000 units; in the coming year, it expects to sell 20,000 units. Could we say that costs in the coming year will double? No, probably not. In fact, we would expect that the cost of making 20,000 units would be less than twice the cost of making 10,000 units. The reason is that, while some costs are *variable* and will double as output doubles, other costs are *fixed* and will not change as output doubles. In order to answer what will happen to costs as output doubles, we need to know about cost behaviour.

**cost behaviour**

The way in which a cost changes in relation to changes in activity usage.

**Cost behaviour** is the general term for describing whether costs change as output changes. Costs react to output changes in many different ways. We will begin by looking at the simplest possibilities—fixed costs, variable costs, and mixed costs.

### Fixed Costs

**fixed cost**

Costs that, *in total*, are constant within the relevant range as the activity output varies.

A cost that stays the same as output changes is a fixed cost. More formally, a **fixed cost** is a cost that, *in total*, remains constant within a relevant range as the level of activity output changes. To illustrate fixed-cost behaviour, consider Reddy Heaters, a company that produces insert heaters for coffeemakers. Although there are many activities performed within the plant, we will look at only one: the pipe-cutting activity. Here machines are used to cut thin metal pipe into 8-centimetre segments. Since one pipe segment is used in each insert heater, we can use the number of heaters produced as the quantifiable output measure for the cutting activity.

For simplicity, assume that the cutting activity uses two resources: (1) the cutting machine and (2) power to operate the cutting machine. Consider the cutting machines: they are leased for $60,000 per year and have the capacity to produce up to 240,000 pipe segments for insert heaters. The cost of leasing the cutting machines is a fixed cost: it stays at $60,000 total cost per year no matter how many segments are cut. This behaviour is illustrated by the following example:

**Reddy Heaters**

| Lease of Machines | Number of Insert heaters | Unit Cost |
|---|---|---|
| $60,000 | 0 | N/A |
| 60,000 | 60,000 | $1.00 |
| 60,000 | 120,000 | 0.50 |
| 60,000 | 180,000 | 0.33 |
| 60,000 | 240,000 | 0.25 |

Two parts of the fixed-cost definition need further discussion: relevant range and the phrase "in total."

**relevant range**

The range over which an assumed cost relationship is valid for the normal operations of a firm.

**Relevant range** is the range over which the assumed cost/output relationship is valid. For the cutting activity, the cutting machines currently leased can produce up to 240,000 insert heaters per year. Thus the relevant range is from 0 units to 240,000 units—the output for which the total cost of leasing remains constant. Reddy Heaters pays $60,000 per year for leasing the equipment regardless of whether it produces 0, 60,000, 120,000, or 240,000 units.

We can gain additional insight into the phrase "in total" by portraying the fixed costs graphically (Exhibit 3–1). As can be seen, for the relevant range, fixed-cost behaviour is illustrated by a horizontal line. Notice that at 120,000 units produced, the leasing cost is $60,000; at 240,000 units produced, the leasing cost is still $60,000. This line visually demonstrates that the total cost remains unchanged as the output varies. We can represent total fixed costs by the following linear equation:

$$\text{Total fixed costs} = \$60,000$$

Notice that total fixed costs do not depend on the output measure (number of insert heaters). They are $60,000 no matter what the output.

**EXHIBIT** **3-1**

Fixed-Cost Behaviour

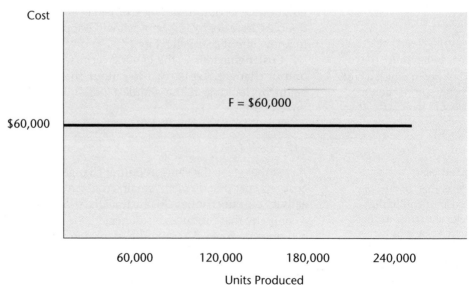

While the total cost of leasing remains unchanged, the cost per insert heater (the unit cost) does change as more units are produced. As the table shows, within the range of 60,000 to 240,000 units, the unit cost of leasing the pipe-cutting machines decreases from $1 to $0.25. Thus, while fixed costs *in total* remain unchanged as output increases, the *unit fixed cost* changes because the fixed costs are being spread out over more output.

A final note on fixed costs is that they can change—but that change does not depend on changes in output. For example, suppose that the company leasing the cutting machines to Reddy Heaters increases the lease payment from $60,000 to $65,000 per year. The cost of the machines would still be fixed, but at the new higher amount. In the graph, the entire cost line would shift up to $65,000. The relevant range would still be from 0 units to 240,000 units. Thus, at 120,000 units produced, the leasing cost is $65,000; at 240,000 units produced, the leasing cost is still $65,000. Again, the cost remains unchanged as the level of output varies.

## Variable Costs

**variable cost**

Costs that, in total, vary in direct proportion to changes in a cost driver.

While fixed costs do not change as output varies, variable costs do change as output changes. A **variable cost** is a cost that, in total, varies in direct proportion to changes in activity output. That is, a variable cost goes up as output goes up and goes down as output goes down.

Let's expand the Reddy Heaters example to include the other resource used by the cutting activity: power. Power cost behaves differently from the cost of the cutting machines. Power is consumed only if output is produced; therefore, as more output is produced, more power is used. Assume that each time a segment for an insert heater is cut, the machine uses 0.1 kilowatt-hour at $2 per kilowatt-hour. The cost of power per insert heater is $0.20 ($2 × 0.1). The cost of power for various levels of activity output follows:

**Reddy Heaters**

| Cost of Power | Number of Insert heaters | Unit Cost |
|---|---|---|
| $ 0 | 0 | N/A |
| 12,000 | 60,000 | $0.20 |
| 24,000 | 120,000 | 0.20 |
| 36,000 | 180,000 | 0.20 |
| 48,000 | 240,000 | 0.20 |

As more insert heaters are produced, the total cost of power increases in direct proportion. For example, as activity output doubles from 60,000 to 120,000 units, the total cost of power doubles from $12,000 to $24,000. Notice also that the unit cost of power is constant.

We can also represent variable costs by a linear equation. Here total variable costs depend on the level of the activity output. This relationship can be described by the following equation:

Total variable costs = Variable cost per unit × Number of units

In the Reddy Heaters example, the cost of power is described by the following equation:

Total variable costs = $0.20 × Number of insert heaters

Exhibit 3–2 graphically illustrates a variable cost. Notice that variable-cost behaviour is a straight line starting at the origin. At zero units processed, total variable cost is zero. However, as units produced increase, the total variable cost also increases. For example, at 120,000 units, the total variable cost is $24,000. We

EXHIBIT    3-2

Variable-Cost Behaviour

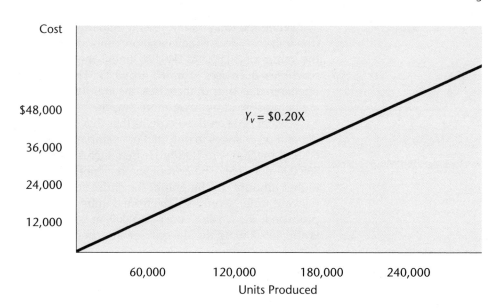

can see that total cost increases in direct proportion to increases in the number of units; the rate of increase is measured by the slope of the line. Here, the slope of the line is 0.20.

## Mixed Costs

**mixed cost**

A cost that has both a fixed and a variable component.

A **mixed cost** is a cost that has both a fixed and a variable component. For example, sales representatives are often paid a salary plus a commission on their sales. Suppose that Reddy Heaters has three sales representatives, each earning a salary of $10,000 per year plus a commission of $0.50 per insert heater sold. The activity is selling insert heaters, and the activity output is units sold. If 100,000 insert heaters are sold, then the total selling cost (associated with the sales representatives) is $80,000—the sum of the fixed salary cost of $30,000 (3 × $10,000) and the variable cost of $50,000 ($0.50 × 100,000). The linear equation for a mixed cost is given by the following:

$$\text{Total cost} = \text{Fixed cost} + \text{Total variable cost}$$

For Reddy Heaters, the selling cost is represented by the following equation:

$$\text{Total cost} = \$30,000 + (\$0.50 \times \text{Units sold})$$

The following table shows the selling cost for different levels of sales activity:

| | | Reddy Heaters | | |
|---|---|---|---|---|
| Insert Heaters Sold | Fixed Cost of Selling | Variable Cost of Selling | Total Cost | Selling Cost per Unit |
| 40,000 | $30,000 | $ 20,000 | $ 50,000 | $1.25 |
| 80,000 | 30,000 | 40,000 | 70,000 | 0.88 |
| 120,000 | 30,000 | 60,000 | 90,000 | 0.75 |
| 160,000 | 30,000 | 80,000 | 110,000 | 0.69 |
| 200,000 | 30,000 | 100,000 | 130,000 | 0.65 |

The graph for our mixed-cost example given in Exhibit 3–3 assumes that the relevant range is 0 units to 200,000 units. Mixed costs are represented by a line that intercepts the vertical axis (at $30,000 for this example). The intercept corresponds to the fixed-cost component, and the slope of the line gives the variable cost per unit of the activity output (the slope is $0.50 for this example).

**EXHIBIT 3-3**

Mixed-Cost Behaviour

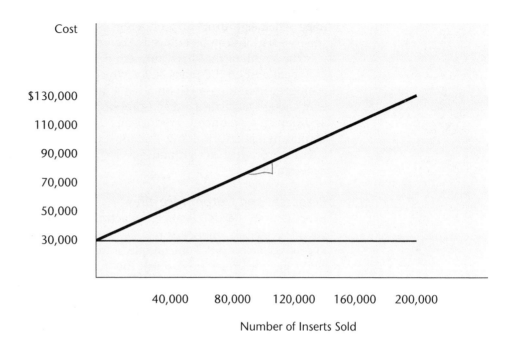

## Classifying Costs According to Behaviour

In our discussion of fixed, variable, and mixed costs, we concentrated on the definitions and took for granted a number of factors that are important for determining whether a cost is fixed or variable. Now it is time to look more closely at the way we can classify costs according to behaviour. To assess cost behaviour, we must first consider the time horizon. Then we must identify the resources needed and output of the activity. Finally, we must measure the inputs and outputs and determine the impact of output changes on the activity cost.

### Time Horizon

Determining whether a cost is fixed or variable depends on the time horizon. According to economics, in the **long run**, all costs are variable; in the **short run**, some costs may be fixed. But how long is the short run? In the Reddy Heaters example, the leasing cost of the cutting machines was fixed for a year, so a year was the length of the short run for that cost. The length of the short run may differ from one cost to another cost.

Consider a process that takes materials and moulds them into the shape of a garden hose. The output is the number of metres of hose. As the amount of hose changes, the direct materials used are relatively easy to adjust (acquiring more as the output increases and less as it decreases). For all practical purposes, the company may treat direct materials as strictly variable, even though for the next few hours (or days) the amount of materials already purchased may be fixed.

What about direct labour? In some settings, a company may be able to hire and lay off its labour relatively quickly—in which case direct labour could be treated as a variable cost. In other cases, a company may not be able to lay off labour for short-term drops in production. For example, there may be contracts

**long run**

A period of time in which all costs are variable.

**short run**

A period of time in which at least one cost is fixed.

with labour unions that make such layoffs impossible, even when there have been permanent changes in the need for labour. Only when the contract is renegotiated can the level of labour be adjusted. In this case, direct labour is a fixed cost rather than a variable cost. The same observation can be made for other forms of labour. For example, salaries of moulding production line supervisors are also difficult to adjust as the activity output varies. It could take months, or even years, to determine whether a drop in production output is permanent and the number of supervisory jobs can be reduced. Accordingly, this cost is typically seen as fixed.

The length of the short-run period depends to some extent on management judgment and on the purpose for which cost behaviour is being estimated. For example, submitting a bid on a one-time, special order may span only a month, long enough to create a bid and produce the order. Other types of decisions, such as dropping a product or product-mix decisions, will affect a much longer period of time. In this case, the costs that must be considered are long-run variable costs, including product design and development, market development, and market penetration.

### Resources and Output Measures

Every activity needs resources to accomplish the task at hand. Resources may include materials, energy or fuel, labour, and capital. These inputs are combined to produce an output. For example, if the activity is moving materials, the inputs could include crates (materials), fuel (energy), a forklift operator (labour), and forklifts (capital). The output would be moved materials. But how do we measure this output? One measure is the number of times the activity is performed. For example, suppose that we are moving raw materials from the storeroom to the assembly line. A good measure of output is the number of moves. The more moves that are made, the higher the cost of moving. Therefore, we could say that the number of moves is a good output measure for material handling. Exhibit 3–4 illustrates the relationship between inputs, activities, output, and cost behaviour.

Another term for output measure is driver. Recall from Chapter 2 that activity drivers are observable causal factors that measure the amount of resources a cost object uses. Activity drivers explain changes in activity costs by measuring changes in activity use or output. Thus, the driver for material handling may be the number of moves; the driver for shipping goods may be the number of units sold; and the driver for laundering hospital bedding may be kilograms of laundry. The choice of driver is tailored not only to the particular organization but also

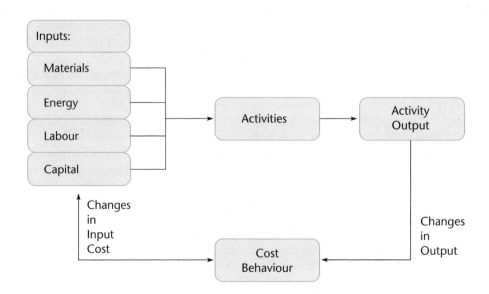

**EXHIBIT   3-4**

Activity Cost Behaviour Model

to the particular activity or cost being measured. Therefore, in order to understand the behaviour of costs, we must first determine the underlying activities and associated drivers that measure activity capacity and usage. The need to understand this cost-activity relationship leads us to determine an appropriate measure of activity output, or activity driver.

There are two general categories of activity drivers: production (or unit-level) drivers and nonunit-level drivers. Production drivers explain changes in costs as the number of units produced changes. Kilograms of direct materials, kilowatt-hours used to run production machinery, and direct labour hours are examples of production drivers. In other words, as kilograms of materials used, kilowatt-hours, and direct labour hours increase, output also increases.

### Nonunit-Level Drivers

Nonunit-level drivers explain changes in cost as factors other than units change. For example, setups are a nonunit-level activity. Every time the plant has to stop producing one product in order to set up the production line to produce a different product, setup costs are incurred. No matter how many units are produced in the new batch, the setup cost remains the same. You have probably run into this type of activity in your personal life. Let's consider a common household production activity—making chocolate chip cookies. Suppose you decide to make two dozen cookies. First you have to set up for cookie baking by taking out a bowl, a spoon, a baking sheet, and the ingredients. Another time, you might decide to make four dozen cookies. You still have to set up, and that activity will probably take the same amount of effort as it took you to set up for two dozen cookies. The point is that setting up is not related to the number of units (cookies). Instead, it is a nonunit-level activity. Other examples of nonunit-level activities include amortization on the plant building, the salary of the production manager, and the cost of operating the purchasing department.

In a functional-based costing system, cost behaviour is assumed to be described by unit-level drivers only. In an activity-based system, both unit-level and nonunit-level drivers are used. Thus the ABC system produces a much richer view of cost behaviour than a functional-based system.

## Activities, Resource Usage, and Cost Behaviour

**Objective** 2

Explain the role of the resource usage model in understanding cost behaviour.

**practical capacity**

The efficient level of activity performance.

Short-run costs often do not adequately reflect all the costs necessary to design, produce, market, distribute, and support a product. In the early 1990s, there were some new insights into the nature of long-run and short-run cost behaviour.[1] These insights relate to activities and the resources needed to perform them.

Capacity is simply the actual or potential ability to do something. So when we talk about capacity for an activity, we are describing the amount of the activity the company can perform. How much capacity is needed depends on the level of performance. Usually, we can assume that the capacity needed corresponds to the level where the activity is performed efficiently. This efficient level of activity performance is called **practical capacity**. On occasion there is excess capacity. To see how this happens and how it affects cost behaviour, we need to look at flexible and committed resources.

---

1. The concepts presented in the remainder of this section are based on Alfred M. King, "The Current Status of Activity-Based Costing: An Interview with Robin Cooper and Robert S. Kaplan," *Management Accounting* (September 1991): pp. 22-26; Robin Cooper and Robert S. Kaplan, "Activity-Based Systems: Measuring the Costs of Resource Usage," *Accounting Horizons* (September 1992): pp. 1-13; and Robert S. Kaplan and Anthony A. Atkinson, *Advanced Management Accounting* (3rd ed.), Prentice-Hall, 1998.

## Flexible Resources

**flexible resources**

Resources that are acquired as used and needed. There is no unused or excess capacity for these resources.

It would be nice if a company could purchase only those resources it needed and could purchase them precisely at the time they were needed. Sometimes that happens. For example, direct materials are frequently purchased at the time and in the amount needed. This kind of a resource is called a *flexible resource*. **Flexible resources** are supplied as needed and used; they are acquired from outside sources, where the terms of acquisition do not require any long-term commitment for any particular amount of the resource. Thus, the company is free to buy only the amount needed. As a result, the quantity of the resource supplied equals the quantity required for production. Materials and energy are examples. There is no unused capacity for this category of resources, since the amount of the resource used just equals the amount acquired.

Since the cost of the resources supplied as needed equals the cost of the resources used, the total cost of the resources increases as the amount of the activity increases (the demand for the resource). So the cost of flexible resources is a variable cost.

## Committed Resources

**committed resources**

Resources that are purchased in advance of usage. These resources may or may not have unused (excess) capacity.

Other resources must be purchased before they are needed. A factory building is a good example. The building must be planned and built before production takes place. **Committed resources** are resources that are supplied in advance of usage; they are acquired by the use of either explicit or implicit contract to obtain a given quantity of resource, regardless of whether the amount of resource available is fully used or not. Committed resources may have unused capacity, since more may be available than are actually used.

Let's look further at committed resources. Many resources are acquired to be used for particular time periods, and before the actual demands for the resource are realized. For example, organizations acquire many multiperiod service capacities by paying cash up front or by entering into an explicit contract that requires periodic cash payments. Buying or leasing buildings and equipment is an example of this form of advance resource acquisition. The annual expense associated with the multiperiod category is independent of actual usage; thus, these costs can be defined as **committed fixed costs** and they provide long-term activity capacity.

**committed fixed costs**

Costs incurred for the acquisition of long-term activity capacity, usually as the result of strategic planning.

A second important example of committed resources concerns organizations that acquire resources in advance through implicit contracts, usually with their salaried and hourly employees. The implicit understanding is that the organization will maintain employment levels even though there may be temporary downturns in the quantity of activity used. As a result, the cost associated with this category of resources is independent of the quantity used—at least in the short run. Thus, in the short run, the amount of the resource cost remains unchanged even though the quantity used may vary, and this resource category can be treated (cautiously) as a fixed cost. We may call these short-term committed resources **discretionary fixed costs**. They are costs incurred for the acquisition of short-term activity capacity.

**discretionary fixed costs**

Costs incurred for the acquisition of short-term capacity or services, usually as the result of yearly planning.

An example of implicit contracting is hiring three receiving clerks, for $90,000, who can supply the capacity of processing 9,000 receiving orders ("receiving orders" is the driver used to measure the receiving activity's capacity and usage).[2] Certainly, none of the three clerks would expect to be laid off if only 6,000 orders were actually processed—unless, of course, the downturn in demand is viewed as

---

2. Receiving refers to the activities involved in bringing purchased materials into the plant. The activities may include inspecting, unpacking, creating a receiving order to match to the invoice, and moving the materials to the storeroom.

permanent. This implicit contracting raises ethical issues. Many companies today are turning to contingent employment to handle variation in demand for labour services. A key reason for the increase in contingent employment includes "buffering core workers against job loss." Apparently, many companies attempt to shield long-time workers from market fluctuations.[3] Suppose that the drop is permanent. In this case, we have an activity with too much capacity; until we reduce the capacity, resource spending will not be reduced. Thus, resource spending changes lag changes in permanent activity output demands.

## Step-Cost Behaviour

**step cost**

A cost function in which cost is defined for ranges of activity use rather than point values. The function has the property of displaying constant cost over a range of activity use and then changing to a different cost level as a new range of activity use is undertaken.

In our discussion of cost behaviour, we have assumed that the cost function is continuous. In reality, some cost functions may be discontinuous, as shown in Exhibit 3–5. This type of cost function is known as a step function. A **step cost** displays a constant level of cost for a range of output and then jumps to a higher level of cost at some point, where it remains for a similar range of output. In Exhibit 3–5, the cost is $100 as long as the output is between 0 and 10 units. If the output is between 10 and 20 units, the cost jumps to $200.

Items that display step-cost behaviour must be purchased in chunks. The width of the step defines the range of activity usage for which that amount of the resource must be acquired. The width of the step in Exhibit 3–5 is 10 units of output. If the width of the step is narrow, as in Exhibit 3–5, the cost of the resource changes in response to fairly small changes in usage. An example of a cost with narrow steps is paint. A house painting company may buy paint in 20-litre pails. Each additional pail used will move the cost of paint to the next level or step. A typical company would use many pails a year, so the step is narrow. If the width of the step is narrow, we can approximate these costs with a strictly variable-cost assumption.

**EXHIBIT** **3-5**

Step-Cost Function

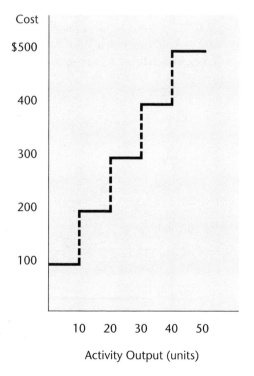

3.  "Contingent Employment on the Rise," *Deloitte & Touche Review* (September 4, 1995): pp. 1-2.

Other types of step costs have fairly wide steps. In reality, many so-called fixed costs are probably best described by a step-cost function. Many committed resources, particularly those that involve implicit contracting, follow a step-cost function. Suppose, for example, that a company hires three sustaining engineers; these are engineers responsible for redesigning existing products to meet customer requirements. Each engineer is paid a salary of $50,000 per year and can process 2,500 engineering change orders per year. The company has acquired the capacity to process 7,500 (3 × 2,500) change orders per year at a total cost of $150,000 (3 × $50,000). The nature of the resource requires that the capacity be acquired in chunks (one engineer hired at a time). The cost function for this example is displayed in Exhibit 3–6. Notice that the width of the steps is 2,500 units—a much wider step than the cost function displayed in Exhibit 3–5.

Step costs with wide steps are assigned to the fixed-cost category. Most of these costs are fixed over the normal operating range of a company. If that range is 5,000 to 7,500 change orders (as shown in Exhibit 3–6), then the company will spend $150,000 on engineering resources. Only if the company wants to increase its capacity for engineering above the 7,500-order level will it increase its spending on engineers.

Frequently, there is excess capacity for activities that are characterized by this type of step behaviour. For example, during the year the company may not actually process 7,500 change orders: that is, all of the available change order-processing capacity may not be used. Suppose 6,000 change orders are processed during the year. We can see that 80 percent (6,000/7,500) of the engineering capacity is actually being used. The engineering department has 20 percent unused or excess capacity. The cost of this unused capacity is $30,000 (0.20 × $150,000). Note that the cost of unused activity occurs because the resource (engineers) must be acquired in lumpy (whole) amounts. Even if the company had anticipated the need for only 6,000 change orders, it would have been difficult to hire the equivalent of 2.4 engineers (6,000/2,500).

The example illustrates that when resources are acquired in advance, there may be a difference between the amount purchased and the amount actually used. This can occur only for activities that require committed resources, with costs that display a fixed-cost behaviour. To show this, let's expand our engineer-

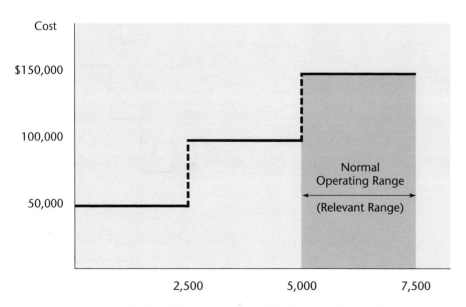

Step-Fixed Costs

Activity Usage: Number of Engineering Change Orders

ing example to include both flexible and committed resources. Recall that there are three engineers, each paid $50,000 and each capable of processing 2,500 change orders. Assume that $90,000 was spent on supplies for the engineering activity and that these supplies are a flexible resource. What is the total cost of one change order?

The cost of a single change order is a combination of its fixed cost (the committed resource—engineering) and its variable cost (the flexible resource—supplies). To calculate the fixed cost per unit, we need to calculate the fixed activity rate. The **fixed activity rate** is simply the total committed cost divided by the *total capacity available*.

**fixed activity rate**

The fixed activity cost divided by the total capacity of the activity driver.

Fixed engineering rate = $150,000/7,500 = $20 per change order

Of course, the **variable activity rate** is the total cost of the flexible resources divided by the *capacity used*.

**variable activity rate**

The total variable activity cost divided by the amount of activity driver used.

Variable engineering rate = $90,000/6,000 = $15 per change order

Therefore, the total cost of one change order is $35. Notice the difference between the 7,500 change orders used to compute the fixed activity rate and the 6,000 orders used to compute the variable activity rate. Because the fixed rate is based on committed resources, we use the capacity available. After all, the three engineers could have processed as many as 7,500 orders. For the variable rate, we use the actual capacity used. This is because the flexible resources are purchased as necessary, so that the $90,000 of supplies relate to the 6,000 change orders actually processed.

Typically, the functional-based management accounting system provides information only about the cost of the resources purchased. An activity-based management accounting system, on the other hand, tells us how much of the activity is used and the cost of its usage. The relationship between resources supplied and resources used is expressed by the following equation:

Resources available = Resources used + Unused capacity

This equation can be expressed in both physical and financial terms. For the engineering order example, the relationship takes the following form when expressed in physical terms:

Available orders = Orders used + Orders unused
7,500 orders = 6,000 orders + 1,500 orders

When the relationship is expressed in financial terms, we simply attach dollar amounts. For the engineering example, this takes the following form:

Cost of orders supplied = Cost of orders used + Cost of unused orders
$240,000 = $210,000 + $30,000

The cost of orders used is $210,000 [($20 + $15) × 6,000]. Of course, the $240,000 is equal to the $150,000 spent on engineers and the $90,000 spent on supplies.

Why is this formulation important? It is important because it gives managers crucial information about their ability to expand or contract production. The $30,000 of excess engineering capacity means that, for example, a new product could be introduced without increasing current spending on engineering salaries, provided that the new product uses no more than 1,500 orders. Of course, the cost of engineering supplies will increase with the introduction of new products at the rate of $15 per change order.

## Implications for Control and Decision Making

The activity-based model just described can improve both managerial control and decision making. Operational control systems encourage managers to pay more attention to controlling resource use and spending. For example, a well-designed operational control system allows managers to assess the changes in resource demands that occur from new product-mix decisions. Adding new, customized products may increase the demands for various overhead activities. If sufficient unused activity capacity does not exist, then resource spending must increase. Similarly, if activity management brings about excess capacity (by finding ways to reduce resource usage), managers must carefully consider what to do with the excess capacity. Eliminating the excess capacity may decrease resource spending and thus improve overall profits. Alternatively, the excess capacity could be used to increase the number and type of products, thereby increasing revenues without increasing resource spending.

The activity-based resource usage model also allows managers to calculate the changes in resource supply and demand resulting from implementing such decisions as whether to make or buy a part, to accept or reject special orders, and to keep or drop product lines. Additionally, the model increases the power of a number of traditional management accounting decision-making models. The impact on decision making is explored in the decision-making chapters found in Part 2. Most of the decision-making models in those chapters depend heavily on knowledge of cost behaviour.

## Methods for Separating Mixed Costs into Fixed and Variable Components

**Objective 3**

Separate mixed costs into their fixed and variable components using the high–low method, the scatterplot method, and the method of least squares.

While some costs can be fairly easily classified as strictly variable, fixed, or step-fixed, others fall into the mixed-cost category. It is necessary to separate such costs into fixed and variable components.

Often the only information available is the total cost of an activity and a measure of activity usage. For example, the accounting system will usually record both the total cost of the maintenance activity for a given period and the number of maintenance hours provided during that period. The accounting records do not reveal how much of the total maintenance cost represents a fixed charge and how much represents a variable charge. Often the total cost is simply recorded with no attempt to segregate the fixed and variable costs.

Since accounting records may reveal only the total cost and the associated activity usage of a mixed-cost item, it is necessary to separate the total cost into its fixed and variable components. Only through a formal effort to separate costs can all costs be classified into the appropriate cost behaviour categories.

There are three widely used methods of separating a mixed cost into its fixed and variable components: the high–low method, the scatterplot method, and the method of least squares. Each method requires us to make the simplifying assumption of a linear cost relationship. Therefore, before we examine each of these methods more closely, let's review the concept of linearity.

### Linearity Assumption

The definition of variable cost assumes a linear relationship between the cost of an activity and its associated driver. For example, suppose that Star Company produces personal computers. Each personal computer uses one floppy disk drive, each of which costs $40. The total variable cost of disk drives can be expressed as:

Total variable cost = \$40 × Units produced

If 100 computers are produced, the total cost of floppy drives is \$4,000 (\$40 × 100). If 200 computers are produced, the total cost is \$8,000 (\$40 × 200). As production doubles, the cost of the drives doubles. In other words, cost increases in direct proportion to the number of units produced. The linear relationship for the computer example is portrayed in Exhibit 3–7. How reasonable is this assumption that costs are linear? Do variable activity costs really increase in direct proportion to increases in the level of the activity driver? If not, then how closely does this assumed linear cost function approximate the underlying cost function?

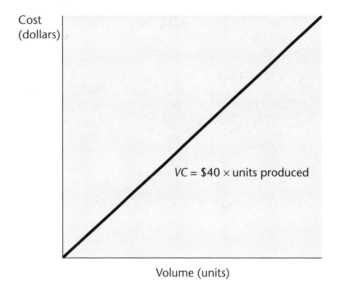

Economists usually argue that variable costs increase at a decreasing rate up to a certain volume, at which point they increase at an increasing rate. This type of nonlinear behaviour is displayed in Exhibit 3–8. Here variable costs increase as the number of units increases, but not in direct proportion. For example, a power supplier that initially has ample capacity may offer prices that decrease per kilowatt-hour to encourage consumption; yet once the power plant capacity has been met, any further demands may produce higher prices to ration a now scarce input

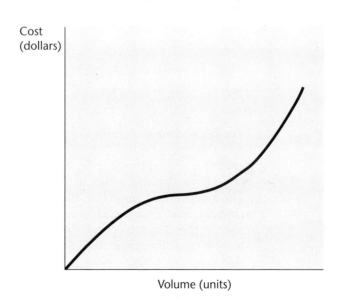

among users. What if the nonlinear view more accurately portrays reality? What do we do then? One possibility is to determine the actual cost function. But every activity could have a different cost function, and this approach could be very time consuming and expensive (if it can even be done). It is much simpler to assume a linear relationship.

If we assume a linear relationship, then our main concern is how closely this assumption approximates the underlying cost function. Exhibit 3–9 gives us some idea of the consequences of assuming a linear cost function. Recall that the relevant range is the range of activity output for which the assumed cost relationships are valid. Here validity refers to how closely the linear cost function approximates the underlying cost function. Note that for units outside the relevant range, the approximation appears to break down.

**EXHIBIT　3-9**

Linear Approximation

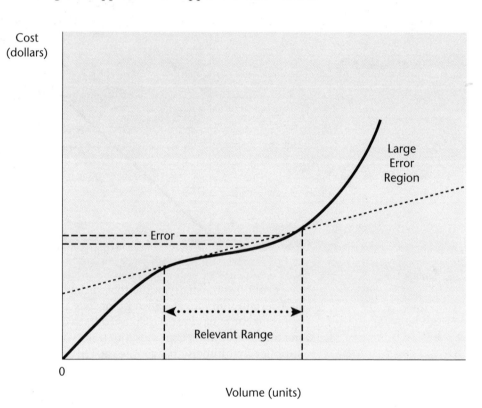

**cost formula**

The linear function $Y = F + VX$, where $Y$ = Total mixed cost, $F$ = Fixed cost, $V$ = Variable cost per unit of activity, and $X$ = Activity level.

**dependent variable**

A variable whose value depends on the value of another variable. For example, $Y$ in the cost formula $Y = F + VX$ depends on the value of $X$.

**independent variable**

A variable whose value does not depend on the value of another variable. For example, in the cost formula $Y = F + VX$, the variable $X$ is an independent variable.

The equation for a linear (or straight-line) mixed-cost function is as follows:

　　　Total mixed cost = Fixed cost + (Variable rate × Activity driver)

This equation is a **cost formula**. Let's take a closer look at each term in the cost formula.

- The **dependent variable** is total mixed cost. It is cost we are trying to predict and total mixed cost is the variable whose value depends on the value of another variable. Its value depends on the values of the parameters and variable on the right-hand side of the equation.
- The **independent variable** is the variable that measures output and explains changes in the cost. It is an activity driver. The choice of an independent variable is related to its economic plausibility. That is, the manager will attempt to find an independent variable that causes or is closely associated with the dependent variable.

**intercept parameter**
The fixed cost, representing the point where the cost formula intercepts the vertical axis. In the cost formula $Y = F + VX$, $F$ is the intercept parameter.

**slope parameter**
The variable cost per unit of activity usage, represented by $V$ in the cost formula $Y = F + VX$.

- The **intercept parameter** corresponds to the fixed cost. Graphically, the intercept parameter is the point at which the mixed-cost line intercepts the cost (vertical) axis (see Exhibit 3–10).
- The **slope parameter** corresponds to the variable cost per unit of activity. Graphically, this represents the slope of the mixed-cost line.

Since accounting records reveal only the total cost and the amount of activity output, those values must be used to estimate the intercept and slope parameters (the fixed cost and the variable rate). With estimates of the fixed cost and the variable rate, the behaviour of the mixed cost can be predicted as activity usage changes.

EXHIBIT **3-10**

Mixed-Cost Behaviour

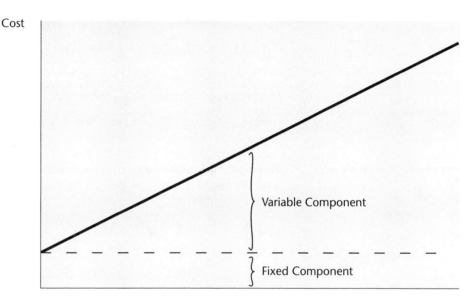

We will examine three methods for estimating the fixed cost and the variable rate: the high–low method, the scatterplot method, and the method of least squares.[4] We will use the same data to illustrate each method so that we can make comparisons. The data have been accumulated for the setup activity of Larson Company's Moncton, New Brunswick, plant. The plant manager believes that setup hours is a good driver for the activity of setting up the production line. Assume that the plant's accounting records show the following setup costs and setup hours for the past five months:

| Month | Setup Cost | Setup Hours |
|---|---|---|
| January | $1,000 | 100 |
| February | 1,250 | 200 |
| March | 2,250 | 300 |
| April | 2,500 | 400 |
| May | 3,750 | 500 |

---

4. For additional discussion of cost estimation, see Anthony A. Atkinson, *Cost Estimation in Management Accounting—Six Case Studies* (Hamilton, Ont.: Society of Management Accountants of Canada, 1987).

## The High–Low Method

From basic geometry, we know that two points are sufficient to determine a line. Once we know two points on a line, then we can determine its equation. Given two points, the slope and the intercept can be determined. The **high–low method** is a method of determining the equation of a straight line by specifying the two points that will be used to compute the slope and intercept parameters. Specifically, the method uses the high and low points. The *high point* is defined as the point with the highest output or activity level. The *low point* is defined as the point with the lowest output or activity level.

**high–low method**

A method for fitting a line to a set of data points using the high and low points in the data set. For a cost formula, the high and low points represent the high and low activity levels. This method is used to break out the fixed and variable components of a mixed cost.

The equation for determining the variable rate (slope parameter) is:

Variable rate = Change in cost/Change in activity
Variable rate = (High cost − Low cost)/(High output − Low output)

The equation for determining the fixed cost (intercept parameter) is:

Fixed cost = Total cost for high point − (Variable rate × High output)

or

Fixed cost = Total cost for low point − (Variable rate × Low output)

Notice that the fixed-cost component can be computed using the total cost at either the high point or the low point.

For Larson, the high point is 500 setup hours at a setup cost of $3,750, or (500, $3,750). The low point is 100 setups at a setup cost of $1,000, or (100, $1,000). Once we identify the high and low points, we can compute the values of the variable rate and the fixed cost:

Variable rate = ($3,750 − $1,000)/(500 − 100) = $2,750/400 = $6.875

and

Fixed cost = $3,750 − ($6.875 × 500) = $312.50

The cost formula using the high–low method is as follows:

Total mixed cost = $312.50 + ($6.875 × Setup hours)

The key point about the total cost formula we have determined is that we can use it to estimate setup costs based on the number of setup hours. If the number of setup hours for June is expected to be 350, this cost formula will predict a total cost of $2,718.75, with fixed costs of $312.50 and variable costs of $2,406.25.

The high–low method has the advantage of objectivity. That is, any two people using the high–low method on a particular data set will arrive at the same answer. In addition, the high–low method allows a manager to get a quick fix on a cost relationship using only two data points. For example, a manager may have only two years' worth of data. Sometimes this will be enough to get a crude approximation of the cost relationship.

The high–low method is usually not as accurate as other methods. Why? First, the high and low points may be *outliers*. Outliers represent atypical cost-activity relationships. If so, the cost formula computed using these two points will not represent what usually takes place. The scatterplot method can help a manager avoid this trap by selecting two points that appear to be representative of the general activity cost pattern. Second, even if these points are not outliers, other pairs of points may clearly be more representative. Again, the scatterplot method allows the choice of the more representative points.

# The Scatterplot Method

**scatterplot method**

A method of fitting a line to a set of data using two points that are selected by judgment. It is used to break out the fixed and variable components of a mixed cost.

**scattergraph**

A plot of (X, Y) data points. For cost analysis, X is activity usage and Y is the associated cost at that activity level.

The **scatterplot method** is a method of determining the equation of a line by plotting the data on a graph. The first step in applying the scatterplot method is to plot the data points so that the relationship between setup costs and activity level can be seen. This plot is referred to as a **scattergraph** and is shown in Exhibit 3–11. The vertical axis is the total setup cost, and the horizontal axis is the number of setup hours.

Inspecting Exhibit 3–11 gives us increased confidence that the assumption of a linear relationship between setup costs and setup hours is reasonable for the indicated range of activity. Thus, one purpose of a scattergraph is to see whether or not the assumed linear relationship is reasonable. Additionally, inspecting the scattergraph may reveal any points that do not seem to fit the general pattern of behaviour. Upon investigation, it may be discovered that these points (the outliers) were due to some unusual occurrences. This knowledge can provide justification for their elimination from the analysis and perhaps lead to a better estimate of the underlying cost function.

A scattergraph can help provide insight concerning the relationship between cost and activity usage. In fact, a scattergraph allows one to visually fit a line to the points on the scattergraph. In doing so, the line should be chosen that appears to best fit the points. In making that choice, a manager or cost analyst is free to use past experience with the behaviour of the cost item. Experience may provide a good intuitive sense of how setup costs behave; the scattergraph then becomes a useful tool for quantifying this intuition. Fitting a line to the points in this way is how the scatterplot method works. Keep in mind that the scattergraph and other statistical aids are tools that can help managers improve their judgment. Using the tools does not restrict the manager from also using judgment to alter any of the estimates produced by formal methods.

Examine Exhibit 3–11 carefully. Based only on the information contained in the graph, how would you fit a line to the points in it? Suppose that you decide that a line passing through points 1 and 3 provides the best fit. Note that the line you decide fits the points does *not* have to pass through any of the plotted points, but the line should best fit all of the points.

| EXHIBIT | 3-11 |
| --- | --- |

Scattergraph for Larson Company

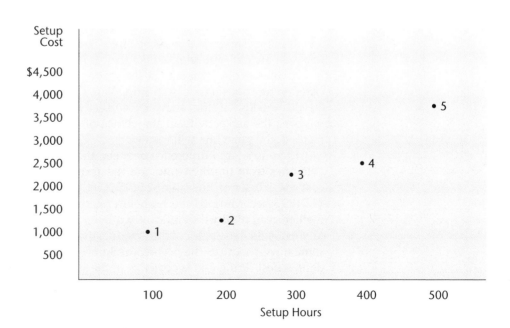

The variable rate can be computed in the following way. First, let point 1 be designated by (100, $1,000) and point 3 by (300, $2,250). Next, use these two points to compute the variable rate (slope):

Variable rate = ($2,250 − $1,000)/(300 − 100) = $1,250/200 = $6.25

Thus, the variable cost per setup hour is $6.25. Given the variable rate, the final step is to compute the fixed-cost component. If we use point 3, the following equation results:

Fixed cost = $2,250 − ($6.25 × 300) = $375

Of course, the fixed-cost component can also be computed using point 1, which produces the same result:

Fixed cost = $1,000 − ($6.25 × 100) = $375

The fixed and variable components of setup cost have now been identified. The cost formula for the setup activity can be expressed as follows:

Total cost = $375 + ($6.25 × Setup hours)

With this formula, the total cost of setups for activity output between 100 and 500 can be predicted and then broken down into fixed and variable components. For example, assume that 350 setup hours are planned for June. Using the cost formula, the predicted cost is $2,562.50 [$375 + ($6.25 × 350)]. Of this total cost, $375 is fixed and $2,187.50 is variable.

We obtained the cost formula for the setup activity by fitting a line to points 1 and 3 in Exhibit 3–11. Judgment was used to select the line. Whereas one person may decide, by inspection, that the best-fitting line is the one that passes through points 1 and 3, others, using their own judgment, may decide that the line should pass through points 2 and 4—or points 1 and 5, or none of the plotted points at all.

A significant advantage of the scatterplot method is that it allows us to see the data. Exhibit 3–12 gives examples of cost behaviour situations that are not appropriate for the simple application of the high–low method. Graph A shows a nonlinear relationship between activity cost and activity usage. An example of this might be a volume discount given on direct materials or evidence of learning by workers (for example, as more hours are worked, the total cost increases at a decreasing rate due to the increased efficiency of the workers). Graph B shows an upward shift in cost if more than $X_1$ units are made. Perhaps this could mean that an additional supervisor must be hired or a second shift run. Graph C shows outliers that are not representative of the overall cost relationship.

A possible disadvantage of the scatterplot method is the lack of an objective criterion for choosing the best-fitting line. The quality of the cost formula depends on the quality of the analyst's subjective judgment. The high–low method removes the subjectivity in the choice of the line. Regardless of who uses the method, the same line will result.

There is a large difference between the fixed-cost components and the variable rates from the high–low and the scatterplot methods. The predicted setup cost for 350 setup hours is $2,562.50 according to the scatterplot method and $2,718.75 according to the high–low method. Which is "right"? Since the two methods can produce significantly different cost formulas, the question of which method is the best naturally arises. Ideally, a method that is objective and, at the same time, produces the best-fitting line is needed. The method of least squares defines best-fitting and is objective in the sense that using the method for a given set of data will always produce the same cost formula.

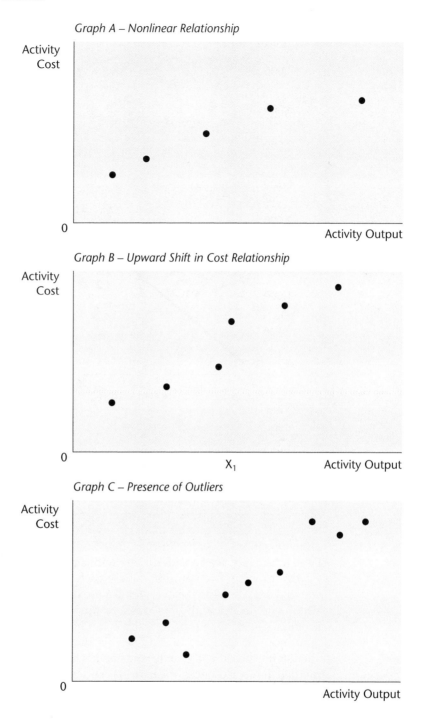

*Graph A – Nonlinear Relationship*

*Graph B – Upward Shift in Cost Relationship*

*Graph C – Presence of Outliers*

## The Method of Least Squares

Up to this point, we have alluded to the concept of a line that best fits the points shown on a scattergraph. What do we mean by a best-fitting line? Intuitively, it is the line to which the data points are closest. But what is meant by closest?

Consider Exhibit 3–13. Here an arbitrary line has been drawn. We can measure the closeness of each point to the line by the point's vertical distance from the line. This vertical distance is the difference between the actual cost and the cost predicted by the line. For point 5, the predicted cost is 5*. The **deviation** is the difference between points 5 and 5* (the vertical distance from the point to the line).

**deviation**

A measure of closeness for the estimated cost line and the observed cost data.

EXHIBIT   3-13

Line Deviations

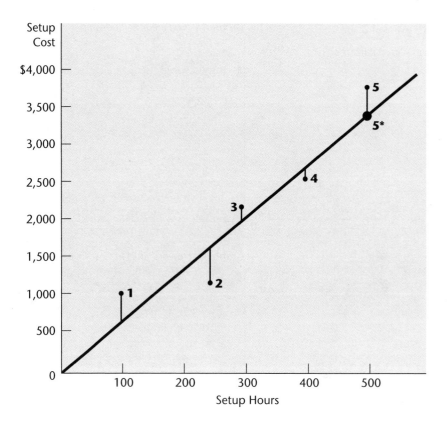

The vertical distance measures the closeness of a single point to the line, but we need a measure of how close all the points are to the line. One possibility is to measure the deviation of all points from the line and then to add all the single measures to obtain an overall measure. However, this overall measure may be misleading. For example, a line with all small positive deviations could result in an overall measure greater than a line with a mix of large positive and large negative deviations, because of the cancelling effect of positive and negative numbers. Intuitively, we consider a line with small deviations to be closer. To correct for this problem, we can first square each single deviation and then sum these squared deviations as the overall measure of closeness. When we square the deviations we are left with only positive numbers, thus we avoid the cancellation problem caused by a mix of positive and negative numbers.

Since our measure of closeness is the sum of the squared deviations, the smaller the measure, the better the line fits the points. For example, the scatterplot method line's closeness measure is 343,750 and the high–low line's closeness measure is 523,438. Thus, the scatterplot line fits the points better than the high–low line. Our earlier claim that the use of judgment in the scatterplot method is superior to the high–low method is supported.

In principle, we could use this closeness measure to rank all possible lines from best to worst. The line that fits the points better than any other line is called the **best-fitting line**. It is the line with the smallest (least) sum of squared deviations. Of course, the number of lines is infinite and ranking all lines is impractical. Fortunately we have the **method of least squares** to identify the best-fitting line. You can learn the manual calculations for the least-squares formula from a statistics textbook. For our purposes, we can use a computer regression program to do the calculations.

**best-fitting line**

The line that fits a set of data points the best, in the sense that the sum of the squared deviations of the data points from the line is the smallest.

**method of least squares**

A statistical method to find a line that best fits a set of data. This method is used to break out the fixed and variable components of a mixed cost.

# Using the Regression Programs

Computing the regression formula manually is tedious, even with only five data points. As the number of data points increases, manual computation becomes impractical. Spreadsheet packages such as Quattro Pro® or Microsoft Excel® have regression routines that will perform the computations.[5] All you need to do is input the data points. The spreadsheet regression programs supply more than the total cost formula. We also receive information that we can use to assess the reliability of the cost equation, a feature that is not available from the scatterplot and high–low methods.

The first step in using the computer to calculate regression coefficients is to enter the data. Exhibit 3–14 shows the computer screen you would see if you entered the Larson Company data on setups into a spreadsheet. It is a good idea to label your variables as is done here. The next step is to run the regression. This step will vary depending on the program you are using, but in Excel and Quattro Pro, the regression routine is located under the "tools" menu.

When the "regression" screen pops up, you can tell the program where the dependent and independent variables are located. Then, you need to tell the program where to place the regression output. The regression output is quickly completed. The regression output for the setup costs is shown in Exhibit 3–15.

Let's look at the information in Exhibit 3–15. First, let's locate the fixed cost and variable rate coefficients. These are highlighted in the exhibit. The fixed cost is the constant—in this case, 125. The variable rate is the ×coefficient—here, 6.75. Now we can construct the setup cost formula for the method of least squares:

$$\text{Setup costs} = \$125 + (\$6.75 \times \text{Setup hours})$$

We can use this formula to predict setup costs for future months, as we did with the formulas for the high–low and scatterplot methods.

Since the regression cost formula is the best-fitting line, it should produce better predictions of setup costs. For 350 setup hours, the setup cost predicted by the least-squares line is \$2,487.50 [\$125 + (\$6.75 × 350)], with a fixed component of \$125 and a variable component of \$2,362.50. Using this prediction as a standard, the scatterplot method more closely approximates the least-squares line than the high-low method.

5.  Quattro Pro is a registered trademark of Novell, Inc. Excel is a registered trademark of Microsoft Corporation. Any reference to Quattro Pro or Excel refers to this footnote.

EXHIBIT   3-14

Spreadsheet Data for Larson Company

| Month | Setup Costs | Setup Hours |
|-------|-------------|-------------|
| Jan | 1,000 | 100 |
| Feb | 1,250 | 200 |
| Mar | 2,250 | 300 |
| Apr | 2,500 | 400 |
| May | 3,750 | 500 |

EXHIBIT   3-15

Regression Output for
Larson Company

| | Regression Output for Larson Company.xls | | | |
|---|---|---|---|---|
| | **A** | **B** | **C** | **D** |
| 1 | | **Regression Output:** | | |
| 2 | **Constant** | | | 125 |
| 3 | **Std Err of Y Est** | | | 299.304749934466 |
| 4 | **R Squared** | | | 0.944300518134715 |
| 5 | **No. of Observation** | | | 5 |
| 6 | **Degrees of Freedom** | | | 3 |
| 7 | | | | |
| 8 | **X Coefficient(s)** | | 6.75 | |
| 9 | **Std Err of Coef.** | | 0.9464847243 | |
| 10 | | | | |
| 11 | | | | |
| 12 | | | | |
| 13 | | | | |
| 14 | | | | |
| 15 | | | | |
| 16 | | | | |
| 17 | | | | |
| 18 | | | | |
| 19 | | | | |
| 20 | | | | |

Sheet1 / Sheet2 / Sheet3 /

## Reliability of Cost Formulas

**Objective 4**

Evaluate the reliability of
a cost equation.

**goodness of fit**

The degree of association
between $Y$ and $X$ (cost
and activity). It is
measured by how much
of the total variability in
$Y$ is explained by $X$.

**coefficient of
determination**

The percentage of total
variability in a dependent
variable (e.g., cost) that is
explained by an
independent variable
(e.g., activity level). It
assumes a value between
0 and 1.

While the computer output in Exhibit 3–15 gives the best-fitting fixed- and variable-cost coefficients, we find its major usefulness in the information it provides
about the reliability of the estimated cost formula. This feature is not provided by
either the scatterplot method or the high–low method. We will use the printout in
Exhibit 3–15 as the basis for our discussion of a statistical assessment of a cost formula's reliability: *goodness of fit*. Although the spreadsheet provides other useful
information for assessing statistical reliability, we will look only at **goodness of
fit**. This measure is important because the best-fitting line may not be a good-fitting line. It may perform miserably when it comes to predicting costs.

### $R^2$—The Coefficient of Determination

Initially, we assume that a single activity driver explains changes (or variability)
in activity cost. Our experience with the Larson Company example suggests that
setup hours can explain changes in setup costs. The scattergraph shown in Exhibit
3–11 confirms this belief because it reveals that setup cost and setup hours seem
to move together. Thus, it seems reasonable that setup hours would explain much
of the variability in setup costs. We can determine statistically just how much
variability is explained by looking at the **coefficient of determination** or $R^2$.

$R^2$ is the percentage of variability in the dependent variable explained by an
independent variable. The higher the percentage of cost variability explained, the
better the fit. Intuitively, we think that more of the variability of the cost is
explained when the data points are closer to the line. $R^2$ always has a value
between 0 and 1.0. The coefficient of determination is labelled "R Squared" and
highlighted in Exhibit 3–15. $R^2$ has a value of 0.9443 in our example, which means
that about 94 percent of the variability in setup cost is explained by the number
of setup hours. We would conclude that the least-squares line for setup costs is a
good-fitting line.

There is no cutoff point for a good versus a bad coefficient of determination.
Clearly, the closer $R^2$ is to 1, the better. However, is 89 percent good enough? How
about 73 percent? Or even 46 percent? The answer is that it depends. If your cost

equation yields a coefficient of determination of 75 percent, you know that your independent variable explains three-quarters of the variability in cost. You also know that some other factor or combination of factors explains the remaining quarter. Depending on your tolerance for error, you may want to improve the equation by trying different independent variables (for example, number of setups rather than setup hours) or by trying multiple regression (explained later in this chapter).

## Coefficient of Correlation

**coefficient of correlation**

The square root of the coefficient of determination, which is used to express not only the degree of correlation between two variables but also the direction of the relationship.

A related measure of goodness of fit is the **coefficient of correlation**, which is the square root of the coefficient of determination. Since square roots can be negative, the value of the coefficient of correlation can range between −1 and +1. If the coefficient of correlation is positive, then the two variables (in this example, setup cost and setup hours) move together in the same direction, and positive correlation exists. Perfect positive correlation would yield a value of 1.00 for the coefficient of correlation. If, on the other hand, the coefficient of correlation is negative, then the two variables move in a predictable fashion but in opposite directions. Perfect negative correlation would yield a coefficient of correlation of −1.00. A coefficient of correlation value close to 0 indicates no correlation. That is, knowledge of the movement of one variable gives us no clue as to the movement of the other variable. Exhibit 3–16 illustrates the concept of correlation.

**EXHIBIT** 3-16

Correlation Illustrated

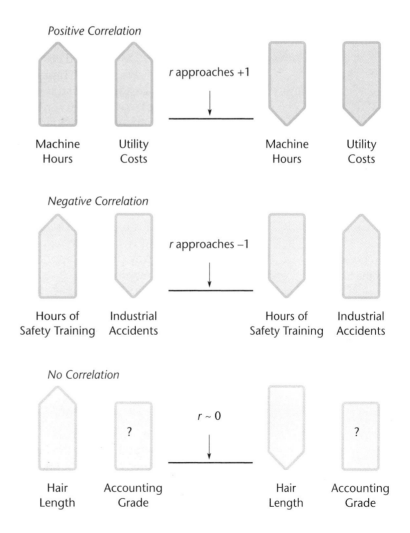

For the Larson Company example, the coefficient of correlation (r) is simply the square root of $R^2$ or 0.97. The square root is positive because the correlation between setup hours and setup cost is positive. In other words, as the number of setup hours increases, the total setup cost also increases. This positive correlation is reflected by a positive sign on the × coefficient shown in Exhibit 3–15. If cost decreases as activity usage increases, then the coefficient of correlation (and the value of the × coefficient) is negative. The sign of the × coefficient reveals the sign of the coefficient of correlation. In the Larson Company example, the very high positive correlation between setup cost and setup hours indicates that setup hours is a good choice for a cost driver.

## Multiple Regression

**Objective 5**

Discuss the role of multiple regression in assessing cost behaviour.

Sometimes obtaining the best cost equation is more complicated than simply identifying one activity driver and regressing activity cost on this driver. The outcome may not produce a cost equation that is good enough for managerial use. In the Larson Company example, 94 percent of the variability in setup cost was explained by changes in setup hours, and that is an excellent result. In other cases, however, a single independent variable may explain much less of the variability in the dependent variable. Then, one possible solution is to search for additional explanatory variables.

In the case of two or more explanatory variables, the linear equation is expanded to include the additional variables:

$$\text{Total cost} = b_0 + b_1X_1 + b_2X_2 + \ldots$$

where

$b_0$ is the fixed cost (intercept)
$b_1$ is the variable rate (slope) for the first independent variable
$X_1$ is the first independent variable
$b_2$ is the variable rate (slope) for the second independent variable
$X_2$ is the second independent variable

and so on.

When there are two or more explanatory variables, neither the high–low method nor the scatterplot method can be used. Fortunately, the extension of the method of least squares is straightforward. Whenever least squares is used to fit an equation involving two or more explanatory variables, the method is called **multiple regression**. Any practical application of multiple regression requires the use of a computer program.

**multiple regression**

The use of the least-squares method to determine the parameters in a linear equation involving two or more explanatory variables.

For example, suppose that the accountant for a factory that produces laser printers in Scarborough, Ontario, is analyzing factory utilities cost. The accountant knows that electricity is used to power the machines and suspects that machine hours would be a good cost driver for utilities cost. Electricity is also used to power the air conditioning; for this reason, the utilities cost rises significantly in the summer. Thus, utilities cost is explained by more than one variable and needs a more complex cost equation:

$$\text{Utilities cost} = \text{Fixed cost} + (b_1 \times \text{Machine hours}) + (b_2 \times \text{Summer})$$

In this equation, machine hours is a continuous variable that takes on values much like those for setup hours in the Larson Company example. "Summer" is a dichotomous or dummy variable; it takes on the values zero and one. That is, a particular month either is or is not in the summer. In Scarborough, summer lasts from May through September. Exhibit 3–17 illustrates 12 months of data for the utilities regression.

Let's take a closer look at the data in Exhibit 3–17. In January, there were 1,340 machine hours, and utilities cost $1,688. January is not a summer month—hence, the variable "summer" takes the value 0. In June, there were 1,432 machine hours, it is a summer month (so "summer" takes the value 1), and total utilities cost was $2,304. The other 10 months of data can be interpreted in the same manner.

When multiple regression is run on these data, the results in Exhibit 3–18 are obtained. The results give rise to the following equation:

Utilities cost = $243.11 + ($1.097 × Machine hours) + ($510.49 × Summer)

This equation can be used to predict the cost of utilities for future months. Suppose that the accountant wants to predict the cost of utilities for the following April and anticipates 1,350 machine hours. The predicted or budgeted cost is $1,724 [$243.11 + (1.097 × 1,350) + ($510.49 × 0)]. The predicted or budgeted cost of utilities for May, based on 1,350 machine hours, is $2,235 [$243.11 + (1.097 × 1,350) + ($510.49 × 1)].

Data for Scarborough Factory Utilities Cost Regression.xls

| Month | Mhrs | Summer | Utilities Cost |
|-------|------|--------|----------------|
| Jan | 1340 | 0 | $1,688 |
| Feb | 1298 | 0 | 1636 |
| Mar | 1376 | 0 | 1734 |
| April | 1405 | 0 | 1770 |
| May | 1500 | 1 | 2390 |
| June | 1432 | 1 | 2304 |
| July | 1322 | 1 | 2166 |
| August | 1416 | 1 | 2284 |
| Sept | 1370 | 1 | 1730 |
| Oct | 1580 | 0 | 1991 |
| Nov | 1460 | 0 | 1840 |
| Dec | 1455 | 0 | 1833 |

Sheet1 / Sheet2 / Sheet3

EXHIBIT 3-18

Multiple Regression Results for Scarborough Factory Utilities Cost

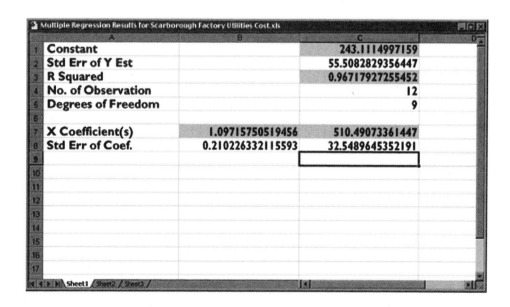

Multiple Regression Results for Scarborough Factory Utilities Cost.xls

| A | B | C |
|---|---|---|
| Constant | | 243.1114997159 |
| Std Err of Y Est | | 55.5082829356447 |
| R Squared | | 0.96717927255452 |
| No. of Observation | | 12 |
| Degrees of Freedom | | 9 |
| | | |
| X Coefficient(s) | 1.09715750519456 | 510.49073361447 |
| Std Err of Coef. | 0.210226332115593 | 32.5489645352191 |

Sheet1 / Sheet2 / Sheet3

Notice that $R^2$ is 0.967, or 96.7 percent. You might try running the regression using just machine hours as the independent variable. The $R^2$ for that regression is much lower, clearly indicating the value of adding the second driver.

## Managerial Judgment

**Objective 6**

Describe the use of managerial judgment in determining cost behaviour.

Managerial judgment is critically important in determining cost behaviour, and is by far the most widely used method in practice.[6] Many managers simply use their experience and past observation of cost relationships to determine fixed and variable costs. This method, however, may take a number of forms. Some managers simply assign particular activity costs to the fixed category and others to the variable category, ignoring the possibility of mixed costs. Thus, a chemical company may regard materials and utilities as strictly variable with respect to kilograms of chemical produced and all other costs as fixed. Even labour, a traditional and common example of a unit-based variable cost, may be fixed for this company. The appeal of this method is simplicity. Before opting for this course, however, management would do well to make sure that each cost is predominantly fixed or variable and that the decisions being made are not highly sensitive to errors in classifying costs.

To illustrate the use of judgment in assessing cost behaviour, consider Elgin Sweeper Company, a leading manufacturer of motorized street sweepers. Using production volume as the cost driver, Elgin revised its chart of accounts to organize costs into fixed and variable components. Elgin's accountants used their knowledge of the company to assign costs, using a decision rule that categorized a cost as fixed if it was fixed 75 percent of the time, and variable if it was variable 75 percent of the time.[7]

Management may instead identify mixed costs and divide these costs into fixed and variable components by deciding just what the fixed and variable parts are—that is, using experience to say that a certain amount of a cost is fixed and that the rest must therefore be variable. For example, a factory may put lease payments for a photocopier into one account and the cost of paper and toner into another. The result is that it is easy to group the lease cost with other fixed costs and to treat the variable costs separately. The variable rate can then be computed using one or more cost/volume data points. This approach has the advantage of accounting for mixed costs but is subject to a similar type of error as the strict fixed/variable dichotomy. That is, management may be wrong in its assessment.

Finally, management may use experience and judgment to refine statistical estimation results. The experienced manager might "eyeball" the data and throw out several points as being highly unusual or might revise the estimation results to take into account projected changes in cost structure or technology. Recently, Martin Color-Fi, a recycler, found that it was paying top prices for discarded plastics. Demand for recyclable plastics has mushroomed, and prices have tripled in the space of a year. What was the reason for the growth in demand? There was a run-up in the price of cotton due to poor crops in China, Pakistan, and India. The cotton shortage led Asian fabric mills to substitute polyester and other synthetics. These synthetic fabrics are made from PET (the polyethylene-terephthalate found in recyclable plastic bottles). Companies like Martin must look forward, not back,

---

6. Maryanne M. Mowen, *Accounting for Costs as Fixed and Variable* (Montvale, N.J.: National Association of Accountants, 1986): pp. 19-20. This practice of using managerial judgment to assign costs to cost behaviour categories has continued in more advanced cost accounting systems.

7. John F. Callan, Wesley N. Tredup, Randy S. Wissinger, "Elgin Sweeper Company's Journey Toward Cost Management," *Management Accounting* (July 1991): pp. 24-27.

to predict the impact of external factors, such as demand for substitute products, on prices and profits.[8] Statistical techniques are highly accurate in depicting the past, but they cannot foresee the future—which is, of course, what management really wants.

The advantage of using managerial judgment to separate fixed and variable costs is its simplicity. In situations in which the manager has a deep understanding of the company and its cost patterns, this method can give good results. However, if the manager does not have good judgment, errors will occur. Therefore, it is important to consider the experience of the manager, the potential for error, and the effect that error could have on related decisions.

8. Stephanie Anderson Forrest, "There's Gold in Those Hills of Soda Bottles," *Business Week*, September 11, 1995: p. 48.

## Summary of Learning Objectives

### 1. Define and describe cost behaviour for fixed, variable, and mixed costs.

Cost behaviour is the way in which a cost changes in relation to changes in activity usage. The time horizon is important in determining cost behaviour because costs can change from fixed to variable depending on whether the decision takes place over the short run or the long run. Variable costs are those that change in total as activity usage changes. Usually, we assume that variable costs increase in direct proportion to increases in activity usage. Fixed costs are those that do not change in total as activity usage changes. Mixed costs have both a variable and a fixed component.

### 2. Explain the role of the resource usage model in understanding cost behaviour

The resource usage model adds to our understanding of cost behaviour. Resources acquired in advance of usage are categorized as committed resources. Resources acquired as used and needed are flexible resources. Some costs, especially discretionary fixed costs, tend to follow a step-cost function. These resources are acquired in lumpy amounts. If the width of the step is sufficiently large, then the costs are viewed as fixed; otherwise, they are approximated by a variable-cost function.

### 3. Separate mixed costs into their fixed and variable components using the high–low method, the scatterplot method, and the method of least squares.

There are three formal methods of decomposing mixed costs: the high–low method, the scatterplot method, and the method of least squares. In the high–low method, the two points chosen are the high and the low points with respect to activity level. These two points are then used to compute the intercept and the slope of the line on which they lie. The intercept gives an estimate of the fixed-cost component, and the slope an estimate of the variable cost per unit of activity. The high–low method is objective and easy. However, if either the high point or the low point is not representative of the true cost relationship, the relationship will be estimated incorrectly.

The scatterplot method involves inspecting a scattergraph (a plot showing total cost at various activity levels) and selecting two points that seem to best represent the relationship between cost and activity. Since two points determine a line, the two selected points can be used to determine the intercept and the slope of the line on which they lie. The scatterplot method is a good way to identify nonlinearity, the presence of outliers, and the presence of a shift in the cost relationship. Its disadvantage is that it is subjective.

The method of least squares uses all of the data points (except outliers) and produces a line that best fits all of the points. The line is best fitting in the sense that it is closest to all the points as measured by the sum of the squared deviations of the points from the line. The method of least squares produces the best fitting line and is therefore recommended over the high–low and scatterplot methods.

### 4. Evaluate the reliability of a cost equation.

The least-squares method has the advantage of offering methods of assessing the reliability of cost equations. The coefficient of determination allows an analyst to compute the amount of cost variability explained by a particular cost driver. The correlation coefficient measures the strength of the association but also indicates the direction of the relationship.

### 5. Discuss the role of multiple regression in assessing cost behaviour.

One driver may not be sufficient in explaining the variability in activity cost behaviour. In such a case, adding additional variables to the equation may increase its ability to predict activity costs as well as

provide insights on how activity costs can be managed.

### 6. Describe the use of managerial judgment in determining cost behaviour.

Managerial judgment can be used alone or in conjunction with the high–low, scatterplot, or least-squares method. Managers use their experience and knowledge of cost and activity-level relationships to identify outliers, understand structural shifts, and adjust parameters due to anticipated changing conditions.

## Key Terms

| | | |
|---|---|---|
| Best-fitting line 90 | Fixed activity rate 81 | Multiple regression 94 |
| Coefficient of correlation 93 | Fixed cost 71 | Practical capacity 77 |
| Coefficient of determination 92 | Flexible resources 78 | Relevant range 72 |
| Committed fixed costs 78 | Goodness of fit 92 | Scattergraph 87 |
| Committed resources 78 | High–low method 86 | Scatterplot method 87 |
| Cost behaviour 71 | Independent variable 84 | Short run 75 |
| Cost formula 84 | Intercept parameter 85 | Slope parameter 85 |
| Dependent variable 84 | Long run 75 | Step cost 79 |
| Deviation 89 | Method of least squares 90 | Variable activity rate 81 |
| Discretionary fixed costs 78 | Mixed cost 74 | Variable cost 73 |

## Review Problems

### I. RESOURCE USAGE AND COST BEHAVIOUR

Kaylin Manufacturing Company has three accounts payable clerks who are responsible for processing purchase invoices. Each clerk is paid a salary of $30,000 and is capable of processing 5,000 invoices per year when working efficiently. In addition to the salaries, Kaylin spends $9,000 per year for forms, postage, cheques, and so on (assuming that 15,000 invoices are processed). During the past year, 12,500 invoices were processed.

### Required:
1. Calculate the activity rate for the purchase order activity. Break the activity into fixed and variable components.
2. Compute the total activity availability and break this into activity usage and unused activity.
3. Calculate the total cost of activity supplied and break this into cost of activity usage and cost of unused activity.

### Solution

1. Activity rate = [(3 × $30,000) + $9,000]/15,000  = $6.60 per invoice
   Fixed rate = $90,000/15,000 = $6.00 per invoice
   Variable rate = $9,000/15,000 = $0.60 per invoice

2. Activity availability = Activity usage + Unused capacity
   15,000 invoices = 12,500 invoices + 2,500 invoices

3. Cost of activity supplied = Cost of activity used + Cost of unused activity
   $90,000 + ($0.60 × 12,500) = ($6.60 × 12,500) + ($6.00 × 2,500)
   $97,500 = $82,500 + $15,000

## II. HIGH–LOW AND METHOD OF LEAST SQUARES

Kim Wilson, controller for Max Enterprises, has decided to estimate the fixed and variable components associated with the company's shipping activity. She has collected the following data for the past six months:

| Packages Shipped | Total Shipping Costs |
|---|---|
| 10 | $ 800 |
| 20 | 1,100 |
| 15 | 900 |
| 12 | 900 |
| 18 | 1,050 |
| 25 | 1,250 |

### Required:

1. Estimate the fixed and variable components for the shipping costs using the high–low method. Using the cost formula, predict the total cost of shipping if 14 packages are shipped.
2. Estimate the fixed and variable components using the method of least squares. Using the cost formula, predict the total cost of shipping if 14 packages are shipped.
3. For the method of least squares, explain what the coefficient of determination is, and compute the coefficient of correlation.

### Solution

1. The estimate of fixed and variable costs using the high–low method is as follows:

   High point is (25, $1,250); Low point is (10, $800)
   Variable rate = ($1,250 − $800)/(25 − 10) = $450/15 = $30 per package
   Fixed cost = $1,250 − ($30 × 25) = $500
   Total cost = $500 + ($30 × Packages shipped)
   Total cost (14 packages shipped) = $500 + ($30 × 14) = $920

2. The computer output using the method of least squares is as follows:

   Constant = $509.912; × Coefficient = $29.405; R-Squared = 0.969
   Total cost = $509.83 + ($29.41 × Packages shipped)
   Total cost (14 packages shipped) = $509.83 + ($29.41 × 14) = $921.57

3. The coefficient of determination ($R^2$) tells us that about 96.9 percent of the variability in the shipping cost is explained by the number of packages shipped. The correlation coefficient ($r$) is the square root of the coefficient of determination, or 0.984.

## Questions for Writing and Discussion

1. Why is knowledge of cost behaviour important for managerial decision making? Give an example to illustrate your answer.

2. How does the length of the time horizon affect the classification of costs as fixed or variable?

3. Explain the difference between resource spending and resource usage.

4. What is the relationship between flexible resources and cost behaviour?

5. What is the relationship between committed resources and cost behaviour?

6. Explain the difference between committed and discretionary fixed costs. Give examples of each.

7. Describe the difference between a variable cost and a step cost with narrow steps.

8. When is it reasonable to treat step costs as if they were variable costs?

9. What is the difference between a step cost with narrow steps and a step cost with wide steps?

10. What is an activity rate?

11. Why do mixed costs pose a problem when it comes to classifying costs into fixed and variable categories?

12. Why is a scattergraph a good first step in decomposing mixed costs into their fixed and variable components?

13. Describe how the scatterplot method breaks out the fixed and variable costs from a mixed cost. Now describe how the high–low method works. How do the two methods differ?

14. What are the advantages of the scatterplot method over the high–low method? the high–low method over the scatterplot method?

15. Describe the method of least squares. Why is this method better than either the high–low method or the scatterplot method?

16. What is meant by the "best-fitting line"?

17. Is the best-fitting line necessarily a good-fitting line? Explain.

18. Describe what is meant by "goodness of fit." Explain the meaning of the coefficient of determination.

19. What is the difference between the coefficient of determination and the coefficient of correlation?

20. When is multiple regression required to explain cost behaviour?

21. Some companies assign mixed costs to either the fixed or variable cost categories without using any formal methodology to separate them. Explain how this practice can be defended.

# Exercises

**3–1**

Cost Behaviour

LO1

The salary paid to a plant supervisor is $80,000 per year. The plant is capable of producing 80,000 kilograms of a chemical per year.

**Required:**
1. Prepare a table that shows how the cost of plant supervision behaves in total and on a per-unit basis as production increases from 0 to 80,000 kilograms, using 20,000-kilogram increments.
2. How would you classify the behaviour of this supervision cost?

**3–2**

Cost Behaviour

LO1

Kilroy Company has determined that the best driver for its delivery activity is "kilometres travelled." The company also discovered that the cost of fuel for its delivery trucks doubled as the kilometres travelled doubled. The fuel cost for 10,000 kilometres was $20,000 and for 20,000 kilometres was $40,000.

**Required:**
1. Prepare a table that shows the total cost of fuel and unit cost for kilometres travelled ranging from 0 to 80,000 kilometres, using increments of 20,000 kilometres.
2. How would you describe the behaviour of the delivery cost?

**3–3**

Cost Behaviour

LO1

Aaron Manufacturing Company produces a variety of products, including some that require the use of a specialized forming machine. Aaron can rent forming machines for $15,000 per year. Each machine can produce as many as 25,000 units per year.

**Required:**
1. Prepare a table that shows the total cost of forming machines rental and the unit cost for units ranging from 0 to 50,000 per year, using increments of 10,000 units.
2. How would you describe the behaviour of the forming machines' rental cost?

**3–4**

Cost Behaviour

LO1, LO2

The University of Saskatchewan Huskies had just won a berth in the Vanier Cup finals, and the students and alumni were excited. Holiday Travel Agency, located close to campus, decided to put together a championship game package. For $16,000, a 737 jet could be chartered to take up to 170 people to and from Toronto, where the game would be played. A block of 75 hotel rooms could be confirmed for $400 each (with a three-night commitment); Holiday Travel must pay for all the rooms in advance and cannot cancel any of them. On the day of the game, a pregame buffet will be catered at $20 per person; each person will receive a game favour package consisting of a sweatshirt, a T-shirt, a commemorative pin with the university and Vanier Cup logos, and two pompoms in the team colours). All items in the favour package can be purchased by Holiday Travel before the trip and will cost the agency $75 per set. Buses will be chartered in Toronto to take the participants to and from the airport and the game. Each bus holds 50 people and can be chartered for $500.

**Required:**

List the resources that are mentioned in the above scenario and for each resource, (1) determine whether it is a flexible resource or a committed resource, and (2) the type of cost behaviour displayed (variable, fixed, mixed, or step cost).

**3–5**

Cost Behaviour

LO1, LO2

Action Figure, Inc., is a manufacturer of moulded plastic action figures that fast-food restaurants purchase to include in children's meal packs. Each action figure is formed in a mould and takes about 25 grams of plastic costing $0.60 per kilogram. Action Figures contracts with an outside supplier to develop new moulds based on current movie and cartoon characters. Each set of moulds costs $4,000 and could be used indefinitely but, practically speaking, has a life of only about three months. After that, children are tired of those figures and want to move on to others. Direct labour and variable overhead cost $0.01 per unit and other facility costs total $10,000 per year. Action Figures, Inc. produces 100,000 action figures from each set of moulds.

**Required:**

1. Categorize each resource as flexible or committed. What is the cost behaviour of each resource?
2. What is the total cost of producing action figures for the year? the per-unit cost?

**3–6**

Cost Behaviour

LO1

Jackson Company manufactures air-conditioning compressors. Based on past experience, Jackson has found that its total cost of moving materials can be represented by the following formula: Cost of moving materials = $90,000 + $0.20 × kilograms of material moved. The activity of moving materials uses forklifts, forklift operators, crates, and fuel (for the forklifts). During 2004, Jackson moved 200,000 kilograms of materials.

**Required:**

1. Identify the activity, its resources (inputs), and its driver (output measure).
2. Identify which resources are likely to vary with the driver over the relevant range. Assume that the relevant range is 150,000 to 250,000 kilograms of materials.
3. What is the total cost of moving materials incurred by Jackson in 2004? the total fixed cost? the total variable cost?
4. What is the cost of moving materials per kilogram moved?
5. What is the fixed cost per kilogram moved?
6. What is the variable cost of moving materials per kilogram moved?
7. Recalculate Requirements 4, 5, and 6 for the following levels of activity: (a) 150,000 kilograms moved and (b) 250,000 kilograms moved. Explain this outcome.

**3–7**

Resource Use and Cost Behaviour

LO2

For the following activities and their associated resources, identify: (1) an activity driver and (2) whether that driver is a flexible resource or a committed resource. Also, label each resource as one of the following with respect to the cost driver: (1) variable, (2) committed fixed, or (3) discretionary fixed.

| Activity | Resource Description |
|---|---|
| Maintenance | Equipment, labour, parts |
| Inspection | Test equipment, inspectors (each inspector can inspect five batches per day), units inspected (process requires destructive sampling)* |
| Packing | Materials, labour (each packer places five units in a box), conveyor belt |
| Processing payables | Clerks, materials, equipment, and facility |
| Assembly | Conveyor belt, supervision (one supervisor for every three assembly lines), direct labour, materials |

* Destructive sampling occurs when it is necessary to destroy a unit as inspection occurs.

**3–8**

Resource Supply and Usage; Activity Rates; Service Organization

LO2

Bex Communications provides cable television service to a number of communities in Alberta, including the town of Lone Wolf. In the Lone Wolf operation, there are 40 service technicians who install cable service and provide repairs. Each technician is salaried at $36,250 per year and works one of two daily eight-hour shifts. Each technician can perform an average of eight service calls per day. There are 250 working days per year. Bex uses 25 trucks for the Lone Wolf operation; each fully equipped to perform installations and repairs on site. Each truck has an amortization cost of $6,000 per year. The 25 trucks allow each technician to have a truck for his/her shift, with five extra trucks in case of breakdown or scheduled maintenance. Last year, supplies, small tools, and fuel cost approximately $840,000; these seem to be highly correlated with the number of service calls. A total of 70,000 service calls were made last year.

**Required:**
1. Classify the resources associated with the cable repair and installation activity into one of the following: (1) committed resources and (2) flexible resources.
2. Calculate the variable activity rate and the fixed activity rate for the repair and installation activity. What is the total cost of one service call?
3. Using the average data given above, what is the largest number of service calls that could be completed per year? This is the total activity availability. Break this total activity availability into activity usage (number of service calls actually made) and unused capacity (calls that could have been made but were not).
4. Calculate the total cost of committed resources used last year, and break this into the cost of service calls made and the cost of unused service call capacity.

**3–9**

Flexible and Committed Resources; Capacity Usage for a Service Organization

LO2

Jana Morgan is about to sign up for cellular telephone service. She is primarily interested in the safety aspect of the phone—that is, she wants to have one available for emergencies. She does not want to use it as her primary phone. Jana has narrowed her options down to two plans:

| | Plan 1 | Plan 2 |
|---|---|---|
| Monthly fee | $ 20 | $ 30 |
| Free local minutes | 60 | 120 |
| | | |
| Additional charges per minute: | | |
| Airtime | $0.25 | $0.20 |
| Long distance | 0.15 | na |

Both plans are subject to a $25 activation fee and a $120 cancellation fee if the service is cancelled before one year. Jana's brother will give her a cell phone that he no longer needs. It is not the latest version (and is not Internet capable), but will work well with both plans.

**Required:**

1. Classify the charges associated with the cellular phone service as (1) committed resources or (2) flexible resources.
2. Assume that Jana will use, on average, 45 minutes per month in local calling. For each plan, split her minute allotment into used and unused capacity. Which plan would be most cost effective? Why?
3. Assume that Jana loves her cell phone and ends up talking frequently with friends while travelling. On average, she uses 60 local minutes a month and 30 long distance minutes. For each plan, split her minute allotment into used and unused capacity. Which plan would be most cost effective? Why?

**3–10**

Separating Fixed and Variable Costs; Service Setting

LO3, LO4

Spreadsheet

Betty Yeager has been operating a dental practice for the past five years. As part of her practice, she provides a dental hygiene service. She has found that her costs for this service increase with patient load. Costs for this service over the past eight months are as follows:

| Month | Patients Served | Total Cost |
|---|---|---|
| May | 320 | $2,000 |
| June | 480 | 2,500 |
| July | 600 | 3,000 |
| August | 200 | 1,900 |
| September | 720 | 4,500 |
| October | 560 | 2,900 |
| November | 630 | 3,400 |
| December | 300 | 2,200 |

**Required:**

1. Prepare a scattergraph based on these data. Use cost for the vertical axis and number of patients for the horizontal. Based on an examination of the scattergraph, does there appear to be a linear relationship between the cost of dental hygiene services and patients served?
2. Compute the cost formula for dental hygiene services using the high–low method. Using the formula, calculate the predicted cost of dental hygiene services for January for 450 patients.
3. Compute the cost formula for dental hygiene services using the method of least squares. Using the regression cost formula, find the predicted cost of dental hygiene services for January for 450 patients. What does the coefficient of determination tell you about the cost formula computed by regression?
4. Which cost formula—the one computed using the high–low method or the one using the least-squares coefficients—do you think is better? Explain.

**3-11**

Separating Fixed and Variable Costs; Service Setting

LO3, LO4

Dan Tanna, the owner of Lube 'n' Go, is interested in determining the fixed and variable costs of performing a standard oil change. Since the oil changes are fairly standard, each one taking about the same amount of time and using about the same amount of grease, paper towels, etc., Dan thinks that the number of oil changes would be a good independent variable. The total monthly cost includes the salaries of the two service persons, amortization on the facility and equipment, utilities, and supplies such as grease and wipes. The cost of oil is not included, as it differs from car to car and is charged to each customer based on the number of litres actually used. Data for the past eight months are as follows:

| Month | Number of Oil Changes | Total Cost |
|---|---|---|
| May | 1,100 | $7,000 |
| June | 1,400 | 7,800 |
| July | 1,380 | 8,200 |
| August | 1,250 | 7,275 |
| September | 890 | 5,580 |
| October | 900 | 5,580 |
| November | 850 | 5,300 |
| December | 700 | 5,000 |

**Required:**

1. Prepare a scattergraph based on these data. Use cost for the vertical axis and number of oil changes for the horizontal axis. Based on an examination of the scattergraph, does there appear to be a linear relationship between the cost of oil changes and the number of oil changes performed?
2. Compute the cost formula for oil changing services using the high-low method. Calculate the predicted cost for January for 800 oil changes using the high-low formula.
3. Compute the cost formula for oil change services using the method of least squares. Using the regression cost formula, what is the predicted cost for January for 800 oil changes? What does the coefficient of determination tell you about the cost formula computed by regression?
4. Which cost formula—the one computed using the high-low method or the one using the least-squares coefficients—do you think is better? Explain.

**3–12**

Separating Fixed and
Variable Costs; Service
Setting

LO3, LO4

Louise McDermott, controller for the Galvin plant of Veromar, Inc., wanted to determine the cost behaviour of moving materials throughout the plant. She accumulated the following data on the number of moves (from 100 to 800, in increments of 100) and the total cost of moving materials at those levels of moves.

| Number of Moves | Total Cost |
|---|---|
| 100 | $ 3,000 |
| 200 | 4,650 |
| 300 | 3,400 |
| 400 | 8,500 |
| 500 | 10,000 |
| 600 | 12,600 |
| 700 | 13,600 |
| 800 | 14,560 |

**Required:**

1. Prepare a scattergraph based on these data. Use cost for the vertical axis and number of moves for the horizontal axis. Based on an examination of the scattergraph, does there appear to be a linear relationship between the total cost of moving materials and the number of moves?
2. Compute the cost formula for moving materials using the high-low method. Calculate the predicted cost per month with 550 moves using the high-low formula.
3. Compute the cost formula for moving materials using the method of least squares. Using the regression cost formula, what is the predicted cost for a month with 550 moves? What does the coefficient of determination tell you about the cost formula computed by regression?

4.  Evaluate the cost formula using the least-squares coefficients. Could it be improved? Try dropping the third data point (300, $3,400) and rerunning the regression. What does the new result tell you about the third data point?

**3–13**

Separation of Mixed
Costs; High-Low and
Least Squares

LO3, LO4

Spreadsheet

Suppose that you have the following data:

| Inspection Cost | Inspection Hours |
| --- | --- |
| $120 | 10 |
| 220 | 20 |
| 320 | 30 |
| 440 | 40 |
| 500 | 50 |

**Required:**

1.  Identify the independent variable and the dependent variable. Which pair is the high point? the low point?
2.  Using the high–low method, prepare a cost formula for inspection cost. What is the estimated inspection cost if 26 inspection hours are budgeted?
3.  Using the method of least squares, prepare a cost formula for inspection cost. What is the estimated inspection cost if 26 inspection hours are budgeted?
4.  Comment on the usefulness of the coefficient of determination in evaluating the reliability of the least-squares equation.

**3–14**

High-Low and Least
Squares

LO3, LO4

Farris, Inc., collected the following data on overhead and direct labour hours for the past 10 months:

| Month | Direct Labour Hours | Overhead Cost |
| --- | --- | --- |
| 1 | 1,000 | $28,000 |
| 2 | 1,200 | 32,300 |
| 3 | 1,100 | 31,015 |
| 4 | 990 | 27,830 |
| 5 | 1,300 | 35,200 |
| 6 | 1,250 | 34,500 |
| 7 | 1,200 | 35,600 |
| 8 | 800 | 23,370 |
| 9 | 1,050 | 29,600 |
| 10 | 1,200 | 33,450 |

**Required:**

1.  Identify the independent variable and the dependent variable. Which pair is the high point? the low point?
2.  Using the high-low method, prepare a cost formula for overhead cost. What is the estimated overhead cost for the next month if 1,120 direct labour hours are budgeted?
3.  Using regression, prepare a cost formula for overhead cost. What is the estimated overhead cost for the next month if 1,120 direct labour hours are budgeted? Comment on the usefulness of the coefficient of determination to evaluate the reliability of the regression equation.

**3–15**

Scatterplot; Method of
Least Squares

LO3

The following data represent the total cost (fixed plus variable) for different machine hours in a division of a manufacturing company.

| Machine Hours | Total Costs |
|---|---|
| 60 | $100 |
| 40 | 80 |
| 80 | 120 |
| 20 | 45 |
| 50 | 90 |

**Required:**
1. Draw a scattergraph for these data using machine hours as the independent variable. Does a linear assumption of cost behaviour seem appropriate?
2. Fit a least-squares regression line to these data, and interpret the $Y$-intercept and the slope of the equation.
3. What is the value of $R^2$ for this least-squares equation? Interpret it.
4. What total cost would you predict for 75 machine hours? Explain.
5. What total cost would you predict for 200 machine hours? Explain. (CGA Canada adapted)

**3–16**

High-Low Method;
Cost Formulas

LO3

Suitor Tool and Die Works needed to make a quick budget estimate for machine-related overhead. During the past year, the high and low levels of machine usage occurred in April and October, respectively. The three overhead activities associated with the machining activity are machine amortization, power usage, and maintenance. The activity driver is machine hours. The total costs of the three activities for the low and high levels follow:

| Activity | Total Cost @ 25,000 Machine Hours | Total Cost @ 40,000 Machine Hours |
|---|---|---|
| Machine amortization | $200,000 | $200,000 |
| Power usage | 4,000 | 6,400 |
| Maintenance | 90,000 | 111,000 |

**Required:**
1. Use the high–low method to calculate the fixed and variable components for each of the three activities. How would you categorize the cost behaviour of each activity?
2. Using your knowledge of cost behaviour, predict the cost of each activity for 32,000 machine hours.
3. Construct a cost formula that can be used to predict the total cost of the three activities combined. Using this formula, predict the total machining cost if 32,000 machine hours are used. In general, when can cost formulas be combined to form a single cost formula?

**3–17**

Method of Least
Squares; Evaluation of
Cost Equation

LO3, LO4

The method of least squares was used to develop a cost equation to predict the cost of purchasing goods. Eighty data points were used for the regression. The following computer output was received:

| | |
|---|---|
| Intercept | $30,500 |
| Slope | $10 |
| Coefficient of correlation | 0.85 |
| Standard error | $1,500 |

The driver used was "number of purchase orders."

$Y = 10x$

**Required:**
1. What is the cost formula?
2. Using the cost formula, predict the cost of purchasing if 10,000 orders are processed.
3. What percentage of the variability in purchasing cost is explained by the number of purchase orders? Do you think the equation will predict well? Why or why not?

**3–18**

Multiple Regression

LO5

Alison Company wants to determine the factors that are associated with overhead. The controller for Alison constructed a multiple regression equation using the following independent variables: direct labour hours, number of setups, and number of purchase orders. The analysis was run using the past 60 months of data. The following printout is obtained:

| Parameter | Estimate | t for $H_0$ Parameter=0 | Pr>t | Standard Error of Parameter |
|---|---|---|---|---|
| Intercept | 1,315 | 65.00 | 0.0001 | 125.000 |
| Direct labour hours | 24 | 3.17 | 0.0050 | 3.256 |
| Number of setups | 670 | 4.90 | 0.0050 | 128.256 |
| Number of purchase orders | 30 | 7.96 | 0.0250 | 5.103 |

$R^2 = 0.92$
$S_e = 150$
Observations: 60

**Required:**
1. Write out the cost equation for Alison's monthly overhead.
2. If Alison budgets 600 direct labour hours, 50 setups, and 120 purchase orders for next month, what is the budgeted overhead cost?
3. Suppose that Alison's engineers found a way to reduce the number of setups by 50 percent. How much could be saved in overhead cost for the following month?

**3–19**

Cost Behaviour Patterns

LO1

The graphs on the following page represent cost behaviour patterns that might occur in a company's cost structure. The vertical axis represents total cost, and the horizontal axis represents activity output.

**Required:**
For each of the following situations, choose the graph that best illustrates the cost pattern involved. Also, for each situation identify the driver that measures activity usage.
1. The cost of power when a fixed fee of $500 per month is charged plus an additional charge of $0.12 per kilowatt-hour used.
2. Commissions paid to sales representatives. Commissions are paid at the rate of 5 percent of sales made up to total annual sales of $500,000, and 7 percent of sales above $500,000.
3. A part purchased from an outside supplier costs $12 per part for the first 3,000 parts and $10 per part for all parts purchased in excess of 3,000 units.
4. The cost of surgical gloves purchased in increments of 100 units (gloves come in boxes of 100 pairs).
5. The cost of tuition at a university that charges $250 per credit hour up to 15 credit hours. Hours taken in excess of 15 are free.
6. The cost of tuition at another university that charges $4,500 per semester for any course load ranging from 12 to 15 credit hours. Students taking fewer than

12 credit hours are charged $375 per credit hour. Students taking more than 15 credit hours are charged $4,500 plus $300 per credit hour in excess of 15.

7. A beauty shop's purchase of soaking solution to remove artificial nails. Each jar of solution can soak off approximately 50 nails before losing effectiveness.

8. The purchase of diagnostics equipment by a company for inspection of incoming orders.

9. Use of disposable gowns by patients in a hospital.

10. The cost of labour at a local fast-food restaurant. Three employees are always on duty during working hours; more employees can be called in during periods of heavy demand to work on an "as-needed" basis.

11. A manufacturer found that the maintenance cost of its heavy machinery was tied to the age of the equipment. Experience indicated that the maintenance cost increased at an increasing rate as the equipment aged.

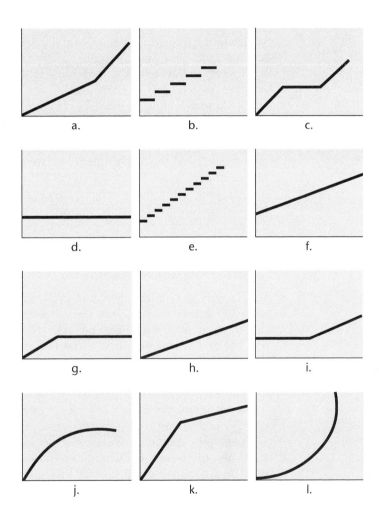

**3–20**

Choose the *best* answer for each of the following questions:

1. Which of the following statements is *true*?
   a. In the short run, all costs are variable.
   b. In the long run, all costs are fixed.
   c. Mixed costs are step costs.
   d. Variable costs change in direct proportion to changes in the amount of the activity.
   e. None of the above.

2. Shorter-term committed resources are termed
   a. committed fixed costs.
   b. flexible resources.
   c. discretionary fixed costs.
   d. nonproduction costs.
   e. period expenses.

3. Which of the following is an advantage of the high-low method?
   a. It is quick and easy to apply.
   b. It enables the analyst to determine whether or not the data are linear.
   c. It gives goodness-of-fit measures.
   d. It eliminates most of the data points.
   e. All of the above.

4. Suppose that regression is run on 30 months of data. The dependent variable is overhead, and the independent variable is machine hours. The coefficient of determination is 0.78. Which of the following is true?
   a. Machine hours and overhead are negatively correlated.
   b. The coefficient of correlation is approximately 0.61.
   c. Machine hours account for about 61 percent of the variation in overhead.
   d. The coefficient of correlation is approximately 0.78.
   e. Factors other than machine hours account for approximately 22 percent of the variation in overhead.

5. An accountant in a factory wants to determine the cost behaviour of manu-facturing overhead. Which of the following is an application of managerial judgment in determining cost behaviour?
   a. The accountant performs a scatterplot analysis and deletes several data points determined to be outliers.
   b. The accountant decides to use only the 12 most recent months of data since significant technological changes make the most recent year differ-ent from the previous five years of operation.
   c. The accountant runs a regression using direct labour hours as the inde-pendent variable. However, she/he adjusts the $\times$ coefficient upwards by 5 percent to reflect anticipated cost increases for the coming year.
   d. The accountant decides to try multiple regression since the coefficient of determination on a simple regression equation is 0.49.
   e. All of the above.

# Problems

**CGA**

**3–21**

*High-Low Method;
Managerial Judgment*

**LO3, LO6**

You have been asked to budget the overhead costs for the month of June 2004. The budget will be based on the costs incurred during the months of May 2003 and September 2003. 2004's fixed costs are expected to be 4 percent higher than in 2003, whereas variable costs will increase by 6 percent. The data for May 2003 and September 2003 are as follows:

|  | May 2003 | September 2003 |
|---|---|---|
| Units produced | 20,000 | 13,000 |
| Units sold | 18,000 | 16,000 |
| Bad debts expense | $ 1,800 | $ 1,600 |
| Amortization of factory equipment | 5,000 | 5,000 |
| Direct labour cost | 200,000 | 130,000 |
| Direct materials used | 120,000 | 78,000 |
| Factory rent | 12,000 | 12,000 |
| Heat, light, and power | 17,000 | 11,400 |
| Indirect labour | 60,000 | 49,500 |
| Insurance on factory | 2,500 | 2,500 |
| President's salary | 16,000 | 16,000 |
| Sales commissions | 18,000 | 16,000 |
| Supplies used | 40,000 | 26,000 |

**Required:**

1. For 2003, prepare a cost formula for overhead cost using the high–low method.
2. Prepare a budget of overhead costs for the month of June 2004 if 17,000 units are expected to be produced and 15,000 are expected to be sold. (CGA Canada adapted)

**3–22**

*Cost Behaviour; High-
Low Method; Pricing
Decision*

**LO1, LO3**

Fonseca, Ruiz, and Dunn is a large, local accounting firm that is located in Hamilton, Ontario. Carlos Ruiz, one of the firm's founders, appreciates the success his firm has enjoyed and wants to give something back to his community. He believes that an inexpensive accounting services clinic could provide basic accounting services for small unincorporated businesses. He wants to price the services at cost.

Since the clinic is brand new, it has no experience to go on. Carlos decided to operate the clinic for two months before determining how much to charge per hour on an ongoing basis. As a temporary measure, the clinic adopted an hourly charge of $25, half the amount charged by Fonseca, Ruiz, and Dunn for professional services.

The accounting services clinic opened on January 1. During January, the clinic had 120 hours of professional service. During February, the activity was 150 hours. Costs for these two levels of activity usage are as follows:

|  | 120 Professional Hours | 150 Professional Hours |
|---|---|---|
| Salaries: |  |  |
| Senior accountant | $2,500 | $2,500 |
| Office assistant | 1,200 | 1,200 |
| Internet and software subscriptions | 700 | 850 |
| Consulting by senior partner | 1,200 | 1,500 |
| Amortization (equipment) | 2,400 | 2,400 |
| Supplies | 905 | 1,100 |
| Administration | 500 | 500 |
| Rent (offices) | 2,000 | 2,000 |
| Utilities | 332 | 365 |

**Required:**

1. Classify each cost as fixed, variable, or mixed, using hours of professional service as the activity driver.
2. Use the high-low method to separate the mixed costs into their fixed and variable components.
3. Luz Mondragon, the senior accountant at the clinic, has estimated that the clinic will average 140 professional hours per month. If the clinic is to be operated as a not-for-profit organization, how much will it need to charge per professional hour? How much of this charge is variable? How much is fixed?
4. Suppose the clinic averages 170 professional hours per month. How much would need to be charged per hour for the clinic to cover its costs? Explain why the per-hour charge decreased as the activity output increased.

**3–23**

Cost Behaviour; Resource Usage Model

LO1, LO2

Rolertyme Company manufactures roller skates. With the exception of the rollers, all parts of the skates are produced internally. Neeta Booth, Rolertyme's president, has decided to make the rollers instead of buying them from external suppliers. The company needs 100,000 sets per year; currently it pays $1.90 per set of rollers.

The rollers can be produced using an available area within the plant. However, equipment for production of the rollers would need to be leased (at $30,000 per year). Additionally, it would cost $0.50 per machine hour for power, oil, and other operating expenses. The equipment will provide 60,000 machine hours per year. Direct materials costs will average $0.75 per set of four, and direct labour costs will average $0.25 per set. Since only one type of roller would be produced, no additional demands would be made on the setup activity.

Other overhead activities (besides machining and setups), however, would be affected. The company's cost management system provides the following information about the current status of the overhead activities that would be affected (the supply and demand figures do not include the effect of roller production on these activities). The lumpy quantity indicates how much capacity must be purchased should any expansion of activity supply be needed. The purchase price is the cost of acquiring the capacity represented by the lumpy quantity. This price also represents the cost of current spending on the existing activity supply (for each block of activity).

| Activity | Activity Driver | Supply | Usage | Lumpy Quantity | Purchase Price |
|---|---|---|---|---|---|
| Purchasing | Orders | 25,000 | 22,000 | 5,000 | $25,000 |
| Inspection | Hours | 10,000 | 9,000 | 2,000 | 30,000 |
| Material handling | Moves | 5,000 | 4,300 | 2,500 | 15,000 |

Production of rollers would place the following demands on the overhead activities:

| Activity | Resource Demands |
|---|---|
| Machine | 50,000 machine hours |
| Purchasing | 2,000 purchase orders (associated with materials used to make the rollers) |
| Inspection | 750 inspection hours |
| Material handling | 500 moves |

Producing the rollers also means that the purchase of outside rollers will cease. Because rollers are no longer being purchased, the number of purchase orders (associated with the outside acquisition of rollers) will drop by 5,000. Similarly, the moves for the handling of incoming orders will decrease by 200. The company has not inspected the rollers purchased from outside suppliers.

**Required:**
1. Classify all resources associated with the production of rollers as flexible resources or committed resources. For committed resources, label them as short-term and long-term commitments. How should we describe the cost behaviour of these short-term and long-term resource commitments? Explain.
2. Calculate the total annual resource spending (for all overhead activities except for setups) that the company will incur after production of the rollers begins. Break this cost into fixed and variable activity costs. In calculating these figures, assume that the company will spend no more than necessary. What is the effect on resource spending caused by production of the rollers (include the effect of materials and labour)?
3. Refer to Requirement 2. For each activity, break down the cost of activity supplied into the cost of activity usage and the cost of unused activity.

**3–24**

High-Low Method;
Scatterplot Method;
Method of Least
Squares

LO3

You have been given the following information about the heat, light, and power costs for the Lily Company.

| Month | Machine Hours | Heat, Light, and Power |
|---|---|---|
| January | 2,800 | $16,100 |
| February | 2,600 | 15,500 |
| March | 2,880 | 16,500 |
| April | 2,760 | 16,100 |
| May | 2,840 | 16,350 |
| June | 2,320 | 14,300 |
| July | 1,840 | 12,400 |
| August | 1,640 | 11,560 |
| September | 2,920 | 16,700 |
| October | 3,400 | 18,600 |
| November | 3,280 | 18,100 |
| December | 2,960 | 16,850 |

**Required:**
1. Using the high-low method, predict what the heat, light, and power cost would be for a month in which 2,500 machine hours are worked.
2. Using the scatterplot method, predict what the heat, light, and power cost would be for a month in which 2,500 machine hours are worked.
3. Using the method of least squares, predict what the heat, light, and power cost would be for a month in which 2,500 machine hours are worked.
4. Compare and evaluate your answers to Requirements 1, 2, and 3. (CGA Canada adapted)

**3–25**

Farnsworth Company has gathered data on its overhead activities and associated costs for the past 10 months. Tracy Heppler, a member of the controller's department, has convinced management that overhead costs can be better estimated and controlled if the fixed and variable components of each overhead activity are known. Tracy has identified 150 different activities and has grouped them into sets based on her belief that they share a common driver. (This classification process has reduced the number of cost formulas needed from 150 to 25.) For example, she has decided that unloading incoming goods, counting goods, and inspecting goods can be grouped together as a more general receiving activity, based on her belief that the costs of the three related activities are all driven by the same driver: number of receiving orders. To confirm her activity classification and driver assignment, she has gathered 10 months of data on the number of receiving orders and on the cost of receiving. Just in case receiving orders is not a good driver, she has also collected data on the kilograms of material received.

| Month | Number of Receiving Orders | Kilograms of Materials Received | Receiving Cost |
|-------|---------------------------|--------------------------------|----------------|
| 1     | 1,000                     | 300,000                        | $18,000        |
| 2     | 700                       | 250,000                        | 15,000         |
| 3     | 1,500                     | 450,000                        | 28,000         |
| 4     | 1,200                     | 320,000                        | 17,000         |
| 5     | 1,300                     | 440,000                        | 25,000         |
| 6     | 1,100                     | 280,000                        | 18,000         |
| 7     | 1,600                     | 550,000                        | 30,000         |
| 8     | 1,400                     | 390,000                        | 24,000         |
| 9     | 1,700                     | 230,000                        | 21,000         |
| 10    | 900                       | 230,000                        | 15,000         |

**Required:**
1. Using the high-low method, prepare a cost formula for the receiving activity using the number of receiving orders as the driver.
2. Using the method of least squares, prepare a cost formula for the receiving activity using the number of receiving orders as the driver. What does the coefficient of determination tell us about the use of receiving orders as the independent variable?
3. Using the method of least squares, prepare a cost formula for the receiving activity using the number of kilograms of material received as the driver. What does the coefficient of determination tell us about the use of kilograms of material received as the independent variable?
4. Run a multiple regression using both the number of receiving orders and the kilograms of material as independent variables. Which of the three regression equations do you think is best? Why?

**3–26**

Kimball Company has a policy of producing to meet customer demand and keeps very little, if any, finished goods inventory (thus, units produced = units sold).

Lately, Kimball's industry is in a recession, and the company is producing well below capacity (and expects to continue doing so for the coming year). The president of Kimball Company has recently implemented a policy that any special orders will be accepted if they cover the costs that the orders cause. She is willing to accept orders that at least cover their variable costs so that the company can keep its employees and avoid layoffs. Also, any orders above variable costs will increase the company's overall profitability.

To help implement the policy, Kimball has developed the following cost formulas using the least squares method:

Material cost = $80X, $r = 0.95$
Labour cost (direct) = $20X, $r = 0.96$
Overhead cost = $350,000 + $100X, $r = 0.75$
Selling cost = $50,000 + $10X, $r = 0.93$
where X = Direct labour hours

**Required:**

1. Compute the total unit variable cost. Suppose that Kimball has an opportunity to accept an order for 20,000 units at $220 per unit. Each unit uses one direct labour hour for production. Should Kimball accept the order? (The order would not displace any of Kimball's regular orders.)
2. Explain the significance of the coefficient of correlation measures ($r$) for the cost formulas. Did these measures have a bearing on your answer in Requirement 1? Should they have a bearing? Why?
3. Suppose that the following multiple regression equation is developed for overhead costs:

$$Y = \$100,000 + \$100X_1 + \$5,000X_2 + \$300X_3$$

where $X_1$ = direct labour hours, $X_2$ = number of setups, and $X_3$ = engineering hours.

The correlation coefficient for the equation is 0.94. Assume that the order of 20,000 units requires 12 setups and 600 engineering hours. Given this new information, should the company accept the special order referred to in Requirement 1? Is there any other information about cost behaviour that you would like to have? Explain.

**3–27**

High-Low Method;
Regression; Multiple
Regression

LO3, LO4, LO5

Weber Valley Regional Hospital has collected data on all of its activities for the past 14 months. Data for cardiac nursing care follow:

| Month | Cost | Hours of Nursing Care |
|---|---|---|
| May 2003 | $ 66,000 | 1,600 |
| June 2003 | 76,500 | 1,900 |
| July 2003 | 78,100 | 1,950 |
| August 2003 | 73,180 | 1,800 |
| September 2003 | 69,500 | 1,700 |
| October 2003 | 64,250 | 1,550 |
| November 2003 | 52,000 | 1,200 |
| December 2003 | 66,000 | 1,600 |
| January 2004 | 110,000 | 1,800 |
| February 2004 | 86,485 | 1,330 |
| March 2004 | 105,022 | 1,700 |
| April 2004 | 100,000 | 1,600 |
| May 2004 | 120,000 | 2,000 |
| June 2004 | 109,500 | 1,790 |

**Required:**

1. Using the high–low method, calculate the variable rate per hour and the fixed cost for the nursing-care activity. Comment on your results.
2. Prepare a scatterplot for the nursing-care activity using the given data. Use one symbol, perhaps an "$x$," for observations occurring in 2003, and another symbol, perhaps a "$y$," for observations occurring in 2004.
3. Upon looking into the events that happened at the end of 2003, you find that the cardiology ward bought a cardiac-monitoring machine for the nursing station. A decision was also made to add a new supervisory position for the evening shift. Monthly amortization on the monitor and the salary of the new

supervisor total $10,000. In addition, the rest of the nursing staff received a raise, and the cost of supplies has increased. Run the following regressions:

   a. Run a regression on the data from 2003 and 2004 using nursing hours as the single independent variable.

   b. Run a regression on the data from 2003 using nursing hours as the single independent variable.

   c. Run a regression on the data from 2004 using nursing hours as the single independent variable.

   d. Create a dummy variable called "changes" that takes the value "0" for observations in 2003 and the value "1" for observations in 2004. Run a multiple regression using nursing hours and "changes" as the independent variables.

4. Which of the four cost formulas should be used to budget the cost of the cardiac nursing-care activity for the remainder of 2004? Explain.

**3–28**

*Comparison of Regression Equations*

**LO1, LO3, LO4, LO5**

Loving Toys Company is attempting to determine cost behaviour of its overhead activities for its Truro, Nova Scotia, plant. One of the major activities is the setup activity. Two possible drivers have been considered: setup hours and number of setups. The plant controller has accumulated the following data for the setup activity to be analyzed using the method of least squares:

| Month | Setup Costs | Setup Hours | Number of Setups |
|---|---|---|---|
| February | $ 7,700 | 2,000 | 70 |
| March | 7,650 | 2,100 | 50 |
| April | 10,052 | 3,000 | 50 |
| May | 9,400 | 2,700 | 60 |
| June | 9,584 | 3,000 | 20 |
| July | 8,480 | 2,500 | 40 |
| August | 8,550 | 2,400 | 60 |
| September | 9,735 | 2,900 | 50 |
| October | 10,500 | 3,000 | 90 |

**Required:**

1. Using the least squares method, estimate a cost equation with setup hours as the only independent variable. If the Truro plant forecasts 2,600 setup hours for the next month, what will the budgeted setup cost be?

2. Using the least squares method, estimate an equation with number of setups as the only independent variable. If the Truro plant forecasts 80 setups for the next month, what will the budgeted setup cost be?

3. Which of the two regression equations do you think does a better job of predicting setup costs? Explain.

4. Run a multiple regression analysis using both setup hours and number of setups as independent variables. Calculate the budgeted cost using the multiple regression equation. Would you recommend using the multiple-driver equation over a single-driver equation? Explain.

**3–29**

Scattergraph; Method
of Least Squares;
Choice of Independent
Variable

LO3, LO4, LO5

Grace Fahran, the executive director of a hospital in Thunder Bay, is preparing a budget for the hospital's finance committee. As part of the budget submission, Grace wants to include an analysis of the overhead cost data over a 30-month period. Total overhead costs include all costs such as supplies, pharmaceutical, and labour costs (including administrative staff and nurses but excluding doctors' salaries). The number of patient admissions includes all patients who are admitted into the hospital, but excluding emergencies and outpatients. The number of administrative staff includes all department heads and support, but excludes nurses and doctors. The following data were obtained for a preliminary analysis:

| Month | Overhead Costs | Patient Admissions | Administrative Staff |
|-------|---------------|--------------------|--------------------|
| 1 | $1,969,000 | 414 | 48 |
| 2 | 1,973,000 | 423 | 48 |
| 3 | 1,975,000 | 419 | 48 |
| 4 | 1,978,000 | 426 | 48 |
| 5 | 1,990,000 | 450 | 46 |
| 6 | 2,014,000 | 432 | 46 |
| 7 | 1,997,000 | 464 | 47 |
| 8 | 2,012,000 | 432 | 48 |
| 9 | 2,023,000 | 458 | 48 |
| 10 | 2,050,000 | 455 | 47 |
| 11 | 2,040,000 | 469 | 47 |
| 12 | 2,063,000 | 475 | 46 |
| 13 | 2,058,000 | 481 | 46 |
| 14 | 2,078,000 | 467 | 49 |
| 15 | 2,050,000 | 480 | 49 |
| 16 | 2,081,000 | 476 | 49 |
| 17 | 2,093,000 | 483 | 48 |
| 18 | 2,086,000 | 479 | 48 |
| 19 | 2,085,000 | 500 | 48 |
| 20 | 2,090,000 | 488 | 47 |
| 21 | 2,090,000 | 495 | 48 |
| 22 | 2,096,000 | 460 | 48 |
| 23 | 2,098,000 | 478 | 47 |
| 24 | 2,105,000 | 482 | 50 |
| 25 | 2,148,000 | 497 | 50 |
| 26 | 2,120,000 | 474 | 50 |
| 27 | 2,099,000 | 511 | 50 |
| 28 | 2,130,000 | 497 | 49 |
| 29 | 2,135,000 | 509 | 51 |
| 30 | 2,132,000 | 516 | 51 |

**Required:**

1. Prepare a scattergraph of overhead costs using the number of administrative staff as the independent variable.
2. Prepare a scattergraph of overhead costs using the number of patient admissions as the independent variable.
3. Based on the scattergraphs prepared in Requirements 1 and 2, which would be the more appropriate choice of independent variable? Explain.

4. Determine an overhead cost equation using the method of least squares with the number of administrative staff as the independent variable.
5. Determine an overhead cost equation using the method of least squares with the number of patient admissions as the independent variable.
6. Compare the goodness of fit for the equations in Requirements 4 and 5.
7. Discuss one factor that would limit the usefulness of the cost equations determined in Requirements 4 and 5. (CGA Canada adapted)

**3–30**

Suspicious Acquisition of Data; Ethical Issues

**LO1**

Bill Lewis, manager of the Thomas Electronics Division, called a meeting with his controller, Brindon Peterson, CMA, and his marketing manager, Patty Fritz. The following is a transcript of the conversation that took place during the meeting.

**Bill**: "Brindon, the variable-costing system that you developed has proved to be a big plus for our division. Our success in winning bids has increased, and as a result, our revenues have increased by 25 percent. However, if we intend to meet this year's profit targets, we are going to need something extra—am I not right, Patty?"

**Patty**: "Absolutely. While we have been able to win more bids, we still are losing too many, particularly to our major competitor, Kilborn Electronics. If I knew more about their bidding strategy, I imagine we could be more successful competing with them."

**Bill**: "Would knowing their variable costs help?"

**Patty**: "Certainly. It would give me their minimum price. With that knowledge, I'm sure we could find a way to beat them on several jobs, particularly for those jobs where we are at least as efficient. It would also help us identify where we are not cost-competitive. With this information, we might be able to find ways to increase our efficiency."

**Bill**: "Well, I have good news. I have some data here in these handouts that reveal bids that Kilborn made on several jobs. I have also been able to obtain the direct labour hours worked for many of these jobs. But that's not all. I have monthly totals for manufacturing costs and direct labour hours for all their jobs for the past ten months. Brindon, with this information, can you estimate what the variable manufacturing cost per hour is? If you can, we can compute the variable costs for each job and the markup that Kilborn is using."

**Brindon**: "Yes, an analysis of the data you're requesting is possible. I have a question, though, before I do this. How did you manage to acquire these data? I can't imagine that Kilborn would willingly release this information."

**Bill**: "What does it matter how the data were acquired? The fact is, we have them, and we have an opportunity to gain a tremendous competitive advantage. With that advantage, we can meet our profit targets, and we will all end the year with a big bonus."

After the meeting, in a conversation with Patty, Brindon learned that Bill was dating Jackie Wilson, a cost accountant (and CMA) who happened to work for Kilborn. Patty speculated that Jackie might be the source of the Kilborn data. Upon learning this information, Brindon expressed some strong reservations to Patty about analyzing the data.

**Required:**
1. Assume that Bill did acquire the data from Jackie Wilson. Comment on Jackie's behaviour. Which of the standards of ethical conduct outlined in Chapter 1 did she violate?
2. Were Brindon's instincts correct—should he have felt some reservations about analyzing the data? Would it be ethical to analyze the data? Do any of the standards of ethical conduct apply? What would you do if you were Brindon? Explain.

## Research Assignment

**3–31**

Cybercase

LO2, LO6

Use the Internet to gather information on one of the theme parks at Walt Disney World: Magic Kingdom, Epcot, Disney-MGM Studios, or Disney's Animal Kingdom (see http://www.disney.com).

Once you have selected your park, list as many resources as possible and classify them as flexible or committed. Discuss the cost behaviour of each. How do you think cost behaviour affected the planning for the theme park?

# Activity-Based Costing

**After studying Chapter 4, you should be able to:**

1. Discuss the importance of unit costs to managers' decisions.

2. Describe functional-based costing approaches.

3. Explain why functional-based costing approaches may produce distorted costs.

4. Explain how an activity-based costing system works.

5. Provide a detailed description of how activities can be grouped into homogeneous cost pool sets to reduce the number of activity rates.

6. Describe activity-based customer and supplier costing.

# Scenario

Ryan Chesser, president and owner of Sharp Paper, Inc., was reviewing the most recent financial reports. Profits had once again declined. The company had failed to achieve its targeted return for the third consecutive year. The company's inability to improve its profits frustrated Ryan. After all, Sharp Paper had been a dominant player in the industry for more than two decades. The company owns three paper mills, which produce coated and uncoated specialty printing papers. Customers have access to a variety of papers differing in finish, colour, weight, and packaging. The company markets more than 400 individual products.

To determine the reasons for the company's declining fortunes, Ryan asked his vice-presidents of production (Jeff Clark) and marketing (Jennifer Woodruff) to do some research on why competitors were winning bids on some major product lines despite aggressive pricing by Sharp. Four weeks after giving the assignment, he received the following report:

MEMO
To:         Ryan Chesser, President
From:       Jeff Clark and
            Jennifer Woodruff
Subject:    Competitive Position
            of Sharp
Date:       February 12, 2004

Our investigation has revealed some rather interesting information—information that we believe can benefit our company. We began by contacting customers who have switched some of their purchases to our competitors. We discovered that the switch usually involved our high-volume products. We have been losing bids on these products even when they were aggressively priced. Often the loss of business was to smaller competitors with less diverse product lines. Their prices were significantly lower than ours, and, in fact, seemed unrealistically low.

Our next effort was focused on determining whether competitors were employing a new technology that might provide significant cost advantages. Virtually all of our small competitors use the same manufacturing processes that we use. No evidence of significant differences in efficiency emerged.

Curiously, our low-volume products appear to be the most profitable. In some cases, we are the only company that produces these specialty products. At times, we even receive referrals from our competitors. But some of our operational managers have urged us to drop some of these low-volume products, arguing that they're more bother than they're worth. Yet these products are being reported as highly profitable. Our initial discussions with Jan Booth, our controller, failed to reveal any logical reasons explaining why the profit margins on the low-volume products were so much greater than those on our high-volume products, which seems counterintuitive given the special processes and handling required for the low-volume products. We were even told that we could increase our margin on the low-volume products by increasing prices. Recent price increases were readily accepted by customers—without any complaints.

Yesterday Jan approached us and indicated that she had given some thought to our questions and concerns. She mentioned the possibility that many of our problems may be rooted in the way we are currently assigning costs to products. She noted that we are using a traditional, functional-based costing system and that it may be causing distortions in product costs. Given the results of our other inquiries, this possibility may be worth further investigation.[1]

**Questions to Think About**

1. What are product costs?

2. What role do product costs play in bids?

3. What is meant by a traditional, functional-based costing system? Why might it cause distortions in product costs?

4. If product costing is the root of the bidding difficulties, why are the smaller, less diverse firms having more success?

5. Why wasn't the controller's office able to explain the high-profit margins on the low-volume products?

6. Assuming that Sharp's problems are founded in the way costs are assigned to products, what can Sharp do to solve the problem?

## Unit Costs

### Objective 1

Discuss the importance of unit costs to managers' decisions.

**unit cost**

The total costs assigned to a product divided by the number of units produced of that product.

Functional-based and activity-based costing systems assign costs to cost objects such as products, customers, materials, suppliers, and marketing channels. Once costs are assigned to a cost object, a unit cost is computed by dividing the total assigned cost by the amount of the particular cost object. Because of their importance, calculation of unit product costs will be discussed first. We will discuss other cost objects later.

Conceptually, computing the unit product cost is simple. The **unit cost** is the total cost associated with the units produced divided by the number of units produced. For example, if a construction company builds 100 subdivision homes of the same size and quality and the total cost for these homes is $6 million, then the cost of each home is $60,000 ($6 million divided by 100 homes). Similarly, if Jiffy-Change, a service firm that specializes in changing oil, works on 400 cars per month and total costs are $4,000, then the cost per car serviced is $10.

Although the concept is simple, the practical reality of the computation can be somewhat more complex. First, what is meant by "total cost"? Does this consist only of production costs? Or production costs plus marketing costs? Or all costs of the organization? Second, how do we measure the costs to be assigned? Do we use actual costs incurred or estimated costs? Third, how do we associate costs with the product? When only one product is produced, this question is triv-

---

1. The setting and the issues in this scenario are based in part on the following three articles: James P. Borden, "Review of Literature on Activity-Based Costing," *Journal of Cost Management for the Manufacturing Industry* (Spring 1990); John K. Shank and Vijay Govindarajan, "Transaction-Based Costing for the Complex Product Line: A Field Study," *Journal of Cost Management for the Manufacturing Industry* (Summer 1988): pp. 31-38; and Robin Cooper, "Does Your Company Need a New Cost System?" *Journal of Cost Management for the Manufacturing Industry* (Spring 1987): pp. 45-49.

ial, because all costs incurred are traceable to that one product. But when more than one product is produced, the answer is more complex.

The first question is answered by defining what is meant by "product cost." Recall that the product cost definition depends on the managerial objective being served. For example, product cost is often defined as production costs: direct materials, direct labour, and overhead. This is a common product cost definition used for external financial reporting. But it is also useful for making many managerial decisions. For example, it can serve as a critical input for establishing bid prices. Furthermore, this common product cost definition can be used to illustrate the differences between functional-based and activity-based cost assignment approaches. We will use this definition of product cost in this chapter.

The second and third questions are concerned with how costs are measured and assigned to products. Total manufacturing costs must be measured, and then these costs must be associated with the units produced. **Cost measurement** consists of determining the dollar amounts of direct materials, direct labour, and overhead used in production. The dollar amounts may be the actual amounts expended for the manufacturing inputs, or they may be estimated amounts. Often, estimated amounts are used to ensure timeliness of cost information or to control costs. The process of associating the costs, once measured, with the units produced is called **cost assignment**. Functional-based and activity-based approaches are two alternative ways of assigning costs to products.

## Importance of Unit Product Costs

A cost accounting system measures and assigns costs so that the unit cost of a product or service can be determined. Unit cost is a critical piece of information for managers of manufacturing and service firms. Unit costs are essential for valuing inventory, determining income, and making a number of important managerial decisions. For example, bidding is a common requirement in the markets for specialized products and services. It is virtually impossible for a manager to submit a meaningful bid without knowing the unit costs of the products or services to be produced. Unit product cost information is vital in a number of other areas as well. Decisions concerning product and service design and the introduction of new products and services are affected by expected unit costs. Managers faced with decisions to make or buy a product or service, accept or reject a special order, or keep or drop a product or service require unit cost information. Because unit cost information is so vital, its accuracy is essential. Distorted unit product costs are not acceptable.

## Supplying Unit Cost Information

To supply unit cost information, a product cost definition, cost measurement, and cost assignment are required. As already mentioned, we will use the traditional product cost definition in this chapter. There are also a number of different ways to measure and assign costs. Two possible measurement systems are *actual costing* and *normal costing*.

**Actual costing** assigns the actual costs of direct materials, direct labour, and overhead to products. In practice, strict actual-cost systems are rarely used, because they cannot provide accurate unit cost information on a timely basis. Interestingly, per-unit computation of the direct materials and direct labour costs is not the source of the difficulty. The amount of actual direct materials and direct labour used for a product can be observed as the units are produced. Thus, actual prime costs can be assigned using direct tracing, and they can be assigned on a timely basis. For these two manufacturing inputs, there are no significant prob-

**cost measurement**

The act of determining the dollar amounts of direct materials, direct labour, and overhead used in production.

**cost assignment**

The process of associating the costs, once measured, with the units produced.

**actual costing**

An approach that assigns actual costs for direct materials, direct labour, and overhead to products.

lems with either accuracy or timeliness. The main problem with using actual costs for the calculation of unit cost is with manufacturing overhead.

Assigning actual overhead costs creates a conflict between timeliness and accuracy. For example, consider a company that produces a single product. In this case, we know that the year's entire overhead costs belong to the units produced during the year. Thus, if we wait until the end of the year, we can compute an accurate cost per unit simply by dividing the year's overhead costs by the year's production. Unfortunately, waiting until the end of the year to compute an overhead rate is unacceptable. Managers need unit cost information throughout the year. Most decisions requiring unit cost information cannot wait until the end of the year.

It is possible to provide more timely unit cost information by using the same procedure for a shorter period—say, a week or a month (for example, by dividing a month's overhead by a month's output). This approach, however, tends to produce unit costs that fluctuate from month to month. This outcome occurs for two major reasons: (1) nonuniform incurrence of overhead, and (2) changes in production volume. Some overhead costs are not incurred uniformly throughout the year; they can differ significantly from one period to the next. Similarly, per-unit overhead costs can fluctuate dramatically because of changes in production volume from period to period.

**Normal costing** assigns the actual costs of direct materials and direct labour to products; however, overhead costs are assigned using predetermined rates. A **predetermined overhead rate** is a rate based on estimated or budgeted data and calculated using the following formula:

$$\text{Predetermined Overhead rate} = \frac{\text{Estimated overhead cost}}{\text{Estimated activity usage}}$$

Virtually all companies use predetermined overhead rates to assign overhead to production. How overhead costs are assigned to products will become clear as we discuss functional-based costing and activity-based costing. Since functional-based costing can be viewed as a special case of activity-based costing, we will discuss it first. Furthermore, by discussing functional-based costing first, we will see the potential advantages of activity-based costing more clearly.

## Functional-Based Product Costing

Functional-based product costing assigns the cost of direct materials and direct labour to products using direct tracing. Overhead costs, on the other hand, pose a different challenge. The physically observable input–output relationship that exists between direct labour, direct materials, and products is simply not available for overhead. Therefore, overhead costs are assigned using driver tracing and allocation. Specifically, functional-based costing uses only *unit-level* activity drivers to assign overhead costs to products.

**Unit-level activity drivers** are factors that cause changes in cost as the number of units produced change. The use of only unit-based drivers to assign overhead costs to products assumes that the overhead consumed by products is highly correlated with the number of units produced. For those overhead costs for which this assumption is valid, the unit-based assignment corresponds to driver tracing; for those overhead costs that do not fit the assumption, the cost assignment is an allocation.

A functional-based predetermined overhead rate requires specification of a unit-level driver, an estimate of the capacity measured by the driver, and an estimate of the expected overhead cost. Examples of unit-level drivers commonly used to assign overhead include the following:

---

**normal costing**

An approach that assigns the actual costs for direct materials and direct labour to products but uses a predetermined rate to assign overhead costs.

**predetermined overhead rate**

An overhead rate computed using estimated data.

**Objective** 2

Describe functional-based costing approaches.

**unit-level activity drivers**

Factors that measure the consumption of unit-level activities by products and other cost objects.

- Units produced
- Direct labour hours
- Direct labour dollars
- Machine hours
- Direct material dollars

**expected activity capacity**

Expected activity output for the coming year.

**normal activity capacity**

The average activity output for a given period.

**theoretical activity capacity**

The activity output possible if the activity is performed with perfect efficiency.

**practical activity capacity**

The activity output produced when the activity is performed efficiently.

After we have identified the unit-level driver, the next step is to determine the activity capacity that the driver measures. Although any reasonable capacity could be chosen, the four usual candidates are expected capacity, normal capacity, theoretical capacity, and practical capacity. These are defined as follows:

- **Expected activity capacity** is the activity output the firm expects to attain for the coming period (often a year).
- **Normal activity capacity** is the average activity output that a firm experiences in the long term (normal volume is computed over more than one period).
- **Theoretical activity capacity** is the absolute maximum activity output that can be realized if everything operates *perfectly*.
- **Practical activity capacity** is the maximum output that can be realized if everything operates *efficiently*.

Of the four choices, the last three have the advantage of using the same activity level period after period. As a result, they each produce less period-to-period fluctuation of the per-unit overhead cost than a rate based on expected capacity for a period.

Using practical or theoretical capacity is often recommended because it avoids assigning unused capacity costs to products and encourages management of any excess capacity. Exhibit 4–1 illustrates these four measures of activity capacity.

## Plantwide Rates

A plantwide overhead rate is the simplest unit-level method for assigning overhead costs. Exhibit 4–2 illustrates how plantwide overhead rates are computed. This calculation consists of two stages. In the first stage overhead costs are accumulated in one large plantwide pool. Overhead costs are assigned to the pool simply by adding all the overhead costs expected to be incurred within the plant

Activity Capacity Measures

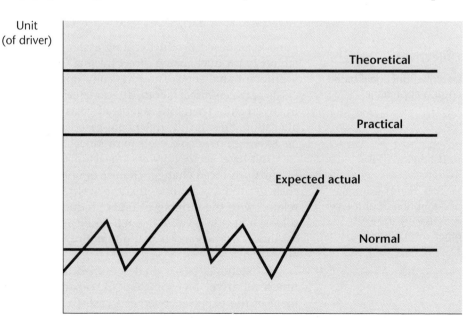

EXHIBIT 4-2

Functional-Based Costing:
Plantwide Rate

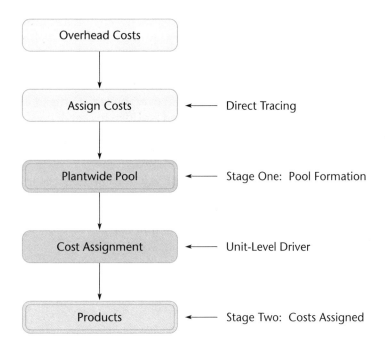

for the period. In a sense, we could argue that the costs are assigned to a very broad macro activity: production. Once costs are accumulated in this pool, we then compute a plantwide rate using a single unit-level driver (often direct labour hours). In the second stage, overhead costs are assigned to products, multiplying the plantwide rate by the actual amount of the unit-level driver used by each product.

### Computation of a Plantwide Rate

We can best illustrate the computation of a plantwide rate with an example. Belring produces two telephones: a cordless phone and a regular model. The company has the following estimated and actual data for 2004:

| | |
|---|---|
| Budgeted overhead | $360,000 |
| Expected activity (in direct labour hours) | 100,000 |
| Actual overhead | $380,000 |
| Actual activity (in direct labour hours) | 100,000 |

Belring bases its plantwide predetermined overhead rate for 2004 on expected direct labour hours (DLH) as follows:

$$\text{Predetermined overhead rate} = \text{Budgeted overhead/Expected activity}$$
$$= \$360,000/100,000 \text{ direct labour hours (DLH)}$$
$$= \$3.60 \text{ per DLH}$$

### Applied Overhead

**applied overhead**

Overhead assigned to production using predetermined rates.

The total overhead assigned to actual production at any point in time is called **applied overhead**. Applied overhead is computed using the following formula:

$$\text{Applied overhead} = \text{Overhead rate} \times \text{Actual activity output}$$

Using the overhead rate, we see that the applied overhead for 2004 is:

$$\text{Applied overhead} = \text{Overhead rate} \times \text{Actual activity}$$
$$= \$3.60 \times 100,000 \text{ DLH}$$
$$= \$360,000$$

**overhead variance**

The difference between actual overhead and applied overhead.

**underapplied overhead**

The amount by which actual overhead exceeds applied overhead.

**overapplied overhead**

The amount by which applied overhead exceeds actual overhead.

The difference between the actual overhead and the applied overhead is called an **overhead variance**. For Belring, the overhead variance is $20,000 ($380,000 – $360,000). If the actual overhead is greater than the applied overhead, the variance is called **underapplied overhead**. Belring has underapplied overhead of $20,000 for 2004. If the actual overhead is less than the applied overhead, the variance is called **overapplied overhead**. Usually, at the end of the period, underapplied overhead is added to cost of goods sold and overapplied overhead is subtracted from cost of goods sold.

### Unit Cost

A product's unit cost is computed as the sum of the product's total prime costs and applied overhead costs, which we then divide by the number of units produced. We will use the following actual data for Belring's two products to illustrate unit-cost computation:

|  | Cordless | Regular |
| --- | --- | --- |
| Units produced | 10,000 | 100,000 |
| Prime costs | $78,000 | $738,000 |
| Direct labour hours | 10,000 | 90,000 |

The unit-cost calculations are summarized in Exhibit 4–3. Notice the role played by the predetermined rate of $3.60 per DLH in calculating the unit cost.

**EXHIBIT**   **4-3**

Unit-Cost Computation: Plantwide Rate

|  | Cordless | Regular |
| --- | --- | --- |
| Prime costs | $ 78,000 | $ 738,000 |
| Applied overhead costs: |  |  |
| $3.60 × 10,000 | 36,000 | — |
| $3.60 × 90,000 | — | 324,000 |
| Total manufacturing costs | $114,000 | $1,062,000 |
| Units produced | 10,000 | 100,000 |
| Unit cost (total costs/units) | $ 11.40 | $ 10.62 |

## Departmental Rates

Exhibit 4–4 illustrates a two-stage framework for using departmental overhead rates. In the first stage, the plantwide overhead costs are divided up and assigned to individual production departments, creating departmental overhead cost pools. In this first stage, departments are the cost objects, and overhead costs are assigned using a combination of direct tracing, driver tracing, and allocation. We describe the detail of how this first-stage cost assignment to departments is done in Chapter 7. Once costs are assigned to individual production departments, then unit-based drivers—such as direct labour hours (for labour-intensive departments) and machine hours (for machine-intensive departments)—are used to compute departmental rates. Products passing through a department are assumed to consume overhead resources in proportion to the department's unit-based driver (such as machine hours or direct labour hours used). Thus, in the second stage, overhead is assigned to products by multiplying the departmental rates by the amount of the driver used in the respective departments. The total overhead assigned to products is simply the sum of the amounts applied in each department.

The rationale for departmental rates is simple. Some producing departments may be more "overhead-intensive" than other producing departments. Thus,

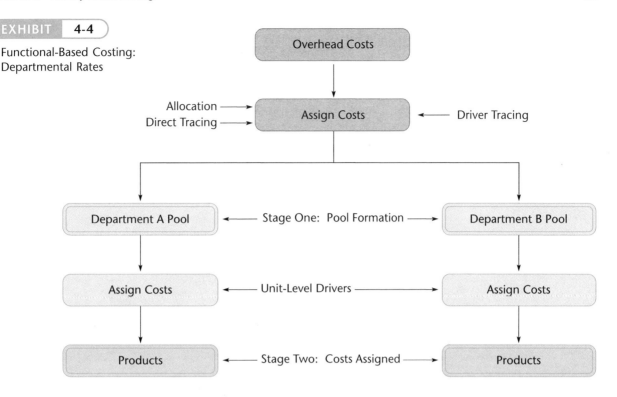

EXHIBIT 4-4

Functional-Based Costing: Departmental Rates

products that spend more time in overhead-intensive departments should be assigned more overhead cost than those that spend less time in these departments. Departmental rates pick up these possible effects, while plantwide rates lose them through averaging.

### Computation of Departmental Rates

We will continue the Belring example to illustrate departmental rates. Belring has two production departments: fabrication and assembly. In fabrication, the major electronic component is made. Other parts are purchased from suppliers and sister divisions. Data relating to the departments for 2004 are given in Exhibit 4–5. Notice that fabrication is machine-intensive (compare machine hours and direct labour hours), whereas assembly tends to be labour-intensive. Observing this, Belring bases its departmental overhead rates on machine hours in fabrication and on direct labour hours in assembly. Two predetermined overhead rates are calculated:

**EXHIBIT 4-5**

Departmental Data

|  | Fabrication | Assembly |
|---|---|---|
| Budgeted overhead | $252,000 | $108,000 |
| Expected and actual usage (direct labour hours): |  |  |
| Cordless | 7,000 | 3,000 |
| Regular | 13,000 | 77,000 |
|  | 20,000 | 80,000 |
| Expected and actual usage (machine hours): |  |  |
| Cordless | 9,000 | 1,000 |
| Regular | 36,000 | 4,000 |
|  | 45,000 | 5,000 |

$$\text{Fabrication rate} = \text{Budgeted fabrication overhead/Expected fabrication machine hours}$$
$$= \$252,000/45,000$$
$$= \$5.60 \text{ per fabrication machine hour}$$

$$\text{Assembly rate} = \text{Budgeted assembly overhead/Expected assembly direct labour hours}$$
$$= \$108,000/80,000$$
$$= \$1.35 \text{ per assembly direct labour hour}$$

### Applied Overhead

Total applied overhead for the year is simply the sum of the amounts applied in each department:

$$\text{Applied overhead} = (\$5.60 \times \text{Actual fabrication machine hours})$$
$$+ (\$1.35 \times \text{Actual assembly direct labour hours})$$
$$= (\$5.60 \times 45,000) + (\$1.35 \times 80,000)$$
$$= \$252,000 + \$108,000$$
$$= \$360,000$$

Notice that the applied overhead equals the budgeted overhead. This happens only when the actual usage is the same as the expected usage, as in this example.

### Unit Cost

Using the departmental rates, the data from Exhibit 4–5, and the earlier information on prime costs and units produced, we show the computation of the unit cost in Exhibit 4–6. Notice that the unit cost of a cordless phone is different when calculated using a plantwide rate compared to when departmental rates are used. Of course the unit cost of a regular phone is also different. We might ask which unit costs are correct. We'll look at how to answer this question next.

|  | Cordless | Regular |
|---|---|---|
| Prime costs | $ 78,000 | $ 738,000 |
| Applied overhead costs: |  |  |
| ($5.60 × 9,000) + ($1.35 × 3,000) | 54,450 | — |
| ($5.60 × 36,000) + ($1.35 × 77,000) | — | 305,550 |
| Total manufacturing costs | $132,450 | $1,043,550 |
| Units produced | 10,000 | 100,000 |
| Unit cost (total costs/units) | $ 13.25 | $ 10.44 |

## Limitations of Functional-Based Accounting Systems

**Objective 3**

Explain why functional-based costing approaches may produce distorted costs.

Plantwide and departmental rates have been used for decades and continue to be used successfully by many organizations. In some settings, however, they do not work well and may actually cause severe product cost distortions. For some companies—particularly those characterized by intense or increasing competition (usually on a worldwide level), continuous improvement and total quality management, total customer satisfaction, and sophisticated technology— product cost distortions can be damaging. As companies operating in this competitive environment adopt new strategies for achieving competitive excellence, their cost accounting systems must often change to keep pace. Specifically, the need for more accurate product costs has forced many companies to take a serious look at their costing procedures. Cost systems that worked reasonably well in the past may no longer be acceptable.

Often organizations experience certain symptoms indicating that their cost accounting system is outdated. Many of these symptoms are present in this chapter's opening scenario involving Sharp Paper Inc. For example, if costs are distorted and severe overcosting of a major high-volume product is the outcome, then bids will be systematically lost, even when the company feels that it is pursuing an aggressive bidding strategy. This can be especially puzzling when the company is confident that it is operating as efficiently as its competitors. Thus, one symptom of an outdated cost system is the inability to explain the outcome of bids. On the flip side, if competitors' prices seem unrealistically low, it should cause managers to wonder about the accuracy of their cost system. Similarly, if somehow an organization's cost system is systematically understating the cost of low-volume specialty products—products that require special processes and handling—then the organization may find that it has a seemingly profitable niche all to itself. Yet it may find operational managers wanting to drop some of these "niche" products. These symptoms of an outdated cost system, along with several others, are listed in Exhibit 4–7.[2]

Organizations that have experienced some or all of these symptoms have found that their plantwide or departmental rates are simply no longer capable of accurately assigning overhead costs to individual products. At least two major factors impair the ability of unit-based plantwide and departmental rates to assign overhead costs accurately: (1) the proportion of nonunit-related overhead costs to total overhead costs is large, and (2) the degree of product diversity is great.

**EXHIBIT  4-7**

Symptoms of an Outdated Functional-Based Costing System

1.  The outcome of bids is difficult to explain.
2.  Competitors' prices appear unrealistically low.
3.  Products that are difficult to produce show high profits.
4.  Operational managers want to drop products that appear profitable.
5.  Profit margins are difficult to explain.
6.  The company has a highly profitable niche all to itself.
7.  Customers do not complain about price increases.
8.  The accounting department spends a lot of time supplying cost data for special projects.
9.  Some departments are using their own accounting system.
10. Product costs change because of changes in financial reporting regulations.

## Nonunit-Related Overhead Costs

When we use either plantwide rates or departmental rates we assume that a product's consumption of overhead resources is related strictly to the number of units produced. For activities that are performed each time a unit of product is produced, this assumption makes sense. But what if there are nonunit-level activities—activities that are unrelated to the number of units produced? Setup costs, for example, are incurred each time a batch of products is produced. A batch may consist of 1,000 or 10,000 units, but the cost of setup is the same. Yet as more setups are done, setup costs increase. The number of setups, not the number of

2.  The list of warning signals is based on Robin Cooper, "You need a New Cost System When... ," *Harvard Business Review* (January-February 1989): pp. 77-82.

**nonunit-level activity drivers**

Factors that measure the consumption of nonunit-level activities by products and other cost objects.

units produced, is a much better measure of the consumption of the setup activity. Similarly, product reengineering costs may depend on the number of different engineering work orders rather than on the number of units produced of any given product. Thus, *nonunit-level drivers* such as setups and engineering hours are needed for accurate cost assignment of nonunit-level activities. **Nonunit-level activity drivers** are factors that measure the consumption of nonunit-level activities by products and other cost objects.

Using only unit-based activity drivers to assign nonunit-related overhead costs can create distorted product costs. The severity of this distortion depends on what proportion of total overhead costs these nonunit-based costs represent. For many companies, this percentage can be significant. Schrader Bellows and John Deere Component Works, for example, experienced nonunit-based overhead cost ratios of about 50 percent and 40 percent, respectively.[3] This suggests that we should exercise some care in assigning nonunit-based overhead costs. However, if nonunit-based overhead costs are only a small percentage of total overhead costs, the distortion of product costs would be quite small. In such a case, using only unit-based activity drivers to assign overhead costs would be acceptable.

## Product Diversity

The presence of significant nonunit overhead costs is a necessary but not sufficient condition for problems to arise with plantwide and departmental rates. If products consume the nonunit overhead activities in the same proportion as the unit-level overhead activities, then no product-costing distortion will occur (with the use of traditional overhead assignment methods). The presence of product diversity is also necessary.

**product diversity**

The situation present when products consume overhead in different proportions.

**Product diversity** simply means that products consume overhead activities in different proportions. There are several reasons that products might consume overhead in different proportions. For example, differences in product size, product complexity, setup time, and size of batches can all cause products to consume overhead at different rates. Regardless of the nature of the product diversity, product cost will be distorted whenever the quantity of unit-based overhead that a product consumes does not vary in direct proportion along with the quantity of nonunit-based overhead that it consumes. The proportion of each activity consumed by a product is defined as the **consumption ratio**. How nonunit overhead costs and product diversity can produce distorted product costs is best illustrated with an example.[4]

**consumption ratio**

Proportion of each activity consumed by a product.

## An Example Illustrating the Failure of Unit-Based Overhead Rates

To illustrate how traditional unit-based overhead rates can distort product costs, we will return to the Belring example, this time providing more detailed information about the overhead activities that define their total overhead cost. The detailed data are provided in Exhibit 4–8 (we will assume that the expected and actual outcomes

---

3.  See Robin Cooper, "Cost Classification in Unit-Based and Activity-Based Manufacturing Cost Systems," *Journal of Cost Management for the Manufacturing Industry* (Fall 1990): pp. 4-14.

4.  See the following publications by Anthony A. Atkinson: "Diagnosing Costing Problems," *CMA Magazine*, Vol. 63, No. 3, April 1989: p. 20; "Manage Activities Instead of Costs," *CMA Magazine*, Vol. 63, No. 4, May 1989: p. 25; and "Activity Costing and Efficiency," *CMA Magazine*, Vol. 63, No. 5, June 1989: p. 8. See also John A. Miller, "Manage Costs? Manage Activities," *CMA Magazine*, March 1989: p. 35; and Paul A. Sharman, "Activity-Based Management: A Growing Practice," *CMA Magazine*, Vol. 67, No. 2, March 1993: pp. 17-22.

EXHIBIT 4-8

Product-Costing Data

| Activity Usage Measures | | | |
|---|---|---|---|
| | **Cordless** | **Regular** | **Total** |
| Units produced per year | 10,000 | 100,000 | 110,000 |
| Prime costs | $78,000 | $738,000 | $816,000 |
| Direct labour hours | 10,000 | 90,000 | 100,000 |
| Machine hours | 10,000 | 40,000 | 50,000 |
| Production runs | 20 | 10 | 30 |
| Number of moves | 60 | 30 | 90 |

| Activity Cost Data (Overhead Activities) | |
|---|---|
| **Activity** | **Activity Cost** |
| Setup | $120,000 |
| Material handling | 60,000 |
| Machining | 100,000 |
| Testing | 80,000 |
| Total | $360,000 |

are the same to simplify our analysis). Because the quantity of regular phones produced is 10 times greater than that of cordless phones, we can label the regular phones a high-volume product and the cordless phones a low-volume product.

For simplicity, only four types of overhead activities are assumed:[5]

- setting up the equipment for each batch
- moving a batch
- machining
- testing

The phones are produced in batches. Different manufacturing configurations are needed for the electronic components associated with each phone. Testing is performed after each department's operations. After fabrication, each component is tested to ensure functionality. After assembly, the entire unit is tested to ensure that it is operational.

### Problems with Costing Accuracy

The activity usage data in Exhibit 4–8 reveal some serious problems with either plantwide or departmental rates for assigning overhead costs. The main problem with either procedure is the assumption that machine hours or direct labour hours drive or cause all overhead costs.

From Exhibit 4–8, we know that producing regular phones, the high-volume product, uses nine times as many direct labour hours as producing cordless phones, the low-volume product (90,000 hours versus 10,000 hours). Thus, if a plantwide rate is used, the regular phones will be assigned nine times more overhead cost than the cordless phones. But is this reasonable? Do unit-based drivers explain the consumption of all overhead activities? In particular, can we reasonably assume that each product's consumption of overhead increases in direct proportion to the direct labour hours used? Let's look at the four overhead activities and see if unit-based drivers accurately reflect the demands of regular and cordless phone production.

When we examine the data in Exhibit 4–8 we see that a significant portion of overhead costs is not driven or caused by direct labour hours. For example, each product's demand for setup and material-handling activities is more logically

---

5. Later in this chapter we will look at how these overhead activities can be identified.

related to the number of production runs and the number of moves, respectively. These nonunit activities represent 50 percent ($180,000/$360,000) of the total overhead costs—a significant percentage. Notice that the low-volume product, cordless phones, requires twice as many runs (20/10) and twice as many moves (60/30) as the regular phones. However, use of direct labour hours, a unit-based activity driver, and a plantwide rate assigns nine times more setup and material-handling costs to the regular phones than to the cordless ones. Thus, product diversity exists, and we should expect product cost distortion because the quantity of unit-based overhead that each product consumes does not vary in direct proportion to the quantity of nonunit-based overhead that it consumes.

The consumption ratios for the two products are calculated in Exhibit 4–9. Consumption ratios are simply the proportion of each activity consumed by a product. The consumption ratios suggest that a plantwide rate based on direct labour hours will overcost the regular phones and undercost the cordless phones.

The problem is only partly solved in this case when departmental rates are used (refer to Exhibit 4–5). In the assembly department, regular phones consume 25.67 times as many direct labour hours as cordless phones do (77,000/3,000). In the fabrication department, regular phones consume 4 times as many machine hours as cordless phones do (36,000/9,000). Thus, the regular phones receive about 25.67 times more overhead than the cordless phones in the assembly department and in the fabrication department they receive 4 times more overhead. As Exhibit 4–6 shows, with departmental rates, the unit cost of the cordless phones increases to $13.25, and the unit cost of the regular phones decreases to $10.44.

**EXHIBIT　4-9**

Product Diversity: Consumption Ratios

| Overhead Activity | Cordless Phones | Regular Phones | Activity Driver |
|---|---|---|---|
| Setups | 0.67[a] | 0.33[a] | Production runs |
| Material handling | 0.67[b] | 0.33[b] | Number of moves |
| Power | 0.20[c] | 0.80[c] | Machine hours |
| Testing | 0.10[d] | 0.90[d] | Direct labour hours |

[a] 20/30 (cordless) and 10/30 (regular)
[b] 60/90 (cordless) and 30/90 (regular)
[c] 10,000/50,000 (cordless) and 40,000/50,000 (regular)
[d] 10,000/100,000 (cordless) and 90,000/100,000 (regular)

### Solving the Problem of Cost Distortion

We can solve the cost distortions just described by using activity rates. That is, rather than assigning the overhead costs to departmental or plantwide pools, why not calculate a rate for each overhead activity and then use this activity rate to assign overhead costs? Using the drivers indicated in Exhibit 4–9 and the data provided in Exhibit 4–8, activity rates are computed below:

Setup rate:　　　　　　$120,000/30 runs = $4,000.00 per run
Material-handling rate: $60,000/90 moves = $666.67 per move
Machining rate:　　　　$100,000/50,000 machine hours = $2.00 per machine hour
Testing rate:　　　　　$80,000/100,000 direct labour hours = $0.80 per direct labour hour

To assign overhead costs, we need to know the amount of activity consumed by each product. These amounts are found in Exhibit 4–8. The calculation of the unit cost for each product using activity rates is given in Exhibit 4–10.

### Comparison of Functional-Based and Activity-Based Product Costs

In Exhibit 4–11, the unit cost from activity-based costing (or ABC) is compared with the unit costs produced by functional-based costing using a plantwide rate

|  | Cordless | Regular |
|---|---|---|
| Prime costs | $ 78,000 | $738,000 |
| Applied overhead costs: |  |  |
| Setups: ($4,000 × 20); ($4,000 × 10) | 80,000 | 40,000 |
| Material handling: ($666.67 × 60); ($666.67 × 30) | 40,000 | 20,000 |
| Machining: ($2 × 10,000); ($2 × 40,000) | 20,000 | 80,000 |
| Testing: ($0.80 × 10,000); ($0.80 × 90,000) | 8,000 | 72,000 |
| Total manufacturing costs | $226,000 | $950,000 |
| Units produced | 10,000 | 100,000 |
| Unit cost (total costs/units) | $ 22.60 | $ 9.50 |

|  | Cordless | Regular | Source |
|---|---|---|---|
| Activity-based unit cost | $22.60 | $ 9.50 | Exhibit 4–10 |
| Functional-based unit cost: |  |  |  |
| Plantwide rate | 11.40 | 10.62 | Exhibit 4–3 |
| Departmental rate | 13.25 | 10.44 | Exhibit 4–6 |

and departmental rates. This comparison clearly illustrates the effects of using only unit-based activity drivers to assign overhead costs. The ABC assignment reflects the pattern of overhead consumption and is therefore the most accurate of the three costs shown in Exhibit 4–11. Activity-based product costing reveals that the functional-based costing undercosts the cordless phones and overcosts the regular phones. In fact, the ABC assignment almost doubles the cost of the cordless phones and decreases the cost of the regular phones by more than $1 per unit—a movement in the right direction, given the pattern of overhead consumption. In a diverse product environment, ABC promises greater accuracy, and given the importance of making decisions based on correct information, a detailed look at ABC is certainly merited.

## Activity-Based Product Costing: Detailed Description

**Objective 4**

Explain how an activity-based costing system works.

**activity-based costing (ABC) system**

A cost system that first traces costs to activities and then traces costs from activities to products.

In Exhibits 4–2 and 4–4, we saw that functional-based overhead costing involves two stages: first, overhead costs are assigned to an organizational unit (plant or departments), and second, overhead costs are then assigned to products. As Exhibit 4–12 illustrates, an **activity-based costing (ABC) system** traces costs first to activities and then to products. The underlying assumption is that activities consume resources and products, in turn, consume activities. Thus, activity-based costing is also a two-stage process.[6] An ABC system, however, emphasizes direct tracing and driver tracing (exploiting cause-and-effect relationships), whereas a functional-based costing system tends to be allocation-intensive (largely ignoring cause-and-effect relationships). As the Exhibit 4–12 model reveals, the focus of activity-based costing is activities. Thus, identifying activities must be the first step in designing an activity-based costing system.

### Identifying Activities and Their Attributes

We usually identify activities by interviewing managers or representatives of functional work areas (departments). We ask a set of key questions and the

6. The two-stage description is a simplification for both the functional-based and the activity-based approaches. In reality, multiple stages are possible. We explore these issues in greater detail in Chapter 7 for both approaches.

EXHIBIT   4-12

ABC: Two-Stage
Assignment

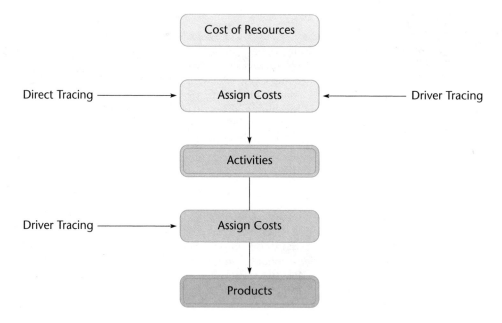

**activity dictionary**

A list of activities
described by specific
attributes, such as name,
definition, classification
as primary or secondary,
and activity driver.

**activity attributes**

Nonfinancial and
financial information
items that describe
individual activities.

**activity drivers**

Factors that measure the
consumption of activities
by products and other
cost objects.

answers provide much of the data needed for an activity-based costing system. We use this interview-derived data to prepare an *activity dictionary*. An **activity dictionary** lists the activities in an organization along with some critical activity attributes. **Activity attributes** are financial and nonfinancial information items that describe individual activities. The attributes included in the activity dictionary depend on the purpose. Examples of activity attributes associated with an activity include types of resources consumed, amount (percentage) of time spent on an activity by workers, cost objects that consume the activity output (reason for performing the activity), a measure of activity output (**activity driver**), and the activity name.

### Key Set of Questions

Information derived from key interview questions serves as the basis for constructing an activity dictionary as well as providing data helpful for assigning resource costs to individual activities. The following list is not exhaustive, but will serve to illustrate the nature of the information-gathering process.

1.  How many employees are in your department? (Activities consume labour.)
2.  What do they do (please describe)? (Activities are people doing things for other people.)
3.  Do people outside your department use any of your department's equipment? (Activities also can be equipment doing work for other people.)
4.  What resources (equipment, materials, energy) are used by each activity? (Activities consume resources in addition to labour.)
5.  What are the outputs of each activity? (Helps identify activity drivers.)
6.  Who and what use the activity output? (Identifies the cost object: products, other activities, customers, etc.)
7.  How much time do workers and equipment spend on each activity? by equipment? (Information needed to assign the cost of labour and equipment to activities.)

### Illustrative Example

Suppose, for example, that a manager of a credit union's credit card department is interviewed and presented with the seven questions just listed. Consider the purpose of and response to each question, in the order indicated.

- *Question 1 (labour resource):* There are six employees, including me.
- *Question 2 (activity identification):* There are four major activities: supervising employees, processing credit card transactions, issuing customer statements, and answering customer questions.
- *Question 3 (activity identification):* Yes. Automatic teller machines (ATMs) service customers who require cash advances.
- *Question 4 (resource identification):* We each have our own computer, printer, and desk. Paper and other supplies are needed to operate the printers. Of course, we each have a telephone as well.
- *Question 5 (potential activity drivers):* Well, for supervising, I manage employees' needs and try to ensure that they carry out their activities efficiently. Processing transactions produces a posting for each transaction in our computer system and serves as a source for preparing the monthly statements. The number of monthly customer statements has to be the product for the issuing activity, and I suppose that customers served is the output for the answering activity. And I guess the number of cash advances would measure the product of the ATM activity, although ATMs really generate more transactions for other products, such as chequing accounts. So perhaps the number of ATM transactions is the real output.
- *Question 6 (identifying potential cost objects):* We have three products: classic, gold, and platinum credit cards. Transactions are processed for these three types of cards, and statements are sent to clients holding these cards. Similarly, answers to questions are directed to clients who hold these cards. As far as supervising, I spend time ensuring the proper coordination and execution of all activities, except for the ATM; I really have no role in managing that particular activity.
- *Question 7 (identifying resource drivers):* I just completed a work survey and have the percentage of time calculated for each worker. All five clerks work on each of the three departmental activities. About 40 percent of their time is spent processing transactions, with the rest of their time split evenly between preparing statements and answering questions. Phone time is used only for answering client questions, and computer time is 70 percent transaction processing, 20 percent statement preparation, and 10 percent answering questions. Furthermore, my own time and that of my computer are 100 percent administrative.

### *Activity Dictionary*

Based on the answers to the survey, an activity dictionary can now be prepared. Exhibit 4–13 illustrates the dictionary for the credit card department. The activity dictionary names the activity (usually by combining an action verb and an object that receives the action), describes the tasks that make up the activity, classifies the activity as primary or secondary, lists the users (cost objects), and identifies a measure of activity output (activity driver). A **primary activity** is an activity that is consumed by a product or customer. A **secondary activity** is one that is consumed by other primary and secondary activities. Ultimately, secondary activities are consumed by a primary activity. For example, the supervising activity is consumed by the following primary activities: processing transactions, preparing statements, and answering phones. The three products—classic, gold, and platinum credit cards—in turn, consume the primary activities. It is not unusual for a typical organization to produce an activity dictionary containing 200 to 300 activities.

**primary activity**

An activity that is consumed by products or customers.

**secondary activity**

An activity that is consumed by primary activities and/or other secondary activities.

## Assigning Costs to Activities

Once activities are identified and described, the next task is determining how much it cost to perform each activity. To do this we must identify the resources

Activity Dictionary: Credit
Card Department

| Activity Name | Activity Description | Activity Type | Cost Object(s) | Activity Driver |
|---|---|---|---|---|
| Supervising employees | Scheduling, coordinating, and evaluating performance | Secondary | Activities within department | Total labour time for each activity |
| Processing transactions | Sorting, keying, and verifying | Primary | Credit cards | Number of transactions |
| Preparing statements | Reviewing, printing, stuffing, and mailing | Primary | Credit cards | Number of statements |
| Answering questions | Answering, logging, reviewing database, and making callbacks | Primary | Credit cards | Number of calls |
| Providing automatic teller machines | Accessing accounts, withdrawing funds | Primary | Credit cards, chequing, and savings accounts | Number of ATM transactions |

being consumed by each activity. Activities consume resources such as labour, materials, energy, and capital. The costs of these resources are found in the general ledger, but how much is spent on each activity is not revealed. It therefore becomes necessary to assign the resource costs to activities using direct tracing and driver tracing. For labour resources, a *work distribution matrix* is often used. A work distribution matrix simply identifies the amount of labour consumed by each activity and is derived from the interview process (or a written survey). For example, the manager of the credit card department disclosed the following about labour usage by the individual activities (see Question 7):

### Percentage of Time on Each Activity

| Activity | Supervisor | Clerks |
|---|---|---|
| Supervising employees | 100% | 0% |
| Processing transactions | 0% | 40% |
| Preparing statements | 0% | 30% |
| Answering questions | 0% | 30% |

The time spent on each activity is the basis for assigning the labour costs to the activity. If the time is 100 percent, then labour is exclusive to the activity and direct tracing can be used to assign the cost (such would be the case for the supervisory labour cost). If the resource is shared by several activities (as is the case for the clerical resource), then we use driver tracing to assign the labour cost. These drivers are called resource drivers. A **resource driver** is a factor that measures the consumption of a resource by activities. Once resource drivers are identified, then we can assign the costs of the resource to the activities. Assume, for example, that the supervisor's salary is $50,000, and each clerk is paid a salary of $30,000 (or $150,000 total clerical cost for five clerks). The amount of labour cost assigned to each activity is given below:

**resource drivers**

Factors that measure the consumption of resources by activities.

| | | |
|---|---|---|
| Supervising employees | $50,000 | (by direct tracing) |
| Processing transactions | $60,000 | (40% × $150,000) |
| Preparing statements | $45,000 | (30% × $150,000) |
| Answering questions | $45,000 | (30% × $150,000) |

Labour, of course, is not the only resource consumed by activities. The interview, for example, reveals that the credit card department uses computers (capital), phones (capital), desks (capital), and paper (materials). The automatic teller activity uses the automatic teller machines (capital) and energy. The costs of these resources must also be assigned to the various activities. They are assigned in the same way as described for labour (using direct tracing and resource drivers). The cost of computers could be assigned using direct tracing for the supervising activity and hours of usage for the remaining activities. From the interview, we know the relative usage of computers for each activity. Suppose the general ledger reveals that the cost per computer is $1,200 per year. Thus, an additional $1,200 would be assigned to the supervising activity, and $6,000 (5 × $1,200) would be assigned to the other activities based on relative usage—70 percent ($4,200) to processing transactions, 20 percent ($1,200) to preparing statements, and 10 percent ($600) to answering questions. Repeating this process for all resources, the total cost of each activity can be calculated. Exhibit 4–14 gives the cost of the activities for the credit card department under the assumption that all resource costs have been assigned (these numbers are assumed because we are not given all the data for their calculation).

EXHIBIT 4-14

Credit Card Department
Activity Costs: First Stage

| | |
|---|---|
| Supervising employees | $ 75,000 |
| Processing transactions | 100,000 |
| Preparing statements | 79,500 |
| Answering questions | 69,900 |
| Providing automatic teller machines | 250,000 |

## Assigning Activity Costs to Other Activities

Assigning costs to activities completes the first stage of activity-based costing. In this first stage, activities are classified as primary and secondary. If there are secondary activities, then intermediate stages exist. In an intermediate stage, the costs of secondary activities are assigned to the activities that consume their output. For example, supervising employees is a secondary activity. The output measure is the total employee time used by each activity (see the activity dictionary, Exhibit 4–13). From the work distribution matrix prepared earlier, we know that the three primary departmental activities use clerical labour in the proportions 40 percent, 30 percent, and 30 percent, respectively. The cost of supervising employees would be assigned to each consuming primary activity using these ratios (which now function as an activity driver). The new costs using the activity driver and the activity costs from Exhibit 4–14 are shown in Exhibit 4–15.

## Assigning Costs to Products

Once the costs of primary activities are determined, then these costs can be assigned to products in proportion to their usage of the activity, as measured by activity drivers. We accomplish this assignment by calculating a predetermined activity rate and multiplying this rate by the actual usage of the activity. From Exhibit 4–13, the activity drivers are identified for each of the four primary activities: number of transactions for processing transactions, number of statements for preparing statements, number of calls for answering questions, and number

EXHIBIT 4-15

Credit Card Department
Activity Costs:
Intermediate Stage

| | | |
|---|---|---|
| Processing transactions | $130,000 | [$100,000 + (0.4 × $75,000)] |
| Preparing statements | 102,000 | [$ 79,500 + (0.3 × $75,000)] |
| Answering questions | 92,400 | [$ 69,900 + (0.3 × $75,000)] |
| Providing automatic teller machines | 250,000 | |

of ATM transactions for the activity of providing automatic teller machines. To calculate an activity rate, the activity capacity of each activity must be determined. To assign costs, we must also determine the amount of each activity consumed by each product. For our purposes, we will assume that total activity usage for all products is equal to the activity capacity. For the credit card example, the following data have been collected:

|  | Classic | Gold | Platinum | Total |
|---|---|---|---|---|
| Number of cards | 5,000 | 3,000 | 2,000 | 10,000 |
| Transactions processed | 600,000 | 300,000 | 100,000 | 1,000,000 |
| Number of statements | 60,000 | 36,000 | 24,000 | 120,000 |
| Number of calls | 10,000 | 12,000 | 8,000 | 30,000 |
| Number of ATM transactions* | 15,000 | 3,000 | 2,000 | 20,000 |

* Remember that the automatic tellers are used for more than credit card cash advances. The total number of ATM transactions is 200,000 and the ATM transactions for the cards is 10 percent of the total transactions from all sources or 20,000 (10% of 200,000).

Using these data and the costs from Exhibit 4–15, the activity rates can be calculated:

**Rate calculations:**

| | |
|---|---|
| Processing transactions | $130,000/1,000,000 = $0.13 per transaction |
| Preparing statements: | $102,000/120,000 = $0.85 per statement |
| Answering questions: | $92,400/30,000 = $3.08 per call |
| Providing ATMs: | $250,000/200,000 = $1.25 per ATM transaction |

Using these rates, costs are assigned as shown in Exhibit 4–16. As should be evident, the assignment process is the same as the one used in the Belring example illustrated in Exhibit 4–10. However, we now know the full story behind the development of the activity rates and usage measures. Furthermore, the credit union setting emphasizes the usefulness of activity-based costing in service organizations.

**EXHIBIT 4-16**

Credit Card Department Activity Costs: Final Stage

|  | Classic | Gold | Platinum |
|---|---|---|---|
| Processing transactions: | | | |
| $0.13 × 600,000; $0.13 × 300,000; $0.13 × 100,000 | $ 78,000 | $ 39,000 | $13,000 |
| Preparing statements: | | | |
| $0.85 × 60,000; $0.85 × 36,000; $0.85 × 24,000 | 51,000 | 30,600 | 20,400 |
| Answering questions: | | | |
| $3.08 × 10,000; $3.08 × 12,000; $3.08 × 8,000 | 30,800 | 36,960 | 24,640 |
| Providing automatic teller machines (ATMs): | | | |
| $1.25 × 15,000; $1.25 × 3,000; $1.25 × 2,000 | 18,750 | 3,750 | 2,500 |
| Total costs | $178,550 | $110,310 | $60,540 |
| Units | 5,000 | 3,000 | 2,000 |
| Unit cost (Total costs/Units) | $ 35.71 | $ 36.77 | $ 30.27 |

# Homogeneous Activity Pools

**Objective 5**

Provide a detailed description of how activities can be grouped into homogeneous sets to reduce the number of activity rates.

In the first stage of activity-based costing, activities are identified, costs are associated with individual activities, and activities are classified as primary and secondary. In the intermediate stage, costs of secondary activities are reassigned to primary activities. In the final stage, costs of primary activities are assigned to products and customers. Assigning costs to other activities (intermediate stage) or assigning costs to products and customers (final stage) requires the use of activity rates. In principle, an activity rate is calculated for each activity. A company may have hundreds of different activities, and thus hundreds of activity rates. Although information technology is certainly capable of handling this volume, there may be some merit to reducing the number of rates, if possible. For example, fewer rates may produce more readable and manageable product cost reports. Fewer rates may also reduce the perceived complexity of an activity-based costing system.

## Process for Reducing the Number of Rates

To reduce the number of overhead rates required and streamline the process, we can group activities into homogeneous sets based on similar characteristics: (1) they are logically related, and (2) they have the same consumption ratios for all products. The costs of the individual activities belonging to each set make up the costs associated with each of these homogeneous sets. The collection of overhead costs associated with each set of activities is called a **homogeneous cost pool**. Since the activities within a homogeneous cost pool have the same consumption ratio, the activity drivers of *each* activity assign costs to products in exactly the same proportions. This means that only one driver is needed to assign the pool's costs, and thus the number of rates can be reduced. Once a cost pool is defined, we can compute the cost per unit of the chosen activity driver by dividing the pool costs by the activity driver's activity capacity. This is called the **pool rate**.

To illustrate this process, consider once again the Belring example. We identified four overhead activities: setups, material handling, machining, and testing. The first criterion for homogeneity is the existence of logical relationships. Setup activities and material-handling activities are performed each time a batch of products is produced. Thus, these two activities are logically related by the more general batch-level production activity. Similarly, testing and machining activities are performed each time a unit of product is produced (recall that each unit is tested). Thus, these two activities are logically related by the more general activity of producing a unit of product. The second criterion for homogeneity is the same consumption ratio for all products. From Exhibit 4–9 we know that the setups and material-handling activities have the same the consumption ratios (0.33 and 0.67). Thus, we are able to reduce two activities to one homogeneous set of activities. This set can now be used to form a homogeneous cost pool. Let's call the set with setups and material handling the batch-level pool. The total cost associated with the pool is simply the sum of the costs assigned to the related activities. The pool rate is the total cost divided by a driver chosen from an activity in the set. We can use the number of production runs as the driver for the batch-level pool. Using the data from Exhibit 4–8, the pool costs and rate follow:

**homogeneous cost pool**

A collection of overhead costs associated with activities that have the same process and the same level, and that can use the same activity driver to assign costs to products.

**pool rate**

The overhead costs for a homogeneous cost pool divided by the practical capacity of the activity driver associated with the pool.

**Batch-Level Pool**

| | |
|---|---|
| Setups | $120,000 |
| Material handling | 60,000 |
| Total | $180,000 |
| Driver | 30 runs |
| Pool rate | $ 6,000 per run |

The unit product costs for regular and cordless phones, using these pool rates to assign the overhead costs, will be the same as those we calculated earlier using individual activity rates (see Exhibit 4–10). This result is shown in Exhibit 4–17. Note that we could also use the number of moves as the batch-level pool driver. This too would yield the same result.

EXHIBIT  4-17

Unit Costs Activity-Based
Costing: Pool Rates

|                                                         | Cordless  | Regular   |
|---------------------------------------------------------|-----------|-----------|
| Prime costs                                             | $ 78,000  | $738,000  |
| Overhead costs:                                         |           |           |
| Batch-level pool:                                       |           |           |
| $6,000 × 20; $6,000 × 10                                | 120,000   | 60,000    |
| Unit-level testing costs:                               |           |           |
| $0.80 × 10,000; $0.80 × 90,000                          | 8,000     | 72,000    |
| Unit-level machining costs:                             |           |           |
| $2.00 × 10,000; $2.00 × 40,000                          | 20,000    | 80,000    |
| Total manufacturing costs                               | $226,000  | $950,000  |
| Units of production                                     | 10,000    | 100,000   |
| Unit cost (Total costs/Units)                           | $   22.60 | $   9.50  |

## Detailed Classification of Activities

The Belring example is quite simple, with only four activities, but we can use the same principle when there are hundreds of activities. In building sets of related activities, activities are classified into one of the following four general activity categories: (1) unit level, (2) batch level, (3) product level, and (4) facility level. Classifying activities into these general categories facilitates product costing because the costs of activities associated with the different levels respond to different types of cost drivers (cost behaviour differs by level). The definition of the activities belonging to each general category clearly illustrates this feature.

**unit-level activities**
Activities that are performed each time a unit is produced.

**batch-level activities**
Activities that are performed each time a batch is produced.

**product-level (sustaining) activities**
Activities that are performed to enable the production of each different type of product.

**facility-level activities**
Activities that sustain a facility's general manufacturing process.

- **Unit-level activities** are those performed each time a unit is produced. For example, machining and assembly are activities performed each time a unit is produced. The costs of unit-level activities vary with the number of units produced.
- **Batch-level activities** are those performed each time a batch of goods is produced. The costs of batch-level activities vary with the number of batches, but they are fixed with respect to the number of units in each batch. Setups, inspections (unless each unit is inspected), production scheduling, and material handling are examples of batch-level activities.
- **Product-level (sustaining) activities** are those performed as needed to support the various products produced by a company. These activities consume inputs that develop products or allow products to be produced and sold. These activities and their costs tend to increase as the number of different products increases. Engineering changes, development of product-testing procedures, marketing a product, and process engineering are examples of product-level activities.
- **Facility-level activities** are those that sustain a factory's general manufacturing processes. These activities benefit the organization at some level but do not provide a benefit for any specific product. Examples include plant management, landscaping, support of community programs, security, property taxes, and plant amortization.

Of the four general levels, the first three—unit level, batch level, and product level—contain product-related activities. For these three levels, it is possible to measure the demands placed on the activities by individual products. Activities within these three levels can be further subdivided on the basis of consumption ratios. Activities with the same consumption ratios can use the same activity driver to assign costs. Thus, in effect, all activities within each of the first three levels that have the same activity driver are grouped together. This final grouping creates a homogeneous set of activities: a collection of activities that are at the same level and use the same activity driver. Exhibit 4–18 illustrates the activity

EXHIBIT 4-18

Formation of
Homogeneous Sets of
Activities

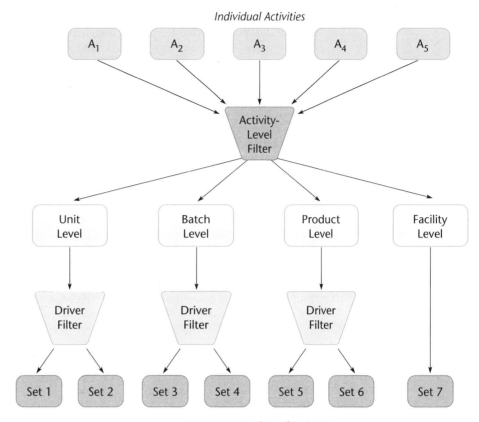

*Individual Activities*

*Homogeneous Sets of Activities*

classification model that creates homogeneous sets of activities. Notice that facility-level activities do not undergo the driver classification.

The fourth general category, facility-level activities, poses a problem for the ABC philosophy of tracing costs to products. Tracing activity costs to individual products depends on the ability to identify the amount of each activity consumed by a product (product demands for activities must be measured). Facility-level activities (and their costs) are common to a variety of products, and it is not possible to identify how individual products consume these activities. A pure ABC system, therefore, would not assign these costs to products. They would be treated as period costs. In effect, these costs are fixed costs—costs that are not driven by any of the cost drivers found in any of the first three categories. In practice, companies that adopt ABC systems usually implement a full-costing (or absorption-costing) approach and allocate these facility-level costs to individual products.[7] Unit-level, batch-level, or product-level cost drivers are often used for the allocation. As a practical matter, assigning these costs may not significantly distort product costs, because they are likely to be small relative to the total costs that are appropriately traced to individual products.

There is, however, a possible exception to this observation about facility-level costs and activity drivers. When a company has organized its production facilities around product lines, then it can be argued that space drivers measure the consumption of facility-level costs. This is because floor space within a plant is dedicated to the production of a single product or subassembly. In this case, area occupied can be viewed as a possible activity driver for facility costs. Assigning facil-

---

7. A study of 31 companies and 51 cost systems revealed that all companies using an ABC system allocated facility-level costs to products. See Robin Cooper, "Cost Classification in Unit-Based and Activity-Based Manufacturing Systems."

ity-level costs on the basis of space drivers can also serve to motivate managers to reduce the space needed for production, thus reducing facility-level costs over time.

## Comparison with Functional-Based Costing

The hierarchical classification of activities allows us to illustrate the fundamental differences between activity-based and functional-based costing systems. In a functional-based system, we assume that only unit-based activity drivers explain the consumption of overhead by products. In a sophisticated functional system, overhead costs are classified as fixed or variable *with respect to unit-based drivers*. Therefore, unit-based costing systems allocate fixed overhead to individual products using fixed overhead rates, and assign variable overhead using variable overhead rates. From the perspective of activity-based costing, the variable overhead is appropriately traced to individual products (for this category, overhead consumption increases as units produced increase). However, assigning fixed overhead costs using unit-based activity drivers can be arbitrary, and may not reflect the activities actually consumed by the products. Many of the costs assigned in the fixed overhead category are in reality batch-level, product-level, and facility-level costs that vary with drivers other than unit-level drivers.

Activity-based costing systems improve product-costing accuracy by recognizing that many of the so-called fixed overhead costs actually vary in proportion to changes other than production volume. If we understand what causes these costs to increase or decrease, we can trace them to individual products. This cause-and-effect relationship allows managers to improve product-costing accuracy, which can significantly improve decision-making. Additionally, this large pool of fixed overhead costs is no longer so mysterious. Knowing the underlying behaviour of many of these costs allows managers to exert more control over the activities that cause the costs.[8]

## ABC Customer and Supplier Costing

**Objective 6**

Describe activity-based customer and supplier costing.

In an activity-based costing system, product-costing accuracy is improved by tracing activity costs to the products that consume the activities. ABC can also be used to more accurately determine the costs of other parts of a company's operations such as management of customers and suppliers. Knowing the costs of customers and suppliers can be vital information to managers for improving a company's profitability. LSI Logic, a high-tech producer of semiconductors, implemented ABC customer costing and discovered that 10 percent of its customers were responsible for 90 percent of its profits. It also discovered that it was actually losing money on about 50 percent of its customers. It worked to convert its unprofitable customers into profitable ones and invited those who would not provide a fair return to take their business elsewhere. As a consequence, its sales decreased but its profits tripled.[9]

---

8. See *Implementing Activity-Based Costing, Management Accounting Guidelines #17*, Society of Management Accountants of Canada, 1993. For more discussion of ABC and its potential application to service organizations, see John Antos, "Activity-Based Management for Service, Not-for-Profit, and Government Organizations," *Journal of Cost Management* (Summer 1992): pp. 13-23; and William Rotch, "Activity-Based Costing in Service Industries," *Journal of Cost Management* (Summer 1990): pp. 4-14. For an example of an application of ABC in a partnership that provides a wide range of engineering and architectural consulting services, see Beth M. Chaffman and John Talbot, "Activity-Based Costing in a Service Organization," *CMA Magazine*, Vol. 64, No. 10, December/January 1991: pp. 15-18.

9. Gary Cokins, "Are All of Your Customers Profitable (To You)?" An online article at http://www.bettermanagement.com/Library as of June 14, 2001.

# Activity-Based Customer Costing

Customers (and distribution channels and markets) are cost objects of fundamental interest. As the LSI Logic experience illustrates, customer management can produce significant profit gains. It is possible to have customer diversity, just as it is possible to have product diversity. Customers can consume customer-driven activities in different proportions. Sources of customer diversity include such things as order frequency, delivery frequency, geographic distance, sales and promotional support, and engineering support requirements. Knowing how much it costs to service different customers can be important information for such purposes as pricing, determining customer mix, and improving profitability. Furthermore, because of diversity of customers, multiple drivers are needed to trace costs accurately. ABC can be useful even to organizations that have only one product or a few homogeneous products, where direct tracing diminishes the value of ABC for product costing.

### Customer Costing versus Product Costing

Assigning the costs of customer service to customers is done in the same way that manufacturing costs are assigned to products. Customer-driven activities such as order entry, order picking, shipping, making sales calls, and evaluating a client's credit are identified and listed in an activity dictionary. The cost of the resources consumed is assigned to activities, and the cost of the activities is assigned to individual customers. The same model and procedures apply to customers as apply to products.[10] We will consider a simple example to illustrate the basics of activity-based customer costing.

### Example

Suppose that Milan Company produces precision parts for 11 major buyers. ABC is used to assign production costs to products. Of the 11 customers, one accounts for 50 percent of the sales, with the other 10 accounting for the remainder of the sales. The 10 smaller customers purchase parts in roughly equal quantities. Orders placed by the smaller customers are about the same size. Data concerning Milan's customer activity follow:

|  | Large Customer | Ten Smaller Customers | Total |
|---|---|---|---|
| Units purchased | 500,000 | 500,000 | 1,000,000 |
| Orders placed | 2 | 200 | 202 |
| Number of sales calls | 10 | 210 | 220 |
| Manufacturing costs | $3,000,000 | $3,000,000 | $6,000,000 |
| Order-filling costs allocated* | $202,000 | $202,000 | $404,000 |
| Sales-force costs allocated* | $110,000 | $110,000 | $220,000 |

* Allocated based on sales volume.

Currently, customer-driven costs are assigned to customers based on units sold, a unit-level driver. ABC improves the assignment by using drivers that better reflect the consumption of the activities by customers: number of orders and number of sales calls. The activity rates are $2,000 per order ($404,000/202

---

10. Although we will not define them, it is also possible to have different levels of customer-driven activities, such as order level, customer level, and channel level. Thus, in principle, it is possible to build homogeneous customer-driven cost pools using level and driver attributes. A detailed discussion of customer-driven costs, including formal definitions of customer-level activities, can be found in Michael C. O'Guin and Stephen A. Rebishke, "Customer-Driven Costs Using Activity-Based Costing," in *Handbook of Cost Management*, ed. Barry Brinker (New York: Warren Gorham Lamont, 1993), pp. B5-1, B5-29.

orders) for order filling and $1,000 per call ($220,000/220 calls) for the sales-force activity. Using this information, the customer-driven costs can be assigned to each group of customers as follows:

| | Large Customer | Ten Smaller Customers | Total |
|---|---|---|---|
| Order-filling costs | $ 4,000 | $400,000 | $404,000 |
| Sales-force costs | $10,000 | $210,000 | $220,000 |

This reveals a much different picture of the cost of servicing each type of customer. The smaller customer is costing more, a difference that is attributable to smaller, more frequent orders and to the evident need of the sales force to engage in more negotiation to make a sale.

What does this tell management that it didn't know before? First, the large customer costs much less to service than the smaller customers and perhaps should be charged less. Second, it raises some significant questions relative to the smaller customers. Is it possible, for example, to encourage these customers to put in larger, less frequent orders? Perhaps offering discounts for larger orders would be appropriate. Why are the smaller customers more difficult to sell to? Why are more calls needed? Are they less informed about the products than the larger customer is? Can we improve profits by influencing our customers to change their buying behaviour?

## Activity-Based Supplier Costing

Activity-based costing can also help a manger identify the true cost of its suppliers. The cost of a supplier is much more than the purchase price of components or materials acquired. Just like customers, suppliers can affect many internal activities of a company and significantly affect the cost of purchasing. A more correct view is one where the costs associated with quality, reliability, and late deliveries are added to the purchase costs. Managers are then able to evaluate suppliers based on total cost, not just purchase price. Activity-based costing is the key to tracing costs related to purchase, quality, reliability, and delivery performance to suppliers.

### Supplier Costing Methodology

Assigning the costs of supplier-related activities to suppliers follows the same pattern as ABC product and customer costing. Supplier-driven activities such as purchasing, receiving, inspecting incoming components, reworking products and warranty work (because of defective components), and expediting products (cost of overnight shipments because of late deliveries from suppliers) are identified and listed in an activity dictionary. The costs of resources consumed are assigned to these activities, and the cost of the activities is assigned to individual suppliers. A simple example will illustrate the basics of ABC supplier costing.

### Example

A purchasing manager uses two suppliers, Murray Company and Plata Associates, as the source of two machine parts: Part A1 and Part B2. The purchasing manager prefers to use Murray because it provides the parts at a lower price; however, the second supplier is used as well to ensure a reliable supply of the parts. Now consider two activities: *repairing products* (under warranty) and *expediting products*. Repairing products occurs because of failure of parts purchased from suppliers. Expediting products takes place due to late delivery of parts by suppliers. Therefore, part failure and late delivery are attributable to suppliers, and the cost of these activities can be assigned to the individual supplier. Warranty repair costs attributable to supplier part failure are assigned to suppliers using the number of failed parts as the driver. The costs of expediting attributable to late deliveries are assigned using the number of late shipments as the driver. Activity cost information and other data needed for supplier costing follow:

**I. Activity Costs Caused by Suppliers (e.g. failed parts or late delivery)**

| Activity | Costs |
| --- | --- |
| Repairing products | $800,000 |
| Expediting products | 200,000 |

**II. Supplier Data**

| | Murray Company | | Plata Associates | | Total |
| --- | --- | --- | --- | --- | --- |
| | **Part A1** | **Part B2** | **Part A1** | **Part B2** | |
| Unit purchase price | $20 | $52 | $24 | $56 | |
| Units purchased | 80,000 | 40,000 | 10,000 | 10,000 | 140,000 |
| Failed units | 1,600 | 380 | 10 | 10 | 2,000 |
| Late shipments | 60 | 40 | 0 | 0 | 100 |

Using the preceding data, we can compute the activity rates for assigning costs to suppliers as follows:

Repair rate = $800,000/2,000 = $400 per failed part
Expediting rate = $200,000/100 = $2,000 per late shipment

Using these rates and the activity data, we compute the total purchasing cost per unit of each component as shown in Exhibit 4-19. We see from these results that the "low-cost" supplier actually costs more when the supplier-related activities of repairing and expediting are considered. If all costs are considered, then the choice becomes clear: Plata Associates is the better supplier with a higher quality product, on-time deliveries, and, consequently, a lower overall cost per unit.

**EXHIBIT 4-19**

Supplier Costing

| | Murray Company | | Plata Associates | |
| --- | --- | --- | --- | --- |
| | **Part A1** | **Part B2** | **Part A1** | **Part B2** |
| Purchase cost: | | | | |
| $20 × 80,000 | $1,600,000 | | | |
| $52 × 40,000 | | $2,080,000 | | |
| $24 × 10,000 | | | $240,000 | |
| $56 × 10,0000 | | | | $560,000 |
| Repairing products: | | | | |
| $400 × 1,600 | 640,000 | | | |
| $400 × 380 | | 152,000 | | |
| $400 × 10 | | | 4,000 | |
| $400 × 10 | | | | 4,000 |
| Expediting products: | | | | |
| $2,000 × 60 | 120,000 | | | |
| $2,000 × 40 | | 80,000 | | |
| $2,000 × 0 | | | 0 | |
| $2,000 × 0 | | | | 0 |
| Total costs | $2,360,000 | $2,312,000 | $244,000 | $564,000 |
| Units | 80,000 | 40,000 | 10,000 | 10,000 |
| Total unit cost | $ 29.50 | $ 57.80 | $ 24.40 | $ 56.40 |

# Summary of Learning Objectives

### 1. Discuss the importance of unit costs to managers' decisions.

Unit costs are important for inventory valuation, income determination, and providing input to a variety of decisions such as pricing, making or buying, and accepting or rejecting special orders. Because of their importance, their accuracy becomes a critical issue.

### 2. Describe functional-based costing approaches.

Functional-based costing assigns direct materials and direct labour using direct tracing; overhead is assigned using a two-stage process. In the first stage, overhead costs are collected in pools, at either the plant level or the departmental level. Once the pools are defined, the costs of the overhead pools are assigned to products using unit-level drivers, the most common being direct labour hours.

### 3. Explain why functional-based costing approaches may produce distorted costs.

Overhead costs have increased in significance over time and in many companies represent a much higher percentage of product costs than direct labour. At the same time, many overhead activities are unrelated to the number of units produced. Functional-based costing systems are not able to assign the costs of these nonunit-related overhead activities properly. Products consume these overhead activities in different proportions than unit-based overhead activities. Because of this difference, assigning overhead using only unit-based drivers can distort product costs. This can be a serious matter if the nonunit-based overhead costs are a significant proportion of total overhead costs.

### 4. Explain how an activity-based costing system works.

Activities are identified and defined through interviews and surveys. This information allows an activity dictionary to be constructed. The activity dictionary lists activities and potential activity drivers, classifies activities as primary and secondary, and provides any other attributes deemed to be important. Resource costs are assigned to primary and secondary activities by using direct tracing and resource drivers. The costs of secondary activities are assigned to primary activities using activity drivers. Finally, the costs of primary activities are assigned to products, customers, and other cost objects. Thus, the cost assignment process is described by the following general steps: (1) identifying the major activities and building an activity dictionary, (2) determining the cost of each activity, (3) identifying a measure for consumption of activity costs (activity drivers), (4) calculating an activity rate, (5) measuring the demands placed on activities by each product, and (6) calculating product costs.

### 5. Provide a detailed description of how activities can be grouped into homogeneous cost pool sets to reduce the number of activity rates.

Homogeneous sets of activities are collections of activities that have the same activity-level classification and the same activity-driver classification. Classifying by level places activities into one of four categories: unit level, batch level, product level, or facility level. Unit-level activities occur each time a unit of product is produced. Batch-level activities occur when batches of products are produced. Product-level activities are incurred to enable production of each different type of product. Facility-level activities sustain a facility's general manufacturing processes. Finally, level-classified activities with the same consumption ratio are combined to form homogeneous sets. Summing the costs associated with activities within homogeneous sets defines homogeneous cost pools. An activity driver for one of the activities in the set is chosen to compute pool rates and assign costs to individual products.

### 6. Describe activity-based customer and supplier costing.

Tracing customer-driven costs to customers can provide significant information to managers. Accurate customer costs allow managers to make better pricing decisions, customer-mix decisions, and other customer-related decisions that improve profitability. Similarly, tracing supplier-driven costs to suppliers can enable managers to choose the true low-cost suppliers, producing a stronger competitive position and improved profitability.

# Key Terms

Activity attributes 134
Activity-based costing (ABC)
  system 133
Activity dictionary 134
Activity drivers 134
Actual costing 122
Applied overhead 125
Batch-level activities 140
Consumption ratio 130
Cost assignment 122
Cost measurement 122

Expected activity capacity 124
Facility-level activities 140
Homogeneous cost pool 139
Nonunit-level activity drivers 130
Normal activity capacity 124
Normal costing 123
Overapplied overhead 126
Overhead variance 126
Pool rate 139
Practical activity capacity 124
Predetermined overhead rate 123

Primary activity 135
Product diversity 130
Product-level (sustaining)
  activities 140
Resource drivers 136
Secondary activity 135
Theoretical activity capacity 124
Underapplied overhead 126
Unit cost 121
Unit-level activities 140
Unit-level activity drivers 123

# Review Problems

## I. PLANTWIDE RATES

Nabors Company produces two types of CD players. For the most recent year, Nabors reports the following data:

| | |
|---|---|
| Budgeted overhead | $180,000 |
| Expected activity (in direct labour hours) | 50,000 |
| Actual activity (in direct labour hours) | 51,000 |
| Actual overhead | $200,000 |

| | Deluxe | Regular |
|---|---|---|
| Units produced | 5,000 | 50,000 |
| Prime costs | $40,000 | $300,000 |
| Direct labour hours | 5,000 | 46,000 |

**Required:**
  1. Calculate a predetermined overhead rate based on direct labour hours.
  2. What is the applied overhead?
  3. What is the underapplied or overapplied overhead?
  4. Calculate the unit cost of each CD player unit.

**Solution:**
  1. Rate = $180,000/50,000 = $3.60 per direct labour hour
  2. Applied overhead = $3.60 × 51,000 = $183,600
  3. Overhead variance = $200,000 − 183,600 = $16,400 underapplied
  4. Unit cost:

|  | Deluxe | Regular |
|---|---|---|
| Prime costs | $40,000 | $300,000 |
| Applied overhead costs: |  |  |
| $3.60 × 5,000; $3.60 × 46,000 | 18,000 | 165,600 |
| Total manufacturing costs | $58,000 | $465,600 |
| Units produced | 5,000 | 50,000 |
| Unit cost (Total costs/Units) | $ 11.60 | $ 9.31 |

## II. DEPARTMENTAL RATES

Nabors Company gathers the following departmental data for a second year:

| Departmental Data | Fabrication | Assembly |
|---|---|---|
| Budgeted overhead | $120,000 | $60,000 |
| Expected and actual activity (direct labour hours): |  |  |
| Deluxe | 3,000 | 2,000 |
| Regular | 8,000 | 43,000 |
| Total direct labour hours | 11,000 | 45,000 |
|  |  |  |
| Expected and actual activity (machine hours): |  |  |
| Deluxe | 2,000 | 5,000 |
| Regular | 18,000 | 5,000 |
| Total machine hours | 20,000 | 10,000 |

In addition to the departmental data, the following information is provided:

|  | Deluxe | Regular |
|---|---|---|
| Units produced | 5,000 | 50,000 |
| Prime costs | $40,000 | $300,000 |

### Required:
1. Calculate departmental overhead rates, using machine hours for fabrication and direct labour hours for assembly.
2. Calculate the applied overhead by product.
3. Calculate unit costs.

### Solution:
1. Departmental rates:
   Fabrication: $120,000/20,000 = $6.00 per machine hour
   Assembly: $60,000/45,000 = $1.333 per labour hour

2. Applied overhead (by product)
   Deluxe: ($6.00 × 2,000) + ($1.333 × 2,000) = $14,666
   Regular: ($6.00 × 18,000) + ($1.333 × 43,000) = $165,319

3. Unit cost:
   Deluxe: ($40,000 + 14,666)/5,000 = $10.93
   Regular: ($300,000 + $165,319)/50,000 = $9.31

## III. ACTIVITY-BASED RATES

Nabors Company gathers the following activity data for a third year:

**Product-Costing Data**

| Activity Usage Measures | Deluxe | Regular | Total |
|---|---|---|---|
| Units produced per year | 5,000 | 50,000 | 55,000 |
| Prime costs | $39,000 | $369,000 | $408,000 |
| Direct labour hours | 5,000 | 45,000 | 50,000 |
| Machine hours | 10,000 | 90,000 | 100,000 |
| Production runs | 10 | 5 | 15 |
| Number of moves | 120 | 60 | 180 |

**Overhead Activity Cost Data:**

| Activity | Activity Cost |
|---|---|
| Setting up equipment | $ 60,000 |
| Material handling | 30,000 |
| Machining | 50,000 |
| Testing | 40,000 |
| Total | $180,000 |

## Required:

1. Calculate the consumption ratios for each activity.
2. Group activities based on the consumption ratios and activity level.
3. Calculate a rate for each pooled group of activities.
4. Using the pool rates, calculate unit product costs.

## Solution:

1. Consumption ratios:

| Overhead Activity | Activity Driver | Deluxe | Regular |
|---|---|---|---|
| Setups | Production runs | 0.67 | 0.33 |
| Material handling | Number of moves | 0.67 | 0.33 |
| Machining | Machine hours | 0.10 | 0.90 |
| Testing | Direct labour hours | 0.10 | 0.90 |

2. Batch-level: setups and material handling
   Unit-level: machining and testing

3. Pool Rates:

| Batch-Level Pool | | Unit-Level Pool | |
|---|---|---|---|
| Setups | $60,000 | Machining | $ 50,000 |
| Material handling | 30,000 | Testing | 40,000 |
| Total | $90,000 | Total | $ 90,000 |
| Runs (1) | 15 | Machine hours (2) | 100,000 |
| Pool rate | $ 6,000 per run | Pool rate | $ 0.90 per machine hour |

(1) We could also use the number of moves as the driver for the batch-level pool.
(2) We could also use direct labour hours as the driver for the unit-level pool.

4. Unit Costs: Activity-Based Costing

| | Deluxe | Regular |
|---|---|---|
| Prime costs | $ 39,000 | $369,000 |
| Applied overhead costs: | | |
| Batch-level pool: | | |
| ($6,000 × 10) ; ($6,000 × 5) | 60,000 | 30,000 |
| Unit-level pool: | | |
| ($0.90 × 10,000); ($0.90 × 90,000) | 9,000 | 81,000 |
| Total manufacturing costs | $108,000 | $480,000 |
| Units produced | 5,000 | 50,000 |
| Unit cost (total costs ÷ units) | $ 21.60 | $ 9.60 |

## Questions for Writing and Discussion

1. Explain why knowing the unit cost of a product or service is important.

2. What is cost measurement? cost assignment?

3. Explain why an actual overhead rate is rarely used for product costing.

4. Describe the two-stage process associated with plantwide overhead rates.

5. Describe the two-stage process for departmental overhead rates.

6. Explain why departmental rates might be chosen over plantwide rates.

7. Explain how a plantwide overhead rate, using a unit-based cost driver, can produce distorted product costs. In your answer, identify two major factors that impair the ability of plantwide rates to assign cost accurately.

8. Explain how low-volume products can be under-costed and high-volume products overcosted if only unit-based cost drivers are used to assign overhead costs.

9. Explain how undercosting low-volume products and overcosting high-volume products can affect a company's competitive position.

10. What are nonunit-related overhead activities? nonunit-level activity drivers? Give some examples.

11. What is meant by "product diversity"?

12. What is an overhead consumption ratio?

13. Explain how departmental overhead rates can produce product costs that are more distorted than those computed using a plantwide rate.

14. Overhead costs are the source of product cost distortions. Do you agree? Explain.

15. What is activity-based product costing?

16. What is an activity dictionary?

17. What is the difference between primary and secondary activities?

18. Explain how costs are assigned to activities.

19. Explain how homogeneous sets of activities are produced. Why are they produced?

20. What is a homogeneous cost pool?

21. What are unit-level activities? batch-level activities? product-level activities? facility-level activities?

22. Why might ABC be useful in a company with only one product?

23. Describe the value of activity-based customer costing.

24. Explain how activity-based costing can help a company identify its true low-cost suppliers.

## Exercises

**4–1**

*Normal versus Actual Costing*

LO1

Nublado Company produces ski boots. At the beginning of the year, the cost manager estimated that overhead costs would be $2,910,000 and that 300,000 units would be produced. Actual data concerning production for the past year follow:

|                | Quarter 1   | Quarter 2 | Quarter 3 | Quarter 4   | Total       |
| -------------- | ----------- | --------- | --------- | ----------- | ----------- |
| Units produced | 100,000     | 40,000    | 20,000    | 140,000     | 300,000     |
| Prime costs    | $2,000,000  | $800,000  | $400,000  | $2,800,000  | $6,000,000  |
| Overhead costs | $800,000    | $600,000  | $900,000  | $700,000    | $3,000,000  |

**Required:**

1. Calculate the unit cost for each quarter and for the year using the following costs:
   a. Actual prime costs
   b. Actual overhead costs
   c. Actual total manufacturing costs
2. What do the calculations in Requirement 1 tell you about actual costing?
3. Using supporting calculations, describe how normal costing would work.

**4–2**

**Plantwide Rates: Overhead Variance**

**LO1, LO2**

Hite Manufacturing uses a normal costing system. Budgeted overhead for the coming year is $4,500,000. Expected actual activity is 1,200,000 direct labour hours. During the year, Hite worked a total of 1,152,000 direct labour hours, and actual overhead totalled $4,200,000.

**Required:**

1. Compute the predetermined overhead rate for Hite Manufacturing.
2. Compute the applied overhead.
3. Compute the overhead variance and label the variance as underapplied or overapplied overhead.
4. Explain why predetermined rates are used.

**4–3**

**Unit Cost; Plantwide Overhead Rate; Applied Overhead,**

**LO1, LO2**

Spreadsheet

Computer Systems Design, which develops specialized software for companies, uses a normal costing system. The following data are available for 2004:

| Budgeted | |
| --- | --- |
| Overhead | $600,000 |
| Machine hours | 25,000 |
| Direct labour hours | 80,000 |

| Actual | |
| --- | --- |
| Units produced | 100,000 |
| Overhead | $595,500 |
| Prime costs | $900,000 |
| Machine hours | 25,050 |
| Direct labour hours | 78,000 |

Overhead is applied on the basis of direct labour hours.

**Required:**

1. What is the predetermined overhead rate?
2. What is the applied overhead for 2004?
3. Was overhead overapplied or underapplied, and by how much?
4. What is the unit cost?

**4–4**

**Using Overhead Cost; Predetermined Plantwide Overhead Rate: Applied Overhead**

**LO1, LO2**

Spreadsheet

Using the information from 4–3, suppose Computer Systems Design applied overhead to production on the basis of machine hours instead of direct labour hours.

**Required:**

1. What is the predetermined overhead rate?
2. What is the applied overhead for 2004?
3. Is overhead overapplied or underapplied, and by how much?
4. What is the unit cost?
5. How can Computer Systems Design decide whether to use direct labour hours or machine hours as the basis for applying factory overhead?

**4–5**

Unit Overhead Cost;
Predetermined
Departmental
Overhead Rates:
Overhead Variance

LO1, LO2

Spreadsheet

Reitmeier Manufacturing, Inc., a producer of precision machine parts, uses a pre-determined overhead rate to apply overhead. Overhead is applied on the basis of machine hours in the drilling department and on the basis of direct labour hours in the assembly department. At the beginning of 2004, the following estimates are provided for the coming year:

|                     | Drilling  | Assembly  |
|---------------------|-----------|-----------|
| Direct labour hours | 10,000    | 100,000   |
| Machine hours       | 140,000   | 10,000    |
| Direct labour cost  | $190,000  | $900,000  |
| Overhead cost       | $300,000  | $196,000  |

Actual results reported for 2004 are as follows:

|                     | Drilling  | Assembly  |
|---------------------|-----------|-----------|
| Direct labour hours | 13,000    | 98,000    |
| Machine hours       | 144,000   | 11,000    |
| Direct labour cost  | $168,000  | $882,400  |
| Overhead cost       | $301,000  | $206,000  |

**Required:**
1. Compute the predetermined overhead rate for each department.
2. Compute the applied overhead for 2004. What is the underapplied or over-applied overhead for each department? for the company?
3. Suppose an order used 2,000 machine hours in drilling and 800 direct labour hours in assembly. If the order was for 4,000 units, what is the overhead cost per unit?

**4–6**

Refer to Exercise 4–5. Suppose that the overhead costs are divided as follows:

|               | Drilling  | Assembly  |
|---------------|-----------|-----------|
| Overhead cost | $316,000  | $180,000  |

**Required:**
1. Compute predetermined overhead rate for the two activities, drilling and assembly.
2. Suppose an order used 2,000 machine hours in drilling and 800 direct labour hours in assembly. If the order was for 4,000 units, what is the overhead cost per unit?

**4–7**

Gator Company has traditionally produced a handcrafted ladies' purse (sold under the label Gator Elegant). A marketing consultant has recommended that a second purse be produced—using lower-quality materials and automation so that it can be produced in larger quantities. This purse will be sold under the label Gator Eminent. Gator decides to produce the second purse. The company buys the equipment for automated production and installs it in a currently unused part of its plant. Gator discovers that a small part of the operation associated with the handcrafted purse can be automated (using the same equipment just purchased) without compromising its claim that the purse is essentially handcrafted. However, the settings on the equipment must be adjusted before it can be used for this purpose (and changed back for production of the other purse). The cost of setting up the equipment is $3,000 per year.

The production equipment is expected to last five years, with a capacity of supplying a total of 25,000 machine hours. The costs associated with the equipment follow:

| | |
|---|---|
| Amortization | $10,000* |
| Operating costs | 8,000 |

\* Amortization is computed on a straight-line basis; book value at the beginning of the year was $50,000.

The controller has collected the expected annual prime costs for each purse, the machine hours, the setup hours, and the expected production.

| | Elegant | Eminent |
|---|---|---|
| Direct labour | $9,000 | $3,000 |
| Direct materials | $3,000 | $3,000 |
| Units | 3,000 | 3,000 |
| Machine hours | 500 | 4,500 |
| Setup hours | 100 | 100 |

**Required:**
1. Do you think that the direct labour costs and direct materials costs are accurately traced to each purse? Explain.
2. The controller has suggested that overhead costs be assigned to each product using a plantwide rate based on direct labour costs. Assume that the setup and equipment costs are the only overhead costs. For each purse, calculate the overhead cost per unit that would be assigned using this approach. Do you think that equipment costs are traced accurately to each purse? setup costs? Explain.
3. Now calculate the overhead cost per unit for each purse using an overhead rate based on machine hours. Do you think equipment costs are traced accurately to each purse? setup costs? Explain.

**4–8**

Formation of an
Activity Dictionary

LO4

A hospital is in the process of implementing an ABC system. A pilot study is being done to assess the effects of the costing change on specific treatments. Of particular interest is the cost of caring for patients who receive inpatient recovery treatment for illness, surgery (noncardiac), and injury. These patients are housed on the hospital's third and fourth floors. These two floors are dedicated to patient care and have only nursing stations and patient rooms. A partial transcript of an interview with the hospital's nursing supervisor is provided below.

1. How many nurses are in the hospital?

   *There are 101 nurses, including me.*

2. Of these 100 nurses, how many are assigned to the third and fourth floors?

   *Fifty nurses are assigned to these two floors.*

3. What do these nurses do (please describe)?

   *Provide nursing care for patients, which, as you know, means answering questions, changing bandages, administering medicine, changing clothes, etc.*

4. And what do you do?

   *I supervise and coordinate all the nursing activity in the hospital. This includes surgery, maternity, the emergency room, and the two floors you mentioned.*

5. What other lodging and care activities are done for the third and fourth floors by persons other than nurses?

   *The patients must be fed. The hospital cafeteria delivers meals. The laundry department picks up dirty clothing and bedding once each shift. The floors also have a physical therapist assigned to provide care on a physician-directed basis.*

6. Does patient care involve the use of any equipment?

   *Yes. Mostly monitoring equipment.*

7. Who or what uses the activity output?

   *Patients. But there are different kinds of patients. On these two floors, we classify patients into three categories according to severity: intensive care, intermediate care, and normal care. The more severe the illness, the more activity used. Nurses spend much more time with intermediate-care patients than with normal-care patients. The more severe patients tend to use more of the laundry service as well. Their clothing and bedding need to be changed more frequently. On the other hand, severe patients use less food. They eat fewer meals. Typically, we measure each patient type by the number of days of hospital stay.*

**Required:**
Prepare an activity dictionary with four categories: activity name, activity description, primary or secondary classification, and activity driver.

**4–9**

*Activity versus Plantwide Overhead Rates: Resource Drivers; Activity Drivers*

**LO3, LO4**

Milan Machining Company has identified the following overhead activities, costs, and activity drivers for the coming year:

| Activity | Expected Cost | Activity Driver | Activity Capacity |
|---|---|---|---|
| Setting up | $60,000 | Number of setups | 300 |
| Inspecting | $45,000 | Inspection hours | 4,500 |
| Grinding | $90,000 | Machine hours | 18,000 |
| Receiving | ? | Number of parts | 50,000 |

The company produces several different machine subassemblies used by other manufacturers. Information on separate batches for two of these subassemblies follows:

|  | Subassembly A | Subassembly B |
|---|---|---|
| Direct materials | $850 | $950 |
| Direct labour | $600 | $600 |
| Units completed | 100 | 50 |
| Number of setups | 1 | 1 |
| Inspection hours | 4 | 2 |
| Machine hours | 20 | 30 |
| Parts used | 20 | 40 |

The company's normal activity is 20,000 direct labour hours. Each batch uses 50 hours of direct labour. Upon investigation, you discover that Receiving employs one worker, who spends 75 percent of her time on the receiving activity and 25 percent of her time on inspecting products. Her salary is $40,000. Receiving also uses a forklift, at a cost of $6,000 per year for amortization and fuel. The forklift is used only in receiving.

**Required:**
Choose the *best* answer for each of the following multiple-choice questions based on the preceding data for Milan Machining Company.

1. The amount of cost assigned to the receiving activity is
   a. $40,000.
   b. $46,000.
   c. $16,000.
   d. $36,000.

2. The activity rate for receiving is
   a. $0.80 per part.
   b. $0.72 per part.
   c. $0.812 per part.
   d. $0.32 per part.
   e. None of the above.

3. The activity rate for setting up equipment is
   a. $200 per setup.
   b. $100 per setup.
   c. $20 per setup.
   d. $30,000 per setup.

4. The activity rate for grinding is
   a. $18,000 per machine hour.
   b. $1.80 per part.
   c. $5.00 per machine hour.
   d. $4,500 per machine hour.
   e. None of the above.

5. The activity rate for inspecting is
   a. $7,500 per inspection hour.
   b. $20 per inspection hour.
   c. $12 per inspection hour.
   d. $10 per inspection hour.
   e. None of the above.

6. The unit cost for Subassembly A, using direct labour hours to assign overhead, is
   a. $20.28.
   b. $21.43.
   c. $14.50.
   d. $42.56.
   e. None of the above.

7. The unit cost for Subassembly A, using activity rates, is
   a. $21.43.
   b. $18.04.
   c. $20.50.
   d. $30.28.
   e. None of the above.

**4–10**

Activity Classification

LO5

Colbie Components produces two types of wafers: Wafer A and Wafer B. A wafer is a thin slice of silicon used as a base for integrated circuits or other electronic components. The dies on each wafer represent a particular configuration designed for use by a particular end product. Colbie makes wafers in batches, with each batch corresponding to a particular type of wafer (A or B). In the wafer inserting and sorting process, dies are inserted and the wafers are tested to ensure that the dies are not defective. Materials are ordered and received just in time for production.

The following activities are listed in Colbie's activity dictionary:

1. Developing test programs
2. Making probe cards
3. Testing products
4. Setting up batches
5. Engineering design
6. Handling wafer lots
7. Inserting dies
8. Purchasing materials
9. Receiving materials
10. Providing utilities (heat, lighting, and so on)
11. Providing space

**Required:**

1. What activities are done each time a wafer is produced (unit-level activities)?
2. What activities are done each time a batch is produced (batch-level activities)?
3. Which activities are done to enable production to take place (product-level activities)?
4. Which activities are done to sustain production processes (facility-level activities)?

**4–11**

*Activity-Based Costing: Homogeneous Cost Pools; Activity Drivers*

LO4, LO5

Tristar Manufacturing produces two types of battery-operated toy cars: sports and police. The cars are produced using one continuous process. Four activities have been identified: machining, setups, receiving, and packing. Resource drivers have been used to assign costs to each activity. The overhead activities, activity costs, and other related data are as follows:

| Product | Machine Hours | Number of Setups | Receiving Orders | Packing Orders |
|---------|--------------|------------------|------------------|----------------|
| Sports  | 20,000       | 200              | 200              | 1,600          |
| Police  | 20,000       | 100              | 400              | 800            |
| Costs   | $80,000      | $24,000          | $18,000          | $30,000        |

**Required:**

1. Classify the overhead activities as unit level, batch level, product level, or facility level.
2. Create homogeneous cost pools. Identify the activities that belong to each pool.
3. Identify the activity driver for each pool, and compute the pool rate.
4. Assign the overhead costs to each product using the pool rates computed in Requirement 3.

**4–12**

*Functional Based Costing; Activity-Based Costing; Pricing*

LO2, LO3, LO4

Spreadsheet

Hammer Company produces a variety of electronic equipment. One of its plants produces two laser printers: the deluxe and the regular. At the beginning of the year, the following data were prepared for this plant:

|                   | Deluxe    | Regular   |
|-------------------|-----------|-----------|
| Quantity          | 100,000   | 800,000   |
| Selling price     | $900.00   | $750.00   |
| Unit prime cost   | $529.00   | $482.75   |
| Unit overhead cost| $47.00    | $117.25   |

Overhead is applied using direct labour hours.

Upon examining the data, the vice-president of marketing was particularly impressed with the per-unit profitability of the deluxe printer and suggested that more emphasis be placed on producing and selling this product. The plant manager objected to this strategy, arguing that the cost of the deluxe printer was understated. He argued that overhead costs could be assigned more accurately by using activity drivers—factors that reflected each product's demands for overhead activities. To convince higher management that overhead rates using activity drivers could produce a significant difference in product costs, he obtained the following projected information from the controller for the production output given:

| Pool Name[a] | Activity Driver | Pool Rate[b] | Deluxe | Regular |
|---|---|---|---|---|
| Setups | Number of setups | $3,000 | 300 | 200 |
| Machining | Machine hours | 200 | 100,000 | 300,000 |
| Engineering | Engineering hours | 40 | 50,000 | 100,000 |
| Packing | Packing orders | 20 | 100,000 | 400,000 |
| Providing space | Machine hours | 1 | 200,000 | 800,000 |

[a] Pools are named according to the nature of the activities found within each pool. Providing space is a collection of facility-level activities. Packing and setups are collections of batch-level activities. Engineering is a collection of product-level activities, and machining is a collection of unit-level activities.

[b] Cost per unit of activity driver.

**Required:**
1. Using the projected data based on functional-based costing, compute gross profit as a percentage of sales, gross profit per unit, and total gross profit for each product.
2. Using the pool rates, compute the overhead cost per unit for each product. Using this new unit cost, compute gross profit percentage, gross profit per unit, and total gross profit for each product.
3. In view of the outcome in Requirement 2, evaluate the suggestion by the vice-president of marketing to switch the emphasis to the deluxe model.

**4–13**

Classification of Activities

LO5

Classify the following activities as unit level, batch level, product level, or facility level. Also identify a potential activity driver for each activity.
1. Setting up equipment
2. Receiving materials
3. Inspecting goods
4. Shipping goods
5. Ordering supplies
6. Scheduling production
7. Administering parts
8. Moving materials
9. Processing customer orders
10. Supervising plant
11. Welding subassemblies
12. Assembling components
13. Testing special-order products
14. Providing heating and air conditioning in the plant
15. Expediting goods
16. Providing plant space

**4–14**

Changing to an ABC
System

LO3

In 1994, Sterling Company changed its cost system. It went from using a single, plantwide overhead rate based on direct labour hours to a system using departmental overhead rates. The departmental overhead rates used direct labour hours, machine hours, and direct material dollars to assign overhead to products. In 2004, Sterling's president, Pamela Jones, was mulling over the possibility of changing to an ABC system. She had heard that the life of a cost system is about 10 years and was worried that the current system was no longer serving the company's needs. She was also convinced, however, that a change to ABC simply because it was a "hot" topic was not the right approach. Any change had to be in the company's best economic interests.

**Required:**

As a consultant to Pamela, identify the factors that should be considered in changing to an ABC system. In your discussion, include a definition of an outmoded or obsolete cost system.

**4–15**

Supplier Costing

LO6

Lumus Company manufactures refrigerators. Lumus produces all the parts necessary for its product except for one electronic component, which is purchased from two local suppliers: Vance, Inc., and Foy Company. Both suppliers are reliable and seldom deliver late; however, Vance sells the component for $23.50 per unit while Foy sells the same component for $21.50. Lumus purchases 80 percent of its components from Foy, because of its lower price. The total annual demand is 2,000,000 components.

Larry Hartley, Vance's vice president of sales, recently met with Jill Linsenmeyer, Lumus's purchasing manager, and urged her to purchase more of its units, arguing that Vance's component is of much higher quality and so should prove to be less costly than its competitor's lower-quality component. Larry offered to supply Vance with all the components needed and asked for a long-term contract. With a five-year contract for 1,600,000 or more units, Vance will sell the component for $22.50 per unit with a contractual provision for an annual product-specific inflationary adjustment. Jill is intrigued by the offer and wonders if the higher-quality component actually does cost less than the lower-quality Foy component. To help assess the cost effect of the two components, the following data were collected for supplier-related activities and suppliers:

### I. Activity data

|  | Activity Cost |
| --- | --- |
| Inspecting components (sampling only) | $ 240,000 |
| Reworking products (due to failed component) | 760,500 |
| Warranty work (due to failed component) | 4,800,000 |

### II. Supplier data:

|  | Vance | Foy |
| --- | --- | --- |
| Unit purchase price | $23.50 | $21.50 |
| Units purchased | 400,000 | 1,600,000 |
| Sampling hours* | 40 | 1,960 |
| Rework hours | 90 | 1,410 |
| Warranty hours | 400 | 7,600 |

*Sampling inspection for Vance's product has been reduced because the reject rate is so low.

**Required:**

Calculate the cost per component for each supplier, taking into consideration the costs of the supplier-related activities and using the current purchase prices and sales volume. What should Jill Linsenmeyer do? Explain.

**4–16**

Emery Company has two classes of customers: category 1 customers and category 2 customers. A category 1 customer places small, frequent orders, and a category 2 customer tends to place larger, less frequent orders. Both types of customer are buying the same product. Emery charges manufacturing cost plus 25 percent for a given order. The 25 percent markup is set large enough to cover nonmanufacturing costs and provide a reasonable return for Emery. Both customer types generated the same sales in units, so Emery's management had assumed that the customer support costs were about the same and priced the goods the same for each customer. Emery recently received some complaints from some of the category 2 customers. Several of these customers are threatening to take their business to other suppliers who allegedly charge less. For example, one customer said that he could buy the same 5,000 units from a competitor for $3 per unit less than Emery's price. This customer wanted a price concession.

A recently hired cost accountant suggested that the problem might have to do with unfair cost assignments and suggested that customer costs be assigned to each customer category using activity-based costing. She collected the following information about customer-related activities and costs for the most recent quarter:

| | Category 1 Customers | Category 2 Customers |
|---|---|---|
| Sales orders | 200 | 20 |
| Sales calls | 20 | 20 |
| Service calls | 100 | 50 |
| Average order size | 500 | 5,000 |
| Manufacturing cost/unit | $100 | $100 |
| | | |
| Customer costs: | | |
| Processing sales orders | $ 880,000 | |
| Selling goods | 320,000 | |
| Servicing goods | 300,000 | |
| Total | $1,500,000 | |

**Required:**
1. Calculate the total revenues per customer category and assign the customer costs to each customer type using revenues as the allocation base.
2. Calculate the customer cost per customer type using activity-based cost assignments. Discuss the merits of offering the category 2 customers a $3 price decrease.

## Problems

**4–17**

Two-Stage Procedure:
Activity-Based Costing

LO5

Mendoza Company has recently decided to convert from functional-based product costing to an activity-based system. The company produces two types of clocks: small and large. The clocks are produced in batches. Information concerning these two products follows:

|  | Small Clock | Large Clock |
|---|---|---|
| Quantity produced | 100,000 | 200,000 |
| Machine hours | 50,000 | 50,000 |
| Direct labour hours | 100,000 | 100,000 |
| Material handling (number of moves) | 2,000 | 4,000 |
| Engineering (hours) | 10,000 | 5,000 |
| Receiving (number of orders processed) | 250 | 500 |
| Setups | 60 | 20 |
| Maintaining (hours used) | 4,000 | 2,000 |
| Kilowatt-hours | 25,000 | 25,000 |
| Inspecting (number of hours) | 3,000 | 1,000 |

Additionally, the following overhead costs are reported for the activities associated with the two products:

| | |
|---|---|
| Material handling | $120,000 |
| Maintaining equipment | 80,000 |
| Producing power | 30,000 |
| Amortization (machines)* | 60,000 |
| Engineering | 100,000 |
| Receiving | 30,000 |
| Setups | 96,000 |
| Inspecting | 60,000 |

  \* Amortization is straight line; book value at the beginning of the year was $600,000. The machine hours reported represent the normal activity level. The remaining life of the machinery is 10 years or 1 million machine hours.

### Required:
1. Classify activities by level and then by driver.
2. Group all overhead costs into homogeneous cost pools. Select an activity driver for each cost pool and compute a pool rate.
3. Using the pool rates calculated in Requirement 2, assign all overhead costs to the two products and compute the overhead cost per unit for each.

**4–18**

Functional-Based
versus Activity-Based
Costing

LO2, LO3, LO4

For years Janeiro Company produced only one product: backpacks. Recently, the company decided to add a line of duffel bags. With this addition, the company began to assign overhead costs using departmental rates. Before adopting this approach, the company used a predetermined plantwide overhead rate based on units produced. Departmental rates meant that overhead costs had to be assigned to each producing department to create overhead pools. Predetermined departmental rates could then be calculated for each overhead cost pool. Surprisingly, after the addition of the duffel-bag line and the switch to departmental rates, the costs of producing the backpacks increased and their profitability dropped.

The marketing manager and the production manager both complained about the increase in the production cost of backpacks. The marketing manager was concerned because the increase in unit costs led to pressure to increase the back-packs' unit selling price. She was resisting this pressure because she was certain that the increase would harm the company's market share. The production manager was also receiving pressure to cut costs, yet he was convinced that nothing different was being done in the way the backpacks were produced. He was also convinced that further efficiency in the manufacture of the backpacks was unlikely. After some discussion, the two managers decided that the problem had to be connected with the addition of the duffel-bag line.

Upon investigation, they were informed that the only real change in product-costing procedures had been in the way overhead costs were assigned. A two-stage procedure was now in use. First, overhead costs are assigned to the two producing departments, patterns and finishing. Some overhead costs are assigned to producing departments using direct tracing and some using driver tracing. For example, the salaries of the producing department's supervisors are assigned using direct tracing, whereas the costs of the factory's accounting department are assigned using driver tracing (the driver being the number of transactions processed for each department). Second, the costs accumulated in the producing departments are assigned to the two products using direct labour hours as a driver (the rate in each department is based on direct labour hours). The managers were assured that great care was being taken to associate overhead costs with individual products. So that they could construct their own example of cost assignment, the controller provided the following information to show how accounting costs are assigned to products:

|  | Department | | |
| --- | --- | --- | --- |
|  | **Pattern** | **Finishing** | **Total** |
| Accounting cost | $48,000 | $72,000 | $120,000 |
| Transactions processed | 32,000 | 48,000 | 80,000 |
| Total direct labour hours | 25,000 | 50,000 | 75,000 |
| Direct labour hours per backpack* | 0.10 | 0.20 | 0.30 |
| Direct labour hours per duffel bag* | 0.40 | 0.80 | 1.20 |

* Hours required to produce one unit of each product

The controller remarked that the cost of operating the accounting department had doubled with the addition of the new product line. The increase came because of the need to process additional transactions, which had also doubled in number.

During the first year of producing duffel bags, the company produced and sold 150,000 backpacks and 25,000 duffel bags. The 150,000 backpacks matched the previous year's output for that product.

**Required:**
1. Compute the amount of accounting cost assigned to each backpack and duffel bag using the departmental rates based on direct labour hours.
2. Compute the amount of accounting cost assigned to a backpack before the duffel-bag line was added using a plantwide rate based on units produced. Is this assignment accurate? Explain.
3. Suppose that the company decided to assign the accounting costs directly to the product lines using the number of transactions as the activity driver. What is the accounting cost per unit of backpacks? per unit of duffel bags?
4. Which way of assigning overhead does the best job, the functional-based approach using departmental rates or the activity-based approach using transactions processed for each product? Explain. Discuss the value of activity-based costing before the duffel-bag line was added.

**4–19**

*Plantwide versus Departmental Rates*

LO2

The Cheetah Company produces custom-made stuffed toy animals and competes in a very competitive marketplace. The company establishes its selling prices as being equal to the cost of production plus a 30 percent markup. The production process consists of two departments:

- The Skins Department, where the outside liners (skins) for each toy animal are handmade from specially ordered materials.
- The Stuffing Department, where the skins are filled by machine with a standard stuffing material to complete the toys.

The two production departments (the Skins and Stuffing Departments) are both served by two other departments (the Purchasing Department and the Cleaning and Maintenance Department). Descriptions of the operations of these departments, and of how their costs are assigned, are given below:

*Purchasing*
- This department purchases all materials and supplies required for all departments.
- Its costs are assigned to the two production departments based on the total amount of materials ordered by each producing department.

*Cleaning and Maintenance*
- This department cleans the entire building and maintains all the equipment in the company.
- Its costs are assigned to the two production departments on the basis of the total square metres each producing department occupies.

**Required:**
1. Should the company use a plantwide overhead rate or departmental overhead rates? Explain your answer.
2. Comment on the company's cost assignment policy and, where necessary, suggest improvements. Justify fully any suggested improvements that you make. (CMA Canada adapted)

**4–20**

*Plantwide versus Departmental Rates; Product-Costing Accuracy; Pool Rates*

LO2, LO3, LO4

Maxwell Company produces small engines for model boats (Engine A and Engine B). Both products pass through two producing departments. Engine A's production is much more labour-intensive than Engine B's. Engine B is by far the more popular of the two engines. The following data have been gathered for these two products:

| | Product Data | |
| --- | --- | --- |
| | Engine A | Engine B |
| Units produced per year | 30,000 | 300,000 |
| Prime costs | $100,000 | $1,000,000 |
| Direct labour hours | 140,000 | 300,000 |
| Machine hours | 20,000 | 200,000 |
| Production runs | 40 | 60 |
| Inspection hours | 800 | 1,200 |

|  | Departmental Data | |
| --- | --- | --- |
|  | **Department 1** | **Department 2** |
| Direct labour hours: | | |
| Engine A | 10,000 | 130,000 |
| Engine B | 30,000 | 270,000 |
| Total | 40,000 | 400,000 |
| Machine hours: | | |
| Engine A | 10,000 | 10,000 |
| Engine B | 170,000 | 30,000 |
| Total | 180,000 | 40,000 |
| Overhead costs: | | |
| Setup costs | $ 90,000 | $ 90,000 |
| Inspection costs | 70,000 | 70,000 |
| Machining | 120,000 | 40,000 |
| Maintenance | 140,000 | 40,000 |
| Total | $420,000 | $240,000 |

### Required:

1. Compute the overhead cost per unit for each product using a plantwide rate based on direct labour hours.
2. Compute the overhead cost per unit for each product using departmental rates. In calculating departmental rates, use machine hours for Department 1 and direct labour hours for Department 2. Repeat, using direct labour hours for Department 1 and machine hours for Department 2. Of the two approaches, which would most likely be chosen? Explain why.
3. Compute the overhead cost per unit for each product using activity-based costing. Form homogeneous cost pools where possible.
4. Using the activity-based product costs as the standard, comment on the ability of departmental rates to improve the accuracy of product costing.

**4–21**

Production-Based
Costing versus
Activity-Based
Costing; Assigning
Costs to Activities;
Resource Drivers

LO3, LO4, LO5

Willow Company produces lawn mowers. One of its plants produces two versions of mowers: a basic model and a deluxe model. The deluxe model has a sturdier frame, a higher-horsepower engine, a wider blade, and mulching capability. At the beginning of the year, the following data were prepared for this plant:

|  | **Basic Model** | **Deluxe Model** |
| --- | --- | --- |
| Expected quantity | 40,000 | 20,000 |
| Selling price | $180 | $360 |
| Prime costs | $80 | $160 |
| Machine hours | 5,000 | 5,000 |
| Direct labour hours | 10,000 | 10,000 |
| Engineering support (hours) | 1,500 | 4,500 |
| Receiving (orders processed) | 250 | 500 |
| Material handling (number of moves) | 2,000 | 4,000 |
| Purchasing (number of requisitions) | 100 | 200 |
| Maintenance (hours used) | 1,000 | 3,000 |
| Paying suppliers (invoices processed) | 250 | 500 |
| Setting up batches (number of setups) | 20 | 60 |

Additionally, the following overhead activity costs are reported:

| Maintaining equipment | $114,000 |
| Engineering support | 120,000 |
| Material handling | ? |
| Setting up equipment | 96,000 |
| Purchasing materials | 60,000 |
| Receiving goods | 40,000 |
| Paying suppliers | 30,000 |
| Providing space | 20,000 |
| Total $ | ? |

Facility-level costs are allocated in proportion to machine hours (an approach that provides a measure of the time the facility is used by each product).

Material handling uses three inputs: two forklifts, propane to operate the forklifts, and three operators. The three operators are paid salaries of $40,000 each. The operators spend 25 percent of their time on the receiving activity and 75 percent on moving goods (material handling). Propane costs $3 per move. Amortization amounts to $6,000 per forklift per year.

**Required:**

1. Calculate the cost of the material-handling activity. Label the cost assignments as driver tracing or direct tracing. Identify the resource drivers.
2. Calculate the cost per unit for each product using direct labour hours to assign all overhead costs.
3. Form homogeneous cost pools and calculate pool rates. Explain why you group activities in pools.
4. Using the pool rates computed in Requirement 3, calculate the cost per unit for each product. Compare these costs with those calculated using functional-based costing. Which cost is the most accurate? Explain.

---

**4–22**

ABC Costing and Cost Behaviour

LO4, LO5

Dulce Sound Company produces several different models of a compact disk player. The company has recently adopted an ABC system. The unit cost expected for the deluxe model, Model FRX, follows:

| Unit-level costs (includes materials and labour) | $120 |
| Batch-level costs | 80 |
| Product-level costs | 40 |
| Facility-level costs | 20 |
| Total unit cost | $260 |

The unit cost is based on an expected volume of 20,000 units. These units will be produced in 20 equal batches. The product-level costs are all from engineering support. The product-level costs are driven by engineering orders. The $40 cost assignment is based on 10 orders. Facility-level costs are allocated on the basis of direct labour hours (one hour per unit produced).

**Required:**

1. Calculate the total manufacturing cost to produce 20,000 units of Model FRX. Present the total cost for each activity category.
2. Now assume that the company has revised its forecast for Model FRX and expects to produce 30,000 units. A decision has been made to handle the increased production by increasing batch size to 3,000 units. The increased production will not require an increase in engineering support. Calculate the total cost to produce the 30,000 units of Model FRX. Present the total cost for each activity category. Explain the outcome.
3. Assume that the revised forecast of 30,000 units is made. Now, however, a decision is made to handle the extra production by increasing the number of batches from 20 to 30. Also, the sales of the extra 10,000 units are possible only if an engineering modification is made. This increases the expected engineer-

ing orders from 10 to 12. Explain why the costs changed from those predicted in Requirement 2.

4. Discuss the value of classifying and reporting costs by activity category.

**4–23**

*Activity-Based Costing; Assigning Resource Costs; Primary and Secondary Activities*

**LO3, LO4**

Longridge Hospital has identified three activities for daily maternity care: occupancy and feeding, nursing, and nursing supervision. The nursing supervisor oversees 150 nurses, 25 of whom are maternity nurses (the other nurses are located in other care areas, such as the emergency room and intensive care). The nursing supervisor has three assistants, a secretary, several offices, computers, phones, and furniture. The three assistants spend 75 percent of their time on the supervising activity and 25 percent of their time as surgical nurses. They each receive a salary of $48,000. The nursing supervisor is paid a salary of $70,000. She spends 100 percent of her time supervising. The secretary receives a salary of $22,000 per year. Other costs directly traceable to the supervisory activity (amortization, utilities, phone, etc.) average $100,000 per year.

Daily care output is measured as "patient days." The hospital has traditionally assigned the cost of daily care by using a daily rate (a rate per patient day). There are actually different kinds of daily care, and rates are structured to reflect these differences. For example, a higher rate is used for an intensive care unit than for a maternity care unit. Within units, however, the daily rates are the same for all patients. Under the traditional, functional approach, the daily rate is computed by dividing the annual costs of occupancy and feeding, nursing, and a share of supervision by the unit's capacity (expressed in patient days). The cost of supervision is assigned to each care area based on the number of nurses. A single cost driver (patient days) is used to assign the costs of daily care to each patient.

A pilot study has revealed that the demands for nursing care vary within the maternity unit, depending on the severity of a patient's case. Specifically, demand for nursing services per day increases with severity. Assume that within the maternity unit there are three levels of increasing severity: normal patients, cesarean patients, and patients with complications. The pilot study provided the following activity and cost information:

| Activity | Annual Cost | Activity Driver | Activity Quantity |
|---|---|---|---|
| Occupancy and feeding | $1,000,000 | Patient days | 10,000 |
| Nursing care (maternity) | 950,000 | Nursing hours | 50,000 |
| Nursing supervision | ? | Number of nurses | 150 |

The pilot study also revealed the following information concerning the three types of patients and their annual demands:

| Patient Type | Patient Days | Nursing Hours |
|---|---|---|
| Normal | 7,000 | 17,500 |
| Cesarean | 2,000 | 12,500 |
| Complications | 1,000 | 20,000 |
| Total | 10,000 | 50,000 |

**Required:**
1. Calculate the cost per patient day using a functional-based approach.
2. Calculate the cost per patient day using an activity-based approach.
3. The hospital processes 1,000,000 kilograms of laundry per year. The cost for the laundry activity is $500,000 per year. In a functional-based costing system, the cost of the laundry department is assigned to each user department in proportion to the kilograms of laundry produced. Typically, maternity produces 200,000 kilograms per year. How much would this change the cost per

patient day calculated in Requirement 1? Describe what information you would need to modify the activity-based calculation in Requirement 2. Under what conditions does an activity-based calculation provide a more accurate cost assignment?

**4–24**

Product-Costing Accuracy; Corporate Strategy; Activity-Based Costing

LO3, LO4, LO5

Pearson Manufacturing produces chemicals for industrial use. One plant specializes in the production of chemicals used in the copper industry. Two compounds are produced: compound X-12 and compound S-15. Compound X-12 was originally developed by Pearson's chemists and played a key role in extracting copper from low-grade ore. The patent for X-12 has expired, and competition for this market has intensified dramatically. Compound X-12 produced the highest volume of activity, and for many years the plant produced only X-12. Five years ago, S-15 was added. Compound S-15 was more difficult to manufacture and required special handling and setups. For the first three years after the addition of the new product, profits increased. In the last two years, however, the plant has faced intense competition, and its sales of X-12 have dropped. In fact, the plant showed a small loss in the most recent reporting period. The plant manager is convinced that competing producers have been guilty of selling X-12 below the cost to produce it—perhaps with the objective of expanding market share. The following conversation between Diane Woolridge, the plant's manager, and Rick Dixon, the divisional marketing manager, reflects the division's concerns about the future of the plant and its products.

**Rick**: "You know, Diane, the divisional manager is very concerned about the plant's trend. He indicated that in this budgetary environment, we can't afford to carry plants that don't show a profit. We shut one down just last month because it couldn't handle the competition."

**Diane**: "Rick, our compound X-12 has a reputation for quality and value—we have a very pure product. It has been a mainstay for years. I don't understand what's happening."

**Rick**: "I just received a call from one of our major customers concerning X-12. He said that a sales representative from another company had offered the chemical at $10 per kilogram—about $6 less than what we ask. It's hard to compete with a price like that. Perhaps the plant is simply obsolete."

**Diane**: "No. I don't agree. We have good technology. I think that we are efficient. And it's costing a little more than $10 per kilogram to produce X-12. I don't see how these companies can afford to sell it so cheaply. I'm not convinced that we should meet the price. Perhaps we should emphasize producing and selling more S-15. Our margin is high on that product, and we have virtually no competition for it. We recently raised the price per kilogram, and our customers didn't blink an eye."

**Rick**: "You may be right. I think we can increase the price even more and not lose business. I called a few customers to see how they would react to a 25 percent increase in price, and they all said that they would still purchase the same quantity as before."

**Diane**: "It sounds promising. However, before we make a major commitment to S-15, I think we had better explore other possible alternatives. The market potential is much less than that for X-12. I want to know how our production costs compare to our competitors' costs. Perhaps we could be more efficient and find a way to earn our normal return on X-12. Besides, my production people hate producing S-15. It's very difficult to produce."

After meeting with Rick, Diane requested an investigation of the production costs and comparative efficiency. Independent consultants were hired. After a three-month assessment, the consulting group provided the following information on the plant's production activities and the costs associated with the two products:

|                            | X-12      | S-15    |
|----------------------------|-----------|---------|
| Production (kilograms)     | 1,000,000 | 200,000 |
| Selling price              | $15.93    | $12.00  |
| Overhead per unit*         | $6.41     | $2.89   |
| Prime cost per kilogram    | $4.27     | $3.13   |
| Number of production runs  | 100       | 200     |
| Receiving orders           | 400       | 1,000   |
| Machine hours              | 125,000   | 60,000  |
| Direct labour hours        | 250,000   | 22,500  |
| Engineering hours          | 5,000     | 5,000   |
| Material handling          | 500       | 400     |

   * Calculated using a plantwide rate based on direct labour hours, which is the current way of assigning the plant's overhead to its products.

The consulting group recommended switching the overhead assignment to an activity-based approach. They maintained that activity-based cost assignment is more accurate and will provide better information for decision making. To facilitate this recommendation, they grouped the plant's activities into homogeneous sets based on common processes, activity levels, and consumption ratios. The costs of these pooled activities follow:

**Overhead Pool:***

| Setup costs              | $ 240,000  |
|--------------------------|------------|
| Machine costs            | 1,750,000  |
| Receiving costs          | 2,100,000  |
| Engineering costs        | 2,000,000  |
| Material-handling costs  | 900,000    |
| Total                    | $6,990,000 |

   * The pools are named for the major activities found within them. All overhead costs within each pool can be assigned using a single driver (based on the major activity after which the pool is named).

**Required:**
1. Verify the overhead cost per unit reported by the consulting group using direct labour hours to assign overhead. Compute the per-unit gross margin for each product.
2. Recompute the unit cost of each product using activity-based costing. Compute the per-unit gross margin for each product.
3. Should the company switch its emphasis from the high-volume product to the low-volume product? Comment on the validity of the plant manager's concern that competitors are selling below the cost of producing compound X-12.
4. Explain the apparent lack of competition for S-15. Comment also on the willingness of customers to accept a 25 percent increase in price for this compound.
5. Describe what actions you would take based on the information provided by the activity-based unit costs.

**4–25**

*Customers as a Cost Object*

**LO6**

A bank has requested an analysis of chequing account profitability by customer type. Customers are categorized according to the size of their account: low balances, medium balances, and high balances. The activities associated with the three different customer categories, and their associated annual costs, are given below.

| Opening and closing accounts | $ 200,000  |
|------------------------------|------------|
| Issuing monthly statements   | 300,000    |
| Processing transactions      | 2,050,000  |
| Customer inquiries           | 400,000    |
| Providing ATM services       | 1,120,000  |
| Total cost                   | $4,070,000 |

Additional information concerning the usage of the activities by the various customers is also provided:

| Account Balance | Low | Medium | High |
|---|---|---|---|
| Number of accounts opened/closed | 15,000 | 3,000 | 2,000 |
| Number of statements issued | 450,000 | 100,000 | 50,000 |
| Number of transactions processed | 18,000,000 | 2,000,000 | 500,000 |
| Number of telephone minutes | 1,000,000 | 600,000 | 400,000 |
| Number of ATM transactions | 1,350,000 | 200,000 | 50,000 |
| Number of chequing accounts | 38,000 | 8,000 | 4,000 |

**Required:**

1. Calculate a cost per account per year by dividing the total cost of processing and maintaining chequing accounts by the total number of accounts. What is the average fee per month that the bank should charge to cover the costs incurred because of chequing accounts?
2. Calculate a cost per customer by customer category using activity rates.
3. Currently the bank offers free chequing to all its customers. However, the bank earns average interest revenues of $90 per account; the interest revenues earned per account by category are $80, $100, and $165 for the low, medium, and high balance accounts, respectively. Calculate the average profit per account (average revenue less average cost from Requirement 1). Now calculate the profit per account using the revenue per customer type and the unit cost per customer type calculated in Requirement 2.
4. After reviewing the analysis from Requirement 3, a bank vice-president recommended eliminating the free chequing feature for low-balance customers. The president expressed reluctance to do so, arguing that the low-balance customers more than make up the loss through cross-sales. He presented a survey showing that 50 percent of the customers would switch banks if a chequing fee were imposed. Explain how you could verify the president's argument using activity-based costing.

**4–26**

ABC and Customer-
Driven Costs

Sorensen Manufacturing produces several types of bolts used in aircraft. The bolts are produced in batches according to customer order. Although there are a variety of bolts, they can be grouped into three product families. Customers can also be grouped into three categories, corresponding to the product family they purchase. The number of units sold to each customer class is the same. The selling prices for the three product families range from $0.50 to $0.80 per unit. Historically, the costs of order entry, processing, and handling were expensed and not traced to individual customer groups. These costs are not trivial: they totalled $4,500,000 for the most recent year. Furthermore, these costs have been increasing over time. Recently, the company started to emphasize a cost reduction strategy; however, any cost reduction decisions had to contribute to the creation of a competitive advantage.

Because of the magnitude and growth of order-filling costs, management decided to explore the causes of these costs. They discovered that the number of customer orders processed was the cost driver for order-filling costs. Further investigation revealed the following cost behaviour for the order-filling activity:

Fixed step-cost component: $50,000 per step (2,000 orders define a step)*
Variable cost component: $20 per order

* Sorensen currently has sufficient steps to process 100,000 orders.

The expected customer orders for the year total 100,000. The expected usage of the order-filling activity and the average size of an order by customer category follow:

|  | Category I | Category II | Category III |
|---|---|---|---|
| Number of orders | 50,000 | 30,000 | 20,000 |
| Average order size | 600 | 1,000 | 1,500 |

As a result of the cost behaviour analysis, the marketing manager recommended the imposition of a charge per customer order. The president of the company concurred. The charge was implemented by adding the cost per order to the price of each order (computed using the projected ordering costs and expected orders). This ordering cost was then reduced as the size of the order increased and eliminated as the order size reached 2,000 units. Within a short time after communicating this new price information to customers, the average order size for all three product families increased to 2,000 units.

### Required:
1. Sorensen has traditionally expensed order-filling costs. What is the most likely reason for this practice?
2. Calculate the order-filling cost per unit for each customer category.
3. Calculate the reduction in order-filling costs produced by the change in pricing strategy (assume that resource spending is reduced as much as possible and that the total units sold remain unchanged). Explain how exploiting customer activity information produced this cost reduction.

**4–27**

**Activity-Based
Supplier Costing**

**LO6**

Levy, Inc., manufactures tractors for agricultural usage. Levy purchases the starters needed for its tractors from two sources: Johnson Starters and Watson Company. The Johnson starter is the more expensive of the two sources and has a price of $1,000. The Watson starter is $900 per unit. Levy produces and sells 44,000 tractors. Of the 44,000 starters needed for the tractors, 8,000 are purchased from Johnson Starters, and 36,000 are purchased from Watson Company. The production manager, Jamie Murray, prefers the Johnson starter. However, Glenys Miller, purchasing manager, maintains that the price difference is too great to buy more than the 8,000 units currently purchased. Glenys also wants to maintain a significant connection with the Johnson source just in case the less expensive source cannot supply the needed quantities. Even though Jamie understands the price argument, he is convinced that the quality of the Johnson starter is worth the price difference.

Frank Wallace, the controller, has decided to use activity costing to resolve the issue. The following data have been collected:

#### I. Activity Cost Data

| | |
|---|---|
| Replacing starters[a] | $1,600,000 |
| Expediting orders[b] | 2,000,000 |
| Warranty work[c] | 3,600,000 |

[a] All units are tested after assembly, and some are rejected because of starter failure. The failed starters are removed and replaced, with the supplier replacing any failed starter. The replaced starter is retested before being sold.

[b] Due to late or failed delivery of starters.

[c] Repair work is for units under warranty and almost invariably is due to starter failure. Repair usually means replacing the starter. This cost plus labour, transportation, and other costs make warranty work very expensive.

**II. Supplier Data**

|  | Watson | Johnson |
|---|---|---|
| Starters replaced by source | 1,980 | 20 |
| Late or failed shipments | 198 | 2 |
| Warranty repairs (by source) | 2,440 | 60 |

**Required:**

1. Calculate the activity-based supplier cost per starter (acquisition cost plus supplier-related activity costs). Which of the two suppliers is the low cost supplier? Explain why this is a better measure of starter cost than the usual purchase costs assigned to the starters.
2. Consider the supplier cost information obtained in Requirement 1. Suppose further that Johnson can only supply a total of 20,000 units. What actions would you advise Levy to undertake with its suppliers?

## Managerial Decision Cases

**4–28**

*Activity-Based Costing; Consideration of Customer-Driven Costs*

**LO4, LO6**

Sharp Paper, Inc., has three paper mills, one of which is located in Kamloops, British Columbia. The Kamloops mill produces 300 different types of coated and uncoated specialty printing papers. This large variety of products was the result of a full-line marketing strategy adopted by Sharp's management. Management was convinced that the value of variety more than offset the extra costs of the increased complexity.

During 2004, the Kamloops mill produced 120,000 tons of coated paper and 80,000 tons of uncoated. Of the 200,000 tons produced, 180,000 were sold. Sixty products account for 80 percent of the tons sold. Thus, 240 products are classified as low-volume products.

Lightweight lime hopsack in cartons (LLHC) is one of the low-volume products. LLHC is produced in rolls, converted into sheets of paper, and then sold in cartons. In 2004, the cost to produce and sell one ton of LLHC was as follows:

| Raw materials: | | |
|---|---|---|
| Furnish (3 different pulps) | 2,225 pounds | $ 450 |
| Additives (11 different items) | 200 pounds | 500 |
| Tub size | 75 pounds | 10 |
| Recycled scrap paper | 296 pounds | (20) |
| Total raw materials | | $ 940 |
| Direct labour | | $ 450 |
| Overhead: | | |
| Paper machine ($100/ton × 2,500 pounds) | | $ 125 |
| Finishing machine ($120/ton × 2,500 pounds) | | 150 |
| Total overhead | | $ 275 |
| Shipping and warehousing | | $ 30 |
| Total manufacturing and selling cost | | $1,695 |

Overhead is applied using a two-stage process. First, overhead is allocated to the paper and finishing machines using the direct method of allocation with carefully selected cost drivers. Second, the overhead assigned to each machine is divided by the budgeted tons of output. These rates are then multiplied by the number of pounds required to produce one good ton.

LLHC sold for $2,400 per ton, making it one of Sharp Paper's most profitable products. A similar examination of some of the other low-volume products revealed that they also had very respectable profit margins. Unfortunately, the performance of the high-volume products was less impressive, with many showing losses or very low profit margins. This situation led Ryan Chesser to call a meeting with his marketing vice-president, Jennifer Woodruff, and his controller, Jan Booth.

**Ryan**: "The above-average profitability of our low-volume specialty products and the poor profit performance of our high-volume products make me believe that we should switch our marketing emphasis to the low-volume line. Perhaps we should drop some of our high-volume products, particularly those showing a loss."

**Jennifer**: "I'm not convinced that the solution you are proposing is the right one. I know our high-volume products are of high quality, and I am convinced that we are as efficient in our production as other firms. I think that somehow our costs are not being assigned correctly. For example, the shipping and warehousing costs are assigned by dividing these costs by the total tons of paper sold. Yet—"

**Jan**: "Jennifer, I hate to disagree, but the $30 per ton charge for shipping and warehousing seems reasonable. I know that our method of assigning these costs is identical to that used by a number of other paper companies."

**Jennifer**: "Well, that may be true, but do these other companies have the variety of products that we have? Our low-volume products require special handling and processing, but when we assign shipping and warehousing costs, we average these special costs across our entire product line. Every ton produced in our mill passes through our mill shipping department and is sent either directly to the customer or to our distribution centre and then eventually to customers. My records indicate quite clearly that virtually all the high-volume products are sent directly to customers, whereas most of the low-volume products are sent to the distribution centre. Now all the products passing through the mill shipping department should receive a share of the $2,000,000 annual shipping costs. I am not convinced, however, that all products should receive a share of the receiving and shipping costs of the distribution centre as currently practised."

**Ryan**: "Jan, is this true? Does our system allocate our shipping and warehousing costs in this way?"

**Jan**: "Yes, I'm afraid it does. Jennifer may have a point. Perhaps we need to re-evaluate our method to assign these costs to the product lines."

**Ryan**: "Jennifer, do you have any suggestions concerning how the shipping and warehousing costs ought to be assigned?"

**Jennifer**: "It seems reasonable to make a distinction between products that spend time in the distribution centre and those that do not. We should also distinguish between the receiving and shipping activities at the distribution centre. All incoming shipments are packed on pallets and weigh 1 ton each (there are 14 cartons of paper per pallet). In 2004, receiving processed 56,000 tons of paper. Receiving employs 15 people at an annual cost of $600,000. Other receiving costs total about $500,000. I would recommend that these costs be assigned using tons processed.

"Shipping, however, is different. There are two activities associated with shipping: picking the order from inventory and loading the paper. We employ 30 people for picking and 10 for loading, at an annual cost of $1,200,000. Other shipping costs total $1,100,000. Picking and loading are more concerned with the number of shipments than with tonnage. That is, a shipment may consist of two or three cartons instead of pallets. Accordingly, the distribution centre's shipping costs should be assigned using the number of shipments. In 2004, for example, we handled 190,000 shipments."

**Ryan**: "These suggestions have merit. Jan, I would like to see what effect Jennifer's suggestions have on the per-unit assignment of shipping and warehousing for LLHC. If the effect is significant, then we will expand the analysis to include all products."

**Jan**: "I'm willing to compute the effect, but I'd like to suggest one additional feature. Currently, we have a policy to carry about 25 tons of LLHC in inventory. Our current cost system totally ignores the cost of carrying this inventory. Since it costs us $1,665 to produce each ton of this product, we are tying up a lot of money in inventory—money that could be invested in other productive opportunities. In fact, the return lost is about 16 percent per year. This cost should also be assigned to the units sold."

**Ryan**: "Jan, that also sounds good to me. Go ahead and include the carrying cost in your computation."

To help in the analysis, Jan gathered the following data for LLHC for 2004:

| | |
|---|---|
| Tons sold | 10 |
| Average cartons per shipment | 2 |
| Average shipments per ton | 7 |

**Required:**

1. Identify the flaws associated with the current method of assigning shipping and warehousing costs to Sharp's products.
2. Compute the shipping and warehousing cost per ton of LLHC sold using the new method suggested by Jennifer and Jan.
3. Using the new costs computed in Requirement 2, compute the profit per ton for LLHC. Compare this with the profit per ton computed using the old method. Do you think that this same effect would be realized for other low-volume products? Explain.
4. Comment on Ryan's proposal to drop some high-volume products and place more emphasis on low-volume products. Discuss the role of the accounting system in supporting this type of decision making.
5. After receiving the analysis of LLHC, Ryan decided to expand the analysis to all products. He also had Jan re-evaluate the way in which mill overhead was assigned to products. After the restructuring was completed, Ryan took the following actions: (a) the prices of most low-volume products were increased, (b) the prices of several high-volume products were decreased, and (c) some low-volume products were dropped. Explain why his strategy changed so dramatically.

**4–29**

Activity-Based Product
Costing and Ethical
Behaviour
LO4, LO5, LO6

Consider the following conversation between Leonard Bryner, president and manager of a company engaged in manufacturing, and Chuck Davis, CMA, the company's controller.

**Leonard**: "Chuck, as you know, our company has been losing market share over the past three years. We have been losing more and more bids, and I don't understand why. At first I thought that other companies were undercutting us simply to gain business, but after examining some of the public financial reports, I believe that they are making a reasonable rate of return. I am beginning to believe that our costs and costing methods are at fault."

**Chuck**: "I can't agree with that. We have good control over our costs. Like most companies in our industry, we use a normal costing system. I really don't see any significant waste in the plant."

**Leonard**: "After talking with some other managers at a recent industrial convention, I'm not so sure that waste by itself is the issue. They talked about activity-based management, activity-based costing, and continuous improvement. They mentioned the use of something called activity drivers to assign overhead. They claimed that these new procedures can help produce more efficiency in manufacturing, better control of overhead, and more accurate product costing. A big deal was made of eliminating activities that added no value. Maybe our bids are too high because these other companies have found ways to decrease their overhead costs and to increase the accuracy of their product costing."

**Chuck**: "I doubt it. For one thing, I don't see how we can increase product-costing accuracy. So many of our costs are indirect costs. Furthermore, everyone uses some measure of production activity to assign overhead costs. I imagine that what they are calling activity drivers is just some new buzzword for measures of production volume. Fads in costing come and go. I wouldn't worry about it. I'll bet that our problems with decreasing sales are temporary. You might recall that we experienced a similar problem about twelve years ago—it was two years before it straightened out."

**Required:**

1. Do you agree with Chuck Davis and the advice that he gave Leonard Bryner? Explain.
2. Do you think that Chuck was well informed—that he was aware of the accounting implications of activity-based costing and that he knew what was meant by activity drivers? Should he have been? Review (in Chapter 1) the standards of ethical conduct for management accountants. Do any of these apply to Chuck's case?

## Research Assignment

**4–30**

Cybercase

LO4, LO5, LO6

There are numerous examples of ABC applications in the real world. A good source of ABC case studies for various industries is found at www.sas.com/solutions/abm/. Access the site and select *Customer Successes*. Choose a manufacturing company and then read about its experience. Next, choose a service company, and read about its implementation of an ABC system. Answer the following questions about the two cases:

1. What reasons were offered for implementing ABC?
2. Describe the implementation procedures.
3. How many activities were identified?
4. What type of benefits (results) did each company achieve?
5. What problems, if any, were mentioned?

# Job-Order Costing

**After studying Chapter 5, you should be able to:**

1. Describe the differences between job-order costing and process costing, and identify the types of organizations that would use each method.

2. Identify and set up the source documents used in job-order costing.

3. Discuss the cost flows associated with job-order costing.

4. Prepare the journal entries associated with job-order costing. (Appendix)

## Scenario

Computrain Company was established five years ago to train employees of companies to use software programs for creating Web pages and providing education over the Internet. Travis Warren, founder and president, saw his company grow from his own occasional consulting with professors at the local university into a company that employed nine people and had sales of $1 million annually. Travis was excited by the growth of his company and saw additional opportunities to provide training at Computrain's headquarters. To accomplish this he added a state-of-the-art training complex. The complex could accommodate 24 trainees, each with his/her own workstation consisting of an instructor's podium with computer, video projector, VCR, and audio capabilities.

One sunny Monday afternoon, Travis invited his accountant, Miranda Spade, to take a tour of the new complex.

*Miranda*: "Travis, this is wonderful! I really like the special touches—the snack area and the lounge with access to phones and e-mail hookups. This will be very appealing to Human Resource department heads. Their people will love coming here for training!"

*Travis*: "That's the idea, Miranda, to become the premier training facility in the region! I know this expansion project was expensive, but I think it was worth it!"

*Miranda*: "You know, that reference to it being worth it started me thinking. Maybe your accounting system will need to be revamped to keep up with the expanded variety of services you are offering."

*Travis*: "What do you mean? Why would adding on to the building cause us to change our accounting system? Won't we just add the value of the project to the property, plant, and equipment account on the balance sheet?"

*Miranda*: "Oh, for sure we'll do that. But what I meant was the scope of your company as well as the variation in the services you offer. Sometimes you call me to help budget the cost of a proposed job in order to submit a bid. It's been pretty simple in the past—just add up the hours we think it will take, decide what professional will handle it, add something for supplies and travel, apply some general overhead, and call it a day. Now, however, with trainees coming here and using the specialized facilities, we'll need to have different overhead rates for different types of jobs. We will definitely need to keep track of costs using a job-order approach. We may need to use some activity-based costing, as well."

*Travis*: "Wait a minute, I'm still not clear on what's happening here.

Figuring the cost of a job seemed pretty simple before. What exactly is a job-order approach? And what is activity-based costing?"

**Miranda**: "OK, Travis, let's look at the Jacob Company's job last month. Bill handled that job. He spent two days at the Jacob's marketing offices in Welland and taught six marketing reps how to build their own Web pages. Bill makes $45,000 per year, so we figured that the cost of the job would be four days' salary for Bill—two days of preparation and two of on-site training. We added some mileage reimbursement, meals, a night at the Fairfield Inn, and supplies—six training manuals. All in all, it amounted to about $975. That job was very similar to one that Jeanna did two months ago for Simbar Company. Even though she trained the Simbar people in a video-capturing software, the costs were about the same.

"Now, though, you are going to bring trainees here. The costs will be very different for taking care of them, as opposed to sending Bill or Jeanna to companies for on-site training. In addition, we should only charge the jobs requiring training here for the use of the training facilities. Plus, I noticed that you are advertising for a systems specialist— someone who can set up hardware. Your jobs are going to include equipment setup as well as training. Again, costs for those jobs will really differ from the simple training jobs."

**Travis**: "I think I'm beginning to catch on. I'm using the costs as a basis for pricing. It is important to know just what my costs are and also to be able to use those costs to justify the price to customers. OK, Miranda, make the changes you think best. Then, I think I'm going to need a training session on our new job-order costing system!"[1]

### Questions to Think About

1. Does Computrain Company produce a product or provide a service? Do these services differ from customer to customer?

2. List some examples of direct materials, direct labour, and overhead for Computrain when it sends someone to provide on-site training. Also, give some examples of each for training at Computrain's new facility. Is Miranda right? Will the accounting system need to change? How?

## Unit Cost in the Job-Order Environment

**Objective 1**

Describe the differences between job-order costing and process costing, and identify the types of organizations that would use each method.

We have seen that companies keep track of total and unit costs for a number of reasons, including the generation of financial statements, the determination of profitability, and the making of decisions (for example, what price to charge). However, we have not yet given much thought to the way that the kinds of products or services produced might affect the kind of accounting system to be used.

Manufacturing and service organizations can be divided into two major types depending on whether or not their products/services are unique. Consider Computrain Company. At first, the company sent trainers to individual companies to provide training to employees on the use of standard software packages. One training session was much like another, and the basic cost of each was the same. It may have changed depending on the number of days spent at the client's company or the travel distance from Computrain, but that was the extent of the difference. Certainly the training sessions differed in terms of what software was being taught, but the underlying cost of training did not change. Therefore, Computrain could consider each training session as fairly similar to the others and not bother to break their costs out separately.

However, as Miranda noted, this accounting system would not work with the variety of services that Travis now plans to offer. Training at Computrain's headquarters will require the use of the specialized facility, as well as maintenance and supplies for the facility. (One thing these facilities provide is lots of candy and snacks to keep the trainees "up" and alert.) Clients desiring hardware customization and setup will place different demands on Computrain, from professional time, to supplies, to the purchasing services required from Computrain's still-to-

---

1. This scenario is based on the actual experiences of a mid-sized consulting firm. The names of the company and people involved have been changed to preserve confidentiality.

be-hired system's specialist. Software might have to be modified, again, placing more demands on Computrain's staff. As a result, Computrain Company must tailor its accounting system to its production processes.

## Job-Order Production and Costing

**job**
One distinct unit or set of units.

Companies operating in job-order industries produce a wide variety of products or jobs that are usually quite distinct from each other. Customized or built-to-order products fit into this category, as do services that vary from customer to customer. A **job**, then, is one distinct unit or set of units. For example, a job may consist of a remodelling project or a set of 20 bookcases for new offices. Common job-order processes include printing, construction, furniture making, automobile repair, and beautician services. Ideally every product or service could be tailored to a specific customer.

Improved technology enables companies to produce even more products to special order. For example, Israeli firm Indigo Ltd. developed a new printing system that made it economical to print very small batches of cans, bottles, labels, and so on. Thus, this process would make it feasible to produce 500 beverage cans for the year-end party for a campus organization.[2]

Job-order systems may be used to produce goods for inventory that are subsequently sold in the general market. Often, however, a job is associated with a particular customer order. The key feature of job-order costing is that the cost of one job differs from that of another job, and must be kept track of separately.

**job-order costing system**
A costing system in which costs are collected and assigned to units of production for each individual job.

For job-order production systems, costs are accumulated by job. This approach to assigning costs is called a **job-order costing system**. In a job-order firm, collecting costs by job provides vital information for management. For example, frequently prices are based on costs in a job-order environment.

## Process Production and Costing

Companies in process industries mass-produce large quantities of similar or homogeneous products. Examples of process manufacturers include food, cement, petroleum, and chemical companies. One litre of paint is the same as another litre; one tube of toothpaste is the same as another tube. The important point here is that the cost of one unit of a product is identical to the cost of another. Service firms can also use a process-costing approach. For example, a bank's cheque-clearing department incurs a uniform cost to clear each cheque, no matter the size of the cheque or the name of the person to whom it is written.

**process-costing system**
A costing system that accumulates production costs by process or by department for a given period of time.

Process companies accumulate production costs by process or by department for a given time period. The output for the process for that period is measured. Unit costs are computed by dividing the process costs for the given period by the output of the period. This approach to cost accumulation is known as a **process-costing system**. Exhibit 5–1 summarizes and contrasts the characteristics of job-order and process costing.

**EXHIBIT    5-1**

Comparison of Job-Order and Process Costing

| Job-Order Costing | Process Costing |
|---|---|
| 1. Wide variety of distinct products | 1. Homogeneous products |
| 2. Costs accumulated by job | 2. Costs accumulated by process or department |
| 3. Unit cost computed by dividing total job costs by units produced on that job | 3. Unit cost computed by dividing process costs for a period by units produced in the period |

2. Peter Coy and Neal Sandler, "A Package for Every Person," *Business Week*, 6 February 1995: p. 44.

## Calculating Unit Cost with Job-Order Costing

While the variety of product cost definitions discussed in Chapter 2 apply to both job-order and process costing, we will use the traditional product-costing definition to illustrate job-order costing procedures. That is, production costs consist of direct materials, direct labour, and overhead. Overhead can be assigned using an activity-based approach or functional-based approaches, depending on the need for product-costing accuracy found within a particular job-order company.[3] It is also important in a job-order environment to use predetermined overhead rates, since the completion of a job rarely coincides with the completion of a fiscal year. Therefore, in the remainder of this chapter, we will use normal costing. Recall that normal costing requires us to cost units of production using actual direct materials cost, actual direct labour cost, and overhead applied using one or more predetermined rates.

The unit cost of a job is simply the total cost of materials used on the job, labour worked on the job, and overhead assigned. Although the concept is simple, the practical reality of the computation can be somewhat more complex, especially when there are products that differ from one another. Initially, to illustrate the unit-cost computation, we use only a single unit-level driver to assign overhead. Later, job-order costing procedures are illustrated using the multiple-driver approach of activity-based costing.

Suppose that Stan Johnson forms a new company, Johnson Leathergoods, which specializes in the production of custom leather products. Stan believes that there is a market for one-of-a-kind leather purses, briefcases, and backpacks. In his company's first month of operation, he obtains two orders: the first is for 20 leather backpacks for a local sporting goods store, and the second is for 10 distinctively tooled briefcases for the coaches of a local football team. Stan agrees to provide these orders at a price of cost plus 50 percent.

Let's look at the computation of unit cost for Stan's first order. The backpacks will require direct materials (leather, thread, buckles), direct labour (cutting, sewing, assembling), and overhead. Assume that overhead is assigned using a single unit-level driver, direct labour hours (a plantwide rate). Suppose that the materials cost $1,000 and the direct labour costs $1,080 (120 hours at $9 per hour). If the predetermined overhead rate is $2 per direct labour hour, then the overhead applied to this job is $240 (120 hours at $2 per hour). Now we can see that the total cost of the backpacks is $2,320, and the unit cost is $116, computed as follows:

| | |
|---|---|
| Direct materials | $1,000 |
| Direct labour | 1,080 |
| Overhead | 240 |
| Total cost | $2,320 |
| Number of units | 20 |
| Unit cost | $ 116 |

Since cost is so closely linked to price in this case, it is easy to see that Stan will charge the sporting goods store $3,480 (cost of $2,320 plus 50 percent of $2,320), or $174 per backpack.

This is a simplified example of how Stan would arrive at the total cost of a single job. But how did he know that materials cost $1,000, or that direct labour for this particular job was $1,080? To determine these amounts, Stan would need to keep track of costs using a variety of source documents. We will examine these source documents next.

---

3. Note that the functional-based unit-level approaches to assigning overhead are simply special cases of the more general ABC system. Unit-level systems can be used effectively whenever any one of three conditions is met: (1) the nonunit-level overhead is a small percentage of the total overhead, (2) the products produced in the job environment have the same overhead consumption ratios, or (3) the cost of using both unit-level and nonunit-level drivers exceeds the benefits.

## Keeping Track of Job Costs with Source Documents

**Objective 2**

Identify and set up the source documents used in job-order costing.

**job-order cost sheet**

A document that is subsidiary to the work-in-process account and on which the total costs of materials, labour, and overhead for a single job are accumulated.

Let's take a closer look at the accounting for job-order production by focusing on the source documents that are used to keep track of the costs of jobs.

### Job-Order Cost Sheet

Every time a new job is started, a job-order cost sheet is prepared. The costing of Stan's backpack job, which lists the total cost of materials, labour, and overhead for a single job, is the simplest example of a job-order cost sheet. A **job-order cost sheet** is prepared for every job; it is a subsidiary record to the Work in Process account and is the primary document for accumulating all costs related to a particular job. Exhibit 5–2 illustrates a simple job-order cost sheet.

Johnson Leathergoods had only two jobs in January, and Stan can easily identify them by calling them "backpacks" and "briefcases." Some companies find that the customer's name is sufficient to identify a job. For example, a construction company may identify its custom houses as the "Smith residence" or the "Malkovich residence." As more and more jobs are produced, a company will usually find it most convenient to number them. Thus, you will see Job 13, Job 22, and Job 44. Perhaps the job number starts with the year, so that the first job of 2004 is 2004-1, the second is 2004-2, and so on. The key point is that each job is unique and must have a uniquely identifiable name. This name, or job-order number, heads the job-order cost sheet.

In a manual accounting system, the job-order cost sheet is a paper document. In automated accounting systems the cost sheet corresponds to a record in a work-in-process master file. The collection of all job cost sheets defines a **work-in-process file**. Work in process consists of all incomplete work. The balance in the Work in Process account at the end of a month would be the total cost of all the job-order cost sheets of the incomplete jobs. In a manual system, the file would be located in a filing cabinet, whereas in an automated system it is stored electronically. In either system, the file of job-order cost sheets serves as a subsidiary work-in-process ledger.

**work-in-process file**

A file that is the collection of all job-order cost sheets.

Both manual and automated systems require the same kind of data in order to accumulate costs and track the progress of a job. A job cost system must have the ability to identify the quantity of direct materials, direct labour, and overhead consumed by each job. In other words, documentation and procedures are needed to associate the manufacturing inputs used by a job with the job itself. This need is satisfied through the use of materials requisitions for direct materials, time tickets for direct labour, and source documents for other activity drivers that might be used in applying overhead.

**EXHIBIT   5-2**

Job-Order Cost Sheet

**Johnson Leathergoods**
**Job Order Cost Sheet**

Job Name:   Backpacks
Date Started:   January 3, 2004
Date Competed:   January 29, 2004

| | | |
|---|---:|---|
| Direct materials | $1,000 | |
| Direct labour | 1,080 | |
| Applied overhead | 240 | |
| Total cost | $2,320 | |
| Number of units | 20 | |
| Unit cost | $116 | |

## Materials Requisitions

The cost of direct materials is assigned to a job by the use of a source document known as a **materials requisition form**, illustrated in Exhibit 5–3. Notice that the form asks for the type, quantity, and unit cost of the direct materials issued and, most importantly, for the job number. Using this form, the cost accounting department can enter the cost of direct materials onto the correct job-order cost sheet.

If the accounting system is automated, this posting may entail directly entering the direct material data at a computer. A program enters the cost of direct materials into the record for each job.

In addition to providing essential information for assigning direct materials costs to jobs, the materials requisition form may also have other data items, such as a requisition number, a date, and a signature. These data items are useful for maintaining proper control over a firm's inventory of direct materials. The signature, for example, transfers responsibility for the materials from the storage area to the person receiving the materials, usually a production supervisor.

No attempt is made to trace the cost of other materials, such as supplies, lubricants, and so on, to a particular job. You will recall that these indirect materials are assigned to jobs through the predetermined overhead rate.

## Job Time Tickets

Direct labour also must be associated with each particular job. A source document known as a **time ticket** (see Exhibit 5–4) is the means by which direct labour costs are assigned to individual jobs. Each day, an employee fills out a time ticket that identifies his or her name, wage rate, and hours worked on each job. These time tickets are collected and transferred to the cost accounting department, where the information is used to post the cost of direct labour to individual jobs. Again, in an automated system, posting involves entering the data into the computer.

Time tickets are used only for direct labourers. Since indirect labour is common to all jobs, these costs belong to overhead and are allocated using one or more predetermined overhead rates.

**EXHIBIT 5-3**

Materials Requisition Form

| | | | Material Requisition Number 12 |
|---|---|---|---|
| Date _____ January 11, 2004 _____ | | | |
| Department _____ Assembly _____ | | | |
| Job Number _____ Briefcases _____ | | | |

| Description | Quantity | Cost/Unit | Total Cost |
|---|---|---|---|
| Buckles | 10 | $3 | $30 |
| | | | |
| | | | |
| | | | |

Authorized Signature _____ *Jim Lawson* _____

EXHIBIT    5-4

Job Time Ticket

| Employee Number | | 4 | | | Job Time Ticket Number 8 |
| Name | | Ed Wilson | | | |
| Date | | January 12, 2004 | | | |

| Start Time | Stop Time | Total Time | Hourly Rate | Amount | Job Number |
|---|---|---|---|---|---|
| 8:00 | 10:00 | 2 | $9 | $18 | Backpacks |
| 10:00 | 11:00 | 1 | $9 | 9 | Briefcases |
| 11:00 | 12:00 | 1 | $9 | 9 | Backpacks |
| 1:00 | 5:00 | 4 | $9 | 36 | Backpacks |

Approved by _Jim Lawson_
Department Supervisor

## Other Source Documents

The use of activity-based costing to assign overhead to jobs clearly requires the company to keep track of more than one activity driver. These other bases must be accounted for as well. That is, the actual amount used of each of the drivers (for example, machine hours, number of purchase orders, number of setups) must be collected and posted to the job cost sheets. If the amount of the driver is already accounted for or easy to accumulate (for example, number of purchase orders), no new source document is needed. However, if the driver is not otherwise being kept track of, a source document must be developed. For example, a source document that will track the machine hours used by each job can be modelled on job time tickets.

All completed job-order cost sheets of a company can serve as a subsidiary ledger for the finished goods inventory. In a manual accounting system, the completed sheets would be transferred from the work-in-process files to the finished goods inventory file. In an automated accounting system, an updating run would delete the finished job from the work-in-process master file and add this record to the finished goods master file. In either case, adding the totals of all completed job-order cost sheets gives the cost of finished goods inventory at any point in time. As finished goods are sold and shipped, the cost records would be pulled (or deleted) from the finished goods inventory file. These records then form the basis for calculating a period's cost of goods sold. We will examine the flow of costs through these accounts next.

## The Flow of Costs Through the Accounts

**Objective 3**

Discuss the cost flows associated with job-order costing.

When we talk about cost flow, we are talking about the way we account for costs from the point at which they are incurred to the point at which they are recognized as an expense on the income statement. Our principal interest in a job-order system is the flow of manufacturing costs. Accordingly, we begin with a description of exactly how the three manufacturing cost elements—direct materials, direct labour, and overhead—flow through Work in Process into Finished Goods and finally into Cost of Goods Sold.

Let's continue to use the simplified job-shop environment provided by our example of Johnson Leathergoods. To start the business, Stan leased a small building and bought the necessary production equipment. Recall that he finalized two orders for January: one for 20 backpacks for a local sporting goods store, and a second for 10 briefcases for the coaches of a local football team. Both orders will be sold for manufacturing cost plus 50 percent. Stan expects to average two orders per month for the first year of operation.

Stan created two job-order cost sheets, one for each order. The first job-order cost sheet is for the backpacks, the second is for the briefcases.

## Accounting for Materials

Since the company is just beginning business, it has no beginning inventories. To produce the orders in January and have a supply of materials on hand at the beginning of February, Stan purchases, on account, $2,500 of raw materials (leather, webbing, thread, buckles, etc.).

Physically, materials are moved to a materials storeroom. In the accounting records, the Materials and Accounts Payable accounts are increased by $2,500.[4] Materials is an inventory account. It is also the controlling account for all materials. When materials are purchased, the cost of these materials "flows" into the raw materials account.

When the production supervisor needs materials for a job, materials are removed from the storeroom. The cost of the materials is removed from the Materials account and added to the Work in Process account. Of course, in a job-order environment, the materials moved from the storeroom to workstations on the plant floor must be "tagged" with the appropriate job name. Suppose that Stan needs $1,000 of materials for the backpacks and $500 for the briefcases.

The job-order cost sheet for backpacks would show $1,000 for direct materials, and the job-order cost sheet for the briefcases would show $500 for direct materials. Exhibit 5–5 summarizes the materials cost flows into these two jobs.

## Accounting for Direct Labour Cost

Since two jobs were in progress during January, Stan must determine not only the total number of direct labour hours worked, but also the time worked on each job. The backpacks required 120 hours at an average wage rate of $9 per hour, for a total direct labour cost of $1,080. For the briefcases, the total was $450, based on 50 hours at an average hourly wage of $9. The summary of the labour cost flows is

---

**EXHIBIT 5-5**

Summary of Materials Cost Flows

**Materials Account**

| | |
|---|---|
| Beginning balance | 0 |
| Purchases | $2,500 |
| Direct materials used | 1,500 |
| Ending balance | $1,000 |

| **Job-Order Cost Sheet** **Job: 20 Backpacks** | | **Job-Order Cost Sheet** **Job: 10 Briefcases** | |
|---|---|---|---|
| Direct materials | $1,000 | Direct materials | $500 |
| Direct labour | | Direct labour | |
| Overhead applied | _____ | Overhead applied | _____ |
| Total cost | | Total cost | |
| Number of units | 20 | Number of units | 10 |
| Unit cost | | Unit cost | |

---

4. See the appendix of this chapter for the journal entries to record these cost flows.

given in Exhibit 5–6. Notice that the direct labour costs assigned to the two jobs exactly equal the total assigned to Work in Process. Remember that the labour cost flows reflect only direct labour cost. Indirect labour is assigned as part of overhead.

## Accounting for Overhead

The use of normal costing means that actual overhead costs are never assigned directly to jobs. Overhead is applied to each individual job using a *predetermined* rate or rates. Actual overhead costs incurred must be accounted for as well, but on an overall (not job-specific) basis. First, we will describe how to account for applied overhead using ABC. Next, we will look at the application of overhead using a plantwide rate. Then, we will discuss accounting for actual overhead.

### ABC and Job-Order Costing

Recall that activity-based costing requires a company to identify production activities and related activity drivers. Then a rate is computed for each activity (or homogeneous sets of activities). Suppose that Stan estimates annual overhead of $9,600, and that this amount can be broken down into three categories: purchasing (locating vendors, preparing purchase documents, and purchasing materials), machining (power, lubricants, and use of machines), and a pool of unit-level activities called "other." Purchasing cost is driven by the number of purchase orders, machining cost is driven by machine hours, and the unit-level pool costs are assigned using number of direct labour hours. The budgeted cost for each activity pool and the expected demands for each driver are as follows:

| Activity Pool | Cost | Cost Driver | Demand |
|---|---|---|---|
| Purchasing | $3,000 | Purchase orders | 100 |
| Machining | $4,200 | Machine hours | 2,800 |
| Other | $2,400 | Direct labour hours | 4,800 |

Activity-based rates would be:

Purchasing: $3,000/100 = $30 per purchase order

Machining: $4,200/2,800 = $1.50 per machine hour

Other: $2,400/4,800 = $0.50 per direct labour hour

In order to assign overhead costs to each job, we must know the demand each job places on the three activity drivers. The demands of the two jobs follow:

**EXHIBIT**  **5-6**

Summary of Direct Labour Cost Flows

| Wages Payable | | | | |
|---|---|---|---|---|
| Direct labour hours | 170 | | | |
| × Wage rate | $ 9 | | | |
| Direct labour cost | $1,530 | | | |

| Job-Order Cost Sheet Job: 20 Backpacks | | Job-Order Cost Sheet Job: 10 Briefcases | |
|---|---|---|---|
| Direct materials | $1,000 | Direct materials | $500 |
| Direct labour | 1,080 | Direct labour | 450 |
| Overhead applied | _____ | Overhead applied | _____ |
| Total cost | | Total cost | |
| Number of units | 20 | Number of units | 10 |
| Unit cost | | Unit cost | |

|  | Backpacks | Briefcases |
|---|---|---|
| Purchase orders | 3 | 1 |
| Machine hours | 60 | 30 |
| Direct labour hours | 120 | 50 |

Overhead assigned to each job is calculated as follows:

|  |  | Backpacks | Briefcases |
|---|---|---|---|
| Purchasing | (3 × $30); (1 × $30) | $ 90 | $ 30 |
| Machining | (60 × $1.50); (30 × $1.50) | 90 | 45 |
| Other | (120 × $0.50); (50 × $0.50) | 60 | 25 |
| Total overhead applied |  | $240 | $100 |

Overhead applied using ABC is posted to the appropriate job-order cost sheet: $240 for the backpack job and $100 for the briefcase job. In normal costing, only applied overhead ever enters the job-order cost sheets and the Work in Process account.

### Applying Overhead Using Functional Approaches

Overhead costs can also be assigned using plantwide overhead rates or departmental overhead rates. The use of a plantwide rate has the virtue of being simple and reduces data collection requirements. To illustrate these two features, recall that total estimated overhead costs for Johnson Leathergoods are $9,600. Assume that direct labour hours is the measure used to calculate a plantwide rate, with 4,800 total budgeted direct labour hours. Accordingly, the predetermined overhead rate is:

$$\text{Overhead rate} = \$9,600/4,800 = \$2 \text{ per direct labour hour}$$

For the backpacks, with a total of 120 hours worked, the amount of applied overhead cost posted to the job-order cost sheet is $240 ($2 × 120). For the briefcases, the applied overhead cost is $100 ($2 × 50). Compared to the ABC assignments, there are fewer calculations. Note also that assigning overhead to jobs requires only a rate and the direct labour hours used by the job. Since direct labour hours are already being collected to assign direct labour cost to jobs, overhead assignment would not require any additional data collection.

Unfortunately, use of a plantwide rate may also significantly reduce the accuracy of cost assignment. The use of a single unit-level driver may not reflect the actual consumption of resources by individual jobs. For example, a third job that requires 6 purchase orders, 200 machine hours, and 100 direct labour hours would have an overhead assignment of $530 [(6 × $30) + (200 × $1.50) + (100 × $0.50)] using ABC, but only $200 (100 × $2) using a unit-level rate. Clearly this job would be undercosted using a single rate, because the impact of increased machine usage and purchasing is ignored when direct labour hours alone is used as the driver. This undercosting could have an adverse effect on product-mix decisions and pricing decisions (among others).

### Accounting for Actual Overhead Costs

We have applied overhead to the two jobs, but what about the actual overhead costs incurred? To illustrate how actual overhead costs are recorded, assume that Johnson Leathergoods incurred the following indirect costs for January:

| Lease payment | $200 |
|---|---|
| Utilities | 50 |
| Equipment amortization | 100 |
| Indirect labour | 65 |
| Total overhead costs | $415 |

Notice that these overhead costs reflect what is spent by account category, not by activity. These resources were used to enable the three activities—purchasing, machining, and other (unit-level) activities—to be performed. For an ABC system, determining the actual cost of activities requires that these costs be unbundled and assigned to individual activities. For example, how much of the indirect labour cost belongs to purchasing? When separate support departments exist, activity costs are traced to them and then assigned to products on the basis of usage. This is discussed in Chapter 7. What is important at this point is to understand that the actual overhead costs never enter the job-order cost sheets or the Work in Process account. The usual procedure is to record actual overhead costs to the Overhead Control account. Then, at the end of the period, actual overhead is reconciled with applied overhead, and any variance is closed to the appropriate accounts. Recall from Chapter 4, an immaterial overhead variance is usually closed to Cost of Goods Sold. For Johnson Leathergoods at the end of January, the actual overhead of $415 and applied overhead of $340 produce underapplied overhead of $75 ($415 – $340).

The flow of overhead costs is summarized in Exhibit 5–7. Note that the total overhead applied from all jobs is entered in the Work in Process account. Therefore, the information in Exhibit 5–7 is pertinent to both ABC and a plantwide overhead rate.

Let's take a moment to recap. So far, we've seen that the cost of a job includes direct materials, direct labour, and applied overhead. We have seen how each cost is entered into the job-order cost sheet and that Work in Process, at any point in time, is the total of the costs on all open job-order cost sheets. Now let's finish a job and follow it out of Work in Process into Finished Goods and Cost of Goods Sold.

## Accounting for Finished Goods

We have already seen what takes place when a job is completed. The direct materials, direct labour, and applied overhead amounts are totalled to yield the manufacturing cost of the job. This job-order cost sheet is then transferred to a finished goods file. Simultaneously, the costs of the completed job are transferred from the Work in Process account to the Finished Goods account.

For example, assume that the backpacks were completed in January with the completed cost sheet shown in Exhibit 5–8. Since the backpacks are completed,

**EXHIBIT   5-7**

Summary of Overhead Cost Flows

| Actual Overhead | | Applied Overhead | |
|---|---|---|---|
| Leases | $200 | Direct labour hours | 170 |
| Utilities | 50 | Overhead rate | $ 2 |
| Equipment amortization | 100 | Total applied overhead | $340 |
| Indirect labour | 65 | | |
| Total actual overhead | $415 | | |

| Job-Order Cost Sheet Job: 20 Backpacks | | Job-Order Cost Sheet Job: 10 Briefcases | |
|---|---|---|---|
| Direct materials | $1,000 | Direct materials | $500 |
| Direct labour | 1,080 | Direct labour | 450 |
| Overhead applied | 240 | Overhead applied | 100 |
| Total cost | | Total cost | |
| Number of units | 20 | Number of units | 10 |
| Unit cost | | Unit cost | |

EXHIBIT 5-8

Summary of Finished
Goods Cost Flows

| Job-Order Cost Sheet Job: 20 Backpacks | | Job-Order Cost Sheet Job: 10 Briefcases | |
|---|---|---|---|
| Direct materials | $1,000 | Direct materials | $500 |
| Direct labour | 1,080 | Direct labour | 450 |
| Overhead applied | 240 | Overhead applied | 100 |
| Total cost | $2,320 | Total cost | $1,050 |
| Number of units | 20 | Number of units | 10 |
| Unit cost | $ 116 | Unit cost* | |

**Finished Goods Account**

| | |
|---|---|
| Backpacks | $2,320 |

\* There is no reason to show the unit costs for the briefcases, since they are still in process.

the total manufacturing costs of $2,320 must be transferred from the Work in Process account to the Finished Goods account.

The completion of a job is an important step in the flow of manufacturing costs. The cost of the completed job must be removed from work in process, added to finished goods, and, eventually, added to the cost of goods sold expense on the income statement. To ensure accuracy in computing these costs, a cost of goods manufactured statement is prepared. The statement of cost of goods manufactured presented in Exhibit 5–9 summarizes the production activity of Johnson Leathergoods for January. It is important to note that applied overhead is used to arrive at the cost of goods manufactured. Both work-in-process and finished goods inventories are carried at normal cost rather than actual cost.

EXHIBIT 5-9

Statement of Cost of
Goods Manufactured

**Johnson Leathergoods Company**
**Statement of Cost of Goods Manufactured**
**For the Month Ended January 31, 2004**

| | | |
|---|---|---|
| Direct materials: | | |
| Beginning raw materials inventory | $ 0 | |
| Purchases of raw materials | 2,500 | |
| Total raw materials available | $2,500 | |
| Ending raw materials | 1,000 | |
| Total raw materials used | | $1,500 |
| Direct labour | | 1,530 |
| Overhead: | | |
| Lease | $ 200 | |
| Utilities | 50 | |
| Amortization | 100 | |
| Indirect labour | 65 | |
| Total actual overhead | $ 415 | |
| Less: Underapplied overhead | 75 | |
| Overhead applied | | 340 |
| Current manufacturing costs | | $3,370 |
| Add: Beginning work in process | | 0 |
| Total manufacturing costs | | $3,370 |
| Less: Ending work in process | | 1,050 |
| Cost of goods manufactured | | $2,320 |

Notice that ending work in process is $1,050. Where did we obtain this figure? Of the two jobs, the backpacks were finished and transferred to finished goods. The briefcases are still in process, however, and the manufacturing costs assigned thus far are direct materials, $500; direct labour, $450; and overhead applied, $100. The total of these costs gives the cost of ending work in process. You may want to check these figures against the job-order cost sheet for briefcases given in Exhibit 5–8.

## Accounting for Cost of Goods Sold

In a job-order company, units can be produced for a particular customer or they can be produced for inventory and later sold. If a job is produced specially for a customer (as with the backpacks), then when that job is shipped to the customer, the cost of the finished job becomes the cost of the goods sold. When the backpacks are completed, we need to recognize that Cost of Goods Sold increases by $2,320 while Work in Process decreases by the same amount. Then we need to recognize the sale by increasing both Sales Revenue and Accounts Receivable by $3,480 (cost plus 50 percent of cost or $2,320 + $1,160).

**normal cost of goods sold**

The cost of goods sold before adjustment for any overhead variance.

A statement of cost of goods sold is usually prepared at the end of each reporting period (for example, monthly and quarterly). Exhibit 5–10 presents such a statement for Johnson Leathergoods for January. Typically, the overhead variance is not material and, therefore, is closed to Cost of Goods Sold. Cost of goods sold before adjustment for an overhead variance is called **normal cost of goods sold**. After the adjustment for the period's overhead variance takes place, the result is called the **adjusted cost of goods sold**. It is this latter figure that appears as an expense on the income statement.

**adjusted cost of goods sold**

The cost of goods sold after all adjustments for overhead variance are made.

However, closing the overhead variance to the Cost of Goods Sold account is often not done until the end of the year. Variances are expected each month because of nonuniform production and nonuniform actual overhead costs. As the year unfolds, these monthly variances should, by and large, offset each other so that the year-end variance is small, assuming that the predetermined overhead rate is reasonable. Nonetheless, to illustrate how the year-end overhead variance would be treated, we will close out the overhead variance experienced by Johnson Leathergoods in January.

Suppose the backpacks had not been ordered by a customer but had been produced for inventory to be sold through a subsequent marketing effort. Then, all 20 units might not be sold at the same time. Assume that on January 31, 15 backpacks were sold. In this case, the cost of goods sold figure is the unit cost times the number of units sold, or $1,740 ($116 × 15). The remainder, or $580 ($116 × 5), would be recorded in Finished Goods Inventory. The unit-cost figure is found on the cost sheet in Exhibit 5–8.

Manufacturing cost flows, however, are not the only cost flows experienced by a company. Nonmanufacturing costs are also incurred. A description of how we account for these costs follows.

## Accounting for Nonmanufacturing Costs

Recall that costs associated with selling and general administrative activities are classified as nonmanufacturing costs. According to the traditional product cost definition, these costs are period costs and are never assigned to the product. They are not part of the manufacturing cost flows. They do not belong to the overhead category and are treated as a totally separate category.

To illustrate how these type of costs are accounted for, assume that Johnson Leathergoods had the following additional costs in January:

**EXHIBIT   5-10**

Statement of Cost of
Goods Sold

| Statement of Cost of Goods Sold | |
| --- | ---: |
| Beginning finished goods inventory | $      0 |
| Cost of goods manufactured | 2,320 |
| Goods available for sale | $2,320 |
| Less: Ending finished goods inventory | 0 |
| Normal cost of goods sold | $2,320 |
| Add: Underapplied overhead | 75 |
| Adjusted cost of goods sold | $2,395 |

| | |
| --- | ---: |
| Advertising circulars | $ 75 |
| Sales commission | 125 |
| Office salaries | 500 |
| Amortization, office equipment | 50 |

We can see that the first two costs fall into the selling expense category and the last two into the administrative expense category. So the selling expense control account would increase by $200 ($75 + $125) and the administrative expense control account would increase by $550 ($500 + $50). Control accounts accumulate all of the selling and administrative expenses for a period. At the end of the period, all of these costs flow to the period's income statement. An income statement for Johnson Leathergoods is shown in Exhibit 5–11.

With the description of the accounting procedures for selling and administrative expenses completed, the basic essentials of a normal job-order costing system are also complete.

**EXHIBIT   5-11**

Income Statement

| Johnson Leathergoods Company<br>Income Statement<br>For the Month Ended January 31, 2004 | | |
| --- | ---: | ---: |
| Sales | | $3,480 |
| Less: Cost of goods sold | | 2,395 |
| Gross margin | | $1,085 |
| Less selling and administrative expenses: | | |
| Selling expenses | $200 | |
| Administrative expenses | 550 | 750 |
| Net income | | $   335 |

*Omit*

# Appendix: Journal Entries Associated with Job-Order Costing

**Objective 4**

Prepare the journal entries associated with job-order costing.

We have looked at the flow of costs through the accounts in a job-order costing system, but how are the transactions actually entered into the accounting system? We do this by making journal entries and posting them to the accounts.

Let's summarize the transactions that occurred during January for Johnson Leathergoods.

1. Materials costing $2,500 were purchased on account.
2. Materials costing $1,500 were requisitioned for use in production.
3. Direct labour costing $1,530 was recognized (that is, not paid in cash but shown as a liability in the wages payable account).

4. Overhead was applied to production at the rate of $2 per direct labour hour. A total of 170 direct labour hours were worked.
5. Actual overhead costs of $415 were incurred.
6. The backpack job was completed and transferred to finished goods.
7. The backpack job was sold at cost plus 50 percent.
8. Underapplied overhead was closed to cost of goods sold.

The journal entries for each of the above transactions are as follows:

|  |  | Debit | Credit |
|---|---|---|---|
| 1. | Materials | 2,500 |  |
|  | Accounts Payable |  | 2,500 |
| 2. | Work in Process | 1,500 |  |
|  | Materials |  | 1,500 |
| 3. | Work in Process | 1,530 |  |
|  | Wages Payable |  | 1,530 |
| 4. | Work in Process | 340 |  |
|  | Overhead Control |  | 340 |
| 5. | Overhead Control | 415 |  |
|  | Lease Payable |  | 200 |
|  | Utilities Payable |  | 50 |
|  | Accumulated Amortization—Equipment |  | 100 |
|  | Wages Payable |  | 65 |
| 6. | Finished Goods | 2,320 |  |
|  | Work in Process |  | 2,320 |
| 7. | Cost of Goods Sold | 2,320 |  |
|  | Finished Goods |  | 2,320 |
|  | Accounts Receivable | 3,480 |  |
|  | Sales Revenue |  | 3,480 |
| 8. | Cost of Goods Sold | 75 |  |
|  | Overhead Control |  | 75 |

Let's look more closely at each of the journal entries. Journal entry (1) shows that the purchase of materials increases the materials account as well as the accounts payable account. In other words, the company has increased both assets (material on hand) and liabilities (accounts payable).

Entry (2) shows the transfer from the materials storeroom to the factory floor. Materials are being used in production. Therefore, the work in process account goes up, but the materials account goes down.

Entry (3) recognizes the use of direct labour in production. The amount of direct labour wages is added to work in process and to the liability account, Wages Payable.

Entry (4) records the application of overhead to the jobs. 170 direct labour hours are worked and the overhead rate is $2 per direct labour hour. Thus $340 of overhead is applied to the jobs. Notice that applying overhead increases the work in process account and is credited to Overhead Control.

Entry (5) shows that the actual overhead incurred is debited to Overhead Control. Various payable accounts are credited.

Entry (6) shows the transfer of the completed backpack job from Work in Process to Finished Goods. We find the appropriate cost by referring to the job-cost sheet for backpacks.

Entry (7) consists of two journal entries. First, we recognize the cost of the backpack job by debiting Cost of Goods Sold for the cost of the job and crediting Finished Goods. This entry reflects the physical movement of the backpacks out of the warehouse and to the customer. The second entry shows the sale. It is important to separate the cost of the job from the sale; two entries are required.

Entry (8) closes the balance in the overhead control account (the difference between the applied overhead and the actual overhead) to Cost of Goods Sold. There is an overhead variance of $75 underapplied. To bring the balance to zero, Overhead Control is credited $75 and Cost of Goods Sold debited $75.

Exhibit 5–12 summarizes the journal entries and posts them to the appropriate accounts.

**EXHIBIT 5-12**

Posting of Journal Entries to Accounts

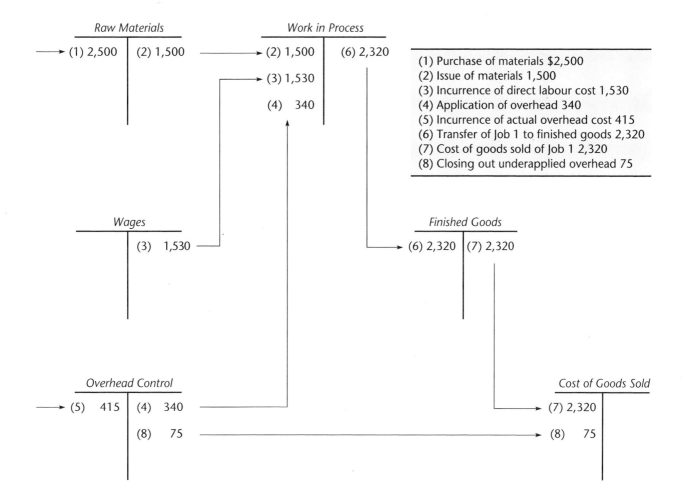

(1) Purchase of materials $2,500
(2) Issue of materials 1,500
(3) Incurrence of direct labour cost 1,530
(4) Application of overhead 340
(5) Incurrence of actual overhead cost 415
(6) Transfer of Job 1 to finished goods 2,320
(7) Cost of goods sold of Job 1 2,320
(8) Closing out underapplied overhead 75

## Summary of Learning Objectives

**1. Describe the differences between job-order costing and process costing, and identify the types of organizations that would use each method.**

Job-order costing and process costing are two major cost assignment systems. Job-order systems are used for companies that produce a wide variety of heterogeneous (unique) products. Process costing is used by companies that mass-produce a homogeneous product.

**2. Identify and set up the source documents used in job-order costing.**

In job-order costing, the key document or record for accumulating manufacturing costs is the job-order cost sheet. Materials requisition forms (for direct materials), time tickets (for direct labour), and source documents for accumulating manufacturing activity information are the source documents needed to assign manufacturing costs to jobs.

**3. Discuss the cost flows associated with job-order costing.**

In job-order costing the cost of each job is accumulated on the job-order cost sheet. The total job cost consists of actual direct materials, actual direct labour, and overhead applied using a predetermined rate (or rates). The balance in work in process consists of the balances of all open (incomplete) jobs. When a job is finished its cost is transferred from Work in Process to Finished Goods and then, when sold, to Cost of Goods Sold.

**4. Prepare the journal entries associated with job-order costing. (Appendix)**

In job-order costing, materials and direct labour are charged to the work in process account (raw materials and payroll are credited, respectively). Overhead costs are assigned to Work in Process using a predetermined rate. Actual overhead costs are accumulated in the overhead control account. The cost of completed units is credited to Work in Process and debited to Finished Goods. When goods are sold, the cost is debited to Cost of Goods Sold and credited to Finished Goods.

## Key Terms

| | | |
|---|---|---|
| Adjusted cost of goods sold  186 | Job-order costing system  176 | Process-costing system  176 |
| Job  176 | Materials requisition form  179 | Time ticket  179 |
| Job-order cost sheet  178 | Normal cost of goods sold  186 | Work-in-process file  178 |

## Review Problems

## I. JOB COST USING PLANTWIDE AND DEPARTMENTAL OVERHEAD RATES

Timter Company uses a normal job-order costing system. The company has two departments through which most jobs pass. Selected budgeted and actual data for the past year follow:

|  | Department A | Department B |
|---|---|---|
| Budgeted overhead | $100,000 | $500,000 |
| Actual overhead | $110,000 | $520,000 |
| Expected activity (direct labour hours) | 50,000 | 10,000 |
| Expected machine hours | 10,000 | 50,000 |
| Actual direct labour hours | 51,000 | 9,000 |
| Actual machine hours | 10,500 | 52,000 |

During the year, several jobs were completed. Data pertaining to one such job, Job 10, follow:

| | |
|---|---|
| Direct materials | $20,000 |
| Direct labour cost: | |
| Department A (5,000 hours × $9) | $45,000 |
| Department B (1,000 hours × $9) | $ 9,000 |
| Machine hours used: | |
| Department A | 100 |
| Department B | 1,200 |
| Units produced | 10,000 |

Timter Company uses a plantwide predetermined overhead rate to assign overhead to jobs. Direct labour hours (DLH) is used to compute the predetermined overhead rate.

### Required:
1. Compute the predetermined overhead rate.
2. Using the predetermined rate, compute the per-unit manufacturing cost for Job 10.
3. Recalculate the unit manufacturing cost for Job 10 using departmental overhead rates. Use direct labour hours for Department A and machine hours for Department B. Explain why this approach provides a more accurate unit cost.

### Solution
1. The predetermined overhead rate is $600,000/60,000 = $10 per DLH. Add the budgeted overhead for the two departments and divide by the total expected direct labour hours (DLH = 50,000 + 10,000).

2. Per unit cost:

| | |
|---|---|
| Direct materials | $ 20,000 |
| Direct labour | 54,000 |
| Overhead ($10 × 6,000 DLH) | 60,000 |
| Total job cost | $134,000 |
| Unit cost ($134,000/10,000) | $ 13.40 |

3. Per unit cost:

The predetermined rate for Department A is $100,000/50,000 = $2 per DLH. The predetermined rate for Department B is $500,000/50,000 = $10 per machine hour.

| | |
|---|---:|
| Direct materials | $20,000 |
| Direct labour | 54,000 |
| Overhead: | |
| Department A ($2 × 5,000) | 10,000 |
| Department B ($10 × 1,200) | 12,000 |
| Total manufacturing costs | $96,000 |
| Unit cost ($96,000/10,000) | $ 9.60 |

Overhead assignment using departmental rates is more accurate because there is a higher correlation with the overhead assigned and the overhead consumed. Notice that Job 10 spends most of its time in Department A, the least overhead-intensive (in terms of cost) of the two departments. Departmental rates reflect this differential time and consumption better than plantwide rates do.

## II. CALCULATION OF WORK IN PROCESS AND COST OF GOODS SOLD WITH MULTIPLE JOBS

Greenthumb Landscape Design designs landscape plans and plants the material for clients. On April 1, 2004, there were three jobs in process: Jobs 68, 69, and 70. During April, two more jobs were started: Jobs 71 and 72. By April 30, Jobs 69, 70, and 72 were completed and sold. The following data were gathered:

| | Job 68 | Job 69 | Job 70 | Job 71 | Job 72 |
|---|---:|---:|---:|---:|---:|
| April 1, Balance | $540 | $1,230 | $990 | — | — |
| Direct material added | 700 | 560 | 75 | $3,500 | $2,750 |
| Direct labour added | 500 | 600 | 90 | 2,500 | 2,000 |

Overhead is applied at the rate of 120 percent of direct labour cost. Jobs are sold at cost plus 40 percent. Operating expenses for April totalled $3,670.

**Required:**

1. Prepare job-order cost sheets for each job as of April 30.
2. Calculate the ending balance in work in process (as of April 30) and cost of goods sold for April.
3. Construct an income statement for Greenthumb Landscape Design for the month of April.

**Solution**

1. Job-order cost sheets:

| | Job 68 | Job 69 | Job 70 | Job 71 | Job 72 |
|---|---:|---:|---:|---:|---:|
| April 1, Balance | $ 540 | $1,230 | $ 990 | — | — |
| Direct material added | 700 | 560 | 75 | $3,500 | $2,750 |
| Direct labour added | 500 | 600 | 90 | 2,500 | 2,000 |
| Applied overhead | 600 | 720 | 108 | 3,000 | 2,400 |
| Totals | $2,340 | $3,110 | $1,263 | $9,000 | $7,150 |

2. Ending balance in work in process (Jobs 68 and 71) = $2,340 + 9,000
$$= \$11,340$$

Cost of goods sold for April (Jobs 69, 70, and 72) = $3,110 + 1,263 + 7,150
$$= \$11,523$$

3.

**Greenthumb Landscape Design**
**Income Statement**
**For the Month Ended April 30, 2004**

| | |
|---|---:|
| Sales ($11,523 ¥ 140%) | $16,132 |
| Cost of goods sold | 11,523 |
| Gross margin | $ 4,609 |
| Less: Operating expenses | 3,670 |
| Operating income | $   939 |

## Questions for Writing and Discussion

1. Explain the differences between job-order costing and process costing.

2. Wilson Company has a predetermined overhead rate of $5 per direct labour hour. The job-order cost sheet for Job 145 shows 1,000 direct labour hours costing $10,000 and materials requisitions totalling $7,500. Job 145 had 500 units completed and transferred to finished goods. What is the cost per unit for Job 145?

3. Why are the accounting requirements for job-order costing more demanding than those for process costing?

4. Give some examples of service organizations that might use job-order costing, and explain why they would do so.

5. Suppose that you and a friend decide to set up a lawnmowing service next summer. Describe the source documents that you would need to account for your activities.

6. How is job-order costing related to profitability analysis? to pricing?

7. What are some differences between a manual job-order costing system and an automated job-order costing system?

8. What is the role of materials requisition forms in a job-order costing system? time tickets? predetermined overhead rates?

## Exercises

**5–1**

*Job-Order Costing versus Process Costing*

**LO1**

Identify each of the following types of businesses as either job-order or process.

a. paint manufacturing
b. auto manufacturing
c. toy manufacturing
d. custom cabinet making
e. airplane manufacturing (e.g. 767s)
f. personal computer assembly
g. furniture making
h. custom furniture making

i. dental services
j. hospital services
k. paper manufacturing
l. auto repair
m. architectural services
n. landscape design services
o. light bulb manufacturing

**5–2**

Job-Order versus
Process Costing

LO1

For each of the following types of industries, give an example of a company that would use job-order costing. Then give an example of a company that would use process costing.

1. auto manufacturing
2. furniture manufacturing
3. auto repair
4. costume making

**5–3**

Applying Overhead to
Jobs; Costing Jobs

LO2, LO3

Corbin Company is an engineering design firm that builds computer-controlled machinery to client specifications. On May 1, Jobs 345 and 346 were in process with the following costs:

|                    | Job 345   | Job 346   |
| ------------------ | --------- | --------- |
| Direct materials   | $ 5,720   | $15,400   |
| Direct labour      | 8,000     | 22,000    |
| Applied overhead   | 6,800     | 8,700     |
| May 1 balance      | $20,520   | $56,100   |

During May, Jobs 347 and 348 were started. Data on May costs for all jobs are as follows:

|                    | Job 345   | Job 346   | Job 347  | Job 348  |
| ------------------ | --------- | --------- | -------- | -------- |
| Direct materials   | $13,960   | $ 7,000   | $ 350    | $4,800   |
| Direct labour      | 13,800    | 10,000    | 1,500    | 4,000    |

Job 346 was completed on May 28, and the client was billed at cost plus 50 percent. All other jobs remained in process.

**Required:**

1. Calculate the overhead rate based on direct labour cost.
2. Calculate the overhead applied to each job during the month of May.
3. Prepare job-order cost sheets for each job as of the end of May.
4. Calculate the balance in Work in Process on May 31.
5. What is the selling price of Job 346?

**5–4**

Applying Overhead to
Jobs; Costing Jobs

LO3

LaSalle, Inc., designs and builds sheds and outbuildings for individual customers. On August 1, there were two jobs in process: Job 214 with a beginning balance of $13,400; and Job 215 with a beginning balance of $9,760. LaSalle applies overhead at the rate of $16 per direct labour hour. Direct labour is paid an average of $10 per hour.

During August, Jobs 216 and 217 were started. Data on August costs for all jobs are as follows:

|                    | Job 214  | Job 215  | Job 216  | Job 217  |
| ------------------ | -------- | -------- | -------- | -------- |
| Direct materials   | $2,200   | $9,000   | $1,500   | $3,450   |
| Direct labour      | 1,800    | 4,000    | 150      | 800      |

Job 214 was completed on August 22, and the client was billed at cost plus 30 percent. All other jobs remained in process.

**Required:**

1. Calculate the overhead applied to each job during the month of August.
2. Prepare job-order cost sheets for each job as of the end of August.
3. Calculate the balance in Work in Process on August 31.
4. What is the selling price of Job 214?
5. Do you suppose that LaSalle has a finished goods account? If so, what jobs would be added to that account?

**5–5**

*Job Cost Calculation*

**LO2, LO3**

Carol Taylor, owner of the Sewing Room, does alterations and sews clothing to order. She just completed 26 dance costumes for a tap class at Encore Dance Studio. The job required materials costing $234, as well as 39 direct labour hours at $10 per hour. Overhead is applied on the basis of direct labour hours at a rate of $4 per hour.

**Required:**

1. What is the total cost of the job? the unit cost?
2. If Carol charges a price that is 1.5 times cost, what price is charged to each member of the dance class?

**5–6**

*Balance of Work in Process and Finished Goods*

**LO3**

Patton Company uses job-order costing. At the end of the month, the following information was gathered:

| Job Number | Total Cost | Completed? | Sold? |
|---|---|---|---|
| 101 | $450 | no | no |
| 102 | 300 | yes | yes |
| 103 | 500 | yes | no |
| 104 | 670 | no | no |
| 105 | 800 | no | no |
| 106 | 230 | yes | no |
| 107 | 150 | yes | yes |
| 108 | 700 | no | no |

The beginning balance of Finished Goods was zero.

**Required:**

1. Calculate the balance in Work in Process at the end of the month.
2. Calculate the balance in Finished Goods at the end of the month.
3. Calculate the Cost of Goods Sold for the month.

**5–7**

*Type of Costing System; Unit Cost; Job Cost*

**LO1, LO3**

Jackson Jewellers has two departments. Department 1 makes class rings for high-school students. Each ring is essentially the same. Department 2 makes custom jewellery to order for clients. Department 2 creates a unique design for each piece and produces it using a variety of gemstones and gold.

On May 14, John Calvin met with Dave Jackson to discuss having a special pin designed for his wife in celebration of their 20th wedding anniversary. Dave created a butterfly design that would take advantage of a pair of matched watermelon tourmalines. To make the pin, gold backing was poured; the tourmalines and several small diamonds were then set into it. In all, direct materials cost $500, direct labour was $250, and overhead was applied at the rate of 100 percent of direct labour cost.

**Required:**

1. Which type of costing is used by Department 1? by Department 2?
2. What was the total cost of the pin for John Calvin's wife?

**5–8**

*Job-Order Costing Using ABC*

**LO2, LO3**

Refer to 5–7. Several months later, Dave met with his accountant to look at a new activity-based costing system. Two activities were identified: security (for gold and gems—includes insurance, amortization on safes, security alarms) and machining (power and amortization on machinery). Other overhead costs were grouped together as "other."

| Activity | Cost | Driver | Driver Amount |
|---|---|---|---|
| Security | $50,000 | Materials cost | $500,000 |
| Machining | 35,000 | Machine hours | 2,000 |
| Other | 74,000 | Direct labour cost | $160,000 |

Dave wondered how this system would affect the costs he had been charging, so he used the Calvin job as an example. This job required direct materials of $500, direct labour of $250, and two machine hours.

**Required:**
1. Calculate the activity rates for security, machining, and other overhead.
2. Using these activity rates, what would the total cost of the Calvin job have been?

**5–9**

ABC and Job-Order Costing

LO2, LO3

Spreadsheet

Trent Company, a job-order costing company, worked on four jobs in July. Data are as follows:

|                      | Job 14    | Job 15   | Job 16    | Job 17   |
|----------------------|-----------|----------|-----------|----------|
| Balance, July 1      | $12,450   | $3,770   | 0         | 0        |
| July activity:       |           |          |           |          |
| Direct materials     | $ 6,000   | $7,900   | $15,350   | $1,000   |
| Direct labour        | $10,000   | $8,500   | $23,000   | $ 900    |
| Machine hours        | 200       | 150      | 1,000     | 10       |
| Material moves       | 50        | 10       | 200       | 5        |
| Purchase orders      | 10        | 40       | 10        | 20       |

ABC is used to apply overhead to jobs. The power rate is $3 per machine hour; the material-handling rate is $25 per move; the purchasing rate is $40 per purchase order. By July 31, Jobs 14 and 15 were completed, and Job 15 was sold. All others remain in process.

**Required:**
1. Prepare job-order cost sheets for each job, showing all costs through July 31.
2. Calculate the balance in Work in Process on July 31.
3. Calculate the cost transferred to Finished Goods during July.
4. Calculate the Cost of Goods Sold for July.

**5–10**

Income Statement for a Job-Order Company

LO3

Refer to 5–9. Trent prices its jobs at cost plus 50 percent. During July, marketing expenses were $2,000, and administrative expenses were $3,500.

**Required:**
Prepare an income statement for Trent Company for the month of July.

**5–11**

Journal Entries; Job Costs

LO2, LO3, LO4

Spreadsheet

The following transactions occurred during the month of April for Kearney Company.

a. Materials costing $3,000 were purchased on account.
b. Materials totalling $1,700 were requisitioned for use in production: $500 for Job 443 and the remainder for Job 444.
c. During the month, direct labour worked 50 hours on Job 443 and 100 hours on Job 444. Direct labour is paid at a rate of $8 per hour.
d. Overhead is applied using a plantwide rate of $7.50 per direct labour hour.
e. Actual overhead for the month was $1,230 and was paid in cash.
f. Job 443 was completed and transferred to Finished Goods.
g. Job 442, which had been completed and transferred to Finished Goods in March, was sold on account for cost ($2,000) plus 25 percent.

**Required:**
1. Prepare journal entries for transactions (a) through (e).
2. Prepare job-order cost sheets for Jobs 443 and 444. Prepare journal entries for transactions (f) and (g).

3. Prepare a statement of cost of goods manufactured for April. Assume that the beginning balance in the raw materials account was $1,400, and the beginning balance in the work in process account was zero.

**5–12**

Overhead Application; Job Cost

LO3, LO4

At the beginning of the year, Paxton Company budgeted overhead of $180,000 and budgeted 15,000 direct labour hours. During the year, Job K456 was completed with the following information: direct materials cost was $2,340, and direct labour cost was $3,600. The average wage for Paxton Company is $10 per hour. Overhead is applied using normal costing and a plantwide rate based on direct labour hours.

By the end of the year, 15,400 direct labour hours had actually been worked, and Paxton Company had incurred the following actual overhead costs for the year:

| | |
|---|---|
| Equipment lease | $ 5,000 |
| Amortization on building | 20,000 |
| Indirect labour | 100,000 |
| Utilities | 15,000 |
| Other overhead | 45,000 |

**Required:**
1. Calculate the overhead rate for the year.
2. Calculate the total cost of Job K456.
3. Is overhead overapplied or underapplied? by how much?

**5–13**

Cost Flows

LO3

For each of the following independent jobs, fill in the missing data. Overhead is applied in Department 1 at the rate of $6 per direct labour hour (DLH). Overhead is applied in Department 2 at the rate of $8 per machine hour. Direct labour wages average $10 per hour in each department.

| | Job 213 | Job 214 | Job 217 | Job 225 |
|---|---|---|---|---|
| Total sales revenue | $ ? | $4,375 | $5,600 | $1,150 |
| Price per unit | 12 | ? | 14 | 5 |
| Material used in production | 365 | ? | 488 | 207 |
| Direct labour cost, Department 1 | ? | 700 | 2,000 | 230 |
| Machine hours, Department 1 | 15 | 35 | 50 | 12 |
| Direct labour cost, Department 2 | 50 | 100 | ? | 0 |
| Machine hours, Department 2 | 25 | 50 | ? | ? |
| Overhead applied, Department 1 | 90 | ? | 1,200 | 138 |
| Overhead applied, Department 2 | ? | 400 | 160 | 0 |
| Total manufacturing cost | 855 | 3,073 | ? | 575 |
| Number of units | ? | 350 | 400 | ? |
| Unit cost | 8.55 | ? | 9.87 | ? |

**5–14**

Calculating Ending Work in Process, Income Statement

LO2, LO3

Brandt Company produces unique metal sculptures. On January 1, there were three jobs in process with the following costs:

| | Job 35 | Job 36 | Job 37 |
|---|---|---|---|
| Direct materials | $100 | $ 340 | $ 780 |
| Direct labour | 350 | 700 | 1,050 |
| Applied overhead | 420 | 840 | 1,260 |
| Total | $870 | $1,880 | $3,090 |

During January, two more jobs were started: Job 38 and Job 39. Direct materials and direct labour costs incurred by each job in process in January are as follows:

|          | Direct Materials | Direct Labour |
|----------|------------------|---------------|
| Job 35   | $400             | $300          |
| Job 36   | 150              | 200           |
| Job 37   | 260              | 150           |
| Job 38   | 800              | 650           |
| Job 39   | 760              | 700           |

Jobs 37 and 38 were completed and sold by January 31.

**Required:**
1. If overhead is applied on the basis of direct labour dollars, what is the overhead rate?
2. Prepare simple job-order cost sheets for each of the five jobs in process during January.
3. What is the balance of Work in Process on January 31? What is the Cost of Goods Sold in January?
4. Suppose that Brandt Company prices its jobs at cost plus 50 percent. In addition, during January selling and administrative costs of $1,200 were incurred. Prepare an income statement for the month of January.

**5–15**

Job Cost

LO2, LO3

Spreadsheet

Parish, Inc., builds custom equipment for manufacturing firms. During May, the following events occurred:

a. Materials were purchased on account for $42,630.
b. Materials totalling $27,000 were requisitioned for use in production: $12,500 for Job 644 and the remainder for Job 648.
c. Direct labour payroll for the month was $26,320, with an average wage of $14 per hour. Job 644 required 780 direct labour hours; Job 648 required 1,100 direct labour hours.
d. Actual overhead of $19,950 was incurred and paid.
e. Overhead is charged to production at the rate of $10 per direct labour hour.
f. Job 644 was completed and transferred to finished goods.
g. Job 648, which was started during May, remained in process at the end of the month.
h. Job 640, which had been completed in March, was sold on account for cost plus 25 percent.

Account balances on May 1 were as follows:

| Direct Materials            | $ 6,070 |
|-----------------------------|---------|
| Work in Process (for Job 644) | 10,000  |
| Finished Goods (for Job 640)  | 6,240   |

**Required:**
1. Prepare simple job-order cost sheets for Jobs 644 and 648.
2. Calculate the May 31 balances of the following:
   a. Direct Materials
   b. Work in Process
   c. Finished Goods

**5–16**

Journal Entries

LO4

Refer to 5–15.

**Required:**
Prepare the journal entries for transactions (a) through (h).

**5–17**

Zavner Company is a job-order costing company that uses activity-based costing to apply overhead to jobs. Zavner identified three overhead activities and their related drivers. Budget information for the year follows:

| Activity | Cost | Driver | Amount of Driver |
|---|---|---|---|
| Engineering design | $120,000 | Engineering hours | 3,000 |
| Purchasing | 80,000 | Number of parts | 10,000 |
| Other | 250,000 | Direct labour hours | 40,000 |

Zavner worked on five jobs in July. Data are as follows:

| | Job 60 | Job 61 | Job 62 | Job 63 | Job 64 |
|---|---|---|---|---|---|
| Balance, July 1 | $32,450 | $40,770 | $29,090 | $ 0 | $0 |
| July activity: | | | | | |
| Direct materials | $26,000 | $37,900 | $25,350 | $11,000 | $13,560 |
| Direct labour | $40,000 | $38,500 | $43,000 | $20,900 | $18,000 |
| Engineering hours | 20 | 10 | 15 | 100 | 200 |
| Number of parts | 150 | 180 | 200 | 500 | 300 |
| Direct labour hours | 2,500 | 2,400 | 2,600 | 1,200 | 1,100 |

By July 31, Jobs 60 and 62 were completed and sold. The remaining jobs were in process.

**Required:**
1. Calculate the activity rates for each of the three overhead activities.
2. Prepare job-order cost sheets for each job showing all costs through July 31. What is the cost of each job by the end of July?
3. Calculate the balance in Work in Process on July 31.
4. Calculate the Cost of Goods Sold for July.

**5–18**

Refer to 5-17. Assume that Zavner uses one plantwide rate based on direct labour hours.

**Required:**
1. Calculate the plantwide overhead rate for Zavner Company.
2. Prepare job-order cost sheets for each job showing all costs through July 31. What is the cost of each job by the end of July?
3. Calculate the balance in Work in Process on July 31.
4. Calculate the Cost of Goods Sold for July.

**5–19**

Reynolds Printing Company specializes in wedding announcements. Reynolds uses an actual job-order cost system. An actual overhead rate is calculated at the end of each month using actual direct labour hours and overhead for the month. Once the actual cost of a job is determined, the customer is billed at actual cost plus 50 percent.

During April, Mrs. Lucky, a good friend of owner Jane Reynolds, ordered three sets of wedding announcements to be delivered May 10, June 10, and July 10, respectively. Reynolds scheduled production for each order on May 7, June 7, and July 7, respectively. The orders were assigned job numbers 115, 116, and 117, respectively.

Reynolds assured Mrs. Lucky that she would attend each of her daughters' weddings. Out of sympathy and friendship, she also offered a lower price. Instead of cost plus 50 percent, she gave Mrs. Lucky a special price of cost plus 25 percent. Additionally, she agreed to wait until the final wedding to bill for the three jobs.

On August 15, Reynolds asked her accountant to bring the completed job-order cost sheets for Jobs 115, 116, and 117. She also gave instructions to lower the price, as had been agreed upon. The cost sheets revealed the following information:

|  | Job 115 | Job 116 | Job 117 |
|---|---|---|---|
| Cost of direct materials | $250.00 | $250.00 | $250.00 |
| Cost of direct labour (5 hours) | 25.00 | 25.00 | 25.00 |
| Cost of overhead | 200.00 | 400.00 | 400.00 |
| Total cost | $475.00 | $675.00 | $675.00 |
| Total price | $593.75 | $843.75 | $843.75 |
| Number of announcements | 500 | 500 | 500 |

Reynolds could not understand why the overhead costs assigned to Jobs 116 and 117 were so much higher than those for Job 115. She asked for an overhead cost summary sheet for the months of May, June, and July, which showed that actual overhead costs were $20,000 for each month. She also discovered that direct labour hours worked on all jobs were 500 hours in May and 250 hours each in June and July.

**Required:**

1. How do you think Mrs. Lucky will feel when she receives the bill for the three sets of wedding announcements?
2. Explain how the overhead costs were assigned to each job.
3. Assume that Reynolds's average activity is 500 hours per month and that the company usually experiences overhead costs of $240,000 each year. Can you recommend a better way to assign overhead costs to jobs? Recompute the cost of each job and its price given your method of overhead cost assignment. Which method do you think is best? Why?

**5–20**

*Overhead Applied to Jobs; Departmental Overhead Rates*

LO3

Watson Products, Inc. uses a normal job-order costing system. Currently, a plant-wide overhead rate based on machine hours is used. Marlon Burke, the plant manager, has heard that departmental overhead rates can offer significantly better cost assignments than a plantwide rate can offer. Watson has the following data for its two departments for the coming year:

|  | Department A | Department B |
|---|---|---|
| Overhead costs (expected) | $50,000 | $22,000 |
| Normal activity (machine hours) | 20,000 | 16,000 |

**Required:**

1. Compute a predetermined overhead rate for the plant as a whole based on machine hours.
2. Compute predetermined overhead rates for each department using machine hours. (Carry your calculations out to three decimal places.)
3. Job 73 used 20 machine hours from Department A and 50 machine hours from Department B. Job 74 used 50 machine hours from Department A and 20 from Department B. Compute the overhead cost assigned to each job using the plantwide rate computed in Requirement 1. Repeat the computation using the departmental rates found in Requirement 2. Which of the two approaches gives the fairer assignment? Why?

**5–21**

Unit Cost; Ending
Work in Process;
Journal Entries

LO3, LO4

During October, Harrison Company worked on two jobs. Data relating to these two jobs follow:

| | Job 34 | Job 35 |
|---|---|---|
| Units in each order | 50 | 100 |
| Units sold | 50 | — |
| Materials requisitioned | $1,240 | $ 985 |
| Direct labour hours | 410 | 583 |
| Direct labour cost | $6,150 | $8,745 |

Overhead is assigned on the basis of direct labour hours at a rate of $12. During October, Job 34 was completed and transferred to finished goods. Job 35 was the only unfinished job at the end of the month.

**Required:**
1. Calculate the per-unit cost of Job 34.
2. Compute the balance in the Work in Process account on October 31.
3. Prepare the journal entries reflecting the completion and sale of Job 34. The selling price is 160 percent of cost.

**5–22**

Predetermined
Overhead Rates;
Variances; Cost Flows

LO3, LO4

Barrymore Costume Company, located in Toronto, sews costumes for plays and musicals. Barrymore considers itself primarily a service company, because it never produces costumes without a firm order and because it purchases materials to the specifications of the particular job. Any finished goods inventory is temporary and is zeroed out as soon as the show producer pays for the order. Overhead is applied on the basis of direct labour cost. During the first quarter of 2004, the following activity took place in each of the accounts that follow:

| **Work in Process** | | | **Finished Goods** | | |
|---|---|---|---|---|---|
| Bal | 17,000 | 245,000 | Bal | 40,000 | 210,000 |
| DL | 80,000 | | | 245,000 | |
| OH | 140,000 | | Bal | 75,000 | |
| DM | 40,000 | | | | |
| Bal | 32,000 | | | | |

| **Overhead** | | | **Cost of Goods Sold** | | |
|---|---|---|---|---|---|
| | 138,500 | 140,000 | | 210,000 | |
| Bal | | 1,500 | | | |

Job 32 was the only job in process at the end of the first quarter. A total of 1,000 direct labour hours at $10 per hour was charged to Job 32.

**Required:**
1. Assume that overhead is applied on the basis of direct labour cost. What was the overhead rate used during the first quarter of 2004?
2. What was the applied overhead for the first quarter? the actual overhead? the underapplied or overapplied overhead?
3. What was the cost of goods manufactured for the quarter?
4. Assume that the overhead variance is closed to the Cost of Goods Sold account. What is the adjusted Cost of Goods Sold?
5. For Job 32, identify the costs incurred for direct materials, direct labour, and overhead.

**5–23**

Choose the *best* answer for each of the following multiple-choice questions.

1. Which of the following statements is *true*?
   a. Job-order costing is used only by manufacturing companies.
   b. The job-order cost sheet is subsidiary to the work in process account.
   c. Job-order costing is simpler to use than process costing because the record keeping requirements are less.
   d. Process costing is used only for services.
   e. All of the above are true.

2. The ending balance of which of the following accounts is calculated by summing the totals of the open (unfinished) job-order cost sheets.
   a. Materials.
   b. Work in Process.
   c. Finished Goods.
   d. Cost of Goods Sold.
   e. Overhead Control.

3. One June 1, Job 17 had a beginning balance of $100. During June, direct materials of $250 and direct labour of $300 were added to the job. Overhead is applied to production at the rate of 70 percent of direct labour cost. Job 17 was completed on June 28 and sold at cost plus 50 percent. The selling price of Job 17 was:
   a. $1,290.
   b. $860.
   c. $650.
   d. $975.
   e. $1,140.

4. If direct materials costing $460 are requisitioned for use on a job, which of the following journal entries is made?
   a. Materials                       460
         Work in process                        460
   b. Materials                       460
         Accounts payable                       460
   c. Work in process                 460
         Accounts payable                       460
   d. Work in process                 460
         Materials                              460
   e. Materials                       460
         Overhead control                       460

5. Greiner's Garage uses a job-order costing system. Overhead is applied to jobs based on direct labour hours. The source document that would give the number of direct labour hours worked on Job 2003-276 is the:
   a. materials requisition form.
   b. labour time ticket.
   c. machine hours usage ticket.
   d. mileage log.
   e. job-order cost sheet.

## Problems

**5–24**

Spade Millhone Detective Agency performs investigative work for a variety of clients. Recently, Reliance Insurance Company asked Spade Millhone to investigate a series of suspicious claims for whiplash. In each case, the claimant was driving on a highway and was suddenly rear-ended by a Reliance-insured car. The claimants were all driving old, uninsured vehicles. The Reliance clients reported that the claimants suddenly changed lanes in front of them and the accidents were unavoidable. Reliance suspected that these "accidents" were the result of insurance fraud: the claimants cruised the highways in virtually worthless cars, attempting to cut in front of other cars. Reliance believed that the injuries were faked.

S. Spade spent 40 hours shadowing the claimants and taking pictures as necessary. His surveillance methods located the office of a doctor used by all the claimants. Spade took pictures of the claimants performing tasks that they had sworn they could no longer perform, due to their whiplash injuries. K. Millhone spent 25 hours using the Internet to research court documents in other provinces. She found a pattern of similar insurance claims for each of the claimants.

The Spade Millhone Detective Agency bills clients for detective time at $100 per hour. Mileage is charged at $0.40 per kilometre. The agency logged 430 kilometres on the Reliance job. The film and developing costs amounted to $80.

**Required:**
1. Prepare a job-order sheet for the Reliance job.
2. Why is overhead not specified in the charges? How does Spade Millhone charge clients for the use of overhead (e.g., the ongoing costs of their office—supplies, paper for notes and reports, telephone, utilities)?
3. The mileage is tallied from a source document. Design a source document for this use, and make up data for it that would total the 430 kilometres driven on the Reliance job.

**5–25**

Courtney Company manufactures specialty tools to customer order. Budgeted overhead for the coming year is as follows:

| | |
|---|---|
| Purchasing | $30,000 |
| Setups | 15,000 |
| Engineering | 20,000 |
| Other | 25,000 |

Previously, Jennifer Langston, Courtney Company's controller, had applied overhead on the basis of machine hours. Expected machine hours for the coming year are 10,000. Jennifer has been reading about activity-based costing, and she wonders whether it might offer some advantages to her company. She decided that appropriate drivers for overhead activities are purchase orders for purchasing, number of setups for setup cost, engineering hours for engineering cost, and machine hours for other. Budgeted amounts for these drivers are 5,000 purchase orders, 1,000 setups, and 500 engineering hours.

Jennifer has been asked to prepare bids for two jobs with the following information:

|                             | Job 1   | Job 2   |
|-----------------------------|---------|---------|
| Direct materials            | $4,500  | $8,600  |
| Direct labour               | $1,000  | $2,000  |
| Number of setups            | 2       | 3       |
| Number of purchase orders   | 15      | 20      |
| Number of engineering hours | 25      | 10      |
| Number of machine hours     | 200     | 200     |

The typical bid price includes a 30 percent markup over full manufacturing cost.

**Required:**
1. Calculate a plantwide rate for Courtney Company based on machine hours. What is the bid price of each job using this rate?
2. Calculate activity rates for the four overhead activities. What is the bid price of each job using these rates?
3. Which bids are more accurate? Why?

**5–26**

Activity-Based Costing and Overhead Rates; Unit Costs

LO2, LO3

Mueller Custom Designs makes cabinets to custom order. Mark Mueller identified the following budgeted overhead activities and drivers:

| Activity          | Cost     | Cost Driver       | Amount  |
|-------------------|----------|-------------------|---------|
| Machine operation | $40,000  | Machine hours     | 10,000  |
| Setups            | $10,000  | Number of setups  | 2,000   |
| Designing costs   | $30,000  | Design hours      | 1,000   |

Frank and Sally Willis were building a large custom house and wanted "lots of storage." Their job had the following data:

| Direct materials      | $6,210 |
|-----------------------|--------|
| Direct labour wages   | $5,000 |
| Machine hours         | 600    |
| Number of setups      | 100    |
| Design hours          | 100    |

Cindy and Ray Gordon were remodelling an older house. They needed some basic cabinets for the kitchen. Mark Mueller suggested a basic design he had built numerous times before. The Gordon job had the following data:

| Direct materials      | $1,500 |
|-----------------------|--------|
| Direct labour wages   | $1,750 |
| Machine hours         | 60     |
| Number of setups      | 1      |
| Design hours          | 0      |

**Required:**
1. Calculate a unit-based overhead rate based on machine hours. What is the total cost of the Willis job using this rate? What is the total cost of the Gordon job using this rate?
2. Calculate activity rates. What is the cost of the Willis job using the three activity rates? What is the cost of the Gordon job using the three activity rates?
3. Of the two costing approaches (unit-based or ABC), which is more accurate and why?

**5–27**

LO3

Ferguson Equipment, Inc., produces custom-designed manufacturing equipment. Ferguson recently received a request to manufacture 40 units of a specialized machine at a price lower than it normally accepts. Marketing manager Emily Dorr indicated that if the order were accepted at that price, the company could expect additional orders from the same customer. In fact, if the company could offer this price in the market generally, she believed that sales of this machine would increase by 50 percent.

Cleon Skowesen, president of Ferguson, was skeptical about accepting the order. The company had a policy of refusing to accept any order that did not provide revenues at least equal to its full manufacturing cost plus 10 percent. The price offered was $2,500 per unit. However, before a final decision was made, Cleon decided to request information on the estimated cost per unit. He was concerned because the company was experiencing increased competition, and the number of new orders was dropping. Also, the controller's office had recently researched the possibility of using activity-based, multiple overhead rates instead of the single rate currently in use. The controller had promised more accurate product costing, and Cleon was curious about how this approach would affect the pricing of this particular machine.

Within 24 hours, the controller assembled the following data:

a. The plantwide overhead rate is based on an expected annual volume of 450,000 direct labour hours and budgeted overhead of $4,068,000.

b. Activity cost pools and activity drivers:

| Activity | Cost | Activity Driver | Activity Amount |
|---|---|---|---|
| Machining | $1,000,000 | Machine hours | 100,000 |
| Material handling | 800,000 | Material moves | 10,000 |
| Inspection and rework | 250,000 | Rework hours | 5,000 |
| Setup | 640,000 | Number of setups | 1,000 |
| Purchasing | 118,000 | Number of purchase orders | 20,000 |
| General factory | 1,260,000 | Direct labour hours | 450,000 |

c. Estimated data for the potential job (based on the production of 40 units) follow:

| | |
|---|---|
| Direct labour (4,100 hours) | $36,900 |
| Direct materials | $24,000 |
| Number of material moves | 6 |
| Number of rework hours | 5 |
| Number of setups | 3 |
| Number of machine hours | 1,000 |
| Number of purchase orders | 20 |

**Required:**

1. Compute the estimated unit cost for the potential job using the current method to assign overhead on a plantwide basis. Given this unit cost, compute the total gross margin earned by the job. Would the job be accepted under normal operating conditions?
2. Calculate activity rates using the activity drivers in (b). Compute the estimated unit cost for the potential job using the activity rates. Given this cost per unit, compute the total gross margin earned by the job. Should the job be accepted?
3. Which approach—the plantwide rate or the activity overhead rates —is best for the company? Explain.

**5–28**

*Job Cost Sheets*

**LO2, LO3**

On July 1, Polk Company had the following balances in its inventory accounts:

| | |
|---|---|
| Raw Materials | $22,000 |
| Work in Process | 7,905 |
| Finished Goods | 0 |

Work in Process on July 1 was made up of three jobs with the following costs:

| | Job 17 | Job 18 | Job 19 |
|---|---|---|---|
| Raw materials | $1,100 | $910 | $1,415 |
| Direct labour | 900 | 850 | 1,050 |
| Applied overhead | 540 | 510 | 630 |

During July, Polk experienced the following transactions:
a. Materials purchased on account: $13,000
b. Materials requisitioned: Job 17, $8,500; Job 18, $7,200; Job 19, $12,300
c. Job time tickets collected and summarized: Job 17, 175 hours at $10 per hour; Job 18, 165 hours at $11 per hour; and Job 19, 225 hours at $10 per hour
d. Overhead is applied on the basis of direct labour cost.
e. Actual overhead: $3,500
f. Jobs 17 and 18 were completed and transferred to the finished goods warehouse.
g. Job 18 was shipped; the customer was billed for 160 percent of the cost.

**Required:**
1. Prepare job-order cost sheets for Jobs 17, 18, and 19. Post the beginning inventory data, and then update the cost sheets for the July activity.
2. Prepare a schedule of inventories on July 31.

**5–29**

*Job-Order Costing: Housing Construction*

**LO2, LO3**

Butter, Inc., is a privately held, family-founded corporation that builds single- and multiple-unit housing. Most projects Butter undertakes involve the construction of multiple units. Butter has adopted a job-order costing system for determining the cost of each unit. Each project's costs are divided into the following five categories:

a. General conditions, including construction site utilities, project insurance, permits and licences, architect's fees, decorating, field office salaries, and cleanup costs.
b. Hard costs, such as subcontractors, direct materials, and labour.
c. Finance costs, including title and registration fees, inspection fees, and taxes and discounts on mortgages.
d. Land costs, which refer to the purchase price of the construction site.
e. Marketing costs, such as advertising, sales commissions, and appraisal fees.

Recently, Butter purchased land for the purpose of developing 20 new single-family houses. The cost of the land was $250,000. Lot sizes vary from 0.125 hectares to 0.25 hectares. The 20 lots occupy a total of 4 hectares.

General condition costs for the project totalled $120,000. This $120,000 is common to all 20 of the units that were constructed on the building site.

Job 3, the third house built in the project, occupied a 0.125 hectare lot and had the following hard costs:

| | |
|---|---|
| Direct materials | $28,000 |
| Direct labour | 36,000 |
| Subcontractor | 44,000 |

For Job 3, finance costs totalled $4,765 and marketing costs $3,800. General condition costs are allocated on the basis of units produced.

**Required:**
1. Which of the five cost categories corresponds to overhead? Do you agree with the way in which this cost is allocated to individual housing units? Can you suggest a different allocation method? Discuss how the other cost categories are treated.
2. Develop a job-order cost sheet for Job 3.

**5–30**

Job-Order Costing: Service Organization

LO3

Price-Gordon Architectural Consultants Ltd. uses a modified job-order costing system to keep track of project costs. During April, the company worked on four projects. The following table provides a summary of the cost of materials used and the number of consulting hours worked on each of the four projects in April:

| Project Number | Cost of Materials | Consulting Hours Worked |
|---|---|---|
| 480 | $120 | 138 |
| 484 | 85 | 145 |
| 485 | 100 | 160 |
| 486 | 150 | 187 |

The records for March showed that 20 hours had been worked and $68 worth of materials had been used on Project 480. Projects 480 and 486 were completed in April, and bills were sent to the clients.

Consultants at Price-Gordon billed clients at $100 per consulting hour. The actual labour cost to the company (based on salary cost) was $40 per hour. Overhead is charged to projects on the basis of the consultants' time spent on the project. Total overhead for the current fiscal year at an expected activity of 10,000 consulting hours is estimated to be $270,000.

**Required:**
1. Determine the product costs associated with Project 480.
2. Determine the cost of work in process on April 30.
3. Prepare the income statement for April. Other expenses for April were $2,341. (CMA Canada adapted)

**5–31**

Plantwide Overhead Rate; Departmental Rates; Effects on Job-Pricing Decisions

LO2, LO3

Alden Peterson, marketing manager for Retlief Company, was puzzled by the outcome of two recent bids. The company's policy was to bid 150 percent of the full manufacturing cost. One job (labelled Job SS) had been turned down by a prospective customer who had indicated that the proposed price was $3 per unit higher than the winning bid. A second job (Job TT) has been accepted by a customer who was amazed that Retlief could offer such favourable terms. This customer revealed that Retlief's price was $43 per unit lower than the next lowest bid.

Alden had been informed that the company was more than competitive in terms of cost control. Accordingly, he began to suspect that the problem was related to cost assignment procedures. Upon investigating, Alden was told that the company uses a plantwide overhead rate based on direct labour hours. The rate is computed at the beginning of the year using budgeted data. Selected budgeted data follow:

| | Department A | Department B | Total |
|---|---|---|---|
| Overhead | $500,000 | $2,000,000 | $2,500,000 |
| Direct labour hours | 200,000 | 50,000 | 250,000 |
| Machine hours | 20,000 | 120,000 | 140,000 |

Alden also discovered that the overhead costs in Department B were higher than those in Department A because B has more equipment, higher maintenance, higher power consumption, higher amortization, and higher setup costs. In addition to the general procedures for assigning overhead costs, Alden was supplied with the following specific manufacturing data on Job SS and Job TT:

| Job SS | Department A | Department B | Total |
|---|---|---|---|
| Direct labour hours | 5,000 | 1,000 | 6,000 |
| Machine hours | 200 | 500 | 700 |
| Prime costs | $100,000 | $20,000 | $120,000 |
| Units produced | | | 14,400 |

| Job TT | Department A | Department B | Total |
|---|---|---|---|
| Direct labour hours | 400 | 600 | 1,000 |
| Machine hours | 200 | 3,000 | 3,200 |
| Prime costs | $10,000 | $40,000 | $50,000 |
| Units produced | | 1,500 | |

**Required:**

1. Using a plantwide overhead rate based on direct labour hours, develop the bid prices for Job SS and Job TT. (Express the bid price on a per-unit basis.)
2. Using departmental overhead rates (use direct labour hours for Department A and machine hours for Department B), develop per-unit bids for Job SS and Job TT.
3. Compute the gross margin that would have been earned had the company used departmental rates in its bids instead of the plantwide rate. Comment.
4. Explain why the use of departmental rates in this case provides a more accurate product cost.

**5–32**

**ABC, Departmental Rates, and Pricing Decisions**

**LO2, LO3**

(A continuation of 5–31 with activity data added.)

Alden had been reading about the increased accuracy of an ABC system and convinced the controller to help in obtaining the following information:

| Overhead | Activities Cost | Activity Category | Activity Driver |
|---|---|---|---|
| Maintenance | $500,000 | Product sustaining | Machine hours |
| Power | 225,000 | Unit level | Kilowatt-hours |
| Setups | 150,000 | Batch level | Setup hours |
| General factory | 625,000 | Facility level | Machine hours* |

*This is an arbitrary allocation. The controller argued that machine hours used by a job would be correlated with the area occupied by the producing departments.

The expected levels of the activity drivers for the year follow:

| | |
|---|---|
| Machine hours | 140,000 |
| Kilowatt-hours | 100,000 |
| Setup hours | 20,000 |

The following activity data for each job are also provided:

| | Job SS | Job TT |
|---|---|---|
| Machine hours | 700 | 3,200 |
| Kilowatt-hours | 400 | 2,500 |
| Setup hours | 20 | 100 |
| Prime costs | $120,000 | $50,000 |
| Units | 14,400 | 1,500 |

**Required:**

1. Calculate the cost of each job using activity-based costing. List the costs of each job by activity category. Calculate the bid price for each job using the normal markup.
2. How do these ABC bid prices compare with the bids that use plantwide and departmental rates? (see 5–31) Does this approach offer any real improvement? Explain.
3. Suppose that the lowest competing bid for Job SS is $14.55. Also assume that the lowest competing bid on Job TT is $85. Now compare the ABC bids with the bids based on departmental rates. What does this comparison imply about the value of ABC as price competition intensifies?

**5–33**

Job-Order Costing, Comprehensive Manufacturing

LO3

Avid Assemblers uses job-order costing to assign costs to products. The company assembles and packages 20 different products to customer specifications. Products are worked on in batches of 30 to 50 units. Each batch is assigned a job number.

On October 1, the company had the following balances recorded.

| Materials | $ 7,800 |
| Work in process | 45,726 |
| Finished goods | 23,520 |

Work in process consisted of the following jobs:

|  | **Job 202** | **Job 204** | **Job 205** |
| --- | --- | --- | --- |
| Direct materials | $ 4,200 | $ 3,190 | $ 2,800 |
| Direct labour | 8,500 | 7,210 | 6,500 |
| Applied overhead | 5,100 | 4,326 | 3,900 |
| Total | $17,800 | $14,726 | $13,200 |
| Number of units | 30 | 50 | 35 |

Finished goods consisted of Job 203, with the following costs:

| Direct materials | $ 7,200 |
| Direct labour | 10,200 |
| Applied overhead | 6,120 |
| Total | $23,520 |
| Number of units | 50 |

Shown below are the direct cost data related to jobs started in October:

|  | **Job 206** | **Job 207** | **Job 208** | **Total** |
| --- | --- | --- | --- | --- |
| Direct materials | $4,180 | $3,600 | $1,200 | $ 8,980 |
| Direct labour | 9,200 | 8,340 | 2,910 | 20,450 |
| Number of units | 40 | 50 | 40 | |

Other information:

1. Direct materials and direct labour added to beginning work in process in October were as follows:

|  | **Job 202** | **Job 204** | **Job 205** | **Total** |
| --- | --- | --- | --- | --- |
| Direct materials | $ 950 | $ 410 | $1,200 | $ 2,560 |
| Direct labour | 2,000 | 3,500 | 4,500 | 10,000 |

2. Overhead is applied at a predetermined rate on the basis of direct labour cost.
3. Actual expenses for October were as follows:

| Supervisory salaries | $4,000 |
|---|---|
| Factory rent | 2,000 |
| Amortization (machines) | 3,000 |
| Indirect labour | 5,000 |
| Supplies (factory) | 1,100 |
| Selling expenses | 8,500 |
| CPP, EI, and other benefits* | 3,200 |

* 80 percent of employer contributions and benefits relates to factory personnel.

4. Purchases of direct materials during October amounted to $8,500. Indirect materials (supplies) are handled in a separate account.
5. Only Jobs 207 and 208 are still in process at closing on October 31. Finished goods consisted only of Job 205 at month end.
6. Avid writes off any over- or underapplied overhead to Cost of Goods Sold in the month it is incurred.

**Required:**
1. What is the predetermined overhead rate used by Avid to apply overhead to jobs?
2. What is the unit cost of Job 204 in October?
3. What are the October 31 balances for the following inventory accounts?
   a. Raw Materials
   b. Work in Process
   c. Finished Goods
4. What is the cost of goods manufactured in October? (You do not have to prepare a statement as part of this Requirement.)
5. Determine the over- or underapplied overhead for October. (CMA Canada adapted)

**5–34**

Job-Order Costing

LO3

The following data were taken from the records of Cougar Enterprises, a Canadian manufacturer that uses a job-order costing system:

**Work in Process, December 1**

| Job Number | 170 | 175 | 180 |
|---|---|---|---|
| Direct materials | $1,800 | $2,400 | $1,500 |
| Direct labour | 1,200 | 2,400 | 600 |
| Applied overhead | 600 | 1,350 | 450 |
| Total | $3,600 | $6,150 | $2,550 |

During December, jobs numbered 170 through 190 were worked on, and the following costs were incurred:

| Job Number | 170 | 175 | 180 | 185 | 190 | Total |
|---|---|---|---|---|---|---|
| Direct materials | $600 | $ 900 | $1,200 | $1,350 | $1,500 | $ 5,550 |
| Direct labour | $750 | $1,500 | $3,000 | $2,250 | $6,000 | $13,500 |
| Direct labour hours | 50 | 100 | 200 | 150 | 400 | 900 |

Additional information:

1. Total overhead costs are applied to jobs on the basis of direct labour hours worked. At the beginning of the year, the company estimated that total overhead costs for the year would be $150,000, and the total labour hours worked would be 12,500.

2. Actual overhead in the Departmental Overhead Control account on December 1 was $160,010. Direct labour hours worked for the previous 11 months (January through November) were 11,250.

3. There were no jobs in finished goods on December 1.

4. Expenses for December were as follows (not yet recorded in the books of account):

| | |
|---|---:|
| Direct materials purchased | $ 7,500 |
| Salaries: | |
|    Production clerk | 1,500 |
|    Supervisor | 2,200 |
| Amortization (plant and equipment) | 2,490 |
| Factory supplies | 1,500 |
| Sales staff salaries | 9,200 |
| Utilities (factory) | 1,800 |
| Administrative expenses | 9,500 |
| Total | $35,690 |

5. The company writes off all over- or underapplied overhead to Cost of Goods Sold at the end of the year.

6. Jobs numbered 170, 180, 185, and 190 were completed during December. Only Job 190 remained in finished goods on December 31.

7. The company charges its customers 250 percent of total manufacturing cost.

8. Cost of goods sold to December 1 was $358,750.

**Required:**
1. Calculate the predetermined overhead rate used to apply overhead to jobs.
2. Prepare job-order cost sheets for each job in process during December.
3. What is the cost of work-in-process inventory at December 31?
4. Prepare a statement of cost of goods manufactured for December.
5. Calculate the normal (unadjusted) gross margin for December.
6. Calculate the over- or underapplied overhead for the year. What effect would this amount have on net income? (CMA Canada adapted)

**5–35**

Activity-Based Costing; Job Costs and Prices

LO3

Mountain View Rentals, located in Banff, Alberta, rents bikes to tourists for bike hiking in the Rocky Mountains. The rental price is tied to cost, so it is important to know the cost of the bikes, labour, and overhead. The bikes can be categorized into three levels, depending on sophistication and anticipated use. The cost per bike-rental-day (the rental of one bike for one day) for the three levels is as follows:

| | |
|---|---:|
| Level 1 | $ 7.50 |
| Level 2 | 12.00 |
| Level 3 | 20.00 |

Since each worker performs a number of tasks (for example, answering the phone, renting bikes, cleaning the shop, and maintaining bikes), there is no separate category for direct labour. Labour is included in overhead. Overhead for last year was $50,000, and it was applied to the jobs based on a unit-level rate of $5 per bike-rental-day. The rental rate is calculated by adding a 40 percent markup to total cost.

Recently, Mountain View Rentals added a picnic catering service that lets customers call the day before to order a picnic lunch to be taken on the bike hike. As a result, budgeted annual overhead increased to $100,000, while budgeted bike-rental-days remained at 10,000.

The addition of the picnic catering service rendered the unit-based overhead application method obsolete, so Mountain View Rentals decided to use a modified activity-based costing system. Major overhead activities identified are purchasing (based on number of purchase orders); power (based on number of kilo-watt-hours); maintenance (based on number of maintenance hours); and other (based on labour hours).

Budgeted activity levels for the coming year are as follows:

| Activity | Cost | Activity | Quantity |
|----------|------|----------|----------|
| Purchasing | $30,000 | Purchase orders | 10,000 |
| Power | 20,000 | Kilowatt-hours | 50,000 |
| Maintenance | 6,000 | Maintenance hours | 600 |
| Other | 44,000 | Labour hours | 22,000 |

Usage by the two different departments of Mountain View Rentals is as follows:

| | Bike Rental | Picnic Catering |
|---|---|---|
| Purchase orders | 7,000 | 3,000 |
| Kilowatt-hours | 5,000 | 45,000 |
| Maintenance hours | 500 | 100 |
| Labour hours | 11,000 | 11,000 |

Once the overhead is assigned to the bike rental segment, an overhead rate based on bike-rental-days is computed. Initially for the catering operation, overhead assigned to catering, using activity rates, is totalled and a single rate based on labour hours is computed.

**Required:**

1. Ignoring the desired shift to an activity-based costing system, calculate a single unit-based rate for last year and this year based on bike-rental-days. Suppose that the Carson family vacations in Banff each year and rents five bikes from Mountain View Rental for a two-day period. Maria and Fred Carson rent Level 3 bikes, while the Carson children rent Level 2 bikes. What was the cost of the Carson family rental last year? this year? What price was charged last year? this year? How do you suppose Maria and Fred feel about this?

2. Calculate activity-based rates for the four activities. How much total overhead is assigned to the bike rental operation? to the catering operation?

3. Suppose that the overhead allocated to the bike rental operation is then applied to jobs on the basis of bike-rental-days, as before. Now, what are this year's cost and price for the Carson rental?

4. Carol and Thurman Estes are honeymooning in Banff and decide to spend one day biking in the mountains. They rent two Level 1 bikes and order a picnic lunch for two. The materials for the picnic cost $12, and it takes one hour to make and pack the picnic. Using the overhead assigned to the catering operation in Requirement 2, calculate a catering overhead rate based on labour hours. What is the total cost of the Estes job?

5. Mountain View Rentals is considering adding Level 4 bikes to its lineup. However, these bikes are high-performance racing bikes and require considerably more maintenance and specialized parts ordering than the Level 1 through 3 bikes. How can activity-based costing help Mountain View decide what the cost of the Level 4 bikes is and whether or not the company should add these bikes to its rental list?

**5–36**

*Job-Order Costing*

LO3

Handy Widget Company does a wide variety of metal work on a custom basis. During the month of June 2004, the company worked on six jobs. A summary of the job cost sheets on these jobs is given below:

| Job Number | Direct Materials | Direct Labour | Applied Overhead | Total Cost |
|---|---|---|---|---|
| 1243 | $ 410 | $ 360 | $ 288 | $ 1,058 |
| 1244 | 850 | 790 | 632 | 2,272 |
| 1245 | 110 | 85 | 68 | 263 |
| 1246 | 1,500 | 1,140 | 912 | 3,552 |
| 1247 | 950 | 850 | 680 | 2,480 |
| 1248* | 70 | 115 | 92 | 477 |
| Total | $4,090 | $3,340 | $2,672 | $10,102 |

* ending work in process

Handy Widget has used the same overhead rate on all jobs. Job 1243 was the only job in process at the beginning of the month. At that time, Job 1243 had incurred direct labour costs of $150 and total costs of $570.

**Required:**
1. What is the apparent predetermined overhead rate being used by Handy Widget?
2. Assume that during June, the overhead was overapplied by $600. What was the actual overhead cost incurred during the month?
3. What was the total amount of direct materials placed into production during June?
4. How much direct labour cost was incurred during June?
5. What was the cost of goods manufactured for June? (CGA Canada adapted)

## Managerial Decision Case

**5–37**

Assigning Overhead to
Jobs; Ethical Issues

LO3

Tonya Martin, CMA, who is the controller of the Parts Division of Gunderson, Inc., was meeting with Doug Adams, the division's manager. The topic of discussion was the assignment of overhead costs to jobs and their impact on the division's pricing decisions. Their conversation follows:

**Tonya**: "Doug, as you know, about 25 percent of our business is based on government contracts, with the other 75 percent being based on jobs from private sources that we have won through bidding. During the last several years, our private business has declined. We have been losing more bids than usual. After some careful investigation, I have concluded that we are overpricing some jobs because of improper assignment of overhead costs. Some jobs are also being underpriced. Unfortunately, the jobs being overpriced are coming from our higher-volume, labour-intensive products; thus, we are losing business."

**Doug**: "I think I understand. Jobs associated with our high-volume products are being assigned more overhead than they should be receiving. Then, when we add our standard 40 percent markup, we end up with a higher price than our competitors, who assign costs more accurately."

**Tonya**: "Exactly. We have two producing departments, one labour-intensive and the other machine-intensive. The labour-intensive department generates much less overhead cost than the machine-intensive department does. Furthermore, virtually all of our high-volume jobs are labour-intensive. We have been using a plantwide rate based on direct labour hours to assign overhead to all jobs. As a result, the high-volume, labour-intensive jobs receive a greater share of the machine-intensive department's overhead than they deserve. This problem can be greatly alleviated by switching to departmental overhead rates. For example, an average high-volume job would be assigned $100,000 of overhead using a plantwide rate and only $70,000 using departmental rates. The change would lower our bidding price on high-volume jobs by an average of $42,000 per job. By increasing the accuracy of our product costing, we can make better pricing decisions and win back much of our private-sector business."

**Doug**: "Sounds good. When can you implement the change in overhead rates?"

**Tonya**: "It won't take long. I can have the new system working within four to six weeks—certainly by the start of the new fiscal year."

**Doug**: "Hold it. I just thought of a possible complication. As I recall, most of our government contract work is done in the labour-intensive department. This new overhead assignment scheme will push down the cost on the government jobs, and we will lose revenues. They pay us full cost plus our standard markup. This business is not threatened by our current costing procedures, but we can't switch our rates for only the private business. Government auditors would question the lack of consistency in our costing procedures."

**Tonya**: "You do have a point. I thought of this issue also. According to my estimates, we will gain more revenues from the private sector than we will lose from our government contracts. Besides, the costs of our government jobs are distorted; in effect, we are overcharging the government."

**Doug**: "They don't know that—and never will, unless we switch our overhead assignment procedures. I think I have the solution. Officially, let's keep our plantwide overhead rate. All of the official records will reflect this overhead-costing approach for both our private and our government business. Unofficially, I want you to develop a separate set of books that can be used to generate the information we need to prepare competitive bids for our private-sector business."

### Required:

1. Do you believe that the solution proposed by Doug Adams is ethical? Explain.
2. Suppose that Tonya Martin decides that Doug's solution is not right. In your opinion, is Tonya supported in this view by the standards of ethical conduct described in Chapter 1? Explain.
3. Suppose that, despite Tonya's objections, Doug insists strongly on implementing the action. What should Tonya do?

# Research Assignments

**5–38**

Research Assignment

LO1, LO2, LO3

Interview an accountant who works for a service organization that uses job-order costing. For a small firm, you may need to talk to an owner or a manager. Examples are a funeral home, insurance firm, repair shop, medical clinic, and dental clinic. Write a paper that describes the job-order cost system used by the firm. Some of the questions that the paper should address are:

a. What service or services does the firm offer?
b. What document or procedure do you use to collect the costs of the services performed for each customer?
c. How do you assign the cost of direct labour to each job?
d. How do you assign overhead to individual jobs?
e. How do you assign the cost of direct materials to each job?
f. How do you determine what to charge each customer?
g. How do you account for a completed job?

As you write the paper, state how the service firm you investigated has adapted the job-order accounting procedures described in this chapter to its particular circumstances. Were the adaptations justified? Explain why or why not. Also, offer any suggestions you might have for improving the approach that you observed.

**5–39**

Cybercase

LO1, LO2, LO3

Healtheon Corporation (www.healtheon.com) is involved in creating Internet solutions for medical recordkeeping. Given that clinics and doctors' offices use a job-order costing system, discuss how the Healtheon software may improve productivity and efficiency. In addition, what problems remain to be solved? Use the Healtheon Web site as well as the following article: George Anders, "Healtheon Struggles in Efforts to Remedy Doctors' Paper Plague," *The Wall Street Journal*, October 2, 1998, pp. A1, A6.

# Process Costing

**After studying Chapter 6, you should be able to:**

1. Describe the basic characteristics and cost flows associated with process manufacturing.

2. Define *equivalent units*, and explain their role in process costing.

3. Prepare a departmental production report using the weighted average method.

4. Explain how process costing is affected by nonuniform application of manufacturing inputs and the existence of multiple processing departments.

5. Prepare a departmental production report using the FIFO method. (Appendix)

## Scenario

Makenzie Gibson, owner of Healthblend Nutritional Supplements, was reviewing last year's income statement. Net income was up 33 percent over the previous year, and Makenzie was pleased. The idea for the company was the result of her recovery from some personal health problems. By working with health care professionals, she had learned to blend a number of different herbs into therapeutic formulas that had brought about an amazing recovery. Hoping to share her discoveries, Makenzie had begun producing some of these same therapeutic formulas in the basement of her home. Now, 10 years later, she was the owner of a multi-million-dollar business housed in a modern facility with more than 60 employees.

Despite her business success, Makenzie was convinced that she could not afford to be complacent. Recently, the owner of a health food store had told her that some other suppliers had dropped competing lines because they were no longer profitable. He had asked Makenzie if all of her products were profitable or if she simply offered the full range as a marketing strategy. She had been forced to admit that she did not know whether all of her products were profitable—in fact, she didn't even know the manufacturing cost of each individual product. All she knew was that overall profits were good.

After some reflection, she decided that knowing individual product costs would be useful for decisions regarding production methods, prices, and the mix of products. So, she contacted Judith Manesfield, manager of a regional CA firm's small business practice section, for help. After several visits by Judith and her staff, Makenzie received the following preliminary report:

**Makenzie Gibson
Healthblend Nutritional
Supplements
Saskatoon, Saskatchewan**

Dear Ms. Gibson:
As you know, your current accounting system does not collect the necessary data for costing out the various products that you produce.

You currently manufacture three major product lines: mineral, herb, and vitamin. Within each product line are a variety of individual products. Each product, regardless of its type, passes through three processes: picking, encapsulating, and bottling. In picking, the ingredients are measured, sifted, and blended. In encapsulating, the powdered mix from the first process is put into capsules. The capsules are then transferred to the bottling department, where they are bottled, after which the bottles are labelled and fitted with safety seals and lids.

Based on the nature of the manufacturing processes, our tentative recommendation is to accumulate costs of manufacturing by process for a given time period and measure the output for that same period. By dividing the costs accumulated for the period by the output for the period, you can obtain a good measure of individual product cost for that process.

The cost system we recommend will require a minimal increase in your bookkeeping activities. With your permission, we will proceed with the development of the cost system. As part of this development, we will conduct several training seminars so that your financial staff can operate the system once it is implemented.

**Questions to Think About**

1. Why do you suppose that Makenzie did not originally implement an accounting system that would give individual product costs?

2. Describe the flow of costs through Healthblend's plant. For each processing department, use a separate work-in-process account.

3. Makenzie recognized that unit-cost information for each product was important in determining individual product profitability. What other managerial decisions would be facilitated by having this type of information?

## Characteristics of Process Manufacturing

**Objective 1**

Describe the basic characteristics and cost flows associated with process manufacturing.

Makenzie Gibson hired the consultant to help her decide how best to cost out Healthblend's products. The consultant first studied Healthblend's methods of production. This is vital, since the production process helps determine the best way of accounting for costs. The study showed that a large number of similar products pass through an identical set of processes. Since each product within a product line passing through the three processes would receive similar "doses" of materials, labour, and overhead, Judith Manesfield saw no need to accumulate costs by batches (a job-costing system). Instead, she recommended accumulating costs by process.

Process costing works well whenever relatively homogeneous products pass through a series of processes and receive similar amounts of manufacturing costs. Large manufacturing plants, such as chemical, food, and tire manufacturers, use process costing.

Let's consider the Healthblend example in more detail. From the consultant's letter, we know that there are three processes. In the picking department, direct labour selects the appropriate herbs, vitamins, minerals, and inert materials (typically some binder, such as cornstarch) for the product to be manufactured. Then the materials are measured and combined in a mixer to blend them thoroughly. When the mix is complete, the resulting mixture is sent to the encapsulation department. In encapsulation, the vitamin, mineral, or herb blend is loaded into a machine that fills half of a gelatin capsule. The filled half is matched to the capsule's other half capsule, and a safety seal is applied. This process is entirely mechanized. Overhead in this department consists of amortization on machinery, maintenance of machinery, supervision, fringe benefits, light, and power. The final department is bottling. Filled capsules are transferred to this department, loaded into a hopper, and automatically counted into bottles. Filled bottles are mechanically capped, and direct labour then manually packs the correct number of bottles into boxes to ship to retail outlets.

Now let's look at Healthblend from an accounting perspective. Suppose that Healthblend has only one picking department, through which all three major product lines pass. Since the product lines differ significantly in the cost of their material inputs, accumulating material costs by process no longer makes any sense. More accurate product costing can be achieved by accumulating material costs by batch. In this case, labour and overhead could still be accumulated by process, but raw materials would be assigned to batches using the usual job-costing approach. Note, however, that even with this change, process costing could still be used for the encapsulating department and the bottling department. In these two departments, each product receives the same amount of material, labour, and overhead.

This example illustrates that some manufacturing settings may need to use a blend of job and process costing. Using job-order procedures to assign material costs to products and a process approach to assign conversion costs is known as **operation costing**. Other blends are possible as well. The example also shows that it is possible to use more than one form of costing within the same organization. This is the case if Healthblend uses operation costing for the picking department and process costing for the other two departments.

The fundamental point is that the cost accounting system should be designed to fit the nature of operations. Job-order and process-costing systems fit pure job and pure process production environments, respectively. There are many settings, however, in which blends of the two costing systems may be suitable. By studying the pure forms of job-order and process costing, we can develop the ability to understand and use any hybrid form.

## Types of Process Manufacturing

In a process operation, units typically pass through a series of manufacturing or producing departments; in each department or process is an operation that brings the product one step closer to completion. In each department, materials, labour, and overhead may be needed. When a particular process is completed, the partly completed goods are transferred to the next department. After passing through the final department, the completed goods are transferred to the warehouse.

Production at Healthblend Nutritional Supplements is an example of **sequential processing**. In a sequential process, units must pass through one process before they can be worked on in later processes. Exhibit 6–1 shows the sequential pattern of the manufacture of Healthblend's minerals, herbs, and vitamins.

Another processing pattern is **parallel processing**, in which two or more sequential processes are required in order to produce a finished good. Partly completed units (for example, two subcomponents) can be worked on simultaneously in different processes and then brought together in a final process for completion. Consider, for example, the manufacture of hard disk drives for personal computers. In one series of processes, write-heads and cartridge disk drives are produced, assembled, and tested. In a second series of processes, printed circuit boards are produced and tested. These two major subcomponents then come together for assembly in the final process. Exhibit 6–2 portrays this type of processing pattern. Notice that processes 1 and 2 can occur independently of (or parallel to) processes 3 and 4.

Other forms of parallel processing also exist. However, regardless of which processing pattern exists within a company, all units produced share a common

**operation costing**

A hybrid costing method that assigns material costs to a product using a job-order approach and assigns conversion costs using a process approach.

**sequential processing**

A processing pattern in which units pass from one process to another in a set order.

**parallel processing**

A processing pattern in which two or more sequential processes are required in order to produce a finished good.

EXHIBIT 6-1

Sequential Processing Illustrated

Picking → Encapsulating → Bottling → Finished Goods

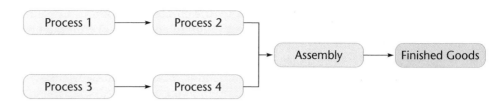

Process 1: Production and assembly of write-head and disk drive
Process 2: Testing of write-head and disk drive
Process 3: Production of circuit board
Process 4: Testing of circuit board

property. Since units are homogeneous and subjected to the same operations for a given process, each unit produced in a period should receive the same unit cost. Understanding how unit costs are computed requires an understanding of the manufacturing cost flows that take place in a process-costing company.

## How Costs Flow Through the Accounts in Process Costing

The manufacturing cost flows for a process-costing system are generally the same as those for a job-order costing system. As raw materials are purchased, the cost of these materials flows into a materials inventory account. Similarly, materials, direct labour, and applied overhead costs flow into a work-in-process account. When goods are completed, the cost of the completed goods is transferred from work in process to the finished goods account. Finally, as goods are sold, the cost of the finished goods is transferred to the cost of goods sold account.

Although job-order and process cost flows are generally similar, some differences exist. In process costing, each producing department has its own work-in-process account. As goods are completed in one department, they are transferred to the next department. Exhibit 6–3 illustrates this process for Healthblend. Notice that a product (let's say, multivitamins) starts out in the picking department, where the proper amounts of vitamin, mineral, and inert materials are mixed. Picking direct labour and applied overhead are recognized and added to the picking Work in Process account. When the mixture is properly blended, it is transferred to the encapsulating department, where capsules are filled. The filled capsules are then transferred to the bottling department. There, the capsules are bottled and then the bottles are packaged. The important point is that as the product is transferred from one department to another, so are all of the costs attached

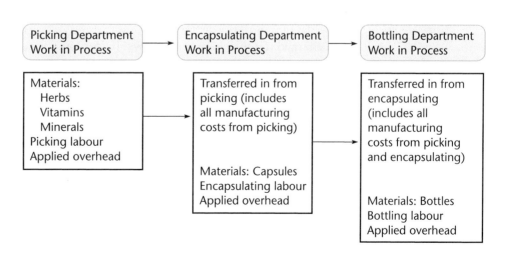

to the product. By the end of the process, all manufacturing costs end up in the final department (bottling, in this case) with the final product.

Let's attach some costs to the various departments and follow them through the accounts. For example, suppose that Healthblend decides to produce 2,000 bottles of multivitamins, with the following costs:

|  | Picking | Encapsulating | Bottling |
|---|---|---|---|
| Direct materials | $1,700 | $1,000 | $ 800 |
| Direct labour | 50 | 60 | 300 |
| Applied overhead | 450 | 500 | 600 |
| Total | $2,200 | $1,560 | $1,700 |

**transferred-in costs**

Costs transferred from a prior process to a subsequent process.

When the multivitamin mixture is transferred to the encapsulating department from the picking department, it takes $2,200 of cost along with it. This $2,200 is **transferred-in cost** to the encapsulating department and is treated as another type of direct materials cost. You could think of the encapsulating department as "buying" the mixture from the picking department. Then encapsulating adds $1,560 of cost from its process and transfers completed capsules plus $3,760 of cost ($2,200 from picking and $1,560 added in encapsulating) to the bottling department. Again, bottling treats the $3,760 of transferred-in cost as a direct materials cost and adds its own cost of $1,700 to come up with a total cost of $5,460. The completed bottles of multivitamins are transferred to the finished goods warehouse along with the $5,460 of manufacturing cost. If there were 2,000 bottles manufactured, each would have a manufacturing cost of $2.73 ($5,460/2,000).

## Accumulating Costs in the Production Report

**production report**

A document that summarizes the manufacturing activity that takes place in a process department for a given period of time.

In process costing, costs are accumulated by department for a period of time. The **production report** is the document that summarizes the manufacturing activity that takes place in a process department for a given time period. A production report contains information on costs transferred in from prior departments as well as costs added in the current department, such as direct materials, direct labour, and overhead; it is subsidiary to the Work in Process account, just as the job-order cost sheet is subsidiary to the Work in Process account in a job-order costing system.

A production report provides information about the physical units processed in a department and about the manufacturing costs associated with them. Thus, a production report is divided into a unit information section and a cost information section. The unit information section has two major subdivisions: (1) units to account for, and (2) units accounted for. Similarly, the cost information section has two major subdivisions: (1) costs to account for, and (2) costs accounted for. A production report traces the flow of units through a department, identifies the costs charged to the department, shows the computation of unit costs, and reveals the disposition of the department's costs for the reporting period.

## Service and Manufacturing Organizations

Any product or service that is basically homogeneous and repetitively produced can take advantage of a process-costing approach. Let's look at three possibilities: services, manufacturing companies with a JIT orientation, and traditional manufacturing companies.

Cheque processing in a bank, teeth cleaning by a dental hygienist, air travel between Calgary and Winnipeg, sorting mail by postal code, and laundering and pressing shirts are examples of homogeneous services that are repetitively produced. Although services cannot be stored, it is possible for organizations engaged in service production to have work-in-process inventories. For example, a batch of tax returns can be partly completed at the end of a period. However, many services are provided so quickly that there are no work-in-process inventories. Tooth cleaning, funerals, surgical operations, sonograms, and carpet cleaning are a few examples where work-in-process inventories would be virtually nonexistent. Therefore, process costing for services is relatively simple. The total costs for the period are divided by the number of services provided to compute unit cost.

Manufacturing companies may also operate without significant work-in-process inventories. Specifically, companies that have adopted a "just in time" (JIT) approach to manufacturing view the carrying of unnecessary inventories as wasteful. These companies try to reduce work-in-process inventories to very low levels. Furthermore, JIT companies usually structure their manufacturing so that process costing can be used to determine product costs.

In many JIT companies, work cells are created that produce a product or subassembly from start to finish. Costs are collected by cell for a time period, and output for the cell is measured for the same period. Unit costs are computed by dividing the costs for the period by the output for the period. There is no ambiguity concerning what costs belong to the period and how output is measured. One of the objectives of JIT manufacturing is simplification. Keep this in mind as you study the process-costing requirements of manufacturing companies that carry work-in-process inventories. The impressive difference between the two settings illustrates one of JIT's significant benefits.

Finally, traditional manufacturing companies may have significant beginning and ending work-in-process inventories. It is the presence of these inventories that leads to much of the complication surrounding process costing. These complications are due to several factors: the presence of beginning and ending work-in-process inventories; different approaches to the treatment of beginning inventory cost; and nonuniform application of manufacturing costs. We will discuss the treatment of these complicating factors in the following sections.

## The Impact of Work-in-Process Inventories on Process Costing

**Objective** 2

Define *equivalent units*, and explain their role in process costing.

The computation of unit cost for the work performed during a period is a key part of the production report. This unit cost is needed both to compute the cost of goods transferred out of a department and to value ending work-in-process inventory.[1] You might think that this is easy—just divide total cost by the number of units produced. However, the presence of work-in-process inventories causes problems.

First, defining a unit of production, given that some units produced during a period are complete while those in ending work-in-process inventory are not, is a problem. This is handled through the concept of equivalent units of production.

Second, how should the costs of beginning work in process be treated? Should they be pooled with current-period costs or separated and transferred out first? Two methods have been developed to handle this problem: the weighted average method and the FIFO method.

### Equivalent Units of Production

By definition, ending work in process is not complete. Thus, a unit completed and transferred out during the period is not identical (or equivalent) to one in ending

---

1. While both manufacturing and service organizations use process costing, typically only manufacturing companies have problems with the valuation of ending inventories of work in process and finished goods. As a result, much of our discussion in this chapter illustrates process manufacturing.

work-in-process inventory, and the cost attached to the two units should not be the same. In computing the unit cost, the output of the period must be measured. A major problem of process costing is making this measurement.

To illustrate the output problem of process costing, assume that Department A had the following data for October:

| | |
|---|---|
| Units, beginning work in process | — |
| Units started | 1,600 |
| Units completed | 1,000 |
| Units, ending work in process (25% complete) | 600 |
| Total manufacturing costs | $11,500 |

What is the output in October for this department? 1,000? 1,600? If we say 1,000 units, we ignore the effort expended on the units in ending work in process. Furthermore, the manufacturing costs incurred in October belong both to the units completed and to the partly completed units in ending work in process. On the other hand, if we say 1,600 units, we ignore the fact that the 600 units in ending work in process are only partly completed. Somehow, output must be measured so that it reflects the effort expended on both completed and partly completed units.

**equivalent units of output**

Complete units that could have been produced given the total amount of manufacturing effort expended during the period.

The solution is to calculate equivalent units of output. **Equivalent units of output** are the complete units that could have been produced given the total amount of manufacturing effort expended for the period under consideration. Determining equivalent units of output for transferred-out units is easy: a unit would not be transferred out unless it was complete. Thus, every transferred-out unit is an equivalent unit. Units remaining in ending work-in-process inventory, however, are not complete. Thus, someone in production must "eyeball" ending work in process to estimate its degree of completion. In the example, the 600 units in ending work in process are 25 percent complete; this is equivalent to 150 fully completed units ($600 \times 25\%$). Therefore, the equivalent units for October would be the 1,000 completed units plus 150 equivalent units in ending work in process—a total of 1,150 units of output.

Knowing the output for a period and the manufacturing costs for the department for that period ($11,500 in this example), we can calculate a unit cost, which in this case is $10 ($11,500/1,150). The unit cost is used to assign a cost of $10,000 ($10 \times 1,000$) to the 1,000 units transferred out and a cost of $1,500 ($10 \times 150$) to the 600 units in ending work in process. This unit cost is $10 per equivalent unit. Thus, when valuing ending work in process, the $10 unit cost is multiplied by the equivalent units, not the actual number of partly completed units.

**weighted average costing method**

A process-costing method that combines beginning inventory costs with current-period costs to compute unit costs. Costs and output from the current period and the previous period are averaged to compute unit costs.

## Two Methods of Treating Beginning Work-in-Process Inventory

The presence of beginning work-in-process inventories also complicates the computation of the unit cost. The work done on these partly completed units represents prior-period work, and the costs assigned to them are prior-period costs. In computing a current-period unit cost for a department, two approaches have evolved for dealing with the prior-period output and prior-period costs found in beginning work in process: the weighted average method and the first-in, first-out (FIFO) method.

The **weighted average costing method** combines beginning inventory costs with current-period costs to compute unit cost. In essence, the costs are pooled, and only one average unit cost is computed and applied to both units transferred out and units remaining in ending inventory.

**FIFO costing method**

A process-costing method that separates units in beginning inventory from those produced during the current period. Unit costs include only current-period costs and production.

The **FIFO costing method**, on the other hand, separates units in beginning inventory from those produced during the current period. It is assumed that units from beginning inventory are completed first, and then transferred out (along with all of the prior-period costs as well as the current-period costs for completing those units). Only then is current-period production started and either completed (and transferred out, along with current costs) or left incomplete as ending work-in-process inventory.

If product costs do not change from period to period, or if there is no beginning work-in-process inventory, the FIFO and weighted average methods yield the same results. The weighted average method is discussed in more detail in the next section. Further discussion of the FIFO method is found in the Appendix.

# Weighted Average Costing

**Objective 3**

Prepare a departmental production report using the weighted average method.

The weighted average costing method treats beginning inventory costs and the accompanying equivalent output as if they belong to the current period. This is done for costs by adding the manufacturing costs in beginning work in process to the manufacturing costs incurred during the current period. The total cost is treated as if it were the current period's total manufacturing cost. Similarly, beginning inventory output and current-period output are merged in the calculation of equivalent units. Under the weighted average method, equivalent units of output are computed by adding units completed to equivalent units in ending work in process. Notice that the equivalent units in beginning work in process are included in the computation. Consequently, these units are counted as part of the current period's equivalent units of output.

## Five Steps in Preparing a Production Report

Recall that the production report summarizes cost and manufacturing activity for a producing department for a given time period. The general pattern is described by the following five steps:

1. Analysis of the flow of physical units
2. Calculation of equivalent units
3. Computation of unit cost
4. Valuation of inventories (goods transferred out and ending work in process)
5. Cost reconciliation

We will follow the five steps in the following example. Doing so gives some structure to the method of accounting for process costs and makes it easier to learn and remember.

## Example of the Weighted Average Method

To illustrate the weighted average method, let's use cost and production data for Healthblend's picking department for July (assume that units are measured in litres):

Production:
| | |
|---|---|
| Units in process, July 1 (75% complete) | 20,000 |
| Units started in July | 40,000 |
| Units completed and transferred out | 50,000 |
| Units in process, July 31 (25% complete) | 10,000 |

Costs:
| | |
|---|---|
| Work in process, July 1 | $ 3,525 |
| Costs added during July | $10,125 |

In the weighted average method, to allocate manufacturing costs to units transferred out and to units remaining in ending work in process, we pool the costs from beginning work in process (BWIP) with the costs added to production during July. These total pooled costs ($3,525 + $10,125 = $13,650) are averaged and assigned to units transferred out and to units in ending work in process (EWIP). On the units side, we concentrate on the degree of completion of all units at the end of the period. We do not care about the percentage of completion of BWIP. We care only about whether these units are complete or not by the end of July. Thus, equivalent units are computed by pooling manufacturing effort from June and July.

Let's take a closer look at the July production in Healthblend's picking department by focusing on the five steps of the weighted average method.

### Step 1: Physical Flow Analysis

The purpose of Step 1 is to trace the physical units of production. Physical units are not equivalent units; they are units that may be in any stage of completion. We can see that there are 60,000 physical units; 20,000 are from BWIP and another 40,000 were started in July. From those 60,000, 10,000 remain in EWIP, 25 percent complete. The analysis of physical flow of units is usually accomplished by preparing a **physical flow schedule** like the one shown in Exhibit 6–4. Notice that the "total units to account for" must equal the "total units accounted for." The physical flow schedule in Exhibit 6–4 is important because it contains the information needed for calculating equivalent units (Step 2).

**physical flow schedule**
A schedule that reconciles units to account for with units accounted for. The physical units are not adjusted for percent of completion.

### Step 2: Calculation of Equivalent Units

Given the information in the physical flow schedule, we can calculate the weighted average equivalent units for July. This calculation is shown in Exhibit 6–5. Notice that July's output is measured as 52,500 units: 50,000 units completed and transferred out, and 2,500 equivalent units from ending inventory (10,000 × 25%).

### Step 3: Computation of Unit Cost

In addition to July output, July manufacturing costs are needed to compute a unit cost. The weighted average method rolls back and includes the manufacturing costs associated with the units in beginning work in process. Thus, the total manufacturing cost for July is defined as $13,650 ($3,525 + $10,125). The manufacturing costs carried over from the prior period ($3,525) are treated as if they were current-period costs.

Given the manufacturing costs for July and the output for the month, we can calculate the unit cost and use it to determine the cost of goods transferred out

**EXHIBIT  6-4**

Physical Flow Schedule

| Units to account for: | |
|---|---|
| Beginning work in process (75% complete) | 20,000 |
| Started during the period | 40,000 |
| Total units to account for | 60,000 |
| Units accounted for: | |
| Completed and transferred out | 50,000 |
| Ending work in process (25% complete) | 10,000 |
| Total units accounted for | 60,000 |

**EXHIBIT  6-5**

Equivalent Units of
Production: Weighted
Average Method

| | |
|---|---:|
| Units completed (100%) | 50,000 |
| Add: Units in ending work in process × fraction completed | |
| 10,000 units × 25% | 2,500 |
| Equivalent units of output | 52,500 |

and the cost of ending work in process. For July, the weighted average method
gives the following unit cost:

$$\text{Unit cost} = \$13,650/52,500 = \$0.26 \text{ per equivalent unit}$$

### Step 4: Valuation of Inventories

With the unit cost of $0.26, the cost of goods transferred to the encapsulating
department is $13,000 (50,000 units × $0.26 per unit), and the cost of ending work
in process is $650 (2,500 equivalent units × $0.26 per unit). Notice that units completed (from Step 1), equivalent units in ending work in process (from Step 2), and
the unit cost (from Step 3) were all needed to value both goods transferred out
and ending work in process.

### Step 5: Cost Reconciliation

The total manufacturing costs assigned to inventories are as follows:

| | |
|---|---:|
| Cost of goods transferred out | $13,000 |
| Cost of goods, ending work in process | 650 |
| Total costs accounted for | $13,650 |

The manufacturing costs to account for are also $13,650.

| | |
|---|---:|
| Cost of beginning work in process | $ 3,525 |
| Costs incurred during the period | 10,125 |
| Total costs to account for | $13,650 |

**cost reconciliation**

The final section of the
production report and the
section that compares the
costs to account for with
the costs accounted for to
ensure that they are
equal.

Thus, the costs to account for are exactly assigned to inventories, and we have
the necessary **cost reconciliation**. Remember, the total costs assigned to goods
transferred out and to ending work in process must agree with the total costs in
beginning work in process and the manufacturing costs incurred during the current period.

### Production Report

Steps 1 through 5 provide all of the information needed to prepare a production
report for the picking department for July. This report is given in Exhibit 6–6.

## Evaluation of the Weighted Average Method

The major benefit of the weighted average method is simplicity. If we treat units in
beginning work in process as belonging to the current period, all equivalent units
belong to the same category when it comes to calculating unit costs. Thus, unit-cost
computations are simplified. The main disadvantage of this method is reduced
accuracy in computing unit costs for current-period output and for units in beginning work in process. If the unit cost in a process is relatively stable from one period
to the next, the weighted average method is reasonably accurate. However, if the
price of manufacturing inputs increases significantly from one period to the next,
the unit cost of current output is understated, and the unit cost of beginning work-
in-process units is overstated. If greater accuracy in computing unit costs is desired,
a company should use the FIFO method to determine unit costs.

EXHIBIT 6-6

Production Report—
Weighted Average
Method (July 2004)

## Healthblend Company
## Picking Department
## Production Report for July 2004
## (Weighted Average Method)

### Unit Information

*Physical Flow*

| Units to account for: | | Units accounted for: | |
|---|---|---|---|
| Beginning work in process | 20,000 | Completed | 50,000 |
| Started | 40,000 | Ending work in process | 10,000 |
| Total units to account for | 60,000 | Total units accounted for | 60,000 |

*Equivalent Units*

| | |
|---|---|
| Completed | 50,000 |
| Ending work in process | 2,500 |
| Total equivalent units | 52,500 |

### Cost Information

Cost to account for:

| | |
|---|---|
| Beginning work in process | $ 3,525 |
| Incurred during the period | 10,125 |
| Total costs to account for | $13,650 |
| Cost per equivalent unit | $0.26    ($13,650/52,500) |

| | Transferred Out | Ending Work in Process | Total |
|---|---|---|---|
| Cost accounted for: | | | |
| Goods transferred out ($0.26 × 50,000) | $13,000 | — | $13,000 |
| Goods in ending work in process ($0.26 × 2,500) | — | $650 | 650 |
| Total costs accounted for | $13,000 | $650 | $13,650 |

# Multiple Inputs and Multiple Departments

**Objective 4**

Explain how process costing is affected by nonuniform application of manufacturing inputs and the existence of multiple processing departments.

Accounting for production using process costing is complicated by nonuniform application of manufacturing inputs and by the presence of multiple processing departments. We will now discuss how process-costing methods address these complications.

## Nonuniform Application of Manufacturing Inputs

Up to this point, we have assumed that work in process being 60 percent complete meant that 60 percent of the materials, labour, and overhead needed to complete the process have been used and that another 40 percent are needed to finish the units. In other words, we have assumed that manufacturing inputs are applied uniformly as the manufacturing process unfolds.

Assuming uniform application of conversion costs (direct labour and overhead) is often reasonable. Direct labour input is usually needed throughout the process, and overhead is often incurred continuously. Direct materials, on the other hand, are not as likely to be applied uniformly. In many instances, materials are added either at the beginning or near the end of the process.

For example, look at the differences in Healthblend's three departments. In the picking and encapsulating departments, all materials are added at the beginning of the process. However, in the bottling department, materials are added both at the beginning (filled capsules and bottles) and at the end (bottle caps and boxes).

Work in process in the picking department that is 50 percent complete with respect to conversion inputs would be 100 percent complete with respect to the material inputs. Work in process in bottling that is 50 percent complete with respect to conversion would be 100 percent complete with respect to bottles and transferred-in capsules, but zero percent complete with respect to bottle caps and boxes.

Different percentage-of-completion figures for manufacturing inputs pose a problem for the calculation of equivalent units. Fortunately, the solution is relatively simple. Equivalent-unit calculations are done for each category of manufacturing input. Thus, there are equivalent units calculated for each category of materials and for conversion cost. The conversion cost category can be broken down into direct labour and overhead, if desired. If direct labour and overhead are applied uniformly, however, this serves no useful purpose.

To illustrate, assume that Healthblend's picking department has the following data for September:

Production:
| | |
|---|---:|
| Units in process, September 1, 50% complete* | 10,000 |
| Units started in September | 70,000 |
| Units completed and transferred out | 60,000 |
| Units in process, September 30, 40% complete* | 20,000 |

Costs:
Work in process, September 1:
| | |
|---|---:|
| Materials | $ 1,600 |
| Conversion costs | 200 |
| Total | $ 1,800 |

Current costs:
| | |
|---|---:|
| Materials | $12,000 |
| Conversion costs | 3,200 |
| Total | $15,200 |

\* With respect to conversion costs

As before, Healthblend uses the weighted average method for process costing. Exhibit 6–7 illustrates Step 1—creating the physical flow schedule. Accounting for the flow of physical units is not affected by the nonuniform application of manufacturing inputs, because physical units may be in any stage of completion.

EXHIBIT   6-7

Physical Flow Schedule
Nonuniform Inputs

| | |
|---|---:|
| Units to account for: | |
| Units in beginning work in process (50% complete) | 10,000 |
| Units started during September | 70,000 |
| Total units to account for | 80,000 |
| | |
| Units accounted for: | |
| Units completed and transferred out | 60,000 |
| Units in ending work in process (40% complete) | 20,000 |
| Total units accounted for | 80,000 |

Nonuniform application of inputs does affect the computation of equivalent units (Step 2). Exhibit 6–8 illustrates this computation. Notice that two categories of input are used to calculate equivalent units. Since all materials are added at the beginning of the process, all units are 100 percent complete with respect to materials. Thus, there are 20,000 equivalent units of materials in ending work in process. However, since only 40 percent of the conversion costs have been applied, there are only 8,000 conversion equivalent units in ending work in process.

**EXHIBIT  6-8**

Equivalent Units of Production: Nonuniform Application

|  | Materials | Conversion |
|---|---|---|
| Units completed | 60,000 | 60,000 |
| Add: Units in ending work in process × Fraction completed: 20,000 × 100%; 20,000 × 40% | 20,000 | 8,000 |
| Equivalent units of output | 80,000 | 68,000 |

When different categories of equivalent units exist, a unit cost for each category must be computed. The cost per completed unit (Step 3) is the sum of these individual unit costs. The computations for the example are shown in Exhibit 6-9.

**EXHIBIT  6-9**

Cost per Equivalent Unit

|  | Materials | Conversion Cost | Total |
|---|---|---|---|
| Beginning work in process | $1,600 | $ 200 | $ 1,800 |
| Incurred during period | 12,000 | 3,200 | 15,200 |
| Total cost | $13,600 | $3,400 | $17,000 |
| Equivalent units (Exhibit 6–8) | 80,000 | 68,000 | n/a |
| Cost per equivalent unit | $ 0.17 | $ 0.05 | $ 0.22 |

Valuation of goods transferred out (Step 4) is accomplished by multiplying the unit cost by the number of units completed:

$$\text{Cost of goods transferred out} = \$0.22 \times 60{,}000 = \$13{,}200$$

Valuation of ending work in process is done by obtaining the cost of each manufacturing input and then summing these individual input costs. For the example, this requires adding the cost of the materials in ending work in process to the conversion costs in ending work in process.

The cost of materials is the unit materials cost multiplied by the material equivalent units in ending work in process. Similarly, the conversion cost in ending work in process is the unit conversion cost multiplied by the conversion equivalent units. Thus, the cost of ending work in process is as follows:

| Materials: $0.17 × 20,000 | $3,400 |
|---|---|
| Conversion: $0.05 × 8,000 | 400 |
| Total cost | $3,800 |

Step 5 reconciles the costs to ensure that the computations are correct.

| Costs to account for: |  |
|---|---|
| Costs from beginning work in process | $ 1,800 |
| Costs incurred during the period | 15,200 |
| Total costs to account for | $17,000 |
| Costs accounted for: |  |
| Cost of goods transferred out | $13,200 |
| Cost of goods in ending work in process | 3,800 |
| Total costs accounted for | $17,000 |

Using the information generated from the five steps, you can prepare a production report (see Exhibit 6–10). As the example has shown, applying manufacturing inputs at different stages of a process poses no serious problems. However, the effort required to compute the costs has increased.

## Multiple Departments

In process manufacturing, some departments receive partly completed goods from prior departments. The usual approach is to treat transferred-in goods as a separate material category when calculating equivalent units.

In dealing with transferred-in goods, two important points should be remembered. First, the cost of this material is the cost of the goods transferred out as computed in the prior department. Second, the units started in the subsequent department correspond to the units transferred out from the prior department.

**EXHIBIT 6-10**

Production Report—
Weighted Average
Method
(September 2004)

**Healthblend Company**
**Picking Department**
**Production Report for September 2004**
**(Weighted Average Method)**

### Unit Information

| Units to account for: | | Units accounted for: | |
|---|---|---|---|
| Beginning work in process | 10,000 | Completed | 60,000 |
| Started | 70,000 | Ending work in process | 20,000 |
| Total units to account for | 80,000 | Total units accounted for | 80,000 |

### Equivalent Units

| | Materials | Conversion Cost |
|---|---|---|
| Completed | 60,000 | 60,000 |
| Ending work in process | 20,000 | 8,000 |
| Total equivalent units | 80,000 | 68,000 |

### Cost Information

| | Materials | Conversion Cost | Total |
|---|---|---|---|
| Costs to account for: | | | |
| Beginning work in process | $ 1,600 | $ 200 | $ 1,800 |
| Incurred during the period | 12,000 | 3,200 | 15,200 |
| Total costs to account for | $13,600 | $3,400 | $17,000 |
| Cost per equivalent unit | $0.17 | $0.05 | $0.22 |

| | Transferred Out | Ending Work in Process | Total |
|---|---|---|---|
| Costs accounted for: | | | |
| Goods transferred out ($0.22 × 60,000) | $13,200 | — | $13,200 |
| Goods in ending work in process: | | | |
| Materials ($0.17 × 20,000) | — | $3,400 | 3,400 |
| Conversion ($0.05 × 8,000) | — | 400 | 400 |
| Total costs accounted for | $13,200 | $3,800 | $17,000 |

For example, let's consider the month of September for Healthblend, restricting our attention to the transferred-in category. Assume that the encapsulating department had 15,000 units in beginning inventory (with transferred-in costs of $3,000) and completed 70,000 units during the month. Further, the picking department completed and transferred out 60,000 units at a cost of $13,200 in September. In constructing a physical flow schedule for the encapsulating department, consider its dependence on the picking department:

| | |
|---|---:|
| Units to account for: | |
|     Beginning work in process | 15,000 |
|     Transferred in during September | 60,000 |
|         Total units to account for | 75,000 |
| | |
| Units accounted for: | |
|     Completed and transferred out | 70,000 |
|     Ending work in process | 5,000 |
|         Total units accounted for | 75,000 |

Equivalent units for the transferred-in category are calculated as follows (ignoring other input categories):

| | |
|---|---:|
| Units completed | 70,000 |
| Add: Units in ending work in process × Fraction completed | |
| (5,000 × 100%*) | 5,000 |
| Equivalent units of output | 75,000 |

* Remember that ending work in process is 100 percent complete with respect to transferred-in costs, not to all costs of the encapsulating department.

To compute the unit cost, we add the cost of the units transferred in from picking in September to the transferred-in costs in beginning work in process and divide by transferred-in equivalent units:

$$\begin{aligned} \text{Unit cost (transferred-in category)} &= (\$13{,}200 + \$3{,}000)/75{,}000 \\ &= \$16{,}200/75{,}000 \\ &= \$0.216 \end{aligned}$$

As has just been shown, the only additional complication introduced in the analysis for a subsequent department is the presence of the transferred-in category. Dealing with this category is similar to handling another material category. However, it must be remembered that the current cost of this "material" is the cost of the units transferred in from the prior process, and the equivalent units transferred in are equal to all units started in the subsequent department.

## Appendix: Production Report—FIFO Costing

**Objective 5**

Prepare a departmental production report using the FIFO method.

Under the FIFO costing method, the equivalent units and manufacturing costs in beginning work in process are excluded from the current-period unit-cost calculation. This method recognizes that the work and costs carried over from the prior period legitimately belong to that period.

If changes occur in the prices of the manufacturing inputs from one period to the next, then FIFO produces a more accurate (that is, more current) unit cost than does the weighted average method. A more accurate unit cost means better cost control, better pricing decisions, and so on. Keep in mind that if the period is as short as a week or a month, however, the unit costs calculated under the two methods are not likely to differ much. In that case, the FIFO method has little, if anything, to offer over the weighted average method. Perhaps for this reason, many companies use the weighted average method.

Since FIFO excludes prior-period work and costs, we need to create two categories of completed units. FIFO assumes that units in beginning work in process are completed first, before any new units are started. Thus, one category of completed units is beginning work-in-process units. The second category is for those units started and completed during the current period.

For example, assume that a department had 20,000 units in beginning work in process and that it completed and transferred out a total of 50,000 units. Of the 50,000 completed units, 20,000 are the units initially found in beginning work in process. The remaining 30,000 were started and completed during the current period.

These two categories of completed units are needed in the FIFO method so that each category can be costed correctly. For the units started and completed in the current period, the unit cost is the total current manufacturing costs divided by the current-period equivalent output. However, for the units from beginning work-in-process, the total associated manufacturing costs are the sum of the prior-period costs plus the costs incurred in the current period to finish the units. Thus, costs from the current period and from beginning inventory are not pooled. Instead, current-period cost is added to beginning inventory cost in order to complete the units on hand at the start of the period.

To illustrate the computations for the FIFO method we will use the same Healthblend data used for the weighted average method when we assumed uniform use of manufacturing inputs. Using the same data highlights the differences between the two methods. The five steps in costing out production follow.

Production:
| | |
|---|---|
| Units in process, July 1 (75% complete) | 20,000 |
| Units started in July | 40,000 |
| Units completed and transferred out | 50,000 |
| Units in process, July 31 (25% complete) | 10,000 |

Costs:
| | |
|---|---|
| Work in process, July 1 | $ 3,525 |
| Costs added during July | $10,125 |

### Step 1: Physical Flow Analysis

The purpose of Step 1 is to trace the physical units of production. As with the weighted average method, in the FIFO method, a physical flow schedule is prepared. This schedule for the FIFO method is shown in Exhibit 6–11. Note that the completed and transferred out are split into two categories: (1) from beginning work in process and (2) started and completed.

### Step 2: Calculation of Equivalent Units

Exhibit 6–12 illustrates the calculation of equivalent units under the FIFO method. From the equivalent-unit computation in Exhibit 6–12, one difference

EXHIBIT  6-11

Physical Flow Schedule

| | | |
|---|---|---|
| Units to account for: | | |
| Beginning work in process (75% complete) | | 20,000 |
| Started during July | | 40,000 |
| Total units to account for | | 60,000 |
| | | |
| Units accounted for: | | |
| Completed and transferred out: | | |
| From beginning work in process | 20,000 | |
| Started and completed | 30,000 | 50,000 |
| Ending work in process (25% complete) | | 10,000 |
| Total units accounted for | | 60,000 |

EXHIBIT   6-12

Equivalent Units of
Production: FIFO Method

| | |
|---|---:|
| Units in beginning work in process × Fraction to be completed | |
| (20,000 × 25%) | 5,000 |
| Add: Units started and completed | 30,000 |
| Add: Units in ending work in process × Fraction complete | |
| (10,000 × 25%) | 2,500 |
| Equivalent units of output | 37,500 |

between weighted average and FIFO becomes immediately apparent. Under FIFO, the equivalent units in beginning work in process, work done in the prior period, are not counted as part of the total equivalent work. Only the equivalent work done *this period* is counted. The equivalent work done this period for the units from the prior period is computed by multiplying the number of units in beginning work in process by the percentage of work remaining. Since in this example the percentage of work done in the prior period is 75 percent, the percentage left to be completed this period is 25 percent, or an equivalent of 5,000 additional units of work.

The effect of excluding prior-period effort is to produce the current-period equivalent output. Recall that under the weighted average method, 52,500 equivalent units were computed for this month. Under FIFO, only 37,500 units are calculated for the same month. These 37,500 units represent current-period output. The difference, of course, is explained by the fact that the weighted average method rolls back and counts the 15,000 equivalent units of prior-period work (20,000 units BWIP × 75%) as belonging to the current period.

### Step 3: Computation of Unit Cost

The additional manufacturing costs incurred in the current period are $10,125. Thus, the current-period unit manufacturing cost is $10,125/37,500, or $0.27. Notice that the costs of beginning inventory are excluded from this calculation. Only current-period manufacturing costs are used.

### Step 4: Valuation of Inventories

Since all equivalent units in ending work in process are current-period units, the cost of ending work in process is simply $0.27 × 2,500, or $675. However, when it comes to valuing goods transferred out, another difference emerges between the weighted average method and FIFO.

Under weighted average, the cost of goods transferred out is simply the unit cost multiplied by the units completed. Under FIFO, however, there are two sources of completed units: 20,000 units from beginning inventory, and 30,000 units started and completed. The cost of the 30,000 units that were started and completed in the current period and transferred out is $8,100 ($0.27 × 30,000). For these units, the use of the current-period unit cost is entirely appropriate.

However, the cost of the beginning work-in-process units that were transferred out is another matter. These units started the period with $3,525 of manufacturing costs already incurred and 15,000 units of equivalent output already completed. To finish these units, the equivalent of 5,000 units was needed. The cost of finishing the units in beginning work in process is $1,350 ($0.27 × 5,000). Adding this $1,350 to the $3,525 in cost carried over from the prior period gives a total manufacturing cost for these units of $4,875. The unit cost of these 20,000 units, then, is about $0.24375 ($4,875/20,000).[2]

---

2. Note that the unit cost from the prior period is $0.235 ($3,525/15,000).

## Step 5: Cost Reconciliation

With the completion of Step 5, the production report can be prepared. This report is shown in Exhibit 6–13. The total costs assigned to production are as follows:

| Goods transferred out: | |
|---|---:|
| Units in beginning work in process | $ 4,875 |
| Units started and completed | 8,100 |
| Goods in ending work in process | 675 |
| Total costs accounted for | $13,650 |

The total manufacturing costs to account for during the period are as follows:

| Beginning work in process | $ 3,525 |
|---|---:|
| Incurred during the period | 10,125 |
| Total costs to account for | $13,650 |

**EXHIBIT 6-13**

Production Report—FIFO Method (July 2004)

**Healthblend Company**
**Picking Department**
**Production Report for July 2004**
**(FIFO Method)**

### Unit Information

| Units to account for: | | |
|---|---:|---|
| Beginning work in process | 20,000 | |
| Started | 40,000 | |
| Total units to account for | 60,000 | |

| | Physical Flow | Equivalent Units |
|---|---:|---:|
| Units accounted for: | | |
| Started and completed | 30,000 | 30,000 |
| Completed from beginning inventory | 20,000 | 5,000 |
| Ending work in process | 10,000 | 2,500 |
| Total units accounted for | 60,000 | 37,500 |

### Cost Information

| Costs to account for: | | |
|---|---:|---|
| Beginning work in process | $ 3,525 | |
| Incurred during the period | 10,125 | |
| Total costs to account for | $13,650 | |
| Current cost per equivalent unit | $0.27 ($10,125/37,500) | |

| | Transferred Out | Ending Work in Process | Total |
|---|---:|---:|---:|
| Costs accounted for: | | | |
| Units in beginning work in process: | | | |
| From prior period | $ 3,525 | — | $ 3,525 |
| From current period ($0.27 × 5,000) | 1,350 | — | 1,350 |
| Units started and completed ($0.27 × 30,000) | 8,100 | — | 8,100 |
| Goods in ending work in process ($0.27 × 2,500) | — | $675 | 675 |
| Total costs accounted for | $12,975 | $675 | $13,650 |

Often the total costs accounted for do not precisely equal the costs to account for, due to rounding error. An easy way to bring the amounts into balance is to adjust the cost of goods transferred out by the amount of the rounding error.

The differences between the weighted average method and the FIFO method consist of the way that equivalent units and unit costs are calculated, and the way unit costs are used to assign costs to the finished goods and work-in-process inventories. In the example, the difference is small; the cost for goods transferred out is $13,000 for the weighted average method (see Exhibit 6–6) and $12,975 for the FIFO method (see Exhibit 6–13). The ending work-in-process inventories are $650 (weighted average) and $675 (FIFO). This reflects the slightly higher current-period unit cost that is applied to a greater extent to ending work-in-process inventory under FIFO. If the difference between current-period and prior-period costs was greater, the difference in the assigned costs would also be greater.

## Summary of Learning Objectives

**1. Describe the basic characteristics and cost flows associated with process manufacturing.**

Cost flows under process costing are similar to those under job-order costing. Raw materials are purchased and charged to the Materials account. Direct materials used in production, direct labour, and overhead applied are charged to the Work in Process account. In a production process with several processes, there is a Work in Process account for each department or process. Goods completed in one department are transferred out to the next department. When units are completed in the final department or process, their cost is transferred from Work in Process to Finished Goods.

**2. Define *equivalent units*, and explain their role in process costing.**

Equivalent units of production are the complete units that could have been produced given the total amount of manufacturing effort expended during the period. The number of physical units is multiplied by the percentage of completion to calculate equivalent units.

**3. Prepare a departmental production report using the weighted average method.**

The production report summarizes the manufacturing activity occurring in a department for a given period. It discloses information concerning the physical flow of units, equivalent units, unit costs, and the disposition of the manufacturing costs associated with the period. Using the weighted average method, beginning inventory costs are combined with current-period costs to compute unit costs. Additionally, equivalent units of production include work done in prior periods.

**4. Explain how process costing is affected by nonuniform application of manufacturing inputs and the existence of multiple processing departments.**

Nonuniform application of productive inputs requires the computation of separate equivalent units and unit costs. This, in turn, requires the determination of separate percentage-of-completion figures for each input. When a company has more than one processing department, the output of one department becomes an input of a succeeding department. The usual method is to handle the transferred-in units and costs as another form of material.

**5. Prepare a departmental production report using the FIFO method. (Appendix)**

A production report prepared according to the FIFO method separates the cost of beginning work in process from the cost of the current period. Beginning work in process is assumed to be completed and transferred out first. Cost from beginning work in process is not pooled with current-period cost in computing unit cost. Additionally, equivalent units of production exclude work done in the prior period.

## Key Terms

Cost reconciliation  225
Equivalent units of output  222
FIFO costing method  222
Operation costing  218

Parallel processing  218
Physical flow schedule  224
Production report  220
Sequential processing  218

Transferred-in costs  220
Weighted average costing
  method  222

## Review Problem

Payson Company, which uses the weighted average method, produces a product that passes through two departments: mixing and cooking. In the mixing department, all materials are added at the beginning of the process. All other manufacturing inputs are added uniformly. The following information pertains to the mixing department for February:

a. Beginning work in process (BWIP), February 1: 100,000 kilograms, 40 percent complete with respect to conversion costs. The costs assigned to this work are as follows:

| | |
|---|---|
| Materials | $20,000 |
| Labour | 10,000 |
| Overhead | 30,000 |

b. Ending work in process (EWIP), February 28: 50,000 kilograms, 60 percent complete with respect to conversion costs.
c. Units started: 320,000 kilograms. The following costs were added during the month:

| | |
|---|---|
| Materials | $211,000 |
| Labour | 100,000 |
| Overhead | 270,000 |

**Required:**
1. Prepare a physical flow schedule.
2. Prepare a schedule of equivalent units.
3. Compute the cost per equivalent unit.
4. Compute the cost of goods transferred out and the cost of ending work in process.
5. Prepare a cost reconciliation.

### Solution

1. Physical flow schedule:

| Units to account for: | | Units accounted for: | |
|---|---|---|---|
| Units, BWIP | 100,000 | Units completed and transferred out* | 370,000 |
| Units started | 320,000 | Units, EWIP | 50,000 |
| Total | 420,000 | Total | 420,000 |

\* 270,000 units started and completed, plus 100,000 units from BWIP

2. Schedule of equivalent units:

| | Materials | Conversion |
|---|---|---|
| Units completed | 370,000 | 370,000 |
| Units, EWIP × Fraction completed: | | |
| 50,000 × 100%; 50,000 × 60% | 50,000 | 30,000 |
| Equivalent units of output | 420,000 | 400,000 |

3. Cost per equivalent unit:

| | | |
|---|---|---|
| Direct materials unit cost | $0.550 | ($20,000 + $211,000)/420,000 |
| Conversion unit cost | $1.025 | ($40,000 + $370,000)/400,000 |
| Total unit cost | $1.575 | |

4. Cost of goods transferred out and cost of ending work in process:

Cost of goods transferred out = $1.575 × 370,000 = $582,750

Cost of EWIP = ($0.55 × 50,000) + ($1.025 × 30,000) = $58,250

5. Cost reconciliation:

| Costs to account for: | | Costs accounted for: | |
|---|---|---|---|
| BWIP | $ 60,000 | Goods transferred out | $582,750 |
| Costs added | 581,000 | EWIP | 58,250 |
| Total to account for | $641,000 | Total costs accounted for | $641,000 |

# Questions for Writing and Discussion

1. Distinguish between sequential processing and parallel processing.

2. Describe the differences between process costing and job-order costing.

3. What are equivalent units? Why are they needed in a process-costing system?

4. Under the weighted average method, how are prior-period costs and output treated? How are they treated under the FIFO method?

5. Under what conditions will the weighted average and FIFO methods give essentially the same results?

6. How is the equivalent-unit calculation affected when materials are added at the beginning or end of the process rather than uniformly throughout the process?

7. Explain why transferred-in costs are a special type of material for the receiving department.

8. What are the similarities in and differences between the manufacturing cost flows for job-order companies and process companies?

9. Describe the five steps in accounting for the manufacturing activity of a processing department, and explain how they interrelate.

10. What is a production report? What purpose does this report serve?

11. In assigning costs to goods transferred out, how do the weighted average and FIFO methods differ?

12. How does the adoption of a JIT approach to manufacturing affect process costing?

13. How would process costing for services differ from process costing for manufactured goods?

## Exercises

**6–1**

*Basic Cost Flows*

**LO1**

Jumpin Jeans produces a variety of styles of jeans in three departments: cutting, sewing, and packaging. During one month, the three departments recorded the following costs:

|  | Cutting | Sewing | Packaging |
|---|---|---|---|
| Direct materials | $5,400 | $ 900 | $225 |
| Direct labour | 150 | 1,800 | 900 |
| Applied overhead | 750 | 3,600 | 900 |

Six hundred pairs of jeans were started and completed during the month. There are no beginning or ending work in process inventories.

**Required:**

1. Prepare a schedule showing, for each department, the direct material cost, direct labour cost, applied overhead cost, cost transferred in from a prior department, and total manufacturing.
2. What is the total unit product cost of a pair of jeans?

**6–2**

*Equivalent Units*

**LO2**

Department B had the following data for November:

| Units in beginning work in process | — |
|---|---|
| Units completed | 500 |
| Units in ending work in process, 30% complete | 300 |
| Total manufacturing cost | $1,652 |

**Required:**

1. Calculate equivalent units of production in ending work-in-process inventory. Calculate total equivalent units of production for Department B for November.
2. What is the unit manufacturing cost for Department B for November?
3. What is the cost of goods transferred out? What is the cost of ending work-in-process inventory?

**6–3**

*Physical Flow; Equivalent Units*

**LO1, LO2, LO3**

Spreadsheet

Jadlow Company manufactures a product that passes through two processes. The following information was obtained for the first department for May:

a. All materials are added at the beginning of the process.
b. Beginning work in process had 13,500 units, 30 percent complete with respect to conversion costs.
c. Ending work in process had 8,100 units, 25 percent complete with respect to conversion costs.
d. Jadlow started in production 16,500 units.

**Required:**
1. How many units were transferred out during the month of May?
2. How many units were started and completed during the month of May?
3. Prepare a physical flow schedule for the month of May.
4. Compute equivalent units for the month of May.

**6–4**

*Weighted Average Method; Valuation of Goods Transferred Out and Ending WIP*

**LO3**

Happy Toddler, Inc., manufactures products that pass through two or more processes. Happy Toddler uses the weighted average method to compute unit costs. During April, equivalent units were computed as follows:

|                                              | Materials | Conversion Cost |
| -------------------------------------------- | --------- | --------------- |
| Units completed                              | 6,000     | 6,000           |
| Units in EWIP × fraction completed:          |           |                 |
| 4,000 × 0%; 4,000 × 60%                       | 0         | 2,400           |
| Equivalent units of output                   | 6,000     | 8,400           |

The unit cost was computed as follows:

| Materials       | $1.30 |
| --------------- | ----- |
| Conversion cost | 0.50  |
| Total           | $1.80 |

**Required:**
1. Determine the cost of ending work in process and the cost of the goods transferred out.
2. If possible, prepare a physical flow schedule.

**6–5**

*Basic Flows; Equivalent Units*

**LO1, LO2**

Shannon Company produces a product that passes through two departments.

Data for June on Department 1 were as follows: beginning work in process was zero; ending work in process had 300 units, 50 percent complete with respect to conversion costs; and 540 units were started. Materials are added at the beginning of the process in Department 1.

Data for June on Department 2 were as follows: beginning work in process was 100 units, 20 percent complete with respect to conversion costs; and ending work in process was 50 units, 40 percent complete with respect to conversion costs. All materials are added at the end of the process in Department 2.

**Required:**
1. For Department 1 for June, calculate the following:
   a. Number of units transferred to Department 2.
   b. Equivalent units of production for materials and for conversion costs.
2. For Department 2 for June, calculate the following:
   a. Number of units transferred out to Finished Goods.
   b. Equivalent units of production for materials and for conversion costs.

**6–6**

*Steps in Preparing a Production Report*

**LO3**

Spreadsheet

Mino Company manufactures chocolate syrup in three departments: cooking, mixing, and bottling. Mino uses the weighted average method. The following are cost and production data for the mixing department for March (assume that units are measured in litres):

| Production:                                    |          |
| ---------------------------------------------- | -------- |
| Units in process, March 1 (60% complete)       | 20,000   |
| Units completed and transferred out            | 50,000   |
| Units in process, March 31 (20% complete)      | 10,000   |
| Costs:                                         |          |
| Work in process, March 1                       | $93,600  |
| Costs added during March                       | $314,600 |

**Required:**
1. Prepare a physical flow analysis for the mixing department for the month of March.
2. Calculate equivalent units of production for the mixing department for the month of March.
3. Calculate unit cost for the mixing department for the month of March.
4. Calculate the cost of units transferred out and the cost of ending work-in-process inventory.
5. Prepare a cost reconciliation for the mixing department for the month of March.

**6–7**

Production Report

LO3

Refer to 6–6. Prepare a production report for the mixing department for the month of March.

**6–8**

Basic Cost Flows

LO1

Choose the *best* answer for each of the following multiple-choice questions:

1. Process costing works well whenever
   a. heterogeneous products pass through a series of processes and receive similar amounts of materials, labour, and overhead.
   b. homogeneous products pass through a series of processes and receive similar amounts of materials, labour, and overhead.
   c. homogeneous products pass through a series of processes and receive similar doses of conversion inputs and different doses of material inputs.
   d. material cost is accumulated by batch and conversion cost is accumulated by process.
   e. None of the above.

2. Operation costing works well whenever
   a. heterogeneous products pass through a series of processes and receive similar amounts of materials, labour, and overhead.
   b. homogeneous products pass through a series of processes and receive similar amounts of materials, labour, and overhead.
   c. homogeneous products pass through a series of processes and receive similar amounts of conversion inputs and different amounts of material inputs.
   d. material cost is accumulated by batch and conversion cost is accumulated by process.
   e. None of the above.

3. Sequential processing is characterized by
   a. a pattern where partially completed units are worked on simultaneously.
   b. a pattern where different partially completed units must pass through parallel processes before being brought together in a final process.
   c. a pattern where partially completed units must pass through one process before they can be worked on in later processes.
   d. a pattern where partially completed units must be purchased from outside suppliers and delivered to the final process in a sequential time mode.
   e. None of the above.

4. The costs transferred from a prior process
   a  to a subsequent process are treated as another type of material cost.
   b. are referred to as transferred-in costs (for the receiving department).
   c. are referred to as the cost of goods transferred out (for the transferring department).
   d. All of the above.
   e. None of the above.

**6–9**

Gilroy, Inc., produces key chains. The key chains are produced in two departments. The data for Department 1 are as follows:

| | |
|---|---:|
| Beginning work in process | 0 |
| Units started | 43,000 |
| Units transferred out | 35,500 |
| Raw materials cost | $16,340 |
| Direct labour cost | $27,126 |
| Overhead applied | $63,294 |

Materials are added at the beginning of the process. Ending inventory is 80
percent complete with respect to labour and overhead.

**Required:**
Prepare a production report for Department 1.

**6–10**

Kirlen Company manufactures soluble plant fertilizer. Department 1 mixes the
chemicals required for the fertilizer. The following Department 1 data are for the
year:

| | |
|---|---:|
| Beginning work in process | 0 |
| Units started | 92,500 |
| Raw materials cost | $277,500 |
| Direct labour cost | $ 50,680 |
| Overhead applied | $ 76,020 |
| Units in ending work in process | 5,000 |

Ending work in process is 100 percent complete with respect to materials and
60 percent complete with respect to conversion.

**Required:**
1. Prepare a physical flow schedule.
2. Calculate equivalent units of production for:
   a. Raw materials
   b. Conversion
3. Calculate unit costs for:
   a. Raw materials
   b. Conversion costs
   c. Total manufacturing costs
4. What is the total cost of units transferred out? What is the cost assigned to
   units in ending inventory?

**6–11**

For the month of December 2004, Pacific Rim Company's records show the following information:

a. The beginning work-in-process inventory consisted of 6,000 units that were
   20 percent complete with respect to both direct materials and conversion
   costs. The balance in the account was $36,820, comprising $18,000 in direct
   materials and $18,820 in conversion costs.
b. The ending work-in-process inventory consisted of 4,000 units that were 70
   percent complete with respect to direct materials and 50 percent complete
   with respect to conversion costs.
c. Costs incurred during December amounted to $156,925 for direct materials
   and $124,180 for conversion costs. During December, 20,000 units were trans-
   ferred to finished goods.
d. Pacific Rim uses the weighted average method.

**Required:**
1. Prepare a physical flow schedule.
2. Calculate the equivalent units of production for:
   a. Direct materials
   b. Conversion
3. Calculate unit costs for:
   a. Direct materials
   b. Conversion
   c. Total manufacturing
4. What is the total cost of units transferred out? What is the cost assigned to units in ending work-in-process inventory? (CGA Canada adapted)

**6–12**

*Equivalent Units—
Weighted Average
Method*

*LO2*

The following are data for four independent process-costing departments.

|                      | A      | B      | C      | D      |
|----------------------|--------|--------|--------|--------|
| Beginning inventory  | 3,200  | 1,000  | 0      | 30,000 |
| Percent completed    | 30%    | 40%    | 0%     | 75%    |
| Units started        | 17,000 | 23,000 | 40,000 | 40,000 |
| Ending inventory     | 4,000  | 0      | 9,000  | 10,000 |
| Percent completed    | 25%    | 0%     | 10%    | 25%    |

**Required:**
Compute the equivalent units of production for each of the four departments using the weighted average method.

**6–13**

*Appendix: Equivalent
Units—FIFO Method*

*LO5*

Using the data from 6–12, compute the equivalent units of production for each of the four departments using the FIFO method.

**6–14**

*Nonuniform Inputs*

*LO4*

Terry Linens, Inc., manufactures bed and bath linens. The bath linens department sews terry cloth into towels of various sizes. Terry Linens uses the weighted average method. All materials are added at the beginning of the process. The following data are for the bath linens department for June:

Production:
  Units in process, June 1, 25% complete*      10,000
  Units completed and transferred out          60,000
  Units in process, June 30, 60% complete*     20,000

Costs:
  Work in process, June 1:
    Materials                         $ 49,000
    Conversion costs                     2,625
      Total                          $ 51,625

  Current costs:
    Materials                         $351,000
    Conversion costs                    78,735
      Total                          $429,735

  * With respect to conversion costs

**Required:**
1. Prepare a physical flow analysis for the bath linens department for the month of June.
2. Calculate equivalent units of production for the bath linens department for the month of June.

3. Calculate unit cost for materials, for conversion, and in total for the bath linens department for the month of June.
4. Calculate the cost of units transferred out and the cost of ending work-in-process inventory.
5. Prepare a cost reconciliation for the bath linens department for the month of June.

**6–15**

Cost of Production
Report; Nonuniform
Inputs

LO3, LO4

Refer to 6–14. Prepare a cost of production report for the bath linens department for the month of June using the weighted average method.

**6–16**

Nonuniform Inputs;
Transferred-In Cost

LO4

Drysdale Dairy produces a variety of dairy products. In Department 12, cream (transferred in from Department 6) and other materials (sugar and flavourings) are mixed and churned to make ice cream. The following data are for Department 12 for August:

Production:

| | |
|---|---:|
| Units in process, August 1, 25% complete* | 40,000 |
| Units completed and transferred out | 120,000 |
| Units in process, August 31, 60% complete* | 30,000 |

Costs:

| | |
|---|---:|
| Work in process, August 1: | |
| Transferred-in from Department 6 | $ 2,100 |
| Materials | 1,500 |
| Conversion costs | 3,000 |
| Total | $ 6,600 |

| | |
|---|---:|
| Current costs: | |
| Transferred-in from Department 6 | $30,900 |
| Materials | 22,500 |
| Conversion costs | 45,300 |
| Total | $98,700 |

\* With respect to conversion costs

Drysdale Dairy uses weighted average costing.

**Required:**
1. How many units were transferred in during the month?
2. Calculate equivalent units for the following categories: transferred-in, materials, and conversion.
3. Calculate unit costs for the following categories: transferred-in, materials, and conversion. Calculate total unit cost.

**6–17**

Appendix: FIFO
Equivalent Units; Unit
Cost

LO5

Halligan Company manufactures a product in four departments. Data for the first department follow:

Production:

| | |
|---|---:|
| Units in process, July 1, 75% complete | 180,000 |
| Units completed and transferred out | 450,000 |
| Units in process, July 31, 25% complete | 90,000 |

Costs:

| | |
|---|---:|
| Work in process, July 1 | $ 580,500 |
| Costs added during the month | 1,501,875 |

Halligan uses FIFO costing.

**Required:**

1. Prepare a physical flow analysis for the first department for the month of July.
2. Calculate equivalent units of production for the first department for the month of July.
3. Calculate the unit cost of production for the first department for the month of July.
4. Calculate the cost of units transferred out and the cost of ending work-in-process inventory for the first department.
5. Prepare a cost reconciliation for the first department for the month of July.

**6–18**

Appendix: FIFO
Production Report

LO5

Refer to 6–17. Prepare a cost of production report for the first department of Halligan Company for the month of July.

**6–19**

Weighted Average
Method; Unit Cost;
Valuation of Goods
Transferred Out and
Ending Work in
Process

LO3

Poston Products, Inc., produces a chemical product that passes through three departments. For the month of May, the following equivalent-unit schedule was prepared for the first department:

|  | Materials | Conversion Cost |
|---|---|---|
| Units completed | 5,000 | 5,000 |
| Units, ending work in process × Fraction completed: | | |
| 6,000 × 100%; 6,000 × 50% | 6,000 | 3,000 |
| Equivalent units of output | 11,000 | 8,000 |

Costs assigned to beginning work in process were materials, $30,000; conversion, $5,000. Manufacturing costs incurred during the month of May were materials, $25,000; conversion, $65,000. Poston Products uses the weighted average method.

**Required:**

1. Compute the unit cost for the month of May.
2. Determine the cost of ending work in process and the cost of goods transferred out.

**6–20**

Appendix: FIFO
Method; Unit Cost;
Valuation of Goods
Transferred Out and
Ending Work in
Process

LO5

Tolliver Company is a manufacturer that uses FIFO to account for its production costs. The product Tolliver makes passes through two processes. Tolliver's controller prepared the following equivalent-unit schedule for October:

|  | Materials | Conversion Cost |
|---|---|---|
| Units started and completed | 8,000 | 8,000 |
| Units, beginning work in process × Fraction completed: | | |
| 2,000 × 0%; 2,000 × 50% | 0 | 1,000 |
| Units, ending work in process × Fraction completed: | | |
| 4,000 × 100%; 4,000 × 25% | 4,000 | 1,000 |
| Equivalent units of output | 12,000 | 10,000 |

Costs in beginning work in process were materials, $6,000; conversion costs, $24,000. Manufacturing costs incurred during October were materials, $72,000; conversion costs, $96,000.

**Required:**

1. Prepare a physical flow schedule for the month of October.
2. Compute the cost per equivalent unit for the month of October.
3. Determine the cost of ending work in process and the cost of goods transferred out.

**6–21**

Weighted Average
Method; Equivalent
Units; Unit Cost;
Multiple Departments

LO2, LO3, LO4

Hogarth, Inc., manufactures a product that passes through three processes. During July, the first department transferred 12,000 units to the second department. The cost of the units transferred into the second department was $20,500. Materials are added uniformly in the second process.

The second department had the following physical flow schedule for July:

| Units to account for: | |
|---|---|
| Units in beginning work in process (40% complete) | 2,000 |
| Units started | ? |
| Total units to account for | ? |

| Units accounted for: | |
|---|---|
| Units in ending work in process (50% complete) | 4,000 |
| Units completed | ? |
| Total units accounted for | ? |

Costs in beginning work in process for the second department were materials, $3,200; conversion costs, $3,120; transferred in, $4,000. Costs added during the month were materials, $16,000; conversion costs, $24,960; transferred in, $20,500.

**Required:**
1. Assuming the use of the weighted average method, prepare a schedule of equivalent units.
2. Compute the unit cost for the month of July.

**6–22**

Appendix: FIFO
Method, Equivalent
Units; Unit Cost;
Multiple Departments

LO2, LO4, LO5

Using the same data found in 6–21, assume that the company uses the FIFO method.

**Required:**
Prepare a schedule of equivalent units and compute the unit cost for the month of July.

**6–23**

Process Costing, Food
Manufacturing

LO1, LO2

Wholesome Bread makes and supplies bread throughout eastern Canada. The production process involves six operations:

a. Flour, milk, yeast, salt, butter, and so on are mixed in a large vat.
b. A conveyor belt transfers the dough to a machine that weighs it and shapes into loaves.
c. The individual loaves are allowed to sit and rise.
d. The dough is moved to a 30-metre-long funnel oven (the dough enters the oven on racks and spends 20 minutes moving slowly through the oven).
e. The bread is removed from the oven, sucked from the pan by a vacuum, and allowed to cool.
f. The bread is sliced and wrapped.

During one week, 4,500 loaves of bread were produced. The total cost of materials (ingredients and wrapping material) was $675. The cost of direct labour and overhead totalled $1,575. There were no beginning or ending work-in-process inventories.

**Required:**
1. Compute the unit cost for the 4,500 loaves of bread produced during the week.
2. Would Wholesome Bread ever need to worry about using the FIFO method or the weighted average method? Why or why not? What implication does this have for the food industry in general?
3. Assume that Wholesome Bread also produces rolls and buns. Also assume that the only difference is that the machine is set to shape the dough differently. What adjustments would need to be made to cost out the three different bread products?

**6–24**

Weighted Average
Method; Physical
Flow; Equivalent
Units; Unit Costs; Cost
Assignment
LO1, LO2, LO3

Spreadsheet

Funnifaces, Inc., manufactures various Halloween masks. Each mask is shaped from a piece of rubber in the moulding department. The masks are then transferred to the finishing department, where they are painted and have elastic bands attached. In April, the moulding department reported the following data:

a. In moulding, all materials are added at the beginning of the process.
b. Beginning work in process consisted of 6,000 units, 20 percent complete with respect to direct labour and overhead. Cost in beginning inventory included direct materials, $1,800; and conversion costs, $552.
c. Costs added to production during the month were direct materials, $3,800; and conversion costs, $8,698.
d. At the end of the month, 18,000 units were transferred out to finishing. Then, 2,000 units remained in ending work in process, 25 percent complete.

**Required:**
1. Prepare a physical flow schedule.
2. Calculate equivalent units of production for direct materials and conversion cost.
3. Compute unit cost.
4. Calculate the cost of goods transferred to finishing at the end of the month. Calculate the cost of ending inventory.

**6–25**

Appendix: FIFO
Method; Physical
Flow; Equivalent
Units; Unit Costs; Cost
Assignment
LO5

Refer to the data in 6–24. Calculate the following using the FIFO method:

**Required:**
1. Prepare a physical flow schedule.
2. Calculate equivalent units of production for direct materials and conversion cost.
3. Compute unit cost.
4. Calculate the cost of goods transferred to finishing at the end of the month. Calculate the cost of ending inventory.

## Problems

**6–26**

Multiple Choice
LO2, LO3, LO4, LO5

Kimbeth Manufacturing Company uses a process-costing system to manufacture Dust Density Sensors for the mining industry. The following information pertains to operations for the month of May 2004.

|  | Units |
| --- | --- |
| Beginning work in process, May 1 | 16,000 |
| Started in production during May | 100,000 |
| Completed production during May | 92,000 |
| Ending work in process, May 31 | 24,000 |

Beginning work in process was 60 percent complete for materials and 20 percent complete for conversion costs. Ending work in process was 90 percent complete for materials and 40 percent complete for conversion costs.

Costs pertaining to May are as follows.

a. Beginning work in process: materials, $54,560; direct labour, $20,320; and overhead, $15,240.
b. Costs incurred during May: materials, $468,000; direct labour, $182,880; and overhead, $390,160.

Choose the *best* answer for each of the following multiple-choice questions. (US–CMA adapted)

1. Using the FIFO method, the equivalent units for materials are
   a. 97,600 units.
   b. 104,000 units.
   c. 107,200 units.
   d. 108,000 units.
   e. 113,600 units.

2. Using the FIFO method, the equivalent units for conversion costs are
   a. 85,600 units.
   b. 88,800 units.
   c. 95,200 units.
   d. 98,400 units.
   e. 101,600 units.

3. Using the FIFO method, the equivalent unit cost of materials is
   a. $4.12.
   b. $4.50.
   c. $4.60.
   d. $4.80.
   e. $5.46.

4. Using the FIFO method, the equivalent unit conversion cost is
   a. $5.65.
   b. $5.82.
   c. $6.00.
   d. $6.20.
   e. $6.62.

5. Using the FIFO method, the total cost of units in ending work in process at May 31, 2004, is
   a. $153,072.
   b. $154,800.
   c. $155,328.
   d. $156,960.
   e. $159,648.

6. Using the weighted average method, the equivalent unit cost of materials for May is
   a. $4.12.
   b. $4.50.
   c. $4.60.
   d. $5.03.
   e. $5.46.

7. Using the weighted average method, the equivalent unit conversion cost for May is
   a. $5.65.
   b. $5.83.
   c. $5.99.
   d. $6.41.
   e. $6.62.

8. Using the weighted average method, the total cost of units in ending work in process at May 31, 2004, is
   a. $86,400.
   b. $153,960.
   c. $154,800.
   d. $155,328.
   e. $156,864.

**6–27**

Weighted Average
Method; Production
Report

LO3

Ellis Company produces a product that passes through two processes: assembly and finishing. All manufacturing costs are added uniformly for both processes. The following information was obtained for the assembly department for November:

a. Work in process, November 1, had 24,000 units (60 percent completed) and the following costs:

| | |
|---|---|
| Direct materials | $93,128 |
| Direct labour | 32,432 |
| Overhead applied | 17,200 |

b. During November, 69,200 units were completed and transferred to the finishing department, and the following costs were added to production:

| | |
|---|---|
| Direct materials | $133,760 |
| Direct labour | 140,640 |
| Overhead applied | 58,752 |

c. On November 30, there were 10,800 partly completed units in process. These units were 70 percent complete.

**Required:**
Prepare a production report for the assembly department for November using the weighted average method of costing. The report should disclose the physical flow of units, equivalent units, and unit costs and should track the disposition of manufacturing costs.

**6–28**

Appendix: FIFO
Method; Production
Report

LO5

Refer to the data in 6–27.

**Required:**
Prepare a production report for the assembly department for November using the FIFO method of costing. The report should contain the same schedules described in 6–27. (*Hint:* Carry the unit-cost computation to four decimal places.)

**6–29**

Weighted Average
Method; Single-
Department Analysis;
Three Cost Categories

LO3, LO4

Tyrone Company produces a variety of stationery products. One product, sealing wax sticks, passes through two processes: blending and moulding. The weighted average method is used to account for production costs. Two ingredients, paraffin and pigment, are added at the beginning of the blending process and are heated and mixed for several hours. After blending, the resulting product is sent to the moulding department, where it is poured into moulds and cooled. The following information relates to the blending process for August:

a. Work in process, August 1, had 20,000 kilograms, 20 percent complete with respect to conversion costs. Costs associated with partly completed units were:

| | |
|---|---|
| Paraffin | $12,000 |
| Pigment | 10,000 |
| Direct labour | 3,000 |
| Overhead applied | 10,000 |

b. Work in process, August 31, had 30,000 kilograms, 70 percent complete with respect to conversion costs.

c. Units completed and transferred out totalled 500,000 kilograms. The following costs were added during the month:

| | |
|---|---|
| Paraffin | $306,000 |
| Pigment | 255,000 |
| Direct labour | 387,750 |
| Overhead applied | 129,250 |

**Required:**
1. Prepare the following: (a) a physical flow schedule, and (b) an equivalent-unit schedule with cost categories for paraffin, pigment, and conversion cost.
2. Calculate the unit cost for each cost category.
3. Compute the cost of ending work in process and the cost of goods transferred out.
4. Prepare a cost reconciliation.

**6–30**

*Physical Flow; Equivalent Units; Unit Costs, Cost Assignment*

**LO3, LO4**

Timepeace Company manufactures a special type of fast-drying paint. You are attempting to verify the following balances, which have been recorded on the Timepeace books at the end of the year:

|                  | Units   | Cost        |
|------------------|---------|-------------|
| Work in process  | 450,000 | $ 991,440   |
| Finished goods   | 300,000 | 1,514,700   |

Materials are added at the beginning of the manufacturing process. Overhead is applied at 50 percent of direct labour costs. There is no beginning finished goods inventory. Beginning and ending work-in-process inventories are 50 percent complete with respect to conversion costs. A physical count revealed that the ending physical units are correct.

Additional information:

|                           | Units     | Materials   | Labour      |
|---------------------------|-----------|-------------|-------------|
|                           |           | Costs       |             |
| Beginning work in process | 300,000   | $ 300,000   | $ 472,500   |
| Units started             | 1,500,000 | —           | —           |
| Units completed           | 1,350,000 | —           | —           |
| Material costs added      | —         | $1,950,000  | —           |
| Labour costs added        | —         | —           | $2,992,500  |

**Required:**
1. Prepare a physical flow schedule.
2. Calculate the equivalent units of production using the weighted average method.
3. Calculate unit costs for: (a) direct materials, (b) direct labour, and (c) applied overhead.
4. What is the total cost of units transferred out? What is the cost assigned to units in ending work-in-process inventory? What is the cost assigned to units in ending finished goods inventory? (CGA Canada adapted)

**6–31**

*Weighted Average Method, Production Report*

**LO3, LO4**

The Chang Manufacturing Company makes wood-finishing stain. The production of stain begins with the blending of various chemicals and ends with the canning of the stain. Canning occurs when the mixture reaches the 90 percent stage of completion. After canning, the cans are transferred to the shipping department. Here the cans are crated and shipped to various customers. Conversion costs are added uniformly throughout the process. Overhead is applied at the rate of $4.00 per direct labour hour. The following are the actual production data for the canning department for April:

April Production Costs
Work in process, April 1:
    Direct materials—chemicals      $ 68,400
    Direct labour ($15 per hour)      18,750
    Applied overhead      5,000

Costs added in April:

| | |
|---|---|
| Direct materials—chemicals | 342,600 |
| Direct materials—cans | 10,500 |
| Direct labour ($15 per hour) | 105,000 |
| Applied overhead | 28,000 |

Units for April:

| | |
|---|---|
| Work-in-process inventory, April 1 (25% complete) | 8,000 litres |
| Transferred to shipping department during April | 40,000 litres |
| Started during April | 42,000 litres |
| Work-in-process inventory, April 30 (80% complete) | 10,000 litres |

**Required:**

Prepare a production report using the weighted average method. (CGA Canada adapted)

**6–32**

*Appendix: FIFO Method, Production Report*

**LO4, LO5**

Using the same data as in 6–31, assume that Chang uses the FIFO method.

**Required:**

1. Prepare a production report using the FIFO method.
2. What are the advantages and disadvantages of using the weighted average method versus the FIFO method? Under what circumstances is it appropriate to use each method? (CGA Canada adapted)

**6–33**

*Weighted Average Method; Single-Department Analysis; Transferred-In Goods*

**LO3, LO4**

Keating Company manufactures a product that passes through three departments. In Department C, materials are added at the end of the process. Conversion costs are incurred uniformly throughout the process. During January, Department C received 20,000 units from Department B. The transferred-in cost of the 20,000 units was $70,350.

The following costs were added by Department C during January:

| | |
|---|---|
| Direct materials | $40,635 |
| Direct labour | 58,500 |
| Overhead applied | 29,400 |

On January 1, Department C had 4,000 units in inventory; these units were 30 percent complete with respect to conversion costs. On January 31, 3,000 units were in inventory, one-third complete with respect to conversion costs. The costs associated with the 4,000 units in beginning inventory were as follows:

| | |
|---|---|
| Transferred in | $14,970 |
| Direct labour | 7,560 |
| Overhead applied | 4,200 |

**Required:**

Prepare a production report using the weighted average method. In preparing the report, follow the five steps outlined in this chapter. (Hint: carry unit costs to three decimal places.)

**6–34**

*Appendix: FIFO Method; Single-Department Analysis; Transferred-In Goods*

**LO4, LO5**

Merrifield, Inc., manufactures a single product that passes through several processes. During the first quarter of the year, the mixing department received 45,000 litres of liquid from the cooking department (transferred in at $28,800). Upon receiving the liquid, the mixing department adds a powder and allows blending to take place for 30 minutes. The product is then passed on to the bottling department.

There were 9,000 litres in process at the beginning of the quarter, 75 percent complete with respect to conversion costs. The costs attached to the beginning inventory were as follows:

| Transferred in | $5,700 |
|---|---|
| Powder | 804 |
| Conversion costs | 1,800 |

Costs added by the mixing department during the first quarter were as follows:

| Powder | $4,200 |
|---|---|
| Conversion costs | 9,080 |

There were 7,875 litres in ending inventory, 20 percent complete with respect to conversion costs.

**Required:**
Prepare a production report for the mixing department using the FIFO method. In preparing the report, follow the five steps outlined in this chapter. Carry unit costs to three decimal places. Round to the nearest dollar in the production report.

**6–35**

Weighted Average Method, Transferred-In Goods

LO3, LO4

Refer to 6–34.

**Required:**
Prepare a production report for the mixing department using the weighted average method.

**6–36**

Weighted Average Method; Two-Department Analysis

LO1, LO3, LO4

Seacrest Company uses a process-costing system. The company manufactures a product that is processed in two departments, A and B. In Department A, materials are added at the beginning of the process; in Department B, additional materials are added at the end of the process. In both departments, conversion costs are incurred uniformly throughout the process. As work is completed, it is transferred out. The following summarizes the production activity and cost for November:

|  | Department A | Department B |
|---|---|---|
| Beginning inventories: |  |  |
| Physical units | 5,000 | 8,000 |
| Costs: |  |  |
| Transferred in | — | $ 45,320 |
| Direct materials | $10,000 | — |
| Conversion costs | $ 6,900 | $ 16,800 |
|  |  |  |
| Current production: |  |  |
| Units started | 25,000 | ? |
| Units transferred out | 28,000 | 33,000 |
| Costs: |  |  |
| Transferred in | — | ? |
| Direct materials | $57,800 | $ 37,950 |
| Conversion costs | $95,220 | $128,100 |
| Percentage completion: |  |  |
| Beginning inventory | 40% | 50% |
| Ending inventory | 80% | 50% |

**Required:**
1. Using the weighted average method, prepare the following for Department A:
   a. A physical flow schedule
   b. An equivalent-units calculation
   c. Calculation of unit costs
   d. Cost of ending work in process and cost of goods transferred out
   e. A cost reconciliation
2. Repeat Requirement 1 for Department B.

**6–37**

Refer to the data in 6–36.

**Required:**

Repeat the Requirements in 6–36 using the FIFO method.

**6–38**

Benson Pharmaceuticals uses a process-costing system to compute the unit costs of the over-the-counter cold remedies that it produces. It has three departments: picking, encapsulating, and bottling. In picking, the ingredients for the cold capsules are measured, sifted, and blended. The mix is transferred out in litre containers. The encapsulating department takes the powdered mix and places it in capsules. One litre of powdered mix converts into 1,500 capsules. After the capsules are filled and polished, they are transferred to bottling where they are placed in bottles, which are then affixed with a safety seal and a lid and labelled. Each bottle receives 50 capsules.

During March, the following results are available for the first two departments:

| | Picking | Encapsulating |
|---|---|---|
| Beginning inventories: | | |
|   Physical units | 10 litres | 4,000 |
|   Costs: | | |
|     Materials | $ 252 | $ 32 |
|     Labour | $ 282 | $ 20 |
|     Overhead applied | $ ? | $ ? |
|     Transferred in | — | $ 140 |
| Current production: | | |
|   Transferred out | 140 litres | 208,000 |
|   Ending inventory | 20 litres | 6,000 |
|   Costs: | | |
|     Materials | $3,636 | $1,573 |
|     Labour | $4,618 | $1,944 |
|     Overhead applied | $ ? | $ ? |
|     Transferred in | — | $ ? |
| Percentage of completion: | | |
|   Beginning inventory | 40% | 50% |
|   Ending inventory | 50% | 40% |

Overhead in both departments is applied as a percentage of direct labour costs. In the picking department, overhead is 200 percent of direct labour. In the encapsulating department, the overhead rate is 150 percent of direct labour.

**Required:**

1. Prepare a production report for the picking department using the weighted average method. Follow the five steps outlined in this chapter.
2. Prepare a production report for the encapsulating department using the weighted average method. Follow the five steps outlined in this chapter.

**6–39**

Refer to the data in 6–38.

**Required:**

Prepare a production report for each department using the FIFO method.

**6–40**

Weighted Average
Method, Multiple-
Department Analysis

LO3, LO4

Strathmore, Inc., manufactures educational toys using a weighted average process-costing system. Plastic is moulded into the appropriate shapes in the moulding department. Moulded components are transferred to the assembly department, where the toys are assembled and additional materials (for example, fasteners, decals) are applied. Completed toys are then transferred to the packaging department, where each toy is boxed.

Strathmore showed the following data on toy production for February:

|  | Moulding | Assembly | Packaging |
|---|---|---|---|
| Beginning inventory: |  |  |  |
|    Units | 500 | — | 150 |
| Costs: |  |  |  |
|    Prior department | — | — | $1,959.00 |
|    Direct materials | $2,500.00 | — | $ 375.00 |
|    Conversion cost | $1,050.00 | — | $ 225.00 |
| Started or transferred in: |  |  |  |
|    Units | 1,000 | ? | ? |
| February costs: |  |  |  |
|    Prior department | — | $14,950.00 | $11,754.00 |
|    Direct materials | $5,000.00 | $ 487.60 | $ 2,407.50 |
|    Conversion cost | $7,660.00 | $ 1,166.00 | $ 2,977.50 |
| Ending inventory, units | 200 | 400 | — |

Beginning and ending work in process for the three departments showed the following degree of completion:

|  | Moulding | Assembly | Packaging |
|---|---|---|---|
| Degree of completion: |  |  |  |
|    BWIP, direct materials | 100% | — | 100% |
|    BWIP, conversion costs | 30% | — | 50% |
|    EWIP, direct materials | 100% | 40% | — |
|    EWIP, conversion costs | 20% | 40% | — |

**Required:**

1. Prepare a physical flow schedule for February for each of the following:
   a. Moulding department
   b. Assembly department
   c. Packaging department
2. Compute equivalent units of production for direct materials and for conversion costs for each of the following:
   a. Moulding department
   b. Assembly department
   c. Packaging department
3. Complete the following unit-cost chart:

|  | Moulding | Assembly | Packaging |
|---|---|---|---|
| Unit prior-department cost* |  |  |  |
| Unit direct material cost |  |  |  |
| Unit conversion cost |  |  |  |
| Total unit cost |  |  |  |

\* Cost transferred in from prior department

4. Determine the cost of ending work in process and the cost of goods transferred out for each of the three departments.
5. Reconcile the costs for each department.

| | |
|---|---|
| **6–41** | Refer to the data in 6–40. |
| ˙ Appendix: FIFO Method, Multiple-Department Analysis | **Required:** |
| LO4, LO5 | Repeat Requirements 2 through 5 using the FIFO method. |

**6–42**

Production Report

LO3

Susan Manners, cost accountant for Lean Jeans, Inc., spent the weekend completing a production report for the inspection department for the month of December. Inspection is the final department in the production of fashion jeans. In that department, each pair of jeans is carefully inspected for quality workmanship. At the end of the inspection process, a slip of paper with "Inspected by _____" is slipped into a back pocket; then the jeans are placed in a bin to be transferred to finished goods.

First thing Monday morning, Susan returned to work and found that someone had accidentally spilled coffee on her report, partly obliterating some of the figures. Susan has only one hour to reconstruct her report.

**Inspection Department**
**Production Report**
**For the Month of December**
**(Weighted Average Method)**

**Unit Information**

| Units to account for: | |
|---|---|
| Beginning inventory | ? |
| Transferred in from assembly | 4,000 |
| Total units to account for | 4,700 |

**Equivalent Units**

| | Physical Flow | Prior Department | Materials | Conversion Costs |
|---|---|---|---|---|
| Units accounted for: | | | | |
| Units completed | ? | ? | ? | ? |
| Units in ending WIP | 900 | — | — | ? |
| Total units accounted for | 4,700 | ? | 3,800 | 4,250 |

**Cost Information**

| | Prior Department | Materials | Conversion Cost | Total |
|---|---|---|---|---|
| Costs to account for: | | | | |
| Beginning WIP | $11,900 | ? | $ 210 | $12,110 |
| Incurred in December | ? | ? | 4,040 | 72,097 |
| Total cost to account for | $79,900 | $57 | $4,250 | $84,207 |
| Unit cost | $17.00 | ? | $1.00 | ? |

| | Transferred Out | Ending WIP | Total |
|---|---|---|---|
| Costs accounted for: | | | |
| Goods transferred out | ? | — | ? |
| Ending inventory: | | | |
| Prior department | — | ? | ? |
| Materials | — | — | — |
| Conversion cost | — | ? | ? |
| Total costs accounted for | $    ? | $15,750 | $84,207 |

**Required:**

Help Susan meet the deadline by filling in the appropriate number for each question mark.

**6–43**

*Weighted Average Method, Incomplete Records*

**LO3, LO4**

Wentworth Processing manufactures a single product in a continuous processing environment. All materials are added at the beginning of the process, and conversion costs are applied uniformly throughout the process. Wentworth has perfected its process to the point that no spoilage occurs. To assign costs to inventories, the company uses weighted average process costing.

During a recent conversion from a manual to a computerized system, Wentworth used a number of part-time clerks to enter data into the new system. As a result of inadequate supervision, certain records were misplaced, causing some accounting information for 2004 to be incomplete. As the accounting supervisor, you must piece together the information to produce the financial reports for 2004. The following information was found on a scrap of paper wedged under the computer:

### Wentworth Processing Information for 2004

| | |
|---|---:|
| Sales (selling price per unit, $40) | $4,080,000 |
| Actual manufacturing overhead | 660,000 |
| Selling and administrative expenses | 328,000 |
| Unit costs of production: | |
|    Direct materials (1 kilogram) | $ 5.00 |
|    Direct labour (1/2 hour) | 6.00 |
|    Overhead | 9.00 |
|     Total | $20.00 |

| | |
|---|---|
| Units transferred to finished goods | 140,000 units |
| Materials purchased | 125,000 kilograms |
| Materials used in process | 136,000 kilograms |

An inventory count at year end (December 31, 2004) revealed that the inventories had the following balances in units:

| | |
|---|---|
| Raw materials | 8,000 kilograms |
| Work in process (35% complete) | 22,000 units |
| Finished goods | 45,000 units |

No record of the opening balance of raw materials or finished goods could be found. Although the January 1, 2004, balance of physical units in work in process was unavailable, it was known that those units were 60 percent complete. The unit cost of production was the same in 2004 as it was in 2003.

**Required:**

Given the preceding information, calculate the following amounts for Wentworth Processing:

1. The opening (January 1, 2004) balance in units and costs of (a) raw materials, (b) work in process, and (c) finished goods.
2. Equivalent units for 2004 for (a) materials and (b) conversion costs.
3. Total cost for 2004 for (a) materials used and (b) conversion applied.
4. Cost of ending work in process, 2004.
5. Cost of units completed and transferred. (CMA Canada adapted)

**6–44**

*Production Report,
Ethical Behaviour*

**LO3**

Consider the following conversation between Gary Means, manager of a division that produces industrial machinery and his controller, Donna Simpson, a CMA and CA:

**Gary**: "Donna, we have a real problem. Our operating cash is too low, and we are in desperate need of a loan. As you know, our financial position is marginal, and we need to show as much income as possible—and our assets need bolstering as well."

**Donna**: "I understand the problem, but I don't see what can be done at this point. This is the last week of the fiscal year, and it looks like we'll report income just slightly above breakeven."

**Gary**: "I know all this. What we need is some creative accounting. I have an idea that might help us, and I wanted to see if you would go along with it. We have 200 partly finished machines in process, about 20 percent complete. That compares with the 1,000 units that we completed and sold during the year. When you computed the per-unit cost, you used 1,040 equivalent units, giving us a manufacturing cost of $1,500 per unit. That per-unit cost gives us cost of goods sold equal to $1.5 million and ending work in process worth $60,000. The presence of the work in process gives us a chance to improve our financial position. If we report the units in work in process as 80 percent complete, this will increase our equivalent units to 1,160. This, in turn, will decrease our unit cost to about $1,345 and cost of goods sold to $1.345 million. The value of our work in process will increase to $215,200. With those financial stats, getting the loan would be a cinch."

**Donna**: "Gary, I don't know. What you're suggesting is risky. It wouldn't take much auditing skill to catch this one."

**Gary**: "You don't have to worry about that. The auditors won't be here for at least six to eight more weeks. By that time, we can have those partly completed units completed and sold. I can bury the labour cost by having some of our loyal employees work overtime for some bonuses. The overtime will never be reported. And as you know, bonuses come out of the corporate budget and are assigned to overhead—next year's overhead. Donna, this will work. If we look good and get the loan to boot, corporate headquarters will treat us well. If we don't do this, we could lose our jobs."

**Required:**

1. Should Donna agree to Gary's proposal? Why or why not? To assist in deciding, review the standards of ethical conduct for management accountants described in Chapter 1. Do any apply?

2. Assume that Donna refuses to cooperate and that Gary accepts this decision and drops the matter. Does Donna have any obligation to report the divisional manager's behaviour to a superior? Explain.

3. Assume that Donna refuses to cooperate; however, Gary insists that the changes be made. Now what should she do? What would *you* do?

4. Suppose that Donna is 63 and that the prospects for employment elsewhere are bleak. Assume again that Gary insists that the changes should be made. Donna also knows that his supervisor, the owner of the company, is his father-in-law. Under these circumstances, would your recommendations for Donna differ? If you were Donna, what would you do?

**6–45**

Process Costing versus
Alternative Costing
Methods, Impact on
Resource Allocation
Decision
LO1, LO3

Golding Manufacturing, a division of Farnsworth Sporting, Inc., produces two different models of bows and eight models of knives. The bow-manufacturing process involves the production of two major subassemblies: the limbs and the handle. The limbs pass through four sequential processes before reaching final assembly: layup, moulding, fabricating, and finishing. In the layup department, limbs are created by laminating layers of wood. In moulding, the limbs are heat-treated, under pressure, to form a strong, resilient limb. In the fabricating department, any protruding glue or other processing residue is removed. Finally, in finishing, the limbs are cleaned with acetone, dried, and sprayed with the final finishes.

The handles pass through two processes before reaching final assembly: pattern and finishing. In the pattern department, blocks of wood are fed into a machine that is set to shape the handles. Different patterns are possible, depending on the machine's setting. After coming out of the machine, the handles are cleaned and smoothed. They then pass to the finishing department, where they are sprayed with the final finishes. In final assembly, the limbs and handles are assembled into different models using purchased parts such as pulley assemblies, weight adjustment bolts, side plates, and string.

Since its inception, Golding has used process costing to assign product costs. A predetermined overhead rate is used, based on direct labour dollars (80 percent of direct labour dollars). Recently, Golding hired a new controller, Karen Jenkins. After reviewing the product-costing procedures, Karen requested a meeting with the divisional manager, Aaron Suhr. The following is a transcript of their conversation.

**Karen**: "Aaron, I have some concerns about our cost accounting system. We make two different models of bows and are treating them as if they were the same product. Now I know that the only real difference between the models is the handle. The processing of the handles is the same, but the handles differ significantly in the amount and quality of wood used. Our current costing does not reflect this difference in material input."

**Aaron**: "Your predecessor is responsible. He believed that tracking the difference in material cost wasn't worth the effort. He simply didn't believe that it would make much difference in the unit cost of either model."

**Karen**: "Well, he may have been right, but I have my doubts. If there is a significant difference, it could affect our views of which model is more important to the company. The additional bookkeeping isn't very stringent. All we have to worry about is the pattern department. The other departments fit what I view as a process-costing pattern."

**Aaron**: "Why don't you look into it? If there is a significant difference, go ahead and adjust the costing system."

After the meeting, Karen decided to collect cost data on the two models: the Deluxe model and the Econo model. She tracked the costs for one week. At the end of the week, she had collected the following data from the pattern department:

a. There were a total of 2,500 bows completed: 1,000 Deluxe models and 1,500 Econo models.
b. There was no beginning work in process; however, there were 300 units in ending work in process: 200 Deluxe and 100 Econo models. Both models were 80 percent complete with respect to conversion costs and 100 percent complete with respect to materials.
c. The pattern department experienced the following costs:

| | |
|---|---|
| Direct materials | $114,000 |
| Direct labour | 45,667 |

    d. On an experimental basis, the requisition forms for materials were modified to identify the dollar value of the materials used by the Econo and Deluxe models:

| | |
|---|---|
| Econo model | $30,000 |
| Deluxe model | 84,000 |

### Required:

1. Compute the unit cost for the handles produced by the pattern department, assuming that process costing is totally appropriate.
2. Compute the unit cost of each handle using the separate cost information provided on materials.
3. Compare the unit costs computed in Requirements 1 and 2. Is Karen justified in her belief that a pure process-costing approach is not appropriate? Describe the costing system that you would recommend.
4. In the past, the marketing manager has requested more money for advertising the Econo line. Aaron has repeatedly refused to grant any increase in this product's advertising budget because its per-unit profit (selling price less manufacturing cost) is so low. Given the results in Requirements 1 through 3, was Aaron justified in his position?

## Research Assignment

**6–46**

Cybercase

LO1, LO4

Go to the Web site for Crayola, Inc. (www.crayola.com). There is a "factory tour" that you can take. Take the factory tours for both crayons and markers. List the departments for each product. Trace the flow of costs through each department to come up with a listing of total manufacturing costs for each of the finished products.

# Support Department Cost Allocation

## Learning Objectives

**After studying Chapter 7, you should be able to:**

1. Describe the difference between support departments and producing departments.

2. Calculate single and multiple charging rates for a support department.

3. Allocate support-department costs to producing departments using the direct, sequential, and reciprocal methods.

4. Calculate departmental overhead rates.

## Scenario

Hamilton and Barry, a large regional public accounting firm, consists of three major departments: audit, tax, and management advisory services (MAS). Gary Premark, head of management advisory services, is talking with Jan McAndrews, partner in charge.

**Jan**: "So far, this has been a good year for MAS, Gary. We're very pleased with the way you increased your client base and billing hours. Our only remaining problem is profitability. As you can see, the total costs of your department rose at a faster pace last year than the year before."

**Gary**: "My profitability is just fine—or would be if I weren't forced to use the inefficient services of this firm. Look at my photocopying costs! These are way out of line! I'd be better off using Kopykats a block away."

**Jan**: "Gary, as you know, we went to an in-house photocopying department to provide convenience and security. If it costs a little more, so be it. Besides, the convenience of just walking down the hall to get your reports and bids copied outweighs any small increase in cost allocation."

**Gary**: "Look, Jan, I don't mind paying a little extra for convenience, but this allocation is much more than a little extra. My department's going to boycott photocopying until this problem gets resolved."

**Jan**: "Don't take that step just yet. Carol Morton is in charge of photocopying. Let's get some answers from her first."

Two days later Gary, Jan, and Carol Morton, executive assistant in charge of the photocopying service, meet in Jan's office.

**Carol**: "Gary, I understand you have some questions about the way photocopying is run. Let me assure you that we work very hard to keep costs down while providing topnotch service. Your department was charged only for the copies you made."

**Gary**: "Carol, I took my total cost allocation and divided by the number of copies. Do you realize that it comes to $0.12 per page? Why are your department's costs so much higher than outside services?"

**Carol**: "Gary, you have to realize that we bought machinery for peak usage. In our firm, that's the month of April—when Tax runs most of its copies. Other months are slower, but I can't trade in the copier on a month-to-month basis. Also, we need at least one person ready to handle your copies or you'll really hit the ceiling. As a result, the per-page charges are higher."

**Gary:** "I think I'm beginning to see what's happening. Still, I'd like to explore different charging systems."
**Jan:** "If there's a problem here, it's a firmwide problem. I can assign Cynthia Bowles, our firm's new co-op student from the University of Regina, to take this on as a special project."

**Questions to Think About**
1. Why do you think that the copying department charges amount to $0.12 per page? List the types of costs incurred for photocopying, and divide them into fixed and variable categories.
2. Jan mentioned the security and convenience of in-house photocopying. How do you think the firm might weigh these factors in

deciding whether or not the cost of in-house copying is "worth it"?
3. Since the firm as a whole has decided to have an in-house copying department, why are copying costs charged to the individual departments? What purpose does the practice of developing support department charging rates serve?

In earlier chapters, we focused on product costs and the way they are assigned to products. The complexity of many modern companies leads the accountant to focus on the assignment of overhead. In Chapter 4, we studied a variety of ways to assign overhead: plantwide rates, departmental rates, and activity-based costing. In this chapter, we explain further the way that support department costs are assigned to producing departments for the calculation of departmental overhead rates.

*Allocation* is simply a means of dividing a pool of cost and assigning it to various subunits. It is important to realize that allocation does not affect the total cost. Total cost is neither reduced nor increased by allocation. However, the amounts of cost assigned to the subunits can be affected by the allocation procedure chosen. Because cost allocation can affect bid prices, the profitability of individual products, and the behaviour of managers, it is an important topic.

## An Overview of Cost Allocation

**Objective 1**

Describe the difference between support departments and producing departments.

**common costs**

The costs of resources used in the output of two or more services or products.

**producing departments**

Units within an organization that are responsible for producing the products or services that are sold to customers.

**support departments**

Units within an organization that provide essential support services for producing departments.

Mutually beneficial costs are called **common costs**. While these common costs may pertain to periods of time, individual responsibilities, sales territories, and classes of customers, this chapter will concentrate on the costs common to departments and to products. For example, the wages paid to security guards at a factory are a common cost of all of the different products manufactured there. The benefits of security are applicable to each product, yet the assignment of security cost to the individual products is an arbitrary process.

## Types of Departments

The first step in cost allocation is to determine just what the cost objects are. In the functional model, they are departments. There are two categories of departments: producing departments and support departments. **Producing departments** are directly responsible for creating the products or services sold to customers. In the opening scenario, examples of producing departments are auditing, tax, and management advisory services. In a manufacturing setting, producing departments are those that work directly on the products being manufactured. **Support departments** provide essential support services for producing departments. These departments are indirectly connected with an organization's services or products. Examples include maintenance, grounds, engineering, housekeeping, personnel, and stores. The Hamilton and Barry photocopying department is a support department.

Once the producing and support departments have been identified, the overhead costs incurred by each department can be determined. Note that this involves tracing costs to the departments, not allocating costs, because the costs are directly associated with the individual department. A factory cafeteria, for example, would have food costs, salaries of cooks and servers, amortization on dishwashers and stoves, and supplies (for example, napkins, plastic forks). Overhead directly associated with a producing department, such as assembly in a furniture-making plant, would include utilities (if measured in that department), supervisory salaries, and amortization on equipment used in that department. Overhead that cannot be easily assigned to a producing or support department is assigned to a catchall department, such as general factory. General factory might include amortization on the factory building, rental of a Santa Claus suit for the factory Christmas party, the plant manager's salary, and telephone service. In this way, all costs are assigned to a department.

Exhibit 7–1 shows how a manufacturing company and a service organization can be divided into producing and support departments. The manufacturing plant, which makes furniture, may be departmentalized into two producing departments (assembly and finishing) and four support departments (materials storeroom, cafeteria, maintenance, and general factory). The service organization,

**EXHIBIT  7-1**

Examples of Departmentalization for a Manufacturing Company and a Service Organization

| **Manufacturing Company: Furniture Maker** | |
| --- | --- |
| **Producing Departments** | **Support Departments** |
| Assembly | Materials storeroom |
|   Supervisory salaries |   Clerk's salary |
|   Small tools |   Amortization on forklift |
|   Indirect materials | Cafeteria |
|   Amortization on machinery |   Food |
| Finishing |   Cooks' salaries |
|   Sandpaper |   Amortization on stoves |
|   Amortization on sanders and buffers | Maintenance |
| |   Janitors' salaries |
| |   Cleaning supplies |
| |   Machine oil and lubricants |
| | General factory |
| |   Amortization on building |
| |   Security and utilities |

| **Service Organization: Bank** | |
| --- | --- |
| **Producing Departments** | **Support Departments** |
| Personal loans | Drive through |
|   Loan processors' salaries |   Tellers' salaries |
|   Forms and supplies |   Amortization on equipment |
| Commercial lending | Data processing |
|   Lending officers' salaries |   Personnel salaries |
|   Amortization on office equipment |   Software |
|   Bankruptcy prediction software |   Amortization on hardware |
| Personal banking | Bank administration |
|   Supplies and postage for statements |   Salary of CEO |
| |   Receptionist's salary |
| |   Telephone costs |
| |   Amortization on bank vault |

a bank, might be departmentalized into three producing departments (personal loans, commercial lending, and personal banking) and three support departments (drive through, data processing, and bank administration). Overhead costs are traced to each department. Note that each kind of factory or service overhead cost must be assigned to one, and only one, department.

## Allocating Costs from Departments to Products

Once the company has been departmentalized, and all overhead costs have been traced to the individual departments, support-department costs are assigned to producing departments and overhead rates are developed to cost products.

Although support departments do not work directly on the products or services that are sold, the costs of providing these support services are part of the total product costs and must be assigned to the products. Departmental overhead rates are necessary when there are multiple products being worked on in each producing department. If there were only one product within a producing department, all the support service costs allocated to that department would belong to that product.

Recall that a predetermined overhead rate is computed by taking total estimated overhead for a department and dividing it by an estimate of an appropriate base. Now we see that a producing department's overhead consists of two parts: overhead directly traced to a producing department, and overhead allocated to the producing department from the support departments. A support department cannot have an overhead rate that assigns overhead costs to units produced, because it does not make a saleable product. That is, products do not pass through support departments. The purpose of support departments is to service producing departments, not the products that pass through the producing departments. For example, maintenance personnel repair and maintain the equipment in the assembly department, not the furniture that is assembled in that department. Exhibit 7–2 summarizes the steps involved.

**EXHIBIT   7-2**

Steps in Allocating
Support-Department
Costs to Producing
Departments

1. Departmentalize the company.
2. Classify each department as a support or producing department.
3. Trace all overhead costs in the company to a support department or producing department.
4. Allocate support-department costs to the producing departments.
5. Calculate predetermined overhead rates for producing departments.
6. Allocate overhead costs to the units of individual products through the predetermined overhead rates.

## Types of Allocation Bases

**causal factors**

Activities or variables
that invoke service costs.
Generally, it is desirable
to use causal factors as
the basis for allocating
service costs.

Producing departments require support services; the costs of support departments are caused by the activities of the producing departments. **Causal factors** are variables or activities within a producing department that bring about support service costs. In choosing a basis for allocating support-department costs, we must identify appropriate causal factors (cost drivers). Using causal factors results in more accurate product costs; furthermore, if the causal factors are known, managers can better control the consumption of support services.

To illustrate the types of cost drivers that can be used, consider the following three support departments: power, personnel, and materials handling. For power costs, a logical allocation base is kilowatt-hours, which can be measured by separate meters for each department. If separate meters do not exist, perhaps machine hours used by each department would provide a good proxy, or means of approximating power usage. For personnel costs, both the number of producing-department employees and the labour turnover (for example, number of new hires) are possible cost drivers. For materials handling, the number of material moves, the hours of material handling used, and the quantity of material moved are all possible cost drivers. Exhibit 7–3 lists some possible cost drivers that can be used to allocate support-department costs. When competing cost drivers exist, managers need to assess which provides the most convincing relationship.

Examples of Possible Cost Drivers for Support Departments

| | |
|---|---|
| Accounting | Payroll |
|   Number of transactions |   Number of employees |
| Cafeteria | Personnel |
|   Number of employees |   Number of employees |
| Data processing |   Number of firings or layoffs |
|   Number of lines entered |   Number of new hires |
|   Number of hours of service |   Direct labour cost |
| Engineering | Power |
|   Number of change orders |   Kilowatt-hours |
|   Number of hours |   Machine hours |
| Maintenance | Purchasing |
|   Machine hours |   Number of orders |
|   Maintenance hours |   Cost of orders |
| Materials storeroom | Shipping |
|   Number of material moves |   Number of orders |
|   Kilograms of material moved | |
|   Number of different parts | |

While the use of a causal factor to allocate common cost is the best, sometimes we cannot find an easily measured causal factor. In that case, we look for a good proxy. For example, the common cost of plant amortization may be allocated to producing departments on the basis of area occupied. Area occupied does not cause amortization; however, it can be argued that the area occupied by a department is a good proxy for the services provided to it by the factory building. The choice of a good proxy to guide allocation depends on the company's objectives for allocation.

## Objectives of Allocation

A number of important objectives are associated with the allocation of support-department costs to producing departments and ultimately to specific products. In a study of cost allocation, Atkinson surveyed practice in Canada and the literature related to allocation.[1] He found that the goals served by allocation, including the allocation of costs of support departments, are diverse, covering such economic and managerial purposes as coordination of decisions and motivation and evaluation of decision makers. These purposes parallel the conceptual themes of managerial decisions and planning and control systems introduced in Chapter 1. It is critical to keep these themes in mind while you study the issues of cost accumulation and cost determination involving support

---

1. See A.A. Atkinson, *Intra-firm Cost and Resource Allocations: Theory and Practice* (Toronto: The Canadian Academic Accounting Association, 1987).

departments. This view is also reflected in the following objectives that have been identified by the IMA:[2]

1. To obtain a mutually agreeable price
2. To compute product-line profitability
3. To predict the economic effects of planning and control
4. To value inventory
5. To motivate managers

Competitive pricing requires an understanding of costs. Only by knowing the costs of each service can a company create meaningful bids. If costs are not accurately allocated, the costs of some services could be overstated, resulting in bids that are too high and a loss of potential business. Alternatively, if the costs are understated, bids could be too low, producing losses on these services.

Good estimates of costs also allow a manager to assess the profitability of individual services. By assessing the profitability of various services, a manager may evaluate the mix of services offered by the company. From this evaluation, it may be decided to drop some services, reallocate resources from one service to another, reprice certain services, or exercise greater cost control in some areas. The validity of any evaluation, however, depends to a great extent on the accuracy of the cost assignments made to individual services.

Of course, the above concepts also apply to costing and evaluation of products. The importance of accurate cost assignments for control and decision-making purposes cannot be overemphasized.

For manufacturing organizations, inventory valuation is often important. Rules of financial reporting (GAAP) require that we assign both direct and indirect manufacturing costs to products unless indirect costs are insignificant. Inventories and cost of goods sold are normally reported on a full-cost basis.

Allocations can be used to motivate managers. If the costs of support departments are not allocated to producing departments, managers may treat these support services as free and overconsume these services. Consumption of a support service may continue until the marginal benefit of the service equals zero. In reality, of course, the marginal cost of a support service is usually greater than zero. If the company allocates support department costs and holds the managers of producing departments responsible for the economic performance of their units, managers will use a support service until the marginal benefit of the service equals its allocated cost. Thus, allocating support department costs helps each producing department select a better level of support service consumption.

There are other behavioural benefits. Allocating support-department costs to producing departments encourages managers of those producing departments to monitor the performance of support departments. Since the costs of the support departments affect the economic performance of their own departments, those managers have an incentive to control support service costs through means other than simple usage of the service. We can see this happening in the opening scenario, as Gary compared the cost of in-house copying with external copy companies. If a support department is not as cost-effective as an outside source, perhaps the company should not continue to supply the support service internally. For example, many university libraries are moving toward the use of outside contractors for photocopying services. They have found that these contractors are more cost-efficient and provide a higher level of service to library users than did the previous method of using professional librarians to make change, keep the

---

2. Statements of Management Accounting (Statement 4B), *Allocation of Service and Administrative Costs* (Montvale, N.J.: NAA, 1985). The NAA is now known as the Institute of Management Accountants (IMA).

copy machines supplied with paper, fix paper jams, and so on. This possibility of comparison should result in a more efficient internal support department. Monitoring by producing-department managers will also encourage support-department managers to be more sensitive to the needs of the producing-departments.

Clearly, then, there are good reasons for allocating support-department costs. The validity of these reasons, however, depends on the accuracy and fairness of the cost assignments made.

In determining how to allocate support-department costs, the guideline of cost–benefit must be considered. In other words, the costs of implementing a particular allocation scheme must be compared to the benefits to be derived. As a result, companies try to use easily measured and easily understood bases for allocation.

## Allocating One Department's Costs to Another Department

**Objective 2**

Calculate single and multiple charging rates for a support department.

Frequently, the costs of a support department are allocated to another department through the use of a charging rate. In this case, we focus on the allocation of one department's costs to other departments. For example, a company's data processing department may serve various other departments. The cost of operating the data processing department is then allocated to the user departments.

### A Single Charging Rate

Let's return to the case of Hamilton and Barry, the accounting firm from this chapter's opening scenario. Recall that the firm developed an in-house photocopying department to serve its three producing departments (audit, tax, and management advisory systems or MAS). The costs of the photocopying department include fixed costs of $26,190 per year (salaries and machine rental) and variable costs of $0.023 per page copied (paper and toner). Estimated usage (in pages) by the three producing departments is as follows:

| | |
|---|---:|
| Audit department | $ 94,500 |
| Tax department | 67,500 |
| MAS department | 108,000 |
| Total | $270,000 |

If a single charging rate is used, the fixed costs of $26,190 will be combined with estimated variable costs of $6,210 (270,000 × $0.023). Total costs of $32,400 are divided by the estimated 270,000 pages to be copied, to yield a rate of $0.12 per page.

The amount charged to the producing departments is solely a function of the number of pages copied. Suppose that the actual usage is audit, 92,000 pages; tax, 65,000 pages; and MAS, 115,000 pages. The total photocopying department charges would be as shown:

| | Number of Pages | Charge per Page | Total Charges |
|---|---|---|---|
| Audit | 92,000 | $0.12 | $11,040 |
| Tax | 65,000 | 0.12 | 7,800 |
| MAS | 115,000 | 0.12 | 13,800 |
| Total | 272,000 | | $32,640 |

Notice that the use of a single rate results in the fixed cost being treated as if it were variable. In fact, to the producing departments, photocopying is strictly variable. Did the photocopying department need $32,640 to copy 272,000 pages? No, it needed only $32,446 [$26,190 + (272,000 × $0.023)]. The extra amount charged is due to the treatment of a fixed cost in a variable manner.[3] In the next section we see how multiple charging rates can address this problem.

## Multiple Charging Rates

Sometimes a single charging rate masks the variety of causal factors that lead to a support department's total costs. The Hamilton and Barry photocopying department is a good example. We saw that a single charging rate was based on the number of pages copied. Then, it looked like every page copied cost $0.12. But this is not true. A large portion of the costs of the photocopying department are fixed; they are not caused by the number of pages copied. Recall that $26,190 per year is spent on wages and rental of the photocopier. Why is this cost incurred? If we ask the photocopying company representative we would discover that the size of the machine rented depends not on the number of pages copied per year, but on monthly peak usage.

When Hamilton and Barry established its photocopying department, it must have surveyed the audit, tax and MAS departments to determine each one's highest monthly usage. Let's assume that the audit and MAS departments have fairly even copying needs throughout the year. In other words, these two departments anticipate needing 202,500 (94,500 + 108,000) copies per year and will average 16,875 per month. Since no one month is higher than the other, peak monthly usage for these two departments is also 16,875 copies. The tax department, however, anticipates a different pattern. Of its 67,500 budgeted yearly copies, it expects to need one-third, or 22,500 copies, in the month of April. Therefore, the peak usage in one month is expected to he 39,375 copies. It is this usage for which the size of the photocopying department is designed.

Now, we can develop two charging rates for the photocopying department. One is the variable rate for toner and paper. This is simply $0.023 per page. Of course, the causal factor is number of pages copied. The second rate is for the fixed cost of equipment rental and wages. This is assigned to the producing departments based on their planned peak usage.

|  | Peak Number of Pages | Proportion of Peak Usage | Total Fixed Costs | Amount Allocated to Each Department |
|---|---|---|---|---|
| Audit | 7,875 | 0.20 | $26,190 | $ 5,238 |
| Tax | 22,500 | 0.57 | 26,190 | 14,928 |
| MAS | 9,000 | 0.23 | 26,190 | 6,024 |
| Total | 39,375 |  |  | $26,190 |

The amount charged to the producing departments is now a function of both the number of pages copied and of the anticipated peak usage. Suppose that the actual usage is Audit, 92,000 pages; Tax, 65,000 pages; and MAS, 115,000 pages. The total photocopying department charges would be as shown.

|  | Number of Pages × $0.023 | Fixed Cost Allocation | Total Charges |
|---|---|---|---|
| Audit | $2,116 | $ 5,238 | $ 7,354 |
| Tax | 1,495 | 14,928 | 16,423 |
| MAS | 2,645 | 6,024 | 8,669 |
| Total | $6,256 | $26,190 | $32,446 |

---

3. Note that the photocopying department would have charged out less than the cost needed if the number of pages copied had been less than the budgeted number of pages. For 268,000 pages the cost charged would be $32,160 [$0.12 × 268,000] but the cost incurred would be $32,354 [$26,190 + ($0.023 × 268,000)].

Notice that the allocation of photocopying department costs is very different when the two charging rates are used. In this case, the tax department absorbs a larger proportion of the cost, because its peak usage is responsible for the size of the department. Notice, too, that the amount charged of $32,446 will now be very close to the actual cost of running the department. With the two charging rates, each one based on a strong causal factor, the allocation of cost to the using departments is clearly based on the amount of cost that they actually cause the support department to incur.

Could there be more than two charging rates? Definitely. However, as a company breaks down support-department resources and causal factors more finely, it may be approaching activity-based costing. The extra precision of charging rates must be balanced against the cost of determining and applying those rates. As always, the company must consider costs and benefits.

## Budgeted versus Actual Cost and Usage

When we allocate support-department costs to the producing departments, should we allocate actual or budgeted costs? The answer is budgeted costs. There are two basic reasons for allocating support-department costs. One is to assign costs to the units produced. In this case, the budgeted support-department costs are allocated to producing departments as a preliminary step in forming the overhead rate. Recall that the overhead rate is calculated at the beginning of the period, when actual costs are not known. Thus, budgeted costs must be used. The second usage of allocated support-department costs is for performance evaluation. In this case, too, budgeted support-department costs are allocated to producing departments.

Managers of support and producing departments are usually held accountable for the performance of their units. Their ability to control costs is an important factor in their performance evaluation. This ability is usually measured by comparing actual costs with planned or budgeted costs. If actual costs exceed budgeted costs, the department may be operating inefficiently, with the difference between the two costs the measure of that inefficiency. Similarly, if actual costs are less than budgeted costs, the unit may be operating efficiently.

A general principle of performance evaluation is that managers should not be held responsible for costs or activities over which they have no control. Since managers of producing departments have significant input regarding the level of support service consumed, they should be held responsible for their share of service costs. This statement, however, has an important qualification: a department's evaluation should not be affected by the degree of efficiency achieved by another department.

This qualifying statement has an important implication for the allocation of support-department costs. Actual costs of a support department should not be allocated to producing departments, because they include efficiencies or inefficiencies achieved by the support department. Managers of producing departments have no control over the degree of efficiency achieved by a support-department manager. By allocating budgeted costs instead of actual costs, no inefficiencies or efficiencies are transferred from one department to another.

Whether budgeted usage or actual usage is used depends on the purpose of the allocation. For product costing, the allocation is done at the beginning of the year on the basis of budgeted usage so that a predetermined overhead rate can be computed. If the purpose is performance evaluation, however, the allocation is done at the end of the period and is based on actual usage. The use of cost information for performance evaluation is covered in more detail in a later chapter.

Let's return to our photocopying example. Recall that annual budgeted fixed costs were $26,190, and the budgeted variable cost per page was $0.023. The three producing departments—audit, tax, and MAS—estimated usage at 94,500 copies, 67,500 copies, and 108,000 copies, respectively. Given these data, we show the cost allocated to each department at the beginning of the year using a single charging rate in Exhibit 7–4.

**EXHIBIT 7-4**

Use of Budgeted Data for Product Costing

| | Number of Copies | × | Total Rate | = | Allocated Cost |
|---|---|---|---|---|---|
| Audit | 94,500 | | $0.12 | | $11,340 |
| Tax | 67,500 | | 0.12 | | 8,100 |
| MAS | 108,000 | | 0.12 | | 12,960 |
| Total | 270,000 | | | | $32,400 |

When the allocation is done for the purpose of budgeting the producing departments' costs, then of course the budgeted support-department costs are used. The photocopying costs allocated to each department would be added to other producing-department costs, including those directly traceable to each department plus other support-department allocations, to compute each department's anticipated spending. In a manufacturing plant, the allocation of budgeted support-department costs to the producing departments would precede the calculation of the predetermined overhead rate.

During the year, each producing department would also be responsible for actual charges incurred based on the actual number of pages copied. Going back to the actual usage assumed previously, we now make a second allocation to measure the actual performance of each department against its budget. The actual photocopying costs allocated to each department for performance evaluation purposes are shown in Exhibit 7–5.

**EXHIBIT 7-5**

Use of Actual Data for Performance Evaluation Purposes

| | Number of Copies | × | Total Rate | = | Allocated Cost |
|---|---|---|---|---|---|
| Audit | 92,000 | | $0.12 | | $11,040 |
| Tax | 65,000 | | 0.12 | | 7,800 |
| MAS | 115,000 | | 0.12 | | 13,800 |
| Total | 272,000 | | | | $32,640 |

## Choosing a Support Department Cost Allocation Method

**Objective 3**

Allocate support-department costs to producing departments using the direct, sequential, and reciprocal methods.

So far, we have considered cost allocation from one support department to several producing departments. We used the direct method of support department cost allocation, in which support-department costs are allocated only to producing departments. This was appropriate in the earlier example because no other support departments existed, thus there was no possibility of interaction among support departments. Many companies, however, have multiple support departments, and they frequently interact. For example, in a factory, personnel and cafeteria serve each other and other support departments as well as the producing departments.

Ignoring these interactions and allocating service costs directly to producing departments may result in unfair and inaccurate cost assignments. For example, power, although a support department, may use 30 percent of the services of the maintenance department. The maintenance costs caused by the power department belong to the power department. Unless these costs are assigned to the power department, its costs are understated. In effect, some of the costs caused by power are "hidden" in the maintenance department, because maintenance costs would be lower if the power department did not exist. As a result, a producing department that is a heavy user of power and an average or below-average user of maintenance may then receive, under the direct method, a cost allocation that is understated.

In determining which support department cost allocation method to use, companies must determine the extent of support-department interaction. In addition, they must weigh the costs and benefits associated with three methods of allocating costs. In the next three sections, the direct, sequential, and reciprocal methods are described and illustrated.

## Direct Method of Allocation

**direct method**

A method that allocates service costs directly to producing departments. This method ignores any interactions that may exist among support departments.

When companies allocate support-department costs only to the producing departments, they are using the **direct method** of allocation. The direct method is the simplest and most straightforward way to allocate support-department costs. Variable support service costs are allocated directly to producing departments in proportion to each department's usage of the service. Fixed costs are also allocated directly to the producing department, but in proportion to the producing department's practical capacity or peak capacity, as in the earlier photocopy example.

Exhibit 7–6 illustrates the lack of support-department reciprocity on cost allocation using the direct method. In Exhibit 7–6, we see that by using the direct

**EXHIBIT  7-6**

Allocation of Support-Department Costs to Producing Departments: Direct Method

Suppose there are two support departments, power and maintenance, and two producing departments, grinding and assembly, each with a "bucket" of directly traceable overhead cost.
Objective: Distribute all maintenance and power costs to grinding and assembly using the direct method.

Direct method—Allocate maintenance and power costs only to grinding and assembly.

After allocation—zero cost in maintenance and power; all overhead cost is in grinding and assembly.

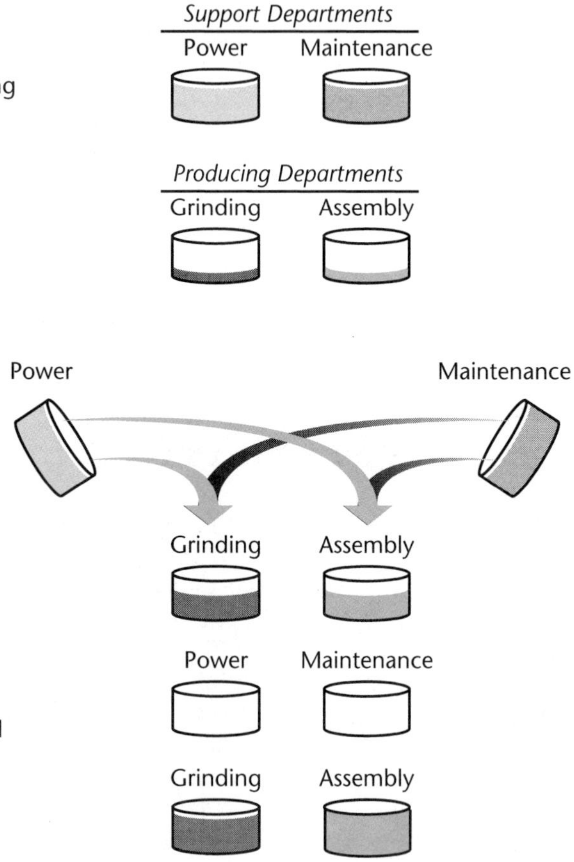

method, we allocate support-department cost to producing departments only. No cost from one support department is allocated to another support department. Thus, no support-department interaction is recognized.

To illustrate the direct method, consider the data in Exhibit 7–7 that show the budgeted activity and budgeted costs of two support departments and two producing departments. Assume that the causal factor for power costs is kilowatt-hours, and the causal factor for maintenance costs is maintenance hours. These

EXHIBIT   7-7

Data for Illustrating
Allocation Methods

|  | Support Departments | | Producing Departments | |
|---|---|---|---|---|
|  | **Power** | **Maintenance** | **Grinding** | **Assembly** |
| Direct costs* | $250,000 | $160,000 | $100,000 | $ 60,000 |
| Normal activity: | | | | |
| Kilowatt-hours | — | 200,000 | 600,000 | 200,000 |
| Maintenance hours | 1,000 | — | 4,500 | 4,500 |

\* For a producing department, direct costs refer only to overhead costs that are directly traceable to the department.

causal factors are used as the bases for allocation. In the direct method, only the kilowatt-hours and the maintenance hours in the producing departments are used to compute the allocation ratios. The direct method allocation ratios and the support department cost allocations based on the data given in Exhibit 7–7 are shown in Exhibit 7–8. (To simplify the illustration, no distinction is made between fixed and variable costs.)

EXHIBIT   7-8

Direct Allocation
Illustrated

| Step 1: Calculate Allocation Ratios | | |
|---|---|---|
|  | **Grinding** | **Assembly** |
| Power[a] | 0.75 | 0.25 |
| Maintenance[b] | 0.50 | 0.50 |

| Step 2: Allocate Support-Department Costs Using the Allocation Ratios | | | | |
|---|---|---|---|---|
|  | Support Departments | | Producing Departments | |
|  | **Power** | **Maintenance** | **Grinding** | **Assembly** |
| Direct costs | $250,000 | $160,000 | $100,000 | $ 60,000 |
| Power[c] | (250,000) | — | 187,500 | 62,500 |
| Maintenance[d] | — | (160,000) | 80,000 | 80,000 |
|  | $ 0 | $ 0 | $367,500 | $202,500 |

a 600,000/(600,000 + 200,000); 200,000/(600,000 + 200,000)
b 4,500/(4,500 + 4,500); 4,500/(4,500 + 4,500)
c Allocation of power based on allocation ratios from Step 1: 0.75 × $250,000; 0.25 × $250,000
d Allocation of maintenance based on allocation ratios from Step 1: 0.50 × $160,000; 0.50 × $160,000

## Sequential Method of Allocation

**sequential (or step) method**

A method that allocates service costs to user departments in a sequential manner. It gives partial consideration to interactions among support departments.

The **sequential (or step) method** of allocation recognizes that interactions among the support departments occur. However, the sequential method does not fully recognize support-department interaction. Cost allocations are performed in step-down fashion, following a predetermined ranking procedure. Usually, the sequence is defined by ranking the support departments in order of the amount of support service rendered, from the greatest to the least. Degree of support service is often measured by the direct costs of each support department: the department with the highest cost is seen as rendering the greatest service.

Exhibit 7–9 illustrates the sequential method. First, the support departments are ranked; here power is first, then maintenance. Then, power costs are allocated to maintenance and the two producing departments. Then, the costs of maintenance are allocated only to producing departments.

EXHIBIT   **7-9**

Allocation of Support-Department Costs to Producing Department: Sequential Method

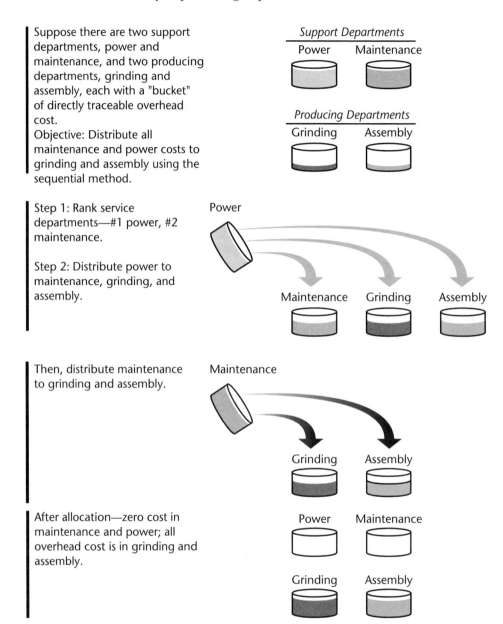

Suppose there are two support departments, power and maintenance, and two producing departments, grinding and assembly, each with a "bucket" of directly traceable overhead cost.
Objective: Distribute all maintenance and power costs to grinding and assembly using the sequential method.

Step 1: Rank service departments—#1 power, #2 maintenance.

Step 2: Distribute power to maintenance, grinding, and assembly.

Then, distribute maintenance to grinding and assembly.

After allocation—zero cost in maintenance and power; all overhead cost is in grinding and assembly.

The costs of the first support department are allocated to all support departments after it in the sequence and to all producing departments. Then the costs of the support department next in sequence are similarly allocated, and so on. In the sequential method, once a support department's costs are allocated, it never receives a subsequent allocation from another support department. In other words, a given support department's costs are never allocated to support departments before it in the sequence. Also, note that the costs allocated from a support department are its direct costs plus any costs it receives in allocations from other support departments. A department's direct costs, of course, are those that are directly traceable to the department.

To illustrate the sequential method, consider the data provided in Exhibit 7–7. Using cost as a measure of service, we see that the support department rendering more service is power. Thus, its costs will be allocated first, followed by those for maintenance.

The allocations obtained with the sequential method are shown in Exhibit 7–10. The first step is to compute the allocation ratios. Note that the allocation ratios for the maintenance department ignore the usage by the power department since its costs cannot be allocated to a support department before it in the allocation sequence. The second step is to allocate the support-department costs using the allocation ratios computed in the first step. Notice that $50,000 of the power department's costs are allocated to the maintenance department. This reflects the fact that the maintenance department uses 20 percent of the power department's output. As a result, the cost of operating the maintenance department increases from $160,000 to $210,000. Also notice that when the costs of the maintenance department are allocated, no costs are allocated back to the power department, even though it uses 1,000 hours of the output of the maintenance department.

The sequential method is more accurate than the direct method because it recognizes some interactions among the support departments. It does not recognize all interactions, however: no maintenance costs were assigned to the power department even though it used 10 percent of the maintenance department's output. The reciprocal method corrects this deficiency.

EXHIBIT 7-10

Sequential Allocation Illustrated

| Step 1: Calculate Allocation Ratios | | | |
|---|---|---|---|
| | **Maintenance** | **Grinding** | **Assembly** |
| Power[a] | 0.20 | 0.60 | 0.20 |
| Maintenance[b] | — | 0.50 | 0.50 |

| Step 2: Allocate Support-Department Costs Using the Allocation Ratios | | | | |
|---|---|---|---|---|
| | **Support Departments** | | **Producing Departments** | |
| | **Power** | **Maintenance** | **Grinding** | **Assembly** |
| Direct costs | $250,000 | $160,000 | $100,000 | $ 60,000 |
| Power[c] | (250,000) | 50,000 | 150,000 | 50,000 |
| Maintenance[d] | — | (210,000) | 105,000 | 105,000 |
| | $   0 | $   0 | $355,000 | $215,000 |

a 200,000/1,000,000; 600,000/1,000,000; 200,000/1,000,000
b 4,500/9,000; 4,500/9,000
c Power allocation based on allocation ratios from Step 1: 0.20 × $250,000; 0.60 × $250,000; 0.20 × $250,000
d Maintenance allocation based on allocation ratios from Step 1: 0.50 × $210,000; 0.50 × $210,000

## Reciprocal Method of Allocation

**reciprocal method**

A method that simultaneously allocates service costs to all user departments. It gives full consideration to interactions among support departments.

The **reciprocal method** of allocation recognizes all interactions among support departments. Under the reciprocal method, one support department's use by another figures in determining the total cost of each support department, where the total cost reflects interactions among the support departments. Then, the new total of support-department costs is allocated to the producing departments. This method fully accounts for support-department interaction.

### Total Cost of Support Departments

To determine the total cost of a support department, so that it reflects interactions with other support departments, we must solve a system of simultaneous linear equations. Each equation, which is a cost equation for a support department, is defined as the sum of the department's direct costs plus the proportion of support service received from other support departments:

$$\text{Total cost} = \text{Direct costs} + \text{Allocated costs}$$

The method is best described using an example, employing the same data used to illustrate the direct and sequential methods. The allocation ratios needed for the simultaneous equations are shown in Exhibit 7–11 and are interpreted as follows: maintenance receives 20 percent of power's output; power receives 10 percent of maintenance's output. Now let $P$ equal the total cost of the power

EXHIBIT   7-11

Data for Illustrating
Reciprocal Method

|                     | Support Departments | | Producing Departments | |
|                     | Power | Maintenance | Grinding | Assembly |
|---------------------|-------|-------------|----------|----------|
| Direct costs:       | $250,000 | $160,000 | $100,000 | $ 60,000 |
| Normal activity:    |       |             |          |          |
| Kilowatt-hours      | —     | 200,000     | 600,000  | 200,000  |
| Maintenance hours   | 1,000 | —           | 4,500    | 4,500    |

| Proportion of Output Used by Department | | | | |
|                   | Power | Maintenance | Grinding | Assembly |
|-------------------|-------|-------------|----------|----------|
| Allocation ratios: |       |             |          |          |
| Power             | —     | 0.20        | 0.60     | 0.20     |
| Maintenance       | 0.10  | —           | 0.45     | 0.45     |

department and $M$ equal the total cost of the maintenance department. As previously indicated, the total cost of a support department is the sum of its direct costs plus the proportion of support service received from other support departments. We can express the cost equation for each support department as follows:

$$P = \text{Direct costs} + \text{Share of maintenance's cost} \qquad (7.1)$$
$$= \$250,000 + 0.10M \text{ (power's cost equation)}$$

$$M = \text{Direct costs} + \text{Share of power's costs} \qquad (7.2)$$
$$= \$160,000 + 0.2P \text{ (maintenance's cost equation)}$$

The direct cost components of each equation are taken from Exhibit 7–11, as are the allocation ratios.

The power cost equation (7.1) and the maintenance cost equation (7.2) can be solved simultaneously to yield the total cost for each support department. Substituting Equation 7.1 into Equation 7.2 gives the following:

$$M = \$160,000 + 0.20(\$250,000 + 0.10M)$$
$$M = \$160,000 + \$50,000 + 0.02M$$

$$0.98M = \$210,000$$
$$M = \$214,286$$

Substituting this value for $M$ into Equation 7.1 yields the total cost for power:

$$P = \$250,000 + 0.1(\$214,286)$$
$$= \$250,000 + \$21,429$$
$$= \$271,429$$

After the equations are solved, the total costs of each support department are known. These total costs, unlike the direct or sequential methods, reflect all interactions between the two support departments.

### Allocation to Producing Departments

Once the total costs of each support department are known, the allocations to the producing departments can be made. These allocations, which are based on the proportion of output used by each producing department, are shown in Exhibit 7–12. Notice that the total costs allocated to the producing departments from power and maintenance equal $410,000, the total direct costs of the two support departments ($250,000 + $160,000). (Actually, the total allocated costs equal $410,001, but the difference is due to a rounding error.)

**EXHIBIT 7-12**

Reciprocal Allocation Illustrated

| | Support Departments | | Producing Departments | |
| --- | --- | --- | --- | --- |
| | **Power** | **Maintenance** | **Grinding** | **Assembly** |
| Direct costs: | $250,000 | $160,000 | $100,000 | $ 60,000 |
| Power[a] | (271,429) | 54,286 | 162,857 | 54,286 |
| Maintenance[b] | 21,429 | (214,286) | 96,429 | 96,429 |
| Total | $ 0 | $ 0 | $359,286 | $210,715 |

[a] Power: 0.20 × $271,429; 0.60 × $271,429; 0.20 × $271,429
[b] Maintenance: 0.10 × $214,286; 0.45 × $214,286; 0.45 × $214,286

## Comparison of the Three Methods

Exhibit 7–13 gives the cost allocations from the power and maintenance departments to the grinding and assembly departments using the three support department cost allocation methods. How different are the results? Does it really matter which method is used?

Depending on the degree of interaction among the support departments, the three allocation methods can give radically different results. In this particular example, the direct method allocated $12,500 more to the grinding department (and $12,500 less to the assembly department). Surely the manager of the assembly department would prefer the direct method, and the manager of the grinding department would prefer the sequential method. Because allocation methods affect the cost responsibilities of managers, it is important for the accountant to understand the consequences of the different methods and to have good reasons for the eventual choice.

It is important to keep a cost–benefit perspective in choosing an allocation method. We must weigh the advantages of better allocation against the increased cost of using a more theoretically preferred method, such as the reciprocal method. For example, about 20 years ago, the controller for an IBM plant decided that the reciprocal method of cost allocation would do a better job of allocating support-department costs. He identified more than 700 support departments and solved the system of equations using a computer. Computationally, he had no problems. However, the producing-department managers did not understand the reciprocal method. They were sure that extra cost was being allocated to their departments; they just were not sure how. After months of meetings with the line

**EXHIBIT 7-13**

Comparison of Support Department Cost Allocations Using the Direct, Sequential, and Reciprocal Methods

| | Direct Method | | Sequential Method | | Reciprocal Method | |
| --- | --- | --- | --- | --- | --- | --- |
| | **Grinding** | **Assembly** | **Grinding** | **Assembly** | **Grinding** | **Assembly** |
| Direct costs | $100,000 | $ 60,000 | $100,000 | $ 60,000 | $100,000 | $ 60,000 |
| Allocated from power | 187,500 | 62,500 | 150,000 | 50,000 | 162,857 | 54,286 |
| Allocated from maintenance | 80,000 | 80,000 | 105,000 | 105,000 | 96,429 | 96,429 |
| Total cost | $367,500 | $202,500 | $355,000 | $215,000 | $359,286 | $210,715 |

managers, the controller threw in the towel and returned to the sequential method—which everyone did understand.

Another factor in allocating support-department cost is the rapid change in technology. Many companies currently find that support department cost allocation is useful for them. However, the move toward activity-based costing and just-in-time manufacturing can virtually eliminate the need for support department cost allocation. In the case of the JIT factory with manufacturing cells, much of the service (for example, maintenance, material handling, and setups) is performed by cell workers. Allocation is not necessary.

## Departmental Overhead Rates and Product Costing

**Objective** 4

Calculate departmental overhead rates.

After allocating all support costs to producing departments, we can then compute an overhead rate for each department. This rate is computed by adding the allocated support-department costs to the overhead costs directly traceable to the producing department and dividing this total by some measure of activity, such as direct labour hours or machine hours.

For example, from Exhibit 7–10, the total overhead costs for the grinding department after allocation of support costs under the sequential method are $355,000. Assume that machine hours are the base for assigning overhead costs to products passing through the grinding department and that the normal level of activity is 71,000 machine hours. The overhead rate for the grinding department is computed as follows:

Overhead rate = $355,000/71,000 machine hours = $5 per machine hour

Similarly, assume that the assembly department uses direct labour hours to assign its overhead. With a normal level of activity of 107,500 direct labour hours, the overhead rate for the assembly department is as follows:

Overhead rate = $215,000/107,500 direct labour hours
            = $2 per direct labour hour

Using these rates, we can determine a product's unit cost. To illustrate, suppose a product requires two machine hours of grinding per unit produced and one hour of assembly. The overhead cost assigned to one unit of this product would be $12 [(2 × $5) + (1 × $2)]. If the same product uses $15 of materials and $6 of labour (totalled from grinding and assembly), then its unit cost is $33 ($12 + $15 + $6).

One might wonder, however, just how accurate this $33 cost is. Is this really what it costs to produce the product in question? Since materials and labour are directly traceable to products, the accuracy of product costs depends largely on the accuracy of the assignment of overhead costs. This, in turn, depends on the degree of correlation between the factors used to allocate support service costs to departments and the factors used to allocate the department's overhead costs to the products. For example, if power costs are highly correlated with kilowatt-hours while machine hours are highly correlated with a product's consumption of the grinding department's overhead costs, then we can have some confidence that the $5 overhead rate accurately assigns costs to individual products. However, if the allocation of support service costs to the grinding department or the use of machine hours is faulty—or both—then product costs will be distorted. The same reasoning can be applied to the assembly department. To ensure accurate product costs, great care should be used in identifying and using causal factors for both stages of overhead assignment.

## Summary of Learning Objectives

**1. Describe the difference between support departments and producing departments.**

Producing departments create the products or services that the company is in business to manufacture and sell. Support departments provide support for the producing departments but do not themselves create a saleable product. Because support departments exist to support a variety of producing departments, the costs of the support departments are common to all producing departments.

The reasons for support-department cost allocations include inventory valuation, product-line profitability, pricing, and planning and control. Allocation can also be used to encourage favourable managerial behaviour.

**2. Calculate single and multiple charging rates for a support department.**

When the costs of one support department are allocated to other departments, a charging rate must be developed. A single rate combines variable and fixed costs of the support department to generate a charging rate.

When multiple rates are used, a separate rate is computed for each type of resource based on a causal factor. Then actual use of each causal factor is multiplied by its rate to get the amount of support department cost to be allocated.

Budgeted, not actual, costs should be allocated so that the efficiencies or inefficiencies of the support departments themselves are not passed on to the producing departments.

**3. Allocate support-department costs to producing departments using the direct, sequential, and reciprocal methods.**

Three methods can be used to allocate support costs to producing departments: the direct method, the sequential method, and the reciprocal method. They differ in the degree of support-department interaction considered. By considering support-department interactions, you can achieve more accurate product costing. The result can be improved planning, control, and decision making.

Two methods of allocation recognize interactions among support departments: the sequential (or step) method and the reciprocal method. These methods allocate support service costs among some (or all) interacting support departments before allocating costs to the producing departments.

**4. Calculate departmental overhead rates.**

Departmental overhead rates are calculated by adding direct departmental overhead costs to those costs allocated from the support departments and dividing the sum by the budgeted departmental base.

## Key Terms

Causal factors 261
Common costs 259
Direct method 268

Producing departments 259
Reciprocal method 271
Sequential (or step) method 269

Support departments 259

## Review Problem

### ALLOCATION OF SUPPORT DEPARTMENT COSTS USING THE DIRECT, SEQUENTIAL, AND RECIPROCAL METHODS

Antioch Manufacturing produces machine parts on a job-order basis. Most business is obtained through bidding. Most companies competing with Antioch bid full cost plus a 20 percent markup. Recently, with the expectation of gaining more sales, Antioch reduced its markup from 25 percent to 20 percent. The company operates two support departments and two producing departments. The budgeted costs and the normal activity levels for each department follow:

|                       | Support Departments | | Producing Departments | |
|-----------------------|----------|----------|----------|----------|
|                       | **A**    | **B**    | **C**    | **D**    |
| Overhead costs        | $100,000 | $200,000 | $100,000 | $50,000  |
| Number of employees   | 8        | 7        | 30       | 30       |
| Maintenance hours     | 2,000    | 200      | 6,400    | 1,600    |
| Machine hours         | —        | —        | 10,000   | 1,000    |
| Labour hours          | —        | —        | 1,000    | 10,000   |

The direct costs of Department A are allocated on the basis of employees; those of Department B, on the basis of maintenance hours. Departmental overhead rates are used to assign costs to products. Department C uses machine hours, and Department D uses labour hours.

The company is preparing to bid on a job (Job K) that requires three machine hours per unit produced in Department C and no time in Department D. The expected prime costs (direct materials and direct labour) per unit are $67.

### Required:

1. Allocate the support costs to the producing departments using the direct method.
2. What will the bid be for Job K if the direct method of allocation is used?
3. Allocate the support costs to the producing departments using the sequential method.
4. What will the bid be for Job K if the sequential method is used?
5. Allocate the support costs to the producing departments using the reciprocal method.
6. What will the bid be for Job K if the reciprocal method is used?

### Solution

1. Allocation of the support costs to the producing departments using the direct method.

|                        | Support Departments | | Producing Departments | |
|------------------------|-----------|-----------|-----------|-----------|
|                        | **A**     | **B**     | **C**     | **D**     |
| Direct costs           | $100,000  | $200,000  | $100,000  | $ 50,000  |
| Department A[a]         | (100,000) | —         | 50,000    | 50,000    |
| Department B[b]         | —         | (200,000) | 160,000   | 40,000    |
| Total                  | $    0    | $    0    | $310,000  | $140,000  |

[a] 30/60 × $100,000; 30/60 × $100,000
[b] 6,400/8,000 × $200,000; 1,600/8,000 × $200,000

2. Department C: Overhead rate = \$310,000/10,000 = \$31 per machine hour.

Product cost and bid price:

| | |
|---|---|
| Prime costs | \$ 67.00 |
| Overhead (3 × \$31) | 93.00 |
| Total unit cost | \$160.00 |
| Bid price (\$160 × 1.2) | \$192.00 |

3. Allocation of support costs to the producing departments using the sequential method requires that a sequence be chosen. Department B's costs are allocated first because its direct costs are greater.

| | Support Departments | | Producing Departments | |
|---|---|---|---|---|
| | A | B | C | D |
| Direct costs | \$100,000 | \$200,000 | \$100,000 | \$ 50,000 |
| Department B[a] | 40,000 | (200,000) | 128,000 | 32,000 |
| Department A[b] | (140,000) | — | 70,000 | 70,000 |
| Total | \$ 0 | \$ 0 | \$298,000 | \$152,000 |

[a] 2,000/10,000 × \$200,000; 6,400/10,000 × \$200,000; 1,600/10,000 × \$200,000
[b] 30/60 × \$140,000; 30/60 × \$140,000

4. Department C: Overhead rate = \$298,000/10,000 = \$29.80 per machine hour.

Product cost and bid price:

| | |
|---|---|
| Prime costs | \$ 67.00 |
| Overhead (3 × \$29.80) | 89.40 |
| Total unit cost | \$156.40 |
| Bid price (\$156.40 × 1.2) | \$187.68 |

5. Allocation of the support costs to the producing departments using the reciprocal method.

Allocation ratios:

| | Proportion of Output Used by Department | | | |
|---|---|---|---|---|
| | A | B | C | D |
| Department A | — | 0.1045 | 0.4478 | 0.4478 |
| Department B | 0.2000 | — | 0.6400 | 0.1600 |

Cost equations:

$$A = \$100,000 + 0.2000B$$
$$B = \$200,000 + 0.1045A$$

Solve simultaneous equations:

$$A = \$100,000 + 0.2(\$200,000 + 0.1045A)$$
$$A = \$100,000 + \$40,000 + 0.0209A$$
$$0.9791A = \$140,000$$
$$A = \$142,988$$

$$B = \$200,000 + 0.1045(\$142,988)$$
$$B = \$214,942$$

Allocation to producing departments:

| | Support Departments | | Producing Departments | |
|---|---|---|---|---|
| | A | B | C | D |
| Direct costs | \$100,000 | \$200,000 | \$100,000 | \$ 50,000 |
| Department B | 42,988 | (214,942) | 137,563 | 34,391 |
| Department A | (142,988)* | 14,942 | 64,030 | 64,030 |
| Total | \$ 0 | \$ 0 | \$301,593 | \$148,421 |

* Note: \$14 difference is the result of rounding.

6. Department C: Overhead rate = $301,593/10,000 = $30.16 per machine hour.

| Product cost and bid price: | |
| --- | --- |
| Prime costs | $ 67.00 |
| Overhead (3 × $30.16) | 90.48 |
| Total unit cost | $157.48 |
| Bid price ($157.48 × 1.2) | $188.98 |

## Questions for Writing and Discussion

1. Describe the two-stage allocation process for assigning support department costs to products in a functional manufacturing environment.

2. Explain how allocating support department costs can be helpful in making pricing decisions.

3. Why are support department costs usually assigned to products for purposes of inventory valuation?

4. Explain how allocating support department costs is useful for planning and control.

5. Assume that a company has decided not to allocate any support department costs to producing departments. Describe the likely behaviour of the managers of the producing departments. Would this be good or bad? Explain why allocation would correct this type of behaviour.

6. Explain how allocating support department costs will encourage support departments to operate more efficiently.

7. Why is it important to identify and use causal factors to allocate support department costs?

8. Identify some possible causal factors for the following support departments:
   a. Cafeteria
   b. Custodial services
   c. Laundry
   d. Receiving, shipping, and stores
   e. Maintenance
   f. Personnel
   g. Accounting

9. Explain why it is better to allocate budgeted support department costs rather than actual support department costs.

10. Explain the difference between the direct method and the sequential method.

11. The reciprocal method of allocation is more accurate than either the direct or sequential methods. Do you agree? Explain.

# Exercises

**7–1**

*Classifying Departments as Producing or Support*

LO1

Classify each of the following departments in a factory as a producing department or a support department:

a. Power
b. Maintenance
c. Finishing
d. Landscaping
e. Payroll
f. Quality control of suppliers
g. Cooking
h. Blending
i. General factory
j. Timekeeping
k. Packaging
l. Data processing
m. Engineering
n. Drilling
o. Cutting

**7–2**

*Identifying Causal Factors*

LO1

For the following support departments, identify one or more causal factors that might be useful for support department cost allocation purposes.

a. Supervision
b. Data processing
c. Quality control
d. Purchasing
e. Receiving
f. Shipping
g. Vending (stocking snack machines throughout the plant)
h. Grounds
i. Building amortization
j. Power and light
k. Employee benefits
l. Housekeeping
m. Equipment repair
n. Heating and cooling

**7–3**

*Classifying Service Organization Departments as Producing or Support*

LO1

Classify each of the following departments in a hospital as a producing department or a support department:

a. Janitorial staff
b. Laundry
c. Courier (runner goes from floor to floor, picking up and deleivering interdepartmental mail and delivering patient specimens to the lab)
d. Landscaping
e. Payroll
f. Operating rooms

g. Laboratory
h. Medical records
i. Admitting
j. Radiology
k. Pediatrics
l. Data processing
m. Supplies
n. Purchasing
o. Billing

**7–4**

*Single Charging Rate*

**LO2**

Broadway Management Company manages five apartment buildings. A local lawyer agreed to provide legal services on an as needed basis for $125 per hour. Based on past experience, Broadway and the lawyer estimated that 100 hours would be needed annually for help with matters such as the wording of leases or the pursuit of a claim against a nonpaying tenant.

Broadway wanted to charge the apartment owners for legal assistance by levying a monthly charge. However, it has no idea how many hours each owner would use. Broadway decided that the number of units in each apartment would be a good proxy for use of legal service and that a single charging rate based on number of units would be reasonable. The number of units for each owner is as follows:

| | |
|---|---:|
| Applewood Court | 100 |
| Evergreen Apartments | 60 |
| Birch Place | 50 |
| Pine Place | 25 |
| Maple Arms | 15 |
| Total | 250 |

By the end of the first year, the actual usage of legal hours was: Applewood Court, 50; Evergreen Apartments, 20; Birch Place, 30; Pine Place, 20; and Maple Arms, 10.

**Required:**
1. Calculate a single charging rate for legal services based on the number of apartment units.
2. What was the total amount charged by the lawyer to Broadway Management Company by the end of the first year? What was the amount charged to each of the apartment owners using the charging rate computed in Requirement 1? How much would have been charged to each apartment owner if actual usage of legal hours had been the basis?
3. Which base is better for charging legal services – number of units, or number of hours of legal service? Why?

**7–5**

*Single Charging Rate*

**LO2, LO3**

Morton Auto Sales has three producing departments: new car sales, used car sales, and service. The service department provides service both to outside customers and to the new and used car sales departments. Morton wants to charge the new and used car sales departments for their use of the service department. It seems fair to charge each department for the cost of actual direct materials used (e.g., oil, engine parts) and to develop a single charging rate for direct labour and overhead.

Assume the following budgeted amounts for the year:

| | |
|---|---:|
| Direct labour cost | $360,000 |
| Direct labour hours | 24,000 |
| Overhead cost | $240,000 |

Actual materials and direct labour hours (DLH) incurred by the service department during the year are as follows:

| | (DLH) Materials | Actual DLH |
|---|---|---|
| New car sales department | $ 2,100 | 1,300 |
| Used car sales department | 7,890 | 4,700 |
| Service department | 86,300 | 19,100 |
| Total | $96,290 | 25,100 |

**Required:**
1. Calculate the single charging rate per hour of labour.
2. Suppose that the used car sales department gets a 1998 Sunbird as a trade-in that needs some general maintenance and some transmission work. The service department spends 8 hours working on the car and uses $478 of parts. Calculate the charge to the used car sales department by the service department.
3. Calculate the total costs charged by the service department to each of the "producing" departments for the year.

**7–6**

Single Charging Rate

LO2

Dottori Company charges all of its departments and manufacturing cells for the use of maintenance services. Budgeted maintenance costs for the year are $156,000, and budgeted maintenance hours are 3,000. By the end of the year, total actual maintenance hours equal 2,960, and actual cost is $154,500.

**Required:**
1. Calculate the billing rate for maintenance.
2. If the small-motor cell required 370 maintenance hours during the year, what was the cell charged for maintenance services?
3. Were the departments and cells (taken as a whole) over- or undercharged for the actual costs of maintenance—and if so, by how much?

**7–7**

Multiple Charging Rates

LO2

Refer to Exercise 7–6. Several departments complained that they were being overcharged for maintenance. The manager of the assembly department said, "I can't understand why my department was charged $520 for maintenance last month. We had one guy in for just a little over a day. What's going on?"

The controller of the plant reviewed the charge to the assembly department for the previous month and verified that it was correct. Then, he took a look at the costs of the maintenance department. Originally, the maintenance department did primarily routine cleaning and oiling of machinery. However, in the past few years, many of the manufacturing cells acquired complex computer-controlled machinery that requires technical support and diagnostic equipment. The budgeted cost of the department can be broken down into $48,000 for salaries and supplies for routine maintenance and the remainder for salaries and amortization on equipment for the more technical equipment maintenance. Budgeted hours of routine maintenance are 2,000, with 1,000 hours for the more technical maintenance.

**Required:**
1. Explain how the controller verified the accuracy of the $520 charged to the assembly department.
2. Calculate two charging rates for the maintenance department: a rate for routine maintenance based on hours needed for routine maintenance; and a rate for technical maintenance based on hours needed for technical maintenance. Assume that the assembly department needed only routine maintenance last month. What would the charge have been under the dual rate system?

3. What does this experience suggest for the determination of charging rates for support departments?

**7–8**

Allocating Support-
Department Cost
Using the Direct
Method

LO3

Spreadsheet

Quillen Company manufactures a product in a factory that has two producing departments (cutting and polishing) and two support departments (maintenance and human resources). The activity driver for maintenance is machine hours, and the activity driver for human resources is number of employees. The following data pertain to Quillen Company:

| | Support Departments | | Producing Departments | |
| --- | --- | --- | --- | --- |
| | Human Resources | Maintenance | Cutting | Polishing |
| Direct costs | $200,000 | $130,000 | $112,400 | $83,400 |
| Normal activity: | | | | |
| Number of employees | — | 10 | 35 | 35 |
| Maintenance hours | 600 | — | 8,000 | 2,000 |

**Required:**
1. Calculate the allocation ratios to be used under the direct method for the human resources and maintenance departments.
2. Allocate the support-department costs to the producing departments using the direct method.

**7–9**

Allocating Support-
Department Cost
Using the Sequential
Method

LO3

Spreadsheet

Refer to 7–8. Under the sequential method, the human resource department costs are allocated first.

**Required:**
1. Calculate the allocation ratios to be used under the sequential method for the human resources and maintenance departments. Carry your calculations out to four digits. (The human resource department will have three allocation ratios—one each for maintenance, cutting, and polishing. The maintenance department will have two allocation ratios—one for each producing department.)
2. Allocate the support-department costs to the producing departments using the sequential method.

**7–10**

Allocating Support-
Department Cost
Using the Reciprocal
Method

LO3

Refer to 7–8.

**Required:**
1. Calculate the allocation ratios to be used under the reciprocal method for the human resources and maintenance departments. Carry your calculations out to four digits. (The human resource department will have three allocation ratios—one each for maintenance, cutting, and polishing. The maintenance department will have three allocation ratios—one each for human resources, cutting, and polishing.)
2. Develop a cost equation for each support department and solve for the total support-department costs.
3. Allocate the support-department costs to the producing departments using the reciprocal method.

**7–11**

Direct Method and
Overhead Rates

LO3, LO4

Gordon Company manufactures pottery in two producing departments: shaping and firing. Three support departments—power, general factory, and human resources—support the production departments. Budgeted data on the five departments follow:

| | Support Departments | | | Producing Departments | |
| | Power | General Factory | Human Resources | Shaping | Firing |
|---|---|---|---|---|---|
| Direct overhead | $90,000 | $167,000 | $84,000 | $75,000 | $234,000 |
| Kilowatt-hours | — | 13,000 | 25,000 | 30,000 | 70,000 |
| Square metres | 2,000 | — | 6,000 | 24,000 | 8,000 |
| Direct labour hours | — | — | — | 4,000 | 6,000 |

Power is allocated on the basis of kilowatt-hours; general factory is allocated on the basis of square metres; and human resources is allocated on the basis of direct labour hours. The company does not break overhead into fixed and variable components.

**Required:**
1. Allocate the overhead costs to the producing departments using the direct method.
2. Using direct labour hours, compute departmental overhead rates.

**7–12**

Sequential Method
and Overhead Rates

LO3, LO4

Refer to the data in 7–11. The company has decided to use the sequential method of allocation instead of the direct method.

**Required:**
1. Allocate the overhead costs to the producing departments using the sequential method.
2. Using direct labour hours, compute departmental overhead rates.

**7–13**

Reciprocal Method and
Overhead Rates

LO3, LO4

Mandelbrot Company produces fractals in two producing departments (generating and colouring) and two support departments (human resources and power). The following budgeted data pertain to these four departments:

| | Support Departments | | Producing Departments | |
| | Human Resources | Power | Generating | Colouring |
|---|---|---|---|---|
| Overhead | $144,000 | $130,000 | $ 50,000 | $ 80,000 |
| Payroll | — | $ 80,000 | $160,000 | $160,000 |
| Kilowatt-hours | 50,000 | — | 200,000 | 150,000 |
| Direct labour hours | — | — | 20,000 | 30,000 |

Costs of the human resources department are allocated on the basis of payroll, and costs of the power department are allocated on the basis of kilowatt-hours.

**Required:**
1. Allocate the overhead costs of the support departments to the producing departments using the reciprocal method.
2. Using direct labour hours, compute departmental overhead rates (to the nearest penny).

**7–14**

*Direct Method and Overhead Rates*

LO3, LO4

Refer to the data in 7–13. The company has decided to simplify its method of allocating support-department costs by switching to the direct method.

**Required:**

1. Allocate the costs of the support departments to the producing departments using the direct method.
2. Using direct labour hours, compute departmental overhead rates (to the nearest penny). Which rate do you consider more accurate—the one using the reciprocal method or the one using the direct method? Explain.

**7–15**

*Sequential Method and Overhead Rates*

LO3, LO4

Refer to the data in 7–13.

**Required:**

1. Allocate the costs of the support departments using the sequential method.
2. Using direct labour hours, compute departmental overhead rates (to the nearest penny). Explain why these rates are generally more accurate than those computed using the direct method.

**7–16**

*Reciprocal Method*

LO3

Trinity Medical Clinic has two support departments and two revenue-producing departments. The clinic's controller has decided to use the reciprocal method to allocate the costs of the support departments (A and B) to the revenue-producing departments (C and D). She has prepared the following cost equations for the two support departments. *A* equals the total cost for the first support department, and *B* equals the total cost for the second support department:

$$A = \$35{,}000 + 0.30B$$
$$B = \$40{,}000 + 0.20A$$

Before the controller was able to complete the allocation, she had to leave to take care of an emergency. In addition to these equations, she left a hastily scribbled note indicating that Department C uses 20 percent of A's output and 40 percent of B's output.

**Required:**

Allocate the costs of the two support departments to each of the two revenue-producing departments using the reciprocal method.

**7–17**

*Choice of Allocation Method*

LO3

Crusher Manufacturing Company has two support departments, power and maintenance. The company is trying to decide whether to use a direct allocation method or a reciprocal allocation method to distribute costs to its two producing departments, assembly and finishing. The usage by each of the four departments for a normal month is:

**Usage of Support Departments: Normal Month**

| | Provider of Support Service | |
| --- | --- | --- |
| User of Service | Power (kilowatt-hours) | Maintenance (hours) |
| Power | 1,000 | 800 |
| Maintenance | 2,000 | — |
| Assembly | 4,000 | 2,500 |
| Finishing | 3,000 | 1,700 |
| Total | 10,000 | 5,000 |

The direct costs of power and maintenance are as follows:

| | | |
|---|---|---|
| Power | | $20,000 |
| Maintenance | | 12,000 |
| | | $32,000 |

As the assistant to the controller, you have been asked to provide some data analysis to help him make his decision on the appropriate allocation method to use.

**Required:**

1. If the company chose to allocate the support-department costs directly to assembly and finishing, how much cost would be allocated to assembly? to finishing? (Show separately the amount allocated from each support department to each producing department in your answer.)
2. Using the reciprocal method, allocate the support-department costs to the appropriate departments, showing the amount allocated from each support department to each of its users.
3. Prepare a short memo to the controller discussing the two possible methods of allocating Crusher's support-department costs. Recommend the best method to be used, and defend your choice. (CMA Canada adapted)

**7–18**

*Direct Method, Overhead Rates, Unit Cost*

**LO3, LO4**

Morris Machine Works has two support departments—power and general factory—and two producing departments—grinding and assembly. Budgeted data for each follows:

| | Power | General Factory | Grinding | Assembly |
|---|---|---|---|---|
| Direct costs | $60,000 | $100,000 | $103,000 | $85,000 |
| Machine hours | — | 1,000 | 8,000 | 2,000 |
| Square metres | 4,000 | — | 2,000 | 6,000 |
| Direct labour hours | 600 | 12,000 | 20,000 | 40,000 |

Power is allocated on the basis of machine hours; general factory is allocated on the basis of square metres.

**Required:**

1. Allocate the support-department costs to producing departments using the direct method.
2. Calculate departmental overhead rates, using machine hours for grinding and direct labour hours for assembly.
3. If a unit has prime costs of $17.50 and spends one hour in grinding and two hours in assembly, what is the unit cost?

**7–19**

*Sequential Method, Overhead Rates, Unit Cost*

**LO3, LO4**

Refer to the data in 7–18.

**Required:**

1. Allocate the support-department costs to producing departments using the sequential method.
2. Calculate departmental overhead rates, using machine hours for grinding and direct labour hours for assembly.
3. If a unit has prime costs of $17.50 and spends one hour in grinding and two hours in assembly, what is the unit cost?

**7–20**

*Reciprocal Method, Overhead Rates, Unit Cost*

**LO3, LO4**

Refer to the data in 7–18.

**Required:**

1. Allocate the support-department costs to producing departments using the reciprocal method.
2. Calculate departmental overhead rates, using machine hours for grinding and direct labour hours for assembly.
3. If a unit has prime costs of $17.50 and spends one hour in grinding and two hours in assembly, what is the unit cost?

**7–21**

*Comparison of Direct, Sequential, and Reciprocal Methods*

**LO3**

The Sedgwick Company has one factory with two production departments (fabricating and assembly) and two support departments (SDX and SDY). The following table provides cost and production/service data:

|                    | SDX     | SDY     | Fabricating | Assembly |
|--------------------|---------|---------|-------------|----------|
| Direct costs       | $6,300  | $5,600  | $20,000     | $37,500  |
| SDX hours used     | —       | 150     | 300         | 450      |
| SDY hours used     | 100     | —       | 500         | 200      |
| Direct labour hours| —       | —       | 1,000       | 1,500    |

**Required:**

1. Determine the amount of support-department costs that would be allocated to fabricating and assembly by the direct method.
2. Determine the amount of support-department costs that would be allocated to fabricating and assembly by the sequential method.
3. Determine the amount of support-department costs that would be allocated to fabricating and assembly by the reciprocal method.
4. Which method do you think most appropriately allocates the support-departments costs to the production departments? Explain why. (CMA Canada adapted)

**7–22**

*Direct Method, Job-Order Costing*

**LO3, LO4**

Osaka Company uses the direct method of allocating support-department costs to production departments. Costs of Department S1 are allocated on the basis of number of employees. Costs of Department S2 are allocated on the basis of machine hours. In Department P1, machine hours are used to assign overhead costs to jobs. In Department P2, direct labour hours are used to assign overhead costs to jobs. The following information is available:

|                      | S1       | S2       | P1        | P2        |
|----------------------|----------|----------|-----------|-----------|
| Direct overhead costs| $50,000  | $25,000  | $200,000  | $300,000  |
| Number of employees  | 50       | 20       | 60        | 120       |
| Machine hours        | —        | —        | 40,000    | 10,000    |
| Direct labour hours  | —        | —        | 20,000    | 60,000    |

| Job 49              | Department P1 | Department P2 |
|---------------------|---------------|---------------|
| Materials cost      | $60           | $45           |
| Direct labour hours | 1             | 2             |
| Machine hours       | 3             | 1             |

**Required:**
Calculate the overhead cost of Job 49. (CGA Canada adapted)

**7–23**

*Sequential Method, Job-Order Costing*

**LO3, LO4**

Refer to the data in 7–22. Assume that Osaka uses the sequential method.

**Required:**

Calculate the overhead cost of Job 49. (CGA Canada adapted)

**7–24**

*Multiple Choice*

**LO1, LO2, LO3, LO4**

Choose the *best* answer for each of the following multiple-choice questions:

1.  Which of the following would most likely be a producing department in a law firm?
    a.  Entertainment Law
    b.  Lexus-Nexus Database Maintenance
    c.  Photocopying
    d.  Paraprofessional Staffing
    e.  Human Resources

2.  If a single charging rate for a support department is used,
    a.  it is multiplied by actual usage of the producing departments to get the total amount charged out by the support department.
    b.  only variable costs are included in calculating the charging rate.
    c.  the support-department costs are allocated only to other support departments.
    d.  only fixed costs are included in calculating the charging rate.
    e.  None of the above.

3.  The method of allocating support-department costs that *best* accounts for support department interaction is the
    a.  direct method.
    b.  sequential method.
    c.  step method.
    d.  reciprocal method.
    e.  All of the above are equally useful in accounting for interactions among the support departments.

## Problems

**7–25**

*Comparison of Methods of Allocation*

**LO3**

Spreadsheet

MedServices Company is divided into two operating departments: Laboratory and Tissue Pathology. The company allocates delivery and accounting costs to each operating department. Delivery costs include the cost of a fleet of vans and drivers that drive throughout the region each day to clinics and doctors' offices to pick up samples and deliver them to the Laboratory and Tissue Pathology Departments. Delivery costs are allocated on the basis of number of samples. Accounting costs are allocated on the basis of the number of transactions processed. No effort is made to separate fixed and variable costs; however, only budgeted costs are allocated. Allocations for the coming year are based on the following data:

| | Support Departments | | Operating Departments | |
|---|---|---|---|---|
| | **Delivery** | **Accounting** | **Laboratory** | **Tissue Pathology** |
| Overhead costs | $240,000 | $270,000 | $345,000 | $456,000 |
| Number of samples | — | — | 70,200 | 46,800 |
| Transactions processed | 2,000 | 200 | 24,700 | 13,300 |

**Required:**
1. Allocate the support-department costs using the direct method.
2. Allocate the support-department costs using the sequential method.
3. Allocate the support-department costs using the reciprocal method.

**7–26**

Comparison of
Methods of Allocation

LO3, LO4

Gojar Uniform Company manufactures a variety of uniforms for city police services. Gojar has two producing departments, cutting and sewing. Usually, the uniforms are ordered in batches of 100.

Two support departments provide support for Gojar's operating units: maintenance and power. Budgeted data for next quarter follow. The company does not separate fixed and variable costs.

| | Support Departments | | Producing Departments | |
|---|---|---|---|---|
| | **Maintenance** | **Power** | **Cutting** | **Sewing** |
| Overhead costs | $240,000 | $380,000 | $65,000 | $ 87,000 |
| Machine hours | — | 30,000 | 40,000 | 10,000 |
| Kilowatt-hours | 20,000 | — | 18,000 | 162,000 |
| Direct labour hours | — | — | 5,000 | 30,000 |

The predetermined overhead rate for cutting is computed on the basis of machine hours; direct labour hours are used for sewing.

Recently, the company was asked to bid on a three-year contract for uniforms for the Calgary Police Service. The prime costs for a batch of 100 sets of uniforms total $1,817.50. It takes two machine hours to produce a batch in the cutting department and 50 direct labour hours to sew the 100 uniforms in the sewing department.

Gojar Uniform Company policy is to bid full manufacturing cost plus 25 percent.

**Required:**
1. Prepare a bid using the direct method.
2. Prepare a bid using the reciprocal method.
3. Which method most accurately reflects the cost of producing the uniforms? Why?

**7–27**

Comparison of
Ranking of Support
Departments Using the
Sequential Method

LO3, LO4

Refer to the data in 7–26.

**Required:**
1. Prepare a bid using the sequential method, allocating maintenance first, then power.
2. Prepare a bid using the sequential method, allocating power first, then maintenance.
3. Was there a difference in the bids calculated in Requirements 1 and 2? Why?

**7–28**

Sequential and Direct
Methods

LO3, LO4

Lilly Candies has three producing departments (mixing, cooking, and packaging) and five support departments. The following is the basic information on all departments (bases represent practical annual levels):

| | Number of Items Processed | Number of Employees | Square Metres Occupied | Machine Hours | Labour Hours |
|---|---|---|---|---|---|
| Cafeteria | 300 | 5 | 5,000 | — | — |
| Personnel | 1,000 | 10 | 7,000 | — | — |
| Custodial services | 200 | 7 | 2,000 | — | — |
| Maintenance | 2,500 | 15 | 16,000 | — | — |
| Cost accounting | — | 13 | 5,000 | — | — |
| Mixing | 2,800 | 20 | 40,000 | 4,000 | 30,000 |
| Cooking | 2,700 | 10 | 30,000 | 10,000 | 20,000 |
| Packaging | 3,000 | 20 | 20,000 | 6,000 | 50,000 |
| Total | 12,500 | 100 | 125,000 | 20,000 | 100,000 |

The budgeted overhead costs for the departments are as follows for the coming year:

| | Fixed | Variable | Total |
|---|---|---|---|
| Cafeteria | $ 20,000 | $ 40,000 | $ 60,000 |
| Personnel | 70,000 | 20,000 | 90,000 |
| Custodial services | 80,000 | — | 80,000 |
| Maintenance | 100,000 | 100,000 | 200,000 |
| Cost accounting | 130,000 | 16,500 | 146,500 |
| Mixing | 120,000 | 20,000 | 140,000 |
| Cooking | 60,000 | 10,000 | 70,000 |
| Packaging | 25,000 | 40,000 | 65,000 |

**Required:**

1. Allocate the support-department costs to the producing departments using the direct method. Use separate rates for fixed and variable costs.
2. Compute predetermined fixed overhead rates and predetermined variable overhead rates. Assume that overhead is applied using direct labour hours for mixing and packaging and machine hours for cooking.
3. Allocate the support-department costs to the producing departments using the sequential method. (*Hint:* Allocate fixed costs in order of descending magnitude of direct fixed costs. Allocate variable costs in order of descending magnitude of direct variable costs.)
4. Compute predetermined fixed and variable overhead rates based on Requirement 3. Overhead is applied using direct labour hours for mixing and packaging and machine hours for cooking.
5. Assume that the prime costs for a batch of chocolate bars total $60,000. The batch requires 1,000 direct labour hours in mixing, 1,500 machine hours in cooking, and 5,000 direct labour hours in packaging. Assume that the selling price is equal to full manufacturing cost plus 30 percent. Compute the selling price of the batch assuming that costs are allocated using the direct method. Repeat, using the sequential method. Comment on the implications of using different allocation methods, assuming that a markup of 30 percent is typical for the industry. Which allocation method do you think should be used?

**7–29**

*Reciprocal Method,*
*Cost of Operating a*
*Support Department*

LO3

Watterman Company has two producing departments (machining and assembly) and two support departments (power and maintenance). The budgeted costs and normal usage are as follows for the coming year:

|  | Power | Maintenance | Machining | Assembly |
|---|---|---|---|---|
| Overhead costs* | $50,000 | $40,000 | $120,000 | $60,000 |
| Kilowatt-hours | — | 100,000 | 300,000 | 100,000 |
| Machine hours | 5,000 | — | 10,000 | 5,000 |

* All overhead costs are variable.

Watterman's president was approached by the electric power company and offered the opportunity to buy power for $0.11 per kilowatt-hour. The president has asked you to determine the cost of producing the power internally so that a response to the offer can be made.

**Required:**

1. Compute the unit cost of kilowatts for overall plant usage. Based on this computation, how would you respond to the offer to buy the kilowatts externally?
2. Now use the reciprocal method to compute the cost of operating the power department. Divide this total cost by the total kilowatts produced by the power department to find a cost per kilowatt-hour. Based on this computation, how would you respond to the offer to buy kilowatts externally?
3. Show that the decision associated with the reciprocal method (Requirement 2) is correct by following two steps: (a) computing the savings realized if the power department is eliminated, and (b) computing the cost per kilowatt-hour saved by dividing the total savings by the kilowatts needed if the power department is eliminated. (*Hint:* Total savings include the direct costs of the power department plus any costs avoided by the maintenance department since it no longer needs to serve the power department. The total kilowatt-hours consumed by the company need to be adjusted since the maintenance department's power needs decrease when it decreases the amount of service it offers.)

**7–30**

*Direct Method,*
*Sequential Method,*
*Overhead Rates*

LO3, LO4

Bright, Inc., has two producing departments and four support departments. It currently uses the direct method of support department cost allocation. Data for the company follow:

|  | Producing Departments | | | Support Departments | | |
|---|---|---|---|---|---|---|
|  | PD1 | PD2 | SD1 | SD2 | SD3 | SD4 |
| Overhead | $183,000 | $212,400 | $30,000 | $35,000 | $40,000 | $100,000 |
| Square metres | 2,000 | 2,000 | 400 | 5,000 | 600 | — |
| Employees | 15 | 45 | — | 12 | 20 | 3 |
| Direct labour hours | 30,000 | 90,000 | — | 24,000 | 20,000 | 6,000 |
| Machine hours | 10,000 | 20,000 | — | — | — | — |

Original Allocation Base
SD1 Machine hours
SD2 Number of employees
SD3 Direct labour hours
SD4 Square metres

Cara James, controller of Bright, Inc., is considering changing to a more accurate method of support department cost allocation. She has discovered the following:

1. SD1 provides its services only to the producing departments, based on machine hours.
2. SD2 provides services to both producing and support departments, based on the number of employees.
3. SD3 provides 15 percent of its service to SD1 and the remainder to PD1 and PD2, based on direct labour hours.
4. SD4 provides services to all other departments, based on area occupied.

Cara has decided to rank the support departments in the following order for purposes of cost allocation: SD4, SD2, SD3, SD1.

**Required:**
1. Allocate support-department costs using the direct method and the original allocation bases.
2. Allocate support-department costs using the sequential method as outlined by Cara James.
3. Calculate overhead rates for PD1 (based on machine hours) and PD2 (based on direct labour hours) using total departmental overhead costs as determined by the direct method.
4. Calculate overhead rates for PD1 (based on machine hours) and PD2 (based on direct labour hours) using total departmental overhead costs as determined by the sequential method.

**7–31**

Fixed and Variable-Cost Allocation

LO2

El Greco's is a chain of restaurants serving Mediterranean (Greek, Italian, and Spanish) food in a family-type atmosphere. The chain has grown from one restaurant in 1995 to five restaurants located in Manitoba and Northwestern Ontario. In 2004, the owner of the company decided to set up a centralized purchasing department to purchase food and other supplies, and to coordinate inventory decisions. The purchasing department was opened in January 2004 by renting space adjacent to corporate headquarters in Winnipeg. All restaurants have been equipped to transfer information to central purchasing on a daily basis.

The purchasing department has budgeted fixed costs of $50,000 per year. Variable costs are budgeted at $16 per hour. Actual costs in 2004 equalled budgeted costs. Further information is as follows:

| | Actual Revenues | | Actual Hours of Purchasing Used in 2004 |
| | 2003 | 2004 | |
| --- | --- | --- | --- |
| Kenora | $337,500 | $390,500 | 1,475 |
| Brandon | 360,000 | 375,000 | 938 |
| Portage la Prairie | 450,000 | 456,000 | 400 |
| Winnipeg (West) | 562,500 | 549,000 | 375 |
| Winnipeg (South) | 540,000 | 550,000 | 562 |

**Required:**
1. Suppose that the total costs of the purchasing department are allocated on the basis of 2003 sales revenue. How much will be allocated to each restaurant?
2. Suppose that El Greco's views 2003 sales figures as a proxy for budgeted capacity of the restaurants. Thus, fixed purchasing department costs are allocated on the basis of 2003 sales, and variable costs are allocated according to 2004 usage multiplied by the variable rate. How much purchasing department cost will be allocated to each restaurant?
3. Comment on the two allocation schemes. Which is better? Explain.

The Davis Company has a computer department that provides its services to two other departments (accounting and research). The computer department was designed with a capacity of 160 hours per month to meet the demands of accounting (50 percent of capacity) and research (50 percent of capacity).

The computer department is expected to incur costs of $180,000 per month plus $200 per hour of usage. During January, the computer department actually incurred costs of $243,750 while providing 70 hours of service to accounting and 80 hours to research.

The company's controller has indicated that she feels the costs of the computer department must be charged to the two departments using its services in order to control the total costs incurred by each department manager and to evaluate the managers' performance. The controller has therefore prepared the following cost allocation:

Rate = Cost of computer department/Total hours used
      = $243,750/150 = $1,625 per hour

Cost Allocation:
| | |
|---|---|
| Accounting department (70 hours @ $1,625) | $113,750 |
| Research department (80 hours @ $1,625) | 130,000 |
| Total cost of computer department | $243,750 |

**Required:**

1. As manager of the research department, comment on the validity and fairness of the method used to allocate the computer department's costs to your department.
2. Describe a more appropriate method of allocating the computer department's costs that might help to alleviate any problems inherent in the method used. (CMA Canada adapted)

**7–33**

Support Department
Cost Allocations,
Plantwide Overhead
Rate versus
Departmental Rates,
Effects on Pricing
Decisions

LO3, LO4

Alden Peterson, marketing manager for Retlief Company, was puzzled by the outcome of two recent bids. The company's policy was to bid 150 percent of the full manufacturing cost. One job (labelled Job SS) had been turned down by a prospective customer, who had indicated that the proposed price was $3 per unit higher than the winning bid. A second job (Job TT) had been accepted by a customer, who was amazed that Retlief could offer such favourable terms. This customer revealed that Retlief's price was $43 per unit lower than the next lowest bid.

Alden knew that Relief Company was more than competitive in terms of cost control. Accordingly, he suspected that the problem was related to cost assignment procedures. Upon investigating, Alden was told that the company used a plantwide overhead rate based on direct labour hours. The rate was computed at the beginning of the year using budgeted data. Selected budgeted data follow:

| | Department A | Department B | Total |
|---|---|---|---|
| Overhead | $500,000 | $2,000,000 | $2,500,000 |
| Direct labour hours | 200,000 | 50,000 | 250,000 |
| Machine hours | 20,000 | 120,000 | 140,000 |

These data led to a plantwide overhead rate of $10 per direct labour hour. In addition, the following specific manufacturing data on Job SS and Job TT were given:

**Job SS**

|  | Department A | Department B | Total |
|---|---|---|---|
| Direct labour hours | 5,000 | 1,000 | 6,000 |
| Machine hours | 200 | 500 | 700 |
| Prime costs | $100,000 | $20,000 | $120,000 |
| Units produced | — | — | 14,400 |

**Job TT**

|  | Department A | Department B | Total |
|---|---|---|---|
| Direct labour hours | 400 | 600 | 1,000 |
| Machine hours | 200 | 3,000 | 3,200 |
| Prime costs | $10,000 | $40,000 | $50,000 |
| Units produced | — | — | 1,500 |

This information led to the original bid prices of $18.75 per unit for Job SS and $60 per unit for Job TT.

Then Alden discovered that the overhead costs in Department B were higher than those of Department A because Department B has more equipment, higher maintenance, higher power consumption, higher amortization, and higher setup costs. So he tried reworking the two bids by using departmental overhead rates. Department A's overhead rate was $2.50 per direct labour hour; Department B's overhead rate was $16.67 per machine hour. These rates resulted in unit prices of $14.67 for Job SS and $101.01 for Job TT.

Alden was still not satisfied, however. He did some reading on overhead allocation methods and learned that proper support department cost allocation can lead to more accurate product costs. He decided to create four support departments and recalculate departmental overhead rates. Information on departmental costs and related items follows:

|  | Maintenance | Power | Setups | General Factory | Dept. A | Dept. B |
|---|---|---|---|---|---|---|
| Overhead | $500,000 | $225,000 | $150,000 | $625,000 | $200,000 | $800,000 |
| Maintenance hours | — | 1,500 | 500 | — | 1,000 | 7,000 |
| Kilowatt-hours | 4,500 | — | 500 | $ 15,000 | 10,000 | 50,000 |
| Direct labour hours | 10,000 | 12,000 | 6,000 | $ 8,000 | 200,000 | 50,000 |
| Number of setups | — | — | — | — | 40 | 160 |
| Square metres | 25,000 | 40,000 | 5,000 | 15,000 | 35,360 | 94,640 |

The following allocation bases (cost drivers) seemed reasonable:

| Support Department | Allocation Base |
|---|---|
| Maintenance | Maintenance hours |
| Power | Kilowatt-hours |
| Setups | Number of setups |
| General factory | Square metres |

### Required:
1. Using the direct method, verify the original departmental overhead rates.
2. Using the sequential method, allocate support-department costs to the producing departments. Calculate departmental overhead rates using direct labour hours for Department A and machine hours for Department B. What would the bids for Job SS and Job TT have been if these overhead rates had been in effect?
3. Which method of overhead cost assignment would you recommend to Alden? Why?

4. Suppose that the best competing bid was $4.10 lower than the original bid price (based on a plantwide rate). Does this affect your recommendation in Requirement 3? Explain.

**7–34**

*Service Organization: Direct and Reciprocal Methods*

**LO3**

In January, a group of Quebec City lawyers and accountants decided to join efforts to provide "one-stop shopping" legal and accounting consulting services to industry and the government. The group established a consulting company, rented office space, and hired both professional and clerical staff.

Following several initial organizational meetings, the partners decided to divide the operation into three parts: the consulting department, the legal department, and the accounting department. The consulting department dealt directly with the clients, providing two distinct services, accounting consulting (AC) and legal consulting (LC). In its first full month of operations, this department recorded its own identifiable costs as $20,000, with 30 percent attributable to accounting consultants and 70 percent to legal consultants. Billings to clients amounted to $30,000 and $20,500 for accounting and legal consulting, respectively. This department made use of the other departments' services in preparing work for the external clients.

The accounting and legal departments provided professional services for each other and for the consulting department on the basis of hours worked according to the following schedule:

|  | Accounting Department | Legal Department | Legal AC | LC |
|---|---|---|---|---|
| Accounting services | — | 20% | 60% | 20% |
| Legal services | 50% | — | 10% | 40% |

The accounting department incurred $8,000 in direct costs in the first month, and the legal department incurred $10,000. Neither department directly bills external clients.

Having completed the first month's activity, the partners are ready to evaluate the performance of the group and of the individual areas. The managing partner is concerned that his organizational structure may be a major determinant of success and has asked you, as an outside consultant, to prepare some performance information for him.

**Required:**
1. Prepare separate income statements for each consulting service using the direct method to allocate the support-department costs.
2. Prepare separate income statements for each consulting service using the reciprocal method to allocate the support-department costs.
3. Prepare a brief memorandum to the managing partner on the performance of the group and individual areas. (CMA Canada adapted)

## Managerial Decision Cases

**7–35**

*Allocation, Pricing, Ethical Behaviour*

**LO1, LO2**

Emma Hanks, manager of a division that produces valves and castings on a special-order basis, was excited about an order received from a new customer. The customer, a friend of Bob Johnson, Emma's supervisor, had placed an order for 10,000 valves. The customer agreed to pay full manufacturing cost plus 25 percent. The order was timely since business was sluggish, and Emma had some concerns about her division's ability to meet its targeted profits. Even with the order, the division would likely fall short in meeting the target by at least $50,000. After examining the cost sheet for the order, however, Emma thought she saw a way to increase the profitability of the job. Accordingly, she called Larry Smith, CMA, the controller of the division.

**Emma:** "Larry, this cost sheet for the new order reflects an allocation of maintenance costs to the grinding department based on maintenance hours used. Currently, 60 percent of our maintenance costs are allocated to grinding on that basis. Can you tell me what the allocation ratio would be if we used machine hours instead of maintenance hours?"

**Larry:** "Sure. Based on machine hours, the allocation ratio would increase from 60 percent to 80 percent."

**Emma:** "Excellent. Now tell me what would happen to the unit cost of this new job if we used machine hours to allocate maintenance costs."

**Larry:** "Hold on. That'll take a few minutes … The cost would increase by $10 per unit."

**Emma:** "And with the 25 percent markup, the revenues on that job would jump by $12.50 per unit. That would increase the division's profitability by $125,000. Larry, I want you to change the allocation base from maintenance hours worked to machine hours."

**Larry:** "Are you sure? After all, if you recall, we spent some time assessing the causal relationships, and we found that maintenance hours reflect the consumption of maintenance cost much better than machine hours. I'm not sure that would be a fair cost assignment. We've used this base for years now."

**Emma:** "Listen, Larry, allocations are arbitrary anyway. Changing the allocation base for this new job will increase its profitability and allow us to meet our targeted profit goals for the year. If we meet or beat those goals, we'll be more likely to get the capital we need to acquire some new equipment. Furthermore, by beating the targeted profit, we'll get our share of the bonus pool. Besides, this new customer has a prosperous business and can easily afford to pay somewhat more for this order."

### Required:

1. Evaluate Emma's position. Do you agree with her reasoning? Explain. What should Emma do?

2. If you were the controller, what would you do? Do any of the standards for ethical conduct for management accountants apply to the controller (see Chapter 1)? Explain.

3. Suppose Larry refused to change the allocation scheme. Emma then issued the following ultimatum: "Either change the allocation or look for another job!" Larry then made an appointment with Bob Johnson and disclosed the entire affair. Bob, however, was not sympathetic. He advised Larry to do as Emma had requested, arguing that the request represented good business sense. Now what should Larry do?

4.  Refer to Requirement 3. Larry decided that he cannot comply with the request to change the allocation scheme. Appeals to higher-level officials have been in vain. Angered, Larry submitted his resignation and called the new customer affected by the cost reassignment. In his phone conversation, Larry revealed Emma's plans to increase the job's costs in order to improve the division's profits. The new customer expressed her gratitude and promptly cancelled her order for 10,000 valves. Evaluate Larry's action. Should he have informed the customer about Emma's intent? Explain.

**7–36**

Direct Method,
Settlement of a
Contract Dispute

LO3, LO4

A government agency contracted with FlyRite Helicopters to provide helicopter services on a requirements contract. After six months, FlyRite discovered that the agency's original estimates of the number of flying hours needed were grossly overstated. FlyRite Helicopters is now making a claim against the agency for defective specifications. The agency has been advised by its legal advisers that its chances in court on this claim would not be strong, and that an out-of-court settlement is therefore in order. As a result of the legal advice, the agency has hired a local CA firm to analyze the claim and prepare a recommendation for an equitable settlement.

The particulars on which the original bid was based follow. The contract was for three different types of helicopters and had a duration of one year. Thus, the data reflect the original annual expectations. Also, the costs and activity pertain only to the contract.

|  | **Aircraft Type** | | |
| --- | --- | --- | --- |
|  | **Hughes 500D** | **206B Jet Ranger** | **206L–1 Long Ranger** |
| Flying hours | 1,200 | 1,600 | 900 |
| Direct costs: | | | |
| Fixed: | | | |
| Insurance | $32,245 | $28,200 | $55,870 |
| Lease payments | 31,000 | 36,000 | 90,000 |
| Pilot salaries | 30,000 | 30,000 | 30,000 |
| Variable: | | | |
| Fuel | $24,648 | $30,336 | $22,752 |
| Minor servicing | 6,000 | 8,000 | 4,500 |
| Lease | — | — | 72,000 |

In addition to the direct costs, the following indirect costs were expected:

|  | **Fixed Costs** | **Variable Costs** |
| --- | --- | --- |
| Maintenance | $26,000 | $246,667 |
| Hangar rent | 18,000 | — |
| General administrative | 110,000 | — |

Maintenance costs and general administrative costs are allocated to each helicopter on the basis of flying hours; hangar rent is allocated on the basis of the number of helicopters. The company has one of each type of aircraft.

During the first six months of the contract, the actual flying hours were as follows:

| **Type** | **Flying Hours** |
| --- | --- |
| 500D | 299 |
| 206B | 160 |
| 206L–1 | 204 |

The agency's revised projection of total hours for the year follows:

| Type | Flying Hours |
|------|--------------|
| 500D | 450 |
| 206B | 600 |
| 206L-1 | 800 |

**Required:**

1. Assume that FlyRite won the contract with a bid of cost plus 15 percent, where cost refers to cost per flying hour. Compute the original bid price per flying hour for each type of helicopter. Next, compute the original expected profit of the contract.

2. Compute the profit (or loss) earned by FlyRite for the first six months of activity. Assume that the actual costs were equal to the planned costs. Also assume that 50 percent of the fixed costs for the year have been incurred. Compute the profit that FlyRite should have earned during the first six months, assuming that 50 percent of the hours originally projected (for each aircraft type) had been flown.

3. Compute the profit (or loss) that the contract would provide FlyRite assuming the original price per flying hour and using the agency's revised projection of hours needed.

4. Assume that the agency has agreed to pay what is necessary so that FlyRite receives the profit originally expected in the contract. This will be accomplished by revising the price paid per flying hour based on the revised estimates of flying hours. What is the new price per flying hour?

**7–37**

*Design of Cost Allocation System*

**LO1, LO2, LO3, LO4**

The Taubner Company manufactures customized office furniture, and each contract is drafted to meet the needs of the individual client. Contracts are obtained through a competitive system of bidding for new jobs.

The company's production facilities consist of the following departments:

**Production Departments**

1. Machining Department: Departmental costs are $600,000 per year, of which 60 percent are fixed costs consisting mainly of amortization of the machinery.

2. Fabrication Department: Departmental costs are $300,000 per year, of which 10 percent are fixed costs. This department assembles the various parts of product and is very labour-intensive due to the wide variety of products produced.

**Support Departments**

1. Computer Facilities: Departmental costs are $200,000 per year, of which 80 percent are fixed costs of the equipment and staff.

2. Product Design Department: Departmental costs are $100,000 per year. The department uses 70 percent of the computer facilities for CAD programs to design the various products and production methods.

3. Purchasing Department: Departmental costs are $40,000 per year, of which 40 percent are fixed costs. The department's main duty is the purchase of materials for the machining department to make furniture.

Karen Bains, Taubner's president, has asked you to prepare a report to her addressing the following issues:

a. Should the company use plantwide or departmental rates for applying the manufacturing overhead to the products?

b. Should the support-department costs be allocated using the direct, the sequential, or the reciprocal method?

c. Should the support-department costs be allocated using variable and fixed charging rates or a single charging rate for total departmental costs?

d.  What would be the most logical base(s) for allocating each support-department cost? What would be the most logical base(s) for allocating the costs of each of the production departments?

**Required:**

Prepare a report to the president addressing the main issues. Where there are alternative methods, be sure to identify the main characteristics of each alternative and to justify your recommended course of action. (CMA Canada adapted)

## Research Assignment

**7–38**

Research Assignment

LO1, LO2

Contact the controller of a local hospital and arrange an interview. Ask the hospital controller the following questions and write up his or her responses:

a.  How many support departments do you have in the hospital? Will you describe several for me?
b.  How many different producing departments are there in the hospital? Will you describe several for me?
c.  How do you assign support-department costs to producing departments?
d.  How many different products are there in the hospital?
e.  How do you assign the costs of the support departments to individual products?
f.  How many different products are costed in your hospital?
g.  How do you determine the cost of a particular product?

## Managerial Decision Making

Part 2 considers how managers make decisions using management accounting information. Managers make decisions daily. Many of their decisions are routine and require little more than being informed. Other decisions have strategic implications, and require more consultation and participation by others in the organization. Some decisions have primarily short-term implications, while others require substantial long-term investments, as when establishing new plants, stores, product or service lines, or processes. The combined forces of intense global competition and rapid technological change have accelerated the frequency of these types of decisions. Almost all major decisions, whether they affect the short term or the long term, deal with a large number of factors. Some of these factors can be easily quantified, for example, the potential impact a decision will have on profit or cash flow, while other more qualitative factors defy quantification, for example, customer satisfaction, quality of products, and competitive posture. The emphasis in Part 2 is primarily, but not exclusively, related to the quantitative aspects of decisions. However, it is important to note that quite often qualitative factors can be as important as quantitative aspects in reaching the ultimate decision.

## Accounting Information and Decision Making

In making any decision, a manager must consider the future consequences of the alternatives available. The information available from traditional accounting records, largely kept for purposes of financial reporting, tends to be historical and less relevant for managerial decisions. Past data, however, can often be used and be relevant as the basis for predicting future consequences such as future costs and revenues.

**Chapter 8** introduces variable costing – a costing and internal reporting system that is consistent with, and highlights, the effects of volume changes on income. It also deals with performance reporting related to segments and assessing customer profitability using activity-based costing.

**Chapter 9** deals directly with short-term decisions and focuses on the interaction of costs, prices, and volume, all of which have an impact on profit and cash flow. In particular, the cost–volume–profit model highlights the impact of volume on profit and cash flow.

**Chapter 10** covers the general case of decision making. It considers the different cash flows associated with different choices. The chapter shows that a focus on past cost information can be misleading. Managers must use different costs for different purposes; the concept of relevant costs—those that are different in the future—is emphasized.

**Chapter 11** deals with the future cash flows associated with capital investment decisions, and with the unique considerations that result from long-term cash flows. These considerations include discounting, income tax effects of capital cost allowance, uncertainty, and inflation.

**Chapter 12** deals with the unique problems and decisions related to inventory management.

## Decision Examples

The following brief cases provide examples of the types of decision situations that are addressed in Part 2:

- During a period of low demand, a manager at first refused to sell her product below its full cost, including its average fixed cost, so as not to lose money on the product. She then discovered that her pricing strategy was costing her many profitable opportunities. Although she could not significantly decrease her fixed costs in the short run, she was rejecting a number of special orders, priced below average full cost but above average variable cost. When she began to accept these special orders, her total contribution margin dramatically increased while her fixed costs remained relatively unaffected, thus increasing her income.

- The Continuing Education Division of a major Canadian university was required to be financially self-supporting. Each program in the division was evaluated financially on the basis of its total contribution (measured as the difference between its revenues and its direct costs). It was subsequently discovered that some programs, with higher total contributions, were actually driving overhead costs higher. By applying ABC, the division controller was able to relate each major type of cost to its cost driver and draw a more accurate picture of the financial performance of each program. As a result, the division recommended corrective actions, including program and course fee changes and the elimination of some less profitable programs.

- A company decided to close down a department because the department income report showed it to be unprofitable. Before the decision was implemented, however, a thorough analysis of differential cash flows was undertaken. The company found that many of the costs that had been assigned to the department would not be eliminated if the department was closed down. These costs continued because they were allocations of common costs from other departments and from the general overhead cost. Contractual obligations also limited the extent of wage savings that would result from the elimination of the department. These factors were not apparent from the department income report alone but became obvious when differential cash-flow analysis was performed.

The cases show that careful consideration of the interdependencies of cost, price, and volume and of their effect on profit and cash flow is required for sound decisions. All of the cases require a full understanding of relevant cost analysis.

# Variable Costing: Segmented Reporting and Performance Evaluation

## Learning Objectives

**After studying Chapter 8, you should be able to:**

1. Explain the differences between variable and absorption costing.

2. Explain how variable costing is useful in evaluating the performance of managers.

3. Prepare a segmented income statement based on a variable-costing approach, and explain how this format can be used with activity-based costing and customer profitability analysis.

4. Explain how variable costing can be used in planning and control.

## Scenario

Kathy Wise had been the manager of the Medical Supplies Division for three years. In the first year, the division's net income had shown a substantial increase over the prior year. Her second year saw an even greater increase. Kathy's boss, the vice-president for operations, was extremely pleased and promised her a $5,000 bonus if the division showed a similar increase in profits for the upcoming year. Kathy was elated. She was completely confident that the goal could be met. Sales contracts were already well ahead of last year's performance, and she knew that there would be no increases in costs.

At the end of the third year, Kathy received the data regarding operations for the first three years. Upon examining the operating data, Kathy was pleased. Sales had increased by 20 percent over the previous year, and costs had been kept stable. However, when she saw the yearly income statements, she was dismayed and perplexed. Instead of seeing a significant increase in income for the third year, she saw a small decrease. Surely, she thought, the accounting department had made an error.

Freda Mathews, controller for the Medical Supplies Division, met with Kathy to explain the anomalous results.

**Freda:** "Kathy, there's been no mistake here. Net income is lower this year than in the past two years. It's easily explained by looking at the changes in inventory."

**Kathy:** "Inventory? What's that got to do with income? We did a terrific job managing inventory this year. It had built up in the past two years, and I got sales up and inventory down. That's good, not bad!"

**Freda:** "Sure, Kathy, from an operating perspective. But you have to realize that inventory carries cost with it. That cost doesn't appear on the income statement until the stuff is sold. Then it flows through income and reduces it."

**Kathy:** "That's crazy! Do you mean that I'm going to lose my bonus even though we sold off our inventory and met cost and revenue projections?"

**Freda:** "Well, Kathy, I'm sorry about your bonus, but the income figures are solid. I'd be happy to spend a little time with you explaining how we account for income. We use absorption costing; it's recommended by GAAP. There is another possibility, variable costing, and it sounds to me like you are implicitly using that method."

**Kathy**: "There are two ways to figure income? Does it make a difference?"

**Freda**: "Oh yes. Variable costing doesn't permit inventory changes to affect income. So your income this year would be higher under variable costing. However, your income the past couple of years would have been lower. So over the long run, it evens out."

**Kathy**: "Hmmm. I wonder if I could get the VP to take a look at variable costing."

**Questions to Think About**

1. Why do companies calculate income? What information does it provide?

2. What costs go into inventory? How can they affect income?

3. What is GAAP, and how does it affect the income statement of the Medical Supplies Division?

4. Why doesn't Kathy understand accounting? Should she?

5. What do you suppose Kathy's chances are for getting the vice-president to consider evaluating her performance on the basis of variable, instead of absorption, costing?

## Variable Costing and Absorption Costing: An Analysis and Comparison

**Objective 1**

Explain the differences between variable and absorption costing.

In the opening scenario, two methods of computing income are identified: one based on variable costing and the other based on full, or absorption, costing. These are costing methods because they refer to the way in which product costs are determined. Recall that product costs are inventoried, whereas period costs are expensed in the period incurred. The difference between variable and absorption costing hinges on the treatment of one particular cost: fixed overhead.

Variable costing stresses the difference between fixed and variable manufacturing costs. This distinction is critical for many decision and control models that are used in management accounting. Studying variable costing provides a good foundation for the application of other important management accounting topics, such as cost–volume–profit analysis, relevant costing, and flexible budgeting.

**variable costing**

A product-costing method that assigns only variable manufacturing costs—direct materials, direct labour, and variable overhead—to production. Fixed overhead is treated as a period cost.

**Variable costing** assigns only variable manufacturing costs to the product; these costs include direct materials, direct labour, and variable overhead. Fixed overhead is treated as a period cost and is excluded from the product cost. The rationale for this is that fixed cost is considered as a cost of capacity or being in business. Once the period is over, any benefits provided by the capacity have expired and should not be inventoried. Under variable costing, fixed overhead for a period is seen as expiring that period and is charged in total against the revenues of the period.[1]

**absorption costing**

A product-costing method that assigns all manufacturing costs to a product.

**Absorption costing** assigns *all* manufacturing costs to the product. Direct materials, direct labour, variable overhead, and fixed overhead define the cost of a product. Thus, under absorption costing, fixed overhead is viewed as a *product* cost, not a period cost. Under this method, fixed overhead is assigned to the product through the use of a predetermined fixed overhead rate and does not expire until the product is sold. In other words, fixed overhead is an inventoriable cost. Exhibit 8–1 illustrates the classification of costs as product or period costs under absorption and variable costing. From Exhibit 8–1, it is clear that the only difference is in the treatment of fixed overhead.

---

1. Variable costing is also known as *direct* costing. Direct costing, however, is a misnomer. Not all variable manufacturing costs are direct costs. For example, variable overhead, by definition, consists of *indirect* manufacturing costs. Clearly, the more descriptive name for this method is variable costing, which is the term we use in this book.

EXHIBIT   8-1

Classification of Costs as
Product or Period Costs
under Absorption and
Variable Costing

|  | **Absorption Costing** | **Variable Costing** |
|---|---|---|
| Product Costs | Direct materials (DM) | Direct materials (DM) |
|  | Direct labour (DL) | Direct labour (DL) |
|  | Variable overhead (VOH) | Variable overhead (VOH) |
|  | Fixed overhead (FOH) |  |
| Period Costs | Selling expense | Fixed overhead (FOH) |
|  | Administrative expense | Selling expense |
|  |  | Administrative expense |

Currently, absorption costing is the most commonly used product-costing method for external reporting.[2] Yet as the dialogue between Kathy and Freda suggests, variable costing can supply vital cost information for decision making and control, information not supplied by absorption costing. For internal application, variable costing is an invaluable managerial tool. Let's look at the way the two costing methods affect inventory valuation and income determination.

## Inventory Valuation

Different product-costing methods will affect the cost of goods stored in inventory. We will use an example to make the inventory valuations of absorption and variable costing more concrete. During the most recent year, Fairchild Company had the following data associated with the product it makes:

| | |
|---|---|
| Units, beginning inventory | — |
| Units produced | 10,000 |
| Units sold (@ $300 per unit) | 8,000 |
| Normal volume[a] | 10,000 |
| Variable costs per unit: | |
|    Direct labour | $100 |
|    Direct materials | 50 |
|    Variable overhead[b] | 50 |
|    Variable selling and administrative | 10 |
| Fixed costs: | |
|    Fixed overhead[b] | $250,000 |
|    Fixed selling and administrative | 100,000 |

[a] This is the average activity level that a company experiences over more than one fiscal period, and is often used as a denominator volume in the allocation of fixed manufacturing overhead.
[b] Assume that estimated and actual overhead are equal.

Recall that the unit product cost obtained under each method differs. Variable costing inventories only variable manufacturing costs, so each unit of product for Fairchild costs $200. Absorption costing includes all manufacturing costs, so each unit of product costs $225. The computations follow:

| | **Variable Costing** | **Absorption Costing** |
|---|---|---|
| Direct labour | $100 | $100 |
| Direct materials | 50 | 50 |
| Variable overhead | 50 | 50 |
| Fixed overhead ($250,000/10,000) | — | 25 |
| Total per unit cost | $200 | $225 |

2. Section 3030.6 of the *CICA Handbook* requires that inventories of work in process and finished goods include the cost of materials, labour, and an appropriate share of overhead. This is usually interpreted as requiring absorption costing, but Section 3030.6 allows for some fixed overhead to be excluded if net income would otherwise be distorted because of fluctuations in production volume. This could be viewed as support for variable costing in some circumstances.
Variable costing is acceptable for income tax purposes in Canada, provided that it is also used for accounting purposes (see *Interpretation Bulletin IT-473* from the Canada Customs and Revenue Agency [CCRA], formerly known as—and still sometimes informally called—Revenue Canada).

Of course, the difference in unit costs affects the amount shown on the balance sheet. Fairchild had no beginning inventory and produced 2,000 units more than it sold. Therefore, ending inventory is 2,000 units (10,000 − 8,000). Under variable costing, the value of ending inventory is $400,000 ($200 × 2,000). Under absorption costing, the value of ending inventory is $450,000 ($225 × 2,000). Note that the only difference between the two approaches is the treatment of fixed overhead. Thus, the unit product cost under absorption costing is always greater than the unit product cost under variable costing.

## Income Statements: Analysis and Reconciliation

Because unit product costs are the basis for cost of goods sold, the variable- and absorption-costing methods can lead to different net income figures. The difference arises because of the amount of fixed overhead recognized as an expense under the two methods. Income statements for the Fairchild example appear in Exhibits 8–2 and 8–3.[3] These income statements reveal that absorption-costing income is $50,000 higher than variable-costing income. As the following analysis shows, this difference is due to some of the period's fixed overhead flowing into inventory when absorption costing is used.

For variable costing (Exhibit 8–2), the variable cost of goods sold is $1.6 million ($200 × 8,000 units sold). The fixed overhead deducted as an expense is $250,000. Thus, the total manufacturing expenses deducted are $1.85 million. The total selling and administrative expenses deducted are $180,000 ($80,000 variable and $100,000 fixed).

EXHIBIT  8-2

Variable-Costing Income Statement

**Fairchild Company**
**Variable-Costing Income Statement**

| | | |
|---|---:|---:|
| Sales | | $2,400,000 |
| Less variable expenses: | | |
| Variable cost of goods sold | $1,600,000 | |
| Variable selling and administrative | 80,000 | 1,680,000 |
| Contribution margin | | $ 720,000 |
| Less fixed expenses: | | |
| Fixed overhead | $ 250,000 | |
| Fixed selling and administrative | 100,000 | 350,000 |
| Net income | | $ 370,000 |

For absorption costing (Exhibit 8–3), the cost of goods sold is $1.8 million ($225 × 8,000 units sold). Of this amount, $200,000 ($25 × 8,000) represents the fixed overhead that was recognized as an expense. The total selling and administrative expenses deducted are still $180,000 ($80,000 variable and $100,000 fixed).

Exhibits 8–2 and 8–3 show that sales, selling expenses, and administrative expenses are always the same. Variable cost of goods sold is always the same. However, the amount of fixed overhead that is expensed differs. Thus, income determined with variable costing is $50,000 less than income determined with absorption costing. For absorption costing, where did the other $50,000 of fixed overhead go?

---

3. Note that while the absorption costing income statement is organized on a functional basis, the variable costing income statement is organized by cost behaviour. The difference between revenue and variable expenses is called a *contribution margin*. We will examine the concept of a contribution margin in more detail in Chapter 9.

| Fairchild Company<br>Absorption-Costing Income Statement | |
| --- | --- |
| Sales | $2,400,000 |
| Less: Cost of goods sold | 1,800,000 |
|    Gross margin | $ 600,000 |
| Less: Selling and administrative expenses | 180,000 |
|    Net income | $ 420,000 |

Under absorption costing, each unit produced was assigned fixed overhead of $25. Of the 10,000 units produced, 2,000 units were not sold. These 2,000 units went into inventory and carried with them $50,000 ($25 × 2,000) of the period's fixed overhead. Only when these 2,000 units are sold will that $50,000 of fixed overhead be recognized as an expense. Thus, under absorption costing, $50,000 of the period's fixed overhead flows into inventory, and its recognition as an expense is deferred to a future period.

Note that none of the selling and administrative costs, either variable or fixed, are assigned to the product under either method. Both methods treat these costs as period costs. Therefore, marketing and administrative costs are never inventoried and never appear on the balance sheet.[4]

## Production, Sales, and Income Relationships

The relationship between variable-costing income and absorption-costing income changes as the relationship between production and sales changes. If more is sold than was produced, variable-costing income is usually greater than absorption-costing income. The reason is just the opposite of that for the Fairchild example. Selling more than was produced means that inventory is being used. Under absorption costing, units coming out of inventory have attached to them fixed overhead from a prior period. In addition, units produced and sold have all of the current period's fixed overhead attached. Thus, the amount of fixed overhead expensed by absorption costing is greater than the current period's fixed overhead by the amount of fixed overhead flowing out of inventory. Accordingly, variable-costing income is greater than absorption-costing income by the amount of fixed overhead flowing out of beginning inventory.

If production and sales are equal, of course, no difference exists between the two reported incomes. Since the units produced are all sold, absorption costing, like variable costing, will recognize the total fixed overhead of the period as an expense. No fixed overhead flows into or out of inventory.

The relationships between production, sales, and the two reported incomes are summarized in Exhibit 8–4.[5] Note that if production is greater than sales, then inventory has increased. If production is less than sales, inventory must have decreased. If production is equal to sales, beginning inventory is equal to ending inventory.

---

4. What is Fairchild's variable cost per unit? $210. What is Fairchild's variable *product* cost per unit? $200. Note the difference; variable product cost does not include the $10 of variable selling and administrative expenses. Total variable cost per unit includes the selling and administrative expenses.

5. The fixed overhead rate will also affect the difference between variable-costing and absorption-costing income. If the fixed overhead rate does not change, the variable-costing income is always greater than absorption-costing income when more is sold than produced. If the fixed overhead rate changes from period to period, the relationship may be reversed in some cases.

Production, Sales, and
Income Relationships

| | If | Then |
|---|---|---|
| 1. | Production > Sales | Absorption net income > Variable net income |
| 2. | Production < Sales | Absorption net income < Variable net income |
| 3. | Production = Sales | Absorption net income = Variable net income |

To illustrate these relationships, consider the following example based on the operating data of Belnip, Inc., in the years 2002, 2003, and 2004.

| | |
|---|---|
| Variable costs per unit: | |
| Direct materials | $4.00 |
| Direct labour | 1.50 |
| Variable overhead (estimated and actual) | 0.50 |
| Variable selling and administrative | 0.25 |

Estimated fixed overhead was $150,000 each year. Actual fixed overhead also was $150,000. Normal production volume is 150,000 units per year. The sales price each year was $10 per unit. Fixed selling and administrative expenses were $50,000 per year. Other operating data (in units) were as follows:

| | 2002 | 2003 | 2004 |
|---|---|---|---|
| Beginning inventory | — | — | 50,000 |
| Production | 150,000 | 150,000 | 150,000 |
| Sales | 150,000 | 100,000 | 200,000 |
| Ending inventory | — | 50,000 | — |

Income statements prepared under variable costing are shown in Exhibit 8–5. Exhibit 8–6 gives the income statements for absorption costing.

In 2002, the net incomes for each method are identical. This means that both methods expensed the same amount of fixed overhead. Under variable costing, we know that the period's total fixed overhead of $150,000 was expensed. Under absorption costing, the fixed overhead is unitized and becomes part of the product cost. Estimated fixed overhead was $150,000 each year. The fixed overhead rate is $1 per unit ($150,000/150,000 units produced) for all three years. The applied fixed overhead is $150,000 ($1 × 150,000) for all three years. Since the actual fixed overhead in every year is also $150,000, there is no fixed overhead variance in any year. Thus, the fixed overhead expensed for any year is simply the overhead rate times the number of units sold. For 2002, the total fixed overhead expensed under absorption costing is $150,000 ($1 × 150,000

Variable-Costing Income
Statements (in thousands
of dollars)

| | 2002 | 2003 | 2004 |
|---|---|---|---|
| Sales | $1,500.0 | $1,000 | $2,000 |
| Less variable expenses: | | | |
| Variable cost of goods sold[a] | 900.0 | 600 | 1,200 |
| Variable selling and administrative[b] | 37.5 | 25 | 50 |
| Contribution margin | $ 562.5 | $ 375 | $ 750 |
| Less fixed expenses: | | | |
| Fixed overhead | 150.0 | 150 | 150 |
| Fixed selling and administrative | 50.0 | 50 | 50 |
| Net income | $ 362.5 | $ 175 | $ 550 |

| | | | |
|---|---|---|---|
| [a] Beginning inventory | — | — | $ 300 |
| Variable cost of goods manufactured | $900 | $900 | $ 900 |
| Goods available for sale | $900 | $900 | $1,200 |
| Less: Ending inventory | — | $300 | — |
| Variable cost of goods sold | $900 | $600 | $1,200 |

[b] $0.25 per unit × Units sold

| EXHIBIT 8-6 | | 2002 | 2003 | 2004 |
|---|---|---|---|---|
| | Sales | $1,500.0 | $1,000 | $2,000 |
| | Less: Cost of goods sold* | 1,050.0 | 700 | 1,400 |
| | Gross margin | $ 450.0 | $ 300 | $ 600 |
| | Less: Selling and administrative expenses | 87.5 | 75 | 100 |
| | Net income | $ 362.5 | $ 225 | $ 500 |

Absorption-Costing
Income Statements (in
thousands of dollars)

| * Beginning inventory | — | — | $ 350 |
|---|---|---|---|
| Cost of goods manufactured | $1,050 | $1,050 | $1,050 |
| Goods available for sale | $1,050 | $1,050 | $1,400 |
| Less: Ending inventory | — | $ 350 | — |
| Cost of goods sold | $1,050 | $ 700 | $1,400 |

units sold). Both methods did indeed recognize the same amount of fixed overhead expense.

In 2003, however, the story is different. From Exhibits 8–5 and 8–6, we see that the absorption-costing income is $50,000 greater than the variable-costing income ($225,000 – $175,000). The difference between the two incomes exists because there is $50,000 less fixed overhead expensed under the absorption-costing method.

Under absorption costing, each unit produced is assigned $1 of fixed overhead. Since 150,000 units were produced but only 100,000 units were sold, 50,000 units were placed in inventory. These 50,000 units carried with them $1 of fixed overhead each, for a total of $50,000. This $50,000 of the current period's fixed overhead will not be recognized as an expense until the units in inventory are sold. Thus, under absorption costing, the period's $150,000 of fixed overhead can be broken down into two categories: $100,000 is expensed, and $50,000 is inventoried.

Under variable costing, however, the total fixed overhead of $150,000 is expensed since it is viewed as a period cost. Because variable costing recognizes $150,000 of fixed overhead expense and absorption costing recognizes only $100,000 of fixed overhead expense, the income reported by absorption costing is $50,000 more.

In 2004, the relationship between the two incomes reverses. The difference is now $50,000 in favour of variable costing. The favourable difference occurs because absorption costing not only recognizes $150,000 of fixed overhead expense for units produced and sold in this period but also recognizes the $50,000 of fixed overhead attached to the units in inventory that were produced in 2003 but sold in 2004. Thus, the total fixed overhead recognized as an expense is $200,000 under absorption costing versus only $150,000 under variable costing.

The key to explaining the difference between the two incomes is an analysis of the flow of fixed overhead. Variable costing always recognizes the period's total fixed overhead as an expense. Absorption costing, on the other hand, recognizes only the fixed overhead attached to the units sold. If production is different from sales, fixed overhead will flow either into or out of inventory. If the amount of fixed overhead in inventory increases, then absorption-costing income is greater than variable-costing income by the amount of the net increase. If the fixed overhead in inventory decreases, then variable-costing income is greater than absorption-costing income by the amount of the net decrease.

Exhibit 8-7 shows the reconciliation of the variable-costing and absorption-costing income based on the flow of fixed overhead costs in and out of inventory.

EXHIBIT 8-7

| | 2002 | 2003 | 2004 |
|---|---|---|---|
| Net income: | | | |
| Absorption costing | $362.5 | $ 225 | $500 |
| Variable costing | 362.5 | 175 | 550 |
| Difference | $ 0 | $ 50 | $(50) |
| | | | |
| Explanation: | | | |
| Units produced | 150 | 150 | 150 |
| Units sold | 150 | 100 | 200 |
| Change in inventory | 0 | 50 | (50) |
| Fixed overhead rate | × $1 | × $1 | × 1 |
| Difference explained* | $ 0 | $ 50 | $(50) |

EXHIBIT 8-7

Reconciliation of Variable and Absorption Costing (in thousands of dollars)

\* In 2002, absorption costing recognized only the period's fixed manufacturing overhead as an expense. No fixed overhead flowed into or out of inventory. In 2003, $50,000 of fixed overhead flowed into inventory, and its recognition as an expense was deferred to a future period. In 2004, $50,000 of fixed manufacturing overhead flowed out of inventory and was recognized as an expense.

## The Treatment of Fixed Overhead in Absorption Costing

The difference between absorption and variable costing centres on the recognition of expense associated with fixed overhead. Under absorption costing, fixed overhead must be assigned to units produced. This presents two problems that we have not yet explicitly considered. First, how do we convert overhead applied on the basis of direct labour hours or machine hours into overhead applied to units produced? Second, what is done when actual overhead does not equal applied overhead?

The first problem is solved relatively easily. Suppose that overhead is applied on the basis of direct labour hours. Further suppose that it takes 0.25 direct labour hours to produce one unit. If the fixed overhead rate is $12 per direct labour hour, then the fixed overhead per unit is $3 (0.25 × $12).

The solution to the second problem requires more thought. First we must calculate the applied fixed overhead and assign it to units produced. Then the total applied amount is compared to actual fixed overhead. If the over- or underapplied amount is immaterial, it is closed to Cost of Goods Sold. Any units going into ending inventory take with them the applied fixed overhead. Variable overhead (which can also be over- or underapplied) is treated in the same fashion. Review Problem II at the end of this chapter illustrates the handling of over- and underapplied fixed and variable overhead.

If the over- or underapplied amount is material, then it is allocated among ending Work in Process, Finished Goods, and Cost of Goods Sold. This complication is beyond the scope of this text.

## Variable Costing and Performance Evaluation of Managers

**Objective 2**

Explain how variable costing is useful in evaluating the performance of managers.

The evaluation of managers is often tied to the profitability of the activities they control. How income changes from one period to the next and how actual income compares to planned income are frequently used as signals of managerial ability. To be a meaningful signal, however, income should reflect managerial effort. For example, if a manager has worked hard and increased sales while holding costs in check, income should increase over the prior period, signalling success. In general terms, if income performance is expected to reflect managerial performance, then managers have the right to expect the following:

1. As sales revenue increases from one period to the next, all other things being equal, income should increase.
2. As sales revenue decreases from one period to the next, all other things being equal, income should decrease.
3. As sales revenue remains unchanged from one period to the next, all other things being equal, income should remain unchanged.

Interestingly, income under variable costing always follows this expected association between sales and income; but under absorption costing, at times, it does not. To illustrate, assume that a division of Myers, Inc., has the following operating data for its first two years. For simplicity, we assume no selling and administrative costs.

| | 2003 | 2004 |
|---|---|---|
| Variable manufacturing costs per unit | $10 | $10 |
| Production (expected and actual units) | 10,000 | 5,000 |
| Units sold ($25 per unit) | 5,000 | 10,000 |
| Fixed overhead (estimated and actual) | $100,000 | $100,000 |

The product cost under variable costing is $10 per unit for both years. If we assume that expected actual volume is used to compute a predetermined fixed overhead rate, the product cost under absorption costing is $20 per unit in 2003 and $30 per unit in 2004 ($10 + $100,000/10,000 for 2003; $10 + $100,000/5,000 for 2004).

The variable-costing and absorption-costing income statements are shown in Exhibit 8–8. Sales increased from 5,000 to 10,000 units. Total fixed costs, the variable manufacturing cost per unit, and the unit sales price are the same for both periods. Thus, the doubling of sales represents the only change from one period to the next. Under variable costing, income increased by $75,000 from 2003 to 2004 (from a loss of $25,000 to a profit of $50,000). However, under absorption costing, despite the increase in sales, net income decreased by $25,000 (from a profit of $25,000 to a profit of $0)!

EXHIBIT   8-8

Variable- and Absorption-Costing Income Statements

| **Variable-Costing Income** | | |
|---|---|---|
| | **2003** | **2004** |
| Sales | $125,000 | $250,000 |
| Less variable expenses: | | |
|   Variable cost of goods sold[a] | 50,000 | 100,000 |
|     Contribution margin | $ 75,000 | $150,000 |
| Less fixed expenses: | | |
|   Fixed overhead | 100,000 | 100,000 |
|   Net income (loss) | $(25,000) | $ 50,000 |

| **Absorption-Costing Income** | | |
|---|---|---|
| | **2003** | **2004** |
| Sales | $125,000 | $250,000 |
| Less cost of goods sold[b] | 100,000 | 250,000 |
| Net income (loss) | $ 25,000 | $ 0 |

[a] $10 × 5,000 in 2003 and $10 × 10,000 in 2004

| [b] Beginning inventory | $ — | $100,000 |
|---|---|---|
|   Cost of goods manufactured | 200,000 | 150,000 |
|     Goods available for sale | $200,000 | $250,000 |
|   Less: Ending inventory | 100,000 | — |
|     Cost of goods sold | $100,000 | $250,000 |

The company improved its sales performance from 2003 to 2004 (twice as many units were sold), fixed costs remained the same, and the unit variable cost was the same; yet absorption costing fails to reveal this improved performance. Variable costing, on the other hand, produces an increase in income corresponding to the improved sales performance. If you were the manager, which income approach would you prefer?

## Variable Costing and Segmented Reporting

**Objective 3**

Prepare a segmented income statement based on a variable-costing approach, and explain how this format can be used with activity-based costing and customer profitability analysis.

**segmented reporting**

The preparation of financial performance reports for each segment of importance within a company.

**segment**

A subunit of a company that is sufficiently important to warrant the production of performance reports.

The usefulness of variable costing for performance evaluation extends beyond evaluating managers. Managers need to be able to evaluate the activities over which they have responsibility. For example, managers must continually evaluate the profit contributions of plants, product lines, and sales territories.[6]

The separation of fixed and variable costs fundamental to variable costing is critical for making accurate evaluations. Implicit in an evaluation is an associated decision—for example, whether to continue to operate a plant or not, or whether to keep or drop a product line. Without a distinction between fixed and variable costs, the evaluation of profit-making activities and the resulting decision may both be erroneous.

Reporting the profit contributions of activities or other units within an organization is called **segmented reporting**. Segmented reports prepared on a variable-costing basis produce better evaluations and decisions than those prepared on an absorption-costing basis.

To evaluate many different activities within a company, a manager needs more than the summary information that appears in a company's income statement. For example, in a company with several divisions operating in different markets, the manager would certainly want to know how profitable each division has been. This knowledge may lead to greater overall profit by eliminating unprofitable divisions, giving special attention to problem divisions, allocating additional funds to the more profitable divisions, and so on. Divisional income statements, however, are not all that a good managerial accounting system should supply. Even finer segmentation is needed for managers to carry out their responsibilities properly. Divisions are made up of different plants. Plants produce products, and information on product profitability is critical. Some products may be profitable; some may not be. Similarly, profit information on sales territories, special projects, individual salespersons, and so on is important.

Managers need to know the profitability of various segments within a company to be able to make evaluations and decisions concerning each segment's continued existence, level of funding, and so on. A **segment** is any profit-making entity within the organization. A report for a segment can provide valuable information on costs that are controllable by the segment's manager. Controllable costs are those costs that can be influenced by a manager. A manager who has no responsibility for a cost should not be held accountable for that cost. For example, divisional managers have no power to authorize corporate-level costs such as research and development and salaries of top managers. Therefore, divisional managers should not be held accountable for the incurrence of those costs. If noncontrollable costs are included in a segment report, they should be separated from controllable costs and labelled as noncontrollable. For example, fixed costs

---

6. This form of disaggregated information is not necessarily the same as that required for publicly listed Canadian companies for external reporting purposes. There are certain rules and guidelines that must be followed for external reporting purposes. The only rule for management accounting purposes is to balance the cost and benefit of information.

common to two or more plants within a division would not be allocated to each plant but instead would be shown as a common cost for the division.

## Segmented Reporting: Absorption-Costing Basis

Should segmented reporting be on a variable-costing basis or an absorption-costing basis? To help answer this question, consider Elcom, Inc., a company that manufactures stereos and video recorders in a single plant and uses absorption costing for both external and internal reporting. Exhibit 8–9 gives the absorption-costing income statements by product line and in total for 2003.

**EXHIBIT   8-9**

Segmented Income Statement, 2003, Absorption-Costing Basis

**Elcom, Inc.**
**Segmented Income Statement, 2003**
**Absorption-Costing Basis**

|  | Stereos | Video Recorders | Total |
|---|---|---|---|
| Sales | $400,000 | $290,000 | $690,000 |
| Less: Cost of goods sold | 350,000 | 300,000 | 650,000 |
| Gross margin | $ 50,000 | $ (10,000) | $ 40,000 |
| Less: Selling and administrative expenses | 30,000 | 20,000 | 50,000 |
| Net income (loss) | $ 20,000 | $ (30,000) | $ (10,000) |

Upon seeing the product-line performance, Devon Lauffer, Elcom's president, decided to stop producing video recorders, reasoning that profits would increase by $30,000. A year later, however, the result was quite different. As the income statement for 2004 in Exhibit 8–10 shows, income actually decreased by $55,000. Why was the outcome so different from what Devon anticipated?

Devon relied on cost information collected by the external financial reporting system. However, the information needed for internal purposes often differs significantly from that required for external reporting. Cost behaviour and the traceability of costs may not be critical concerns for reporting results to external parties, but they are vital to managers who are attempting to make strategic decisions.

Devon discovered that many fixed costs that had been allocated to the video recorders were not eliminated when that product line was dropped. Since both stereos and video recorders were produced in the same plant, much of the fixed overhead was common to the two products. This includes amortization on the plant, taxes, insurance, and the plant manager's salary, among other items. When the video recorders were dropped, all these common fixed overhead costs were loaded entirely on the stereo product line. Similarly, some fixed selling and administrative costs previously assigned to the video recorder line were then fully assigned to the stereo line.

**EXHIBIT   8-10**

Income Statement, 2004, Absorption-Costing Basis

**Elcom, Inc.**
**Income Statement, 2004**
**Absorption-Costing Basis**

| | |
|---|---|
| Sales | $400,000 |
| Less: Cost of goods sold | 430,000 |
| Gross margin | $ (30,000) |
| Less: Selling and administrative expenses | 35,000 |
| Net income (loss) | $ (65,000) |

## Segmented Reporting: Variable-Costing Basis

A segmented income statement using variable costing provides the essential cost information for assessing the role of the video recorder line. Exhibit 8–11 gives the segmented income statement using variable costing for 2003.

**EXHIBIT 8-11**

Segmented Income Statement, 2003, Variable-Costing Basis

**Elcom, Inc.**
**Segmented Income Statement, 2003**
**Variable-Costing Basis**

|  | Stereos | Video Recorders | Total |
|---|---|---|---|
| Sales | $400,000 | $290,000 | $690,000 |
| Less variable expenses: |  |  |  |
| Variable cost of goods sold | 300,000 | 200,000 | 500,000 |
| Variable selling and administrative | 5,000 | 10,000 | 15,000 |
| Contribution margin | $ 95,000 | $ 80,000 | $175,000 |
| Less direct fixed expenses: |  |  |  |
| Direct fixed overhead | 30,000 | 20,000 | 50,000 |
| Direct selling and administrative | 10,000 | 5,000 | 15,000 |
| Segment margin | $ 55,000 | $ 55,000 | $110,000 |
| Less common fixed expenses: |  |  |  |
| Common fixed overhead |  |  | 100,000 |
| Common selling and administrative |  |  | 20,000 |
| Net income (loss) |  |  | $(10,000) |

Segmented income statements using variable costing have one feature in addition to the variable-costing income statements already shown. Fixed expenses are broken down into two categories: *direct* fixed expenses and *common* fixed expenses. This additional subdivision highlights controllable versus non-controllable costs and enhances the manager's ability to evaluate each segment's contribution to overall company performance.

**direct fixed expenses**

Fixed costs that are directly traceable to a given segment and, consequently, disappear if the segment is eliminated.

**Direct fixed expenses** are fixed expenses that are directly traceable to a segment (a product line in this example). These are sometimes referred to as *avoidable fixed expenses* or *traceable fixed expenses*, because they vanish if the segment is eliminated. These fixed expenses are caused by the existence of the segment itself. In the Elcom example, amortization on equipment used in producing video recorders and the salary of the production supervisor of the video recorder production line are examples of direct fixed expenses.

**common fixed expenses**

Fixed expenses that cannot be directly traced to individual segments and that are unaffected by the elimination of any one segment.

**Common fixed expenses** are jointly caused by two or more segments. These expenses persist even if one of the segments to which they are common is eliminated. In the Elcom example, plant amortization and the salary of the plant supervisor are common fixed expenses. Elimination of the video recorder line did not eliminate the plant and its associated amortization. Similarly, the plant supervisor was still needed to oversee the production of the stereo product line.

Fixed costs that are direct for one segment definition may be indirect, or common, for another segment definition. For example, suppose that the stereo product line is segmented into two sales territories. In that case, the amortization on the equipment used to produce stereos is common to both territories but directly traceable to the product segment itself.

Now let's examine Exhibit 8–11 to see whether this form of segmented income statement is more useful than the absorption-costing format. Notice that both stereos and video recorders have large positive contribution margins ($95,000 for stereos and $80,000 for video recorders). Both products are providing revenue above variable costs that can be used to help cover the company's fixed

**segment margin**

The contribution a segment makes to cover common fixed costs and variable costs and provide for profit after direct fixed costs and variable costs are deducted from the segment's sales revenue.

costs. However, some of the company's fixed costs are caused by the segments themselves. Thus, the real measure of each segment's profit contribution is what is left over after these direct fixed costs are covered.

The profit contribution each segment makes toward covering a company's common fixed costs is called the **segment margin**. A segment should at least be able to cover both its own variable costs and its own direct fixed costs. A negative segment margin drags down the company's total profit, making it time to consider dropping the product. Ignoring any effect a segment may have on the sales of other segments, we see that the segment margin measures the change in a company's profits that would occur if the segment were eliminated.

From Exhibit 8–11, we see that the video recorder line contributes $55,000 toward covering Elcom's common fixed costs. If the line is dropped, total profit decreases by $55,000—exactly what happened, as shown in Exhibit 8–10. Dropping the video recorder line was a disastrous decision, and Exhibit 8–11 shows why.

The correct decision is to retain both product lines. Both are making equal contributions to the company's profitability. Dropping either product simply aggravates the problem, unless the dropped product is replaced by a product with a higher segment margin. Since both products have large positive contribution margins, other solutions to the net loss are needed. Accounting can help by focusing on a more detailed analysis of costs using activity-based costing.

## Segmented Reporting: Activity-Based Costing Approach

An activity-based costing approach, with its insight into unit-, batch-, product-, and facility-level costs, may give management a more accurate feel for profits attributable to different product lines. Elcom's overhead costs can be further analyzed by determining activities and drivers.

For example, suppose that the common fixed overhead includes material handling and maintenance. Also suppose that direct fixed overhead includes setup costs. Elcom figures that the annual cost of these activities is as follows:

| | |
|---|---|
| Material handling | $20,000 |
| Maintenance costs | 8,000 |
| Setups | 18,000 |

Now Elcom has some idea of where to focus attention. Material handling is a nonvalue-added activity, as are setups. Any reduction in these can go directly to the bottom line. Perhaps a reconfiguration of the plant will lead to lower material-handling costs, or perhaps a new agreement with suppliers can lead to having materials delivered directly to the line. Similarly, a change in the configuration of the assembly process might lead to quicker, cheaper setups. Finally, noticing that maintenance costs $8,000 might lead to a re-examination of the way in which maintenance is done. A JIT approach to manufacturing could result in line workers performing maintenance during downtime.

An activity-based approach shows the complexity of the manufacturing operation and reminds managers that a decrease in power costs can be achieved only with a decrease in machine usage (perhaps by the use of more efficient machinery). Similarly, a decrease in setup costs can come about only through streamlining or eliminating setup activity. Reducing activities reduces actual costs and leads to increased profits.

## Segmented Reporting and Customer Profitability Analysis

While customers are clearly important to profit, some are more profitable than others. Companies that assess the profitability of various customer groups can more accurately target their markets and increase profits. The first step in determining customer profitability is to identify the customer. The second step is to determine which customers add value to the company.

The identification of a company's customer may seem obvious. Grocery stores and automobile repair shops can easily identify their customers, and may even know them by name. However, frequently the company is part of a complex chain of customer relationships. For example, Weldcraft Products, Inc., produces welding torches, which are sold to distributors, retail stores, and, eventually, companies and individuals who use the torches to weld. Weldcraft determined that its main customer is distributors and redistributed its activities so that Weldcraft salespeople now spend much of their time with distributors.[7]

Once customer groups have been identified, the second step is to determine which customer groups are most profitable, eliminate the unprofitable customers, and retain and add to the base of profitable customers.

Some customers are so unprofitable that they should not be kept. Rice Lake Products, Inc., manufactures movable owl and geese decoys. The company sold both to specialty stores and to Wal-Mart. However, the Wal-Mart sales, at $19 each, infuriated the specialty stores that charged $20. Even worse from the viewpoint of Rice Lake Products was that the profit on a Wal-Mart sale averaged just $0.50, whereas the profit on a specialty store sale amounted to $4. The reason for the difference was that Wal-Mart required special packaging and promotion, and returned product that did not sell. Rice Lake Products chose to concentrate on sales to specialty stores.[8]

Sometimes, a company may need to add an initially unprofitable customer group. Banks offer incentives to get students to open bank accounts. While the accounts may be unprofitable during the student's school and university years, they become profitable later on as the student graduates, gains employment, and remains as a bank customer.

It is generally more costly to win a customer than to keep a customer. Recruiting a customer may require advertising, sales calls, the drafting of proposals, and the generation of prospective customer lists. All of these activities are costly. Keeping existing customers happy also requires effort. For example, many stores provide free gift wrapping as a service to the customer who has already made a purchase. Companies must have profitability data to understand the profit contribution of customer relationships, to match the costs of increased service with the benefits. Many companies are now taking a customer life-cycle approach, by recognizing that a loyal customer will yield significant revenue over the years. For example, the lifetime revenue stream of a pizza eater can be $8,000. For more expensive products, like a Cadillac, the amount approaches $332,000.[9]

Relational databases and improved accounting systems can greatly assist the effort to track customer profitability. Profitability analysis of various customer classes requires information on the product, marketing, and administrative activ-

---

7.  Ellen Graham, "Meat and Potatoes: Sometimes the Most Successful Courses Are the Most Basic," *The Wall Street Journal*, 10 September 1993: p. R5.

8.  Christie Brown, "A Great Way to Retire," *Forbes*, 9 October 1995: pp. 96-97.

9.  James L. Heskett, Thomas O. Jones, Gary W. Loveman, W. Early Sasser, Jr., and Leonard A. Schlesinger, "Putting the Service-Profit Chain to Work," *Harvard Business Review* (March/April 1994): pp. 164-174.

ities used to serve each class. Let's analyze Barton, Inc., a manufacturer of highly realistic model horses sold to three classes of customer: large discount chains, small independent toy stores, and hobbyists. Each model is made of high-density plastic, from a detailed mould. A team of designers ensures that the design is accurate for the breed depicted. Colour pigments are deep and rich. While Barton produces many designs, they all incur roughly the same manufacturing costs. Exhibit 8–12 provides manufacturing and marketing data.

Each class of customer places different demands on Barton. The large discount chains purchase 63 percent of the output. They receive price discounts averaging $1.25 per unit and are linked to Barton through electronic data interchange (EDI). As a result, when supplies at the chains run low, an order is transmitted electronically to Barton's factory and another shipment of models dispatched. No commissions are paid on chain store sales. However, Barton must pay each chain store outlet $1,500 per year for shelf space (this ensures premium shelf position within the stores). There are 75 outlets. Barton pays shipping costs. The chain stores are not particular about which models are shipped; therefore, Barton typically sends whatever is in stock at the time. There is no special packaging involved.

The independent toy stores are smaller and typically stock upscale toys with a heavily educational flavour. About 35 percent of Barton's production is sold to them. No price discounts are given to these stores, and no shelf space is paid for. However, a sales commission of $0.75 per unit sold is paid to the independent wholesale jobbers who sell to the stores. The stores pay any shipping costs from Barton's factory. The independent toy stores prefer models with a story attached. For example, a series of models of Indian war horses with accompanying explanatory booklets and special packaging are quite popular. Therefore, Barton attempts to ship all models with special packaging to the independents.

The final 2 percent of Barton's sales take place at summer fairs. Each summer Barton stages five model fairs around the United States. Fun and colourful, the fairs are designed to display the Barton models, to provide a meeting opportunity for model horse hobbyists, and to generate interest in the Barton product. Barton reserves meeting rooms at a hotel for two days, invites local area hobbyists to put on shows and demonstrations, and sets up a series of trading booths for model horse fanciers. Several of Barton's staff (designers, the president, and the vice-president of marketing) attend to chat with customers, answer questions, and display (and sell) the latest models. To generate additional interest in the fairs, a special model available only at that summer's fairs is designed and produced. The special model requires 150 hours of design time (at $14 per hour) and one setup (costing $1,000).

**EXHIBIT 8-12**

Cost Information for Barton, Inc.

| Manufacturing expenses: | |
| --- | --- |
| Units produced | 500,000 |
| Average price per model | $15 |
| Direct materials per unit | $5 |
| Direct labour cost | $2 |
| Overhead per unit | $1 |
| | |
| Marketing expenses: | |
| Commissions (per model sold) | $0.75 |
| Special packaging per unit | $0.20 |
| EDI costs per year | $100,000 |
| Fair expense | $75,000 |
| Shipping | $157,500 |
| Shelf space charges | $112,500 |

Given this information, Barton can analyze profitability by customer class. Exhibit 8–13 provides profit statements for each class of customer. The chain stores yield the most revenue, but these must be adjusted for discounts. Expenses directly attributable to the chain store outlets include shelf space payments, shipping charges, and the cost of the EDI equipment and personnel. The independent toy stores receive no price discount, but do require special packaging and the payment of commissions. The fairs have the lowest revenue, with expenses consisting of fair expense special design, and setup.

**EXHIBIT** **8-13**

Customer Analysis for Barton, Inc.

| Profit for Chain Stores | |
|---|---:|
| Sales | $4,725,000 |
| Less: Discounts | 393,750 |
| Net sales | $4,331,250 |
| Less: Cost of goods sold | 2,520,000 |
| Gross profit | $1,811,250 |
| Less: Shelf space | 112,500 |
| Less: Shipping | 157,500 |
| Less: EDI | 100,000 |
| Profit | $1,441,250 |

| Profit for Independent Toy Stores | |
|---|---:|
| Sales | $2,625,000 |
| Less: Cost of goods sold | 1,400,000 |
| Gross profit | $1,225,000 |
| Less: Commissions | 131,250 |
| Less: Special packaging | 35,000 |
| Profit | $1,058,750 |

| Profit for Fairs | |
|---|---:|
| Sales | $150,000 |
| Less: Cost of goods sold | 80,000 |
| Gross profit | $ 70,000 |
| Less: Fair expense | 75,000 |
| Less: Design time | 2,100 |
| Less: Setup | 1,000 |
| Loss | $ (8,100) |

Clearly, the chain stores are the most profitable, followed by the independent toy stores. The fairs are unprofitable. A customer profitability analysis can give Barton's management a better idea of which customers to emphasize and where cost cutting might occur. For example, the fairs are money losers on the basis of sales. Perhaps management might consider them a promotional activity and not a customer class at all. In fact, the fairs' major objective is to stimulate interest in the entire Barton line, not merely to sell 10,000 models. Therefore, the entire cost of the fairs could be added to overall marketing expense.

These activity-based data can also give management a good idea of the cost of expanding into one area and away from another. For example, should Barton sell to one more chain outlet if it is at capacity? Each chain outlet averages sales of 4,200 models (315,000/75 outlets). These 4,200 models would not be sold to the independent toy stores. The analysis is as follows:

Profit from Adding One More Chain Outlet:

| | |
|---|---:|
| Revenue from additional outlet | $63,000 |
| Less: discount | 5,250 |
| Net additional revenue | $57,750 |
| Less: Cost of goods sold | 33,600 |
| Less: Shipping | 2,100 |
| Less: Shelf space | 1,500 |
| Profit from added outlet | $20,550 |

Profit from Selling 4,200 Models to Independent Toy Stores:

| | |
|---|---:|
| Revenue | $63,000 |
| Less: Cost of goods sold | 33,600 |
| Less: Special packaging | 840 |
| Less: Commission | 3,150 |
| Profit from independents | $25,410 |

Barton should continue to sell to the independent toy stores, because the chain outlets are less profitable.

Activity-based accounting can provide data on these marketing activities, which are important in customer profitability analysis. However, it is important to remember that activities alone do not cause costs. Other factors—such as time, business volumes, and earlier decisions—may lead to efficiencies or inefficiencies.

## Variable Costing for Planning and Control

**Objective 4**

Explain how variable costing can be used in planning and control.

Financial planning requires managers to estimate future sales, future production levels, future costs, and so on. Sales forecasts determine production plans, which in turn determine the level of expenditures required for raw materials, direct labour, and manufacturing overhead. Because sales forecasts are not certain, management may wish to look at several different levels of sales to assess the range of possibilities facing the company. Knowledge of cost behaviour is fundamental to achieving this outcome. Fixed costs do not vary with volume changes, so distinguishing between fixed and variable costs is essential to making an accurate cost assessment at the different possible sales and production volumes.

Once management has chosen one expected sales and production level for the coming year, the costs that should occur can also be determined. The financial plan, then, consists of the expected activity levels and the associated expected costs. This plan can be used to monitor the actual performance as it unfolds.

If actual performance is different from what was expected, corrective action may be necessary. By comparing actual outcomes with the expected outcomes and taking corrective action when necessary, managers exercise control. For the control process to work, though, cost behaviour must be known.

Suppose the financial plan called for 12,000 units to be produced for the year, and the utility cost planned for the year is $18,000. At the end of the first month, the company has produced 3,000 units and spent $4,500 on utilities. Are utility costs being incurred as planned?

Under an absorption-costing approach, the planned utility cost per unit produced is $1.50 ($18,000/12,000). Therefore, for 3,000 units, the company should spend $4,500 ($1.50 × 3,000). Since the expected utility cost for 3,000 units was $4,500, and the actual cost was $4,500, the plan appears to be unfolding as expected. Unfortunately, this calculation ignores cost behaviour. It assumes that all costs are variable. In reality, the utility cost is a flat fee of $1,000 per month plus $0.50 per kilowatt-hour. If it takes one kilowatt-hour to produce one unit of output, the expected cost for the 3,000 units produced in one month is $2,500 ($1,000 + $0.50 × 3,000 units). The company should have spent $2,500 on utilities to produce 3,000 units, but it spent $4,500. The plan is not unfolding as it should.

The correct signal about the planned utility cost is given when cost behaviour is considered. Once again, we see the importance of the distinction between fixed and variable costs. Since this distinction is fundamental to variable costing, we must conclude that variable costing is superior to absorption costing for internal purposes.

## Summary of Learning Objectives

### 1. Explain the differences between variable and absorption costing.

Variable and absorption costing differ in their treatment of fixed overhead. Variable costing treats fixed overhead as a period expense. Thus, unit production cost under variable costing consists of direct materials, direct labour, and variable overhead. Absorption costing treats fixed overhead as a product cost. Thus, unit production cost under absorption costing consists of direct materials, direct labour, variable overhead, and a share of fixed overhead.

A variable-costing income statement separates expenses according to cost behaviour. First, variable expenses of manufacturing, marketing, and administration are subtracted from sales to yield the contribution margin. Then all fixed expenses are subtracted from the contribution margin to yield variable-costing net income. An absorption-costing income statement separates expenses according to function. First, the cost of goods sold is subtracted from sales to yield gross profit (or gross margin). Then marketing and administrative expenses are subtracted from gross profit to yield absorption-costing net income.

### 2. Explain how variable costing is useful in evaluating the performance of managers.

By separating costs according to behaviour, variable costing enhances the traceability and controllability of costs. Variable costing preserves the correspondence between effort and outcome that is necessary for good evaluation of management performance.

### 3. Prepare a segmented income statement based on a variable-costing approach, and explain how this format can be used with activity-based costing and customer profitability analysis.

A segmented income statement takes the following form:

|  | Segment X | Segment Y | Company |
|---|---|---|---|
| Sales | XXX | YYY | CCC |
| Less variable expenses | XX | YY | CC |
| Contribution margin | XXX | YYY | CCC |
| Less direct fixed expenses | XX | YY | CC |
| Segment margin | XX | YY | CC |
| Less common fixed expenses |  |  | CC |
| Net income (loss) |  |  | CC |

The use of variable costing emphasizes the cost behaviour of each segment so that management can properly evaluate each segment's contribution to the company's overall performance.

Activity-based costing can be used with the segmented income statement to provide more insight into unit-level, batch-level, and product-level costs. Customer profitability can be assessed by treating each customer group as a segment and determining the activities associated with each group.

### 4. Explain how variable costing can be used in planning and control.

Variable costing requires management to distinguish between fixed and variable costs. This distinction is important in determining budgeted costs, and comparing actual outcomes against expectations.

## Key Terms

Absorption costing 303
Common fixed expenses 313
Direct fixed expenses 313

Segment 311
Segmented reporting 311
Segment margin 314

Variable costing 303

## Review Problems

### I. ABSORPTION AND VARIABLE COSTING, SEGMENTED INCOME STATEMENTS

Fine Leathers Company produces a women's wallet and a men's wallet. Selected data for the past year follow:

|  | Women's Wallets | Men's Wallets |
|---|---|---|
| Production (units) | 100,000 | 200,000 |
| Sales (units) | 90,000 | 210,000 |
| Selling price | $5.50 | $4.50 |
| Direct labour hours | 50,000 | 80,000 |
| Manufacturing costs: |  |  |
|    Direct materials | $ 75,000 | $100,000 |
|    Direct labour | 250,000 | 400,000 |
|    Variable overhead | 20,000 | 24,000 |
|    Fixed overhead: |  |  |
|      Direct | 50,000 | 40,000 |
|      Common | 20,000 | 20,000 |
| Nonmanufacturing costs: |  |  |
|    Variable selling | $ 30,000 | $ 60,000 |
|    Direct fixed selling | 35,000 | 40,000 |
|    Common fixed selling | 25,000 | 25,000 |

*(Handwritten annotations: "= Sales" next to Sales (units); "= Var Selling exp" next to $60,000; "= Fixed selling" next to Common fixed selling 25,000)*

Common overhead totals $40,000 and is divided equally between the two products. Common fixed selling cost totals $50,000 and is divided equally between the two products. Budgeted fixed overhead for the year, $130,000, equalled the actual fixed overhead. Fixed overhead is assigned to products using a plantwide rate based on expected direct labour hours, which were 130,000. The company had 10,000 men's wallets in inventory at the beginning of the year. These wallets had the same unit cost as the men's wallets produced during the year.

**Required:**

1. Compute the unit product cost for the women's and men's wallets using the variable-costing method. Compute the unit product cost using absorption costing.
2. Prepare an income statement using absorption costing.

3. Prepare an income statement using variable costing.
4. Reconcile the difference between the two income statements.
5. Prepare a segmented income statement using products as segments.

## Solution

1. The unit product cost for a women's wallet is as follows:

| | |
|---|---|
| Direct materials ($75,000/100,000) | $0.75 |
| Direct labour ($250,000/100,000) | 2.50 |
| Variable overhead ($20,000/100,000) | 0.20 |
| Variable cost per unit | $3.45 |
| Fixed overhead (50,000 × $1.00)/100,000 | 0.50 |
| Absorption cost per unit | $3.95 |

The unit product cost for a men's wallet is as follows:

| | |
|---|---|
| Direct materials ($100,000/200,000) | $0.50 |
| Direct labour ($400,000/200,000) | 2.00 |
| Variable overhead ($24,000/200,000) | 0.12 |
| Variable cost per unit | $2.62 |
| Fixed overhead (80,000 × $1.00)/200,000 | 0.40 |
| Absorption cost per unit | $3.02 |

In absorption costing, the fixed overhead unit cost is assigned using the predetermined fixed overhead rate of $1.00 per direct labour hour ($130,000/130,000). For example, the women's wallets used 50,000 direct labour hours, so they receive $1.00 × 50,000, or $50,000, of fixed overhead. This total, when divided by the units produced, gives the $0.50 per unit fixed overhead cost.

Notice that the only difference between the variable and absorption unit costs is the assignement of the fixed overhead cost. Finally, observe that variable nonmanufacturing costs are not part of the unit cost for variable costing or absorption costing. For both approaches, only manufacturing costs are used to compute the unit costs.

2. The income statement under absorption costing is as follows:

| | | |
|---|---|---|
| Sales | $1,440,000 | [($5.50 × 90,000) + ($4.50 × 210,000)] |
| Less: Cost of goods sold | 989,700 | [($3.95 × 90,000) + ($3.02 × 210,000)] |
| Gross margin | $ 450,300 | |
| Less: Selling expenses* | 215,000 | |
| Net income | $ 235,300 | |

* This is the sum of selling expenses for both products.

3. The income statement under variable costing is as follows:

| | | |
|---|---|---|
| Sales | $1,440,000 | [($5.50 × 90,000) + ($4.50 × 210,000)] |
| Less variable expenses: | | |
| Variable cost of goods sold | 860,700 | [($3.45 × 90,000) + ($2.62 × 210,000)] |
| Variable selling expenses | 90,000 | |
| Contribution margin | $489,300 | |
| Less fixed expenses: | | |
| Fixed overhead | 130,000 | |
| Fixed selling | 125,000 | |
| Net income | $234,300 | |

4. Reconciliation is as follows:

Absorption NI – Variable NI= $235,300 – $234,300 = $1,000

Thus, variable-costing income is $1,000 less than absorption-costing income. This difference can be explained by the net change in fixed overhead found in inventory under absorption costing.

Women's wallets:

| | |
|---|---|
| Units produced | 100,000 |
| Units sold | 90,000 |
| Increase in inventory | 10,000 |
| Unit fixed overhead | $0.50 |
|     Increase in fixed overhead | $5,000 |

Men's wallets:

| | |
|---|---|
| Units produced | 200,000 |
| Units sold | 210,000 |
| Decrease in inventory | (10,000) |
| Unit fixed overhead | $0.40 |
|     Decrease in fixed overhead | $(4,000) |

The net change is a $1,000 ($5,000 − $4,000) increase in fixed overhead in inventories. Thus, under absorption costing, there is a net flow of $1,000 of the current period's fixed overhead into inventory. Since variable costing recognized all of the current period's fixed overhead as an expense, variable-costing income should be $1,000 lower than absorption costing, as it is.

5. Segmented income statement:

| | Women's Wallets | Men's Wallets | Total |
|---|---|---|---|
| Sales | $495,000 | $945,000 | $1,440,000 |
| Less variable expenses: | | | |
|     Variable cost of goods sold | 310,500 | 550,200 | 860,700 |
|     Variable selling expenses | 30,000 | 60,000 | 90,000 |
|         Contribution margin | $154,500 | $334,800 | $489,300 |
| Less direct fixed expenses: | | | |
|     Direct fixed overhead | 50,000 | 40,000 | 90,000 |
|     Direct selling expenses | 35,000 | 40,000 | 75,000 |
|         Segment margin | $ 69,500 | $254,800 | $324,300 |
| Less common fixed expenses: | | | |
|     Common fixed overhead | | | 40,000 |
|     Common selling expenses | | | 50,000 |
|         Net income | | | $234,300 |

## II.  ABSORPTION AND VARIABLE COSTING WITH OVER- AND UNDERAPPLIED OVERHEAD

Bellingham, Inc., has just completed its first year of operations. The unit costs on a normal costing basis are as follows:

Manufacturing costs (per unit):

| | |
|---|---|
|     Direct materials (2 kilograms × $2) | $ 4.00 |
|     Direct labour (1.5 hours × $9) | 13.50 |
|     Variable overhead (1.5 hours × $2) | 3.00 |
|     Fixed overhead (1.5 hours × $3) | 4.50 |
|         Total | $25.00 |

Selling and administrative costs:

| | |
|---|---|
|     Variable | $5/unit |
|     Fixed | $190,000 |

During the year, the company had the following activity:

| | |
|---|---|
| Units produced | 24,000 |
| Units sold | 21,500 |
| Unit selling price | $42 |
| Direct labour hours worked | 36,000 |

Actual fixed overhead was $12,000 less than budgeted fixed overhead. Budgeted variable overhead was $5,000 less than actual variable overhead. The company used an expected actual activity level of 36,000 direct labour hours to compute the predetermined overhead rates. Any overhead variances are closed to Cost of Goods Sold.

**Required:**

1. Compute the unit cost using (a) absorption costing, and (b) variable costing.
2. Prepare an absorption-costing income statement.
3. Prepare a variable-costing income statement.
4. Reconcile the difference between the two income statements.

**Solution**

1. Unit cost using absorption costing, and variable costing:

| **Absorption Unit Cost** | | **Variable Unit Cost** | |
|---|---|---|---|
| Direct materials | $ 4.00 | Direct materials | $ 4.00 |
| Direct labour | $13.50 | Direct labour | $13.50 |
| Variable overhead | $ 3.00 | Variable overhead | $ 3.00 |
| Fixed overhead | $ 4.50 | Total | $20.50 |
|    Total | $25.00 | | |

2. Absorption-costing income statement:

**Bellingham, Inc.**
**Absorption-Costing Income Statement**

| | | |
|---|---|---|
| Sales (21,500 × $42) | | $903,000 |
| Cost of goods sold (21,500 × $25.00) | $537,500 | |
| Less: Overapplied overhead* | 7,000 | 530,500 |
| Gross margin | | $372,500 |
| Less: Selling and administrative expenses | | 297,500 |
|    Net income | | $ 75,000 |

\* The budgeted fixed overhead rate of $3 per direct labour hour was computed based on 36,000 direct labour hours. Therefore, budgeted fixed overhead must have been $108,000. Since actual fixed overhead was $12,000 less than budgeted, actual fixed overhead must be $96,000. Similarly, the variable overhead rate of $2 per direct labour hour implies budgeted variable overhead of $72,000 ($2 × 36,000 direct labour hours). Since actual variable overhead was $5,000 higher than budgeted overhead, actual variable overhead must be $77,000. Both variable and fixed overhead were applied on the basis of direct labour hours. Since 36,000 hours were worked, total applied overhead amounts to $180,000. Actual overhead was $173,000 (actual fixed cost of $96,000 plus actual variable cost of $77,000). Applied overhead $180,000 less actual overhead $173,000 equals overapplied overhead $7,000.

3. Variable-costing income statement:

**Bellingham, Inc.**
**Variable-Costing Income Statement**

| | | |
|---|---|---|
| Sales (21,500 × $42) | | $903,000 |
| Variable cost of goods sold (21,500 × $20.50) | $440,750 | |
| Add: Underapplied variable overhead* | 5,000 | 445,750 |
| Variable selling expenses (21,500 × $5) | | 107,500 |
|    Contribution margin | | $349,750 |
| Less: Fixed overhead | $ 96,000 | |
| Less: Selling and administrative expenses | 190,000 | 286,000 |
|    Net income | | $ 63,750 |

\* Note that the underapplied variable overhead is simply the actual variable overhead of $77,000 minus the applied variable overhead of $72,000 ($2 × 36,000 direct labour hours). Note also that actual fixed overhead is charged on the income statement, not applied fixed overhead.

4. Reconciliation of the difference between the two income statements:

Absorption NI − Variable NI = Fixed overhead rate × (Production − Sales)

$$\$75,000 - \$63,750 = \$4.50 \times (24,000 - 21,500)$$
$$\$11,250 = \$4.50 \times (2,500)$$
$$\$11,250 = \$11,250$$

## Questions for Writing and Discussion

1. What is the only difference between the way costs are assigned under variable and absorption costing?

2. A company's variable manufacturing costs are $10 per unit, its variable selling expenses are $2 per unit, and its fixed overhead rate is $5 per unit. What is the per-unit inventory cost of the product under absorption costing? under variable costing?

3. Why is variable costing a more descriptive term for the product-costing method popularly known as direct costing?

4. If production is greater than sales, why is absorption-costing income greater than variable-costing income?

5. If sales are greater than production, why is variable-costing income greater than absorption-costing income?

6. Assume that a company has a fixed overhead rate of $8 per unit produced. During the year, the company produced 10,000 units and sold 8,000. What is the difference between absorption costing income and variable costing income?

7. The fixed overhead expense recognized on an income statement was $100,000. The fixed overhead for the period was $80,000. Was the income statement prepared using absorption costing or variable costing? Explain.

8. Why is variable costing better than absorption costing for the evaluation of managerial performance?

9. Why is variable costing better than absorption costing for the evaluation of segment performance?

10. Why is variable costing better than absorption costing for planning and controlling costs?

11. What is the difference between a direct fixed cost and a common fixed cost? Why is this difference important?

12. What is the difference between segment margin and contribution margin?

13. Explain how income under absorption costing can increase from one period to the next although unit sales, selling prices, and costs have remained the same.

14. How would a segment be identified within a company?

15. How is activity-based costing applied to segmented reporting?

16. Explain how treating customer groups as segments can be useful to a company.

# Exercises

**8–1**

Unit Costs, Inventory
Valuation, Variable
and Absorption
Costing

LO1

Richard Company produced 25,000 units during its first year of operations and sold 21,500 units at $16 per unit. The company chose to use practical activity—at 25,000 units—to compute its predetermined overhead rate. Manufacturing costs are as follows:

| | |
|---|---|
| Expected and actual fixed overhead | $65,000 |
| Expected and actual variable overhead | 26,500 |
| Direct labour | 132,500 |
| Direct materials | 162,500 |

**Required:**
1. Calculate the unit cost and the cost of finished goods inventory under absorption costing.
2. Calculate the unit cost and the cost of finished goods inventory under variable costing.
3. What is the dollar amount that would be used to report the cost of finished goods inventory to external parties? Why?

**8–2**

Income Statements,
Variable and
Absorption Costing

LO1

Spreadsheet

The following information pertains to Morina, Inc., for 2004:

| | |
|---|---|
| Beginning inventory, units | — |
| Units produced | 15,000 |
| Units sold | 13,800 |
| Ending inventory, units | 1,200 |
| Variable costs per unit: | |
|    Direct materials | DM $9.00 |
|    Direct labour | DL 4.00 |
|    Variable overhead | VOH 1.50 |
|    Variable selling expenses | 3.50 |
| Fixed costs per year: | |
|    Fixed overhead | FOH $48,000   3.20 |
|    Fixed selling and administrative | 22,000 |

There are no work-in-process inventories. Normal activity is 15,000 units. Expected and actual overhead costs are the same.   *estimated*

**Required:**
1. Without preparing an income statement, indicate what the difference will be between variable-costing income and absorption-costing income.
2. Assume that the selling price per unit is $30. Prepare an income statement (a) using variable costing and (b) using absorption costing.

**8–3**

Income Statements and
Company Performance,
Variable and
Absorption Costing

LO1, LO2

Irvine Company had the following operating data for its first two years of operations:

| | |
|---|---|
| Variable cost per unit: | |
|    Direct materials | $4 |
|    Direct labour | 2   VC |
|    Variable overhead | 1 |
| Fixed costs per year: | |
|    Fixed overhead | $120,000 |
|    Selling and administrative | 24,300 |

Spreadsheet

Irvine produced 20,000 units in the first year and sold 16,000. In the second year, it produced 16,000 units and sold 20,000 units. The selling price per unit each year was $24. Irvine uses an actual-cost system for product costing.

**Required:**
1. Prepare income statements for both years using absorption costing. Has company performance, as measured by income, improved or declined from Year 1 to Year 2?
2. Prepare income statements for both years using variable costing. Has the company's performance, as measured by income, improved or declined from Year 1 to Year 2?

**8–4**

Inventory Valuation

LO1

Refer to Exercise 8–3.

**Required:**
1. Calculate the fixed overhead rate for Year 1.
2. Calculate the Year 1 value of ending inventory under absorption costing and under variable costing.

**8–5**

Absorption Costing, Variable Costing, Reconciliation with Fixed Overhead Variance

LO1

Denham Company uses a predetermined overhead rate based on normal capacity expressed in units of output. Normal capacity is 75,000 units, and the expected fixed overhead cost for the year is $300,000.

During the year, Denham produced 74,000 units and sold 72,000 units. There was no beginning finished goods inventory. The variable-costing income statement for the year follows:

| | |
|---|---:|
| Sales (72,000 units × $21) | $1,512,000 |
| Less variable costs: | |
| Variable cost of goods sold | 756,000 |
| Variable selling expenses | 360,000 |
| Contribution margin | $  396,000 |
| Less fixed costs: | |
| Fixed overhead | 300,000 |
| Fixed selling and administrative | 84,000 |
| Net income | $    12,000 |

Any under- or overapplied overhead is closed to Cost of Goods Sold. Variable cost of goods sold is already adjusted for any variable overhead variance.

**Required:**
1. Denham Company needs an income statement based on absorption costing for external reporting. Using the provided information, prepare this statement.
2. Explain the difference between the income reported by variable costing and by absorption costing.

**8–6**

Segmented Income Statements, Product-Line Analysis

LO3, LO4

Cocino Company produces blenders and coffee makers. During the past year, 100,000 blenders and 25,000 coffee makers were produced and sold. Fixed costs for Cocino totalled $250,000, of which $90,000 can be avoided if the blenders are not produced and $45,000 can be avoided if the coffee makers are not produced. Revenue and variable-cost information follow:

| | Blenders | Coffee Makers |
|---|---|---|
| Variable expenses per appliance | $20 | $43 |
| Selling price per appliance | $22 | $45 |

**Required:**

1. Prepare product-line income statements. Segregate direct and common fixed costs.
2. What would be the effect on Cocino's profit if the coffee-maker line were dropped? the blender line?
3. What would be the effect on company profits if an additional 10,000 blenders could be produced (using existing capacity) and sold for $20.50 on a special-order basis? Assume that existing sales would be unaffected by the special order.

**8–7**

Product-Line Analysis
with Complementary
Effects

LO3, LO4

FunTime Company produces three lines of greeting cards: scented, musical, and regular. A segmented income statement for the past year is as follows:

|  | Scented | Musical | Regular | Total |
|---|---|---|---|---|
| Sales | $10,000 | $15,000 | $25,000 | $50,000 |
| Less: Variable expenses | 7,000 | 12,000 | 12,500 | 31,500 |
| Contribution margin | $ 3,000 | $ 3,000 | $12,500 | $18,500 |
| Less: Direct fixed expenses | 4,000 | 5,000 | 3,000 | 12,000 |
| Segment margin | $(1,000) | $(2,000) | $ 9,500 | $ 6,500 |
| Common fixed expenses |  |  |  | 7,500 |
| Net profit (loss) |  |  |  | $(1,000) |

Louise LaFortune, FunTime's president, is concerned about her company's financial performance and is seriously considering dropping both the scented and musical product lines. However, before making a final decision, she consults Jim Dorn, FunTime's vice-president of marketing.

**Required:**

1. Jim believes that if FunTime increased advertising by $1,000 ($250 for the scented line and $750 for the musical line), sales of those two lines would increase by 30 percent. If you were Louise, how would you react to this information?
2. Jim warns Louise that eliminating the scented and musical lines would lower the sales of the regular line by 20 percent. Given this information, would it be profitable to eliminate the scented and musical lines?
3. Suppose that eliminating either line reduces sales of the regular cards by 10 percent. Would a combination of increased advertising (the option described in Requirement 1) and eliminating one of the lines be beneficial? Identify the best combination for the company.

**8–8**

Absorption Costing,
Variable Costing,
Income Statements,
Inventory Valuation,
Income Reconciliation

LO1

Emby Company produces and sells wooden pallets. The operating costs for the past year were as follows:

Variable costs per unit:
Direct materials $2.45
Direct labour 2.10
Variable overhead 0.25 4.8
Variable selling 0.30
Fixed costs per year:
Fixed overhead $180,000
Selling and administrative 56,000

During the year, Emby produced 200,000 wooden pallets and sold 208,000 at $9.00 each. Emby had 11,300 pallets in beginning finished goods inventory; costs have not changed from last year to this year. An actual-cost system is used for product costing.

**Required:**

1. What is the per-unit inventory cost that will be reported on Emby's balance sheet at the end of the year? What will be the reported income?
2. What would the per-unit inventory cost be under variable costing? Does this differ from the unit cost computed in Requirement 1? Why? What would income be using variable costing?
3. Reconcile the difference between the variable-costing and the absorption-costing income figures.

**8–9**

*Absorption Costing, Variable Costing, Income Statements, Inventory Valuation, Income Reconciliation*

**LO1**

Refer to Exercise 8–8. Suppose Emby Company had sold 196,700 pallets during the year.

**Required:**

1. What is the absorption-costing income? What is the variable costing income?
2. Reconcile the difference between the variable-costing and the absorption-costing income figures.

**8–10**

*Variable Costing, Absorption Costing, Income Statements, Inventory Valuation, Underapplied Fixed Overhead*

**LO1**

During its first year of operations, Sugarsmooth, Inc., produced 55,000 jars of hand cream based on a formula containing 10 percent glycolic acid. Unit sales were 53,500 jars. Fixed overhead was applied at $0.50 per unit produced. Fixed overhead was underapplied by $10,000. This fixed overhead variance was closed to Cost of Goods Sold. There was no variable overhead variance. The results of the year's operations are as follows (on an absorption-costing basis):

| | |
|---|---:|
| Sales (53,500 units × $8.50) | $454,750 |
| Less: Cost of goods sold | 170,500 |
| Gross margin | $284,250 |
| Less: Selling and administrative (all fixed) | 120,000 |
| Net income | $164,250 |

**Required:**

1. Give the cost of the company's ending inventory under absorption costing. What is the cost of the ending inventory under variable costing?
2. Prepare a variable-costing income statement. Reconcile the difference between the two income figures.

**8–11**

*Customer Profitability*

**LO3**

Refer to 8–10. At the end of the first year of operations, Sugarsmooth is considering expanding its customer base. In its first year, it sold to small drugstores and supermarkets. Now, Sugarsmooth wants to add large discount stores and small beauty shops. Working together, the company controller and marketing manager have accumulated the following information:

a. Anticipated sales to discount stores would be 20,000 units at a discounted price of $6.75 each. Higher costs of shipping and return penalties would be incurred. Shipping would amount to $45,000 per year, and return penalties would average 1 percent of sales. In addition, a clerk would need to be hired solely to handle the discount stores' accounts. The clerk's salary and benefits would be $30,000 per year.

b. Anticipated sales to beauty shops would be 10,000 units, at a price of $9 each. A commission of 10 percent of sales would be paid to the independent jobbers who sell to the shops. In addition, an extra packing expense of $0.50 per unit would be incurred, because the shops require fewer bottles per carton.

c. The fixed overhead expenses and the fixed selling and administrative expenses would remain unchanged; all are treated as common costs.

**Required:**

1. Prepare a segmented variable-costing income statement for next year. The segments correspond to customer groups: drugstores and supermarkets, discount stores, and beauty shops.
2. Are all three customer groups profitable? Should Sugarsmooth expand its marketing base?

**8–12**

Variable Costing and Absorption Costing, Net Income and Inventory Valuation

LO1, LO2

During October, the Meerkat Company Ltd. produced 10,000 units. The beginning inventory on October 1 was 4,000 units. During October, 12,000 units were sold for $720,000. October cost information is available on a per-unit basis and is consistent with cost patterns of previous months:

| | |
|---|---|
| Direct materials | $5.00 |
| Direct labour | 9.00 |
| Variable overhead | 6.00 |
| Fixed overhead | 7.00 |
| Variable selling expense | 1.00 |
| Fixed selling and administrative expense | 2.00 |

**Required:**

1. Using variable costing, produce an income statement for October.
2. If Meerkat switched to absorption costing, would its October net income be higher or lower? By how much?
3. Calculate the cost of ending inventory under (a) variable costing, and (b) absorption costing. (CMA Canada adapted)

**8–13**

Variable and Absorption Costing, Net Income

LO1

Summerside Company uses absorption costing but has heard about variable costing. Data for Summerside Company and its industrial product are:

| | |
|---|---|
| Selling price per unit | $20.00 |
| Costs per unit: | |
| Direct labour | $3.00 |
| Direct materials | 5.00 |
| Variable overhead | 4.00 |
| Monthly expenses: | |
| Fixed overhead | $480,000 |
| Administrative expenses | 280,000 |
| Selling expenses | 250,000 |

The denominator used in arriving at the fixed overhead rate was 300,000 units. The company's cost behaviour pattern is consistent between periods. In November, Summerside Company reports the following:

| | |
|---|---|
| Sales | 315,000 units |
| Beginning inventory | 25,000 units |
| Production | 300,000 units |

**Required:**

1. Prepare a November income statement using absorption costing.
2. Prepare a November income statement using variable costing.
3. Reconcile and explain the reason for any difference in net income between absorption costing and variable costing. (CMA Canada adapted)

**8–14**

Variable and
Absorption Costing,
Overhead Variances

LO1

During its first year of operations, Rose Company produced a product with the following variable costs per unit:

| | |
|---|---|
| Direct materials | $15.00 |
| Direct labour | 20.00 |
| Variable overhead | 8.00 |

These variable costs are from the company's normal costing system. The budgeted fixed overhead was $260,000. Practical capacity is 20,000 units, but expected production was 13,000 units. Rose's predetermined overhead rate is based on expected annual production. During the year, 14,000 units were produced and 10,500 units were sold. Actual manufacturing costs included $115,000 of variable overhead costs and $265,000 of fixed overhead costs. Rose assigns any overhead variance to Cost of Goods Sold at the end of the year.

**Required:**

1. Compute the amount of Cost of Goods Sold for the year if Rose used absorption costing.
2. Compute the amount of Cost of Goods Sold for the year if Rose used variable costing.
3. Explain the difference in net income reported by variable costing and absorption costing. (CGA Canada adapted)

**8–15**

Variable-Costing and
Absorption-Costing
Income Statement Net
Income

LO1

The Grenada Company is comparing absorption costing with variable costing. An examination of its records provides the following information about 2004:

| | |
|---|---|
| Budgeted production (units) | 40,000 |
| Actual production (units) | 42,000 |
| Sales (units) | 45,000 |
| Inventory, January 1, 2004 (6,000 units) | $33,000 |
| Sales price per unit | $10.00 |
| Variable manufacturing cost per unit | 4.00 |
| Variable selling expenses per unit | 1.00 |
| Fixed overhead (actual and budgeted) | 60,000 |
| Fixed selling and administrative expenses | 20,000 |

Any overhead variance is treated as a period cost and is closed to cost of goods sold.

**Required:**

1. Prepare a variable-costing income statement for 2004.
2. Prepare an absorption-costing income statement for 2004.
3. Reconcile the variable-costing net income with the absorption-costing net income. (CGA Canada adapted)

**8–16**

Variable-Costing and
Absorption-Costing,
Income Statements

LO1

The Manning Company manufactures personal time organizers. The following are the company's operating data for 2003 and 2004:

| | 2003 | 2004 |
|---|---|---|
| Units produced | 60,000 | 50,000 |
| Units sold | 54,000 | 54,000 |
| Selling price per unit | $250 | $250 |
| Variable costs per unit: | | |
|   Direct materials | 80 | 80 |
|   Direct labour | 40 | 40 |
|   Variable overhead | 35 | 35 |
|   Variable selling expenses | 30 | 30 |
| Fixed overhead (total) | 2,500,000 | 2,500,000 |
| Fixed selling and administrative expenses (total) | 300,000 | 300,000 |

There was no finished goods inventory on January 1, 2003. The company uses actual costing and the FIFO method for inventories.

**Required:**

1. Prepare income statements for 2003 and 2004 using absorption costing.
2. Prepare income statements for 2003 and 2004 using variable costing.
3. Reconcile the absorption-costing and variable-costing net income amounts for 2003 and 2004. (CGA Canada adapted)

**8–17**

Segmented Income Statements, Absorption Costing, Variable Costing, Regional Analysis

LO3, LO4

Spreadsheet

Copper Company sells its products in eastern and western Canada. Major plants are located in each region. Based on a recent quarterly income statement, the company's president has expressed some concern regarding performance in the Eastern Region. The income statement (prepared on an absorption-costing basis) follows:

**Copper Company**
**Income Statement**
**(dollars in thousands)**

|  | Western Region | Eastern Region | Total |
|---|---|---|---|
| Sales | $15,000 | $12,000 | $27,000 |
| Less: Cost of goods sold | 8,000 | 10,000 | 18,000 |
| Gross margin | $ 7,000 | $ 2,000 | $ 9,000 |
| Less: Selling and administrative | 2,000 | 2,500 | 4,500 |
| Net income (loss) | $ 5,000 | $ (500) | $ 4,500 |

Copper sold all of the units produced during the quarter. There were no beginning or ending finished goods inventories. Twenty percent of the cost of goods sold represents fixed overhead costs. Of total fixed overhead costs, 30 percent are traceable directly to the Western Region and 20 percent to the Eastern Region. The remaining fixed overhead costs, common to both regions, are allocated equally between them. All selling and administrative costs are fixed. Of the total, $2 million representing common costs are divided equally between the two regions. Of the remaining selling and administrative fixed costs, 40 percent are traceable directly to the Western Region and 60 percent to the Eastern Region.

**Required:**

1. Prepare a variable-costing segmented income statement for the quarter. Should Copper consider eliminating the Eastern Region?
2. Express the contribution margin and the segment margin computed in Requirement 1 as a percentage of sales. Now assume that each region increases its sales activity in the next quarter by 10 percent. Assuming the same cost relationships, prepare a new variable-costing segmented income statement. Recompute the contribution margin and segment margin ratios. What happened? Explain.

**8–18**

Unit Cost, Inventory Valuation, Absorption and Variable Costing, Contribution Margin

LO1, LO4

Wetzel Company manufactures stackable plastic cubes that are used for storage in dorm rooms. In January 2004, Wetzel began producing multicoloured cubes. During January, 9,000 were produced and 8,800 were sold at $6.20 each. The following costs were incurred:

| Direct materials | $ 6,300 |
|---|---|
| Direct labour | 4,950 |
| Variable overhead | 5,850 |
| Fixed overhead | 27,000 |

A selling commission of 10 percent of sales price was paid. Administrative expenses, all fixed, amounted to $13,470.

**Required:**
1. Calculate the unit cost and cost of ending inventory under absorption costing.
2. Calculate the unit cost and cost of ending inventory under variable costing.
3. What is the contribution margin per unit?
4. Wetzel believes that multicoloured cubes will take off after one year of sales. It believes January 2005 sales should be twice as high as January 2004 sales. Costs are estimated to remain unchanged. What is the planned net income for Wetzel for January 2005? Did you use variable or absorption costing to determine this answer?

**8–19**

Net Income,
Absorption and
Variable Costing

LO1

Refer to Exercise 8–18.

**Required:**
1. Prepare an absorption-costing income statement for Wetzel Company for January 2004.
2. Prepare a variable-costing income statement for Wetzel Company for January 2004.
3. Reconcile the difference between the two net incomes.

**8–20**

Inventory Valuation
under Absorption and
Variable Costing,
Variable-Costing Net
Income

LO1

Frost Company manufactured 18,000 units during the year and sold 21,050. Frost's accountant prepared the following income statement:

| | | |
|---|---|---|
| Sales (21,050 × $28) | | $589,400 |
| Cost of goods sold (21,050 × $21) | | 442,050 |
| Gross profit | | $147,350 |
| Marketing expense | $23,155 | |
| Administrative expense | 65,000 | 88,155 |
| Net income | | $ 59,195 |

Marketing expenses are strictly variable. Administrative expenses are entirely fixed. The fixed overhead rate is $5 per unit. Beginning inventory was 6,400 units, with a cost of $21 per unit.

**Required:**
1. Prepare a variable-costing income statement for Frost Company.
2. What was the value of ending inventory under absorption costing?
3. What was the value of ending inventory under variable costing?

**8–21**

Calculating Unit and
Total Costs under
Absorption Costing

LO1

Three independent companies, Company A, Company B, and Company C, use absorption costing. (See top of following page.) There are no overhead variances. Prices have stayed constant for all relevant time periods.

**Required:**
Replace each question mark with the correct amount.

**8–22**

Inventory Valuation
and Net Income under
Variable Costing

LO1

Refer to 8–21.

**Required:**
1. What are the net incomes for Companies A, B, and C using variable costing?
2. What are the values of ending inventory for Companies A, B, and C using variable costing?

|  | A | B | C |
|---|---|---|---|
| Unit information: |  |  |  |
| Price | $22 | $? | $? |
| Direct materials | 4 | 2 | 6 |
| Direct labour | 3 | 4 | 1 |
| Variable overhead | 1 | 1 | 1 |
| Fixed overhead | $ ? | 3 | 1 |
| Contribution margin | 14 | $? | $? |
| Gross profit | 9 | $? | $? |
| Units sold | 2,000 | 7,600 | ? |
| Units produced | 2,000 | 8,000 | ? |
| Beginning inventory, units | 500 | 0 | 3,000 |
| Total information: |  |  |  |
| Sales | $? | $114,000 | $136,000 |
| Cost of goods sold | $? | $? | $ 72,000 |
| Gross profit | $? | $ 38,000 | $? |
| Variable marketing | $? | $ 9,500 | $ 24,000 |
| Fixed marketing | $5,000 | $ 8,000 | $? |
| Fixed administrative | $3,000 | $? | $ 8,300 |
| Net income | $? | $ 500 | $ 16,700 |
| Value of ending inventory | $6,500 | $? | $ 9,000 |

**8–23**

*Variable and Absorption Costing*

**LO1**

Telster Company manufactures underwater pumps for water gardens. The pumps are sold for $85 each. Cost of goods sold is $60; of that amount, $24 is for direct materials. Variable overhead is applied at twice the rate of direct labour cost. Total fixed overhead is $41,400. Production was 12,000 units for this year due to the need to increase inventory by 2,000 units. No pumps were in inventory at the beginning of the year. Selling and administrative costs, all fixed, were $137,000.

**Required:**

1. Compute direct labour cost per unit, variable overhead cost per unit, and fixed overhead cost per unit. What is the unit manufacturing cost per unit?
2. What was absorption-costing net income for Telster Company for the year? What was variable-costing net income?
3. What was the value of ending inventory under absorption costing? Under variable costing?

**8–24**

*Variable and Absorption Costing, Performance Evaluation*

**LO1, LO4**

Selwyn Shroode was hired in early 2004 to manage the Mixed Manufacturing Division and improve its profit picture. His appointment specified a bonus of 10 percent of income as well as a promotion to corporate vice-president if profits in 2004 exceeded $1,000,000. The following are partial 2003 and 2004 absorption-costing income statements (in thousands):

|  | 2003 | | 2004 | |
|---|---|---|---|---|
| Sales (1,000,000 units) |  | $10,000 |  | $10,000 |
| Cost of goods sold: |  |  |  |  |
| Beginning inventory | $ 0 |  | $ 0 |  |
| Manufacturing costs | 7,000 |  | 10,000 |  |
| Ending inventory | 0 | 7,000 | 5,000 | 5,000 |
| Gross margin |  | $ 3,000 |  | $ 5,000 |
| Selling and administrative expenses |  | 3,000 |  | 3,000 |
| Net income before income tax |  | $ 0 |  | $ 2,000 |

Manufacturing costs had the same cost behaviour in both years.

**Required:**
1. How many units were produced in 2003? In 2004?
2. Use the high–low method to determine the fixed and variable components of manufacturing costs.
3. Prepare variable-costing income statements for each year.
4. Comment on Shroode's performance. Should Shroode get a bonus?

**8–25**

**Customer Profitability**

**LO3**

Woolywear, Inc., manufactures knitted gloves, hats, and scarves. For several years, Woolywear sold its products to small specialty shops. Recently, the company landed a large contract (amounting to half of its output) with Giga-Mart. Cost information for Woolywear is as follows:

| | |
|---|---|
| Units produced and sold | 100,000 |
| Average selling price (per unit) | $   9.00 |
| Manufacturing costs: | |
|     Direct material (per unit) | $   1.75 |
|     Direct labour (per unit) | 1.50 |
|     Overhead (per unit) | 3.00 |
| Marketing expenses: | |
|     Commissions (per unit) | $   0.90 |
|     Special design (per unit) | 2.00 |
|     Delivery expense | 80,000 |
|     Shipping expense | 20,000 |
|     Return penalties | 3,000 |

The specialty stores require special designs, forcing Woolywear to incur additional setup and materials costs. These amount to about $2 per unit. The shipping expense is for shipment to the specialty stores, as are the commissions. Giga-Mart orders do not incur any commissions; however, the discount giant does require a $1 discount on the unit price and just-in-time deliveries. The delivery expense averages $80,000 per year. Also, Giga-Mart levies return penalties if any order does not meet its specifications. These penalties are incurred on about 15 percent of the orders and amount to 5 percent of sales price.

**Required:**
Compute the profit earned by Woolywear for the specialty shops and for Giga-Mart.

**8–26**

**Multiple Choice Questions**

**LO1, LO2, LO3, LO4**

Choose the *best* answer for each of the following multiple-choice questions:

1. Any difference between absorption-costing income and variable-costing income is due to the differing treatment of
   a. selling and administrative expense.
   b. overhead.
   c. prime cost.
   d. fixed overhead.
   e. There is no difference between the two income figures.

2. If there is a decrease in inventory from the beginning of the period to the end of the period, absorption-costing income will be
   a. greater than variable-costing income.
   b. equal to variable-costing income.
   c. less than variable-costing income.
   d. twice as large as variable-costing income.
   e. None of the above.

3.  When variable costing is used to develop segmented income statements,
    a.  all fixed overhead is expensed together.
    b.  only segment fixed overhead is expensed.
    c.  segment direct fixed overhead and selling expense are subtracted from contribution margin to yield segment margin.
    d.  common fixed overhead is allocated to the segments based on sales.
    e.  Variable costing cannot be used to develop segmented income statements.

4.  For a company with fixed overhead, the value of ending inventory under variable costing is
    a.  less than the value of ending inventory under absorption costing.
    b.  more than the value of ending inventory under absorption costing.
    c.  equal to the value of ending inventory under absorption costing.
    d.  composed of direct materials, direct labour, variable overhead, and a portion of fixed overhead.
    e.  composed of prime cost only.

5.  Fixed costs common to two or more plants within a division
    a.  are allocated among the plants in accordance with the relative amount of manufacturing cost.
    b.  are added to prime cost and subtracted from sales to yield contribution margin.
    c.  are added to other operating expenses and labelled administrative expense on the income statement.
    d.  are divided among the plants in accordance with relative sales.
    e.  are shown as a common cost for the division.

6.  For planning and control purposes within the company,
    a.  absorption costing gives better information.
    b.  variable costing is better because it considers cost behaviour.
    c.  variable costing is better because it is acceptable for external reporting.
    d.  absorption costing cannot be used.
    e.  variable and absorption costing are equally useful.

## Problems

**8–27**

*Variable-Costing and Absorption-Costing Income Statements*

**LO1**

Eckel Company manufactures heavy-duty motors. Sales for last year totalled $643,200. Cost of goods sold amounted to 45 percent of sales. Of the total, 20 percent represented fixed overhead costs. Selling expenses were equally split between fixed and variable components. Administrative expenses, all fixed, totalled $60,000. Net income for last year was $170,400. Eckel produced and sold 53,600 motors last year.

**Required:**
1.  Prepare an absorption-costing income statement for Eckel Company for last year.
2.  Prepare a variable-costing income statement for Eckel Company for last year.
3.  What is the total variable cost per motor? What is the variable production cost per motor?

**8–28**

Variable Costing,
Budgeted Income

LO1, LO4

Nguyen Inc. manufactures medical equipment. Nguyen's income statement is as follows:

| | |
|---|---:|
| Sales | $2,340,700 |
| Variable cost of goods sold | 1,076,722 |
| Variable selling expense | 117,035 |
| Contribution margin | $1,146,943 |
| Fixed overhead | 550,000 |
| Fixed selling and administrative | 244,000 |
| Net income | $ 352,943 |

Nguyen believes that it can increase the average price of its products by 8 percent next year. No change in quantity of products sold is forecast. Variable selling expenses will increase by 2 percent, and administrative expenses will increase by $10,500. Variable production costs will decrease by 4 percent; fixed production costs will be unchanged.

**Required:**

1. Prepare a budgeted variable-costing income statement for next year.
2. Suppose that Nguyen's controller believes that a more conservative estimate of the coming year's activity is a 6 percent increase in prices, no change in variable production costs, an increase in variable selling expenses of 5 percent, and an increase in administrative expenses of $15,000. Prepare a budgeted variable-costing income statement based on the more conservative figures.

**8–29**

Variable Costing,
Targeted Net Income

LO1, LO4

Madengrad Company manufactures a single electronic product called Precisionmix. This unit is a batch-density monitoring device that attaches to the large industrial mixing machines used in flour, rubber, petroleum, and chemical manufacturing. Precisionmix sells for $900 per unit. The following variable costs are incurred to produce each Precisionmix device:

| | |
|---|---:|
| Direct labour | $180 |
| Direct materials | 240 |
| Variable overhead | 105 |
| Variable product cost | $525 |
| Marketing cost | 75 |
| Total variable cost | $600 |

Madengrad's annual fixed costs are $6,600,000. Except for an operating loss incurred in the year of incorporation, the company has been profitable over the last five years. Madengrad is forecasting sales of 21,500 units for next year and has budgeted production at that level.

**Required:**

1. Prepare a pro forma variable-costing income statement for Madengrad Company for next year.
2. Madengrad has just learned of a significant change in production technology that will cause a 10 percent increase in total annual fixed costs and a 20 percent unit labour cost increase as a result of needing higher-skilled direct labour. However, this change permits the replacement of a costly imported component with a domestic component. The effect is to reduce unit material costs and variable overhead costs by 25 percent. No change in selling price is forecast. Prepare a variable-costing income statement for Madengrad Company for next year assuming that it invests in the new production technology. (US CMA adapted)

**8–30**

*Segment Analysis,
Addition of a New
Product*

LO3

Sandia Company currently produces two products, A and B. The company has sufficient floor space to manufacture an additional product, with two (C and D) currently under consideration. Only one of the two products can be chosen. The expected annual sales and associated costs for each product are as follows:

| | Product C | Product D |
|---|---|---|
| Sales | $100,000 | $125,000 |
| Variable costs as a percentage of sales: | | |
| Production | 54% | 65% |
| Selling and administrative | 12% | 5% |
| Direct fixed expenses | $15,000 | $11,250 |

The company's common fixed costs are allocated to each product line on the basis of sales revenues. The following income statement for last year's operations is also available:

| | Product A | Product B | Total |
|---|---|---|---|
| Sales | $250,000 | $375,000 | $625,000 |
| Less variable expenses: | | | |
| Cost of goods sold | 100,000 | 250,000 | 350,000 |
| Selling and administrative | 20,000 | 65,000 | 85,000 |
| Contribution margin | $130,000 | $ 60,000 | $190,000 |
| Less: Direct fixed expenses | 10,000 | 55,000 | 65,000 |
| Segment margin | $120,000 | $ 5,000 | $125,000 |
| Less: Common fixed expenses | | | 75,000 |
| Net income | | | $ 50,000 |

**Required:**

1. Prepare an income statement that reflects the impact on the company's profits of adding Product C. Repeat for Product D. Which of the two would you recommend adding?
2. Suppose that Products C and D could both be added if either A or B were dropped. Would you drop one of the current products to add both C and D? If so, which would you drop? Why?

**8–31**

*Variable-Costing and
Absorption-Costing
Income Statements*

LO1, LO2, LO4

The following information was taken from the records of Jarrett Company Ltd. during its first six months of operations, which ended May 31, 2004:

| | |
|---|---|
| Production | 27,000 units |
| Sales | 22,000 units |
| Selling price | $15 per unit |
| Production costs incurred: | |
| Direct materials used | $ 67,500 |
| Direct labour | 101,250 |
| Variable overhead | 54,000 |
| Fixed overhead | 189,000 |
| Selling and administrative expenses: | |
| Variable (commissions) | 5% of sales |
| Fixed | $ 30,000 |

All ending inventories are complete. Since Jarrett is a new company, its president is interested in installing a proper costing system. He is aware of two alternatives available to him: a full (absorption-based) system, or a variable-costing-based system.

**Required:**

1. To assist the president in his decision, prepare two income statements for the six months ended May 31, 2004.

2. Reconcile the two net incomes, showing your calculations.
3. Advise the president on which statement approach you feel he should use, pointing out the advantages and disadvantages of each. (CMA Canada adapted)

**8–32**

*Variable Costing,*
*Absorption Costing*

**LO1**

The Moonbeam Company used absorption costing in producing the following income statement for 2004:

| | | |
|---|---:|---:|
| Sales (6,000 units) | | $240,000 |
| Cost of goods sold: | | |
| Inventory, January 1 (1,500 units) | $ 42,000 | |
| Cost of goods manufactured (6,700 units) | 187,600 | |
| Cost of goods available for sale | $229,600 | |
| Less: inventory, December 31 | 61,600 | |
| Cost of goods sold | | 168,000 |
| Gross profit | | $ 72,000 |
| Operating expenses: | | |
| Selling | $ 24,000 | |
| Administrative | 43,000 | 67,000 |
| Net Income | | $ 5,000 |

An analysis of the costs indicates the following:
- the selling costs are all variable;
- 85% of the administrative costs are fixed; and
- 40% of all manufacturing costs are fixed.

**Required:**
1. Produce an income statement using variable costing.
2. Under what circumstances would a difference arise between net income under absorption costing and net income under variable costing? Reconcile the two net incomes, showing your calculations. (CMA Canada adapted)

**8–33**

*Absorption Costing*
*and Inventory Changes*

**LO1, LO2, LO4**

B.T. Company Ltd. prepared the following budgeted income statement based on production and sales estimates of 20,000 units:

| | | |
|---|---:|---:|
| Sales | | $400,000 |
| Cost of goods sold: | | |
| Direct materials | $ 80,000 | |
| Direct labour | 60,000 | |
| Variable overhead | 40,000 | |
| Fixed overhead* | 100,000 | |
| Total cost of goods sold | | 280,000 |
| Gross profit | | $120,000 |
| Selling and administrative expenses: | | |
| Variable | $ 30,000 | |
| Fixed | 40,000 | |
| Total selling and administration | | 70,000 |
| Net income | | $ 50,000 |

\* Relevant range of 15,000 to 50,000 units.

During 2004, the company produced 25,000 units and sold 20,000 units. All costs and revenues behaved precisely as expected, but net income was $70,000 instead of the $50,000 expected.

**Required:**
1. Prepare B.T. Company's income statement for 2004.
2. Why is net income different from that expected? Explain the difference using the actual figures given.
3. What costing system or method would avoid this difference in net income? Explain. (CMA Canada adapted)

**8–34**

Blades Products was organized as a new division of Amalgamated Stuff, Inc., to produce in-line roller skates. With the continuing popularity of physical fitness, the divisional manager expected a good response to the product. In the first year of operations, Blades reported the following net income to its shareholders:

**Blades Products
Income Statement
For the Year Ended December 31, 2003**

| | | |
|---|---|---|
| Sales (@ $85) | | $42,500,000 |
| Less: Cost of goods sold (@ $65)[a] | | 32,500,000 |
| Gross margin | | $10,000,000 |
| Less: Selling and administrative[b] | | 5,125,000 |
| Net income | | $ 4,875,000 |

| | |
|---|---|
| [a] Direct materials | $24 |
| Direct labour | 12 |
| Variable overhead | 15 |
| Fixed overhead | 14 |
| Total | $65 |

[b] $6.25 per unit variable; $2,000,000 fixed

In 2003, Blades produced 100,000 units more than it sold, because sales were less than expected. The divisional manager believed the sales slump was due to a soft economy and was confident that second-year sales would be 20 percent higher. Overhead is applied on the basis of units produced using expected actual activity. Any under- or overapplied overhead is closed to Cost of Goods Sold. For 2003, there was no under- or overapplied overhead.

For 2004, fixed costs and unit variable costs remained the same; the selling price also remained unchanged. Budgeted fixed costs equalled actual fixed costs. In 2004, Blades produced 500,000 units and sold 600,000 units. Production was 100,000 less than expected, because of unanticipated equipment problems. However, the divisional manager was not displeased: the 20 percent sales increase had been achieved, and production costs were completely in line with plans.

**Required:**

1. Prepare the 2004 income statement required for shareholders. Did income increase or decrease? What do you think the reaction of the parent company, Amalgamated Stuff, Inc., would be to this income statement? What would the divisional manager's reaction be?
2. Prepare variable-costing income statements for 2003 and 2004. How do you suppose Amalgamated Stuff, Inc., would react now?
3. Reconcile and explain the differences between the variable-costing and absorption-costing income figures for 2003 and 2004.
4. Which type of income statement (variable- or absorption-costing) do you think the divisional manager would prefer? Why?

**8–35**

Beldar Company produces and sells a single product. Cost data for the product follow:

| | |
|---|---|
| Unit variable costs: | |
| Direct materials | $4 |
| Direct labour | 2 |
| Variable overhead | 2 |
| Variable selling | 1 |
| Total | $9 |

Fixed costs per year:*

| | |
|---|---|
| Overhead | $ 960,000 |
| Selling and administrative | 300,000 |
| Total | $1,260,000 |

\* Fixed costs are incurred uniformly throughout the year.

During the first three months, the company produced and sold the following units:

| | Units Produced | Units Sold |
|---|---|---|
| Month 1 | 50,000 | 40,000 |
| Month 2 | 40,000 | 40,000 |
| Month 3 | 40,000 | 30,000 |

The company uses an actual-cost system to assign the costs of production. The selling price of the product is $14 per unit. A FIFO inventory system is used.

**Required:**

1. What is the unit cost for each month under absorption costing? under variable costing?
2. Without preparing income statements, determine the difference between absorption-costing and variable-costing income for each of the three months.
3. Prepare income statements using absorption costing and variable costing for each of the three months. Reconcile the net income figures.

**8–36**

Segmented Income
Statements, Analysis
of Proposals to
Improve Profits

**LO2, LO3**

Harris, Inc., has two divisions. One produces and sells paper diapers; the other produces and sells paper napkins and paper towels. A segmented income statement for the most recent quarter follows:

| | Diaper Division | Napkin and Towel Division | Total |
|---|---|---|---|
| Sales | $500,000 | $750,000 | $1,250,000 |
| Less: Variable expenses | 425,000 | 460,000 | 885,000 |
| Contribution margin | $ 75,000 | $290,000 | $ 365,000 |
| Less: Direct fixed expenses | 85,000 | 110,000 | 195,000 |
| Segment margin | $(10,000) | $180,000 | $ 170,000 |
| Less: Common fixed expenses | | | 130,000 |
| Net income | | | $ 40,000 |

On seeing the quarterly statement, Rebekkah Cornfield, the president of Harris, Inc., was distressed. "The Diaper Division is killing us," she complained. "It's not even covering its own fixed costs. I'm beginning to believe that we should shut down that division. This is the seventh consecutive quarter it has failed to provide a positive segment margin. I was certain that Fran Simmons could turn it around. But this is her third quarter, and she hasn't done much better than the previous divisional manager."

"Well, before you get too excited about the situation, perhaps you should evaluate Fran's most recent proposals," remarked Tom Ferguson, the company's vice-president of finance. "She wants to lease some new production equipment and at the same time increase the advertising budget by $25,000 per quarter. She has made some improvements in the design of the diaper and wants to let the public know about them. According to her marketing people, sales should increase by 10 percent if the right advertising is done—and done quickly. The new production machinery will increase the rate of production, decrease labour costs, and reduce the division's waste of materials. Fran claims that variable costs will be reduced by 30 percent. The cost of the lease is $105,000 per quarter."

Upon hearing this news, Rebekkah calmed down considerably: in fact, she was somewhat pleased. After all, she was the one who had selected Fran, and she had a great deal of confidence in Fran's judgment and abilities.

**Required:**

1. Assuming that Fran's proposals are sound, do you think Rebekkah Cornfield should be pleased with the prospects for the Diaper Division? Prepare a segmented income statement for the next quarter that reflects the implementation of Fran's proposals. Assume that the Napkin and Towel Division's sales increase by 5 percent for the next quarter and that the same cost relationships hold.

2. Suppose that everything materializes as Fran projected except for the 10 percent increase in sales—no change in sales revenues take place. Are the proposals still sound? What if the variable costs are reduced by 40 percent instead of 30 percent with no change in sales?

**8–37**

Variable-Costing, Absorption-Costing, Income Statements, Reconciliation

**LO1**

The Epsol Company has the following average revenues and costs based on the production and sale of 30,000 units per year:

| Selling price | | $25.00 per unit |
|---|---|---|
| Manufacturing costs: | | |
| Direct materials | $4.00 | |
| Direct labour | 5.00 | |
| Variable overhead | 2.00 | |
| Fixed overhead | 3.00 | |
| Total manufacturing costs | | $14.00 per unit |
| Selling and administrative: | | |
| Variable selling | $1.00 | |
| Fixed administrative | 6.00 | |
| Total selling and administrative | | $7.00 per unit |

The company actually produced 32,000 units but sold only 29,000 units in the year ended February 29, 2004. They did not have a beginning inventory of finished goods. All revenues and costs behaved as expected during the year ended February 29, 2004.

**Required:**

1. Prepare an income statement for the year ended February 29, 2004, assuming that Epsol uses normal absorption costing, with any overhead variances closed to Cost of Goods Sold.

2. Prepare an income statement for the year ended February 29, 2004, assuming the company uses variable costing.

3. Explain why there is, or should be, a difference in the net operating income between the two systems (use the data given to explain the dollar amount of the difference as fully as possible). (CMA Canada adapted)

**8–38**

Variable and Absorption Costing, Overhead Variances

**LO1, LO2**

The Woods Company uses a normal absorption-costing system, with overhead being applied based on the expected capacity to be used in the year. Any overhead variances are closed to Cost of Goods Sold at the end of the year. The company has the following income statement for the year ending December 31, 2004, based on the production and sales of 20,000 units:

| | | |
|---|---|---|
| Sales (20,000 units × $40) | | $800,000 |
| Cost of goods sold (40% fixed) | $550,000 | |
| Add: Underapplied overhead for the year | 55,000 | |
| Adjusted cost of goods sold | | 605,000 |
| Gross profit margin | | $195,000 |
| Selling and administrative expenses (80% fixed) | | 180,000 |
| Operating income | | $ 15,000 |

The company expected to produce and sell 22,000 units in 2005, but a change in demand resulted in actual production of 23,000 units and sales of 22,500 units. All revenues and expenses behaved as expected for the year (the same as in 2004).

**Required:**

1. What was the company's expected production level in 2004, assuming that all revenues and expenses behaved as expected in that year?
2. What is the company's actual operating income for 2005 if they use their present costing system? variable costing?
3. Explain why operating income would normally be different between the two systems, and state exactly how much the difference should be.
4. What advantages would there be in using variable costing instead of normal absorption costing? (CMA Canada adapted)

**8–39**

Performance Evaluation, Absorption Costing Compared with Variable Costing

LO1, LO2

Reread the opening scenario for this chapter. The following represent three years of operating data and income statements that Kathy Wise received.

|  | Operating Data | | |
| --- | --- | --- | --- |
|  | **Year 1** | **Year 2** | **Year 3** |
| Production | 10,000 | 11,000 | 9,000 |
| Sales (in units) | 8,000 | 10,000 | 12,000 |
| Unit selling price | $10 | $10 | $10 |
| Unit costs: |  |  |  |
|    Fixed overhead* | $2.90 | $3.00 | $3.00 |
|    Variable overhead | 1.00 | 1.00 | 1.00 |
|    Direct materials | 1.90 | 2.00 | 2.00 |
|    Direct labour | 1.00 | 1.00 | 1.00 |
| Variable selling | 0.40 | 0.50 | 0.50 |
| Actual fixed overhead | $29,000 | $30,000 | $30,000 |
| Other fixed costs | $9,000 | $10,000 | $10,000 |

\* The predetermined fixed overhead rate is based on expected actual units of production and expected fixed overhead. Expected production each year was 10,000 units. Any under- or overapplied fixed overhead is closed to Cost of Goods Sold.

|  | Income Statements | | |
| --- | --- | --- | --- |
|  | **Year 1** | **Year 2** | **Year 3** |
| Sales revenue | $80,000 | $100,000 | $120,000 |
| Less: Cost of goods sold* | 54,400 | 67,000 | 86,600 |
| Gross margin | $25,600 | $ 33,000 | $ 33,400 |
| Less: Selling and administrative | 12,200 | 15,000 | 16,000 |
| Net income | $13,400 | $ 18,000 | $ 17,400 |

\* Assume a LIFO inventory flow.

Recall that Kathy was pleased with the operating data, but she was dismayed and perplexed by the income statements. Instead of seeing a significant increase in income for the third year, she saw a small decrease. Kathy's initial reaction was that the accounting department had made an error.

**Required:**

1. Explain to Kathy why she lost her $5,000 bonus.
2. Prepare variable-costing income statements for each of the three years. Reconcile the differences between the absorption-costing and variable-costing incomes.
3. If you were the vice-president of Kathy's company, which income statement (variable-costing or absorption-costing) would you prefer to use for evaluating Kathy's performance? Why?

**8–40**

Wilmont Company's executive committee was meeting to select a new vice-president of operations. The leading candidate was Howard Kimball, manager of Wilmont's largest division. Howard had been divisional manager for three years. The president of Wilmont, Gus Olsen, was impressed with the significant improvements in the division's profits since Howard had assumed command. In the first year of operations, divisional profits had increased by 20 percent. They had shown significant improvements for the following two years as well. To bolster support for Howard, the company's president circulated the following divisional income statements (dollars in thousands):

|  | 2003 | 2004 | 2005 |
|---|---|---|---|
| Sales | $30,000 | $32,000 | $34,000 |
| Less: Cost of goods sold[a] | 26,250 | 26,900 | 27,900 |
| Gross margin | $ 3,750 | $ 5,100 | $ 6,100 |
| Less: Selling and administrative expenses[b] | 3,000 | 3,600 | 3,800 |
| Net income | $ 750 | $ 1,500 | $ 2,300 |

[a] Assumes a FIFO inventory flow.
[b] All costs are fixed.

"As you can see," Gus observed at a meeting, "Howard has increased profits by a factor of three since 2003. That's by far the most impressive performance of any divisional manager. We could certainly use someone with that kind of drive. I definitely believe that Howard should be the new vice-president."

"I'm not quite as convinced that Howard's performance is as impressive as it appears," responded Theo Petrou, the vice-president of finance. "I could hardly believe that Howard's division could show the magnitude of improvement revealed by the income statements, so I asked the division's controller to supply some additional information. As the data suggest, the profits realized by Howard's division may be attributable to a concerted effort to produce for inventory. In fact, I believe it can be shown that the division is actually showing a loss each year and that real profits have declined by as much as 15 percent since 2003." Theo then presented the following information:

|  | 2003 | 2004 | 2005 |
|---|---|---|---|
| Sales (units) | 150,000 | 160,000 | 170,000 |
| Production* | 200,000 | 250,000 | 300,000 |
| Actual (and budgeted) fixed overhead | $15,000,000 | $15,000,000 | $15,000,000 |
| Fixed overhead rate | $75 | $60 | $50 |
| Unit variable production costs | $100 | $105 | $110 |

* Represents both expected and actual production. Fixed overhead rates are computed using expected actual production.

**Required:**
1. Explain what Theo Petrou meant by "produce for inventory."
2. Recast the income statements in a variable-costing format. Now how does the division's performance appear?
3. Reconcile the differences in the income figures using the two methods for each of the three years.
4. If you were a shareholder, how could you detect income increases that are caused mainly by production for inventory?

**8–41**

Inventory Changes and
Absorption-Costing
Net Income,
Comparison to
Variable Costing
LO1, LO4

The Lion Company has prepared the following income statements at two levels of sales:

| | 10,000 units | 15,000 units |
|---|---|---|
| Units produced and sold | 10,000 units | 15,000 units |
| Sales | $120,000 | $180,000 |
| Direct material | 14,000 | 21,000 |
| Direct labour | 37,500 | 56,250 |
| Variable overhead | 18,750 | 28,125 |
| Fixed overhead* | 12,000 | 12,000 |
| Sales salaries | 30,000 | 30,000 |
| Sales commissions (2% of sales) | 2,400 | 3,600 |
| Administrative costs* | 25,000 | 25,000 |
| Net income (loss) | $ (19,650) | $ 4,025 |

\* Relevant range of 5,000 units to 40,000 units.

**Required:**

1. During 2004, the company actually sold 15,000 units, and all revenues and costs behaved as expected, but the company's net income was actually $7,025 using absorption costing. How many units did the company produce during 2004?

2. If the company used a variable-costing system, would the discrepancy between expected and actual net income occur? Explain why or why not. (CMA Canada adapted)

**8–42**

During November 2004, the Canberra Company produced 7,000 units. Inventory at November 1, 2004, was 3,000 units. During November, 9,000 units were sold for $450,000. Canberra uses a normal absorption-costing system with the following costs per unit:

| | |
|---|---|
| Direct materials | $ 6.00 |
| Direct labour | 14.00 |
| Variable overhead | 7.00 |
| Fixed overhead | 5.00 |
| | $32.00 |

Other information available for November 2004 is as follows:
- Variable selling expenses were $2.00 per unit.
- Fixed selling and administrative expenses were $20,000.
- The activity base for the predetermined rate was 8,000 units.
- Actual overhead was $91,000.
- Overhead variances are closed to Cost of Goods Sold each month.

**Required:**

1. Prepare an income statement for November 2004, using variable costing.

2. Reconcile the variable-costing net income with the reported net income, using absorption costing. (CGA Canada adapted)

**8–43**

Shown below is the income statement for Lampton Green Industries for 2004, when 12,000 units of product were sold:

**Lampton Green Industries**
**Income Statement**
**For the Year Ended December 31, 2004**

| | | |
|---|---:|---:|
| Sales | | $540,000 |
| Cost of goods sold: | | |
|    Materials | $102,000 | |
|    Direct labour | 84,000 | |
|    Variable overhead | 75,000 | |
|    Fixed overhead | 85,800 | 346,800 |
| Unadjusted gross margin | | $193,200 |
| Underapplied overhead | | 8,580 |
| Gross margin | | $184,620 |
| Variable selling and administration | $ 63,000 | |
| Fixed selling and administration | 80,000 | 143,000 |
|    Net income | | $ 41,620 |

During 2004, 12,800 units were produced. On January 1, 2004, there were 950 units in finished goods and no units in process. On December 31, 2004, there were no units in process. Lampton Green uses a normal absorption-costing system to value inventories. There was no underapplied variable overhead in 2004. All overhead variances are closed to cost of goods sold on the income statement.

**Required:**
1. Determine the total amount of fixed manufacturing overhead incurred in 2004.
2. What was the total contribution margin for 2004?
3. If Lampton Green had used variable costing, what would net income be for 2004?
4. Explain the difference in net income under absorption costing from that calculated using variable costing. Show your calculations.
5. What is the value of ending inventory under absorption costing? under variable costing? (CMA Canada adapted)

**8–44**

Variable-Costing and
Absorption-Costing
Net Income

LO1

On January 1, 2003, Jaskyl Company started operations. For the first two years, Jaskyl used an absorption-costing system. The following are condensed income statements for 2003 and 2004.

| | 2003 | 2004 |
|---|---:|---:|
| Sales revenue | $1,000,000 | $1,200,000 |
| Expenses (including cost of goods sold and administrative expenses) | 850,000 | 950,000 |
|    Income before income taxes | $ 150,000 | $ 250,000 |
| Number of units sold | 20,000 | 30,000 |

The variable costs consisted of 50 percent direct materials, 25 percent direct labour, and 25 percent variable overhead. Selling and administrative expenses were all fixed. There were 8,000 units in finished goods inventory at December 31, 2003, and 10,000 units at December 31, 2004. In 2003 and 2004, actual fixed overhead was $180,000 and $260,000, respectively. Overhead is applied on the basis of direct labour cost. In 2003, there was overapplied overhead of $30,000; in 2004, there was underapplied overhead of $20,000. These amounts were due entirely to fixed overhead and were closed to Cost of Goods Sold.

**Required:**
1. What would be the reported net income for 2003 and 2004 if variable costing were used?
2. For 2004, prepare a variable-costing income statement (break down expenses in as much detail as possible). (CGA Canada adapted)

**8–45**

Comparison of
Variable and
Absorption Costing,
Predetermined
Overhead Rates

LO1

Camilleri, Inc., has just completed its first year of operations. The unit costs on a normal costing basis are as follows:

Manufacturing costs (per unit):
| | |
|---|---|
| Direct materials (1.5 kilograms × $2) | $ 3.00 |
| Direct labour (2 hours × $9) | 18.00 |
| Variable overhead (2 hours × $2.50) | 5.00 |
| Fixed overhead (2 hours × $3.25) | 6.50 |
| Total | $32.50 |

Nonmanufacturing costs:
| | |
|---|---|
| Variable | 15% of sales |
| Fixed | $230,000 |

During the year, the company had the following activity:

| | |
|---|---|
| Units produced | 30,000 |
| Units sold | 27,400 |
| Unit selling price | $50 |
| Direct labour hours worked | 60,000 |

Actual fixed overhead was $10,000 greater than budgeted fixed overhead. Actual variable overhead was $5,000 greater than budgeted variable overhead. The company used an expected actual activity level of 60,000 direct labour hours to compute the predetermined overhead rates. Any overhead variances are closed to Cost of Goods Sold.

**Required:**
1. Compute the unit cost using (a) absorption costing, and (b) variable costing.
2. Prepare an absorption-costing income statement.
3. Prepare a variable-costing income statement.
4. Reconcile the difference between the two income statements.

**8–46**

Comprehensive
Review Problem:
Variable Costing,
Absorption Costing,
Segmented Reporting

LO1, LO3

The Clock Division of Thurmond Company produces both wall clocks and table clocks. The clocks are sold in two regions, the West and the East. The table below gives the division's sales (in units) during 2004.

| | West | East | Total |
|---|---|---|---|
| Wall clocks | 100,000 | 250,000 | 350,000 |
| Table clocks | 250,000 | 520,000 | 770,000 |

Production data for 2004 are as follows (there were no beginning or ending work-in-process inventories):

| | Wall Clocks | Table Clocks |
|---|---|---|
| Production | 300,000 | 800,000 |
| Direct labour hours | 30,000 | 40,000 |
| Manufacturing costs: | | |
| Direct materials | $450,000 | $720,000 |
| Direct labour | 210,000 | 200,000 |
| Variable overhead | 60,000 | 90,000 |
| Fixed overhead* | 360,000 | 540,000 |

* Common fixed overhead of $280,000 has been allocated to the two products on the basis of actual direct labour hours and is included in each total.

The selling prices are $4.50 for wall clocks and $3 for table clocks. Variable nonmanufacturing costs are 20 percent of the selling price for wall clocks and 30 percent of the selling price for table clocks. Total fixed nonmanufacturing costs are $300,000, with one-third common to both products and one-third traceable directly to each product. Of the fixed costs (both manufacturing and nonmanufacturing), 20 percent are common to both sales regions, 40 percent are traceable directly to the West, and 40 percent are traceable directly to the East.

Overhead is applied on the basis of direct labour hours. Normal volume is 75,000 hours (300,000 wall clocks, 900,000 table clocks), and the preceding actual overhead figures correspond to the budgeted figures used to compute the predetermined overhead rate. Any under- or overapplied overhead is closed to Cost of Goods Sold. Assume that any beginning finished goods inventory has the same unit costs as current production. The company uses FIFO to value inventories.

### Required:

1. Compute the unit costs for each product using (a) absorption costing, and (b) variable costing.
2. Prepare absorption-costing and variable-costing income statements for 2004. Reconcile the difference between the two income figures.
3. Prepare a segmented income statement on a variable-costing basis where segments are defined as products.
4. Prepare a segmented income statement on a variable-costing basis where segments are defined as sales regions.

## Managerial Decision Cases

**8–47**

*Choice of Costing System*

**LO1, LO2, LO4**

Lougheed Custom Furniture Manufacturers Ltd. has been expanding rapidly over the past two years. During that time, the company's accounting staff consisted of one bookkeeper who was assisted frequently by the company's auditors. Because of the recent expansion, Lougheed's president, Ron Stokes, believes that it is necessary to hire a controller and also to expand the accounting staff by two additional clerks. At the same time, Stokes believes that the current accounting system should be revised to make it more flexible for planning and control purposes.

The current system at Lougheed is simple. Actual costs of material, labour, and overhead items are accumulated as incurred. Periodic inventory counts are made annually for financial statement preparation. Inventories are costed at average annual cost.

Furniture production at Lougheed is a combination of standard frames and springs and custom covering. The furniture design (that is, frame, springs, and so on) is limited to several types, whereas the upholstery for the furniture is custom-made to order.

Stokes believes that some form of job-order costing, perhaps with a predetermined overhead rate, may be advisable. Also, he wonders whether the company could benefit from a variable-costing system of the sort described to him at a recent managerial seminar. Since Stokes is considering entering the institutional market (that is, hotels, hospitals) on a special-order basis, he believes that a new system that would give him a better idea of his costs would be beneficial.

Stokes discussed the subject with his bookkeeper, Ravi Singh, who was not as enthusiastic about the changes. Singh argued that variable costing provided results as arbitrary as absorption costing and, moreover, did not give the full cost of products, something that was needed for pricing and financial reporting. Job-order costing, Singh felt, was too time consuming.

Stokes decided to hire a consultant to recommend a new accounting system for Lougheed.

**Required:**

As the consultant, prepare a short report analyzing the costs and benefits of an appropriate accounting system for Lougheed, considering the nature of the business described. (CMA Canada adapted)

**8–48**

Ethical Issues,
Absorption Costing,
Performance
Measurement
LO1, LO2

Ruth Swazey, division controller and CMA, was upset by a recent memo she had received from the divisional manager, Anton Grebov. Ruth was scheduled to present the division's financial performance at headquarters in one week. In the memo, Anton had given Ruth some instructions for this upcoming report. In particular, she had been told to emphasize the significant improvement in the division's profits over last year. Ruth, however, didn't believe that there was any real underlying improvement in the division's performance and was reluctant to say otherwise. She knew that the increase in profits was a result of Anton's conscious decision to produce for inventory.

In an earlier meeting, Anton had convinced his plant managers to produce more than they knew they could sell. He argued that if they deferred some of this period's fixed costs, reported profits would jump. He pointed out two significant benefits. First, by increasing profits, the division could exceed the minimum level needed so that all the managers would qualify for the annual bonus. Second, by meeting the budgeted profit level, the division would be better able to compete for much-needed capital. Ruth had objected but had been overruled. The most persuasive counterargument was that the increase in inventory could be liquidated in the coming year as the economy improved. Ruth, however, considered this event unlikely. From past experience, she knew that it would take at least two years of improved market demand before the division's productive capacity was exceeded.

**Required:**

1. Discuss the behaviour of Anton Grebov, the divisional manager. Was the decision to produce for inventory an ethical one?
2. What should Ruth Swazey do? Should she comply with the directive to emphasize the increase in profits? If not, what options does she have?
3. In Chapter 1, ethical standards for management accountants were discussed. Identify any standards that apply in this situation.

**8–49**

Variable Costing
versus Absorption
Costing
LO1, LO2, LO4

Norma Richardson, manager of a division specializing in concrete pipe and concrete blocks, had just been rebuffed by Eric Hipple, the company's president. Eric had called a meeting of all divisional managers to discuss the downturn in business the company had been experiencing during the past two years. Eric had come down hard on the managers, pointing out that their jobs would be on the line if some immediate improvements were not forthcoming.

Norma, acting as spokesperson for the divisional managers, had tried to explain to Eric why revenues and profits were declining. In the divisional managers' view, business was suffering because residential and commercial construction was down. With the slump in the construction business, competition had intensified. Norma indicated that her division had lost several bids to competitors who were bidding below the full cost of the product. Since company policy prohibited divisional managers from accepting any jobs below full cost, these bids were lost. Norma, on behalf of the managers, requested a change in the company policy concerning bids. She proposed that the floor for bids be changed to variable cost rather than full cost. In times of economic distress, bids that covered at least their variable costs would make a positive contribution toward covering fixed costs and help maintain the divisions' profits.

Norma also proposed that divisional income statements be changed to a variable-costing basis so that a better picture of divisional performance would be available. Additionally, income statements for individual products, organized on a variable-costing basis, would provide better information concerning product performance and would facilitate bidding.

Upon hearing the request, Eric Hipple flatly turned it down. Eric was convinced that all costs must be covered or the company would go under. "It's impossible to sell a product for less than what it costs and stay in business. Those companies that do so will be the first ones to go bankrupt. Also, I want to see the income produced by your divisions when all costs are considered—not just variable costs. I don't believe in variable costing. If any of you can prove to me that variable costing is a better approach, I would consider changing."

Upon returning home, Norma decided to prepare more formal arguments to convince Eric of the value of variable costing. To help in building her case, she had the divisional controller supply the following information concerning the concrete block line.

| | |
|---|---|
| Last quarter's production (and sales) | 100,000 |
| Productive capacity | 140,000 |
| Unit manufacturing cost: | |
|    Direct materials | $0.22 |
|    Direct labour | 0.14 |
|    Variable overhead | 0.09 |
|    Fixed overhead* | 0.10 |
|      Total | $0.55 |
| Nonmanufacturing costs: | |
|   Selling costs: | |
|    Fixed | $10,000 |
|    Variable | 5% of sales |
|   Administrative (all fixed) | $20,000 |

\* Based on the productive capacity of 140,000 units.

Total fixed overhead costs were $14,000 (budgeted and actual). Variable overhead was incurred as expected. Overhead variances are closed to Cost of Goods Sold. The average selling price for the 100,000 units sold was $0.90.

**Required:**

1. Prepare absorption-costing and variable-costing income statements for the last quarter's results. Will this information help Norma in building her case?
2. Suppose that Norma consults her marketing manager and finds that the division could have produced and sold 30,000 more concrete blocks with a unit selling price of $0.54. Compute the gross margin on the sale of these additional 30,000 blocks, assuming a price of $0.54. Now compute the total contribution margin on the 30,000 blocks. Discuss why the two figures differ.
3. Prepare absorption-costing and variable-costing income statements that reflect the sale of the additional 30,000 units at $0.54. Which figure in Requirement 2, gross margin or contribution margin, gave the best indication of the impact of the 30,000 additional units on the division's profits? Explain.
4. What approach would you take to convince Eric that variable costing is a useful managerial tool? Does he have any basis for his contention that a company must cover its full costs and that income statements should reflect all costs, not just variable costs? Explain.

## Research Assignment

**8–50**

Choose one or more of the following Web sites:

- www.generalmills.com
- www.pepsico.com
- www.ual.com
- www.deere.com
- www.ahp.com

Identify the types of segments for which it would be useful for the company to have income information. Now, check the company's annual report. Is the income statement reported by segment? Do the segments match your earlier identification? Why or why not? Next check the format of the income statement given in the annual report. Is it an absorption-costing or variable-costing income statement?

# Cost–Volume–Profit Analysis: A Managerial Planning Tool

**After studying Chapter 9, you should be able to:**

1. Determine the number of units that must be sold to break even or to earn a targeted profit.

2. Determine the amount of revenue required to break even or to earn a targeted profit.

3. Apply cost–volume–profit analysis in a multiple-product setting.

4. Prepare a profit–volume graph and a cost–volume–profit graph, and explain the meaning of each.

5. Explain the impact of risk, uncertainty, and changing variables on cost–volume–profit analysis.

6. Discuss the impact of activity-based costing on cost–volume–profit analysis.

## Scenario

For years, Janet McFarland's friends and family raved about her home-made jellies and salsas. Janet traditionally canned several litres of salsa, ladled it into decorative small jars, wrapped them, and sent them as gifts. Her friends said, "You ought to sell this stuff—you'd make a fortune!" So Janet decided to give it a try.

First, she decided to concentrate on one product, a green cactus salsa that had gotten rave reviews. She scouted sources of jars, lids, and labels. In addition, Janet got in touch with her local agricultural extension office and learned a considerable amount about laws regulating food

sales. One surprise was that she was required to obtain an expert confirmation of the ingredients in her salsa. Usually, Janet added a little of this and a little of that until it tasted right. She found out that this casual approach would not work. Foods were required to be labelled with the name of each ingredient, in order of amount. Suddenly, it mattered whether ancho or poblano chilis were used, and in what proportion. Janet needed a standardized recipe. She located a professional food chemist to analyze the recipe and certify the proportion of ingredients.

Janet travelled to a number of grocery stores and gift shops in the area. Several were willing to stock her product on consignment, plac-

ing a few jars by the cash register; others guaranteed shelf space but required a shelf charge for it. She figured that travelling to the stores, checking on sales and stock, and visiting prospective customers would take about one day a week.

Before starting production, Janet consulted with Bob Ryan, her family accountant.

**Janet**: "Bob, I'm really excited about this opportunity—it all seems to be falling into place."

**Bob**: "I'm happy for you, too, Janet. But first let's do some planning. I need to look at the costs and selling price you anticipate."

**Janet**: "I think I can charge $3.50 per jar. It's a new product, and I want to build a market for it. The costs I've come up with are on this sheet. They aren't as high as they could be, since I'm going to start slowly and cook small batches at a time in our kitchen."

**Bob** (after a couple of minutes of figuring): "Janet, do you realize that at a price of $3.50, and with the variable costs you described, you'll lose money? You can't do that."

**Janet**: "What if I sell more jars? Will that help?"

**Bob**: "No, that will just make it worse. Let's go back to the drawing board and see if there's a way to decrease those variable costs and/or increase the price. Otherwise, you would be better off never getting involved with this business."

### Questions to Think About

1. What kinds of variable and fixed costs do you think Janet will incur?

2. Give Bob's initial assessment that the variable costs are higher than the price, what is wrong with Janet's thought that selling more is the way to go?

3. How important is breakeven analysis to a company? Do you suppose that large companies as well as small companies do breakeven analysis?

4. Why is the concept of breaking even important? Doesn't Janet want to make a profit?

5. Janet doesn't know what price to charge. How could she get a better idea?

Cost–volume–profit analysis (CVP analysis) is a powerful tool for planning and decision making. Because CVP analysis emphasizes the interrelationships of costs, quantity sold, and price, it brings together all of the company's financial information. CVP analysis can be a valuable tool for identifying the extent and magnitude of the economic trouble a division is facing and for helping to pinpoint the necessary solution. For example, SAAB was on the brink of collapse in 1990 when General Motors bought a 50 percent share in the company. Over the last few years, SAAB has cut costs dramatically and lowered its breakeven point from 130,000 cars to 80,000 cars.[1]

We can use CVP analysis to address many issues—such as the number of units that must be sold to break even; the impact of a given reduction in fixed costs on the breakeven point; and the impact of an increase in price on profit. Additionally, CVP analysis allows managers to do a sensitivity analysis by examining the impact of various price or cost levels on profit.

While this chapter deals with the mechanics and terminology of CVP analysis, you should keep in mind that CVP analysis is an integral part of financial planning and decision making. Every accountant and manager should be thoroughly conversant with its concepts, not just the mechanics.

## Breakeven Point in Units

### Objective 1

Determine the number of units that must be sold to break even or to earn a targeted profit.

**breakeven point**

The point where total sales revenue equals total costs; the point of zero profits.

Since we are interested in how revenues, expenses, and profits behave as volume changes, it is natural to begin by finding the company's breakeven point in units sold. The **breakeven point** is the point at which total revenue equals total cost—the point of zero profit. To find the breakeven point in units, we focus on operating income. We will first discuss the way to find the breakeven point, and then see how our approach can be expanded to determine the number of units that must be sold to earn a targeted profit.

The company's first step in implementing a units-sold approach to CVP analysis is the determination of just what a unit is. For manufacturing companies, the answer is obvious. Procter & Gamble may define a unit as a bar of Ivory soap. Service organizations face a more difficult choice. Air Canada may define a unit

1. James Bennet, "Eurocars: On the Road Again," *New York Times*, 20 August 1995, 3: pp. 1, 10.

as a passenger kilometre, or as a one-way trip. Each company will define a unit consistent with its particular circumstances.

The next step centres on the separation of costs into fixed and variable components. CVP analysis focuses on the factors that effect a *change* in the components of profit. Because we are looking at CVP analysis in terms of units sold, we need to determine the fixed and variable components of cost and revenue with respect to units. This assumption will be relaxed when we incorporate activity-based costing into CVP analysis. It is important to realize that we are focusing on the company as a whole. Therefore, the costs we are talking about are *all* of the company's costs—manufacturing, marketing, and administrative. Thus, variable costs refer to all costs that increase as more units are sold, including direct materials, direct labour, variable overhead, and variable selling and administrative costs. Similarly, fixed costs include fixed overhead and fixed selling and administrative expenses.

## Using Operating Income in CVP Analysis

The income statement is a useful tool for organizing the company's costs into fixed and variable categories. The income statement can be expressed as a narrative equation:

Operating income = Sales revenues − Variable expenses − Fixed expenses

**operating income**
Revenues minus expenses from the company's normal operations. Income taxes are excluded.

Note that we are using the term operating income to denote income or profit *before* income taxes. **Operating income** includes only revenues and expenses from the company's normal operations. We will use the term **net income** to mean operating income minus income taxes.

**net income**
Operating income less income taxes.

Once we have a measure of units sold, we can expand the operating-income equation by expressing sales revenues and variable expenses in terms of unit dollar amounts and number of units. Specifically, sales revenue is expressed as the unit selling price multiplied by the number of units sold, and total variable costs are the unit variable cost multiplied by the number of units sold. With these expressions, the operating-income equation becomes:

Operating income = (Price × Units) − (Variable cost per unit × Units) − Total fixed cost

Suppose you are asked how many units must be sold to break even or earn a zero profit. You can answer this question by setting operating income to zero and then solving the operating-income equation for the number of units.

We will use the following example to illustrate how to solve for the breakeven point in units. Assume that Whittier Company manufactures a mulching lawn mower. For the coming year, the company's projected income statement is:

| | |
|---|---|
| Sales (1,000 units × $400) | $400,000 |
| Less: Variable expenses | 325,000 |
| Contribution margin | $ 75,000 |
| Less: Fixed expenses | 45,000 |
| Operating income | $ 30,000 |

We see that for Whittier Company, the price is $400 per unit, and the variable cost is $325 ($325,000/1,000 units). Fixed cost is $45,000. At the breakeven point, then, the operating-income equation would take the following form:

$$0 = (\$400 \times \text{Units}) - (\$325 \times \text{Units}) - \$45,000$$
$$0 = (\$75 \times \text{Units}) - \$45,000$$
$$\$75 \times \text{Units} = \$45,000$$
$$\text{Units} = 600$$

Therefore, Whittier must sell 600 lawn mowers to just cover all fixed and variable expenses. We can check this answer by preparing an income statement based on 600 units sold.

| | |
|---|---|
| Sales (600 units × $400) | $240,000 |
| Less: Variable expenses | 195,000 |
| Contribution margin | $ 45,000 |
| Less: Fixed expenses | 45,000 |
| Operating income | $     0 |

Indeed, selling 600 units does yield a zero profit.

An important advantage of the operating-income approach is that all further CVP equations are derived from the variable-costing income statement. Any CVP problem can be solved by using this approach.

## Shortcut to Calculating Breakeven Units

**contribution margin**

Sales revenue minus total variable cost.

We can more quickly calculate breakeven units by focusing on the contribution margin. The **contribution margin** is sales revenue minus total variable cost. At breakeven, the contribution margin equals the fixed expenses. If we substitute the unit contribution margin for price minus unit variable cost in the operating-income equation and solve for the number of units, we obtain the following fundamental breakeven equation:

Number of units = Fixed cost/Unit contribution margin

Using Whittier Company as an example, we can see that the contribution margin per unit can be computed in one of two ways. One way is to divide the total contribution margin by the units sold for a result of $75 per unit ($75,000/1,000). A second way is to compute price minus variable cost per unit. Doing so yields the same result, $75 per unit ($400 – $325).

To calculate the breakeven number of units for Whittier Company, the breakeven equation is:

Number of units = $45,000/($400 – $325)
= $45,000/$75 per unit
= 600 units

Of course, the answer is identical to that computed using the operating-income equation.

## Unit Sales Needed to Achieve Targeted Profit

While the breakeven point is useful information, most companies would like to earn an operating income greater than zero. CVP analysis gives us a way to determine how many units must be sold to earn a particular targeted income. Targeted operating income can be expressed as a dollar amount (for example, $20,000) or as a percentage of sales revenue (for example, 15 percent of revenue). Both the operating-income approach and the contribution margin approach can be easily adjusted to allow for targeted income.

### *Targeted Income as a Dollar Amount*

Assume that Whittier Company wants to earn an operating income of $60,000. How many mulching mowers must be sold to achieve this result? The income statement can be used to find out:

$ 60,000 = ($400 × Units) – ($325 × Units) – $45,000
$105,000 = $75 × Units
Units = 1,400

If instead the breakeven equation is used, targeted profit of $60,000 is added to the fixed cost before solving for the number of units.

$$\text{Units} = (\$45{,}000 + \$60{,}000)/(\$400 - \$325)$$
$$= \$105{,}000/\$75$$
$$= 1{,}400$$

Whittier must sell 1,400 lawn mowers to earn a before-tax profit of $60,000. The following income statement verifies this outcome:

| | |
|---|---:|
| Sales (1,400 units × $400) | $560,000 |
| Less: Variable expenses | 455,000 |
|    Contribution margin | $105,000 |
| Less: Fixed expenses | 45,000 |
|    Operating income | $ 60,000 |

Another way to check this number of units is to use the breakeven point. As just shown, Whittier must sell 1,400 lawn mowers, or 800 more than the break-even volume of 600 units, to earn an operating income of $60,000. The contribution margin per lawn mower is $75. Multiplying $75 by the 800 lawn mowers *above* breakeven produces the targeted operating income: $60,000 ($75 × 800). This outcome demonstrates that contribution margin per unit for each unit above breakeven is equivalent to operating income per unit. Since the breakeven point had already been computed, the number of lawn mowers to be sold to yield a $60,000 operating income could have been calculated by dividing the unit contribution margin into the target operating income and adding the resulting amount to the breakeven volume.

In general, assuming that fixed costs remain the same, the impact on a company's operating income resulting from a change in the number of units sold can be assessed by multiplying the unit contribution margin by the change in units sold. For example, if 1,500 lawn mowers instead of 1,400 are sold, how much more operating income will be earned? The change in units sold is an increase of 100 lawn mowers, and the unit contribution margin is $75. Thus, operating income will increase by $7,500 ($75 × 100).

### Targeted Income as a Percentage of Sales Revenue

Assume that Whittier Company wants to know the number of lawn mowers that it must sell to earn a profit equal to 15 percent of sales revenue. Sales revenue is price multiplied by the quantity sold. Thus, the targeted operating income is 15 percent of price times quantity. Using the income statement (which is simpler in this case), we have the following:

$$0.15 \times (\$400 \times \text{Units}) = (\$400 \times \text{Units}) - (\$325 \times \text{Units}) - \$45{,}000$$
$$\$60 \times \text{Units} = (\$400 \times \text{Units}) - (\$325 \times \text{Units}) - \$45{,}000$$
$$\$60 \times \text{Units} = (\$75 \times \text{Units}) - \$45{,}000$$
$$\$15 \times \text{Units} = \$45{,}000$$
$$\text{Units} = 3{,}000$$

Does a volume of 3,000 lawn mowers achieve a profit equal to 15 percent of sales revenue? For 3,000 lawn mowers, the total revenue is $1.2 million ($400 × 3,000). The profit can be computed without preparing a formal income statement. Remember that above breakeven, the contribution margin per unit is the increase in profit per unit. The breakeven volume is 600 lawn mowers. If 3,000 lawn mowers are sold, then 2,400 (3,000 − 600) lawn mowers above the breakeven point are sold. Operating income, therefore, is $180,000 ($75 × 2,400), which is 15 percent of sales ($180,000/$1,200,000).

## After-Tax Profit Targets

When calculating the breakeven point, income taxes play no role. This is because the taxes paid on zero income are zero. However, when the company needs to know how many units it must sell to earn a particular net income, some additional consideration is needed. Recall that net income is operating income after income taxes, and that our targeted income figure was expressed in before-tax terms. As a result, when the income target is expressed as net income, we must add back the income taxes to obtain operating income.

To illustrate this idea, we will assume that taxes are computed as a percentage of income. After-tax profit is computed by subtracting the tax from the operating income (or before-tax profit).

$$\text{Net income} = \text{Operating income} - \text{Taxes}$$
$$= \text{Operating income} - (\text{Tax rate} \times \text{Operating income})$$
$$= \text{Operating income}\,(1 - \text{Tax rate})$$

or

$$\text{Operating income} = \text{Net income}/(1 - \text{Tax rate})$$

Thus, to convert the after-tax profit to before-tax profit, we simply divide the after-tax profit by (1 − Tax rate).

Suppose that Whittier Company wants to achieve a net income of $48,750 and that its tax rate is 35 percent. To convert the after-tax profit target into a before-tax profit target, we complete the following steps:

$$\$48,750 = \text{Operating income} - (0.35 \times \text{Operating income})$$
$$\$48,750 = 0.65 \times \text{Operating income}$$
$$\text{Operating income} = \$75,000$$

In other words, with a tax rate of 35 percent, Whittier Company must earn $75,000 before taxes to have $48,750 after taxes.[2] With this conversion, we can now calculate the number of units that must be sold:

$$\text{Units} = (\$45,000 + \$75,000)/\$75$$
$$\text{Units} = \$120,000/\$75$$
$$\text{Units} = 1,600$$

Let's check this answer by preparing an income statement based on sales of 1,600 lawn mowers.

| | |
|---|---|
| Sales (1,600 × $400) | $640,000 |
| Less: Variable expenses | 520,000 |
| Contribution margin | $120,000 |
| Less: Fixed costs | 45,000 |
| Operating income | $ 75,000 |
| Less: Taxes (35% tax rate) | 26,250 |
| Net income | $ 48,750 |

---

2. To practise the after-tax to before-tax conversion, calculate how much before-tax income Whittier would need to have $48,750 after-tax income if the tax rate were 40 percent. (Answer: $81,250)

## Breakeven Point in Sales Dollars

**Objective 2**

Determine the amount of revenue required to break even or to earn a targeted profit.

In some cases, managers may prefer to use sales revenues as the measure of sales activity instead of units sold. A units-sold measure can be converted to a sales revenue measure simply by multiplying the unit selling price by the units sold. For example, the breakeven point for Whittier Company was computed at 600 mulching mowers. Since the selling price for each lawn mower is $400, the breakeven volume in sales revenue is $240,000 ($400 × 600).

Any answer expressed in units sold can be easily converted to one expressed in sales revenues, but we can compute the answer more directly by developing a separate formula for the sales revenue case. In this case, the important variable is sales dollars, so both the revenue and the variable costs must be expressed in sales dollars instead of units. Since sales revenue is always expressed in dollars, measuring that variable is no problem. Let's look more closely at variable costs and see how we can express them in terms of sales dollars.

To calculate the breakeven point in sales dollars, variable costs are defined as a percentage of sales rather than as an amount per unit sold. In our example, Whittier Company's selling price is $400 per unit and its variable cost is $325 per unit. Thus we can express Whittier's variable cost as 0.8125 of the selling price or 81.25 percent. This 81.25 percent is the **variable-cost ratio**. It is simply the proportion of each sales dollar that must be used to cover variable costs.[3] The percentage of sales dollars remaining after variable costs are covered is the **contribution margin ratio**. The contribution margin ratio is the proportion of each sales dollar available to cover fixed costs and provide for profit. It makes sense that the complement of the variable-cost ratio is the contribution margin ratio. After all, the proportion of the sales dollar left after variable costs are covered should be the contribution margin component.

Where do fixed costs fit into this? Since the contribution margin is revenue remaining after variable costs are covered, it must be the revenue available to cover fixed costs and contribute to profit. There are three possibilities: fixed cost can equal contribution margin; fixed cost can be less than contribution margin; or fixed cost can be greater than contribution margin. When fixed cost is equal to contribution margin, profit is zero and the company is at breakeven. When fixed cost is less than contribution margin, the company earns a profit. Finally, when fixed cost is greater than contribution margin, the company faces an operating loss.

Let's turn to some examples based on Whittier Company to illustrate the sales revenue approach. Whittier Company's variable-costing income statement for 1,000 lawn mowers follows:

**variable-cost ratio**

Variable costs divided by sales revenues. It is the proportion of each sales dollar needed to cover variable costs.

**contribution margin ratio**

Contribution margin divided by sales revenue. It is the proportion of each sales dollar available to cover fixed costs and provide for profit.

|  | **Dollars** | **Percent of Sales** |
|---|---|---|
| Sales | $400,000 | 100.00% |
| Less: Variable expenses | 325,000 | 81.25% |
| Contribution margin | $ 75,000 | 18.75% |
| Less: Fixed expenses | 45,000 |  |
| Operating income | $ 30,000 |  |

Note that sales revenue, variable costs, and contribution margin are expressed as a percent of sales. The variable cost ratio is 0.8125 ($325,000/$400,000); the contribution margin ratio is 0.1875 (computed either as 1 − 0.8125, or $75,000/$400,000). Fixed costs are $45,000.

---

3.  We can also calculate the variable cost ratio from the information in Whittier Company's variable-costing income statement. The projected income statement for 1,000 units shows variable expenses of $325,000 for sales of $400,000. Thus, variable expenses are 81.25 percent of revenues ($325,000/$400,000). Repeat this calculation for the income statement with 1,400 units. Can you explain why it is the same answer?

Given the information in this income statement, how much sales revenue must Whittier earn to break even?

$$\text{Operating income} = \text{Sales} - \text{Variable costs} - \text{Fixed costs}$$
$$0 = \text{Sales} - (\text{Variable cost ratio} \times \text{Sales}) - \text{Fixed costs}$$
$$0 = \text{Sales} - (1 - \text{Variable cost ratio}) - \text{Fixed costs}$$
$$0 = \text{Sales} - (1 - 0.8125) - \$45,000$$
$$\text{Sales} \times (0.1875) = \$45,000$$
$$\text{Sales} = \$240,000$$

Thus, Whittier must earn revenues totalling $240,000 in order to break even. To check this answer, prepare an income statement based on revenue of $240,000 and verify that it yields zero profit. Note that $(1 - 0.8125)$ is the contribution margin ratio. We can skip a couple of steps by recognizing that *Sales – (Variable cost ratio × Sales)* is equal to *Sales × Contribution margin ratio*.

What about the breakeven equation used to determine the breakeven point in units? We can use that approach here as well. At the breakeven point, operating income is:

$$\text{Sales} = \text{Variable cost} + \text{Fixed cost}$$
$$\text{Sales} = \text{Variable cost ratio} \times \text{Sales} + \text{Fixed cost}$$
$$\text{Sales} - (\text{Variable cost ratio} \times \text{Sales}) = \text{Fixed cost}$$
$$\text{Sales} \times (1 - \text{Variable cost ratio}) = \text{Fixed cost}$$
$$\text{Sales} \times \text{Contribution margin ratio} = \text{Fixed cost}$$
$$\text{Sales} = \text{Fixed cost}/\text{Contribution margin ratio}$$

Again using Whittier Company data, the breakeven sales dollars would be computed as ($45,000/0.1875) or $240,000. This is the same answer, arrived at by a slightly different approach.

## Profit Targets and Sales Revenue

Consider the following question: How much sales revenue must Whittier generate to earn a before-tax profit of $60,000? This question is similar to the one we asked earlier with regard to units, but this time the question is phrased directly in terms of sales revenue. To answer the question, add the targeted operating income of $60,000 to the $45,000 of fixed cost, and divide the total by the contribution margin ratio:

$$\text{Sales} = (\$45,000 + \$60,000)/0.1875$$
$$= \$105,000/0.1875$$
$$= \$560,000$$

Whittier must earn revenues equal to $560,000 to achieve a profit target of $60,000. Since breakeven is $240,000, additional sales of $320,000 ($560,000 – $240,000) must be earned above breakeven. Note that multiplying the contribution margin ratio by revenues above breakeven yields the profit of $60,000 (0.1875 × $320,000). Above breakeven, the contribution margin ratio is a profit ratio; therefore, it represents the proportion of each sales dollar assignable to profit. In this example, every sales dollar earned above breakeven increases profits by $0.1875.

In general, assuming that fixed costs remain unchanged, the contribution margin ratio can be used to find the profit impact of a change in sales revenue. To obtain the total change in profits from a change in revenues, simply multiply the contribution margin ratio times the change in sales. For example, if sales revenues are $540,000 instead of $560,000, how will the expected profits be affected? A decrease in sales revenues of $20,000 will cause a decrease in profits of $3,750 (0.1875 × $20,000).

## Comparison of the Two Approaches

For a single-product setting, converting the breakeven point in units to breakeven in sales revenue is simply a matter of multiplying the unit selling price by the units sold. Then why bother with a separate formula for the sales revenue approach? There are two reasons. First, the formula for sales revenue allows us to solve directly for revenue if that is what is desired. Second, the sales revenue approach is much simpler to use in a multiple-product setting, as we will see in the next section.

## Multiple Product Analysis

**Objective 3**

Apply cost–volume–profit analysis in a multiple-product setting.

Cost–volume–profit analysis is fairly simple in the single-product setting. However, most companies produce and sell a number of different products or services. Even though the conceptual complexity of CVP analysis does increase with multiple products, the operation is reasonably straightforward. Let's see how we can adapt the formulas we used in a single-product setting to the multiple-product setting by expanding the Whittier Company example.

Suppose Whittier Company has decided to offer two models of lawn mowers: a mulching mower that will sell for $400, and a riding mower that will sell for $800. The marketing department is convinced that 1,200 mulching mowers and 800 riding mowers can be sold during the coming year. The following projected income statement based on the sales forecast is prepared:

| | Mulching Mower | Riding Mower | Total |
|---|---|---|---|
| Sales | $480,000 | $640,000 | $1,120,000 |
| Less: Variable expenses | 390,000 | 480,000 | 870,000 |
| Contribution margin | $ 90,000 | $160,000 | $ 250,000 |
| Less: Direct fixed expenses | 30,000 | 40,000 | 70,000 |
| Product margin | $ 60,000 | $120,000 | $ 180,000 |
| Less: Common fixed expenses | | | 26,250 |
| Operating income | | | $ 153,750 |

Note that direct fixed expenses have been separated from common fixed expenses. Direct fixed expenses are those fixed costs that can be traced to each segment and that would be avoided if the segment did not exist. Common fixed expenses are the fixed costs that are not traceable to the segments and that would remain even if one of the segments was eliminated.

## Breakeven Point in Units

Whittier's management is somewhat apprehensive about adding a new product line and wants to know how many of each model must be sold to break even. One possible response to this question is to use the equation we developed earlier in which fixed costs were divided by the contribution margin. This equation presents some immediate problems, however. It was developed for a single-product analysis. For two products, there are two unit contribution margins. The mulching mower has a contribution margin per unit of $75 ($400 – $325), and the riding mower has one of $200 ($800 – $600).[4]

---

4. We derive the variable cost per unit from the income statement. For the riding mower, total variable costs are $480,000 based on sales of 800 units. This yields a per-unit variable cost of $600 ($480,000/800). A similar computation produces the per-unit variable cost for the mulching mower.

One possible solution is to apply the analysis separately to each product line. We would then obtain individual breakeven points with profit defined as product margin. Breakeven for the mulching mower is as follows:

Mulching mower breakeven units = Fixed cost/Contribution margin
= $30,000/$75
= 400 units

We can compute a breakeven for the riding mower as well:

Riding mower breakeven units = Fixed cost/Contribution margin
= $40,000/$200
= 200 units

Thus, 400 mulching mowers and 200 riding mowers must be sold to achieve a breakeven product margin. But a breakeven product margin covers only direct fixed costs; the common fixed costs are not covered. Selling these numbers of lawn mowers would result in a loss equal to the common fixed costs. We have not identified a breakeven point for the company as a whole. Somehow the common fixed costs must be factored into the analysis.

We could allocate the common fixed costs to each product line (in proportion to sales, for example) before computing a breakeven point to resolve this difficulty. The problem with this approach is that allocation of the common fixed costs is arbitrary. We would find a different breakeven point for every different allocation. Thus, no meaningful breakeven volume is readily apparent.

Another possible solution is to convert the multiple-product problem into a single-product problem. If we can do this, then we can apply all of the single-product CVP methodology directly. The key to this conversion is to identify the expected *sales mix*, in units. **Sales mix** is the relative combination of products being sold by a company.

**sales mix**

The relative combination of products (or services) being sold by an organization.

### Determining the Sales Mix

The sales mix can be measured in units sold or in proportion of revenue. For example, if Whittier plans on selling 1,200 mulching mowers and 800 riding mowers, then the sales mix in units is 1,200:800. Usually, the sales mix is reduced to the smallest possible whole numbers. Thus, the relative mix 1,200:800 can be reduced to 12:8 and further to 3:2. That is, for every three mulching mowers sold, two riding mowers are sold.

Alternatively, the sales mix can be represented by the percentage of total revenue contributed by each product. In that case, the mulching mower revenue is $480,000 and the riding mower revenue is $640,000. The mulching mower accounts for 42.86 percent of total revenue, and the riding mower accounts for the remaining 57.14 percent.

It may seem as though the two sales mixes are different. The sales mix in units is 3:2; that is, of every five mowers sold, 60 percent are mulching mowers and 40 percent are riding mowers. However, the revenue-based sales mix is 42.86 percent for the mulching mowers. What is the difference? The sales mix in revenue takes the sales mix in units and weights it by price. Therefore, even though the underlying proportion of mowers sold remains 3:2, the lower-priced mulching mowers are weighted less heavily when price is factored in. For CVP analysis, we will use the sales mix expressed in units.

A number of different sales mixes can be used to define the breakeven volume. For example, a sales mix of 2:1 will define a different breakeven point than a 1:1 sales mix. Fortunately, every sales mix need not be considered. Can Whittier really expect a sales mix of 2:1 or 1:1? For every two mulching mowers sold, does Whittier expect to sell a riding mower? Or for every mulching mower, can Whittier really sell one riding mower? According to Whittier's marketing study, a sales mix of 3:2 can be expected. That is the ratio that should be used; others can be ignored. The sales mix we expect to prevail should be used for CVP analysis.

### Sales Mix and CVP Analysis

When we define a particular sales mix, we convert a multiple-product problem into a single-product CVP format. We can use the 3:2 sales mix to define a single product as a *package* containing three mulching mowers and two riding mowers.[5] To use the single-product breakeven-point-in-units approach, we must calculate the package's selling price and the variable cost per package. To compute these package values, the sales mix, the individual product prices, and the individual variable costs are needed. Given the individual product data found in the projected income statement, we can compute the package values as follows:

| Product | Price | Unit Variable Cost | Unit Contribution Margin | Sales Mix | Package Unit Contribution Margin |
|---|---|---|---|---|---|
| Mulching | $400 | $325 | $ 75 | 3 | $225[a] |
| Riding | 800 | 600 | 200 | 2 | 400[b] |
| Package total | | | | | $625 |

[a] The number of these units in the package (3) multiplied by its unit contribution margin ($75).
[b] The number of these units in the package (2) multiplied by its unit contribution margin ($200).

Given the package contribution margin, we can use the breakeven equation to determine the number of packages that are needed to break even. From Whittier's projected income statement, we know that the total fixed costs for the company are $96,250. Thus, the breakeven point is as follows:

$$\text{Breakeven packages} = \text{Fixed cost/Package contribution margin}$$
$$= \$96,250/\$625$$
$$= 154 \text{ packages}$$

Whittier must sell 462 mulching mowers (3 × 154) and 308 riding mowers (2 × 154) to break even. An income statement verifying this solution is presented in Exhibit 9–1.

For a given sales mix, we can use CVP analysis as if the company were selling a single product. However, actions that change the prices of individual products can affect the sales mix because consumers may buy relatively more or less of the product. Accordingly, pricing decisions may involve a new sales mix and must reflect this possibility. Keep in mind that a new sales mix will affect the units of each product that need to be sold in order to achieve a desired profit target. If the sales mix for the coming period is uncertain, it may be necessary to look at several different mixes. In this way, a manager can gain some insight into the possible outcomes facing the company.

The complexity of the breakeven-point-in-units approach increases dramatically as the number of products increases. Imagine performing this analysis for a company with several hundred products. Fortunately, this task seems more overwhelming than it actually is. Computers can easily handle a problem with this much data. Furthermore, many companies simplify the problem by analyzing product groups rather than individual products. Another way to handle the increased complexity is to switch from the units-sold approach to the sales revenue approach. The latter approach can accomplish a multiple-product CVP analysis using only the summary data found in an organization's income statement. The computational requirements are much simpler.

---

5.  Of course, individual customers may purchase different mixes of mulching and riding mowers. We use the overall sales mix in our analysis.

EXHIBIT 9-1

Breakeven Solution
Income Statement

|  | Mulching Mower | Riding Mower | Total |
|---|---|---|---|
| Sales | $184,800 | $246,400 | $431,200 |
| Less: Variable expenses | 150,150 | 184,800 | 334,950 |
| Contribution margin | $ 34,650 | $ 61,600 | $ 96,250 |
| Less: Direct fixed expenses | 30,000 | 40,000 | 70,000 |
| Segment margin | $ 4,650 | $ 21,600 | $ 26,250 |
| Less: Common fixed expenses |  |  | 26,250 |
| Operating income |  |  | $ 0 |

## Sales Dollars Approach

To illustrate the breakeven point in sales dollars, we will use the same examples. However, the only information we need is the projected income statement for Whittier Company as a whole.

| Sales | $1,120,000 |
|---|---|
| Less: Variable expenses | 870,000 |
| Contribution margin | $ 250,000 |
| Less: Fixed expenses | 96,250 |
| Operating income | $ 153,750 |

Notice that this income statement corresponds to the total column of the more detailed income statement we examined previously. The projected income statement rests on the assumption that 1,200 mulching mowers and 800 riding mowers will be sold (a 3:2 sales mix). The breakeven point in sales revenue also rests on the expected sales mix. (As with the units-sold approach, each different sales mix will produce a different result.)

We can address the usual CVP questions. For example, how much sales revenue must be earned to break even? To answer this question, we divide the total fixed cost of $96,250 by the contribution margin ratio of 0.2232 ($250,000/$1,120,000):

$$\text{Breakeven sales} = \text{Fixed cost/Contribution margin ratio}$$
$$= \$96,250/0.2232$$
$$= \$431,228[6]$$

The breakeven point in sales dollars implicitly uses the assumed sales mix but we avoid the requirement of building a package contribution margin. No knowledge of individual product data is needed. The computational effort is similar to that used in the single-product setting. Moreover, the answer is still expressed in sales revenue. Unlike the breakeven point in units, the answer to CVP questions using sales dollars is still expressed in a single summary measure. The sales revenue approach, however, does sacrifice information concerning individual product performance.

---

6. The sales volume is slightly overstated because of rounding in the contribution margin ratio. The exact answer is $431,200 (obtained by multiplying the package selling price [$2,800] by the 154 packages needed to break even). We can use more decimal places in the contribution margin ratio to calculate the exact answer, but the difference is unlikely to be significant to a manager's decision.

## Graphical Representation of CVP Relationships

**Objective 4**

Prepare a profit–volume graph and a cost–volume–profit graph, and explain the meaning of each.

We may better understand CVP relationships if we see them portrayed visually. A graphical representation can help managers see the difference between variable cost and revenue. It may also help them understand quickly what impact an increase or decrease in sales will have on the breakeven point. We present two basic graphs: the *profit–volume graph* and the *cost–volume–profit graph*.

### The Profit–Volume Graph

**profit–volume graph**

A graph that depicts the relationship between profits and sales volume.

A **profit–volume graph** visually portrays the relationship between profits and sales volume. The profit–volume graph is the graph of the operating-income equation:

Operating income = (Price × Units) – (Unit variable cost × Units) – Fixed cost

In this graph, the dependent variable is operating income; the independent variable is units. Usually, the values of the independent variable are measured along the horizontal axis and the values of the dependent variable along the vertical.

To make this discussion more concrete, we will use a simple set of data. Assume that Tyson Company produces a single product with the following cost and price data:

| | |
|---|---|
| Total fixed costs | $100 |
| Variable costs per unit | 5 |
| Selling price per unit | 10 |

Using these data, we can express operating income as:

$$\text{Operating income} = (\$10 \times \text{Units}) - (\$5 \times \text{Units}) - \$100$$
$$= (\$5 \times \text{Units}) - \$100$$

We can graph this relationship by plotting units along the horizontal axis and operating income (or loss) along the vertical axis. Two points are needed to graph a linear equation. While any two points will do, we often choose the points that correspond to zero sales volume and zero profits. When units sold are zero, Tyson experiences an operating loss of $100 (or a profit of –$100). The point corresponding to zero sales volume, therefore, is (0, –$100). In other words, when no sales take place, the company suffers a loss equal to its total fixed costs. When operating income is zero, the units sold are equal to 20. The point corresponding to zero profits (breakeven) is (20, $0). These two points, plotted in Exhibit 9–2, define the profit–volume graph.

We can use the graph in Exhibit 9–2 to assess Tyson's operating income (or loss) at any level of sales activity. For example, we can read the operating income associated with the sale of 40 units from the graph by (1) drawing a vertical line from the horizontal axis to the profit line, and (2) drawing a horizontal line from the profit line to the vertical axis. As we see in Exhibit 9–2, the operating income associated with sales of 40 units is $100. But the profit–volume graph, while easy to interpret, fails to reveal how costs change as sales volume changes. An alternative approach to graphing can provide this detail.

**cost–volume–profit graph**

A graph that depicts the relationships among costs, volume, and profits. It consists of a total revenue line and a total cost line.

### The Cost–Volume–Profit Graph

The **cost–volume–profit graph** depicts the relationships among cost, volume, and profits. To obtain the more detailed relationships, it is necessary to graph two

EXHIBIT 9-2

Profit–Volume Graph

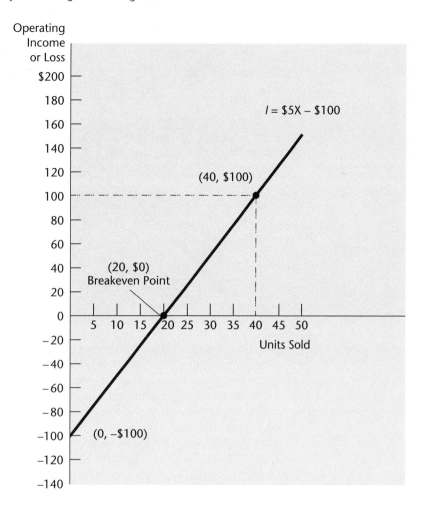

separate lines: the total revenue line and the total cost line. These two lines are represented, respectively, by the following two equations:

Revenue = Price × Units
Total cost = (Unit variable cost × Units) + Fixed cost

Using the Tyson Company example, we see that the revenue and cost equations are as follows:

Revenue = $10 × Units
Total cost = ($5 × Units) + $100

To portray both equations in the same graph, the vertical axis is measured in dollars and the horizontal axis in units sold.

Two points are needed to graph each equation. We will use the same *x*-coordinates as in the profit–volume graph. For the revenue equation, setting number of units equal to 0 results in revenue of $0; setting number of units equal to 20 results in revenue of $200. Therefore, the two points for the revenue equation are (0, $0) and (20, $200). For the cost equation, units sold of 0 and units sold of 20 produce the points (0, $100) and (20, $200). The graph of each equation appears in Exhibit 9–3.

Note that the total revenue line begins at the origin and rises with a slope equal to the selling price per unit (a slope of 10). The total cost line intercepts the vertical axis at a point equal to total fixed costs and rises with a slope equal to the variable cost per unit (a slope of 5). When the total revenue line lies below the total cost line, a loss region is defined. Similarly, when the total revenue line lies

EXHIBIT  9-3

Cost–Volume–Profit Graph

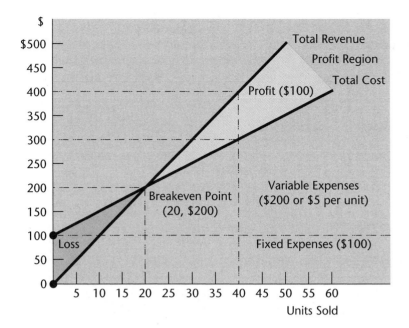

above the total cost line, a profit region is defined. The point where the total revenue line and the total cost line intersect is the breakeven point. To break even, Tyson Company must sell 20 units and, thus, receive $200 total revenues.

Now let's compare the information available from the CVP graph with that available from the profit–volume graph. To make this comparison, consider the sale of 40 units. Recall that the profit–volume graph in Exhibit 9–2 revealed that this sale will produce profits of $100. Now examine Exhibit 9–3 again. The CVP graph also shows profits of $100, but it reveals more as well. The CVP graph discloses that total revenues of $400 and total costs of $300 are associated with the sale of 40 units. Furthermore, the total costs can be broken down into fixed costs of $100 and variable costs of $200. The CVP graph provides revenue and cost information not provided by the profit–volume graph. Unlike the profit–volume graph, some computation is needed to determine the profit associated with a given sales volume. Nonetheless, because of the greater information content, managers are likely to find the CVP graph a more useful tool.

## ✳Assumptions of Cost–Volume–Profit Analysis

The profit–volume and cost–volume–profit graphs just illustrated rely on some important assumptions. Some of these assumptions are as follows:

1. The analysis assumes a linear revenue function and a linear cost function.
2. The analysis assumes that price, total fixed costs, and unit variable costs (a) can be accurately identified, and (b) remain constant over the relevant range.
3. The analysis assumes that all production is sold.
4. For multiple-product analysis, the sales mix is assumed to be known.
5. The selling prices and costs are assumed to be known with certainty.

### Linear Functions

Our first assumption, linear cost and revenue functions, deserves additional consideration. Let's look at the underlying total revenue and total cost functions identified in economics. In Exhibit 9–4, Panel A portrays curvilinear revenue and cost functions. As quantity sold increases, revenue also increases, but eventually it begins to rise less steeply than before. This pattern is explained quite simply by the need to decrease price for more units to be sold. The total cost function is more complicated, rising steeply at first, then levelling off somewhat (as increasing returns to scale develop), and then rising steeply again (as decreasing returns to scale develop). How can we deal with these complicated relationships?

### Relevant Range

Fortunately, we do not need to consider all possible ranges of production and sales for a company. Remember that CVP analysis is a short-run decision-making tool. (We know it is short run in orientation because some costs are fixed.) It is only necessary to determine the current operating range, or relevant range, for which the linear cost and revenue relationships are valid. In Exhibit 9–4, Panel B illustrates a relevant range from 5,000 to 15,000 units. Note that the cost and revenue relationships are roughly linear in this range, allowing us to use our linear CVP equations. Of course, if the relevant range changes, different fixed and variable costs and different prices must be used.

**EXHIBIT  9-4**

The Relevant Range

Panel A: Curvilinear CVP Relationships

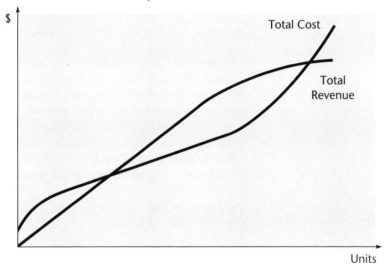

Panel B: Relevant Range and Linear CVP Relationships

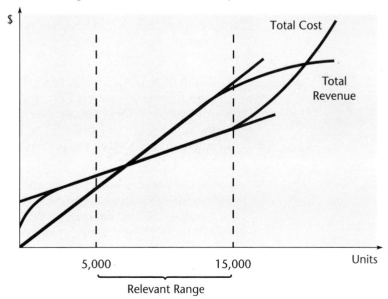

Our second assumption is linked to the definition of relevant range. Once a relevant range has been identified, the cost and price relationships are assumed to be known and constant.

### Production Equal to Sales

Our third assumption is that all production is sold. This means that there is no change in the quantity of inventory over the period. It makes sense that inventory has no impact on breakeven analysis. Breakeven analysis is a short-run decision-making technique, so it is concerned with covering all costs related to a particular time period. Inventory embodies costs from a previous period and is therefore not considered. This, of course, is also what we saw when we examined variable-costing net income.

### Constant Sales Mix

In single-product analysis, the sales mix is obviously constant—the one product is 100 percent of sales. Multiple-product breakeven analysis also requires a constant sales mix. However, it is virtually impossible to predict the sales mix with certainty. Typically, this constraint is handled in practice through sensitivity analysis. By using the capabilities of spreadsheet analysis, the sensitivity of variables to a variety of sales mixes can be readily assessed.

### Prices and Costs Known with Certainty

In actuality, companies seldom know prices, variable costs, and fixed costs with certainty. A change in one variable usually affects the value of others. CVP analysis is used to obtain insight into the relationships among crucial variables that affect profitability. This kind of insight helps the manager in planning, budgeting, and decision making. Often there is a probability distribution to contend with. Furthermore, there are formal ways of explicitly building uncertainty into the CVP model. Exploration of these issues is introduced in the next section.

## Changes in the CVP Variables

**Objective 5**

Explain the impact of risk, uncertainty, and changing variables on cost–volume–profit analysis.

Because companies operate in a dynamic world, they must be aware of changes in prices, variable costs, and fixed costs. They must also account for the effect of risk and uncertainty. We will now examine the effect of changes in price, unit contribution margin, and fixed cost on the breakeven point and look at how managers can handle risk and uncertainty within the CVP framework.

Suppose that Whittier Company recently conducted a market study that revealed three different alternatives:

1. Alternative 1: An $8,000 increase in advertising expenditures will increase sales from 1,600 units to 1,725 units.
2. Alternative 2: A price decrease from $400 to $375 per lawn mower will increase sales from 1,600 units to 1,900 units.
3. Alternative 3: Decreasing prices to $375 and increasing advertising expenditures by $8,000 will increase sales from 1,600 units to 2,600 units.

Should Whittier maintain its current price and advertising policies, or should it select one of the three alternatives described by the marketing study?

Consider the first alternative. What is the effect on profits if advertising costs increase by $8,000 and sales increase by 125 units? This question can be answered by employing the contribution margin per unit. We know that the unit contribution margin is $75. Since units sold increase by 125, the incremental increase in total contribution margin is $9,375 ($75 × 125 units). However, since fixed costs increase by $8,000, the incremental increase in operating income is only $1,375

($9,375 – $8,000). Exhibit 9–5 summarizes the effects of the first alternative. ˹
that we need to look only at the incremental increase in total contribution margin
and fixed expenses to compute the increase in total operating income.

| | Before the Increased Advertising | With the Increased Advertising |
|---|---|---|
| Units sold | 1,600 | 1,725 |
| Unit contribution margin | × $75 | × $75 |
| Total contribution margin | $120,000 | $129,375 |
| Less: Fixed expenses | 45,000 | 53,000 |
| Operating income | $ 75,000 | $ 76,375 |

| | Difference in Operating Income |
|---|---|
| Change in sales volume | 125 |
| Unit contribution margin | × $75 |
| Change in contribution margin | $9,375 |
| Less: Increase in fixed expenses | 8,000 |
| Increase in operating income | $1,375 |

For the second alternative, fixed expenses do not increase. Thus, it is possible
to answer the question by looking only at the effect on total contribution margin.
For the current price of $400, the contribution margin per unit is $75. If 1,600 units
are sold, the total contribution margin is $120,000 ($75 × 1,600). If the price is
dropped to $375, then the contribution margin drops to $50 per unit ($375 – $325).
If 1,900 units are sold at the new price, then the new total contribution margin is
$95,000 ($50 × 1,900). Dropping the price results in an operating income decline of
$25,000 ($120,000 – $95,000). The effects of the second alternative are summarized
in Exhibit 9–6.

The third alternative calls for a decrease in the unit selling price and an
increase in advertising costs. As with the first alternative, we can assess this alternative's impact on operating income by looking at the incremental effects on contribution margin and fixed expenses. The incremental profit change can be found
by (1) computing the incremental change in total contribution margin, (2) computing the incremental change in fixed expenses, and (3) adding the two results.

| | Before the Proposed Price Change | With the Proposed Price Decrease |
|---|---|---|
| Units sold | 1,600 | 1,900 |
| Unit contribution margin | × $75 | × $50 |
| Total contribution margin | $120,000 | $95,000 |
| Less: Fixed expenses | 45,000 | 45,000 |
| Operating income | $ 75,000 | $50,000 |

| | Difference in Operating Income |
|---|---|
| Change in contribution margin ($95,000 – $120,000) | $(25,000) |
| Less: Change in fixed expenses | 0 |
| Decrease in operating income | $(25,000) |

As shown, the current total contribution margin (for 1,600 units sold) is $120,000. Since the new unit contribution margin is $50, the new total contribution margin is $130,000 ($50 × 2,600 units). Thus, the incremental increase in total contribution margin is $10,000 ($130,000 − $120,000). However, to achieve this incremental increase in contribution margin, an incremental increase of $8,000 in fixed costs is needed. The net effect is an incremental increase in operating income of $2,000. The effects of the third alternative are summarized in Exhibit 9–7.

Of the three alternatives identified by the marketing study, the one that promises the most benefit is the third. It increases total operating income by $2,000. The first alternative increases operating income by only $1,375, and the second actually decreases operating income by $25,000.

These examples are all based on a units-sold approach. However, we could just as easily have applied a sales revenue approach. The resulting answers would be the same.

**EXHIBIT   9-7**

Summary of the Effects of Alternative 3

| | Before the Proposed Price and Advertising Change | With the Proposed Price Decrease and Advertising Increase |
|---|---|---|
| Units sold | 1,600 | 2,600 |
| Unit contribution margin | × $75 | × $50 |
| Total contribution margin | $120,000 | $130,000 |
| Less: Fixed expenses | 45,000 | 53,000 |
| Operating income | $ 75,000 | $ 77,000 |

| | Difference in Operating Income |
|---|---|
| Change in contribution margin ($130,000 − $120,000) | $10,000 |
| Less: Change in fixed expenses ($53,000 − $45,000) | 8,000 |
| Increase in operating income | $ 2,000 |

## Introducing Risk and Uncertainty

An important assumption of CVP analysis is that prices and costs are known with certainty. However, this is seldom the case. Risk and uncertainty are unavoidable in business decision making and cannot simply be ignored. Formally, risk differs from uncertainty: under risk, the probability distributions of the variables are known, whereas under uncertainty, they are not known. For our purposes, however, the terms will be used interchangeably.

How do managers deal with risk and uncertainty? There are a variety of methods. First, management must realize the uncertain nature of future prices, costs, and quantities. Next, managers move from considering a breakeven point to considering what might be called a breakeven band. In other words, given the uncertain nature of the data, a company might break even, for example, when 1,800 to 2,000 units are sold instead of at the point estimate of 1,900 units. Further, managers may engage in sensitivity or what-if analysis. In this, a computer spreadsheet is helpful, allowing managers to set up the breakeven (or targeted profit) relationships and then check to see the impact that varying costs and prices have on quantity sold. Two concepts useful to management are *margin of safety* and *operating leverage*. Both of these may be considered measures of risk. Each requires knowledge of fixed and variable costs.

### Margin of Safety

The **margin of safety** is the units sold (or expected to be sold) or the revenue earned (or expected to be earned) above the breakeven volume. For example, if a company's breakeven volume is 200 units and the company is currently selling

**margin of safety**

The units sold or expected to be sold or sales revenue earned or expected to be earned above the breakeven volume.

500 units, then the margin of safety is 300 units (500 – 200). The margin of safety can be expressed in sales revenue as well. If the breakeven revenue is $200,000 and current revenue is $350,000, then the margin of safety is $150,000.

The margin of safety can be viewed as a crude measure of risk. There are always events, unknown when plans are made, that can lower sales below the original expected level. If a company's margin of safety is large given the expected sales for the coming year, the risk of suffering losses should sales take a downward turn is less than if the margin of safety is small. Managers who face a low margin of safety may wish to consider actions to increase sales or decrease costs. These steps will increase the margin of safety and lower the risk of incurring losses.

### Operating Leverage

In physics, a lever is a simple machine used to multiply force. Basically, the lever multiplies the effort applied, thereby creating more work. Operating leverage is concerned with the relative mix of fixed costs and variable costs in an organization. It is sometimes possible to trade off fixed costs for variable costs. As variable costs decrease, the unit contribution margin increases, making the contribution of each unit sold that much greater. In such a case, the effect of fluctuations in sales on profitability increases. Thus, companies that have achieved lower variable costs by increasing the proportion of fixed costs will benefit with greater increases in profits as sales increase than will companies with a lower proportion of fixed costs. Fixed costs are being used as leverage to increase profits. Unfortunately, it is also true that companies with a higher operating leverage will also experience greater reductions in profits if sales decrease. Therefore, **operating leverage** is the use of fixed costs to extract higher percentage changes in operating income as sales activity changes.

The greater the degree of operating leverage, the greater will be the effect of changes in sales activity on operating income. Because of this phenomenon, the mix of costs that an organization chooses can have a considerable influence on its operating risk and operating income.

The **degree of operating leverage (DOL)** is measured for a given level of sales by taking the ratio of contribution margin to operating income, as follows:

Degree of operating leverage = Contribution margin/Operating income

If fixed costs are used to lower variable costs such that contribution margin increases, then the degree of operating leverage increases—signalling an increase in risk.

To illustrate the application of these concepts, consider Cedilla Company, a company which is planning to add a new product line. In adding the line, Cedilla can choose to rely heavily on automation or on labour. If the company chooses to emphasize automation rather than labour, fixed costs will be higher and unit variable costs will be lower. Relevant data for a sales level of 10,000 units follow:

**operating leverage**

The use of fixed costs to extract higher percentage changes in profits as sales activity changes. Leverage is achieved by increasing fixed costs while lowering variable costs.

**degree of operating leverage (DOL)**

A measure of the sensitivity of profit change to changes in sales volume. It measures the percentage change in profits resulting from a percentage change in sales.

|  | Automated System | Manual System |
|---|---|---|
| Sales | $1,000,000 | $1,000,000 |
| Less: Variable expenses | 500,000 | 800,000 |
| Contribution margin | $  500,000 | $  200,000 |
| Less: Fixed expenses | 375,000 | 100,000 |
| Operating income | $  125,000 | $  100,000 |
| Unit selling price | $100 | $100 |
| Unit variable expense | 50 | 80 |
| Unit contribution margin | 50 | 20 |

The degree of operating leverage for the automated system is 4.0 ($500,000/$125,000). The degree of operating leverage for the manual system is 2.0 ($200,000/$100,000). What happens to operating income in each system if sales increase by 40 percent? The following income statements show the resulting change:

|  | **Automated System** | **Manual System** |
|---|---|---|
| Sales | $1,400,000 | $1,400,000 |
| Less: Variable expenses | 700,000 | 1,120,000 |
| Contribution margin | $ 700,000 | $ 280,000 |
| Less: Fixed expenses | 375,000 | 100,000 |
| Operating income | $ 325,000 | $ 180,000 |

Operating income for the automated system would increase by $200,000 ($325,000 – $125,000), a 160 percent increase. This can be calculated by multiplying the 40 percent sales increase by the degree of operating leverage (40% × 4.0 = 160%). In the manual system, operating income increases by only $80,000 ($180,000 – $100,000), an 80 percent increase (40% × 2.0). The automated system has a greater percentage increase because it has a higher degree of operating leverage.

In choosing between the two systems, the effect of operating leverage is a valuable piece of information. As the 40 percent increase in sales illustrates, this effect can bring a significant benefit to Cedilla. However, the effect is a two-edged sword. As sales decrease, the automated system will also show much higher percentage decreases. Moreover, the increased operating leverage is available under the automated system because of the presence of increased fixed costs. The breakeven point for the automated system is 7,500 units ($375,000/$50), whereas the breakeven point for the manual system is 5,000 units ($100,000/$20). Thus, the automated system has greater operating risk. The increased risk, of course, provides a potentially higher profit level (as long as units sold exceed 9,167).[7]

In choosing between the automated and the manual systems, Cedilla's manager must assess the likelihood that sales will exceed 9,167 units. If, after careful study, there is a strong belief that sales will easily exceed this level, the choice is obvious: the automated system. On the other hand, if sales are unlikely to exceed 9,167 units, the manual system is preferable. Exhibit 9–8 summarizes the relative differences between the manual and the automated systems in terms of some of the CVP concepts.

## Sensitivity Analysis and CVP

**sensitivity analysis**

The "what-if" process of altering certain key variables to assess the effect on the original outcome.

The pervasiveness of personal computers and spreadsheets has placed sensitivity analysis within reach of most managers. An important tool, **sensitivity analysis** is a "what-if" technique that examines the impact changes in underlying assumptions will have on an answer. It is relatively simple to input data on prices, variable costs, fixed costs, and sales mix and to set up formulas to calculate breakeven points and expected profits. Then the data can be varied as desired to see what impact changes have on the expected income.

In the preceding example on operating leverage, the Cedilla Company analyzed the impact on profit of using an automated versus a manual system. The computations were done by hand, an approach that makes it cumbersome to introduce much variation. Using the power of a computer, it would be an easy matter to change the sales price in $1 increments between $75 and $125, with related assumptions about quantity sold. At the same time, variable and fixed costs could be adjusted. For example, suppose that the automated system has

---

7. We can compute this benchmark by setting the operating income equations equal and solving for units: $50 × units – $375,000 = $20 × units – $100,000; units = 9,167.

EXHIBIT 9-8

Differences between
Manual and Automated
Systems

|  | Manual System | Automated System |
|---|---|---|
| Price | Same | Same |
| Variable cost | Relatively higher | Relatively lower |
| Fixed cost | Relatively lower | Relatively higher |
| Contribution margin | Relatively lower | Relatively higher |
| Breakeven point | Relatively lower | Relatively higher |
| Margin of safety | Relatively higher | Relatively lower |
| Degree of operating leverage | Relatively lower | Relatively higher |
| Downside risk | Relatively lower | Relatively higher |
| Upside potential | Relatively lower | Relatively higher |

fixed costs of $375,000, but that those costs could easily range up to twice as high in the first year, coming back down in the second and third years as bugs are worked out of the system and workers learn to use it. Again, a spreadsheet can effortlessly handle the many computations.

Finally, while the spreadsheet is wonderful for cranking out numerical answers, it cannot do the most difficult job in CVP analysis. That job is determining the data to be entered in the first place. The accountant must be cognizant of the company's cost and price distributions, as well as of the impact of changing economic conditions on these variables. The fact that variables are seldom known with certainty is no excuse for ignoring the impact of uncertainty on CVP analysis. Fortunately, sensitivity analysis can also give managers a feel for the degree to which a poorly forecasted variable will affect an answer.

## CVP Analysis and Activity-Based Costing

**Objective 6**

Discuss the impact of activity-based costing on cost–volume–profit analysis.

Conventional CVP analysis assumes that all costs of the company can be divided into two categories: those that vary with sales volume (variable costs) and those that do not (fixed costs). Further, costs are assumed to be a linear function of sales volume. However, many companies now realize that this fixed-versus-variable distinction is too simplistic.

In an activity-based costing system, costs are divided into unit- and nonunit-based categories. Activity-based costing acknowledges that some costs vary with units produced and some costs do not. However, while activity-based costing acknowledges that nonunit-based costs are fixed with respect to production volume changes, it also argues that many nonunit-based costs vary with respect to other activity drivers.

The use of activity-based costing does not mean that CVP analysis is less useful. In fact, it becomes more useful, since it provides more accurate insights concerning cost behaviour. These insights produce better decisions. However, within an activity-based framework, CVP analysis must be modified. To illustrate, assume that Serif Company's costs can be explained by three variables: a unit-level activity driver (units sold), a batch-level activity driver (number of setups), and a product-level activity driver (engineering hours). We can express the ABC cost equation as follows:

$$\text{Total cost} = \text{Fixed cost} + (\text{Unit variable cost} \times \text{Number of units}) \\ + (\text{Setup cost} \times \text{Number of setups}) + (\text{Engineering cost} \\ \times \text{Number of engineering hours})$$

Operating income, as before, is total revenue minus total cost. This is expressed as:

$$\text{Operating income} = \text{Total revenue} - [\text{Fixed cost} + (\text{Unit variable cost} \\ \times \text{Number of units}) + (\text{Setup cost} \times \text{Number of setups}) \\ + (\text{Engineering cost} \times \text{Number of engineering hours})]$$

We can use the contribution margin approach to calculate the breakeven point in units. At breakeven, operating income is zero, and the number of units that must be sold to achieve breakeven is as follows:

$$\text{Breakeven units} = [\text{Fixed cost} + (\text{Setup cost} \times \text{Number of setups}) \\ + (\text{Engineering cost} \times \text{Number of engineering hours})]/ \\ (\text{Price} - \text{Unit variable cost})$$

When we compare the ABC breakeven point with the conventional breakeven point we see two significant differences. First, the fixed costs differ. Some costs previously identified as being fixed may actually vary with nonunit-level drivers—in this case, setups and engineering hours. Second, the numerator of the ABC breakeven equation has two nonunit-level variable-cost terms: one for batch-related activities and one for product-sustaining activities.

## Example Comparing Conventional and ABC Analysis

To make this discussion more concrete, a comparison of conventional cost–volume–profit analysis with activity-based costing is useful. Assume that Galliard Company wants to compute the units that must be sold to earn a before-tax income of $20,000. The analysis is based on the following data:

| Activity Driver | Variable Cost | Level of Activity Driver |
|---|---|---|
| Units sold | $ 10 | — |
| Setups | 1,000 | 20 |
| Engineering hours | 30 | 1,000 |
| Other data: | | |
|   Total fixed costs (conventional) | | $100,000 |
|   Total fixed costs (ABC) | | 50,000 |
|   Unit selling price | | 20 |

Using CVP analysis, the units that Galliard must sell to earn an operating income of $20,000 are computed as follows:

$$\begin{aligned}
\text{Number of units} &= (\text{Targeted income} + \text{Fixed cost})/(\text{Price} - \text{Unit variable cost}) \\
&= (\$20,000 + \$100,000)/(\$20 - \$10) \\
&= \$120,000/\$10 \\
&= 12,000 \text{ units}
\end{aligned}$$

Using the ABC equation, the units that Galliard must sell to earn an operating income of $20,000 are computed as follows:

$$\begin{aligned}
\text{Number of units} &= [\$20,000 + \$50,000 + (\$1,000 \times 20) + (\$30 \times 1,000)]/(\$20 - \$10) \\
&= \$120,000/\$10 \\
&= 12,000 \text{ units}
\end{aligned}$$

The number of units that Galliard Company must sell is identical under both approaches. The reason is simple. The total fixed-cost pool under conventional costing consists of nonunit-based variable costs plus costs that are fixed regardless of the activity driver. ABC breaks out the nonunit-based variable costs. These costs are associated with certain levels of each activity driver. For the batch-level activity driver, the level is 20 setups; for the product-level variable, the level is 1,000 engineering hours. As long as the activity levels for the nonunit-based cost drivers remain the same, the results for the conventional and ABC computations will be the same. But these levels can change; as a result, the information provided by the two approaches can be significantly different. The ABC equation for CVP analysis is a richer representation of the underlying cost behaviour and can provide important strategic insights. To see this, let's use the same data to look at a different application.

## Strategic Implications: Conventional CVP Analysis versus ABC Analysis

Suppose that after the conventional CVP analysis, Galliard Company's marketing department indicates that selling 12,000 units is not possible. In fact, only 10,000 units can be sold. The company's president then directs its product design engineers to find a way to reduce the cost of making the product. The engineers have also been told that the conventional cost equation, with fixed costs of $100,000 and unit variable costs of $10, holds. The variable cost of $10 per unit consists of the following: direct labour, $4; direct materials, $5; and variable overhead, $1. To comply with the request to reduce the breakeven point, engineering produces a new design that requires less labour. The new design would reduce the direct labour cost by $2 per unit, but would not affect materials or variable overhead. Thus, the new variable cost is $8 per unit, and the breakeven point is calculated as follows:

$$\text{Number of units} = \text{Fixed cost}/(\text{Price} - \text{Unit variable cost})$$
$$= \$100,000/(\$20 - \$8)$$
$$= 8,333 \text{ units}$$

The projected income if 10,000 units are sold is as follows:

| | |
|---|---|
| Sales ($20 × 10,000) | $200,000 |
| Less: Variable expenses ($8 × 10,000) | 80,000 |
| Contribution margin | $120,000 |
| Less: Fixed expenses | 100,000 |
| Operating income | $ 20,000 |

Excited, Galliard's president approves the new design. A year later, she discovers that the expected increase in income did not materialize. In fact, a loss is realized. Why? The answer is provided by an ABC approach to CVP analysis.

The original ABC cost relationship for the Galliard example follows:

$$\text{Total cost} = \$50,000 + (\$10 \times \text{Units}) + (\$1,000 \times \text{Setups})$$
$$+ (\$30 \times \text{Engineering hours})$$

Suppose that the new design requires a more complex setup, increasing the cost per setup from $1,000 to $1,600. Also suppose that the new design, because of increased technical content, requires a 40 percent increase in engineering support (from 1,000 hours to 1,400 hours). The new cost equation, including the reduction in unit-level variable costs, follows:

$$\text{Total cost} = \$50,000 + (\$8 \times \text{Units}) + (\$1,600 \times \text{Setups})$$
$$+ (\$30 \times \text{Engineering hours})$$

The breakeven point, setting operating income equal to zero and using the ABC equation, is calculated as follows (assume that 20 setups are still performed):

$$\text{Number of units} = [\$50,000 + (\$1,600 \times 20) + (\$30 \times 1,400)]/(\$20 - \$8)$$
$$= \$124,000/\$12$$
$$= 10,333 \text{ units}$$

And the income for 10,000 units is as follows (recall that a maximum of 10,000 can be sold):

| Sales ($20 × 10,000) | | $200,000 |
|---|---|---|
| Less: Unit-based variable expenses ($8 × 10,000) | | 80,000 |
|    Contribution margin | | $120,000 |
| Less: Nonunit-based variable expenses: | | |
|    Setups ($1,600 × 20) | $32,000 | |
|    Engineering support ($30 × 1,400) | 42,000 | 74,000 |
|    Traceable margin | | $ 46,000 |
| Less: Fixed expenses | | 50,000 |
|    Operating income (loss) | | $ (4,000) |

How could the engineers have been off by so much? Didn't they know that the new design would increase setup cost and engineering support? Yes and no. They were probably aware of the increases in these two variables, but the conventional cost equation diverted attention from figuring out just how much impact changes in those variables would have. The information conveyed by the conventional equation to the engineers gave the impression that any reduction in labour cost—as long as it didn't affect materials or variable overhead—would reduce total costs, since changes in the level of labour activity would not affect the fixed costs. The ABC equation, however, indicates that a reduction in labour input that adversely affects setup activity or engineering support might be undesirable. With more insight, better design decisions can be made. Providing ABC cost information to the design engineers would probably have led them down a different path—one that would have been more advantageous to the company.

## Summary of Learning Objectives

**1. Determine the number of units that must be sold to break even or to earn a targeted profit.**
In a single-product setting, the breakeven point can be computed in units by dividing the total fixed costs by the contribution margin per unit. In essence, sufficient units must be sold to just cover all fixed and variable costs of the company.

**2. Determine the amount of revenue required to break even or to earn a targeted profit.**
Breakeven revenue is computed by dividing the total fixed costs by the contribution margin ratio. Targeted profit is added to fixed costs in the numerator to calculate the amount of revenue needed to yield this targeted profit.

**3. Apply cost–volume–profit analysis in a multiple-product setting.**
Multiple-product analysis requires that we make an assumption concerning the expected sales mix. Given a particular sales mix, a multiple-product problem can be converted into a single-product analysis. However, we should remember that the answers change as the sales mix changes. If the sales

mix changes in a multiple-product company, the breakeven point will also change. In general, increases in the sales of products with high contribution margins will decrease the breakeven point, while increases in the sales of products with low contribution margins will increase the breakeven point.

**4. Prepare a profit–volume graph and a cost–volume–profit graph, and explain the meaning of each.**
CVP analysis is based on several assumptions that must be considered when applying it to business problems. The analysis assumes linear revenue and cost functions, no finished goods ending inventories, and a constant sales mix. CVP analysis also assumes that selling prices and fixed and variable costs are known with certainty. These assumptions form the basis for simple graphical analysis using the profit–volume graph and the cost–volume–profit graph.

**5. Explain the impact of risk, uncertainty, and changing variables on cost–volume–profit analysis.**
Measures of risk and uncertainty, such as the margin

of safety and operating leverage, can be used to give managers more insight into CVP answers. Sensitivity analysis provides still more insight into the effect of changes in underlying variables on CVP relationships.

### 6. Discuss the impact of activity-based costing on cost–volume–profit analysis.

CVP can be used with activity-based costing, but the analysis must be modified. Under ABC, a type of sensitivity analysis is used. Fixed costs are separated from costs that vary with particular cost drivers. At this stage, it is easiest to organize variable costs as unit-level, batch-level, and product-level. Then the impact of decisions on batches and products can be examined within the CVP framework.

The subject of cost–volume–profit analysis lends itself naturally to the use of numerous equations. Some of the more common equations used in this chapter are summarized in Exhibit 9–9.

---

**EXHIBIT 9-9**

Summary of Important Equations

1. Sales revenue = Price × Units
2. Operating income = (Price × Units) − (Unit variable cost × Units) − Fixed cost
3. Breakeven point in units = Fixed cost/(Price − Unit variable cost)
4. Contribution margin ratio = Contribution margin/Sales
   or = (Price − Unit variable cost)/Price
5. Variable cost ratio = Total variable cost/Sales
   or = Unit variable cost/Price
6. Breakeven point in sales dollars = Fixed cost/Contribution margin ratio
   or = Fixed cost/(1 − Variable cost ratio)
7. Margin of safety = Sales − Breakeven sales
8. Degree of operating leverage = Total contribution margin/Operating income
9. Percentage change in profits = Degree of operating leverage × % change in sales
10. Income taxes = Tax rate × Operating income
11. After-tax income = Operating income − (Tax rate × Operating income)
12. Before-tax income = After-tax income/(1 − Tax rate)
13. ABC total cost = Fixed cost + (Unit variable cost × Number of units) + (Batch-level cost × Batch driver) + (Product-level cost × Product driver)
14. ABC breakeven units = [Fixed cost + (Batch-level cost × Batch driver) + (Product-level cost × Product driver)]/(Price − Unit variable cost)

---

## Key Terms

| | | |
|---|---|---|
| Breakeven point 353 | Degree of operating leverage (DOL) 371 | Operating leverage 371 |
| Contribution margin 355 | Margin of safety 370 | Profit–volume graph 364 |
| Contribution margin ratio 358 | Net income 354 | Sales mix 361 |
| Cost–volume–profit graph 364 | Operating income 354 | Sensitivity analysis 372 |
| | | Variable-cost ratio 358 |

## Review Problems

### I. BREAKEVEN ANALYSIS

Cutlass Company's projected operating income for the coming year is as follows:

|                          | Total      | Per Unit |
|--------------------------|------------|----------|
| Sales                    | $200,000   | $20      |
| Less: Variable expenses  | 120,000    | 12       |
| Contribution margin      | $ 80,000   | $ 8      |
| Less: Fixed expenses     | 64,000     |          |
| Operating income         | $ 16,000   |          |

**Required:**

1. Compute the breakeven point in units.
2. How many units must be sold to earn an operating income of $30,000?
3. Compute the contribution margin ratio. Using that ratio, compute the additional operating income that Cutlass would earn if sales were $25,000 more than expected.
4. Suppose Cutlass would like to earn operating income equal to 20 percent of sales revenue. How many units must be sold for this goal to be realized? Prepare an income statement to prove your answer.
5. For the projected level of sales, compute the margin of safety.

**Solution**

1. The breakeven point is computed as follows:

$$\text{Units} = \text{Fixed cost}/(\text{Price} - \text{Unit variable cost})$$
$$= \$64,000/(\$20 - \$12)$$
$$= \$64,000/\$8$$
$$= 8,000 \text{ units}$$

2. The number of units that must be sold to earn an operating income of $30,000 is computed as follows:

$$\text{Units} = (\$64,000 + \$30,000)/\$8$$
$$= \$94,000/\$8$$
$$= 11,750 \text{ units}$$

3. The contribution margin ratio is $8/$20 = 0.40. With additional sales of $25,000, the additional operating income would be 0.40 × $25,000 = $10,000.
4. To find the number of units that must be sold to generate an operating income equal to 20 percent of sales, let target income equal (0.20 × Price × Units) and solve for units:

$$\text{Operating income} = (\text{Price} \times \text{Units}) - (\text{Unit variable cost} \times \text{Units}) - \text{Fixed cost}$$
$$0.2 \times \$20 \times \text{Units} = (\$20 \times \text{Units}) - (\$12 \times \text{Units}) - \$64,000$$
$$\$4 \times \text{Units} = \$64,000$$
$$\text{Units} = 16,000$$

The income statement is as follows:

| | |
|---|---|
| Sales (16,000 × $20) | $320,000 |
| Less: Variable expenses (16,000 × $12) | 192,000 |
| Contribution margin | $128,000 |
| Less: Fixed expenses | 64,000 |
| Operating income | $ 64,000 |

5. The margin of safety is 10,000 – 8,000 = 2,000 units, or $40,000 in sales revenues.

## II. BREAKEVEN ANALYSIS WITH ABC

Dory Manufacturing Company produces T-shirts screen-printed with the logos of various sports teams. Each shirt is priced at $10. Costs are as follows:

| Cost Driver | Unit Variable Cost | Level of Cost Driver |
|---|---|---|
| Units sold | $ 5 | — |
| Setups | 450 | 80 |
| Engineering hours | 20 | 500 |

Other data:

| | |
|---|---|
| Total fixed costs (conventional) | $96,000 |
| Total fixed costs (ABC) | 50,000 |

### Required:

1. Compute the breakeven point in units using conventional analysis.
2. Compute the breakeven point in units using activity-based analysis.
3. Suppose that Dory could reduce the setup cost by $150 per setup and the number of engineering hours needed to 425. How many units must be sold to break even in this case?

### Solution

1. Breakeven units = Fixed cost/(Price – Unit variable cost)
   = $96,000/($10 – $5)
   = 19,200 units

2. Breakeven units = [Fixed cost + (Setups × Setup cost) + (Engineering hours ×
                     Engineering cost)]/(Price – Unit variable cost)
   = [$50,000 + ($450 × 80) + ($20 × 500)]/($10 – $5)
   = 19,200 units

3. Breakeven units = [$50,000 + ($300 × 80) + ($20 × 425)]/($10 – $5)
   = $82,500/$5
   = 16,500 units

# Questions for Writing and Discussion

1. Explain how CVP analysis can be used for managerial planning.

2. Describe the difference between the units-sold approach to CVP analysis and the sales revenue approach.

3. Define the term *breakeven point*.

4. Explain why contribution margin per unit becomes profit per unit above the breakeven point.

5. If the contribution margin per unit is $7 and the breakeven point is 10,000 units, how much oper-ating income will a company make if 15,000 units are sold?

6. What is the variable cost ratio? the contribution margin ratio? How are the two ratios related?

7. Suppose a company has fixed costs of $20,000 and a contribution margin ratio of 0.4. How much sales revenue must the company have in order to break even?

8. Suppose a company with a contribution margin ratio of 0.3 increased its advertising expenses by $10,000 and found that sales increased by

$30,000. Was it a good decision to increase advertising expenses?

9. Define the term *sales mix* and give an example to support your definition.

10. Explain how CVP analysis developed for single products can be used in a multiple-product setting.

11. Assume that a company has two products—A and B. Last year, 2,000 units of A and 1,000 units of B were sold. The same sales mix is expected for the coming year. Total fixed expenses are $30,000, and the unit contribution margins are $10 for A and $5 for B. How many units of A and how many units of B must be sold to break even?

12. Makeba Company has a contribution margin ratio of 0.6. The breakeven point is $100,000. During the year, Makeba earned total revenues of $200,000. What was Makeba's operating income?

13. Explain how a change in sales mix can change a company's breakeven point.

14. Define the term *margin of safety*. Explain how it can be used as a crude measure of operating risk.

15. Explain what is meant by the term *operating leverage*. What impact does increased leverage have on risk?

16. How can sensitivity analysis be used in conjunction with CVP analysis?

17. Why does the activity-based costing approach to CVP analysis offer more insight than the conventional approach?

18. A company has a positive profit, $p$, at a given volume of sales, $x$. If $x$ doubles (within the relevant range), would profit be equal to $2p$, greater than $2p$, or less than $2p$? Explain.

# Exercises

**9–1**

**Breakeven Terminology**

**LO1**

Match a term from Column A with the correct definition in Column B.

| Column A | Column B |
|---|---|
| 1. Contribution margin | a. Sales minus total variable costs minus total fixed costs |
| 2. Contribution margin ratio | b. Total fixed costs divided by the contribution margin per unit |
| 3. Variable cost ratio | c. Contribution margin per unit divided by price |
| 4. Break-even units | d. Total variable cost divided by total revenue |
| 5. Operating income | e. Price minus variable cost per unit |

**9–2**

**Breakeven Terminology**

**LO1**

Suppose that Adams Company sells a product for $16. Unit costs are as follows:

| | |
|---|---|
| Direct materials | $3.90 |
| Direct labour | 1.40 |
| Variable overhead | 2.10 |
| Variable selling expenses | 1.60 |

Total fixed overhead is $52,000 per year, and total fixed selling and administrative expenses are $37,950.

**Required:**
Match a term from Column A with the correct number based on the above information for Adams Company in Column B.

| Column A | Column B |
|---|---|
| 1. Contribution margin | a. 12,850 |
| 2. Contribution margin ratio | b. 0.5625 |
| 3. Variable cost ratio | c. $9.00 |
| 4. Breakeven units | d. 0.4375 |
| 5. Prime cost per unit | e. $3.50 |
| 6. Conversion cost per unit | f. $7.00 |
| 7. Variable cost per unit | g. $5.30 |

**9–3**

*Breakeven in Units*

**LO1**

The controller of Dorian Company prepared the following projected income statement:

| | | |
|---|---|---|
| Sales (2,000 units × $25) | $50,000 | 25 |
| Less: Variable expenses | 30,000 | 15 |
| Contribution margin | $20,000 | 10 |
| Less: Fixed expenses | 18,000 | |
| Operating income | $ 2,000 | |

**Required:**
1. Calculate the breakeven number of units. _1500_
2. Prepare an income statement for Dorian at breakeven.
3. How many units must Dorian sell to earn operating income equal to $15,000?

**9–4**

*Contribution Margin Ratio, Variable-Cost Ratio, Breakeven in Sales Revenue*

**LO2**

Refer to 9–3 for data.

**Required:**
1. What is the contribution margin per unit for Dorian Company? What is the contribution margin ratio?
2. What is the variable-cost ratio for Dorian Company?
3. Calculate the breakeven revenue.
4. How much revenue must Dorian make to earn operating income equal to $15,000?

**9–5**

*Targeted Income as a Function of Sales*

**LO1**

Refer to 9–3 for data.

**Required:**
1. How many units must Dorian sell to earn operating income equal to 20 percent of revenue?
2. Prepare an income statement based on the number of units you calculated in Requirement 1 to prove your answer.

**9–6**

*After-tax Break Even*

**LO1**

Refer to 9–3 for data.

**Required:**
1. Assuming a tax rate of 40 percent, what is the before-tax income that Dorian must earn to have after-tax income equal to $7,200? How many units must Dorian sell to earn after-tax income equal to $7,200?
2. Assuming a tax rate of 50 percent, what is the before-tax income that Dorian must earn to have after-tax income equal to $7,200? How many units must Dorian sell to earn after-tax income equal to $7,200?
3. Assuming a tax rate of 30 percent, what is the before-tax income that Dorian must earn to have after-tax income equal to $7,200? How many units must Dorian sell to earn after-tax income equal to $7,200?

**9–7**

*Multiple-Product Breakeven*

LO3

Lacy Company manufactures two products. In the coming year, Lacy expects to sell 1,000 units of Product A and 3,000 units of Product B. A budgeted income statement for next year follows:

|  | Product A | Product B | Total |
|---|---|---|---|
| Sales | $10,000 | $36,000 | $46,000 |
| Less: Variable expenses | 6,000 | 27,000 | 33,000 |
| Contribution margin | $ 4,000 | $ 9,000 | $13,000 |
| Less: Direct fixed expenses | 1,500 | 3,200 | 4,700 |
| Product margin | $ 2,500 | $ 5,800 | $ 8,300 |
| Less: Common fixed expenses |  |  | 3,100 |
| Operating income |  |  | $ 5,200 |

**Required:**
1. What is the sales mix for Lacy Company?
2. Calculate the number of units of Product A and the number of units of Product B that Lacy must sell to break even.
3. Without forming a product package, calculate the breakeven revenue for Lacy Company.

**9–8**

*Margin of Safety and Degree of Operating Leverage*

LO5

Anjou Company has prepared the following income statement for the year:

| | |
|---|---|
| Sales ($50 × 8,000 units) | $400,000 |
| Less: Variable expenses | 140,000 |
| Contribution margin | $260,000 |
| Less: Fixed expenses | 119,925 |
| Operating income | $140,075 |

**Required:**
1. What is the margin of safety in sales dollars? in units?
2. What is the degree of operating leverage for Anjou Company?

**9–9**

*CVP and Activity-Based Costing*

LO6

The controller of Fremont Company collected the following data for one of Fremont's plants:

| Activity Driver | Variable Cost | Level of Activity Driver |
|---|---|---|
| Units sold | $ 10 | — |
| Setups | $600 | 50 |
| Engineering hours | 60 | 500 |

Other data:

| | |
|---|---|
| Total fixed costs (conventional) | $100,000 |
| Total fixed costs (ABC) | 40,000 |
| Unit selling price | 20 |

**Required:**
1. Calculate the breakeven point in units using the traditional approach.
2. Calculate the breakeven point in units using the ABC approach.
3. If Fremont's engineers can reduce the variable cost of a setup by $100, what will the new breakeven point in units be under the ABC approach? under the traditional approach?

**9–10**

*Units Sold to Break Even, Targeted Income*

**LO1**

Loewen Company produces and sells multivitamins to retailers for $2.72 per bottle. The variable costs per bottle are as follows:

| | |
|---|---|
| Ingredients | $0.45 |
| Bottle and cap | 0.10 |
| Direct labour | 0.58 |
| Variable overhead | 0.62 |
| Selling | 0.17 |

Fixed manufacturing costs total $136,000 per year. Administrative costs (all fixed) total $14,000.

**Required:**
1. Compute the number of bottles that Loewen must sell to break even.
2. How many bottles must Loewen sell to earn an operating income of $12,600?
3. What is the unit variable cost? What is the unit variable manufacturing cost? Which is used in cost–volume–profit analysis and why?

**9–11**

*After-Tax Profit, Margin of Safety*

**LO2, LO5**

Refer to 9–10.

**Required:**
1. Assuming a tax rate of 40 percent, how many bottles must be sold to earn an after-tax profit of $25,200?
2. Assuming a tax rate of 30 percent, how many bottles have to be sold to earn an after-tax profit of $25,200?
3. Assuming a tax rate of 50 percent, how many bottles have to be sold to earn an after-tax profit of $25,200?
4. Suppose that Loewen expects to sell 215,000 bottles. What is the margin of safety in bottles? What is the margin of safety in dollars?

**9–12**

*Units Sold, After-Tax Profit, Margin of Safety*

**LO2, LO5**

Popfresh, Inc., manufactures and sells packaged prepopped popcorn to retailers and movie theatres. The popcorn is packaged in 500-gram bags and sold to retailers for $1.25 per bag. The variable costs per bag are as follows:

| | |
|---|---|
| Corn | $0.65 |
| Vegetable oil | 0.10 |
| Miscellaneous ingredients | 0.03 |
| Selling | 0.17 |

Fixed manufacturing costs total $250,000 per year. Administrative costs (all fixed) total $50,000.

**Required:**
1. Compute the number of bags of popcorn that must be sold for Popfresh to break even.
2. How many bags of popcorn must be sold for Popfresh to earn an operating income of $150,000?
3. Assume a tax rate of 40 percent. How many bags of popcorn must be sold to earn an after-tax profit of $324,000?
4. Suppose that Popfresh expects to sell 1.2 million bags of popcorn. What is the margin of safety?

**9–13**

Contribution Margin, Unit Amounts

LO1, LO2

Information on four independent companies follows. Calculate the correct amount for each question mark.

|  | A | B | C | D |
|---|---|---|---|---|
| Sales | $5,000 | $   ? | $   ? | $9,000 |
| Total variable expenses | 4,000 | 11,700 | 9,750 | ? |
| Contribution margin | $1,000 | $ 3,900 | $   ? | $   ? |
| Total fixed costs | ? | 4,000 | ? | 750 |
| Operating income (loss) | $  500 | $   ? | $  400 | $2,850 |
| Units sold | ? | 1,300 | 125 | 90 |
| Price per unit | $    5 | ? | $ 130 | ? |
| Variable cost per unit | ? | $    9 | ? | ? |
| Contribution margin per unit | ? | $    3 | ? | ? |
| Contribution margin ratio | ? | ? | 40% | ? |
| Breakeven in units | ? | ? | ? | ? |

**9–14**

CVP, Margin of Safety

LO2, LO5

Daley Company had revenues of $930,000 last year, with total variable costs of $353,400 and fixed costs of $310,000.

**Required:**
1. What is the variable-cost ratio for Daley? What is the contribution margin ratio?
2. What is the breakeven point in sales revenue?
3. What was the margin of safety for Daley last year?
4. Daley is considering starting a multimedia advertising campaign that is supposed to increase sales by $7,500 per year. The campaign will cost $5,000. Is the advertising campaign a good idea? Explain.

**9–15**

CVP

LO1, LO2

Solve the following independent problems.
1. Thiessen Company's breakeven point is 1,500 units. Variable cost per unit is $300; total fixed costs are $120,000 per year. What price does Thiessen charge?
2. Jesper Company charges a price of $3.50; total fixed costs are $160,000 per year; and the breakeven point is 128,000 units. What is the variable cost per unit?

**9–16**

Breakeven, Targeted Operating Income

LO2

The Heidleweiss Co. Ltd. has a maximum capacity of 210,000 units per year. Variable manufacturing costs are $11 per unit. Fixed overhead is $540,000 per year. Variable selling costs are $3 per unit; fixed selling costs are $252,000 per year. Sales price is $20 per unit.

**Required:**
1. What is the breakeven point expressed in dollar sales?
2. How many units must be sold to earn a targeted operating income of $60,000 per year?
3. How many units must be sold to earn a targeted operating income of 10 percent of sales? (CGA Canada adapted)

**9–17**

Contribution Margin, CVP, Margin of Safety

LO1, LO2, LO5

Candyland, Inc., produces a particularly rich praline fudge. Each 250-gram box sells for $5.60. Variable unit costs are as follows:

| | |
|---|---|
| Pecans | $0.70 |
| Sugar | 0.35 |
| Butter | 1.85 |
| Other ingredients | 0.34 |
| Box, packing material | 0.76 |
| Selling commission | 0.20 |

Spreadsheet

Fixed overhead cost is $32,300 per year. Fixed selling and administrative costs are $12,500 per year. Candyland sold 35,000 boxes last year.

**Required:**
1. What is the contribution margin per unit for a box of praline fudge? What is the contribution margin ratio?
2. How many boxes must be sold to break even? What is the breakeven sales revenue?
3. What was Candyland's operating income last year?
4. What was the company's margin of safety?
5. Suppose that Candyland raises the price to $6.20 per box, but anticipated sales will drop to 31,500 boxes. What will be the new breakeven point in units? Should Candyland raise the price? Explain.

**9–18**

After-Tax Profit Target

LO1

The Wencam Company produced and sold 55,000 units during 2003. The following amounts were obtained from its financial statements for the year ended December 31, 2003:

| | |
|---|---|
| Sales | $2,475,000 |
| Direct materials used | 476,500 |
| Direct labour costs | 805,750 |
| Variable overhead incurred | 269,500 |
| Fixed overhead incurred* | 347,600 |
| Variable selling and administrative costs | 129,250 |
| Fixed selling and administrative costs | 187,200 |

\* The relevant range for fixed costs is 10,000 units to 85,000 units.

Expectations for 2004 include the following:

- Variable and fixed costs are expected to behave in the same manner as indicated above, but costs are expected to increase in general by 8 percent.
- The selling price will be raised by 6 percent.
- The company's 2004 income tax rate is expected to be 35 percent.

**Required:**
How many units must Wencam sell in 2004 in order to earn an after-tax income of $211,250? Show all calculations. (CMA Canada adapted)

**9–19**

CVP, Prices

LO1

The Brisbane Company has budgeted the following costs for 2004:

| | Total Cost | Unit Cost |
|---|---|---|
| Direct materials | $ 160,000 | $ 2.00 |
| Direct labour | 320,000 | 4.00 |
| Variable overhead | 80,000 | 1.00 |
| Fixed overhead | 400,000 | 5.00 |
| Variable selling | 240,000 | 3.00 |
| Fixed administrative | 600,000 | 7.50 |
| | $1,800,000 | $22.50 |

**Required:**
1. What price would Brisbane have to charge in order to produce an after-tax profit of $144,000 if the company's tax rate is 40 percent?
2. At a sales price of $25.00, what is Brisbane's breakeven point in units?
3. If 70,000 units were produced and sold, what price would Brisbane have to charge in order to have an operating income equal to 10 percent of sales? (CGA Canada adapted)

**9–20**

Sales Revenue
Approach, Variable-
Cost Ratio,
Contribution Margin
ratio, Margin of Safety

LO2, LO5

Lane Company produces and sells an economy line of ski parkas. The budgeted income statement for the coming year is as follows:

| | |
|---|---|
| Sales | $315,000 |
| Less: Variable expenses | 141,750 |
|    Contribution margin | $173,250 |
| Less: Fixed expenses | 63,000 |
|    Operating income | $110,250 |
| Less: Taxes | 33,075 |
|    Net income | $ 77,175 |

**Required:**
1. What is Lane's variable-cost ratio? What is its contribution margin ratio?
2. Suppose Lane's actual revenues are $30,000 more than budgeted. By how much will operating income increase? Give the answer without preparing a new income statement.
3. How much sales revenue must Lane earn in order to break even? What is the expected margin of safety?
4. How much sales revenue must Lane generate to earn an operating income of $91,000?
5. How much sales revenue must Lane generate to earn an after-tax profit of $56,000? Prepare a variable-costing income statement to verify the accuracy of your answer.

**9–21**

CVP Analysis with
Target Profits

LO1, LO2

Tom Flannery has developed a new recipe for fried chicken and plans to open a takeout restaurant in Edmundston. His father-in-law has agreed to invest $500,000 in the operation, provided Tom can convince him that profits will be at least 20 percent of sales revenues. Tom estimated that total fixed expense would be $24,000 per year and that variable expense would be approximately 40 percent of sales revenues.

**Required:**
1. How much sales revenue must be earned to produce operating income equal to 20 percent of sales revenue? Prepare a variable-costing income statement to verify your answer.
2. If Tom plans on selling 12-piece buckets of chicken for $10 each, how many buckets must he sell to earn an operating income equal to 20 percent of sales? 25 percent of sales? Prepare a variable-costing income statement to verify the second answer.
3. Suppose Tom's father-in-law meant that the after-tax net income had to be 20 percent of sales revenue. Under this assumption, how much sales revenue must be generated by Tom's chicken business? (Assume that the tax rate is 40 percent.)

**9–22**

CVP, Margin of Safety

LO1, LO2, LO5

Commonwealth Computer Company manufactures and sells a line of computers to computer stores across Canada. The company has experienced a moderate but steady growth in sales for the last three years. In order to compete with major computer manufacturers and increase market share, Commonwealth's president is planning to cut the unit selling price by 15 percent, effective January 1, 2004.

The following are actual cost data and projected sales volumes for 2003 and 2004:

| | |
|---|---:|
| Selling price per unit for 2003 | $ 2,100 |
| Actual sales units (January 1 to September 30, 2003) | 35,000 |
| Forecasted sales units (October 1 to December 31, 2003) | 10,000 |
| Unit variable costs: | |
|   Direct materials | $ 475 |
|   Direct labour | 225 |
|   Variable overhead | 180 |
|   Selling expenses | 140 |
|     Total variable cost per unit | $ 1,020 |
| Fixed cost per year: | |
|   Manufacturing | $7,500,000 |
|   Selling | 6,400,000 |
|   Administrative | 4,375,000 |
| Income tax rate | 45% |

It is anticipated that sales units for 2004 will increase by 5 percent to 47,250 units. The cost structure will remain the same, with no changes in inventory levels.

**Required:**
1. Determine the following for 2003:
   a. Contribution margin ratio
   b. Breakeven point in units and sales dollars
   c. Projected net income (after tax)
   d. Margin of safety
2. Determine the following for 2004:
   a. Contribution margin ratio
   b. Breakeven point in units and sales dollars
   c. Projected net income (after tax)
   d. Margin of safety (CGA Canada adapted)

**9–23**

Operating Leverage

LO5

Spreadsheet

Income statements for two different companies in the same industry are as follows:

| | Company A | Company B |
|---|---:|---:|
| Sales | $500,000 | $500,000 |
| Less: Variable costs | 400,000 | 200,000 |
|   Contribution margin | $100,000 | $300,000 |
| Less: Fixed costs | 50,000 | 250,000 |
|   Operating income | $ 50,000 | $ 50,000 |

**Required:**
1. Compute the degree of operating leverage for each company.
2. Compute the breakeven point for each company. Explain why Company B's breakeven point is higher.
3. Suppose that both companies experience a 50 percent increase in revenues. Compute the percentage change in profits for each company. Explain why the percentage increase in Company B's profits is so much larger than that in Company A's.

**9–24**

CVP Analysis with
Multiple Products

LO3

Spreadsheet

Gernon Company produces scientific and business calculators. For the coming year, Gernon expects to sell 20,000 scientific calculators and 100,000 business calculators. A segmented income statement for the two products is given below.

|  | Scientific | Business | Total |
|---|---|---|---|
| Sales | $500,000 | $2,000,000 | $2,500,000 |
| Less: Variable costs | 240,000 | 900,000 | 1,140,000 |
| Contribution margin | $260,000 | $1,100,000 | $1,360,000 |
| Less: Direct fixed costs | 120,000 | 960,000 | 1,080,000 |
| Segment margin | $140,000 | $ 140,000 | $ 280,000 |
| Less: Common fixed costs |  |  | 145,000 |
| Operating income |  |  | $ 135,000 |

**Required:**

1. Compute the number of scientific calculators and the number of business calculators that Gernon must sell in order to break even.
2. Using information from only the "Total" column of the income statement, compute the sales revenue that must be generated for the company to break even.

**9–25**

Multiple Product
Breakeven, Breakeven
Sales Revenue, Margin
of Safety

LO2, LO3, LO5

Serenity Products Incorporated produces and sells yoga-related training products: how-to videotapes and a basic equipment set (a nonskid mat, blocks, a strap, and a small pillow). Last year, Serenity sold 10,000 videos and 5,000 equipment sets. Information on the two products is as follows:

|  | Videotape | Equipment Set |
|---|---|---|
| Price | $12.00 | $15.00 |
| Variable cost per unit | 4.00 | 6.00 |

Total fixed costs are $70,000.

**Required:**

1. What is the sales mix of videotapes and equipment sets?
2. Compute the breakeven quantity of each product.
3. Prepare an income statement for Serenity for last year. What is the overall contribution margin ratio? the overall breakeven sales revenue?
4. Compute the margin of safety for last year.

**9–26**

Multiple Product
Breakeven, Breakeven
Sales Revenue, Margin
of Safety

LO2, LO3, LO5

Refer to 9–25. Suppose that in the coming year, Serenity plans to produce an extra-thick yoga mat for sale to health clubs. The company estimates that 20,000 mats can be sold at a price of $18 with a variable cost per unit of $13. Fixed cost must be increased by $48,350 (making total fixed costs $118,350). Assume that the anticipated sales of the other products, as well as their prices and variable costs, remain the same.

**Required:**

1. What is the sales mix of videotapes, equipment sets, and yoga mats?
2. Compute the breakeven quantity of each product.
3. Prepare an income statement for Serenity for the coming year. What is the overall contribution margin ratio? the overall breakeven sales revenue?
4. Compute the margin of safety for the coming year.

**9–27**

**Changes in Breakeven Points with Changes in Unit Prices**

**LO1, LO2, LO5**

The income statement for Roy, Inc., is as follows:

| | |
|---|---|
| Sales | $600,000 |
| Less: Variable expenses | 228,000 |
| Contribution margin | $372,000 |
| Less: Fixed expenses | 295,000 |
| Operating income | $ 77,000 |

Roy produces and sells a single product. The above income statement is based on sales of 100,000 units.

**Required:**
1. Compute the breakeven point in units and in revenues.
2. Suppose that the selling price increases by 10 percent. Will the breakeven point increase or decrease? Recompute it.
3. Ignoring Requirement 2, suppose that the variable cost per unit increases by $0.35. Will the breakeven point increase or decrease? Recompute it.
4. Can you predict whether the breakeven point will increase or decrease if both the selling price and the unit variable cost increase? Recompute the breakeven point incorporating both of the changes in Requirements 2 and 3.
5. Assume that total fixed costs increase by $50,000. (Assume no other changes from the original data.) Will the breakeven point increase or decrease? Recompute it.

**9–28**

**CVP and Profit–Volume Graphs**

**LO4, LO5**

Bryant Company produces and sells one product. The selling price is $10, and the unit variable cost is $6. Total fixed costs are $10,000.

**Required:**
1. Prepare a CVP graph with units sold as the horizontal axis and dollars as the vertical axis. Label the breakeven point on the horizontal axis.
2. Prepare CVP graphs for each of the following independent scenarios:
   a. Fixed costs increase by $5,000.
   b. Unit variable cost increases to $7.
   c. Unit selling price increases to $12.
   d. Fixed costs increase by $5,000, and variable cost is $7.
3. Prepare a profit–volume graph using the original data. Repeat the scenarios in Requirement 2.
4. Which of the two graphs do you think provides the most information? Why?

**9–29**

**Basic CVP Concepts**

**LO1, LO2, LO5**

Suriname Company produces a single product. The projected income statement for the coming year is as follows:

| | |
|---|---|
| Sales (50,000 units × $45) | $2,250,000 |
| Less: Variable costs | 1,305,000 |
| Contribution margin | $ 945,000 |
| Less: Fixed costs | 812,700 |
| Operating income | $ 132,300 |

**Required:**
1. Compute the unit contribution margin and the units that must be sold to break even. Suppose that 30,000 units are sold above breakeven. What is the operating income?
2. Compute the contribution margin ratio and the breakeven point in dollars. Suppose that revenues are $200,000 more than expected. What would the total operating income be?
3. Compute the margin of safety.

4. Compute the degree of operating leverage. Compute the new operating income if sales are 20 percent higher than expected.
5. How many units must be sold to earn an operating income equal to 10 percent of sales?
6. Assume that the tax rate is 40 percent. How many units must be sold to earn an after-tax profit of $180,000?

**9–30**

*Multiple-Product Breakeven*

**LO3**

Parker Pottery produces a line of vases and a line of ceramic figurines. Each line uses the same equipment and labour; hence, there are no traceable fixed costs. Common fixed costs equal $30,000. Parker's accountant has begun to assess the profitability of the two lines and has gathered the following data for last year:

|  | Vases | Figurines |
|---|---|---|
| Price | $40 | $70 |
| Variable cost | 30 | 42 |
| Contribution margin | $10 | $28 |
| Number of units | 1,000 | 500 |

**Required:**
1. Compute the number of vases and the number of figurines that must be sold for the company to break even.
2. Parker Pottery is considering upgrading its factory to improve the quality of its product. If the upgrade—which will cost $5,260—is successful, the projected sales of vases will be 1,500; figurine sales will increase to 1,000 units. What is the new breakeven point in units for each of the products?

**9–31**

*Multiple Choice*

**LO1, LO2, LO3, LO4, LO5, LO6**

Choose the *best* answer for each of the following multiple-choice questions:

1. If the variable cost per unit goes up,

|  | **Contribution margin** | **Breakeven point** |
|---|---|---|
| a. | increases | increases |
| b. | increases | decreases |
| c. | decreases | decreases |
| d. | decreases | increases |
| e. | decreases | remains unchanged |

2. To determine the amount of revenue required to earn a targeted profit, the
   a. fixed cost must be divided by contribution margin.
   b. fixed cost must be divided by contribution margin ratio.
   c. total of fixed cost plus targeted profit must be divided by contribution margin ratio.
   d. targeted profit must be divided by contribution margin ratio.
   e. targeted profit must be divided by variable cost ratio.

3. Breakeven revenue for the multiple-product firm can be calculated by
   a. dividing the total fixed costs by the overall contribution margin ratio.
   b. dividing the segment fixed costs by the overall contribution margin ratio.
   c. dividing the total fixed costs by the package contribution margin.
   d. multiplying the total fixed cost by the contribution margin ratio.
   e. Breakeven revenue can only be computed for a single-product firm.

4. In the cost–volume–profit graph,
   a. the breakeven point is found where the total revenue curve crosses the x-axis.
   b. the area of profit is to the left of the breakeven point.

    c. the area of loss cannot be determined from this graph.
    d. Both the total revenue curve and the total cost curve appear on this graph.
    e. Neither the total revenue curve nor the total cost curve appear on this graph.

5. An important assumption of cost–volume–profit analysis is that
    a. both costs and revenues are linear functions.
    b. all cost and revenue relationships are seen within the relevant range.
    c. there is no change in inventories.
    d. sales mix remains constant.
    e. All of the above.

6. The use of fixed costs to extract higher percentage changes in profits as sales activity changes is referred to as
    a. margin of safety.
    b. operating leverage.
    c. degree of operating leverage.
    d. sensitivity analysis.
    e. variable cost reduction.

7. When activity-based costing is applied to cost–volume–profit analysis,
    a. the contribution margin becomes price minus variable cost per unit, per batch, and per product.
    b. the units needed to achieve a targeted income cannot be computed.
    c. fixed costs include batch costs, product-level costs, and facility-level costs.
    d. the denominator includes batch costs, product-level costs, and facility-level costs.
    e. Activity-based costing is never used in cost–volume–profit analysis.

## Problems

**9–32**

Basic CVP Concepts

LO1, LO2, LO3

Fisper Company produces a variety of industrial products. One division makes solvents. The division's projected income statement for the coming year is as follows:

| | |
|---|---|
| Sales (128,000 units × $50) | $6,400,000 |
| Less: Variable expenses | 4,480,000 |
| Contribution margin | $1,920,000 |
| Less: Fixed expenses | 1,000,000 |
| Operating income | $ 920,000 |

**Required:**
1. Compute the contribution margin per unit, and calculate the breakeven point in units (round to the nearest unit). Calculate the contribution margin ratio and the breakeven sales revenue.
2. The divisional manager has decided to increase the advertising budget by $100,000. This change will increase sales revenues by $1 million. By how much will operating income increase or decrease as a result of this action?
3. Suppose sales revenues exceed the estimated amount on the income statement by $315,000. Without preparing a new income statement, by how much is operating income underestimated?

4. Refer to the original data. How many units must Fisper sell to earn an after-tax profit of $630,000? Assume a tax rate of 40 percent.
5. Compute the margin of safety based on the original income statement.
6. Compute the degree of operating leverage based on the original income statement. If sales revenues are 20 percent greater than expected, what is the percentage increase in operating income?

**9–33**

Multiple-Product Analysis, Change in Sales Mix

LO3

Unicorn Enterprises produces two strategy games, Mystical Wars and Magical Dragons. The projected income for the coming year, segmented by product line, follows:

|  | **Wars** | **Dragons** | **Total** |
|---|---|---|---|
| Sales | $300,000 | $2,500,000 | $2,800,000 |
| Less: Variable expenses | 100,000 | 500,000 | 600,000 |
| Contribution margin | $200,000 | $2,000,000 | $2,200,000 |
| Less: Direct fixed expenses | 28,000 | 1,500,000 | 1,528,000 |
| Product margin | $172,000 | $ 500,000 | $ 672,000 |
| Less: Common fixed expenses |  |  | 100,000 |
| Operating income |  |  | $ 572,000 |

The selling prices are $30 for Mystical Wars and $50 for Magical Dragons.

**Required:**
1. Compute the number of games of each kind that must be sold for Unicorn Enterprises to break even.
2. Compute the revenue that Unicorn must earn to produce an operating income of 10 percent of sales revenues.
3. Assume that the marketing manager changes the sales mix of the two games so that the ratio is three Mystical Wars games to five Magical Dragons games. Repeat Requirements 1 and 2.
4. Refer to the original data. Suppose that Unicorn can increase the sales of Magical Dragons with increased advertising. The extra advertising would cost an additional $45,000, and some of the potential purchasers of Mystical Wars would switch to Magical Dragons. In total, sales of Magical Dragons would increase by 15,000 units and sales of Mystical Wars would decrease by 5,000 units. Would Unicorn be better off with this strategy?

**9–34**

CVP Equation, Basic Concepts, Solving for Unknowns

LO1, LO2

Azucar Company produces combination shampoos and conditioners in individual-use bottles for hotels. Each bottle sells for $0.36. The variable costs for each bottle (materials, labour, and overhead) total $0.27. The total fixed costs are $54,000. During the most recent year, 830,000 bottles were sold. The president of Azucar, not fully satisfied with the product's profit performance, was considering the following options to increase profitability: (1) increase promotional spending; (2) increase the quality of the ingredients and, simultaneously, increase the selling price; (3) increase the selling price; (4) combinations of the three.

**Required:**
1. The sales manager is confident that she has developed an advertising campaign that could increase sales volume by 50 percent and meet the company president's goal to increase this year's operating income by 50 percent over last year's. What amount does the sales manager plan to spend on advertising?
2. Assume that the company has a plan to imprint the name of the purchasing hotel on each bottle. This will increase variable costs to $0.30. How much must the selling price be increased to maintain the same breakeven point?

3. Azucar increases its selling price to $0.40. Sales volume drops from 830,000 to 700,000 bottles. Was the decision to increase the price a good one? Compute the sales volume that would be needed at the new price for the company to earn the same operating income as last year.

**9–35**

CVP, Target Income, Prices

**LO1, LO2**

Laraby Company produces a single product in its Halifax factory. It sold 25,000 units last year with the following results:

| | |
|---|---|
| Sales | $625,000 |
| Variable costs | 375,000 |
| Contribution margin | $250,000 |
| Fixed costs | 150,000 |
| | |
| Operating income | $100,000 |
| Income taxes | 45,000 |
| Net income | $ 55,000 |

In an attempt to improve its product in the coming year, Laraby is considering replacing a component part that has cost $2.50 with a new and better part costing $4.50 per unit. A new machine will also be needed to increase plant capacity. The machine, which would cost $18,000, would have a useful life of six years and no salvage value.

**Required:**
1. What was Laraby Company's breakeven point in number of units last year?
2. How many units of product would Laraby have had to sell last year to earn $77,000 in net income after taxes?
3. If Laraby holds the sales price constant and makes the suggested changes, how many units of product must be sold in the coming year to break even?
4. If Laraby holds the sales price constant and makes the suggested changes, how many units of product must be sold in the coming year to make the same net income after taxes as last year?
5. If Laraby wishes to maintain the same contribution margin ratio after implementing the changes, what selling price per unit of product must it charge next year to cover the increased materials costs? (CGA Canada adapted)

**9–36**

CVP, Changes in Price and Costs

**LO1, LO2, LO5**

Nico's Pizza, Inc., is a new company currently studying various alternatives in regard to opening pizza outlets. The only available data was formulated by a hired consultant who, unfortunately, died quite suddenly. A summary of the information that the consultant developed follows:

**Average selling price per pizza: $7.50**

| Normal monthly costs* | Fixed | Variable |
|---|---|---|
| Cost of pizzas sold | $    0 | $5,500 |
| Manager's salary | 2,000 | 0 |
| Wages | 2,000 | 0 |
| Rent | 1,500 | 500 |
| Utilities | 500 | 200 |
| Insurance and commissions | 1,000 | 0 |
| Total cost | $7,000 | $6,200 |

* Note: Costs are based on budgeted sales of 2,000 pizzas per month.

The above information represents estimates for the operation of a pizza outlet. Nico's is interested in opening the outlets as soon as possible and has asked you to comment on various alternatives.

**Required:**

1. Compute the breakeven point for a pizza outlet in terms of both sales dollars and number of pizzas sold each month.
2. As a promotion to attract business, the company is considering whether to offer a special price during the first month of operations. This move would, in effect, reduce the average selling price to $5 per pizza. How many additional pizzas will have to be sold by a pizza outlet at the promotional selling price compared with the normal average selling price to earn operating income of $2,500 during the first month?
3. As a potential incentive program for the outlet manager, Nico's is considering implementing a change in the method of compensation as proposed by the consultant. Instead of paying the outlet manager a fixed wage of $2,000 per month, the company is considering an incentive plan of $1,000 per month plus 8 percent of monthly revenue. Under this alternative compensation method and using the normal average selling price per pizza, calculate how many pizzas will have to be sold to achieve operating income of $2,000 per month. (CMA Canada adapted)

**9–37**

*CVP, Multiple Products*

**LO3, LO5**

Klamic Ceramics (KC) manufactures and sells ceramic flowerpots. As a result of competitive forces (for example, plastic substitutes), KC has been selling its only product at a price of $10 each. In 2003, its first year of operations, KC determined that at a normal volume of 80,000 units per year, the following costs would apply:

| | |
|---|---|
| Materials | $2.00 |
| Direct labour | 3.50 |
| Applied overhead | 2.50 |
| Total cost | $8.00 |

Annual fixed overhead costs total $180,000. Annual fixed selling and administrative costs total $20,000.

Klamic's owners, Jack and Katie Brown, have recently been offered positions in other companies, which would commence in January 2004. Consequently, Jack and Katie have spent much of the current month (December 2003) attempting to determine whether they could jointly have a higher income by working for other companies. Their salaries would total $70,000 before taxes.

For 2003, Jack considered introducing a new product. After some research, he established that an increasing demand for ceramic lawn ornaments existed in the community. Average variable costs for the ornaments would total $7, and the average selling price would be $12. Additional moulds and a part-time worker would increase total fixed costs to $245,000 per year.

**Required:**

1. Calculate the breakeven point for the ceramic flowerpot production for 2003.
2. Jack estimated that production and sales in 2004 would be 80,000 flowerpots. Determine whether Jack and Katie would be better off by remaining self-employed by comparing KC's operating income to the couple's joint salaries while working elsewhere. Show supporting calculations.
3. If the company plans to produce and sell 50,000 flowerpots and 30,000 lawn ornaments in 2004, what is the breakeven revenue for both products combined?
4. After some discussions with a local advertising agency, Katie determined that if KC spent $15,000 on additional marketing efforts, it would be able to increase sales of lawn ornaments in 2004 to 40,000 units. To accommodate producing 40,000 lawn ornaments, KC would be able to produce and sell a maximum of 40,000 flowerpots. Assuming KC decides to go ahead with the above marketing plan, determine the impact this decision would have on the company's breakeven point in dollar sales in 2004. (CMA Canada adapted)

**9–38**

We-Care Lawn Service is a lawn-care company operating in Kelowna. We-Care offers chemical fertilization, insect control, and weed and crabgrass control for its customers' lawns and foundations. Four chemical applications are given per growing period, which lasts from April through October. Four chemicals are used in the applications: dacthal for crabgrass control, trimel for weed control, urea fertilizer, and Dursban insecticide. In the first application, dacthal accounts for 75 percent of the chemical cost, followed by 10 percent for trimel, 10 percent for urea, and 5 percent for Dursban; in the remaining three applications, dacthal is not used—it is ineffective after May 31.

We-Care offers two services: residential and commercial. The price charged per residential application is $13.50. The average residential lot is 0.1 hectares. Commercial applications are for any area larger than a hectare and are priced at $40 per hectare per application.

We-Care's variable costs consist of chemicals, direct labour, operating expenses for its truck, and operating supplies. For the first application, the cost of chemicals is $40 per hectare; for the remaining applications, chemicals cost $10 per application per hectare. We-Care has one employee, who is classified as direct labour. He is paid $6 per hour. Residential lawns should be sprayed at a rate of three lawns per hour (including travel time). Commercial applications are sprayed at a rate of 45 minutes per hectare. Operating expenses for the truck average $13.78 per hectare per residential application and $5 per hectare per commercial application. Operating supplies average $4.13 per hectare per application, regardless of the type of service. Fixed costs for the year follow:

| | |
|---|---|
| Truck lease | $12,337 |
| Amortization, equipment | 1,747 |
| Truck insurance | 1,339 |
| Telephone | 1,200 |
| Tax and licence | 1,085 |
| Advertising | 10,000 |
| Salary of supervisor | 12,000 |
| Total | $39,708 |

Based on last year's experience, We-Care services two hectares of residential property for every hectare of commercial property. The owner expects the same sales mix for the coming year.

**Required:**

1. Assume that every customer receives all four applications. Compute the hectares of residential applications and the hectares of commercial applications that must be serviced for We-Care to break even. Given the hectares of residential service, compute the average number of residential customers.

2. Given the breakeven point computed in Requirement 1, determine the labour hours needed to service the breakeven volume. Is one employee sufficient? Assume that the employee works 8 hours per day and a total of 140 days during the 7-month growing season. What volume is needed before a second employee is hired? Discuss the effect on CVP analysis if additional employees are needed.

3. Assume that 60 percent of all residential customers receive only the first application, with the remaining 40 percent receiving all four. All commercial customers receive all four applications. Redo the breakeven analysis. (Hint: There are now two types of residential customers, producing a mix of three services.)

**9–39**

*Basics of the Sales
Revenue Approach*

**LO2, LO5**

Dalhart Company produces plastic mailboxes. A projected income statement follows:

| | |
|---|---|
| Sales | $560,400 |
| Less: Variable costs | 257,784 |
| Contribution margin | $302,616 |
| Less: Fixed costs | 150,000 |
| Operating income | $152,616 |

**Required:**

1. Compute the contribution margin ratio for the mailboxes.
2. How much revenue must Dalhart earn in order to break even?
3. What volume of sales must be earned if Dalhart wants to earn an after-tax income equal to 8 percent of sales? Assume that the tax rate is 34 percent.
4. What is the effect on the contribution margin ratio if the unit selling price and unit variable cost each increase by 10 percent?
5. Suppose that management has decided to pay a 3 percent commission on all sales. The projected income statement does not reflect this commission. Recompute the contribution margin ratio assuming that the commission will be paid. What effect does this change have on the breakeven point?
6. If the commission is paid as described in Requirement 5, management expects sales revenues to increase by $80,000. Is it a sound decision to implement the commission? Support your answer with appropriate computations.

**9–40**

*CVP Analysis, Sales
Revenue Approach,
Pricing, After-Tax
Profit Target*

**LO2**

Kline Consulting is a service organization that specializes in the design, installation, and servicing of mechanical, hydraulic, and pneumatic systems. For example, some manufacturing companies, with machinery that cannot be turned off for servicing, need a system for lubricating the machinery during use. To deal with this type of problem for a client, Kline designed a central lubricating system that pumps lubricants intermittently to bearings and other moving parts.

Kline's operating results for last year are as follows:

| | |
|---|---|
| Sales | $802,429 |
| Less: Variable expenses | 430,000 |
| Contribution margin | $372,429 |
| Less: Fixed expenses | 154,750 |
| Operating income | $217,679 |

Next year, the company expects variable costs to increase by 5 percent and fixed costs by 4 percent.

**Required:**

1. What is the contribution margin ratio for last year?
2. Compute Kline's breakeven point for last year in dollars.
3. Suppose that Kline would like to see a 6 percent increase in operating income next year. What percentage (on average) must Kline raise its bids to cover the expected cost increases and obtain the desired operating income? Assume that Kline expects the same mix and volume of services each year.
4. Next year, how much revenue must be earned for Kline to earn an after-tax profit of $175,000? Assume a tax rate of 34 percent.

**9–41**

Artistic Woodcrafting, Inc., began in 2000 as a one-person cabinetmaking operation. Business soon expanded, and employees were added. By 2003, sales volume totalled $850,000, and sales were expected to be $1.6 million for 2004. Unfortunately, the cabinetmaking business is highly competitive. More than 200 cabinetmaking shops in the area are all competing for the same business.

Artistic currently offers two different quality grades of cabinets: Grade I and Grade II, with Grade I being of higher quality. The average unit selling prices, unit variable costs, and direct fixed costs are as follows:

|  | Unit Price | Unit Variable Cost | Direct Fixed Costs |
|---|---|---|---|
| Grade I | $3,400 | $2,686 | $95,000 |
| Grade II | 1,600 | 1,328 | 95,000 |

Common fixed costs (fixed costs not traceable to either cabinet) are $35,000. Currently, for every three Grade I cabinets sold, seven Grade II cabinets are sold.

**Required:**

1. Calculate the number of Grade I and Grade II cabinets that are expected to be sold during 2004.
2. Calculate the number of Grade I and Grade II cabinets that must be sold for the company to break even.
3. Artistic Woodcrafting can buy computer-controlled machines that will make doors, drawers, and frames. If the machines are purchased, the variable costs for each type of cabinet will decrease by 9 percent, but common fixed costs will increase by $44,000 per year. Compute the effect on operating income in 2004, and calculate the new breakeven point.
4. Refer to the original data. Artistic Woodcrafting is considering adding a retail outlet. This change will increase common fixed costs by $70,000 per year. As a result of adding the retail outlet, the additional publicity and emphasis on quality will allow the company to change the sales mix to 1:1. The retail outlet is also expected to increase sales by 30 percent. Calculate the effect on the company's expected operating income for 2004, and calculate the new breakeven point.

**9–42**

Junior's Executive Jet Service is planning to run commuter flights between Toronto and Ottawa from Monday through Friday each week. Junior believes that he can charge $150 per customer (round trip) per flight and earn an operating income of $2,000 per round trip if he can fill 80 percent of each 70-seat aircraft. At 100 percent capacity, his total operating income would be $3,750 per round trip. Junior can schedule his flights either every hour or every two hours between 7:00 a.m. and 6:00 p.m. (thus making either 6 or 12 round-trip flights per day). Junior believes that he will operate at 70 percent capacity if he schedules flights hourly and 85 percent capacity if he schedules flights every two hours.

**Required:**

1. What is the breakeven point (in number of customers) per round-trip flight?
2. What is the breakeven point (in number of customers) per week if 6 round-trip flights are scheduled per day?
3. What is the breakeven point (in number of customers) per week if 12 round-trip flights are scheduled per day?
4. Should Junior schedule flights every hour or every two hours? Provide appropriate analysis. (CGA Canada adapted)

**9–43**

Multiple Products,
Breakeven Analysis,
Operating Leverage

LO3, LO5

Carlyle Lighting Products produces two different types of lamps: a floor lamp and a desk lamp. Floor lamps sell for $30, desk lamps for $20. The projected income statement for the coming year follows:

| Sales | $600,000 |
|---|---|
| Less: Variable expenses | 400,000 |
| Contribution margin | $200,000 |
| Less: Fixed expenses | 150,000 |
| Operating income | $ 50,000 |

Carlyle's owner estimates that 60 percent of the sales revenues will be produced by floor lamps, with the remaining 40 percent by desk lamps. Floor lamps are also responsible for 60 percent of the variable expenses. Of the fixed expenses, one-third are common to both products, and one-half are directly traceable to the floor lamp product line.

**Required:**
1. Compute the sales revenue that Carlyle must earn to break even.
2. Compute the number of floor lamps and desk lamps that Carlyle must sell to break even.
3. Compute the degree of operating leverage for Carlyle Lighting Products. Now assume that the actual revenues will be 40 percent higher than the projected revenues. By what percentage will operating income increase with this change in sales volume?

**9–44**

Multiple-Product
Breakeven

LO3

Polaris, Inc., manufactures two types of metal stampings for the automobile industry: door handles and trim kits. Fixed costs equal $146,000. Each door handle sells for $12 and has variable costs of $9; each trim kit sells for $8 and has variable costs of $5.

**Required:**
1. What are the contribution margin per unit and the contribution margin ratio for door handles and for trim kits?
2. If Polaris sells 20,000 door handles and 40,000 trim kits, what is its operating income?
3. How many door handles and how many trim kits must Polaris sell to break even?
4. Assume that Polaris has the opportunity to rearrange its plant to produce only trim kits. If this is done, fixed costs will decrease by $35,000, and 70,000 trim kits can be produced and sold in a year. Is this a good idea? Explain.

**9–45**

CVP, Margin of Safety

LO1, LO2, LO5

Victoria Company produces a single product. Last year's income statement is as follows:

| Sales (29,000 units) | $1,218,000 |
|---|---|
| Less: Variable expenses | 812,000 |
| Contribution margin | $ 406,000 |
| Less: Fixed expenses | 300,000 |
| Operating income | $ 106,000 |

**Required:**
1. Compute the breakeven point in units and sales dollars.
2. What was the margin of safety for Victoria Company last year?
3. Suppose that Victoria Company is considering an investment in new technology that will increase fixed costs by $250,000 per year but will lower variable costs to 45 percent of sales. Units sold will remain unchanged. Prepare a

budgeted income statement, assuming that Victoria makes this investment. What is the new breakeven point in units and sales dollars, assuming that the investment is made?

**9–46**

Multiplant Breakeven

LO2, LO3

The PTO Division of the Galva Manufacturing Company produces power take-off units for the farm equipment business. The PTO Division, headquartered in Neepawa, Manitoba, has a newly renovated plant in Neepawa and an older, less automated plant in Yorkton, Saskatchewan. Both plants produce the same power take-off units for farm tractors that are sold to most domestic and foreign tractor manufacturers.

The PTO Division expects to produce and sell 192,000 power take-off units during the coming year. The divisional production manager has the following data available regarding the unit costs, unit prices, and production capacities for the two plants.

|  | Neepawa | Yorkton |
|---|---|---|
| Selling price | $150.00 | $150.00 |
| Variable manufacturing cost | $72.00 | $88.00 |
| Fixed manufacturing cost | 30.00 | 15.00 |
| Commission (5%) | 7.50 | 7.50 |
| General and administrative expense | 25.50 | 21.00 |
| Total unit cost | $135.00 | $131.50 |
| Unit profit | $ 15.00 | $ 18.50 |
| Production rate per day | 400 units | 320 units |

All fixed costs are based on a normal year of 240 working days. When the number of working days exceeds 240, variable manufacturing costs increase by $3 per unit in Neepawa and $8 per unit in Yorkton. Capacity for each plant is 300 working days.

Galva Manufacturing charges each of its plants a per-unit fee for administrative services such as payroll, general accounting, and purchasing, because Galva considers these services to be a function of the work performed at the plants. For each of the plants, a fee of $6.50 represents the variable portion of the general and administrative expense.

Wishing to maximize the higher unit profit at Yorkton, PTO's production manager has decided to manufacture 96,000 units at each plant. This production plan results in Yorkton's operating at capacity and Neepawa's operating at its normal volume. Galva's corporate controller is not happy with this plan; he wonders if it might be better to produce relatively more at the automated plant in Neepawa.

**Required:**
1. Determine the annual breakeven units for each of PTO's plants.
2. Calculate the operating income that would result from the division production manager's plan to produce 96,000 units at each plant.
3. Calculate the operating income that would result from sales of 192,000 power take-off units if 120,000 of them were produced at the Neepawa plant and the remainder at the Yorkton plant. (US CMA adapted)

**9–47**

CVP Analysis, Assumptions

LO2, LO6

Marston Corporation manufactures pharmaceutical products that are sold through a network of sales agents located in Canada and the United States. The agents are currently paid an 18 percent commission on sales; this percentage was used when Marston prepared the following pro forma income statement for the fiscal year ending June 30, 2004.

**Marston Corporation**
**Pro Forma Income Statement**
**For the Year Ending June 30, 2004**
**(dollars in thousands)**

| | | |
|---|---:|---:|
| Sales | | $26,000 |
| Cost of goods sold | | |
| Variable | $11,700 | |
| Fixed | 2,870 | 14,570 |
| Gross profit | | $11,430 |
| Selling and administrative costs | | |
| Commissions | $ 4,680 | |
| Fixed advertising cost | 750 | |
| Fixed administrative cost | 1,850 | 7,280 |
| Operating income | | $ 4,150 |
| Fixed interest cost | | 650 |
| Income before income taxes | | $ 3,500 |
| Income taxes (40%) | | 1,400 |
| Net income | | $ 2,100 |

Since the completion of the above statement, Marston has learned that its agents are requesting an increase in the commission rate to 23 percent for the upcoming year. As a result, Marston's president has decided to investigate the possibility of hiring his own sales staff in place of the network of sales agents and has asked Tom Ross, Marston's controller, to gather information on the costs associated with this change.

Ross estimates that Marston will have to hire eight salespeople to cover the current market area, and the annual payroll cost for each of these employees will average $80,000, including fringe benefit expense. Travel and entertainment expense is expected to total $600,000 for the year, and the annual cost of hiring a sales manager and sales secretary will be $150,000. In addition to their salaries, the eight salespeople will each earn commissions at the rate of 10 percent on the first $2 million in sales and 15 percent on all sales over $2 million. For planning purposes, Ross expects that all eight salespeople will exceed the $2 million mark and that sales will be at the level previously projected. Ross believes that Marston should also increase its advertising budget by $500,000.

**Required:**
1. Calculate Marston Corporation's breakeven point in sales dollars for the fiscal year ending June 30, 2004, if the company hires its own sales force and increases its advertising costs.
2. If Marston Corporation continues to sell through its network of sales agents and pays the higher commission rate, determine the estimated volume in sales dollars for the fiscal year ending June 30, 2004, that would be required to generate the same net income as that projected in the pro forma income statement presented above.
3. Describe the general assumptions underlying breakeven analysis that might limit its usefulness in this case. (US CMA adapted)

## Managerial Decision Cases

**9–48**

Ethics and a CVP Application

LO1

Danna Lumus, the marketing manager for a division that produces a variety of paper products, was considering the divisional manager's request for a sales forecast for a new line of paper napkins. The divisional manager was gathering data so that he could choose between two different production processes. The first process would have a variable cost of $10 per case produced and fixed costs of $100,000. The second process would have a variable cost of $6 per case and fixed costs of $200,000. The selling price would be $30 per case. Danna had just completed a marketing analysis that projected annual sales of 30,000 cases.

Danna was reluctant to report the forecast of 30,000 cases to the divisional manager. She knew that the first process was labour-intensive, whereas the second was largely automated, with little labour and no requirement for an additional production supervisor. If the first process were chosen, Jerry Jovanovic, a good friend, would be appointed as the line supervisor. If the second process were chosen, Jerry and an entire line of labourers would be laid off. After some consideration, Danna revised the projected sales downward to 22,000 cases.

She believed that the revision downward was justified. Since it would lead the divisional manager to choose the manual-oriented system, it showed a sensitivity to the needs of current employees—a sensitivity that she was afraid her divisional manager did not possess. He was too focused on quantitative factors in his decision making and usually ignored the qualitative aspects.

**Required:**
1. Compute the breakeven point for each process.
2. Compute the sales volume for which the two processes are equally profitable. Identify the range of sales for which the manual process is more profitable than the automated process. Identify the range of sales for which the automated process is more profitable than the manual process. Why did the divisional manager want the sales forecast?
3. Discuss Danna's decision to alter the sales forecast. Do you agree with her decision? Did she act ethically? Was her decision justified since it helped a number of employees keep their jobs? Should the impact on employees be factored into decisions? In fact, is it unethical *not* to consider the impact of decisions on employees?

**9–49**

Service Organization, Multiple Products, Breakeven, Pricing and Scheduling Decisions

LO1, LO2, LO3

Utah Metropolitan Ballet is located in Salt Lake City. The company is housed in the Capitol Theater, one of three buildings that make up the Bicentennial Arts Center in downtown Salt Lake City. The ballet company features five different ballets per year. For the upcoming season, the five ballets to be performed are *The Dream, Petrushka, The Nutcracker, Sleeping Beauty,* and *Bugaku.*

The president and general manager has tentatively scheduled the following number of performances for each ballet for the coming season:

| | |
|---|---|
| Dream | 5 |
| Petrushka | 5 |
| Nutcracker | 20 |
| Sleeping Beauty | 10 |
| Bugaku | 5 |

To produce each ballet, costs must be incurred for costumes, props, rehearsals, royalties, guest artist fees, choreography, salaries of production staff, music, and wardrobe. These costs are fixed for a particular ballet regardless of the number of performances. These direct fixed costs are given below for each ballet.

| Dream | Petrushka | Nutcracker | Sleeping Beauty | Bugaku |
|-------|-----------|------------|-----------------|--------|
| $275,500 | $145,500 | $70,500 | $345,000 | $155,500 |

Other fixed costs are incurred as follows:

| | |
|---|---|
| Advertising | $ 80,000 |
| Insurance | 15,000 |
| Administrative salaries | 222,000 |
| Office rental, phone, and so on | 84,000 |
| Total | $401,000 |

For each performance of each ballet, the following costs also are incurred:

| | |
|---|---|
| Utah Symphony | $3,800 |
| Auditorium rental | 700 |
| Dancers' payroll | 4,000 |
| Total | $8,500 |

The auditorium in which the ballet is presented has 1,854 seats, which are classified as A, B, and C. The A seats offer the best viewing, followed by the B seats and then the C seats. Information concerning the different types of seats is given below:

| | A Seats | B Seats | C Seats |
|---|---------|---------|---------|
| Quantity | 114 | 756 | 984 |
| Price | $35 | $25 | $15 |
| Percentage sold for each performance:* | | | |
| *Nutcracker* | 100% | 100% | 100% |
| All others | 100% | 80% | 75% |

* Based on past experience, the same percentages are expected for the coming season.

## Required:

1. Compute the expected revenues from the performances that have been tentatively scheduled. Prepare a variable-costing income statement for each ballet.
2. Calculate the number of performances of each ballet required to produce the revenues needed to cover each ballet's direct fixed expenses.
3. Calculate the number of performances of each ballet required for the company as a whole to break even. If you were the president and general manager, how would you alter the tentative schedule of performances?
4. Suppose that it is possible to offer a matinee of the popular *Nutcracker*. Seats would sell for $5 less than in the evening, and the auditorium rental would cost $200 less. The president and general manager believes that five matinee performances are feasible and that 80 percent of each type of seat can be sold. What effect will the matinee have on the company's operating income on the overall breakeven point?
5. Suppose that no additional evening performances can be offered beyond those tentatively scheduled. Assume that the company will offer five matinee performances of *The Nutcracker* and that no additional performances are feasible. Also, the company expects to receive $60,000 in government grants and contributions from supporters of the fine arts. Will the company break even? If not, what actions could the company take to bring revenues in line with costs?

## Research Assignment

**9–50**

Research Assignment

LO1, LO3

Interview the owner of a small business (for example, dry cleaner, shoe repair, CA firm) about the revenue he or she needs to break even. Has the business owner calculated this amount? Does he or she have a "feel" for the business's variable and fixed costs? Write up the results of your interview.

# Tactical Decision Making

**After studying Chapter 10, you should be able to:**

1. Describe the tactical decision-making model.

2. Explain how the activity resource usage model is used in assessing relevancy.

3. Apply the tactical decision-making concepts in a variety of management situations.

4. Choose the optimal product mix when faced with one constrained resource.

5. Explain the impact of cost on pricing decisions.

6. Use linear programming to find the optimal solution to a problem of multiple constrained resources. (Appendix)

## Scenario

Gunn Products, Inc., manufactures potentiometers. A potentiometer is a device that adjusts electrical resistance. Potentiometers are used in switches and knobs, for example, to control the volume on a radio or to raise or lower the lights using a dimmer switch. Currently, all parts necessary for the assembly of the products are produced internally. The company, in operation for five years, has a single plant located in Penticton, British Columbia. The facilities for the manufacture of potentiometers are leased, with five years remaining on the lease. All equipment is owned by the company. Because of increases in demand, production has been expanded significantly over the five years of operation, straining the capacity of the leased facilities. Currently, the company needs more warehousing and office space, as well as more space for the production of plastic mouldings. The current output of these mouldings, used to make potentiometers, needs to be expanded to accommodate the increased demand for the main product.

Len Gunn, owner and president of Gunn Products, has asked his vice-president of marketing, John Gunn, and his vice-president of finance, Linda Thayn, to meet and discuss the problem of limited capacity. This is the second meeting the three have had concerning the problem. In the first meeting, Len rejected Linda's proposal to build the company's own plant. He believed that it was too risky to invest the capital necessary to build a plant at this stage of the company's development. The combination of leasing a larger facility and subleasing the current plant was also considered but was rejected; subleasing would be difficult, if not impossible. At the end of the first meeting, Len asked John to explore the possibility of leasing another facility comparable to the current one. He also assigned Linda the task of identifying other possible solutions. As the second meeting began, Len asked John to give a report on the leasing alternative.

"After some careful research," John responded, "I'm afraid that the idea of leasing an additional plant is not a very good one. Although we have some space problems, our current level of production doesn't justify another plant. In fact, I expect it will be at least five years before we need to be concerned about expanding into another facility like the one we have now. My market studies reveal a modest growth in sales over the next five years. All this growth can be absorbed by our current production capacity. The large increases in demand that we experienced for the past five years are not likely to be repeated. Leasing another plant would be an overkill solution."

"Even modest growth will aggravate our current space problems," Len observed. "As you both know, we are already operating three production shifts. But, John, you are right—except for plastic mouldings, we could expand production, particularly during the graveyard shift. Linda, I hope that you have been successful in identifying some other possible solutions. Some fairly quick action is needed."

"Fortunately," Linda replied, "I believe that I have two feasible alternatives. One is to rent an additional building to be used for warehousing. By transferring our warehousing needs to the new building, we will free up internal space for offices and for expanding the production of plastic mouldings. I have located a building within two kilometres of our plant that we could use. It has the capacity to handle our current needs and the modest growth that John mentioned. The second alternative may be even more attractive. We currently produce all the parts that we use to manufacture potentiometers, including shafts and bushings. In the last several months, the market has been flooded with these two parts. Prices have tumbled as a result. It might be better to buy shafts and bushings instead of making them. If we stop internal production of shafts and bushings, that would free up the space we need. Well, Len, what do you think? Are these alternatives feasible? Or should I continue my search for additional solutions?"

"I like both the alternatives," responded Len. "In fact, they are exactly the types of solutions we are looking for. All we have to do now is choose the one that's best for our company. A key factor that must be examined is the cost of each alternative. Linda, you're the financial chief—prepare a report that details the costs that have an impact on this decision."[1]

### Questions to Think About

1. Describe the decision to be made by Gunn; is it a strategic or a tactical decision?

2. What cost do you think Len is referring to in the last paragraph of the scenario? Give examples.

3. Assume that Gunn Products accepts Linda's first alternative. Are there any noncost factors that should be considered? What about her second alternative?

One of the major roles of the management information system is supplying cost and revenue data that serve as the basis for user actions. Although a variety of user actions are possible, one of the more important actions that can be taken by users is tactical decision making. How cost and revenue data can be used to make tactical decisions is the focus of this chapter.

## Tactical Decision Making

**Objective** 1

Describe the tactical decision-making model.

**tactical decision making**

Choosing among alternatives with an immediate or limited end in view.

**Tactical decision making** consists of choosing among alternatives with an immediate or limited end in view. Accepting a special order for less than the normal selling price to utilize idle capacity and increase this year's profits is an example. Thus, some tactical decisions tend to be *short run* in nature; however, it should be emphasized that short-run decisions often have long-run consequences. Consider a second example. Suppose that a company is considering producing a component instead of buying it from suppliers. The immediate objective may be to lower the cost of making the main product. Yet this tactical decision may be a small part of the overall strategy of establishing a cost leadership position for the company. Thus, tactical decisions are often *small-scale actions* that serve a larger purpose.

---

1. This scenario is based on a company whose name was changed (along with the names of its executives) to preserve confidentiality.

**strategic decision making**

Choosing among alternative strategies so that a long-term competitive advantage is established.

The overall objective of **strategic decision making** is to select among alternative strategies so that a long-term competitive advantage is established. Tactical decision making should support this overall objective, even if the immediate objective is short run (accepting a one-time order to increase profits) or small scale (making instead of buying a component). Thus, *sound* tactical decision making means that the decisions made not only achieve the limited objective but also serve a larger purpose. In fact, no tactical decision should be made that does not serve the overall strategic goals of an organization. A good example of a company that has made tactical decisions that are in accordance with its strategic goals is Hyatt Hotels Corporation.[2] In the early 1990s, steep costs jeopardized a number of Hyatt's management contracts. It was necessary to reduce the cost structure fast. However, Hyatt attacked only the costs that guests did not particularly care about (for example, turndown service, in which the bedcovers are turned down at night and a mint is left on the pillow). Services that were important to business travellers, whom Hyatt courted, were expanded (for example, in-room fax machines).

## Model for Making Tactical Decisions

How does a company go about making good tactical decisions? We can describe a general approach to making tactical decisions. The following six steps describe the recommended decision-making process:[3]

1. Recognize and define the problem.
2. Identify alternatives as possible solutions to the problem; eliminate alternatives that are clearly not feasible.
3. Identify the costs and benefits associated with each feasible alternative. Classify costs and benefits as relevant or irrelevant, and eliminate irrelevant ones from consideration.
4. Total the relevant costs and benefits for each alternative.
5. Assess the qualitative factors.
6. Select the alternative with the greatest overall benefit.

**decision model**

A specific set of procedures that, when followed, produces a decision.

These six steps define a simple decision model. A **decision model** is a set of procedures that, if followed, will lead to a decision. Exhibit 10–1 depicts the sequence of steps to be followed.

### Step 1: Define the Problem

The first step is to recognize and define a specific problem. For example, the members of Gunn's management team all recognized the need for additional space for warehousing, offices, and the production of plastic mouldings. The amount of space needed, the reasons for the need, and how the additional space would be used are all important dimensions of the problem. However, the central question is *how* to acquire the additional space.

### Step 2: Identify the Alternatives

Step 2 is to list and consider possible solutions. Gunn Products identified the following possible solutions:

1. Build a new facility, with sufficient capacity to handle current and immediately foreseeable needs.

---

2. Richard A. Melcher, "Why Hyatt Is Toning Down the Glitz," *Business Week* (27 February 1995): pp. 92, 94.

3. The decision model we describe here has six steps. There is nothing special about this particular listing. You may find it useful to break down the steps into eight or ten segments. Alternatively, you could use a three-step model: (1) identify the decision; (2) identify the alternatives and their associated relevant costs; and (3) make the decision. The key point is to find a comfortable way for you to remember the important steps in the decision-making model.

EXHIBIT 10-1

Tactical Decision-Making
Model for Gunn Products'
Space Problem

| Step 1 | Define the problem. | Increase capacity for warehousing and production. |
|--------|--------------------|--------------------------------------------------|
| Step 2 | Identify the alternatives. | 1. Build new facility.<br>2. Lease larger facility; sublease current facility.<br>3. Lease additional facility.<br>4. Lease warehouse space.<br>5. Buy shafts and bushings; free up needed space. |
| Step 3 | Identify the costs and benefits associated with each feasible alternative. | Alternative 4:<br>   Variable production costs   $345,000<br>   Warehouse lease   135,000<br>Alternative 5:<br>   Purchase price   $460,000 |
| Step 4 | Total the relevant costs and benefits for each feasible alternative. | Alternative 4:   $480,000<br>Alternative 5:   460,000<br>   Differential cost   $ 20,000 |
| Step 5 | Assess the qualitative factors. | 1. Quality of external supplier<br>2. Reliability of external supplier<br>3. Price stability<br>4. Labour relations and community image |
| Step 6 | Make the decision. | Continue to produce shafts and bushings internally; lease warehouse. |

2. Lease a larger facility, and sublease its current facility.
3. Lease an additional, similar facility.
4. Lease an additional building that would be used for warehousing only, thereby freeing up space for expanded production.
5. Buy shafts and bushings externally, and use the space made available (previously used for producing these parts) to solve the space problem.

As part of this step, Gunn must eliminate alternatives that are not feasible. The first alternative was eliminated because it carried too much risk for the company. The second alternative was rejected because subleasing was not a viable option. The third was eliminated because it went too far in solving the space problem, and, presumably, was too expensive. The fourth and fifth alternatives were feasible; they were within the cost and risk constraints and solved the space needs of the company. Notice that Len linked the tactical decision (find more space) to the company's overall growth strategy by rejecting alternatives that involved too much risk at this stage of the company's development.

### Step 3: Identify the Costs and Benefits Associated with Each Feasible Alternative

In Step 3, the costs and benefits associated with each feasible alternative are identified. At this point, clearly irrelevant costs can be eliminated from consideration.[4] The management accountant is responsible for gathering necessary data.

---

4. It is fine to include irrelevant costs and benefits in the analysis as long as they are included in all of the alternatives. The reason we usually exclude irrelevant items is that focusing only on the relevant costs and benefits reduces the amount of data to be collected and presented.

Assume that Gunn Products determines that the costs of making the shafts and bushings include the following:

| | |
|---|---|
| Direct materials | $130,000 |
| Direct labour | 150,000 |
| Variable overhead | 65,000 |
| Total variable production cost | $345,000 |

If Gunn Products selects Alternative 4 rather than Alternative 5, these costs will still be incurred to internally manufacture the shafts and bushings. In addition, a warehouse must be leased to solve the space problem if Gunn continues to manufacture the shafts and bushings internally. An appropriate warehouse has been located for $135,000 per year. The second alternative is to purchase the shafts and bushings externally and use the freed-up production space. An outside supplier has offered to supply sufficient product for $460,000 per year.

It should be mentioned that when the cash-flow patterns become complicated for competing alternatives, it becomes difficult to produce a stream of equal cash flows for each alternative. In such a case, more sophisticated procedures can and should be used for the analysis. These procedures are discussed in Chapter 11, which deals with the long-run investment decisions referred to as *capital expenditure decisions*.

### Step 4: Total the Relevant Costs and Benefits for Each Feasible Alternative

It is clear now that Alternative 4 (continue producing internally, and lease more space) costs $480,000, whereas Alternative 5 (purchase outside, and use internal space) costs $460,000. The comparison follows:

| **Alternative 4** | | **Alternative 5** | |
|---|---|---|---|
| Variable cost of production | $345,000 | Purchase price | $460,000 |
| Warehouse lease | 135,000 | | |
| Total | $480,000 | | |

The differential cost is $20,000 in favour of Alternative 5.

### Step 5: Assess the Qualitative Factors

Decision making is based on an evaluation of quantitative and qualitative factors. Typically, the quantitative factors are determined by the differences in net cash flows that would result from different decisions (differential cash flows). In addition, there are other factors that bear upon the decision and that are usually referred to as qualitative. But qualitative factors can also be measured. Examples of qualitative factors that can be quantified are a ranking of suppliers that is based on quality and service, a rating of customer acceptance of different new products, and an opinion poll that clarifies whether a community prefers jobs or ecological preservation when considering a new logging or mining operation. Although it is more difficult and perhaps undesirable to attempt to measure these factors strictly in dollar terms,[5] in some cases, qualitative factors can be far more important than cash-flow considerations in decision making.

---

5. We can use four measurement scales to quantify qualitative factors: (a) nominal (such as high, low; male, female; acceptable, unacceptable); (b) ordinal, where it is possible to rank but where the difference between rank 1 and rank 2 is not equal to the difference between rank 2 and rank 3 (such as: strongly agree, agree, neutral, disagree, strongly disagree); (c) interval, where the measurement scale assigns equal value to intervals between assigned numbers (such as temperatures, aptitude scores); and (d) ratio, where there is a natural zero (such as the quantity of inventory, time to transport an important raw material). We can classify the factors considered in decision making into those that are monetary (measured in dollars) or nonmonetary (nondollar measures), and those that are not quantified. The choice to quantify or not to quantify a qualitative factor should be based on the cost and benefit considerations of the quantification. Attempts at quantification should be tempered by good judgment.

For example, in the make-or-buy decision facing Gunn Products, Len Gunn would likely be concerned with such qualitative considerations as the quality of the shafts and bushings purchased externally, the reliability of supply sources, the expected stability of prices over the next several years, labour relations, community image, and so on. To illustrate the possible impact of qualitative factors on the make-or-buy decision, consider the first two factors, quality and reliability of supply.

If the quality of shafts and bushings is significantly less if purchased externally than what is available internally, then the quantitative advantage from purchasing may be more fictitious than real. Settling for lower-quality materials may reduce the quality of the potentiometers, thus harming sales. Because of this, Gunn Products may choose to continue to produce the parts internally.

Similarly, if supply sources are not reliable, production schedules could be interrupted, and deliveries to customers could be late. These factors can increase labour costs and overhead and hurt sales. Again, depending on the perceived tradeoffs, Gunn Products may decide that producing the parts internally is better than purchasing them, even if relevant cost analysis gives the initial advantage to purchasing.

How should qualitative factors be handled in the decision-making process? First, they must be identified. Second, the decision maker may try to quantify them. For example, possible unreliability of the outside supplier might be quantified as the probable number of days late multiplied by the labour cost of downtime in Gunn's plant. Finally, truly qualitative factors, such as the impact of late orders on customer relations, must be taken into consideration in the final step of the decision-making model—the selection of the alternative with the greatest overall benefit.

### Step 6: Make the Decision

Once all relevant costs and benefits for each alternative have been assessed, and the qualitative factors weighed, a decision can be made. It is relatively easy to select an alternative when both quantitative and qualitative factors support that choice. It is also easy not to select an alternative when both quantitative and qualitative factors do not support that choice. However, it is quite difficult to make a decision when the quantitative and qualitative factors lead to different conclusions. Here, as in most cases requiring managerial decisions, judgment is crucial in assessing the appropriate tradeoffs between the quantitative and qualitative aspects of the decision. This boils down to juxtaposing the financial criterion versus the nonfinancial factors. What did Len decide for Gunn Products? Given the relatively small difference in costs of the two alternatives, and the weight Gunn Products assigns to ensuring quality and full employment, the decision was made to make the shafts and bushings internally and lease the warehouse.

### Relevant Costs Defined[6]

**relevant costs**

Future costs that change across alternatives.

**Relevant costs** are future costs that differ across alternatives. All decisions relate to the future; accordingly, only future costs can be relevant to decisions. However, to be relevant, a cost must also differ from one alternative to another. If a future cost is the same for more than one alternative, it has no effect on the decision. Such a cost is an *irrelevant cost*. The ability to identify relevant and irrelevant costs is an important decision-making skill.

---

6. "Relevant cost analysis" is a widely used term, but its use connotes a narrower meaning than is intended. Our analysis includes not only costs but also benefits, qualitative factors as well as quantifiable factors. When we use relevant cost analysis, we are referring to this wider meaning.

### Relevant Costs Illustrated

To illustrate the concept of relevant costs, consider Gunn's make-or-buy alternatives. The cost of direct labour used to produce shafts and bushings is $150,000 per year (based on normal volume). Should this cost be a factor in the decision? Is the direct labour cost a future cost that differs across the two alternatives? It is certainly a future cost. To produce the shafts and bushings for another year requires the services of direct labourers, who must be paid. But does it differ across the two alternatives? If shafts and bushings are purchased from an external supplier, no internal production is needed. The services of the direct labourers can be eliminated, reducing the direct labour cost for shafts and bushings under this alternative to zero. Thus, the cost of direct labour differs across alternatives ($150,000 for the make alternative and $0 for the buy alternative). It is, therefore, a relevant cost.

Implicit in this analysis is the use of a past cost to estimate a future cost. The most recent cost of direct labour for normal activity was $150,000. This past cost was used as the estimate of next year's cost. Although past costs are never relevant, they are often used to predict what future costs will be.

### Illustration of an Irrelevant Past Cost

Gunn Products uses machinery to manufacture shafts and bushings. This machinery was purchased five years ago and is being amortized at an annual rate of $125,000. Is this $125,000 a relevant cost? In other words, is amortization a future cost that differs across the two alternatives?

**sunk cost**

A cost for which the outlay has already been made and that cannot be affected by a future decision.

Amortization represents an allocation of a cost already incurred. It is a **sunk cost**, a cost that cannot be affected by any future action. Although we allocate this sunk cost to future periods and call that allocation *amortization*, none of the original cost is avoidable. Sunk costs are past costs. They are always the same across alternatives and are therefore always irrelevant.

It would be expected, therefore, that rational decision makers would not use sunk costs in decision making. There is some evidence, however, that decision makers do in fact use sunk costs in their decisions.[7] Typically, the evidence is that decision makers continue their commitment to a project even in the face of negative feedback, presumably because of the sunk cost.[8]

---

7. For example, see Barry M. Staw, "Knee-Deep in the Big Muddy: A Study of Escalating Commitment to a Chosen Course of Action," *Organization Behaviour and Human Performance*, 1976 (16): pp. 27-44; Arkes and Blumer, "The Psychology of Sunk Costs," *Organization Behaviour and Human Decision Processes*, 1985 (35): pp. 124-140; Nabil Elias, "Entrapment and the Sunk Cost Phenomena: More than Self-Justification," Working Paper, Faculty of Management, University of Manitoba, 1988; and Nabil Elias and Mohamed Ibrahim, "Entrapment, Sunk Cost, and Marginal Analysis: An Identification of Issues," Paper presented at the 15th Congress of the European Accounting Association, Madrid, Spain, April 1992.

8. Is it necessary to conclude that decision makers are irrational? Possible rational reasons for the use of sunk costs in decision making include the following:

   1. Performance evaluation systems tend to be oriented toward the short term and are retrospective in their outlook. Managers may desire to cover up previously made but failing investment decisions (now seen as past mistakes) in the hope that they will advance or be promoted before the full effects of these decisions become known. Managers are often concerned about how past costs or performance will appear to their superiors.

   2. Generally accepted accounting principles (including accrual accounting) in financial performance measurement are primarily based on historical (sunk) cost accounting. Externally reported results may affect management's performance bonuses and influence management's objectives. Sunk costs can therefore play a role in managerial decisions.

   3. When sunk costs are used by decision makers as inputs in cost prediction models, this use may give the appearance that sunk costs are being used in decision models as well.

In choosing between the two alternatives, the original cost of the machinery used to produce shafts and bushings and its associated amortization are not factors. However, it should be noted that the machinery's salvage value (what Gunn could receive for selling the machinery now) would be relevant and would be included as a benefit of purchasing from outside suppliers. To simplify the Gunn example, assume that the salvage value of the machinery is zero.

### *Illustration of an Irrelevant Future Cost*

Assume that the cost to lease the current factory used by Gunn, $340,000, is allocated to different production departments, including the department that produces shafts and bushings, which receives $12,000 of the cost. Is this $12,000 cost relevant to the make-or-buy decision facing Gunn?

The lease payment is a future cost, since it must be paid during each of the next five years. But does the cost differ across the make-and-buy alternatives? Whatever option Gunn chooses, the factory lease payment must be made—it is the same across both alternatives. The amount of the payment allocated to the remaining departments may change if production of shafts and bushings is stopped, but the level of the total payment is unaffected by the decision. It is therefore an irrelevant cost.

The example illustrates the importance of identifying allocations of common fixed costs. Allocations of common fixed costs can be safely classified as irrelevant since any choice does not affect the level of cost. The only effect may be a reallocation of those common fixed costs to fewer cost objects or segments.

Examine all three cost examples for the production of shafts and bushings to see which are relevant in deciding whether or not to continue production. Of the three, only direct labour cost is relevant, since it is the only one that occurs if production continues but stops if production stops.

|  | Cost to Make | Cost Not to Make | Differential Cost |
|---|---|---|---|
| Direct labour | $150,000 | — | $150,000 |
| Amortization | 125,000 | $125,000 | — |
| Allocated lease | 12,000 | 12,000 | — |
|  | $287,000 | $137,000 | $150,000 |

The same concepts apply to benefits. One alternative may produce an amount of future benefits different from another alternative (for example, differences in future revenues). If future benefits differ across alternatives, then they are relevant and should be included in the analysis.

## Ethics in Tactical Decision Making

In tactical decision making, ethical concerns revolve around the way in which decisions are implemented, and the possible sacrifice of long-run objectives for short-run gain. Relevant costs are used in making tactical decisions—decisions that have an immediate view or limited objective in mind. However, decision makers should always maintain an ethical framework. Reaching objectives is important, but how you get there is perhaps more important. Unfortunately, many managers have the opposite view. Part of the reason for the problem is the extreme pressure to perform that many managers feel. Often the individual who is not a top performer may be laid off or demoted. Under such conditions, the temptation is often to engage in questionable behaviour today and let the future take care of itself.

For example, laying off employees to increase profits in the short run could loosely qualify as a tactical decision. However, if the only benefit is an increase in short-run profits, and there is no evidence that the decision supports the company's longer-term strategic objectives, then the decision can be questioned. In fact, the workload may not decrease at all, but the number of people available to carry out the work has decreased. Pressure may then be exerted by managers on the remaining employees to work unreasonable amounts of overtime. Is this right?

All companies should have a clear mission and goals. For example, if marketing enthusiastically touts the product's high quality and reliability while engineering and production are busily reducing the quality of the materials and reliability of the design, problems are sure to surface. Customers may see this inconsistency as an ethical lapse.

Debates about what is right and what is wrong can be endless. As was pointed out in Chapter 1, ethical standards have been developed to provide guidance for individuals. Additionally, many companies are hiring full-time ethics officers. Often these officers set up "hot lines" so that employees can call and register complaints or ask about the propriety of certain actions. However, some ethical problems can be avoided simply by using common sense and not focusing solely on the short term at the expense of the long term.

## Relevancy, Cost Behaviour, and the Activity Resource Usage Model

**Objective** 2

Explain how the activity resource usage model is used in assessing relevancy.

The space problem Gunn Products faced was a very simple example of tactical decision making. Most tactical decisions require more complicated analysis—in particular, they require more extensive consideration of cost behaviour. Earlier work on relevant costing emphasized the importance of variable versus fixed costs. Usually, variable costs were relevant and fixed costs were not. For example, the variable costs of production were relevant to the Gunn Products make-or-buy decision. The amortization expense and factory lease were not relevant. However, activity-based costing allows further consideration of variable costs with respect to both unit-based and nonunit-based cost drivers.

The key point is that changes in supply and demand for activity resources must be considered when assessing relevance. If changes in demand and supply for resources across alternatives bring about changes in resource spending, then the changes in resource spending are the relevant costs that should be used in assessing the relative desirability of the two alternatives.

Recall from Chapter 3 that the activity-based resource usage model reminds us to consider both flexible and committed resources. These categories can help us to identify relevant costs, thereby facilitating relevant cost analysis.

### Flexible Resources

Some resources can be easily purchased in the amount needed and at the time of use. For example, electricity used to run stoves that boil fruit in the production of jelly is a resource acquired as used and needed. Thus, for this resource category, if the demand for an activity changes across alternatives, then resource spending will change and the cost of the activity is relevant to the decision. This type of resource spending is typically referred to as a variable cost. The key point is that the amount of resource demanded by the company equals the amount of resource supplied.

Now suppose that the jelly producer is asked by a customer to produce a special order of jelly for promotional purposes. The jelly producer must consider the following two alternatives: (1) accept the special, one-time order, and (2) reject the special order. If accepting the order increases the demand for kilowatt-hours (electricity's cost driver), then the cost of electricity will differ across alternatives. Thus, electricity is relevant to the decision.

## Committed Resources

Committed resources are purchased before they are used. Therefore, there may or may not be unused capacity that will affect tactical decision making. We will consider two types of committed resources: those that can be altered in the short run and those that provide capacity for multiple periods.

### Committed Resources for the Short Run

Some committed resources are acquired in advance of usage through implicit contracting; they are usually acquired in lumpy amounts. (Graphically, we usually think of this cost as step-variable or step-fixed.) This category often represents resource spending associated with an organization's salaried and hourly employees. The implicit understanding is that the organization will maintain employment levels even though there may be temporary downturns in the quantity of an activity used. This means that an activity may have unused capacity available. Thus, an increase in demand for an activity across alternatives may not mean that the activity cost will increase (because all the increased demand is absorbed by the unused activity capacity). For example, assume that a company has five manufacturing engineers who supply a capacity of 10,000 engineering hours (2,000 hours each). The cost of this activity capacity is $250,000, or $25 per hour. Suppose that this year, the company expects to use only 9,000 engineering hours for its normal business. This means that the engineering activity has 1,000 hours of unused capacity. In deciding to reject or accept a special order that requires 500 engineering hours, the cost of engineering would be irrelevant. The order can be filled using unused engineering capacity, and the resource spending is the same for each alternative ($250,000 will be spent whether the order is accepted or not).

However, if a change in demand across activities produces a change in resource supply, then the activity cost will change and, thus, be relevant to the decision. A change in resource supply means a change in resource spending and, consequently, a change in activity cost. A change in resource spending can occur in one of two ways: (1) the demand for the resource exceeds the supply (increasing resource spending); or (2) the demand for the resource drops permanently, and supply exceeds demand enough that activity capacity can be reduced (decreasing resource spending).

To illustrate the first change, consider once again the engineering activity and the special-order decision. Suppose that the special order requires 1,500 engineering hours. This exceeds the resource supply. To meet the demand, the organization would need to hire a sixth engineer or perhaps use a consulting engineer. Either way, resource spending increases if the order is accepted; thus, the cost of engineering is now a relevant cost.

To illustrate the second type of change, suppose that the company's manager is considering purchasing a component used for production instead of making it. Assume the same facts about engineering capacity: 10,000 hours available and 9,000 used. If the component is purchased, then the demand for engineering hours will drop from 9,000 to 7,000. This is a permanent reduction, because engineering support will no longer be needed for manufacturing the component. Unused capacity is now 3,000 hours: 2,000 permanent and 1,000 temporary. Furthermore, since engineering capacity is acquired in chunks of 2,000, this means that the company can reduce activity capacity and resource spending by laying off one engineer. The resource supply is reduced to 8,000 hours. If an engineer's salary is $50,000, then engineering cost would differ by $50,000 across the make-or-buy alternatives. This cost is therefore relevant to the decision. However, if the demand for the engineering activity drops by less than 2,000 hours, the increase in unused capacity is not enough to reduce resource supply and resource spending; in this case, the cost of the engineering activity would not be relevant.

### Committed Resources for Multiple Periods

Often resources are acquired in advance for multiple periods, before the resource demands are known. Leasing or buying a building is an example. Buying multi-period activity capacity is often done by paying cash up front. In this case, an annual expense may be recognized, but no additional resource spending is needed. Up-front resource spending is a sunk cost and, thus, never relevant. Periodic resource spending, such as leasing, is essentially independent of resource usage. Even if a permanent reduction of activity usage is experienced, it is difficult to reduce resource spending because of formal contractual commitments.

For example, assume that a company leases a plant for $100,000 per year for ten years. The plant is capable of producing 20,000 units of a product—the level expected when the plant was leased. After five years, suppose that the demand for the product drops and the plant needs to produce only 15,000 units each year. The lease payment of $100,000 still must be paid each year, even though production activity has decreased. Now suppose that demand increases beyond the 20,000-unit capability. In this case, the company may consider acquiring or leasing an additional plant. Here, resource spending could change across alternatives. The decision, however, to acquire long-term activity capacity is not in the realm of tactical decision making. This is not a short-term or small-scale decision. Decisions involving multiperiod capabilities are called *capital investment decisions* and are discussed in Chapter 11. Exhibit 10–2 summarizes the activity resource usage model's role in assessing relevancy.

**EXHIBIT　10-2**

Activity Resource Usage Model and Assessing Relevancy

| Resource Category | Demand and Supply Relationships | Relevancy |
|---|---|---|
| Flexible Resources | Supply = Demand | |
| | a. Demand Changes | a. Relevant |
| | b. Demand Constant | b. Not Relevant |
| Committed Resources (Short-Term) | Supply − Demand = Unused Capacity | |
| | a. Demand Increase < Unused Capacity | a. Not Relevant |
| | b. Demand Increase > Unused Capacity | b. Relevant |
| | c. Demand Decrease (Permanent) | |
| |    1. Activity Capacity Reduced | 1. Relevant |
| |    2. Activity Capacity Unchanged | 2. Not Relevant |
| Committed Resources (Multiperiod Capacity) | Supply − Demand = Unused Capacity | |
| | a. Demand Increase < Unused Capacity | a. Not Relevant |
| | b. Demand Decrease (Permanent) | b. Not Relevant |
| | c. Demand Increase > Unused Capacity | c. Capital Decision |

## Illustrative Examples of Relevant Cost Applications

**Objective 3**

Apply the tactical decision-making concepts in a variety of management situations.

Relevant costing is of value in solving many different types of problems. Traditionally, these applications include decisions to make or buy a component; keep or drop a segment or product line; accept a special order at less than the usual price; and process a joint product further or sell it at the split-off point. Of course, this is not an exhaustive list. However, many of the same decision-making principles apply to a variety of problems.

### Make-or-Buy Decisions

Managers are often faced with the decision of whether to make or buy components used in manufacturing. Indeed, management should periodically evaluate

**make-or-buy decisions**

Relevant cost analyses that focus on whether a component should be made internally or purchased externally.

past decisions concerning production. Conditions upon which prior decisions were based may have changed, and as a result, a different approach may be required. Periodic evaluations, of course, are not the only source of these **make-or-buy decisions**. Frequently, as with Gunn Products, the decision is motivated by an indirectly related, underlying problem.

To illustrate more fully the cost analysis of a make-or-buy problem, assume that Kopp Manufacturing currently produces an electronic component used in one of its printers. In one year, Kopp will switch production to another type of printer, and the electronic component will no longer be used. However, for the coming year, Kopp must produce 10,000 of these parts to support the production requirements for the old printer.

Kopp has been approached by a potential supplier of the component. The supplier will build the electronic component to Kopp's specifications for $4.75 per unit. The offer sounds very attractive, since the full manufacturing cost per unit is $8.20. Should Kopp Manufacturing make or buy the component?

The problem and the feasible alternatives are both readily identifiable. Since the horizon for the decision is only one period, there is no need to be concerned about periodically recurring costs. Relevant costing is particularly useful for short-run analysis. We simply need to identify the relevant costs, total them, and make a choice (assuming no overriding qualitative concerns).

First, let's look at the costs associated with the production of these 10,000 parts. The full absorption cost is computed as follows:

|  | Total Cost | Unit Cost |
|---|---|---|
| Rental of equipment | $12,000 | $1.20 |
| Equipment amortization | 2,000 | 0.20 |
| Direct materials | 10,000 | 1.00 |
| Direct labour | 20,000 | 2.00 |
| Variable overhead | 8,000 | 0.80 |
| General fixed overhead | 30,000 | 3.00 |
| Total | $82,000 | $8.20 |

Most of the equipment is rented. However, one specialized piece of machinery had to be custom-made and was purchased. Rental equipment can be returned at any time without penalty; the company is charged only for the time the equipment is held. The specialized machinery will not be fully amortized at the end of the year; however, the company plans to scrap it, since it cannot be sold. The company recently purchased sufficient materials for 5,000 components. There is no alternative use for the materials. Variable overhead is applied to the electronic component at $0.40 per direct labour dollar. General fixed overhead for the plant totals $1 million. General fixed overhead is assigned to products based on the space occupied by each product. The manufacturing facilities for the component under consideration occupy 6,000 of the plant's 200,000 square metres. Thus, $30,000 of the general fixed overhead is allocated to the electronic component ($0.03 \times \$1,000,000$).

Of these cost items, amortization can be eliminated from the analysis; it is a sunk cost. Since the direct materials already purchased have no alternative use, half of the total cost of direct materials is also a sunk cost. General overhead is not relevant either. The $30,000 is an allocation of a common fixed cost that will continue even if the component is purchased externally.

All other costs are relevant. The cost of renting the equipment is relevant, since it will not be needed if the part is bought externally. Similarly, the cost of direct labour, the cost of the remaining 5,000 units of direct materials, and the cost of variable overhead are all relevant costs; they would not be incurred if the component were bought externally.

Now let's focus on the purchase of the component. Of course, the purchase cost is relevant. If the component were made, this cost would not be incurred. Are there any other costs associated with an outside purchase? A check with the receiving dock elicits the information that the receiving and inspecting crew is at capacity. An additional purchase of this magnitude would require hiring an additional half-time employee for the year at a cost of $8,500. The purchasing department has sufficient excess capacity to handle the purchase of the component, so no additional cost would be incurred there.

A listing of the total relevant costs for each alternative follows:

|  | Alternatives | | Differential |
| --- | --- | --- | --- |
|  | **Make** | **Buy** | **Cost to Make** |
| Rental of equipment | $12,000 | — | $ 12,000 |
| Direct materials | 5,000 | — | 5,000 |
| Direct labour | 20,000 | — | 20,000 |
| Variable overhead | 8,000 | — | 8,000 |
| Purchase cost | — | $47,500 | (47,500) |
| Half-time employee | — | 8,500 | (8,500) |
| Total relevant cost | $45,000 | $56,000 | $(11,000) |

The analysis shows that making the product is $11,000 cheaper than buying it. The supplier's offer should be rejected.

The same analysis can be done on a unit-cost basis. Once the relevant costs are identified, relevant unit costs can be compared. For this example, these costs are $4.50 ($45,000/10,000) for the make alternative and $5.60 ($56,000/10,000) for the buy alternative.

## Keep-or-Drop Decisions

**keep-or-drop decisions**

Relevant cost analyses that focus on keeping or dropping a segment of business.

Often a manager needs to determine whether or not a segment, such as a product line, should be kept or dropped. Segmented reports prepared on a variable-costing basis provide valuable information for these **keep-or-drop decisions**. Both the segment's contribution margin and its segment margin are useful in evaluating a segment's performance. However, while segmented reports provide useful information for keep-or-drop decisions, relevant costing describes how the information should be used to arrive at a decision.

To illustrate, consider Norton Materials, Inc., which produces concrete blocks, bricks, and roofing tile. The company's controller has prepared the following estimated income statement for 2004 (in thousands of dollars):

|  | **Blocks** | **Bricks** | **Tile** | **Total** |
| --- | --- | --- | --- | --- |
| Sales revenue | $500 | $800 | $150 | $1,450 |
| Less: Variable expenses | 250 | 480 | 140 | 870 |
| Contribution margin | $250 | $320 | $ 10 | $ 580 |
| Less direct fixed expenses: | | | | |
| Salaries | $ 37 | $ 40 | $ 35 | $ 112 |
| Advertising | 10 | 10 | 10 | 30 |
| Amortization | 53 | 40 | 10 | 103 |
| Total | $100 | $ 90 | $ 55 | $ 245 |
| Segment margin | $150 | $230 | $ (45) | $ 335 |
| Less: Common fixed expenses | | | | 125 |
| Net income | | | | $ 210 |

The projected performance of the roofing tile line shows a negative segment margin. This would represent the third consecutive year of poor performance for that line. The president of Norton Materials, Tilman Blackburn, concerned about this poor performance, is trying to decide whether to drop or keep the roofing tile line.

Tilman's first reaction is to take steps to increase the sales revenue of roofing tiles. He is considering an aggressive sales promotion coupled with an increase in the selling price. The company's marketing manager thinks that this approach would be fruitless, however: the market is saturated and the level of competition too keen to hold out any hope for increasing the company's market share. An increase in the selling price would almost certainly result in a decrease in sales revenue.

Increasing the product line's profitability through cost cutting is not feasible either. Costs were cut during the past two years to reduce the loss to its current anticipated level. Any further reductions would lower the product's quality and adversely affect sales.

With no hope for improving the line's profit performance beyond its projected level, Tilman has decided to drop it. He reasons that the company will lose a total of $10,000 in contribution margin but save $45,000 by dismissing the line's supervisor and eliminating its advertising budget. (The amortization cost of $10,000 is not relevant, since it represents an allocation of a sunk cost.) Thus, dropping the product line has a $35,000 advantage over keeping it. Before finalizing the decision, Tilman decides to notify the marketing manager and the production supervisor. The following memo is sent to both individuals:

**MEMO**

| | |
|---|---|
| **TO:** | Debora Sachs, Marketing, and Trevor Molinaro, Production |
| **FROM:** | Tilman Blackburn, President |
| **SUBJECT:** | Tentative Decision Concerning the Production of Roofing Tiles |
| **DATE:** | March 14, 2004 |

Since there is no realistic expectation of improving the profitability of the roofing tile line, I have reluctantly decided to discontinue its production. I realize that this decision will have a negative impact on the community, since our workforce will need to be reduced. I am also sympathetic to the disruption this may cause in the personal lives of many employees.

However, we must be prepared to take actions that are in the best interests of the company. By eliminating the roofing tile line, we can improve the company's cash position by $35,000 per year. To support this decision, I am including the following analysis (focusing only on the tile segment):

| | Keep | Drop | Differential Amount to Keep |
|---|---|---|---|
| Sales | $150 | $— | $150 |
| Less: Variable expenses | 140 | — | 140 |
| Contribution margin | $ 10 | $— | $ 10 |
| Less: Advertising | 10 | — | 10 |
| Less: Cost of supervision | 35 | — | 35 |
| Total relevant benefit (loss) | $ (35) | $ 0 | $ (35) |

I have included only future costs and benefits that differ across the two alternatives. Amortization on the tile equipment is not relevant, since it is simply an allocation of a sunk cost. Also, the level of common fixed costs is unchanged regardless of whether we keep or drop the tile line.

At this point, I view the decision as tentative and welcome any response. Perhaps I am overlooking something that would affect the decision. Please respond as soon as possible.

### Keep or Drop with Complementary Effects

In response to the memo, the marketing manager writes that dropping the roofing tile line would lower sales of blocks by 10 percent and of bricks by 8 percent. She explains that many customers buy roofing tile at the same time they purchase blocks or bricks. Some will go elsewhere if they cannot buy both products at the same location.

Shortly after receiving this response, Tilman decides to repeat the analysis, factoring in the effect that dropping the tile line would have on the sales of the other two lines. He decides to use total company sales and total costs for each alternative. As before, amortization and common fixed costs are excluded from the analysis on the basis of irrelevancy.

Dropping the product line reduces total sales by $264,000: $50,000 (0.10 × $500,000) for blocks, $64,000 (0.08 × $800,000) for bricks, and $150,000 for roofing tiles. Similarly, total variable expenses are reduced by $203,400: $25,000 (0.10 × $250,000) for blocks, $38,400 (0.08 × $480,000) for bricks, and $140,000 for tiles. Thus, total contribution margin is reduced by $60,600 ($264,000 − $203,400).

Since dropping the tile line saves only $45,000 in supervision costs and advertising, the net effect is a disadvantage of $15,600 ($45,000 − $60,600). The following is a summary of the analysis using the new information (in thousands):

|  | Keep | Drop | Differential Amount to Keep |
|---|---|---|---|
| Sales | $1,450 | $1,186.0 | $264.0 |
| Less: Variable expenses | 870 | 666.6 | 203.4 |
| Contribution margin | $ 580 | $ 519.4 | $ 60.6 |
| Less: Advertising | 30 | 20.0 | 10.0 |
| Less: Cost of supervision | 112 | 77.0 | 35.0 |
| Total | $ 438 | $ 422.4 | $ 15.6 |

Tilman is pleased to find the outcome favouring production of the roofing tile. The unpleasant task of dismissing some of his workforce is no longer necessary. However, just as he is preparing to write a second memo announcing his new decision, he receives Trevor Molinaro's written response to his first memo.

### Keep or Drop with Alternative Use of Facilities

The production supervisor's response is somewhat different. He agrees that roofing tile should be eliminated but suggests that it be replaced with the production of floor tile. He gives assurances that existing machinery could be converted to produce this new product with little or no cost. He has also contacted the marketing manager about the marketability of floor tile, and he includes this assessment in his response.

The marketing manager sees the market for floor tile as stronger and less competitive than that for roofing tile. However, the other two lines would still lose sales at the same rate; producing floor tile would not change that result. The following estimated financial statement for floor tile is also submitted (in thousands of dollars):

| Sales | $100 |
|---|---|
| Less: Variable expenses | 40 |
| Contribution margin | $ 60 |
| Less: Direct fixed expenses | 55 |
| Segment margin | $ 5 |

Tilman Blackburn is now faced with a third alternative: replacing the roofing tile with floor tile. Should the roofing tile line be kept, or should it be dropped and replaced with the floor tile?

From his prior analysis, Tilman knows that dropping the roofing tile would decrease the company's contribution margin by $60,600. Producing the floor tile would generate $60,000 more in contribution margin, according to the estimate. Dropping the roofing tile line and replacing it with floor tile, then, would cause a $600 net decrease in total contribution margin ($60,600 – $60,000). The same outcome can be developed by directly comparing the relevant benefits and costs of the two alternatives (dollars expressed in thousands).

|  | Keep | Drop and Replace | Differential Amount to Keep |
|---|---|---|---|
| Sales | $1,450 | $1,286.0[a] | $164.0 |
| Variable expenses | (870) | (706.6)[b] | (163.4) |
| Contribution margin | $ 580 | $ 579.4 | $ (0.6) |

[a] ($1,450 – $150 – $50 – $64) + $100
[b] ($870 – $140 – $25 – $38.4) + $40

The Norton Materials example again illustrates the tactical decision-making process. First, a problem was identified and defined (the poor performance of the roofing tile product line). Next, possible solutions were listed, and those that were not feasible were eliminated. For example, increasing sales or further decreasing costs were both rejected. Three feasible solutions were examined: (1) keeping the product line, (2) dropping it, and (3) dropping the product line and replacing it with another product. An analysis of the costs and benefits of the feasible alternatives led to the selection of the preferred alternative (keeping the product line).

The example provides some insights beyond the simple application of the decision model. The initial analysis, which focused on two feasible alternatives, led to a tentative decision to drop the product line. Additional information provided by the marketing manager led to a reversal of the first decision. Before that decision could be implemented, the president was made aware of a third feasible alternative, which required additional analysis.

Often managers do not have all the information necessary to make the best decision. They also may not be able to identify all feasible solutions. Managers benefit from gathering all the information available before finalizing a decision. They should attempt to identify as many feasible solutions as possible. As the example clearly illustrates, limited information can result in poor decisions. If the set of feasible solutions is too narrow, the best solution may never be selected simply because the manager has not thought of it. Managers can benefit from obtaining input from others who are familiar with the problem. By doing so, they can expand both the set of information and the set of feasible solutions. The result is improved decision making.

## Special-Order Decisions

**special-order decisions**

Relevant cost analyses that focus on whether a specially priced order should be accepted or rejected.

Price discrimination laws require that companies sell identical products at the same price to competing customers in the same market. These restrictions do not apply to competitive bids or to noncompeting customers. Bid prices can vary to customers in the same market, and companies often have the opportunity to consider special orders from potential customers in markets not ordinarily served. **Special-order decisions** focus on whether a specially priced order should be accepted or rejected. These orders can often be attractive, especially when the company is operating below its maximum productive capacity.

Suppose, for example, that an ice-cream company is operating at 80 percent of its productive capacity. The company has a capacity of 20 million one-litre units. The company produces only premium ice cream. The total costs associated with producing and selling 16 million units are as follows (in thousands of dollars):

|                          | Total     | Unit Cost |
|--------------------------|-----------|-----------|
| Variable costs:          |           |           |
| Dairy ingredients        | $11,200   | $0.70     |
| Sugar                    | 1,600     | 0.10      |
| Flavourings              | 2,400     | 0.15      |
| Direct labour            | 4,000     | 0.25      |
| Packaging                | 3,200     | 0.20      |
| Commissions              | 320       | 0.02      |
| Distribution             | 480       | 0.03      |
| Other                    | 800       | 0.05      |
| Total variable costs     | $24,000   | $1.50     |
| Fixed costs:             |           |           |
| Salaries                 | $   960   | $0.060    |
| Amortization             | 320       | 0.020     |
| Utilities                | 80        | 0.005     |
| Taxes                    | 32        | 0.002     |
| Other                    | 160       | 0.010     |
| Total fixed costs        | $ 1,552   | $0.097    |
| Total costs              | $25,552   | $1.597    |
| Wholesale selling price  | $32,000   | $2.000    |

An ice-cream distributor from a region not normally served by the company has offered to buy 2 million units at $1.55 per unit, provided that its own label can be attached to the product. The distributor has also agreed to pay the transportation costs. Since the distributor approached the company directly, there is no sales commission. As the manager of the ice-cream company, would you accept this order or reject it?

The offer of $1.55 is well below the normal selling price of $2.00; in fact, it is even below the total unit cost. Even so, accepting the order may be profitable. The company does have idle capacity, and the order will not displace other units being produced to sell at the normal price. Additionally, many of the costs are not relevant; fixed costs will continue regardless of whether the order is accepted or rejected.

If the order is accepted, a benefit of $1.55 per unit will be realized that otherwise wouldn't. However, all of the variable costs except for distribution ($0.03) and commissions ($0.02) will also be incurred, producing a cost of $1.45 per unit. The net benefit is $0.10 ($1.55 – $1.45) per unit. The relevant cost analysis can be summarized as follows:

|                   | Accept      | Reject | Differential Benefit to Accept |
|-------------------|-------------|--------|-------------------------------|
| Revenues          | $3,100,000  | $—     | $3,100,000                    |
| Dairy ingredients | (1,400,000) | —      | (1,400,000)                   |
| Sugar             | (200,000)   | —      | (200,000)                     |
| Flavourings       | (300,000)   | —      | (300,000)                     |
| Direct labour     | (500,000)   | —      | (500,000)                     |
| Packaging         | (400,000)   | —      | (400,000)                     |
| Other             | (100,000)   | —      | (100,000)                     |
| Total             | $ 200,000   | $ 0    | $ 200,000                     |

We see that for this company, accepting the special order will increase profits by $200,000 ($0.10 × 2,000,000).

# Decisions to Sell or Process Further

**joint products**

Products that are inseparable prior to a split-off point. All manufacturing costs up to the split-off point are joint costs.

**split-off point**

The point at which products become distinguishable after passing through a common process.

**sell-or-process further**

Relevant cost analysis that focuses on whether a product should be processed beyond the split-off point.

**Joint products** have common processes and costs of production up to a split-off point. At that point, they become distinguishable. For example, certain minerals such as copper and gold may both be found in a given ore. The ore must be mined, crushed, and treated before the copper and gold are separated. The point of separation is called the **split-off point**. The costs of mining, crushing, and treatment are common to both products.

Often joint products are sold at the split-off point. Sometimes it is more profitable to process a joint product further, beyond the split-off point, prior to selling it. Determining whether to **sell or process further** is an important decision that a manager must make.

To illustrate, consider Appletime Corporation. Appletime is a large corporate farm that specializes in growing apples. Each plot produces approximately 1,000 kilograms of apples. The trees in each plot must be sprayed, fertilized, watered, and pruned. When the apples are ripened, workers are hired to pick them. The apples are then transported to a warehouse, where they are washed and sorted. The approximate cost of all these activities (including processing) is $300 per 1,000 kilograms per year.

Apples are sorted into three grades (A, B, and C), which are determined by size and blemishes. Large apples without blemishes (bruises, cuts, wormholes, and so on) are sorted into one bin and classified as Grade A. Small apples without blemishes are sorted into a second bin and classified as Grade B. All remaining apples are placed in a third bin and classified as Grade C. Every 1,000 kilograms of apples produce 400 kilograms of Grade A, 300 kilograms of Grade B, and 300 kilograms of Grade C.

Grade A apples are sold to large supermarkets for $0.80 per kilogram. Grade B apples are packaged in plastic. Each bag contains 2.5 kilograms of apples and is sold to supermarkets for $1.30. The cost of each plastic bag is $0.05. Grade C apples are processed further and made into applesauce. The sauce is sold in 500-millilitre cans for $0.75 each. The cost of processing is $0.20 per kilogram of apples. The final output is 500 cans. Exhibit 10–3 summarizes the process. Keep in mind that the processing costs occur only if further processing takes place. Hence, processing costs are relevant.

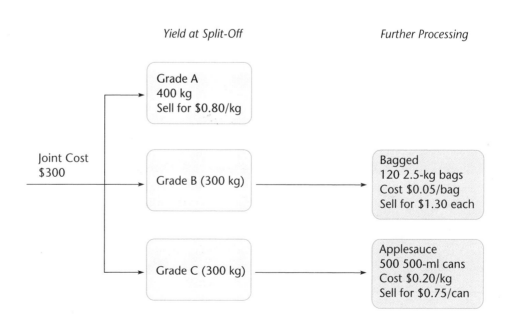

**EXHIBIT 10-3**

Appletime's Joint Process

*Yield at Split-Off*

*Further Processing*

Joint Cost $300

Grade A
400 kg
Sell for $0.80/kg

Grade B (300 kg)

Bagged
120 2.5-kg bags
Cost $0.05/bag
Sell for $1.30 each

Grade C (300 kg)

Applesauce
500 500-ml cans
Cost $0.20/kg
Sell for $0.75/can

A large supermarket chain recently requested that Appletime supply 500-millilitre cans of apple pie filling, for which the chain was willing to pay $0.90 per can. Appletime determined that the Grade B apples would be suitable for this purpose and estimated that it would cost $0.40 per kilogram to process the apples into pie filling. The output would be 500 cans.

In deciding whether to sell Grade B apples at split-off or to process them further and sell them as pie filling, the common costs of spraying, pruning, and so on are not relevant. The company must pay the $300 per 1,000 kilograms for these activities regardless of whether it sells at split-off or processes further. However, the revenues earned at split-off are likely to differ from the revenues that would be received if the Grade B apples were sold as pie filling. Therefore, revenues are a relevant consideration.

Since there are 300 kilograms of Grade B apples at split-off, Appletime sells 120 2.5-kilogram bags at a price of $1.30 each—$156 in total. Total cost of bagging the apples is $6 ($0.05 × 120). Thus, the total net revenues at split-off are $150 ($156 – $6). If the apples are processed into pie filling, the total revenues are $450 ($0.90 × 500). Therefore, the incremental revenues from processing further are $294 ($450 – $156). The costs of further processing are $120 ($0.40 × 300 kilograms), which is $114 greater than the cost of bagging the apples. Since revenues increase by $294 and costs by only $114, the net benefit of processing further is $180. Thus, Appletime should process the Grade B apples into pie filling. The analysis is summarized as follows:

| | Sell | Process Further | Differential Amount to Process Further |
|---|---|---|---|
| Revenues | $156 | $ 450 | $ 294 |
| Processing cost | (6) | (120) | (114) |
| Total | $150 | $ 330 | $ 180 |

## Product-Mix Decisions

**Objective 4**

Choose the optimal product mix when faced with one constrained resource.

In the example above, of every 1,000 kilograms of apples harvested, 400 were Grade A, 300 were Grade B, and 300 were Grade C. Although the relative amounts of each type of apple can be influenced to some extent by the procedures followed in spraying, watering, fertilizing, and so on, the mix of apples is largely beyond Appletime's control. However, many organizations have total discretion in choosing their product mix. Moreover, decisions about product mix can have a significant impact on an organization's profitability.

Each mix represents an alternative that carries with it an associated profit level. A manager should choose the alternative that maximizes total profits. Since fixed costs do not vary with activity level, the total fixed costs of a company would be the same for all possible mixes and therefore are not relevant to the decision. Hence, a manager needs to choose the alternative that maximizes total contribution margin.

Assume, for example, that Jorgenson Company produces two types of gears: X and Y, with unit contribution margins of $25 and $10, respectively. If the company possesses unlimited resources and the demand for each product is unlimited, the product-mix decision is simple—produce an infinite number of each product. Unfortunately, every company faces limited resources and limited demand for each product. These limitations are called **constraints**. A manager must choose the optimal mix given the constraints found within the company.

Assuming that Jorgenson can sell all that is produced, some may argue that only Gear X should be produced and sold—it has the larger contribution margin.

**constraints**

Mathematical expressions that express resource limitations.

However, this solution is not necessarily the best. The selection of the optimal mix is significantly affected by the relationships of the constrained resources to the individual products. These relationships affect the quantity of each product that can be produced, and consequently the total contribution margin that can be earned. This point is most vividly illustrated with one resource constraint.

## One Constrained Resource

Assume that each gear must be notched by a special machine. The company owns eight machines that together provide 40,000 hours of machine time per year. Gear X requires two hours of machine time, and Gear Y requires half an hour of machine time. Assume that there are no other constraints. What is the optimal mix of gears? Since each unit of Gear X requires two hours of machine time, 20,000 units of Gear X can be produced per year (40,000/2). At $25 per unit, Jorgenson can earn a total contribution margin of $500,000. On the other hand, Gear Y requires only 0.5 hours of machine time per unit; therefore, 80,000 (40,000/0.5) gears can be produced. At $10 per unit, the total contribution margin is $800,000. Producing only Gear Y yields a higher profit level than producing only Gear X—even though the unit contribution margin for Gear X is 2.5 times larger than that for Gear Y.

The contribution margin per unit of each product is not the critical concern. The contribution margin per unit of *scarce resource* is the deciding factor. The product yielding the highest contribution margin per machine hour should be selected. Gear X earns $12.50 per machine hour ($25/2), but Gear Y earns $20 per machine hour ($10/0.5). Thus, the optimal mix is 80,000 units of Gear Y and none of Gear X.

## Multiple Constrained Resources

The presence of only one constrained resource is unrealistic. All organizations face multiple constraints: limitations of raw materials, limitations of labour inputs, limited demand for each product, and so on. Solving the product-mix problem in the presence of multiple constraints is considerably more complicated and requires the use of a specialized mathematical technique known as *linear programming*, which is defined and illustrated in the Appendix to this chapter.

## Pricing

**Objective 5**

Explain the impact of cost on pricing decisions.

One of the more difficult decisions faced by a company is pricing. This section examines the impact of cost on price, and the accountant's role in gathering the needed information.

### Cost-Based Pricing

Demand is one side of the pricing equation; supply is the other side. Since revenue must cover cost for the company to make a profit, many companies start with cost to determine price. That is, they calculate product cost and add the desired profit. The mechanics of this approach are straightforward. Usually, there is some base cost and a markup. The **markup** is a percentage applied to the base cost; it includes desired profit and any costs not included in the base cost. Companies that bid for jobs routinely base bid price on cost.

Consider Elvin Company, owned and operated by Clare Elvin, which assembles and installs computers to customer specifications. Costs of the components

**markup**

The percentage applied to a base cost; it includes desired profit and any costs not included in the base cost.

and other direct materials are easy to trace. Direct labour cost is similarly easy to trace to each job. Assemblers receive, on average, $15 per hour. Last year, Elvin's total direct labour cost was $140,000. Overhead, consisting of utilities, small tools, building space, and so on, amounted to $80,000. Elvin Company's income statement for last year is as follows:

| | | |
|---|---|---|
| Revenues | | $856,500 |
| Cost of goods sold: | | |
| Direct materials | $489,750 | |
| Direct labour | 140,000 | |
| Overhead | 84,000 | 713,750 |
| Gross profit | | $142,750 |
| Selling and administrative expenses | | 25,000 |
| Operating income | | $117,750 |

Suppose that Clare wants to earn approximately the same amount of operating income on each job as was earned last year. She could calculate a markup on cost of goods sold by summing selling and administrative expenses and operating income, then dividing by cost of goods sold:

$$\text{Markup on COGS} = \text{(Selling and administrative expenses} + \text{Operating income)/COGS}$$
$$= (\$25,000 + \$117,750)/\$713,750$$
$$= 0.20$$

The markup on cost of goods sold is 20 percent. Thus, if Clare determines selling price by charging 120 percent of cost of goods sold, she should realize the same level of operating income as last year. Notice that the 20 percent markup covers both operating income and selling and administrative costs. The markup is not pure profit.

The markup can be calculated using a variety of bases. Clearly for Elvin Company, the cost of purchased materials is the largest component. Last year, the markup on materials amounted to 74.9 percent of all other costs and profit:

$$\text{Markup on direct materials} = \text{(Direct labour + Overhead + Selling and administrative expenses + Operating income)/Direct materials}$$
$$= (\$140.000 + \$84,000 + \$25,000 + \$117,750)/\$489,750$$
$$= 0.749$$

A markup percentage of 74.9 percent of direct materials cost would also yield the same amount of operating income, assuming the level of operations and other expenses remained stable. The choice of base and markup percentage generally rests on convenience. If Clare finds that the labour varies in rough proportion to the cost of materials (for example, more expensive components take more time to set up) and that the cost of materials is easier to track than the cost of goods sold, then materials might be the better base.

To see how the markup can be used in bidding, suppose that Clare has the opportunity to bid on a job for a local insurance company. The job requires Elvin Company to assemble 100 computers according to certain specifications. She estimates the following costs:

| | |
|---|---|
| Direct materials (computer components, software, cables) | $100,000 |
| Direct labour (100 × 6 hours × $15) | 9,000 |
| Overhead (@ 60 percent of direct labour cost) | 5,400 |
| Estimated cost of goods sold | $114,400 |
| Plus 20 percent markup on COGS | 22,880 |
| Bid price | $137,280 |

Thus, Elvin Company's initial bid price is $137,280. Note that this is the first pass at a bid. Clare can adjust the bid based on her knowledge of competition for the job and other factors. The markup is a guideline, not an absolute rule.

If Elvin Company bids every job at cost plus 20 percent, is it guaranteed a profit? No, not at all. If very few jobs are won, the entire markup will go toward selling and administrative expenses, the costs not explicitly included in the bidding calculations.

Markup pricing is often used by retail stores, and their typical markup is 100 percent of cost. Thus, if a sweater is purchased by Graham Department Store for $24, the retail price marked is $48 [$24 + (1.00)($24)]. Of course, the 100 percent markup is not pure profit. It goes toward the salaries of the clerks, payment for space and equipment (cash registers and so on), utilities, advertising, and so on. A major advantage of markup pricing is that standard markups are easy to apply. It is very easy to apply a uniform markup to cost and then adjust prices as needed if less is demanded than anticipated.

## Target Costing and Pricing

**target costing**

A method of determining the cost of a product or service based on the price (target price) that customers are willing to pay.

We just examined the way in which companies use cost to determine price. Working backward shows how price can determine cost. **Target costing** is a method of determining the cost of a product or service based on the price (target price) that customers are willing to pay. This is also referred to as *price-driven costing*.

Most North American companies, and nearly all European companies, set the price of a new product as the sum of the costs and the desired profit. The rationale is that the company must earn sufficient revenues to cover all costs and yield a profit. Peter Drucker writes, "This is true but irrelevant: Customers do not see it as their job to ensure manufacturers a profit. The only sound way to price is to start out with what the market is willing to pay."[9]

Target costing is a method of working backward from price to find cost. The marketing department determines what characteristics and price for a product are most acceptable to consumers. Then it is the job of the company's engineers to design and develop the product such that cost and profit can be covered by that price. Japanese companies have been doing this for years; North American companies also often use target costing. For example, Borland International, Inc., used target costing in developing its 1993 version of Quattro Pro for Windows spreadsheet software. Priced at $49[10] (compared with $495 for Lotus and Microsoft versions), it was designed to appeal to new spreadsheet users. "When we were developing the product, we anticipated the pricing and the people it would attract. We thought of features for that audience."[11] Those features included clear instructions, preformatted spreadsheets for 50 common tasks, and interactive on-screen tutorials. Soothing first-time users wasn't the only reason for Quattro Pro's inclusion of built-in help. At $49, the company could not afford numerous calls for technical advice.

Returning to the Elvin Company example, suppose that Clare finds that the insurance company will not consider any bid over $100,000. Her cost-based bid was $137,280. Is she out of the running? No: not if she can tailor her bid to the customer's desired price. Recall that the original bid called for $100,000 of direct

---

9. Peter Drucker, "The Five Deadly Business Sins," *The Wall Street Journal* (21 October 1993): p. A22.

10. Prices are quoted in U.S. dollars.

11. Quotation by Joe Ammirato, group manager of the spreadsheet business unit at Borland, as reported by Lawrence M. Fisher, "Using 'Usability' to Sell Spreadsheets to the Masses," *New York Times* (6 February 1994): p. 12F.

materials and $9,000 of direct labour. Clearly, adjusting the materials will yield the greatest savings. Working with the customer specifications, Clare must determine whether or not a less expensive set of components will achieve the insurance company's objectives.

Suppose that the insurance company has specified sufficient hard-disk space on each drive to accommodate particular software, and that the minimum required is 1.2 gigabytes. Clare's original bid specified 3-gigabyte hard drives. If she reduces the hard-disk space to 1.5 gigabytes and uses a marginally slower drive, she could save $25,000. Substituting a slightly more expensive monitor (a $20 increase) that does not require the installation of screensaver software would result in saving $30 per computer on software and 15 minutes of direct labour time (at $15 per hour) to install it. The net reduction is $13.75 [($30 + $3.75) − $20] for each of the 100 computers. So far, Clare has developed the following costs:

| Direct materials ($100,000 − $25,000) | $75,000 |
|---|---|
| Direct labour (100 × 5.75 hours × $15) | 8,625 |
| Total prime cost | $83,625 |

Recall that Elvin Company applies overhead at the rate of 60 percent of direct labour cost. However, Clare must think carefully about this job. Perhaps somewhat less overhead will be incurred, because purchasing is reduced (no need to purchase screensaver software) and testing is reduced (the smaller hard drives require fewer hours of testing). Perhaps overhead for this job will amount to $4,313 (50 percent of direct labour). That would make the cost of the job $87,938 ($4,313 + $83,625).

Still, not all costs have been covered. There is the administrative cost and desired profit. If the standard markup of 20 percent is applied, the bid would be $105,526. This is still too high. Now Clare must determine if further cuts are possible, or if she wants to decrease desired profit and administrative expenses. As you can see, target costing is an iterative process. Clare will go through the cycle until she either achieves the target cost or determines that she cannot. Note, however, that given the customer's price ceiling, Clare still has a chance of winning the bid.

A further issue might cause concern. Is there anything ethically wrong with changing the components from the initial bid to the target-costed bid? No: the new components meet customer specifications and are clearly described in the bid. In fact, Clare's initial bid was overspecified. If the customer wants a Chevrolet, the bidder need not provide a Rolls-Royce, especially at Chevrolet prices. However, if in Clare's professional opinion the insurance company should upgrade its specifications, she could point that out. For example, if she knows that the insurance company's word-processing program is due for an upgrade that will require more hard-disk space, she could inform the company of that and encourage an increase in specified disk space.

Target costing involves much more up-front work than cost-based pricing. However, additional work must be done if the cost-based price turns out to be higher than what customers will accept. Then the arduous task of bringing costs into line to support a lower price, or the opportunity cost of missing the market altogether, begins. For example, the North American consumer electronics market is virtually nonexistent because cost-based pricing led to increasingly higher prices. Japanese (and later Korean) companies practising target costing offered lower prices and won the market.

Target costing can be used most effectively in the design and development stage of the product life cycle. At that point, the product's features as well as its costs are still fairly easy to adjust.

## Legal Aspects of Pricing

Customers and costs are important economic determinants of price. The Canadian government also has an important impact on pricing. The basic principle behind much pricing regulation is that competition is good and should be encouraged. Therefore, collusion by companies to set prices and the deliberate attempt to drive competitors out of business are prohibited. In general, cost is an important justification for price.

### Predatory Pricing

**predatory pricing**

The practice of setting prices below cost for the purpose of injuring competitors and eliminating competition.

The practice of setting prices below cost for the purpose of injuring competitors and eliminating competition is called **predatory pricing**. It is important to note that pricing below cost is not necessarily predatory pricing. Companies frequently price an item below cost—loss leaders or weekly specials in a grocery store, for example. In Canada, the 1986 Competition Act culminated a process of revisions of laws that were put in motion in 1888. Paragraph 34(1)(c) of the Competition Act deals directly with predatory pricing:

> *34(1) Every one engaged in a business who . . .*
> *(c) engages in a policy of selling products at prices unreasonably low, having the effect or tendency of substantially lessening competition or eliminating a competitor, or designed to have such effect; is guilty of an indictable offence and is liable to imprisonment for two years.*

A conviction under this paragraph is based on two conditions—prices must be unreasonably low, and such prices have the effect of reducing competition. Because price competition is so highly valued, it is usually difficult to prove predatory pricing.

Predatory pricing on the international market is called dumping. For years, U.S. automobile manufacturers have accused Japanese companies of dumping. Companies found guilty of dumping products in the United States and Canada are subject to trade restrictions and stiff tariffs—which act to increase the price of the good. The defence against a charge of dumping is demonstrating that the price is indeed above or equal to cost.

### Price Discrimination

The 1986 Competition Act also includes provisions that outlaw price discrimination. Price discrimination refers to the charging of different prices to different customers for essentially the same product.

Paragraph 34(1)(a) states:

> *34(1) Every one engaged in a business who*
> *(a) is a party or privy to, or assists in, any sale that discriminates to his knowledge, directly or indirectly, against competitors of a purchaser of articles from him in that any discount, rebate, allowance, price concession or other advantage that, at the time the articles are sold to such purchaser, is not available to such competitors in respect of a sale of articles of like quality and quantity; is guilty of an indictable offence and is liable to imprisonment for two years.*

It should be noted that not all price discrimination is an offence. For example, price discrimination based on quantities of goods purchased is not an offence. Canadian law does not require a seller to demonstrate a cost difference to support quantity discounts (if more items are purchased, the price charged per item declines) if the discount pricing structures are available to competing buyers.[12]

---

12. Montrose Sommers, James Barnes, William Stanton, and Charles Futrell, *Fundamentals of Marketing*, Fifth Canadian Edition (Toronto: McGraw-Hill Ryerson Limited, 1989): pp. 326-29.

## Fairness and Pricing

Community standards of fairness have an important effect on prices. For example, should hardware stores raise the price of snowshovels the morning after a heavy snowfall? They could, but generally they do not. Their customers believe that a price increase at such a time would be taking unfair advantage. Whether we characterize the store's reluctance to raise prices in this situation as fairness or as an act in the long-term best interests of the company, the result is the same.

**price gouging**

A subjective term referring to the practice of setting an "excessively" high price.

**Price gouging** is said to occur when companies with market power price products "too high." How high is too high? Surely cost is a consideration. Any time price just covers cost, gouging does not occur. This is why so many companies go to considerable trouble to explain their cost structure and point out costs consumers may not realize exist. Pharmaceutical companies, for example, emphasize the research and development costs associated with new drugs. When a high price is clearly not supported by cost, buyers take offence. For example, after Hurricane Andrew in 1992, some companies and individuals sold ice for very high prices. Floridians faced by those prices were outraged that some suppliers would take advantage of the disaster to profiteer.

It is easy to see that cost as a justification for price underlies community standards of fairness. Ethics are founded on a sense of fairness. So unethical behaviour in pricing is related to taking unfair advantage of customers. Cost-related price increases are the best defence against customer rebellion.

## Appendix: Linear Programming

**Objective 6**

Use linear programming to find the optimal solution to a problem of multiple constrained resources.

**linear programming**

A method that searches among possible solutions until it finds the optimal solution.

**Linear programming** is a method that searches among possible solutions until it finds the optimal solution. The theory of linear programming permits many solutions to be ignored. In fact, all but a finite number of solutions are eliminated by the theory, with the search then limited to the resulting finite set.

To illustrate how linear programming can be used to solve a problem of multiple constrained resources, consider the earlier example of the product mix for Jorgenson Company. Assume that there are demand constraints for both Gear X and Gear Y. For Gear X, no more than 15,000 units can be sold and for Gear Y no more than 40,000 units. As before, the objective is to maximize Jorgenson's total contribution margin subject to the constraints faced by Jorgenson.

The objective can be expressed mathematically. Let $X$ be the number of units produced and sold of Gear X, and let $Y$ stand for Gear Y. Since the unit contribution margins are \$25 and \$10 for X and Y, respectively, the total contribution margin ($Z$) can be expressed as:

$$Z = \$25X + \$10Y \tag{10.1}$$

**objective function**

The function to be optimized, usually a profit function; thus, optimization usually means maximizing profits.

Equation 10.1 is called the **objective function**.

Jorgenson also has three constraints. One is the limited machine hours available for production, and the other two reflect the demand limitations for each product. Consider the machine-hour constraint first. Two machine hours are used for each unit of Gear X, and 0.5 machine hours are used for each unit of Gear Y. Thus, the total machine hours used can be expressed as $2X + 0.5Y$. The maximum of 40,000 machine hours available can be expressed mathematically as follows:

$$2X + 0.5Y \leq 40,000 \tag{10.2}$$

The two demand constraint limitations can also be expressed mathematically:

$$X \leq 15,000 \tag{10.3}$$

$$Y \leq 40,000 \tag{10.4}$$

Jorgenson's problem is to select the number of units of $X$ and $Y$ that maximize total contribution margin subject to the constraints in Equations 10.2, 10.3, and 10.4. This problem can be expressed in the following way, which is the standard formulation for a linear programming problem (often referred to as a *linear programming model*):

$$\text{Max. } Z = \$25X + \$10Y$$

subject to

$$2X + 0.5Y \leq 40{,}000$$
$$X \leq 15{,}000$$
$$Y \leq 40{,}000$$
$$X \geq 0$$
$$Y \geq 0$$

The last two constraints are called *nonnegativity constraints* and simply reflect the reality that negative quantities of a product cannot be produced. All constraints, taken together, are referred to as the **constraint set**.

A **feasible solution** is a solution that satisfies the constraints in the linear programming model. The collection of all feasible solutions is called the **feasible set of solutions**. For example, producing and selling 10,000 units of Gear X and 20,000 units of Gear Y would be a feasible solution and a member of the feasible set. This product mix uses 30,000 machine hours [$(2 \times 10{,}000) + (0.5 \times 20{,}000)$], which is under the limit for machine hours. Additionally, the company can sell the indicated amounts, since they do not exceed the demand constraints for each product. If this mix is selected, the company would earn a contribution margin totalling $450,000 [($25 \times 10{,}000$) + ($10 \times 20{,}000$)].

However, the mix of 10,000 units of X and 20,000 units of Y is not the best mix. One better solution would be to produce and sell 12,000 units of X and 30,000 units of Y. This mix uses 39,000 machine hours [$(2 \times 12{,}000) + (0.5 \times 30{,}000)$] and produces a total contribution margin of $600,000 [($25 \times 12{,}000$) + ($10 \times 30{,}000$)]. This feasible solution is better than the first, because it produces $150,000 more in contribution margin and profits. There are, however, even better feasible solutions. The objective is to identify the best. The best feasible solution—the one that maximizes the total contribution margin—is called the **optimal solution**.

When there are only two products, the optimal solution can be identified by graphing. Since solving the problem by graphing provides considerable insight into the way linear programming problems are solved, the Jorgenson problem will be solved in this way.

Four steps are followed in solving the problem graphically.

1. Graph each constraint.
2. Identify the feasible set of solutions.
3. Identify all corner-point values in the feasible set.
4. Select the corner point that yields the largest value for the objective function.

The graph of each constraint for the Jorgenson problem is shown in Exhibit 10–4. The nonnegativity constraints put the graph in the first quadrant. The other constraints are graphed by assuming that equality holds. Since each constraint is a linear equation, the graph is obtained by identifying two points on the line, plotting those points, and connecting them.

A feasible area for each constraint (except for the nonnegativity constraints) is determined by everything that lies below (or to the left) of the resulting line. The *feasible set* or *region* is the intersection of each constraint's feasible area. The feasible set is shown by the figure *ABCDE*; it includes the boundary of the figure.

There are five corner points: *A, B, C, D,* and *E*. Their values, obtained directly from the graph, are (0,0) for *A*, (15,0) for *B*, (15,20) for *C*, (10,40) for *D*, and (0,40)

**constraint set**

The collection of all constraints that pertain to a particular optimization problem.

**feasible solution**

A product mix that satisfies all constraints.

**feasible set of solutions**

The collection of all feasible solutions.

**optimal solution**

The feasible solution that produces the best value for the objective function (the largest value if seeking to maximize the objective function; the minimum otherwise).

Graphical Solution
(Coordinates represent
thousands).

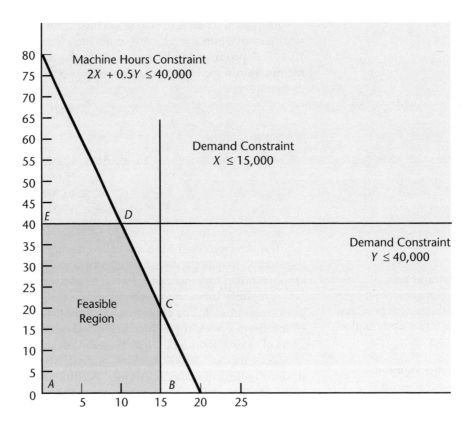

for $E$. The impact of these values on the objective function is as follows (expressed in thousands):

| Corner Point | X-value | Y-value | Z = $25X + $10Y |
|---|---|---|---|
| A | 0 | 0 | $   0 |
| B | 15 | 0 | 375 |
| C | 15 | 20 | 575 |
| D | 10 | 40 | 650* |
| E | 0 | 40 | 400 |

* Optimal solution

The optimal solution calls for producing and selling 10,000 units of Gear X and 40,000 units of Gear Y. No other feasible solution will produce a larger contribution margin. It has been shown in the literature on linear programming that the optimal solution will always be one of the corner points. This is because if a solution other than a corner point is considered, there will be always a corner-point solution that includes more of at least one of the products and at least the same amount of the other. Accordingly, the corner-point solution has a larger total contribution margin. Once the graph is drawn and the corner points are identified, finding the solution is simply a matter of computing the value of each corner point and selecting the one with the greatest value.

Graphical solutions are not practical with more than two or three products. Fortunately, an algorithm called the **simplex method** can be used to solve larger linear programming problems. This algorithm is available for use on computers to solve these larger problems.

The linear programming model is an important tool for making product-mix decisions, though it requires very little independent managerial decision making. The mix decision is made by the linear programming model itself. Assuming that the linear programming model is a reasonable representation of reality, the main

**simplex method**

An algorithm that
identifies the optimal
solution for a linear
programming problem.

role for management is to ensure that accurate data are used as input to the model. This includes the ability to recognize the irrelevancy of fixed costs for this type of decision and the ability to assess the accounting and technological inputs accurately (for example, the unit selling prices, the unit costs, and the amount of resource consumed by each product as it is produced).

Objectives that include more than one goal (goal programming) and applications where constraints are nonlinear (nonlinear programming) are beyond the scope of this book.

## Summary of Learning Objectives

### 1. Describe the tactical decision-making model.

The decision-making model described in this chapter consists of six steps: recognizing and defining the problem, identifying alternatives, determining the costs and benefits of each alternative, comparing relevant costs and benefits for each alternative, assessing qualitative factors, and making the decision. In using cost analysis to choose among alternatives, managers should take steps to ensure that all important feasible alternatives are being considered.

### 2. Explain how the activity resource usage model is used in assessing relevancy.

The activity resource usage model breaks costs into two groups: flexible resources and committed resources. Flexible resources are acquired as used and needed: supply equals demand. If demand changes, the cost is relevant. Committed resources are acquired in advance; therefore, they may have unused capacity. The cost may or may not be relevant. If committed resources have sufficient unused capacity, their cost is not relevant. If there is not sufficient excess capacity, the additional cost is relevant.

### 3. Apply the tactical decision-making concepts in a variety of management situations.

Several examples illustrating the application of the relevant-costing model were given within the chapter. Applications were illustrated for make-or-buy decisions, keep-or-drop decisions, special-order deci-

sions, and sell-or-process-further decisions. Product-mix decisions were also discussed. The list of applications is by no means exhaustive but was provided to illustrate the scope and power of relevant-costing analysis.

### 4. Choose the optimal product mix when faced with one constrained resource.

In dealing with a resource constraint, it is important to phrase the product contribution margin in terms of contribution margin per unit of constrained resource.

### 5. Explain the impact of cost on pricing decisions.

Costs are important inputs into the pricing decision. Cost-based pricing uses a markup based on a subset of costs. Target costing works backward from a price acceptable to consumers to find the cost necessary to manufacture the product. The Competition Act prohibits price discrimination.

### 6. Use linear programming to find the optimal solution to a problem of multiple constrained resources. (Appendix)

Linear programming is a method that locates the optimal solution in a set of feasible solutions. The graphical method may be used with two products. When more than two products are involved, the simplex method is used.

## Key Terms

## Review Problem

Rianne Company produces a light fixture with the following unit cost:

| | |
|---|---|
| Direct materials | $2 |
| Direct labour | 1 |
| Variable overhead | 3 |
| Fixed overhead | 2 |
| Unit cost | $8 |

The production capacity is 300,000 units per year. Because of a depressed housing market, the company expects to produce only 180,000 fixtures for the coming year. The company also has fixed selling costs totalling $500,000 per year and variable selling costs of $1 per unit sold. The fixtures normally sell for $12 each.

At the beginning of the year, a customer from a geographic region outside the area normally served by the company offered to buy 100,000 fixtures for $7 each. The customer also offered to pay all transportation expenses. Since there would be no sales commissions involved, this order would not have any variable selling expenses.

### Required:

Should the company accept the order? Provide both qualitative and quantitative justification for your decision. Assume that no other orders are expected beyond the regular business and the special order.

### Solution

The company is faced with a problem of idle capacity. Accepting the special order would bring production up to near capacity. There are two options: accept or reject the order. If the order is accepted, the company could avoid laying off employees and would enhance and maintain its community image. However, the order is considerably below the normal selling price of $12. Because the price is so low, the company needs to assess the potential impact of the sale on its regular customers and on the company's profitability. Considering the fact that the customer is located in a region not usually served by the company, the likelihood of creating an adverse impact on regular business is not high. Thus, the qualitative factors seem to favour acceptance.

The only remaining consideration is the profitability of the special order. To assess profitability, the company should identify the relevant costs and benefits of each alternative. This analysis is as follows:

|  | **Accept** | **Reject** |
|---|---|---|
| Revenues | $700,000 | $— |
| Direct materials | (200,000) | — |
| Direct labour | (100,000) | — |
| Variable overhead | (300,000) | — |
| Total benefits | $100,000 | $ 0 |

Accepting the order would increase profits by $100,000 (the fixed overhead and selling expenses are all irrelevant since they are the same across both alternatives). Conclusion: The order should be accepted since both qualitative and quantitative factors favour this alternative.

## Questions for Writing and Discussion

1. What is the difference between tactical and strategic decisions?

2. Explain why amortization on an existing asset is always irrelevant.

3. Give an example of a future cost that is not relevant.

4. Explain why relevant costs need to be expressed on a periodically recurring basis.

5. Relevant costs always determine which alternative should be chosen. Do you agree? Explain.

6. Give an example of a fixed cost that is relevant.

7. What is the difference, if any, between a relevant cost and a differential cost?

8. When, if ever, is amortization a relevant cost?

9. What role do past costs play in relevant-costing decisions?

10. Can direct materials ever be irrelevant in a make-or-buy decision? Explain.

11. Discuss the importance of complementary effects in a keep-or-drop decision.

12. What are some ways a manager can expand his or her knowledge of the feasible set of alternatives?

13. Should joint costs be considered in a sell-or-process-further decision? Explain.

14. Suppose that a product can be sold at split-off for $5,000 or processed further at a cost of $1,000 and then sold for $6,400. Should the product be processed further?

15. Why are fixed costs never relevant in a product-mix decision?

16. Suppose that a company produces two products. Should the company always place the most emphasis on the product with the largest contribution margin per unit? Explain.

17. Why would a company ever offer a price on a product that is below its full cost?

18. When can a company legally offer different prices for the same product?

19. "Rational managers are not influenced by sunk costs," said the economics professor. "But managers are influenced by sunk costs," responded his organizational behaviour colleague—whereupon the economics professor asked, "Do you mean that managers are irrational? There goes the whole foundation of economics!" Briefly answer the economics professor.

20. Discuss the purpose of linear programming.

21. What is an objective function? a constraint? a constraint set?

22. What is a feasible solution? a feasible set of solutions?

23. Explain the procedures for graphically solving a linear programming problem. What solution method is usually used when the problem includes more than two or three products?

## Exercises

**10–1**

*Model for Making
Tactical Decisions*

**LO1**

The model for making tactical decisions that we described in the chapter has six steps. These steps are listed, out of order, below. Put the steps in the correct order, starting with the step that would be taken first.

A.  Select the alternative with the greatest overall benefit.
B.  Identify the costs and benefits associated with each feasible alternative.
C.  Assess qualitative factors.
D.  Recognize and define the problem.
E.  Identify alternatives as possible solutions to the problem.
F.  Total the relevant costs and benefits for each alternative.

**10–2**

*Make-or-Buy Decision*

**LO3**

Zorro Manufacturing had always made its components in-house. However, Simpson Component Works had recently offered to supply one component, P7-43, at a price of $12 each. Zorro uses 4,100 units of Component P7-43 each year. The absorption cost per unit of this component is as follows:

| | |
|---|---|
| Direct materials | $7.42 |
| Direct labour | 2.38 |
| Variable overhead | 1.75 |
| Fixed overhead | 3.00 |
| Total | $14.55 |

The fixed overhead is an allocated expense; none of it would be eliminated if production of Component P7-43 stopped.

**Required:**
1.  What are the alternatives facing Zorro Manufacturing with respect to production of Component P7-43?
2.  List the relevant costs for each alternative. Which alternative is better?

**10–3**

*Keep-or-Drop Decision*

**LO3**

Uintah Company produces three products: A, B, and C. A segmented income statement, with amounts given in thousands, follows:

| A | B | C | Total |
|---|---|---|---|
| Sales revenue | $700 | $1,800 | $200 | $2,700 |
| Less: Variable expenses | 350 | 1,000 | 140 | 1,490 |
| Contribution margin | $350 | $ 800 | $ 60 | $1,210 |
| Less: Direct fixed expenses | 100 | 300 | 70 | 470 |
| Segment margin | $250 | $ 500 | $ (10) | $ 740 |
| Less: Common fixed expenses | | | | 340 |
| Operating income | | | | $ 400 |

Direct fixed expenses include amortization on equipment dedicated to the product lines of $20,000 for A, $120,000 for B, and $30,000 for C. None of the equipment can be sold.

**Required:**
1.  What impact on profit would result from dropping Product C?
2.  Now suppose that 10 percent of the customers for Product B choose to buy from Uintah because it offers a full range of products, including Product C. If

C were no longer available from Uintah, these customers would go elsewhere to purchase B. Now what is the impact on profit if Product C is dropped?

**10–4**

*Special-Order Decision; Flexible and Committed Resources*

**LO3**

Dexter Company has been approached by a new customer with an offer to purchase 2,300 units of Dexter's product at a price of $6.90 each. The new customer is geographically separated from Dexter's other customers, and there would be no effect on existing sales. Dexter normally produces 12,000 units, but plans to produce and sell only 9,000 in the coming year. The normal sales price is $11 per unit. Unit-cost information is as follows:

| | |
|---|---|
| Direct materials | $1.75 |
| Direct labour | 2.80 |
| Variable overhead | 1.40 |
| Fixed overhead | 2.00 |
| Total | $7.95 |

If Dexter accepts the order, no fixed manufacturing activities will be affected, because there is sufficient excess capacity.

**Required:**

1. Should Dexter accept the special order? By how much will profit increase or decrease if the order is accepted?
2. Suppose that Dexter's distribution centre at the warehouse is operating at full capacity and would need to add capacity costing $1,000 for every 5,000 units to be packed and shipped. Should Dexter accept the special order? By how much will profit increase or decrease if the order is accepted?

**10–5**

*Keep or Buy Decision; Sunk Costs*

**LO1, LO3**

Heather Alburty purchased a two-year-old previously owned Grand Am for $8,900. Since purchasing the car, she has spent the following amounts on parts and labour:

| | |
|---|---|
| New stereo system | $1,200 |
| Trick paint | 400 |
| New wide racing tires | 800 |
| Total | $2,400 |

Unfortunately, the new stereo doesn't completely drown out the sounds of a grinding transmission. Apparently, the Grand Am needs a considerable amount of work to make it reliable transportation. Heather estimates that the needed repairs include the following:

| | |
|---|---|
| Transmission overhaul | $2,000 |
| Water pump | 400 |
| Master cylinder work | 1,100 |
| Total | $3,500 |

In a visit to a used car dealer, Heather has found a one-year-old Neon in mint condition for $9,400. Heather has advertised and found that she can sell the Grand Am for only $6,400. If she buys the Neon, she will pay cash, but she would need to sell the Grand Am.

**Required:**

1. In trying to decide whether to repair the Grand Am or buy the Neon, Heather is distressed because she already has spent $11,300 on the Grand Am. The investment seems too much to give up. How would you react to her concern?
2. Assuming that Heather would be equally happy with the Grand Am or the Neon, should she buy the Neon or should she repair the Grand Am?

**10–6**

Make-or-Buy Decision

LO3

Spreadsheet

Fontaro Company is currently manufacturing Part K96, producing 35,000 units annually. The part is used in the production of several products made by Fontaro. The cost per unit for K96 is as follows:

| | |
|---|---|
| Direct materials | $ 6.00 |
| Direct labour | 2.00 |
| Variable overhead | 1.50 |
| Fixed overhead | 3.00 |
| Total | $12.50 |

 NJF drop

Of the total fixed overhead assigned to K96, $77,000 is direct fixed overhead (the lease of production machinery and salary of a production line supervisor—neither of which will be needed if the line is dropped). The remaining fixed overhead is common fixed overhead. An outside supplier has offered to sell the part to Fontaro for $11. There is no alternative use for the facilities currently used to produce the part.

**Required:**

1. Should Fontaro Company make or buy Part K96?
2. What is the most Fontaro would be willing to pay an outside supplier?
3. If Fontaro bought the part, by how much would operating income increase or decrease?

**10–7**

Make-or-Buy Decision

LO3

Refer to Exercise 10–6. Now suppose that *all* of the fixed overhead is common fixed overhead.

**Required:**

1. Should Fontaro Company make or buy Part K96?
2. What is the most Fontaro would be willing to pay an outside supplier?
3. If Fontaro bought the part, by how much would operating income increase or decrease?

**10–8**

Make-or-Buy Decision

LO3

Rocky Company Ltd. currently produces 10,000 units per year of XL500, which is a component of the company's major products. XL500 has the following unit costs:

| | |
|---|---|
| Direct materials | $ 16.50 |
| Direct labour | 37.80 |
| Indirect costs: | |
|   Indirect labour (variable) | 12.60 |
| + Heat and power (variable) | 3.20 |
|   Fixed overhead | 53.50 |
|    Total cost per unit | $123.60 |

Rocky Company expects future annual demand for XL500 to increase to 15,000 units starting next year, which is within present capacity. A supplier has offered to supply 15,000 units of XL500 at $105 per unit.

If Rocky decided to purchase the required XL500, they could avoid fixed costs of $13.75 per unit based on their current production of 10,000 units per year. They could rent out the vacant area resulting from discontinuing production of XL500 for $200,000 per year plus heat and power.

**Required:**

1. How much could the company gain or lose per year if it purchased the required XL500? Show all calculations.
2. Briefly explain three qualitative factors that would be relevant to the decision to make or buy. (CMA Canada adapted)

Currently, Pomona Company manufactures and sells a variety of power washers, one of which is a small portable model designed for sale to households. Pomona makes 40,000 of these portable power washers per year at a full cost of $71 each. The breakdown of the manufacturing cost is as follows:

| | |
|---|---|
| Direct materials | $25.00 |
| Direct labour | 33.50 |
| Variable overhead | 5.50 |
| Fixed overhead | 7.00 |

Schering Company offered to sell Pomona the portable power washer for $65. Schering will imprint Pomona's name on the housing, and Pomona can continue to sell the portable power washer as part of its full line of products.

**Required:**
1. If Pomona buys the portable power washer from Schering, by how much will operating income increase or decrease?
2. Now suppose that Pomona's controller has completed an activity-based costing study of the factory. He has calculated the following activity rates: materials handling, $25 per move; purchasing, $15 per purchase order; setups, $200 per setup; engineering, $50 per engineering hour; and maintenance, $5 per maintenance hour. The portable power washer line uses 2,200 moves, 4,000 purchase orders, 800 setups, 1,000 engineering hours, and 7,000 maintenance hours. If Pomona buys the portable power washers from Schering, by how much will operating income increase or decrease?

Spreadsheet

Willem Vanderburg, president of Vanderburg Corporation, had just received the following variable-costing income statement:

| | Product A | Product B |
|---|---|---|
| Sales | $100,000 | $250,000 |
| Less: Variable expenses | 50,000 | 145,000 |
| Contribution margin | $ 50,000 | $105,000 |
| Less: Fixed expenses | 80,000 | 110,000 |
| Operating income (loss) | $(30,000) | $ (5,000) |

Willem was distressed, since this was the fifth consecutive quarter in which both products had shown a loss. Upon careful review, Willem discovered that $70,000 of the total fixed costs were common to both products; the common fixed costs are allocated to the individual products on the basis of sales revenues. He was also told that if either product is dropped, the sales of the other product will increase: Product A's by 50 percent if B is dropped and B's by 10 percent if A is dropped.

**Required:**
1. Prepare a segmented income statement in proper form for the past quarter.
2. Assume that Willem will choose among one of the following alternatives:
   a. Keep both products.
   b. Drop both products.
   c. Drop Product A.
   d. Drop Product B.
   Which is the best alternative? Provide supporting computations.

**10–11**

Special-Order
Decision; Flexible and
Committed Resources;
Qualitative Aspects

LO3

Randy Stone, the manager of Specialty Paper Products Company, was agonizing over an offer for an order requesting 5,000 calendars. Specialty Paper Products was operating at 70 percent of its capacity and could use the extra business; unfortunately, the order's offering price of $4.20 per calendar was below the cost of producing the calendars. Louis Nadeau, the company's controller, was opposed to taking a loss on the deal. But Yatika Isaacs, the company's personnel manager, argued in favour of accepting the order even though a loss would be incurred: it would avoid the problem of layoffs and would help maintain the company's community image. The full cost to produce a calendar follows:

| | |
|---|---|
| Direct materials | $1.15 |
| Direct labour | 2.00 |
| Variable overhead | 1.10 |
| Fixed overhead | 1.00 |
| Total | $5.25 |

Later that day, Louis and Yatika met over coffee. Louis sympathized with Yatika's concerns and suggested that the two of them rethink the special-order decision. He offered to determine relevant costs if Yatika would list the activities to be affected by a layoff. Yatika eagerly agreed and came up with the following activities: a loss of productivity equivalent to 1 percent of total payroll; notification costs to lay off approximately 20 employees; increased costs of rehiring and retraining workers when the downturn was over. Louis determined that these activities would cost the following amounts:

- Total payroll is $1,460,000 per year.
- Layoff paperwork is $25 per laid-off employee.
- Rehiring and retraining is $150 per new employee.

**Required:**
1. Assume that the company would accept the order only if it increases total profits. Should the company accept or reject the order? Provide supporting computations.
2. Consider the new information regarding activity costs associated with the layoff. Should the company accept or reject the order? Provide supporting computations.

**10–12**

Sell-or-Process-Further
Decision; Basic
Analysis

LO3

Shenista, Inc., produces four products (Alpha, Beta, Delta, and Gamma) from a common input. The joint costs for a typical quarter follow:

| | |
|---|---|
| Direct materials | $95,000 |
| Direct labour | 43,000 |
| Overhead | 85,000 |

The revenues from each product are as follows: Alpha, $100,000; Beta, $93,000; Delta, $40,000; and Gamma, $30,000.

Management is considering processing Delta beyond the split-off point, which would increase the sales value of Delta to $75,000. However, to process Delta further means that the company must rent some special equipment costing $15,400 per quarter. Additional materials and labour also needed would cost $8,500 per quarter.

**Required:**
1. What is the operating income earned by the four products for one quarter?
2. Should the division process Delta further or sell it at split-off? What effect does the decision have on quarterly operating income?

**10–13**

Spreadsheet

Kohata Company produces two products (Juno and Hera) that use the same material input. Juno uses 2 kilograms of the material for every unit produced, and Hera uses 5 kilograms. Currently, Kohata has 16,000 kilograms of the material in inventory. All of the material is imported. For the coming year, Kohata plans to import an additional 8,000 kilograms to produce 2,000 units of Juno and 4,000 units of Hera. The unit contribution margin is $30 for Juno and $60 for Hera.

Kohata Company has received word that the source of the material has been shut down by embargo. Consequently, the company will not be able to import the 8,000 kilograms it planned to use in the coming year's production. There is no other source of the material.

**Required:**
1. Compute the total contribution margin that the company would earn if it could manufacture 2,000 units of Juno and 4,000 units of Hera.
2. Determine the optimal usage of the company's inventory of 16,000 kilograms of the material. Compute the total contribution margin for the product mix that you recommend.

**10–14**

Zanbrow Company produces two products that use the same material input. Product A uses 2 kilograms of the material for every unit produced, and Product B uses 5 kilograms. Currently, Zanbrow has 6,000 kilograms of the material in inventory and will not be able to obtain more for the coming year. The maximum demand (sales) for A is estimated at 1,000 units, and for B it is estimated at 2,000 units. The detail of each product's unit contribution margin follows:

|  | Product A | Product B |
| --- | --- | --- |
| Selling price | $81 | $139 |
| Less variable expenses: |  |  |
| Direct materials | 20 | 50 |
| Direct labour | 21 | 14 |
| Variable overhead | 10 | 15 |
| Contribution margin | $30 | $ 60 |

Assume that Product A uses 3 direct labour hours for every unit produced and that Product B uses 2 hours. A total of 6,000 direct labour hours is available for the coming year.

**Required:**
1. Formulate the linear programming problem faced by Zanbrow Company. To do so, you must derive mathematical expressions for the objective function and for the material and labour constraints.
2. Solve the linear programming problem using the graphical approach.
3. Compute the total contribution margin produced by the optimal mix developed in Requirement 2.

**10–15**

The Bruning Company has the following budgeted income statement for the month of May, 2004:

| Sales (40,000 units) | | $2,000,000 |
|---|---|---|
| Cost of goods sold: | | |
| Direct materials | $300,000 | |
| Direct labour | 400,000 | |
| Variable overhead | 200,000 | |
| Fixed overhead | 600,000 | |
| Total cost of goods sold | | 1,500,000 |
| Gross profit margin | | 500,000 |
| Selling and administrative costs: | | |
| Sales commissions (2% of sales) | $ 40,000 | |
| Delivery costs | 20,000 | |
| Sales salaries | 120,000 | |
| Administrative salaries | 100,000 | |
| Office rental | 70,000 | |
| Total selling and administrative | | 350,000 |
| Operating income | | $ 150,000 |

The plant has a maximum capacity of 50,000 units; this capacity can be increased at a cost of $60,000 per increment of 2,000 units.

A company salesperson has brought an offer from a new customer to purchase the product at a price of $35 per unit. The customer will pick up the order at Bruning's factory.

**Required:**
1. Analyze the consequences for Bruning if it accepts the new order and:
   a. the customer wishes to purchase only 8,000 units.
   b. the customer wishes to purchase only 14,000 units.
2. What qualitative factors should the company consider in making this type of decision? (CMA Canada adapted)

**10–16**

Keep-or-Buy Decision; Identification of Relevant Costs and Benefits

LO2, LO3

( multiply by 6)

Foster Company is currently using manufacturing machinery that some company officers believe is outdated. They are urging the president to acquire the latest computerized equipment, maintaining that output will increase and operating costs decrease. The company president has commissioned a report that compares costs and revenues of the existing equipment with that of the new equipment. The report is as follows:

| | Old | New |
|---|---|---|
| Cost of acquisition | $280,000 | $540,000 |
| Accumulated amortization[a] | $100,000 | — |
| Annual operating cost | $63,000 | $50,000 |
| Annual maintenance | $8,500 | $4,000 |
| Salvage value[b] | — | — |
| Output | 100,000 units | 120,000 units |
| Output selling price | $100 | $100 |

[a] Using the straight-line method. Expected life for both machines is six years.
[b] At the end of the six years. Currently, the old machinery does have market value, and if it is sold now, a six-year note will be paid off, saving the company annual payments of $16,500.

**Required:**
Identify all costs and benefits relevant to the decision to keep or buy. Ignore taxes.

<table>
<tr><td>

**10–17**

</td><td>

Lastivika Company produces two products from a joint process. Joint costs are $70,000 for one batch, which yields 1,000 litres of cavasol and 4,000 litres of perosol. Cavasol can be sold at the split-off point for $26 or can be processed further, into cavasette, at a manufacturing cost of $2,300 (for the 1,000 litres) and sold for $32 per litre.

If cavasette is sold, additional distribution costs of $0.90 per litre and sales commission of 10 percent of sales will be incurred. In addition, Lastivika's legal department is concerned about potential liability issues with cavasette—issues that do not arise with cavasol.

**Required:**
1. Considering only gross profit, should cavasol be sold at the split-off point or processed further?
2. Taking a value-chain approach (by considering distribution, marketing, and after-the-sale costs), determine whether or not cavasol should be processed into cavasette.

</td></tr>
</table>

**10–18**

Moulder Company produces two models of an industrial product that require the use of a laser-operated drilling machine. The laser-operated drilling machines owned by the company provide a total of 12,000 hours per year. Model 33-K requires six hours of machine time, and Model 20-ST requires three hours of machine time. Model 33-K has a contribution margin of $21 per unit, and Model 20-ST has a contribution margin of $12 per unit.

**Required:**
1. Calculate the optimal number of units of each model that should be produced, assuming that an unlimited number of each model can be sold.
2. Calculate the optimal number of units of each model that should be produced, assuming that no more than 3,000 units of each model can be sold.

**10–19**

O'Connor Company produces two models of machine housings that require the use of a special lathe. The six lathes owned by the company provide a total of 12,000 hours per year. Model 14-D requires 4 hours of machine time, and Model 33-P requires 2 hours of machine time. Model 14-D has a contribution margin of $12 per unit, and Model 33-P has a contribution margin of $10.

**Required:**
1. Calculate the optimal number of units of each model that should be produced, assuming that an unlimited number of each model can be sold.
2. Calculate the optimal number of units of each model that should be produced, assuming that no more than 5,000 units of each model can be sold.

**10–20**

Refer to Exercise 10–19. Assume that no more than 2,000 units of Model 14-D can be sold and that no more than 5,000 units of Model 33-P can be sold.

**Required:**
1. Formulate the linear programming problem faced by O'Connor Company. To do so, you must derive mathematical expressions for the objective function and for the lathe constraint.
2. Solve the linear programming problem using the graphical approach.
3. Compute the total contribution margin produced by the optimal mix developed in Requirement 2.

**10–21**

Jamil Khan, owner of Khan, Inc., is preparing a bid on a job that requires $1,800 of direct materials, $1,600 of direct labour, and $800 of overhead. Jamil normally applies a standard markup based on cost of goods sold to arrive at an initial bid price. He then adjusts the price as necessary in view of other factors (for example, competitive pressure). Last year's income statement is as follows:

| Sales | $130,000 |
|---|---|
| Cost of goods sold | 48,100 |
| Gross margin | $ 81,900 |
| Selling and administrative expenses | 46,300 |
| Operating income | $ 35,600 |

**Required:**

1. Calculate the markup Jamil will use.
2. What is Jamil's initial bid price?

**10–22**

Sealing Company manufactures three types of floppy disk storage units. Each of the three types requires the use of a special machine that has a total operating capacity of 15,000 hours per year. Information on the three types of storage units is as follows:

|  | **Basic** | **Standard** | **Deluxe** |
|---|---|---|---|
| Selling price | $9.00 | $30.00 | $35.00 |
| Variable cost | $6.00 | $20.00 | $10.00 |
| Machine hours required | 0.10 | 0.50 | 0.75 |

Sealing Company's marketing director has assessed demand for the three types of storage units and believes that the company can sell as many units as it can produce.

**Required:**

1. How many of each type of unit should be produced and sold to maximize the company's contribution margin? What is the total contribution margin for your selection?
2. Now suppose that Sealing Company believes that it can sell no more than 12,000 of the deluxe model but up to 50,000 each of the basic and standard models at the selling prices estimated. What product mix would you recommend, and what would be the total contribution margin?

**10–23**

Discuss the costs that would be relevant to decision making in each of the following independent situations:

1. In pricing a special one-time-only order, where the order would make use of idle capacity for a company operating below its breakeven point.

2. In pricing a special one-time-only order, where the order would make use of capacity that would normally be required for regular production.

3. In pricing regular production orders for a company where production is fully automated and therefore has a very high proportion of fixed costs.

4. In making a decision on whether to produce or buy a component for the company's main product line. (CMA Canada adapted)

**10–24**

Multiple Choice

LO1, LO2, LO3, LO4,
LO5, LO6

Choose the *best* answer for each of the following multiple-choice questions:

1. Small-scale actions that serve a larger purpose are called
   a. qualitative factors.
   b. strategic decisions.
   c. minor alternatives.
   d. tactical decisions.
   e. borderline decisions.

2. A characteristic of a flexible resource is that
   a. supply equals demand.
   b. there is unused capacity in the short run.
   c. there is unused capacity in the long run.
   d. unused capacity is charged to administrative expense.
   e. None of the above.

3. Which of the following factors should be considered in a make-or-buy decision?
   a. The variable costs of manufacturing.
   b. The purchase price if the item is bought outside.
   c. The fixed overhead that is traced directly to the item.
   d. All of the above.
   e. None of the above.

4. The product mix problem with multiple constraints can be solved by using
   a. tactical decision making.
   b. strategic decision making.
   c. linear programming.
   d. goal programming.
   e. cost–volume–profit analysis.

5. A method of determining the cost of a product or service based on the price that customers are willing to pay is called
   a. linear programming.
   b. target costing.
   c. cost-plus pricing.
   d. common costing.
   e. segment costing.

6. The practice of selling goods in other countries below cost is called
   a. predatory pricing.
   b. dumping.
   c. price discrimination.
   d. cost-plus pricing.
   e. None of the above.

# Problems

**10–25**

Comparison of
Alternatives
LO1, LO2, LO3

Alice Knapp is the director of the Newkirk Drug Counselling Centre. She and her staff design programs to assist clients to become and stay drug-free. Most clients are referred to the centre through their probation officers. The centre is funded through a combination of provincial and federal grants. Alice anticipates that funding will last for another two to three years. After that, the Centre will in all probability cease to exist.

The centre has just been informed that it will lose the lease on its office in two months. Alice is considering three other sites. Information on the sites is as follows:

*Site 1:* This site is a 160-square-metre office in downtown Newkirk. Other lessees include a law company, a bail bond agency, and two insurance agencies. Monthly rent is $475. The office has no interior walls, and permanent partitions cannot be installed. However, private meetings between caseworker and client are crucial. Therefore, Alice believes that she must rent movable partitions to surround each caseworker's desk for $85 per month.

*Site 2:* This site is a 200-square-metre office in a strip mall in a suburban area of Newkirk. It is close to caseworkers' homes but relatively farther from clients' homes. The monthly rent is $500. The office has been subdivided into three smaller offices. One would be suitable for the reception area, another would serve as Alice's office, and the third would accommodate the caseworkers. Permanent partitions could be installed in the caseworkers' office at a cost of $1,500.

*Site 3:* A former client's parents have heard about the Centre's need for space. They have offered to donate a house that they previously used as a rental home. This site is an older house in Newkirk that is located in a rapidly commercializing district. The house provides plenty of space and privacy for all caseworkers. However, the plumbing and electrical services are not up to standard and must be repaired before the Centre can move in. Additionally, city regulations on handicapped access must be followed, so ramps and handrails must be built. Alice has received estimates on the work needed and figures that the total cost will be $15,000.

**Required:**
1. Determine the relevant costs associated with each site. Does it matter whether the centre will exist for two or three years? Explain.
2. Write a memo to Alice summarizing the qualitative and quantitative aspects of each site.

**10–26**

Make-or-Buy Decision;
Qualitative
Considerations
LO1, LO2, LO3

Hetrick Dentistry Services operates in a large metropolitan area. Currently, Hetrick has its own dental laboratory to produce porcelain and gold crowns. The unit costs to produce the crowns are as follows:

|                   | Porcelain | Gold  |
|-------------------|-----------|-------|
| Raw materials     | $ 70      | $130  |
| Direct labour     | 27        | 27    |
| Variable overhead | 8         | 8     |
| Fixed overhead    | 22        | 22    |
| Total             | $127      | $187  |

Fixed overhead is detailed as follows:

| | |
|---|---|
| √Salary (supervisor) | $26,000 |
| N/A Amortization | 5,000 |
| √ Rent (lab facility) | 32,000 |

Overhead is applied on the basis of direct labour hours. These rates were computed using 5,500 direct labour hours.

A local dental laboratory has offered to supply Hetrick with all the crowns it needs. Its price is $125 for porcelain crowns and $150 for gold crowns; however, the offer is conditional on supplying both types of crowns—it will not supply just one type for the price indicated. If the offer is accepted, the equipment used by Hetrick's laboratory will be scrapped (it is old and has no market value), and the lab facility will be closed. Hetrick uses 2,000 porcelain crowns and 600 gold crowns per year.

**Required:**

1. Should Hetrick continue to make its own crowns, or should they be purchased from the external supplier? What is the effect of purchasing (in dollars)?
2. What qualitative factors should Hetrick consider in making this decision?
3. Suppose that the lab facility is owned rather than rented and that the $32,000 is amortization rather than rent. What effect does this have on the analysis in Requirement 1?
4. Refer to the original data. Assume that the volume of crowns used is 3,400 porcelain and 600 gold. Should Hetrick make or buy the crowns? Explain the outcome.

**10–27**

Sell-or-Process Further Decision

LO1, LO2, LO3

Zanda Drug Corporation buys three chemicals that are processed to produce two type of analgesics used as ingredients for popular over-the-counter drugs. The purchased chemicals are blended for two to three hours and then heated for fifteen minutes. The results of the process are two separate analgesics, depryl and pencol, which are sent to a drying room until their moisture content is reduced to 6 to 8 percent. For every 1,300 kilograms of chemicals used, 600 kilograms of depryl and 600 kilograms of pencol are produced. After drying, depryl and pencol are sold to companies that process them into their final form. The selling prices are $12 per kilogram for depryl and $30 per kilogram for pencol. The costs to produce 600 kilograms of each analgesic are as follows:

| | |
|---|---|
| Chemicals | $8,500 |
| Direct labour | 6,735 |
| Overhead | 9,900 |

The analgesics are packaged in 20-kilogram bags and shipped. The cost of each bag is $1.30. Shipping costs are $0.10 per kilogram.

Zanda could process depryl further by grinding it into a fine powder and then moulding the powder into tablets. The tablets can be sold directly to retail drug stores as a generic brand. If this route were taken, the revenue received per bottle of tablets would be $4, with 10 bottles produced by every kilogram of depryl. The costs of grinding and tableting total $2.50 per kilogram of depryl. Bottles cost $0.40 each. Bottles are shipped in boxes that hold 25 at a shipping cost of $1.60 per box.

**Required:**

1. Should Zanda sell depryl at split-off, or should depryl be processed and sold as tablets?
2. If Zanda normally sells 265,000 kilograms of depryl per year, what will be the difference in profits if depryl is processed further?

10 = Kg

**10–28**

**Keep-or-Drop Decision**

**LO3**

AudioMart is a retailer of radios, stereos, and televisions. The store carries two portable sound systems that have radios, compact disk players, and speakers. System A, of slightly higher quality than System B, costs $20 more. With rare exceptions, the store also sells a headset when a system is sold. The headset can be used with either system. Variable-costing income statements for the three products follow:

|  | System A | System B | Headset |
|---|---|---|---|
| Sales | $45,000 | $ 32,500 | $8,000 |
| Less: Variable expenses | 20,000 | 25,500 | 3,200 |
| Contribution margin | $25,000 | $ 7,000 | $4,800 |
| Less: Fixed costs* | 10,000 | 18,000 | 2,700 |
| Operating income | $15,000 | $(11,000) | $2,100 |

* This includes common fixed costs totalling $18,000, allocated to each product in proportion to its revenues.

The owner of the store is concerned about the profit performance of System B and is considering dropping it. If the product is dropped, sales of System A will increase by 30 percent and sales of headsets will drop by 25 percent.

**Required:**

1. Prepare segmented income statements for the three products using a more useful format.
2. Prepare segmented income statements for System A and the headsets assuming that System B is dropped. Should B be dropped?
3. Suppose that a third system, System C, with a similar quality to System B, could be acquired. Assume that with C, the sales of A would remain unchanged; however, C would produce only 80 percent of the revenues of B, and sales of the headsets would drop by 10 percent. The contribution margin ratio of C is 50 percent, and its direct fixed costs would be identical to those of B. Should System B be dropped and replaced with System C?

**10–29**

**Dropping a Product**

**LO3**

The president of Hoboe Company Ltd. has been presented with the following summary of the three products Hoboe manufactures:

|  | Product A | Product B | Product C | Total |
|---|---|---|---|---|
| Sales | $15,750 | $12,500 | $22,500 | $50,750 |
| Cost of goods sold | 17,460 | 6,225 | 10,450 | 34,135 |
| Gross profit | $ (1,710) | $ 6,275 | $12,050 | $16,615 |
| Selling and administrative | 5,090 | 3,125 | 4,050 | 12,265 |
| Net income | $(6,800) | $ 3,150 | $ 8,000 | $ 4,350 |
| | | | | |
| Sales price per unit | $3.50 | $5.00 | $7.50 | |
| Variable cost of goods sold per unit | 3.25 | 1.25 | 1.50 | |
| Variable selling and administrative expense per unit | 0.35 | 0.20 | 0.30 | |

The president is thinking of discontinuing the production and sale of Product A.

**Required:**

1. Advise the president whether Product A should be discontinued. Show appropriate calculations to support your recommendation.
2. If Product A is discontinued, Hoboe's sales department predicts that the sales of Product C will decrease. At what point would your recommendation in Requirement 1 change? Explain. (CGA Canada adapted)

**10–30**

Merv Murningham, manager of an electronics division, is considering an offer by Jaya Sellers, manager of a sister division. Jaya's division is operating below capacity and has just been given an opportunity to produce 8,000 units of one of its products for a customer in a market not normally served. The opportunity involves a product that uses an electrical component produced by Merv's division. Each unit that Jaya's department produces requires two of these components. However, the price that the customer is willing to pay is well below the price usually charged; to make a reasonable profit on the order, Jaya needs a price concession from Merv's division. Jaya has offered to pay full manufacturing cost for the parts. So that Merv will know that everything is aboveboard, Jaya has supplied the following unit-cost and price information concerning the special order, excluding the cost of the electrical component:

| | |
|---|---:|
| Selling price | $32 |
| Less costs: | |
| Direct materials | 17 |
| Direct labour | 7 |
| Variable overhead | 2 |
| Fixed overhead | 3 |
| Operating profit | $ 3 |

The normal selling price of the electrical component is $2.30 per unit. Its full manufacturing cost is $1.85 ($1.05 variable and $0.80 fixed). Jaya has argued that paying $2.30 per component would wipe out most of the operating profit and result in a net loss for her division. Merv is interested in the offer because his division is also operating below capacity (the order would not use all his excess capacity).

**Required:**
1. Should Merv accept the order at a selling price of $1.85 per unit? By how much will his division's operating profit be changed if the order is accepted? By how much will the profits of Jaya's division change if Merv agrees to supply the part at full cost?
2. Suppose that Merv offers to supply the component at $2. In offering the price, Merv says that it is a company offer not subject to negotiation. Should Jaya accept this price and produce the special order? If Jaya accepts the price, what is the change in operating profit for Merv's division?
3. Assume that Merv's division is operating at full capacity and that Merv refuses to supply the part for less than the full price. Should Jaya still accept the special order? Explain.

**10–31**

Small Bear Ltd. operates in Vancouver manufacturing teddy bears. Small Bear currently produces 45,000 teddy bears a year but has the capacity to produce 50,000. It is early in 2004 and Small Bear has received a special order from a retailer in Seattle for 8,000 teddy bears that will be sold in Seattle.

Small Bear's 2003 income statement is as follows:

| | | |
|---|---:|---:|
| Sales (45,000 teddy bears) | | $900,000 |
| Cost of goods sold: | | |
| Direct materials | $270,000 | |
| Direct labour | 225,000 | |
| Manufacturing overhead | 210,000 | 705,000 |
| Gross profit | | $195,000 |
| Selling expenses | $125,000 | |
| Administrative expenses | 20,000 | 145,000 |
| Net income | | $ 50,000 |

Small Bear's variable manufacturing overhead is $3 per bear, and its variable selling expense is $2 per bear. The administrative expense is fixed but will increase by $1,000 if the special order is accepted. There will be no variable selling expense associated with the special order, and the variable manufacturing overhead per bear will remain constant.

Small Bear's direct labour cost per bear for the special order will increase by 5 percent, while its direct materials cost per bear for the special order will increase 10 percent. Fixed manufacturing overhead and fixed selling expenses will not change.

**Required:**

If the Seattle retailer has offered to pay $18 per bear for the special order, should Small Bear accept the order? Show all calculations. Note: All funds are in Canadian dollars. (CGA Canada adapted)

**10–32**

*Pricing of Special Orders*

**LO2, LO3, LO4**

Altaco Ltd. manufactures one product in its Edmonton factory. The company's general manager, Ellen Ismail, has just received a special request from a customer for 10,000 units of this product to be produced and delivered this month. The customer has suggested a selling price of $3 per unit. Ellen is unsure whether she should accept this offer. The company normally produces and sells 50,000 units per month, and capacity is 70,000 units per month. The normal selling price is $4 per unit.

Ellen approached Oscar Giterman, the plant accountant, with the issue. Oscar was unable to provide a proper analysis at that time because he had a meeting to attend. However, after quickly reviewing his files, he provided the following schedule of cost information:

| Level of Activity (units of production per month) | Average Unit Cost |
|---|---|
| 40,000 | $3.675 |
| 50,000 | 3.500 |
| 60,000 | 3.383 |
| 70,000 | 3.400 |

As he rushed off for his meeting, Oscar indicated that if production exceeds 62,000 units per month, an additional supervisor must be hired and costs will increase by $7,700 per month.

**Required:**

*Note:* All requirements are independent situations. Expected activity levels do not include the 10,000 units in the special order that Ellen is considering.

1. Assume that Altaco already expects to be working at a level of 50,000 units for the month. Calculate the minimum price that the company could charge for this special order without reducing its expected net income.
2. If the company expects to produce and sell 55,000 units this month, calculate the minimum price that the company could charge the customer for this special-order job without reducing its expected net income.
3. Assume that the company expects to produce and sell 65,000 units this month. Should Ellen accept the customer's order? Support your decision with appropriate calculations. (CMA Canada adapted)

**10–33**

Home Security, Inc., manufactures cabinets for use in its home security systems and for sale to outsiders. Management expects that during the third quarter of 2004—the three months ending September 30—the cabinet facility will be operating at 80 percent of normal capacity. Because management desires a higher utilization of capacity, it would consider accepting a special order. Data for Home Security cabinets now being manufactured are as follows:

| | |
|---|---|
| Regular selling price to outsiders | $18.00 |
| Cost per unit: | |
| Raw materials | $ 5.00 |
| Direct labour—0.5 hour at $12 | 6.00 |
| Overhead—0.25 machine hour at $8 | 2.00 |
| Total costs | $13.00 |

Home Security has received special-order inquiries from two companies, as follows:

a. First Alarm Ltd. would like to order a cabinet similar to that produced by Home Security. The First Alarm cabinet requirement is for 25,000 to be shipped by October 1, 2004, for a price of $12 each. The cost data for this order would be similar to those for the Home Security cabinets, with one exception. According to the specifications provided by First Alarm, the special cabinet requires raw materials that will cost only $4.50 per cabinet. Management estimates that the remaining costs, labour time and machine time, will be the same as for the Home Security cabinet.

b. Bar-the-Door, Inc., has submitted another special order to Home Security for 8,000 cabinets at $15 per cabinet. These too would have to be shipped by October 1, 2004. However, the Bar-the-Door cabinet is different from any cabinet in the Home Security line. The estimated unit costs of this cabinet are as follows:

| | |
|---|---|
| Raw materials | $ 6.50 |
| Direct labour—0.5 hour at $12.00 | 6.00 |
| Overhead—0.5 hour at $8.00 | 4.00 |
| Total costs | $16.50 |

In addition, Home Security will incur $3,600 in additional setup costs and will have to purchase a special device costing $5,200 to manufacture these cabinets; this device would be discarded once the special order is completed.

Home Security's manufacturing capabilities are limited to the total machine hours available. The maximum plant capacity available under normal operating conditions is 87,000 machine hours per year or 7,250 machine hours per month. Home Security has firm orders for 80 percent of the available capacity. The budgeted fixed overhead for 2004 amounts to $417,600. All manufacturing overhead costs are applied to production at the predetermined rate of $8 per hour based on plant capacity.

Home Security will have the entire third quarter—July 1, 2004, to September 30, 2004—to work on the special orders. It is not expected that any repeat business will be generated from either special order. It is Home Security's policy not to subcontract any portion of an order when special orders are not expected to generate repeat sales.

**Required:**

Should Home Security accept either special order? Justify your answer, and show your calculations. (CMA Canada adapted)

**10–34**

Pricing of a Special
Order

LO2, LO3, LO4

The General Rubber Tire Company Ltd. has been approached by a volume buyer with an offer to purchase 50,000 tires at $43 per tire. Delivery must be made within 30 days and variable selling costs will be $2 per tire. The productive capacity of General Rubber is 320,000 tires per month, and 10,000 tires are currently on hand. At the regular price, sales of 300,000 tires are expected for this month. The sales manager believes that 40 percent of sales lost during this month could be recovered later in the year.

Unit price and cost data of regular tires are as follows:

| | |
|---|---|
| Selling price | $66.00 |
| Product costs | 45.00 |
| Gross margin | $21.00 |
| Selling and administration | 15.00 |
| Profit per unit | $ 6.00 |

A recent analysis has shown that regular sales have a variable selling cost of $12 per unit and that the contribution margin is $18 per unit.

**Required:**

1. Determine whether General Rubber Tire should accept or reject the special order. (Support your answer with an appropriate analysis.)
2. What price could General Rubber Tire charge if the order is sold for zero profit?
3. What other factors should be considered before accepting the order?
4. Assume that the company has 500 defective tires on hand that could be sold as scrap for $2 each. The company has decided instead to retread these tires at a cost of $6 each and then attempt to sell them as "seconds." What is the lowest price that General Rubber Tire should accept for the retread tires? Explain your answer. (CMA Canada adapted)

**10–35**

Keep or Drop a
Division

LO2, LO3, LO4

Ira Shumard, president and general manager of Danbury Company, is concerned about the future of one of the company's largest divisions. The division's most recent quarterly income statement is as follows:

| | |
|---|---|
| Sales | $3,751,500 |
| Less: Cost of goods sold | 2,722,400 |
| Gross profit | $1,029,100 |
| Less: Selling and administrative | 1,100,000 |
| Net profit (loss) | $ (70,900) |

Ira is giving serious consideration to shutting down the division, since this is the ninth consecutive quarter that it has shown a loss. To help him in his decision, the following additional information has been gathered:

a. The division produces one product at a selling price of $100 to outside parties.
b. The division sells 50 percent of its output to another division within the company for $83 (full manufacturing cost plus 25 percent). The internal price is set by company policy. If the division were shut down, the user division would buy the part externally for $100 per unit.
c. The fixed overhead assigned per unit is $20.
d. There is no alternative use for the facilities if shut down. The facilities and equipment would be sold and the proceeds invested to produce an annuity of $100,000 per year.
e. Of the fixed selling and administrative expenses, 30 percent represent allocated expenses from corporate headquarters.

f. Variable selling expenses are $5 per unit sold for units sold externally. These expenses are avoided for internal sales. There are no variable administrative expenses.

**Required:**

1. Prepare an income statement that more accurately reflects the division's profit performance.
2. Should Ira shut down the division? What would be the effect on the company's profits if the division were closed?

**10–36**

Plant Shutdown or
Continue to Operate;
Qualitative
Considerations

LO2, LO3, LO4

GianAuto Corporation manufactures automobiles, vans, and trucks. Among the various GianAuto plants around Canada and the United States is the Denver cover plant, where vinyl covers and upholstery fabric are sewn. These are used to cover interior seating and other surfaces of GianAuto products.

Oriana Vosilo is the plant manager for the Denver cover plant. The plant was the first GianAuto plant in the region. As other area plants were opened, Oriana, in recognition of her management ability, was given the responsibility of managing them. Oriana functions as a regional manager, although the budget for her and her staff is charged to the Denver plant.

Oriana has just received a report indicating that GianAuto could purchase the entire annual output of the Denver cover plant from outside suppliers for $30 million. Oriana was astonished at the low outside price, because the budget for the Denver plant's operating costs was set at $52 million. Oriana believes that the Denver plant will have to close down operations in order to realize the $22 million in annual cost savings.

The budget (in thousands) for the Denver plant's operating costs for the coming year follows:

| | | |
|---|---:|---:|
| Materials | | $12,000 |
| Labour: | | |
|   Direct | $13,000 | |
|   Supervision | 3,000 | |
|   Indirect plant | 4,000 | 20,000 |
| Overhead: | | |
|   Amortization—Equipment | $ 5,000 | |
|   Amortization—Building | 3,000 | |
|   Pension expense | 4,000 | |
|   Plant manager and staff | 2,000 | |
|   Corporate allocation | 6,000 | 20,000 |
|     Total budgeted costs | | $52,000 |

Additional facts regarding the plant's operations are as follows:

a. Due to the Denver plant's commitment to using high-quality fabrics in all its products, the purchasing department was instructed to place blanket orders with major suppliers to ensure the receipt of sufficient materials for the coming year. If these orders were cancelled as a consequence of the plant closing, termination charges would amount to 15 percent of the cost of direct materials.

b. Approximately 400 plant employees will lose their jobs if the plant is closed. This includes all direct labourers and supervisors as well as the plumbers, electricians, and other skilled workers classified as indirect plant workers. Some would be able to find new jobs, but many others would have difficulty. All employees would have difficulty matching the Denver plant's base pay of $16.45 per hour, the highest in the area. A clause in the Denver plant's contract with the union may help some employees: the company must provide employment assistance to its former employees for 12 months after a plant closing. The estimated cost of administering this service would be $1 million for the year.

c. Some employees would probably elect to take early retirement, because the Denver plant has an excellent pension plan. In fact, $3 million of next year's pension expense would continue whether the Denver plant is open or not.

d. Oriana and her staff would not be affected by the closing of the Denver plant. They would still be responsible for administering three other area plants.

e. The Denver cover plant considers equipment amortization to be a variable cost and uses the units-of-production method to amortize its equipment; the Denver plant is the only GianAuto plant to use this amortization method. However, the Denver plant uses the customary straight-line method to amortize its building.

### Required:

1. Prepare a quantitative analysis to help in deciding whether or not to close the Denver cover plant. Explain how you treated the nonrecurring relevant costs.
2. Consider the analysis in Requirement 1 and add to it the qualitative factors that you believe are important to the decision. What is your decision? Would you close the plant? Explain. (US CMA adapted)

---

**10–37**

*Equipment Purchase; Drop Product*

LO1, LO2, LO3, LO4

Triangle Ltd. manufactures and sells three different products: Isosceles, Equilateral, and Scalene. Projected income statements by production line for the next year are presented below:

|  | Isosceles | Equilateral | Scalene | Total |
|---|---|---|---|---|
| Unit sales | 10,000 | 500,000 | 125,000 | 635,000 |
| Revenue | $925,000 | $1,000,000 | $575,000 | $2,500,000 |
| Less variable cost of units sold | 285,000 | 350,000 | 150,000 | 785,000 |
| Less fixed cost of units sold | 304,200 | 289,000 | 166,800 | 760,000 |
| Gross margin | $335,800 | $ 361,000 | $258,200 | $955,000 |
| Less variable administrative expenses | 270,000 | 200,000 | 80,000 | 550,000 |
| Less fixed administrative expenses | 125,800 | 136,000 | 78,200 | 340,000 |
| Net income (loss) before income taxes | $ (60,000) | $ 25,000 | $100,000 | $ 65,000 |

The fixed administrative expenses are allocated to products in proportion to revenues. The fixed cost of units sold is allocated to products by various allocation bases, such as square metres for factory rent, machine hours for repairs, and so on.

Triangle's management is concerned about the loss for the Isosceles product and is considering two alternative courses of corrective action:

*Alternative A.* The company would purchase some new machinery for the production of Isosceles. This new machinery would involve an immediate cash outlay of $650,000. Management expects that the new machinery would reduce variable production costs so that the total variable costs (production and administrative) for Isosceles would be 52 percent of Isosceles revenues. The new machinery would increase the total fixed costs and expenses (production and administrative) allocated to Isosceles to $480,000 per year. There would be no additional fixed costs and expenses allocated to the Equilateral and Scalene products.

*Alternative B.* The company would discontinue the manufacture of Isosceles. Selling prices for Equilateral and Scalene would not change. Management expects that Scalene's production and revenues would increase by 50 percent. Some of the production machinery devoted to Isosceles could be sold at scrap value, which would equal its removal cost. The removal of this machinery would reduce the fixed costs and expenses allocated to Isosceles by $30,000 per year. The remaining fixed costs and expenses allocated to Isosceles include $155,000 of rent expense per year. The space previously used for Isosceles can be rented to an outside organization for $157,500 per year.

**Required:**
1. Prepare a schedule analyzing the effects of Alternative A and Alternative B on projected net income before income taxes.
2. Assume that the immediate cash outlay for the new machine in Alternative A is $700,000 and that all other data remain unchanged. What effect will this have on your analysis? Explain.
3. Explain the term *relevant costs*. How do historical (sunk) costs pertain to decision making when using the relevant cost approach? (CMA Canada adapted)

**10–38**

Appendix: Product-Mix Decision; Single and Multiple Constraints; Basics of Linear Programming

LO4, LO6

Paper Products, Inc., produces table napkins and facial tissues. The manufacturing process is highly mechanized; both products are produced by the same machinery by using different settings. For the coming period, 200,000 machine hours are available. Management is trying to decide on the quantities of each product to produce. The following data are available (for napkins, one unit is one package of napkins; for facial tissue, one unit is one box of tissue):

|                          | Napkins | Tissue |
|--------------------------|---------|--------|
| Machine hours per unit   | 1.00    | 0.50   |
| Unit selling price       | $2.50   | $3.00  |
| Unit variable cost       | $1.50   | $2.25  |

**Required:**
1. Determine the units of each product that should be produced in order to maximize profits.
2. Because of market conditions, the company can sell no more than 150,000 packages of napkins and 300,000 boxes of tissue. Do the following:
   a. Formulate the problem as a linear programming problem.
   b. Determine the optimal product mix using a graph.
   c. Compute the maximum profit given the optimal product mix.

**10–39**

Keep or Drop; Product Mix

LO2, LO3, LO4

Olat Corporation produces three gauges. These gauges measure density, permeability, and thickness and are known as *D-gauges*, *P-gauges*, and *T-gauges*, respectively. For many years, Olat has been profitable and has operated at capacity (which is 82,000 direct labour hours). In the last two years, however, prices on all gauges were reduced and selling expenses increased to meet competition and keep the plant operating at full capacity. Third-quarter results (in thousands), as shown below, are representative of recent experience.

|                                | D-gauge | P-gauge | T-gauge | Total   |
|--------------------------------|---------|---------|---------|---------|
| Sales                          | $900    | $1,600  | $ 900   | $3,400  |
| Less: Cost of goods sold       | 770     | 1,048   | 950     | 2,768   |
| Gross profit                   | $130    | $ 552   | $ (50)  | $ 632   |
| Less: Selling and administrative | 185   | 370     | 135     | 690     |
| Net income (loss)              | $(55)   | $ 182   | $(185)  | $ ( 58) |

Mel Carlo, Olat's president, is concerned about the results of the company's pricing, selling, and production policies. After reviewing the third-quarter results, he asked his management staff to consider the following three-point course of action:

- Discontinue production of the T-gauge. T-gauges would not be returned to the line of products unless the problems with the gauge can be identified and resolved.
- Increase quarterly sales promotion by $100,000 on the P-gauge to increase sales volume by 25 percent.
- To accommodate the increased demand for P-gauges, cut production of the D-gauge by 50 percent and reduce traceable advertising and promotion costs for this line by $20,000 each quarter.

Kirk Spears, Olat's controller, suggested that a more careful study of the financial relationships be made to determine the possible effects on the company's operating results as a consequence of these proposed actions. Mel agreed, and JoAnn Brower, the company's assistant controller, was given the assignment. She gathered the following information:

- All three gauges are manufactured with common equipment and facilities.
- The quarterly general selling and administrative expenses are allocated to the three product lines in proportion to their dollar sales volumes.
- Special selling expenses (advertising and shipping) are incurred on each gauge as follows:

|  | Advertising per quarter | Shipping per unit |
|---|---|---|
| D-gauge | $100,000 | $ 4 |
| P-gauge | 210,000 | 10 |
| T-gauge | 40,000 | 10 |

- The unit manufacturing costs for the three products are as follows:

|  | D-gauge | P-gauge | T-gauge |
|---|---|---|---|
| Raw materials | $17 | $ 31 | $ 50 |
| Direct labour* | 20 | 40 | 60 |
| Variable overhead | 30 | 45 | 60 |
| Fixed overhead | 10 | 15 | 20 |
| Total | $77 | $131 | $190 |

\* The wage rate averages $10 per hour.

The unit sales prices for the three products are $90 for the D-gauge, $200 for the P-gauge, and $180 for the T-gauge.

The company is manufacturing at capacity and selling all that it produces.

**Required:**
1. Prepare a variable-costing segmented income statement for the three product lines.
2. Should the T-gauge line be dropped as Mel suggests? Explain.
3. Evaluate Mel's remaining two suggestions (combined with his first). Was Mel correct in promoting the P-gauge rather than the D-gauge? Explain. (US CMA adapted)

**10–40**

Appendix: Product-
Mix Decisions

LO6

Calen Company manufactures and sells three products. Each product passes through three separate departments. Both labour and machine time are applied to the products as they pass through each department. The nature of the machine processing and of the labour skills required in each department is such that neither machines nor labour can be switched from one department to another.

Calen's management is attempting to plan its production schedule for the next several months. The planning is complicated by the fact that labour shortages exist in the community and some machines will be down several months for repairs.

Following is information regarding available machine and labour time by department and the machine hours and direct labour hours required per unit of product. These data should be valid for at least the next six months.

|  |  | Department |  |  |
|---|---|---|---|---|
| **Monthly Capacity** |  | **1** | **2** | **3** |
| Labour hours available |  | 3,700 | 4,500 | 2,750 |
| Machine hours available |  | 3,000 | 3,100 | 2,700 |
| **Product** | **Input per Unit Produced** |  |  |  |
| 401 | Labour hours | 2 | 3 | 3 |
|  | Machine hours | 1 | 1 | 2 |
| 402 | Labour hours | 1 | 2 | — |
|  | Machine hours | 1 | 1 | — |
| 403 | Labour hours | 2 | 2 | 2 |
|  | Machine hours | 2 | 2 | 1 |

The sales department believes that the monthly demand for the next six months will be as follows:

| Product | Units Sold |
|---|---|
| 401 | 500 |
| 402 | 400 |
| 403 | 1,000 |

Ending inventory levels will not be increased or decreased during the next six months. The unit cost and price data for each product are as follows:

|  | Product | | |
|---|---|---|---|
|  | **401** | **402** | **403** |
| Unit costs: |  |  |  |
| Direct materials | $  7 | $ 13 | $ 17 |
| Direct labour | 66 | 38 | 51 |
| Variable overhead | 27 | 20 | 25 |
| Fixed overhead | 15 | 10 | 32 |
| Variable selling | 3 | 2 | 4 |
| Total unit cost | $118 | $ 83 | $129 |
| Unit selling price | $196 | $123 | $167 |

## Required:

1. Calculate the monthly requirement for machine hours and direct labour hours for producing Products 401, 402, and 403 to determine whether the factory can meet the monthly sales demand.
2. Determine the quantities of 401, 402, and 403 that should be produced monthly to maximize profits. Prepare a schedule that shows the contribution to profits of your product mix.
3. Assume that the machine hours available in Department 3 are 1,500 instead of 2,700. Calculate the optimal monthly product mix using the graphing approach to linear programming. Prepare a schedule that shows the contribution to profits from this optimal product mix. (US CMA adapted)

**10–41**

Among its many products, Phylex Corporation manufactures three types of electrical components, designated A, B, and C. From its records, it has determined that the three products use two types of materials (metal and plastic) that are purchased at the cost of $0.40 for one unit of metal and $0.50 for each unit of plastic. Because of contracts with its suppliers, Phylex can obtain up to 18,000 units of metal and 15,000 units of plastic per month at these prices. The three products require machining, inspection, and some final assembly. Available capacity for electrical component production includes 1,420 direct labour hours (at a cost of $15.60 per hour) and 168 machine hours per month (at a cost of $570 per machine hour). Supervisors undertake inspections on a sampling basis as part of their duties. Inspection time is not considered to be part of direct labour cost. All labour used in producing the electrical components is part of the permanent skilled labour force at Phylex, and therefore is considered a fixed cost.

An engineering study developed the following requirements for Products A, B, and C:

|  | A | B | C |
|---|---|---|---|
| Materials: |  |  |  |
| Metal | 3 units | 6 units | 8 units |
| Plastic | 4 units | 2 units | 2 units |
| Direct labour | 4 minutes | 6 minutes | 6.5 minutes |
| Machining | 4 minutes | 6 minutes | 10 minutes |

Under a recently negotiated contract, Phylex has agreed to supply 400 units per month of Product C for the next six months. The company's sales staff estimated that at a price of $62 per unit, 2,800 units of Product A could be sold; at a price of $84, 2,100 units of Product B could be sold; and at $120 (the same as the contract price), up to 300 units of Product C (excluding the contract sale) could be sold. Selling costs are 5 percent of the product selling price.

The production manager and the controller met to determine the most profitable sales and production mix for Phylex for the next six months. They decided to use linear programming.

**Required:**
Formulate the objective function and constraint functions for the linear program. Be sure to define your variables. Do not solve the linear program. (CGA Canada adapted)

**10–42**

Seung Company produces two products, A and B. The segmented income statement for a typical quarter is given below.

|  | Product A | Product B | Total |
|---|---|---|---|
| Sales | $150,000 | $80,000 | $230,000 |
| Less: Variable expenses | 80,000 | 46,000 | 126,000 |
| Contribution margin | $ 70,000 | $34,000 | $104,000 |
| Less: Direct fixed expenses* | 20,000 | 38,000 | 58,000 |
| Segment margin | $ 50,000 | $ (4,000) | $ 46,000 |
| Less: Common fixed expenses |  |  | 30,000 |
| Net income |  |  | $ 16,000 |

* Includes amortization.

Product A uses a subassembly that is purchased from an external supplier for $25 per unit. Each quarter, 2,000 subassemblies are purchased. All units produced are sold, and there are no ending inventories of subassemblies. Seung is considering making the subassembly rather than buying it. Unit variable manufacturing costs are as follows:

| Direct materials | $2 |
| Direct labour | 3 |
| Variable overhead | 2 |

Two alternatives exist to supply the productive capacity:

a. Lease the needed space and equipment at a cost of $27,000 per quarter for the space and $10,000 per quarter for a supervisor. There are no other fixed expenses.
b. Drop Product B. The equipment could be adapted with virtually no cost and the existing space utilized to produce the subassembly. The direct fixed expenses, including supervision, would be $38,000, $8,000 of which is amortization on equipment. If Product B is dropped, there will be no effect on the sales of Product A.

**Required:**
1. Should Seung Company make or buy the subassembly? If it makes the subassembly, which alternative should be chosen? Explain and provide supporting computations.
2. Suppose that dropping Product B will decrease sales of Product A by 6 percent. What effect does this have on the decision?
3. Assume that dropping Product B decreases sales of Product A by 6 percent and that 2,800 subassemblies are required per quarter. As before, assume that there are no ending inventories of subassemblies and that all units produced are sold. Assume also that the per-unit sales price and variable costs are the same as in Requirement 1. Include the leasing alternative in your consideration. Now what is the correct decision?

**10–43**

Make-or-Buy Decision

LO2, LO3

Sportway, Inc., is a wholesale distributor supplying a wide range of moderately priced sporting equipment to large chain stores. About 60 percent of Sportway's products are purchased from other companies, while the remainder of the products are manufactured by Sportway. The company's plastics department is currently manufacturing moulded fishing tackle boxes. Sportway is able to manufacture and sell 8,000 tackle boxes annually, making full use of its direct labour capacity at available work stations. Presented below are the selling price and costs associated with Sportway's tackle boxes:

| Selling price per box | | $86.00 |
| Costs per box: | | |
| Moulded plastic | $ 8.00 | |
| Hinges, latches, handle | 9.00 | |
| Direct labour ($15/hour) | 18.75 | |
| Manufacturing overhead | 12.50 | |
| Selling and administrative | 17.00 | 65.25 |
| Profit per box | | $20.75 |

Because Sportway believes that it could sell 12,000 tackle boxes if it had sufficient manufacturing capacity, the company has looked into the possibility of purchasing the tackle boxes for distribution. Maple Products, a steady supplier of quality products, would be able to provide up to 9,000 tackle boxes per year at a price of $68 per box delivered to Sportway's facility.

Bart Orazem, Sportway's product manager, has suggested that the company could make better use of its plastics department by manufacturing skateboards. To support his position, Bart obtained a market study that indicates an expanding market for skateboards and a need for additional suppliers. Bart believes that Sportway could expect to sell 17,500 skateboards annually at a price of $45 per skateboard. His estimate of the costs to manufacture the skateboards is presented below:

| Selling price per skateboard | | $45.00 |
|---|---|---|
| Costs per skateboard: | | |
| Moulded plastic | $5.50 | |
| Wheels, hardware | 7.00 | |
| Direct labour ($15/hour) | 7.50 | |
| Manufacturing overhead | 5.00 | |
| Selling and administrative | 9.00 | 34.00 |
| Profit per skateboard | | $11.00 |

In the plastics department, Sportway uses direct labour hours as the application base for manufacturing overhead. Included in the manufacturing overhead for the current year is $50,000 of factorywide fixed manufacturing overhead that has been allocated to the plastics department. For each unit of product that Sportway sells, regardless of whether the product has been purchased or is manufactured by Sportway, an allocated $6 fixed cost per unit for distribution is included in the selling and administrative costs. Total selling and administrative costs for the purchased tackle boxes would be $10 per unit.

### Required:

1. In order to maximize the company's profitability, prepare an analysis based on the data presented that will show which product or products Sportway should manufacture and/or purchase and will also show the associated financial impact. Support your answer with appropriate calculations.
2. Discuss some qualitative factors that might have an impact on Sportway's decision. (US CMA adapted)

**10–44**

Make-or-Buy Decision

LO2, LO3

Sarbec Company needs a total of 125 tonnes of sheet steel (50 tonnes of 5-centimetre width and 75 tonnes of 10-centimetre width) for a customer's job. Sarbec can purchase the sheet steel in these widths directly from Jensteel Corporation, a steel manufacturer, or it can purchase sheet steel from Jensteel that is 60 centimetres wide and have it slit into the desired widths by Precut, Inc. Both vendors are local and have previously supplied materials to Sarbec.

Precut specializes in slitting sheet steel that is provided by a customer into any desired width. When negotiating a contract, Precut tells its customers that there is a scrap loss in the slitting operation but that this loss has never exceeded 2.5 percent of input tonnes. Precut recommends that if a customer has a specific tonnage requirement, it should supply an adequate amount of steel to yield the desired quantity. Precut's charges for steel slitting are based on good output, not input handled.

The 60-centimetre-wide sheet steel is one of Jensteel's regular stock items and can be shipped to Precut within 5 days after receipt of Sarbec's purchase order. If Jensteel is to do the slitting, shipment to Sarbec would be scheduled for 15 days after receipt of the order. Precut has quoted delivery at 10 days after receipt of the sheet steel. In prior dealings, Sarbec has found both Jensteel and Precut to be reliable vendors with high-quality products.

Sarbec has received the following price quotations from Jensteel and Precut:

| **Jensteel Corporation Rates** | | | |
|---|---|---|---|
| Size | Gauge | Quantity | Cost per Tonne |
| 5 centimetres | 14 | 50 tonnes | $210 |
| 10 centimetres | 14 | 75 tonnes | $200 |
| 60 centimetres | 14 | 125 tonnes | $180 |

### Precut, Inc., Steel-Slitting Rates

| Size | Gauge | Quantity | Price per Tonne |
|------|-------|----------|-----------------|
| 5 centimetres | 14 | 50 tonnes | $18 |
| 10 centimetres | 14 | 75 tonnes | $15 |

### Freight and Handling Charges

| Destination | Cost per Tonne |
|-------------|----------------|
| Jensteel to Sarbec | $10.00 |
| Jensteel to Precut | 5.00 |
| Precut to Sarbec | 7.50 |

In addition to the above information, Precut has informed Sarbec that if it purchases 100 output tonnes of each width, the per-tonne slitting rates would be reduced 12 percent. Sarbec knows that the same customer will be placing a new order in the near future for the same material and estimates that it would have to store the additional tonnage for an average of two months at a carrying cost of $1.50 per month for each tonne. There would be no change in Jensteel's prices for additional tonnes delivered to Precut.

**Required:**

1. Prepare an analysis that will show whether Sarbec Company should:
   a. Purchase the required slit steel directly from Jensteel Corporation.
   b. Purchase the 60-centimetre-wide sheet steel from Jensteel and have it slit by Precut, Inc., into 50 output tonnes 5 centimetres wide and 75 output tonnes 10 centimetres wide.
   c. Take advantage of Precut's reduced slitting rates by purchasing 100 output tonnes of each width.
2. Ignoring your answer to Requirement 1, present three qualitative reasons why Sarbec Company may favour the purchase of the slit steel directly from Jensteel Corporation. (US CMA adapted)

## Managerial Decision Cases

**10–45**

*Make or Buy; Ethical
Considerations*

**LO1, LO2, LO3**

Valerie McDonald, CMA and controller for Murray Manufacturing, Inc., was having lunch with Quentin Branch, manager of the company's power department. Over the past six months, Valerie and Quentin had developed a romantic relationship and were making plans for marriage. To keep company gossip at a minimum, Valerie and Quentin had kept the relationship very quiet, and no one in the company was aware of it. The topic of the luncheon conversation centred on a decision concerning the company's power department that Pascal Dallaire, the company's president, was about to make.

**Valerie**: "Quentin, in our last executive meeting, we were told that a local utility company offered to supply power and quoted a price per kilowatt-hour that they said would hold for the next three years. They even offered to enter into a contractual agreement with us."

**Quentin**: "This is news to me. Is the bid price a threat to my area? Can they sell us power cheaper than we make it? And why wasn't I informed about this matter? I should have some input. This burns me. I think I should give Pascal a call this afternoon and lodge a strong complaint."

**Valerie**: "Calm down, Quentin. The last thing I want you to do is call Pascal. He made us all promise to keep this whole deal quiet until a decision has been made.

He did not want you involved, because he wanted to make an unbiased decision. You know that the company is struggling somewhat, and it is looking for ways to save money."

**Quentin**: "Yeah, but at my expense? And at the expense of my department's workers? At my age, I doubt that I could find a job that pays as well and has the same benefits. How much of a threat is this offer?

**Valerie**: "Colin Lacy, my assistant controller, prepared an analysis while I was on vacation. It showed that internal production is cheaper than buying, but not by much. Pascal asked me to review the findings and submit a final recommendation for next Wednesday's meeting. I've reviewed Colin's analysis, and it's faulty. He overlooked the interactions between your department and other service departments. When these are considered, the analysis is overwhelmingly in favour of purchasing the power. The savings are about $300,000 per year."

**Quentin**: "If Pascal hears that, my department's gone. Valerie, you can't let this happen. I'm three years away from having a vested retirement. And my workers—they have home mortgages, kids in college, families to support. No, it's not right. Valerie, just tell him that your assistant's analysis is on target. He'll never know the difference."

**Valerie**: "Quentin, what you're suggesting doesn't sound right either. Would it be ethical for me to fail to disclose this information?"

**Quentin**: "Ethical? Do you think it's right to lay off employees who have been loyal, faithful workers simply to fatten the pockets of the owners of this company? The Murrays are already so rich that they don't know what to do with their money. I think that it's even more unethical to penalize me and my workers. Why should we have to bear the consequences of some bad marketing decisions? Anyway, the effects of those decisions are nearly gone, and the company should be back to normal within a year or so."

**Valerie**: "You may be right. Perhaps the well-being of you and your workers is more important than saving $300,000 for the Murrays."

**Required:**
1. Should Valerie have told Quentin about the impending decision concerning the power department? In revealing this information, did Valerie violate any of the ethical standards described in Chapter 1?
2. Should Valerie provide Pascal with the correct data concerning the power department? Or should she protect its workers? What would you do if you were Valerie?

**10–46**

Centralize versus Decentralize

LO1, LO2, LO3

Central University, a Saskatchewan university with approximately 13,000 students, is in the middle of a budget crisis. For the third consecutive year, government funding for higher education has remained essentially unchanged (the university is currently in its 2002–03 academic year). Yet utilities, employee benefits, insurance, and other operating expenses have increased. Moreover, the faculty are becoming restless, and some members have begun to leave for higher-paying opportunities elsewhere.

The president and the academic vice-president have announced their intention to eliminate some academic programs and to reduce others. The savings that result would be used to cover the increase in operating expenses and for raises for the remaining faculty. Needless to say, the possible dismissal of tenured faculty has aroused a great deal of concern throughout the university.

With this background, the president and academic vice-president called a meeting of all deans and department heads to discuss the budget for the coming year. As the budget was presented, the academic vice-president noted that Continuing Education, a separate, centralized unit, has accumulated a deficit of $504,000 over the past several years, which must be eliminated during the coming fiscal year. Continuing Education has responsibility for all noncredit offerings. Additionally, it has nominal responsibility for credit courses offered in the evening on campus and for credit courses offered off-campus. However, all scheduling and staffing of these evening and off-campus courses is done by the heads of the academic departments. What courses are offered and who staffs them must be approved by the head of each department. The vice-president noted that allocating the deficit equally among the seven faculties would create a hardship on some of the faculties, wiping out their entire operating budget except for salaries.

After some discussion of alternative ways to allocate the deficit, the head of the accounting department suggested an alternative solution: decentralize Continuing Education, allowing each faculty to assume responsibility for its own continuing education programs. In this way, the overhead of a centralized continuing education unit could be avoided.

The academic vice-president responded that the suggestion would be considered, but it was received with little enthusiasm. The vice-president observed that Continuing Education was now generating more revenues than costs—and that the trend was favourable.

A week later, at a meeting of the Deans' Council, the vice-president reviewed the role of Continuing Education. He pointed out that only the dean of Continuing Education holds tenure. If Continuing Education were decentralized, her salary ($50,000) would continue; however, she would return to her academic department, and the university would save $20,000 of instructional wages, since fewer temporary faculty would be needed in her department. All other employees in the unit are classified as staff. According to the vice-president, one of the main contributions of the Continuing Education Department to the evening and off-campus programs is advertising. He estimates that $30,000 per year is being spent.

After reviewing this information, the vice-president made available the following information pertaining to the department's performance for the past several years (the 2005–06 data were projections). He once again defended keeping a centralized department, emphasizing the favourable trend revealed by the accounting data. (All numbers are expressed in thousands.)

| | 2002–03 | 2003–04 | 2004–05 | 2005–06 |
|---|---|---|---|---|
| Tuition revenues: | | | | |
| Off-campus | $ 300 | $   400 | $   400 | $   410 |
| Evening | —[a] | 525 | 907 | 1,000 |
| Noncredit | 135 | 305 | 338 | 375 |
| Total | $ 435 | $ 1,230 | $ 1,645 | $ 1,785 |
| Operating costs: | | | | |
| Administration | $(132) | $  (160) | $  (112) | $  (112) |
| Off-campus: | | | | |
| Direct[b] | (230) | (270) | (270) | (260) |
| Indirect | (350) | (410) | (525) | (440) |
| Evening | (—)[a] | (220) | (420) | (525) |
| Noncredit | (135) | (305) | (338) | (375) |
| Total | $(847) | $(1,365) | $(1,665) | $(1,712) |
| Income (loss) | $(412) | $  (135) | $   (20) | $   73 |

[a] In 2002–03, the department had no responsibility for evening courses. Beginning in 2003, it was given the responsibility to pay for any costs of instruction incurred when temporary or adjunct faculty were hired to teach evening courses. Tuition revenues earned by evening courses also began to be assigned to the department at the same time.

[b] Instructional wages.

The dean of the Faculty of Management is unimpressed by the favourable trend identified by the academic vice-president. The dean maintains that decentralization would still be in the university's best interests. He argues that although decentralization would not fully solve the deficit, it would provide a sizable contribution each year to the operating budgets for each of the seven faculties. The academic vice-president disagrees vehemently. He is convinced that Continuing Education is now earning its own way and will continue to produce additional resources for the university.

**Required:**

You have been asked by the president of Central University to assess which alternative, centralization or decentralization, is in the best interests of the university. The president is willing to decentralize provided that significant savings can be produced and that the mission of the Continuing Education Department will still be carried out. Prepare a memo to the president that details your analysis and reasoning and recommends one of the two alternatives. Provide both qualitative and quantitative reasoning in the memo.

# Research Assignments

**10–47**

Research Assignment

LO1, LO2, LO5

"Dumping" is an accusation that is often made against foreign companies. Japanese automobile companies, for example, have been accused of this practice.

**Required:**

Go to the library or on the Internet and find out the following:
1. What is dumping?
2. Why do international trade agreements usually prohibit dumping? Do you agree that its prohibition is good for the domestic consumer? Explain.
3. Explain how the relevant-costing principles learned in this chapter relate to dumping.
4. Provide several examples of companies accused of dumping. See if you can determine the outcome of an accusation made against one of the companies. Why do you suppose that international companies pursue dumping even though it's prohibited? What are the ethical implications?

**10–48**

Cybercase

LO1, LO3

After the acquisition of Canadian Airlines by Air Canada in 2000, Air Canada announced several new routes that neither airline had serviced before. Check Air Canada's website (www.aircanada.ca) for recent examples of tactical decisions. Write a brief paper discussing the types of cost and revenue information that would be used in making this sort of tactical decision.

# Capital Investment Decisions

## Learning Objectives

**After studying Chapter 11, you should be able to:**

1. Explain what a capital investment decision is, and distinguish between independent and mutually exclusive capital investment projects.

2. Compute the payback period and accounting rate of return for a proposed investment, and explain their roles in capital investment decisions.

3. Use net present value (NPV) analysis for capital investment decisions involving independent projects.

4. Use the internal rate of return (IRR) to assess the acceptability of independent projects.

5. Explain why NPV is better than IRR for capital investment decisions involving mutually exclusive projects.

6. Explain the role and value of postaudits.

7. Convert gross cash flows to after-tax cash flows.

8. Describe capital investment in an advanced manufacturing environment.

## Scenario

TastyFood Corporation, a large food-store chain, is considering investing in an automated deposit processing system for all of its stores. An investment of $2 million would provide the system for all 150 existing stores as well as for the 30 stores to be opened by the beginning of the following year. The president of TastyFood has assigned the responsibility of assessing the investment to a special capital acquisitions committee. The committee's first act was to design a pilot study to test such a system in seven stores for a nine-month period.

At the end of the nine months, Maryanne Weiss, chair of the capital acquisitions committee and vice-president of finance, scheduled a committee meeting to evaluate the outcome of the pilot study. Besides Maryanne, the committee included Sandor Tokaj, controller; Noah Kimball, vice-president of operations; and Paula Summers, area supervisor for the seven stores where the pilot study was conducted.

"As you recall," Maryanne remarked, "we met more than nine months ago and agreed to implement a pilot study before committing ourselves to an automated deposit system. Because of her close scrutiny of the project, Paula has agreed to give us a summary of the benefits observed in the pilot study."

"I'm extremely pleased with the results of the pilot study," Paula replied, "as I think you will be. To quantify the financial impact of this project, I have classified the benefits into four categories: immediate, near-term, indirect, and potential for future. Immediate benefits are available in a store as soon as the equipment is operational. Near-term benefits will be realized only after the local system is connected to the store computer. Indirect benefits accrue from the project but are more difficult to quantify. Potential future benefits can result from the system's ability to interface directly with the accounting system. This handout describes some of the specific benefits found in each category."

## SPECIFIC BENEFITS BY CATEGORY

### Immediate Benefits:

*Bank Charge Reduction.* The automated system reduces the charges for processing cheques, since it encodes the dollar amount on all cheques prior to depositing them.

*Productivity Gains.* The amount of additional payroll required during the busy season is reduced.

*Forms Cost Reduction.* Nearly 3 million documents used per year to process deposits manually are eliminated.

### Near-Term Benefits:

*Reduction of Cash Shortages.* Once the system is connected to the store computer, a cash variance analysis can be provided the next day. Currently, this analysis is performed manually at headquarters and is several weeks old by the time it arrives in the store. Quicker response to cash shortages should reduce annual losses.

### Indirect Benefits:

*Greater Data Integrity.* Reducing manual calculations will result in greater data integrity. This will decrease time spent on correcting deposit information errors.

*Lower Training Costs.* Since the system is simpler with fewer forms, new cashiers and new store openings should require less training time.

### Potential Future Benefits:

*Interfacing Abilities.* Processing data through the store computer to the host computer at headquarters can save time in both the sales audit and cash/banking calculations by eliminating manual entries and expediting bank reconciliations.

"After seeing these benefits, I'm convinced that automatic deposits are a good idea," observed Noah Kimball. "I move that we attach Paula's handout to a recommendation to implement the automated system for the entire company. Then we can get back to more pressing matters."

"Wait a minute!" interjected Sandor. "While the description of the benefits of the automated system is impressive, we shouldn't be too hasty in our decisions. After all, we are talking about investing $2 million. We need to be certain that this is a sound investment."

"But that's the whole point, Sandor. The benefits make it clear that the investment is sound. Why waste any more time deliberating over an obvious conclusion? What do you say, Maryanne? Can we vote on this matter and adjourn?"

"Well, Noah, we can—if you will first answer the following questions. How much will this investment increase our company's profits? What effect will it have on our overall value? Will the investment earn at least the return required by company policy? How long will it take us to recover the investment through the savings alluded to in Paula's handout? Only when we know the answers to these questions can we accurately assess the investment's soundness. The pilot study provides us with the fundamental information we need to estimate the future cash savings associated with automation. Once we have these estimates, we can use financial models to assess the proposed investment. Sandor, for our next meeting, please bring estimates of the cash flows over the life of the proposed system. I will come prepared to discuss the financial models that will help us assess the financial merits of the investment."[1]

### Questions to Think About

1. What role should qualitative factors play in capital investment decisions?

2. How do we measure the financial benefits of long-term investments?

3. Why are cash flows important for assessing an investment's financial merits?

4. What role do inflation and taxes play in assessing cash flows?

5. Should the cash flows of intangible factors be estimated?

---

1. The facts of this case are based on an actual food store chain; however, the name of the chain has been changed.

# Types of Capital Investment Decisions

Explain what a capital investment decision is, and distinguish between independent and mutually exclusive capital investment decisions.

**capital investment decisions**

The process of planning, setting goals and priorities, arranging financing, and identifying criteria for making long-term investments.

**capital budgeting**

The process of making capital investment decisions.

**independent projects**

Projects that, if accepted or rejected, will not affect the cash flows of another project.

**mutually exclusive projects**

Projects that, if accepted, preclude the acceptance of competing projects.

**Capital investment decisions** are concerned with the process of planning, setting goals and priorities, arranging financing, and using certain criteria to select long-term assets. Capital investment decisions are similar to the decisions discussed in previous chapters, but with a major difference: a longer planning horizon (since capital investment decisions usually provide benefits over a number of years). Relevant cost analysis, which summarizes the decision's financial effects, must take into account the time value of money.[2] This is the focus of this chapter. The financial models, some incorporating the time value of money, that Maryanne was planning to discuss in her next committee meeting are introduced and explained.

Because capital investment decisions place large amounts of resources at risk for long periods of time and simultaneously affect the company's future development, they are among the most important decisions that managers make. Every organization has limited resources, which should be used to maintain or enhance its long-run profitability. Poor capital investment decisions can be disastrous. For example, if a company fails to invest in automated manufacturing when competitors do, it may suffer significant losses in market share because of being unable to compete on the basis of quality, cost, and delivery time. Competitors with more modern facilities may produce more output at lower cost and higher quality. Thus, making the right capital investment decision is absolutely essential for long-term survival.

The process of making capital investment decisions is often referred to as **capital budgeting**. Two types of capital budgeting projects will be considered: *independent projects* and *mutually exclusive projects*. **Independent projects** are projects that, if accepted or rejected, do not affect the cash flows of other projects. Suppose a company is considering the addition of a new product line that would require significant outlays for working capital and equipment. If no other new product lines are being considered, and if the new product line is not complementary with existing product lines, the decision involving the new product line stands alone. Since it is independent of other proposals, the project can be evaluated on its own merits.

The second type of capital budgeting project requires a company to choose among several alternatives that will provide the same basic service. Accepting one option precludes accepting any other. Thus, **mutually exclusive projects** are those projects that, if accepted, preclude accepting all other competing projects. For example, TastyFood was considering replacing its existing manual deposit processing system with an automated system. Part of the company's deliberation would concern different types of automated systems. If three different automated systems were being considered, there are four alternatives in all—the current system plus the three potential new systems. Once one system is chosen, the other three are excluded; they are mutually exclusive.

Notice that one of the competing alternatives in the scenario is maintaining the status quo (the manual system). Of course, at times replacing an old system is mandatory and not discretionary if the company wishes to remain in business (for example, equipment in the old system may be worn out). In such a situation, going out of business could be an alternative, especially if none of the new investment alternatives is profitable.

Capital investment decisions are often concerned with investments in long-term capital assets. With the exception of land, these assets depreciate over their lives, and the original investment is used up as the assets are employed. In gen-

---

2. The time value of money is the notion that a dollar now is worth more than a dollar to be received one period from now. Basic concepts are reviewed in the appendix to this chapter.

eral terms, a sound capital investment will earn back its original capital outlay over its life and will at the same time provide a reasonable return on the original investment. Thus, one task of a manager is to decide whether or not a capital investment will earn back its original outlay and provide a reasonable return. By making this assessment, a manager can decide on the acceptability of independent projects and compare competing projects on the basis of their economic merits.

But what is meant by "reasonable return"? It is generally agreed that any new project must cover the opportunity cost of the funds invested. For example, if a company takes money from a money market fund that is earning 3 percent and invests it in a new project, then the project must provide at least a 3 percent return (the return that could have been earned had the money been left in the money market account). Of course, in reality, funds for investment come from different sources—each representing a different opportunity cost. The return that must be earned is a blend of the opportunity costs of the different sources. Thus, if a company uses two sources of funds, one with an opportunity cost of 5 percent and the other with an opportunity cost of 3 percent, then the return that must be earned is somewhere between 3 percent and 5 percent, depending on the relative amounts used from each source. Furthermore, it is usually assumed that managers should select projects that promise to maximize the wealth of the company's owners.

To make a capital investment decision, a manager must estimate the quantity and timing of cash flows, assess the risk of the investment, and consider the project's expected impact on the company's profits. One of the most difficult tasks is estimating the cash flows. Projections must be made years into the future, and forecasting is far from a perfect science. Obviously, as the accuracy of cash-flow forecasts increases, the reliability of the decision improves.

In making projections, managers must identify and quantify the benefits associated with the proposed project(s). For example, an automated cash deposit system can produce the following benefits (relative to a manual system): reduced bank charges, productivity gains, reduced cost of forms, greater data integrity, lower training costs, and savings in time required for bank/cash reconciliations. The dollar amount of these benefits must be assessed.

Although forecasting future cash flows is a critical part of the capital investment decision process, we won't consider forecasting methods here. Consequently, cash flows are assumed to be known; our focus will be on making capital investment decisions *given* these cash flows.

Managers must set goals and priorities for capital investments and identify some basic criteria for the acceptance or rejection of proposed investments. In this chapter, we will study four basic methods to guide managers in accepting or rejecting potential investments. The methods include both nondiscounting and discounting decision approaches (two methods are discussed for each approach). The discounting models are applied to both independent and mutually exclusive capital investment decisions.

## Nondiscounting Models

**Objective 2**

Compute the payback period and accounting rate of return for a proposed investment, and explain their roles in capital investment decisions.

The basic capital investment decision models can be classified into two major categories: nondiscounting models and discounting models. **Nondiscounting models** ignore the time value of money, whereas discounting models explicitly consider it. Although many accounting theorists disparage the nondiscounting models because they ignore the time value of money, many companies continue to use these models in making capital investment decisions. However, the use of discounting models has increased over the years, and few companies use only

**nondiscounting models**

Capital investment models that identify criteria for accepting or rejecting projects without considering the time value of money.

**payback period**

The time required for a project to return its investment.

one model—indeed, many companies seem to use both types of models.[3] This suggests that both approaches supply useful information to managers as they struggle to make a capital investment decision.

## Payback Period

The **payback period** is the time required for a company to recover its original investment and is a nondiscounting approach. When a project's annual cash flows are expected to be the same each year, the following formula can be used to compute its payback period:

Payback period = Original investment/Annual cash inflow

For example, if a company's original investment is $80,000, and it expects the project to generate even annual cash flows of $40,000, the payback period is two years ($80,000/$40,000).

If, however, the cash flows are uneven, we compute the payback period by adding the annual cash flows until the original investment is recovered. If a fraction of a year is needed, we will assume that cash flows occur evenly within each year. For example, suppose a car wash facility requires an investment of $100,000 and has a life of five years, with the following expected annual cash flows:

| | Year 1 | Year 2 | Year 3 | Year 4 | Year 5 |
|---|---|---|---|---|---|
| Cash flow | $30,000 | $40,000 | $50,000 | $60,000 | $70,000 |

The payback period for the project is 2.6 years, as shown in Exhibit 11–1. Notice that in Year 3, when only $30,000 is needed and $50,000 is available, we find the amount of time required to earn the $30,000 by dividing the amount needed by the annual cash flow.

One way to use the payback period is to set a maximum payback period for all projects and to reject any project that exceeds this level. Why would a company use the payback period in this way? Some analysts suggest that the payback period can be used as a rough measure of risk, with the notion that the longer it takes for a project to pay for itself, the riskier it is. Also, companies with riskier

**EXHIBIT 11-1**

Payback Analysis: Uneven Cash Flows

| Year | Unrecovered Investment (beginning of year) | Annual Cash Flow |
|---|---|---|
| 1 | $100,000 | $30,000 |
| 2 | 70,000 | 40,000 |
| 3 | 30,000* | 50,000 |
| 4 | — | 60,000 |
| 5 | — | 70,000 |

\* At the beginning of Year 3, $30,000 is needed to recover the investment. Since a net cash flow of $50,000 is expected, only 0.6 year ($30,000/$50,000) is needed to recover the $30,000. Thus, the payback is 2.6 years (2.0 + 0.6).

3. Surveys show that from the 1950s to the 1980s, the use of discounting models as the primary evaluation method for capital projects increased from 9 to 80 percent. A more recent survey in the United States and Canada shows that more than 90 percent of companies used a discounting method. See A.A. Robichek and J.G. McDonald, "Financial Planning in Transition, Long Range Planning Service," Report 268 (Menlo Park, CA.: Stanford Research Institute, January 1966); J.D. Blazouske, I. Carlin, and S.H. Kim, "Capital Budgeting Practices in Canada," *CMA Magazine* 62(2) (March 1988): pp. 51-54; and Janet D. Payne and Will Carrington Heath, "Comparative Practice in the US and Canada: Capital Budgeting and Risk Assessment," *Financial Practice and Education* 9(1) (Spring/Summer 1999): pp. 16-25.

cash flows could require a shorter payback period for investment projects. Companies with liquidity problems may be more interested in projects with quick paybacks. Another critical concern is obsolescence. In some industries, the risk of obsolescence is high; companies within these industries would be interested in recovering funds rapidly.

Another reason, less beneficial to the company, may also be at work. Many managers making capital investment decisions may choose investments with short payback periods out of self-interest. If a manager's performance is measured using such short-run criteria as annual net income, he or she may choose projects with quick paybacks to show improved net income as quickly as possible. For example, divisional managers are often responsible for making capital investment decisions and are evaluated on divisional profits. The tenure of divisional managers, however, is typically short—three to five years would be common. Consequently, such managers have an incentive to shy away from investments that promise healthy long-run returns but relatively meagre returns in the short run. These problems can be eliminated by appropriate capital budgeting policies and a budget review committee.

The payback period can be used to choose among competing alternatives. Under this approach, the investment with the shortest payback period is preferred over investments with longer payback periods. However, this use of the payback period is less defensible, because this measure suffers from two major deficiencies: (1) it ignores the investments' performance beyond the payback period, and (2) it ignores the time value of money.

These two significant deficiencies are easily illustrated. Assume that an engineering company is considering two different types of CAD (computer-aided design) systems, CAD-A and CAD-B. Each system has a five-year life, requires an initial outlay of $150,000, and displays the following annual cash flows:

| Investment | Year 1 | Year 2 | Year 3 | Year 4 | Year 5 |
|---|---|---|---|---|---|
| CAD-A | $90,000 | $ 60,000 | $50,000 | $50,000 | $50,000 |
| CAD-B | 40,000 | 110,000 | 25,000 | 25,000 | 25,000 |

Both investments have payback periods of two years. Thus, for a manager who uses the payback period to choose among competing investments, the two investments would be equally desirable.

There are two reasons why CAD-A should be preferred over CAD-B. First, CAD-A provides a much larger dollar return for the years beyond the payback period ($150,000 versus $75,000). Second, CAD-A returns $90,000 in the first year, while CAD-B returns only $40,000. The extra $50,000 that CAD-A provides in the first year could be put to productive use, such as investing it in another project. It is better to have a dollar now than to have it a year from now, because the dollar on hand can be invested to provide a return one year from now.

In summary, the payback period provides managers with information that can be used:

1. to help control the risks associated with the uncertainty of future cash flows,
2. to help minimize an investment's impact on a company's liquidity problems,
3. to help control the risk of obsolescence.

However, the method suffers significant deficiencies: it ignores a project's total profitability and the time value of money. While computing the payback period may be useful to a manager, relying on it alone for a capital investment decision would be unwise.

## Accounting Rate of Return

**accounting rate of return**

The rate of return obtained by dividing the average accounting net income by the original investment (or by average investment).

The accounting rate of return is also a nondiscounting model. The **accounting rate of return** measures the return on a project in terms of income, rather than cash flow. The accounting rate of return is computed by the following formula:

$$\text{Accounting rate of return} = \text{Average income}/\text{Original investment} \\ \text{(or average investment)}$$

Income is not equivalent to cash flows, because we use accounting accruals and deferrals in computing it. A project's average income is calculated by adding the net income for each year of the project and then dividing this total by the number of years.[4]

Investment can be defined as original investment or as average investment. Letting $I$ equal original investment and $S$ equal salvage value, and assuming that investment is uniformly consumed, we can define average investment as follows:[5]

$$\text{Average investment} = (I + S)/2$$

To illustrate how the accounting rate of return is computed, assume that an investment requires an initial outlay of $100,000. The life of the investment is five years, with the following cash flows:

|  | Year 1 | Year 2 | Year 3 | Year 4 | Year 5 |
|---|---|---|---|---|---|
| Cash flow | $30,000 | $30,000 | $40,000 | $30,000 | $50,000 |

Assume that the asset has no salvage value after these five years and that all revenues earned within a year are collected in that year. Total cash flow for the five years is $180,000, making average cash flow $36,000 ($180,000/5). Average amortization is $20,000 ($100,000/5). Average net income is the difference between these two amounts: $16,000 ($36,000 − $20,000). Using average net income and original investment, we see that the accounting rate of return is 16 percent ($16,000/$100,000). If average investment is used instead of original investment, the accounting rate of return is 32 percent ($16,000/$50,000).

Debt contracts often require that a company maintain certain financial accounting ratios, which can be affected by the income reported and by the level of long-term assets. Accordingly, the accounting rate of return may be used as a screening measure to ensure that any new investment will not adversely affect these ratios. Additionally, because bonuses to managers are often based on accounting income or return on assets, managers may have a personal interest in seeing that any new investment contributes significantly to net income. A manager seeking to maximize personal income will select investments that return the highest net income per dollar invested.

Unlike the payback period, the accounting rate of return does consider a project's profitability; like the payback period, it ignores the time value of money. Ignoring the time value of money is a critical deficiency in this method: doing so can lead a manager to choose investments that do not maximize profits.

The use of discounting models requires an understanding of present value concepts, which are reviewed in this chapter's appendix. Review these concepts and make sure that you understand them before studying the discounting capital investment models.

---

4. Average net income can be approximated by subtracting average amortization from average cash flow. The approximation is exact if we assume that all revenues earned in a period are collected and that amortization is the only noncash expense.

5. The average investment formula is derived from the definition of the average value of a function and requires the use of calculus.

## Discounting Models: The Net Present Value Method

**Objective** 3

Use net present value (NPV) analysis for capital investment decisions involving independent projects.

**discounting models**

Capital investment models that explicitly consider the time value of money in identifying criteria for accepting or rejecting proposed projects.

**net present value (NPV)**

The difference between the present value of a project's cash inflows and the present value of its cash outflows.

**discount rate**

The rate of return used to compute the present value of future cash flows.

**Discounting models** explicitly consider the time value of money, and therefore incorporate the concept of discounting cash inflows and outflows. Two discounting models will be considered: net present value (NPV) and internal rate of return (IRR).

### NPV Defined

**Net present value (NPV)** is the difference in the present value of the cash inflows and outflows associated with a project:

$$NPV = [\Sigma CF_t/(1 + i)_t] - I$$
$$= [\Sigma CF_t \times df_t] - I$$
$$= P - I$$

where

$I$ = The present value of the project's cost (usually the initial outlay)
$CF_t$ = The net cash flow to be received in period $t$, with $t = 1 \ldots n$.
$n$ = The useful life of the project
$I$ = The rate of return
$t$ = The time period
$P$ = The present value of the project's future cash flows
$Df_t = 1/(1 + i)^t$, the discount factor

NPV measures an investment's profitability. If NPV is positive, it measures the increase in wealth. For a company, this means that the size of a positive NPV measures the increase in the value of the company resulting from an investment. To use the NPV method, a *required rate of return* must be defined. The required rate of return is the minimum acceptable rate of return. It is also referred to in certain contexts as the **discount rate**, the *hurdle rate*, and the *cost of capital*.

A positive net present value signals that:

1. the initial investment has been recovered,
2. the required rate of return has been achieved, and
3. a return in excess of (1) and (2) has been received.

If NPV is greater than zero, the investment is profitable and acceptable. If NPV equals zero, the decision maker is indifferent between accepting or rejecting the investment proposal. If NPV is less than zero, the investment should be rejected because it is earning less than the required rate of return.

### An Example Illustrating Net Present Value

Majestic Company has developed new earphones for portable CD players that it believes are superior to anything on the market. The company's marketing manager is excited about the new product's prospects after completing a detailed market study that revealed expected annual revenues of $300,000. The earphones have a projected life cycle of five years. The equipment for producing the earphones would cost $320,000. After five years, that equipment could be sold for $40,000. In addition to equipment, working capital is expected to increase by $40,000 because of increases in inventories and receivables. The company expects to recover the investment in working capital at the end of the project's life. Annual cash operating expenses are estimated at $180,000. Assuming that the required rate of return is 12 percent, should the company manufacture the new earphones?

To answer this question, two steps must be taken: (1) the cash flows for each year must be identified, and (2) the NPV must be computed using the cash flows from Step 1. The solution to the problem is given in Exhibit 11–2. Notice that two approaches can be used in Step 2 to compute NPV. Step 2A computes NPV by using a separate discount factor for each year. Step 2B simplifies the computation by using a single discount factor for the even cash flows occurring in Years 1 to 4.[6]

**EXHIBIT    11-2**

Cash Flows and NPV
Analysis

| STEP 1. CASH-FLOW IDENTIFICATION | | |
|---|---|---|
| Year | Item | Cash Flow |
| 0 | Equipment | $(320,000) |
| | Working capital | (40,000) |
| | Total | $(360,000) |
| 1–4 | Revenues | $ 300,000 |
| | Operating expenses | (180,000) |
| | Total | $ 120,000 |
| 5 | Revenues | $ 300,000 |
| | Operating expenses | (180,000) |
| | Salvage | 40,000 |
| | Recovery of working capital | 40,000 |
| | Total | $ 200,000 |

| STEP 2A. NPV ANALYSIS | | | |
|---|---|---|---|
| Year | Cash Flow[a] | Discount Factor | Present Value |
| 0 | $(360,000) | 1.000 | $(360,000) |
| 1 | 120,000 | 0.893 | 107,160 |
| 2 | 120,000 | 0.797 | 95,640 |
| 3 | 120,000 | 0.712 | 85,440 |
| 4 | 120,000 | 0.636 | 76,320 |
| 5 | 200,000 | 0.567 | 113,400 |
| Net present value | | | $ 117,960 |

| STEP 2B. NPV ANALYSIS | | | |
|---|---|---|---|
| Year | Cash Flow | Discount Factor | Present Value |
| 0 | $(360,000) | 1.000 | $(360,000) |
| 1–4 | 120,000 | 3.037 | 364,440 |
| 5 | 200,000 | 0.567 | 113,400 |
| Net present value | | | $ 117,840[b] |

[a] From Step 1
[b] The NPV differs because of rounding.

## Discounting Models: Internal Rate of Return

**Objective** 4

Use the internal rate of return (IRR) to assess the acceptability of independent projects.

The internal rate of return (IRR) method is another discounting model. The **internal rate of return** is defined as the interest rate that sets the present value of a project's net cash flows equal to the present value of the project's cost. In other words,

---

6. The even cash flows for Years 1 to 4 are called an annuity. See the appendix to this chapter for more detail. Discount factors for single payments and annuities can be calculated by using a financial calculator or any of many computer programs.

**internal rate of return (IRR)**

The rate of return that equates the present value of a project's cash inflows with the present value of its cash outflows (i.e., it sets the net present value equal to zero). Also, the rate of return being earned on funds that remain internally invested in a project.

it is the interest rate that sets the project's NPV at zero. The following equation can be used to determine a project's IRR:

$$I = \sum CF_t/(1 + i)^t$$

The left-hand side of the equation is the initial investment, and the right-hand side is the present value of the future net cash flows. We know the values for $I$, $CF_t$, and $t$. Thus, we can find the IRR (the interest rate, $i$, in the equation).[7] Once a project's IRR is computed, it is compared with the company's required rate of return. If the IRR is greater than the required rate, the project is deemed acceptable; if the IRR is equal to the required rate of return, acceptance or rejection of the investment is equal; if the IRR is less than the required rate of return, the project is rejected.

The internal rate of return is the most widely used of the capital investment techniques.[8] One reason for its popularity may be that it is a rate of return, a concept that managers are comfortable using. Another possibility is that managers may believe (in most cases, incorrectly) that the IRR is the true or actual compounded rate of return being earned by the initial investment. Whatever the reasons for its popularity, a basic understanding of the IRR is necessary.

## Example: Multiple-Period Setting with Uniform Cash Flows

To illustrate how to compute the IRR in a multiple-period setting, assume that a company has an opportunity to invest $120,000 in new equipment that will produce net cash flows of $49,950 at the end of each year for the next three years. The IRR is the interest rate that equates the present value of the three equal receipts of $49,950 to the investment of $120,000. Since the series of cash flows is uniform, a single discount factor can be used to compute the annuity's present value. Letting $df$ be this discount factor and $CF$ be the annual cash flow, the IRR equation is:

$$I = CF(df)$$

Solving for $df$, we obtain the following:

$$df = I/CF$$
$$= \text{Investment/Annual cash flow}$$

The discount factor for the company's investment is 2.402 [$120,000/$49,950]. Since the life of the investment is three years, the interest rate corresponding to 2.402 is 12 percent, which is the IRR. Financial calculators or spreadsheet programs are commonly used to calculate IRR.

## Multiple-Period Setting: Uneven Cash Flows

If the cash flows are not uniform, the IRR equation must be solved using a financial calculator or a software package or by trial and error. To illustrate solution by trial and error, assume that a $10,000 investment in a computer system produces clerical savings of $6,000 and $7,200 over two years. The IRR is the interest rate that sets the present value of these two cash inflows equal to $10,000:

$$P = \$6,000/(1 + i) + \$7,200/(1 + i)^2$$
$$= \$10,000$$

---

7. We can use a financial calculator or a computer program to calculate IRR.

8. Blazouske, Carlin, and Kim (see note 3) found that IRR was used as the primary technique by more than 60 percent of the companies that used a discounting method.

To solve the above equation by trial and error, we start by selecting a possible value for $i$. Given this first guess, we compute the present value of the future cash flows and then compare the present value to the initial investment. If the present value is greater than the initial investment, the interest rate is too low; if the present value is less than the initial investment, the interest rate is too high. Our next guess is adjusted accordingly.

Assume that our first guess is 18 percent. Using $i$ equal to 0.18, we find the discount factors for Years 1 and 2: 0.847 and 0.718, respectively. These discount factors produce the following present value for the two cash inflows:

$$P = \$6,000 \times 0.847 + \$7,200 \times 0.718$$
$$= \$10,252$$

Since $P$ is greater than \$10,000, the interest rate selected is too low. A higher guess is needed. If our next guess is 20 percent, we obtain the following:

$$P = \$6,000 \times 0.833 + \$7,200 \times 0.694$$
$$= \$9,995$$

Since this value is reasonably close to \$10,000, we can say that the IRR is approximately 20 percent. (The IRR is, in fact, exactly 20 percent: the present value is slightly less than the investment because of rounding in the discount factors.)

## Mutually Exclusive Projects

Up to this point, we have focused on independent projects. Many capital investment decisions, however, involve mutually exclusive projects. How NPV and IRR analysis are used to choose among competing projects is, of course, an interesting question. An even more interesting question to consider is whether NPV and IRR differ in their ability to help managers make wealth-maximizing decisions in the presence of competing alternatives. For example, we already know that nondiscounting models can produce erroneous choices because they ignore the time value of money. Because of this deficiency, the discounting models are judged superior. Similarly, it can be shown that the NPV model is generally preferred over the IRR model when choosing among mutually exclusive alternatives.

## NPV Compared with IRR

NPV and IRR both yield the same decision for independent projects: for example, if the NPV is greater than zero, then the IRR is also greater than the required rate of return—both models signal the correct decision. However, for competing projects, the two models can produce different results. Intuitively, we believe that for mutually exclusive projects, the project with the highest NPV or the highest IRR should be chosen. Since it is possible for the two models to produce different rankings of mutually exclusive projects, the model that consistently reveals the wealth-maximizing project should be preferred.

NPV differs from IRR in two major ways. First, NPV assumes that each cash inflow received is reinvested at the required rate of return, whereas IRR assumes that each cash inflow is reinvested at the computed IRR. Assuming that cash inflows will be reinvesting at the required rate of return is more realistic and produces more reliable results when comparing mutually exclusive projects. Second, NPV measures profitability in absolute terms, whereas IRR measures it in relative terms. NPV measures the amount by which the company's value changes.

Because NPV measures the impact that competing projects have on the company's value, choosing the project with the largest NPV is consistent with maximizing the wealth of shareholders. On the other hand, IRR does not consistently result in choices that maximize wealth. As a relative measure of profitability, IRR has the virtue of accurately measuring the rate of return of funds that remain internally invested. However, maximizing IRR will not necessarily maximize the value of the company because IRR cannot, by nature, consider the absolute dollar contributions of projects. In the final analysis, what counts are the total dollars earned—the absolute profits—not the relative profits. Accordingly, NPV, not IRR, should be used for choosing among competing, mutually exclusive projects, or among competing projects when capital funds are limited.

An independent project is acceptable if its NPV is positive. For mutually exclusive projects, the project with the largest NPV is chosen. There are three steps in selecting the best project from several competing projects: (1) assessing the cash-flow pattern for each project, (2) computing the NPV for each project, and (3) identifying the project with the greatest NPV. We will use the following example to illustrate NPV analysis for competing projects.

## Example: Mutually Exclusive Projects

Hintley Corporation has committed to improve its environmental performance. One environmental project identified a manufacturing process as the source of both liquid and gaseous residues. After six months of research, the Engineering Department announced that it is possible to redesign the process to prevent the production of contaminating residues. Hintley is considering two different process designs. Both designs are more expensive to operate than the current process; however, the designs have significant benefits because Hintley will no longer need to operate and maintain expensive pollution control equipment to treat and dispose of toxic liquid wastes and pay the annual fines for exceeding allowable contaminant releases. Increased sales to environmentally conscious customers are factored into the benefit estimates. Design B is more elaborate than Design A and will require a larger investment and greater annual operating costs; however, it will also generate greater annual revenues. The projected annual revenues, annual costs, capital outlays, and project life for each design (in after-tax cash flows) follow:

|  | Design A | Design B |
|---|---|---|
| Annual revenues | $179,460 | $239,280 |
| Annual operating costs | 119,460 | 169,280 |
| Equipment (purchased before Year 1) | 180,000 | 210,000 |
| Project life | 5 years | 5 years |

The company must decide which design to choose. Assume that the company's cost of capital is 12 percent.

Design A requires an initial outlay of $180,000 and has an annual net cash flow of $60,000 (revenues of $179,460 minus costs of $119,460). Design B, with an initial outlay of $210,000, has an annual net cash flow of $70,000 ($239,280 − 169,280). With this information, we can describe the cash-flow pattern for each project and compute NPV. These are shown in Exhibit 11–3. Based on NPV analysis, Design B is more profitable; it has the larger NPV. Accordingly, the company should select Design B over Design A.

Interestingly, Designs A and B have identical internal rates of return. As shown in Exhibit 11–3, both designs have a discount factor of 3.000. A discount factor of 3.000 and a life of five years give an IRR of about 20 percent. Even though both projects have an IRR of 20 percent, the company should not consider the two designs equally desirable. The analysis above has just shown that Design B produces a larger NPV, and will therefore increase the company's value more than Design A will. Hence, Design B should be chosen. This illustrates the conceptual superiority of NPV over IRR for analysis of competing projects.

### CASH-FLOW PATTERN

| Year | Design A | Design B |
|---|---|---|
| 0 | $(180,000) | $(210,000) |
| 1 | 60,000 | 70,000 |
| 2 | 60,000 | 70,000 |
| 3 | 60,000 | 70,000 |
| 4 | 60,000 | 70,000 |
| 5 | 60,000 | 70,000 |

### DESIGN A: NPV ANALYSIS

| Year | Cash Flow | Discount Factor | Present Value |
|---|---|---|---|
| 0 | $(180,000) | 1.000 | $(180,000) |
| 1–5 | 60,000 | 3.605 | 216,300 |
| Net present value | | | $ 36,300 |

### DESIGN A: IRR ANALYSIS

$$\text{Discount factor} = \frac{\text{Initial investment}}{\text{Annual cash flow}}$$

$$= \frac{\$180,000}{60,000}$$

$$= 3.00$$

A *df* of 3.000 for five years implies an IRR of 20% (approximately).

### DESIGN B: NPV ANALYSIS

| Year | Cash Flow | Discount Factor | Present Value |
|---|---|---|---|
| 0 | $(210,000) | 1.000 | $(210,000) |
| 1–5 | 70,000 | 3.605 | 252,350 |
| Net present value | | | $ 42,350 |

### DESIGN B: IRR ANALYSIS

$$\text{Discount factor} = \frac{\text{Initial investment}}{\text{Annual cash flow}}$$

$$= \frac{\$210,000}{70,000}$$

$$= 3.00$$

A *df* of 3.000 for five years implies an IRR of 20% (approximately).

## Capital Investment and Ethical Issues

Capital investment decisions often offer great temptation for misrepresentations. Divisional mangers must often compete for scarce resources. With this competition comes the temptation to engage in deceptive behaviour. Examples of such behaviour are numerous. Managers have been guilty of deliberately overestimating cash inflows and underestimating cash outlays so that a pet project might have the NPV or IRR necessary to be approved. This is particularly tempting when the project's early cash flows are expected to be good, whereas its later cash flows are expected to be poor. Adjusting the estimates of the poor cash flows upward may produce an approved project that has good performance in its early years and poor performance in its later years. Other possibilities also exist. For example, a manager may need approval for any capital expenditure above a certain level. Suppose that a manager acquired a computer system by purchasing it in pieces, where the cost of each piece was less than the manager's capital expenditure approval limit. Was this right?

Managers need to realize that how objectives are reached is almost as important as (and maybe more important than) merely reaching the objectives. Furthermore, companies should structure their performance evaluation systems so that the reward system does not provide strong incentives for unethical behaviour. As observed in an article on ethics, "No code of ethics and no amount of cajolery by the chief executive will have much effect if promotions go regularly to the people who pile up big numbers by cutting corners."[9] In the same article, another interesting observation was made—one that is particularly appropriate for the capital expenditure framework. A positive net present value means that the company's value should increase. According to the article, James Burke, CEO for Johnson & Johnson, identified a group of companies that paid a lot of attention to ethical standards. From 1950 to 1990, the market value of this group of companies grew at 11.3 percent annually, compared with 6.2 percent growth in the Dow Jones industrials. Perhaps ethical behaviour pays off on the bottom line!

## Postaudit of Capital Projects

**Objective 6**

Explain the role and value of postaudits.

**postaudit**

A follow-up analysis of an investment decision, comparing actual benefits and costs with expected benefits and costs.

A key element in the capital investment decision process is a follow-up analysis of a capital project once it is implemented. This analysis is called a *postaudit*. A **postaudit** compares the actual benefits with the estimated benefits and compares the actual operating costs with estimated operating costs; it evaluates the investment's overall outcome and proposes corrective action if any is needed.[10] The following real-world case illustrates the usefulness of a postaudit.

### Honley Medical Company: An Illustrative Application

Allen Manesfield and Jenny Winters were discussing a persistent and irritating problem present in the process of producing intravenous needles (IVs). Both Allen and Jenny are employed by Honley Medical, which specializes in the production of medical products and has three divisions: the IV Products Division, the Critical Care Monitoring Division, and the Specialty Products Division. Allen and Jenny both are associated with the IV Products Division—Allen as the senior production engineer and Jenny as the marketing manager.

The IV Products Division produces needles of five different sizes. During one stage of the manufacturing process, the needle itself is inserted into a plastic hub and bonded using epoxy glue. According to Jenny, the use of epoxy to bond the needles was causing the division all kinds of problems. In many cases, the epoxy was not bonding correctly. Rejects were high, and the division was receiving a large number of complaints from its customers. Corrective action was needed to avoid lost sales.

After some discussion and analysis, a recommendation was made to use induction welding in lieu of epoxy bonding. In induction welding, the needles are inserted into the plastic hub, and an RF generator is used to heat the needles. The RF generator works on the same principle as a microwave oven. As the needles get hot, the plastic melts and the needles are bonded.

---

9.  Kenneth Labich, "The New Crisis in Business Ethics," Fortune (20 April 1992): pp. 167-76.

10. Postaudits of capital projects are the subject of CMA Canada's Management Accounting Guideline 1, Post Appraisal of Capital Expenditure, 1984.

Switching to induction welding required an investment in RF generators and the associated tooling; the IV Division justified the investment based on the savings associated with the new system. Induction welding promised to reduce the cost of direct materials by eliminating the need to buy and use epoxy. Savings of direct labour costs were also predicted, because the new process was much more automated. Adding to these savings were the avoidance of daily cleanup costs and the reduction in rejects. Allen presented a formal NPV analysis showing that the welding system was superior to the epoxy system. The purchase was approved by headquarters.

## One Year Later

**Jenny**: "Allen, I'm quite pleased with induction welding for bonding needles. In the year since the new process was implemented, we've had virtually no complaints from our customers. The needles are firmly bonded."

**Allen**: "I wish that positive experience were true for all other areas as well. Unfortunately, implementing the process has uncovered some rather sticky and expensive problems that I simply didn't anticipate. The Internal Audit Department recently completed a postaudit of the project, and now my feet are being held to the fire."

**Jenny**: "That's too bad. What's the problem?"

**Allen**: "You mean problems. Let me list a few for you. One is that the RF generators interfered with the operation of other equipment. To eliminate this interference, we had to install filtering equipment. But that's not all. We also discovered that our maintenance staff didn't know how to maintain the new equipment. Now we are faced with the need to initiate a training program to upgrade the skills of our maintenance people. Upgrading skills also implies higher wages. Although the RF bonding process is less messy, it is also more complex. The manufacturing people complained to the internal auditors about that. They maintain that a simple process, even if it's messy, is to be preferred—especially now that demand for the product is increasing by leaps and bounds."

**Jenny**: "What did the internal auditors conclude?"

**Allen**: "They observed that many of the predicted savings did take place, but that some significant costs were not foreseen. Because of some of the unforeseen problems, they have recommended that I look carefully at the possibility of moving back to using epoxy. They indicated that NPV analysis using actual data appears to favour that process. With production expanding, the acquisition of additional RF generators and filtering equipment, plus the necessary training, is simply not as attractive as returning to epoxy bonding. This conclusion is reinforced by the fact that the epoxy process is simpler and by the auditors' conclusion that the mixing of the epoxy can be automated, avoiding the quality problem we had in the first place."

**Jenny**: "Well, Allen, you can't really blame yourself. You had a real problem and took action to solve it. It's difficult to foresee all the problems and hidden costs of a new process."

**Allen**: "Unfortunately, the internal auditors don't totally agree. In fact, neither do I. I probably jumped too quickly. In the future, I intend to think through new projects more carefully."

## Benefits of a Postaudit

In the case of the RF bonding decision, some of the estimated benefits did materialize: complaints from customers decreased, rejects were fewer, and direct labour and materials costs decreased. However, the investment was greater than expected because filtering equipment was needed, and actual operating costs were much higher because of the increased maintenance cost and the increased complexity of the process. Overall, the internal auditors concluded that the investment was a poor decision. The corrective action they recommended was to abandon the new process and return to epoxy bonding.[11]

Companies that perform postaudits of capital projects experience a number of benefits. First, by evaluating profitability, postaudits ensure that resources are used wisely. If the project is doing well, it may call for additional funds and additional attention. If the project is not doing well, corrective action may be needed to improve performance, or perhaps the project may even be abandoned.

A second benefit of the postaudit is its impact on the behaviour of managers. If managers are held accountable for the results of a capital investment decision, they are more likely to make such decisions in the company's best interests. Additionally, postaudits supply feedback to managers that should help improve future decision making. Consider Allen's reaction to the postaudit of the RF bonding process. Certainly, he would be expected to be more careful and more thorough in making future investment recommendations. In the future, Allen will probably consider more than one alternative, such as automating the mixing of the epoxy. Also, for those alternatives being considered, he will probably be especially alert to the possibility of hidden costs, such as increased training requirements for a new process.

The case also reveals that the postaudit was performed by the internal audit staff. Generally, more objective results are obtainable if the postaudit is done by an independent party. Since considerable effort is expended to ensure as much independence as possible for the internal audit staff, that group is usually the best choice for this task.

Postaudits, however, are costly. Moreover, even though they may provide significant benefits, they have other limitations. Most obvious is the fact that the assumptions driving the original analysis may often be invalidated by changes in the actual operating environment. Accountability must be qualified to some extent by the impossibility of foreseeing every possible eventuality.

## Computation and Adjustment of Cash Flows

**Objective** 7

Convert gross cash flows to after-tax cash flows.

An important step in capital investment analysis is determining the cash-flow pattern for each project being considered. In fact, the computation of cash flows may be the most critical step in the capital investment process. Erroneous estimates may result in erroneous decisions, regardless of the sophistication of the decision models being used. The Honley Medical Company case described in the previous section illustrates this point vividly. If the cash flows associated with the inductive welding process had been more accurately forecast, a better decision could have been made.

Two steps are needed to compute cash flows: (1) forecasting revenues, expenses, and capital outlays; and (2) adjusting these gross cash flows to after-tax cash flows through a careful analysis of the relevant tax factors. Of the two steps, the more challenging is the first. Forecasting is technically demanding, and its methodology is typically studied in market research and management science courses.[12] Once gross cash flows are estimated, they should be adjusted for sig-

---

11. The company did abandon inductive welding and returned to epoxy bonding, which was improved by automating the mixing. The simplicity of the epoxy process was a major qualitative factor in deciding to return to the old, improved process.

12. There is a detailed discussion of determining cash-flow patterns in CMA Canada's *Management Accounting Guideline 2, Estimating Cash Flows for Capital Expenditure Decisions,* 1985.

nificant inflationary effects. Finally, straightforward applications of tax law can be used to compute the after-tax flows. At this level of analysis, we assume that gross cash flows are available, and focus on adjusting forecasted cash flows to improve their accuracy and relevance.

## Adjusting Forecasts for Inflation

In recent years, inflation in Canada has been relatively modest, so the need to adjust cash flows for inflation may not be critical. However, companies that operate in the international environment may face different circumstances: inflation can be very high in some countries, and its effect on capital investment decisions can be dramatic. Venezuela, for example, has experienced double-digit inflation rates in recent years. Thus, it is important to know how to adjust the capital investment models for inflationary effects—particularly given the fact that many Canadian companies make capital investment decisions within many different national environments. In an inflationary environment, financial markets react by increasing the cost of capital to reflect inflation. Thus, the cost of capital is composed of two elements:

1. the real rate,
2. the inflationary element (investors demand a premium to compensate for the loss in general purchasing power of the dollar or local currency).

Since the required rate of return used in capital investment analysis reflects an inflationary component at the time NPV analysis is performed, inflation must also be considered in predicting the operating cash flows. If the operating cash flows are not adjusted to account for inflation, an erroneous decision may result. In adjusting predicted cash flows, specific price change indexes should be used if possible. If that is not possible, a general price index should be used.

Note, however, that cash inflows due to the tax effects of amortization, which are discussed later in this section, need *not* be adjusted for inflation as long as the national tax law for the country in question requires that amortization (or its equivalent) be based on the *original* dollar investment.

To illustrate, assume that a subsidiary of a Canadian company operating in Hungary is considering a project that requires an investment of 5,000,000 forints (the Hungarian currency) and is expected to produce annual cash inflows of 2,900,000 forints for the coming two years. The required rate of return is 20 percent, which includes an inflationary component. The general inflation rate is expected to average 15 percent for the next two years. Net present value analysis with and without the adjustment of predicted cash flows for inflation is given in Exhibit 11–4. As the analysis shows, failing to adjust predicted cash flows for inflation leads to a decision to reject the project, whereas adjusting for inflation leads to a decision to accept it. Thus, failure to adjust the predicted cash flows for inflationary effects can lead to an incorrect conclusion.

## Conversion of Gross Cash Flows to After-Tax Cash Flows

Once gross cash flows are predicted with the desired degree of accuracy, the analyst must adjust these cash flows for taxes. To analyze tax effects, cash flows are usually broken into two categories:

1. the initial cash outflows needed to acquire the assets of the project, and
2. the cash flows produced over the life of the project.

**EXHIBIT**  **11-4**

The Effects of Inflation on
Capital Investment

| WITHOUT INFLATIONARY ADJUSTMENT | | | |
|---|---|---|---|
| **Year** | **Cash Flow** | **Discount Factor** | **Present Value** |
| 0 | (5,000,000) | 1.000 | (5,000,000) |
| 1–2 | 2,900,000 | 1.528 | 4,431,200 |
| Net present value | | | (568,800) |

| WITH INFLATIONARY ADJUSTMENT | | | |
|---|---|---|---|
| **Year** | **Cash Flow\*** | **Discount Factor** | **Present Value** |
| 0 | (5,000,000) | 1.000 | (5,000,000) |
| 1 | 3,335,000 | 0.833 | 2,778,055 |
| 2 | 3,835,250 | 0.694 | 2,661,664 |
| Net present value | | | 439,719 |

\* Adjustment for one year of inflation: 1.15 × 2,900,000; adjustment for two years of inflation
1.15 × 1.15 × 2,900,000
*Note:* All cash flows are expressed in forints.

Cash outflows and cash inflows adjusted for tax effects are called after-tax
cash outflows and inflows. After-tax cash flow includes provisions for after-tax
revenues, after-tax operating expenses, and the tax implications of amortization.

### After-Tax Cash Flows: Year 0

The after-tax cash flow in Year 0 (the initial out-of-pocket outlay) is simply the difference between the initial cost of the project and any cash inflows directly associated with it. The project's gross cost includes such things as the cost of land, the
cost of equipment (including transportation and installation), taxes on gains from
the sale of assets, and increases in working capital. Cash inflows occurring at the
time of acquisition include cash from the sale of assets and tax savings from losses
on the sale of assets.

Under current Canadian tax law, all costs relating to the acquisition of assets
other than land must be capitalized and written off over the useful life of the
assets. In Canada, a capital cost allowance (similar to the accounting amortization
concept) based on this capitalized cost is used to write off a portion each year.
Capital cost allowance and operating expenses (other than amortization) are
deducted from revenues when computing taxable income during each year of the
asset's life. However, at the point of acquisition, there is no taxable income related
to the asset, so the principal tax implications are related to the recognition of gains
or losses on the sale of existing assets.

The sale of assets may produce additional tax payable because of a taxable
gain, and the cash inflow from the sale would be reduced accordingly. Losses on
the sale of assets are noncash expenses that may reduce taxable income. More
details about the tax implications from the sale of assets are discussed later in this
section.

### After-Tax Cash Flows: Life of the Project

Managers must also estimate the annual after-tax cash flows expected over the
life of the project. If the project generates revenue, the principal source of cash
flows is from operations. Operating cash flows can be assessed from the project's
income statement. The annual after-tax flows are the sum of the project's after-tax
profits and its noncash expenses. In terms of a simple formula, this computation
can be represented as follows:

$$\text{After-tax cash flows} = \text{After-tax net income} + \text{Noncash expenses}$$
$$CF = NI + NC$$

where            $CF$ = After-tax cash flows
                 $NI$ = After-tax net income
                 $NC$ = Noncash expenses

**capital cost allowances (CCAs)**

Deduction for Canadian income tax purposes related to the capital cost of fixed assets.

The most common examples of noncash expenses are amortization and losses. For income tax purposes in Canada, amortization is not allowed as a deduction in determining taxable income: **capital cost allowances (CCAs)** are used instead. For the purposes of our current discussion, we will treat CCA and amortization as the same for now. We will cover the special features of the CCA system later in this section.

At first glance, it may seem odd that noncash expenses are included in computing after-tax cash flows. Noncash expenses are not cash flows, but will affect cash flows by reducing cash tax payments. Shielding income from taxation creates actual cash savings. We illustrate the use of the income statement to determine after-tax cash flows in the following example. We also use the example to show how noncash expenses can increase cash inflows by saving taxes.

Assume that Spear Corporation plans to purchase a machine that costs $300,000. The machine will produce a new product that is expected to increase the company's annual revenues (and cash inflows) by $300,000. Expenses (and cash outflows) for materials, labour, and other operating costs will be $125,000 per year. The machine has a life of three years and will be amortized on a straight-line basis for accounting and tax purposes. The machine will have no salvage value at the end of three years. The project's projected income statement is as follows:

| | |
|---|---:|
| Revenues | $300,000 |
| Less: Cash operating expenses | 125,000 |
| Less: Amortization | 100,000 |
| Income before taxes | $ 75,000 |
| Less: Taxes (@ 40%)[13] | 30,000 |
| Net income | $ 45,000 |

Cash flow can be computed from the income statement as follows:

$$CF = NI + NC$$
$$= \$45,000 + \$100,000$$
$$= \$145,000$$

The income approach to determining operating cash flows can be used to assess the after-tax cash flows, as illustrated above. Following is an approach known as the decompostion method.

$$CF = [(1 - \text{Tax rate}) \times \text{Revenues}] - [(1 - \text{Tax rate}) \times \text{Cash expenses}] + [\text{Tax rate} \times \text{Noncash expenses}]$$

We will look at each of the terms on the right hand side of this equation.

1.  *[(1 – Tax rate) × Revenues]* gives the after-tax cash flows from cash revenues. For our example, cash revenues are projected to be $300,000. The company can therefore expect to keep $180,000 of the revenues received [(1 – 0.4) × $300,000] with tax of $120,000 to be paid.

---

13. An important element of adjusting for taxes is identifying the appropriate rate to apply. In Canada, corporate tax is a combination of federal and provincial taxes (along with other factors). We will assume a simple tax rate. For a detailed discussion of tax rates, see, for example, W.J. Buckwold, *Canadian Income Taxation: Planning and Decision Making*, Third Edition, Whitby, ON: McGraw-Hill Ryerson, 1999.

2. *[(1 − Tax rate) × Cash expenses]* is the after-tax cash flows from cash operating expenses. Because cash expenses can be deducted from revenues to arrive at taxable income, the effect is to shield part of the revenues from taxation. This shielding saves taxes and reduces the effective cash outflows associated with a given expenditure. In our example, the company has cash operating expenses of $125,000. The after-tax cash outflow is $75,000 [(1 − 0.4) × $125,000]. The deductibility of the operating expenses produces tax savings of $50,000.

3. *[Tax rate × Noncash expenses]* is the cash inflow from tax savings produced by the noncash expenses. Noncash expenses, such as amortization, also shield revenues from taxation. In our example, amortization shields revenues of $100,000 from being taxed and thus saves taxes of $40,000; this effect is known as the *amortization tax shield*.

A summary of the three items is given below:

| After-tax revenues | $180,000 |
| After-tax cash expenses | (75,000) |
| Amortization tax shield | 40,000 |
| After-tax cash flow | $145,000 |

The decomposition approach yields the same outcome as the income approach but more directly demonstrates the cash-flow consequences of the noncash expenses. Remember that in this section, we have assumed that amortization (for accounting net income) and the capital cost allowance (for taxable income) are determined in the same way. Next, we will consider how our analysis changes when the particulars of the CCA system are included.

## Cash-Flow Consequences of Capital Cost Allowances (CCAs)

The capital cost allowance provisions of the Canadian income tax system are different from accounting amortization in some significant ways. When a capital property asset is acquired, it is assigned to a capital asset class along with other assets of a similar type. We calculate the CCA allowed for a particular class in a tax year by multiplying the balance of capital cost in the class, after adding new purchases of assets and deducting disposals of assets during the tax year, by the appropriate CCA rate. There are currently more than 40 separate classes, each with a specific maximum rate. A sample of CCA classes and the applicable maximum CCA rates is given in Exhibit 11–5.

Two features of the capital cost allowance system are important for determining the appropriate after-tax or net cash flows for capital investment purposes.

1. The capital cost allowance system is generally a declining-balance system: a constant percentage or rate is applied to the remaining balance in the capital

**EXHIBIT** 11-5

Sample of Capital Cost Allowance Classes and Maximum Rates

| Class | Examples of Assets Included | Maximum Rate |
|---|---|---|
| Class 1 | Buildings and other structures | 4% |
| Class 7 | Boats, ships | 15% |
| Class 8 | Equipment and machinery | 20% |
| Class 9 | Aircraft | 25% |
| Class 10 | Computer equipment, trucks | 30% |
| Class 12 | Small tools, computer software | 100% |
| Class 33 | Timber resource property | 15% |
| Class 37 | Amusement park buildings and equipment | 15% |

cost allowance class.[14] Unlike the uniform amount under straight-line amortization, the size of the tax shield will change each year, and separate calculations of CCA tax shield are required for each year.

2. The capital costs of each class are combined in a single cost pool. As a consequence, if there are other asset items in the class, a particular project may continue to affect the company's cash flows even after the project is completed (and its associated assets are retired). This effect is caused because the balance in the cost pool for the class determines the allowable CCA. When an asset item is retired, the cost pool is reduced by the proceeds from its retirement, to a maximum of the asset item's original capital cost. A project will continue to have a tax shield effect if the proceeds are less than the original cost and if some other asset remains in the class.[15]

To illustrate these factors, we will again consider Spear Corporation's plan to purchase a machine with a capital cost of $300,000, but now we will calculate CCA using a 30 percent rate instead of straight-line amortization. We need to calculate CCA and tax payable for each of the three years. Remember that annual cash flows are $300,000, and cash operating expenses are $125,000. The calculation of after-tax cash flows is shown in Exhibit 11–6.[16]

Now assume that Spear Corporation has a required rate of return of 10 percent and that the machine will have a zero salvage value after three years. The net present value analysis for the project, based on the after-tax cash flows from Exhibit 11–6, is given in Part A of Exhibit 11-7.

We can find the amount of the CCA tax shield by comparing the project's NPV with CCA to the project's NPV without CCA. The NPV without CCA is shown in Part B of Exhibit 11–7.

The project's NPV is $(38,865) without CCA, but $27,817 with CCA. The difference, $66,682, is the present value of the CCA tax shield. We can calculate this amount directly, as shown below:

| Year | CCA[a] | Tax Savings[b] | Discount Factor | Present Value |
|------|--------|----------------|-----------------|---------------|
| 1 | $90,000 | $36,000 | 0.909 | $ 32,724 |
| 2 | 63,000 | 25,200 | 0.826 | 20,815 |
| 3 | 44,100 | 17,640 | 0.751 | 13,248 |
| | Net Present Value | | | $66,787[c] |

[a] From Exhibit 11–6
[b] CCA × 40%
[c] The small difference from $66,682 is due to rounding in the discount factors.

---

14. There are a few exceptions to this general discussion (e.g., lease improvements and passenger vehicles), but a more detailed discussion is beyond the scope of this book.

15. If the proceeds from disposal are less than the asset's "unamortized" cost, there will be a tax shield effect from the remaining capital cost (after the proceeds are deducted from the class). The remaining capital cost will result in a higher CCA tax shield in future years if there are other assets in the class. The remaining capital cost is a *terminal loss* if the asset was the only asset in the class. Terminal losses are deducted from taxable income and an immediate tax shield realized.

If the proceeds on disposal are greater than the "unamortized" capital cost of the asset, the balance in the capital cost pool may be negative. This is a *recapture of CCA*, which is added to taxable income for the year. If the class includes other assets, the balance in the pool may still be positive but the CCA tax shield in future years is reduced.

If the proceeds from disposal exceed the original capital cost of the asset, there will also be a *taxable capital gain*.

16. A further complication of the CCA system is that allowable CCA is limited to one-half the normal amount in the year of acquisition. We will ignore this requirement here but consider it later in this section.

EXHIBIT 11-6

After-Tax Cash Flow with CCA

| CCA Calculation | Year 1 | Year 2 | Year 3 |
|---|---|---|---|
| Capital cost, beginning of year | $300,000 | $210,000 | $147,000 |
| Less CCA, 30% × capital cost, beginning of year | 90,000 | 63,000 | 44,100 |
| Capital cost, end of year | $210,000 | $147,000 | $102,900 |

| After-Tax Income Calculation | Year 1 | Year 2 | Year 3 |
|---|---|---|---|
| Revenues | $300,000 | $300,000 | $300,000 |
| Less operating expenses | 125,000 | 125,000 | 125,000 |
| Less CCA (from above) | 90,000 | 63,000 | 44,100 |
| Taxable income | $ 85,000 | $112,000 | $130,900 |
| Less tax payable (40%) | 34,000 | 44,800 | 52,360 |
| After-tax income | $ 51,000 | $ 67,200 | $ 78,540 |

| After-Tax Cash-Flow Calculation | Year 1 | Year 2 | Year 3 |
|---|---|---|---|
| After-tax income (from above) | $ 51,000 | $ 67,200 | $ 78,540 |
| Plus noncash expense (CCA) | 90,000 | 63,000 | 44,100 |
| After-tax cash flow | $141,000 | $130,200 | $122,640 |

However, our analysis is still not complete, because there is unused (for CCA purposes) capital cost related to the project of $102,900 at the end of Year 3, as shown in Exhibit 11–6. We need to consider two cases:

1.  The first case is when there are no other assets in the CCA class. This case will result in a terminal loss of $102,900 in Year 3. The calculation of after-tax cash

EXHIBIT 11-7

NPV With and Without CCA

| PART A | | | |
|---|---|---|---|
| Net Present Value—With CCA | | | |
| Year | After-Tax Cash Flow | Discount Factor | Present Value |
| 0 | $(300,000) | 1.000 | $(300,000) |
| 1 | 141,000 | 0.909 | 128,169 |
| 2 | 130,200 | 0.826 | 107,545 |
| 3 | 122,640 | 0.751 | 92,103 |
| Net Present Value | | | $27,817 |

| PART B | | | |
|---|---|---|---|
| Cash Flows—Without CCA | | | |
| | Year 1 | Year 2 | Year 3 |
| Operating cash flow[a] | $175,000 | $175,000 | $175,000 |
| Less tax payable (40%) | 70,000 | 70,000 | 70,000 |
| After-tax cash flow | $105,000 | $105,000 | $105,000 |

| Net Present Value—Without CCA | | | |
|---|---|---|---|
| Year | After-Tax Cash Flow | Discount Factor | Present Value |
| 0 | $(300,000) | 1.000 | $(300,000) |
| 1–3 | 105,000 | 2.487 | 261,135 |
| Net Present Value | | | $ (38,865) |

[a] $300,000 − $125,000 = $175,000

flow for Year 3 will change, because the tax payable will be lower as shown below:

| | |
|---|---:|
| Taxable operating income (from Exhibit 11–6) | $130,900 |
| Less terminal loss | 102,900 |
| Taxable income | $ 28,000 |
| Tax payable (@ 40%) | $ 11,200 |

The after-tax cash flow in Year 3 will be as follows:

$$\text{After-tax cash flow} = \text{Gross cash flow} - \text{Tax payable}$$
$$= \$175,000 - \$11,200$$
$$= \$163,800$$

The complete NPV analysis, including the terminal loss, is given below:

| Year | After-Tax Cash Flow[a] | Discount Factor | Present Value |
|:---:|:---:|:---:|:---:|
| 0 | $(300,000) | 1.000 | $(300,000) |
| 1 | 141,000 | 0.909 | 128,169 |
| 2 | 130,200 | 0.826 | 107,545 |
| 3 | 163,800 | 0.751 | 123,014 |
| Net Present Value | | | $ 58,728 |

[a] From Exhibit 11–6, modified in Year 3

NPV increases to $58,728 from $27,817, because the terminal loss in Year 3 is a tax shield and reduces the tax payable by $41,160, which has a present value of $30,911.

2. The second case is when there are other assets in the class. In this case, the allowable CCA in future years (and the associated tax shield) will be higher. We can calculate the present value of the remaining tax shield as follows:

| Year | CCA[a] | Tax Shield[b] | Discount Factor | Present Value |
|:---:|:---:|:---:|:---:|:---:|
| 4 | $30,870 | $12,348 | 0.683 | $ 8,434 |
| 5 | 21,609 | 8,644 | 0.621 | 5,368 |
| 6 | 15,126 | 6,051 | 0.564 | 3,413 |
| ...... | ... | ... | ... | |
| 18 | 209 | 84 | 0.180 | 15 |
| 19 | 147 | 59 | 0.164 | 10 |
| 20 | 103 | 41 | 0.149 | 6 |
| etc. | ... | ... | ... | ... |
| Present Value of Remaining CCA Tax Shield | | | | $23,190 |

[a] 30% × Capital Cost, Beginning of Year
[b] 40% × CCA

Notice that very little is added to the tax shield in Year 20 and beyond. The present value of the remaining CCA tax shield is $23,190, for a total NPV for the project of $51,007 [$27,817 + 23,190].

### An Alternative CCA Tax Shield Approach

We can use an alternative analysis based on the decomposition of the operating cash flows illustrated in the previous section. This approach, the formula method, highlights the present value of the CCA tax shield and offers a simpler calculation.[17] From Exhibit 11–7, the NPV of the after-tax cash flows, ignoring the tax

---

17. With the widespread use of spreadsheet programs and customized capital budgeting programs, the major benefit of the formula approach is separating the CCA tax shield from other cash flows. Simplifying the calculation is now less important.

shield effect of CCA, is $(38,865) and represents the first two terms of the after-tax cash-flow equation. The present value of the CCA tax shield, the third term, is calculated using the following formula.

Present value of CCA tax shield $= (R \times C \times T)/(R + i)$

where
$R$ = the CCA rate
$C$ = the original capital cost of the project
$T$ = the tax rate
$i$ = required rate of return

For our example, the CCA tax shield is as follows:

Present value of CCA tax shield $= (30\% \times \$300,000 \times 40\%)/(30\% + 10\%)$
$= \$90,000$

The machine's NPV, calculated using the CCA tax shield formula, is $(38,865) + $90,000 = $51,135. Rounding accounts for the small difference between this answer and the NPV of $51,007 that we calculated using the direct method.

As we have seen, CCA will affect the amount of tax payable and, therefore, the after-tax cash flows of projects with investments in capital assets. We have looked at two ways to account for the tax shield effect of CCA. In our first analysis, the direct method, we include the tax shield effect of CCA directly when determining the after-tax cash flows over the life of the project. We need to make adjustments for any continuing tax shield after the project ends. In our second analysis, the formula method, we decompose the operating cash flows and prepare an NPV analysis of the project ignoring CCA, and then use the CCA tax shield formula to calculate the present value of the CCA tax shield for the project. So far, our focus has been on the fundamental impact of CCA on capital investment decisions. There are other features of Canadian income tax rules that affect our analysis. We will modify our example for Spear Corporation to illustrate two of these features, the *one-half rule* and the *nonzero salvage value.*

## The One-Half Rule

**one-half rule**

The rule that restricts the amount of CCA that can be claimed in the year of acquisition to one half of the CCA for the class.

The **one-half rule** restricts the amount of CCA that can be claimed in the year of acquisition to one-half of the CCA rate for the class. In our previous analyses, whether calculating the CCA effect on NPV directly or employing the tax shield formula, we used a full amount of CCA in the first year. If the one-half rule is applied, however, we must adjust our analyses.

1. For the direct calculation method, the adjustment is straightforward: reduce the amount of CCA in the first year, and adjust the following years accordingly. We see the adjustment in the CCA amounts, after-tax cash flows, and NPV for our Spear Corporation example in Exhibit 11–8. Note that the total NPV of $46,904 is less than the NPV of $51,007 that we calculated without the one-half rule. The effect of the one-half rule is to decrease the project's NPV, because some of the tax shield is deferred during the first year.

2. If we use the formula approach, the CCA tax shield formula must be adjusted to include the one-half rule. The formula including the one-half rule is given below:

Present value of CCA tax shield $= [(R \times C \times T)/(R + i)] \times [(1 + 0.5 \times i)/(1 + i)]$

where
$R$ = the CCA rate
$C$ = the original capital cost of the project
$T$ = the tax rate
$i$ = required rate of return

EXHIBIT  11-8

NPV Effect of CCA One-Half Rule

| CCA Calculation | Year 1 | Year 2 | Year 3 |
|---|---|---|---|
| Capital cost, beginning of year | $300,000 | $255,000 | $178,500 |
| Less CCA, 30% × capital cost, beginning of year | 45,000 | 76,500 | 53,550 |
| Capital cost, end of year | $255,000 | $178,500 | $124,950 |

| Tax Payable Calculation | Year 1 | Year 2 | Year 3 |
|---|---|---|---|
| Operating cash flow | $175,000 | $175,000 | $175,000 |
| Less CCA | 45,000 | 76,500 | 53,500 |
| Taxable income | $130,000 | $ 98,500 | $121,450 |
| Tax payable (40%) | $ 52,000 | $ 39,400 | $ 48,580 |

| Cash-Flow Calculation | Year 1 | Year 2 | Year 3 |
|---|---|---|---|
| Cash flow | $175,000 | $175,000 | $175,000 |
| Less tax payable | 52,000 | 39,400 | 48,580 |
| After-tax cash flow | $123,000 | $135,600 | $126,420 |

### NET PRESENT VALUE CALCULATION

| Year | Cash Flow | Discount Factor | Present Value |
|---|---|---|---|
| 0 | $(300,000) | 1.000 | $(300,000) |
| 1 | 123,000 | 0.909 | 111,807 |
| 2 | 135,600 | 0.826 | 112,006 |
| 3 | 126,420 | 0.751 | 94,941 |
| Net Present Value | | | $  18,754 |

### PRESENT VALUE OF CCA TAX SHIELD AFTER DISPOSAL OF ASSET*

| Year | CCA | Tax Shield | Discount Factor | Present Value |
|---|---|---|---|---|
| 4 | $37,485 | $14,994 | 0.683 | $10,241 |
| 5 | 26,240 | 10,496 | 0.621 | 6,517 |
| 6 | 18,368 | 7,347 | 0.564 | 4,144 |
| ... | ... | ... | ... | ... |
| 18 | 254 | 102 | 0.180 | 18 |
| 19 | 178 | 71 | 0.164 | 12 |
| 20 | 125 | 50 | 0.149 | 7 |
| etc. | ... | ... | ... | ... |
| Present Value | | | | $28,150 |

### Summary of NPV

| | |
|---|---|
| NPV (Years 0 – 3) | $18,754 |
| NPV (Years 4 – ∞) | 28,150 |
| Total NPV | $46,904 |

*Assuming other assets remain in the class and zero salvage value

The formula includes a second term that accounts for the fact that only half of the acquisition cost is taken into the pool in the first year. The calculation of the present value of the CCA tax shield using this formula is shown below:

$$PV = [(30\% \times \$300,000 \times 40\%)/(30\% + 10\%)] \times [(1 + 0.5 \times 10\%)/(1 + 10\%)]$$
$$= \$85,909$$

The net present value of the after-tax cash flows (excluding the CCA tax shield effect) was $(38,865) (see Exhibit 11–7). Adding the present value of the tax shield gives a total NPV for the project of $47,044 (the small difference between the approaches is due to rounding).

### Nonzero Salvage Value

In our examples so far, we have assumed that salvage value is zero. Zero salvage value is also implicit in the CCA tax shield formulas. A nonzero salvage value generates a cash flow at the time of disposal and will have to be included in the NPV analysis. A nonzero salvage value also has three potential tax effects:

1. When a capital asset is sold, the balance in the capital cost pool is reduced by the lesser of the salvage value or the original capital cost. The effect is to reduce the amount of the CCA tax shield, because the remaining CCA pool is reduced.
2. Deducting the salvage value may cause the pool's balance to be negative, triggering a recapture of CCA and an immediate tax payable.
3. If the salvage value is greater than the original capital cost, a capital gain results, generating an additional tax payable.

We can include the tax effects of (2) and (3) by adjusting the cash flows in the year in which the asset is retired. If we use the direct approach, the reduction in tax shield from (1) is automatically accomplished when the CCA pool is reduced. If we use the formula approach, the following adjustment must be subtracted from the present value of the CCA tax shield (calculated with our original assumption of a zero salvage value):

CCA Adjustment for Salvage Value $= [(R \times S \times T)/(R + i)] \times [1/(1 + i)_n]$

where

$R$ = the CCA rate
$S$ = the salvage value of the project
$T$ = the tax rate
$i$ = required rate of return
$n$ = the period of sale on retirement

This adjustment is the tax shield related to the salvage value (the first term) discounted from the time of sale to the present (the second term). For our example, assume that on January 1 of Year 4, Spear Corporation will sell the machine for a salvage value of $40,000. Assume also that there are other assets in the class and that the one-half rule is applied. Because the salvage value is less than the remaining capital cost, there is no capital gain or recapture of capital cost allowance. The salvage value creates a cash flow of $40,000 at the beginning of Year 4. The adjustment to the CCA tax shield for salvage value is shown as follows:

$$[(30\% \times \$40,000 \times 40\%)/(30\% + 10\%)] \times [1/(1 + 10\%)^3] = \$9,016$$

The project's NPV is calculated from the NPV of net cash flows (excluding the CCA tax shield), the present value of the salvage value, and the present value of the CCA tax shield with an adjustment for the salvage value. A summary of the NPV calculation follows:

| | |
|---|---:|
| NPV of net cash flows (from Exhibit 11–7) | $(38,865) |
| PV of salvage value ($40,000 × 0.751) | 30,040 |
| PV of CCA tax shield (unadjusted) | 85,909 |
| PV of salvage value adjustment to CCA tax shield | (9,016) |
| Total NPV | $ 68,068 |

Income tax rules have a profound effect on capital investment decisions, and it is important to correctly incorporate tax effects into the analysis. In this section we have illustrated the common effects due to CCA, but as tax rules with respect to capital property change, it will be necessary to alter the analysis and consult with tax professionals to ensure that future cash-flow implications are accounted for correctly.

## Capital Investment: The Advanced Manufacturing Environment

**Objective 8**

Describe capital investment in an advanced manufacturing environment.

In an advanced manufacturing environment, long-term investments are generally concerned with the automation of manufacturing. Before any commitment to automation is made, however, a company should first make the most efficient use of existing technology. Many benefits can be realized by redesigning and simplifying the current manufacturing process. An example often given to support this thesis is automation of material handling. Automation of this operation can cost millions—and it is usually unnecessary, because greater efficiency can be achieved by eliminating inventories and simplifying material transfers through the implementation of a JIT system.

Once the benefits from redesign and simplification are achieved, however, it becomes apparent where automation can generate additional benefits. Many companies can improve their competitive positions by adding such features as robotics, flexible manufacturing systems, and completely integrated manufacturing systems. The ultimate commitment to automation is the construction of greenfield factories. Greenfield factories are new factories designed and built from scratch; they represent a strategic decision by a company to completely change the way it manufactures.

Although discounted cash-flow analysis (using net present value and internal rate of return) remains preeminent in capital investment decisions, the new manufacturing environment demands that more attention be paid to the inputs used in discounted cash-flow models. How investment is defined, how operating cash flows are estimated, how salvage value is treated, and how the discount rate is chosen all must be carefully specified.

There is also another important dimension. Contemporary investment management involves both *financial* and *nonfinancial* criteria. It is critical that a company's investment management process be linked with its strategies. Analyses involving advanced manufacturing technology should consider the contributions made by such technologies toward supporting such strategies as product enhancement, diversification, and risk reduction. For example, advanced technology may contribute to product enhancement by allowing a company more flexibility in responding to fluctuating demand. Improving quality is also a product enhancement feature. Some product enhancement features are readily quantified. It may be possible to estimate the cost savings attributable to improved quality. Other factors may be more difficult to quantify. Assessing the cost savings or increased revenues from increased flexibility may be quite difficult. Yet the increased flexibility may be as critical for the company as the improved quality. Thus, consideration of nonfinancial factors is important. Of course, every possible effort should be made to quantify all factors affecting the investment decision.

### How Investment Differs

Investment in automated manufacturing processes is much more complex than investment in the standard manufacturing equipment of the past. For standard equipment, the direct costs of acquisition represent virtually the entire investment. For automated manufacturing, the direct costs can represent as little as 50 or 60 percent of the total investment; software, engineering, training, and implementation are a significant percentage of the total costs. Thus, great care must be exercised to assess the actual cost of an automated system. It is easy to overlook the peripheral costs, which can be substantial.

# How Estimates of Operating Cash Flows Differ

Estimates of operating cash flows from investments in standard equipment have typically relied on directly identifiable benefits, such as direct savings from labour, power, and scrap. Indirect benefits and savings were ignored because they were viewed as immaterial.

In the new manufacturing environment, however, the indirect benefits can be material and critical to the project's viability. Greater quality, more reliability, reduced lead time, improved customer satisfaction, and an enhanced ability to maintain market share are all important benefits of an advanced manufacturing system. Reduction of labour in support areas, such as production scheduling and stores, is another indirect benefit. More effort is needed to measure these indirect benefits in order to assess the potential value of investments more accurately.

We can illustrate the importance of considering indirect benefits with an example. Suppose that a company is evaluating a potential investment in a flexible manufacturing system (FMS). The company can continue producing with its conventional equipment, which is expected to last 10 years, or switch to the new system, which is also expected to have a useful life of 10 years. The company's discount rate is 12 percent. The data pertaining to the investment are presented in Exhibit 11–9.

Using these data, we can compute the net present value of the proposed system as follows:

| | |
|---|---|
| PV ($4,000,000 × 5.650[a]) | $22,600,000 |
| Less investment | 18,000,000 |
| NPV | $ 4,600,000 |

[a] Discount factor for an interest rate of 12 percent and a life of 10 years

The NPV is positive and large in magnitude, and it clearly signals the acceptability of the FMS. This outcome, however, is strongly dependent on explicit

**EXHIBIT 11-9**

Investment Data: Direct and Indirect Benefits

| | FMS | Status Quo |
|---|---|---|
| Investment (current outlay): | | |
| Direct costs | $10,000,000 | — |
| Software, engineering | 8,000,000 | — |
| Total current outlay | $18,000,000 | $ 0 |
| Net after-tax cash flow | $ 5,000,000 | $1,000,000 |
| Less: After-tax cash flow for status quo | 1,000,000 | n/a |
| Incremental benefit | $ 4,000,000 | n/a |

| Incremental Benefit Explained | | |
|---|---|---|
| Direct benefits: | | |
| Direct labour | $1,500,000 | |
| Scrap reduction | 500,000 | |
| Setups | 200,000 | $2,200,000 |
| Indirect benefits: | | |
| Quality savings: | | |
| Rework | $ 200,000 | |
| Warranties | 400,000 | |
| Maintenance of competitive position | 1,000,000 | |
| Production scheduling | 110,000 | |
| Payroll | 90,000 | 1,800,000 |
| Total | | $4,000,000 |

recognition of indirect benefits. If those benefits are eliminated, then the direct savings total $2.2 million, and the NPV is negative:

| | |
|---|---|
| PV ($2,200,000 × 5.650) | $12,430,000 |
| Less investment | 18,000,000 |
| NPV | $(5,570,000) |

The increase in use of activity-based costing has made identifying indirect benefits easier with the use of cost drivers. Once they are identified, they can be included in the analysis if they are material.

Exhibit 11–9 reveals the importance of measuring all indirect benefits. One of the most important indirect benefits is maintaining or improving a company's competitive position. A key question that needs to be asked is what will happen to the company's cash flows if the investment is not made? That is, if the company chooses to forgo an investment in technologically advanced equipment, will it be able to continue to compete with other companies on the basis of quality, delivery, and cost? This question becomes especially relevant if competitors choose to invest in advanced equipment. If a company's competitive position deteriorates, its current cash flows will decrease.

If cash flows decrease if the investment is not made, this decrease should show up as an incremental benefit for the advanced technology. In Exhibit 11–9, the company estimates this competitive benefit as $1,000,000. Estimating this benefit requires some serious strategic planning and analysis, but its effect can be critical. If this benefit had been ignored or overlooked, then the NPV would have been negative, and the investment alternative rejected. This calculation is shown below:

| | |
|---|---|
| PV ($3,000,000 × 5.650) | $16,950,000 |
| Less investment | 18,000,000 |
| NPV | $(1,050,000) |

## Salvage Value

Earlier in this chapter, we saw that salvage value can have a number of tax implications for a company. But terminal or salvage value is often ignored in investment decisions. The usual reason offered is the difficulty of estimating this value. Because of this uncertainty, the effect of salvage value is often ignored or heavily discounted. This approach may be unwise, however, because salvage value could make the difference between investing or not investing. Given a highly competitive environment, companies cannot afford to make incorrect decisions.

A much better approach to dealing with uncertainty is to use sensitivity analysis. Sensitivity analysis (often referred to as **what-if analysis**) changes the assumptions on which the capital investment analysis relies and assesses their effect on the cash-flow pattern. This approach can be used to address such questions as what the effect would be if cash reserves were 5 percent less? 5 percent more? Although sensitivity analysis is time consuming if done manually, it can be done rapidly and easily using many common computer programs.

To illustrate the potential effect of salvage value, assume that the after-tax annual operating cash flow of the project shown in Exhibit 11–9 is $3.1 million instead of $4 million. The NPV without salvage value is as follows:

| | |
|---|---|
| PV ($3,100,000 × 5.650) | $17,515,000 |
| Less investment | 18,000,000 |
| NPV | $ (485,000) |

Without the salvage value, the project would be rejected. The NPV with a salvage value of $2 million, however, is a positive result, meaning that the investment should be made.

**what-if analysis**

A method to deal with uncertainty where the assumptions on which the analysis is based are changed and their effect assessed (see sensitivity analysis).

| | |
|---|---|
| PV ($3,100,000 × 5.650) | $17,515,000 |
| PV of salvage value ($2,000,000 × 0.322) | 644,000 |
| Total PV | $18,159,000 |
| Less investment | 18,000,000 |
| NPV | $ 59,000 |

But what if the salvage value is less than expected? Suppose that the worst possible salvage value is $1,600,000. What is the effect of this information on the decision? The NPV can be recalculated under this new (what-if) scenario:

| | |
|---|---|
| PV ($3,100,000 × 5.650) | $17,515,000 |
| PV of salvage value ($1,600,000 × 0.322) | 515,200 |
| Total PV | $18,030,200 |
| Less investment | 18,000,000 |
| NPV | $ 30,200 |

Thus, under a pessimistic scenario the NPV is still positive. This example illustrates how sensitivity analysis can be used to deal with the uncertainty surrounding salvage value. It can also be used for other uncertain cash-flow variables.

## Discount Rates

Being overly conservative with discount rates can prove even more damaging. In theory, if future cash flows are known with certainty, the correct discount rate is a company's cost of capital. In practice, future cash flows are uncertain, and managers often choose a discount rate higher than the cost of capital to deal with that uncertainty. If the rate chosen is excessively high, it will bias the selection process toward short-term investments.

To illustrate the effect of an excessive discount rate, consider the project in Exhibit 11–9 once again. Assume that the correct discount rate is 12 percent but that the company uses 18 percent. The NPV using an 18 percent discount rate is calculated as follows:

| | |
|---|---|
| PV ($4,000,000 × 4.494[a]) | $17,976,000 |
| Less investment | 18,000,000 |
| NPV | $ (24,000) |

[a] Discount rate for 18 percent and 10 years

The project would be rejected. With a higher discount rate, the discount factor decreases in magnitude more rapidly than does the discount factor for a lower rate (compare the discount factor for 12 percent, 5.650, with the factor for 18 percent, 4.494). The effect of a higher discount factor is to place more weight on earlier cash flows and less weight on later cash flows, thereby favouring short-term over long-term investments. This outcome makes it more difficult for automated manufacturing systems to appear as viable projects, since the cash returns required to justify the investment are received over a longer period of time.

## Appendix: Time Value of Money Concepts

An important feature of money is that it can be invested and can earn interest. A dollar today is not the same as a dollar tomorrow. This fundamental principle is the backbone of discounting models. Discounting models rely on the relationships between current and future dollars. Thus, to use discounting models, we must understand these relationships.

## Future Value

Suppose that a bank advertises a 4 percent annual interest rate. If a customer invests $100 at this rate, then after one year she will receive the original $100 plus $4 interest, or $104. This result can be expressed by the following equation, where $F$ is the future amount, $P$ is the initial or current outlay, and $i$ is the interest rate:

$$F = P(1 + i)$$

For our example, $F = \$100(1 + 0.04) = \$100(1.04) = \$104$.

Now suppose that the same bank offers a 5 percent rate if the customer leaves the original deposit, plus any interest, on deposit for two years. How much will the customer receive at the end of the two years?

Again, assume that she invests $100. Using the future value equation, she will earn $105 at the end of Year 1 [$F = \$100(1 + 0.05) = \$105$]. If she leaves this amount in the account for a second year, we can use the equation again, with $P$ now equal to $105. At the end of the second year, then, the total is $110.25 [$F = \$105(1 + 0.05) = \$110.25$]. In the second year, she earns interest on both the original deposit and the interest earned in the first year. The earning of interest on interest is referred to as **compounding interest**. The value that accumulates by the end of an investment's life, assuming a specified compound return, is the **future value**. The future value of the $100 deposit in our second example is $110.25.

We have a more direct way to compute the future value. The first application of the future value equation can be expressed as $F = \$105 = \$100(1.05)$, the second application can be expressed as $F = \$105(1.05) = \$100(1.05)(1.05) = \$100(1.05)^2 = P(1 + i)^2$. This suggests the following formula for computing amounts for $n$ periods into the future:

$$F = P(1 + i)^n$$

## Present Value

Often a manager needs to compute not the future value but the amount that must be invested *now* in order to earn some given future value. The amount that must be invested now to produce the future value is known as the **present value** of the future amount. For example, how much must be invested now in order to earn $363 two years from now, assuming that the interest rate is 10 percent? Or, put another way, what is the present value of $363 to be received two years from now?

In this example, the future value, the years, and the interest rate are all known; the problem is to find the current outlay that will produce that future amount. Let $P$ be the variable representing the current outlay (the present value of $F$). Thus, to compute the present value of a future outlay, we need only solve the future value equation for $P$:

$$P = F/(1 + i)^n$$

Using this equation, we can compute the present value of $363 as follows:

$$P = \$363/(1 + 0.1)^2$$
$$= \$363/1.21$$
$$= \$300$$

The present value, $300, is what the future amount of $363 is worth today. All other things being equal, having $300 today is the same as having $363 two years from now. Put another way, if a company requires a 10 percent rate of return, $300 is the most the company will be willing to pay today for any investment that yields $363 two years from now.

**compounding interest**
Paying interest on interest.

**future value**
The value that will accumulate by the end of an investment's life if the investment earns a specified compounded return.

**present value (PV)**
The current value of a future cash flow. It represents the amount that must be invested now if the future cash flow is to be received, assuming compounding at a given rate of interest.

The process of computing the present value of future cash flows is referred to as discounting; thus, we say we have discounted the future value of $363 to its present value of $300. The interest rate used to discount the future cash flow is the discount rate. The expression

$$1/(1 + i)^n$$

is the discount factor. Calling the discount factor *df*, the present value formula can be expressed as:

$$P = F(df)$$

For example, the discount factor for $i = 10$ percent and $n = 2$ is 0.826.[18] With the discount factor, the present value of $363 is computed as follows:

$$P = F(df)$$
$$= \$363 \times 0.826$$
$$= \$300 \text{ (rounded)}$$

### Present Value of an Uneven Series of Cash Flows

**annuity**

A series of future cash flows.

We can use the discount factors to compute the present value of any future cash flow or series of future cash flows. A series of future cash flows is called an **annuity**. We can find the present value of an annuity by computing the present value of each future cash flow and then summing these values. For example, suppose that an investment is expected to produce the following annual cash flows: $110, $121, and $133.10. Assuming a discount rate of 10 percent, we can compute the present value of this series of cash receipts as in Exhibit 11-10.

EXHIBIT 11-10

Present Value of an Uneven Series of Cash Flows

| Year | Cash Receipt | Discount Factor | Present Value |
|------|-------------|-----------------|---------------|
| 1 | $110.00 | 0.909 | $100.00 |
| 2 | 121.00 | 0.826 | 100.00 |
| 3 | 133.10 | 0.751 | 100.00 |
| | | | $300.00 |

### Present Value of a Uniform Series of Cash Flows

If the series of cash flows is even, the computation of the annuity's present value is simplified. Assume, for example, that an investment is expected to return $100 per year for three years. Assuming a discount rate of 10 percent, we can compute the annuity's present value as in Exhibit 11–11.

As with the uneven series of cash flows, the present value in Exhibit 11–10 was computed by calculating the present value of each cash flow separately and then summing them. However, in the case of an annuity that displays uniform cash flows, the computations can be reduced from three to one, as the sum of the individual discount factors (2.486) can be thought of as a discount factor for an annuity of uniform cash flows.

EXHIBIT 11-11

Present Value of Uniform Series of Cash Flows

| Year | Cash Receipt | Discount Factor | Present Value |
|------|-------------|-----------------|---------------|
| 1 | $100 | 0.909 | $ 90.90 |
| 2 | 100 | 0.826 | 82.60 |
| 3 | 100 | 0.751 | 75.10 |
| | | 2.486 | $248.60 |

18. The discount factor is $df = 1/(1 + i)^n = 1/(1 + 0.1)^2 = 0.826$. We can easily calculate discount factors with a financial calculator or with formulas in many computer programs.

## Summary of Learning Objectives

**1. Explain what a capital investment decision is, and distinguish between independent and mutually exclusive capital investment projects.**

Capital investment decisions are concerned with the acquisition of long-term assets and usually involve a significant outlay of funds. There are two types of capital investment projects: independent and mutually exclusive. Independent projects are projects whose acceptance or rejection does not affect the cash flows of other projects. Mutually exclusive projects are projects that, if accepted, preclude the acceptance of all other competing projects.

**2. Compute the payback period and accounting rate of return for a proposed investment, and explain their roles in capital investment decisions.**

Managers make capital investment decisions by using formal models to decide whether to accept or reject proposed projects. These decision models are classified as nondiscounting and discounting, depending on whether they address the question of the time value of money. There are two nondiscounting models: the payback period and the accounting rate of return.

The payback period is the time required for a company to recover its initial investment. For even cash flows, it is calculated by dividing the investment by the annual cash flow. For uneven cash flows, the cash flows are summed until the investment is recovered. If only a fraction of a year is needed, then it is assumed that the cash flows occur evenly within each year. The payback period ignores the time value of money and the profitability of projects, because it does not consider the cash inflows available beyond the payback period. However, it does supply some useful information. The payback period is useful in assessing and controlling risk, minimizing an investment's impact on a company's liquidity, and controlling the risk of obsolescence.

The accounting rate of return is computed by dividing the average income expected from an investment by either the original investment or the average investment. Unlike the payback period, it does consider the profitability of a project; however, it too ignores the time value of money. Managers may find the accounting rate of return useful for screening new investments to ensure that certain financial accounting ratios (specifically, any accounting ratios that may be monitored to ensure compliance with debt contracts) are not adversely affected.

**3. Use net present value (NPV) analysis for capital investment decisions involving independent projects.**

NPV is the difference between the present value of future cash flows and the initial investment outlay. To use this model, a required rate of return (usually the cost of capital) must be identified. The NPV method uses the required rate of return to compute the present value of a project's cash inflows and outflows. If the present value of the inflows is greater than the present value of the outflows, the net present value is greater than zero, and the project is profitable; if the NPV is less than zero, the project is not profitable and should be rejected.

**4. Use the internal rate of return (IRR) to assess the acceptability of independent projects.**

The IRR is computed by finding the interest rate that equates the present value of a project's cash inflows with the present value of its cash outflows. If the IRR is greater than the required rate of return (cost of capital), the project is acceptable; if the IRR is less than the required rate of return, the project should be rejected.

**5. Explain why NPV is better than IRR for capital investment decisions involving mutually exclusive projects.**

In evaluating mutually exclusive or competing projects, managers have a choice of using NPV or IRR. When managers must choose among competing projects, the NPV model correctly identifies the best investment alternative. Using IRR, on the other hand, may at times lead to choosing an inferior project. Thus, since NPV always provides the correct signal, it should be used.

**6. Explain the role and value of postaudits.**

A postaudit of a capital project is an important step in the capital investment decision process. Postaudits evaluate a project's actual performance in relation to its expected performance. A postaudit may lead to corrective action to improve the project's performance, or the project may even be abandoned. Postaudits also serve as an incentive for managers to make capital investment decisions prudently.

### 7. Convert gross cash flows to after-tax cash flows.

Accurate and reliable cash-flow forecasts are absolutely critical for capital investment decisions. Managers should assume responsibility for the accuracy of cash-flow projections. All cash flows in a capital investment analysis should be after-tax cash flows. There are two different but equivalent ways to compute after-tax cash flows: the income method and the decomposition method.

Although amortization is not a cash flow, it does have cash-flow implications, because tax laws allow capital cost allowances (CCAs) to be deducted in computing taxable income, and this has the effect of shielding revenue from taxation. There are two ways to calculate the tax shield effect of CCA: the direct method and the formula method. To reflect income tax more accurately, the one-half rule and nonzero salvage value must also be considered when calculating the effect of CCA on a project's net present value.

### 8. Describe capital investment in an advanced manufacturing environment.

Capital investment in an advanced manufacturing environment is affected by the way in which inputs are determined. Much greater attention must be paid to the investment outlays, because peripheral items can require substantial resources. Furthermore, in assessing benefits, indirect items such as quality and maintaining competitive position can be deciding factors. Choice of the required rate of return is also critical. The tendency of companies to use required rates of return that are much greater than the cost of capital should be avoided. Also, since the salvage value of an automated system can be considerable, that value should be estimated and included in the analysis.

---

## Key Terms

Accounting rate of return 470
Annuity 495
Capital budgeting 466
Capital cost allowances (CCA) 482
Capital investment decisions 466
Compounding interest 494
Discount rate 471

Discounting models 471
Future value 494
Independent projects 466
Internal rate of return (IRR) 473
Mutually exclusive projects 466
Net present value (NPV) 471
Nondiscounting models 468

One-half rule 487
Payback period 468
Postaudit 477
Present value (PV) 494
What-if analysis 492

---

## Review Problems

### I. BASICS OF CAPITAL INVESTMENT DECISIONS (IGNORE TAXES FOR THIS PROBLEM.)

Sebastian Ebro is investigating the possibility of acquiring an ice-cream franchise. To acquire the franchise requires an initial outlay of $300,000 (the purchase includes building and equipment). To raise the capital, Sebastian will sell stock valued at $200,000 (the stock pays dividends of $24,000 per year) and borrow $100,000. The loan for $100,000 would carry an interest rate of 6 percent. Sebastian figures that his cost of capital is 10 percent [(2/3 × 0.12) + (1/3 × 0.06)]. This weighted cost of capital is the discount rate that he will use for capital investment decisions.

The franchise will produce an annual cash inflow of $50,000. Sebastian expects to operate the business for 20 years, after which he will turn it over to one of his children.

**Required:**

1. Compute the payback period.
2. Assuming that amortization is $14,000 per year, compute the accounting rate of return (on total investment).
3. Compute the NPV of the franchise.
4. Compute the IRR of the franchise.
5. Should Sebastian acquire the franchise?

## Solution

1. The payback period is $300,000/$50,000, or six years.
2. The accounting rate of return is ($50,000 – $14,000)/$300,000, or 12 percent.
3. The discount factor for an annuity with $i$ at 10 percent and $n$ at 20 years is 8.514 (this can be calculated with a financial calculator). Thus, the NPV is (8.514 × $50,000) – $300,000, or $125,700.
4. The discount factor associated with the IRR is 6.00 ($300,000/$50,000). With a financial calculator, the IRR is 15.8 percent.
5. Since the NPV is positive and the IRR is greater than Sebastian's cost of capital, the franchise is a sound investment. This conclusion, of course, assumes that the cash-flow projections are accurate.

## II. CAPITAL INVESTMENT WITH COMPETING PROJECTS (CCA TAX SHIELD)

Blalock Manufacturing has decided to acquire a new parcel van to transport packages from its warehouse to the airport. The choice has been narrowed to two models. The following information has been gathered for each model:

|  | Model A | Model T |
|---|---|---|
| Acquisition cost | $20,000 | $25,000 |
| Annual operating costs | $3,500 | $2,000 |
| Capital cost allowance rate | 30% | 30% |
| Expected salvage value | $4,000 | $5,000 |

Blalock's cost of capital is 14 percent. The company plans to use the van for five years and then sell it for its salvage value. Assume that the tax rate is 40 percent and that Blalock has other assets in the same capital cost class.

**Required:**

1. Compute the after-tax operating cash flows for each model.
2. Compute the NPV for each model, and make a recommendation.

## Solution

1. First, we will calculate the capital cost allowance and CCA tax shield for each model:

| | Model A | | | Model T | | |
|---|---|---|---|---|---|---|
| Year | Capital Cost beginning | CCA (a) | CCA Tax Shield (b) | Capital Cost beginning | CCA (a) | CCA Tax Shield (b) |
| 1(c) | $20,000 | $3,000 | $1,200 | $25,000 | $3,750 | $1,500 |
| 2 | 17,000 | 5,100 | 2,040 | 21,250 | 6,375 | 2,550 |
| 3 | 11,900 | 3,570 | 1,428 | 14,875 | 4,463 | 1,785 |
| 4 | 8,330 | 2,499 | 1,000 | 10,412 | 3,124 | 1,250 |
| 5 | 5,831 | 1,749 | 700 | 7,288 | 2,187 | 874 |

a Capital cost (beginning of year) × CCA rate
b CCA × tax rate
c CCA is calculated at 50% of the usual rate in the first year.

We can calculate after-tax operating cash flows as follows:

**Model A**

| Year | (1 – Tax rate) × Cash expenses | CCA Tax Shield | After-tax cash flows |
|------|-------------------------------|----------------|----------------------|
| 1 | $(2,100) | $1,200 | $ (900) |
| 2 | (2,100) | 2,040 | (60) |
| 3 | (2,100) | 1,428 | (672) |
| 4 | (2,100) | 1,000 | (1,100) |
| 5 | (2,100) | 700 | (1,400) |

[a] (1 – 0.4) × 3,500

**Model T**

| Year | (1 – Tax rate) × Cash expenses | CCA Tax Shield | After-tax cash flows |
|------|-------------------------------|----------------|----------------------|
| 1 | $(1,200) | $1,500 | $ 300 |
| 2 | (1,200) | 2,550 | 1,350 |
| 3 | (1,200) | 1,785 | 585 |
| 4 | (1,200) | 1,250 | 50 |
| 5 | (1,200) | 874 | (326) |

[a] (1 – 0.4) × 2,000

2. NPV computation:
Given the after-tax operating cash flows from Requirement 1, we can calculate the present value of each model directly from net cash flows.

| | | Model A | | Model T | |
|------|-----------------|-----------|------------------|-----------|------------------|
| Year | Discount Factor | Cash Flow | Present Value | Cash Flow | Present Value |
| 0 | 1.000 | $(20,000) | $(20,000) | $(25,000) | $(25,000) |
| 1 | 0.877 | (900) | (789) | 300 | 263 |
| 2 | 0.769 | (60) | (46) | 1,350 | 1,038 |
| 3 | 0.675 | (672) | (454) | 585 | 395 |
| 4 | 0.592 | (1,100) | (651) | 50 | 30 |
| 5 | 0.519 | (1,400) | (727) | (326) | (169) |
| Salvage Value[a] | 0.519 | 4,000 | 2,076 | 5,000 | 2,595 |
| Remaining CCA[b] | – | 82 | 11 | 102 | 13 |
| NPV | | | $(20,580) | | $(20,835) |

[a] Assume that salvage value is received at the beginning of Year 6.
[b] Because there are other assets in the cost pool, any remaining capital cost after the asset is sold will continue as a tax shield. The remaining capital cost for Model A is $20,000 – $15,918 – $4,000 = $82, and that for Model T is $25,000 – $19,898 – $5,000 = $102.

The present value is calculated by determining the CCA for years beyond Year 5 and then discounting. Model A should be chosen, since it has the highest (least negative) NPV, indicating that it is the least costly of the two parcel vans. Note also that the net present values are negative, so that this choice is the least costly investment.

We can also calculate the NPV for each model by analyzing the direct cash flows and tax shield effects separately (using the CCA tax shield formula).

First, the NPV for each model, without the CCA tax shield, is calculated as follows:

|       |                    | **Model A** | | **Model T** | |
|-------|--------------------|------------|------------------|------------|------------------|
| Year  | Discount Factor    | Cash Flow  | Present Value    | Cash Flow  | Present Value    |
| 0     | 1.000              | $(20,000)  | $(20,000)        | $(25,000)  | $(25,000)        |
| 1     | 0.877              | (2,100)    | (1,842)          | (1,200)    | (1,052)          |
| 2     | 0.769              | (2,100)    | (1,615)          | (1,200)    | (923)            |
| 3     | 0.675              | (2,100)    | (1,418)          | (1,200)    | (810)            |
| 4     | 0.592              | (2,100)    | (1,243)          | (1,200)    | (710)            |
| 5     | 0.519              | (2,100)    | (1,090)          | (1,200)    | (623)            |
| Salvage Value | 0.519      | 4,000      | 2,076            | 5,000      | 2,595            |
| NPV   |                    |            | $(25,132)        |            | $(26,523)        |

We can calculate the present value of the CCA tax shield by using a formula that includes the adjustment for salvage value and the one-half rule.

Present value of CCA tax shield – Present value of salvage value adjustment:

$$[(R \times C \times T)/(R + i)] \times [(1 + 0.5i)/(1 + i)] - [(R \times S \times T)/(R + i)] \times [1/(1 + i)^n]$$

where

$R$ = the CCA rate
$C$ = the original capital cost
$T$ = the tax rate
$i$ = the discount rate
$n$ = the period of sale
$S$ = the salvage value

For Model A, the CCA tax shield has a present value of $4,553, calculated as follows:

| | |
|---|---|
| $[0.3 \times \$20,000 \times 0.4]/[0.3 + 0.14] \times [(1 + 0.5 \times 0.14)/(1 + 0.14)]$ | $5,120 |
| less $[0.3 \times \$4,000 \times 0.4]/[0.3 + 0.14] \times [1/(1 + 0.14)^5]$ | 567 |
| Present value of CCA tax shield | $4,553 |

For Model T, the CCA tax shield has a present value of $5,692, calculated as follows:

| | |
|---|---|
| $[0.3 \times \$25,000 \times 0.4]/[0.3 + 0.14] \times [(1 + 0.5 \times 0.14)/(1 + 0.14)]$ = | $6,400 |
| less $[0.3 \times \$5,000 \times 0.4]/[0.3 + 0.14] \times [1/(1 + 0.14)^5]$ = | 708 |
| Present value of CCA tax shield | $5,692 |

To summarize, the NPV of each model is as follows:

| | **Model A** | **Model T** |
|---|---|---|
| NPV without CCA tax shield | $(25,132) | $(26,523) |
| PV of CCA tax shield | 4,553 | 5,692 |
| NPV [a] | $(20,579) | $(20,831) |

[a] The differences between these answers and those for the previous analysis are due to rounding

1. Explain the difference between independent projects and mutually exclusive projects.

2. Explain why the timing and quantity of cash flows are important in capital investment decisions.

3. The time value of money is ignored by both the payback period and the accounting rate of return. Explain why this is a major deficiency in these two models.

4. What is the payback period? Compute the payback period for an investment requiring an initial outlay of $80,000 with expected annual cash inflows of $30,000.

5. Name and discuss three possible reasons why the payback period is used to help make capital investment decisions.

6. What is the accounting rate of return? Compute the accounting rate of return on original investment for an investment that requires an initial outlay of $300,000 and promises an average net income of $100,000.

7. What is meant by the term *future value*?

8. What are discounted cash flows? What is the discount rate? the discount factor?

9. What is meant by the term *present value*?

10. Compute the present value of an annuity that has uniform cash inflows if the discount rate is 8 percent and the annual cash inflow produced by the annuity is $32,000. The expected life of the annuity is four years.

11. The net present value is the same as the profit of a project expressed in present dollars. Do you agree? Explain.

12. What is the cost of capital? What role does it play in capital investment decisions?

13. What role does the required rate of return play for the NPV model? for the IRR model?

14. The IRR is the true or actual rate of return being earned by the project. Do you agree or disagree? Discuss.

15. Explain how the NPV is used to determine whether a project should be accepted or rejected.

16. Explain the relationship between NPV and a company's value.

17. Compute the IRR for a project that requires an investment of $299,100 and provides a return of $100,000 per year for four years.

18. What method would you choose to use to make a capital investment decision? Why?

19. Explain what a postaudit is and how it can provide useful input for future capital investment decisions, especially those involving advanced technology.

20. Explain why NPV is generally preferred over IRR when choosing among competing or mutually exclusive projects. Why would managers continue to use IRR to choose among mutually exclusive projects?

21. Suppose that a firm must choose between two mutually exclusive projects, both of which have negative NPVs. Explain how a company can legitimately choose between two such projects.

22. Why is it important to have accurate projections of cash flows for potential capital investments?

23. Describe why it is important for a manager to conduct a careful review of the assumptions and methods used in forecasting cash flows.

24. Why is it necessary to adjust future cash flows for inflation?

25. Explain what sensitivity analysis is. How can it help in capital investment decisions?

26. What are the main tax implications that should be considered in Year 0?

27. Assume that a project's annual after-tax net income is $40,000. Annual amortization for the project is $10,000. What is the project's annual after-tax operating cash inflow?

28. Assume that a project has annual cash expenses of $20,000 and annual amortization of $10,000. The tax rate is 34 percent. Using the decomposition method, compute the project's annual after-tax cash flow. (Assume that the project has no direct revenues and that straight-line amortization is used for tax purposes.)

29. Discuss the differences between amortization (for accounting purposes) and capital cost allowance (for tax purposes).

30. Why is a formula useful for calculating the present value of the CCA tax shield?

31. What is the one-half rule? What is the effect of this rule on the CCA tax shield?

32. What effect does salvage value have on the CCA tax shield?

33. Explain the important factors to consider for capital investment in the advanced manufacturing environment.

## Exercises

**11–1**

*Payback Period; Accounting Rate of Return*

LO2

A new laundromat facility costs $200,000 and has a life of five years with no salvage value. The facility will generate the following annual cash flows:

| Year | 1 | 2 | 3 | 4 | 5 |
|------|---|---|---|---|---|
| Cash flow | $ 60,000 | $80,000 | $100,000 | $120,000 | $140,000 |

**Required:**
1. Compute the payback period.
2. Compute the accounting rate of return using the original investment.

**11–2**

*NPV*

LO3

A new product is expected to produce annual revenues of $500,000. The product has a life cycle of five years. Equipment for producing the product will cost $550,000. After five years, this equipment can be sold for $80,000. Working capital will increase by $60,000, because inventories and receivables will increase. Annual cash operating expenses are estimated at $380,000. The required rate of return is 12 percent. Assume that there are no income taxes.

**Required:**
1. Compute the annual cash flows.
2. Calculate the NPV for the project.

**11–3**

*IRR; Uniform Cash Flows*

LO4

A proposed project requires an investment of $300,000 and will produce annual after-tax cash flows of $124,875. The project life is three years.

**Required:**
Compute the IRR.

**11–4**

*Mutually Exclusive Projects*

LO5

A company is considering two different product designs: Design A and Design B. The after-tax cash flows for each design follow:

|  | Design A | Design B |
|---|---|---|
| Annual revenues | $300,000 | $400,000 |
| Operating expenses | 210,000 | 295,000 |
| Investment | 269,190 | 314,055 |
| Product life | 5 years | 5 years |

The required rate of return is 12 percent.

**Required:**
1. Compute the NPV for each project.
2. Compute the IRR for each project.
3. Which design should be chosen? Explain.

**11–5**

After-Tax Cash Flows

LO7

A company has revenues of $900,000, cash expenses of $500,000, and annual amortization of $100,000. The tax rate is 40 percent. (Assume that straight line amortization is used for tax purposes.)

**Required:**
1. Compute the annual after-tax cash flow using an income statement approach.
2. Compute the annual after-tax cash flows for each item on the income statement.

**11–6**

Basic Concepts

LO1, LO2, LO3, LO4

Each of the following parts is independent (ignore taxes).
1. Leif Alton has just invested $200,000 as a part owner of a funeral home. He expects to receive an income of $60,000 per year from the investment. What is the payback period for Leif?
2. Cora Javier placed $40,000 in a three-year savings plan. The plan pays 6 percent, and she cannot withdraw the money early without a penalty. Assume that Cora leaves the money in the plan for the full three years. How much money will she have?
3. King Manufacturing is considering the purchase of a robotics material-handling system. The cash benefits will be $240,000 per year. The system costs $1,360,000 and will last 10 years. Compute the NPV assuming a discount rate of 12 percent. Should the company buy the robotics system?
4. Perry Rowe has just invested $100,000 in a company. He expects to receive $16,100 per year for the next eight years. His cost of capital is 6 percent. Compute the internal rate of return. Did Perry make a good decision?

**11–7**

Present Value
Computations

LO3

Complete the following cases, each independent of the others (ignore taxes).
1. Two independent projects have the following cash flows:

|            | Year 1    | Year 2    | Year 3   | Year 4   |
|------------|-----------|-----------|----------|----------|
| Project I  | $ 5,000   | $ 5,000   | $5,000   | $5,000   |
| Project II | 30,000    | 20,000    | 5,000    | 5,000    |

   Compute the present value of each project, assuming a discount rate of 16 percent.

2. Suppose a couple want to have $50,000 in a fund six years from now to provide support for their daughter's university education. How much must they invest now in order to have the desired amount if the investment can earn 8 percent? 12 percent? 16 percent?

3. Some new equipment promises to save $40,000 per year in operating expenses. The life of the machine is 10 years. Assume that the company's cost of capital is 12 percent. What is the most the company should pay for the new equipment?

4. A seller is asking $343,300 for some flexible manufacturing equipment, which is expected to last five years and to generate equal annual savings (because of reductions in labour costs, material waste, and so on). What is the minimum savings in operating expenses that must be earned each year to justify the acquisition? Assume that the buyer's cost of capital is 14 percent.

**11–8**

Kimmer Optical is considering an investment in equipment that will be used to grind lenses. The outlay required is $800,000. The equipment will last five years, with no salvage value. The expected cash flows associated with the project are given below:

| | Year 1 | Year 2 | Year 3 | Year 4 | Year 5 |
|---|---|---|---|---|---|
| Cash revenues | $1,300,000 | $1,300,000 | $1,300,000 | $1,300,000 | $1,300,000 |
| Cash expenses | 1,000,000 | 1,000,000 | 1,000,000 | 1,000,000 | 1,000,000 |

Assume that there are no taxes.

**Required:**
1. Compute the project's payback period.
2. Compute the project's accounting rate of return (a) on initial investment, and (b) on average investment.
3. Compute the project's net present value, assuming a required rate of return of 10 percent.
4. Compute the project's internal rate of return.

**11–9**

Note: The first two parts are related; each of the last three is independent of all other parts. Ignore taxes.

1. Kwon Wei is considering investing in one of the two following projects. Either project will require an investment of $10,000. The expected cash flows are given below.

| | Year 1 | Year 2 | Year 3 | Year 4 | Year 5 |
|---|---|---|---|---|---|
| Project A | $3,000 | $4,000 | $5,000 | $10,000 | $10,000 |
| Project B | 3,000 | 4,000 | 6,000 | 3,000 | 3,000 |

     What is the payback period for each project? If rapid payback is important, which project should be chosen? Which would you choose?

2. Calculate the accounting rate of return on original investment for each project in Requirement 1. Which project should be chosen based on the accounting rate of return?

3. Wilma Geisler is retiring and has two options: she can take her retirement pension as a lump sum of $225,000, or she can receive $24,000 per year for 20 years. Wilma's required rate of return is 8 percent. Assume that Wilma will live for another 20 years. Should she take the lump sum or the annuity?

4. Darryl Bowen is interested in investing in some tools and equipment so that he can do independent drywalling. The cost of the tools and equipment is $20,000. Darryl estimates that the return from owning his own equipment will be $6,000 per year. The tools and equipment will last six years. Assuming a required rate of return of 8 percent, calculate the NPV of the investment. Should Darryl invest?

5. Zara Folson, the owner of a small manufacturing company, is evaluating what appears to be an attractive opportunity. She has been offered the chance to acquire another small company's equipment that would allow her company to produce a part currently purchased externally. Zara estimates that the savings from internal production would be $25,000 per year. She estimates that the equipment would last 10 years. The owner is asking $130,400 for the equipment. Her company's cost of capital is 10 percent. Calculate the project's internal rate of return. Should Zara acquire the equipment?

**11–10**

The Delta Company is planning a project that is expected to last for six years. During that time, the project is expected to generate net cash flows of $85,000 per year. The project will require the purchase of a machine for $310,000. This new machine is expected to have a salvage value of $20,000 at the end of six years. (Amortization will be calculated on a straight-line basis.) In addition to its annual operating costs, the machine will require an overhaul costing $55,000 at the end of Year 4. The company currently has a minimum desired rate of return of 12 per-cent. Using this information, the company's accountant has prepared the follow-ing analysis:

| | | |
|---|---:|---:|
| Annual cash inflow | | $85,000 |
| Less: Annual amortization | $48,333 | |
| Annual average cost of overhaul | 9,167 | 57,500 |
| Average annual net income | | $27,500 |

Return on investment = 27,500/310,000 = 8.87%

Therefore, the accountant recommends that the project be rejected, because it does not meet the company's minimum desired rate of return. Assume that there are no taxes.

**Required:**
1. What criticism(s) would you make of the accountant's evaluation of the project?
2. Use present value analysis to determine whether or not the project should be accepted. (CMA Canada adapted)

**11–11**

Timtell Transport is considering investment in two independent loading and packaging equipment projects. Each project would require an investment of $200,000. In both cases, assume that the equipment would last five years with no salvage value. The cash inflows associated with each project are given below:

| | Year 1 | Year 2 | Year 3 | Year 4 | Year 5 |
|---|---|---|---|---|---|
| Project A | $120,000 | $60,000 | $ 80,000 | $ 40,000 | $ 20,000 |
| Project B | 20,000 | 20,000 | 120,000 | 160,000 | 180,000 |

Assume that there are no taxes.

**Required:**
1. Assuming a discount rate of 12 percent, compute the net present value of each project.
2. Compute the payback period for each project. Assume that Timtell's manager accepts only projects with a payback period of three years or less. Offer some reasons why this may be a rational strategy, even though the NPV computed in Requirement 1 may indicate otherwise.
3. Compute the accounting rate of return for each project using (a) initial investment and (b) average investment.

**11–12**

Drury Legal Services is considering an investment that requires an outlay of $200,000 and promises $231,000 of cash inflow one year from now. The company's cost of capital is 10 percent. Ignore taxes.

**Required:**
1. Break the $231,000 future cash inflow into three components: (a) the return of the original investment, (b) the cost of capital, and (c) the profit earned on the investment. Now compute the present value of the profit earned on the investment.

2. Compute the NPV of the investment. Compare this result with the present value of the profit computed in Requirement 1. What does this comparison tell you about the meaning of NPV?

**11–13**

NPV; Cost of Capital; Basic Concepts

LO3

Spreadsheet

Royal Electronics Company has an opportunity to invest in a new product line that will have a three-year life cycle. The investment requires a current $250,000 outlay. The capital will be raised by borrowing $150,000 and by issuing new stock for $100,000. The $150,000 loan will have interest payments of $7,500 at the end of each of the three years, with the principal being repaid at the end of Year 3. The stock issue carries with it an expectation of a 17.5 percent return, expressed in the form of dividends at the end of each year ($17,500 in dividends will be paid each of the next three years). The sources of capital for this investment represent the same proportion and costs that the company typically holds. Finally, the project will produce cash inflows of $125,000 per year for the next two years. Ignore taxes.

**Required:**

1. Compute the cost of capital for the project.
2. Compute the NPV for the project. Explain why it is not necessary to subtract the interest payments and the dividend payments from the annual inflow of $125,000 in carrying out this computation.

**11–14**

Solving for Unknowns

LO3, LO4

Solve each of the following independent cases (ignore taxes).

1. Romas Company is investing $120,000 in a project that will yield a uniform series of cash inflows over the next four years. If the internal rate of return is 14 percent, how much cash inflow per year can be expected?

2. Daw's Video Repair has decided to invest in some new electronic equipment. The equipment will have a three-year life and will produce a uniform series of cash savings. The net present value of the equipment is $1,750, using a discount rate of 8 percent. The internal rate of return is 12 percent. Determine the investment and the amount of cash savings realized each year.

3. A new lathe costing $60,096 will produce savings of $12,000 per year. How many years must the lathe last if an IRR of 18 percent is realized?

4. The NPV of a project is $3,927. The project has a life of four years and produces the following cash flows:

| Year 1 | Year 2 | Year 3 | Year 4 |
|--------|--------|--------|--------|
| $10,000 | $12,000 | $15,000 | $? |

The cost of the project is two times the cash flow produced in Year 4. The discount rate is 10 percent. Find the cost of the project and the cash flow for Year 4.

**11–15**

Flexible Manufacturing System; Payback; NPV

LO2, LO3, LO8

Isabel Anders, president of Torront Company, is considering the purchase of a flexible manufacturing system. The benefits/savings associated with the system are described below:

| | |
|---|---|
| Increased quality | $80,000 |
| Decrease in operating costs | 90,000 |
| Increase in on-time deliveries | 30,000 |

The system will cost $1,229,000 and will last 10 years. The company's cost of capital is 12 percent. Ignore taxes.

**Required:**

1. Calculate the payback period for the system. Assume that Torront has a policy of accepting only projects with a payback of five years or less. Should the system be acquired?
2. Calculate the project's NPV. Should the system be purchased—even if it does not meet the payback criterion?
3. The project manager has reviewed the projected cash flows. He points out that two items have been missed. First, the system would have a salvage value of $100,000 at the end of 10 years. Second, the increased quality and delivery performance would allow Torront to increase its market share by 20 percent. This would produce an additional annual benefit of $50,000. Recalculate the payback period and NPV given this new information. Does the decision change?

**11–16**

Implementation of an ABC System; Payback; NPV

LO2, LO3

Keith Yearwood was certain that the current cost accounting system was costing the company money. Over time, the system had become less useful. Products had been added, and overhead had become a much greater percentage of total manufacturing costs. Keith believed that overhead costs were not being accurately assigned to products, thereby causing distorted product costs. In harmony with these views, Keith had hired a consultant to review the company's accounting system. The consultant recommended the installation of an activity-based costing system. The justification was straightforward. The cost of errors from the current system was high. The consultant estimated the following annual cost of inaccurate cost information:

| | |
|---|---|
| Special studies | $ 50,000 |
| Lost bids | 150,000 |
| Suboptimal product mix | 60,000 |
| Poor marketing (mostly related to new products) | 140,000 |
| Total | $400,000 |

These costs, the consultant explained, could be avoided with the installation of a more accurate cost system. The consultant recommended an ABC system. The cost of implementing the system was estimated as follows:

| | |
|---|---|
| Acquisition of PCs and associated software | $ 425,000 |
| Mainframe upgrade and software development | 500,000 |
| System redesign | 375,000 |
| Training | 450,000 |
| Total investment | $1,750,000 |

The company's cost of capital is 14 percent. The ABC system is projected to have a life of 10 years. Ignore taxes.

**Required:**

1. Compute the payback period for the ABC system.
2. Compute the NPV of the ABC system. Should the system be implemented?

**11–17**

NPV versus IRR

LO5

Spreadsheet

A company is considering two different modifications to its current manufacturing process. The cash flows associated with the two investments are shown below:

| Year | Project I | Project II |
|---|---|---|
| 0 | $(100,000) | $(100,000) |
| 1 | — | 63,857 |
| 2 | 134,560 | 63,857 |

The company's cost of capital is 10 percent. Ignore taxes.

**Required:**
1. Compute the NPV and the IRR for each investment.
2. Show that the project with the larger NPV is the correct choice for the company.

**11–18**

After-Tax Cash Flows

LO7

Steiner Corporation is evaluating two independent projects. One involves recycling, and the other involves the acquisition of some maintenance equipment. The projects' expected annual operating revenues and expenses are given below.

| Project A (recycling project): | |
|---|---|
| Revenues | $180,000 |
| Less cash expenses | 90,000 |
| Less amortization | 30,000 |
| Income before taxes | $ 60,000 |
| Less taxes | 24,000 |
| Net income | $ 36,000 |

| Project B (maintenance equipment): | |
|---|---|
| Cash expenses | $ 60,000 |
| Amortization | 10,000 |

**Required:**
Compute the after-tax cash flows for each project. Assume that the tax rate is 40 percent and that amortization is deductible for tax purposes.

**11–19**

NPV; CCA Tax Shield

LO7

A trucking company is planning to buy special equipment for its maintenance operation. The cost of the equipment is $12,000, and the equipment will have a five-year life and a zero salvage value. The CCA rate is 20 percent, and there are other assets in the class. The tax rate is 38 percent; the cost of capital is 12 percent.

**Required:**
1. Calculate the present value of the CCA tax shield (including the one-half rule).
2. Calculate the present value of the CCA tax shield, assuming that the equipment has a $2,500 salvage value when sold at the beginning of Year 6.

**11–20**

Lease or Buy; NPV; CCA

LO5, LO7

Megan Emond, owner of a small company, has decided that she needs to have regular access to a car for local errands and occasional business trips. Megan is trying to decide between buying or leasing the car. The purchase cost is $30,000. The annual operating costs are estimated at $5,000. If the car is leased, a five-year lease will be acquired. The lease requires a refundable deposit of $1,000 and annual lease payments of $8,000. Operating costs, in addition to the lease payment, total $4,500 per year. The company's cost of capital is 10 percent, and its tax rate is 40 percent. If the car is purchased, it will be included with other assets in a class with a maximum CCA rate of 30 percent. Ignore the one-half rule.

**Required:**
Using NPV analysis, determine whether the car should be leased or purchased.

**11–21**

NPV; Inflation

LO7

Thistle Bus Company is planning to undertake a project that will have a two-year life. The project requires an initial outlay of $40,000; it will generate cash inflows of $22,000 and $24,000, respectively, in the two years. The company's cost of capital is 12 percent. During the coming two years, inflation is expected to average 5 percent per year. The cash flows have not been adjusted for inflation. The cost of capital, however, reflects an inflationary component. Ignore taxes.

**Required:**
1. Compute the NPV using the unadjusted cash flows.
2. Compute the NPV using cash flows adjusted for inflationary effects.

**11–22**

After-Tax Cash Flows;
CCA

LO7

As vice-president of Irwin Ltd., you must decide whether or not the following investment proposal should be accepted. Irwin has the opportunity to invest in a new auto-painting business that would require the purchase of a paint-sealing machine for $120,000. The machine is expected to last four years, with a salvage value of $10,000. Your staff has prepared the following budgeted income statement for each of the four years, based on expected contracts for 450 cars per year:

| Revenues: | | |
|---|---|---|
| Paint-sealing fees earned | | $90,000 |
| Operating expenses: | | |
| Machine operator's salary | $22,000 | |
| Variable machine supplies expense | 6,000 | |
| Building rental expenses | 3,300 | |
| Variable sealant expense | 7,000 | |
| Amortization expense | 27,500 | |
| Variable machine cleaning (after sealing) | 9,000 | |
| Total operating expenses | | 74,800 |
| Net operating income | | $15,200 |

Your analysis of the above shows the following:
- The machine has a capacity of 2,000 paint jobs per year.
- The machine will be included in a class with other assets. The maximum CCA rate is 20 percent.
- An inventory of supplies and parts costing $5,000 will have to be maintained.
- All cash flows occur at the end of the year.
- The company has an income tax rate of 45 percent.

**Required:**
Should Irwin purchase the machine assuming a minimum rate of return of 12 percent? Support your answer with calculations. (CMA Canada adapted)

**11–23**

After-Tax Cash Flows;
CCA

LO7

The Craddock Company is considering the purchase of a machine costing $780,000. This machine has an expected useful life of five years and an expected salvage value of $30,000. It will be amortized for accounting purposes using the straight-line method. A CCA rate of 25 percent will be used for tax purposes. Assume that there are other assets in the CCA class. The machine is expected to reduce variable costs of production by 20 percent; however, hiring a machine operator for $30,000 per year would be required. The machine will increase the company's production capacity to 50,000 units per year (from the present capacity of 30,000 units). The company's income statement for last year, when the company produced 30,000 units and sold 25,000 units, was as follows:

| | |
|---|---|
| Sales | $950,000 |
| Less: Cost of goods sold (20% of which are fixed) | 575,000 |
| Gross profit | $375,000 |
| Less: Operating expenses: | |
| Variable selling and administration | 250,000 |
| Fixed selling and administration | 100,000 |
| Net income | $ 25,000 |

The income tax rate is 38 percent.

**Required:**

Using the net present value method, determine whether or not the company should purchase the machine, assuming that sales demand is expected to be 50,000 units per year for the next five years and that the company's minimum desired rate of return is 10 percent. (CMA Canada adapted)

**11–24**

Discount Rates;
Advanced
Manufacturing
Environment

LO8

A company is considering two competing investments. The first is for a standard piece of production equipment; the second is for some computer-aided manufacturing (CAM) equipment. The investment and after-tax operating cash flows are shown below.

| Year | Standard Equipment | CAM |
|------|------|------|
| 0 | $(500,000) | $(2,000,000) |
| 1 | 300,000 | 100,000 |
| 2 | 200,000 | 200,000 |
| 3 | 100,000 | 300,000 |
| 4 | 100,000 | 400,000 |
| 5 | 100,000 | 400,000 |
| 6 | 100,000 | 400,000 |
| 7 | 100,000 | 500,000 |
| 8 | 100,000 | 1,000,000 |
| 9 | 100,000 | 1,000,000 |
| 10 | 100,000 | 1,000,000 |

The company uses a discount rate of 18 percent for all of its investments. The company's cost of capital is 10 percent.

**Required:**

1. Calculate the net present value for each investment using a discount rate of 18 percent.
2. Calculate the net present value for each investment using a discount rate of 10 percent.
3. Which rate should the company use to compute the net present value? Explain.

**11–25**

Quality; Market Share;
Advanced
Manufacturing
Environment

LO8

Refer to 11–24. Assume that the company's cost of capital is 14 percent.

**Required:**

1. Calculate the NPV of each alternative using the 14 percent rate.
2. Now assume that if the standard equipment is purchased, the company's competitive position will deteriorate because of lower quality (relative to competitors who have automated). Marketing estimates that the loss in market share will decrease the projected after-tax cash inflows by 50 percent for Years 3 through 10. Recalculate the NPV of the standard equipment given this outcome. What is the decision now? Discuss the importance of assessing the effect of indirect benefits.

**11–26**

Basic Concepts

LO1, LO2, LO3, LO4,
LO5, LO6, LO7, LO8

Choose the *best* answer for each of the following multiple-choice questions:

1. Mutually exclusive capital investment projects are those that
   a. if accepted or rejected do not affect the cash flows of other projects.
   b. if accepted do affect the cash flows of other projects.
   c. if accepted preclude the acceptance of all other competing projects.
   d. if rejected preclude the acceptance of all other competing projects.
   e. if accepted will produce a positive payback period.

2. The payback period suffers from which of the following deficiencies?
   a. It is only a rough measure of the uncertainty of future cash flows.
   b. It helps control the risk of obsolescence.
   c. It ignores the time value of money.
   d. It ignores the performance of a project beyond the payback period.
   e. Both c and d.

3. If the present value is positive, it signals that the
   a. initial investment has been recovered.
   b. required rate of return has been earned.
   c. value of the company has decreased.
   d. All of the above.
   e. Only a and b.

4. Which of the following is *not* true regarding the IRR?
   a. The IRR is the interest rate that sets the net present value of a project's cash inflows equal to the present value of the project's cost.
   b. The IRR is the interest rate that sets NPV = 0.
   c. The IRR is the most widely used capital investment technique.
   d. If the IRR is greater than the required rate of return, the project is acceptable.
   e. The popularity of IRR may be attributable to the fact that it is a rate of return, a concept that managers are comfortable using.

5. Postaudits of capital projects are useful because
   a. they are not very costly.
   b. they help ensure that resources are used wisely.
   c. the assumptions underlying the original analyses are often invalidated by changes in the actual operating environment.
   d. they have no significant limitations.
   e. All of the above.

6. For competing projects, NPV is preferred to IRR because
   a. maximizing IRR may not maximize the wealth of the company's owners.
   b. in the final analysis, total dollars earned, not relative profitability, are what count.
   c. choosing the project with the largest NPV maximizes the wealth of shareholders.
   d. assuming that cash flows are reinvested at the required rate of return is more realistic than assuming that cash flows are reinvested at the computed IRR.
   e. All of the above.

7. In countries where inflation is high, you should
   a. adjust the cost of capital to equal the inflation rate.
   b. use the real rate of return as the discount rate.
   c. adjust operating cash flows to account for inflation.
   d. adjust cash inflows due to the tax shield effect of capital cost allowances.
   e. always use a general price index to adjust cash flows for inflation.

8. Capital investment decisions involving automated technology
   a. are the same as any other long-term investment decisions.
   b. should use both financial and nonfinancial criteria.
   c. pay more attention to inputs used in discounted cash-flow analysis.
   d. Both b and c.
   e. Both a and b.

## Problems

**11–27**

*Basic NPV Analysis*

**LO1, LO3**

Ross Liddel, marketing manager, was arguing for the introduction of a new product—a stair stepper. The company was already a major player in the exercise equipment market, and he felt that the new product bearing the company's brand name would be well accepted. He knew, however, that the acceptance of the new product would depend on the economic feasibility of acquiring the equipment needed to produce the product. The equipment would cost $300,000, and its cash operating expenses would total $60,000 per year. The equipment would last for seven years but would need a major overhaul costing $20,000 at the end of the fifth year. At the end of seven years, the equipment would be sold for $24,000. An increase in working capital totalling $30,000 would also be needed at the beginning of the project. This would be recovered at the end of the seven years.

The stair steppers would sell for $170 per unit and would cost $80 per unit to produce (in addition to the operating expenses of the equipment). Ross expects to sell 1,500 units per year. The cost of capital is 10 percent. Ignore taxes.

**Required:**
1. Prepare a schedule of cash flows for the proposed project.
2. Compute the NPV of the project. Should the new product be produced?

**11–28**

*Cash Flows; Basic NPV Analysis*

**LO3**

The Cone Company currently sells 25,000 units a year at a price of $90 per unit. These units are produced using a machine that was purchased five years ago at a cost of $600,000. It currently has a book value of $300,000; however, due to its specialized nature, it has a market value today of only $35,000. The machine, expected to last another five years, after which it will have no expected salvage value, gives rise to the following production costs:

| | |
|---|---|
| Direct materials (5 kilograms @ $1.50/kilogram) | $ 7.50 |
| Direct labour (4 hours @ $15.00/hour) | 60.00 |
| Variable overhead (4 hours @ $1.20/hour) | 4.80 |
| Fixed overhead (4 hours @ $1.60/hour)[a] | 6.40 |
| Total cost per unit | $78.70 |

[a] Based on an annual activity of 100,000 direct labour hours

The company expects the following changes for next year:
- The selling price will increase by 10 percent.
- Direct labour rates will increase by 15 percent.
- Sales are expected to increase to 26,000 units (within the capacity of present facilities) and remain at that level.

Management is currently considering the replacement of Cone's old machine with a new one that would cost $750,000. The new machine is expected to last five years, with a salvage value of $30,000 expected at that time (straight-line amortization used). By using the new machine, management expects to cut variable direct labour hours to 3.5 hours per unit, but the company will have to hire an operator for the machine at $45,000 per year. The company has a minimum desired rate of return of 10 percent. Ignore taxes.

**Required:**
1. Determine the cash flows associated with the machine replacement decision.
2. Determine, by using the net present value approach, whether or not the company should purchase the new machine. (CMA Canada adapted)

**11–29**

*Payback; NPV;
Managerial Incentives;
Ethical Behaviour*

**LO2, LO3**

Dominic Ferrara, manager of a credit union branch, was pleased with his branch's performance over the past three years. Each year the branch's profits had increased, and he had earned a sizable bonus (bonuses are a linear function of the branch's reported income). He had also received considerable attention from higher management. A vice-president had told him in confidence that if his performance over the next three years matched that of his first three, he would be promoted.

Determined to fulfil these expectations, Dominic made sure that he personally reviewed every capital request. He wanted to be certain that any funds invested would provide good, solid returns (the branch's cost of capital is 10 percent). At the moment, he is reviewing two independent requests. Proposal A involves automating a cheque-processing operation that is currently labour-intensive. Proposal B centres on developing and marketing several new electronic tellers. Proposal A requires an initial outlay of $90,000, and Proposal B requires $130,000. Both projects could be funded given the status of the branch's capital budget. Both have an expected life of six years, and the two projects have the following projected cash flows after implementation:

| Year | Proposal A | Proposal B |
|---|---|---|
| 1 | $60,000 | $(15,000) |
| 2 | 50,000 | (10,000) |
| 3 | 20,000 | (5,000) |
| 4 | 15,000 | 85,000 |
| 5 | 10,000 | 110,000 |
| 6 | 5,000 | 135,000 |

After careful consideration of each investment, Dominic approves the funding of Proposal A and rejects Project B. Ignore taxes.

**Required:**
1. Compute the NPV for each proposal.
2. Compute the payback period for each proposal.
3. According to your analysis, which proposal(s) should be accepted? Explain.
4. Explain why Dominic accepted only Proposal A. Considering the possible reasons for rejecting Project B, would you judge his behaviour to be ethical? Explain.

**11–30**

*Basic IRR Analysis*

**LO1, LO4**

Leshow Company was approached by a local furnace company with the proposition of replacing its old heating system with a modern, more efficient unit. The cost of the new system was quoted at $193,320, but it would save $40,000 per year in fuel costs. The estimated life of the new system is 10 years, with no salvage value. Excited over the possibility of saving $40,000 per year and having a more reliable unit, Leshow's president requested an analysis of the project's economic viability. All capital projects are required to earn at least the company's cost of capital, which is 10 percent. Assume that there are no tax effects.

**Required:**
1. Calculate the project's internal rate of return. Should Leshow acquire the new furnace?
2. Suppose that fuel savings are less than claimed. Calculate the minimum annual cash savings that must be realized for the project to earn a rate equal to the company's cost of capital.
3. Suppose that the life of the furnace is overestimated by two years. Repeat Requirements 1 and 2 under this assumption.
4. Explain the implications of the answers for Requirements 1, 2, and 3.

**11–31**

*NPV; Uncertainty*

**LO1, LO3**

PrairieJet Airlines is interested in acquiring a new aircraft to service a new route. The route would be from Winnipeg to Chicago. The aircraft would fly one round trip daily, except for scheduled maintenance days. There are 15 maintenance days scheduled each year. The aircraft's seating capacity is 150. Flights are expected to be fully booked. The average revenue per passenger per flight (one-way) is $200. Annual operating costs of the aircraft are given below:

| | |
|---|---|
| Fuel | $1,400,000 |
| Flight personnel | 500,000 |
| Food and beverages | 100,000 |
| Maintenance | 400,000 |
| Other | 100,000 |
| Total | $2,500,000 |

The aircraft will cost $100,000,000 and has an expected life of 20 years. The company requires a 14 percent return. Ignore taxes.

**Required:**
1. Calculate the NPV for the aircraft. Should PrairieJet buy it?
2. In management discussions regarding the proposal, PrairieJet's marketing manager states his belief that the assumption of 100 percent booking is unrealistic. He believes that the actual booking rate will be somewhere between 70 percent and 90 percent, with the most likely rate being 80 percent. Recalculate the NPV using an 80 percent seating capacity. Should the aircraft be purchased?
3. Calculate the average seating rate that would be needed so that NPV = 0.
4. Suppose that the price per passenger could be increased by 10 percent without any effect on demand. What is the average seating rate now needed to achieve an NPV = 0? What would you now recommend?

**11–32**

*Review of Capital Investment Procedures*

**LO1, LO2, LO3, LO4**

Dr. Hanna White, a dentist, had just returned from a conference where she learned about a new procedure for performing root canals, which reduces the time to complete them by 50 percent. Given her patient-load pressures, Hanna was anxious to try out the new technique. By decreasing the time she spent on root canals, she could increase her total revenues by performing more services within a work period. Unfortunately, in order to implement the new procedure, some special equipment costing $74,000 was needed. The equipment had an expected life of four years, with a salvage value of $6,000. Hanna estimated that her cash revenues would increase by the following amounts:

| | Year 1 | Year 2 | Year 3 | Year 4 |
|---|---|---|---|---|
| Revenue increase | $19,800 | $27,000 | $32,400 | $32,400 |

She also expected additional cash expenses amounting to $3,000 per year. Her cost of capital is 12 percent. Ignore taxes.

**Required:**

1. Compute the payback period for the new equipment.
2. Compute the accounting rate of return using both original investment and average investment.
3. Compute the NPV and IRR for the project. Should Hanna purchase the new equipment? Should she be concerned about payback or the accounting rate of return in making this decision?
4. Before finalizing her decision, Hanna decided to call two dentists who had been using the new procedure for the past six months. These conversations revealed a somewhat less glowing report than she had received at the conference. The new procedure turned out to reduce the required time by about 25 percent, rather than the advertised 50 percent. Hanna estimated that the net operating cash flows of the procedures would be cut by 33 percent because of the extra time and cost involved. Using this information, recompute the NPV and the IRR of the project. What would you now recommend?

**11–33**

Replacement Decision; NPV; CCA

LO1, LO5, LO7

Dinocare Travel Agency is considering replacing its existing computer system with a new one manufactured by a different company. The old computer was acquired three years ago, has a remaining life of five years, and will have a salvage value of $10,000. The old computer is one of many assets included in a class with a maximum CCA rate of 30 percent. The unamortized capital cost of the old computer is $200,000. The cash operating costs of the existing computer (including software, personnel, and other supplies) total $100,000 per year. The new computer system has an initial cost of $500,000 and will have cash operating costs of $50,000 per year. The new computer system will have a life of five years and will have a salvage value of $100,000 at the end of the fifth year. If the new computer is purchased, the old one will be sold for $50,000. Dinocare needs to decide whether to keep the old computer or buy the new one. The cost of capital is 12 percent. The tax rate is 40 percent.

**Required:**

Compute the NPV of each alternative. Should Dinocare keep the old computer or buy the new one?

**11–34**

Machine Replacement; After-Tax Cash Flows

LO7

Tyler Company Ltd. had the following income statement for the year ended December 31, 2004, when the company produced and sold 18,000 units:

| | |
|---|---|
| Sales | $720,000 |
| Less: Cost of goods sold | 576,000 |
| Gross profit | $144,000 |
| Less: Operating expenses: | |
| Variable selling | $ 14,400 |
| Fixed selling | 23,000 |
| Variable administrative | 21,600 |
| Fixed administrative | 43,800 |
| Net income (before taxes) | $ 41,200 |

Cost of goods sold can be broken down as follows:

| | |
|---|---|
| Direct materials | 35% |
| Direct labour | 42% |
| Variable overhead (incurred in relationship to direct labour costs) | 14% |
| Fixed overhead (relevant range of 8,000 to 25,000 units) | 9% |

The company is considering the purchase of a machine costing $150,000 with an expected useful life of five years and a salvage value of $25,000. The machine would have a maximum capacity of 25,000 units per year and is expected to reduce direct labour costs by 25 percent; however, it would require an additional supervisor at a cost of $40,000 per year. The machine would be amortized over the five years using the straight-line method for both accounting and tax purposes. Production and sales for the next five years are expected to be as follows:

|  | 2005 | 2006 | 2007 | 2008 | 2009 |
|---|---|---|---|---|---|
| Units produced | 18,000 | 18,000 | 20,000 | 20,000 | 20,000 |

**Required:**
Assume that Tyler has a minimum desired rate of return of 16 percent and an income tax rate of 38 percent. Should the company purchase the machine? Round amounts to the nearest dollar, and show all calculations. (CMA Canada adapted)

**11–35**

Lease versus Buy; CCA

LO1, LO5, LO7

Moore Company is trying to decide whether it should purchase or lease a new piece of equipment to be used in manufacturing a new product. If purchased, the new machine will cost $100,000 and will be used for 10 years. Its salvage value is estimated at $20,000. The machine will be added to existing assets in a CCA class with a maximum CCA rate of 20 percent. The annual maintenance and operating costs will be $20,000. Annual revenues are estimated at $55,000.

If the machine is leased, the company will need to make annual lease payments of $20,700. The first lease payment and a deposit of $5,000 are due immediately. The last lease payment is to be paid at the beginning of Year 10. The deposit is refundable at the end of the tenth year. In addition, under a normal contract, the company must pay for all maintenance and operating costs, although the leasing company does offer a service contract that will provide annual maintenance (on leased machines only). The contract must be paid up front and costs $30,000. Moore estimates that the contract will reduce its annual maintenance and operating costs by $10,000. Moore's cost of capital is 14 percent. The tax rate is 40 percent.

**Required:**
1. Prepare schedules showing the after-tax cash flows for each alternative. (Prepare schedules for the lease alternative with and without the service contract; assume that the service contract is amortized on a straight-line basis for the 10 years and that the annual lease payments are deductible for tax purposes.) Include all revenues and costs associated with each alternative.
2. Compute the NPV for each alternative, assuming that Moore does not purchase the service contract. Should the machine be purchased or leased? For this analysis, was it necessary to include all of the costs and revenues for each alternative? Explain.
3. Compute the NPV for the lease alternative assuming that the service contract is purchased. Does this change your decision about leasing? What revenues and costs could be excluded without affecting the conclusion?

**11–36**

Advanced Manufacturing Environment

LO7, LO8

"I know that it's the thing to do," insisted Latifah Kincaid, vice-president of finance for Colgate Manufacturing. "If we are going to be competitive, we need to build this completely automated plant."

"I'm not so sure," replied Greg Vitkus. "The savings from labour reductions and increased productivity are only $4 million per year. The price tag for this factory—and it's a small one—is $45 million. That gives a payback period of more than 11 years. That's a long time to put the company's money at risk."

"Yeah, but you're overlooking the savings that we'll get from the increase in quality," interjected Cameron Bay, production manager. "With this system, we can decrease our waste and our rework time significantly. Those savings are worth another million dollars per year."

"Another million will only cut the payback to nine years," retorted Greg. "Raffi, you're the marketing manager—do you have any insights?"

"Well, there are other factors to consider, such as service quality and market share. I think that increasing our product quality and improving our delivery service will make us a lot more competitive. I know for a fact that two of our competitors have decided against automation. That'll give us a shot at their customers, provided that our product is of higher quality and we can deliver it faster. I estimate that it'll increase our net cash benefits by another $6 million."

"Wow! Now that's impressive," Greg exclaimed, nearly convinced. "The payback is now getting down to a reasonable level."

"I agree," said Latifah, "but we do need to be sure that it's a sound investment. I know that estimates for construction of the facility have gone as high as $49.8 million. I also know that the expected residual value, after the 20 years of service we expect to get, is $5 million. Also, you're using before-tax cash flows. We need after-tax cash flows. I think I had better see if this project can cover our 14 percent cost of capital."

"Now wait a minute, Latifah," Greg demanded. "You know that I usually insist on a 20 percent rate of return, especially for a project of this magnitude."

**Required:**
1. Compute the NPV of the project using the original savings and investment figures. Do the calculation for discount rates of 14 percent and 20 percent. Assume that straight-line amortization is used for tax purposes. The tax rate is 40 percent.
2. Compute the NPV of the project using the additional benefits noted by the production and marketing managers. Also, use the original cost estimate of $45 million. Again, do the calculation for both possible discount rates.
3. Compute the NPV of the project again using all estimates of cash flows, including the possible initial outlay of $49.8 million. Do the calculation using discount rates of 14 percent and 20 percent.
4. If you were making the decision, what would you do? Explain.

**11–37**

After-Tax Cash Flows; NPV

LO7

Thayn Thompson, divisional manager, has been pushing headquarters to grant approval for the installation of a new flexible manufacturing system. Finally, in the last executive meeting, Thayn was told that if he could show how the new system would increase the company's value, it would be approved. Thayn gathered the following information:

|  | Old System | Flexible System |
| --- | --- | --- |
| Initial investment | — | $1,250,000 |
| Annual operating costs | $350,000 | $95,000 |
| Annual amortization | $100,000 | ? |
| Tax rate | 34% | 34% |
| Cost of capital | 12% | 12% |
| Expected life | 10 years | 10 years |
| Salvage value | none | none |

With the exception of the cost of capital, the above information ignores the rate of inflation, which has been 4 percent per year and is expected to continue at this level for the next decade. (Assume that straight-line amortization is deductible for tax purposes.)

**Required:**
1. Compute the NPV for each system, ignoring inflation.
2. Compute the NPV for each system adjusting the future cash flows for the rate of inflation.
3. Comment on the importance of adjusting cash flows for inflationary effects.

**11–38**

After-Tax Cash Flows; NPV

LO7

The Roofer Company produces a product with the following unit costs based on a level of 5,000 units per year (present capacity):

| | |
|---|---|
| Direct materials (3 kilograms @ $2.80/kilogram) | $ 8.40 |
| Direct labour (8 hours @ $15/hour) | 120.00 |
| Variable overhead (8 hours @ $4/hour) | 32.00 |
| Fixed overhead (8 hours @ $2.50/hour) | 20.00 |
| Total cost per unit | $180.40 |

The product's selling price is $270.00 per unit, and the company incurs the following additional costs:

| | |
|---|---|
| Variable selling and administrative | $3.00 per unit |
| Fixed selling and administrative | $60,000 per year |

Roofer is considering the purchase of a machine that would cost $650,000 and would last for four years, with an expected salvage value of $20,000. If purchased, the machine would reduce direct labour hours by 20 percent per unit and would increase the company's capacity by 2,000 units per year. However, the machine would require an inventory of spare parts and supplies costing $13,000 to be maintained and would require additional power costs of $1.50 per direct labour hour of use. The investment in spare parts and supplies would be fully recoverable at the end of the machine's useful life. The machine would be amortized using the straight-line method for both accounting and tax purposes. The company's tax rate is 38 percent.

**Required:**
Assume that Roofer has a minimum desired rate of return of 12 percent, and sales demand is expected to be 6,000 units per year for the next four years. Should the company purchase the new machine? (CMA Canada adapted)

**11–39**

NPV; CCA; Postaudit; Sensitivity Analysis

LO5, LO6, LO7

Rutherford Products, Inc., is evaluating a new design for one of its manufacturing processes. The new design will eliminate the production of a toxic solid residue. The system's initial cost is estimated at $860,000, including computerized equipment and installation. There is no expected salvage value. The new system has a useful life of eight years and is projected to produce cash operating savings of $270,000 per year over the old system (reducing labour costs and the costs of processing and disposing of toxic waste). In addition to the operating savings, the new system will produce a CCA tax shield that is absent under the old system. The equipment will be in a CCA class with other assets of a similar type. The maximum CCA rate is 30 percent. The tax rate is 34 percent, and the cost of capital is 16 percent.

**Required:**
1. Compute the NPV of the new system.
2. One year after implementation, Rutherford's internal audit staff notes the following about the new system: (1) the cost of acquiring the system was $60,000 more than expected, due to higher installation costs; and (2) the annual cost savings were $20,000 less than expected, because labour cost was higher than expected. Using the changes in expected costs and benefits, compute the NPV as if this information had been available one year ago. Did the company make the right decision?

3. After the results mentioned in the postaudit were reported, Rutherford's marketing manager responded in a memo that revenues had increased by $100,000 per year because of increased purchases by environmentally sensitive customers. Describe the effect this information has on the analysis in Requirement 2.
4. Why would a postaudit be beneficial to Rutherford Products?

**11–40**

*Make or Buy; After-Tax Cash Flows*

**LO7**

The Springster Company manufactures a product called Radids, a major component of which is called Rads. Currently, the company purchases 20,000 units per year of Rads from a supplier at a cost of $53 per unit. The company is considering manufacturing the Rads that it now purchases and has compiled the following data:

- This process would require the purchase of a special machine costing $40,000. This machine would be used for four years, at which time it would be sold for $8,000, and it would be amortized using the straight-line method for financial accounting purposes. The machine would be included with other assets in a class with a CCA rate of 25 percent.
- Direct materials for the Rads would consist of 5 kilograms at a cost of $3 per kilogram. The manufacture of Radids, the major product, currently uses this same material, and the scrap from this production, which would fill 10 percent of the amount required for Rads, is presently sold for $1 per kilogram.
- Direct labour would be two hours per unit of Rads, with an average labour rate of $8 per hour (fringe benefit costs average 10 percent).
- Supervision of the production of Rads would be handled by a manager who is currently paid $30,000 per year. He would continue with his present duties as well as supervising the production of Rads (expected to occupy 15 percent of his time) and would therefore be paid an additional $5,000 per year.
- Variable overhead costs for the production of Rads are expected to total $3.50 per direct labour hour.
- The main factory is rented for $80,000 per year for 5,000 square metres. The production of Rads should require an area of 500 square metres that is presently idle.
- Other fixed overhead costs (all cash) would be applied at the rate of $6 per labour hour.
- In order to fulfil fluctuations in demand, an initial inventory of 1,000 units of Rads would have to be purchased and maintained.
- Springster's minimum desired rate of return is 12 percent, and the income tax rate is 38 percent.

**Required:**
Use present value analysis to determine whether Springster should continue to purchase the required Rads or manufacture them, assuming that demand is expected to increase by 10 percent annually from Years 2 through 4. Show all calculations to the nearest dollar. (CMA Canada adapted)

**11–41**

*CCA; Competing Projects*

**LO5, LO7**

Nigel Day, owner of a repair shop, has unused space in the building he purchased several years ago. Initially, Nigel offered only the basic auto repair services, but since the business has grown, he is now considering the possibility of using the empty space to offer one of two additional services. Specifically, he is planning to add either an engine overhaul service or a diesel engine repair service. In either case, equipment must be purchased and skilled labour hired. The revenues and costs associated with each alternative are shown below.

| | Overhaul Service | Diesel Service |
|---|---|---|
| Revenues | $120,000 | $250,000 |
| Labour costs | 24,000 | 30,000 |
| Material costs | 20,190 | 100,000 |
| Tax rate | 40% | 40% |

To set up the overhaul service, an initial investment of $280,000 in equipment is required. The equipment investment for the diesel service is $420,000. In each case, the useful life of the equipment is 10 years, with no salvage value expected. Assume that straight-line amortization is used for tax purposes. The cost of capital is 16 percent.

### Required:

1. Prepare a schedule of after-tax cash flows for each alternative.
2. Compute the NPV and the IRR for each alternative. Which alternative would you recommend? Do the NPV and the IRR measures recommend the same investment? Will this always be the case?
3. Someone tells Nigel that he should be using CCA instead of straight-line amortization in the analysis. Recompute the NPV for the diesel service alternative using a CCA rate of 20 percent. By how much did the NPV change?

**11–42**

*Alternative Use of Space; CCA; After-Tax Cash Flows*

**LO5, LO7**

The Eagle Crest Company is considering alternative uses for the unused basement area in its plant. One alternative is to sublet the area to a third party at a rate of $6,000 per year. But Eagle Crest's president is hesitant to do this, since the basement represents a third of the total building. The building costs the company $60,000 per year to rent; therefore, the company would be losing money on the sublet rental. An alternative use for the area is to start up production and sales of a new product line. This option would require the purchase of new machinery at a cost of $250,000. The company's lease expires in five years, at which time the company expects to move to its own premises.

The new product line is expected to be obsolete in five years, at which time the machinery would have an expected salvage value of $30,000. Demand is expected to remain constant for the first four years, but is expected to drop by 60 percent in the final year. Eagle Crest's president has prepared the following income statement for the new product line for the first year, when the department must establish and maintain a finished goods inventory of 5,000 units:

| | | | |
|---|---|---|---|
| Sales (20,000 units) | | | $260,000 |
| Cost of goods sold: | | | |
|   Finished goods—January 1, 2003 | | $　　0 | |
| Cost of goods manufactured: | | | |
|   Direct materials | $60,000 | | |
|   Direct labour | 80,000 | | |
|   Supervisor | 30,000 | | |
|   Plant rental | 20,000 | | |
|   Amortization of machinery | 44,000 | | |
| Cost of goods manufactured | | 234,000 | |
| Cost of goods available for sale | | $234,000 | |
| Less: Finished goods—December 31, 2003 | | 46,800 | |
|     Total cost of goods sold | | | 187,200 |
| Gross profit | | | $ 72,800 |
| | | | |
| Operating costs: | | | |
|   Variable selling | | $ 26,000 | |
|   Head office cost allocation (20% of sales) | | 52,000 | |
|     Total operating costs | | | 78,000 |
|       Department income (loss) | | | $ (5,200) |

**Required:**

1. Use the net present value method to determine the company's optimal course of action assuming that its minimum desired rate of return is 14 percent. Assume also that Eagle Crest will have other assets in the CCA class (at a rate of 25 percent) and that the company's income tax rate is 38 percent.

2. What annual rental rate would be required for subletting the basement area to make the company indifferent as to whether or not it should purchase the machine? (CMA Canada adapted)

**11–43**

Advanced
Manufacturing
Environment

LO7, LO8

Meikle Manufacturing, Inc. produces trash compactors, microwave ovens, and electric ranges. Because of increasing competition, Meikle is considering making an investment in a computer-aided manufacturing (CAM) system. Since competition is most keen for microwaves, the microwave production line has been selected for initial evaluation. The CAM system for the microwave line would replace an existing system (purchased a year ago for $6 million). Although the existing system will be fully amortized in nine years, it is expected to last another ten years. The CAM system would also have a useful life of ten years.

The existing system is capable of producing 100,000 microwave ovens per year. The accounting department has provided the following sales and production data for the existing system:

| | |
|---|---|
| Sales per year (units) | 100,000 |
| Selling price | $300 |
| Costs per unit: | |
| Direct materials | $ 80 |
| Direct labour | 90 |
| Volume-related overhead | 20 |
| Direct fixed overhead | 40[a] |

[a] All cash expenses with the exception of amortization, which is $6 per unit.
  The existing equipment is being amortized using straight-line with no salvage value.

The CAM system will cost $34 million to purchase, plus an estimated $20 million in software and implementation. (Assume that all investment outlays occur at the beginning of the first year.) If the CAM equipment is purchased, the old equipment can be sold for $3 million.

The CAM system will require fewer parts for production and will produce with less waste. Because of this, the direct materials cost per unit will be reduced by 25 percent. Automation will also require fewer support activities; as a consequence, volume-related overhead will be reduced by $5 per unit, and direct fixed overhead (other than amortization) will decrease by $17 per unit. Direct labour will be reduced by $66\frac{2}{3}$ percent. Assume, for simplicity, that the new investment will be amortized on a pure straight-line basis for tax purposes with no salvage value.

Meikle's cost of capital is 12 percent, but management chooses to use 18 percent as the required rate of return when evaluating investments. The tax rate is 40 percent.

**Required:**

1. Compute the net present value for the old system and the CAM system. Which system should Meikle choose?

2. Repeat the net present value analysis of Requirement 1 using 12 percent as the discount rate.

3. Upon seeing the projected sales for the old system, Meikle's marketing manager comments, "Sales of 100,000 units per year cannot be maintained in the current competitive environment for more than one year unless we buy the CAM system. The CAM system will allow us to compete on the basis of qual-

ity and lead time. If we keep the old system, our sales will drop by 10,000 units per year." Repeat the net present value analysis using this new information and a 12 percent discount rate.

4. An industrial engineer for Meikle noticed that salvage value for the CAM equipment had not been included in the analysis. He estimated that the equipment could be sold for $4 million at the end of 10 years. He also estimated that the equipment of the old system would have no salvage value at the end of 10 years. Repeat the net present value analysis using this information, the information in Requirement 3, and a 12 percent discount rate.

5. Given the outcomes of the previous four requirements, comment on the importance of providing accurate inputs for assessing capital investments in CAM systems.

## Managerial Decision Cases

**11–44**

Payback; NPV; IRR

LO2, LO3, LO4

Shaftel Ready Mix is a processor and supplier of concrete, aggregate, and rock products. One division of the company operates in the intermountain western United States. Currently, Shaftel has 14 cement-processing plants and a labour force of more than 375 employees. With the exception of cement powder, all raw materials (for example, aggregates and sand) are produced internally by the company. U.S. demand for concrete and aggregates has been growing steadily, and in the west, the growth rate has been above the national average. Because of this growth, Shaftel has more than tripled its gross revenues over the past 10 years.

Of the intermountain states, Arizona has been experiencing the most growth. Processing plants have been added over the past several years, and the company is considering the addition of yet another plant (to be located in Scottsdale). A major advantage of having another plant in Arizona is the ability to operate year-round, a feature not found in such states as Utah and Wyoming.

In setting up the new plant, land would have to be purchased and a small building constructed. Equipment and furniture would not need to be purchased; these items would be transferred from a plant that had been opened in Wyoming during the oil-boom period and closed a few years after the end of that boom. However, the equipment needs some repair and modifications before it can be used. It has a book value of $200,000, and the furniture has a book value of $30,000. Neither has any outside market value. Other costs—such as those related to the installation of a silo, a well, electrical hookups, and so on—will be incurred. No salvage value is expected. The summary of the initial investment costs by category is as follows:

| | |
|---|---|
| Land | $ 20,000 |
| Building | 135,000 |
| Equipment: | |
|     Book value | 200,000 |
|     Modifications | 20,000 |
| Furniture (book value) | 30,000 |
| Silo | 20,000 |
| Well | 80,000 |
| Electrical hookups | 27,000 |
| General setup | 50,000 |
|     Total initial outlay | $582,000 |

Estimates concerning the operation of the Scottsdale plant are given below:

| | |
|---|---|
| Life of plant and equipment | 10 years |
| Expected annual sales (in cubic yards) | 35,000 |
| Selling price (per cubic yard) | $45.00 |
| Variable costs (per cubic yard): | |
|    Cement | $12.94 |
|    Sand/gravel | 6.42 |
|    Fly ash | 1.13 |
|    Admixture | 1.53 |
|    Driver labour | 3.24 |
|    Mechanics | 1.43 |
|    Plant operations (batching and cleanup) | 1.39 |
|    Loader operator | 0.50 |
|    Truck parts | 1.75 |
|    Fuel | 1.48 |
|    Other | 3.27 |
|      Total variable cost | $35.08 |
| | |
| Fixed costs (annual): | |
|    Salaries | $135,000 |
|    Insurance | 75,000 |
|    Telephone | 5,000 |
|    Amortization | 58,200* |
|    Utilities | 25,000 |
|      Total fixed cost | $298,200 |

\* Straight-line amortization is calculated using all initial investment costs over a 10-year period, assuming no salvage value.

After reviewing the above data, Karl Flemming, vice-president of operations, argues against the proposed plant. Karl is concerned because the plant would earn significantly less than the normal 8.3 percent return on sales. All other plants in the company are earning between 7.5 and 8.5 percent on sales. Karl also notes that it would take more than five years to recover the total initial outlay of $582,000. In the past, Shaftel has always insisted that an investment's payback period be no more than four years. The company's cost of capital is 10 percent. Ignore tax effects.

**Required:**

1. Prepare a variable-costing income statement for the proposed plant. Compute the ratio of net income to sales. Is Karl correct that the return on sales is significantly lower than the company average?
2. Compute the payback period for the proposed plant. Is Karl right that the payback period is greater than four years? Explain. Suppose that you were told that the equipment being transferred from Wyoming could be sold for its book value. Would this affect your answer?
3. Compute the NPV and the IRR for the proposed plant. Would your answer be affected if you were told that the furniture and equipment could be sold for their book values? If so, repeat the analysis with this effect considered.
4. Compute the cubic yards of cement that must be sold for the new plant to break even. Using this breakeven volume, compute the NPV and the IRR. Would the investment be acceptable? If so, explain why an investment that promises to do nothing more than break even can be viewed as acceptable.
5. Compute the volume of cement that must be sold for the IRR to equal Shaftel's cost of capital. Using this volume, compute the company's expected annual income. Explain this result.

**11–45**

Capital Investment and Ethical Behaviour

LO3

Manny Correia, CMA and controller of Wakeman Enterprises, had been given permission to acquire a new computer and software for the company's accounting system. The capital investment analysis had shown an NPV of $100,000; however, the initial estimates of acquisition and installation costs had been made on the basis of tentative costs without any formal bids. Manny now has two formal bids—one that would allow the company to meet the original projected NPV, and one that would reduce the projected NPV by $50,000. The second bid involves a system that would increase both the initial cost and the operating cost.

Normally, Manny would take the first bid without hesitation. However, Todd Downing, the owner of the company presenting the second bid, was a close friend. Manny had called Todd and explained the situation, offering Todd an opportunity to alter his bid and win the job. Todd thanked Manny and then made a counteroffer.

**Todd**: "Listen, Manny, this job at the original price is the key to a successful year for me. The revenues will help me gain approval for the loan I need for renovation and expansion. If I don't get that loan, I see hard times ahead. The financial stats for loan approval are so marginal that reducing the bid price may blow my chances."

**Manny**: "Losing the bid altogether would be even worse, don't you think?"

**Todd**: "True. However, I have a suggestion. If you grant me the job, I will have the capability of adding personnel. I know that your son is looking for a job, and I can offer him a good salary and a promising future. Additionally, I'll be able to take you and your wife on that vacation to Hawaii that we've been talking about."

**Manny**: "Well, you have a point. My son is having an awful time finding a job, and he has a wife and three kids to support. My wife is tired of having them live with us. She and I could use a vacation. I doubt that the other bidder would make any fuss if we turned it down. Its offices are out of province, after all."

**Todd**: "Out of province? All the more reason to turn it down. Given the province's economy, it seems almost criminal to take business outside. Those are the kinds of business decisions that cause problems for people like your son."

**Required:**

Evaluate Manny's ethical behaviour. Should Manny have called Todd in the first place? What if Todd had agreed to meet the lower bid price—would there have been any problems? Identify the standards of ethical conduct (refer to Chapter 1) that Manny may be violating, if any.

# Research Assignment

**11–46**

*Analytical Hierarchy*

**LO1, LO8**

The capital expenditure approach you have studied in this chapter relies on quantitative financial measures such as payback, net present value, and the internal rate of return. Some have argued that these traditional capital expenditure models should be only a starting point in the analysis. Other criteria, such as cycle time (the time it takes to convert materials into a finished good) and flexibility, may be important considerations in a capital expenditure decision, yet such factors are not captured by IRR or NPV. In fact, there have been efforts to build formal frameworks that allow explicit consideration of multiple criteria. One of these frameworks is an analytical hierarchy process. This approach is described in the following article: David E. Stout, Matthew J. Liberatore, and Thomas F. Monahan, "Decision Support Software for Capital Budgeting," *Management Accounting* (July 1991): pp. 50-53.

**Required:**

Read the above article, and write a paper that describes how the method works. In your paper, offer a critique of the method. What is your opinion of the approach? Is it better than the traditional models, or do you think there are ways that the traditional models can capture such criteria as cycle time and flexibility? Do you think that managers would really use this methodology? Explain.

# Inventory Management

*handwritten: 1. Omit pages 540-545*

# Scenario

Michelle Anderson, president and owner of Anderson Parts, Inc., had just finished reading the report prepared by Henry Jensen, a special consultant attached to the management advisory section of a national public accounting firm. The recommendations in the report were somewhat surprising, and Michelle was looking forward to her meeting with him to discuss them. Her thoughts were interrupted by Henry's arrival.

**Michelle**: "Have a seat, Henry. I have to confess that your recommendations are intriguing. If you can convince me that they'll work, you'll have more than earned your fee."

**Henry**: "I think I can provide a lot of support for those recommendations. When we first met, you mentioned that your company had lost 20 percent of its market share over the past five years. In your industry, as in

many others, much of that loss is because of the gains made by foreign competitors. Foreign producers are offering a higher-quality product at a lower price and with better delivery performance."

**Michelle**: "I am aware of that. You remember that in our first meeting I said as much. I was certain at that time that the solution was automation and was prepared to sink millions into that approach. I was convinced that automating would improve quality, lower manufacturing costs, and cut down our lead time for production. Because so much money was involved, I hired you to tell us how to automate and exactly what type of equipment to buy. Instead you're telling me that I shouldn't automate—at least not right away—but instead simplify our purchasing and manufacturing by installing something called a just-in-time system. Your report also mentions that I should look at the theory of constraints. Do you really believe that this will bring the benefits I'm

seeking? Are you speaking from experience?"

**Henry**: "Absolutely. Case after case has shown us that 80 percent of the competitive benefits from automation can be achieved by implementing JIT—and at a significantly decreased cost. First implement JIT; then you can see where automation will be of the most benefit. The strategy we recommend is first simplify, automate, integrate, and continuously seek ways of improving. Continuous improvement is essential. A method called the theory of constraints offers an ongoing way of improving performance. One of its major byproducts is inventory reduction."

**Michelle**: "It sounds promising. But can you be more specific? What benefits have other companies experienced?"

**Henry**: "Well, Michelle, your company manufactures machine parts. Another company in your same line of business was having a difficult time competing. It needed 24 weeks to produce one of its products from start to finish, whereas a Japanese competitor produced and delivered the same part in 6 weeks. After installing a JIT system, the company was able to produce the part in only 20 days. In some cases, however, the theory of constraints can offer even more."

**Michelle**: "Henry, that's hard to believe. Yet I know that a lot of the business we have lost is because we have such poor delivery performance compared with that of some of our competitors. You're telling me that we can make dramatic improvements in our lead time with our existing technology?"

**Henry**: "Yes, but that isn't all. Reducing lead time leads to other benefits. Methods like JIT purchasing and manufacturing and the theory of constraints can reduce your inventories—raw materials, work in process, and finished goods—to much lower levels. Companies often tie up as much as 40 percent of their assets in inventory. That's a lot of nonproductive capital. As you might imagine, decreasing lead time allows a company to reduce its inventories, freeing up a lot of capital to be used elsewhere. Other inventory-related costs are also avoided, and reducing or avoiding these costs can make your company more competitive."

**Michelle**: "Intriguing. I would like to know more."

**Questions to Think About**
1. Why do companies carry inventory?
2. What are inventory-related costs?
3. What can be done to minimize inventory costs?
4. How does JIT reduce inventories?
5. What are the weaknesses of JIT?
6. How does the theory of constraints reduce inventories?
7. Why is effective management of inventory so important?

## Traditional Inventory Management

**Objective 1**

Describe the traditional inventory management model.

Managing the levels of inventory is fundamental to establishing a long-term competitive advantage. Quality, product engineering, prices, overtime, excess capacity, ability to respond to customers (due-date performance), lead times, and overall profitability are all affected by inventory levels. In general, companies that maintain higher inventory levels than their competitors tend to be in a worse competitive position.

The focus of this chapter is how inventory policy can be used to aid in establishing a competitive advantage. First, we review the traditional inventory management model—the model that has been the mainstay of manufacturing companies for decades. Learning the basics of this model and its underlying conceptual foundation will help us understand where it can still be appropriately applied. Understanding traditional inventory management also provides the necessary background for grasping the advantages of inventory management methods that are used in the advanced manufacturing environment, such as JIT and the theory of constraints.

### Inventory-Related Costs

In a world of certainty—where the demand for a product is known with certainty for a given period of time (usually a year)—two major costs are associated with inventory. If the inventory is purchased from an outside source, then these inventory-related costs are known as *ordering costs* and *carrying costs*. If the inventory is produced internally, then the costs are called *setup costs* and *carrying costs*.

**ordering costs**

The costs of placing and receiving an order.

- **Ordering costs** are the costs of placing and receiving an order. Examples include the costs of processing an order (clerical costs and documents), the cost of insurance for shipment, and unloading costs.

**setup costs**

The cost of preparing equipment and facilities so that they can be used for production.

**carrying costs**

The costs of holding inventory.

**stock-out costs**

The costs of insufficient inventory.

- **Setup costs** are the costs of preparing equipment and facilities so that they can be used to produce a particular product or component. Examples are wages of idled production workers, the cost of idled production facilities (lost income), and the costs of test runs (labour, materials, and overhead).
- **Carrying costs** are the costs of carrying inventory. Examples include insurance, obsolescence, the opportunity cost of funds tied up in inventory, handling costs, and storage space.

Ordering costs and setup costs are similar in nature—both represent costs that must be incurred to acquire inventory. They differ only in the nature of the prerequisite activity (filling out and placing an order versus configuring equipment and facilities). Thus, in the discussion that follows, any reference to ordering costs can be viewed as a reference to setup costs.

If demand is not known with certainty, a third category of inventory costs—called *stock-out costs*—exists.

- **Stock-out costs** are the costs of not having a product available when demanded by a customer. Examples are lost sales (both current and future), the costs of expediting (increased transportation charges, overtime, and so on), and the costs of interrupted production.

Maximizing profits requires that inventory-related costs be minimized. But minimizing *carrying costs* favours ordering or producing in small lot sizes, whereas minimizing *ordering costs* favours large, infrequent orders (minimization of setup costs favours long, infrequent production runs). Thus, minimizing carrying costs encourages small or no inventories, and minimizing ordering or setup costs encourages larger inventories. These two sets of costs must be balanced so that the *total* cost of carrying and ordering can be minimized.

## Traditional Reasons for Holding Inventory

Several reasons are given to explain why organizations invest in inventory. A recurring theme is that inventory is a *buffer* between supply and demand although there are other reasons as well.

1. Dealing with uncertainty in demand is a major reason for holding inventory. Even if the ordering or setup costs were negligible, organizations still carry inventory because of stock-out costs. If the demand for products is greater than expected, inventory can serve as a buffer, giving organizations the ability to meet delivery dates (thus keeping customers satisfied).

2. Inventories of parts and raw materials are often viewed as necessary because of supply uncertainties. That is, inventory buffers of parts and materials are needed to keep production flowing in case of late deliveries or no deliveries (strikes, bad weather, and bankruptcy are examples of uncertain events that can cause an interruption in supply).

3. Unreliable production processes may also create a demand for producing extra inventory. For example, a company may decide to produce more units than needed to meet demand because the production process usually yields a large number of nonconforming units.

4. Buffers of inventories may be required to continue supplying customers or processes with goods in the case of manufacturing equipment failure.

5. Organizations may acquire larger inventories than normal to take advantage of quantity discounts or to avoid anticipated price increases.

## Economic Order Quantity: The Traditional Inventory Model

In developing an inventory policy, two basic questions must be addressed:

1. How much should be ordered (or produced)?
2. When should the order be placed (or the setup done)?

### Order Quantity and Total Ordering and Carrying Costs

If demand is known, managers need be concerned only with ordering (or setup) and carrying costs in choosing an order quantity or a lot size for production. The total ordering (or setup) and carrying cost is described by the following equation:

$$TC = PD/Q + CQ/2$$
$$= \text{Ordering cost} + \text{Carrying cost}$$

where   $TC$ = total ordering(or setup) and carrying costs
   $P$ = cost of placing and receiving an order (or setting up a production run)
   $D$ = known annual demand
   $Q$ = number of units ordered in each order (or the lot size for production)
   $C$ = cost of carrying one unit of stock for one year

This inventory model can be applied to any organization, including retail, service, and manufacturing organizations. To illustrate the application for a service organization, assume the following for a part used in the repair of refrigerators (the part is purchased from external suppliers):

$$P = \$25 \text{ per order}$$
$$D = 10{,}000 \text{ units}$$
$$Q = 1{,}000 \text{ units}$$
$$C = \$2 \text{ per unit}$$

The ordering cost is the number of orders ($D/Q$) times the cost per order ($P$). The number of orders per year is demand ($D$) divided by the size of an order ($Q$); in this case, 10 (10,000/1,000). The total ordering cost [($D/Q$) × $P$] is $250 (10 × $25).

The total carrying cost for the year is the average inventory on hand ($Q/2$) by the carrying cost per unit ($C$).[1] For an order of 1,000 units with a carrying cost of $2 per unit, the average inventory is 500 (1,000/2) and the carrying cost for the year ($CQ/2$) is $1,000 ($2 × 500).

An order quantity of 1,000 with a total cost of $1,250, however, may not be the best choice. Another order quantity may produce a lower total cost. The objective is to find the order quantity that minimizes the total cost. This order quantity is called the **economic order quantity (EOQ)**. The EOQ model is an example of a push inventory system. In a push system, the acquisition of inventory is initiated in anticipation of future demand—not in reaction to present demand. Fundamental to the analysis is the assessment of $D$, the future demand.

**economic order quantity (EOQ)**

The amount that should be ordered (or produced) to minimize the total ordering (or setup) and carrying costs.

## Computing EOQ

Since EOQ is the quantity that minimizes total inventory cost, a formula for computing this quantity is easily derived:[2]

---

1. Assuming an average inventory of $Q/2$ is equivalent to assuming that inventory is consumed uniformly.

2. $d(TC)/dQ = C/2 - DP/Q^2 = 0$, which implies that $Q^2 = 2DP/C$ and $Q = \sqrt{2DP/C}$.

*[Handwritten notes in margin:*

$D$ = annual demand   $P$ = order or setup cost
$TC$ = Total Cost (order/carry)   $C$ = carrying cost
$Q$ = Quantity (order/setup)

$$TC = \frac{PD}{Q} + \frac{CQ}{2}$$

Economic Order Quantity = $\sqrt{2PD/C}$
(EOQ) = how much to order

*]*

$$EOQ = \sqrt{2PD/C}$$

Use the data from the preceding example, the EOQ can be computed:

$$EOQ = \sqrt{(2 \times 25 \times 10,000)/2} = \sqrt{250,000} = 500$$

An order quantity of 500 requires 20 orders (10,000/500) and an average inventory of 250 (500/2), with a total cost of $1,000. The total ordering cost is $500 (20 × $25). The total carrying cost of $500 (250 × $2). Notice that the carrying cost equals the ordering cost. This is always true for the simple EOQ model. Also notice that an order quantity of 500 is less costly than an order quantity of 1,000 ($1,000 versus $1,250).

## Reorder Point

The EOQ answers the question of how much to order (or produce). Knowing when to place an order (or initiate a setup for production) is also an essential part of any inventory policy. The **reorder point** is the point in time when a new order should be placed (or setup started). It is a function of the EOQ, the lead time, and the rate at which inventory is depleted. Lead time is the time required to receive the economic order quantity once an order is placed or a setup is initiated.

To avoid stock-out costs and to minimize carrying costs, an order should be placed so that it arrives just as the last item in inventory is used. Knowing the rate of usage and the **lead time** allows us to compute the reorder point (ROP) that accomplishes these objectives:

$$ROP = \text{Rate of usage} \times \text{Lead time}$$

To illustrate, we will continue the refrigerator part example. Assume that the producer uses 50 parts per day and that the lead time is four days. If so, an order should be placed when the inventory level of the refrigerator part drops to 200 units (4 × 50). Exhibit 12–1 provides a graphical illustration. Note that the inventory is depleted just as the order arrives and that the quantity on hand jumps back up to the EOQ level.

### Demand Uncertainty and the Reorder Point

If the demand for the part or product is not known with certainty, the possibility of stock-out exists. For example, if the refrigerator part were used at a rate of 60 parts a day instead of 50, the company would use 200 parts after three and one-third days. Since the new order would not arrive until the end of the fourth day, repair activity requiring this part would be idled for two-thirds of a day. To avoid this problem, organizations often choose to carry safety stock. **Safety stock** is extra inventory carried to serve as insurance against fluctuations in demand. Safety stock is computed by multiplying the lead time by the difference between the maximum rate of usage and the average rate of usage. For example, if the maximum usage of the refrigerator part is 60 units per day, the average usage is 50 units per day, and the lead time is four days, the safety stock is computed as follows:

| | |
|---|---|
| Maximum usage | 60 |
| Average usage | 50 |
| Difference | 10 |
| Lead time | 4 |
| Safety stock | 40 |

With the presence of safety stock, the reorder point is computed as follows:

$$ROP = (\text{Average rate of usage} \times \text{Lead time}) + \text{Safety stock}$$

**reorder point**
The point in time at which a new order (or setup) should be initiated.

**lead time**
For purchasing, the time to receive an order after it is placed. For manufacturing, the time to produce a product from start to finish.

**safety stock**
Extra inventory carried to serve as insurance against fluctuations in demand.

*[Handwritten notes in margin:*

ROP (reorder point)
= (lead time × avg. rate of use) + safety stock

↳ or → ROP = (lead time × average rate of use) + (max rate of use − average rate of use)

*]*

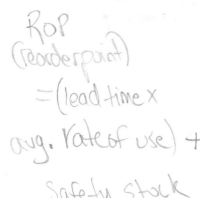

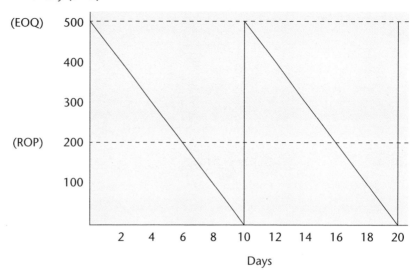

Inventory (units)

For the refrigerator part example, the reorder point with safety stock is computed as follows:

$$ROP = (50 \times 4) + 40 = 240 \text{ units}$$

Thus, an order is automatically placed whenever the inventory level drops to 240 units.

### A Manufacturing Example

The service repair setting involved the purchase of inventory. The same concepts can be applied to settings where inventory is manufactured. To illustrate, consider Benson Company, a large manufacturer of farm implements with several plants throughout Canada. Each plant produces all subassemblies necessary to assemble a particular farm implement. One large plant in Saskatchewan produces ploughs. The manager of this plant is trying to determine the size of the production runs for the blade fabrication area. He is convinced that the current lot size is too large and wants to identify the quantity that should be produced to minimize the sum of the carrying and setup costs. He also wants to avoid stock-outs, since any stock-out would shut down the assembly department.

To help him in his decision, the controller has supplied the following information:

| | |
|---|---|
| Average demand for blades | 320 per day |
| Maximum demand for blades | 340 per day |
| Annual demand for blades | 80,000 |
| Unit carrying cost | $5 |
| Setup cost | $12,500 |
| Lead time | 20 days |

Based on this information, the economic order quantity and the reorder point are computed in Exhibit 12–2. As the computation illustrates, the blades should be produced in batches of 20,000 and a new setup should be started when the supply of blades drops to 6,800.

**EXHIBIT 12-2**

EOQ and Reorder Point
Illustrated

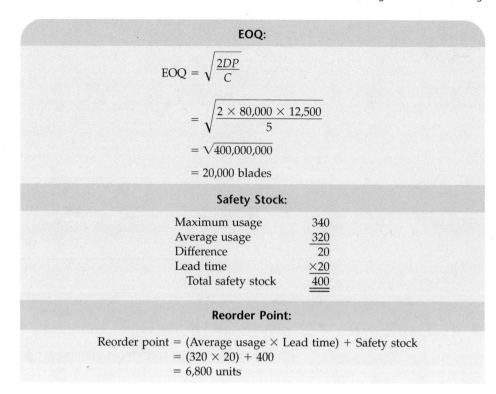

**EOQ:**

$$EOQ = \sqrt{\frac{2DP}{C}}$$

$$= \sqrt{\frac{2 \times 80,000 \times 12,500}{5}}$$

$$= \sqrt{400,000,000}$$

$$= 20,000 \text{ blades}$$

**Safety Stock:**

| | |
|---|---|
| Maximum usage | 340 |
| Average usage | 320 |
| Difference | 20 |
| Lead time | ×20 |
| Total safety stock | 400 |

**Reorder Point:**

Reorder point = (Average usage × Lead time) + Safety stock
$$= (320 \times 20) + 400$$
$$= 6,800 \text{ units}$$

## EOQ and Inventory Management

The traditional approach to managing inventory has been referred to as a *just-in-case system*.[3] In some settings, a just-in-case inventory system is entirely appropriate. For example, hospitals need inventories of medicines, drugs, and other critical supplies on hand at all times so that life-threatening situations can be handled. Using an economic order quantity coupled with safety stock would seem eminently sensible in such an environment. Relying on a critical drug to arrive just in time to save a heart attack victim is simply not practical. Furthermore, many smaller retail stores, manufacturers, and services may not have the buying power to command alternative inventory management systems, such as just-in-time purchasing.

As the plough blade example illustrates, the EOQ model is very useful in identifying the optimal tradeoff between inventory carrying costs and setup costs. It is also useful in helping to deal with uncertainty by using safety stock. The historical importance of the EOQ model in many industries can be better appreciated by understanding the nature of the traditional manufacturing environment. This environment has been characterized by the mass production of a few standardized products that typically have a very high setup cost. The production of the plough blades fits this pattern. The high setup cost encouraged a large batch size: 20,000 units. The annual demand of 80,000 units can be satisfied using only four batches. Thus, production runs for these companies tended to be quite long. Furthermore, diversity was viewed as being costly and was avoided. Producing variations of the product can be quite expensive, especially since additional, special features would usually demand even more expensive and frequent setups—the reason for the standardized products.

---

3. Eliyahu M. Goldratt and Robert E. Fox, *The Race* (Croton-on-Hudson, N.Y.: North River Press, 1986).

## JIT Inventory Management

**Objective** 2

Describe JIT inventory management.

The manufacturing environment for many of these traditional large-batch, high-setup-cost companies has changed dramatically in the past 10 to 20 years. For one thing, the competitive markets are no longer defined by national boundaries. Advances in transportation and communication have contributed significantly to the creation of global competition. Advances in technology have contributed to shorter life cycles for products, and product diversity has increased. Foreign companies offering higher-quality, lower-cost products *with specialized features* have created tremendous pressures for large-batch, high-setup-cost companies to increase both quality and product diversity while simultaneously reducing total costs. These competitive pressures have led many companies to abandon the EOQ model in favour of a JIT approach.

JIT has two strategic objectives: to increase profits and to improve a company's competitive position. These two objectives are achieved by controlling costs (enabling better price competition and increased profits), improving delivery performance, and improving quality. JIT offers increased cost efficiency and simultaneously has the flexibility to respond to customer demands for better quality and more variety.

JIT manufacturing and purchasing represent the continual pursuit of productivity through the elimination of waste. Nonvalue-added activities are a major source of waste. Nonvalue-added activities are either unnecessary, or necessary but inefficient and improvable. Eliminating nonvalue-added activities is a major thrust of JIT, but it is also a basic objective of any company following the path of continuous improvement—regardless of whether or not JIT is being used. Inventories are particularly viewed as representing waste. They tie up resources such as cash, space, and labour. They also conceal inefficiencies in production and increase the complexity of a company's information system. Thus, even though JIT focuses on more than inventory management, control of inventory is an important benefit. In this chapter, the inventory dimension of JIT is emphasized.

### A Pull System

JIT maintains that goods should be pulled through the system by present demand rather than pushed through the system on a fixed schedule based on anticipated demand. Many fast-food restaurants, like McDonald's, use a pull system to control their finished goods inventory. When a customer orders a hamburger, it is taken from the rack. When the number of hamburgers gets too low, then the cooks make new hamburgers. Customer demand pulls the materials through the system. This same principle is used in manufacturing settings. Each operation produces only what is necessary to satisfy the demand of the succeeding operation. The material or subassembly arrives just in time for production to occur so that demand can be met.

One effect of JIT is to reduce inventories to very low levels. The pursuit of insignificant levels of inventories is vital to the success of JIT. This idea of pursuing insignificant inventories, however, necessarily challenges the traditional reasons for holding inventories. These reasons are no longer viewed as valid.

### Setup and Carrying Costs: The JIT Approach

JIT takes a radically different approach to minimizing total carrying and setup costs. The traditional approach accepts the existence of setup costs and then finds the order quantity that best balances the two categories of costs. JIT, on the other hand, does not accept setup costs (or ordering costs) as a given; rather, JIT attempts to drive these costs to zero. If setup costs and ordering costs become insignificant, the only remaining cost to minimize is carrying cost. This is accomplished by reducing inventories to very low levels.

### Long-Term Contracts, Continuous Replenishment, and Electronic Data Interchange

Ordering costs are reduced by developing close relationships with suppliers. Negotiating long-term contracts for the supply of outside materials will obviously reduce the number of orders and the associated ordering costs. Retailers have found a way to reduce ordering costs by adopting an arrangement known as *continuous replenishment*. With **continuous replenishment**, a manufacturer assumes the inventory management function for the retailer. The manufacturer tells the retailer when and how much stock to reorder. The retailer reviews the recommendation and approves the order if it makes sense. Wal-Mart and Procter & Gamble, for example, use this arrangement.[4] The arrangement has reduced inventories for Wal-Mart, and it has also reduced stock-out problems. Additionally, Procter & Gamble's goods are often sold before Wal-Mart has to pay for them. Procter & Gamble, on the other hand, has become a preferred supplier, has more and better shelf space, and also has less demand uncertainty. The ability to project demand better allows Procter & Gamble to produce and deliver continuously in smaller lots—a goal of JIT manufacturing. Similar arrangements can be made between manufacturers and their suppliers.

The process of continuous replenishment is facilitated by electronic data interchange. **Electronic data interchange (EDI)** allows suppliers access to a buyer's on-line database.[5] By knowing the buyer's production schedule (in the case of a manufacturer), the supplier can deliver the needed parts where they are needed just in time for their use. EDI involves no paper—no purchase orders or invoices. The supplier uses the production schedule that is in the database to determine its own production and delivery schedules. When the parts are shipped, an electronic message is sent from the supplier to the buyer that a shipment is en route. When the parts arrive, a bar code is scanned with an electronic wand; this action initiates payment for the goods. Clearly, EDI requires a close working arrangement between the supplier and the buyer—they almost operate as one company rather than two separate companies. General Motors' Saturn plant uses an EDI arrangement with its component suppliers. This approach has enabled both suppliers and Saturn to reduce overhead.[6]

### Reducing Setup Times

Reducing setup times requires a company to search for new, more efficient ways to accomplish setup. Fortunately, experience has indicated that dramatic reductions in setup times can be achieved. Upon adopting a JIT system, Harley-Davidson reduced setup times by more than 75 percent on the machines evaluated.[7] In some cases, Harley-Davidson was able to reduce the setup times from hours to minutes. Other companies have experienced similar results.

**continuous replenishment**

A system where a manufacturer assumes the inventory management function for the retailer.

**electronic data interchange (EDI)**

An inventory management method that allows suppliers access to a buyer's on-line database.

---

4. Michael Hammer and James Champy, *Reengineering the Corporation* (New York: HarperBusiness, 1993).

5. For more discussion on EDI, see *Implementing Electronic Data Exchange*, Management Accounting Guideline 24, CMA Canada (Hamilton, Ont., 1994), *The Role of Management Accounting in Electronic Data Exchange*, CMA Canada, 1992, and John W. Yu, "The Paperless EDI Environment," *CGA Magazine*, September 1993: pp. 40-42, 74-75 .

6. Hammer and Champy, pp. 90-91.

7. Gene Schwind, "Man Arrives Just in Time to Save Harley-Davidson," *Materials Handling Engineering* (August 1984): pp. 28-35.

# Due-Date Performance: The JIT Solution

Due-date performance is a measure of a company's ability to respond to customer needs. In the past, finished goods inventories have been used to ensure that a company is able to meet a requested delivery date. JIT solves the problem of due-date performance not by building inventory but by dramatically reducing lead times. Shorter lead times increase a company's ability to meet requested delivery dates and to respond quickly to the demands of the market. Thus, the company's competitiveness is improved. JIT cuts lead times by reducing setup times, improving quality, and using cellular manufacturing.

Manufacturing cells reduce travel distance between machines and inventory; they can also have a dramatic effect on lead time. For example, in a traditional manufacturing system, one company took two months to manufacture a valve. Grouping the lathes and drills used to make the valves into U-shaped cells reduced the lead time to two or three days.

# Avoidance of Shutdown and Process Reliability: The JIT Approach

Most shutdowns occur for one of three reasons: machine failure, defective material or subassembly, or unavailability of a raw material or subassembly. Holding inventories is one traditional solution to all three problems. Those espousing the JIT approach claim that inventories do not solve the problems but cover up or hide them. JIT proponents use the analogy of rocks in a lake. The rocks represent the three problems, and the water represents inventories. If the lake is deep (that is, if inventories are high), then the rocks are never exposed, and managers can pretend that they do not exist. Once inventories are reduced to zero, the rocks are exposed and can no longer be ignored. JIT solves the three problems by emphasizing total preventive maintenance and total quality control and by building the right kind of relationship with suppliers.

### Total Preventive Maintenance

**total preventive maintenance**

A program of preventive maintenance that has zero machine failures as its standard.

Zero machine failures is the goal of **total preventive maintenance**. By paying more attention to preventive maintenance, a company can avoid most machine breakdowns. This objective is easier to attain in a JIT environment because of the interdisciplinary labour philosophy. It is not uncommon for a cell worker to be trained to maintain the machines he or she operates. Because of the pull-through nature of JIT, it is also not unusual for a cell worker to have idle manufacturing time. Some of this time can be used productively by having the cell workers involved in preventive maintenance.

### Total Quality Control

The problem of defective parts is solved by striving for zero defects. Because JIT manufacturing does not rely on inventories to replace defective parts or materials, the emphasis on quality for both internally produced and externally purchased materials increases significantly. Decreasing defective parts also diminishes the justification for holding inventories due to unreliable processes.

### The Kanban System

**Kanban system**

An information system that controls production on a demand-pull basis through the use of cards or markers.

To ensure that parts or materials are available when needed, the **Kanban system** is employed. This information system controls production through the use of markers or cards.

The cards or markers used in a Kanban system are plastic, cardboard, or metal plates measuring 10 centimetres by 20 centimetres. The Kanban card is usually placed in a vinyl sack and attached to the part or a container holding the needed parts.

A basic Kanban system uses three cards: a withdrawal Kanban, a production Kanban, and a vendor Kanban. The first two control the movement of work among the manufacturing processes, while the third controls the movement of parts between the processes and outside suppliers.

**withdrawal Kanban**

A marker or card that specifies the quantity that a subsequent process should withdraw from a preceding process.

**production Kanban**

A card or marker that specifies the quantity that the Kanban system should produce.

**vendor Kanbans**

Cards or markers that signal to a supplier the quantity of materials that need to be delivered and the time of delivery.

- A **withdrawal Kanban** specifies the quantity that a subsequent process should withdraw from the preceding process.
- A **production Kanban** specifies the quantity that the preceding process should produce.
- **Vendor Kanbans** are used to notify suppliers to deliver more parts; they also specify when the parts are needed.

The three Kanbans are illustrated in Exhibits 12–3, 12–4, and 12–5.

We can illustrate how Kanban cards are used to control the work flow with a simple example. Assume that two processes are needed to manufacture a product. The first process (CB Assembly) builds and tests printed circuit boards (using a U-shaped manufacturing cell). The second process (Final Assembly) puts eight circuit boards into a subassembly purchased from an outside supplier. The final product is a personal computer.

Exhibit 12–6 provides the plant layout corresponding to the manufacture of the personal computers. Refer to this exhibit as the steps involved in using Kanbans are outlined.

Consider first the movement of work between the two processing areas. Assume that eight circuit boards are placed in a container and that one such container is located in the CB stores area. Attached to this container is a production Kanban (P-Kanban). A second container with eight circuit boards is located near

**EXHIBIT 12-3**

Withdrawal Kanban

| Item No. | 15670T07 | Preceding Process |
| --- | --- | --- |
| Item Name | Circuit Board | CB Assembly |
| Computer Type | TR6547 PC | |
| Box Capacity | 8 | Subsequent Process |
| Box Type | C | Final Assembly |

**EXHIBIT 12-4**

Production Kanban

| Item No. | 15670T07 | Process |
| --- | --- | --- |
| Item Name | Circuit Board | CB Assembly |
| Computer Type | TR6547 PC | |
| Box Capacity | 8 | |
| Box Type | C | |

EXHIBIT **12-5**

Vendor Kanban

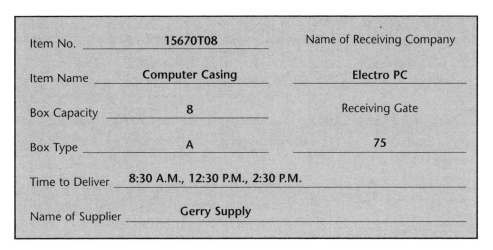

| | |
|---|---|
| Item No. **15670T08** | Name of Receiving Company |
| Item Name **Computer Casing** | **Electro PC** |
| Box Capacity **8** | Receiving Gate |
| Box Type **A** | **75** |
| Time to Deliver **8:30 A.M., 12:30 P.M., 2:30 P.M.** | |
| Name of Supplier **Gerry Supply** | |

EXHIBIT **12-6**

Kanban Process

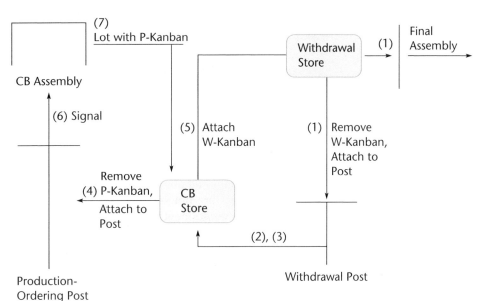

the Final Assembly line (the withdrawal store) with a withdrawal Kanban (W-Kanban). Now assume that the production schedule calls for the immediate assembly of a computer.

The Kanban setups can be described as follows:

1. A worker from the Final Assembly line goes to the withdrawal store, removes the eight circuit boards, and places them into production. The worker also removes the withdrawal Kanban and places it on the withdrawal post.
2. The withdrawal Kanban on the post signals that the Final Assembly unit needs an additional eight circuit boards.
3. A worker from Final Assembly (or a material handler called a carrier) removes the withdrawal Kanban from the post and carries it to CB stores.
4. At the CB stores area, the carrier removes the production Kanban from the container of eight circuit boards and places it on the production-ordering post.
5. The carrier next attaches the withdrawal Kanban to the container of parts and carries the container back to the Final Assembly area. Assembly of the next computer can begin.
6. The production Kanban on the production-ordering post signals the workers of the CB Assembly to begin producing another lot of circuit boards. The production Kanban is removed and accompanies the units as they are produced.

7. When the lot of eight circuit boards is completed, the units are placed in a container in the CB stores area with the production Kanban attached. The cycle is then repeated.

The use of Kanbans ensures that the subsequent process (Final Assembly) withdraws the circuit boards from the preceding process (CB Assembly) in the necessary quantity at the appropriate time. The Kanban system also controls the preceding process by allowing it to produce only the quantities withdrawn by the subsequent process. In this way, inventories are kept at a minimum, and the components arrive just in time to be used.

Essentially, the same steps are followed for a purchased subassembly. The only difference is the use of a vendor Kanban in place of a production Kanban. A vendor Kanban on a vendor post signals to the supplier that another order is needed. As with the circuit boards, the subassemblies must be delivered just in time for use. A JIT purchasing system requires the supplier to deliver small quantities on a frequent basis. These deliveries could be weekly, daily, or even several times a day. This system calls for a close working relationship with suppliers. Long-term contractual agreements tend to ensure supply of materials.

## Discounts and Price Increases: JIT Purchasing versus Holding Inventories

Traditionally, inventories are carried so that a company can take advantage of quantity discounts and hedge against future price increases of the items purchased. The objective is to lower the cost of inventory. The JIT solution is to negotiate long-term contracts with a few chosen suppliers located as close to the production facility as possible and to establish more extensive supplier involvement. Suppliers are not selected on the basis of price alone. Performance—the quality of the component and the supplier's ability to deliver as needed—and commitment to JIT purchasing are vital considerations. Other benefits of long-term contracts exist. They stipulate prices and acceptable quality levels. Long-term contracts also dramatically reduce the number of orders placed, which helps drive down the ordering cost.

## JIT's Limitations

JIT is not an approach that can simply be purchased and plugged in with immediate results. Its implementation should be more of an evolutionary process than a revolutionary process. Patience is needed. JIT is often referred to as a program of simplification—yet this does not imply that it is simple or easy to implement. Time is required, for example, to build sound relationships with suppliers. Insisting on immediate changes in delivery times and quality may not be realistic and may cause confrontations between a company and its suppliers. Partnership, not coercion, should be the basis of supplier relationships. To achieve the benefits that are associated with JIT purchasing, a company may be tempted to unilaterally redefine its supplier relationships. Unilaterally redefining supplier relationships by extracting concessions and dictating terms may create supplier resentment and may actually cause suppliers to retaliate. In the long run, suppliers may seek new markets, find ways to charge higher prices than those that would exist with a preferred supplier arrangement, or seek regulatory relief. These actions may destroy many of the JIT benefits extracted by the impatient company.

Workers also may be affected by JIT. Sharp reductions in inventory buffers may cause a regimented work flow and high levels of stress among production workers. A deliberate pace of inventory reduction may be required to allow workers to develop a sense of autonomy and to encourage their participation in broader improvement efforts. Forced and dramatic reductions in inventories may indeed reduce costs—but it may also cause problems: lost sales and stressed workers. If the workers perceive JIT as a way of simply squeezing more out of them, then JIT efforts may be doomed. Implementing JIT is not easy, and it requires careful and thorough planning and preparation. Companies should expect some struggle and frustration.

The most glaring deficiency of JIT is the absence of inventory to buffer production interruptions. Current sales are constantly being threatened by an unexpected interruption in production. In fact, if a problem occurs, JIT's approach consists of trying to find and solve the problem before any further production activity occurs. Retailers who use JIT tactics also face the possibility of shortages (JIT retailers order what they need now, not what they expect to sell; the idea is to flow goods through the channel as late as possible, keeping inventories low and decreasing the need for markdowns). If demand increases well beyond the retailer's supply of inventory, the retailer may be unable to make order adjustments quickly enough to avoid lost sales and irritated customers. Yet despite the downside, retailers seem to be strongly committed to JIT. Apparently, losing sales on surprise hits is less costly than carrying high levels of inventory.

The JIT manufacturing company is also willing to place current sales at risk to achieve assurance of future sales. This assurance comes from higher quality, faster response time, and lower operating costs. Even so, we must recognize that a sale lost today is a sale lost forever. Installing a JIT system so that it operates with very little interruption is not a short-run project. Thus, permanent loss of sales is a real cost of installing a JIT system.

An alternative and perhaps complementary approach is the theory of constraints (TOC). In principle, TOC can be used in conjunction with JIT manufacturing; after all, JIT manufacturing environments also have constraints. Furthermore, the TOC approach has the very appealing quality of protecting current sales while also striving to increase future sales by increasing quality, lowering response time, and decreasing operating costs.

# Theory of Constraints

**Objective 3**

Describe the theory of constraints and explain how it can be used to manage inventory.

Every company faces limited resources and limited demand for each product. These limitations are called *constraints*. The theory of constraints recognizes that the performance of any organization is limited by its constraints. The theory of constraints then develops a specific approach to managing constraints in a way that supports the objective of continuous improvement. According to TOC, if performance is to be improved, an organization must identify its constraints, exploit the constraints in the short run, and, in the longer term, find ways to overcome the constraints.

## Basic Concepts

TOC focuses on three measures of organizational performance: *throughput, inventory,* and *operating expenses.*

**throughput**

The rate at which an organization generates money through sales.

- **Throughput** is the rate at which an organization generates money through sales.[8] In operational terms, throughput is the difference between sales revenue and unit-level variable costs such as materials and power. Direct labour is typ-

---

8. This follows the definition offered by Eliyahu M. Goldratt and Robert E. Fox in *The Race* (see footnote 3, p. 532). Other definitions and basic concepts of the theory of constraints are also based on the developments of Goldratt and Fox.

**inventory**

The money an organization spends in turning raw materials into throughput.

**operating expenses**

The money an organization spends in turning inventories into throughput.

ically viewed as a fixed unit-level expense and is not usually included in the definition. With this understanding, throughput corresponds to contribution margin.

- **Inventory** is all the money the organization spends in turning raw materials into throughput.
- **Operating expenses** are defined as all the money the organization spends in turning inventories into throughput.

Based on these three measures, management's objectives can be expressed as increasing throughput, minimizing inventory, and decreasing operating expenses.

If these objectives are achieved, financial measures of performance will be affected: net income and return on investment will increase, and cash flow will improve. Increasing throughput and decreasing operating expenses have always been emphasized as key elements in improving these three financial measures of performance. However the role of minimizing inventory in achieving these improvements has been traditionally regarded as less important.

TOC recognizes that lowering inventory decreases carrying costs—and therefore decreases operating expenses and improves net income. TOC, however, argues that lowering inventory helps produce a competitive edge through better products, lower prices, and faster response to customer needs.

### Better Products

Better products mean higher quality. It also means that the company is able to improve products and provide these improved products quickly to the market. The relationship between low inventories and quality has been described in the JIT section. Essentially, low inventories allow defects to be detected more quickly and the cause of the problem to be assessed. Improving products is also a key competitive element. New or improved products need to reach the market quickly—before competitors can provide similar features. This goal is facilitated with low inventories. Low inventories allow new product changes to be introduced more quickly because the company has fewer old products (in stock or in process) that would need to be scrapped or sold before the new product is introduced.

### Lower Prices

High inventories mean that more productive capacity is needed, thus more investment in equipment and space. Since lead time and high work-in-process inventories are usually correlated, high inventories may often be the cause of overtime. Overtime, of course, increases operating expenses and lowers profitability. Lower inventories reduce carrying costs, per-unit investment costs, and other operating expenses such as overtime and special shipping charges. Lowering investment and operating costs increases the unit margin of each product, providing more flexibility in pricing decisions. Lower prices are possible (or higher product margins occur) due to these cost decreases.

### Responsiveness

Delivering goods on time and producing goods with shorter lead times than the market dictates are important competitive tools. Delivering goods on time is related to a company's ability to forecast the time required to produce and deliver goods. High inventories may obscure the actual time required to produce and fill an order. Lower inventories allow actual lead times to be more carefully observed, and more accurate delivery dates can then be provided. Shortening lead times is also crucial in gaining a competitive advantage. Shortening lead times is equivalent to lowering work-in-process inventories. A company carrying

10 days of work-in-process inventories has an average production lead time of 10 days. If the company can reduce lead time from 10 days to 5 days, then the company should now be carrying only 5 days' worth of work-in-process inventories.

As lead times are reduced, it is also possible to reduce finished goods inventories. For example, if a product's lead time is 10 days and the market requires delivery on demand, then the company must carry, on average, 10 days of finished goods inventory (plus some safety stock to cover demand uncertainty). Suppose that the company is able to reduce lead time to 5 days. In this case, finished goods inventory should also be reduced to 5 days. Thus, the levels of inventories signal the organization's ability to respond. High levels relative to those of competitors translate into a competitive disadvantage.

## TOC Steps

The theory of constraints uses five steps to achieve its goal of improving organizational performance:

1. Identify the organization's constraint(s).
2. Exploit the binding constraint(s).
3. Subordinate everything else to the decisions made in Step 2.
4. Elevate the binding constraint(s).
5. Repeat the process.

### Step 1: Identify the Organization's Constraint(s)

**external constraints**

Limiting factors imposed on the firm from external sources (such as market demand).

**internal constraints**

Limiting factors found within the firm (such as machine time availability).

**loose constraints**

Constraints whose limited resources are not fully used by a product mix.

**binding constraints**

Constraints whose resources are fully utilized.

Constraints can be classified as *external* or *internal*. **External constraints** are limiting factors imposed on the company from external sources (such as market demand). **Internal constraints** are limiting factors found within the company (such as machine-time availability). Although resources and demands may be limited, some product mixes may not meet all the demand or use all of the available resources. Constraints whose limited resources are not fully used are **loose constraints**. **Binding constraints** are those constraints whose available resources are fully utilized.

In Step 1 of the TOC process, then, internal and external constraints are identified. The optimal product mix is identified as the mix that maximizes throughput subject to all the organization's constraints. The optimal mix reveals how much of each constrained resource is used and which of the organization's constraints are binding.

Decisions about product mix can have a significant impact on an organization's profitability. Each mix represents an alternative that carries with it an associated profit level. A manager should choose the alternative that maximizes total profits. The usual approach is to assume that only unit-based variable costs are relevant to the product-mix decision. Thus, assuming that nonunit-level costs are the same for different mixes of products, the optimal mix is the one that maximizes total contribution margin.

Assume, for example, that Confer Company produces two types of machine parts: X and Y, with unit contribution margins of $300 and $600, respectively. Assuming that Confer can sell all that is produced, some may argue that only Part Y should be produced and sold, because it has the larger contribution margin. However, this solution is not necessarily the best. The selection of the optimal mix can be significantly affected by the relationships of the constrained resources to the individual products. These relationships affect the quantity of each product that can be produced and, consequently, the total contribution margin that can be earned. This point is illustrated by looking at a situation where there is one binding internal resource constraint.

### One Binding Internal Constraint

Assume that each part must be drilled by a special machine. The company owns machines which provide 120 drilling hours per week. Part X requires 1 hour of drilling, and Part Y requires 3 hours of drilling. Assuming no other binding constraints, what is the optimal mix of parts? Since each unit of X requires 1 hour of drilling, 120 units of X can be produced per week (120/1). At $300 per unit, Confer can earn a total contribution margin of $36,000 per week. On the other hand, Y requires 3 hours of drilling per unit; therefore, 40 (120/3) parts can be produced. At $600 per unit, the total contribution margin is $24,000 per week. Producing only X yields a higher profit level than producing only Y—even though the unit contribution margin for Y is two times larger than that for X.

The contribution margin per unit of each product is not the critical concern. The contribution margin per unit of *scarce resource* is the deciding factor. The product yielding the highest contribution margin per drilling hour should be selected. Part X earns $300 per machine hour ($300/1), while Part Y earns only $200 per machine hour ($600/3). Thus, the optimal mix is 120 units of Part X and none of Part Y, producing a total contribution margin of $36,000 per week. Notice that since this product mix uses up all 120 machine hours, the machine-hour constraint is binding.

### Internal Binding Constraint and External Binding Constraint

The contribution margin per unit of scarce resource can also be used to identify the optimal product mix when an external binding constraint exists. For example, assume the same internal constraint of 120 drilling hours, but also assume that Confer can sell at most 30 units of Part X and 100 units of Part Y. The internal constraint allows Confer to produce 120 units of Part X, but this is no longer a feasible choice, because only 30 units of X can be sold. Thus, we now have a binding external constraint, one that affects the earlier decision to produce and sell only Part X. Since the contribution per unit of scarce resource (machine hour) is $300 for Part X and $200 for Part Y, it still makes sense to produce as much of X as possible before producing any of Y. Confer should first produce 30 units of X, using 30 machine hours. This leaves 90 machine hours, allowing the production of 30 units of Y. The optimal mix is now 30 units of X and 30 units of Y, producing a total contribution margin of $27,000 per week ($300 × 30 + $600 × 30).

### Step 2: Exploit the Binding Constraint(s)

One way to make the best use of binding constraints is to ensure that the optimal product mix is produced. Making the best use of binding constraints, however, is more extensive than simply ensuring production of the optimal mix. This step is the heart of TOC's philosophy of short-run constraint management and is directly related to TOC's goal of reducing inventories and improving performance.

In most organizations, there are only a few binding resource constraints. The major binding constraint is defined as the **drummer**. Assume, for example, that there is only one internal binding constraint. By default, this constraint becomes the drummer. The drummer constraint's production rate sets the production rate for the entire plant. Downstream processes fed by the drummer constraint are naturally forced to follow its rate of production. Scheduling for downstream processes is easy. Once a part is finished at the drummer process, the next process begins its operation. Similarly, each subsequent operation begins when the prior operation is finished. Upstream processes that feed the drummer constraint are scheduled to produce at the same rate as the drummer constraint. Scheduling at the drummer rate prevents the production of excessive upstream work-in-process inventories.

For upstream scheduling, there are two additional features that TOC uses in managing constraints to lower inventory levels and improve organizational per-

**drummer**

The major binding contraint in an organization.

**time buffer**

The inventory needed to keep the constrained resource busy for a specified time interval.

formance: buffers and ropes. First, an inventory buffer is established in front of the major binding constraint. The inventory buffer is referred to as the **time buffer**. A time buffer is the inventory needed to keep the constrained resource busy for a specified time interval. The purpose of a time buffer is to protect the organization's throughput from any disruption that can be overcome within the specified time interval. For example, if it takes one day to overcome most interruptions that occur upstream from the drummer constraint, then a two-day buffer should be sufficient to protect throughput from any interruptions. Thus, in scheduling, the operation immediately preceding the drummer constraint should produce the parts needed by the drummer resource two days in advance of their planned usage. Any other preceding operations are scheduled backward in time to produce so that their parts arrive just in time for subsequent operations.

**ropes**

Actions taken to tie the rate at which raw material is released into the plant (at the first operation) to the production rate of the constrained resource.

**Ropes** are actions taken to tie the rate at which raw material is released into the plant (at the first operation) to the production rate of the constrained resource. The objective of a rope is to ensure that the work-in-process inventory will not exceed the level needed for the time buffer. Thus, the drummer rate is used to limit the rate of raw material release and effectively controls the rate at which the first operation produces. The rate of the first operation then controls the rates of subsequent operations. The TOC inventory system is often called the **Drum–Buffer–Rope (DBR) System**. Exhibit 12–7 illustrates the DBR structure for a general setting.

**Drum–Buffer–Rope (DBR) system**

The TOC (theory of constraints) inventory management system that relies on the drum beat of the major constrained resources, time buffers, and ropes to determine inventory levels.

The Confer Company example can be expanded to provide a specific illustration of the DBR system. Assume that there are three sequential processes: grinding, drilling, and polishing. Each of these processes has a limited amount of resources. Demand for each type of machine part produced is also limited (30 for Part X and 100 for Part Y, as indicated earlier). Assume that the only internal binding constraint is drilling and that the optimal product mix consists of 30 units of Part X and 30 units of Part Y (per week). This is the most that the drilling process can handle. The other two processes represent loose constraints and are therefore capable of producing more per week of each part than the optimal mix calls for. Since the drilling process feeds the polishing process, we can define the drilling constraint as the drummer for the plant. Assume that the demand for each part is uniformly spread out over the week. This means that the production rate should be 6 per day of each part (for a 5-day workweek). A 2-day time buffer would require 24 completed parts from the grinding process: 12 for Part X and 12 for Part Y. To ensure that the time buffer does not increase at a rate greater than 6 per day for each part, raw materials should be released to the grinding process in such a way that only 6 of each part can be produced each day (this is the rope—tying the release of materials to the production rate of the drummer constraint). Exhibit 12–8 summarizes the specific DBR details for the Confer Company.

### Step 3: Subordinate Everything Else to the Decisions Made in Step 2

The drummer constraint essentially sets the capacity for the entire plant. All remaining departments should be subordinated to the needs of the drummer constraint. This principle requires many companies to change the way they view things. For example, the use of efficiency measures at the departmental level may no longer be appropriate. Consider the Confer Company once again. Encouraging maximum productive efficiency for the grinding department would produce excess work-in-process inventories. For example, assume that the capacity of the grinding department is 80 units per week. Assuming that the two-day buffer is in place, we soon find out that if it worked at capacity, the grinding department would add 20 units per week to the buffer in front of the drilling department. Over a period of a year, the potential exists for building very large work-in-process inventories (1,000 units of the two parts would be added to the buffer over a 50-week period). Polishing, of course, must produce at the rate of

EXHIBIT   12-7

Drum–Buffer–Rope
System; General
Description

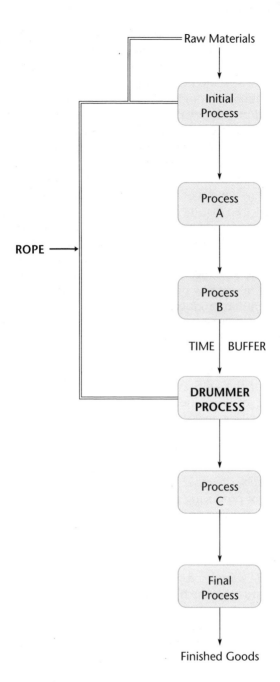

drilling, because it follows drilling in the sequential production process. Thus, the
only concern for polishing is that it can handle the output of drilling.

### Step 4: Elevate the Binding Constraint(s)

Once actions have been taken to make the best possible use of the existing constraints, the next step is to embark on a program of continuous improvement by
reducing the limitations that the binding constraint(s) place on the organization's
performance. Suppose, for example, that Confer Company adds a half shift for
the drilling department, increasing the drilling hours from 120 to 180 per week.
With 60 additional drilling hours, Confer can increase production of Part Y from
30 to 50 units, an additional 20 units per week (recall that Part Y uses 3 hours per
unit, yielding the 20 additional units (60/3)). Since Part Y has a unit contribution
margin of $600, this will increase throughput by $12,000 per week ($600 × 20),

Drum–Buffer–Rope:
Confer Company

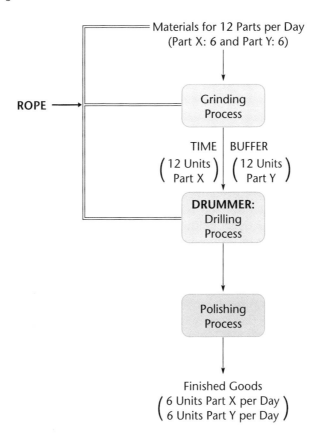

assuming that grinding and polishing can handle an increase of 20 units of Y per week. We know, for example, that grinding has 80 hours per week available and that X and Y each use 1 hour of grinding. Currently, 60 hours are being used. An increase of 20 units is possible.

Now assume that polishing has 160 hours available and that Part X uses 2 hours per unit and Part Y 1 hour per unit. For the current product mix (30 of X and 30 of Y), 90 hours are being used. To increase production of Y by 20 units, 20 more hours are needed—certainly possible. Thus, moving from a mix of 30 units of X and 30 units of Y to a mix of 30 of X and 50 of Y is possible. Is the half shift worth it? This question is answered by comparing the cost of adding the half shift with the increased throughput of $12,000 per week. If the cost of adding the half shift is $50 per hour, then the incremental cost is $3,000 per week, and the decision to add the half shift is a good one.

### Step 5: Repeat the Process

Eventually, the drilling resource constraint will be elevated to a point where the constraint is no longer binding. Suppose, for example, that the company adds a full shift for the drilling operation, increasing the resource availability to 240 hours. Both the drilling and polishing constraints are capable of producing more of Part Y, but the grinding process cannot (grinding can produce a maximum of 80 units per week of any combination of X and Y). Thus, the new drummer constraint is grinding. Once the new drummer constraint is identified, then the TOC process is repeated. The objective is to continually improve performance by managing constraints.

# Summary of Learning Objectives

## 1. Describe the traditional inventory management model.

The traditional approach uses inventories to manage the tradeoffs between ordering (setup) costs and carrying costs. The optimal tradeoff defines the economic order quantity. Traditional reasons for holding inventories include: due-date performance, avoiding shutdowns (protecting sales), hedging against future price increases, and taking advantage of discounts. JIT and TOC, on the other hand, argue that inventories are costly and are used to cover up fundamental problems that need to be corrected so that the organization can become more competitive.

## 2. Describe JIT inventory management.

JIT uses long-term contracts, continuous replenishment, and EDI to reduce or even eliminate ordering costs. Engineering efforts are made to reduce setup times drastically. Once ordering costs and setup costs are reduced to minimal levels, it becomes possible to reduce carrying costs by reducing inventory levels. JIT carries small buffers in front of each operation and uses a Kanban system to regulate production. Production is tied to market demand. If an interrup-

tion occurs, throughput tends to be lost because of the small buffers. Yet future throughput tends to increase, because efforts are being made to improve such things as quality, productivity, and lead time.

## 3. Describe the theory of constraints and explain how it can be used to manage inventory.

TOC identifies an organization's constraints and exploits them so that throughput is maximized, and inventories and operating costs are minimized. Identifying the optimal product mix is part of this process. The major binding constraint is identified and is used to set the plant's productive rate. Release of raw materials into the first process (operation) is regulated by the drummer constraint. A time buffer is located in front of critical constraints. This time buffer is sized so that it protects throughput from any interruptions. As in JIT, the interruptions are used to locate and correct the problem. However, unlike JIT, the time buffer serves to protect throughput. Furthermore, because buffers are located only in front of critical constraints, TOC may actually produce smaller inventories than JIT.

# Key Terms

Binding constraints 541
Carrying costs 528
Continuous replenishment 534
Drum–Buffer–Rope (DBR)
  System 543
Drummer 542
Economic order quantity (EOQ) 529
Electronic data interchange (EDI) 534
External constraints 541

Internal constraints 541
Inventory 540
Kanban system 535
Lead time 530
Loose constraints 541
Operating expenses 540
Ordering costs 527
Production Kanban 536
Reorder point 530

Ropes 543
Safety stock 530
Setup costs 528
Stock-out costs 528
Throughput 539
Time buffer 543
Total preventive maintenance 535
Vendor Kanban 536
Withdrawal Kanban 536

## Review Problems

### I. INVENTORY COSTS; EOQ; REORDER POINT

A local TV repair shop uses 36,000 units of a part each year (an average of 100 units per working day). It costs $20 to place and receive an order. The shop orders in lots of 400 units. It cost $4 to carry one unit per year in inventory.

**Required:**

1. Calculate the total annual ordering cost.
2. Calculate the total annual carrying cost.
3. Calculate the total annual inventory cost.
4. Calculate the EOQ.
5. Calculate the total annual inventory cost using the EOQ inventory policy.
6. How much is saved per year using the EOQ versus an order size of 400 units?
7. Compute the reorder point, assuming that the lead time is three days.
8. Suppose that the usage of the part can be as much as 110 units per day. Calculate the safety stock and the new reorder point.

### Solution

1. Total annual ordering cost:

$$
\begin{aligned}
\text{Ordering cost} &= PD/Q \\
&= \$20 \times 36{,}000/400 \\
&= \$1{,}800
\end{aligned}
$$

2. Total annual carrying cost:

$$
\begin{aligned}
\text{Carrying cost} &= CQ/2 \\
&= \$4 \times 400/2 \\
&= \$800
\end{aligned}
$$

3. Total cost:

$$
\begin{aligned}
\text{Total cost} &= \text{Ordering cost} + \text{Carrying cost} \\
&= \$1{,}800 + \$800 \\
&= \$2{,}600
\end{aligned}
$$

4. EOQ:

$$
\begin{aligned}
\text{EOQ} &= \sqrt{2PD/C} \\
&= \sqrt{(2 \times 20 \times 36{,}000/4)} \\
&= \sqrt{360{,}000} \\
&= 600
\end{aligned}
$$

5. Total cost (with EOQ):

$$
\begin{aligned}
\text{Total cost} &= (PD/Q) + (CQ/2) \\
&= (\$20 \times 36{,}000/600) + (\$4 \times 600/2) \\
&= \$1{,}200 + \$1{,}200 \\
&= \$2{,}400
\end{aligned}
$$

6. Savings:

$$
\$2{,}600 - \$2{,}400 = \$200
$$

7. Reorder point:

$$\text{Reorder point} = \text{Average rate of usage} \times \text{Lead time}$$
$$= 100 \times 3$$
$$= 300 \text{ units}$$

8. Reorder point (with safety stock):

$$\text{Safety stock} = (\text{Maximum usage} - \text{Average usage}) \times \text{Lead time}$$
$$= (110 - 100) \times 3$$
$$= 30 \text{ units}$$
$$\text{Reorder point} = 300 + 30$$
$$= 330 \text{ units (or } 110 \times 3 = 330 \text{ units)}$$

## II. OPTIMAL MIX

Two types of gears are produced: A and B. Gear A has a unit contribution margin of $200, and Gear B has a unit contribution margin of $400. Gear A uses 2 hours of grinding time, and Gear B uses 5 hours of grinding time. There are 200 hours of grinding time available per week. This is the only constraint.

**Required:**
1. Is the grinding constraint an internal constraint or an external constraint?
2. Determine the optimal product mix. What is the total contribution margin?
3. Suppose that there is an additional demand constraint: market conditions will allow the sale of only 80 units of each gear. Now what is the optimal product mix? the total contribution margin?

### Solution

1. The grinding constraint is an internal constraint.

2. Optimal mix (one constraint):

    Gear A: $200/2 = $100 per grinding hour

    Gear B: $400/5 = $80 per grinding hour

    Since Gear A earns more contribution margin per unit of scarce resource than Gear B does, only Gear A should be produced and sold (based on the fact that the company can sell all it wants of either product).

    Optimal product mix: Gear A: 100 units (200/2); Gear B: 0 units

    Total contribution margin = $200 \times 100 + $400 \times 0 = $20,000 per week

3. Optimal mix (two constraints):
    The company should produce and sell 80 units of Gear A using 160 hours $(80 \times 2)$ and 8 units of Gear B $[(200 - 160)/5]$.

    The total contribution margin = $200 \times 80 + $400 \times 8 = $19,200 per week.

## III. DRUMMERS AND INVENTORY MANAGEMENT SYSTEMS

Traditional and JIT inventory management systems also have drummers—factors that determine the plant's production rate. For a traditional just-in-case system, the drummer is the excess capacity of the first operation. For JIT, the drummer is market demand.

**Required:**
1. Explain why the drummer of a just-in-case system is identified as the excess capacity of the first operation.
2. Explain how market demand drives the JIT production system.
3. Explain how a drummer constraint is used in the TOC approach to inventory management.

4. What are the advantages and disadvantages of the three types of drummers?

## Solution

1. In a traditional inventory system, local efficiency measures encourage the manager of the first operation to keep the department's workers busy. Raw materials are therefore released to satisfy this objective. This practice is justified because the inventory may be needed just in case the demand is greater than expected, or just in case the first operation has downtime or other problems.

2. In a JIT system, when the final operation delivers its goods to a customer, a backward-rippling effect triggers the release of raw materials into the factory. First, the last process removes the buffer inventory from the withdrawal store; this leads to a P-Kanban being placed on the production post of the preceding operation. That operation then begins production, withdrawing the parts that it needs from its withdrawal store, leading to a P-Kanban being placed on the production post of its preceding operation. This process repeats itself all the way back to the first operation.

3. A drummer constraint sets the factory's production rate to match its own production rate. This is automatically true for operations that succeed the drummer constraint. For preceding operations, the rate is controlled by tying the drummer constraint's production rate to that of the first operation. A time buffer is also set in front of the drummer constraint to protect throughput in the event of interruptions.

4. The excess capacity drummer will typically build excess inventories. This serves to protect current throughput. However, it ties up a lot of capital and tends to cover up problems such as poor quality, bad delivery performance, and inefficient production. Because it is costly and covers up certain critical production problems, the just-in-case approach may threaten future throughput by damaging a company's competitive position. JIT reduces inventories dramatically—using only small buffers in front of each operation as a means of regulating production flow and signalling when production should occur. JIT has the significant advantage of uncovering problems and eventually correcting them. However, discovering problems usually means that current throughput will be lost while the problems are being corrected. Future throughput tends to be protected, however, because the company is taking actions to improve its operations. TOC uses time buffers in front of the critical constraints. These buffers are large enough to keep the critical constraints operating while other operations may be down. Once the problem is corrected, the other resource constraints usually have sufficient excess capacity to catch up. Thus, current throughput is protected. Furthermore, future throughput is also protected, because TOC uses the same approach as JIT— namely, uncovering and correcting problems. TOC can be viewed as an improvement on JIT methods—correcting the lost-throughput problem while maintaining the other JIT features.

## Questions for Writing and Discussion

1.  What are ordering costs? Provide examples.

2.  What are setup costs? Illustrate with examples.

3.  What are carrying costs? Illustrate with examples.

4.  What are stock-out costs?

5.  Explain why, in the traditional view of inventory, carrying costs increase as ordering costs decrease.

6.  Discuss the traditional reasons for carrying inventory.

7.  What is the economic order quantity?

8.  Suppose that a raw material has a lead time of three days and that the average usage of the material is 12 units per day. What is the reorder point? If the maximum usage is 15 units per day, what is the safety stock?

9.  Explain how safety stock is used to deal with demand uncertainty.

10. What approach does JIT take to minimize total inventory costs?

11. Explain how long-term contractual relationships with suppliers can reduce the acquisition cost of raw materials.

12. What is EDI, and what relationship does it have to continuous replenishment?

13. One reason for inventory is to prevent shutdowns. How does the JIT approach to inventory management deal with this potential problem?

14. Explain how the Kanban system helps reduce inventories.

15. What is a constraint? an internal constraint? an external constraint?

16. What are loose constraints? binding constraints?

17. Define and discuss the three measures of organizational performance used by the theory of constraints.

18. Explain how lowering inventory produces better products, lower prices, and better responsiveness to customer needs.

19. What are the five steps that TOC uses to improve organizational performance?

20. What is a Drum–Buffer–Rope System?

## Exercises

**12–1**

*Ordering and Carrying Costs*

**LO1**

Snowgo Company uses 48,000 carburetors each year in its production of snowmobile engines. The cost of placing an order is $250. The cost of holding one unit of inventory for one year is $6. Currently, Snowgo places twelve orders of 4,000 carburetors each year.

**Required:**
1.  Compute the annual ordering cost.
2.  Compute the annual carrying cost.
3.  Compute the cost of Snowgo's current inventory policy.

**12–2**

Refer to the data in 12–1.

**Required:**
1. Compute the economic order quantity.
2. Compute the ordering cost and the carrying cost for the EOQ.
3. How much money does using the EOQ policy save the company over the policy of purchasing 4,000 carburetors per order?

**12–3**

Spreadsheet

Quito Mining Company uses 720,000 litres of sulphuric acid each year. The cost of placing an order is $5, and the carrying cost for 1 litre of acid is $0.05.

**Required:**
1. Compute the economic order quantity for sulphuric acid.
2. Compute the carrying cost and the ordering cost for the EOQ.

**12–4**

Spreadsheet

Grof Company manufactures radios. One part that it orders from an outside supplier is a potentiometer. Information pertaining to the potentiometer is as follows:

| | |
|---|---|
| Economic order quantity | 180,000 units |
| Average daily usage | 12,000 units |
| Maximum daily usage | 18,000 units |
| Lead time | 4 days |

**Required:**
1. What is the reorder point, assuming that no safety stock is carried?
2. What is the reorder point, assuming that safety stock is carried?

**12–5**

Power Manufacturing produces two different types of engines: one for riding lawn mowers and one for jet skis. In order to produce the different engines, equipment must be set up. Each setup configuration corresponds to a particular type of engine. The setup cost per batch of lawn mower engines is $2,000; the setup cost for the jet-ski engines is $2,400 per batch. The cost of carrying lawn mower engines in inventory is $2 per engine per year; for jet-ski engines, this cost is $3 per engine per year. During the coming year, the company expects to produce 162,000 lawn mower engines and 250,000 jet-ski engines. The company hopes to sell an average of 648 lawn mower engines per workday and an average of 500 jet-ski engines per workday. It takes Power two days to set up the equipment for production of either engine. Once the equipment is set up, Power can produce 2,000 engines per workday. There are 250 workdays available per year. The lead time is 11 days for lawn mower engines and 12 days for jet-ski engines.

**Required:**
1. Compute the number of lawn mower engines that should be produced per setup to minimize total setup and carrying costs for this product.
2. Compute the total setup and carrying costs associated with the economic order quantity for lawn mower engines.
3. What is the reorder point for lawn mower engines?
4. Repeat Requirements 1 through 3 for jet-ski engines.
5. Using the economic order batch size, find out whether it is possible for Power to produce the amount that can be sold of each engine. Does scheduling have a role here? Explain. Is this a push- or pull-system approach to inventory management? Explain.

**12–6**

EOQ; Setup Cost; Setup Time

LO1, LO2

Refer to 12–5. Suppose that Power was able to reduce the setup time from 2 days to 0.5 days and that, as a consequence, setup cost are reduced to 25 percent of their current level (for both products). Engineering predicts that within one year, setup time and costs can be further reduced (0.5 days to 0.05 days, and costs to $100).

**Required:**

1. Calculate the EOQ for lawn mower engines for the new setup time (0.5 days). Repeat for the projected setup time and costs.
2. Is reducing the setup time to 0.05 days (and setup costs to $100) associated with JIT? How?

**12–7**

Safety Stock

LO1

Pinegar Manufacturing produces a component used in its production of cell phones. The time required to set up and produce a batch of the components is six days. The average daily usage is 750 components, and the maximum daily usage is 875 components.

**Required:**

Compute the reorder point, assuming that Pinegar carries safety stock. How much safety stock does the company carry?

**12–8**

Reasons for Carrying Inventory

LO1, LO2, LO3

The following reasons have been offered for holding inventories:

a. To satisfy customer demand (for example, to meet delivery dates).
b. To avoid shutting down manufacturing facilities because of
   (i)   machine failure,
   (ii)  defective parts,
   (iii) unavailable parts, or
   (iv)  late delivery of parts.
c. To buffer against unreliable production processes.
d. To take advantage of discounts.
e. To hedge against future price increases.

**Required:**

1. Explain how the JIT approach responds to each of these reasons and, consequently, argues for maintaining insignificant levels of inventories.
2. The theory of constraints (TOC) criticizes the JIT approach to inventory management, arguing that it fails to protect throughput. Explain what this means, and describe how TOC addresses this issue.

**12–9**

Kanban Cards

LO2

Explain the use of each of the following cards in the Kanban system:

1. The withdrawal Kanban
2. The production Kanban
3. The vendor Kanban

**12–10**

JIT Limitations

LO2

Many companies have viewed JIT as a panacea—a knight in shining armour promising rescue from sluggish profits, poor quality, and productive inefficiency. JIT is often lauded for its beneficial effects on employee morale and self-esteem. Yet JIT may also cause a company to struggle and may produce a good deal of frustration. In some cases, JIT appears to deliver less than its reputation warrants.

**Required:**

Discuss some of the limitations and problems that companies may encounter when implementing a JIT system.

<table>
<tr><td></td><td>Marvel Company has the capability of producing three types of rods used in the manufacture of different kinds of hydraulic cylinders. All three rods can be shaped and cut on the same machine. Marvel owns one of these machines, which has a total operating capacity of 20,000 hours per year. Information on each of the three rods follows:</td></tr>
</table>

**12–11**

*Product-Mix Decisions; Single Constraint*

LO3

Marvel Company has the capability of producing three types of rods used in the manufacture of different kinds of hydraulic cylinders. All three rods can be shaped and cut on the same machine. Marvel owns one of these machines, which has a total operating capacity of 20,000 hours per year. Information on each of the three rods follows:

|  | Type I | Type II | Type III |
|---|---|---|---|
| Selling price | $40.00 | $60.00 | $75.00 |
| Unit variable cost | $20.00 | $44.00 | $34.00 |
| Machine hours required | 0.50 | 0.20 | 1.50 |

Marvel's marketing manager has determined that the company can sell all that it can produce of each of the three products.

**Required:**
1. How many of each product should be sold to maximize total contribution margin? What is the total contribution margin for this product mix?
2. Suppose that Marvel can sell no more than 75,000 units of each type at the prices indicated. What product mix would you recommend, and what would be the total contribution margin?

**12–12**

*Drum-Buffer-Rope System*

LO3

Goicoechea, Inc., manufactures two models of bows: regular and deluxe. The company sells all the bows it produces. Bows are produced in three processes: laminating, moulding, and finishing. In laminating, limbs are created by laminating layers of wood. In moulding, the limbs are heat-treated, under pressure, to form a strong, resilient limb. In finishing, any protruding glue is removed, and the limbs are cleaned with acetone, dried, and sprayed with final finishes. Recently, Goicoechea implemented a TOC approach for its Kelowna plant. One binding constraint was identified, and the optimal product mix was determined. The following diagram reflects the TOC outcome.

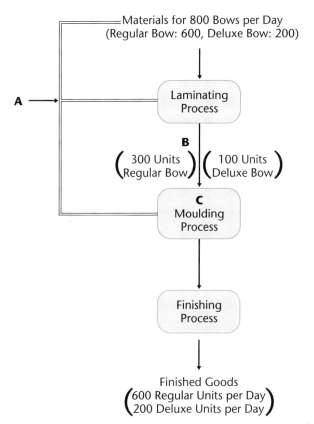

**Required:**
1. What is the daily production rate? What process sets this rate?
2. How many days of buffer inventory is Goicoechea carrying? How is this time buffer determined?
3. Explain what the letters A, B, and C represent in the diagram. Discuss each of their roles in the TOC system.

**12–13**

Various Topics

LO2

Choose the *best* answer for each of the following multiple-choice questions:

1. Which of the following *best* describes a JIT system?
   a. It is a demand-pull system.
   b. It requires suppliers to deliver parts and materials just in time for production.
   c. It emphasizes total quality management.
   d. It increases the number of costs that are directly traceable to a product.
   e. All of the above.

2. A JIT system is characterized by
   a. a small supplier base.
   b. departmental structure.
   c. centralized service.
   d. specialized labour.
   e. None of the above.

3. In a JIT system, which of the following costs would be typically assigned to a plant using direct tracing?
   a. Plant amortization.
   b. Salary of the plant supervisor.
   c. Landscaping.
   d. Material handling.
   e. Cafeteria services.

4. A marker or card that controls movement of work among the manufacturing processes is referred to as a
   a. processing Kanban.
   b. vendor Kanban.
   c. production Kanban.
   d. production-ordering Kanaban.
   e. kaizen Kanban.

# Problems

**12–14**

*EOQ and Reorder Point*

**LO1**

Italia Pizzeria is a popular pizza restaurant near a college campus. Brandon Thayn, an accounting student, works for Italia Pizzeria. After several months at the restaurant, Brandon began to analyze the efficiency of the business, particularly its inventory practices. He noticed that the owner had more than 50 items regularly carried in inventory. Of these items, the most expensive to buy and carry was cheese. Cheese was ordered in blocks at $17.50 per block. Annual usage totals 14,000 blocks.

Upon questioning the owner, Brandon discovered that the owner did not use any formal model for ordering cheese. It took five days to receive a new order when placed, which was done whenever the inventory of cheese dropped to 200 blocks. The size of the order was usually 400 blocks. The cost of carrying one block of cheese is 10 percent of its purchase price. It costs $40 to place and receive an order.

Italia Pizzeria stays open seven days a week and operates fifty weeks a year. The restaurant closes for the last two weeks of December.

**Required:**
1. Compute the total cost of ordering and carrying the cheese inventory under the current policy.
2. Compute the total cost of ordering and carrying cheese if the restaurant were to change to the economic order quantity. How much would the restaurant save per year by switching policies?
3. If the restaurant uses the economic order quantity, when should it place an order? (Assume that the amount of cheese used per day is the same throughout the year.) How does this timing compare with the current reorder policy?
4. Suppose that storage space allows a maximum of 600 blocks of cheese. Discuss the inventory policy that should be followed under this restriction.
5. Suppose again that the maximum storage is 600 blocks of cheese and that cheese can be held for a maximum of 10 days. The owner will not hold cheese any longer, since doing so can interfere with the pizzas' flavour and quality. Under these conditions, evaluate the owner's current inventory policy.

**12–15**

*EOQ with Safety Stock*

**LO1**

Parry Chiropractic Clinic uses an EOQ model to order supplies. Lately, several chiropractors have been complaining about the availability of X-ray film. During the past three months, the clinic has had to place five rush orders because of stock-outs. Because of the problem, the supply officer has decided to review the current inventory policy. The following data have been gathered:

| | |
|---|---|
| Cost of placing and receiving an order | $90 |
| Cost of carrying one package | $3.65 |
| Average usage per day | 20 packages |
| Maximum usage per day | 30 packages |
| Lead time for an order | 4 days |
| Annual demand | 7,300 packages |

The clinic currently does not carry any safety stock. The clinic operates 365 days each year.

**Required:**

1. Compute the economic order quantity and the reorder point. What is the total ordering and carrying cost for the clinic's current inventory policy?
2. Assume that the clinic has decided to carry safety stock. Compute how much should be carried to ensure no stock-outs. Compute the total ordering and carrying cost for this policy. Will the reorder point change? If so, what will it be?

**12–16**

*EOQ; Safety Stock; Setup Costs*

**LO1, LO2**

Geneva Company produces safety goggles for coal miners. Goggles are produced in batches according to model and size. Although the setup and production times vary for each model, the smallest lead time is 6 days. The most popular model, Model SG4, takes 2 days for setup; its production rate is 750 units per day. The expected annual demand for the model is 36,000 units. However, demand for this model can reach 45,000 units. The cost of carrying one SG4 unit is $3 per unit. The setup cost is $6,000. Geneva chooses its batch size based on the economic order quantity criterion. Expected annual demand is used to compute the EOQ.

Recently, Geneva has encountered some stiff competition—especially from foreign sources. Some of the company's foreign competitors have been able to produce and deliver the goggles to retailers in half the time it takes Geneva to do so. For example, a large retailer recently requested a delivery of 12,000 SG4 goggles with the stipulation that delivery occur within 7 working days. Geneva had 3,000 units of SG4 in stock. It informed the potential customer that it could deliver 3,000 units immediately and the other 9,000 units in about 14 working days—with the possibility of interim partial orders being delivered. The customer declined the offer, indicating that the total order had to be delivered within 7 working days so that its stores could take advantage of some special local conditions. The customer expressed regret and indicated that it would place this order with one of Geneva's competitors, a company that could satisfy the time requirements.

**Required:**

1. Calculate the optimal batch size for Model SG4 using the EOQ model. Was Geneva's response to the customer right? Would it take the time indicated to produce the number of units wanted by the customer? Explain with supporting computations.
2. Upon learning of the lost order, Geneva's marketing manager grumbled about the company's inventory policy. "We lost the order because we didn't have sufficient inventory. We need to carry more units in inventory to deal with unexpected orders like these." Do you agree? How much additional inventory would have been needed to meet the customer's requirements? In the future, should Geneva carry more inventory? Can you think of other solutions?
3. Fenton Gray, Geneva's head of industrial engineering, reacted differently to the lost order. "Our problem is more complex than insufficient inventory. I know that our foreign competitors carry much less inventory than we do. What we need to do is decrease the lead time. I have been studying this problem, and my staff has found a way to reduce the setup time for Model SG4 from 2 days to 1.5 hours. Using this new procedure, we can reduce setup cost to about $94. Also, by rearranging the plant layout for this product—creating what are called manufacturing cells—we can increase the production rate from 750 units per day to about 2,000 units per day. This is done simply by eliminating a lot of move time and waiting time—both nonvalue-added activities."

   Assume that Fenton's estimates are on target. Compute the new optimal batch size (using the EOQ formula). What is the new lead time? Given this new information, find out whether Geneva would have been able to meet the customer's time requirements. Assume that there are 8 hours available in each workday.

4. Suppose that the setup time and cost are reduced to 0.5 hour and $10, respectively. What is the batch size now? As setup time approaches zero and the setup cost becomes negligible, what does this imply? Assume, for example, that it takes 5 minutes to set up and costs about $0.864 per setup.

**12–17**

*Reorder Point with Demand Uncertainty*

LO1

(Note: this question requires knowledge of statistics.)

The Old Orchard Battery Distributor Company supplies automotive batteries to retail auto parts stores. The company is developing an EOQ system to assist in the management of its battery inventory. The EOQ demand distribution and purchase lead time for each type of battery have been determined.

David Kellogg, the owner of Old Orchard, has asked Marvin Rollins, his materials manager, for assistance in determining a reorder point for each type of battery. Kellogg would like the reorder points set high enough to minimize stockouts, thereby maximizing customer service. Rollins can demonstrate a reorder point by using the demand data on the RJ47 battery shown below. Rollins recalls that a product's reorder point is equal to its demand during the purchase lead time plus a safety stock.

| RJ47 Demand During Lead Time | RJ47 Demand Probability |
|---|---|
| 100 | 0.03 |
| 200 | 0.05 |
| 300 | 0.20 |
| 400 | 0.40 |
| 500 | 0.25 |
| 600 | 0.07 |

The purchase lead time for the battery is six weeks.

**Required:**
1. For the RJ47 battery, calculate the expected demand during the lead time.
2. For the RJ47 battery, calculate the reorder point given David Kellogg's desire to minimize stockouts.
3. Without prejudice to your answer in Requirement 2, assume that the reorder point is 400. What is the probability of a stockout? (US CMA adapted)

**12–18**

*Kanban System; EDI*

LO2

Packer Company produces a product that requires two processes. In the first process, a subassembly is produced (Subassembly A); in the second process, this subassembly and a subassembly purchased from outside (Subassembly B) are assembled to produce the final product. For simplicity, assume that the assembly of one unit takes the same time as the production of Subassembly A. Subassembly A is placed in a container and sent to an area called the subassembly stores (SB stores) area. A production Kanban is attached to this container. A second container, also with one subassembly, is located near the assembly line (this second container is called the withdrawal store). This container has attached to it a withdrawal Kanban.

**Required:**
1. Explain how withdrawal and production Kanban cards are used to control the work flow between the two processes. How does this approach minimize inventories?
2. Explain how vendor Kanban cards can be used to control the flow of the purchased subassembly. What implication does this have for supplier relationships? What role, if any, do continuous replenishment and EDI play in this process?

**12–19**

Product-Mix Decision;
Single and Multiple
Constraints

LO3

Morning Beverages, Inc., produces two instant breakfast drinks: Rich Instant and Diet Instant. Rich Instant has more ingredients and therefore requires more machine time for grinding and mixing. The manufacturing process is highly mechanized; the same equipment produces both products by using different settings. For the coming period, 800,000 machine hours are available. Management is trying to decide on the quantities of each product to produce. The following data are available:

|                          | Rich Instant | Diet Instant |
|--------------------------|:------------:|:------------:|
| Machine hours per unit   | 2.00         | 1.00         |
| Unit selling price       | $5.00        | $6.00        |
| Unit variable cost       | $3.00        | $4.50        |

**Required:**

1. Determine the units of each product that should be produced in order to maximize profits. What is the total contribution margin earned by this optimal product mix?
2. Because of market conditions, the company can sell no more than 500,000 packages of Rich Instant and 600,000 packages of Diet Instant. Now what is the optimal product mix? the total contribution margin?

**12–20**

Optimal Product Mix

LO3

Wilson Company manufactures and sells three components in a factory of three departments. The components are used as replacement parts in jet aircraft. After machining in each department, the components are subjected to stress tests. The nature of the machine processing and of the labour skills required for stress testing is such that neither machines nor test labour can be switched from one department to another. Wilson's management is planning its production schedule for the next several months. Planning is complicated by the facts that labour shortages exist in the community and that some machines will be down for several months while undergoing repairs.

Following is information regarding available machine and test time by department, along with the machine hours and test hours required for each component. These data are valid for at least the next six months.

|                        |                        | Department |       |       |
|------------------------|------------------------|:----------:|:-----:|:-----:|
| **Monthly Capacity**   |                        | **A**      | **B** | **C** |
| Test hours available   |                        | 7,400      | 9,000 | 5,500 |
| Machine hours available|                        | 6,000      | 6,200 | 5,400 |
| Component              | Input per Unit Produced |           |       |       |
| 12-L                   | Test hours             | 2          | 3     | 3     |
|                        | Machine hours          | 1          | 1     | 2     |
| 16-M                   | Test hours             | 1          | 2     | —     |
|                        | Machine hours          | 1          | 1     | —     |
| 40-S                   | Test hours             | 2          | 2     | 2     |
|                        | Machine hours          | 2          | 2     | 1     |

The monthly demand for the next six months will be as follows:

| Component | Units Sold |
|-----------|:----------:|
| 12-L      | 1,000      |
| 16-M      | 800        |
| 40-S      | 2,000      |

Inventory levels will not be increased or decreased during the next six months. The unit cost and price data for each component are as follows:

|  | Component | | |
|---|---|---|---|
|  | 12-L | 16-M | 40-S |
| Unit costs: | | | |
| Direct material | $ 14 | $ 26 | $ 34 |
| Test labour | 66 | 38 | 51 |
| Variable overhead | 27 | 20 | 25 |
| Fixed overhead | 15 | 10 | 32 |
| Variable selling | 3 | 2 | 4 |
| Total unit cost | $125 | $ 96 | $146 |
| Unit selling price | $203 | $136 | $184 |

**Required:**
1. Calculate the monthly requirement for machine hours and test hours for producing components 12-L, 16-M, and 40-S to determine whether the factory can meet the monthly sales demand.
2. Determine the quantities of each component that should be produced monthly to maximize profits. Prepare a schedule that shows the contribution to profits of your recommended product mix. (US CMA adapted)

**12–21**

Identifying and Exploiting Constraints; Constraint Elevation

LO3

Covey Company produces two metal parts used in industrial equipment (Part A and Part B). The company has three processes: moulding, grinding, and finishing. In moulding, moulds are created and molten metal is poured into the shell. Grinding removes the gates that allowed the molten metal to flow into the mould's cavities. In finishing, rough edges caused by the grinders are removed by small handheld pneumatic tools. In moulding, the setup time is 1 hour. The other two processes require no setup time. The demand for Part A is 300 units per day, and the demand for Part B is 500 units per day. The minutes required per unit for each product follow:

| Product | Minutes Required per Unit of Product | | |
|---|---|---|---|
|  | Moulding | Grinding | Finishing |
| Part A | 10 | 20 | 30 |
| Part B | 20 | 30 | 40 |

The company operates one 8-hour shift. The moulding process employs 24 workers (who each work 8 hours). Two hours of their time, however, is used for setups (assuming that both products are being produced). The grinding process has sufficient equipment and workers to provide 24,000 grinding minutes per shift.

The finishing department is labour-intensive and employs 70 workers, who each work 8 hours per day. The only significant unit-level variable costs are materials and power. For Part A, the variable cost per unit is $80; for Part B, it is $100. Selling prices for A and B are $180 and $220, respectively. Covey's policy is to use two setups per day: an initial setup to produce all that is scheduled for A and a second setup (changeover) to produce all that is scheduled for B. The amount scheduled does not necessarily correspond to each product's daily demand.

**Required:**
1. Calculate the time (in minutes) needed each day to meet the daily market demand for Part A and Part B. What is the major internal constraint facing Covey Company?
2. Describe how Covey should exploit its major binding constraint. Specifically, identify the product mix that will maximize daily throughput.

3. Assume that manufacturing engineering has found a way to reduce the moulding setup time from 1 hour to 10 minutes. Explain how this improvement affects the optimal product mix and the daily throughput.

**12–22**

*Theory of Constraints; Internal Constraints*

**LO3**

Young Company produces two subassemblies used by aircraft manufacturers: Sub A and Sub B. Sub A is made up of two components, one manufactured internally and one purchased from external suppliers. Sub B is made up of three components, one manufactured internally and two purchased from suppliers. The company has two processes: fabrication and assembly. In fabrication, the internally produced components are made. Each component takes 20 minutes to produce. In assembly, it takes 30 minutes to assemble the components for Sub A and 40 minutes to assemble the components for Sub B. Young Company operates one shift per day. Each process employs 100 workers, each of whom works 8 hours per day.

Sub A earns a unit contribution margin of $20, and Sub B earns a unit contribution margin of $24 (calculated as the difference between revenue and the cost of materials and energy). Young can sell all that it produces of either part. There are no other constraints. Young can add a second shift of either process. Although a second shift would also work 8 hours, there is no mandate that it must employ the same number of workers. The labour cost per hour for fabrication is $8, and the labour cost per hour for assembly is $7.

**Required:**

1. Identify the constraints facing Young. How many binding constraints are possible? What is Young's optimal product mix? What daily contribution margin is produced by this mix?
2. What is the drummer constraint? How much excess capacity does the other constraint have? Assume that a 1.5-day buffer inventory is needed to deal with any production interruptions. Describe the drummer–buffer–rope concept, using the Young data to illustrate the process.
3. Explain why the use of local labour efficiency measures will not work in Young's TOC environment.
4. Suppose that Young decides to elevate the binding constraint by adding a second shift of 50 workers (for assembly only). Would elevation of Young's binding constraint improve its system performance? Explain with supporting computations.

**12–23**

*TOC; Internal and External Constraints*

**LO3**

Bountiful Manufacturing produces two types of bike frames (X and Y). Both frames pass through four processes: cutting, welding, polishing, and painting. With the exception of polishing, each of the processes employs 20 workers, each of whom works 8 hours each day. Polishing employs 26 workers. Frame X sells for $80 per unit, and Frame Y sells for $110 per unit. Raw materials cost is the only unit-level variable cost. The materials cost for Frame X is $40 per unit, and the materials cost for Frame Y is $50 per unit. Bountiful's accounting system has provided the following additional information about its operations and products:

| Resource Name | Resource Available | Frame X Resource Usage (per unit) | Frame Y Resource Usage (per unit) |
|---|---|---|---|
| Cutting labour | 9,600 minutes | 30 minutes | 20 minutes |
| Welding labour | 9,600 minutes | 30 minutes | 60 minutes |
| Polishing labour | 12,480 minutes | 30 minutes | 30 minutes |
| Painting labour | 9,600 minutes | 20 minutes | 30 minutes |
| Market demand: | | | |
|   Frame X | 200 per day | 1 unit | — |
|   Frame Y | 100 per day | — | 1 unit |

Bountiful's management has determined that any production interruptions can be corrected within two days.

**Required:**

1. Assuming that Bountiful can meet daily market demand, compute the potential daily profit. Now compute the minutes needed for each process to meet the daily market demand. Can Bountiful meet daily market demand? If not, where is the bottleneck?
2. Determine the optimal product mix and the maximum daily contribution margin (throughput).
3. Explain how a DBR system would work for Bountiful.
4. Suppose that Bountiful's engineering department has proposed a process design change that will increase the polishing time for Frame X from 30 to 46 minutes per unit and decrease its welding time from 30 to 20 minutes per unit. The cost of process redesign would be $20,000. Evaluate this proposed change. What step in the TOC process does this proposal represent?

## Managerial Decision Case

**12–24**

Ethical Issues

LO2

Mac Ericson and Tammy Ferguson met at a conference two months ago and began dating. Mac is the controller of Longley Enterprises, and Tammy is a marketing manager for Sharp Products. Longley is a major supplier for Piura Products, a major competitor of Sharp's. Longley has entered into a long-term agreement to supply certain materials to Piura. Piura has been developing a JIT purchasing and manufacturing system. As part of its development, Piura and Longley have established EDI capabilities. The following conversation took place during a luncheon engagement:

**Tammy**: "Mac, I understand that you have EDI connections with Piura. Is that right?"

**Mac**: "Sure. It's part of the partners-in-profit arrangement that we've worked so hard to get. It's working real well. Knowing Piura's production schedule helps us stabilize our own schedule. It has actually cut some of our overhead costs. It has also decreased Piura's costs. I estimate that both companies have decreased their production costs by about 7 to 10 percent."

**Tammy**: "That's interesting. You know, I have a real chance of getting promoted to VP of marketing ..."

**Mac**: "Hey, that's great. When will you know?"

**Tammy**: "It all depends on this deal that I am trying to cut with Balboa—if I win the contract, then I think I have it. My main problem is Piura. If I knew what their production schedule was, I could get a pretty good idea as to how long it would take them to deliver. I could then make sure that we beat their delivery offer—even if we had to work overtime and do all kinds of expediting. I know that how fast we can deliver is very, very important to Balboa. Our quality is as good as Piura's, but they tend to beat us on delivery time. My boss would love to kick Piura. They have beaten us too many times recently. I'm wondering if you'd be willing to help me out."

**Mac**: "Tammy, you know that I'd help if I could, but Piura's production schedule is confidential information. If word got out that I had leaked that kind of stuff to you, I would be history."

**Tammy**: "Well, no one would ever know. Besides, I have already had a chat with Tom Anderson, who is our CEO. Our VP of finance is retiring. He knows about you and your capabilities. I think he'd be willing to hire you—especially if he knew that you had helped swing this Balboa deal. You could increase your salary by 40 percent."

**Mac**: "I don't know. I have my doubts about the propriety of all this. It might look kind of funny if I were to take over as VP of finance not long after Piura loses the Balboa deal. But a VP position and a big salary increase are tempting. It's unlikely that I'll ever have a shot at the VP position in my company."

**Tammy**: "Think it over. If you are interested, I'll arrange a dinner with Tom. He said that he'd like to meet you. He knows a little about this. I'm sure that he has the ability to keep it quiet. I don't think there is much risk."

### Required:

1. Based on this information, do you think Mac has violated any of the standards of ethical conduct outlined in Chapter 1?
2. Suppose that Mac decides to provide information in exchange for the VP position. What ethical standards has he violated?

## Research Assignment

**12–25**

*Cybercase*

**LO3**

The theory of constraints is a method for bringing about continuous improvement (the five TOC steps are a continuous improvement loop). In effect, TOC addresses three questions: (1) what to change, (2) what to change to, and (3) how to cause the change. The answers to these questions have to do with what is called the "thinking process." There are specific thinking process tools suggested: the current reality tree, the evaporative cloud, the future reality tree, the negative branches, the prerequisite tree, and the transition tree. Supporters of TOC claim that the method can bring about significant improvements in lead time, inventory, and financial performance. Furthermore, some advocate changing to what is called "constraint accounting." These issues create some significant opportunities for TOC-related Internet research.

### Required:

1. Search the Internet for definitions of the thinking process and of the thinking process tools listed above.
2. Search the Internet and find examples of three companies that have successfully used the theory of constraints. List some of the benefits achieved by these companies. Is TOC more than an inventory management method?
3. Search the Internet and find information on constraint accounting. What is constraint accounting? Is it an alternative to activity- and functional-based accounting? Explain.

## Planning and Control

Topics dealing with managerial decision making were covered in Part 2. The discussion was based on the assumption that a company always makes an optimal decision after examining the differential cash flow effects of the decision. This assumption, however, ignores two facts: decisions are made by many different people throughout the organization; and the total differential cash flow calculus, from the corporate point of view, may not be known to each decision maker. Even when decision makers have companywide information, they may still be motivated to make decisions in their own best interest. Sometimes these decisions are also good for the company, but other times the interests of the decision maker conflict with those of the organization. Suboptimization of corporate interests can result.

It is also important to keep in mind that different parts of the organization often have different objectives. Different managers may also have different views as to what the most important objectives are. For example, a marketing manager may be less concerned about the effect accepting a rush order will have on production costs than a production manager. The production manager would be responsible for changing the production schedule and incurring additional costs for setup and overtime. Therefore, he or she may be more concerned with increased production costs than with possible long-term effects on customer relations. The coordination of such conflicting objectives and the communication of necessary information are achieved through company policies and planning and budgeting processes. After plans are completed, it is important to determine from time to time whether actual performance is on target and, if it is not, to take appropriate corrective actions. All these activities have implications for management control systems.

## Management Control Systems

A management control system is a planning and control system that is aimed at the efficient and effective allocation and use of resources in an organization. Any system can be viewed in terms of a structure and a process. For example, to understand a transportation system requires an understanding of both structure (highways, freeways, and bridges) and process (the types of vehicles travelling, the flow of traffic, and bottlenecks). Understanding planning and control systems requires a knowledge of the structures within which planning and control processes occur. Organizational structure forms the foundation for assigning responsibility for decisions—that is, for establishing a responsibility structure. Cost, revenue,

profit, and investment centres are examples of responsibility structure. Decentralized organizations generally call for greater delegation of responsibility and authority than centralized organizations—that is, for movement from responsibility only for costs toward responsibility for investment. It follows that both organizational structure and responsibility structure are important contextual determinants of effective management controls.

Since planning and control occur within given structures in an organization, their study requires us to examine the processes used in formulating strategy, setting objectives, and developing budgets, and includes the consideration of environmental influences. Typically, the budgeting process is a major component of a management control system; that being said, the control process does not stop when the budget is approved. Actual performance must be tracked and compared to the budget, differences between actual and budgeted amounts must be analyzed, and appropriate corrective action must be taken as warranted. Other financial and nonfinancial information reflecting efficiency and effectiveness is also an important element of management control. Effective control systems need to be closely linked to an organization's strategy. Strategies and operating environments differ among organizations; so, then, should the control systems. In other words, control systems should be designed to fit the organizational circumstances.

## Conflicting Interests and Management Incentives

The potential for conflict between corporate interests and an individual manager's interests requires a close examination of the effects of the management control system on individual managers. Management control is more complicated than control of a mechanical process because managers have the freedom to make choices. It is possible that some of these choices may be suboptimal from a corporate perspective; yet it is also possible that the apparently suboptimal corporate behaviour may be the most efficient way of balancing the interests of different constituencies. *Agency theory* provides a useful framework for examining these issues. Agency theory is concerned with economic behaviour related to agency relationships. Many agency relationships exist in organizations, and their management is a rich area of study.

The typical agency relationship is between, for example, the owners or shareholders of a company (known as the principal) and management (called the agent). Both parties are assumed to be self-interested, and the managers are assumed to be effort averse. Effort aversion implies that managers prefer to work less, other things equal, and must be compensated for additional effort. This reflects a basic conflict of interest. Also, managers know the level of their effort, whereas the owners cannot directly or indirectly observe managerial effort. This information asymmetry in the agency relationship can cause problems for management control. Information asymmetry can result in what is known as the "moral hazard" problem, where the manager has an incentive to expend less effort than is desirable from the company's point of view. To address problems like this, agency theorists have studied how various control mechanisms, such as incentive compensation, can better align the interests of managers and owners.

Part 3 of this book focuses on the design and effective use of various management planning and control mechanisms. Chapter 13 deals with budgeting—an important planning and coordination tool—including its behavioural dimensions. Chapter 14 focuses on the analysis of variances between actual and budgeted performance; such analysis can point to necessary corrective actions. Chapter 15 is concerned with the measurement, reporting, and control of quality costs and productivity. Chapter 16 deals with evaluating the performance of profit and investment centres—in particular, transfer pricing issues and their behavioural implications. Finally, Chapter 17 focuses on strategic performance evaluation and control, and calls for integrated performance management systems that strike a proper balance between financial and nonfinancial performance criteria and measures.

## Examples of the Importance of Planning and Control

The importance of planning and control can be illustrated by the following examples:

1. Over 80 percent of new small businesses fail within the first three years, mainly because of poor planning—especially poor cash flow planning.
2. The price charged by a profit division of a particular company included its variable and fixed costs plus a mark-up. This price was seen as a strictly variable cost by another division that was a "customer." Decisions made by the buying division did not take into account the behaviour of costs from the corporate point of view—only from the divisional point of view. The consequence was short-term suboptimization.
3. A company had an excellent process in place for setting its budget. However, the company's management was incapable of making decisions based on an analysis of actual results against the budget when disputes arose regarding responsibility for budget variances. In other words, the company succeeded in using the budget as a planning tool but not as a control tool.
4. A company was determined to cut the "slack" in its budget. It found out the hard way that this was not easy to accomplish. Most employees were so unhappy with budget cutting that this process resulted in the loss of the commitment that the employees had previously felt. Employees felt more secure in a budget environment that allowed some slack to exist, and they felt threatened when their actions were more transparent to management in the absence of slack. As a result, the company lost its competitive edge and many employees lost their jobs.

# Budgeting for Planning and Control

**After studying Chapter 13, you should be able to:**

1. Define *budgeting* and discuss its role in planning, control, and decision making.

2. Define and prepare a *master budget*, identify its major components, and explain the interrelationships of its various components.

3. Describe flexible budgeting and identify the features that a budgetary system should have to encourage managers to engage in goal-congruent behaviour.

4. Describe activity-based budgeting.

## Scenario

By all outward appearances, Dr. Roger Jones was a successful dentist. He owned his own office building, which he leased to the professional corporation that housed his dental practice. The revenues from his practice exceeded $750,000 each year, providing him with a salary of $150,000 a year. He and his family lived in a large home in a prestigious neighbourhood.

However, Dr. Jones had just received a registered letter from the Canada Customs and Revenue Agency (CCRA) threatening to impound his business and sell its assets for failure to remit income tax withholdings and pay employment insurance premiums for the past six months. Furthermore, the professional corporation was having difficulty paying its suppliers. The corporation owed one supplier more than $200,000; it had arranged to make interest payments on the amount, but it had missed even some of these. The corporation had been experiencing these kinds of difficulties repeatedly for the past five years.

In the past, Dr. Jones had solved similar problems by borrowing money on the equity in his personal residence or his office building. There was still enough equity in the office building to solve the employment insurance problem. A visit to a local bank resulted in a refinancing agreement that provided sufficient capital to pay the overdue taxes and premiums, as well as the associated penalties and interest.

This time, however, Dr. Jones was not satisfied with the short-run solution to his financial difficulties. His latest loan had exhausted his personal financial resources, and he could not tolerate further problems. His first action was to dismiss his receptionist/bookkeeper, reasoning that part of the blame was hers for failing to properly manage his financial resources. He called Lawson, Johnson, and Day, a local CA firm, and requested that a consultant determine the cause of his recurring financial difficulties. Jeanette Day, a partner in the CA firm, spent a week examining the records of the practice and interviewing Dr. Jones extensively. She delivered the following report:

Dr. Roger Jones
1091 West Apple Avenue
Cambridge, Ontario
Dear Dr. Jones:

The cause of your current financial difficulties is the absence of proper planning and control. Currently, many of your expenditure decisions are made in a haphazard and arbitrary manner. Affordability is seldom, if ever, considered. Because of this, resources are often committed beyond the capabilities of the practice. To meet these additional commitments, your bookkeeper has been forced to postpone payments for essential operating expenses, such as employment insurance premiums, supplies, and laboratory services.

The following examples illustrate some of the decisions that have contributed to your financial troubles:

1. *Salary decisions.* You have been granting 5 percent increases each year whether or not the business could successfully absorb these increases. Also, your salary is 10 percent higher than that of dentists with comparable practices.

2. *Withdrawal decisions.* For the past five years, you have withdrawn from cash receipts approximately $1,000 per month. Such withdrawals have been treated as a loan from the corporation to you, the president of the corporation.

3. *Equipment acquisition decisions.* During the past five years, the corporation has acquired a van, a video recorder, a refrigerator, and a microcomputer system. Some of these items were cash acquisitions, and some are being paid on an instalment basis. None of them was essential to the mission of your corporation.

These decisions, and others like them, have adversely affected both your personal financial status and the financial well-being of the corporation. The mortgage payments for your personal residence and your office building have increased by 50 percent over the past five years. Additionally, the liabilities of the corporation have increased by 200 percent for the same period.

To solve your financial problems, I recommend the instalation of a formal budgeting system. A comprehensive financial plan is needed, so that you know what you can accomplish and afford.

My firm would be pleased to assist you in designing and implementing the recommended system. For it to be successful, you and your staff need to be introduced to the elementary principles of budgeting. As a part of this implementation, we will offer three two-hour seminars on budgeting. The first will describe the basic philosophy of budgeting, the second will teach you how to prepare budgets, and the third will explore the use of budgets for planning, control, and performance evaluation.

Sincerely,

**Jeanette Day, CA**

**Note:** This scenario is based on the experience of a real organization. The names have been changed to preserve confidentiality.

**Questions to Think About**
1. Why did Dr. Jones fire his bookkeeper? Were his financial problems her fault? Explain why or why not.

2. How would a formal budgeting system help Dr. Jones solve his financial difficulties?

3. Many small businesses do not budget, reasoning that they are small enough to keep track of all revenues and expenditures mentally. Comment on this idea.

4. Do you budget? Explain why or why not.

## Description of Budgeting

**Objective** 1

Define *budgeting* and discuss its role in planning, control, and decision making.

All organizations should prepare budgets. Every for-profit and not-for-profit entity, regardless of its size, can benefit from the planning and control provided by budgets. As the scenario for Dr. Jones shows, budgeting is also vital for small organizations.

### Budgeting and Planning and Control

Planning and control are inextricably linked. Planning involves looking ahead and determining what actions should be taken to realize particular goals, whereas control involves looking backward, determining what actually happened and comparing actual results with the previously planned outcomes. These compar-

**feedforward control**

Control processes and mechanism focused on planning for future performance.

**feedback control**

Control processes and mechanism focused on explaining past performance.

**budgets**

Plans of action expressed in financial terms.

**strategic plan**

The long-term plan for future activities and operations, usually involving at least five years.

isons can then be used to adjust the budgets and to plan for future periods, looking forward again. This suggests why future-oriented planning has sometimes been referred to as **feedforward control** and historically-oriented control as **feedback control**. Both feedback and feedforward control are part of a traditional, continuous planning–control cycle.

Exhibit 13–1 illustrates a typical planning and control cycle. Budgets form a key component of planning. **Budgets** are financial plans for the future. They identify objectives and the actions needed to achieve them. Before a budget is prepared, however, an organization should develop a strategic plan. The **strategic plan**, which usually covers at least five years, identifies strategies for future activities and operations. The overall strategy can then be translated first into long-term objectives and then into short-term objectives. The short-term objectives form the basis for the budgets. Note that there should be a tight linkage between the budgets and the strategic plan. In developing this linkage, management should ensure that all attention is not focused on the short term, and that the budgets are also consistent with the long-term objectives and the strategic plan. This is important because the typical budget, which covers a period of one year, is short-term in nature.

To illustrate the planning process, let's consider again the case of Dr. Roger Jones. Assume that his strategic plan is to increase the size and profitability of his business by building a practice that has a reputation for quality and timely service. A key element in achieving this strategy is the addition of a dental laboratory to his building so that crowns, bridges, and dentures can be made locally. That is his long-term objective. To add the laboratory, he needs more money. Because of his financial status, he will have to obtain the capital by increasing revenues. After some careful calculation, he concludes that he must increase his annual revenues by 10 percent. This is a short-term objective.

How can these long-term and short-term objectives be achieved? Suppose that Dr. Jones finds that his fees for fillings and crowns are below the average in

EXHIBIT   13-1

Planning, Control, and Budgets

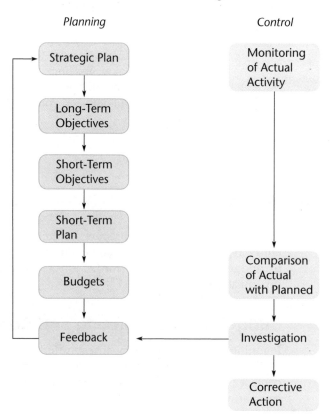

his community and decides that the 10 percent increase can be achieved by increasing these fees. He now has a short-term plan. A sales budget would outline the quantity of fillings and crowns expected for the coming year, the new per-unit fee, and the total fees expected. Thus, the sales budget becomes the concrete plan of action needed to achieve the 10 percent increase in revenues.

The control component of the cycle has four steps: monitoring actual activity, comparing actual results with the plan, investigating significant differences, and taking necessary corrective actions. The feedback obtained from these control processes may lead Dr. Jones to revise his future strategies and long-term plans. As the year unfolds, he can compare the actual revenues received with the budgeted revenues (monitoring and comparing). If actual revenues are less than planned, he should determine why (investigation). Then he can act to remedy the shortfall—perhaps by working longer hours or by increasing fees for other dental services (corrective action). The reasons for the shortfall may also lead to an alteration of future plans (feedback).

## Purposes of Budgeting

A budgetary system offers an organization several advantages:

1. It forces managers to plan.
2. It provides resource information that can be used to improve decision making.
3. It provides a standard for performance evaluation.
4. It improves communication and coordination.

Budgeting forces management to plan for the future. It encourages managers to develop an overall direction for the organization, foresee problems, and develop future policies. If Dr. Jones had spent time planning, he would have known the capabilities of his practice and where the resources of the business should be used.

Budgets improve decision making. For example, if Dr. Jones had known the expected revenues and the costs of supplies, lab fees, utilities, salaries, and so on, he might have lowered the rate of salary increases, avoided borrowing money from the corporation, and limited the purchase of nonessential equipment. These better decisions might in turn have prevented his problems and resulted in a better financial status for both Dr. Jones and his business.

**control**

The process of setting standards, receiving feedback on actual performance, and taking corrective action whenever actual performance has deviated significantly from planned performance.

Budgets also set standards for control of a company's resources and can motivate employees. **Control** is achieved by comparing actual results with budgeted results on a periodic basis (e.g., monthly). A large difference between the actual and planned results signals that the system is out of control. Steps should be taken to find out why and then correct the situation. For example, if Dr. Jones knows how much amalgam should be used in a filling and what the cost should be, he can evaluate his use of this resource. If he finds that he is using more amalgam than expected, he may discover that he is often careless with it and that extra care will produce significant savings. The same principle applies to other resources used by Dr. Jones, as well as to all resources used by larger corporations.

Budgets also serve as a communication and coordination mechanism. A budget formally communicates the organization's plan to each employee. In this way, all employees are made aware of their role in achieving its objectives. Since budgets for the organization's various areas and activities must work together to achieve organizational objectives, budgets promote coordination. Managers can see the needs of other areas and may as a result be encouraged to promote organizational interests. The role of communication and coordination becomes even more significant as an organization grows.

## Dimensions of Budgeting

There are two main dimensions to budgeting:

1. Budget preparation.
2. The use of budgets to implement the organization's plans.

The first of these dimensions is concerned with the processes and mechanics of budget estimates and calculations. The second dimension involves the use of budgets as a control tool, and is also concerned with the behavioural reactions of individuals to the budgetary system. When budgets are used for decision making, performance evaluation, communication, and coordination purposes, human behaviour can be affected. It follows that the success or failure of budgeting depends on how well management handles the behavioural aspects. The rest of this chapter deals with these two dimensions.

## Budget Preparation

**Objective 2**

Define and prepare a *master budget*, identify its major components, and explain the inter-relationships of its various components.

**continuous budget**

A moving 12-month budget with a future month added as the current month expires.

**budget director**

The individual responsible for coordinating and directing the overall budgeting process.

**budget committee**

A committee responsible for setting budgetary policies and goals, reviewing and approving the budget, and resolving any differences that may arise in the budgetary process.

**master budget**

The collection of all area and activity budgets representing a firm's comprehensive plan of action.

Most organizations prepare the budget for the coming year during the last four or five months of the current year. However, some organizations have developed a continuous budgeting philosophy. A **continuous budget** is a moving 12-month budget. As a month expires in the budget, an additional month in the future is added so that the company always has a 12-month plan on hand. Proponents of continuous budgeting maintain that it forces managers to plan continuously.

But a typical budget covers one year corresponding to the company's fiscal year. Annual budgets are broken down into quarterly budgets, and quarterly budgets are broken down into monthly budgets. The use of shorter time periods allows managers to compare actual data with budgeted data more often, so that problems can be detected and solved sooner.

## Directing and Coordinating

Someone must be responsible for directing and coordinating an organization's overall budgeting process. In large organizations, the controller is usually also the **budget director**, who works under the direction of the budget committee. The **budget committee** provides policy guidelines and budgetary goals, reviews the budget, resolves differences during the budget preparation process, approves the final budget, and monitors the organization's actual performance as the year unfolds. The organization's president appoints the committee members, who are usually the president, the vice-presidents, and the controller.

## Master Budget

The **master budget** is a comprehensive financial plan for the organization as a whole, and consists of various individual budgets. The master budget can be divided into operating and financial budgets. **Operating budgets** describe the company's income-generating activities: sales, production, and finished goods inventories. The ultimate outcome is a budgeted (or pro forma) income statement. **Financial budgets** detail the inflows and outflows of cash and the overall financial position. Planned cash inflows and outflows appear in the cash budget. The expected financial position at the end of the budget period is shown in a budgeted (or pro forma) balance sheet. Because many of the financing activities are not known until the operating budgets are known, the operating budget is prepared first.

**operating budgets**
Budgets associated with the income-producing activities of an organization.

**financial budgets**
The portions of the master budget that include the cash budget, the budgeted balance sheet, the budgeted statement of cash flows, and the capital budget.

To illustrate master budget preparation, throughout this chapter we use the operating budgets and financial budgets for Canblock, Inc., a manufacturer of concrete blocks and pipes with plants in several Western Canadian cities.

## Preparing the Operating Budget

The operating budget consists of a budgeted income statement and the following supporting schedules:

Schedule 1.   Sales budget
Schedule 2.   Production budget
Schedule 3.   Direct materials purchases budget
Schedule 4.   Direct labour budget
Schedule 5.   Overhead budget
Schedule 6.   Selling and administrative expenses budget
Schedule 7.   Ending finished goods inventory budget
Schedule 8.   Cost of goods sold budget

The sales forecast is the basis for the sales budget, which in turn is the basis for all other operating budgets and most financial budgets. Accordingly, the accuracy of the sales forecast strongly affects the soundness of the entire master budget.

Creating the sales forecast is usually the responsibility of the marketing department. One approach to forecasting sales is the *bottom-up approach*, which requires individual salespeople to submit sales predictions. These are then aggregated to form a total sales forecast. The accuracy of this sales forecast can be improved by considering other factors such as the general economic climate, competition, advertising, pricing policies, and so on. Some companies supplement the bottom-up approach with other, more formal approaches, such as time-series analysis, correlation analysis, and econometric models.

### Sales Budget

**sales budget**
A budget that describes expected sales in units and dollars for the coming period.

The first step in the budgeting process is the preparation of a sales budget. The **sales budget** is a sales projection for a future period, typically one year, approved by the budget committee. It describes expected sales in both units and dollars. Usually, an initial sales forecast is presented to the budget committee for approval. The budget committee may decide that the forecast is either too pessimistic or too optimistic, and revise it appropriately. For example, if the budget committee decides that the forecast is too pessimistic and not consistent with the organization's strategic plan, it may recommend specific actions to increase sales beyond the forecast level, such as increasing promotional activities and hiring additional salespeople.

Schedule 1 illustrates the sales budget for Canblock's concrete block line. For simplicity, we assume that Canblock has only one product: a standard block measuring $20 \times 20 \times 40$ cm. For a multiple-product company, the sales budget would need to reflect the total sales for each product in units and sales dollars.

Note that the sales budget reveals that Canblock's sales fluctuate seasonally. Most sales (75 percent) take place in the spring and summer quarters. Also note that the budget reflects an expected increase in selling price from $0.70 to $0.80, beginning in the summer quarter. Because of the price change, an average price of $0.75 per unit is used for the year as a whole.

### Production Budget

**production budget**
A budget that shows how many units must be produced to meet sales needs and satisfy ending inventory requirements.

A production budget can be prepared after the sales budget has been finalized. The **production budget** describes how many units must be produced in order to meet the sales needs and satisfy the ending inventory requirements. From

**Schedule 1**
**Canblock, Inc.**
**Sales Budget (in thousands)**
**For the Year Ended December 31, 2005**

| | Quarter | | | | |
|---|---|---|---|---|---|
| | 1 | 2 | 3 | 4 | Year |
| Units | 2,000 | 6,000 | 6,000 | 2,000 | 16,000 |
| Unit selling price | × $0.70 | × $0.70 | × $0.80 | × $0.80 | × $0.75 |
| Sales | $1,400 | $4,200 | $4,800 | $1,600 | $12,000 |

Schedule 1, we know how many concrete blocks are needed to satisfy the sales demand for each quarter and for the year. If there were no beginning or ending inventories, the concrete blocks to be produced would equal the units sold. In a JIT environment, for example, units sold equal units produced, since a customer order triggers production. However, the production budget must commonly incorporate beginning and ending inventories, since traditional manufacturing companies use inventories as a buffer against uncertainties in demand or production. Assume that a company policy requires 100,000 concrete blocks to be available in inventory at the beginning of the first and fourth quarters and 500,000 blocks at the beginning of the second and third quarters. This policy is equivalent to budgeting 100,000 concrete blocks as ending inventory for the third and fourth quarters and 500,000 concrete blocks as ending inventory for the first and second quarters.

To compute the units to be produced, both unit sales and units of beginning and ending finished goods inventory are needed. These are calculated as follows:

Units to be produced = Expected unit sales + Units in ending inventory – Units in beginning inventory

This formula is the basis for the production budget in Schedule 2. Let's go through the first column of Schedule 2, the production needs for the first quarter. We see that Canblock anticipates sales of 2 million concrete blocks. Also, the company wants 500,000 blocks in ending inventory at the end of the first quarter. Thus, 2.5 million blocks are needed during the first quarter. Where will the 2.5 million blocks come from? Beginning inventory can provide 100,000 blocks, leaving 2.4 million blocks to be produced during the quarter. Notice that the production budget is expressed in terms of units. A similar process applies to the calculation of the units to be produced for the other three quarters and for the

**Schedule 2**
**Canblock, Inc.**
**Production Budget (in thousands)**
**For the Year Ended December 31, 2005**

| | Quarter | | | | |
|---|---|---|---|---|---|
| | 1 | 2 | 3 | 4 | Year |
| Sales (Schedule 1) | 2,000 | 6,000 | 6,000 | 2,000 | 16,000 |
| Desired ending inventory | 500 | 500 | 100 | 100 | 100 |
| Total needs | 2,500 | 6,500 | 6,100 | 2,100 | 16,100 |
| Less: Beginning inventory | 100 | 500 | 500 | 100 | 100 |
| Units to be produced | 2,400 | 6,000 | 5,600 | 2,000 | 16,000 |

year as a whole. Note also that the beginning inventory for the year is the beginning inventory of the first quarter and that the ending inventory for the year is the ending inventory of the fourth quarter.

### *Direct Materials Budget*

After the production budget is completed, the budgets for direct materials, direct labour, and overhead can be prepared. The **direct materials purchases budget** depends on the expected use of materials in production and the firm's raw materials inventory needs.

The amount of direct materials needed for production depends on the number of units to be produced. Suppose a lightweight concrete block (a single unit of output) requires cement, sand, gravel, shale, pumice, and water. For simplicity, we will treat all raw materials jointly, as if there were only one raw material input, and assume that 13 kilograms of raw material are needed per block. If Canblock wants to produce 2.4 million blocks in the first quarter, it will need 31,200,000 kilograms of raw material (13 kilograms × 2.4 million blocks).

Once expected usage is computed, the purchases in units can be computed as follows:

Purchases = Direct materials needed for production
+ Desired direct materials ending inventory
− Direct materials beginning inventory

The quantity of direct materials in inventory is determined by the company's inventory policy. Canblock's policy is to have 2,500 metric tonnes, or 2,500,000 kilograms, of raw material in the ending inventory for the third and fourth quarters, and 4,000 metric tonnes, or 4,000,000 kilograms, for the first and second quarters.

The direct materials purchases budget for Canblock is presented in Schedule 3. Note how similar it is to the production budget. Again, let's go through the first quarter of Schedule 3. The 2.4 million blocks to be produced are multiplied by 13 kilograms to yield the total raw materials needed for production. Then, the desired ending inventory of 4,000,000 kilograms is added. We see that 35,200,000 kilograms of raw materials are required during the first quarter. Of these total needs, 2,500,000 kilograms are provided by the beginning inventory, meaning that the remaining 32,700,000 kilograms must be purchased.

**direct materials purchases budget**
A budget that outlines the expected usage of materials for production and purchases of the direct materials required.

**Schedule 3**
**Canblock, Inc.**
**Direct Materials Purchases Budget (in thousands)**
**For the Year Ended December 31, 2005**

| | Quarter | | | | |
| --- | --- | --- | --- | --- | --- |
| | 1 | 2 | 3 | 4 | Year |
| Units to be produced (Schedule 2) | 2,400 | 6,000 | 5,600 | 2,000 | 16,000 |
| Direct materials per unit (kg) | × 13 | × 13 | × 13 | × 13 | × 13 |
| Production needs (kg) | 31,200 | 78,000 | 72,800 | 26,000 | 208,000 |
| Desired ending inventory (kg) | 4,000 | 4,000 | 2,500 | 2,500 | 2,500 |
| Total needs | 35,200 | 82,000 | 75,300 | 28,500 | 210,500 |
| Less: Beginning inventory[a] | (2,500) | (4,000) | (4,000) | (2,500) | (2,500) |
| Direct materials to be purchased (kg) | 32,700 | 78,000 | 71,300 | 26,000 | 208,000 |
| Cost per kilogram | × $0.02 | × $0.02 | × $0.02 | × $0.02 | × $0.02 |
| Total purchase cost | $654 | $1,560 | $1,426 | $520 | $4,160 |

[a]Canblock follows the inventory policy of having 4 million kilograms of raw material on hand at the end of the first and second quarters and 2.5 million kilograms on hand at the end of the third and fourth quarters.

Multiplying the 32,700,000 kilograms by the cost of $0.02 per kilogram gives Canblock the expected cost of raw materials purchases of $654,000 for the first quarter. Of course, there would be a separate direct materials purchases budget for each type of raw material used.

### Direct Labour Budget

**direct labour budget**

A budget showing the total direct labour hours needed and the associated cost for the number of units in the production budget.

The **direct labour budget** shows the total direct labour hours needed and the associated cost for the number of units in the production budget. As with direct materials, the budgeted hours of direct labour are determined by the relationship between labour and outputs. For example, if a batch of 100 concrete blocks requires 1.5 direct labour hours, the direct labour time per block is 0.015 hours.

Given the direct labour used per unit of output, and the units to be produced from the production budget, the direct labour budget can be prepared, as shown in Schedule 4.

In the direct labour budget, the wage rate of $10 per hour is the *average* wage paid to the direct labourers associated with the production of the concrete blocks. The average rate incorporates the different wage rates paid to individual workers.

**Schedule 4**
**Canblock, Inc.**
**Direct Labour Budget (in thousands)**
**For the Year Ended December 31, 2005**

| | Quarter | | | | |
| --- | --- | --- | --- | --- | --- |
| | 1 | 2 | 3 | 4 | Year |
| Units to be produced (Schedule 2) | 2,400 | 6,000 | 5,600 | 2,000 | 16,000 |
| Direct labour time per unit (hr.) | × 0.015 | × 0.015 | × 0.015 | × 0.015 | × 0.015 |
| Total hours needed | 36 | 90 | 84 | 30 | 240 |
| Average wage per hour | × $10 | × $10 | × $10 | × $10 | × $10 |
| Total direct labour cost | $360 | $900 | $840 | $300 | $2,400 |

### Overhead Budget

**overhead budget**

A budget that reveals the planned expenditures for all indirect manufacturing items.

The **overhead budget** shows the expected cost of all indirect manufacturing items. Unlike direct materials and direct labour, overhead items display no readily identifiable input–output relationship. Instead, there are a series of activities and related drivers. In order to focus on budgeting issues, we will simplify by ignoring the various activities, cost pools, and cost drivers. Instead, we will use traditional overhead rates, classified into variable and fixed components. At the end of the chapter, we will revisit activity-based budgeting issues.

Past experience can be used as a guide to determine how overhead costs vary. Individual variable overhead items are identified (e.g., supplies and utilities), and the amount expected to be spent for each item per unit of activity is estimated. Individual rates are then added to obtain a total variable overhead rate. For our example, let's assume that two overhead cost pools are created: one for overhead activities that vary with direct labour hours, and one for all other activities, which are fixed. The variable overhead rate is $8 per direct labour hour, and the total budgeted fixed overhead is $1.28 million ($320,000 per quarter). Using this information and the budgeted direct labour hours from the direct labour budget (Schedule 4), we can prepare an overhead budget; see Schedule 5.

### Selling and Administrative Expenses Budget

**selling and administrative expenses budget**

A budget that outlines planned expenditures for nonmanufacturing activities.

The **selling and administrative expenses budget** outlines planned expenditures for nonmanufacturing activities. As with overhead, selling and administrative

**Schedule 5
Canblock, Inc.
Overhead Budget (in thousands)
For the Year Ended December 31, 2005**

| | Quarter | | | | |
| | 1 | 2 | 3 | 4 | Year |
|---|---|---|---|---|---|
| Budgeted direct labour hours (Schedule 4) | 36 | 90 | 84 | 30 | 240 |
| Variable overhead rate | × $8 × | $8 × | $8 × | $8 × | $8 |
| Budgeted variable overhead | $288 | $ 720 | $672 | $240 | $1,920 |
| Budgeted fixed overhead[a] | 320 | 320 | 320 | 320 | 1,280 |
| Total overhead | $608 | $1,040 | $992 | $560 | $3,200 |

[a]Includes $200,000 of amortization in each quarter.

expenses can be broken down into fixed and variable components. Such items as sales commissions, freight, and supplies vary with sales activity and total $0.05 per unit of sales. The fixed selling and administrative expenses per quarter are $69,000. The selling and administrative expenses budget is illustrated in Schedule 6.

**Schedule 6
Canblock, Inc.
Selling and Administrative Expenses Budget (in thousands)
For the Year Ended December 31, 2005**

| | Quarter | | | | |
| | 1 | 2 | 3 | 4 | Year |
|---|---|---|---|---|---|
| Planned sales in units (Schedule 1) | 2,000 | 6,000 | 6,000 | 2,000 | 16,000 |
| Variable selling and administrative expenses per unit | × $0.05 | × $0.05 | × $0.05 | × $0.05 | × $ 0.05 |
| Total variable expenses | $ 100 | $300 | $ 300 | $ 100 | $ 800 |
| Fixed selling and administrative expenses: | | | | | |
| Salaries | $ 35 | $ 35 | $ 35 | $ 35 | $ 140 |
| Advertising | 10 | 10 | 10 | 10 | 40 |
| Amortization | 15 | 15 | 15 | 15 | 60 |
| Insurance | 4 | 4 | 4 | 4 | 16 |
| Travel | 5 | 5 | 5 | 5 | 20 |
| Total fixed expenses | $ 69 | $ 69 | $ 69 | $ 69 | $ 276 |
| Total selling and administrative expenses | $ 169 | $ 369 | $ 369 | $ 169 | $1,076 |

## Ending Finished Goods Inventory Budget

**ending finished goods inventory budget**

A budget that describes planned ending inventory of finished goods in units and dollars.

The **ending finished goods inventory budget** supplies information needed for the balance sheet; it also serves as an important input for preparing the cost of goods sold budget. To prepare this budget, we must calculate the unit cost of producing each concrete block, using information from Schedules 3, 4, and 5. The unit cost of a concrete block and the cost of the planned ending inventory are shown in Schedule 7.

**Schedule 7**
**Canblock, Inc.**
**Ending Inventory Budget (in thousands)**
**For the Year Ended December 31, 2005**

Unit-cost computation:

| | |
|---|---|
| Direct materials (13 kilograms @ 0.02) | $0.26 |
| Direct labour (0.015 hours @ $10) | 0.15 |
| Overhead: | |
| Variable (0.015 hours @ $8) | 0.12 |
| Fixed (0.015 hours @ $5.33[a]) | 0.08 |
| Total unit cost | $0.61 |

$$^a \quad \frac{\text{Budgeted fixed overhead (Schedule 5)}}{\text{Budgeted direct labour hours (Schedule 4)}} = \frac{\$1,280}{240} = \$5.33$$

| | Units | Unit Cost | Total |
|---|---|---|---|
| Finished goods: Concrete block | 100,000 | $0.61 | $61,000 |

## Cost of Goods Sold Budget

**cost of goods sold budget**

The estimated costs for the units sold.

After we have calculated the budgeted direct materials, direct labour, overhead, and ending inventory, we can prepare a cost of goods sold budget. Assuming that the beginning finished goods inventory is valued at $55,000, we can prepare the **cost of goods sold budget** using Schedules 3, 4, 5, and 7. The cost of goods sold budget, shown in Schedule 8, is the last schedule we need in order to prepare a budgeted income statement.

**Schedule 8**
**Canblock, Inc.**
**Cost of Goods Sold Budget (in thousands)**
**For the Year Ended December 31, 2005**

| | |
|---|---|
| Direct materials used (Schedule 3)[a] | $4,160 |
| Direct labour used (Schedule 4) | 2,400 |
| Overhead (Schedule 5) | 3,200 |
| Budgeted manufacturing costs | $9,760 |
| Beginning finished goods | 55 |
| Goods available for sale | $9,815 |
| Less: Ending finished goods (Schedule 7) | 61 |
| Budgeted cost of goods sold | $9,754 |

[a] Production needs $\times$ $0.02 = 208,000 $\times$ $0.02.

## Budgeted Income Statement

After completing the cost of goods sold budget, Canblock has all the operating budgets it needs to prepare an estimate of operating income. However, the operating income is usually *not* equivalent to the net income. To obtain the net income, an interest expense and corporate income taxes must be deducted from the operating income. The budgeted income statement for Canblock is shown in Schedule 9. The interest expense deduction is obtained from the cash budget (see Schedule 10 in the next section). The amount of income tax in this example is assumed to be $650,000; in practice, of course, it will depend on the current Canadian tax laws. The budgeted income statement and the eight schedules together constitute the operating budget.

| Schedule 9 |
| :--: |
| Canblock, Inc. |
| **Budgeted Income Statement (in thousands)** |
| **For the Year Ended December 31, 2005** |

| | |
| :-- | --: |
| Sales (Schedule 1) | $12,000 |
| Less: Cost of goods sold (Schedule 8) | 9,754 |
| Gross margin | $ 2,246 |
| Less: Selling and administrative expenses (Schedule 6) | 1,076 |
| Operating income | $ 1,170 |
| Less: Interest expense (Schedule 10) | 54 |
| Income before taxes | $ 1,116 |
| Less: Income taxes | 650 |
| Net income | $    466 |

## Preparing the Financial Budget

After all components of the operating budget have been prepared, a financial budget can be prepared. Besides the operating budgets, the master budget typically includes the following three financial budgets:

1. Cash budget
2. Budgeted balance sheet
3. Capital expenditures budget

The master budget also contains a plan for acquiring long-term assets—that is, assets with a time horizon longer than the one-year operating period. Some of these assets may be purchased during the coming year; others may be acquired in future periods. This part of the master budget is referred to as the *capital budget*. Only the cash budget and the budgeted balance sheet are illustrated in this chapter. Capital budgeting was covered in Chapter 11.

### Cash Budget

**cash budget**

A detailed plan that outlines all sources and uses of cash.

A **cash budget** shows the budgeted cash inflows and outflows from operations, capital investments, and financing. Knowledge of cash flows is critical to managing a business. A business can be successful in producing and selling products, but it can still fail due to the timing of cash inflows and outflows. By knowing when cash deficiencies and surpluses are likely to occur, a manager can plan to borrow cash as necessary and to repay the loans during periods of excess cash. Bank loan officers use a company's cash budget to document the company's cash needs, as well as its ability to repay. Because cash flow is an organization's lifeblood, the cash budget is one of the most important budgets in the master budget. A basic framework for a cash budget is illustrated in Exhibit 13–2.

**EXHIBIT   13-2**

The Cash Budget

| | |
| :-- | :-- |
| Beginning cash balance | xxx |
| Add: Cash receipts | xxx |
| Cash available | xxx |
| Less: Cash disbursements | xxx |
| Less: Minimum cash balance | xxx |
| Cash surplus (deficit) | xxx |
| Add: Cash from loans | xxx |
| Less: Loan repayments | xxx |
| Add: Minimum cash balance | xxx |
| Ending cash balance | xxx |

Cash available consists of the beginning cash balance and the expected cash receipts. Expected cash receipts include all sources of cash for the period. The principal source of cash is sales. Because a significant proportion of sales is usually on credit, a major task of an organization is to determine the pattern of collection for its accounts receivable. It can use past experience to determine what percentages of accounts receivable, on average, are paid during the month of sale and the months following the sale. For example, assume that a company has the following accounts receivable collection experience:

| | |
|---|---|
| Percentage collected during the month of sale | 30% |
| Percentage collected during the month after the sale | 60% |
| Percentage collected during the second month after the sale | 10% |

Thus, if sales on account in May are $100,000, cash collections from May credit sales are $30,000 (30 percent) in May, $60,000 (60 percent) in June, and $10,000 (10 percent) in July. Notice that all accounts receivable are expected to be collected. However, if the company experiences, let's say, 3 percent uncollectible accounts, then 3 percent of sales is ignored for the purpose of cash budgeting.

The cash disbursements section lists all planned cash outlays for the period. Typical cash disbursements include payments to be made during the period for materials, labour, overhead, administrative expenses, and income taxes. All expenses that do not result in a cash outlay are excluded from the cash budget. For example, amortization charges are never included, since they do not require a cash outlay. Furthermore, interest payments on short-term debt, although a cash outlay, are typically not included in the disbursements section; instead they are shown in the financing section.

The cash surplus or deficit line compares the cash available with the cash needed. Cash needed is the total cash disbursements plus the minimum cash balance required by company policy. The minimum cash balance is simply the lowest amount of cash on hand that the company finds acceptable. Consider your own chequing account. You probably try to keep at least some cash in the account, perhaps because a minimum balance avoids service charges or allows you to make an unplanned purchase. Similarly, companies also require minimum cash balances. The amount is determined by each company's needs and policies. If the total cash available is less than the cash needed, a deficit exists, and the company needs a short-term loan. On the other hand, if the cash available is greater than the cash needed, a surplus exists, and the company can repay past loans or make temporary investments.

The final section of the cash budget consists of loans and repayments. If a deficit exists, the section shows the amount that must be borrowed. If surplus cash is available, it shows planned repayments, including interest expense. The last line of the cash budget is the planned ending cash balance. Remember that the minimum cash balance was subtracted when the cash surplus or deficit was calculated. However, since the minimum cash balance is not a disbursement, it must be added back to obtain the planned ending cash balance.

To illustrate the cash budget, assume the following additional information for Canblock:

a. A minimum cash balance of $100,000 is required at the end of each quarter.
b. Money can be borrowed and repaid in multiples of $100,000 at an annual interest rate of 12 percent. Interest payments are made only for the amount of principal repaid. All borrowing occurs at the beginning of the quarter and all repayments at the end of the quarter.
c. One half of all sales are for cash; 70 percent of credit sales are collected during the quarter of sale and the remaining 30 percent during the following quarter. The sales for the fourth quarter of 2004 were $2 million.

d. Purchases of raw materials are made on account; 80 percent of purchases are paid during the quarter of purchase and the remaining 20 percent during the following quarter. The purchases for the fourth quarter of 2004 were $500,000.

e. Budgeted amortization is $200,000 per quarter for overhead and $15,000 per quarter for selling and administration expenses. Insurance premiums of $16,000 are paid in the third quarter.

f. The capital budget for 2005 reveals a plan to purchase additional equipment to handle increased demand at a plant in Kitimat, British Columbia. The cash outlay for the equipment, $600,000, will occur during the first quarter. The company plans to finance the acquisition of the equipment with operating cash, supplemented with a short-term loan if necessary.

g. Corporate income taxes of approximately $650,000 will be paid at the end of the fourth quarter.

h. Beginning cash balance is $120,000.

Given this information, we can calculate the cash budget for Canblock. Much of the information needed to prepare the cash budget comes from the operating budgets. In fact, Schedules 1, 3, 4, 5, and 6 contain important input. However, these schedules by themselves do not provide all the necessary information. The collection pattern for revenues and the payment pattern for materials must also be known before the cash flow for sales and purchases on credit can be determined.

Exhibit 13–3 displays the pattern of cash inflows from both cash and credit sales. Let's look at the cash receipts for the first quarter of 2005. Budgeted cash sales for the quarter are $700,000 ($0.50 × $1,400,000; Schedule 1). Collections on account during the first quarter relate to credit sales made during the last quarter of 2004 and the first quarter of 2005. Credit sales for the fourth quarter of 2004 were $1,000,000 ($0.50 × $2,000,000), and $300,000 of these sales ($0.30 × $1,000,000) remain to be collected in the first quarter of 2005. Seventy percent of the first-quarter credit sales of $700,000, or $490,000, will be collected during that quarter. Similar computations are also made for the remaining quarters.

| EXHIBIT 13-3 | Source | Quarter 1 | Quarter 2 | Quarter 3 | Quarter 4 |
|---|---|---|---|---|---|
| Cash Receipts Pattern for 2005: Canblock, Inc. | Cash sales | $ 700,000 | $2,100,000 | $2,400,000 | $ 800,000 |
| | Received on account from: | | | | |
| | Quarter 4, 2004 | 300,000 | | | |
| | Quarter 1, 2005 | 490,000 | 210,000 | | |
| | Quarter 2, 2005 | | 1,470,000 | 630,000 | |
| | Quarter 3, 2005 | | | 1,680,000 | 720,000 |
| | Quarter 4, 2005 | | | | 560,000 |
| | Total cash receipts | $1,490,000 | $3,780,000 | $4,710,000 | $2,080,000 |

The total cash receipts for each quarter from Exhibit 13–3 are then added to the beginning quarterly cash balances in the cash budget, shown in Schedule 10, to calculate the total cash available for each quarter. The total cash needs are determined next by adding the total disbursements and the minimum desired cash balance. The minimum cash balance serves as a cushion against any unanticipated cash needs. Note that all noncash expenses, such as amortization, are not included in disbursements. Recall that the overhead expenses in Schedule 5 included amortization of $200,000 per quarter. The selling and administrative expenses in Schedule 6 included amortization of $15,000 and insurance of $4,000 per quarter. Because insurance premiums are paid in the third quarter, insurance expense must be removed from disbursements in the first, second, and fourth quarters, and $16,000 (4 × $4,000) must be added in the third quarter. Only the net amount of overhead appears in the cash budget.

## Schedule 10
## Canblock, Inc.
## Cash Budget (in thousands)
## For the Year Ended December 31, 2005

| | Quarter | | | | | |
| | 1 | 2 | 3 | 4 | Year | Source[a] |
|---|---|---|---|---|---|---|
| Beginning cash balance | $ 120 | $ 169 | $ 162 | $ 985 | $ 120 | |
| Collections: | | | | | | |
| Cash sales | 700 | 2,100 | 2,400 | 800 | 6,000 | c, 1 |
| Credit sales: | | | | | | |
| Current quarter | 490 | 1,470 | 1,680 | 560 | 4,200 | c, 1 |
| Prior quarter | 300 | 210 | 630 | 720 | 1,860 | c, 1 |
| Total cash available | $1,610 | $3,949 | $4,872 | $3,065 | $12,180 | |
| Less disbursements: | | | | | | |
| Raw materials: | | | | | | |
| Current quarter | $ 523 | $1,248 | $1,141 | $ 416 | $ 3,328 | d, 3 |
| Prior quarter | 100 | 131 | 312 | 285 | 828 | d, 3 |
| Direct labour | 360 | 900 | 840 | 300 | 2,400 | 4 |
| Overhead | 408 | 840 | 792 | 360 | 2,400 | e, 5 |
| Selling and administrative | 150 | 350 | 366 | 150 | 1,016 | e, 6 |
| Income taxes | — | — | — | 650 | 650 | g, 9 |
| Equipment | 600 | — | — | — | 600 | f |
| Total disbursements | $2,141 | $3,469 | $3,451 | $2,161 | $11,222 | |
| Minimum cash balance | 100 | 100 | 100 | 100 | 100 | a |
| Total cash needs | $2,241 | $3,569 | $3,551 | $2,261 | $11,322 | |
| Excess (deficiency) of cash available over needs | $ (631) | $ 380 | $1,321 | $ 804 | $ 858 | |
| Financing: | | | | | | |
| Borrowings | 700 | — | — | — | 700 | |
| Repayments | — | (300) | (400) | — | (700) | b |
| Interest[b] | — | (18) | (36) | — | (54) | b |
| Total financing | $ 700 | $ (318) | $ (436) | — | $ (54) | |
| Ending cash balance[c] | $ 169 | $ 162 | $ 985 | $ 904 | $ 904 | |

[a] Letters refer to the information in points a to h. Numbers refer to schedules already developed.
[b] Interest payments are $6/12 \times 0.12 \times \$300$ and $9/12 \times 0.12 \times \$400$, respectively. Since borrowings occur at the beginning of the quarter and repayments at the end of the quarter, the first principal repayment takes place after six months, and the second principal repayment takes place after nine months.
[c] Total cash available minus total disbursements plus (or minus) total financing.

The difference between the total cash available and the total cash needed represents either a surplus (positive difference) or a deficit (negative difference). For the first quarter, a deficit of $631,000 is predicted; it is financed by borrowing $700,000 (the closest multiple of $100,000). This results in an ending cash balance of $169,000 after the minimum cash balance is added back. A similar process is repeated for the other quarters, with the ending cash balance for each quarter becoming the beginning balance for the next quarter. In this example, enough cash is generated in the second and third quarters to cover all disbursements and minimum cash balances and to repay the first-quarter loan with interest.

The cash budget for Canblock underscores the importance of breaking down the annual budget into smaller, in this case quarterly, periods. The cash budget for the year gives the impression that sufficient operating cash will be available to finance the acquisition of new equipment. Quarterly information, however, shows the need to borrow $700,000 as a result of the acquisition of new equipment and the timing of cash flows. To obtain even more detailed estimates of cash needs, most companies prepare monthly cash budgets; some even prepare weekly and daily budgets.

Another significant piece of information emerges from Canblock's cash budget. By the end of the third quarter, the company has an accumulated cash balance of $985,000. It is not wise to allow this much cash to sit idly in a bank account. Management should consider paying dividends and making investments. At the very least, the excess cash should be invested in short-term marketable securities. After the plan for the use of excess cash is finalized, the cash budget should be revised to reflect this plan. Budgeting is a dynamic process. As new information becomes available during the budget process, budgets are revised to incorporate this information.

### Budgeted Balance Sheet

The budgeted balance sheet uses information contained in the current balance sheet and in the master budget schedules. The balance sheet for Canblock for 2004 is shown in Exhibit 13–4. It provides some beginning balances used for the budgeted balance sheet for 2005, which is presented in Schedule 11.

The cash amount on the budgeted balance sheet is the fourth-quarter balance of $904,000 from Schedule 10. The accounts receivable of $240,000 consist of 30 percent of credit sales for the fourth quarter ($0.50 \times \$1,600,000 = \$800,000$) from Schedule 1. The raw materials inventory of $50,000 is the ending inventory of 2,500,000 kilograms from Schedule 3 at $0.02 per kilogram. The finished goods inventory of $61,000 was calculated in Schedule 7. The value of land, $2,500,000, comes from the 2004 balance sheet, as there was no change. The building and equipment amount of $9,600,000 comes from the 2004 balance sheet, $9,000,000,

---

**EXHIBIT 13-4**

Balance Sheet: Canblock, Inc., December 31, 2004

**Canblock, Inc.**
**Balance Sheet**
**December 31, 2004**
**(in thousands)**

### Assets

| | | |
|---|---:|---:|
| Current assets: | | |
| Cash | $ 120 | |
| Accounts receivable | 300 | |
| Raw materials inventory | 50 | |
| Finished goods | 55 | |
| Total current assets | | $ 525 |
| Property, plant, and equipment: | | |
| Land | $2,500 | |
| Building and equipment | 9,000 | |
| Accumulated amortization | (4,500) | |
| Total property, plant, and equipment | | 7,000 |
| Total assets | | $7,525 |

### Liabilities and Shareholders' Equity

| | | |
|---|---:|---:|
| Current liabilities: | | |
| Accounts payable | | $ 100 |
| Shareholders' equity: | | |
| Common stock, no par | $ 600 | |
| Retained earnings | 6,825 | |
| Total shareholders' equity | | 7,425 |
| Total liabilities and shareholders' equity | | $7,525 |

## Schedule 11
## Canblock, Inc.
## Budgeted Balance Sheet (in thousands)
## December 31, 2005

### Assets

| | | |
|---|---:|---:|
| Current assets: | | |
| Cash | $ 904[a] | |
| Accounts receivable | 240[b] | |
| Raw materials inventory | 50[c] | |
| Finished goods | 61[d] | |
| Total current assets | | $1,255 |
| Property, plant, and equipment: | | |
| Land | $2,500[e] | |
| Building and equipment | 9,600[f] | |
| Accumulated amortization | (5,360)[g] | |
| Total property, plant, and equipment | | 6,740 |
| Total assets | | $7,995 |

### Liabilities and Shareholders' Equity

| | | |
|---|---:|---:|
| Current liabilities: | | |
| Accounts payable | | $ 104[h] |
| Shareholders' equity: | | |
| Common stock, no par | $ 600[i] | |
| Retained earnings | 7,291[j] | |
| Total shareholders' equity | | 7,891 |
| Total liabilities and shareholders' equity | | $7,995 |

[a] Ending balance from Schedule 10.
[b] 30 percent of fourth-quarter credit sales (0.30 × $800,000)—see Schedules 1 and 10.
[c] From Schedule 3, 2,500 × $0.02.
[d] From Schedule 7.
[e] From the December 31, 2004, balance sheet.
[f] December 31, 2004, balance ($9,000,000) plus new equipment acquisition of $600,000 (see the 2004 ending balance sheet and Schedule 10).
[g] From the December 31, 2004, balance sheet, Schedule 5, and Schedule 6 ($4,500,000 + $800,000 + $60,000).
[h] 20 percent of fourth-quarter purchases (0.20 × $520,000)—see Schedules 3 and 10.
[i] From the December 31, 2004, balance sheet.
[j] $6,825,000 + $466,000 (December 31, 2004, balance plus net income from Schedule 9).

plus the acquisition of new equipment of $600,000 from Schedule 10. The accumulated amortization of $5,360,000 consists of the 2004 balance of $4,500,000, plus amortization on the new and old equipment for the budget year of $800,000 (4 × $200,000) from Schedule 5 and $60,000 from Schedule 6. The accounts payable of $104,000 represent unpaid fourth-quarter purchases of raw materials (0.20 × $520,000) from Schedule 3. The amount of common stock remains unchanged from 2004. Finally, the retained earnings of $7,291,000 consist of the 2004 balance of $6,825,000, plus the budgeted net income of $466,000 from Schedule 9.

The Canblock budgeting example demonstrates clearly the interdependencies among the various budgets that constitute the master budget. A diagram summarizing these interrelationships is provided in Exhibit 13–5. It emphasizes the flow of the budgeting process and the order in which the various budgets can be prepared. The ultimate outcome of the master budget preparation process is the budgeted balance sheet; each budget provides supporting calculations for one or more items required for the budgeted balance sheet.

EXHIBIT   13-5

The Master Budget and
Its Interrelationships

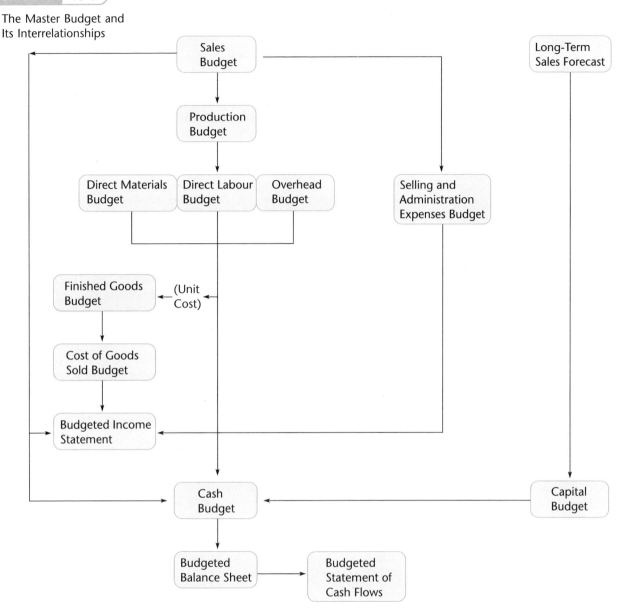

## Using Budgets for Performance Evaluation

**Objective** 3

Describe flexible
budgeting and identify
the features that a
budgetary system should
have to encourage
managers to engage in
goal-congruent behaviour.

Budgets are useful control vehicles. However, their use in performance evaluation requires two important considerations. The first relates to determining an
appropriate basis for comparing budgets with actual results. The second relates
to the behavioural impact of budgets.

### Static Budgets versus Flexible Budgets

Budgets can be used for both planning and control. In planning, companies prepare a master budget based on their best estimate of the level of activity to be
achieved during the coming year. However, the actual level of activity does not
usually equal the budgeted level. For this reason, budgeted amounts cannot be

compared with actual results. To address this problem, companies should also prepare a flexible budget for performance evaluation purposes.

### Static Budgets

**static budget**

A budget for a particular level of activity.

The master budget developed for Canblock is an example of a static budget. A **static budget** is a budget for a particular level of activity. Canblock developed budgets based on expected annual sales of 16 million units. Because static budgets depend on a particular level of activity, they are not very useful for performance reporting. To illustrate this, suppose that Canblock's first-quarter sales were greater than expected: 2.6 million concrete blocks were sold instead of the 2 million blocks budgeted in Schedule 1. Because of the increased sales, production increased. Instead of producing 2.4 million units (Schedule 2), Canblock produced 3 million units.

A performance report comparing the actual production costs with the planned production costs for the first quarter is shown in Exhibit 13–6. Note that it breaks down the budgeted overhead amounts into individual items. For simplicity, Schedule 5 ignored such details.

According to the report, unfavourable variances occurred for direct materials, direct labour, supplies, indirect labour, and rent. However, there is something fundamentally wrong with the report. Actual costs for the production of 3 million concrete blocks are being compared with planned costs for the production of 2.4 million. Because direct materials, direct labour, and variable overhead are variable costs, we would expect them to be greater at a higher activity level. Thus, even if cost control were perfect for the production of 3 million units, unfavourable variances would be produced for at least some variable costs. To create a meaningful performance report, we must compare actual costs and expected costs at the *same* level of activity. Since actual output often differs from planned output, we need some method of computing what the costs should have been for the actual output level.

### Flexible Budgets

**flexible budget**

A budget that can specify costs for a range of activity.

A budget that enables a company to compute expected costs for a range of activity is called a **flexible budget**. Flexible budgeting has three major uses:

**EXHIBIT** 13-6

Performance Report: Production Costs (in thousands) for Quarter 1

| | Actual | Budget | Variance |
|---|---|---|---|
| Units produced | 3,000 | $ 2,400 | 600 F[a] |
| Direct materials cost | $ 927.30 | $ 624.00[b] | $303.30 U[c] |
| Direct labour cost | 450.00 | 360.00[d] | 90.00 U |
| Overhead:[e] | | | |
| Variable: | | | |
|   Supplies | 80.00 | 72.00 | 8.00 U |
|   Indirect labour | 220.00 | 168.00 | 52.00 U |
|   Power | 40.00 | 48.00 | (8.00) F |
| Fixed: | | | |
|   Supervision | 90.00 | 100.00 | (10.00) F |
|   Amortization | 200.00 | 200.00 | 0.00 |
|   Rent | 30.00 | 20.00 | 10.00 U |
|     Total | $2,037.30 | $1,592.00 | $445.30 |

[a] F means that the variance is favourable.
[b] From Schedule 3 (31,200 kilograms × $0.02).
[c] U means that the variance is unfavourable.
[d] From Schedule 4.
[e] Schedule 5 provides the aggregate amount of budgeted overhead (e.g., the aggregate variable overhead is 0.015 × 2,400,000 × $8 = $288,000, and the total budgeted fixed overhead is $320,000).

1. To prepare the budget before the fact for the expected level of activity.
2. To compute, after the fact, what costs should have been for the actual level of activity. Once expected costs are known for the actual level of activity, a performance report comparing the expected and actual costs can be prepared.
3. To help managers deal with uncertainty by allowing them to see the expected outcomes for a range of activity. It can be used to generate financial results for a number of plausible scenarios.

Flexible budgeting can provide managers with frequent feedback. Such feedback is necessary for them to exercise control and carry out effectively the organization's plans.

To compute the expected cost at different levels of activity, we need to know the cost behaviour pattern of each item in the budget. That is, we need to know the variable cost per unit of activity as well as the fixed cost per item. Let's prepare a flexible budget for Canblock, one that measures activity level by the number of blocks produced. From Schedule 7, we know the variable costs for direct materials ($0.26 per unit), direct labour ($0.15 per unit), and variable overhead ($0.12 per unit). To increase the detail in the flexible budget, let's assume that supplies, indirect labour, and power have variable costs per unit of $0.03, $0.07, and $0.02, respectively. These three individual variable overhead items total $0.12. From Schedule 5, we also know that budgeted fixed overhead is $320,000 per quarter. Exhibit 13–7 displays a flexible budget for production costs at three levels of activity.

Note from Exhibit 13–7 that total budgeted production costs increase as the activity level increases. The increase occurs because variable costs change. This is why flexible budgets are sometimes referred to as **variable budgets**. Flexible budgets are powerful control tools because they allow management to compute what the costs *should* be for any level of activity. Exhibit 13–7 reveals what the costs should have been for the actual level of activity of 3 million units. Now we can provide management with a useful performance report—one that compares actual and budgeted costs for the actual level of activity. This report is provided in Exhibit 13–8.

The revised performance report in Exhibit 13–8 paints a much different picture than the one in Exhibit 13–6. By comparing budgeted costs for the actual level of activity with actual costs for the same level, management can immediately identify a problem area—expenditures for direct materials are excessive.

**variable budgets**
See *flexible budget*.

**EXHIBIT 13-7**

Flexible Production Budget (in thousands)

| Production Costs | Variable Cost per Unit | Range of Production (units) 2,400 | 3,000 | 3,600 |
|---|---|---|---|---|
| Variable: | | | | |
| Direct materials | $0.26 | $ 624 | $ 780 | $ 936 |
| Direct labour | 0.15 | 360 | 450 | 540 |
| Variable overhead: | | | | |
| Supplies | 0.03 | 72 | 90 | 108 |
| Indirect labour | 0.07 | 168 | 210 | 252 |
| Power | 0.02 | 48 | 60 | 72 |
| Total variable costs | $0.53 | $1,272 | $1,590 | $1,908 |
| Fixed overhead: | | | | |
| Supervision | | $ 100 | $ 100 | $ 100 |
| Amortization | | 200 | 200 | 200 |
| Rent | | 20 | 20 | 20 |
| Total fixed costs | | $ 320 | $ 320 | $ 320 |
| Total production costs | | $1,592 | $1,910 | $2,228 |

EXHIBIT 13-8

Actual versus Flexible
Performance Report:
Production Costs (in
thousands) for Quarter 1

|  | Actual | Flexible Budget[a] | Variance | |
|---|---|---|---|---|
| Units produced | 3,000 | 3,000 | — | |
| Production costs: | | | | |
| Direct materials | $ 927.30 | $ 780.00 | $147.30 | U |
| Direct labour | 450.00 | 450.00 | 0.00 | |
| Variable overhead: | | | | |
| Supplies | 80.00 | 90.00 | (10.00) | F |
| Indirect labour | 220.00 | 210.00 | 10.00 | U |
| Power | 40.00 | 60.00 | (20.00) | F |
| Total variable costs | $1,717.30 | $1,590.00 | $127.30 | U |
| Fixed overhead: | | | | |
| Supervision | $ 90.00 | $ 100.00 | $(10.00) | F |
| Amortization | 200.00 | 200.00 | 0.00 | |
| Rent | 30.00 | 20.00 | 10.00 | U |
| Total fixed costs | $ 320.00 | $ 320.00 | 0.00 | |
| Total costs | $2,037.30 | $1,910.00 | $127.30 | U |

[a] From Exhibit 13–7.

**flexible budget variance**

The sum of price variances and efficiency variances in a performance report comparing actual costs to expected costs predicted by a flexible budget.

The other unfavourable variances seem relatively small. With this knowledge, management can search for the causes of the excess expenditures and take action to prevent similar problems in the future.

The difference between the actual amount and the flexible budget amount is the **flexible budget variance**. The flexible budget makes it possible to assess a manager's efficiency. In addition, it is often desirable to establish whether a manager has accomplished his or her goals. The static budget is important for this purpose, since it represents certain goals that the company wants to achieve. A manager is *effective* if he or she achieves or exceeds the goals described in the static budget. Any differences between the flexible budget and the static budget are attributable to differences in volume. They are called *volume variances*. A five-column performance report that reveals both the flexible budget variances and the volume variances can be used. Exhibit 13–9 provides an example of such a report for Canblock.

As the report in Exhibit 13–9 reveals, production volume was 600,000 units greater than the original budgeted volume. Thus, the manager exceeded the original budgeted goal. This volume variance is labelled *favourable* because it exceeds the original production goal. Recall that the *reason* for the extra production was that the demand for the product was greater than expected. Thus, the increase in production over the original estimate was truly favourable. On the other hand, the budgeted variable costs are greater than expected because of the increased production. This difference is labelled *unfavourable*, because the costs are greater than expected; however, the increase in costs is a result of an increase in production. For this particular example, the manager's effectiveness is not in question: the main issue is how well the manager controls costs, as revealed by the flexible budget variances.

### Flexible Revenue and Expense Budgets

The above discussion highlighted the usefulness of flexible budgets in evaluating manufacturing and nonmanufacturing cost performance. However, an operating budget encompasses revenues as well as costs. Flexible budgets assist in the process of evaluating not only cost performance but also profit performance. Exhibit 13–10 provides an example of a profit performance report. Actual sales and production for Canblock's second quarter were 5.4 million concrete blocks at

EXHIBIT   13-9

Managerial Performance
Report: Production Costs
(in thousands) for
Quarter 1

| | Actual Results | Flexible Budget | Flexible Budget Variances[a] | Static Budget | Volume Variance[b] |
|---|---|---|---|---|---|
| Units produced | 3,000 | 3,000 | — | 2,400 | 600  F |
| Production costs: | | | | | |
| Direct materials | $ 927.30 | $ 780.00 | $147.30  U | $ 624.00 | $156.00  U |
| Direct labour | 450.00 | 450.00 | — | 360.00 | 90.00  U |
| Supplies | 80.00 | 90.00 | (10.00) F | 72.00 | 18.00  U |
| Indirect labour | 220.00 | 210.00 | 10.00  U | 168.00 | 42.00  U |
| Power | 40.00 | 60.00 | (20.00) F | 48.00 | 12.00  U |
| Supervision | 90.00 | 100.00 | (10.00) F | 100.00 | — |
| Amortization | 200.00 | 200.00 | — | 200.00 | — |
| Rent | 30.00 | 20.00 | 10.00  U | 20.00 | — |
| Total costs | $2,037.30 | $1,910.00 | $127.30  U | $1,592.00 | $318.00  U |

[a] Actual results minus flexible budget.
[b] Flexible budget minus static budget.

an average selling price of $0.75, and the budget was 6 million blocks at $0.70. The exhibit provides actual results for that second quarter and compares them to the static budget and the flexible budget.

The last column in Exhibit 13–10 shows that in the second quarter, the effect of sales volume on profit, other things constant, was $72,000, unfavourable. We can verify this by multiplying the decrease in sales (5,400,000 – 6,000,000) by the budgeted contribution margin ($0.70 – $0.58 = $0.12).[1] In Exhibit 13–10, this is shown in two steps: the decrease in revenue resulting from the decrease in volume (600,000 units × $0.70 = $420,000, unfavourable), less the decrease in vari-

EXHIBIT   13-10

Profit Performance Report
(in thousands) for
Quarter 2

| | Actual Results | Flexible Budget | Flexible Budget Variances[a] | Static Budget | Volume Variance[b] |
|---|---|---|---|---|---|
| Sales (units) | 5,400 | 5,400 | — | 6,000 | 600  U |
| Sales revenue | $4,050[c] | $3,780[d] | $270  F | $4,200[e] | $420  U |
| Variable expenses: | | | | | |
| Production | $2,950 | $2,862[f] | $ 88  U | $3,180[f] | $318  F |
| Selling and administrative | 280 | 270[g] | 10  U | 300[g] | 30  F |
| Total variable expenses | $3,230 | $3,132 | $ 98  U | $3,480 | $348  F |
| Contribution margin | $ 820 | $ 648 | $172  F | $ 720 | $ 72  U |
| Fixed expenses: | | | | | |
| Production | $ 340 | $ 320[h] | $ 20  U | $ 320[h] | $ — |
| Selling and administrative | 72 | 69[i] | 3  U | 69[i] | — |
| Total fixed expenses | $ 412 | $ 389 | $ 23  U | $ 389 | $ — |
| Net income | $ 408 | $ 259 | $149  F | $ 331 | $ 72  U |

[a] Actual results minus flexible budget.
[b] Flexible budget minus static budget.
[c] 5,400 × $0.75.
[d] 5,400 × $0.70.
[e] From Schedule 1.
[f] From Exhibit 13–7; 5,400 × $0.53; 6,000 × $0.53.
[g] From Schedule 6; 5,400 × $0.05; 6,000 × $0.05.
[h] From Schedule 5.
[i] From Schedule 6.

1. The budgeted variable cost of $0.58 per unit consists of variable production costs of $0.53 ($0.26 + $0.15 + $0.12) from Schedule 7, plus variable selling and administrative costs of $0.05 from Schedule 6.

able costs resulting from the decrease in volume (600,000 units × $0.58 = $348,000, favourable)—a total of $72,000, unfavourable.[2]

The flexible budget variances column of Exhibit 13–10 shows that the effect of the selling price increase on profits, other things remaining constant, is $270,000, favourable. We can verify this by multiplying the increase in selling price ($0.75 − $0.70) by the actual volume sold (5,400,000 units). It also shows cost performance effects. For variable production expenses, this amounts to $88,000, unfavourable, since the actual variable costs exceeded the flexible budget amount; for variable selling and administrative expenses, the flexible budget variance is $10,000, unfavourable.[3] Finally, the column also shows an unfavourable variance of $23,000 for fixed costs, consisting of a $20,000 unfavourable variance for production and a $3,000 unfavourable variance for selling and administrative expenses. The total of the last column and the middle column of Exhibit 13–10 is equal to the difference between the actual profit ($408,000) and the static budget profit ($331,000)—a difference of $77,000, favourable. A summary of these variances is as follows.

| | | |
|---|---:|---|
| Profit volume variance | $ 72,000 | U |
| Sales price variance | 270,000 | F |
| Variable cost variances | 98,000 | U |
| Fixed cost variances | 23,000 | U |
| Total master (static) budget variance | $ 77,000 | F |

Note that the flexible budget is important in that it separates the effects of sales and production volume changes from the effects of price and cost changes. The above example illustrates the use of variance analysis as an analytical tool for separating the effects of each factor on the planned outcome (budgeted profit). The results of this analysis can help determine appropriate corrective actions. A detailed variance analysis is the subject of Chapter 14.

## The Behavioural Dimension of Budgeting

Budgets are often used to judge the actual performance of managers. Bonuses, salary increases, and promotions are affected by a manager's ability to achieve or exceed budgeted goals. Since a manager's financial status and career can be affected, budgets can have significant behavioural effects. Whether that effect is positive or negative depends to a large extent on how budgets are used.

Positive behaviour occurs when the goals of individual managers are aligned with the goals of the organization, and the manager is motivated to achieve them. The alignment of managerial and organizational goals is often referred to as **goal congruence**. As well, a manager must exert effort to achieve the organization's goals. If the budget is improperly administered, managers may undermine the organization's goals and engage in **dysfunctional behaviour**. Dysfunctional behaviour is individual behaviour that is in basic conflict with the organization's goals.

Ethics is a theme that runs through the behavioural dimension of budgeting. Emphasis on budget performance in managerial performance evaluation and compensation can lead to unethical actions. All dysfunctional actions relating to

**goal congruence**
The alignment of a manager's personal goals with those of the organization.

**dysfunctional behaviour**
Individual behaviour that conflicts with the goals of the organization.

---

2.  A variance's effect on profit can be determined by the sign of the variance. For example, comparing actual amounts minus budgeted amounts, and assigning positive signs to revenues and negative signs to expenses, the profit volume variance = (5,400,000 − 6,000,000) × ($0.70 − $0.58) = −600,000 × $0.12 = −$72,000 or $72,000U. Similarly, the flexible budget variance for variable expenses is −$3,230,000 − (−$3,132,000) = −$98,000 or $98,000U.

3.  The variable production cost variance can be broken down further into material, labour, and variable manufacturing overhead variances. Each of these variances can de decomposed even further to isolate the effect of input price, efficiency, and so on. This analysis is the subject of Chapter 14.

budgets can have an unethical aspect. For example, a manager who deliberately underestimates sales or overestimates costs for the purpose of making the budget easier to achieve is engaging in unethical behaviour. It is the company's responsibility to create budgetary incentives that encourage ethical behaviour, and it is the manager's responsibility to demonstrate such behaviour.

An ideal budgetary system is one that achieves complete goal congruence and simultaneously motivates managers to achieve the organization's goals in an ethical manner. An ideal budgetary system probably does not exist; that being said, research and practice have identified some key features that can promote positive behaviour. These features include frequent feedback on performance, monetary and nonmonetary incentives, participative budgeting, realistic standards, controllability of costs, and multiple measures of performance.

### Frequent Feedback on Performance

Managers need to know how they are performing as the year unfolds. When they are provided with frequent, timely, and useful performance reports, they know how successful their efforts have been; they can also take corrective actions and change plans as necessary. Flexible budgets allow management to see whether actual costs and revenues are in line with the budgeted amounts. Selective investigation of significant variances, both negative and positive, allows managers to focus only on the areas that need attention, and to recognize and reward exceptional performance. This process is called *management by exception.*

### Monetary and Nonmonetary Incentives

A sound budgetary system encourages goal-congruent behaviour. The methods an organization uses to influence managers to work harder to achieve its goals are called **incentives**. Traditional organizational theory assumes that individuals are motivated mainly by monetary rewards, resist work, and are inefficient and wasteful. Thus, **monetary incentives** are offered in an attempt to control the tendency of managers to shirk and to waste resources; they relate salary increases, bonuses, and promotions to budgetary performance.

Dismissal is the ultimate economic sanction for poor performance. But actually, individuals are motivated by more than economic factors. Also important are psychological and social factors such as recognition, responsibility, self-esteem, and the nature of work itself. Thus, **nonmonetary incentives**—including job enrichment, increased responsibility and autonomy, nonmonetary recognition programs, and so on—can be used to enhance a budgetary control system.

### Participative Budgeting

**Participative budgeting** allows managers considerable input into the budget process. It ensures that budgets are not imposed on them. This approach is referred to as **bottom-up budgeting**, as opposed to **top-down budgeting**, whereby budgets are set unilaterally by top management. Typically, overall objectives are communicated to the manager, who helps develop a budget that will accomplish these objectives. Participative budgeting communicates a sense of responsibility to managers and fosters creativity. When a manager helps create the budget, the budget goals probably become that manager's personal goals; the result, presumably, is greater goal congruence and better performance. Furthermore, the increased responsibility and challenge inherent in the process act as nonmonetary incentives that can improve performance.

However, participative budgeting has three potential problems:

1. Standards may be set too high or too low.
2. The budget may include "slack."
3. Managers may practise "pseudoparticipation."

**incentives**
The positive or negative measures taken by an organization to induce a manager to exert effort toward achieving the organization's goals.

**monetary incentives**
Economic rewards used to motivate managers.

**nonmonetary incentives**
Psychological and social rewards used to motivate managers.

**participative budgeting**
An approach to budgeting that allows managers who will be held accountable for budgetary performance to participate in the budget's development.

**bottom-up budgeting**
A participative budgeting process that allows managers considerable input into the budget levels and processes.

**top-down budgeting**
A budgeting process in which budgets are set unilaterally by top management.

When managers are allowed to participate in budgeting, some of them may set the budget too loose or too tight. Since budgeted goals tend to become the manager's goals, these errors or misjudgments could result in decreased performance. If the goals are too easy to achieve, the manager will not have to exert significant effort and for that reason may lose interest. Similarly, when a budget is too tight, the manager will fail to achieve the standards and become frustrated as a result. For example, when performance has been poor and significant pressure for improvement exists, the manager may be tempted to set overoptimistic budgets, in the hope that things will improve. The challenge is to get managers to set high but achievable goals. It has been suggested that a 50 percent chance of budget achievement provides the highest level of motivation.

Loose standards provide managers with an opportunity to build slack into budgets. **Budgetary slack** (or *padding the budget*) exists when a manager deliberately underestimates revenues or overestimates costs. Either approach increases the likelihood of budget achievement and thereby reduces risk. Top management should carefully review the budgets proposed by managers, providing input where needed, in order to decrease the negative effects of building slack into the budgets. However, some budget slack can also have beneficial effects by providing flexibility and making it possible to capitalize on new and unforeseen opportunities—especially in uncertain operating environments.

The third problem with participation arises when top management assumes total control of the budget process, seeking only superficial participation from lower-level managers. This practice is called **pseudoparticipation**. Top management is simply obtaining formal acceptance of the budget from managers; it is not seeking and valuing real input. In these circumstances, none of the potential behavioural benefits of participation may be realized. On the contrary, pseudoparticipation can be demoralizing and result in dysfunctional behaviours.

### Realistic Standards

Budgeted objectives are used to gauge performance. Accordingly, they should be based on realistic conditions and expectations. Budgets should reflect operating realities such as actual levels of activity, seasonal variations, efficiencies, and general economic trends. Flexible budgets are used to ensure that budgeted costs can be realistically compared with costs for the actual level of activity. Interim budgets should reflect seasonal effects. Toys "R" Us, for example, would expect much higher sales in the quarter that includes Christmas than in other quarters. Budgetary cuts should be based on *planned* increases in efficiency and not simply on arbitrary across-the-board reductions. Cuts that are made without any formal evaluation may impair the ability of some units to carry out their missions. General economic conditions also need to be considered. Budgeting for a significant increase in sales when a recession is projected is not only foolish but potentially dangerous.

### Controllability of Costs

Managers should be held accountable only for costs over which they have a reasonable degree of control. **Controllable costs** are costs whose level a manager can influence significantly. For example, divisional managers have no power to authorize corporate costs such as R&D expenditures and management salaries, so they should not be held accountable for those costs. If noncontrollable costs are included in the budgets of managers to help them understand that these costs also need to be covered, they should be separated from controllable costs and identified as *noncontrollable* for managerial evaluation purposes.

---

**budgetary slack**

The process of padding the budget by overestimating costs and underestimating revenues.

---

**pseudoparticipation**

A budgetary system in which top management solicits inputs from lower-level managers and then ignores those inputs. Thus, in reality, budgets are dictated from above.

---

**controllable costs**

Costs that managers have the power to influence.

### Multiple Measures of Performance

Organizations often make the mistake of using budgets as their only measure of managerial performance. Financial measures of performance are important, but too much emphasis on them can lead to dysfunctional behaviour called *milking* or *myopia*. **Myopic behaviour** occurs when a manager takes actions that improve short-term budgetary performance but harm long-term performance. For example, to meet budgeted cost or profit objectives, managers might fail to promote deserving employees, or they might reduce expenditures for preventative maintenance, advertising, and new product development. Using financial *and* nonfinancial measures that take into account the long-term *and* short-term perspectives can alleviate this problem. Budgetary measures by themselves are inadequate. Chapter 17 examines the use of multiple measures and integrated performance measurement systems.

**myopic behaviour**

Managerial actions that improve budgetary performance in the short run at the expense of the long-run welfare of the program.

## Activity-Based Budgeting

**Objective 4**

Describe activity-based budgeting.

**activity-based budgeting system**

In activity-based budgeting, the workload (demand) for each activity is estimated and the resources required to sustain this workload are established.

Companies that have implemented an ABC system may also wish to install an **activity-based budgeting system**. A budgetary system at the activity level can be a useful approach to supporting continuous improvement and process management. Furthermore, because activities consume resources—and therefore are the causes of costs—activity-based budgeting may be a much more powerful planning and control tool than traditional, functional-based budgeting. Activity-based budgeting can be used to emphasize cost reduction through the elimination of unnecessary activities, and to improve the efficiency of necessary activities.

### Static Activity Budgets

Activities cause costs by consuming resources. However, the amount of resources consumed depends on the demand for the activity's output. Thus, building an activity-based budget involves three steps:

1. Identify activities within the organization.
2. Estimate demand for each activity's output.
3. Estimate the costs of the resources required for the activity output.

If an organization has implemented an ABC or ABM system, Step 1 has already been accomplished. Assuming that such a system has been implemented, activity-based budgeting mainly involves estimating the workload (or demand) for each activity and then budgeting the resources required to sustain this workload. The workload for each activity must be set to support the sales and production activities expected for the coming period.

Thus, like functional-based budgeting, activity-based budgeting begins with sales and production budgets. Direct materials and direct labour budgets are also compatible with the ABC framework, because these inputs are directly traceable to individual products. The main difference between traditional and activity-based budgeting is the treatment of the overhead and the selling and administration expenses.

In functional-based budgeting, budgets for overhead and for selling and administrative expenses are typically presented by cost elements. (See Exhibit 13–6 for an example of a detailed overhead budget.) These cost elements are classified as variable or fixed, and production or sales output measures provide the basis for determining cost behaviour. Furthermore, these budgets are usually constructed by budgeting for a cost item within a department (or function) and then rolling these items upward into the master overhead budget. For example, the cost of supervision in the overhead budget in Exhibit 13–6 is the sum of all supervision costs for various departments. In contrast, activity-based budgeting identifies the overhead, selling, and administrative *activities* and then builds a budget for each activity, based on the resources needed to provide the required activity output levels. Costs are classified as variable or fixed with respect to the *activity* of output measure.

Consider, for example, the activity of purchasing materials. The demand for this activity is a function of the materials requirements of the various products and services produced. An activity driver, such as the number of purchase orders, measures the activity output. Suppose that materials requirements, as expressed by the materials purchases budget, create a demand for 15,000 purchase orders. To execute the purchasing activity, resources such as purchasing agents, supplies, office space, and office equipment are needed. Assuming that a purchasing agent can process 3,000 orders per year, five agents are needed. Similarly, five desks, five computers, and office space for five agents are required.

Of the resources consumed by the purchasing activity, supplies are a flexible resource and, therefore, a variable cost, whereas the other resources consumed are committed resources and, therefore, display a fixed-cost behaviour (or a step-fixed behaviour, in the case of salaries and amortization). But there is an important difference that should be mentioned: fixed and variable purchasing costs are defined with respect to the *number of purchase orders* and not direct labour hours, units produced, or other measures of production output. The cost behaviour of each activity is defined with respect to *its* output measure, which is often different from that of the production-based drivers used in traditional functional-based budgeting.

Knowing the output measure provides significant insight for controlling activity costs. In an activity-based framework, controlling costs translates into managing activities. For example, when products are redesigned so that they use more common components, the number of purchase orders can be decreased. When the number of purchase orders is decreased, flexible resource demand is reduced. Furthermore, decreasing the number of purchase orders also reduces the activity capacity needed. Thus, activity costs will decrease. This is an example of activity-based management.

## Activity Flexible Budgeting

**activity flexible budgeting**

The prediction of what activity costs will be as activity usage changes.

The ability to identify changes in activity costs as activity output changes allows managers to plan and monitor activity improvement more carefully. **Activity flexible budgeting** can predict what activity costs will be as activity output changes. Variance analysis within an activity framework makes it possible to improve traditional budgetary performance reporting. It also enhances the ability to manage activities.

In functional-based budgeting, budgeted costs for the actual level of activity are obtained by assuming that a single unit-based driver—for example, units of product or direct labour hours—drives all costs. A cost formula is developed for each cost item as a function of units produced or direct labour hours. Exhibit 13–7 provides an example of a traditional flexible budget using units of product as the driver. Exhibit 13–11 presents a flexible budget based on direct labour hours. However, if costs vary with respect to more than one driver and if the drivers are not highly correlated with direct labour hours, the predicted costs can be misleading.

The solution, of course, is to build flexible budget formulas for more than one driver. Cost estimation procedures, such as the high–low and least-squares methods, can be used to estimate and validate the cost formulas for each activity. In

**EXHIBIT 13-11**

Flexible Budget: Direct Labour Hours

| | Cost Formula | | Direct Labour Hours | |
|---|---|---|---|---|
| | **Fixed** | **Variable** | **10,000** | **20,000** |
| Direct materials | — | $10 | $100,000 | $200,000 |
| Direct labour | — | 8 | 80,000 | 160,000 |
| Maintenance | $ 20,000 | 3 | 50,000 | 80,000 |
| Machining | 15,000 | 1 | 25,000 | 35,000 |
| Inspections | 120,000 | — | 120,000 | 120,000 |
| Setups | 50,000 | — | 50,000 | 50,000 |
| Purchasing | 220,000 | — | 220,000 | 220,000 |
| Total | $425,000 | $22 | $645,000 | $865,000 |

principle, the variable-cost component for each activity should correspond to resources acquired as needed (flexible resources), and the fixed-cost component should correspond to resources acquired in advance of usage (committed resources). This multiple-formula approach allows managers to predict more accurately what costs ought to be for different levels of activity usage, as measured by the activity output measure. These costs can then be compared with the actual costs to help assess budgetary performance.

Exhibit 13–12 illustrates an activity flexible budget. Note that the budgeted amounts for materials and labour are the same as those reported in Exhibit 13–11; they use the same activity output measure. The budgeted amounts for the other items differ significantly from the traditional amounts, because their activity output measures differ.

**EXHIBIT 13-12**

Activity Flexible Budget

| | Driver: Direct Labour Hours | | | |
|---|---|---|---|---|
| | **Formula** | | **Level of Activity** | |
| | **Fixed** | **Variable** | **10,000** | **20,000** |
| Direct materials | $ — | $10 | $100,000 | $200,000 |
| Direct labour | — | 8 | 80,000 | 160,000 |
| Subtotal | $ 0 | $18 | $180,000 | $360,000 |

| | Driver: Machine Hours | | | |
|---|---|---|---|---|
| | **Fixed** | **Variable** | **8,000** | **16,000** |
| Maintenance | $20,000 | $ 5.50 | $64,000 | $108,000 |
| Machining | 15,000 | 2.00 | 31,000 | 47,000 |
| Subtotal | $35,000 | $ 7.50 | $95,000 | $155,000 |

| | Driver: Number of Setups | | | |
|---|---|---|---|---|
| | **Fixed** | **Variable** | **25** | **30** |
| Inspections | $80,000 | $2,100 | $132,500 | $143,000 |
| Setups | — | 1,800 | 45,000 | 54,000 |
| Subtotal | $80,000 | $3,900 | $177,500 | $197,000 |

| | Driver: Number of Orders | | | |
|---|---|---|---|---|
| | **Fixed** | **Variable** | **15,000** | **25,000** |
| Purchasing | $211,000 | $1 | $226,000 | $236,000 |
| Total | | | $678,500 | $948,000 |

Assume that the first activity level for each driver in Exhibit 13–12 corresponds to the actual activity usage levels. Exhibit 13–13 compares the budgeted costs for the actual activity usage levels with the actual costs. One item is on target; the other seven items are mixed. The net outcome is a favourable variance of $21,500.

The performance report in Exhibit 13–13 compares the total budgeted costs for the actual level of activity with the total actual costs for each activity. It is also possible to compare the actual fixed activity costs with the budgeted fixed activity costs, and the actual variable activity costs with the budgeted variable activity costs. For example, assume that the actual fixed inspection costs are $82,000—due to a midyear salary adjustment, reflecting a more favourable union agreement than anticipated—and that the actual variable inspection costs are $43,500. The variable and fixed budget variances for the inspection activity are computed as follows:

| Activity | Actual Cost | Budgeted Cost | Variance |
|---|---|---|---|
| Inspection: | | | |
| Fixed | $ 82,000 | $ 80,000 | $2,000 U |
| Variable | 43,500 | 52,500 | 9,000 F |
| Total | $125,500 | $132,500 | $7,000 F |

Breaking each variance into fixed and variable components provides more insight into the source of the variation in the planned and actual expenditures.

**EXHIBIT  13-13**

Activity-Based
Performance Report

| | Actual Costs[a] | Budgeted Costs | Budget Variance |
|---|---|---|---|
| Direct materials | $101,000 | $100,000 | $ 1,000 U |
| Direct labour | 80,000 | 80,000 | — |
| Maintenance | 55,000 | 64,000 | 9,000 F |
| Machining | 29,000 | 31,000 | 2,000 F |
| Inspections | 125,500 | 132,500 | 7,000 F |
| Setups | 46,500 | 45,000 | 1,500 U |
| Purchasing | 220,000 | 226,000 | 6,000 F |
| Total | $657,000 | $678,500 | $21,500 F |

[a] Actual levels of drivers: 10,000 direct labour hours, 8,000 machine hours, 25 setups, and 15,000 orders.

## Summary of Learning Objectives

**1. Define *budgeting* and discuss its role in planning, control, and decision making.**

Budgeting is the process of creating a financial plan of action. Budgeting plays a key role in planning, control, and decision making. Budgets also improve communication and coordination—a role that becomes increasingly important as organizations grow.

**2. Define and prepare a *master budget*, identify its major components, and explain the interrelationships of its various components.**

The master budget is an organization's comprehensive financial plan. It consists of the operating and financial budgets. The operating budget consists of the budgeted income statement and several supporting schedules. The sales budget (Schedule 1) consists of the anticipated quantity and price of all products to be sold. The production budget (Schedule 2) gives the expected production in units to meet the forecasted sales and desired ending inventory goals, given the existing beginning inventory. The direct materials purchases budget (Schedule 3) gives the necessary purchases during the year for every type of raw material to meet production and desired ending inventory goals. The direct labour budget (Schedule 4) and overhead budget (Schedule 5) give the amounts of these resources necessary for the coming year's production. The overhead budget may be broken down into fixed and variable components to facilitate the budget preparation. The selling and administrative expenses budget (Schedule 6) gives the forecasted costs for these functions. The finished goods inventory budget (Schedule 7) and the cost of goods sold budget (Schedule 8) detail production costs for the expected ending inventory and the units sold, respectively. The budgeted income statement (Schedule 9) outlines the net income to be realized if budgeted plans materialize.

The financial budget includes the cash budget, the capital expenditures budget, and the budgeted bal-

ance sheet. The cash budget (Schedule 10) is simply the beginning balance in the cash account, plus anticipated receipts, minus anticipated disbursements, plus or minus any necessary borrowing. The budgeted balance sheet (Schedule 11) gives the anticipated ending balances of the asset, liability, and equity accounts if budgeted plans hold.

**3. Describe flexible budgeting and identify the features that a budgetary system should have to encourage managers to engage in goal-congruent behaviour.**

The success of a budgetary system is affected by human factors. To discourage dysfunctional behaviour, organizations should avoid overemphasizing budgets as a control mechanism. Other areas of performance should be evaluated besides budget performance. Budget control can be improved by using flexible budgets and a participative budgeting approach, by setting realistic budget objectives, by providing frequent feedback on performance, by holding managers accountable only for controllable outcomes, and by providing nonmonetary as well as monetary rewards.

**4. Describe activity-based budgeting.**

Activity-based budgeting identifies activities, demands for activity output, and the cost of resources needed for the activity output. The most unique feature of an activity-based approach is that it includes a detailed listing of activities and their expected costs for the overhead, selling, and administrative categories. Activity-based budgeting is potentially more accurate than traditional budgeting, because it focuses on output measures for each activity and thus allows a manager to understand cost behaviour at a much more detailed level. Activity flexible budgeting is also more accurate, because it uses cost formulas that depend on each activity's output measures.

# Key Terms

Activity-based budgeting system  591
Activity flexible budgeting  592
Bottom-up budgeting  589
Budget committee  570
Budget director  570
Budgetary slack  590
Budgets  568
Cash budget  577
Continuous budget  570
Control  569
Controllable costs  590
Cost of goods sold budget  576
Direct labour budget  574
Direct materials purchases budget  573

Dysfunctional behaviour  588
Ending finished goods inventory
  budget  575
Feedback control  568
Feedforward control  568
Financial budgets  571
Flexible budget  584
Flexible budget variance  586
Goal congruence  588
Incentives  589
Master budget  570
Monetary incentives  589
Myopic behaviour  591
Nonmonetary incentives  589

Operating budgets  571
Overhead budget  574
Participative budgeting  589
Production budget  571
Pseudoparticipation  590
Sales budget  571
Selling and administrative expenses
  budget  574
Static budget  584
Strategic plan  568
Top-down budgeting  589
Variable budgets  585

# Review Problems

## I.  OPERATING BUDGETS

Young Metal Products produces coat racks. The projected sales and inventory data for the first quarter of the coming year are as follows:

| | |
|---|---|
| Unit sales | 100,000 |
| Unit price | $15 |
| Beginning inventory (units) | 8,000 |
| Ending inventory (units) | 12,000 |

The coat racks are moulded and then painted. Each rack requires 4 kilograms of metal, which costs $2.50 per kilogram. The beginning inventory of raw materials is 4,000 kilograms. The company wants to have 6,000 kilograms of metal in inventory at the end of the quarter. Each rack requires 30 minutes of direct labour time at $9 per hour.

**Required:**
  1.  Prepare a sales budget for the first quarter.
  2.  Prepare a production budget for the first quarter.
  3.  Prepare a direct materials purchases budget for the first quarter.
  4.  Prepare a direct labour budget for the first quarter.

### Solution
  1.  **Sales Budget**
      **For the First Quarter**

| | |
|---|---:|
| Units | 100,000 |
| Unit price | × $15 |
| Sales | $1,500,000 |

2. **Production Budget**
   **For the First Quarter**

| | |
|---|---:|
| Sales (in units) | 100,000 |
| Desired ending inventory | 12,000 |
| Total needs | 112,000 |
| Less: Beginning inventory | 8,000 |
| Units to be produced | 104,000 |

3. **Direct Materials Purchases Budget**
   **For the First Quarter**

| | |
|---|---:|
| Units to be produced | 104,000 |
| Direct materials per unit (kilograms) | x 4 |
| Production needs (kilograms) | 416,000 |
| Desired ending inventory (kilograms) | 6,000 |
| Total needs (kilograms) | 422,000 |
| Less: Beginning inventory (kilograms) | 4,000 |
| Materials to be purchased (kilograms) | 418,000 |
| Cost per kilogram | x $2.50 |
| Total purchase cost | $1,045,000 |

4. **Direct Labour Budget**
   **For the First Quarter**

| | |
|---|---:|
| Units to be produced | 104,000 |
| Labour: Hours per unit | x 0.5 |
| Total hours needed | 52,000 |
| Cost per hour | x $9 |
| Total direct labour cost | $468,000 |

## II. CASH BUDGET

Boston, Inc., expects to receive $45,000 from sales in March. In addition, it expects to sell property worth $3,500. Payments for materials and supplies are expected to be $10,000, direct labour payroll $12,500, and other cash expenditures $14,900. On March 1, the cash account balance is $1,230.

### Required:
1. Prepare a cash budget for Boston, Inc., for March.
2. Assume that the company requires a minimum cash balance of $15,000 and that it can borrow from the bank in multiples of $1,000 at the annual interest rate of 12 percent. What will the adjusted ending cash balance be for March? How much interest will the company owe in April, assuming that the entire amount borrowed in March will be paid back?

### Solution
1. **Cash Budget for March**

| | |
|---|---:|
| Beginning cash balance | $ 1,230 |
| Cash sales | 45,000 |
| Sale of property | 3,500 |
| Total cash available | $49,730 |
| Less disbursements: | |
|   Materials and supplies | $10,000 |
|   Direct labour payroll | 12,500 |
|   Other expenditures | 14,900 |
|     Total disbursements | $37,400 |
| Ending cash balance | $12,330 |

2.

| | |
|---|---:|
| Unadjusted ending cash balance | $12,330 |
| Plus: borrowing | 3,000 |
| Adjusted ending cash balance | $15,330 |

In April, interest owed will be $(1/12 \times 0.12 \times \$3,000) = \$30$.

## III. COMPREHENSIVE OPERATIONAL AND CASH BUDGETS

Sunfun Ltd., a medium-sized manufacturing company located in Montreal, makes lounge chairs for patios and solariums. It has designed a popular model made from durable composite polymer material that is also aesthetic and ergonomic. Terry Coleridge, Sunfun's budget director, is ready to begin preparing a master budget for 2005 based on the following information compiled by his staff:

a. The projected quarterly unit sales for 2005 are as follows:

| | |
|---|---|
| First quarter | 20,000 |
| Second quarter | 60,000 |
| Third quarter | 80,000 |
| Fourth quarter | 40,000 |

b. The selling price is $100 per unit. Eighty percent of the sales are on a cash basis, the remainder on credit. Seventy percent of the credit sales are collected during the quarter in which the sales occurred; 30 percent of the credit sales are collected the following quarter. There are no bad debts.

c. The planned beginning inventory of finished goods on January 1, 2005, is expected to be 2,000 units. The desired ending inventory for each quarter is 10 percent of the sales for the following quarter. The unit sales for the first quarter of 2006 are expected to be the same as the sales for the first quarter of 2005.

d. Each chair requires 1.5 hours of direct labour at $13 per hour and 2 units of direct materials at $20 per unit.

e. All direct materials are purchased on credit. Sixty percent of the purchases are paid during the quarter of acquisition, the remainder during the following quarter.

f. The quarterly production pattern has been quite stable. Sunfun's policy is to have 25,000 units of materials on hand at the end of the first and fourth quarters and 40,000 units at the end of the second and third quarters.

g. Wages and salaries are paid on the fifteenth and thirtieth of each month, immediately following each pay period in which they are earned.

h. Fixed overhead costs are $200,000 for each quarter. Of this total, one half is amortization. All other fixed overhead costs are paid in cash during the quarter in which they are incurred. The fixed overhead rate per unit is calculated using the annual budgeted fixed overhead costs and production volume.

i. Variable overhead costs are budgeted at $2 per direct labour hour. All variable overhead costs are paid during the quarter in which they are incurred.

j. Fixed selling and administrative expenses are $60,000 per year, including $20,000 amortization. They are incurred uniformly throughout the year. Budgeted variable selling and administrative expenses are $1 per unit sold. All selling and administrative expenses are paid during the quarter in which they are incurred.

k. Sunfun plans to pay quarterly dividends of $200,000.

l. Sunfun plans to purchase new production equipment in early January 2005, at a cost of $4,000,000. It will have a useful life of 10 years. It plans to make a down payment of $1,000,000 and issue a 7 percent, 10 year note payable for the balance. The annual interest and principal payments will be due on each anniversary date, starting in 2006.

m. For short-term cash needs, Sunfun will borrow at an annual rate of 6 percent in multiples of $100,000 and repay at the end of the first quarter in which cash becomes available.

n. An estimated income tax liability is 45 percent of the before-tax net income, payable at the end of the year.

o. The balance sheet on December 31, 2004, is as follows:

### Assets

| | |
|---|---|
| Cash | $ 280,000 |
| Accounts receivable | 210,000 |
| Direct materials inventory | 500,000 |
| Finished goods inventory | 133,000 |
| Plant and equipment | 14,600,000 |
| Total assets | $15,723,000 |

### Liabilities and Shareholders' Equity

| | |
|---|---|
| Accounts payable[a] | $ 600,000 |
| Capital stock | 14,000,000 |
| Retained earnings | 1,123,000 |
| Total liabilities and shareholders' equity | $15,723,000 |

[a]For purchase of direct materials only

## Required:

Prepare a master budget for each quarter of 2005 and for the year in total, including the following:

1. Sales budget
2. Production budget
3. Direct materials purchases budget
4. Direct labour budget
5. Overhead budget
6. Selling and administrative expenses budget
7. Ending finished goods inventory budget for 2005
8. Cost of goods sold budget for 2005
9. Cash budget
10. Budgeted income statement for 2005
11. Budgeted balance sheet for 2005

## Solution

### Schedule 1: Sales Budget (units in thousands)

| | Qtr 1 | Qtr 2 | Qtr 3 | Qtr 4 | Total |
|---|---|---|---|---|---|
| Units | 20 | 60 | 80 | 40 | 200 |
| Unit price | × $100 | × $100 | × $100 | × $100 | × $100 |
| Total sales | $2,000 | $6,000 | $8,000 | $4,000 | $20,000 |

### Schedule 2: Production Budget (units)

| | Qtr 1 | Qtr 2 | Qtr 3 | Qtr 4 | Total |
|---|---|---|---|---|---|
| Sales (Sch. 1) | 20,000 | 60,000 | 80,000 | 40,000 | 200,000 |
| Desired ending inventory | 6,000 | 8,000 | 4,000 | 2,000 | 2,000 |
| Total needs | 26,000 | 68,000 | 84,000 | 42,000 | 202,000 |
| Less: Beginning inventory | 2,000 | 6,000 | 8,000 | 4,000 | 2,000 |
| Production | 24,000 | 62,000 | 76,000 | 38,000 | 200,000 |

### Schedule 3: Direct Materials Purchases Budget (in thousands)

| | Qtr 1 | Qtr 2 | Qtr 3 | Qtr 4 | Total |
|---|---|---|---|---|---|
| Production | 24 | 62 | 76 | 38 | 200 |
| Materials/unit | × 2 | × 2 | × 2 | × 2 | × 2 |
| Production needs | 48 | 124 | 152 | 76 | 400 |
| Desired ending inventory | 25 | 40 | 40 | 25 | 25 |
| Total needs | 73 | 164 | 192 | 101 | 425 |
| Less: Beginning inventory | 25 | 25 | 40 | 40 | 25 |
| Purchases | 48 | 139 | 152 | 61 | 400 |
| Cost per unit | × $20 | × $20 | × $20 | × $20 | × $20 |
| Purchase cost | $960 | $2,780 | $3,040 | $1,220 | $8,000 |

### Schedule 4: Direct Labour Budget (in thousands)

| | Qtr 1 | Qtr 2 | Qtr 3 | Qtr 4 | Total |
|---|---|---|---|---|---|
| Production | 24 | 62 | 76 | 38 | 200 |
| Hours per unit | × 1.5 | × 1.5 | × 1.5 | × 1.5 | × 1.5 |
| Hours needed | 36 | 93 | 114 | 57 | 300 |
| Cost per hour | × $13 | × $13 | × $13 | × $13 | × $13 |
| Total cost | $468 | $1,209 | $1,482 | $741 | $3,900 |

### Schedule 5: Overhead Budget (in thousands)

| | Qtr 1 | Qtr 2 | Qtr 3 | Qtr 4 | Total |
|---|---|---|---|---|---|
| Budgeted hours | 36 | 93 | 114 | 57 | 300 |
| Variable rate | × $2 | × $2 | × $2 | × $2 | × $2 |
| Variable overhead | $ 72 | $186 | $228 | $114 | $600 |
| Fixed overhead | 200 | 200 | 200 | 200 | 800 |
| Total overhead | $272 | $ 386 | $428 | $314 | $1,400 |

### Schedule 6: Selling and Administrative Expenses Budget (in thousands)

| | Qtr 1 | Qtr 2 | Qtr 3 | Qtr 4 | Total |
|---|---|---|---|---|---|
| Budgeted sales | 20 | 60 | 80 | 40 | 200 |
| Variable rate | × $1 | × $1 | × $1 | × $1 | × $1 |
| Variable expenses | $20 | $60 | $80 | $40 | $200 |
| Fixed expenses | 15 | 15 | 15 | 15 | 60 |
| Total expenses | $35 | $75 | $95 | $55 | $260 |

### Schedule 7:  Ending Finished Goods Inventory Budget

Unit cost computation:

| | |
|---|---|
| Direct materials (2 units @ $20) | $40.00 |
| Direct labour (1.5 hours @ $13) | 19.50 |
| Overhead: | |
| Variable (1.5 hours @ $2) | 3.00 |
| Fixed ($800,000/200,000) | 4.00 |
| Total unit cost | $66.50 |

Budgeted Finished Goods Ending Inventory = 2,000 × $66.50 = $133,000

### Schedule 8:  Cost of Goods Sold Budget

| | |
|---|---|
| Direct materials used (Sch. 3) | $ 8,000,000 |
| Direct labour used (Sch. 4) | 3,900,000 |
| Overhead (Sch. 5) | 1,400,000 |
| Budgeted manufacturing costs | $13,300,000 |
| Add: | |
| Beginning finished goods inventory[a] | 133,000 |
| Goods available for sale | $13,433,000 |
| Less: | |
| Ending finished goods inventory (Sch. 7) | 133,000 |
| Budgeted cost of goods sold | $13,300,000 |

[a] 2,000 × $66.50 = $133,000

### Schedule 9: Cash Budget (in thousands)

|  | Qtr 1 | Qtr 2 | Qtr 3 | Qtr 4 | Total |
|---|---|---|---|---|---|
| Beginning cash balance | $ 280 | $ 24 | $1,260 | $4,104 | $ 280 |
| Collections: | | | | | |
| Credit sales: | | | | | |
| Current quarter[a] | 1,880 | 5,640 | 7,520 | 3,760 | 18,800 |
| Prior quarter[b] | 210 | 120 | 360 | 480 | 1,170 |
| Cash available | $2,370 | $5,784 | $9,140 | $8,344 | $20,250 |
| | | | | | |
| Less disbursements: | | | | | |
| Direct materials: | | | | | |
| Current quarter (60%) | $ 576 | $1,668 | $1,824 | $ 732 | $ 4,800 |
| Prior quarter (40%) | 600 | 384 | 1,112 | 1,216 | 3,312 |
| Direct labour | 468 | 1,209 | 1,482 | 741 | 3,900 |
| Overhead[c] | 172 | 286 | 328 | 214 | 1,000 |
| Selling and admin.[d] | 30 | 70 | 90 | 50 | 240 |
| Dividends | 200 | 200 | 200 | 200 | 800 |
| Income taxes[e] | — | — | — | 2,895 | 2,895 |
| Equipment | 1,000 | — | — | — | 1,000 |
| Total cash needs | $3,046 | $3,817 | $5,036 | $6,048 | $17,947 |
| | | | | | |
| Cash surplus (deficit) | ($ 676) | $1,967 | $4,104 | $2,296 | $ 2,303 |
| Bank loan | 700 | — | — | — | 700 |
| Repayment | — | (700) | — | — | (700) |
| Interest | — | (7) | — | — | (7) |
| Ending cash balance | $ 24 | $1,260 | $4,104 | $2,296 | $ 2,296 |

[a](Current quarter sales × 80%) + (Current quarter sales × 20% × 70%)
[b](Prior quarter sales × 20% × 30%)
[c]Net of amortization of $100,000 per quarter
[d]Net of amortization of $5,000 per quarter
[e]45% × Budgeted pre-tax income from the income statement below

### 10. Budgeted Income Statement
### For the Year Ending 12/31/2005

| | |
|---|---|
| Sales (Sch. 1) | $20,000,000 |
| Less: Cost of goods sold (Sch. 8) | 13,300,000 |
| Gross margin | $ 6,700,000 |
| Less: Selling & administrative expenses (Sch. 6) | 260,000 |
| Income before interest and taxes | $ 6,440,000 |
| Less: Interest expense (Sch. 9) | 7,000 |
| Income before taxes | $6,433,000 |
| Less: Income taxes (Sch. 9) | 2,895,000 |
| Net income | $ 3,538,000 |

### 11. Budgeted Balance Sheet
### 12/31/2005

| | |
|---|---:|
| Assets: | |
| Cash (Sch. 9) | $ 2,296,000 |
| Accounts receivable[a] | 240,000 |
| Direct materials inventory[b] | 500,000 |
| Finished goods inventory (Sch. 8) | 133,000 |
| Plant and equipment[c] | 18,180,000 |
| Total assets | $21,349,000 |
| Liabilities and Shareholders' Equity: | |
| Accounts payable[d] | $ 488,000 |
| Notes payable | 3,000,000 |
| Capital stock | 14,000,000 |
| Retained earnings[e] | 3,861,000 |
| Total liabilities and shareholders' equity | $21,349,000 |

[a]Fourth-quarter sales $4,000,000 × 20% × 30% = $240,000
[b]25,000 units × $20 = $500,000

| | |
|---|---:|
| [c]Beginning plant and equipment | $14,600,000 |
| Add: New equipment | 4,000,000 |
| Less: Amortization expense ($100,000 × 4 + $20,000) | (420,000) |
| Ending plant and equipment | $18,180,000 |

[d]Fourth-quarter purchases $1,220,000 × 40% = $488,000

| | |
|---|---:|
| [e]Beginning retained earnings | $1,123,000 |
| Plus: Net income | 3,538,000 |
| Less: Dividends paid | (800,000) |
| Ending retained earnings | $3,861,000 |

## Questions for Writing and Discussion

1. Define the term *budget*. How are budgets used in planning?

2. Define *control*. How are budgets used to control?

3. Explain how both small and large organizations can benefit from budgeting.

4. Discuss the main objectives of budgeting.

5. What is a master budget? An operating budget? A financial budget?

6. Explain the role of a sales forecast in budgeting. What is the difference between a sales forecast and a sales budget?

7. All budgets depend on the sales budget. Is this true? Explain.

8. How do master budgets differ for manufacturing, merchandising, and service organizations?

9. Discuss the differences between static and flexible budgets. Why are flexible budgets superior to static budgets for performance reporting?

10. Explain why mixed costs must be broken down into their fixed and variable components before a flexible budget can be developed.

11. Why is goal congruence important?

12. Why is it important for a manager to receive frequent feedback on his or her performance?

13. Discuss the roles of monetary and nonmonetary incentives. Do you believe that nonmonetary incentives are needed? Explain why or why not.

14. What is participative budgeting? Discuss its main advantages.

15. Easy budget targets can lead to diminished performance. Do you agree? Explain.

16. What is the role of top management in participative budgeting?

17. Explain why a manager may have an incentive to build slack into the budgets.

18. Explain how a manager can "milk the firm" to improve budgetary performance.

19. Identify performance measures other than budgets that can be used to discourage myopic behaviour. Discuss how you would use these measures.

20. How important are the behavioural aspects of a budgetary control system? Explain.

21. In an era of budgetary cuts, across-the-board cuts harm good programs more than bad programs. Do you agree? What approach to budget cutting would you recommend? Why?

22. Explain how an activity-based budget is prepared.

23. What is the difference between an activity flexible budget and a functional-based (traditional) flexible budget?

# Exercises

**13–1**

*Sales Budget*

**LO1, LO2**

Fresh-n-Clean, Inc., produces two laundry products: detergent and a powdered presoak. Both products are sold in 2-litre boxes. Detergent sells for $3.00 per box and presoak for $3.50 per box. Projected sales (in boxes) are as follows:

|  | Detergent | Presoak |
|---|---|---|
| First quarter, 2004 | 40,000 | 50,000 |
| Second quarter, 2004 | 55,000 | 50,000 |
| Third quarter, 2004 | 62,000 | 60,000 |
| Fourth quarter, 2004 | 70,000 | 70,000 |
| First quarter, 2005 | 45,000 | 55,000 |

The vice-president of sales believes that the projected sales are realistic and can be achieved by the company.

**Required:**
1. Prepare a sales budget for each quarter of 2004 and for the year in total. Show sales by product and in total for each period.
2. How can Fresh-n-Clean use this sales budget?

**13–2**

*Production Budget*

**LO2**

Refer to Exercise 13–1. Fresh-n-Clean prepares a production budget for each product. The beginning inventory of detergent on January 1 was 2,000 boxes. The company's policy is to have 10 percent of the next quarter's sales of detergent in ending inventory. The beginning inventory of presoak on January 1 was 3,200 boxes. The company's policy is to have 20 percent of the next quarter's sales of presoak in ending inventory.

**Required:**
Prepare a production budget for each product by quarter and for the year in total.

**13–3**

Pretty-Kitty, Inc., produces a variety of products for pets. Among them is a 200-gram can of cat food. The sales budget for the first four months of next year is as follows:

|            | Unit Sales | Dollar Sales |
|------------|------------|--------------|
| January    | 100,000    | $75,000      |
| February   | 120,000    | 90,000       |
| March      | 110,000    | 82,500       |
| April      | 100,000    | 75,000       |

Company policy requires that ending inventory for each month be 35 percent of the next month's sales. At the beginning of January, the inventory of cat food is 18,000 cans.

**Required:**

Prepare a production budget for the first quarter of the year. Show the number of cans that should be produced each month as well as for the quarter in total.

**13–4**

Refer to Exercise 13–3. Suppose that two raw materials required for making Pretty-Kitty's cat food are protein meal and cans. Each can of cat food requires a can and 100 grams of protein meal, which is mixed with water. Company policy requires that the ending inventory of raw materials for each month be 20 percent of the next month's production needs. This policy was met on January 1.

**Required:**

1. Prepare separate direct materials purchases budgets for cans and protein meal for January and February.
2. Can you prepare a direct materials purchases budget for March? Explain why or why not.

**13–5**

Carson, Inc. produces office supplies, including pencils. Pencils are bundled in packages of four, which are sold for $0.50. The sales budget for the first four months of the year for this product is as follows:

|            | Unit Sales | Dollar Sales |
|------------|------------|--------------|
| January    | 200,000    | $100,000     |
| February   | 240,000    | 120,000      |
| March      | 220,000    | 110,000      |
| April      | 200,000    | 100,000      |

Company policy requires that ending inventories for each month be 15 percent of next month's sales. However, at the beginning of January, due to greater sales in December than anticipated, the beginning inventory of pencils is only 18,000 packages.

**Required:**

Prepare a production budget for the first quarter of the year. Show the number of units that should be produced each month as well as for the quarter in total.

**13–6**

Lester Company produces a variety of labels, including iron-on name labels, which are sold to parents of schoolchildren. The schools require students to have their name on every article of clothing. The labels are sold in rolls of 1,000; each roll requires about 25 metres of paper strip. Each metre of paper strip costs $0.17. The company has budgeted the following production levels:

| | Units (Rolls) |
|---|---|
| March | 5,000 |
| April | 25,000 |
| May | 35,000 |
| June | 6,000 |

The company's inventory policy requires that enough paper strip be in ending monthly inventory to satisfy 20 percent of the following month's production needs. Inventory of paper strip at the beginning of March equals exactly the amount needed to satisfy this inventory policy.

**Required:**

Prepare a direct materials purchases budget for March, April, and May, showing purchases in units and in dollars for each month and in total.

**13–7**

*Direct Labour Budget*

LO2

Refer to the production budget in Exercise 13–6. Each roll of labels requires, on average, 0.03 direct labour hours. The average hourly direct labour rate is $8 per hour.

**Required:**

Prepare a direct labour budget for March, April, and May, showing the hours needed and the direct labour costs for each month and in total.

**13–8**

*Sales Budget*

LO2

Garland, Inc., manufactures six models of moulded plastic waste containers. Garland's budgeting team is finalizing the sales budget for the coming year. Sales in units and dollars for last year were as follows:

| Model | Number Sold | Price | Revenue |
|---|---|---|---|
| W–1 | 16,800 | $ 9 | $151,200 |
| W–2 | 18,000 | 15 | 270,000 |
| W–3 | 25,200 | 13 | 327,600 |
| W–4 | 16,200 | 10 | 162,000 |
| W–5 | 2,400 | 22 | 52,800 |
| W–6 | 1,000 | 26 | 26,000 |
| Total | | | $989,600 |

In looking over the previous year's sales figures, Garland's sales budgeting team recalls the following:

a. Model W–1's costs are rising faster than its price can rise. Garland is preparing to phase out this model; to that end, it plans to slash its advertising budget and to raise its price by 50 percent. The unit sales forecast for Model W–1 is 20 percent of the previous year's unit sales.

b. Models W–5 and W–6 were introduced on November 1 of the previous year. These are brightly coloured, heavy-duty, wheeled garbage containers designed for household use. Garland estimates that demand for both models will continue at the previous year's rate.

c. A competitor has announced plans to introduce an improved version of Model W–3. Garland believes that this model's price must be cut 20 percent to maintain unit sales at the previous year's level.

d. It is assumed that unit sales of all other models will increase by 10 percent, prices remaining constant.

**Required:**

Prepare a sales budget by product and in total for Garland, Inc., for the coming year.

**13–9**

Production Budget;
Direct Materials
Purchases Budget

LO2

Spreadsheet

Jenna Mitchell, owner of Jenna's Jams and Jellies, produces homemade-style jellies using fruits indigenous to her locality. She has estimated the following sales of 500-gram jars of fruit jelly for the rest of the year and January of next year:

| September | 100 |
|---|---|
| October | 150 |
| November | 170 |
| December | 225 |
| January | 100 |

Jenna likes to have 20 percent of the next month's sales needs on hand at the end of each month. This requirement was met on August 31. Materials needed for each jar of jelly are as follows:

| Fruit | 0.5 | kilograms |
|---|---|---|
| Sugar | 0.5 | kilograms |
| Pectin | 100 | grams |
| Jar sets | 1 | |

The materials inventory policy is to have 5 percent of the next month's fruit needs on hand, as well as 50 percent of the next month's production needs for all other materials. The relatively low inventory level for fruit is designed to prevent spoilage. Materials inventory on September 1 met this policy.

**Required:**

1. Prepare a production budget for September, October, November, and December.
2. Prepare a direct materials purchases budget for all materials used in the production of fruit jelly for September, October, and November. (Round all answers to the nearest whole unit.)
3. Why can't you prepare a direct materials purchases budget for December?

**13–10**

Direct Materials
Purchases Budget;
Budgeted Income
Statement

LO2

The following data relate to the operation of David Company Ltd., a retail store:

| **Sales Forecast 2006** | |
|---|---|
| April | $ 70,000 |
| May | 60,000 |
| June | 80,000 |
| July | 100,000 |
| August | 120,000 |

a. Cost of sales averages 40 percent of sales. Other variable costs are 20 percent of sales.
b. Inventory is maintained at twice the budgeted sales requirements for the following month.
c. Fixed costs are $20,000 per month.
d. The income tax rate is estimated to be 40 percent.

**Required:**

1. Prepare a direct materials purchases budget in dollars for June.
2. Prepare a budgeted income statement for June. (CGA Canada adapted)

**13–11**

Cash Receipts Budget

LO2

Andrea's Shop sells china, silverware, and kitchenware. A popular service is the wedding registry service, which includes free gift wrapping and delivery of gifts to local brides. Andrea accepts cash, cheques, and Visa, MasterCard, and American Express credit cards. These methods of payment have the following characteristics:

| | |
|---|---|
| Cash | Payment is immediate; no fee is charged. |
| Cheque | Payment is immediate; the bank charges $0.25 per cheque; 1 percent of cheque revenue is from "bad" cheques that Andrea cannot collect. |
| Visa/MasterCard | Andrea accumulates these credit card receipts throughout the month and submits them in one bundle for payment on the last day of the month. The money is credited to Andrea's account by the fifth day of the following month. A fee of 1.5 percent is charged by the credit card company. |
| American Express | Andrea accumulates these receipts throughout the month and mails them for payment on the last day of the month. American Express credits Andrea's account by the sixth day of the following month. A fee of 3.5 percent is charged by American Express. |

During a typical month, Andrea has sales of $24,000, broken down as follows:

| | |
|---|---|
| American Express | 20% |
| VISA/MasterCard | 50% |
| Cheque | 5% (average cheque is $37.50) |
| Cash | 25% |

**Required:**
If Andrea estimates sales of $30,000 in April and $60,000 in May, what are her planned net cash receipts for May?

**13–12**

*Cash Budget*

**LO2**

Spreadsheet

The owner of 24–7 Convenience Store has asked you to prepare a cash budget for June. After examining the company's records, you find the following:

a. Cash balance on June 1 is $345.
b. Actual sales for April and May are as follows:

| | April | May |
|---|---|---|
| Cash sales | $10,000 | $15,000 |
| Credit sales | 25,000 | 35,000 |
| Total sales | $35,000 | $50,000 |

c. Credit sales are collected over a three-month period: 50 percent in the month of sale, 30 percent in the second month, and 15 percent in the third month. The sales collected in the third month are subject to a 1.5 percent late fee, but only half of the affected customers pay the late fee, and the owner does not think it is worthwhile to try to collect from the other half. The remaining sales are uncollectible.
d. Inventory purchases average 60 percent of a month's total sales. Of these purchases, 40 percent are paid in the month of purchase. The remaining 60 percent are paid for in the following month.
e. Salaries and wages are $8,700 a month, including a salary of $4,500 paid to the owner.
f. Rent is $1,200 per month.
g. Taxes to be paid in June are $5,500.

The owner also tells you that he expects cash sales of $20,000 and credit sales of $40,000 for June. No minimum cash balance is required. The owner does not have access to short-term loans.

**Required:**
1. Prepare a cash budget for June. Include supporting schedules for cash collections and cash payments.

2. Did the business show a negative cash balance for June? Assuming that the owner has no hope of establishing a line of credit for the business, what recommendations would you make to the owner for dealing with a negative cash balance?

**13–13**

*Overhead Budget;
Flexible Budget*

**LO2, LO3**

Lyman, Inc., manufactures machine parts in its St. John's plant. Lyman has developed the following flexible budget for overhead for the coming year. Activity level is measured in direct labour hours.

|  | Variable-Cost Formula | Activity Level (hours) | | |
|---|---|---|---|---|
|  |  | 20,000 | 30,000 | 40,000 |
| Variable costs: |  |  |  |  |
| Maintenance | $1.00 | $ 20,000 | $ 30,000 | $ 40,000 |
| Supplies | 0.50 | 10,000 | 15,000 | 20,000 |
| Power | 0.10 | 2,000 | 3,000 | 4,000 |
| Total variable costs | $1.60 | $ 32,000 | $ 48,000 | $ 64,000 |
| Fixed costs: |  |  |  |  |
| Amortization |  | $  7,200 | $  7,200 | $  7,200 |
| Salaries |  | 64,800 | 64,800 | 64,800 |
| Total fixed costs |  | $ 72,000 | $ 72,000 | $ 72,000 |
| Total overhead costs |  | $104,000 | $120,000 | $136,000 |

The plant produces two different types of parts. The production budget for October is 48,000 units for Part 301 and 18,000 units for Part 414. Part 301 requires 15 minutes of direct labour time, and Part 414 requires 20 minutes. Fixed overhead costs are incurred uniformly throughout the year.

**Required:**
Prepare an overhead budget for October.

**13–14**

*Activity-Based Budget;
Static and Flexible
Budget*

**LO4**

Jamison, Inc., uses three forklifts to move materials from Receiving to Stores. The forklifts are also used to move materials from Stores to the production area. The forklifts are obtained through an operating lease that costs $8,000 per year per forklift. Jamison employs 10 forklift operators, who receive an average salary of $40,000 per year, including benefits. Each move requires the use of a crate. The crates are used to store the parts and are emptied only when the parts are used in production. Crates are disposed of after one cycle (two moves); a cycle is defined as Receiving to Stores to Production. Each crate costs $2. Fuel for a forklift costs $1.20 per litre. A litre of gas is used for every 20 moves. Forklifts can make three moves per hour and are available for 280 days per year, 24 hours per day. The remaining time is downtime for various reasons. Each operator works 40 hours per week and 50 weeks per year.

**Required:**
1. Prepare an annual budget for the activity of moving materials, assuming that all activity capacity is used. Identify which resources you would treat as fixed costs and which as variable costs.
2. Assume that Jamison uses only 90 percent of the activity capacity. What is the budget for this level of activity?
3. Suppose that a redesign of the plant layout reduces the demand for moving materials by 75 percent. What would be the budget for this new activity level?

**13–15**

Overhead Budget;
Flexible Budget

LO2, LO3

Regina Johnson, controller for Pet-Care Company, is in the process of developing a flexible budget for overhead costs. The company produces two types of dog food. One, BasicDiet, is a standard mixture for healthy dogs. The second, SpecDiet, is a reduced-protein formulation for older dogs with health problems. The two dog foods use common raw materials in different proportions. The company expects to produce 100,000 (20 kilogram) bags of each product during the coming year. BasicDiet requires 0.25 direct labour hours per bag, and SpecDiet requires 0.30. Regina has developed the following fixed and variable costs for each of the four overhead items:

| Overhead Item | Fixed Cost | Variable Rate per DLH |
|---|---|---|
| Maintenance | $17,000 | $0.40 |
| Power | — | 0.50 |
| Indirect labour | 26,500 | 1.60 |
| Rent | 18,000 | — |

**Required:**
1. Prepare an overhead budget for the expected activity level for the coming year.
2. Prepare an overhead budget for production that is 10 percent higher than expected (for both products), and another for production that is 20 percent lower than expected.

**13–16**

Performance Report

LO3

Refer to the information given in Exercise 13–15. Assume that Pet-Care actually produced 120,000 bags of BasicDiet and 100,000 bags of SpecDiet. The actual overhead costs incurred were as follows:

| | |
|---|---|
| Maintenance | $ 40,500 |
| Power | 31,700 |
| Indirect labour | 119,000 |
| Rent | 18,000 |

**Required:**
1. Prepare a performance report for the period.
2. Based on the report, would you judge any of the variances to be significant? Can you suggest some possible reasons for the variances?

**13–17**

Cash Receipts and
Payments Budgets

LO2

The following information pertains to Telnor Corporation's sales revenue:

| | November 2005 (Actual) | December 2005 (Actual) | January 2006 (Budgeted) |
|---|---|---|---|
| Cash sales | $ 80,000 | $100,000 | $ 60,000 |
| Credit sales | 240,000 | 360,000 | 180,000 |
| Total sales | $320,000 | $460,000 | $240,000 |

Management estimates that 5 percent of credit sales are uncollectible. Of the credit sales that are collected, 60 percent are collected during the month of sale and the remainder during the month following the sale. Purchases of inventory each month are 70 percent of the next month's projected total sales. All purchases of inventory are on account; 25 percent are paid during the month of purchase and the remainder during the month following the purchase.

**Required:**
1. What are the budgeted cash collections in December 2005 from November 2005 credit sales?
2. What are the total budgeted cash receipts in January 2006?
3. What is the budgeted amount of cash payments for inventory purchases in December 2005? (US CMA adapted)

**13–18**

LO3

An effective budget converts an organization's goals and objectives into data. The budget serves as a blueprint for management plans. The budget is also the basis for control. Management performance can be evaluated by comparing actual results with the budget.

Thus, preparing the budget is essential for the successful operation of an organization. Finding the resources to implement the budget—that is, getting from the starting point to the ultimate goal—requires the extensive use of human resources. How managers perceive their roles in the budgeting process is important to the successful use of the budget as an effective tool for planning, communication, and control.

**Required:**

1. Discuss the behavioural implications of planning and control under the following approaches:
   a. An imposed budgetary approach.
   b. A participative budgetary approach.
2. Communication plays an important role in the budgetary process, whether a participative or an imposed budgetary approach is used.
   a. Discuss the differences between communication flows in these two budgetary approaches.
   b. Discuss the behavioural implications associated with the communication process for each approach. (US CMA adapted)

**13–19**

LO3

Budgeted overhead costs for two different levels of activity, measured in labour hours, are as follows:

|             | Direct Labour Hours | |
|-------------|----------|----------|
|             | **1,000** | **2,000** |
| Maintenance | $10,000  | $16,000  |
| Amortization | 5,000   | 5,000    |
| Supervision | 15,000   | 15,000   |
| Supplies    | 1,400    | 2,800    |
| Power       | 750      | 1,500    |
| Other       | 8,100    | 8,200    |

**Required:**
Prepare a flexible budget for the activity level of 1,650 direct labour hours.

**13–20**

LO2

EMP & Associates, a legal firm, has found from past experience that 30 percent of its services are paid in cash. The remaining 70 percent are on credit. An ageing schedule for accounts receivable reveals the following pattern:

a. Ten percent of fees on credit are paid during the month the service is rendered.
b. Seventy percent of fees on credit are paid during the month following the performance of service.
c. Seventeen percent of fees on credit are paid during the second month following the performance of service.
d. Three percent of fees on credit are never collected.

Fees on credit that have not been paid until the second month following the performance of the service are considered overdue and are subject to a 2 percent late charge. The firm has developed the following forecast of fees:

| | |
|---|---|
| May | $228,000 |
| June | 255,000 |
| July | 204,000 |
| August | 240,000 |
| September | 300,000 |

**Required:**

Prepare a schedule of cash receipts for August and September.

**13–21**

*Cash Budget*

LO2

Finnco Company purchased direct materials on account as follows:

| | |
|---|---|
| June | $20,000 |
| July | $25,000 |
| August | $30,000 |

The company pays 25 percent of accounts payable during the month of purchase and the remaining 75 percent during the following month.

Direct labour costs were $40,000 in July and $50,000 in August. The company has discovered that typically 90 percent of direct labour costs are paid in cash during the month in which costs are incurred; the remainder is paid during the following month. Overhead costs in August were $70,000, including $5,500 amortization.

The company borrowed $10,000 on May 1. Interest on the principal payment accrues at the rate of 12 percent per year. The loan, plus all interest owing, was repaid on August 31.

**Required:**

Prepare a schedule of cash payments for August.

**13–22**

*Multiple Choice*

LO1, LO2, LO3, LO4

Choose the single *best* answer for each of the following multiple-choice questions:

1. Which of the following is an advantage of budgeting?
   a. It forces managers to plan.
   b. It can improve decision making.
   c. It can provide a standard for performance evaluation.
   d. It can improve communication and coordination.
   e. All of the above.

2. Which of the following budgets is not part of the operating budget?
   a. Sales budget.
   b. Overhead budget.
   c. Ending finished goods inventory budget.
   d. Cash budget.
   e. None of the above.

3. A flexible budget
   a. can be used only for planning purposes.
   b. is the basis for the master budget.
   c. can help managers deal with uncertainty.
   d. cannot be used in manufacturing companies.
   e. always shows at least two levels of activity.

4. A budget based on the predicted usage of unit-level and non-unit-level drivers is a(n)
   a. static budget.
   b. flexible budget.
   c. operating budget.
   d. financial budget.
   e. activity flexible budget.

# Problems

**13–23**

Operating Budget;
Comprehensive
Analysis

LO2

Algonquin Manufacturing Company produces a subassembly used in the production of jet aircraft engines. The assembly is sold to engine manufacturers and to aircraft maintenance facilities. Projected sales for the coming four months in units are as follows:

| January | 40,000 |
| February | 50,000 |
| March | 60,000 |
| April | 60,000 |

The following data pertain to production policies and manufacturing specifications:

a. Finished goods inventory on January 1 is 32,000 units, each costing $148.71. The desired ending inventory for each month is 80 percent of next month's sales.

b. The data on materials used are as follows:

| Direct Materials | Per-Unit Usage | Unit Cost |
|---|---|---|
| Metal | 10 kilograms | $8 |
| Components | 6 kilograms | $2 |

c. The inventory policy dictates that sufficient materials be on hand at the beginning of the month to produce 50 percent of that month's estimated sales. This is exactly the amount of material on hand on January 1.

d. The direct labour used per unit of output is four hours. The average direct labour cost per hour is $9.25.

e. Overhead each month is estimated using a flexible budget formula. Activity is measured in direct labour hours.

| | Fixed-Cost Component | Variable-Cost Component |
|---|---|---|
| Supplies | — | $1.00 |
| Power | — | 0.50 |
| Maintenance | $ 30,000 | 0.40 |
| Supervision | 16,000 | — |
| Amortization | 200,000 | — |
| Taxes | 12,000 | — |
| Other | 80,000 | 1.50 |

f. Monthly selling and administrative expenses are also estimated using a flexible budget formula. Activity is measured in units sold.

| | Fixed Costs | Variable Costs |
|---|---|---|
| Salaries | $50,000 | — |
| Commissions | — | $2.00 |
| Amortization | 40,000 | — |
| Shipping | — | 1.00 |
| Other | 20,000 | 0.60 |

g. The unit selling price of the subassembly is $180.

h. All sales and purchases are for cash. The cash balance on January 1 equals $400,000. If the company develops a cash shortage by the end of the month, sufficient cash is borrowed to cover the shortage. Any cash borrowed is repaid at the end of the quarter with the interest due. Cash borrowed at the end of the quarter is repaid at the end of the following quarter. The annual interest rate is 12 percent. No money is owed at the beginning of January.

**Required:**
Prepare a monthly operating budget for the first quarter with the following schedules:

1. Sales budget
2. Production budget
3. Direct materials purchases budget
4. Direct labour budget
5. Overhead budget
6. Selling and administrative expenses budget
7. Ending finished goods inventory budget
8. Cost of goods sold budget
9. Budgeted income statement
10. Cash budget

**13–24**

*Cash Budget;*
*Budgeted Balance*
*Sheet*

**LO2**

Spreadsheet

Ryan Richards, controller for TopMart Retailers, has assembled the following data to assist in the preparation of a cash budget for the third quarter of 2005:

a. Sales:

| | |
|---|---|
| May (actual) | $100,000 |
| June (actual) | 120,000 |
| July (estimated) | 90,000 |
| August (estimated) | 100,000 |
| September (estimated) | 135,000 |
| October (estimated) | 110,000 |

b. Each month, 30 percent of sales are for cash and 70 percent are on credit. The collection pattern for credit sales is 20 percent during the month of sale, 50 percent during the following month, and 30 percent during the second month following the sale.

c. Each month, the ending inventory is exactly 50 percent of the cost of next month's sales. The markup on goods is 25 percent of cost.

d. Inventory purchases are paid during the month following the purchase.

e. Recurring monthly expenses are as follows:

| | |
|---|---|
| Salaries and wages | $10,000 |
| Amortization on plant and equipment | 4,000 |
| Utilities | 1,000 |
| Other | 1,700 |

f. Property taxes of $15,000 are due and payable on July 15, 2005.

g. Advertising fees of $6,000 must be paid on August 20, 2005.

h. A lease on a new storage facility is scheduled to begin on September 2, 2005. Monthly payments are $5,000.

i. The company has a policy of maintaining a minimum cash balance of $10,000. If necessary, it will borrow to meet its short-term needs. All borrowing occurs at the beginning of the month. All principal and interest payments are made at the end of the month. The annual interest rate is 9 percent. The company must borrow in multiples of $1,000.

j. The partially completed balance sheet on June 30, 2005, is as follows:

| | | | |
|---|---|---|---|
| Cash | $ ? | | |
| Accounts receivable | ? | | |
| Inventory | ? | | |
| Plant and equipment | 425,000 | | |
| Accounts payable[a] | | $ ? | |
| Common stock | | 210,000 | |
| Retained earnings | | 268,750 | |
| Total | $ ? | $ ? | |

[a]Accounts payable is for inventory purchases only.

**Required:**
1. Complete the balance sheet given in (j).
2. Prepare a cash budget for each month in the third quarter and for the quarter in total. (The third quarter begins on July 1.) Provide a supporting schedule of cash collections.
3. Prepare a budgeted balance sheet as of September 30, 2005.

**13–25**

Cash Budget

LO2

The partially completed trial balance for Nepean Trade Fair on April 1 includes the following information:

| | Debits | Credits |
|---|---|---|
| Cash | $ 6,000 | |
| Accounts receivable | 19,500 | |
| Allowance for bad debts | | $2,400 |
| Merchandise inventory | 12,000 | |
| Accounts payable (merchandise) | | 9,000 |

Purchases are payable within 10 days. Assume that one-third of the purchases of any month are due and paid during the following month. The cost of merchandise purchased is $10 per unit. The company's policy is to have an inventory equal to 50 percent of the following month's unit sales on hand at the end of each month.

Sales terms include a 1 percent discount for payments made by the end of the calendar month in which the sales occurred. Past experience indicates that 60 percent of the billings will be collected during the month of sale, 30 percent during the following month, and 6 percent during the second following month. The remaining 4 percent will be uncollectible.

Sales data are as follows:

| | |
|---|---|
| Selling price per unit | $ 15 |
| February actual sales revenue | 15,000 |
| March actual sales revenue | 45,000 |
| April estimated sales revenue | 36,000 |
| May estimated sales revenue | 27,000 |
| Total estimated sales revenue for the year | 450,000 |

The fiscal year begins on February 1. Excluding bad debts, the total budgeted selling and administrative expenses for the year are estimated to be $70,500, of which $21,000 represents fixed expenses, including $9,000 amortization. Fixed expenses are incurred uniformly throughout the year. The balance of the selling and administrative expenses varies with sales. Expenses are paid as incurred.

**Required:**
Prepare a cash budget for April. (CGA Canada adapted)

| | |
|---|---|
| **13–26** | The balance sheet of Victoria Company on December 31, 2004, is as follows: |

| | |
|---|---:|
| Cash | $ 25,600 |
| Accounts receivable (net of allowance for doubtful accounts of $6,400) | 121,600 |
| Inventory | 51,200 |
| Fixed assets (net of accumulated amortization of $192,000) | 128,000 |
| Total assets | $326,400 |
| | |
| Accounts payable (for inventory purchases) | $264,000 |
| Common shares | 40,000 |
| Retained earnings | 22,400 |
| Total liabilities and shareholders' equity | $326,400 |

Cash Budget;
Budgeted Income
Statement

LO2

Projected sales are $352,000 for January and $384,000 for February. The gross profit percentage is 25 percent. Cash collections for accounts receivable are estimated to be 50 percent during the month of sale, and 48 percent during the following month. The remaining 2 percent are uncollectible. Purchases of inventory each month are 75 percent of the next month's projected sales and are paid in full during the following month. Amortization is $16,000 per month. Other expenses, $52,800 per month, are paid in cash during the month in which they are incurred.

**Required:**

Prepare a cash budget and budgeted income statement for January 2005. (CGA Canada adapted)

**13–27**

Cash Collections;
Cash Disbursements

LO2

Laurier Medical Products, Ltd., has provided you with the following information for July, August, and September 2006 for cash budgeting purposes:

a. Balances on July 1 are expected to be as follows:

| | |
|---|---|
| Cash | $5,500 |
| Accounts receivable | 437,000 |
| Inventories | 309,400 |
| Accounts payable | 133,055 |

b. The budget is based on the following assumptions:
- Each month's sales are billed on the last day of the month.
- Customers are allowed a 3 percent discount for payments made within 10 days of the billing date. Receivables are recorded at the gross amount.
- Sixty percent of the billings are collected within the discount period, 25 percent are collected by the end of the month after the sale, 9 percent are collected by the end of the second month after the sale, and 6 percent remain uncollectible.
- Fifty-four percent of all purchases of material and selling and administrative expenses are paid during the month in which they are incurred. The remainder is paid during the following month.
- Each month's ending inventory in units is 130 percent of the next month's sales in units.
- The cost of each unit of inventory is $20.
- Selling and administrative expenses, of which $2,000 is amortization, are $16,000, plus 9 percent of the month's sales.

c. Actual and projected sales are as follows:

| | Sales | Units |
|---|---|---|
| May | $354,000 | 11,800 |
| June | 363,000 | 12,100 |
| July | 357,000 | 11,900 |
| August | 342,000 | 11,400 |
| September | 360,000 | 12,000 |
| October | 366,000 | 12,200 |

**Required:**

Calculate the following:

1.  Budgeted cash disbursements for August 2006.
2.  Budgeted cash collections for July 2006.
3.  Budgeted number of units of inventory to be purchased during September 2006. (CMA Canada adapted)

**13–28**

*Cash Budget; Budgeted Income Statement*

**LO2**

Maple Leaf Supply Company buys and sells a product line with an average selling price of $20 per unit. All sales are on credit, with a 2 percent discount available to customers who pay their accounts by the end of the month of purchase. On average, 80 percent of the customers pay within the discount period, 4 percent never pay their account, and the others pay during the month following the sale. The accountant recognizes the estimated bad debts at the end of each month.

Purchases of the product occur evenly throughout the month at an average price of $9 per unit. The targeted ending inventory is 200 units. All purchases are on account, due within 10 days after the purchase, with no discounts. As a result, two-thirds of the purchases are paid during the month in which the purchase occurred and one-third during the following month.

Other information:

1.  Rent and utilities of $1,200 are paid on the 20th of each month, and employee salaries of $6,700 are paid on the 28th of each month.
2.  Office supplies are purchased in January, April, July, and October for use in each quarter. The quarterly outlays have been $4,200.
3.  Office equipment, with an expected five-year life, was purchased at the beginning of 2004. Its net book value is currently $9,350. The company uses straight-line amortization.
4.  Monthly sales in units were are follows:

| | Estimated | Actual |
|---|---|---|
| December 2005 | 1,300 | 1,400 |
| January 2006 | 1,600 | 1,400 |
| February 2006 | 1,200 | 1,200 |
| March 2006 | 850 | — |
| April 2006 | 900 | — |

The cash balance on March 1, 2006, is $2,350. The company has a good credit rating, and it can borrow to cover short-term cash needs.

**Required:**

1.  Prepare a schedule of budgeted cash receipts and disbursements for March 2006. Will the company need a loan?
2.  Prepare a budgeted income statement for March 2006. (CMA Canada adapted)

**13–29**

Participative Budgeting; Not-for-Profit Setting

LO3

Scott Weidner, Deputy Minister of a provincial department of social services, recognizes the importance of the budgetary process for planning, control, and motivation. He believes that a properly implemented process of participative budgeting and management by exception will motivate the employees to improve productivity in their departments. Based on this philosophy, he has implemented the following budgetary procedures:

1. An appropriation target figure is given to each department manager. This amount represents the maximum funding that each department can expect to receive for the next fiscal year.
2. Department managers develop their individual budgets within the following spending constraints, as directed by the controller's office:
   a. Requests for spending cannot exceed the appropriated target.
   b. All fixed expenditures should be included in the budget. Fixed expenditures include such items as contracts and salaries at current levels.
   c. All projects directed by the federal government should be included in the budget in their entirety.
3. The controller's office consolidates the requests from various programs into one budget for the entire department.
4. On final budget approval by the legislature, the controller's office allocates the funds to various programs, based on directives from the deputy minister. However, a specified percentage of each program's appropriation is held back in anticipation of potential budget cuts and special funding needs. The amount and use of this contingency fund is left to the discretion of each program manager.
5. Each program manager is allowed to adjust his or her budget when necessary to operate within the reduced appropriation level. However, as stated in the original directive, specific projects authorized by the federal government must remain intact.
6. The budget is used as a basis for management-by-exception reporting. Excessive expenditures by account for each program are highlighted on a monthly basis. Program managers are expected to account for all expenditures that exceed the budget, and fiscal responsibility is an important factor in the performance evaluation of program managers. Scott believes that the policy of allowing managers to participate in the budget process and holding them accountable for the results is essential, especially during the times of limited resources. He also believes that it motivates managers to improve the efficiency and effectiveness of their programs, because they have provided input into the budgetary process and are required to justify any unfavourable performance.

**Required:**
1. Discuss the advantages and limitations of participative budgeting.
2. Identify deficiencies in Scott Weidner's outline for a budgetary process. Recommend how each deficiency identified can be corrected. (US CMA adapted)

**13–30**

Cash Budget

LO2

The controller of Manotik Company is gathering data to prepare a cash budget for July 2005. The following information is available:

a. Of all sales, 30 percent are cash sales.
b. Of credit sales, 60 percent are collected during the month of sale. Half of the credit sales collected during the month are paid within 10 days of the invoice and receive a 2 percent cash discount. Twenty percent of credit sales are collected during the following month and the balance during the second following month. There are almost no bad debts.

c. Actual sales for the second quarter (April–June) and budgeted sales for the third quarter (July–September) are as follows:

| | Sales |
|---|---|
| April | $ 460,000 |
| May | 600,000 |
| June | 1,000,000 |
| July | 1,140,000 |
| August | 1,200,000 |
| September | 1,134,000 |

d. The company sells all that it produces each month. The cost of raw materials is 24 percent of sales. The company requires a monthly ending inventory equal to the next month's production requirements. Fifty percent of raw material purchases are paid during the month of purchase, the remaining 50 percent during the following month.

e. Wages are $110,000 each month and are paid during the month in which they are incurred.

f. Budgeted monthly operating expenses are $336,000, of which $50,000 is amortization and $6,000 is expired prepaid insurance. The annual premium of $72,000 is paid on January 1.

g. Dividends of $140,000, declared on June 30, will be paid on July 15.

h. Old equipment will be sold for $25,200 on July 4.

i. On July 13, new equipment will be purchased for $168,000.

j. The company maintains a minimum cash balance of $20,000.

k. The cash balance on July 1 is $27,000.

**Required:**

Prepare a cash budget for July, including a supporting schedule of cash collections from sales.

**13–31**

Revision of Operating Budget; Cost of Goods Sold Budget; Budgeted Income Statement

LO2

Mary Campeau founded Macam Company five years ago. The company produces modems for the telecommunications industry, and business has expanded rapidly. Bob Wells, the controller, prepared a budget for the fiscal year ending August 31, 2006. The budget was based on the prior year's sales and production activity, because Mary believed that the sales growth experienced during the prior year would not continue at the same pace. The budgeted income statement and cost of goods sold budget for 2006 are as follows:

**Budgeted Income Statement (in thousands)**
**For the Year Ending August 31, 2006**

| | |
|---|---|
| Net sales | $31,248 |
| Less: Cost of goods sold | 20,765 |
| Gross margin | $10,483 |
| Less: Operating expenses | 5,400 |
| Income before taxes | $ 5,083 |

**Budgeted Cost of Goods Sold (in thousands)**
**For the Year Ending August 31, 2006**

| | | |
|---|---|---|
| Direct materials: | | |
| Materials inventory, September 1, 2005 | $ 1,360 | |
| Materials purchased | 14,476 | |
| Available for use | 15,836 | |
| Less: Materials inventory, August 31, 2006 | 1,628 | |
| Direct materials used | | $14,208 |
| Direct labour | | 1,134 |
| Overhead: | | |
| Indirect materials | $1,421 | |
| General | 3,240 | 4,661 |
| Cost of goods manufactured | | $20,003 |
| Finished goods, September 1, 2005 | | 1,169 |
| Total goods available | | $21,172 |
| Less: Finished goods, August 31, 2006 | | 407 |
| Cost of goods sold | | $20,765 |

On December 5, 2005, Mary and Bob met to discuss the first-quarter operating results. Bob believed that several changes should be made to the budget assumptions that had been used to prepare the budgeted statements. He prepared the following notes summarizing the changes, which had become known after the first-quarter results were compiled.

a. Actual first-quarter production was 35,000 units. The estimated production for the fiscal year should be increased from 162,000 to 170,000, with the production for the remaining nine months of the fiscal year scheduled in equal segments.

b. The planned ending inventory for finished goods of 3,300 units at the end of the fiscal year remains unchanged. The finished goods inventory of 9,300 units as of September 1, 2005, had dropped to 9,000 units by November 30, 2006. The finished goods inventory at the end of the fiscal year will be valued at the average manufacturing costs for the year.

c. Direct materials sufficient to produce 16,000 units were on hand at the beginning of the fiscal year. The plan to have the equivalent of 18,500 units of production in direct materials inventory at the end of the fiscal year remains unchanged. Direct materials inventory is valued on a LIFO basis. Direct materials equivalent to 37,500 units of output were purchased for $3.3 million during the first quarter of the fiscal year. The suppliers have informed the company that direct materials prices will increase by 5 percent on March 1, 2006. Direct materials needed for the remainder of the fiscal year will be purchased evenly throughout the last nine months.

d. Based on historical data, projected indirect materials costs are 10 percent of the cost of direct materials used.

e. One half of general manufacturing overhead and all selling and general and administrative expenses are fixed.

**Required:**

Based on the new information, prepare the revised budgeted income statement and cost of goods sold budget for the year ending August 31, 2006. (US CMA adapted)

**13–32**

*Performance Reporting; Behavioural Considerations*

**LO1, LO3**

Espanola Power Tools, Inc., is a manufacturer of small industrial tools with annual sales of approximately $3.5 million. Sales growth has been steady during the year, and there is no evidence of cyclical demand. Production has increased gradually during the year and has been evenly distributed throughout each month. The company has a sequential processing system. The four manufacturing departments—casting, machining, finishing, and packaging—are all in the same building. Fixed overhead is assigned using a plantwide rate.

The company has always been able to compete with other manufacturers of small tools. However, its market has expanded only in response to product innovation. Thus, research and product development are very important and have helped the company expand and maintain its market share.

Carla Sutherland, the controller, has designed and implemented a new budget system in response to concerns voiced by George Doni, the president. Carla has prepared an annual budget, divided into 12 montly components. This budget can be used to assist in the timely evaluation of monthly performance.

George is visibly upset when he receives the May performance report for the machining department: "How can they be efficient enough to produce nine extra units every working day and still miss the budget by $300 per day?" Gene Jordan, supervisor of the machining department, cannot understand "all the red ink"— he knows his department operated more efficiently in May than it had in months. "I was expecting a pat on the back," he exclaims, "and instead the boss tore me apart, and I don't even know why!"

**Espanola Power Tools, Inc.**
**Machining Department Performance Report**
**For the Month Ended May 31, 2005**

|  | Budgeted | Actual | Variance |
|---|---|---|---|
| Volume in units | 3,000 | 3,185 | 185 F |
| Variable manufacturing costs: |  |  |  |
|   Direct materials | $24,000 | $ 24,843 | $ 843 U |
|   Direct labour | 27,750 | 29,302 | 1,552 U |
|   Variable overhead | 33,300 | 35,035 | 1,735 U |
|   Total variable costs | $85,050 | $ 89,180 | $4,130 U |
| Fixed manufacturing costs: |  |  |  |
|   Indirect labour | $ 3,300 | $ 3,334 | $ 34 U |
|   Amortization | 1,500 | 1,500 | — |
|   Taxes | 300 | 300 | — |
|   Insurance | 240 | 240 | — |
|   Other | 930 | 1,027 | 97 U |
|   Total fixed costs | $ 6,270 | $ 6,401 | $ 131 U |
| Corporate costs: |  |  |  |
|   Research and development | $ 2,400 | $ 3,728 | $1,328 U |
|   Selling and administrative | 3,600 | 4,075 | 475 U |
|   Total corporate costs | $ 6,000 | $ 7,803 | $1,803 U |
| Total costs | $97,320 | $103,384 | $6,064 U |

**Required:**

1. Review the May performance report. Use the information given in the report and elsewhere to:
   a. discuss the strengths and weaknesses of the new budgetary system, *and*
   b. identify the weaknesses of the performance report, explaining how it should be revised to eliminate each weakness.
2. Prepare a revised report for the machining department using the May data.
3. What other changes would you make to improve the company's budgetary system? (US CMA adapted)

**13–33**

*Functional versus Flexible Budgets*

**LO3, LO4**

Amy Clarke, a production manager, was upset with the latest performance report, which indicated that she was $100,000 over budget. Given the efforts that she and her employees had made, she was sure the company had met or exceeded the budget. Now she was not only upset but also genuinely puzzled over the results. Three items—direct labour, power, and setups—were over budget. The actual costs for these three items are as follows:

| | |
|---|---:|
| Direct labour | $210,000 |
| Power | 135,000 |
| Setups | 140,000 |
| Total | $485,000 |

Amy knew that her operation had produced more units than originally budgeted, so naturally, more power and labour had been used. She also knew that scheduling uncertainties had led to more setups than planned. When she pointed this out to Gary Grant, the controller, he assured her that the budgeted costs had been adjusted for the increase in productive activity. Curious, Amy questioned Gary about the methods used to make the adjustment.

**Gary**: "If the actual level of activity differs from the original planned level, we adjust the budget by using budget formulas—formulas that allow us to predict the costs for different levels of activity."

**Amy**: "The approach sounds reasonable. But I'm sure something's wrong here. Tell me exactly how you adjusted the costs of direct labour, power, and setups."

**Gary**: "First, we obtain formulas for the individual items in the budget by using the method of least squares. We assume that cost variations can be explained by variations in productive activity, where activity is measured by direct labour hours. Here is a list of the cost formulas for the three items you mentioned. The variable $X$ is the number of direct labour hours."

$$\text{Direct labour cost} = \$10X$$
$$\text{Power cost} = \$5,000 + \$4X$$
$$\text{Setup cost} = \$100,000$$

**Amy**: "I think I see the problem. Power costs don't have a lot to do with direct labour hours. They have more to do with machine hours. As production increases, machine hours increase more rapidly than direct labour hours do. Also …"

**Gary**: "You know, you have a point. The coefficient of determination for power cost is only about 50 percent. That leaves a lot of unexplained cost variation. But the coefficient for labour is much better—it explains about 96 percent of the cost variation. Setup costs, of course, are fixed."

**Amy**: "Well, as I was about to say, setup costs also have very little to do with direct labour hours. And I might add that they are certainly not fixed—at least not all of them. Because of the scheduling changes, we had to do more setups than our original plan called for. And we have to pay our people when they work extra hours. It seems like we're always paying overtime. I wonder if we simply don't have enough people for the setup activity. Also, there are supplies used for each setup, and they aren't cheap. Did you build these extra costs of increased setup activity into your budget?"

**Gary**: "No, we assumed that setup costs were fixed. I see now that some of them could vary as the number of setups increases. Amy, let me see if I can develop some cost formulas based on better explanatory variables. I'll get back to you in a few days."

Assume that after a few days, Gary develops the following cost formulas, all with a coefficient of determination greater than 90 percent:

Direct labour cost = $10X$, where $X$ = Direct labour hours
Power cost = $68,000 + 0.9Y$, where $Y$ = Machine hours
Setup cost = $98,000 + $400Z$, where $Z$ = Number of setups

The actual measures of each of the activity drivers are as follows:

| | |
|---|---|
| Direct labour hours | 20,000 |
| Machine hours | 90,000 |
| Number of setups | 110 |

**Required:**
1. Prepare a performance report for direct labour, power, and setups using the direct-labour-based formulas.
2. Prepare a performance report for direct labour, power, and setups using the multiple-cost-driver formulas that Gary developed.
3. Of the two approaches, which provides the more accurate picture of Amy's performance? Explain why.

**13–34**

*Activity Flexible Budgeting*

LO4

Billy Adams, controller for Westward, Inc., prepared the following budget for manufacturing costs at two different levels of activity for 2005:

**Direct labour Hours**

| | Level of Activity | |
|---|---|---|
| | **50,000** | **100,000** |
| Direct materials | $  300,000 | $  600,000 |
| Direct labour | 200,000 | 400,000 |
| Amortization (plant) | 100,000 | 100,000 |
| Subtotal | $  600,000 | $1,100,000 |

**Machine Hours**

| | Level of Activity | |
|---|---|---|
| | **200,000** | **300,000** |
| Equipment maintenance | $  360,000 | $  510,000 |
| Machining | 112,000 | 162,000 |
| Subtotal | $  472,000 | $  672,000 |

**Material Moves**

| | Level of Activity | |
|---|---|---|
| | **20,000** | **40,000** |
| Materials handling | $  165,000 | $  290,000 |

**Number of Batches Inspected**

| | Level of Activity | |
|---|---|---|
| | **100** | **200** |
| Inspections | $  125,000 | $  225,000 |
| Total | $1,362,000 | $2,287,000 |

During 2005, the company used a total of 80,000 direct labour hours and 250,000 machine hours, made 32,000 moves, and performed 120 batch inspections. The following actual costs were incurred:

| | |
|---|---|
| Direct materials | $440,000 |
| Direct labour | 355,000 |
| Amortization | 100,000 |
| Equipment Maintenance | 425,000 |
| Machining | 142,000 |
| Materials handling | 232,500 |
| Inspections | 160,000 |

The company applies overhead using rates based on direct labour hours, machine hours, number of moves, and number of batches. The second level of activity (the far-right column in the preceding table) is the practical level of activity (i.e., the available activity for resources acquired in advance of usage). It is used to compute predetermined overhead pool rates.

**Required:**
1. Prepare a performance report for manufacturing costs in 2005.
2. Assume that one of the products is budgeted to use 10,000 direct labour hours, 15,000 machine hours, and 500 moves, and will be produced in five batches. A total of 10,000 units will be produced during the year. Calculate the budgeted unit manufacturing cost.
3. One manager said: "Budgeting at the activity level makes a lot of sense. It really helps us manage costs better. But the above budget really needs to provide more detailed information. For example, I know the materials-handling activity involves using forklifts and operators, and this information is lost when we only report the total cost of the activity for various levels of output. We have four forklifts, each capable of providing 10,000 moves a year. We lease these forklifts for five years, at $10,000 per year. Furthermore, for our two shifts, we need up to eight operators if we run all four forklifts. Each operator is paid a salary of $30,000 per year. Also, I know that fuel costs about $0.25 per move."

   Based on these comments, explain how this additional information could help the company manage its costs better. Assuming that these are the only three items, expand the detail of the flexible budget for materials handling to reveal the cost of these three resources for 20,000 moves and 40,000 moves, respectively. (You may wish to review the concepts of flexible, committed, and discretionary resources from Chapter 3).

**13–35**

*Master Budget;*
*Comprehensive*
*Review*

LO2

Corella Resources, Inc,. is a high-technology company that produces a mass storage system. The system's design is unique and represents a breakthrough in the industry. It combines the positive features of both floppy and hard disks. The company is completing its fifth year of operations and is starting to prepare its master budget for 2005. The budget will detail each quarter's activity and the activity for the year in total. The master budget will be based on the following information:

a. Fourth-quarter sales for 2004 are 55,000 units.
b. Unit sales by quarter for 2005 are projected as follows:

| | |
|---|---|
| First quarter | 65,000 |
| Second quarter | 70,000 |
| Third quarter | 75,000 |
| Fourth quarter | 90,000 |

The selling price is $400 per unit. All sales are credit sales. The company collects 85 percent of all sales within the quarter in which they are realized; the other 15 percent are collected in the following quarter. There are no bad debts.
c. There is no beginning inventory of finished goods. The company is planning the following ending finished goods inventories for each quarter:

| | |
|---|---|
| First quarter | 13,000 units |
| Second quarter | 15,000 units |
| Third quarter | 20,000 units |
| Fourth quarter | 10,000 units |

d. Each mass storage unit requires five hours of direct labour and three units of direct materials. Labourers are paid $10 per hour, and one unit of direct materials costs $80.

e. There are 65,700 units of direct materials in beginning inventory as of January 1, 2005. At the end of each quarter, the company plans to have 30 percent of the direct materials needed for next quarter's unit sales on hand. The company will end the year with the same amount of direct materials inventory as in this year's beginning inventory.

f. The company buys direct materials on account. Half of the purchases are paid during the quarter of acquisition, the remaining half are paid during the following quarter. Wages and salaries are paid on the 15th and 30th of each month.

g. Fixed overhead costs are $1 million each quarter. Of this total, $350,000 represents amortization. All other fixed expenses are paid in cash during the quarter they are incurred. The fixed overhead rate is computed by dividing the year's total fixed overhead by the year's expected actual units produced.

h. Budgeted variable overhead is $6 per direct labour hour. All variable overhead expenses are paid for during the quarter they are incurred.

i. Fixed selling and administrative expenses are $250,000 per quarter, including $50,000 amortization.

j. Budgeted variable selling and administrative expenses are $10 per unit sold. All selling and administrative expenses are paid during the quarter they are incurred.

k. The balance sheet as of December 31, 2004, is as follows:

| Assets | |
| --- | --- |
| Cash | $ 250,000 |
| Direct materials inventory | 5,256,000 |
| Accounts receivable | 3,300,000 |
| Plant and equipment | 33,500,000 |
| Total assets | $42,306,000 |

| Liabilities and Shareholders' Equity | |
| --- | --- |
| Accounts payable[a] | $ 7,248,000 |
| Capital stock | 27,000,000 |
| Retained earnings | 8,058,000 |
| Total liabilities and shareholders' equity | $42,306,000 |

[a]For purchase of direct materials only

l. The company will pay quarterly dividends of $300,000. At the end of the fourth quarter, equipment valued at $2 million will be purchased.

**Required:**

Prepare a master budget for each quarter of 2005 and for the year in total. The following components must be included:

a. Sales budget
b. Production budget
c. Direct materials purchases budget
d. Direct labour budget
e. Overhead budget
f. Selling and administrative expenses budget
g. Ending finished goods inventory budget
h. Cost of goods sold budget
i. Cash budget
j. Budgeted income statement (using absorption costing)
k. Budgeted balance sheet

**13–36**

*Flexible Budgeting*

**LO3, LO4**

Patterson Company employs flexible budgeting to evaluate the performance of its activities. The selling expenses flexible budgets for three representative monthly activity levels are as follows:

**Representative Monthly Flexible Budgets for Selling Expenses**

| | | | |
|---|---|---|---|
| Activity measures: | | | |
| Unit sales volume | 400,000 | 425,000 | 450,000 |
| Dollar sales volume | $10,000,000 | $10,625,000 | $11,250,000 |
| Number of orders | 4,000 | 4,250 | 4,500 |
| Number of salespeople | 72 | 72 | 72 |
| Monthly expenses: | | | |
| Advertising and promotion | $ 1,200,000 | $ 1,200,000 | $ 1,200,000 |
| Administrative salaries | 57,000 | 57,000 | 57,000 |
| Sales salaries | 75,600 | 75,600 | 75,600 |
| Sales commissions | 300,000 | 318,750 | 337,500 |
| Sales travel | 170,000 | 175,000 | 180,000 |
| Sales office expense | 490,000 | 498,750 | 507,500 |
| Shipping expense | 675,000 | 712,500 | 750,000 |
| Total | $ 2,967,600 | $ 3,037,600 | $ 3,107,600 |

The following assumptions were used to develop the selling expenses flexible budgets:

a. Patterson's planned sales force during the year consists of an average of 72 salespeople.
b. Salespeople are paid a monthly salary plus commission on gross dollar sales.
c. The travel costs are best characterized as a step-variable cost. The fixed portion is related to the number of salespeople; the variable portion tends to fluctuate with gross dollar sales.
d. Sales office expense is a mixed cost, with the variable portion related to the number of orders processed.
e. Shipping expense is a mixed cost, with the variable portion related to the number of units sold.

A sales force of 80 people generated a total of 4,300 orders resulting in a sales volume of 420,000 units in November. The gross dollar sales amounted to $10.9 million. The selling expenses incurred for November were as follows:

| | |
|---|---|
| Advertising and promotion | $1,350,000 |
| Administrative salaries | 57,000 |
| Sales salaries | 84,000 |
| Sales commissions | 327,000 |
| Sales travel | 185,000 |
| Sales office expense | 497,200 |
| Shipping expense | 730,000 |
| Total | $3,230,200 |

**Required:**

1. Explain why the selling expenses flexible budgets presented would not be appropriate for evaluating Patterson Company's November selling expenses. Indicate how the flexible budget would have to be revised.
2. Prepare a selling expenses report for November that Patterson Company can use to evaluate its control over selling expenses. The report should have a line for each selling expense item showing the appropriate budgeted amount, the actual selling expense, and the monthly dollar variation. (US CMA adapted)

**13–37**

ArtDecor Corporation, a rapidly expanding art dealership, is in the process of planning for 2006. Joan Caldwell, the marketing director, has completed the following sales forecast for 2006 and is confident that it represents realistic growth estimates.

| Month | Forecasted Sales |
|---|---|
| January | $1,800,000 |
| February | $2,000,000 |
| March | $1,800,000 |
| April | $2,200,000 |
| May | $2,500,000 |
| June | $2,800,000 |
| July | $3,000,000 |
| August | $3,000,000 |
| September | $3,200,000 |
| October | $3,200,000 |
| November | $3,000,000 |
| December | $3,400,000 |

George Brownell, the assistant controller, is responsible for formulating the cash flow projection and has collected the following additional information:

a. The company has experienced an excellent record in accounts receivable collection and expects this trend to continue. Sixty percent of billings are collected during the month following the sale, 40 percent during the second month following the sale. Uncollectible accounts are nominal and ignored in this analysis.

b. The purchase of inventory is the largest expenditure. The cost of these items equals 50 percent of sales. Sixty percent of inventory is received one month prior to sale and 40 percent during the month of sale.

c. Prior experience shows that 80 percent of accounts payable are paid during the month following the purchase, the remaining 20 percent during the second following month.

d. Hourly wages, including fringe benefits, are 20 percent of the current month's sales. They are paid during the month they are incurred.

e. General and administrative expenses are incurred and paid uniformly throughout the year, except property taxes, which are paid in four equal instalments at the end of each quarter. Estimated G & A expenses are as follows:

| | |
|---|---|
| Salaries | $ 480,000 |
| Promotion | 660,000 |
| Property taxes | 240,000 |
| Insurance | 360,000 |
| Utilities | 300,000 |
| Amortization | 600,000 |
| Total | $2,640,000 |

f. Income taxes are paid during the first month of each quarter, based on the income for the prior quarter. The income tax rate is 40 percent. The estimated net income for the first quarter of 2006 is $612,000.

g. A corporate policy requires maintaining an end-of-month cash balance of $100,000. Cash is invested or borrowed monthly, as necessary, to maintain this balance.

**Required:**

1. Prepare schedules of budgeted cash receipts and disbursements by month, for the second quarter of 2006. Ensure that all receipts and disbursements,

including loans and investments, are presented on a monthly basis. Ignore the interest expense and interest income associated with any loans and investments.

2. Discuss why cash budgeting is especially important for a rapidly expanding company such as ArtDecor. (US CMA adapted)

**13–38**

*Cash Budget*

LO2

Jennifer Johnson decided to start a business that would require the purchase of assets at the total cost of $200,000. She started her business with a cash investment of $50,000 and, on January 1, 2006, took out a loan for $150,000. The terms of the loan stipulated that interest, at the annual rate of 9 percent, would be payable at the end of each month, and that a principal payment of $30,000 would be payable at the end of each quarter. The company manufactures a product with the following budgeted revenues and expenses, based on a monthly volume of 5,000 units:

| | | |
|---|---:|---:|
| Selling price per unit | | $150 |
| Manufacturing costs per unit: | | |
| Direct materials | | $ 20 |
| Direct labour | | 30 |
| Variable overhead: | | |
| Utilities | $ 5 | |
| Supplies | 6 | |
| Indirect labour | 4 | 15 |
| Fixed overhead: | | |
| Factory rent | 10 | |
| Amortization | 15 | 25 |
| Total manufacturing cost | | $ 90 |
| | | |
| Selling and administrative costs: | | |
| Sales commissions | $8 per unit | |
| Bad debt expenses | $3 per unit | |
| Office rentals | $12,000 per month | |
| Equipment amortization | $5,000 per month | |

Other information:

a. Expected sales:

| | |
|---|---:|
| January 2006 | $360,000 |
| February 2006 | 450,000 |
| March 2006 | 480,000 |
| April 2006 | 600,000 |

b. All sales are on credit; terms 2/10, net 30. The collection of accounts receivable is expected to display the following pattern:
   - 30 percent collected during the month of sale (80 percent of customers will earn a discount).
   - 30 percent collected during the month following the sale.
   - 38 percent collected two months following the sale.
   - 2 percent are uncollectible.

c. A direct materials inventory of $2,000 will be maintained at all times. All direct materials purchases are expected to incur uniformly throughout the month, with all payments made during the month of purchase.

d. To meet fluctuations in customer demand, a finished goods inventory equal to 100 units, plus 10 percent of the unit demand expected during the following month, will be maintained.

e. Wages payable at the end of each month average $7,500.

f. A minimum cash balance of $10,000 is maintained at all times.

**Required:**

Prepare a cash budget for the quarter ending on March 31, 2006. Include any supporting schedules that are appropriate, and indicate what financing (if any) may be required. (CMA Canada adapted)

**13–39**

Cash Disbursements

LO2

Hosking Company has the following inventory policies that have been adhered to in the past:

Finished goods: 200 units plus 20 percent of the units expected to be sold during the next month

Direct materials: 1,000 kilograms plus 10 percent of the materials required for production during the next month

The company had the following costs for 2005:

Direct materials: 2 kilograms per unit @ $3 per kilogram
Direct labour: $12 per unit

Manufacturing overhead:

- Indirect supplies of $6,000 used each month.
- Amortization of plant equipment of $15,000 per month.
- Production supervision of $14,000 per month.
- Insurance on plant of $1,000 per month (annual policy paid on January 1 of each year).

Selling and administrative expenses:

- Uncollectible accounts expense of $2 per unit sold.
- Salaries of $40,000 per month.

**Required:**

Calculate the budgeted cash disbursements for January 1, 2006, assuming the following:

- All purchases of direct materials are paid during the month of purchase.
- Accrued salaries and wages payable will increase by $2,400 per month.
- Indirect supplies on hand are expected to increase by $900 per month.
- Sales are expected to be 30,000 units in January, 25,000 units in February, and 20,000 units in March.
- All other costs are expected to remain at the 2005 level. (CMA Canada adapted)

## Managerial Decision Cases

**13–40**

*Budgetary Performance; Rewards; Ethical Behaviour*

LO3

Linda Ellis, a division manager, is evaluated and rewarded based on budgetary performance. She, her assistants, and the plant managers are eligible to receive a bonus, providing that actual divisional profits are between budgeted profits and 120 percent of budgeted profits. The bonuses are based on a fixed percentage of actual profits. Profits above 120 percent of budgeted profits earn a bonus at the 120 percent level. In other words, there is an upper limit on possible bonus payments. If the actual profits are less than budgeted profits, no bonuses are awarded. Consider the following actions taken by Linda:

a. Linda tends to overestimate expenses and underestimate revenues. This approach facilitates the divison's ability to attain budgeted profits. Linda believes this action is justified because it increases the likelihood of receiving bonuses and helps keep the managers' morale high.

b. Suppose that toward the end of the fiscal year, Linda sees that the division will not achieve budgeted profits. Accordingly, she instructs the sales department to defer the closing of several sales agreements to the following fiscal year. She also decides to write off some inventory that is nearly worthless. Deferring revenues to next year and writing off the inventory in a no-bonus year increases the chances of a bonus for next year.

c. Assume that toward the end of the year, Linda sees that actual profits will likely exceed the 120 percent limit. She takes actions similar to those described in (b).

**Required:**

1. Comment on the ethics of Linda's behaviour. Are her actions right or wrong? What role does the company play in encouraging her actions?

2. Suppose you are the division's marketing manager and you receive instructions to defer the closing of sales until the next fiscal year. What do you do?

3. Suppose you are a plant manager and you know your budget has been padded by the division manager. Further suppose that the padding is common knowledge among the plant managers, who support it because it increases the ability to achieve the budget and receive a bonus. What do you do?

4. Suppose you are the division controller and you receive instructions from the division manager to accelerate the recognition of some expenses that legitimately belong to a future period. What do you do?

**13–41**

*Cash Budget*

LO2

The opening scenario to this chapter described the financial difficulties facing Dr. Roger Jones. According to the analysis of a consultant, those difficulties have been caused by the absence of proper planning and control. To assist you in preparing a plan of action that will help his dental practice regain financial stability, Dr. Jones has provided you with the following financial information for a typical month:

|  | Average Fee | Quantity |
|---|---|---|
| Fillings | $ 50 | 90 |
| Crowns | 300 | 19 |
| Root canals | 170 | 8 |
| Bridges | 500 | 7 |
| Extractions | 45 | 30 |
| Cleaning | 25 | 108 |
| X-rays | 15 | 150 |

|                                | Costs    |
| ------------------------------ | -------- |
| Salaries:                      |          |
| Two dental assistants          | $ 1,900  |
| Receptionist/bookkeeper        | 1,500    |
| Hygienist                      | 1,800    |
| Public relations (Mrs. Jones)  | 1,000    |
| Personal salary                | 6,500    |
| Total salaries                 | $12,700  |
|                                |          |
| Other Costs:                   |          |
| Benefits                       | 1,344    |
| Building lease                 | 1,500    |
| Dental supplies                | 1,200    |
| Janitorial                     | 300      |
| Utilities                      | 400      |
| Phone                          | 150      |
| Office supplies                | 100      |
| Lab fees                       | 5,000    |
| Loan payments                  | 570      |
| Interest payments              | 500      |
| Miscellaneous                  | 500      |
| Amortization                   | 700      |
| Total other costs              | 12,264   |
| Total costs                    | $24,964  |

Benefits include Dr. Jones's share of employment insurance and a supplemental health insurance premium for all employees. Although all revenues billed in a month are not collected, the cash flowing into the business is approximately equal to the month's billings because of collections from prior months. The dental office is open Monday through Thursday from 8:30 a.m. to 4:00 p.m., and on Friday from 8:30 a.m. to 12:30 p.m. A total of 32 hours are worked each week. Additional hours could be worked, but Dr. Jones is reluctant to work them because of other personal endeavours that he enjoys.

Dr. Jones has noted that the two dental assistants and the receptionist are not fully utilized. He estimates that they are busy about 65 to 70 percent of the time. Dr. Jones's wife spends about five hours each week on a monthly newsletter that is sent to all patients. She also maintains a birthday list and sends cards to the patients on their birthdays.

Dr. Jones spends about $2,400 yearly on informational seminars. These seminars are targeted at dentists and teach them how to increase their revenues. As a result of one of these seminars Dr. Jones has decided to invest in promotion and public relations.

### Required:
1. Prepare a monthly cash budget for Dr. Jones. Does he have a significant cash flow problem? How would you use the budget to show Dr. Jones why he is having financial difficulties?
2. Using the cash budget prepared in Requirement 1 and the information given in the case, recommend actions to solve Dr. Jones's financial problems. Prepare a cash budget that reflects these recommendations and that demonstrates to Dr. Jones that the problems can be corrected. Do you think Dr. Jones will accept your recommendations? Do any of the behavioural principles discussed in this chapter have a role in this type of setting? Explain.

## Research Assignments

**13–42**

Cybercase

LO1, LO2

The Government of Canada, just like private for-profit companies, must prepare a budget each year. However, unlike the budgets of private companies, the government's budget and its details are available to the public. The entire budgetary process is established by law. The government makes available a considerable amount of information concerning the federal budget. Most of this information can be found on the Internet. Using Internet resources, answer the following questions:

1. When is the federal budget prepared?
2. Who is responsible for preparing the federal budget?
3. How is the final federal budget determined? Explain in detail how the government creates its budget.
4. What percentage of the gross domestic product (GDP) is represented by the federal budget?
5. What are the revenue sources for the federal budget? Indicate the percentage contribution from each major source.
6. How does Canada's spending as a percentage of GDP compare to spending by other countries?
7. How are deficits financed?

**13–43**

Research Assignment

LO1, LO2

A formal master-budgeting process is important to many companies. Locate a manufacturing plant in your community that has its headquarters elsewhere. Interview the plant's controller regarding the master budget process. Ask when the process starts each year, what schedules and budgets are prepared at the plant level, how the controller forecasts the amounts, and how these schedules and budgets fit with the overall corporate budget.

# Standard Costing: A Managerial Control Tool

**After studying Chapter 14, you should be able to:**

1. Explain how unit standards are set and why standard cost systems are adopted.

2. Explain the purpose of a standard cost sheet.

3. Describe the basic concepts underlying variance analysis, and explain when variances should be investigated.

4. Compute the materials and labour variances, and explain how they are used for control.

5. Compute the variable and fixed overhead variances, and explain their meaning.

6. Use variance analysis as an analytical tool for profitability analysis. (Appendix A)

7. Prepare journal entries for materials and labour variances and describe the accounting for overhead variances. (Appendix B)

## Scenario

Millie Anderson, manager of Honley Medical's IV Products Division, was more than satisfied with her division's performance the previous year. At the start of the year, the division had introduced a new line of polyurethane catheters, and sales had more than tripled. The market's reaction to the new catheter was a virtual replay of the company's history: Honley Medical was establishing a dominant position in the IV market.

Nearly 30 years earlier, Lindell Honley, the founder of Honley Medical, had perceived the need for something other than a metal needle for long-term insertion into veins. Metal needles were irritating and could damage the vein. Based on this, Honley had developed a catheter using teflon, a lubricated plastic that was easy to insert into the vein. The development was well received by the medical community and produced a new and successful company, which gradually expanded its activities into a variety of medical products.

For years, the new technology allowed Honley to dominate the market, but when the patent expired, other companies entered the market with their own teflon catheters, increasing competition. Prices were driven down, and profit margins began eroding.

The eroding profit margins had prompted Millie and other high-level managers to examine the continued viability of the teflon catheters. After many years, the medical profession had noted that after 24 hours of catheter use, an infection tended to develop around the point of insertion. Researchers at Honley Medical had discovered that the problem was one of incompatibility between the teflon and the patient's blood and tissue. Further studies showed that different plastics produced different reactions. Research began immediately to find a material that was more biocompatible than teflon. The outcome was polyurethane catheters. The new catheter could be left in for 72 hours, compared to 24 hours for the teflon catheters.

Millie knew that history would eventually repeat itself—that eventually other companies would start producing catheters with the same degree of biocompatibility. In fact, Honley's research scientists estimated that competitors would have a competing catheter on the market within three years. This time, Millie was determined to protect the division's market share. Since most patients have little need for a catheter beyond 72 hours, further improvements in biocompatibility were not likely to yield the same market benefits as in the past. Price competition would become more important. Competing on price meant that cost control would become critical. In the past, because of its dominant position, the division had not been very concerned with manufacturing costs. Millie believed that by implementing cost control measures now, the division would be better able to compete on price when competition resurfaced in a few years. She consulted with Reed McCourt, the division's controller.

**Millie:** "Reed, is our budgetary system the only attempt we make to control manufacturing costs?"

**Reed:** "Yes, but it really isn't a very good effort. Budgets are based on last year's costs plus some allowance for inflation. We've never tried to identify what the costs ought to be. Nor have we held managers responsible for cost control. Our profitability has always been good and resources plentiful. My guess is that we spend more than necessary simply because we've been so successful."

**Millie:** "Well, resources wouldn't be so plentiful now if we hadn't developed the polyurethane catheter. And I'm afraid that resources won't be plentiful in the future unless we take actions now to control our manufacturing costs. If we can be more profitable now by using better cost control, we ought to use it. I want my plant and production managers to recognize their responsibilities in this area. Any suggestions?"

**Reed:** "We need to inject more formality into the budgetary system. First, budgets should reflect what costs should be, not what they have been. Second, we can encourage managers to be cost conscious by having them help identify efficient levels of costs on which the budget will be based, and then tying bonuses and promotions into the system. But I think we can gain cost control by going one step farther and establishing a standard cost system."

**Millie:** "Doesn't that involve specifying unit price and quantity standards for materials and labour?"

**Reed:** "That's essentially correct. Using the unit price and quantity standards, we can establish budgeted costs for labour, materials, and overhead for each unit produced. The standards are based on efficiency expectations and will demand less resource usage than our traditional incremental budgetary approach. The unit price and quantity standards are used to develop budgets. Then, once actual costs are known, we use them to break down the budget variances into price and efficiency variances. A standard cost system provides more detailed control information than a budgetary system using normal costing. We can hold our managers responsible for meeting the established standards."

**Millie:** "I think our division needs this type of system. It's about time our managers become cost conscious."

### Questions to Think About

1. What was motivating Millie to implement a more formal cost control system?

2. Why does a standard cost system provide more detailed control information?

3. How can standards be used to control costs?

# Unit Standards

### Objective 1

Explain how unit standards are set and why standard cost systems are adopted.

Both Millie and Reed recognized the need to encourage operating managers to control costs. Cost control often means the difference between success and failure, or between strong and weak profitability. Millie was certain that cost control meant her managers had to be cost conscious and assume responsibility for this important objective. Reed suggested that the way to control costs and involve managers was by establishing a formal budget control system.

In Chapter 13 we saw how budgets provide benchmarks, which can be used to control and evaluate managerial performance. However, budgets are aggregate measures of performance. They identify the revenues and costs an organization should experience in total if plans are executed as expected. By comparing the actual costs and revenues with the corresponding budgeted amounts at the same level of activity, companies can measure managerial efficiency.

The process just described provides significant information for control. However, companies can enhance control by developing standards for *unit* amounts as well as for total amounts. The groundwork for unit standards already exists within the framework of flexible budgeting. For flexible budgeting to work, the budgeted variable cost per unit of input for each unit of output must be known for every item in the budget. The budgeted variable input cost per unit of output is a unit standard. Unit standards are the foundation on which a flexible budget is built.

In determining the unit standard cost for a particular input, two decisions must be made:

1. How much of the input should be used per unit of output? (*quantity decision*)
2. How much should be paid for the quantity of the input to be used? (*pricing decision*)

**quantity standard**

The quantity of input allowed per unit of output.

The quantity decision produces **quantity standards**; the pricing decision produces **price standards**. The unit standard cost can be computed by multiplying these two standards.

For example, a soft drink company may decide that it should use 0.1 litres of fructose for every 355-millilitre can of cola (the quantity standard) and that the price of the fructose should be $2.50 per litre (the price standard). The standard cost of the fructose per can of cola is then $0.25 (0.1 × $2.50). The standard cost per unit of fructose can be used to predict what the total cost of fructose should be as the activity level varies. It thus becomes a flexible budget formula. If 10,000 cans of cola are produced, the total expected cost of fructose is $2,500 ($0.25 × 10,000); if 15,000 cans are produced, the total expected cost of fructose is $3,750 ($0.25 × 15,000).

**price standard**

The price that should be paid per unit of input.

## How Standards Are Developed

Historical experience, engineering studies, and input from operating personnel are three potential sources of quantitative standards. Historical experience can provide a guideline for setting standards, but it should be used cautiously. If processes are operating inefficiently (which they often are), adopting past input–output relationships will only perpetuate these inefficiencies.

For example, the IV division of Honley Medical had never emphasized cost control and had operated in a resource-rich environment. The divisional manager and the controller were both certain that significant inefficiencies existed. Engineering studies can determine the most efficient way to operate and can provide rigorous guidelines. However, engineered standards are often too rigorous for operating personnel to achieve. Since operating personnel are accountable for meeting the standards, they should have plenty of say in setting them. The principles pertaining to participative budgeting also apply to setting unit standards.

Price standards are the joint responsibility of operations, purchasing, personnel, and accounting. Operations determines the quality of inputs required; personnel and purchasing then acquire the input quality requested at the lowest price. Market forces, trade unions, and other external forces limit the range of choices for price standards. In setting price standards for materials and labour inputs, the purchasing department must consider discounts, freight, and quality; the personnel department must consider payroll taxes, fringe benefits, and qualifications. The accounting department is responsible for recording the price standards and for preparing reports that compare actual performance with the standards.

# Types of Standards

**ideal standards**

Standards that reflect perfect operating conditions.

**currently attainable standards**

Standards that reflect an efficient operating state; they are rigorous but attainable.

Standards are generally classified as either *ideal* or *currently attainable*. **Ideal standards** demand maximum efficiency and can be achieved only if everything operates perfectly—no provision is made for machine breakdowns, slack, or lack of skill. **Currently attainable standards** can be achieved under efficient operating conditions—provision is made for normal breakdowns, interruptions, less-than-perfect skills, and so on. These standards are demanding but reasonably achievable.

Of the two types, currently attainable standards offer the most behavioural benefits. If standards are too tight and never achievable, workers become frustrated and performance levels decline. Challenging but achievable standards tend to result in higher performance levels, especially when the people who are subject to the standards have participated in their creation.

# Why Standard Cost Systems Are Adopted

There are two major reasons for adopting a standard cost system: to improve planning and control, and to facilitate product costing.

## *Planning and Control*

Standard cost systems enhance planning and control and improve performance measurement. Unit standards are a fundamental requirement for a flexible budgeting system, which is a key feature of a meaningful planning and control system. Budgetary control systems compare actual costs with budgeted costs by computing variances (i.e., the differences between the actual and planned costs for the actual level of activity). By developing unit price and quantity standards, we can decompose an overall variance into two components: a *price or rate variance* and a *usage or efficiency variance*.

**efficiency variances**

See usage (efficiency) variance.

By performing this decomposition, a manager acquires more information. If the variance is unfavourable, the manager can tell whether it is attributable to discrepancies between planned prices and actual prices, or discrepancies between planned usage and actual usage, or both. Because managers have more control over the usage of inputs than over their prices, **efficiency variances** provide specific signals regarding the need for corrective action and where that action should be focused. So in principle, the use of efficiency variances enhances operational control. Also, by breaking down the price variance, over which managers have little control, the system provides an improved measure of managerial efficiency.

However, the benefits of operational control may not extend to the advanced manufacturing environment. The use of a standard cost system for operational control in such an environment can lead to dysfunctional behaviour. For that reason, the detailed computation of variances—at least at the operational level—is discouraged in that environment. Nonetheless, standards are still useful in the advanced manufacturing environment for planning purposes—for example, for establishing bids. Also, variances may still be computed and presented in reports to higher-level managers so that the financial dimension can be monitored.

Finally, it should be mentioned that many companies still use conventional manufacturing systems. Among these, standard cost systems are still widely used. In one survey of manufacturing companies, 87 percent of the responding companies used a standard cost system.[1] The same survey revealed that significant numbers of respondents were calculating variances at the operational level. For example, about 40 percent of the companies using a standard cost system reported labour variances for small work crews or individual workers.

---

1. Bruce R. Gaumnitz and Felix P. Kollaritsch, "Manufacturing Variances: Current Practice and Trends," *Journal of Cost Management* (Spring 1991): pp. 58–64.

*Product Costing*

In a *standard cost* system, costs are assigned to products using quantity and price standards for all three manufacturing costs: direct materials, direct labour, and overhead. In contrast, a *normal cost* system predetermines overhead costs for the purpose of product costing, but assigns actual direct materials and direct labour costs to products. Overhead is assigned using a budgeted rate and actual activity. At the other end of the cost assignment spectrum, an *actual cost* system assigns the actual costs of all three manufacturing inputs to products. Exhibit 14–1 summarizes these three cost assignment approaches. Standard product costing has several advantages over both normal costing and actual costing. One, of course, is greater capacity for control. Standard cost systems also provide readily available unit-cost information that can be used for pricing decisions. This is especially helpful for companies that do a significant amount of bidding and for those paid on a cost-plus basis.[2]

**EXHIBIT  14-1**

Cost Assignment Approaches

| | Manufacturing Costs | | |
|---|---|---|---|
| | **Direct Materials** | **Direct Labour** | **Overhead** |
| Actual cost system | Actual | Actual | Actual |
| Normal cost system | Actual | Actual | Budgeted |
| Standard cost system | Standard | Standard | Standard |

Other simplifications are also possible. For example, if a process-costing system uses standard costing to assign product costs, there is no need to compute a unit cost for each equivalent unit-cost category. A standard unit cost would exist for each category. Also, there is no need to distinguish between the FIFO and weighted average methods of accounting for beginning inventory costs, because both methods use the same standard costs. A standard process-costing system normally follows the equivalent unit calculation of the FIFO approach. Because current equivalent units of work are calculated, companies can compare current actual production costs with standard costs for control purposes.[3]

## Standard Product Costs

**Objective 2**

Explain the purpose of a standard cost sheet.

**standard cost per unit**

The per-unit cost that should be achieved given materials, labour, and overhead standards.

**standard cost sheet**

A listing of the standard costs and standard quantities of direct materials, direct labour, and overhead that should apply to a single product.

In manufacturing firms, standard costs are developed for materials, labour, and overhead. Using these costs, we can compute the **standard cost per unit**. The **standard cost sheet** provides the details underlying the standard unit cost. To illustrate this, consider the standard cost sheet for a 400-gram bag of corn chips produced by the Crunchy Chips Company. The production of corn chips begins by steaming and soaking corn kernels overnight in a lime solution. This process softens the kernels so that they can be shaped into a sheet of dough. The dough is then cut into small triangular chips. Next, the chips are toasted in an oven and dropped into a deep fryer. After cooking, the chips pass under a salting device and are inspected for quality. Substandard chips are sorted and discarded. The chips that pass inspection are bagged by a packaging machine. Then the bagged chips are packed by hand into shipping boxes.

2.  For example, Canblock, Inc., the concrete and pipe company mentioned in Chapter 13, conducts the vast majority of its business through bidding and uses a standard cost system to estimate costs and facilitate the bidding process.

3.  If you have not read Chapter 6 yet, you may not fully understand this example. However, the main point is still relevant—namely, that standard costing can bring useful computational savings.

Four materials are used to process corn chips: yellow corn, cooking oil, salt, and lime. The package into which the chips are placed is also classified as a direct material. Crunchy Chips has two types of direct labourers: machine operators and inspectors. Variable overhead consists of three costs—gas, electricity, and water—and is applied using direct labour hours. Fixed overhead is applied using direct labour hours. The standard cost sheet is provided in Exhibit 14–2. Note that it should cost $0.56 to produce a 400-gram package of corn chips. Note also that the company uses 500 grams of corn to produce a 400-gram package of chips. There are two reasons for this. First, since some chips are always discarded during the inspection process, the company plans for a normal amount of waste. Second, the company wants to have more than 400 grams in each package to increase customer satisfaction and to avoid any problems with fair packaging laws.

Exhibit 14–2 reveals other important insights. The standard usage for variable and fixed overhead is tied to the direct labour standards.[4] For variable overhead, the rate is $3.85 per direct labour hour. Since one package of corn chips uses 0.0078 direct labour hours, the variable overhead cost assigned to a package of corn chips is $0.03 ($3.85 × 0.0078). For fixed overhead, the rate is $32.05 per direct labour hour, making the fixed overhead cost per package of corn chips $0.25 ($32.05 × 0.0078). Nearly half the production costs are fixed, which indicates a capital-intensive operation. Indeed, the production process is highly automated.

The standard cost sheet also reveals the quantity of each input that should be used to produce one unit of output. The unit quantity standards can be used to compute the total amount of inputs allowed for the actual output. This computation is an essential component in computing efficiency variances. A manager should be able to compute the **standard quantity of materials allowed** ($SQ$) and the **standard hours allowed** ($SH$) for the actual output. This computation must be done for every class of direct material and direct labour. Assume, for example, that 100,000 packages of corn chips are produced during the first week of March. How much yellow corn should have been used for the actual output of 100,000 packages? The unit quantity standard is 500 grams of yellow corn per package (see Exhibit

**standard quantity of materials allowed**

The quantity of materials that should have been used to produce the actual output (Unit materials standard × Actual output).

**standard hours allowed**

The direct labour hours that should have been used to produce the actual output (Unit labour standard × Actual output).

---

EXHIBIT 14-2

**EXHIBIT** 14-2

Standard Cost Sheet for Corn Chips

| Description | Standard Price | Standard Usage | Standard Cost[a] | Subtotal |
|---|---|---|---|---|
| Direct materials: | | | | |
| Yellow corn | $0.216/kilogram | 500 grams | $0.108 | |
| Cooking oil | $1.00/litre | 62 millilitres | 0.062 | |
| Salt | $0.20/kilogram | 25 grams | 0.005 | |
| Lime | $4.00/litre | 1 millilitre | 0.004 | |
| Bags | $0.044/bag | 1 bag | 0.044 | |
| Total direct materials | | | | $0.223 |
| Direct labour: | | | | |
| Inspection | $7/hour | 0.0070 hours | $0.049 | |
| Machine operators | $10/hour | 0.0008 hours | 0.008 | |
| Total direct labour | | | | 0.057 |
| Overhead: | | | | |
| Variable overhead | $3.85/hour | 0.0078 hours | $0.030 | |
| Fixed overhead | $32.05/hour | 0.0078 hours | 0.250 | |
| Total overhead | | | | 0.280 |
| Total standard unit cost | | | | $0.560 |

[a]Calculated by multiplying price times usage.

---

4. We refer here to a conventional costing environment for the sake of simplicity, as most standard costing systems exist in such an environment.

14–2). For 100,000 packages, the standard quantity of yellow corn allowed is computed as follows:

$$SQ = \text{Unit quantity standard} \times \text{Actual output}$$
$$= 500 \times 100,000$$
$$= 50,000,000 \text{ grams} = 50,000 \text{ kilograms}$$

The computation of standard direct labour hours allowed can be illustrated using machine operators. From Exhibit 14–2, we know that the unit quantity standard is 0.0008 hours per package produced. Thus, if 100,000 packages are produced, we can compute the standard hours allowed as follows:

$$SH = \text{Unit quantity standard} \times \text{Actual output}$$
$$= 0.0008 \times 100,000$$
$$= 80 \text{ direct labour hours}$$

Standard costs can also be used by service and nonprofit organizations. For example, the Canada Customs and Revenue Agency (CCRA) could set standard processing times for different categories of tax returns. If the standard processing time is 3 minutes for a simple return, and the standard price of labour is $9 per hour, then the standard cost of processing a simple return is $0.45 ($9 × 3/60). Another example: Provincial governments classify illnesses into diagnostic related groups (DRGs), which are then used to predetermine the hospital costs that should be incurred for an average case. The costs include patient days, food, medicine, supplies, use of equipment, and so on. Provincial governments pay the hospital the standard cost of the DRG. If the cost of the patient's treatment is greater than the DRG allows, the hospital suffers a deficit. If the cost of the patient's treatment is less than the DRG reimbursement, the hospital gains a surplus. Supposedly, the average hospital breaks even. Although service and nonprofit organizations can and do use standard costing, its use is more common in manufacturing organizations. That is why we are using a manufacturing setting—the Crunchy Chips Company—to illustrate standard costing.

## Variance Analysis: General Description

**Objective 3**

Describe the basic concepts underlying variance analysis, and explain when variances should be investigated.

**total flexible budget variance**

The difference between the actual cost of the input and the planned cost for the actual output.

**price (rate) variance**

The difference between the actual and standard unit price of an input multiplied by the number of inputs used.

A flexible budget can be used to identify the costs that should have been incurred for the actual level of activity. This figure is obtained by multiplying the amount of input allowed for the actual output by the standard unit price. Letting $SP$ be the standard unit price of an input and $SQ$ the standard quantity of inputs allowed for the actual output, the planned or budgeted input cost is $SP \times SQ$. The actual input cost is $AP \times AQ$, where $AP$ is the actual price per unit of input and $AQ$ is the actual quantity of input used.

### Price and Efficiency Variances

The **total flexible budget variance** is simply the difference between the actual and planned cost of the input for the actual output. For convenience, the total flexible budget variance for all variable cost items is sometimes referred to as the *budget variance* or, simply, the *total variance*. It is calculated as follows:

$$\text{Total variance} = (AP \times AQ) - (SP \times SQ)$$

In a standard cost system, the total variance is broken down into price (or rate) and usage (or efficiency) variances. **Price (rate) variance** is the difference between the actual and standard unit price of an input multiplied by the number of inputs used. **Usage (efficiency) variance** is the difference between the actual

**usage (efficiency) variance**

The difference between standard quantities and actual quantities multiplied by standard price.

and the standard quantity of inputs multiplied by the standard unit price. As mentioned earlier, by breaking down the total flexible budget variance into these two components, managers can better analyze and control the total variance. They can then identify the origins of cost increases and take corrective actions. Dividing the total variance into price and efficiency components is accomplished by subtracting and adding $SP \times AQ$ to the right-hand side of the total variance equation, as follows:

$$
\begin{aligned}
\text{Total variance} &= \text{Price variance} + \text{Usage variance} \\
&= (AP - SP)AQ + (AQ - SQ)SP \\
&= [(AP \times AQ) - (SP \times AQ)] + [(SP \times AQ) - (SP \times SQ)] \\
&= (AP \times AQ) - (SP \times AQ) + (SP \times AQ) - (SP \times SQ) \\
&= (AP \times AQ) - (SP \times SQ)
\end{aligned}
$$

Exhibit 14–3 presents a three-pronged diagram that describes this process. This graphical approach is an alternative way of presenting variance analyses and may be easier to understand than the formula approach.

Usually, the total variance is divided into the price and usage components for direct materials. The corresponding variances for direct labour are labelled the rate and efficiency variances, respectively. The treatment of overhead is discussed later in this chapter.

**unfavourable (U) variances**

Variances produced whenever the actual input amounts are greater than the budgeted or standard allowances.

**favourable (F) variances**

Variances produced whenever the actual amounts are less than the budgeted or standard allowances.

**Unfavourable (U) variances** occur when actual prices or usage of inputs is greater than standard prices or usage. When the opposite occurs, **favourable (F) variances** are obtained. Favourable and unfavourable variances are not equivalent to "good" and "bad" variances. The terms merely indicate the relationship of the actual prices or quantities to the standard prices or quantities. Whether the variances are good or bad depends on *why* they occurred. The reasons for the variances must be investigated.

## The Decision to Investigate

Actual performance is rarely exactly equal to standard performance, and wise management does not expect it to be. Random variations around the standards are to be expected. For this reason, management should have an acceptable range of performance in mind. When variances are within this range, it is

**EXHIBIT 14-3**

Variance Analysis: General Description

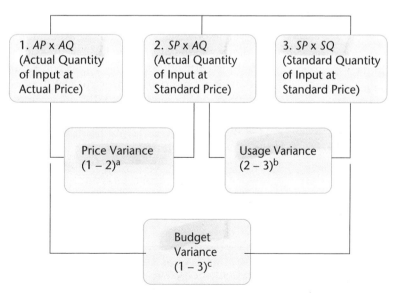

<sup>a</sup> Price Variance = $(AP \times AQ) - (SP \times AQ) = (AP - SP) \times AQ$
<sup>b</sup> Usage Variance = $(SP \times AQ) - (SP \times SQ) = (AQ - SQ) \times SP$
<sup>c</sup> Budget Variance = $(AP \times AQ) - (SP \times SQ)$

assumed that they have been caused by random factors. When a variance falls outside this range, the deviation is likely to have been caused by nonrandom factors—either factors that managers could have controlled, or factors that they could not. If the factors could not have been controlled, management needs to revise the standard.

An example from the pharmaceutical industry will drive home the importance of variance investigation.[5] Drugs must contain a certain amount of the active ingredient, plus or minus a small percentage. For example, aspirin that claims to have 5 grains per tablet must actually have somewhere between 90 and 110 percent of the specified amount. The U.S. Food and Drug Administration (FDA) is responsible for ensuring the safety and efficacy of drugs sold in the United States, whether they are manufactured domestically or in foreign countries. In 1991, an anonymous letter alerted the FDA to manufacturing problems with an antibiotic produced by a Canadian firm, Novopharm, Ltd. Basically, the drug was too strong and had the potential to destroy beneficial bacteria along with harmful bacteria. The FDA investigated and found that the blending process was "out of control." As a result, the firm stopped shipping that drug until the process was corrected. The problem could likely have been corrected earlier, had material usage variances been analyzed thoroughly.

Now that we understand why variance investigation is important, we need to understand when to investigate. Like all activities, the investigating and "correcting" of variances has an associated cost. As a general principle, an investigation should be undertaken only if the anticipated benefits are greater than the expected costs. However, assessing the costs and benefits of a variance investigation is not easy. A manager must consider whether the variance will recur. If it probably will, the process may be permanently out of control, in which case periodic savings may be achieved if corrective action is taken. But how can we tell if the variance is going to recur unless we conduct an investigation? And how can we know the cost of corrective action before we have determined the cause of the variance?

It is difficult to assess the costs and benefits of variance analysis on a case-by-case basis. For this reason, many companies have adopted the general guideline of investigating variances only if they fall outside an acceptable range. It follows that for variances to warrant investigation, they must be large enough to have been caused by something other than random factors, and to justify the costs of investigating and taking corrective action.

How do managers determine whether variances are significant? How is the acceptable range established? The acceptable range is the standard plus or minus an allowable deviation. The top and bottom measures of the allowable range are called the **control limits**. The upper control limit is the standard plus the allowable deviation, and the lower control limit is the standard minus the allowable deviation. Management usually determines the allowable deviation from the standard subjectively, using past experience, intuition, and judgment.[6] Exhibit 14–4 illustrates the concept of control limits. The assumed standard is $100,000; the allowable deviation is plus or minus $10,000. The upper limit is $110,000, and the lower limit is $90,000. An investigation is conducted whenever an observation falls outside these limits, as would be the case for the sixth observation.

The control limits are often expressed both as a percentage of the standard and as an absolute dollar amount. For example, the allowable deviation may be

**control limits**

The maximum allowable deviation from a standard.

---

5. The examples given here are taken from an article by Christopher Drew, "Medicines from Afar Raise Safety Concerns," *The New York Times*, 29 October 1995: pp. A1, A16.

6. Gaumnitz and Kollaritsch, in "Manufacturing Variances: Current Practices and Trends," report that about 45 to 47 percent of responding companies to one survey used dollar and percentage controls limits. Most other companies used judgment instead of any formal control limits.

EXHIBIT 14-4

Control Chart

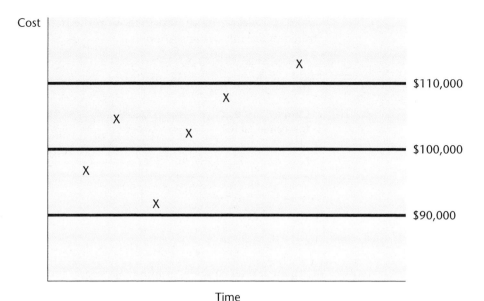

expressed as the lesser of 10 percent of the standard amount or $10,000. In other words, even if the dollar amount is less than $10,000, an investigation is required if the deviation is more than 10 percent of the standard amount.

Formal statistical procedures can also be used to set the control limits. This approach involves less subjectivity and allows a manager to assess the likelihood that the variance was caused by random factors. In practice, the use of such formal procedures has gained little acceptance to date.[7]

Finally, it is important to note that variance investigations should be conducted at an appropriate level. For example, the total flexible budget variance may be small, within control limits, and thus not investigated. However, the price and usage variances may be large in different directions and offset each other. A failure to investigate the latter two variances can conceal significant opportunities for cost savings and efficiency improvement.

## Variance Analysis: Materials and Labour

**Objective 4**

Compute the materials and labour variances, and explain how they are used for control.

The total variance measures the difference between the actual cost of materials and labour and their budgeted costs for the actual level of activity. To illustrate this, consider these selected data for Crunchy Chips Company for the first week of March:[8]

Actual production: 48,500 bags of corn chips
Actual corn usage: 20,500 kilograms
Actual price paid per kilogram of corn: $0.252
Actual hours of inspection: 360 hours
Actual wage rate: $7.35 per hour

Using the above actual data and the unit standards from Exhibit 14–2, we can develop a performance report for the first week of March (see Exhibit 14–5). As has been mentioned, the total variance can be divided into price and usage vari-

---

7. According to Gaumnitz and Kollaritsch, only about 1 percent of companies use formal statistical procedures.

8. To keep the example simple, only one material (corn) and one type of labour (inspection) are illustrated. A complete analysis for the company would include all material and labour categories.

ances, providing more information to the manager. This analysis will be illustrated in the following sections.

|  | Actual Costs | Budgeted Costs[a] | Total Variance |
|---|---|---|---|
| Corn | $5,166.00 | $5,238.00 | $ 72.00 Favourable (F) |
| Inspection labour | 2,646.00 | 2,376.50 | 269.50 Unfavourable (U) |

[a] The standard quantities for materials and labour are computed as follows (using unit quantity standards from Exhibit 14–2): materials, 500 × 48,500 = 24,250,000 grams = 24,250 kilograms; labour, 0.007 × 48,500 = 339.5 hours. Multiplying these standard quantities by the unit standard prices given in Exhibit 14–2 produces the budgeted amounts appearing in this column: $0.216 × 24,250 = $5,238 for materials; $7 × 339.5 = $2,376.50 for labour.

## Direct Materials Variances

Both the three-pronged columnar approach and the formula approach are used to calculate materials price and usage variances in this section.

### The Columnar Approach

Exhibit 14–6 provides an overview of the columnar (graphical) approach to the materials variance calculations for Crunchy Chips. The price and usage variances are shown only for corn. Further explanations about the calculations are provided in later sections, using the formula approach.

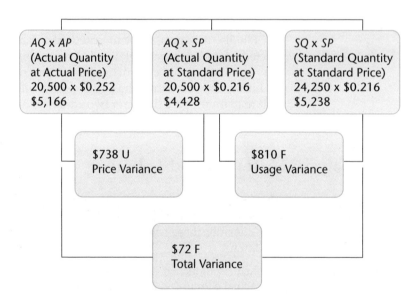

SP = $0.216 (from Exhibit 14–2)
SQ = 24,250 kg (from Exhibit 14–5, footnote a)

**materials price
variance**

The difference between
the actual price paid per
unit of materials and the
standard price allowed
per unit multiplied by the
actual quantity of
materials purchased.

### Materials Price Variance: Formula Approach

The materials price variance can be calculated separately. The **materials price variance (MPV)** measures the difference between what should have been paid for raw materials and what was actually paid. A simple formula for computing this variance is as follows:

$$MPV = (AP \times AQ) - (SP \times AQ)$$

or, after factoring, as follows:[9]

$$MPV = (AP - SP) \times AQ$$

where

$AP$ = the actual price per unit
$SP$ = the standard price per unit
$AQ$ = the actual quantity of material used

### Computation of the Materials Price Variance

Crunchy Chips purchased and used 20,500 kilograms of yellow corn during the first week of March. The purchase price was $0.252 per kilogram. Thus, $AP$ is $0.252, $AQ$ is 20,500 kilograms, and $SP$ (from Exhibit 14–2) is $0.216. Using this information, we can compute the materials price variance as follows:

$$
\begin{aligned}
MPV &= (AP - SP) \times AQ \\
&= (\$0.252 - \$0.216) \times 20,500 \\
&= \$0.036 \times 20,500 \\
&= \$738 \text{ U}
\end{aligned}
$$

$$
\begin{aligned}
\text{Percentage of } SP \times AQ &= \$738/(\$0.216 \times 20,500) \\
&= \$738/\$4,428 = 17\% \text{ (rounded)}
\end{aligned}
$$

### Responsibility for the Materials Price Variance

The purchasing agent is usually held responsible for the materials price variance. Admittedly, the price of materials itself is largely beyond his or her control. However, prices can also be influenced by quality, quantity discounts, location of supplier, and so on—factors over which the agent may have some control. In such circumstances, the use of price variances to evaluate the performance of the purchasing agent can lead to some undesirable behaviours. For example, if the purchasing agent feels pressured to produce favourable variances, he or she may purchase low-quality materials or excess inventory when prices are low.

### Analysis of the Materials Price Variance

The first step in variance analysis involves deciding whether the variance is significant. If it is immaterial, no further steps need be taken. Assume that an unfavourable materials price variance of $738 (17 percent of the standard cost) is judged to be material. The next step is to find out why it occurred. For the Crunchy Chips example, the investigation revealed that a higher-quality corn was purchased because of a shortage of the usual grade on the market. Once the reason is known, corrective action can be taken if necessary—and if possible. In this situation, no corrective action is needed. The company has no control over the supply shortage. It will simply have to wait until market conditions improve.

### Timing of the Price Variance Computation

The materials price variance can be computed at two points:

1. When raw materials are purchased.
2. When raw materials are issued for use in production.

It is better to compute the price variance at the point of purchase. This is because it is better to have information on variances earlier than later. The more

---

9. The materials price variance usually calculated includes the combined effect of both price and usage variations, since the difference between the actual quantity used and the standard quantity allowed also affects the total price. It is also possible to compute a pure price variance as $(AP - SP) \times SQ$, and a combined price-usage variance as $(AP - SP) \times (AQ - SQ)$. They total the price variance described here.

timely the information, the more likely it is that proper action can be taken. Old information is often useless. Materials may sit in inventory for weeks or months before they are needed in production. By the time the materials price variance is computed, signalling a problem, it may be too late to take corrective action. And even if corrective action is still possible, the delay may cost the company thousands of dollars.

For example, suppose a new purchasing agent is unaware that a quantity discount is available for a raw material. If the materials price variance is calculated for the first purchase that agent makes, the resulting unfavourable signal can lead to quick corrective action. Here, the action would be to remind the agent to take the discount on future purchases. If the materials price variance is not computed until the material is issued to production, it may be several weeks—or even months—before the problem is discovered.

When the materials price variance is computed at the point of purchase, $AQ$ needs to be redefined as the actual quantity of materials *purchased*, or $AQP$, rather than actual materials used. The materials price variance on materials purchased is called the **materials purchase price variance**. Since the materials purchased may differ from the materials used, the overall materials budget variance is not necessarily the sum of the materials price variance and the materials usage variance. When all materials purchased are used in production during the period in which the variances are calculated, the two variances will equal the total variance.

Recognizing the materials purchase price variance at the point of purchase also means that the raw materials inventory is carried at standard cost. In a standard costing system, actual costs are not entered into the inventory account.

**materials purchase price variance**

The materials price variance based on materials purchased.

### *Direct Materials Usage Variance: Formula Approach*

The **materials usage variance** (*MUV*) measures the difference between the direct materials actually used and the direct materials that should have been used for the actual output. The formula for computing this variance is as follows:

$$MUV = (SP \times AQ) - (SP \times SQ)$$

or, after factoring, as follows:[10]

$$MUV = (AQ - SQ) \times SP$$

where

**materials usage variance**

The difference between the direct materials actually used and the direct materials allowed for the actual output multiplied by the standard price.

> $AQ$ = the actual quantity of materials used
> $SQ$ = the standard quantity of materials allowed for the actual output
> $SP$ = the standard price per unit

### *Computation of the Materials Usage Variance*

When materials are issued to production, the materials usage variance can be calculated. Crunchy Chips used 20,500 kilograms of yellow corn to produce 48,500 bags of corn chips. Therefore, $AQ$ is 20,500. From Exhibit 14–2, $SP$ is $0.216 per kilogram of yellow corn. $SQ$ is the product of the unit quantity standard and the actual units produced. From Exhibits 14–2 and 14–5, the unit standard is 500 grams of yellow corn for every bag of corn chips, and $SQ$ is 500 × 48,500, or 24,250,000 grams, or 24,250 kilograms. Thus, the materials usage variance is computed as follows:

---

10. The usage variance calculated this way is a pure variance, because it is affected only by variations in quantity.

$$MUV = (AQ - SQ) \times SP$$
$$= (20{,}500 - 24{,}250) \times (\$0.216)$$
$$= (-3{,}750 \times \$0.216)$$
$$= \$810 \text{ F}$$
$$\text{Percentage of } SQ \times SP = \$810/(24{,}250 \times \$0.216)$$
$$= \$810/\$5{,}238 = 15\% \text{ (rounded)}$$

### Responsibility for the Materials Usage Variance

The production manager is generally responsible for materials usage. The manager can ensure that standards are met by minimizing scrap, waste, and rework. As with the price variance, the use of materials usage variances to evaluate performance can lead to undesirable behaviours. For example, a production manager feeling pressure to produce a favourable variance might allow a defective unit to be transferred to finished goods. Although this action avoids the problem of wasted materials, it may create customer relations problems. Also, the cause of the variance can be attributable to others outside the production area, as discussed in the next section.

### Analysis of the Materials Usage Variance

Investigation at Crunchy Chips revealed that the favourable materials usage variance was the result of the higher-quality corn acquired by the purchasing department. Here, the favourable variance is essentially assignable to purchasing. Since the materials usage variance is favourable—and larger than the unfavourable price variance—the overall result of the change is favourable.

If management anticipates the favourable usage variance to persist, the higher quality of corn should be purchased regularly, and the price and quantity standards should be revised to reflect this decision. As this example reveals, standards are not static. As improvements in production take place and as conditions change, standards need to be revised to reflect changes in the operating environment.

## Direct Labour Variances

The rate and efficiency variances for labour (equivalent to price and usage variances for materials) are calculated in this section using the columnar and formula approaches.

### Columnar Approach

The three-pronged graphical presentation in Exhibit 14–7 illustrates inspection labour at the Crunchy Chips plant. The standard rate ($SR$) is $7 per hour (from Exhibit 14–2); standard hours ($SH$) are 339.5 hours (from Exhibit 14–5). Further explanations about detailed variance calculations, using the formula approach, are provided in the following sections.

### Labour Rate Variance: Formula Approach

**labour rate variance**

The difference between the actual hourly rate paid and the standard hourly rate multiplied by the actual hours worked.

The **labour rate variance** ($LRV$) computes the difference between what was paid to direct labourers and what should have been paid:

$$LRV = (AR \times AH) - (SR \times AH)$$

or, after factoring:

$$LRV = (AR - SR) \times AH$$

where

EXHIBIT   14-7

Labour Variances:
Columnar Approach

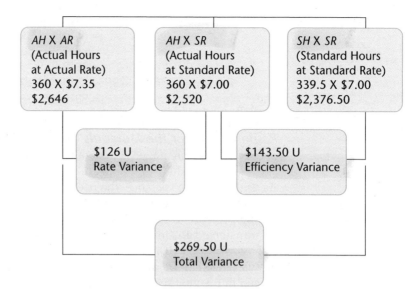

$AR$ = the actual hourly wage rate
$SR$ = the standard hourly wage rate
$AH$ = the actual direct labour hours used

### Computation of the Labour Rate Variance

Direct labour activity for Crunchy Chips's inspectors will be used to illustrate the computation of the labour rate variance. During the first week of March, 360 hours were used for inspection. The actual hourly wage paid to inspectors was $7.35. From Exhibit 14–2, the standard wage rate is $7. Thus, $AH$ is 360, $AR$ is $7.35, and $SR$ is $7. The labour rate variance is computed as follows:

$$LRV = (AR - SR)\ AH$$
$$= (\$7.35 - \$7)360$$
$$= \$0.35 \times 360$$
$$= \$126\ U$$
$$\text{Percentage of } SR \times AH = \$126/(\$7 \times 360)$$
$$= \$126/\$2,520 = 5\%$$

### Responsibility for the Labour Rate Variance

Labour rates are largely determined by labour markets and union contracts. Actual wage rates rarely differ from the standard rates. However, a variance can sometimes occur—for example, because more skilled labourers with a higher wage rate are used for less skilled tasks. Unexpected overtime can also cause a labour rate variance.

Wage rates for a particular labour activity often differ among workers because of different levels of seniority. Instead of using labour rate standards for each level, an average wage standard is often chosen. As the seniority mix changes, the average rate changes. This situation results in a labour rate variance. It also calls for a revised standard to reflect the new seniority mix. Production managers cannot typically control labour rate variances in this situation, so they should not be held responsible for them.

However, production managers may be able to significantly influence the *use* of labour. A production manager often deliberately assigns more skilled workers to less skilled tasks (or vice versa). Also, that manager may control the use of casual and part-time employees. The responsibility for the labour rate variance is usually assigned to those managers who decide how labour is used.

### Analysis of the Labour Rate Variance

A 5 percent variance is not likely to be considered significant, but let us assume for illustrative purposes that an investigation is conducted. The cause of the variance at Crunchy Chips is found to be the use of more highly paid and skilled machine operators as inspectors. This substitution became necessary after two inspectors resigned suddenly. The corrective action is to hire and train two new inspectors.

### Labour Efficiency Variance: Formula Approach

labour efficiency variance

The difference between the actual direct labour hours used and the standard direct labour hours allowed multiplied by the standard hourly wage rate.

The **labour efficiency variance** ($LEV$) measures the difference between the labour hours that were actually used and the labour hours that should have been used, calculated as follows:

$$LEV = (AH \times SR) - (SH \times SR)$$

or, after factoring:

$$LEV = (AH - SH)SR$$

where

$AH$ = the actual direct labour hours used
$SH$ = the standard direct labour hours that should have been used
$SR$ = the standard hourly wage rate

### Computation of the Labour Efficiency Variance

Crunchy Chips used 360 direct labour hours for inspection while producing 48,500 bags of corn chips. From Exhibit 14–2, we know that 0.007 hours per bag of chips at a cost of $7 per hour should have been used. The standard hours allowed for inspection are 339.5 (0.007 × 48,500). Thus, $AH$ is 360, $SH$ is 339.5, and $SR$ is $7. The labour efficiency variance is computed as follows:

$$
\begin{aligned}
LEV &= (AH - SH)\ SR \\
&= (360 - 339.5) \times \$7 \\
&= 20.5 \times \$7 \\
&= \$143.50 \text{ U}
\end{aligned}
$$

$$
\begin{aligned}
\text{Percentage of } SH \times SR &= \$143.50/(339.5 \times \$7) \\
&= \$143.50/\$2,376.50 = 6\% \text{ (rounded)}
\end{aligned}
$$

### Responsibility for the Labour Efficiency Variance

Generally speaking, production managers are responsible for the productive use of direct labour. However, as is true of all variances, once the cause is discovered, responsibility may be assigned elsewhere. For example, frequent breakdowns of machinery may cause interruptions and nonproductive use of labour. But these breakdowns may be caused by lack of proper maintenance. If so, the maintenance manager should be held responsible for the unfavourable labour efficiency variance.

If too much emphasis is placed on the labour efficiency variance, production managers may be tempted to engage in dysfunctional behaviours. For example, to avoid using additional labour hours to rework defective units, a production manager could deliberately transfer defective units to finished goods.

### Analysis of the Labour Efficiency Variance

Assume that the $143.50 unfavourable variance was considered to be significant and its cause was investigated. The investigation revealed that more shutdowns of the process occurred because the duties of the machine operators were split between machine operations and inspection. (Recall that this reassignment was necessary because two inspectors resigned unexpectedly.) This resulted in more idle time for inspection. Also, the machine operators were unable to meet the standard output per hour for inspection because they lacked experience in the sorting process. The corrective action to solve the problem is the same as that recommended for the unfavourable rate variance—hire and train two new inspectors.

### Sum of LRV and LEV

From Exhibit 14–7, the total labour variance is $269.50 unfavourable. It is the sum of the unfavourable labour rate variance and the unfavourable labour efficiency variance ($126.00 + $143.50).

## Variance Analysis: Overhead Costs

**Objective 5**

Compute the variable and fixed overhead variances, and explain their meaning.

For direct materials and direct labour, total variances are broken down into price (rate) and usage (efficiency) variances. The total overhead variance—the difference between applied and actual overhead—is also broken down into component variances. The number of component variances computed depends on the method of variance analysis used. A common method divides overhead into two categories—fixed and variable—and isolates component variances for each category. The total variable overhead variance is divided into the variable overhead spending variance and the variable overhead efficiency variance. Similarly, the total fixed overhead variance is divided into the fixed overhead spending variance (also called the fixed overhead flexible budget variance) and the fixed overhead denominator variance (also called the volume variance).[11]

### Variable Overhead Variances[12]

To illustrate the variable overhead variances, let's consider the activities of Crunchy Chips Company for the first week of March, 2005. The following data were gathered for this period:

| | |
|---|---|
| Variable overhead rate (standard) | $3.85  per direct labour hour |
| Actual variable overhead costs | $1,600 |
| Actual hours worked | 400[a] |
| Bags of chips produced | 48,500 |
| Hours allowed for production | 378.3[b] |
| Applied variable overhead | $1,456[c] |

[a] includes both inspection and machine operator labour
[b] 0.0078 (from Exhibit 14–2) × 48,500
[c] $3.85 × 378.3 (rounded to nearest dollar); overhead is applied using hours allowed.

### Total Variable Overhead Flexible Budget Variance

The total variable overhead flexible budget variance (also called the total variable overhead variance) is the difference between the actual and applied variable overhead. The total variable overhead variance is computed as follows:

---

11. The denominator variance is often called the volume variance. In this book we discourage the use of the term "volume variance" without a qualifier. The denominator variance refers to the production volume variance and measures the effect of the denominator volume, used to allocate fixed manufacturing overhead, on the under- or overallocation of fixed manufacturing costs. In contrast, the profit volume variance measures the effect of sales volume on profit.

12. The analysis in this example assumes a traditional costing environment with labour hours as the cost driver for variable overhead items. However, other unit- and non-unit-based drivers are also possible, especially in an activity-based costing environment.

$$\text{Total variable overhead variance} = \$1,600 - \$1,456$$
$$= \$144 \text{ U}$$

The total variable overhead variance can be divided into the spending and efficiency variances. Just as for materials and direct labour variances, both the three-pronged and formula approaches can be used. The computations using the three-pronged columnar approach are illustrated in Exhibit 14–8. Further details about the variance calculations, using the formula approach, are provided in the following sections.

EXHIBIT  14-8

Variable Overhead
Flexible Budget Variances:
Columnar Approach

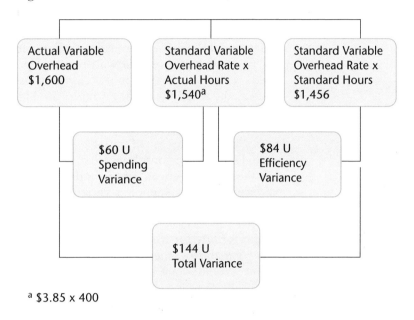

ᵃ $3.85 x 400

### Variable Overhead Spending Variance

**variable overhead spending variance**
The difference between the actual variable overhead and the budgeted variable overhead based on the actual hours used to produce the actual output.

The **variable overhead spending variance** measures the aggregate effect of differences in the actual variable overhead rate ($AVOR$) and the standard variable overhead rate ($SVOR$). The actual variable overhead rate is simply actual variable overhead divided by actual hours. For our example, this rate is $4 ($1,600/400 hours). The formula for computing the variable overhead spending variance is as follows:

$$\text{Variable overhead spending variance} = (AVOR \times AH) - (SVOR \times AH)$$
$$= (AVOR - SVOR) \times AH$$
$$= (\$4 - \$3.85) \times 400$$
$$= \$0.15 \times 400$$
$$= \$60 \text{ U}$$

### Comparison with the Materials and Labour Price Variances

The variable overhead spending variance is similar, but not identical, to the materials and labour price and rate variances. Variable overhead is not a homogeneous input—it can consist of a large number of individual items such as indirect materials, indirect labour, electricity, and maintenance. The standard variable overhead rate represents the weighted cost per direct labour hour that should be incurred for all variable overhead items. The difference between what should have been spent per hour and what was actually spent per hour is a type of price variance.

A variable overhead spending variance can arise because prices for individual variable overhead items have changed. Assume for the moment that the price changes of overhead items are the only cause of the spending variance. If the spending variance is unfavourable, price increases for variable overhead items are the cause; and if the spending variance is favourable, price decreases are dominating.

If price changes were the only source of the variable overhead spending variance, it would be completely analogous to the materials and labour price variances. However, the spending variance is also affected by how efficiently overhead items are used. Waste or inefficiency in the use of variable overhead items increases the actual variable overhead cost. The increased cost is in turn reflected in the increased actual variable overhead rate. Thus, even if the actual prices of the individual overhead items were equal to the budgeted prices, an unfavourable variable overhead spending variance could occur.

For example, more kilowatt-hours of power may be used than should be used, but this difference is not captured by a change in direct labour hours. Instead, the additional kilowatt-hours used increase the total cost of power—and thus the total cost of variable overhead. Similarly, improved efficiency can decrease the actual variable overhead costs and decrease the variable overhead rate. Therefore, the use of variable overhead items can affect the spending variance. Efficient use contributes to a favourable spending variance; inefficent use has the opposite effect. The net effect depends on which state dominates. The variable overhead spending variance is clearly a result of both price and efficiency factors.

### Responsibility for the Variable Overhead Spending Variance

Many variable overhead items are affected by several responsibility centres. For example, utilities are a joint cost. To the extent that the consumption of variable overhead can be traced to a responsibility centre, responsibility can be assigned.[13]

Controllability is a prerequisite for assigning responsibility. Price changes of variable overhead items are essentially beyond the control of supervisors. However, if price changes are small, the spending variance is mainly a matter of efficient use of overhead in production, which is controllable by production supervisors. Accordingly, responsibility for the variable overhead spending variance is generally assigned to production departments.

### Analysis of the Variable Overhead Spending Variance

The $60 unfavourable variance simply reveals that in aggregate, Crunchy Chips spent more on variable overhead than expected. Even if the variance were insignificant, it would reveal nothing about how well the costs of individual variable overhead items were controlled. Control of variable overhead requires line-by-line analysis for each individual item. Exhibit 14–9 presents a performance report that provides the line-by-line information essential for proper control of variable overhead. Variable overhead in this example consists of three items: gas, electricity, and water.

From Exhibit 14–9, it is clear that two of the three items present no control problems for the company. Electricity is the only item showing an unfavourable variance. In fact, it is the cause of the overall variable overhead spending variance. If the variance is significant, an investigation may be warranted. This investigation may reveal that the power company raised the price of electricity. If so, the cause of the variance is beyond the company's control. The correct response is to revise the budget formula to reflect the increased cost of electricity.

---

13. If a company installs meters to measure the consumption of utilities for each responsibility centre, responsibility can be assigned. However, the cost of assigning responsibility can exceed potential benefits. The alternative is allocation. Unfortunately, allocations can be arbitrary, and it is often difficult to identify accurately the amount actually consumed.

EXHIBIT 14-9

Flexible Budget
Performance Report

| | **Crunchy Chips Company**<br>**Flexible Budget Performance Report**<br>**For the Week Ended March 8, 2005** | | | |
|---|---|---|---|---|
| | Cost<br>Formula[a] | Actual<br>Costs | Budget[b] | Spending<br>Variance |
| Gas | $3.00 | $1,190 | $1,200 | $ 10 F |
| Electricity | 0.78 | 385 | 312 | 73 U |
| Water | 0.07 | 25 | 28 | 3 F |
| Total cost | $3.85 | $1,600 | $1,540 | $60 U |

[a]Per direct labour hour
[b]Computed using the cost formula and an activity level of 400 actual direct labour hours

However, if the price of electricity has remained unchanged, the usage of electricity has to be greater than expected. For example, the company may find that there were more startups and shutdowns of machinery than normal, causing an increased consumption of electricity. Here, further investigation is needed to avoid abnormal shutdowns in the future.

### Variable Overhead Efficiency Variance

**variable overhead efficiency variance**

Assuming that direct labour hours are used to apply overhead costs, the difference between the actual direct labour hours used and the standard hours allowed multiplied by the standard variable overhead rate.

It is assumed that variable overhead varies in proportion to changes in the direct labour hours used as the production volume changes. The **variable overhead efficiency variance** measures the change in variable overhead consumption that occurs because of efficient (or inefficient) use of direct labour. The efficiency variance is computed using the following formula:

$$\text{Variable overhead efficiency variance} = (AH - SH) \times SVOR$$
$$= (400 - 378.3) \times \$3.85$$
$$= 21.7 \times \$3.85$$
$$= \$84U \text{ (rounded)}$$

### Responsibility for the Variable Overhead Efficiency Variance

The variable overhead efficiency variance is directly related to the direct labour efficiency or usage variance. If variable overhead is truly proportional to direct labour consumption, then, like the labour usage variance, the variable overhead efficiency variance is caused by efficient or inefficient use of direct labour. If more (or fewer) direct labour hours are used than the standard calls for, the total variable overhead cost increases (or decreases).

The validity of the measure depends on the validity of the relationship between variable overhead costs and direct labour hours. In other words, do variable overhead costs *really* change in proportion to changes in direct labour hours? If they do, responsibility for the variable overhead efficiency variance should be assigned to the individual who is responsible for the use of direct labour: the production manager.

### Analysis of the Variable Overhead Efficiency Variance

At Crunchy Chips, the reasons for the unfavourable variable overhead efficiency variance are the same as those for the unfavourable labour usage variance. More hours were used than the standard called for, because of excessive idle time for inspectors and because of the use of inexperienced machine operators as substitute inspectors. More information about the effect of labour usage on variable overhead is provided by a line-by-line analysis of individual variable overhead items. This can be accomplished by comparing the budget allowance for the actual hours used with the budget allowance for the standard hours allowed for each item. The performance report in Exhibit 14–9 is extended in Exhibit 14–10 to include this comparison for all three variable overhead costs.

Exhibit 14–10 reveals that the cost of gas is affected most by inefficient use of labour. This can be explained by the need to keep the cooking oil hot (assuming that gas is used for cooking), even though the cooking process is slowed down by the subsequent sorting process. The column labelled "Budget for Standard Hours" gives the amount that should have been spent on variable overhead for the actual output. The total of all items in this column is the applied variable overhead, the amount assigned to production in a standard cost system. Note that in a standard cost system, variable overhead is applied using the hours allowed for the actual output (*SH*), while in a normal costing system, variable overhead is applied using actual hours (see Chapter 4). Although not shown in Exhibit 14–10, the difference between actual costs and the budget for standard hours is the total variable overhead variance ($144, underapplied). Thus, the underapplied variable overhead variance is the sum of the spending and efficiency variances.

**EXHIBIT  14-10**

Performance Report—
Variable Overhead

| | | | **Crunchy Chips Company** Performance Report For the Week Ended March 8, 2005 | | | | |
|---|---|---|---|---|---|---|
| **Cost** | **Cost Formula[a]** | **Actual Costs** | **Budget for Actual Hours** | **Spending Variance[b]** | **Budget for Standard Hours[c]** | **Efficiency Variance[d]** |
| Gas | $3.00 | $1,190 | $1,200 | $10 F | $1,135 | $65 U |
| Electricity | 0.78 | 385 | 312 | 73 U | 295 | 17 U |
| Water | 0.07 | 25 | 28 | 3 F | 26 | 2 U |
| Total | $3.85 | $1,600 | $1,540 | $60 U | $1,456 | $84 U |

[a] Per direct labour hour
[b] Spending variance = Actual costs − Budget for actual hours
[c] Computed using the cost formula and an activity level of 378.3 standard hours. Rounded to the nearest dollar.
[d] Efficiency variance = Budget for actual hours − Budget for standard hours

## Fixed Overhead Variances

The Crunchy Chips Company example can be extended to illustrate the computation of fixed overhead variances. The additional data needed for this purpose are as follows:

### Budgeted/Planned Fixed Overhead Items

| | |
|---|---|
| Budgeted fixed overhead | $749,970 |
| Practical activity level (direct labour hours) | 23,400[a] |
| Standard fixed overhead rate | $32.05[b] |

[a] Hours allowed to produce 3,000,000 bags of chips: 0.0078 × 3,000,000
[b] $749,970/23,400

### Actual Fixed Overhead Items

| | |
|---|---|
| Actual production (bags of chips) | 2,750,000 |
| Actual fixed overhead cost | $749,000 |
| Standard hours allowed for actual production | 21,450[a] |

[a] 0.0078 (from Exhibit 14–2) × 2,750,000

### Total Fixed Overhead Variance

The total fixed overhead variance is the difference between actual fixed overhead and applied fixed overhead. The applied fixed overhead is obtained by multiplying the standard fixed overhead rate by the standard hours allowed for the actual output. Thus, the applied fixed overhead is as follows:

$$\text{Applied fixed overhead} = \text{Standard fixed overhead rate} \times \text{Standard hours}$$
$$= \$32.05 \times 21{,}450$$
$$= \$687{,}473 \text{ (rounded)}$$

The total fixed overhead variance is the difference between the actual fixed overhead and the applied fixed overhead:

$$\text{Total fixed overhead variance} = \$749{,}000 - \$687{,}473$$
$$= \$61{,}527 \text{ underapplied}$$

To help managers understand why fixed overhead was underapplied by $61,527, the total variance can be broken down into two variances: the fixed overhead spending variance and the fixed overhead denominator (or volume) variance. The two variances are illustrated in Exhibit 14–11 and further explained in the next section.

**EXHIBIT   14-11**

Fixed Overhead Variances

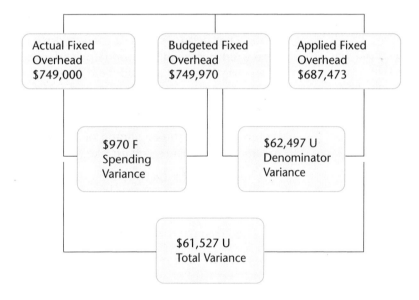

### Fixed Overhead Spending Variance

**fixed overhead spending variance**

The difference between actual fixed overhead and applied fixed overhead.

The **fixed overhead spending variance** is defined as the difference between the actual fixed overhead and the budgeted fixed overhead. For Crunchy Chips Company, the spending variance is favourable, because less was spent on fixed overhead items than was budgeted.

### Responsibility for the Fixed Overhead Spending Variance

Fixed overhead is made up of a number of individual items, such as salaries, amortization, taxes, and insurance. Many fixed overhead items result from long-term investments and are not subject to change in the short term. Consequently, fixed overhead costs are often beyond the immediate control of management. Since many fixed overhead costs are affected mainly by long-term decisions, and not by changes in production levels, the budget variance is usually small. For example, amortization, salaries, taxes, and insurance costs are not likely to be much different than planned.

### Analysis of the Fixed Overhead Spending Variance

Because fixed overhead is made up of many individual items, a line-by-line comparison of budgeted costs with actual costs provides more information about the causes of the spending variance. Exhibit 14–12 provides such a report. The fixed overhead in this example consists of amortization, salaries, taxes, and insurance. The report reveals that the fixed overhead spending variance is essentially in line with expectations. The fixed overhead spending variances, both on a line-item basis and in the aggregate, are relatively small.

**EXHIBIT 14-12**

Performance Report—
Fixed Overhead

| | Crunchy Chips Company Performance Report For the Year Ended 2005 | | |
|---|---|---|---|
| **Fixed Overhead Items** | **Actual Cost** | **Budgeted Cost** | **Variance** |
| Amortization | $530,000 | $530,000 | $ — |
| Salaries | 159,370 | 159,970 | 600 F |
| Taxes | 50,500 | 50,000 | 500 U |
| Insurance | 9,130 | 10,000 | 870 F |
| Total fixed | $749,000 | $749,970 | $970 F |

### Fixed Overhead Denominator Variance

**fixed overhead denominator variance**

The difference between budgeted fixed overhead and applied fixed overhead.

The **fixed overhead denominator variance** is the difference between budgeted fixed overhead and applied fixed overhead. The denominator variance measures the effect of the actual output departing from the output used at the beginning of the year to compute the predetermined standard fixed overhead rate. To see this, let $SH(D)$ represent the standard hours allowed for the denominator volume (the volume used at the beginning of the year to compute the predetermined fixed overhead rate). The standard fixed overhead rate ($SFOR$) is computed as follows:

$$SFOR = \text{(Budgeted fixed overhead)}/SH(D)$$
$$= \$749,970/23,400$$
$$= \$32.05$$

The fixed overhead denominator variance can then be computed as follows:

Fixed overhead denominator variance = Budgeted fixed overhead
$$- \text{Applied fixed overhead}$$
$$= SFOR \times SH(D) - SFOR \times SH$$
$$= SFOR \times (SH(D) - SH)$$
$$= \$32.05 \times (23,400 - 21,450)$$
$$= \$62,497 \text{ U (rounded)}$$

Thus, for a fixed overhead denominator variance to occur, the denominator hours, $SH(D)$, must differ from the standard hours allowed for the actual volume, $SH$. At the beginning of the year, Crunchy Chips had the capacity to produce 3,000,000 bags of chips, using 23,400 direct labour hours. The actual outcome was 2,750,000 bags produced, using 21,450 standard hours. Thus, as fewer units were produced than expected, an unfavourable fixed overhead denominator variance arose.

But what is the meaning of this variance? The variance occurs because the actual output volume differs from the predicted output volume. At the beginning of the year, if management had used 2,750,000 bags of corn chips as the denominator volume, the denominator variance would not have existed. In this view, the denominator variance is seen as a prediction error—a measure of management's inability to select the correct volume over which to spread fixed overhead.

If, however, the denominator volume represented the amount that management believed *could* be produced and sold, the denominator variance conveys more significant information. If the actual volume is less than the denominator volume, the denominator variance signals to management that a loss in volume has occurred. That loss is not equivalent, however, to the dollar value of the denominator variance. The loss is equal to the lost contribution margin on the units that were not produced and sold. However, the denominator variance is positively correlated with the lost contribution margin.

For example, suppose that the contribution margin per standard direct labour hour is $40. By producing only 2.75 million bags of chips instead of 3 million bags, the company lost sales of 250,000 bags. This is equivalent to 1,950 hours (0.0078 × 250,000). At $40 per hour, the loss is $78,000. The unfavourable denominator variance of $62,497 signals this loss, but in this case understates it. In this sense, the denominator variance is a measure of capacity utilization, but it is clearly less useful than the profit volume variance calculated here. The denominator variance is analogous to the cost of unused capacity described in Chapter 3.

### Responsibility for the Denominator Variance

The assumption that the denominator variance measures capacity utilization implies that the general responsibility for this variance should be assigned to the production department. Sometimes, however, investigation into the reasons for a significant denominator variance may reveal the cause to be factors beyond the control of the production function. Here, specific responsibility can be assigned elsewhere. For example, if a purchasing agent acquires a raw material of lower quality than usual, significant rework time may result, causing lower production and an unfavourable denominator variance. In this case, responsibility for the variance rests with purchasing, not production.

## Summary of Manufacturing Cost Flexible Budget Variances

The following is a summary of the flexible budget variances discussed in this chapter, including common alternative names found in practice. Each variable cost has a price dimension and an input quantity dimension.

| Cost Item | Price Dimension | Quantity Dimension |
|---|---|---|
| Materials | Price variance (based on usage) | Quantity variance |
| | Purchase price variance (based on purchases) | Usage variance |
| | | Efficiency variance |
| Labour | Price variance | Quantity variance |
| | Rate variance | Usage variance |
| | | Efficiency variance |
| Variable overhead | Rate variance | Quantity variance |
| | Spending variance | Usage variance |
| | | Efficiency variance |
| Fixed overhead | Price variance | Not applicable |
| | Spending variance | Not applicable |
| | Flexible budget variance | Not applicable |

The fixed overhead denominator variance is not a flexible budget variance, and it is unique to fixed overhead. The denominator variance results from the difference between the flexible budget and applied fixed overhead, and is due solely to the denominator used in prorating fixed overhead on the basis of some output measure (such as units produced) or input measure (such as labour hours or machine hours). Thus it can be influenced by market factors, since companies may adjust the production volume in response to unexpected changes in demand for their products during the budget period.

The adoption of a standard costing system with variances calculated for the four categories can help the IV Products Division of Honley Medical, introduced in the opening scenario, to improve cost control and hold managers responsible for cost control. It can also provide a basis for managerial evaluation and reward systems. Improving cost control is especially important and timely for the future profitability of that company, as it expects competition to increase in the future.

## Appendix A: Profitability Analysis

**Objective 6**

Use variance analysis as an analytical tool for profitability analysis.

In Chapter 13, the discussion of flexible budgeting was followed by an example of profitability analysis, where performance reports were used to identify problem areas as well as efficiencies. This appendix expands the profitability analysis by considering variations in actual and budgeted sales volume, prices, and mix, as well as in market share.

Consider the following example for Virtuality, Ltd., a manufacturer of two types of helmets used on virtual reality architectural design and other applications. Virtuality sells these products in the Canadian market. Exhibit 14–13 provides selected information about the company's annual budget and actual results for its two products. Assume that Virtuality has no inventories and that it uses variable costing.

The budgeted sales volume was based on an expected industry volume for products A and B (combined) of 4,500 units. Actual industry volume was 4,950 units. Although products A and B serve different needs, they are considered substitute products, in the sense that a customer is likely to buy either a unit of A or a unit of B, but not both.

**total profit variance**

The difference between actual and budgeted profit.

This example provides an analysis of variances that identifies the effect of each factor on profit. Using the data provided in Exhibit 14–13, Exhibit 14–14 shows that budgeted operating profit was $1,230,000 and that actual profit was $1,660,500. This results in a **total profit variance**—the difference between actual and budgeted profit (using the static budget)—in the amount of $430,500F. The concepts of cost variance analysis can be applied to provide insight into the effect of various changes on profit. It is clear that the actual sales volume was higher for A by 30 units but lower for B by 15 units. This raises the question of the sales volume effect on revenues and variable costs. Furthermore, selling prices were higher by $500 for A but lower by $500 for B. Unit variable costs were lower by $500 for both A and B. Finally, fixed costs were higher than budgeted by $12,000. Each of these factors has an effect on profits. To show more clearly the impact of

**EXHIBIT 14-13**

Product Contribution Margins and Total Fixed Costs: Virtuality Ltd.

| | Budgeted | Actual |
|---|---|---|
| Sales of product A (in units) | 360 | 390 |
| Sales of product B (in units) | 240 | 225 |
| Total sales (in units) | 600 | 615 |
| Selling price per unit of A | $ 10,000 | $ 10,500 |
| Variable cost per unit of A | 7,000 | 6,500 |
| Contribution margin per unit of A | $ 3,000 | $ 4,000 |
| Selling price per unit of B | $ 5,000 | $ 4,500 |
| Variable cost per unit of B | 2,500 | 2,000 |
| Contribution margin per unit of B | $ 2,500 | $ 2,500 |
| Total fixed costs | $450,000 | $462,000 |

each of these factors or causes on the bottom line, a series of variances are computed to measure each factor's effects on profits while holding other factors constant. The first stage of this analysis is shown in Exhibit 14–14.

The following is a breakdown of the effect of each factor on profit as shown in Exhibit 14–14.

**sales price variance**

Measures the direct effect of the change in selling prices on profit.

1. *Sales price variance* The **sales price variance** measures the direct effect of the change in selling prices on profit. Actual selling prices were $500 higher than budgeted for A and $500 lower for B. Based on the actual units sold, this is a variance in profit of $82,500F (390 × $500 = $195,000F for A and 225 × $500 = $112,500U for B). Note that the sales price variance is equal to the flexible budget variance in Exhibit 14–14.

2. *Profit volume variance (gross)* This variance measures the effect of the sales volume changes on profits—an increase of 30 units for A and a decrease of 15 units for B—other things constant. The sales volume changes affect both revenues and variable costs. The profit volume variance for revenues is $225,000F (30 × $10,000 = $300,000F for A, and 15 × $5,000 = $75,000U for B). The profit volume variance for variable costs is $172,500U (30 × $7,000 = $210,000U for A, and 15 × $2,500 = $37,500F for B). Together, the effect is $52,500F. This variance can also be calculated directly from the standard unit contribution margins (30 × $3,000 = $90,000F for A, and 15 × $2,500 = $37,500U for B, for a total of $52,500 F).

3. *Variable cost flexible budget variance* Actual unit variable costs were $500 lower than budgeted for both A and B. These unit cost differences account for $307,500F of the profit variance (390 × $500 = $195,000F for A, and 225 × $500 = $112,500F for B).

4. *Fixed cost flexible budget variance* Because fixed costs are not affected by sales volume, the variance is the difference between the actual fixed costs and the budgeted fixed costs, or $12,000U.

These variances account for the total profit variance of $430,500F, as shown in the following summary:

| | |
|---|---:|
| Sales price variance | $ 82,500 F |
| Profit volume variance (gross) | 52,500 F |
| Variable cost flexible budget variance | 307,500 F |
| Fixed cost flexible budget variance | 12,000 U |
| Total profit variance | $430,500 F |

**EXHIBIT** 14-14

Comparison of Actual and Budget Profits: Virtuality Ltd.

| | Actual Results | Flexible Budget[a] | Flexible Budget Variance[b] | Static Budget | Profit Volume Variance[c] |
|---|---:|---:|---:|---:|---:|
| Sales revenue | $5,107,500[d] | $5,025,000[e] | (1)$ 82,500 F | $4,800,000[f] | $225,000 F |
| Variable costs | 2,985,000[g] | 3,292,500[h] | (3) 307,500 F | 3,120,000[i] | 172,500 U |
| Contribution margin | $2,122,500 | $1,732,500 | $390,000 F | $1,680,000 | (2)$ 52,500 F |
| Fixed costs | 462,000 | 450,000 | (4) 12,000 U | 450,000 | — |
| Profit | $1,660,500 | $1,282,500 | $378,000 F | $1,230,000 | $ 52,500 F |

[a] Based on actual sales and budgeted prices and costs
[b] Actual results minus flexible budget
[c] Flexible budget minus static budget
[d] (390 × $10,500) + (225 × $4,500)
[e] (390 × $10,000) + (225 × $5,000)

[f] (360 × $10,000) + (240 × $5,000)
[g] (390 × $6,500) + (225 × $2,000)
[h] (390 × $7,000) + (225 × $2,500)
[i] (360 × $7,000) + (240× $2,500)

Note: The difference between the actual profit, $1,660,500, and the static budget profit, $1,230,000, is the total profit variance, $430,500F.

The variances can be analyzed in greater detail. Variable cost variances can be decomposed into manufacturing and nonmanufacturing. The manufacturing cost variances can be decomposed further into material, labour, and overhead variances, with each also broken down into price and quantity components. Similarly, it is possible to analyze the profit volume variance (gross) in more detail. The concept is the same: to isolate the effect of one factor, such as sales volume, while holding the other factors, such as sales mix or selling price, constant. An application of this analysis is illustrated in the next section.

### Detailed Analysis of the Profit Volume Variance

**profit volume variance (gross)**

Consists of a profit volume variance (net) and a sales mix variance.

**profit volume variance (net)**

Measures the effect on profit of the difference in total sales volume between the budget and the actual volume, with other factors—including sales mix and contribution margin per unit—remaining constant.

**sales mix variance**

Measures the effect of the change from the budgeted sales mix.

**industry volume variance**

A difference in profit due to the difference between budgeted sales volume based on expected industry sales volume and budgeted sales volume based on actual industry sales volume.

**market share variance**

A difference in profit due to the difference between the budgeted market share and the actual market share.

The **profit volume variance (gross)** can be broken down into a **profit volume variance (net)** and a **sales mix variance** as follows:

1. *Profit volume variance (net)* This variance measures the profit effect of the increase in total sales volume, from the budget of 600 units to the actual volume of 615 units, with other factors (including sales mix and contribution margin per unit) being held constant. From Exhibit 14–14, the average standard contribution margin for the budgeted sales mix is $1,680,000/600 = $2,800. The net profit effect of sales volume changes is (615 − 600) × $2,800 = $42,000F.

2. *Sales mix variance* This variance measures the effect of the change from the budgeted sales mix. From Exhibit 14–14, the average standard contribution margin for the actual sales mix is $1,732,500/615 = $2,817.07. The profit effect of the change from the budgeted sales mix is ($2,817.07 − $2,800) × 615 = $10,500F (rounded).

The total of the profit volume variance (net) and the sales mix variance is equal to the profit volume variance (gross) of $52,500F ($42,000F + $10,500F = $52,500F).

Another level of analysis is also possible. The profit volume variance (net) can be broken down into an **industry volume variance** and a **market share variance** as follows:

1. *Industry volume variance* Assume that Virtuality, Ltd., based its sales budget on an industry volume of 4,500 units and expected to sell a total of 600 units. If the actual industry sales were 4,950 units, or 10 percent higher than expected, Virtuality's sales should increase by 600 × 10 percent = 60 units, all other factors being held constant. The effect on profit of the increase in industry sales is 60 × $2,800 (average standard contribution margin for the budgeted sales mix) = $168,000F.

2. *Market share variance* Virtuality's actual market share was 12.4 percent (615/4,950) and not the expected 13.3 percent (600/4,500). Had Virtuality maintained its market share, it would have obtained 660 units (4,950 × 13.3 percent) instead of 615 units. The profit effect of the decrease in the company's market share is (660 − 615) × $2,800 = $126,000U.

The total of the industry volume and market share variances is equal to the profit volume variance (net) of $42,000F ($168,000F + $126,000U = $42,000F). The total profit variance of $430,500F is equal to the difference between the actual profit and the static budget profit in Exhibit 14–14. The results of the profit volume variance calculations are summarized in Exhibit 14–15.

Exhibit 14–16 further summarizes the calculations of the variances in Exhibit 14–15 in a diagram that emphasizes the sequence in which the variances should be calculated. It starts with the static profit budget on the left and adjusts the budget in successive steps, one factor at a time, ending with the actual profit. This generates a series of variances that account for the difference between the budgeted and actual profits.

EXHIBIT 14-15

Profit Variance Analysis:
Virtuality, Ltd.

| | | |
|---|---|---|
| Industry volume variance | $168,000 F | |
| Market share variance | 126,000 U | |
|   Profit volume variance (net) | | $42,000 F |
| Sales mix variance | | 10,500 F |
|   Profit volume variance (gross) | | $ 52,500 F |
| Sales price variance | | 82,500 F |
| Fixed cost flexible budget variance | | 12,000 U |
| Variable cost flexible budget variance | | 307,500 F |
|   Total profit variance | | $430,500 F |

The sequence of changing factors can affect the resulting variances. It is important to isolate exogenous factors first: volume, mix, and price, in that order. After that, the cost variances will reflect the actual volume, mix, and price. The change in industry volume is generally less controllable than the change in market share. Thus, the sequence of variance calculations should proceed from industry volume to market share variances.

As stated before, this example illustrates the use of profitability variance analysis for Virtuality, Ltd. Note, however, that no single template is appropriate for all organizations, and that organizations need to create their own customized approaches to profitability variance analysis.

# Appendix B: Accounting for Variances

**Objective 7**

Prepare journal entries for materials and labour variances, and describe the accounting for overhead variances.

To illustrate the recording of variances, assume that the materials price variance is computed at the time materials are purchased. With this assumption, a general rule for a firm's inventory accounts is that all inventories are carried at standard cost. Actual costs are never entered into an inventory account. In recording variances, unfavourable variances are always debits, and favourable variances are always credits.

## Entries for Direct Materials Variances

### Materials Purchase Price Variance

The entry to record the purchase of materials is given below (assuming an *unfavourable MPV* and that *AQP* is materials purchased).

| | | |
|---|---|---|
| Materials | $SP \times AQ$ | |
| Materials purchase price variance | $(AP - SP) \times AQ$ | |
|   Accounts payable | | $AP \times AQ$ |

For example, if *AP* is $0.252 per kilogram of corn, *SP* is $0.216, and 20 500 kilograms are purchased, the entry would be as follows:

| | | |
|---|---|---|
| Materials | $4,428 | |
| Materials purchase price variance | 738 | |
|   Accounts payable | | $5,166 |

Note that the raw materials are carried in the inventory account at standard cost.

### Materials Usage Variance

The general form for the entry to record the issuance and usage of materials, assuming a *favourable MUV*, is as follows:

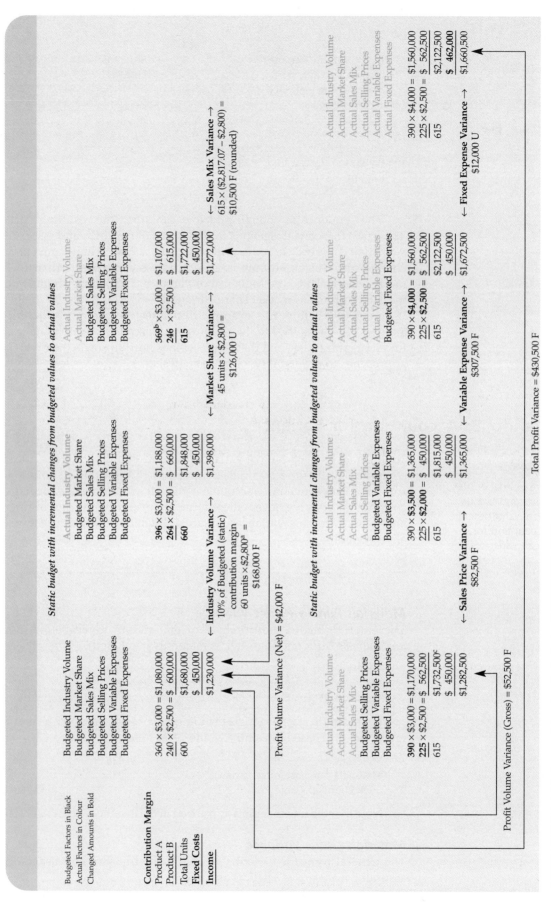

**EXHIBIT 14-16**

Profitability Analysis for Virtuality Ltd.

Budgeted Factors in Black
Actual Factors in Colour
Changed Amounts in Bold

*Static budget with incremental changes from budgeted values to actual values*

| | Budgeted Industry Volume | Actual Industry Volume | Actual Industry Volume |
|---|---|---|---|
| | Budgeted Market Share | Budgeted Market Share | Actual Market Share |
| | Budgeted Sales Mix | Budgeted Sales Mix | Budgeted Sales Mix |
| | Budgeted Selling Prices | Budgeted Selling Prices | Budgeted Selling Prices |
| | Budgeted Variable Expenses | Budgeted Variable Expenses | Budgeted Variable Expenses |
| | Budgeted Fixed Expenses | Budgeted Fixed Expenses | Budgeted Fixed Expenses |

**Contribution Margin**

| | | | |
|---|---|---|---|
| Product A | 360 × $3,000 = $1,080,000 | 396 × $3,000 = $1,188,000 | 369ᵇ × $3,000 = $1,107,000 |
| Product B | 240 × $2,500 = $600,000 | 264 × $2,500 = $660,000 | 246 × $2,500 = $615,000 |
| Total Units | 600 / $1,680,000 | 660 / $1,848,000 | 615 / $1,722,000 |
| Fixed Costs | $450,000 | $450,000 | $450,000 |
| Income | $1,230,000 | $1,398,000 | $1,272,000 |

← Industry Volume Variance → 10% of Budgeted (static) contribution margin 60 units × $2,800ª = $168,000 F

← Market Share Variance → 45 units × $2,800 = $126,000 U

← Sales Mix Variance → 615 × ($2,817.07 − $2,800) = $10,500 F (rounded)

Profit Volume Variance (Net) = $42,000 F

*Static budget with incremental changes from budgeted values to actual values*

| | Actual Industry Volume | Actual Industry Volume | Actual Industry Volume | Actual Industry Volume |
|---|---|---|---|---|
| | Actual Market Share | Actual Market Share | Actual Market Share | Actual Market Share |
| | Actual Sales Mix | Actual Sales Mix | Actual Sales Mix | Actual Sales Mix |
| | Budgeted Selling Prices | Actual Selling Prices | Actual Selling Prices | Actual Selling Prices |
| | Budgeted Variable Expenses | Budgeted Variable Expenses | Actual Variable Expenses | Actual Variable Expenses |
| | Budgeted Fixed Expenses | Budgeted Fixed Expenses | Budgeted Fixed Expenses | Actual Fixed Expenses |

| | | | | |
|---|---|---|---|---|
| 390 × $3,000 = $1,170,000 | 390 × $3,500 = $1,365,000 | 390 × $4,000 = $1,560,000 | 390 × $4,000 = $1,560,000 |
| 225 × $2,500 = $562,500 | 225 × $2,000 = $450,000 | 225 × $2,500 = $562,500 | 225 × $2,500 = $562,500 |
| 615 / $1,732,500ᶜ | 615 / $1,815,000 | 615 / $2,122,500 | 615 / $2,122,500 |
| $450,000 | $450,000 | $450,000 | $462,000 |
| $1,282,500 | $1,365,000 | $1,672,500 | $1,660,500 |

← Sales Price Variance → $82,500 F

← Variable Expense Variance → $307,500 F

← Fixed Expense Variance → $12,000 U

Profit Volume Variance (Gross) = $52,500 F

Total Profit Variance = $430,500 F

ª Average budgeted contribution margin based on standard mix = $1,680,000 / 600 = $2,800
ᵇ Actual volume of 615: 60% (360/600) from A and 40% (240/600) from B
ᶜ Average budgeted contribution margin based on actual mix = $1,732,500 / 615 = $2,817

| | | |
|---|---|---|
| Work in process | $SQ \times SP$ | |
| Materials usage variance | | $(AQ - SQ) \times SP$ |
| Materials | | $AQ \times SP$ |

Here, $AQ$ is the materials issued and used, not necessarily equal to the materials purchased. Note that only standard quantities and standard prices are used to assign costs to Work in Process; no actual costs enter this account.

For example, if $AQ$ is 20,500 kilograms of corn, $SQ$ is 24,250 kilograms, and $SP$ is \$0.216 per kilogram, the entry would be as follows:

| | | |
|---|---|---|
| Work in process | \$5,238 | |
| Materials usage variance | | \$ 810 |
| Materials | | 4,428 |

Note that the favourable usage variance appears as a credit entry.

## Entries for Direct Labour Variances

Unlike the direct materials variances, both types of labour variances are recorded in a single entry. The general form of this entry is given below (assuming an *unfavourable* labour rate variance and an *unfavourable* labour efficiency variance).

| | | |
|---|---|---|
| Work in Process | $SH \times SR$ | |
| Labour efficiency variance | $(AH - SH) \times SR$ | |
| Labour rate variance | $(AR - SR) \times AH$ | |
| Accrued payroll | | $AH \times AR$ |

Note again that only standard hours and standard rates are used to assign costs to Work in Process. Actual prices or quantities are not used.

To give a specific example, assume that $AH$ is 360, $SH$ is 339.5, $AR$ is \$7.35, and $SR$ is \$7. The following general ledger entry would be made:

| | | |
|---|---|---|
| Work in process | \$2,376.50 | |
| Labour efficiency variance | 143.50 | |
| Labour rate variance | 126.00 | |
| Accrued payroll | | \$2,646.00 |

## Disposition of Materials and Labour Variances

At the end of the year, the variances for materials and labour are usually closed to Cost of Goods Sold. This practice is acceptable provided that variances are not material in amount. With the use of the above data, the entries would take the following form:

| | | |
|---|---|---|
| Cost of goods sold | \$1007.50 | |
| Materials purchase price variance | | \$738.00 |
| Labour efficiency variance | | 143.50 |
| Labour rate variance | | 126.00 |
| | | |
| Materials usage variance | 810.00 | |
| Cost of goods sold | | 810.00 |

If the variances are material, they should be prorated among various accounts if management desires to maintain the firm's financial statements on an actual costing basis. The materials purchase price variance is prorated among Materials Inventory, Materials Usage Variance, Work in Process, and Cost of Goods Sold. The remaining materials and labour variances are prorated among Work in Process, Finished Goods, and Cost of Goods Sold. Typically, materials variances are prorated on the basis of the cost of materials balances in each of these accounts, and labour variances on the basis of the labour balances in the accounts.

## Overhead Variances

Although overhead variances can be recorded following a pattern similar to the one described for labour and materials, these variances are more generally treated as part of a periodic overhead analysis. Applied overhead is accumulated in the applied accounts, and actual overhead is accumulated in the control accounts. Periodically (e.g., monthly), performance reports that provide overhead variance information are prepared. At the end of the year, the applied accounts and control accounts are closed out and the variances isolated. The overhead variances are then disposed by closing them to Cost of Goods Sold if they are not material, or by prorating them among Work in Process, Finished Goods, and Cost of Goods Sold if they are material.

## Summary of Learning Objectives

### 1. Explain how unit standards are set and why standard cost systems are adopted.

A standard cost system budgets quantities and costs on a unit basis. Unit budgets are established for labour, materials, and overhead. Standard costs, therefore, are the amount that should be expended to produce a product or service. Standards are set using historical experience, engineering studies, and input from operating personnel, marketing, and accounting. Currently attainable standards are those which can be achieved under efficient operating conditions. Ideal standards are those achievable under maximum efficiency—that is, under ideal operating conditions. Standard cost systems are adopted to improve planning and control and to facilitate product costing. By comparing actual outcomes with standards, and by breaking down the variance into price and quantity components, this approach provides detailed feedback to managers. This information allows managers to exercise a greater degree of cost control than that found in a normal or actual cost system. Decisions such as those related to bidding are also made more easily when a standard cost system is in place.

### 2. Explain the purpose of a standard cost sheet.

The standard cost sheet provides the details for computing the standard cost per unit. It shows the standard costs for materials, labour, variable, and fixed overhead. It also reveals the quantity of each input that should be used to produce one unit of output. Using these unit quantity standards, the standard quantity of materials allowed and the standard hours allowed for the actual output can be computed. These computations play an important role in variance analysis.

### 3. Describe the basic concepts underlying variance analysis, and explain when variances should be investigated.

The budget variance is the difference between the actual costs and the planned costs. In a standard cost system, the budget variance is broken down into price and usage variances. Breaking the budget variances into price and usage variances provides managers with more ability to analyze and control the total variance. Variances should be investigated if they are material and if the benefits of corrective action are greater than the costs of investigation and correction. Because of difficulties in assessing costs and benefits on a case-by-case basis, many companies set up formal control limits—a dollar amount, a percentage, or both. Others use judgment to assess the need to investigate.

### 4. Compute the materials and labour variances, and explain how they are used for control.

The materials and labour price (rate) and usage (efficiency) variances can be computed using either a three-pronged columnar approach or formulas. The materials price variance (Exhibit 14–6) is the difference between what should have been paid for materials and what was paid (generally associated with the purchasing activity). The materials usage variance is the difference between the standard cost of the materials that should have been used and the amount that was used (generally associated with the production activity). The labour rate variance (Exhibit 14–7) is caused by the actual wage rate differing from the standard wage rate. It is the difference between the wages that were paid and those which should have been paid. The labour efficiency variance is the difference between the cost of the labour that was used and the cost of the labour that should have been used. When a significant variance is signalled, investigation is called for and corrective action should be taken, if possible, to put the system back in control.

## 5. Compute the variable and fixed overhead variances, and explain their meaning.

The variable overhead spending variance (Exhibit 14–8) is the difference between the actual variable overhead cost and the budgeted variable overhead cost for the actual hours worked. It is a budget variance, and it results from price changes and the efficient or inefficient use of variable overhead inputs. The variable efficiency variance is the difference between budgeted variable overhead at actual hours and applied variable overhead. Because the application base used in most chapter examples is labour hours, the efficiency variance is strictly attributable to the efficiency of labour usage, and assumes that all variable overhead items vary by direct labour hours. The fixed overhead spending variance (Exhibit 14–11) is the difference between the actual fixed overhead costs and the budgeted fixed overhead costs. Thus it is simply a budget variance. The denominator variance is the difference between the budgeted fixed overhead and the applied fixed overhead. It occurs when the actual production volume is different from the expected production volume used to determine the fixed overhead rate, and is thus a measure of capacity utilization.

## 6. Use variance analysis as an analytical tool for profitability analysis (Appendix A).

The same concepts used to analyze cost variances can be used to identify the effects of different factors on profit. Variances related to sales volume, prices, variable costs, and fixed costs can be isolated. In turn, these variances can be decomposed into several components. For example, the profit volume variance (gross) can be decomposed into profit volume (net) and sales mix variances (for multiproduct companies), and the profit volume variance (net) can be decomposed into industry volume and market share components. This analysis allows managers to identify the factors that have contributed significantly to profits.

## 7. Prepare journal entries for materials and labour variances, and describe the accounting for overhead variances (Appendix B).

Assuming that the materials price variance is computed at the point of purchase, all inventories are carried at standard cost. Actual costs are never entered into an inventory account. Accounts are created for materials price and usage variances and for labour rate and efficiency variances. Unfavourable variances are always debits; favourable variances are always credits. Overhead variances are generally not journalized. Instead, periodic overhead variance reports are prepared. At the end of the year, overhead variances are isolated. Immaterial variances are closed to the cost of goods sold and material variances prorated among the cost of goods sold, work in process, and finished goods inventory.

## Key Terms

Control limits 640
Currently attainable standards 635
Efficiency variances 635
Favourable (F) variances 639
Fixed overhead denominator
  variance 654
Fixed overhead spending variance 653
Ideal standards 635
Industry volume variance 658
Labour efficiency variance 647
Labour rate variance 645
Market share variance 658

Materials price variance 642
Materials purchase price
  variance 644
Materials usage variance 644
Price (rate) variance 638
Price standards 634
Profit volume variance (gross) 658
Profit volume variance (net) 658
Quantity standards 634
Sales mix variance 658
Sales price variance 657
Standard cost per unit 636

Standard cost sheet 636
Standard hours allowed 637
Standard quantity of materials
  allowed 637
Total flexible budget variance 638
Total profit variance 656
Unfavourable (U) variances 639
Usage (efficiency) variance 639
Variable overhead efficiency
  variance 651
Variable overhead spending
  variance 649

## Review Problem

### MATERIALS, LABOUR, AND OVERHEAD VARIANCES

Wangsgard Manufacturing has the following standard cost sheet for one of its products:

| | |
|---|---|
| Direct materials (2 metres @ $5) | $10 |
| Direct labour (0.5 hours @ $10) | 5 |
| Variable overhead (0.5 hours @ $4) | 2 |
| Fixed overhead (0.5 hours @ $2[a]) | 1 |
| Standard unit cost | $18 |

[a] Rate based on expected activity of 2,500 hours

During the most recent year, the following actual results were recorded:

| | |
|---|---|
| Production | 6,000 units |
| Direct materials (11,750 metres purchased and used) | $61,100 |
| Direct labour (2,900 hours) | 29,580 |
| Variable overhead | 10,500 |
| Fixed overhead | 6,000 |

### Required:

Compute the following variances:
1. Materials price and usage variances
2. Labour rate and efficiency variances
3. Variable overhead spending and efficiency variances
4. Fixed overhead spending and denominator variances

### Solution

1. Materials Variances:

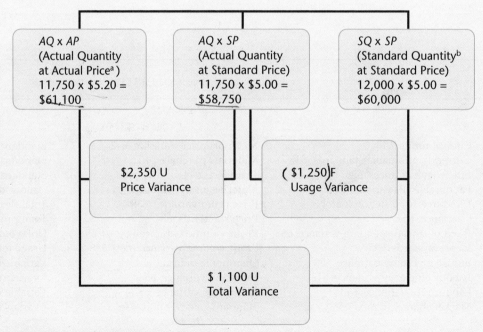

[a] $61,100/11,750 = $5.20 = actual price
[b] 2 x 6,000 = 12,000 metres = standard quantity

Or, using formulas:

$$MPV = (AP - SP) \times AQ$$
$$= (\$5.20 - \$5.00) \times 11{,}750$$
$$= \$2{,}350 \text{ U}$$

$$MUV = (AQ - SQ) \times SP$$
$$= (11{,}750 - 12{,}000) \times \$5.00$$
$$= \$1{,}250 \text{ F}$$

2. Labour Variances:

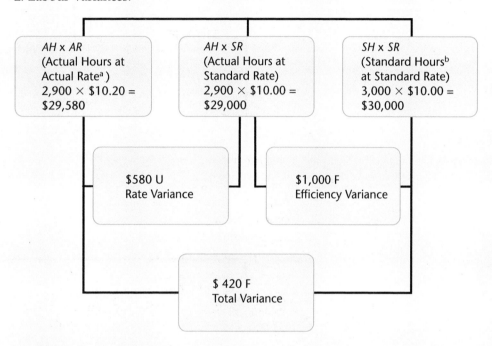

[a] $29,580/2,900 = \$10.20 =$ actual price
[b] $0.5 \times 6,000 = 3,000 =$ standard hours

Or, using formulas:

$$LRV = (AR - SR) \times AH$$
$$= (\$10.20 - \$10.00) \times 2{,}900$$
$$= \$580 \text{ U}$$

$$LEV = (AH - SH) \times SR$$
$$= (2{,}900 - 3{,}000) \times \$10.00$$
$$= \$1{,}000 \text{ F}$$

3. Variable Overhead Variances:

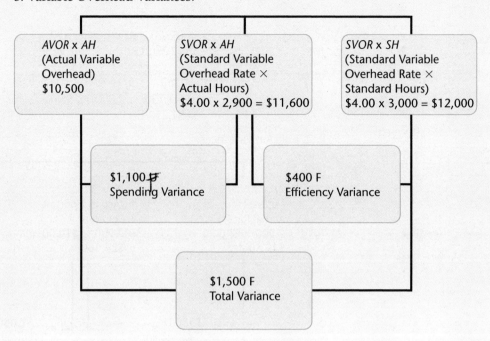

4. Fixed Overhead Variances:

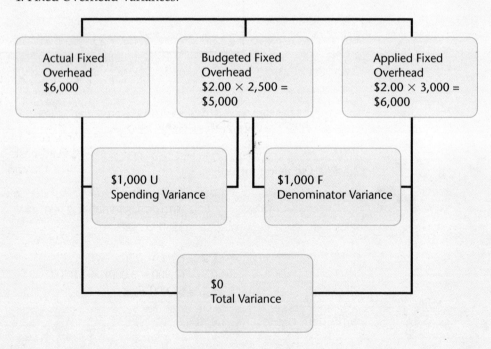

## Questions for Writing and Discussion

1. Discuss the difference between budgets and standard costs.

2. Describe the relationship that unit standards have with flexible budgeting.

3. What is the *quantity decision*? The *pricing decision*?

4. Why is historical experience often a poor basis for establishing standards?

5. Should standards be set by engineering studies? Explain why or why not.

6. What are ideal standards? And what are currently attainable standards? Of the two, which are usually adopted? Explain why.

7. Explain why standard cost systems are adopted.

8. How does standard costing improve the control function?

9. Discuss the differences among actual costing, normal costing, and standard costing.

10. What is the purpose of a standard cost sheet?

11. The budget variance for variable production costs is broken down into quantity and price variances. Explain why the quantity variance is more useful for control purposes than the price variance.

12. When should a standard cost variance be investigated?

13. What are control limits, and how are they set?

14. Explain why the materials price variance is often computed at the point of purchase rather than at the point of issue.

15. The materials usage variance is always the responsibility of the production supervisor. Do you agree or disagree? Explain.

16. The labour rate variance is never controllable. Do you agree or disagree? Explain.

17. Suggest some possible causes for an unfavourable labour efficiency variance.

18. Explain why the variable overhead spending variance is not a pure price variance.

19. The variable overhead efficiency variance has nothing to do with efficient use of variable overhead. Do you agree or disagree? Explain.

20. Explain why the fixed overhead spending variance is usually very small.

21. What is the cause of an unfavourable denominator variance? Does the denominator variance convey any meaningful information to managers?

22. Which variance is more important for control of fixed overhead costs—the spending variance or the denominator variance? Explain.

## Exercises

**14–1**

Setting Standards and Assigning Responsibility

LO1

Greenlief Publishing, Ltd., is a rapidly expanding company specializing in the reproduction of instructional materials. Ralph Greenlief, the owner and manager, is committed to providing a quality product at a fair price and with reliable, prompt delivery. Expanding sales have been attributed to this philosophy. As the business grows, however, Ralph has experienced difficulties in supervising the operations personally. So he has started to establish an organizational structure that will improve management control.

Recently, Ralph has designated the operating departments as cost centres and transferred control over departmental operations to the individual departmental managers. However, quality control still reports directly to Ralph, and so do the finance and accounting functions. A materials manager has been hired to purchase all materials and to oversee inventory handling (receiving, storage, etc.) and record keeping. The materials manager is also responsible for maintaining an adequate inventory based on planned production levels.

The loss of personal control over the operations has caused Ralph to look for more efficient methods for evaluating performance. A new cost accountant has proposed using a standard cost system. Such a system would allow for materials, labour, and overhead variances to be calculated and reported to Ralph.

**Required:**
1. Assume that the company will implement a standard cost system and establish standards for materials, labour, and overhead.
   a. Who should be involved in setting the standards for each cost component?
   b. What factors should be considered in establishing the standards for each cost component?
2. Describe the basis for assigning responsibility under a standard cost system. (US CMA adapted)

---

**14–2**

**Computation of Inputs Allowed; Materials and Labour**

**LO2**

During the year, Sask Farm Machinery Company produced 45,000 mechanical components for a combine manufacturer. The materials and labour standards are as follows:

| | |
|---|---|
| Direct materials (3 components @ $8) | $24.00 |
| Direct labour (0.8 hours @ $12) | 9.60 |

**Required:**
1. Compute the standard hours allowed for the production of 45,000 units.
2. Compute the standard number of components allowed for the production of 45,000 units.

---

**14–3**

**Materials and Labour Variances**

**LO4**

Spreadsheet

Okanagan Fruit Processing, Inc., produces fruit juices. Recently, the company adopted the following standards per litre of its grape juice:

| | |
|---|---|
| Direct materials (1 litre @ $1.28) | $1.28 |
| Direct labour (0.03 hours @ $7) | 0.21 |
| Standard prime cost | $1.49 |

During the first week of operation, the company obtained the following results:
a. Production: 8,000 litres
b. Materials purchased: 8,400 litres at $1.15
c. There are no beginning or ending inventories of raw materials
d. Direct labour: 250 hours at $7.50

**Required:**
1. Compute the price and usage variances for direct materials.
2. Compute the rate and efficiency variances for direct labour.

---

**14–4**

**Overhead Variances**

**LO5**

Spreadsheet

Anderson, Inc. has gathered the following data on last year's operations:

Units produced: 28,000
Direct labour: 20,000 hours @ $9
Actual fixed overhead: $280,000
Actual variable overhead: $92,000

Anderson employs a standard cost system. During the year, the following rates were used: standard fixed overhead rate, $12 per hour; standard variable overhead rate, $4.05 per hour. The labour standard requires 0.75 hours per unit produced. These rates were based on a standard normal volume of 22,500 direct labour hours.

**Required:**
1. Compute the fixed overhead spending and denominator variances.
2. Compute the variable overhead spending and efficiency variances.

### 14–5

*Decomposition of Budget Variances; Materials and Labour*

**LO4**

Canhide Corporation produces high-quality leather purses. The company uses a standard cost system and has set the following standards for materials and labour:

| | |
|---|---|
| Leather (6 strips @ $8) | $48 |
| Direct labour (1.5 hours @ $12) | 18 |
| Total prime cost | $66 |

During the year, Canhide produced 10,000 leather purses. Actual leather purchased was 61,000 strips at $7.96 per strip. There were no beginning or ending inventories of leather. Actual direct labour was 15,600 hours at $12.50 per hour.

**Required:**
1. Compute the costs of leather and direct labour that should have been incurred for the production of 10,000 leather purses.
2. Compute the total budget variances for materials and labour.
3. Break down the total materials variance into a price variance and a usage variance.
4. Break down the total labour variance into a rate variance and an efficiency variance.

### 14–6

*Materials and Labour Variances; Journal Entries*

**LO4, LO7**

One of the product lines of Learning Technology, Inc., is whiteboards. These boards are popular in classrooms and corporate conference rooms. The standard costs of materials and labour are as follows:

Direct materials: 10 kilograms @ $8.25
Direct labour: 3.5 hours @ $9.65

During the first month of the year, 3,200 boards were produced. The actual costs and usage of materials and labour are as follows:

| | |
|---|---|
| Materials purchased: | 36,000 kilograms @ $8.35 |
| Materials used: | 31,800 kilograms |
| Direct labour hours: | 11,520 hours |
| Direct labour costs: | $112,896 |

**Required:**
1. Compute the materials price and usage variances.
2. Compute the labour rate and efficiency variances.
3. Prepare journal entries for material and labour transactions and variances (Appendix B).

### 14–7

*Overhead Application; Overhead Variances*

**LO5**

Thunder Electric plans to produce 2,400,000 power drills next year. Each drill requires 0.5 standard hours of labour for completion. The company uses direct labour hours to assign overhead costs to products. The total budgeted overhead is $2,700,000; the standard fixed overhead rate $0.55 *per unit produced*. Actual results for the year are as follows:

| | |
|---|---|
| Actual production (units) | 2,360,000 |
| Actual direct labour hours | 1,190,000 |
| Actual variable overhead | $1,410,000 |
| Actual fixed overhead | $1,260,000 |

**Required:**
1. Compute the applied fixed overhead.
2. Compute the fixed overhead spending and volume variances.
3. Compute the applied variable overhead.
4. Compute the variable overhead spending and efficiency variances.

**14–8**

*Investigation of Variances*

LO3

Polkow Company investigates materials usage variances (MUV) any time the amount exceeds the lesser of $8,000 or 10 percent of the standard cost. Reports for the past five weeks provided the following information:

| Week | MUV | Standard Materials Cost |
|---|---|---|
| 1 | $7,000 F | $80,000 |
| 2 | 7,800 U | 75,000 |
| 3 | 6,000 F | 80,000 |
| 4 | 9,000 U | 85,000 |
| 5 | 7,000 U | 69,000 |

**Required:**
1. Using the rule provided, identify the cases that will be investigated.
2. Investigation reveals that the cause of an unfavourable materials usage variance is the use of lower-quality materials than are normally used. Who is responsible? What corrective action will likely be taken?
3. Investigation reveals that a significant unfavourable materials usage variance is attributable to a new approach to manufacturing that takes less labour time but causes more material waste. On examining the labour efficiency variance, you discover that it is favourable and that it is larger than the unfavourable materials usage variance. Who is responsible? What action should be taken?

**14–9**

*Overhead Application; Overhead Variances*

LO5

Manitoulin Manufacturing Company produces a single product and uses a standard cost system. The direct labour standard indicates that four direct labour hours should be used for each unit of product. The normal production volume is 120,000 units per year. The budgeted overhead for 2005 is as follows:

| | |
|---|---|
| Fixed overhead | $1,440,000 |
| Variable overhead (at normal volume) | 960,000 |

The company applies overhead on the basis of direct labour hours. In 2005 the company produced 119,000 units, used 487,900 direct labour hours, and incurred fixed overhead costs of $1,500,000 and actual variable overhead costs of $950,000.

**Required:**
1. Calculate the standard fixed overhead rate and the standard variable overhead rate.
2. Compute the applied fixed overhead and the applied variable overhead. What is the total fixed overhead variance? The total variable overhead variance?
3. Break down the total fixed overhead variance into a spending variance and a denominator variance. Discuss the significance of each.
4. Compute the variable overhead spending and efficiency variances. Discuss the significance of each.

**14–10**

*Basic Variance Calculations*

**LO4, LO5**

Labrador Company uses a costing system with standard costs developed for each of its products. One product, X–29, has the following standard cost:

| | |
|---|---:|
| Direct materials (6 kilograms @ $2.40/kilogram) | $14.40 |
| Direct labour (3 hours @ $16/hour) | 48.00 |
| Variable overhead (3 hours @ $4.50/hour) | 13.50 |
| Fixed overhead (3 hours @ $2.80/houra) | 8.40 |
| Standard cost per unit of X–29 | $84.30 |

a Based on an annual activity of 7,500 direct labour hours

The company identifies the material purchase price variance when materials are purchased, and it calculates all possible variances for overhead. Actual results for X–29 production in 2005 were as follows:

- Started and completed 2,450 units of X–29. There were no beginning or ending inventories of work in process.
- Direct material purchases were 15,000 kilograms at the total cost of $38,250. A total of 14,680 kilograms were issued to production.
- Direct labour costs were $122,430 for 7,420 hours.
- Variable overhead costs were $33,675.
- Fixed overhead costs were $22,500.

**Required:**

Calculate all possible cost variances based on the information provided. (CMA Canada adapted)

**14–11**

*Materials, Labour, and Overhead Variances*

**LO4, LO5**

Spreadsheet

At the beginning of 2005, Kanata Company had the following standard cost for one of its products:

| | |
|---|---:|
| Direct materials (5 kilograms @ $1.60) | $ 8 |
| Direct labour (2.0 hours @ $9) | 18 |
| Fixed overhead (2.0 hours @ $2) | 4 |
| Variable overhead (2.0 hours @ $1.50) | 3 |
| Standard cost per unit | $33 |

Kanata computes its overhead rates using practical volume, which is 72,000 units. The actual results for 2005 are as follows:

a. Units produced: 70,000
b. Materials purchased: 372,000 kilograms at $1.55
c. Materials used: 369,000 kilograms
d. Direct labour: 145,000 hours at $8.95
e. Fixed overhead: $240,000
f. Variable overhead: $220,000

**Required:**

1. Compute price and usage variances for materials.
2. Compute the labour rate and efficiency variances.
3. Compute the fixed overhead spending and denominator variances.
4. Compute the variable overhead spending and efficiency variances.

**14–12**

*Basic Variance Analysis*

**LO4, LO5**

Carleton Corporation manufactures and sells a single product for $20. The company uses a standard costing system, with all variances separated as soon as possible. The standards, which are updated each month, were as follows on November 1:

| Direct materials (1 kilogram @ $2/kilogram) | $ 2.00 |
|---|---|
| Direct labour (1.6 hours @ $8/hour) | 12.80 |
| Variable manufacturing overhead (1.6 hours @ $2/hour) | 3.20 |
| Fixed manufacturing overhead (1.6 hours @ $1/hour[a]) | 1.60 |
| Total standard cost per unit | $19.60 |

[a] Overhead is applied based on direct labour hours. The combined overhead application rate is $3 per direct labour hour.

Normal production capacity is 60,000 units, or 96,000 direct labour hours, per year. Actual results for November are as follows:

| Units produced | 5,100 |
|---|---|
| Direct materials purchased (@ $2.10/kilogram) | $10,920 |
| Direct materials used in production (kilograms) | 5,300 |
| Direct labour costs (8,200 hours) | $67,240 |
| Variable manufacturing overhead | $16,560 |
| Fixed manufacturing overhead | $ 8,190 |

### Required:
Calculate all possible cost variances for November based on the information provided. (CMA Canada adapted)

**14–13**

*Variances, Performance Evaluation, and Behaviour*

**LO1**

Nellie Hentel is furious. She is nearly ready to dismiss Tom Nenonen, the purchasing agent. Just a month earlier, she had awarded him a salary increase and a bonus for his performance. She had been especially pleased with his ability to meet or come below the standard prices. Now she has discovered that he was able to do so only by purchasing a huge quantity of raw materials. It will take several months to use that inventory, and the company has only limited storage space. "We have hardly enough storage space for the *regular* materials!" she exclaims. She also knows that a lot of capital is tied up in that inventory—capital that could have been used to finance new products.

Her interview with Tom is frustrating. He argues in his own defence that he was meeting the standards she wanted him to meet and that it should not matter how he met them. He also points out that quantity purchases were the only way he could have met the price standards, and that if he had not met them, an unfavourable variance would have been realized.

### Required:
1. Why did Tom purchase the large quantity of materials? Do you think this behaviour was the objective of the price standard? If not, what are its objectives?
2. Suppose that Tom is right and that the only way he could have met the price standards was through taking quantity discounts. Also assume that using quantity discounts is not a desirable practice for this company. What would you do to solve this dilemma?
3. Should Tom be dismissed? Explain.

**14–14**

*Basic Materials and Labour Variances*

**LO4**

Mazzuca Company produces concrete planters for gardens. The following standards for producing one unit have been established:

| Direct material (5 kilograms @ $0.90) | $ 4.50 |
|---|---|
| Direct labour (1.5 hours @ $7.00) | 10.50 |
| Standard prime cost | $15.00 |

During December, 53,000 kilograms of material are purchased and used in production, and 10,000 units are produced, with the following actual prime costs:

| Direct materials | $ 42,000 |
| Direct labour | $102,000 (for 14,900 hours) |

**Required:**

Compute the materials and labour variances, labelling each variance as favourable or unfavourable.

**14–15**

Incomplete Data; Variance Analysis

LO4, LO5

Lanark Company uses a standard costing system. For the most recent quarter, the following variances have been computed:

| Variable overhead efficiency variance | $ 8,000 U |
| Labour efficiency variance | 20,000 U |
| Labour rate variance | 6,000 U |

Lanark applies variable overhead using a standard rate of $2 per direct labour hour allowed. Four direct labour hours are allowed per unit produced. The company makes only one product. During the quarter, Lanark used 20 percent more direct labour hours than should have been used.

**Required:**

1. What were the actual direct labour hours worked? the total hours allowed?
2. What was the standard hourly rate for direct labour? the actual hourly rate?
3. How many units were actually produced?

**14–16**

Setting Standards

LO1

Choose the single *best* answer for each of the following multiple-choice questions:

1. Standards set by engineering studies
   a. can determine the most efficient way of operating.
   b. can provide very rigorous guidelines.
   c. may not be achievable by operating personnel.
   d. often do not allow operating personnel to have much input.
   e. All of the above.

2. To determine the standard cost per unit of output for a particular input, the manager must
   a. know the price per unit of input.
   b. know the quantity of input used per unit of output.
   c. know the total budgeted output.
   d. All of the above.
   e. Only a and b.

3. A currently attainable standard is one that
   a. relies on maximum efficiency.
   b. is based only on historical experience.
   c. can be achieved under efficient operating conditions.
   d. makes no allowances for normal breakdowns, interruptions, lack of skills, etc.
   e. Both a and d.

4. The main objective(s) of a standard costing system is (are)
   a. to enhance operational control.
   b. to imitate most other companies.
   c. to encourage purchasing managers to take advantage of purchase discounts.
   d. to allow the use of the weighted-average method for process manufacturers.
   e. All of the above.

# Problems

### 14–17

Basic Variance
Calculations and
Interpretation

LO1, LO4, LO5

Global Trading Company assembles one of its products in its Mexico plant. It uses a standard cost system to control costs and has set the selling price at 150 percent of the standard cost. The standard costs per unit based on a monthly production of 1,200 units are as follows:

| | |
|---|---|
| Raw materials | 12 parts per unit at $1.12 per part |
| Direct labour | 2 hours per unit at $5.50 per hour |
| Manufacturing overhead: | |
| Variable | $1.40 per direct labour hour |
| Fixed | $4.10 per direct labour hour |

In June 2005, 1,000 units were started and completed. The following additional information is also available for June:

a. Inventory: none (on June 1 or on June 30)
b. Raw materials: 14,000 parts used; total cost, $14,280
c. Direct labour costs: $16,000
d. Actual direct labour hours: 2,500
e. Manufacturing overhead incurred: variable, $3,600; fixed, $10,000

**Required:**
1. Determine the following:
   a. The unit selling price
   b. All possible variances for June 2005 based on the information provided.
2. Comment on the possible causes of each overhead variance.
3. Explain why it is preferable to compare actual data to standards rather than to historical data. (CMA Canada adapted)

### 14–18

Basics of Variance
Analysis; Materials,
Labour, and Overhead

LO4, LO5

You have been given the following information for Kuhmo Company:

| | |
|---|---|
| Standard material price | $5 per kilogram |
| Direct labour costs incurred | $65,570 for 7,900 hours |
| Variable overhead applied | $2 per direct labour hour |
| Finished goods produced | 4,000 units |
| Standard direct labour hours per unit | 2 hours |
| Actual fixed overhead | $29,000 |
| Materials purchased | 15,000 kilograms for $73,500 |
| Denominator activity | 10,000 direct labour hours |
| Standard direct labour rate | $8 per hour |
| Materials used | 12,300 kilograms |
| Fixed overhead spending variance | $1,000 favourable |
| Standard quantity of material per unit | 3 kilograms |
| Variable overhead costs incurred | $16,200 |

**Required:**
Compute all possible materials, labour, and overhead variances. (CGA Canada adapted)

Renegades Company manufactures football helmets. The following unit standards have been established:

| | Standard Quantity | Standard Price (Rate) | Standard Cost |
|---|---|---|---|
| Direct materials | 1.20 kilograms | $ 6.00 | $ 7.20 |
| Direct labour | 0.32 hours | 10.00 | 3.20 |
| Variable overhead | 0.32 hours | 2.50 | 0.80 |
| Total | | | $11.20 |

During the first week of July, the company had the following actual results:

| | |
|---|---|
| Units produced | 40,000 |
| Actual labour costs | $140,000 |
| Actual labour hours | 13,200 |
| Materials purchased and used | 46,000 kilograms @ $6.10 |
| Actual variable overhead costs | $53,000 |

The purchasing agent located a new source of slightly higher-quality material, and this material was used during the first week in July. A new manufacturing process was also implemented on a trial basis. The new process required a slightly higher level of skilled labour, and it was expected to reduce materials usage by 0.025 kilograms per unit. The higher-quality material has no effect on labour utilization.

**Required:**

1. Compute the materials price and usage variances. Assume that the 0.025 kilograms reduction of materials occurred as expected and that the remaining effects are attributable to the higher-quality material. Would you recommend that the purchasing agent continue to buy this material? Or should the previous, lower-quality material be purchased? Assume that the quality of the end product is not affected significantly.
2. Compute the labour rate and efficiency variances. Assuming that the labour variances are attributable to the new manufacturing process, should that process be continued or discontinued? In answering, consider the new process's materials reduction effect as well. Explain.
3. Refer to Requirement 2. Suppose the industrial engineer argues that the new process should not be evaluated after only one week. His reasoning is that it will take at least that long for the workers to become efficient with the new approach. Suppose the production is the same in the second week, that the actual labour hours are 12,000, and that labour costs are $124,000. Should the new process be adopted? Assume that the variances are attributable to the new process. Assuming the production of 40,000 units per week, what are the projected annual savings, including the materials reduction effect?

Oakpantry, Ltd., is a small manufacturer of wooden household items. Ellen Acland, the controller, plans to implement a standard cost system and has collected the necessary information.

One of the products is a wooden cutting board. Each cutting board requires 0.4 metres of precut (2 centimetre × 30 centimetre) wood and 12 minutes of direct labour time for preparing and cutting the wood. The cutting boards are inspected after they are cut. Because the cutting boards are made of natural wood with imperfections, one out of six boards is usually rejected. The rejected boards are scrapped. The good boards are sanded and oiled; then four rubber "feet" are attached. This process requires 15 minutes of direct labour. The lumber costs $9.50 per metre, and each foot costs $0.05. The direct labour rate is $8 per hour.

**Required:**

1. Develop standard costs for the direct cost components. The standard cost should identify the standard quantity, standard rate, and standard cost per unit for each direct cost component.
2. Identify the advantages of implementing a standard cost system.
3. Explain the role of the following people in developing standards:
   a. Purchasing manager
   b. Industrial engineer
   c. Cost accountant
4. Assume that the standards have been set and that the following actual results occur during the first month under the new standard cost system:
   a. Actual good units produced: 10,000
   b. Wood purchased: 4,800 metres @ $10.10
   c. Wood used: 4,800 metres
   d. Rubber footpads purchased and used: 51,000 @ $0.048
   e. Direct labour: 5,550 hours @ $8.05

   Compute price and usage variances for materials and labour. (US CMA adapted)

**14–21**

*Basic Variance Analysis*

**LO4, LO5**

Cupar Company manufactures a product that has the following standard unit costs:

| | |
|---|---|
| Direct materials (2.5 kilograms @ $4) | $10.00 |
| Direct labour (3 hours @ $8) | 24.00 |
| Variable manufacturing overhead (3 hours @ $1.50) | 4.50 |
| Fixed manufacturing overhead (3 hours @ $2.50) | 7.50 |

The denominator activity for 2005 was 16,000 units or 48,000 hours. During 2005, the company produced 15,750 units and incurred the following costs:

| | |
|---|---|
| Direct materials purchased (40,000 kilograms) | $164,000 |
| Direct materials used in production (39,000 kilograms) | 156,000 |
| Direct labour (48,200 hours) | 385,600 |
| Manufacturing overhead incurred: | |
| Variable overhead | 73,500 |
| Fixed overhead | 121,600 |

**Required:**

1. Calculate all direct materials, direct labour, variable overhead, and fixed overhead variances.
2. Provide some possible causes for the variable overhead spending variance, and explain the fixed overhead denominator variance. (CGA Canada adapted)

**14–22**

*Setting a Direct Labour Standard; Learning Effects*

**LO1, LO2**

Laurentian Company produces customized parts for mining equipment. The parts are custom made; however, most follow a fairly standard pattern. Recently, a new customer has ordered a new part that is significantly different from the parts the company usually manufactures. Laurentian has to buy new equipment to manufacture the part, as well as retrain some of its workers. The customer's initial order is for 15,000 units. If the new part proves satisfactory, the company will place several additional orders of the same size over the next few years.

Laurentian uses a standard cost system and needs to develop standard costs for the new part. To date, management has set the following standards: 4 kilograms of material per part at $3 per kilogram, standard labour rate of $11 per hour, standard variable overhead rate of $6 per hour, and standard fixed overhead rate of $2 per hour. The only remaining decision is the labour usage standard. The Engineering Department has estimated the following relationship between the parts produced and the average direct labour hours used:

| Cumulative Average | |
| --- | --- |
| Units Produced | Time per Unit |
| 20 | 1.00 hour |
| 40 | 0.80 hours |
| 80 | 0.64 hours |
| 160 | 0.512 hours |
| 320 | 0.448 hours |

As more parts are produced, the employees become more efficient in manufacturing the part, and the average time per part declines. The Engineering Department estimates that all learning effects will have been achieved by the time 160 units are produced, and that no further efficiency improvement will occur beyond this level.

**Required:**

1. Assuming no further improvement in labour time per unit is possible past 160 units, explain why the cumulative average time per unit is lower at 320 units than at 160 units.
2. What standard would you set for direct labour usage per unit? Explain.
3. Using the standard you set in Requirement 2, prepare a standard cost sheet that shows the standard unit cost for the new part.
4. Given the standard you set in Requirement 2, would you expect favourable or unfavourable labour and variable overhead efficiency variances for production of the first 160 units? Explain.

**14–23**

*Variance Analysis; Materials, Labour, and Overhead*

**LO2, LO4, LO5**

Cambrian Electrical Company manufactures specialized electrical equipment. The standard cost to assemble a unit of one product is as follows:

Direct materials:
    8 sheets of sheet metal @ $1.50 a sheet
    2 spools of copper wire @ $2.50 a spool
Direct labour rate: $16 per hour
Manufacturing overhead rate (variable and fixed combined):
    $4.25 per direct labour hour

Overhead is applied based on standard direct labour hours. The flexible budget reveals that the total overhead is $17,000 for 1,000 units produced and $19,000 for 1,200 units produced. The production budget for the previous month called for 4,400 direct labour hours and $11,000 variable overhead costs. During the past month 1,050 units were produced at the following costs:

| | |
| --- | --- |
| Direct materials purchased: | |
| 9,000 sheets of sheet metal | $13,050 |
| 2,200 spools of copper wire | $5,566 |
| Direct materials used: | |
| 8,000 sheets of sheet metal | |
| 2,150 spools of copper wire | |
| Direct labour (4,100 hours) | $66,010 |
| Overhead costs: | |
| Variable | $10,750 |
| Fixed | $7,850 |

**Required:**
1. What is the standard assembly time per unit?
2. What is the standard absorption cost?
3. Calculate the following variances for the past month:
   a. Materials price
   b. Materials efficiency
   c. Direct labour rate
   d. Direct labour efficiency
   e. Variable overhead spending
   f. Variable overhead efficiency
   g. Fixed overhead spending
   h. Fixed overhead denominator (CGA Canada adapted)

**14–24**

Variance Analysis;
Revision of Standards

LO4, LO5

The Windsor plant of Precision Manufacturing, Ltd., produces a subassembly for the auto industry. The plant uses a standard costing system for production costing and control. The standard cost for the subassembly is as follows:

| | |
|---|---|
| Direct materials (3.0 kilograms @ $10) | $30.00 |
| Direct labour (1.6 hours @ $12) | 19.20 |
| Variable overhead (1.6 hours @ $10) | 16.00 |
| Fixed overhead (1.6 hours @ $6) | 9.60 |
| Standard unit cost | $74.80 |

During the year, the Windsor plant had the following actual production activity:

a. Production was 50,000 units.
b. A total of 130,000 kilograms of raw materials was purchased at $9.40 per kilogram.
c. The beginning inventory of raw materials was 30,000 kilograms, valued at $10 per kilogram. There was no ending inventory.
d. 82,000 direct labour hours were used, at a total cost of $1,066,000.
e. Actual fixed overhead costs were $556,000.
f. Actual variable overhead costs were $860,000.

The Windsor plant's practical activity is 60,000 units per year. Standard overhead rates are computed based on practical activity measured in standard direct labour hours.

**Required:**
1. Compute the materials price and usage variances. Which variance is more controllable? To whom would you assign responsibility for the usage variance in this case? Explain.
2. Compute the labour rate and efficiency variances. Who is usually responsible for the labour efficiency variance? What are some possible causes for this variance?
3. Compute the variable overhead spending and efficiency variances.
4. Compute the fixed overhead spending and denominator variances. Interpret the denominator variance. What can be done to reduce this variance?
5. Assume that the purchasing manager had purchased lower-quality raw material this year than in the past. Would you recommend that the plant continue to use this cheaper raw material? If so, which standards would likely need revision to reflect this decision? Assume that the product's quality is not adversely affected.

**14–25**

Topaz RV Manufacturing, Ltd., a producer of recreational vehicles, decided to begin making a major subassembly, which it uses in its jet skis. The company leased two large buildings (one in Ste-Foy, Quebec, the other in Calgary, Alberta) under a 10-year renewable lease. The two plants were the same size, and each had 10 production lines. New equipment was purchased for each line, and workers were hired to operate the equipment. The company also hired production line supervisors for each plant. Each supervisor could direct up to two production lines per shift. Two shifts were run at each plant. The practical production capacity of each plant was 300,000 subassemblies per year. Two standard direct labour hours were allowed for each subassembly. The costs for leasing, equipment amortization, and supervision for each plant were as follows:

| | |
|---|---:|
| Supervision (10 supervisors @ $50,000) | $ 500,000 |
| Building lease (annual payment) | 800,000 |
| Equipment amortization (annual) | 1,100,000 |
| Total fixed overhead costs[a] | $2,400,000 |

[a]For simplicity, assume these are the only fixed overhead costs.

Soon after opening the plants, the company discovered that demand for the product in the region covered by the Ste-Foy plant is less than anticipated. By the end of the first year, only 240,000 units sold were from that plant. The Calgary plant had sold 300,000 units, as expected. The actual fixed overhead costs at the end of the first year were $2,500,000 for each plant.

**Required:**
1. Calculate a fixed overhead rate based on standard direct labour hours.
2. Calculate the fixed overhead spending and denominator variances for the Ste-Foy and Calgary plants. What is the most likely cause for the spending variance? Why are the denominator variances different for the two plants?
3. Suppose that, from now on, the sales for the Ste-Foy plant are expected to be no more than 240,000 units. What actions would you take to manage the capacity costs (fixed overhead costs)?
4. Calculate the fixed overhead cost per subassembly for each plant. Do they differ? Should they differ? Explain. Do activity-based costing concepts help in analyzing this issue?

**14–26**

Koolkare Company manufactures two models of icemakers: small and regular. The standard quantities of labour and materials per unit for 2005 are as follows:

| | Small | Regular |
|---|:---:|:---:|
| Direct materials (grams) | 340 | 560 |
| Direct labour (hours) | 0.2 | 0.30 |

The standard price paid per kilogram of direct materials is $3.20. The standard labour rate is $8. Overhead is applied on the basis of direct labour hours. A plantwide rate is used. Budgeted overhead for the year is as follows:

| | |
|---|---|
| Fixed overhead | $720,000 |
| Variable overhead | 960,000 |

The company expects to use 24,000 direct labour hours in 2005. Standard overhead rates are computed using this activity level. For every small icemaker produced, the company produces two regular icemakers. Actual operating data for the two models in 2005 are as follows:

a. Units produced: small, 35,000; regular, 70,000.
b. Direct materials purchased and used: 56,000 kilograms @ $3.10 (13,000 for small; 43,000 for regular). There were no beginning or ending raw materials inventories.

c. Direct labour: 29,600 hours at the total cost of $229,400 (7,200 hours for small; 22,400 hours for regular).
d. Variable overhead costs: $1,215,000.
e. Fixed overhead costs: $700,000.

**Required:**
1. Compute the standard unit cost of each model.
2. Compute the materials price and usage variances for each model.
3. Compute the labour rate and efficiency variances.
4. Compute the fixed and variable overhead variances.
5. Assume that you know only the combined total direct materials and the total direct labour hours used for both models. Can you compute the total materials and labour usage variances? Explain.

**14–27**

Incomplete Data;
Variance Calculation

LO4, LO5

Henderson Company uses a standard costing system for its only product, with all variances separated as soon as possible. The standard cost per unit for 2005 is as follows:

| | |
|---|---:|
| Direct materials (5 kilograms @ $17 per kilogram) | $ 85 |
| Direct labour (10 hours @ $14/hour) | 140 |
| Variable overhead (10 hours @ $2.50/hour) | 25 |
| Fixed overhead (10 hours @ $3.80/hour) | 38 |
| Total standard cost per unit | $288 |

Unfortunately, a fire destroyed most of the company's records on December 31, 2005, and only the following information remained available:

a. Purchases of materials were 95,000 kilograms at the total cost of $1,726,000.
b. Production for the year was 16,000 units.
c. Variable overhead costs were $403,620, with a favourable efficiency variance of $3,625.
d. The actual fixed manufacturing overhead costs were $515,000, and there was a favourable denominator variance of $95,000.
e. The direct materials usage variance was $4,318, favourable.
f. There were no beginning or ending work-in-process inventories.
g. The actual average direct labour rate was $14.30 per hour.

**Required:**
1. Calculate all other possible variances based on the information provided.
2. What was the company's denominator level of activity? (CMA Canada adapted)

**14–28**

Incomplete Data;
Overhead Analysis

LO2, LO4, LO5

Watts Company produces surge protectors. To help control costs, the company employs a standard cost system and uses a flexible budget to predict overhead costs at various levels of activity. For the most recent year, the company used the standard overhead rate of $18 per direct labour hour. The rate was computed using practical activity. Budgeted overhead costs were $396,000 for 18,000 direct labour hours and $540,000 for 30,000 direct labour hours. During the year, Watts had the following actual results:

a. Actual production: 100,000 units
b. Fixed overhead denominator variance: $20,000 U
c. Variable overhead efficiency variance: $18,000 F
d. Actual fixed overhead costs: $200,000
e. Actual variable overhead costs: $310,000

**Required:**
1. Calculate the fixed overhead rate.
2. Determine the fixed overhead spending variance.
3. Determine the variable overhead spending variance.
4. Determine the standard hours allowed per unit of product.
5. If the standard labour rate is $9.50 per hour, compute the labour efficiency variance.

**14–29**

Comprehensive
Variance Analysis;
Incomplete Data

LO4, LO5

Pollara, Inc., uses a flexible budget and standard costs to aid in planning and control. At a level of 50,000 direct labour hours, budgeted variable overhead is $40,000. For flexible budgeting purposes, the company uses a variable overhead rate of 16 percent of the standard direct labour hour cost. The following are selected results for March:

| | |
|---|---:|
| Actual direct labour costs incurred | $330,000 |
| Variable overhead flexible budget variance | 9,000 U |
| Variable overhead efficiency variance | 2,400 U |
| Direct materials purchase price variance | 12,000 F |
| Direct materials efficiency variance | 19,000 U |

The standard price per kilogram of direct material is $0.95. The standard allowance is 1 kilogram of direct material for each unit of finished product. Eighty thousand units were produced during March. There was no beginning or ending work in process. In March, the purchase price variance was $0.08 per kilogram. The actual wage rate in March exceeded the standard average wage rate by $0.50 per hour.

**Required:**
Compute the following:
1. Standard direct labour cost per hour.
2. Total number of kilograms of material purchased.
3. Total number of kilograms of excess material usage.
4. Price paid per kilogram of direct materials purchased in March.
5. Variable overhead spending variance.
6. Actual labour rate per hour.
7. Actual number of hours worked.
8. Total number of standard hours allowed for the units produced.
9. Actual variable overhead costs. (CGA Canada adapted)

**14–30**

Control Limits;
Variance Investigation

LO2, LO3, LO4, LO5

Nina Rico Laboratories produces a perfume called Sweet Dreams. The standard manufacturing cost for a bottle of perfume is as follows:

| | |
|---|---:|
| Direct materials: | |
| Liquids (125 millilitres @ $8.40 per litre) | $1.05 |
| Bottles (1 @ $0.05) | 0.05 |
| Direct labour (0.2 hours @ $12.50) | 2.50 |
| Variable overhead (0.2 hours @ $4.70) | 0.94 |
| Fixed overhead (0.2 hours @ $1) | 0.20 |
| Standard cost per unit | $4.74 |

Management investigates only the variances that exceed the lesser of 10 percent of the standard cost for each cost category or $20,000. The previous quarter, 250,000 bottles of perfume were produced. Actual activity for the quarter is as follows:
a. A total of 34,000 litres of liquids were purchased, mixed, and processed. Evaporation was higher than expected. No inventories of liquids are maintained. The average price paid per litre was $9.15.

b.  The price per bottle was $0.048, and 250,000 bottles were purchased and used.
c.  Direct labour hours used were 48,250, with the total cost of $622,425.
d.  Variable overhead costs were $239,000.
e.  Fixed overhead costs were $50,500.

The normal production volume is 250,000 bottles per quarter. The standard overhead rates are computed using normal volume. All overhead costs are incurred uniformly throughout the year.

**Required:**

1.  Calculate the upper and lower control limits for each manufacturing cost category.
2.  Compute the total materials variance and break it into price and usage variances. Should these variances be investigated?
3.  Compute the total labour variance and break it into rate and efficiency variances. Should these variances be investigated?
4.  Compute all overhead variances. Should any of them be investigated? Would you recommend a different approach to deal with overhead? Explain.

**14–31**

*Flexible Budget:
Overhead Variances*

LO3, LO4, LO5

Concordia Company produces a single product. Overhead is applied to production based on standard direct labour hours. The following schedule shows monthly overhead costs at different activity levels:

| Direct Labour Hours | Overhead Costs |
|---|---|
| 3,000 | $30,000 |
| 4,000 | 35,000 |
| 5,000 | 40,000 |
| 6,000 | 45,000 |

The standard cost per unit is as follows:

| | |
|---|---|
| Direct labour, 4 hours @ $25 | $100.00 |
| Direct materials, 10 kilograms @ $6 | 60.00 |
| Overhead | 32.00 |
| Total standard cost | $192.00 |

During May, the company produced 1,200 units, used 5,100 direct labour hours, and incurred overhead costs of $40,400, of which $15,100 were fixed.

**Required:**

1.  Prepare an analysis of overhead variances for May to the extent possible with the information provided.
2.  As the controller of the company, prepare a brief report to the president discussing how well control over overhead costs was maintained during May. Indicate who should be held responsible for the variances you calculated. (CMA Canada adapted)

**14–32**

*Flexible Budget;
Standard Cost
Variances*

LO1, LO4, LO5

Shumaker Company manufactures a line of high-top basketball shoes. At the beginning of the year, the planned production and costs were as follows:

| | |
|---|---|
| Production and sales (pairs of shoes) | 55,000 |
| Standard cost per pair: | |
| Direct materials | $15 |
| Direct labour | 12 |
| Variable overhead | 6 |
| Fixed overhead | 3 |
| Total unit cost | $36 |

During the year, 50,000 pairs were produced and sold. The following actual costs were incurred:

| | |
|---|---|
| Direct materials | $775,000 |
| Direct labour | 590,000 |
| Variable overhead | 310,000 |
| Fixed overhead | 180,000 |

There were no beginning or ending inventories of raw materials. The materials price variance was $5,000, unfavourable. In producing the 50,000 units, 63,000 labour hours were used, 5 percent more hours than the standard allowed for the actual output. Overhead costs are applied to production using direct labour hours.

**Required:**
1. Using a flexible budget, prepare a performance report comparing the expected costs of actual production with the actual costs.
2. Determine the following:
   a. Materials usage variance
   b. Labour rate variance
   c. Labour usage variance
   d. Fixed overhead spending and denominator variances
   e. Variable overhead spending and efficiency variances

**14–33**

Control Limits;
Variance Investigation

LO3, LO4

The management of Golding Company has determined that the cost of investigating a variance produced by its standard cost system ranges from $2,000 to $3,000. If a problem is discovered, the average benefit from taking corrective action usually outweighs the cost of the investigation. Past experience from the investigation of variances has revealed that corrective action is rarely needed for deviations within 8 percent of the standard cost. Golding produces a single product, which has the following materials and labour standards:

| | |
|---|---|
| Direct materials (8 kilograms @ $0.25) | $2 |
| Direct labour (0.4 hours @ $7.50) | 3 |

There are no beginning or ending raw material inventories. The actual production and costs are as follows:

| | April | May | June |
|---|---|---|---|
| Production (units) | 90,000 | 100,000 | 110,000 |
| Direct materials: | | | |
| Cost | $189,000 | $218,000 | $230,000 |
| Usage (kilograms) | 723,000 | 870,000 | 885,000 |
| Direct labour: | | | |
| Cost | $270,000 | $323,000 | $360,000 |
| Usage (hours) | 36,000 | 44,000 | 46,000 |

**Required:**
1. What upper and lower control limits would you use for materials variances? for labour variances?
2. Compute the materials and labour variances for April, May, and June. Identify those which require investigation.
3. Prepare a control chart for each type of variance. Let the horizontal axis be time and the vertical axis variances measured as a percentage deviation from standard. Draw horizontal lines that identify upper and lower control limits. Plot the labour and materials variances for April, May, and June. Explain how you can use these graphs to help you analyze variances.

**14–34**

Standard Process
Costing; Cost Variance
Analysis

LO4, LO5

The Laval Company manufactures a single product. The standard unit cost information for the product is as follows:

| Direct materials: | |
|---|---|
| Material Y (10 kilograms @ $0.50) | $ 5.00 |
| Material W (5 metres @ $0.75) | 3.75 |
| Direct labour (3 hours @ $6) | 18.00 |
| Variable overhead (3 hours @ $1.50) | 4.50 |
| Fixed overhead (3 hours @ $1) | 3.00 |

The company has chosen 10,000 units (30,000 standard direct labour hours) as the denominator activity level for August 2005. Following are the operating data for August 2005:

a. There were no units in process at the beginning of August 2005.
b. The number of units completed during August was 9,000.
c. The work-in-process inventory at the end of August was 500 units. These units were 60 percent complete with respect to their conversion costs. All Material Y, but only 60 percent of Material W, had been issued for these units.
d. Actual direct labour costs were $195,000, at a rate of $6.50 per hour.
e. Materials issued to production: Material Y, 95,000 kilograms @ $0.55; Material W, 55,000 metres @ $0.75.
f. The company incurred variable overhead costs of $43,000 and fixed overhead costs of $31,000 in August.

**Required:**

1. Determine the following variances:
   a. Direct materials price variances for Materials Y and W
   b. Direct materials quantity variances for Materials Y and W
   c. Direct labour rate variance
   d. Direct labour efficiency variance
   e. Variable overhead spending variance
   f. Variable overhead efficiency variance
   g. Fixed overhead spending variance
   h. Fixed overhead denominator variance
2. Explain the relationship between direct labour efficiency variance and variable overhead efficiency variance. (CGA Canada adapted)

**14–35**

Standard Costing;
Planned Variances

LO2, LO4

As part of its cost control program, Heffernan Company uses a standard cost system for all products. The standard cost for each product is established at the beginning of the fiscal year, and the standards are not revised until the beginning of the next fiscal year. Changes in costs arising from changes in input prices and usage are recognized as planned variances in monthly operating budgets.

The following labour standards were established for one product for the fiscal year beginning June 1, 2005:

| Assembler A labour (5 hours @ $10 per hour) | $ 50 |
|---|---|
| Assembler B labour (3 hours @ $11 per hour) | 33 |
| Machinist labour (2 hours @ $15 per hour) | 30 |
| Standard cost per 100 units | $113 |

The labour standard was based on work completed by a team consisting of five Assembler A's, three Assembler B's, and two machinists. This team represents the most efficient use of the skills of the employees. The standard also assumed that the quality of materials used in prior years would be available for the coming year.

For the first seven months of the fiscal year, actual manufacturing costs were within the standards. However, the company has experienced a significant increase in orders, and the number of skilled workers is not sufficient to meet the increased production. So effective in January, the production teams will consist of eight Assembler A's, one Assembler B, and one machinist. The reorganized teams will work more slowly than the normal teams. As a result, only 80 units will be produced in the same time period in which 100 units would normally be produced. Defective work has never been a cause for rejected units in the final inspection, and it is not expected to be a cause for rejections with the reorganized teams.

Furthermore, a major supplier has notified the company that lower-quality materials will be supplied beginning January 1. Normally, one unit of raw materials is required for each good unit produced, and no units are lost due to defective materials. The company estimates that defective materials will cause the rejection of 10 percent of units produced, when lower-quality materials are used.

**Required:**
1. Determine the number of units of lower-quality material needed to produce 54,000 good units.
2. How many hours of each class of labour must be used to produce 54,000 good units?
3. Compute the planned labour variance that should be included in the January operating budget because of the reorganization of labour teams and the use of lower-quality materials. (US CMA adapted)

---

**14–36**

*Variance Analysis;*
*Incomplete Data*

**LO4, LO5**

KleenAir, Ltd., uses a standard costing system and manufactures a product called DustTrap. The standard unit manufacturing and selling and administrative costs are as follows:

| Manufacturing costs: | |
|---|---|
| Direct materials (15 m @ $2/metre) | $30 |
| Direct labour (4 hours @ $8/hour) | 32 |
| Total manufacturing overhead[a] | 20 |
| | $82 |
| | |
| Selling and administrative costs: | |
| Variable | $10 |
| Fixed | 0 |
| | $10 |

[a] Applied at 5/8 of a direct labour hour. The ratio of variable to fixed overhead is 3:1.

The following information relates to June:

| | |
|---|---|
| Normal volume (in direct labour hours) | 2,500 |
| Actual cost of 20,000 metres of direct materials | $39,500.00 |
| Material usage variance | $900.00 F |
| Actual direct labour costs | $22,620.50 |
| Actual production (units) | 700 |
| Total manufacturing overhead costs | $13,287.50 |
| Actual direct labour rate per hour | $8.05 |

**Required:**
1. What is the standard unit cost of DustTrap?
2. Compute the standard variable overhead rate per direct labour hour.
3. Compute the total budgeted fixed manufacturing overhead for June.
4. Compute the following:
   a. Purchase price variance
   b. Labour rate variance
   c. Actual direct material used in metres
   d. Labour efficiency variance
   e. Variable overhead efficiency variance
   f. Fixed overhead denominator variance (CGA Canada adapted)

**14–37**

Overhead Variances;
Incomplete Data

LO5

Alanis Morris is a recently hired cost accountant for Capital Corporation, which produces a single product. The product requires a standard direct labour input of 2.5 hours per unit. Total overhead is applied to production using a predetermined rate per standard direct labour hour.

Before leaving for vacation, Alanis's supervisor asked her to prepare an analysis of total overhead costs for January. She suddenly realizes that she only has the following analysis for November and December to use as a starting point:

|  | December | November |
|---|---|---|
| Actual overhead costs | $27,500 | $25,100 |
| Standard direct labour hours allowed | 8,250 | 7,000 |
| Overhead variances: |  |  |
| Spending | $400 U | $200 F |
| Efficiency | 100 U | 800 U |
| Denominator | 1,050 F | 700 U |

**Required:**
1. Determine the following:
   a. Predetermined overhead rate
   b. Flexible budget formula
   c. Denominator volume
2. Prepare an analysis of overhead costs for January, in as much detail as possible, assuming that 3,100 units were actually produced and that the total overhead costs incurred were $25,850. (CMA Canada adapted)

**14–38**

Incomplete Data;
Variance Analysis;
Standard Costs

LO2, LO4, LO5

Gatineau Company has recently acquired Madera Enterprises, a small manufacturing firm. Madera has very poor internal controls. A master disk with some fundamental cost data for the past year has been accidentally erased, and no backup exists. Linda Bois, the internal auditor, has been assigned the task of reconstructing the cost records. She finds a computer printout containing the following cost information for Madera:

- Direct materials: 5,000 kilograms purchased and used, $51,000
- Production: 20,000 units
- Direct labour costs: $34,320 for 4,400 hours
- Fixed overhead costs: $23,000
- Variable overhead costs: $46,000

|  | Cost Variances |
|---|---|
| Materials price | $ 1,000 U |
| Materials usage | 10,000 F |
| Labour efficiency | 3,200 U |
| Variable overhead efficiency | 4,000 U |
| Variable overhead spending | 2,000 U |
| Underapplied fixed overhead | 3,000 U |
| Denominator variance | 4,000 U |

Linda interviews Madera's controller, who tells her that he bases overhead rates on expected actual activity and normally calculates two variances for variable overhead and two for fixed overhead.

Before Linda can analyze this information, she has to take an emergency leave. She asks you to complete the analysis.

**Required:**
1. Compute the standard unit cost, showing the fixed and variable overhead as separate items.
2. Compute the fixed overhead spending variance.

3. Compute the labour rate variance.
4. Determine the expected actual activity used to compute the predetermined fixed overhead rate.

**14–39**

Incomplete Data;
Overhead Variances

LO4, LO5

For the production of Magic-Glue, Sure-Stix Company uses the following standards based on the production of 100,000 cases and the use of 300,000 direct labour hours for its 2005 fiscal year:

| | | |
|---|---:|---:|
| Direct materials (4 litres for each case) | | $300,000 |
| Direct labour | | 2,700,000 |
| Manufacturing overhead: | | |
|    Variable | $300,000 | |
|    Fixed | 600,000 | 900,000 |
| Total standard cost (100,000 cases) | | $3,900,000 |

Other information:
a. Manufacturing overhead is applied on the basis of direct labour hours. The denominator activity is 300,000 direct labour hours.
b. During 2005, Sure-Stix produced 97,000 cases of Magic-Glue and used 293,000 direct labour hours and 394,000 litres of direct materials.
c. There was no beginning inventory of direct materials.
d. Based on the purchase of 440,000 litres of direct materials, the purchase price variance was $5,500, unfavourable.
e. The direct labour rate variance was $29,300, favourable.

**Required:**
1. What is the actual price per litre of the direct materials purchased?
2. What is the actual prime cost of a case of Magic-Glue during 2005?
3. Actual overhead costs during 2005 were $937,600, of which $316,000 was variable. Calculate the overhead variances. (CGA Canada adapted)

**14–40**

Variance Analysis;
Incomplete Data

LO4, LO5

Bay of Funday Boat Builders, Ltd., was hit by an extremely high tide that destroyed some accounting records. As the cost accountant, you were able to reconstruct the following information for October:

| | |
|---|---:|
| Direct materials (4 m @ $4.50 per metre) | $18 |
| Direct labour (3 hours @ $12 per hour) | 36 |
| Variable overhead (3 hours @ $2 per hour) | 6 |
| Fixed overhead (3 hours @ $5 per hour) | 15 |

You were also able to derive the following other information for October:
a. The direct materials price variance is $4,750F. The price variance is isolated when materials are issued to production. The average actual cost of material issued was $4.40 per metre. The direct materials standard cost of the units produced was $207,000.
b. The actual direct labour rate was $12.20 per hour, and 33,400 hours were worked.
c. Actual variable overhead was $67,400, and actual fixed overhead was $156,200. The fixed overhead spending variance was $1,300F.

**Required:**
1. What is the company's denominator activity level for October?
2. Determine the remaining variances for direct materials, direct labour, and overhead.
3. Describe an alternative method for calculating the direct materials price variance, and explain why that method would be preferable to the company's present method. (CMA Canada adapted)

**14–41**

Incomplete Data;
Variance Analysis

LO4, LO5

You have the following information about Rapala Company, which uses a standard costing system for its only product:

a. In November 2005, 5,000 units were produced.
b. The annual overhead budget includes $750,000 for variable and $1,050,000 for fixed overhead items. Budgeted production for the year is 50,000 units. Overhead is applied on the basis of direct labour hours.
c. The materials standard per unit is 5 litres at $4.
d. The direct labour standard per unit is 3 hours at $10.
e. The actual price paid for materials was $3.98.
f. The actual direct labour rate was $10.50.
g. Actual fixed overhead costs were $88,000.
h. The following variances have already been computed:

| | |
|---|---|
| Materials price | $ 600 F |
| Materials quantity | 1,600 U |
| Labour rate | 7,400 U |
| Variable overhead spending | 1,800 U |

**Required:**
Calculate the following for November 2005:
1. The quantity of materials purchased
2. The quantity of materials used
3. The actual direct labour hours worked
4. Labour efficiency variance
5. Variable overhead efficiency variance
6. Actual variable overhead
7. Fixed overhead spending variance
8. Fixed overhead denominator variance (CGA Canada adapted)

**14–42**

Variance Analysis;
Incomplete Data

LO4, LO5

NR-ON Company recently had a fire in its accounting office that destroyed part of its accounting records for July. The company uses a standard cost system, with the direct materials purchase price variance isolated when the materials are purchased. A search of the remaining records revealed the following unit standards for July:

| | |
|---|---|
| Direct materials (15 kilograms @ $4 per kilogram) | $60 |
| Direct labour (3 hours @ $9 per hour) | 27 |
| Variable overhead (3 hours @ $5 per hour) | 15 |
| Fixed overhead (3 hours @ $10 per hour) | 30 |

The files with the variance analysis for July were partly destroyed, but it was possible to reconstruct the following information:

a. The actual average direct materials price was $4.20 per kilogram.
b. The direct materials usage variance was $3,080, unfavourable.
c. Direct materials inventories decreased by 3,500 kilograms in July.
d. The standard direct labour cost was $324,000.
e. The direct labour rate variance was $3,800, favourable.
f. The actual variable overhead costs were $197,000, and the variable overhead spending variance was $7,000, favourable.
g. The actual fixed overhead costs were the same as budgeted.
h. The total overhead costs were underapplied by $77,000 in July.

**Required:**
Calculate the following for July:
1. Total units produced
2. Direct materials purchase price variance

3. Actual average direct labour rate
4. Direct labour efficiency variance
5. Variable overhead efficiency variance
6. Denominator variance
7. Denominator activity level used to establish the standards for July. (CMA Canada adapted)

**14–43**

Profitability Analysis; Variance Analysis as an Analytical Tool (Appendix A)

LO6

Sennen, Ltd. manufactures two types of appliances that are sold on national markets. The budgeted and actual results for these two products for the past year are as follows:

| | Sennen, Ltd. | | Industry | |
|---|---|---|---|---|
| | **Budgeted** | **Actual** | **Budgeted** | **Actual** |
| Units of Product A | 12,000 | 13,000 | 100,000 | 120,000 |
| Units of Product B | 8,000 | 7,500 | 50,000 | 45,000 |
| Selling price per unit of A | $200 | $210 | | |
| Variable cost per unit of A | $140 | $130 | | |
| Selling price per unit of B | $100 | $90 | | |
| Variable cost per unit of B | $50 | $40 | | |
| Total fixed cost | $600,000 | $620,000 | | |

**Required:**
1. Prepare actual and budgeted income statements.
2. Analyze, by cause, the effect of each variable on profit. (*Hint:* Calculate a variance for each of the following: industry volume, market share, sales mix, sales price, variable cost, and fixed cost.)
3. Comment on the company's performance.

**14–44**

Profitability Analysis; Variance Analysis as an Analytical Tool (Appendix A)

LO6

Toyworld manufactures and sells two types of toys: Type A and Type B. The master budget for 2005 showed a budgeted variable-costing income of $69,000. At the end 2005, the actual variable-costing income was $64,400. As the president of Toyworld, you want to analyze the company's profitability. Your assistant has provided you with the following information:

| | Master Budget | | | Actual | | |
|---|---|---|---|---|---|---|
| | **A** | **B** | **Total** | **A** | **B** | **Total** |
| Selling price, per unit | $20 | $30 | — | $21 | $32 | — |
| Variable manufacturing cost, per unit | $11 | $18 | — | $12 | $20 | — |
| Variable marketing and administrative expenses, per unit | $1 | $1 | — | $1.10 | $1.10 | — |
| Total fixed manufacturing costs | — | — | $34,500 | — | — | $36,000 |
| Total fixed marketing and administrative expenses | — | — | $40,000 | — | — | $44,000 |
| Sales volume, in units | 9,000 | 6,500 | 15,500 | 10,000 | 6,000 | 16,000 |
| Industry volume of similar toys | — | — | 77,500 | — | — | 64,000 |

**Required:**
1. Calculate the profit volume variance (gross).
2. Calculate the sales mix variance and the profit volume variance (net).
3. Separate the profit volume variance (net) into two components, reflecting the changes in industry volume and market share.
4. Calculate the sales price variance.
5. Calculate the variable cost flexible budget variances.

6.  Calculate the fixed cost flexible budget variances.
7.  Based on Requirements 1 to 6 above, reconcile the budgeted and actual operating incomes.
8.  Comment on Toyworld's performance based on your reconciliation in Requirement 7.

## Managerial Decision Cases

**14–45**

*Standard Costing*

**LO1, LO2, LO3**

McOcean, Ltd. is a frozen-food processor, located in Halifax, that specializes in seafood dishes. Since its founding in 1982, the company has developed a loyal clientele willing to pay premium prices for its high-quality products. In the past two years the company has experienced rapid sales growth in the Atlantic region and has fielded many inquiries about supplying its products nationally. To meet this demand, the company has expanded its processing capacity; the result of this has been increased production and distribution costs. In addition, the company has encountered pricing pressure from national competitors.

The company wants to keep expanding, so Jim Gordon, the CEO, has engaged a consultant to help determine the best course of action. The consultant is recommending the implementation of a standard cost system. Mr. Gordon now meets with his management team to discuss the consultant's recommendations, and assigns to this team the task of establishing standard costs. After discussing the situation with their staff, the management team meets to discuss the matter at more length. The following are key points raised at the meeting:

- Jane Morgan, the purchasing manager, notes that meeting expanded production will mean that more supplies will have to be obtained from sources other than the traditional suppliers. This will entail increased raw material and shipping costs and may result in lower-quality supplies. These increased costs will have to be covered by the processing department if current costs are to be maintained or reduced.
- Stan Walters, the processing manager, counters that the need to accelerate processing cycles to increase production, coupled with the possibility of receiving lower-grade supplies, could result in decreased quality and higher spoilage and rejection rates. In these circumstances, he will not be able to maintain or reduce per-unit labour utilization, and he will find it more difficult to forecast future unit labour content.
- Tom Lopez, the production engineer, advises that the equipment will have to be properly maintained and thoroughly cleaned at prescribed daily intervals; otherwise, the quality and unique fresh taste of the products will almost certainly be affected.
- Jack Reid, the vice-president of sales, states that if quality cannot be maintained, the company cannot expect to increase sales to the projected levels.

When Mr. Gordon hears of these problems, he advises the managers that if they cannot agree on the standards, he will ask the consultant to set the standards, and everyone will have to live with the outcome.

**Required:**
1.  List the major advantages of using a standard cost system.
2.  List disadvantages that can result from the use of a standard cost system.
3.  Identify the key individuals who should participate in setting standards, and describe the benefits of their participation in the standard-setting process.

4. What characteristics of a standard cost system make it an effective tool for cost control?

5. What could be the consequences if Mr. Gordon has the consulting firm set the standards? (US CMA adapted)

**14–46**

*Establishment of Standards; Variance Analysis*

**LO1, LO2, LO4**

Crunchy Chips was established in 1960 by Paul Golding and his wife Nancy. Paul assumed responsibility for buying potatoes and selling chips; Nancy assumed responsibility for production.

Over the past 30 years, the company has prospered and established its distribution channels in five provinces, with production facilities located in New Brunswick, Ontario, and Saskatchewan. In 1990, Paul Golding retired and his son, Edward, took control of the business. By 2005 the company was facing stiff competition from large snack food companies. A management consultant advised Edward that the plants needed to gain better control over production costs, and recommended a standard cost system. To help the consultant establish appropriate standards, Edward sent her the following memo:

| | |
|---|---|
| **To:** | **Diana Craig, CMA** |
| **From:** | **Edward Golding, President, Crunchy Chips** |
| **Subject:** | **Production Process and Costs** |
| **Date:** | **September 28, 2005** |

As promised, this memo provides information on the production process and costs for our potato chips.

The manufacturing process is almost completely automated. It begins when potatoes are placed in a large vat for automatic washing. After washing, the potatoes move to an automatic peeler. The peeled potatoes pass by inspectors, who cut out deep eyes and other blemishes. After inspection, the potatoes are automatically sliced and dropped into cooking oil for frying. The frying process is closely monitored by an employee. After frying, the chips pass under a salting device and travel past inspectors, who remove discoloured, undersized, and broken chips. The good chips then continue on the conveyor belt to a packaging machine, which bags them in 454-gram bags. After sealing, the bags are placed in boxes and shipped. Each box holds 15 bags.

The raw potato pieces (eyes and blemishes), peelings, and rejected finished chips are sold to animal feed producers for $0.35 per kilogram. We use this revenue to reduce the cost of potatoes and would like the price standard for potatoes to reflect this.

We purchase high-quality potatoes at a cost of $0.54 per kilogram. Each potato weighs, on average, 120 grams Under efficient operating conditions, it takes four potatoes to produce one 454-gram bag of plain chips. Although we label bags as containing 454 grams, we actually place 460 grams in each bag. We plan to continue this policy to ensure customer satisfaction. Besides potatoes, other raw materials used are cooking oil, salt, bags, and boxes. Cooking oil costs $1.35 per litre, and we use 100 millilitres of oil per one bag of chips. Salt is so inexpensive that we add it to overhead. Bags cost $0.11 each, and boxes $0.52 each.

Our plants produce 8.8 million bags of chips per year. A recent engineering study has revealed that we need the following direct labour hours to produce this quantity, assuming that our plants operate at optimum efficiency:

| | |
|---|---|
| Raw potato inspection | 3,200 |
| Finished chip inspection | 12,000 |
| Frying monitor | 6,300 |
| Boxing | 16,600 |
| Machine operators | 6,300 |

I'm not sure we can achieve the level of efficiency advocated by the study. In my opinion, plants are operating efficiently if the hours allowed are up to 10 percent higher. The hourly labour rates negotiated with the union are as follows:

| | |
|---|---|
| Raw potato inspectors | $8.60 |
| Finished chip inspectors | 6.15 |
| Frying monitor | 8.00 |
| Boxing | 6.50 |
| Machine operators | 7.50 |

Overhead is applied based on direct labour dollars. We have found that variable overhead averages about 116 percent of our direct labour cost. Our fixed overhead is budgeted at $1,135,216 for the coming year.

**Required:**
1. Discuss the benefits of a standard cost system for Crunchy Chips.
2. Discuss the president's concern about using the labour standards set in the engineering study. Which standards would you recommend?
3. Develop a standard cost sheet for Crunchy Chips's plain potato chips.
4. Suppose the level of production was 8.8 million bags of potato chips for the year as planned. If 4,300,000 kilograms of potatoes were used, compute the materials usage variance for potatoes.

**14–47**

*Standard Costing and Ethical Behaviour*

**LO1, LO3**

Pat James, the purchasing manager for the Regina plant of Megasound Electronics, was considering the purchase of a component from a new supplier. The component's purchase price, $0.90, compared favourably with the standard price of $1.10. Given the quantity that would be purchased, Pat knew that the favourable price variance would help offset an unfavourable variance for another component. By offsetting the unfavourable variance, he would make his overall performance report look impressive—good enough to help him qualify for the annual bonus. More importantly, a good performance rating this year would help him secure a position at divisional headquarters at a significant salary increase.

Purchase of the part, however, presented Pat with a dilemma. Consistent with his past behaviour, Pat made inquiries regarding the reliability of the new supplier and the part's quality. Reports were basically negative. The supplier had a reputation for making the first two or three deliveries on schedule but being unreliable later. Worse, the part itself was of questionable quality. The number of defective units was only slightly higher than for other suppliers, but the life of the component was 25 percent shorter.

If the part were purchased, no problems with deliveries would surface for several months. The problem of shorter life would cause eventual customer dissatisfaction and perhaps some loss of sales, but the part would last at least 18 months in normal use. If all went well, Pat expected to be at headquarters within 6 months. He saw very little personal risk associated with a decision to purchase the part from the new supplier. By the time any problems surfaced, they would belong to his successor. With this rationalization, Pat decided to purchase the component from the new supplier.

**Required:**
1. Do you agree with Pat's decision? Explain why or why not. How important was Pat's assessment of his personal risk in the decision? Should it be a factor?
2. Do you think the use of standards and the practice of holding individuals accountable for their achievement played a major role in Pat's decision?
3. Review the discussions of ethical standards for management accountants in Chapter 1 (see footnote 10 for website addresses). Even though Pat is not a management accountant, identify the standards that might apply to his situation. Should every company adopt a set of ethical standards that apply to its employees, regardless of their specialty?

# Research Assignment

**14–48**

LO1, LO3, LO4, LO5

The usefulness of standard costing has been challenged in recent years. Some claim that its use is an impediment to the objective of continuous improvement—an objective that many feel is vital in today's competitive environment. Write a short report analyzing the role and value of standard costing in today's manufacturing environment. In the report, address the following questions:

1. What are the major criticisms of standard costing?
2. Will standard costing disappear? Or will it still play a role in the new manufacturing environment? If so, what is that role?
3. Given the criticisms, can you explain why its use continues to be so prevalent? Will this use eventually change?
4. If standard costing is no longer completely suitable for some manufacturing environments, what control approaches are being used to supplement or replace the traditional standard costing systems?

In preparing your report, you may find the following references useful. However, do not restrict your literature search to these references. They are provided simply to help you get started.

Robin Cooper and Robert S. Kaplan, "Activity-Based Systems: Measuring the Costs of Resource Usage," *Accounting Horizons* (September 1992): pp. 1-13.

Carole B. Cheatham and Leo R. Cheatham, "Redesigning Cost Systems: Is Standard Costing Obsolete?" *Accounting Horizons* (December 1996): pp. 23-31.

Bruce R. Gaumnitz and Felix P. Kollaritsch, "Manufacturing Variances: Current Practice and Trends," *Journal of Cost Management* (Spring 1991): pp. 58-64.

Robert S. Kaplan, "Limitations of Cost Accounting in Advanced Manufacturing Environments," in Robert S. Kaplan (ed.), *Measures for Manufacturing Excellence* (Boston: Harvard Business School Press, 1990).

Mike Lucas, "Standard Costing and Its Role in Today's Manufacturing Environment," *Management Accounting* (April 1997): pp. 32-34.

# Quality Costs and Productivity: Measurement, Reporting, and Control

**After studying Chapter 15, you should be able to:**

1. Identify and describe the four types of quality costs.

2. Prepare a quality cost report, and explain the difference between the conventional acceptable quality level (AQL) view and the zero-defects view of quality cost control.

3. Explain why quality cost information is needed and how it is used.

4. Explain what productivity is, and calculate the impact of productivity changes on profits.

# Scenario

Russell Walsh, president of Ladd Lighting Corporation, had just returned from a productivity seminar, excited and encouraged by what he had heard. He immediately called a meeting with Sarah Burke, the production quality manager, and Dennis Schmitt, the controller and vice-president of finance.

**Russell**: "I'm convinced we can become more competitive by increasing productivity and improving quality. Something needs to be done, given the direction our profits have been heading over the past several years."

**Dennis**: "I agree we need to do something. But improving quality will cost, and I'm not sure that spending more on quality will help much. After all, right now we spend a lot on quality-related activities. Pouring more money into quality may not be the answer."

**Russell**: "I don't intend to spend more on quality—just the opposite. According to experts, and backed up by the experience of many cases, improving quality *decreases* quality costs. Most quality-related costs are incurred because of poor quality. It costs us when we do things wrong, in terms of rework, scrap, repairs, and so on. By controlling quality costs, we can improve profitability and become more competitive.

"The Ritz-Carlton Hotel Company, L.L.C., a winner of the Malcolm Baldrige National Quality Award in the service category in 1992 and 1999, has more than doubled its pretax return on investment and earnings since 1995. Sunny Fresh Foods, a 1999 award winner in the small business category, reports that its return on gross investment tripled over a five-year period, while its operating profits increased an average of 25 percent per year over the same period. Both companies also claim that their quality improvement efforts have significantly improved customer satisfaction."[1]

**Sarah**: "I can see how this would make Ladd Lighting more competitive. As I have always maintained, it costs us when we do things wrong."

**Russell**: "Exactly. I now understand what you were saying—poor quality is what costs. Several cases were dis-

---

1. For a detailed profile of each company, see www.nist.gov/public_affairs/bald99/ritz.htm *and* www.nist.gov/public_affairs/bald99/sunnyfresh.htm (as of August 11, 2001).

cussed at the conference. One example given was that of Tennant Company, a manufacturer of industrial floor maintenance products. Tennant's quality improvement efforts have been remarkable. But the most exciting thing about Tennant's experience is the effect of the improved quality on its profitability. When the quality improvement program began, Tennant estimated that its cost of doing things wrong was as high as 17 percent of sales. Within a six-year period, this cost had dropped to 8 percent of sales. Based on annual sales of $136 million, savings from improved quality totalled $12.24 million."[2]

**Dennis**: "I'm impressed by the savings that could be achieved through improved quality. But I'm not sure what role you envision for me, other than being aware of the importance of a quality improvement program. Sarah's department has been responsible for quality cost reporting."

**Russell**: "I envision your role as being much more extensive than simple awareness. We need a solid, reliable quality cost reporting system, and I expect you to assume responsibility for its development and operation. Our company needs quality information to help our managers make quality improvement decisions. We also need to monitor and control the programs we implement. Sarah, do you have any problems with this arrangement?"

**Sarah**: "None at all. It seems sensible that the controller's office be responsible for collecting and reporting quality costs. I know that other companies have similar arrangements. The quality department should be responsible for analyzing and controlling these costs. Besides, I have a feeling that given the increased emphasis on quality, my department will have plenty to do without worrying about a cost reporting system."

**Questions to Think About**

1. Why has measurement of productivity and quality become so important?
2. What are quality costs?
3. How can improving quality reduce quality costs?
4. What kind of quality cost reports should be prepared by the accounting department?
5. What is meant by "productivity"?
6. How is productivity measured?

## Measuring the Costs of Quality

**Objective** 1

Identify and describe the four types of quality costs.

By attending a productivity seminar, Russell Walsh discovered that paying more attention to quality can increase profitability. Quality improvement can increase profitability in two ways:

1. By increasing customer demand
2. By decreasing costs

In a tightly competitive market, increased demand and cost savings can mean the difference between surviving and thriving. Consequently, the importance of quality management has been widely recognized in recent years. The Baldrige National Quality Award was created by law in the United States to recognize American companies that excel in quality management and achievement.[3] The award categories include manufacturing, small business, service, educational, and health entities. For example, the award winners in 2000 included Dana Corporation (Spicer Driveshaft Division) and Karlee Company in manufacturing, Operations Management International, Inc., in services, and Los Alamos National Bank in the small business category.

The costs of quality can be substantial, as well as a source of significant savings. Studies indicate that costs of quality are typically 20 to 30 percent of sales.[4]

---

2. Lawrence Carr and Thomas Tyson, "Planning Quality Cost Expenditures," *Management Accounting* (October 1992): pp. 52-56.

3. The Malcolm Baldrige National Quality Award was created by U.S. Public Law 100-107 in 1987.

4. Michael R. Ostrenga, "Return on Investment Through the Costs of Quality," *Journal of Cost Management* (Summer 1991): pp. 37-44.

Yet quality experts maintain that the optimal quality cost level should be about 2 to 4 percent of sales. This difference between actual and optimal figures represents a veritable gold mine of opportunities. Improving quality can produce significant improvements in profitability.

In the past two decades, quality has become an important competitive dimension for both service and manufacturing organizations. Quality is an integrating theme for all organizations. Foreign companies' ability to sell higher-quality products at lower prices has cost many North American companies market share. In an effort to combat this stiff competition, more and more North American companies have been paying attention to quality and productivity, especially given the potential to reduce costs and improve product quality simultaneously. Some have called the push for increased quality a "second industrial revolution."[5] The quality revolution has been going on long enough for some to believe that quality has shifted from a strategic advantage to competitive necessity.[6]

For example, the senior management of IBM identified poor quality as the root cause of its problems. In an effort to solve these problems, the company implemented a quality program called "Market-Driven Quality." According to the former IBM chairman, quality improvement is a survival issue for today's businesses.[7] Other North American companies have strived to meet the quality expectations of consumers. For example, Standard Aero of Winnipeg embarked on an impressive quality management program.[8] It recognized that airplane owners routinely sent their engines to be overhauled—a process that took two months in the shop and required a stock of spare engines that cost more than $1 million each. As one feature of its comprehensive quality programs, the company decided to cut the overhaul time from 2 months to 15 days. As a result of increased productivity and the implementation of total quality management, Standard Aero's 4.5 percent sales increase produced a tenfold increase in earnings.[9]

In response to the globalization of markets, the International Organization for Standardization (ISO), which has 145 member nations, has developed the ISO 9000 series of quality assurance and management standards. The Canadian Standards Association (CSA) is the Canadian member of the ISO. ISO 9000 has gained wide acceptance internationally, especially in Europe. More and more North American companies that sell products internationally now follow ISO 9000. The Society of Management Accountants of Canada has issued a Management Accounting Guideline to provide practical guidance for implementing required quality systems and for becoming ISO 9000 registered.[10]

5.  James P. Simpson and David L. Muthler, "Quality Costs: Facilitating the Quality Initiative," *Journal of Cost Management* (Spring 1987): pp. 25-34.

6.  Robert S. Kaplan and David P. Norton, *The Balanced Scorecard* (Boston: Harvard Business School Press, 1996): pp. 87-88.

7.  Lawrence Carr and Thomas Tyson, "Planning Quality Expenditures," *Management Accounting* (October 1992): pp. 52-56.

8.  Paul Sharman, "World-Class Productivity at Standard Aero," *CMA Magazine* (April 1991): pp. 7-12.

9.  These results are also found for other industries. For example, J.M. Schneider, Inc., responded to declining demand in the meat-packing industry by adopting a program of continuous improvement. See Douglas Dodds, "Making It Better ... and Better," *CMA Magazine* (February 1992): pp. 16-21. Service organizations are examined in H. David Sherman, *Service Organization Productivity Management*, A Research Monograph, The Society of Management Accountants of Canada, 1988.

10. The Society of Management Accountants of Canada, *Becoming ISO 9000 Registered*, Management Accounting Guideline 25 (Hamilton, Ont., 1994).

As companies implement quality improvement programs, the need arises to monitor and report on the progress of these programs.[11] Managers need to know what quality costs are and how they are changing over time. Reporting and measuring quality performance is absolutely essential to the success of an ongoing quality improvement program. A fundamental prerequisite for such reporting is measuring the costs of quality. To measure these costs, an operational definition of *quality* is needed.

## Quality Defined

The typical dictionary definition of *quality* refers to the "degree or grade of excellence." In this sense, quality is a relative measure of goodness. But defining quality as goodness is so general that it offers no operational content. How do we build an operational definition? We do so by "adopting a customer focus." Operationally, a **quality product or service** is one that meets or exceeds customer expectations. In effect, quality is customer satisfaction. But what is meant by "customer expectations"? Customer expectations can be described by quality attributes, or what are often referred to as "dimensions of quality."[12] Thus, a quality product or service is one that meets or exceeds customer expectations on the following eight dimensions:

1. Performance
2. Aesthetics
3. Serviceability
4. Features (quality of design)
5. Reliability
6. Durability
7. Quality of conformance
8. Fitness of use

The first four dimensions describe important quality attributes but are difficult to measure. **Performance** refers to how consistently and how well a product functions. For services, the inseparability principle means that the service is performed in the presence of the customer. Thus, the performance dimension for services can be further defined by the attributes of responsiveness, assurance, and empathy. *Responsiveness* is simply the willingness to help customers and provide prompt, consistent service. *Assurance* refers to the knowledge and courtesy of employees and their ability to convey trust and confidence. *Empathy* means providing caring, individualized attention to customers.

**Aesthetics** is concerned with the appearance of tangible products (e.g., style and beauty) as well as the appearance of the facilities, equipment, personnel, and communication materials associated with services. **Serviceability** measures the ease of maintaining and/or repairing the product.

**Features (quality of design)** refer to characteristics of a product that differentiate functionally similar products. For example, first-class air travel and economy air travel reflect different design qualities. First-class air travel typically offers more leg room, better meals, and more luxurious seats. Obviously, the product features are different for the two classes of service. Higher design quality with more expensive product features is usually reflected in higher costs and revenues.

**quality product or service**
A product that meets or exceeds customer expectations.

**performance**
The measure of how consistent and well a product functions.

**aesthetics**
A quality attribute that is concerned with the appearance of tangible products (e.g., style and beauty) as well as the appearance of the facilities, equipment, personnel, and communications materials associated with services.

**serviceability**
The ease of maintaining and/or repairing a product.

**features (quality of design)**
Characteristics of a product that differentiate functionally similar products.

---

11. The Society of Management Accountants of Canada, *Managing Quality Improvements*, Management Accounting Guideline 14 (Hamilton, Ont., 1992).

12. These dimensions are based on Edwin S. Schecter, *Managing for World Class Quality* (Milwaukee: ASQC Quality Press, 1992), and Leonard L. Berry and A. Parasurman, *Marketing Services: Competing Through Quality* (New York: The Free Press, Macmillan, 1991): p. 16.

**reliability**

The probability that the product or service will perform its intended function for a specified length of time.

**durability**

The length of time a product functions.

**quality of conformance**

Conforming to the design requirements of the product.

**fitness of use**

The suitability of a product for carrying out its advertised functions.

**defective product**

A product or service that does not conform to specifications.

**zero defects**

A quality performance standard that requires all products and services to be produced and delivered according to specifications.

**costs of quality**

Costs incurred because poor quality may exist or because poor quality does exist.

A market for both services exists, and the quality of design helps an airline target the appropriate markets.

**Reliability** is the probability that the product or service will perform its intended function for a specified length of time. **Durability** is defined as the length of time a product functions. **Quality of conformance** is a measure of how a product meets its specifications. For example, the specifications for a machined part may be a drilled hole that is 5 centimetres in diameter, plus or minus 0.25 centimetres. Parts that fall within this range are defined as conforming parts. **Fitness of use** relates to the suitability of the product for carrying out its advertised functions. If there is a fundamental design flaw, the product may fail in the field even if it conforms to its specifications. Product recalls are often the result of fitness-of-use failures.

Improving quality entails improving one or more of the eight quality dimensions while maintaining performance on the remaining dimensions. Providing a higher-quality product than a competitor means outperforming the competitor on at least one dimension while matching performance on the remaining dimensions.

Although all eight dimensions are important and can affect customer satisfaction, the quality attributes that are measurable tend to receive more emphasis. Conformance, in particular, is strongly emphasized. In fact, many quality experts believe that "quality *is* conformance" is the best operational definition. There is some logic to this position. Product specifications should explicitly consider such things as reliability, durability, fitness of use, and performance. Implicitly, a conforming product is reliable, durable, fit for use, and performs well. The product should be produced as the design specifies it—that is, specifications should be met. Furthermore, conformance is the basis for defining what is meant by a nonconforming, or defective, product.

A **defective product** is one that does not conform to specifications. **Zero defects** means that all products conform to specifications. But what is meant by "conforming to specifications"? The *traditional view* of conformance assumes that there is an acceptable range of values for each specification or quality characteristic. A target value is defined, and upper and lower limits are set to define acceptable product variation for a given quality characteristic. Any unit that falls within the limits is deemed nondefective. For example, losing or gaining zero minutes per month may be the target value for a watch, and any watch that keeps time correctly within plus or minus two minutes per month is judged acceptable. In contrast, the *robust quality view* of conformance emphasizes fitness of use. *Robustness* means hitting the target value every time. There is no range in which variation is acceptable. A nondefective watch in the robust setting would be one that does not gain or lose *any* minutes during the month. Since evidence exists that product variation can be costly, the robust zero-defects definition of conformance is superior to the traditional definition.

## Costs of Quality Defined

Quality-linked activities are activities performed because poor quality may or does exist. The costs of performing these activities are referred to as costs of quality. Thus, the **costs of quality** are the costs that exist because poor quality may or does exist.[13] This definition implies that quality costs are associated with two sub-

---

13. This definition is from Wayne J. Morse, Harold P. Roth, and Kay M. Poston, *Measuring, Planning, and Controlling Quality Costs* (Montvale, N.J.: National Association of Accountants, 1987): p.19. Another way of looking at quality costs involves determining how much is spent on discovering, scrapping, and correcting errors. See Mohammed Beheiry, "New Thoughts on an Old Concept: The Cost of Quality," *CMA Magazine* (June 1991): pp. 24-25.

**control activities**

Activities performed by an organization to prevent or detect poor quality (because poor quality may exist).

**control costs**

Costs incurred from performing control activities.

**failure activities**

Activities performed by an organization or its customers in response to poor quality (poor quality does exist).

**failure costs**

The costs incurred by an organization because failure activities are performed.

**prevention costs**

Costs incurred to prevent defects in products or services being produced.

**appraisal costs**

Costs incurred to determine whether products and services are conforming to requirements.

**internal failure costs**

Costs incurred because products and services fail to conform to requirements, where lack of conformity is discovered prior to external sale.

**external failure costs**

Costs incurred because products fail to conform to requirements after being sold to outside parties.

**observable quality costs**

Quality costs that are available from an organization's accounting records.

categories of quality-related activities: control activities and failure activities. **Control activities** are performed by an organization to prevent or detect poor quality (because poor quality *may* exist). Thus, control activities consist of prevention and appraisal activities. **Control costs** are the costs of performing control activities.

**Failure activities** are performed by an organization or its customers in response to poor quality (because poor quality *does* exist). If the response to poor quality occurs before delivery of a defective product (e.g., a nonconforming, unreliable, or nondurable product) to a customer, the activities are classified as internal failure activities. Otherwise, they are classified as external failure activities. **Failure costs** are the costs incurred by an organization through its performance of failure activities. Note that the definitions of failure activities and failure costs imply that customer response to poor quality can impose costs on an organization. The definitions of quality-related activities also imply four categories of quality costs:

1. Prevention costs
2. Appraisal costs
3. Internal failure costs
4. External failure costs

**Prevention costs** are incurred to prevent poor quality in the products or services being produced. As prevention costs increase, we would expect the costs of failure to decrease. Examples of prevention costs are quality engineering, quality training programs, quality planning, quality reporting, supplier evaluation and selection, quality audits, quality circles, field trials, and design reviews.

**Appraisal costs** are incurred to determine whether products and services conform to their requirements or customer needs. Examples of appraisal costs are the costs of inspecting and/or testing raw materials, inspecting packaging, supervising appraisal activities, approving products and processes, and inspecting and testing equipment. Two of these terms require further explanation.

*Product approval* involves sampling from batches of finished goods to determine whether they meet an acceptable quality level; if so, the goods are accepted. *Process approval* involves sampling goods while in process to determine whether the process is in control and producing acceptable goods; if not, the process is shut down until corrective action can be taken. The main objective of the appraisal function is to prevent nonconforming goods from being shipped to customers.

**Internal failure costs** are incurred because products and services do not conform to specifications or customer needs. Such nonconformance is detected by appraisal activities prior to shipping or delivering the goods to outside parties. Examples of internal failure costs are scrap, rework, downtime due to defects, reinspection, retesting, and design changes. These costs disappear if no defects exist.

**External failure costs** are incurred because products and services fail to conform to requirements or to satisfy customer needs after delivery. Of all costs of quality, this category can be the most devastating. For example, costs of recalls can be very high and result in the loss of consumer confidence. Other examples of external failure costs include lost sales due to poor product performance; returns and allowances due to poor quality; warranty, repair, and product liability costs; and lost market share. External failure costs, like internal failure costs, disappear if no defects exist.

## Measuring Quality Costs

Quality costs can also be classified as observable or hidden. **Observable quality costs** are those which are available from an organization's accounting records.

**hidden quality costs**
Opportunity costs resulting from poor quality.

**Hidden quality costs** are opportunity costs arising from poor quality. Opportunity costs are not usually recognized in the accounting records.

Consider, for example, all the examples of quality costs listed in the previous section. With the exception of lost sales, customer dissatisfaction, and lost market share, all quality costs are observable and should be available from the accounting records. Note also that all hidden costs are in the external failure category. These hidden quality costs can be significant and should be estimated. Although estimating hidden quality costs is not easy, three methods have been suggested:

1. Multiplier method
2. Market research method
3. Taguchi quality loss function

### The Multiplier Method

The multiplier method assumes that the total failure costs are simply some multiple of measured failure costs:

$$\text{Total external failure costs} = k(\text{Measured external failure costs})$$

where $k$ is the multiplier effect. The value of $k$ is based on experience. For example, Westinghouse Electric reports a value of $k$ between 3 and 4.[14] Thus, if the measured external failure costs are \$2 million, the actual external failure costs are between \$6 million and \$8 million. Including hidden costs in the amount of external failure costs allows management to determine more accurately the appropriate level of resource spending for prevention and appraisal activities. Specifically, with an increase in failure costs, we would expect management to increase its investment in control costs.

### The Market Research Method

Formal market research methods can be used to assess the effects of poor quality on sales and market share. Customer surveys and interviews with members of a company's sales force can provide significant insights into the magnitude of a company's hidden costs. Market research results can be used to project future profit losses attributable to poor quality.

### The Taguchi Quality Loss Function

The traditional zero-defects definition assumes that hidden quality costs exist only for units that fall outside the upper and lower specification limits. The **Taguchi loss function** assumes that any variation from the target value of a quality characteristic causes hidden quality costs. Furthermore, the hidden quality costs increase quadratically as the actual value deviates from the target value. The Taguchi quality loss function (see Exhibit 15–1) can be described by the following equation:

$$L(y) = k(y - T)^2$$

**Taguchi loss function**
A function that assumes that any variation from the target value of a quality characteristic causes hidden quality costs.

where

$k$ = a proportionality constant dependent on the organization's external failure cost structure
$y$ = actual value of quality characteristic
$T$ = target value of quality characteristic
$L$ = quality loss

---

14. T.L. Albright and P.R. Roth, "The Measurement of Quality Costs: An Alternative Paradigm," *Accounting Horizons* (June 1992): pp. 15-27. This article also describes the three approaches to measuring hidden quality costs.

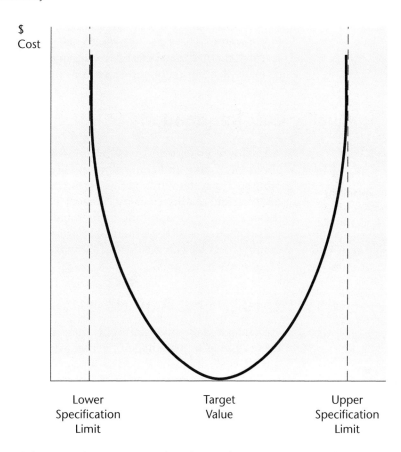

EXHIBIT 15-1

The Taguchi Quality Loss Function

Exhibit 15–1 demonstrates that the quality cost is zero at the target value and increases symmetrically, at an increasing rate, as the actual value varies from the target value. Assume, for example, that $k = \$400$ and $T = 10$ cm in diameter. Exhibit 15–2 illustrates the computation of the quality loss for four units. Note that the cost quadruples when the deviation from the target doubles (from units 2 to 3). Note also that the average deviation squared and the average loss per unit can be computed. These averages can be used to compute the total expected hidden quality costs for a product. If, for example, the total units produced are 2,000 and the average squared deviation is 0.025, the expected cost per unit is $10 (0.025 × $400), and the total expected loss for the 2,000 units would be $20,000 ($10 × 2,000).

To apply the Taguchi loss function, $k$ must be estimated. The value for $k$ is computed by dividing the estimated cost at one of the specification limits by the squared deviation of the limit from the target value:

$$k = c/d^2$$

where

$c$ = loss at the lower or upper specification limit
$d$ = distance of limit from target value

EXHIBIT 15-2

Quality Loss Computation Illustrated

| Unit | Actual Diameter ($y$) | $y - T$ | $(y - T)^2$ | $k(y - T)^2$ |
|------|------------------------|---------|-------------|---------------|
| 1 | 9.9 | −0.10 | 0.010 | $ 4 |
| 2 | 10.1 | 0.10 | 0.010 | 4 |
| 3 | 10.2 | 0.20 | 0.040 | 16 |
| 4 | 9.8 | −0.20 | 0.040 | 16 |
| Total | | | 0.100 | $40 |
| Average | | | 0.025 | $10 |

This means we must still estimate the loss for a given deviation from the target value. The first two methods, the multiplier method and the market research method, can be used to help make this estimate. Once we know $k$, we can estimate the hidden quality costs for any level of variation from the target value.

## Reporting Quality Cost Information

**Objective 2**

Prepare a quality cost report, and explain the difference between the conventional acceptable quality level (AQL) view and the zero-defects view of quality cost control.

A quality cost reporting system is essential for an organization that is serious about improving and controlling quality costs. The first and simplest step in creating such a system involves assessing current actual quality costs. A detailed listing of actual quality costs by category can provide two important insights. First, it can reveal the magnitude of the quality costs in each category, thus allowing managers to assess their financial impact. Second, it can show the distribution of quality costs by category, thus allowing managers to assess the relative importance of each category.

### Quality Cost Reports

We can assess the financial significance of quality costs more easily by expressing these costs as a percentage of actual sales. Exhibit 15–3, for example, reports the quality costs of Jensen Products for the fiscal year 2005.[15] According to the report, quality costs represent almost 12 percent of sales. Given the rule of thumb that

**EXHIBIT 15-3**

Quality Cost Report

| | Jensen Products Quality Cost Report For the Year Ended March 31, 2005 | | |
|---|---|---|---|
| | **Quality Costs** | | **Percentage (%) of Sales[a]** |
| Prevention costs: | | | |
| Quality training | $35,000 | | |
| Reliability engineering | 80,000 | $115,000 | 4.11 |
| Appraisal costs: | | | |
| Materials inspection | $20,000 | | |
| Product acceptance | 10,000 | | |
| Process acceptance | 38,000 | 68,000 | 2.43 |
| Internal failure costs: | | | |
| Scrap | $50,000 | | |
| Rework | 35,000 | 85,000 | 3.04 |
| External failure costs: | | | |
| Customer complaints | $25,000 | | |
| Warranty | 25,000 | | |
| Repair | 15,000 | 65,000 | 2.32 |
| Total quality costs | | $333,000 | 11.90[b] |

[a] Actual sales of $2,800,000.
[b] $333,000/$2,800,000 = 11.89 percent; (difference is due to rounding error.)

15. The quality cost report given in Exhibit 15–3 parallels the format used by ITT, except for minor differences. The ITT report combines the internal and external categories into one failure category, and it has a third column expressing quality costs as a percentage of a measure other than sales. For more details, see Morse, Roth, and Poston, *Measuring, Planning, and Controlling Quality Costs*: pp. 78-81.

quality costs should be no more than about 2.5 percent, Jensen Products has ample opportunity to improve profits by decreasing quality costs. However, this reduction in costs should come through improvement of quality. Reducing quality costs without any effort to improve quality could be disastrous.

Additional insight concerning the relative distribution of quality costs can be obtained by constructing a pie chart. Exhibit 15–4 provides such a chart, using the quality costs reported in Exhibit 15–3. Managers, of course, are responsible for assessing the optimal level of quality and for determining the relative expenditures in each category.

There are two views of optimal quality costs:

1. The traditional view, which calls for an *acceptable quality level.*
2. The contemporary view, referred to as *total quality control.*

Each view offers managers insights about how quality costs ought to be managed.

EXHIBIT 15-4

Relative Distribution of Quality Costs: Jensen Products

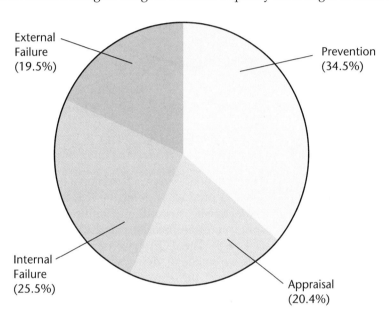

Quality Cost Function: Acceptable Quality Level (AQL) View

The acceptable quality view assumes that there is a tradeoff between control costs and failure costs. As control costs increase, failure costs should decrease. As long as the decrease in failure costs is greater than the corresponding increase in control costs, a company should continue increasing its efforts to prevent or detect nonconforming units. Eventually, a point is reached at which any additional increase in these efforts costs more than the corresponding reduction in failure costs. This point represents the minimum level of total quality costs. It is the optimal balance between control costs and failure costs, and it defines the **acceptable quality level (AQL).** This theoretical relationship is illustrated in Exhibit 15–5.

Exhibit 15–5 shows two cost functions: one for control costs and one for failure costs. The percentage of defective units increases as the amount spent on prevention and appraisal activities decreases. In contrast, failure costs increase as the number of defective units increases. The total quality cost function indicates that total quality costs decrease as quality improves—up to a point. After that point, no further improvement is possible. The model identifies an optimal level of defective units, and the company can work to achieve this level. This level of allowable defective units is the *acceptable quality level.*

**acceptable quality level (AQL)**

An approach to quality control that permits or allows defects to occur provided that they do not exceed a predetermined level.

EXHIBIT 15-5

AQL Quality Cost Graph

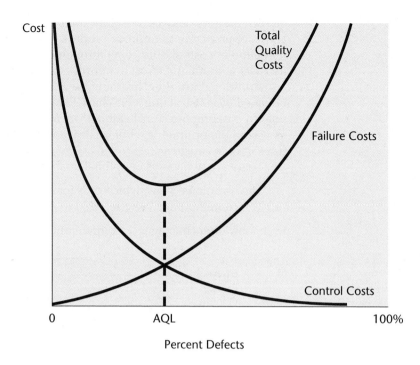

## Quality Cost Function: Zero-Defects View

The AQL perspective is based on a traditional defective product definition. In this sense, a product is defective if it falls outside the tolerance limits for a quality characteristic. Accordingly, failure costs are incurred only if the product fails to conform to specifications, and an optimal tradeoff exists between failure and control costs. The AQL view permits—in fact, it encourages—the production of a given number of defective units. This model prevailed in the quality control world until the late 1970s, when the AQL model was challenged by the *zero-defects model*. Essentially, the zero-defects model made the claim that it is cost-beneficial to reduce nonconforming units to zero. Companies producing fewer and fewer nonconforming units became more competitive than companies that continued applying the traditional AQL model.

In the mid-1980s, the zero-defects model was taken one step farther by the *robust quality model*, which challenged the definition of a defective unit. According to the robust view, a loss can occur from products that vary from a target value, and the greater the distance from the target the greater the loss. Furthermore, the loss is incurred even if the deviation is within the specification limits. In other words, variation from the ideal is costly, and specification limits serve no useful purpose—in fact, they may be deceptive. The zero-defects model understates the quality costs as well as potential savings from further quality improvements. The robust quality model has tightened the definition of a defective unit, refined the view of quality costs, and intensified the race for quality improvements by companies.

For companies operating in an intensely competitive environment, quality can provide an important competitive advantage. If the robust quality view is correct, companies can decrease the number of defective units, robustly defined, and simultaneously decrease total quality costs. This outcome appears to occur in companies that strive for a robust zero-defect state with zero tolerance. The optimal level of quality costs occurs when products meet their target values. The quest to find ways to achieve the target value creates a dynamic quality environment, as opposed to the static quality environment of the AQL model.

### Dynamic Nature of Quality Costs

The discovery that tradeoffs among quality cost categories can be managed differently from what is implied by the relationships portrayed in Exhibit 15–5 is analogous to the discovery that inventory cost tradeoffs can be managed differently from what the traditional inventory model (EOQ) implied. Essentially, as companies increase their prevention and appraisal costs and reduce their failure costs, they discover that they can cut back on prevention and appraisal costs. What initially appears to be a tradeoff turns into a permanent reduction in costs for *all* quality cost categories. Exhibit 15–6 illustrates the changes in quality cost relationships. It shows a total quality cost function that is consistent with the quality cost relationships described earlier. However, there are some key differences. First, control costs do not increase without limit as a robust zero-defect state is approached. Second, control costs may increase and then decrease as the robust state is approached. Third, failure costs can be driven to zero.

Suppose, for example, that a company has decided to improve the quality of its raw materials by implementing a supplier selection program. The objective of the program is to identify suppliers who are willing to meet certain quality standards. As the company implements the program, it may incur additional costs (e.g., review of suppliers, communication with suppliers, contract negotiations), and other prevention and appraisal costs may initially continue at their current levels. But once the program is fully implemented and evidence of failure cost reduction surfaces (e.g., less rework, fewer customer complaints, fewer repairs), the company may reduce the number of inspections of raw materials and the level of product acceptance activities. The net effect is a reduction of quality costs in all categories and an increase in quality as well!

This example is consistent with the strategy for reducing quality costs recommended by the American Society for Quality Control. The strategy is quite simple:

1. Attack failure costs directly in an attempt to drive them to zero.
2. Invest in "right" prevention activities to bring about improvement.
3. Reduce appraisal costs according to results achieved.
4. Continuously evaluate and redirect prevention efforts to gain further improvement.

EXHIBIT   15-6

Contemporary Quality
Cost Graph

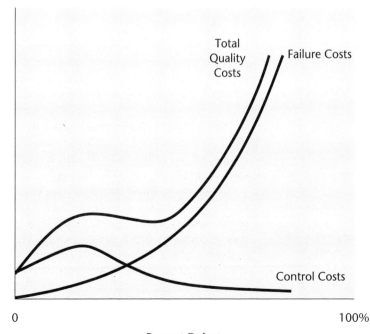

This strategy is based on the following premises:

1. A root cause exists for each failure.
2. Causes are preventable.
3. Prevention is always cheaper.[16]

### Activity-Based Management and Optimal Quality Costs

Activity-based management classifies activities as value-added and nonvalue-added, then keeps only those which add value. The same general principle can be applied to quality-related activities. Appraisal and failure activities and their associated costs are nonvalue-added and should therefore be eliminated. Prevention activities—performed efficiently—can be classified as value-added and should therefore be retained. Initially, however, prevention activities may not be performed efficiently, and activity reduction and activity selection (and perhaps even activity sharing) can be used to achieve the desired value-added state.

For example, Grede Foundries, Inc., the world's largest foundry company, has been tracking all four categories of quality costs for more than 15 years. Yet it does not report prevention costs as part of its final cost-of-quality figures, because it does not want its managers to reduce quality costs by cutting prevention activities. It feels strongly that spending money on prevention activities pays off. For example, it has found that a 1 percent reduction in scrap reduces external defects by about 5 percent.[17]

Once the activities are identified for each category, resource drivers can be used to improve cost assignment to individual activities. Root cost drivers can also be identified, especially for failure activities, and used to help managers understand what is causing the costs of activities. This information can be used to reduce quality costs to the level shown in Exhibit 15–6.

In effect, activity-based management supports the robust zero-defect view of quality costs. There is no optimal tradeoff between control and failure costs. The latter are nonvalue-added costs and should be reduced to zero by eliminating the associated nonvalue-added activities. Other control activities may be value-added but performed inefficiently. The costs caused by inefficiency are nonvalue-added and should also be reduced.

## Trend Analysis

Quality cost reports reveal the magnitude of quality costs and their distribution among the four categories, thus indicating opportunities for improvement. Once quality improvement measures are undertaken, it is important to determine whether quality costs are being reduced as planned. Quality cost reports do not reveal whether improvement has occurred over time. To ascertain this, it is useful to have a picture of how the quality improvement program has performed since its inception. Has the multiple-period trend—the overall change in quality costs—moved in the right direction? Have significant quality gains been made in each period?

**multiple-period quality trend report**

A graph that plots quality costs (as a percentage of sales) against time.

Answers to these questions can be obtained from a trend chart or graph that tracks the change in quality costs through time. Such a graph is called a **multiple-period quality trend report**. By plotting quality costs as a percentage of sales over time, a company can assess the overall trend of its quality program. Assume that a company implemented a quality improvement program at the beginning of 2002 and incurred the following quality costs:

---

16. Jack Campanella, ed., *Principles of Quality Costs* (Milwaukee: ASQC Quality Press, 1990): p. 12.

17. Nancy Chase, "Counting Costs, Reaping Returns," *Quality Magazine* (October 1998), www.qualitymag.com/articles/oct98/1098fl.html.

| | Quality Costs | Actual Sales | Costs as a Percentage (%) of Sales |
|---|---|---|---|
| 2001 | $440,000 | $2,200,000 | 20.0 |
| 2002 | 423,000 | 2,350,000 | 18.0 |
| 2003 | 412,500 | 2,750,000 | 15.0 |
| 2004 | 392,000 | 2,800,000 | 14.0 |
| 2005 | 280,000 | 2,800,000 | 10.0 |

The trend graph is shown in Exhibit 15–7, with 2001 being year 0, 2002 being year 1, and so on. Years are plotted on the horizontal axis and percentages of sales on the vertical axis. The ultimate quality cost objective of 3 percent—the target percentage—is represented as a horizontal line on the graph. The graph reveals that there has been a steady downward trend in quality costs expressed as a percentage of sales, but also that there is still ample room for improvement toward the long-term target percentage.

Additional insight can be obtained by plotting the trend for each individual quality category. Assume that the costs for each category are expressed as a percentage of sales for each year, as follows:

| | Prevention | Appraisal | Internal Failure | External Failure |
|---|---|---|---|---|
| 2001 | 2.0% | 2.0% | 6.0% | 10.0% |
| 2002 | 3.0 | 2.4 | 4.0 | 8.6 |
| 2003 | 3.0 | 3.0 | 3.0 | 6.0 |
| 2004 | 4.0 | 3.0 | 2.5 | 4.5 |
| 2005 | 4.1 | 2.4 | 2.0 | 1.5 |

The graph showing the trend for each category is provided in Exhibit 15–8. It shows that the company has had dramatic success in reducing external and internal failure costs. Appraisal costs have increased and then decreased. Prevention costs, however, have doubled as a percentage. Note also that the relative distribution of costs has changed. In 2001, failure costs were 80 percent of the total quality costs (0.16/0.20). In 2005, they are 35 percent of the total (0.035/0.10). The usefulness of such quality cost information for decision making and planning should not be underestimated.

**EXHIBIT 15-7**

Multiple-Period Trend Graph: Total Quality Costs

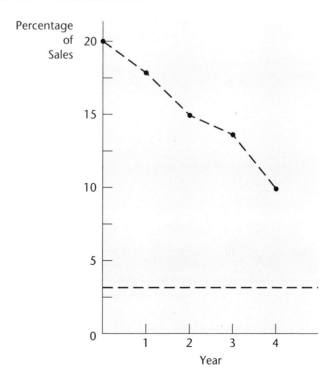

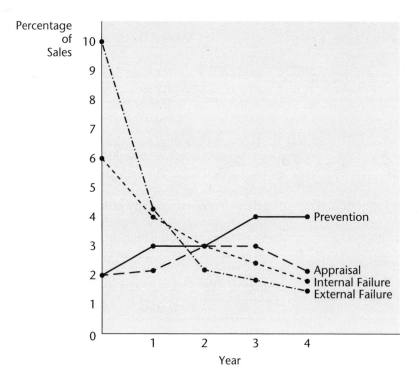

**EXHIBIT** 15-8

Multiple-Period Trend Graph: Individual Quality Cost Categories

# Using Quality Cost Information

### Objective 3

Explain why quality cost information is needed and how it is used.

The principal objective of reporting quality costs is to improve and facilitate managerial planning, control, and decision making. For example, in deciding whether to implement a supplier selection program to improve the quality of materials, a manager needs to assess current quality costs as well as projected program costs and savings by item and by category. When the costs and savings will occur must also be estimated. A capital budgeting analysis can then be completed to assess the merits of the proposed program. If the program is implemented, it is also important to monitor the program through proper performance reporting procedures.

The implementation and evaluation of quality programs is only one use of quality cost information. The following two scenarios illustrate the use of such information for two other purposes: strategic pricing decisions, and profitability analysis of new products.

## Scenario A: Strategic Pricing

Leola Wise, a marketing manager, muttered to herself as she reviewed the latest market share data for her company's low-priced electronic measurement instruments. Once again the share had dropped! Japanese firms were continuing to put pressure on this product line.

Anticipating this outcome, Leola had begun preparing a proposal for a significant price decrease for this line of products. A price decrease of $3 was needed to recapture the lost market share. The new price less the desired profit per unit produced a target cost that was less than the current actual cost of producing and selling the lower-level instruments. To continue producing this line, a cost reduction strategy was needed to re-establish the competitive position.

In the last executive meeting, the discussion had focused on how to achieve cost reductions. Ben Blackburn, the chief engineer, had indicated that process redesign could offer about half the needed cost reduction. Leola had suggested that the company adopt a total quality control position and work to reduce the cost of the lower-level instruments by decreasing quality costs.

To determine the potential magnitude of the cost reductions, she asked Earl Simpson, the controller, what the quality costs were for the lower-level instruments. Earl admitted that the costs were not tracked separately. For example, the cost of scrap was buried in the work-in-process account. But he promised to have some cost estimates—even if not complete—by the end of the month. His report is as follows:

**MEMO**

| | |
|---|---|
| **To:** | **Leola Wise** |
| **From:** | **Earl Simpson** |
| **Subject:** | **Quality Costs** |

As requested, I have assembled some quality cost estimates for the measurement instrument line. I have not included any costs of lost sales due to nonconforming products, as you are probably in a better position to assess them.

Estimated quality costs:

| | |
|---|---|
| Inspection of raw materials | $ 200,000 |
| Scrap | 800,000 |
| Rejects | 500,000 |
| Rework | 400,000 |
| Product inspection | 300,000 |
| Warranty work | 1,000,000 |
| Total costs | $3,200,000 |

On receiving the memo, Leola immediately called the quality control department and arranged a meeting with its manager, Art Smith. Art indicated that implementing total quality initiatives would reduce quality costs by 50 percent within 18 months. He had already begun planning the implementation of a new quality program. With this information, and using a volume of 1,000,000 units, Leola calculated that a 50 percent reduction in the quality costs associated with the lower-level instruments would reduce costs by about $1.60 per unit ($1,600,000/1,000,000).

This cost reduction constitutes slightly more than half of the necessary $3 reduction in the selling price (15 percent of $20). Based on this outcome, Leola decided to implement the price reduction in three phases: a $1 reduction immediately, a $1 reduction in 6 months, and the final reduction of $1 in 12 months. This phased reduction would likely prevent any further erosion of market share and would start increasing it sometime during the second phase. Phasing in the price reductions would give the quality department time to reduce costs so that large losses could be avoided.

Scenario A illustrates that quality cost information can contribute significantly to strategic decisions. It also shows that improving quality is not a panacea. The cost reductions may not be large enough to bear the full price reduction, and other productivity gains may be needed to ensure the long-term viability of products.

## Scenario B: New Product Analysis

Tara Anderson, the marketing manager, and Brittany Fox, the design engineer, of VKP Enterprises were both unhappy. They had been certain that their proposal for a new product was going to be approved. Instead, they received the following report from the controller's office.

**New Product Analysis, Project #675**

**Estimated product life cycle**: 2 years
**Projected sales potential**: 50,000 units (life cycle)
**Projected life-cycle income statement**:

| | | |
|---|---|---:|
| Sales (50,000 @ $60) | | $3,000,000 |
| Cost of inputs: | | |
| | Materials | 800,000 |
| | Labour | 400,000 |
| | Scrap | 150,000 |
| | Inspection | 350,000 |
| | Repair work | 200,000 |
| | Product development | 500,000 |
| | Selling | 300,000 |
| Total costs | | $2,700,000 |
| | Life-cycle income | $ 300,000 |

**Decision**: Reject
**Reason(s)**: Life-cycle income is less than the required return on sales of 18 percent.

"You know," Tara remarked, "I can't quite believe this report. Why don't we ask Bob how he came up with these figures?"

"I agree," said Brittany. "I'll arrange a meeting for tomorrow. I'll ask him to provide more detail than just the aggregate figures shown in the report."

The next day, the following conversation took place just after Tara and Brittany had reviewed the detailed cost projections supplied by Bob Brown, the assistant controller.

**Brittany**: "Bob, I would like to know why there is a three-dollar-per-unit scrap cost. And the inspection costs—they seem high, too. Can you explain these costs?"

**Bob**: "Sure. The scrap cost is comparable to what we have for other products. Also, as you know, we have a 10 percent destructive sampling requirement for these types of products."

**Brittany**: "Well, I think you've overlooked the new design features of this new product. Its design virtually eliminates any waste—especially when you consider that the product will be made on a numerically controlled machine."

**Tara**: "Also, this two-dollar-per-unit charge for repair work should be eliminated. The new design Brittany is proposing solves the failure problems we've had with related products. It also means that $100,000 of fixed costs associated with the repair activity can be eliminated. Furthermore, because of the new design, destructive sampling is not required, and we need one less inspector than you've budgeted."

**Bob**: "Brittany, how certain are you that this new design will eliminate some of these quality problems?"

**Brittany**: "I'm absolutely positive. The early prototypes did exactly as we expected. The results of those tests are included in the proposal. You must not have read the prototype results."

**Bob**: "Right, I didn't. Eliminating scrap reduces the unit-level variable costs by $3 per unit. I also see where the repair and inspection activities are overcosted. We need only one inspector, with a salary of $50,000. And eliminating the repair activity saves $200,000. That means the projected life-cycle profits are $650,000 more than I've projected, which in turn means the return on sales is more than 30 percent."

Scenario B illustrates the importance of classifying quality costs by behaviour. It also reinforces the importance of identifying and reporting quality costs separately. The new product was designed to reduce its quality costs, and only by knowing the quality costs assigned could Brittany and Tara have discovered the error in the life-cycle income analysis.

Reporting quality costs so that they can be used for decision making is just one objective of a good quality costing system. Another objective is controlling quality costs—a factor critical in helping expected outcomes of decisions to materialize.

# Productivity: Measurement and Control

**Objective 4**

Explain what productivity is, and calculate the impact of productivity changes on profits.

**productivity**

The efficient production of output, using the least quantity of inputs possible.

**total productive efficiency**

The point at which technical and price efficiency are achieved.

**technical efficiency**

The point at which, for any mix of inputs that will produce a given output, no more of any one input is used than is absolutely necessary.

**input tradeoff efficiency**

The least-cost, technically efficient mix of outputs.

**Productivity** is concerned with producing output efficiently. Specifically, it addresses the relationship between outputs and the inputs used to produce those outputs. Usually, different combinations or mixes of inputs can be used to produce a given level of output. **Total productive efficiency** is the point at which two conditions are satisfied:

1. For any mix of inputs to produce a given output, no more inputs are used than are necessary to produce that output.
2. Given the mixes that satisfy the first condition, the least costly mix is chosen.

The first condition is driven by technical relationships and is referred to as **technical efficiency**. Viewing activities as inputs, the first condition requires eliminating all nonvalue-added activities and performing value-added activities with the minimal quantities needed to produce the given output. The second condition is driven by relative input price relationships, and is referred to as **input tradeoff efficiency**. Input prices determine the relative proportions of each input that should be used. Deviation from these fixed proportions creates input tradeoff inefficiency.

Productivity improvement programs attempt to move toward a state of total productive efficiency. Technical improvements in productivity can be achieved by using fewer inputs to produce the same outputs or by producing more outputs using the same or relatively fewer inputs.

For example, in 1992, Lantech, a wrapping-machine producer, produced 8 wrapping machines per day with 50 workers—an average of 0.16 machines per worker. By 1998, the output had increased to 14 machines per day using 20 workers—an average of 0.7 machines per worker. Using 1992 productivity standards, about 87.5 workers would have been needed to produce 14 machines. Thus, the output increased and fewer workers were needed. [18]

Exhibit 15–9 illustrates the three ways to improve technical efficiency. The output is tons of steel, and the inputs are labour (number of workers) and capital (investment in equipment). Note that the relative proportions of the inputs are held constant so that all productivity improvement is attributable to technical efficiency.

Productivity improvement can also be achieved by trading more costly inputs for less costly inputs. Exhibit 15–10 illustrates the possibility of improving productivity by increasing input tradeoff efficiency. Most individuals think of technical efficiency in connection with productivity improvement; however, input tradeoff efficiency can also offer significant opportunities for increasing overall economic efficiency.

Choosing the right combination of inputs can be as critical as choosing the right quantity of inputs. Note in Exhibit 15–10 that Input Combination I produces the same output as Input Combination II—but that the cost is $5 million less. Total measures of productivity are usually a combination of changes in technical and input tradeoff efficiency.

18. Melissa Larson, "Are You Ready for Kaizen?" *Quality Magazine* (June 1998), www.qualitymag.com/articles/jun98/0698fl.html.

**EXHIBIT   15-9**

Technical Efficiency

**Current Productivity**

Inputs:

Labour

Capital

Output:

**Same Output, Fewer Inputs**

Inputs:

Labour

Capital

Output:

**More Outputs, Same Inputs**

Inputs:

Labour

Capital

Output:

**More Outputs, Fewer Inputs**

Inputs:

Labour

Capital

Output:

**EXHIBIT   15-10**

Input Tradeoff Efficiency

**Technically Efficient Combination I:**
**Total Cost of Inputs = $20,000,000**

Labour

Capital

**Technically Efficient Combination II:**
**Total Cost of Inputs = $25,000,000**

Labour

Capital

## Partial Productivity Measurement

**productivity measurement**

The assessment of productivity changes.

**Productivity measurement** is simply a quantitative assessment of productivity changes. The objective is to assess whether productive efficiency has increased or decreased. Productivity measurement can be actual or prospective. *Actual* productivity measurement allows managers to assess, monitor, and control changes. *Prospective* measurement is forward-looking and serves as input for strategic decision making. Specifically, prospective measurement allows managers to compare the relative benefits of different input combinations and then choose the inputs and input mix that provide the greatest benefits. Productivity measures can be developed for each input separately or for all inputs jointly. Measuring productivity for one input at a time is called **partial productivity measurement**.

**partial productivity measurement**

A ratio that measures productive efficiency for one input.

### Partial Productivity Measurement Defined

The productivity of a single input is typically measured by calculating the ratio of the output to the input:

$$\text{Productivity ratio} = \text{Output/Input}$$

**operational productivity measure**

A measure that is expressed in physical terms.

**financial productivity measure**

A productivity measure in which inputs and outputs are expressed in dollars.

Because the productivity of only one input is being measured, the measure is called a *partial productivity measure*. If both the output and input are measured in physical quantities, the measure is an **operational productivity measure**. If either the output or the input is expressed in dollars, the measure is a **financial productivity measure**. Assume, for example, that in 2004, Kankul Company produced 120,000 motors for air-conditioning units and used 40,000 hours of labour. The labour productivity ratio is 3 motors per hour (120,000/40,000). This is an operational measure, since the units are expressed in physical terms. If the selling price of each motor is $50 and the cost of labour is $12 per hour, then output and input can be expressed in dollars. The labour productivity ratio, expressed in financial terms, is $12.50 of revenue per dollar of labour cost ($6,000,000/$480,000).

### Partial Productivity Measures and Measuring Changes in Productive Efficiency

**base period**

A prior period used to set the benchmark for measuring productivity changes.

The labour productivity ratio of 3 motors per hour gives an indication of Kankul's productivity in 2004. But by itself, the ratio conveys little information about productive efficiency or changes in productivity. It is possible, however, to make a statement about increasing or decreasing productive efficiency by measuring changes in productivity. To do so, we compare the actual current productive measure to the same productivity measure from a prior period. This prior period, referred to as the **base period**, sets a benchmark, or standard, for measuring changes in productive efficiency.

The prior period can be any period desired. It could, for example, be the preceding year, the preceding week, or the period during which the last batch of products was produced. For strategic evaluations, the base period usually chosen is a prior year. For operational control, the base period tends to be close to the current period—perhaps the preceding batch of products or the preceding week.

Assuming that 2004 is the base period, the labour productivity standard is 3 motors per hour. Further assume that late in 2004, Kankul implemented a new procedure that was expected to use less labour. In 2005, there were 150,000 motors produced, using 37,500 hours of labour. The labour productivity ratio for 2005 is 4 motors per hour (150,000/37,500). The *change* in productivity is a 1-unit-per-hour increase in productivity from 3 units per hour in 2004 to 4 units per hour in 2005. The change is a significant improvement in labour productivity and provides evidence supporting the efficacy of the new process.

### Advantages of Partial Productivity Measures

Partial productivity measures allow managers to focus on the use of a particular input. Partial operational measures are easy to interpret and use for assessing the productivity of operating personnel. Labourers, for instance, can relate to units produced per hour or units produced per kilogram of material. Since partial operational measures deal with specific inputs over which operational personnel have reasonable control, such measures can provide meaningful and understandable feedback to operational personnel. This increases the likelihood that they will accept the measures. Furthermore, operational standards are often short-term, such as the productivity ratios of prior batches of goods. Using such standards, management can track productivity trends on a timely basis.

### Disadvantages of Partial Productivity Measures

Partial productivity measures, used in isolation, can be misleading. A decline in the productivity of one input may be necessary to increase the productivity of another. Such a tradeoff is desirable if overall costs decline, but the effect would be missed by using either partial measure.

For example, changing a process so that direct labourers take less time to assemble a product may increase scrap and waste while leaving total output unchanged. Labour productivity has increased, but productive use of materials has declined. If the increase in the cost of waste and scrap outweighs the savings of the decreased labour, overall productivity has declined.

Two important conclusions can be drawn from this example. First, because the possibility of tradeoffs exists, we need a total measure of productivity. Only by looking at the total productivity effect of all inputs can managers accurately draw any conclusions about overall productivity. Second, because of possible tradeoffs, a total measure of productivity must assess the aggregate financial consequences; it should therefore be a financial measure.

## Total Productivity Measurement

**total productivity measurement**

The assessment of productive efficiency for all inputs combined.

Measuring productivity for all inputs at once is called **total productivity measurement**. In practice, it may not be necessary to measure the effect of all inputs. Many companies measure the productivity of only those factors which are thought to be relevant indicators of organizational performance and success. Thus, in practice, total productivity measurement focuses on a limited number of inputs that, in total, indicate organizational success. In either case, total productivity measurement requires the development of a multifactor measurement approach.

A common multifactor approach suggested in the productivity literature (but rarely found in practice) is the use of aggregate productivity indexes. Aggregate indexes are complex and difficult to interpret and have not been widely accepted. Two approaches that have gained some acceptance are *profile measurement* and *profit-linked productivity measurement*.

### Profile Productivity Measurement

**profile measurement**

A series or vector of separate and distinct partial operational measures.

Producing a product involves numerous critical inputs, such as labour, materials, capital, and energy. **Profile measurement** provides a series or a vector of separate and distinct partial operational measures. Profiles can be compared over time to provide information about productivity changes.

To illustrate the profile approach, let's return to the Kankul Company example. As before, Kankul implements a new production and assembly process in 2005 that affects both labour and materials. The following data for 2004 and 2005 are available:

|  | 2004 | 2005 |
|---|---|---|
| Number of motors produced | 120,000 | 150,000 |
| Labour hours used | 40,000 | 37,500 |
| Materials used (kilograms) | 1,200,000 | 1,428,571 |

Exhibit 15–11 provides productivity ratio profiles for each year. As you can see, the productivity increased for both labour and materials, from 3 to 4 for labour and from 0.100 to 0.105 for materials. The profile comparison provides enough information for a manager to conclude that the new assembly process has improved overall productivity. The ratios, however, do not reveal the *value* of this improvement. Although profile analysis can provide managers with useful insights about changes in productivity, it does not always reveal the nature of the overall change in productivity.

EXHIBIT 15-11

Productivity
Measurement: Profile
Analysis with No
Tradeoffs

|  | Partial Productivity Ratios | |
|---|---|---|
|  | 2004 Profile[a] | 2005 Profile[b] |
| Labour productivity ratio | 3.000 | 4.000 |
| Materials productivity ratio | 0.100 | 0.105 |

[a] Labour: 120,000/40,000; materials: 120,000/1,200,000
[b] Labour: 150,000/37,500; materials: 150,000/1,428,571

In some cases, profile analysis will not provide any clear indication of the overall productivity change. To illustrate this, assume that 1,700,000 kilograms of materials were used in 2005, but all other data remain unchanged. The revised productivity profiles for 2004 and 2005 are presented in Exhibit 15–12. The comparison of productivity profiles provides a mixed signal: productivity for labour has increased from 3 to 4, but productivity for materials has decreased from 0.100 to 0.088.

EXHIBIT 15-12

Productivity
Measurement: Profile
Analysis with Tradeoffs

|  | Partial Productivity Ratios | |
|---|---|---|
|  | 2004 Profile[a] | 2005 Profile[b] |
| Labour productivity ratio | 3.000 | 4.000 |
| Materials productivity ratio | 0.100 | 0.088 |

[a] Labour: 120,000/40,000; materials: 120,000/1,200,000
[b] Labour: 150,000/37,500; materials: 150,000/1,700,000

The new process has caused a tradeoff in the two productivity measures. Furthermore, while a profile analysis reveals that the tradeoff exists, it does not reveal whether the tradeoff is favourable or unfavourable. If the financial effect of the productivity changes is positive, the tradeoff is favourable; otherwise, it is unfavourable. The value of the productivity change would constitute an overall measure of productivity and allow management to assess the financial impact of the change in the assembly process.

### Profit-Linked Productivity Measurement

Assessing the effects of productivity changes on current profits is one way to value productivity changes. Some of the profit change from the base period to the current period is likely attributable to productivity changes. The measurement of such changes is defined as **profit-linked productivity measurement**.

**profit-linked
productivity
measurement**

The assessment of the amount of profit change (from the base period to the current period) attributable to productivity changes.

The assessment of the effect of productivity changes on profits in the current period can help managers understand the financial impact of productivity changes. Linking productivity changes to profits can be accomplished as follows:

1.  Calculate the cost of inputs that would have been used in the absence of any productivity change for the current period.
2.  Calculate the actual cost of inputs used.
3.  Compare the costs in Steps 1 and 2. The difference in the costs is the amount by which profits changed as a result of productivity changes.

First, the inputs that would have been used for the current period in the absence of a productivity change must be calculated. Let $PQ$ represent this productivity-neutral quantity of inputs. To determine $PQ$ for a particular input, divide the output in the current period by the input's base period productivity ratio:

$$PQ = \text{Current output/Base period productivity ratio}$$

To illustrate the application of this profit-linked rule, let's return to the Kankul example with input tradeoffs, supplemented with some additional cost information, as follows:

|                                | 2004      | 2005      |
| ------------------------------ | --------- | --------- |
| Number of motors produced      | 120,000   | 150,000   |
| Labour hours used              | 40,000    | 37,500    |
| Materials used (kilograms)     | 1,200,000 | 1,700,000 |
| Unit selling price (motors)    | $50       | $48       |
| Wages per labour hour          | $11       | $12       |
| Cost per kilograms of material | $ 2       | $ 3       |

Current 2005 output is 150,000 motors. The base period productivity ratios in Exhibit 15–12 were 3 and 0.10 for labour and materials, respectively. Using this information, we can compute the productivity-neutral quantity for each input as follows:

$$PQ \text{ (labour)} = 150,000/3 = 50,000 \text{ hours}$$
$$PQ \text{ (materials)} = 150,000/0.10 = 1,500,000 \text{ kilograms}$$

$PQ$ represents the labour and materials inputs that would have been used in 2005, assuming no productivity change. The total cost is the sum of the labour and material costs, computed by multiplying each individual input quantity ($PQ$) by its current price ($P$), as follows:[19]

| Cost of labour (50,000 × $12)       | $  600,000 |
| ----------------------------------- | ---------- |
| Cost of materials: (1,500,000 × $3) | 4,500,000  |
| Total $PQ$ cost                     | $5,100,000 |

The total actual cost of inputs is the sum of the labour and material costs, obtained by multiplying the actual quantity ($AQ$) by the current input price ($P$) for each input, as follows:

| Cost of labour (37,500 × $12)      | $  450,000 |
| ---------------------------------- | ---------- |
| Cost of materials (1,700,000 × $3) | 5,100,000  |
| Total current cost                 | $5,550,000 |

Finally, the productivity effect on profits is computed by subtracting the total current cost from the total $PQ$ cost.

---

19. Base period prices are often used to value productivity changes. It has been shown, however, that current input prices should be used for accurate profit-linked productivity measurement. See Don R. Hansen, Maryanne Mowen, and Lawrence Hammer, "Profit-Linked Productivity Measurement," *Journal of Management Accounting Research* (Fall 1992): pp. 79-98.

$$\text{Profit-linked productivity effect} = \text{Total } PQ \text{ cost} - \text{Total current cost}$$
$$= \$5,100,000 - \$5,550,000$$
$$= \$450,000 \text{ decrease in profits}$$

The calculation of the profit-linked effect is summarized in Exhibit 15–13. It reveals that the net effect of the process change was unfavourable. Profits declined by $450,000 because of the productivity changes. Note also that profit-linked productivity effects can be assigned to individual inputs. The increase in labour productivity created a $150,000 increase in profits; however, the drop in materials productivity caused a $600,000 *decrease* in profits.

EXHIBIT **15-13**

Profit-Linked Productivity
Measurement

|  | (1) | (2) | (3) | (4) | (2) – (4) |
|---|---|---|---|---|---|
| Input | $PQ^a$ | $PQ \times P$ | $AQ$ | $AQ \times P$ | $(PQ \times P) - (AQ \times P)$ |
| Labour | 50,000 | $600,000 | 37,500 | $450,000 | $150,000 |
| Materials | 1,500,000 | 4,500,000 | 1,700,000 | 5,100,000 | (600,000) |
| Total |  | $5,100,000 |  | $5,550,000 | $(450,000) |

[a] Labour: 150,000/3; materials: 150,000/0.10

Most of the profit decrease came from an increase in materials usage. Apparently, waste, scrap, and spoiled units are much greater with the new process. Thus, the profit-linked measure provides partial measurement effects, as well as the total measurement effect. The total profit-linked productivity measure is the sum of the individual partial measures.

This property makes the profit-linked measure ideal for assessing tradeoffs. A much clearer picture of the effects of the changes in productivity thereby emerges. Unless waste and scrap can be brought under better control, Kankul ought to return to its old assembly process. Of course, it is possible that the learning effects of the new process have not yet been fully captured and that further improvements in labour productivity may be observed later. As labour becomes more proficient at the new process, it is possible that the materials usage could also decrease.

## Price Recovery Component

**price-recovery
component**

The difference between
the total profit change
and the profit-linked
productivity change.

The profit-linked measure computes the amount of profit change from the base period to the current period attributable to productivity changes. It generally does not equal the total profit change between the two periods. The difference between the total profit change and the profit-linked productivity change is called the **price recovery component**. It is the change in revenues less a change in the costs of inputs, assuming no productivity changes. Thus it measures the ability of revenue changes to cover changes in the cost of inputs, assuming no productivity change. To calculate the price recovery component, we must calculate the change in profits for each period, as follows:

|  | 2005 | 2004 | Difference |
|---|---|---|---|
| Revenues[a] | $7,200,000 | $6,000,000 | $ 1,200,000 |
| Costs[b] | 5,550,000 | 2,840,000 | 2,710,000 |
| Income | $1,650,000 | $3,160,000 | $(1,510,000) |

[a] $48 × 150,000; $50 × 120,000
[b] ($12 × 37,500) + ($3 × 1,700,000); ($11 × 40,000) + ($2 × 1,200,000)

$$\text{Price recovery} = \text{Profit change} - \text{Profit-linked productivity change}$$
$$= (\$1,510,000) - (\$450,000)$$
$$= (\$1,060,000)$$

The increase in revenues is not sufficient to cover the increase in the cost of inputs. The decrease in productivity simply aggravated the price recovery problem. Note, however, that increases in productivity can be used to offset price recovery losses.

## Quality and Productivity

Improving quality may improve productivity, and vice versa. For example, if rework is reduced by producing fewer defective units, less labour and fewer materials are used to produce the same output. Reducing the number of defective units improves quality, and reducing the amount of inputs used improves productivity.

Since most quality improvements reduce the amount of resources used to produce and sell an organization's output, most quality improvements will improve productivity. Thus, quality improvements will generally be reflected in productivity measures. However, there are other ways to improve productivity. A company may produce a good with few or no defects but still have an inefficient process.

For example, consider a product that passes through two 5-minute processes. Assume that no defects exist. One unit requires 10 minutes to pass through both processes. Currently, units are produced in batches of 1,200. Process 1 produces 1,200 units. The batch is then conveyed by forklift to another location, where the units pass through Process 2. Thus, for each process, a total of 6,000 minutes, or 100 hours, are needed to produce a batch. The 1,200 finished units require a total of 200 hours (100 hours for each process) plus conveyance time of 15 minutes.

By redesigning the manufacturing process, the company can improve efficiency. Suppose that the second process is relocated close enough to the first process that as soon as a unit is completed by the first process, it can be passed to the second process. In this way, the first and second processes can be working at the same time. The startup of the second process no longer has to wait for the completion of 1,200 units plus conveyance time. The total time to produce 1,200 units is now 6,000 minutes, plus the waiting time for the first unit of 5 minutes. Thus, the production time for 1,200 units has been reduced from 200 hours and 15 minutes to 100 hours and 5 minutes, and more output can be produced with fewer inputs.

## Summary of Learning Objectives

### 1. Identify and describe the four types of quality costs.

To understand quality costs, it is first necessary to understand what is meant by quality. There are two types of quality: quality of design and quality of conformance. The quality of design is concerned with quality differences that arise for products with the same function but different specifications. In contrast, the quality of conformance is concerned with meeting the specifications required by the product. Quality costs are incurred when products fail to meet design specifications (and are therefore associated with quality of conformance). There are four categories of quality costs: prevention, appraisal, internal failure, and external failure. Prevention costs are those incurred to prevent poor quality. Appraisal costs are those incurred to detect poor quality. Internal failure costs are those incurred when products fail to conform to requirements, and this lack of conformity is discovered before an external sale. External failure costs are those incurred when products fail to conform to requirements after a sale is made.

### 2. Prepare a quality cost report, and explain the difference between the conventional acceptable quality level (AQL) view and the zero-defects view of quality cost control.

A quality cost report is prepared by listing costs for

each item within each of the four major quality cost categories. There are two views concerning the optimal distribution of quality costs: the AQL view and the zero-defects view. The AQL view holds that a tradeoff exists between costs of failure and prevention, and appraisal costs. This tradeoff produces an optimal level of performance called the acceptable quality level. AQL is the level at which the number of defects allowed minimizes total quality costs. In contrast, the zero-defects view promotes total quality control. Total quality control maintains that the conflict between failure and appraisal and prevention costs is more conjectural than real. The actual optimal level of defects is the zero-defect level, and companies should be striving to achieve this level of quality. Although quality costs do not vanish at this level, they are much lower than the optimum envisioned by the AQL view.

### 3. Explain why quality cost information is needed and how it is used.

Quality cost information is needed to help managers control quality performance and to serve as input for decision making. It can be used to evaluate the overall performance of quality improvement programs. It can also be used to help improve a variety of managerial decisions—for example, strategic pricing and new product analysis. Perhaps the most important observation is that quality cost information is fundamental to a company's pursuit of continuous improvement. Quality is one of the major competitive dimensions for world-class companies.

### 4. Explain what productivity is, and calculate the impact of productivity changes on profits.

Productivity is concerned with the efficient use of inputs in the production of outputs. Partial measures of productivity evaluate the efficient use of single inputs. Total measures of productivity assess the efficiency of all inputs. Profit-linked productivity effects are calculated by using the profit linkage rule. Essentially, the profit-linked effect is computed by taking the difference between the cost of inputs that would have been used without any productivity change and the cost of the actual inputs used. Because possible input tradeoffs exist, it is essential to asess the financial effect of productivity changes in order to determine their overall effects.

## Key Terms

## Review Problems

### I. QUALITY

At the beginning of 2005, Kare Company initiated a quality improvement program. Considerable effort was expended to reduce the number of defective units produced. By the end of the year, reports from the production manager revealed that both scrap and rework had decreased. The president was pleased but wanted an assessment of the financial impact of these improvements. To make this assessment, the following financial data were collected for the preceding and current years:

|                    | 2004         | 2005         |
| ------------------ | ------------ | ------------ |
| Sales              | $10,000,000  | $10,000,000  |
| Scrap              | 400,000      | 300,000      |
| Rework             | 600,000      | 400,000      |
| Product inspection | 100,000      | 125,000      |
| Product warranty   | 800,000      | 600,000      |
| Quality training   | 40,000       | 80,000       |
| Materials inspection | 60,000     | 40,000       |

### Required:

1. Classify the costs as prevention, appraisal, internal failure, and external failure costs.
2. Compute the quality costs as a percentage of sales for each year. By how much has profit increased because of quality improvements? If the quality costs for 2005 could be reduced to 2.5 percent of sales, how much additional profit would be available through quality improvements?
3. Prepare a quality cost report for 2005.

### Solution

1. Appraisal costs: product inspection and materials inspection; prevention costs: quality training; internal failure costs: scrap and rework; external failure costs: warranty.
2. For 2004—total quality costs: $2,000,000; percentage of sales: 20 percent ($2,000,000/$10,000,000). For 2005—total quality costs: $1,545,000; percentage of sales: 15.45 percent ($1,545,000/$10,000,000). Profit has increased by $455,000. If quality costs dropped to 2.5 percent of sales, $1,295,000 in profit improvement would be possible ($1,545,000 − $250,000).

3.

**Kare Company**
**Quality Cost Report**
**For the Year Ended 2005**

|  | Quality Costs | | Percentage of Sales |
|---|---|---|---|
| Prevention costs: | | | |
| Quality training | $ 80,000 | $ 80,000 | 0.80 |
| Appraisal costs: | | | |
| Product inspection | $125,000 | | |
| Materials inspection | 40,000 | 165,000 | 1.65 |
| Internal failure costs: | | | |
| Scrap | $300,000 | | |
| Rework | 400,000 | 700,000 | 7.00 |
| External failure costs: | | | |
| Product warranty | $600,000 | 600,000 | 6.00 |
| Total quality costs | | $1,545,000 | 15.45 |

## II. PRODUCTIVITY

Bearing Company made some changes at the end of 2004 that it hoped would improve the efficiency of input usage. At the end of 2005, the president wants to assess the effect of the changes on productivity. The data needed for the assessment are as follows:

|  | 2004 | 2005 |
|---|---|---|
| Output (units) | 5,000 | 6,000 |
| Output prices | $10 | $10 |
| Materials (kilograms) | 4,000 | 4,200 |
| Materials unit price | $3 | $4 |
| Labour (hours) | 2,500 | 2,400 |
| Labour rate per hour | $8 | $8 |
| Power (kilowatt-hours) | 1,000 | 1,500 |
| Price per kilowatt-hour | $2 | $3 |

### Required:

1. Compute the partial operational measures for each input for both 2004 and 2005. What can be said about productivity improvement?
2. Prepare an income statement for each year, and calculate the total change in profits.
3. Calculate the profit-linked productivity measure for 2005. What can be said about the productivity program?
4. Calculate the price recovery component. What does this tell you?

### Solution

1. Partial measures:

|  | 2004 | 2005 |
|---|---|---|
| Materials | 5,000/4,000 = 1.25 | 6,000/4,200 = 1.43 |
| Labour | 5,000/2,500 = 2.00 | 6,000/2,400 = 2.50 |
| Power | 5,000/1,000 = 5.00 | 6,000/1,500 = 4.00 |

Efficiency increased for materials and labour and decreased for power. The outcome is mixed, and no statement about overall productivity improvement can be made without considering the tradeoff.

2. Income statements:

|  | 2004 | 2005 |
|---|---|---|
| Sales | $50,000 | $60,000 |
| Costs | 34,000 | 40,500 |
| Income | $16,000 | $19,500 |

Total change in profits: $19,500 − $16,000 = $3,500 increase

3. Profit-linked measurement:

|  | (1) | (2) | (3) | (4) | (2) - (4) |
|---|---|---|---|---|---|
| Input | $PQ^a$ | $PQ \times P$ | $AQ$ | $AQ \times P$ | $(PQ \times P) - (AQ \times P)$ |
| Materials | 4,800 | $19,200 | 4,200 | $16,800 | $2,400 |
| Labour | 3,000 | 24,000 | 2,400 | 19,200 | 4,800 |
| Power | 1,200 | 3,600 | 1,500 | 4,500 | (900) |
|  |  | $46,800 |  | $40,500 | $6,300 |

$^a$ Materials: 6,000/1.25; labour: 6,000/2; power: 6,000/5

The increase in efficiency for materials and labour more than offsets the increased usage of power. Thus, the productivity program is considered successful.

4. Price recovery:

Price recovery component = Profit change − Profit-linked productivity change
= $3,500 − $6,300
= ($2,800)

Without productivity improvement, profits would have declined by $2,800. The increase of $10,000 in revenues would not have offset the increase in the costs of inputs. The costs of inputs without a productivity increase would have been $46,800 (Requirement 3, column 2). The increase in the input costs without productivity would have been $12,800 ($46,800 − $34,000). It is $2,800 higher than the increase in revenues. The profitability increase occurred due to productivity.

## Questions for Writing and Discussion

1. Explain what is meant by "quality."

2. What is reliability? What is durability?

3. What is quality of conformance?

4. Explain the difference between the traditional and robust views of conformance.

5. Why are quality costs the costs of doing things wrong?

6. Identify and discuss the four kinds of quality costs.

7. Explain why external failure costs can be more devastating to a company than internal failure costs.

8. What are hidden quality costs? Provide an example.

9. What are the three methods for estimating hidden quality costs?

10. Discuss the value of a quality cost report.

11. What is the difference between the AQL model and the zero-defects model?

12. What is the difference between the zero-defects model and the robust quality model?

13. Explain the purpose of multiple-period trend analysis for quality costs.

14. Define total productive efficiency.

15. Explain the difference between partial and total measures of productivity.

16. Discuss the advantages and disadvantages of partial measures of productivity.

17. How can a manager measure productivity improvement?

18. What is profit-linked productivity measurement?

19. Explain why profit-linked productivity measurement is important.

20. What is the price-recovery component?

21. Can productivity improvements be achieved without improving quality? Explain.

22. Why is it important for managers to be concerned with both productivity and quality?

23. What are the differences between quality and productivity? Similarities?

## Exercises

**15–1**

Quality Costs

LO 1

Choose the *best* answer for each of the following multiple choice questions:

1. The *best* operational definition of quality is
   a. how consistently and well a product functions.
   b. the probability that a product performs its functions as intended for a specified length of time.
   c. how well the product meets its specifications.
   d. the suitability of the product for carrying out its intended functions.
   e. None of the above.

2. Conforming to specifications means that the specifications of a product
   a. fall within an acceptable range of values.
   b. exactly meet their targeted values.
   c. include all essential aspects except serviceability.
   d. are strictly controlled by quality audits.
   e. Both a and b, depending on whether the traditional or robust view of conformance is emphasized.

3. The costs of quality are costs that exist
   a. to ensure that good quality is achieved.
   b. because poor quality may or does exist.
   c. to prevent poor quality.
   d. to determine whether products or services are conforming to their requirements.
   e. All of the above.

4. The costs associated with supplier evaluation and selection are
   a. prevention costs.
   b. appraisal costs.
   c. internal failure costs.
   d. external failure costs.
   e. None of the above.

5. The costs associated with rework are
   a. prevention costs.
   b. appraisal costs.
   c. internal failure costs.
   d. external failure costs.
   e. None of the above.

**15–2**

Quality Cost
Classification

LO1

Classify the following quality activities as prevention costs, appraisal costs, internal failure costs, or external failure costs:

1. Customers do not want second-class products. However, if they are sent slightly defective products, they may be willing to keep them, provided they are given a price reduction.
2. Components from suppliers are carefully inspected.
3. Workers sand and stain a piece of wood, which later warps. It is then discarded as useless.
4. An automobile company recalls a model to repair a defective transmission.
5. A tire manufacturer is sued for deaths caused by a defective tire.
6. Designs are verified and reviewed to evaluate the quality of new products.
7. New personnel are trained in quality circle methods.
8. Work is stopped to correct a process malfunction (discovered using statistical process control procedures).
9. Returned products are packaged and shipped.
10. Rework is reinspected.
11. A defective product is replaced with a good one.
12. An internal audit is done to ensure that quality policies are being followed.
13. A product is redesigned to reduce the number of worker mistakes leading to a defective product.
14. Purchase orders are corrected to reflect the correct items and quantities.
15. Adjustments are made to accounts receivable to compensate for returned goods and price concessions.
16. New products are tested to ensure that they function as intended.
17. Field service personnel are sent to repair products on site.
18. Software is corrected for defects.
19. Suppliers are evaluated to assess whether they are capable of providing non-defective components.
20. Subassemblies are inspected.
21. Customer complaints are processed.
22. Prototypes are inspected and tested.
23. A worker accidentally drills a hole in a steel plate. The hole must be repaired for the plate to be useful.

**15–3**

During 2005 and 2006, Huntington Company reported sales of $6,000,000 for each year. The company listed the following quality costs for the past two years. Assume that all changes in the quality costs are due to a quality improvement program.

| | 2005 | 2006 |
|---|---|---|
| Design review | $ 150,000 | $ 300,000 |
| Recalls | 200,000 | 100,000 |
| Reinspection | 100,000 | 50,000 |
| Materials inspection | 60,000 | 40,000 |
| Quality training | 40,000 | 100,000 |
| Process acceptance | — | 50,000 |
| Scrap | 145,000 | 35,000 |
| Lost sales (estimated) | 300,000 | 200,000 |
| Product inspection | 50,000 | 30,000 |
| Returned goods | 155,000 | 95,000 |
| Total | $1,200,000 | $1,000,000 |

**Required:**
1. Prepare a quality cost report for 2005 and 2006.
2. How much was invested in prevention and appraisal activities (additional control costs) in 2006? What return did this investment generate? What reduction in failure costs was achieved?
3. Management believes it is possible to reduce quality costs to 2.5 percent of sales. Assuming that sales continue at the $6,000,000 level, calculate the additional profit potential. Is the expectation of improving quality and reducing quality costs to 2.5 percent of sales realistic? Explain.

**15–4**

Hillary Enterprises had sales of $120 million in 2000 and $150 million in 2006. A quality improvement program had been implemented in 2000. Overall conformance quality was targeted for improvement. Assume that any changes in quality costs are attributable to improvements in quality. The quality costs for 2000 and 2006 are as follows:

| | 2000 | 2006 |
|---|---|---|
| Internal failure costs | $ 9,000,000 | $ 450,000 |
| External failure costs | 12,000,000 | 300,000 |
| Appraisal costs | 5,400,000 | 1,125,000 |
| Prevention costs | 3,600,000 | 1,875,000 |
| Total quality costs | $30,000,000 | $3,750,000 |

**Required:**
1. Compute the quality costs/sales ratio for each year. Is this type of improvement possible?
2. Calculate the relative distribution of quality costs by category for 2000 (quality costs by category/total quality costs). What do you think of the relative cost distribution? How do you think quality costs will be distributed as the company approaches a zero-defects state?
3. Calculate the relative distribution of costs by category for 2006. What do you think of the level and distribution of quality costs? Do you think further reductions are possible?

**15–5**

Tradeoffs among
Quality Cost
Categories

LO2, LO4

Kumara Company has sales of $10 million and quality costs of $1,200,000. The company is embarking on a major quality improvement program. During the next three years, it intends to attack failure costs by increasing its appraisal and prevention costs. The "right" prevention activities will be selected, and appraisal costs will be reduced according to the results achieved. For next year, management is considering six activities: quality training, process control, product inspection, supplier evaluation, redesign of two major products, and prototype testing. To encourage managers to reduce nonvalue-added quality costs and select the right activities, the company establishes a bonus pool of 10 percent of the total reduction in quality costs.

Current quality costs and the costs of these six activities are provided in the following table. Each activity is added sequentially so that its effect on the cost categories can be assessed. For example, after quality training is added, the control costs increase to $400,000, and the failure costs drop to $1,300,000. Even though the activities are presented sequentially, they are totally independent of one another. Thus, only beneficial activities can be selected.

|  | Control Costs | Failure Costs |
| --- | --- | --- |
| Current quality costs[a] | $ 200,000 | $1,800,000 |
| Quality training | 400,000 | 1,300,000 |
| Process control | 650,000 | 900,000 |
| Product inspection | 750,000 | 820,000 |
| Supplier evaluation | 900,000 | 250,000 |
| Prototype testing | 1,200,000 | 150,000 |
| Engineering redesign | 1,250,000 | 50,000 |

[a] All current control costs are appraisal costs.

**Required:**

1. Identify the control activities that should be implemented, and calculate the total quality costs associated with this selection. Assume that an activity is selected only if it increases the bonus pool.
2. Given the activities selected in Requirement 1, calculate the following:
   a. Reduction in total quality costs
   b. Percentage distribution for control and failure costs
   c. Amount of this year's bonus pool
3. A quality engineer complains about the incentive system. Basically, he contends that the bonus should be based only on the reductions of failure and appraisal costs. This method would encourage investment in prevention activities and eventually eliminate failure and appraisal costs. After nonvalue-added costs are eliminated, focus could be placed on prevention costs. If this approach were adopted, which activities would be selected? Do you agree with this approach? Explain.

**15–6**

Quality Cost Report;
Taguchi Quality Loss
Function

LO1, LO2

Spreadsheet

At the end of 2006, Vanier Metal Works began to focus on its quality costs. As a first step, it identified the following sales and quality-related costs:

|  | 2006 |
| --- | --- |
| Sales (50,000 units @ $60) | $3,000,000 |
| Scrap | 90,000 |
| Rework | 120,000 |
| Training program | 36,000 |
| Consumer complaints | 60,000 |
| Warranty | 120,000 |
| Test labour | 90,000 |
| Inspection labour | 75,000 |
| Supplier evaluation | 9,000 |

**Required:**

1. Prepare a quality cost report by quality cost category.
2. Calculate the relative distribution percentages for each quality cost category. Comment on the distribution.
3. Using the Taguchi quality loss function, an average loss per unit is $9. What are the hidden costs of external failure? How does this affect the relative distribution? What effect will the hidden-cost information have on a quality improvement program?

**15–7**

Taguchi Quality Loss Function

LO1

Neste Company manufactures a product that has a target value of 20 grams. Specification limits are 20 grams plus or minus 0.5 grams. The value of $K$ is $80. A sample of five units produced the following measures:

| Unit | Measured Weight |
|------|-----------------|
| 1 | 20.20 |
| 2 | 20.50 |
| 3 | 20.30 |
| 4 | 19.50 |
| 5 | 19.75 |

A total of 12,500 units were produced in April.

**Required:**

1. Calculate the loss for each unit. Calculate the average loss for the sample of five.
2. Using the average loss, calculate the hidden quality costs for April.

**15–8**

Multiple-Year Trend Reports

LO2

Golden Company implemented a quality improvement program at the beginning of 2002. The controller has computed quality costs as a percentage of sales for the past five years as follows:

| | Prevention | Appraisal | Internal Failure | External Failure | Total |
|------|-----------|-----------|------------------|------------------|-------|
| 2002 | 3% | 4% | 9% | 13% | 29% |
| 2003 | 4 | 5 | 8 | 11 | 28 |
| 2004 | 5 | 6 | 6 | 8 | 25 |
| 2005 | 6 | 5 | 4 | 6 | 21 |
| 2006 | 7 | 2 | 1 | 2 | 12 |

**Required:**

1. Prepare a trend graph for total quality costs. Comment on the success of the quality improvement program.
2. Prepare a trend graph showing each quality cost category. What does the graph indicate about the success of the quality improvement program? Does this graph supply more insight than the total cost trend graph? What does the graph reveal about the distribution of quality costs in 2002? in 2006?

**15–9**

Productivity Measurement; Partial Measure

LO4

Daryl Company produces a product that uses two inputs: energy and labour. The previous month, 100 units were produced, which required 80 units of energy and 320 hours of labour. An engineering study has revealed that the output of 100 units can be produced using either of the following two combinations of inputs:

| | Energy | Labour |
|---------------|--------|--------|
| Combination A | 50 | 200 |
| Combination B | 80 | 125 |

Energy costs are $18 per unit used; the labour rate is $15 per hour.

**Required:**

1. Calculate the output/input ratio for each input of Combination A. Does this represent a productivity improvement over the current use of inputs? What is the total dollar value of the improvement? Classify this as a technical or input tradeoff efficiency improvement.
2. Calculate output/input ratios for each input of Combination B. Does this represent a productivity improvement over the current use of inputs? Compare these ratios to those of Combination A. What has happened?
3. Compute the cost of producing the 100 units of output using Combination B. Compare this to the cost using Combination A. Does moving from Combination A to Combination B represent a productivity improvement? Explain.

**15–10**

Interperiod Measure of Productivity; Basic Computations

LO4

Spreadsheet

The following data pertain to the last two years of operation at Chelsea, Inc.:

|                              | 2004    | 2005    |
| ---------------------------- | ------- | ------- |
| Output                       | 16,000  | 20,000  |
| Power (quantity used)        | 2,000   | 2,000   |
| Materials (quantity used)    | 4,000   | 4,500   |
| Unit price (power)           | $1.00   | $2.00   |
| Unit price (materials)       | $4.00   | $5.00   |
| Unit selling price           | $2.00   | $2.50   |

**Required:**

1. Compute the partial operational productivity ratios for each year. Did productivity improve? Explain.
2. Compute the profit-linked productivity measure. By how much did profits increase due to productivity?
3. Calculate the price recovery component for 2005. Explain its meaning.

**15–11**

Productivity Measurement: Tradeoffs

LO4

Spreadsheet

Masterkraft Company installed an automated manufacturing system to reduce the use of materials and labour. A year later, management wants to evaluate the productivity change. The president is especially interested in knowing whether the tradeoff among capital, labour, and materials was favourable. Data relating to output, labour, materials, and capital are provided for the year before and the year after the implementation.

|                         | Year Before | Year After |
| ----------------------- | ----------- | ---------- |
| Output                  | 200,000     | 240,000    |
| Input quantities:       |             |            |
| Materials (kilograms)   | 50,000      | 40,000     |
| Labour (hours)          | 10,000      | 4,000      |
| Capital                 | $10,000     | $600,000   |
| Input prices:           |             |            |
| Materials               | $2          | $2         |
| Labour                  | $5          | $5         |
| Capital                 | 15%         | 15%        |

**Required:**

1. Compute the partial productivity measures for materials, labour, and capital for each year. What caused the change in labour and materials productivity?

2. Calculate the change in profits attributable to the change in productivity of the three inputs. Assuming that they are the only three inputs, evaluate the decision to automate.

**15–12**

*Productivity Measurement: Technical and Price Efficiency Illustrated*

LO4

At the end of the fiscal year, the manager of Lawson Company was reviewing two competing proposals for process changes in the machining department. The changes would affect the input usage. The accounting department provided the following information about the inputs used to produce 50,000 units of output during the year:

|  | Quantity | Unit Prices |
|---|---|---|
| Materials | 90,000 kilograms | $ 8 |
| Labour | 40,000 hours | 10 |
| Energy | 20,000 kilowatt-hours | 2 |

Each proposal offers a process design that is different from the one currently used. Neither proposal would cost anything to implement. Both proposals estimate the following input usage for the production of 60,000 units during next year:

|  | Proposal A | Proposal B |
|---|---|---|
| Materials | 90,000 kilograms | 100,000 kilograms |
| Labour | 40,000 hours | 30,000 hours |
| Energy | 20,000 kilowatt-hours | 20,000 kilowatt-hours |

Input prices are expected to remain unchanged.

**Required:**
1. Compute the partial operational productivity measures for the year and for each proposal. Does either proposal improve technical efficiency? Explain. Can you make a recommendation about either proposal by using only the physical measures?
2. Calculate the profit-linked productivity measure for each proposal. Which proposal results in a better outcome? How does this relate to the concept of input tradeoff efficiency? Explain.

**15–13**

*Productivity and Quality*

LO4

As part of an ongoing effort to improve quality, Sohee Biotechnology, Inc., is thinking about acquiring an automated system that would decrease the number of units scrapped because of poor quality. The production manager is pushing for the acquisition, because he believes that productivity will be greatly enhanced— especially regarding labour and materials. Output and input data before and after acquisition are as follows:

|  | Current | After Acquisition |
|---|---|---|
| Output (units) | 10,000 | 10,000 |
| Output selling price | $40 | $40 |
| Input quantities: |  |  |
| Materials (kilograms) | 40,000 | 35,000 |
| Labour (hours) | 20,000 | 15,000 |
| Capital | $20,000 | $100,000 |
| Energy (kilowatt-hours) | 10,000 | 25,000 |
| Input prices: |  |  |
| Materials | $4.00 | $4.00 |
| Labour | $9.00 | $9.00 |
| Capital | 10% | 10% |
| Energy | $2.00 | $2.50 |

**Required:**

1. Calculate the partial operational ratios for materials and labour under each alternative. Is the production manager right in thinking that materials and labour productivity increases with the automated system?
2. Compute the partial productivity ratios for all four inputs. Does the system improve productivity?
3. Determine the amount by which profits will change if the system is adopted. Are the tradeoffs among the inputs favourable? Comment on the system's ability to improve productivity.

**15–14**

Basics of Productivity Measurement

LO4

Kang Company gathered the following data for the past two years:

|  | Base Year | Current Year |
|---|---|---|
| Output | 150,000 | 180,000 |
| Output prices | $20 | $20 |
| Input quantities: |  |  |
|   Materials (kilograms) | 200,000 | 180,000 |
|   Labour (hours) | 50,000 | 90,000 |
| Input prices: |  |  |
|   Materials | $5 | $6 |
|   Labour | $8 | $8 |

**Required:**

1. Calculate the partial operational productivity measures for each year.
2. Prepare income statements for each year. Calculate the total change in income.
3. Calculate the change in profits attributable to productivity changes.
4. Calculate the price recovery component. Explain its meaning.

## Problems

**15–15**

Classification of Quality Costs

LO1

Classify the following quality costs as prevention, appraisal, internal failure, or external failure.

1. Prototype inspection and testing.
2. Reinspection of reworked product.
3. Packaging and shipping repaired goods.
4. Loss of customer goodwill due to inferior-quality products.
5. Grinding bumps off a poorly welded steel plate.
6. Maintenance of inspection equipment.
7. Design verification and review to evaluate the quality of new products.
8. Design and development of quality equipment.
9. Quality training program for new personnel.
10. Correcting an improperly filled out purchase order.
11. Purchasing replacement parts to repair a product that breaks down while under warranty.
12. Internal audit assessing the effectiveness of the quality system.
13. Replacing a component that was improperly inserted and damaged.
14. Machine jammed and damaged because of an incorrectly sized subassembly.

15. Quality reporting.
16. Proofreading.
17. Cost to incinerate scrap.
18. Setup for testing.
19. Lending engineers to help improve processes and products of suppliers.
20. Developing a new quality improvement program.
21. Extra overhead costs incurred due to returned products.
22. Supervision of in-process inspection.
23. Inspection of parts purchased from suppliers.
24. Customer complaint department.
25. Outside laboratory evaluation of product quality.

**15–16**

Various Quality and
Productivity Concepts

LO1, LO2, LO3, LO4

Match the following, using each item only once:

1. Hidden quality costs
2. Technical efficiency
3. Failure activities
4. Profit-linked productivity
5. Fitness of use
6. Base period
7. Zero defects
8. Operational productivity measures
9. Durability
10. Input tradeoff efficiency
11. External failure costs
12. Appraisal costs
13. Financial productivity measure
14. Profile measurement

a. Activities performed because poor quality exists
b. Length of time a product functions
c. Lost sales because of poor quality
d. Vector of partial productivity measures
e. Costs of detecting poor quality
f. Revenue/labour cost
g. Lowest-cost technically efficient inputs
h. Units produced/kilograms of material used
i. No nonconforming products
j. Product does intended functions
k. Standard for productivity measurement
l. Profit change due to productivity change
m. No more input used than necessary
n. Costs not recorded in accounting records

**15–17**

Quality Cost Summary

LO1, LO2, LO3, LO4

Linda Timo, the president of Ontor Company, has recently returned from a conference. While there, she learned that many North American companies have made significant progress in improving quality and reducing quality costs. Many of these companies have been able to reduce quality costs from between 20 and 30 percent of sales to between 2 and 3 percent. However, she is sceptical. Even if the quality experts are right, she is sure her company's quality costs are much lower than those of competitors—probably less than 5 percent. But if she is wrong, she has been overlooking an opportunity to significantly improve profits and strengthen her company's competitive position.

She reflects on the comment of one quality expert: "Quality has become a condition of entry to the market. If the product is not good, you will quickly go out of business." The quality issue is at least worth exploring. Moreover, it might be risky *not* to assess her company's quality performance. She knows that her company produces most of the information it needs for quality cost reporting—but there has never been a need for formal analysis.

The conference has convinced Linda that quality improvement can increase profitability significantly. So she contacts the controller and requests a preliminary estimate of the current quality costs. She also asks the controller to classify quality costs into four categories: prevention, appraisal, internal failure, and external failure costs. The controller gathers the following information for 2005:

a. Sales revenue is $20,000,000, and net income is $4,000,000.
b. Customers returned 60,000 units needing repair. Average repair cost is $7 per unit.

c.  Ten inspectors are employed to inspect the final products, at an annual salary of $30,000 each.
d.  Each year, around 300,000 units are rejected in the final inspection. Of these units, 80 percent can be recovered through rework. The cost of rework is $3 per unit. The remainder is scrap.
e.  Total scrap is 60,000 units. All scrap is quality-related. The cost of scrap is about $15 per unit.
f.  A customer cancelled an order that would have increased profits by $500,000. The reason for cancellation was poor product performance. The company loses at least this amount each year for this reason.
g.  The company employs eight full-time employees in its complaint department. Each earns $25,000 a year.
h.  The company gave sales allowances totalling $250,000 to customers with substandard products.
i.  The company requires all new employees to take its three-hour quality training program. The estimated annual cost of the program is $160,000.
j.  The final inspection requires testing equipment, with annual operating and maintenance costs of $240,000.

**Required:**
1.  Prepare a simple quality cost report, classifying costs by category. Comment on the quality costs/sales ratio.
2.  Discuss the distribution of quality costs among the four categories. Are they properly distributed? Explain.
3.  Discuss how the company can improve its overall quality and at the same time reduce total quality costs. Consider the strategy advocated by the American Society for Quality Control.
4.  Suppose the company decides that a five-year program will reduce quality costs to 2.5 percent of sales and that control costs will be 80 percent of total quality costs. Calculate the income increase if sales remain at $20,000,000. Also, calculate the total amount spent on control and failure costs.
5.  Refer to Requirements 1 and 4. Suppose that Linda decides to provide a bonus pool for employees, allowing them to share the benefits of quality improvements. If the bonus pool is 20 percent of quality cost reductions, how much will be put in the bonus pool for the five-year period? What are the benefits of such a pool? Suppose a manager suggests basing the bonus only on the reductions of appraisal and failure costs. Explain why he might suggest this modification. Do you agree with his suggestion?
6.  Hidden quality costs are estimated by applying a multiplier of 3. What are the actual external failure costs? What other methods are available for estimating hidden quality costs? What effect does this estimation have on a quality improvement strategy? Finally, should reductions in these costs be included in the bonus pool mentioned in Requirement 5? If these reductions were included, what would the effect on the bonus pool be?

**15–18**

Quality Costs; Pricing
Decisions; Market
Share

LO3

Asko Company manufactures furniture, with an economy line of kitchen tables as one product line. Last year, the company produced and sold 100,000 units for $100 per unit. Sales are on a bid basis, but the company has always been able to win sufficient bids until this year, when it lost a significant number of bids. Concerned, Larry Franklin, the president, called a meeting of the executive committee: Megan Johnson, marketing manager; Fred Davis, quality manager; Kevin Jones, production manager; and Helen Jackson, controller.

**Larry**: "I don't understand why we're losing bids. Megan, do you have an explanation?"

**Megan**: "Yes, as a matter of fact. Two competitors have lowered their price to $92 per unit. That's too big a difference for most of our buyers to ignore. If we want to keep selling our 100,000 units per year, we'll need to lower our price to $92. Otherwise, our sales will drop to between 20,000 and 25,000 per year."

**Helen**: "The unit contribution margin is $10. Lowering the price to $92 will cost us $8 per unit. Based on a sales volume of 100,000, we'd make $200,000 in contribution margin. If we keep the price at $100, our contribution margin will be $200,000 to $250,000. If we have to lose, let's just take the lower market share. It's better than lowering our prices."

**Megan**: "Perhaps. But the same thing could happen to some of our other product lines. My sources tell me that these two companies are on the tail end of a major quality improvement program—one that allows them significant savings. We need to rethink our whole competitive strategy to stay in business. Ideally, we should match the price reduction and reduce costs to recapture the lost contribution margin."

**Fred**: "I think I have something to offer. We're about to embark on a new quality improvement program of our own. I've brought the following estimates of the current quality costs for this economy line. As you can see, these costs are about 16 percent of current sales. That's excessive, and we believe they can be reduced to about 4 percent of sales over time."

| | |
|---|---|
| Scrap | $ 700,000 |
| Rework | 300,000 |
| Rejects (sold as seconds to discount houses) | 250,000 |
| Returns (due to poor workmanship) | 350,000 |
| Total costs | $1,600,000 |

**Larry**: "This sounds good. Fred, how long will it take you to achieve this reduction?"

**Fred**: "Because all these costs vary with the sales level, I'll express their reduction rate in those terms. Our best guess is that we can reduce these costs by about 1 percent of sales per quarter. So it should take about 12 quarters, or three years, to achieve the full benefit. Keep in mind that this is with an improvement in quality."

**Megan**: "This offers us some hope. If we meet the price immediately, we can maintain our market share. Furthermore, if we can reduce the price below $92, we can increase our market share. I estimate that we can increase sales by about 10,000 units for every dollar of price reduction below $92. Kevin, how much extra capacity do we have for this line?"

**Kevin**: "We can handle an extra 30,000 or 40,000 tables per year."

**Required:**
1. Assume that the company immediately reduces its bid price to $92. How long will it be before the unit contribution margin is restored to $10, assuming that quality costs are reduced as expected and that sales are maintained at 100,000 units per year (25,000 per quarter)?
2. Assume that the company holds the price at $92 until the 4 percent target is achieved. At this level of quality costs, should the price be reduced? If so, by how much? What is the increase in contribution margin? Assume that the price can be reduced only in $1 increments.
3. Assume that the company immediately reduces the price to $92 and begins the quality improvement program. Suppose it does not wait until the end of the three-year period before reducing prices. Instead, prices will be reduced when it is profitable to do so. Assume that prices can be reduced only in $1 increments. When should the first future price change occur (if ever)?
4. Discuss the different perspectives of the five stakeholders concerning the price decrease and the short-run contribution margin analysis done by the

controller. Did quality cost information play an important role in the company's strategic decision making?

**15–19**

Quality Costs;
Cost–Volume–Profit
Analysis

LO2, LO3

At the end of 2001, Westwood Electronics hired Milton Ridelle to manage one of its struggling divisions. Milton had a reputation for turning around troubled businesses. In 2002, the division had sales of $100 million, a unit-level variable cost ratio of 0.8, and total fixed costs of $24 million. The division produced only one product. Milton obtained the following quality cost report for 2002:

| | Fixed | Variable (unit-level) |
|---|---|---|
| Prevention | $ 800,000 | — |
| Appraisal | 1,200,000 | $ 4,000,000 |
| Internal failure | 2,000,000 | 8,000,000 |
| External failure | 4,000,000 | 20,000,000 |
| Total | $8,000,000 | $32,000,000 |

Milton was astonished by the high level of quality costs. He had heard of companies with quality costs as high as 60 percent of sales, but he had never personally seen any exceeding 20 to 30 percent of sales. This division's level of 40 percent was clearly out of line. He immediately implemented a program aimed at improving conformance quality. At the end of 2003, the following quality costs were reported:

| | Fixed | Variable (unit-level) |
|---|---|---|
| Prevention | $ 4,000,000 | — |
| Appraisal | 4,000,000 | $ 4,000,000 |
| Internal failure | 2,000,000 | 4,000,000 |
| External failure | 4,000,000 | 14,000,000 |
| Total | $14,000,000 | $22,000,000 |

Revenues and other costs were unchanged for 2003.

Milton estimates that by 2007, the defect rate will be 0.1 percent, compared to 2 percent for 2002, and quality costs will be reduced to $2 million, distributed as follows:

| | Fixed | Variable (unit-level) |
|---|---|---|
| Prevention | $ 800,000 | — |
| Appraisal | 800,000 | — |
| Internal failure | — | $ 80,000 |
| External failure | — | 320,000 |
| Total | $1,600,000 | $400,000 |

**Required:**
1. Calculate the breakeven point in revenues for 2002. How much was the division losing?
2. Calculate the breakeven point for 2003. Explain the change.
3. Calculate the breakeven point for 2007, assuming that revenues and other costs remain unchanged. Is it possible to reduce quality costs as dramatically as portrayed?
4. Assume that from 2002 to 2007, the division was forced to cut selling prices and that total revenues dropped to $60 million. Calculate the income (loss) that would be reported under the 2002 cost structure. Now calculate the income (loss) that would be reported under the 2007 quality cost structure

(assuming all other costs remain unchanged). Discuss the strategic significance of quality cost management.

**15–20**

In September 2003, Wolfville Lumber Company received a report from an external consulting group on its quality costs. The consultants reported that the company's quality costs were about 25 percent of its sales revenues. Somewhat shocked by the magnitude of the costs, Frank Roosevelt, the president, launched a quality improvement program. The program was scheduled for implementation in January 2004. The program's goal was to reduce quality costs to 2.5 percent by the end of 2006, by improving overall quality.

In 2004, management decided to reduce quality costs to 22 percent of sales revenues. It felt that the amount of reduction was reasonable and realistic. To monitor the quality improvement program, the president directed Pamela Golding, the controller, to prepare quarterly performance reports comparing budgeted and actual quality costs. He told Pamela that improving quality should reduce quality costs by 1 percent of sales for each of the first three quarters and 2 percent for the last quarter. Projected sales are $5 million per quarter. Pamela prepared the following budgets for the first two quarters of the year:

|  | **Quarter 1** | **Quarter 2** |
|---|---|---|
| Sales | $5,000,000 | $5,000,000 |
| Quality costs: |  |  |
| Warranty | $ 300,000 | $ 250,000 |
| Scrap | 150,000 | 125,000 |
| Incoming materials inspection | 25,000 | 50,000 |
| Product acceptance | 125,000 | 150,000 |
| Quality planning | 40,000 | 60,000 |
| Field inspection | 30,000 | 0 |
| Retesting | 50,000 | 40,000 |
| Allowances | 65,000 | 50,000 |
| New product review | 10,000 | 10,000 |
| Rework | 130,000 | 100,000 |
| Complaint adjustment | 60,000 | 20,000 |
| Downtime (defective parts) | 50,000 | 40,000 |
| Repairs | 50,000 | 35,000 |
| Product liability | 85,000 | 60,000 |
| Quality training | 30,000 | 70,000 |
| Quality engineering | 0 | 40,000 |
| Design verification | 0 | 20,000 |
| Process control measurement | 0 | 30,000 |
| Total budgeted costs | $1,200,000 | $1,150,000 |
| Quality costs/sales ratio | 24% | 23% |

**Required:**

1. Assume that the company reduces quality costs as indicated. What is the amount of quality costs as a percentage of sales for the year? for the end of the fourth quarter? Will the company achieve its goal of reducing quality costs to 22 percent of sales?

2. Prepare a reorganized quarterly budget that classifies quality costs into prevention, appraisal, internal failure, and external failure costs. Also, identify each cost as variable or fixed, assuming that none are mixed costs.

3. Compare the two quarterly budgets. What do they reveal about the company's quality improvement plans?

**15–21**

*Distribution of Quality Costs*

**LO2**

The Consumer Products Division of Abit-Tibbits Company produces paper diapers, napkins, and towels. The divisional manager has decided that quality costs can be minimized by distributing quality costs evenly among the four quality categories and reducing them to no more than 5 percent of sales. He has just received the following quality cost report:

**Consumer Products Division**
**Quality Cost Report**
**For the Year Ended December 31, 2005**

|  | Diapers | Napkins | Towels | Total |
|---|---|---|---|---|
| Prevention: |  |  |  |  |
| Quality training | $ 3,000 | $ 2,500 | $ 2,000 | $   7,500 |
| Quality engineering | 3,500 | 1,000 | 2,500 | 7,000 |
| Quality audits | — | 500 | 1,000 | 1,500 |
| Quality reporting | 2,500 | 2,000 | 1,000 | 5,500 |
| Total | $ 9,000 | $ 6,000 | $ 6,500 | $ 21,500 |
| Appraisal: |  |  |  |  |
| Inspection, materials | $ 2,000 | $ 3,000 | $ 3,000 | $   8,000 |
| Process acceptance | 4,000 | 2,800 | 1,200 | 8,000 |
| Product acceptance | 2,000 | 1,200 | 2,300 | 5,500 |
| Total | $ 8,000 | $ 7,000 | $ 6,500 | $ 21,500 |
| Internal failure: |  |  |  |  |
| Scrap | $10,000 | $ 3,000 | $ 2,500 | $ 15,500 |
| Disposal costs | 7,000 | 2,000 | 1,500 | 10,500 |
| Downtime | 1,000 | 1,500 | 2,500 | 5,000 |
| Total | $18,000 | $ 6,500 | $ 6,500 | $ 31,000 |
| External failure: |  |  |  |  |
| Allowances | $10,000 | $ 3,000 | $ 2,750 | $ 15,750 |
| Customer complaints | 4,000 | 1,500 | 3,750 | 9,250 |
| Product liability | 1,000 | — | — | 1,000 |
| Total | $15,000 | $ 4,500 | $ 6,500 | $ 26,000 |
| Total quality costs | $50,000 | $24,000 | $26,000 | $100,000 |

Assume that all prevention costs are fixed and that the remaining quality costs are variable.

**Required:**

1. Assume that the sales revenue for the year is $2 million, with sales for each product as follows: diapers, $1 million; napkins, $600,000; towels, $400,000. Evaluate the distribution of costs for the division as a whole and for each product line. What recommendations do you have for the divisional manager?

2. Assume instead that the total sales are $1 million, with the following breakdown: diapers, $500,000; napkins, $300,000; towels, $200,000. Evaluate the distribution of costs for the division as a whole and for each product line. Do you think that it is possible to reduce quality costs to 5 percent of sales for each product line and for the division as a whole and, simultaneously, to achieve an equal distribution of quality costs? What recommendations do you have?

3. Assume the total sales are $1 million, with the following breakdown: diapers, $500,000; napkins, $180,000; towels, $320,000. Evaluate the distribution of quality costs. What recommendations do you have?

4. Discuss the importance of the quality cost report by segment.

**15–22**

In 2001, Eric Donaldson, president of Thompson Electronics, received a report indicating that quality costs were 21 percent of sales. Faced with growing pressures from imported goods, Eric resolved to take measures to improve the overall quality of the company's products. After hiring a consultant, the company began an aggressive program of total quality control in 2002. At the end of 2005, Eric requested an analysis of the progress the company had made in reducing and controlling quality costs. The accounting department assembled the following data:

|  | Sales | Prevention | Appraisal | Internal Failure | External Failure |
|---|---|---|---|---|---|
| 2001 | $500,000 | $ 5,000 | $10,000 | $40,000 | $50,000 |
| 2002 | 600,000 | 20,000 | 20,000 | 50,000 | 60,000 |
| 2003 | 700,000 | 30,000 | 25,000 | 30,000 | 40,000 |
| 2004 | 600,000 | 35,000 | 35,000 | 20,000 | 25,000 |
| 2005 | 500,000 | 35,000 | 15,000 | 8,000 | 12,000 |

**Required:**
1. Compute the quality costs as a percentage of sales by category and in total for each year.
2. Explain why quality costs increased in total and as a percentage of sales in 2002.
3. Prepare a multiple-year trend graph for quality costs, both by total costs and by category. Using the graph, assess the progress made in reducing and controlling quality costs. Does the graph provide evidence that quality has improved? Explain.

**15–23**

Norcan Leather Products produces handcrafted leather belts. Almost all manufacturing costs are for materials and labour. Over the past several years, profits have declined because the costs of inputs have increased. Barry Norton, the president, has indicated that the price of belts cannot be increased; thus, the only way to improve or at least stabilize profits is by increasing overall productivity. At the beginning of 2005, Barry implemented a productivity program. To encourage productivity improvement, he established a bonus pool of 10 percent of productivity gains. He wants to know how much profits have increased from the previous year as a result of the program. The cost analyst has gathered the following data:

|  | 2004 | 2005 |
|---|---|---|
| Unit selling price | $32 | $32 |
| Output produced and sold | 100,000 | 120,000 |
| Materials used (kilograms) | 200,000 | 200,000 |
| Labour used (hours) | 50,000 | 50,000 |
| Unit price of materials | $8 | $9 |
| Unit price of labour | $9 | $10 |

**Required:**
1. Compute the partial productivity ratios for each year. Comment on the effectiveness of the productivity improvement program.
2. Compute the increase in profits attributable to increased productivity.
3. Calculate the price recovery component, and comment on its meaning. Ignore the bonus cost in this calculation.

**15–24**

In 2005, Brandon Products, Inc., used the following input combination to produce 2,000 units of output:

| Materials | 2,200 kilograms |
|---|---|
| Labour | 2,000 hours |

Assume that the following combination is optimal for 2,000 units of output but unknown to the company:

| | |
|---|---|
| Materials | 1,000 kilograms |
| Labour | 4,000 hours |

The cost of materials is $40 per kilogram and the labour rate is $10 per hour for both 2005 and 2006. In 2006 the company produced 2,000 units, with the following input combination:

| | |
|---|---|
| Materials | 1,200 kilograms |
| Labour | 5,000 hours |

**Required:**
1. Compute the partial productivity ratios for each of the following:
   a. The actual inputs used in 2005.
   b. The actual inputs used in 2006.
   c. The optimal input combination.
   Did productivity increase in 2006, as measured by the partial productivity ratios?
2. Compute the cost of productive inefficiency, in relation to the optimal input combination, for 2005.
3. By how much did profits increase because of improvements in productive efficiency from 2005 to 2006?
4. How much additional improvement in profits is possible after 2006, assuming that input costs and output remain unchanged?

**15–25**

Productivity
Measurement; Partial
and Total Measures;
Price Recovery

LO4

The industrial division of Cantco Company recently engaged in a vigorous effort to increase productivity. Over the past several years, competition had intensified. To maintain its market share, the division had to decrease its price by $2.50 per unit by the end of 2006. The price decrease, however, necessitated an equal increase in productive efficiency. If divisional profits dropped by $2.50 per unit, the division's survival would be in question. To assess the outcome of the productivity improvement program, the controller gathered the following data:

| | 2005 | 2006 |
|---|---|---|
| Output | 400,000 | 500,000 |
| Input quantities: | | |
|    Materials (kilograms) | 100,000 | 100,000 |
|    Labour (hours) | 400,000 | 200,000 |
|    Capital | $4,000,000 | $10,000,000 |
|    Energy (kilowatt-hours) | 100,000 | 300,000 |
| Input prices: | | |
|    Materials | $2 | $3 |
|    Labour | $8 | $10 |
|    Capital | 15% | 10% |
|    Energy | $2 | $2 |

**Required:**
1. Calculate the partial productivity ratios for each year. Has productivity improved? Explain.
2. Calculate the profit change attributable to productivity changes.
3. Calculate the cost per unit for 2005 and 2006. Was the division able to decrease its unit cost by at least $2.50? Comment on the relationship between competitive advantage and productive efficiency.

**15–26**

Andy Lund, the production manager, arranged a meeting with Will Rogers, the plant manager. Andy had some questions about the recently implemented operational measures.

**Andy**: "Will, my questions are more to satisfy my curiosity than anything else. At the beginning of the year, we began some new procedures that require us to work toward increasing output per kilogram of material and decreasing output per labour hour. As instructed, I've been tracking these operational measures for each batch we've produced this year. Here's a copy of the trend report for the first five batches of this year. Each batch consisted of 10,000 units."

| Batches | Materials Usage (kilograms) | Ratio | Labour Usage (hours) | Ratio |
|---|---|---|---|---|
| 1 | 4,000 | 2.50 | 2,000 | 5.00 |
| 2 | 3,900 | 2.56 | 2,020 | 4.95 |
| 3 | 3,750 | 2.67 | 2,150 | 4.65 |
| 4 | 3,700 | 2.70 | 2,200 | 4.55 |
| 5 | 3,600 | 2.78 | 2,250 | 4.44 |

**Will**: "Andy, this report is very encouraging. The trend is exactly what we hoped for. I'll bet we meet our goal of getting the targeted batch productivity measures. Let's see, those goals were 3 units per kilogram for materials and 4 units per hour for labour. Last year's figures were 2.50 for materials and 5 for labour. Things are looking good. I guess tying bonuses and raises to improving these productivity stats was a good idea."

**Andy**: "Maybe so, but I don't understand why you want to make these tradeoffs between materials and labour. The materials cost only 5 dollars a kilogram, and labour costs 10 dollars an hour. It seems like you're increasing the cost of this product."

**Will**: "It may seem that way, but it's not so. There are other factors to consider. You know we've been talking about quality improvement. The new procedures produce products that conform to the product specifications. More labour time is needed to achieve this, and as we take more time, we waste fewer materials. But the real benefit is the reduction in our external failure costs. Every defect in a batch of 10,000 units costs us $1,000—warranty work, lost sales, and so on. If we can reach the materials and labour productivity goals, our defects will drop from 20 per batch to 5 per batch."

**Required:**
1. Discuss the advantages of using only operational measures of productivity for controlling shop-level activities.
2. Assume that the batch productivity statistics are met by the end of the year. Calculate the change in a batch's profits during the year attributable to changes in materials and labour productivity.
3. Assume that three inputs are evaluated: materials, labour, and quality. Quality is measured by the number of defects per batch. Calculate the change in a batch's profits during the year attributable to changes in productivity of all three inputs. Do you agree that quality is an input? Explain.

**15–27**

Patricia Parker, the president of Marco Company, meets with two of her plant managers. She tells them that the demand for their products is about to increase by 50 percent next year over this year's output of 10,000 litres. A major foreign source of raw materials has been shut down by a civil war. It will be years before that source is available again. As a result, the price of materials is expected to quadruple. Many less efficient competitors will be leaving the business, increasing demand and output prices. In fact, output prices may soon double.

In discussing the situation with the plant managers, Patricia reminds them that a new automated process will allow them to increase productivity. Available for the new fiscal year, this process will decrease evaporation substantially by using more machine hours. There are, however, only two other feasible settings beyond the current setting. The current input usage for the 10,000-litre output (current setting) and the input usage for the other two settings, based on the output of 15,000 litres, are as follows:

|  | **Current** | **Setting A** | **Setting B** |
|---|---|---|---|
| Input quantities: |  |  |  |
| Materials (litres) | 25 000 | 15 000 | 30 000 |
| Equipment (machine hours) | 6,000 | 15,000 | 7,500 |

The current prices for this year's inputs are $3 per litre for materials and $12 per machine hour for equipment. The materials price will change for next year as explained, but the $12 rate per machine hour will remain unchanged. The chemical currently sells for $20 per litre.

Based on separate productivity analyses, one plant manager chooses Setting A and the other Setting B. The manager who chooses Setting B justifies his decision by noting that it is the only setting that clearly signals an increase in both partial measures of productivity. The other manager agrees that Setting B is an improvement but believes that Setting A is even better.

**Required:**
1. Calculate the partial measures of productivity for the current year and for the two settings. Which of the two settings signals an increase in productivity for both inputs?
2. Calculate the profits that will be realized under each setting for the coming year. Which setting provides a greater profit increase?
3. Calculate the profit change for each setting attributable to productivity changes. Which setting offers greater productivity improvement? By how much? Explain why this happened. (Hint: Look at tradeoffs.)

## Managerial Decision Cases

**15–28**

Quality Cost
Performance Reports

LO2

Thomkins Press is in its fourth year of a five-year quality improvement program. The program began at the beginning of 2002 with an internal study of quality costs. A five-year plan was developed to lower quality costs to 10 percent of sales by the end of 2006. Sales and quality costs for each year are as follows:

|  | **Sales Revenues** | **Quality Costs** |
|---|---|---|
| 2002 | $10,000,000 | $2,000,000 |
| 2003 | 10,000,000 | 1,800,000 |
| 2004 | 11,000,000 | 1,815,000 |
| 2005 | 12,000,000 | 1,680,000 |
| 2006 (budgeted) | 12,000,000 | 1,320,000 |

Quality costs by category can be expressed as a percentage of sales, as follows:

|  | **Prevention** | **Appraisal** | **Internal Failure** | **External Failure** |
|---|---|---|---|---|
| 2002 | 1.0% | 3.0% | 7.0% | 9.0% |
| 2003 | 2.0 | 4.0 | 6.0 | 6.0 |
| 2004 | 2.5 | 4.0 | 5.0 | 5.0 |
| 2005 | 3.0 | 3.5 | 4.5 | 3.0 |
| 2006 | 3.5 | 3.5 | 2.0 | 2.0 |

The 2006 budget for quality costs is as follows:

Prevention costs:

| | |
|---|---:|
| Quality planning | $ 150,000 |
| Quality training | 20,000 |
| Quality improvement (special project) | 80,000 |
| Quality reporting | 10,000 |

Appraisal costs:

| | |
|---|---:|
| Proofreading | 500,000 |
| Other inspection | 50,000 |

Failure costs:

| | |
|---|---:|
| Correction of typos | 150,000 |
| Rework (because of customer complaints) | 75,000 |
| Plate revisions | 55,000 |
| Press downtime | 100,000 |
| Waste (because of poor work) | 130,000 |
| Total quality costs | $1,320,000 |

All prevention costs are fixed, and all other quality costs are variable.

During 2006, the company had $12 million in sales. Actual quality costs for 2005 and 2006 are as follows:

| | 2005 | 2006 |
|---|---:|---:|
| Quality planning | $140,000 | $150,000 |
| Quality training | 20,000 | 20,000 |
| Special project | 120,000 | 100,000 |
| Quality reporting | 12,000 | 12,000 |
| Proofreading | 580,000 | 520,000 |
| Other inspection | 80,000 | 60,000 |
| Correction of typos | 200,000 | 165,000 |
| Rework | 131,000 | 76,000 |
| Plate revisions | 83,000 | 58,000 |
| Press downtime | 123,000 | 102,000 |
| Waste | 191,000 | 136,000 |

**Required:**

1. Prepare a quality cost performance report for 2006 that compares actual and budgeted quality costs. Comment on the company's ability to achieve its quality goals for the year.
2. Prepare a quality performance report for 2006 that compares the actual costs for 2005 and 2006. How much did profits change because of improved quality?
3. Prepare a graph showing the trend in total quality costs as a percentage of sales for the five-year period.
4. Prepare a graph showing the trend for all four quality cost categories from 2002 to 2006. How does this graph show that the reduction in total quality costs is attributable to quality improvements?

**15–29**

Quality Performance and Ethical Behaviour

LO1, LO4

Western Manufacturing Company rewards its managers for their ability to meet budgeted quality cost reductions. The bonus is increased if the productivity goal is met or exceeded. The productivity goal is computed by multiplying the units produced by the prevailing market price and then dividing this measure of output by the total cost of the inputs used. Additionally, if plants as a whole meet the budgeted targets, the production supervisors and workers receive salary and wage increases. Matt Ashton, the manager of a plant in Alberta, feels obligated to do everything he can to provide this increase to his employees. Accordingly, he has decided to take the following actions during the last quarter of the year to meet the plant's budgeted targets and increase the productivity ratio:

a. Decrease inspections of the process and final product by 50 percent and transfer inspectors temporarily to quality training programs. Matt believes that this move will increase the inspectors' awareness of the importance of quality, and that decreasing inspection will result in significantly less downtime and less rework. By increasing the output and decreasing the costs of internal failure, the plant will be able to meet the budgeted reductions for internal failure costs, and simultaneously increase its productivity measure. Also, the increase in the costs of quality training will help the plant meet the budgeted level of prevention costs.

b. Delay replacing and repairing defective products until the beginning of the following year. While this may increase customer dissatisfaction somewhat, Matt believes that most customers expect some inconvenience. Besides, the policy of promptly dealing with dissatisfied customers can always be reinstated in three months. In the meantime, the action will significantly reduce the costs of external failure, and allow the plant to meet its budgeted target.

### Required:

1. Evaluate Matt's behaviour, taking into account his concern for his employees. Is he justified in pursuing the actions described in the problem? If not, what should he do instead?
2. Assume that the company views Matt's behaviour as undesirable. What can it do to discourage it?
3. Assume that Matt is a CMA. Refer to the ethical code for management accountants discussed in Chapter 1. Are any ethical standards being violated?

## Research Assignments

**15–30**

Library and
Cyberspace Research

LO1, LO2, LO3

Listed below are articles that describe some early quality improvement efforts by five companies:

- Corning Incorporated: Keith H. Hammonds, "Corning's Class Act: How Jamie Houghton Reinvented the Company," *Business Week* (May 13, 1991): pp. 68-73.
- Federal Express: American Management Association, *Blueprint for Service Quality: The Federal Express Approach*, 1991.
- Motorola: Keki R. Bhote, "Motorola's Long March to the Malcolm Baldrige National Quality Award," *National Productivity Review* VIII (4) (Autumn 1989): pp. 365-75.
- Solectron: "What Drives Quality?" *Internal Auditor Magazine* (April 1992): pp. 39-45.
- Southern Pacific: Gus Welty, "Southern Pacific's Quality Comeback," *Railway Age* (November 1992): pp. 30-34.

### Required:

Write a three- to five-page report that compares and contrasts the experiences of three of the five companies. At least one of the three companies should be a service company. Include a discussion of how the companies defined quality, and describe how quality was measured, if at all. Were the financial effects measured? Were quality costs mentioned? Finally, conduct a library and/or Internet search on one of the companies. Determine whether the quality achievements have been maintained and whether quality is still emphasized.

**15–31**

LO1

1. Go to www.qualitymag.com and, using the resources of that site, summarize three cases involving companies that have improved their quality perform- ance during the most recent year.
2. Conduct Internet research on "QNet." Write two paragraphs describing QNet's role in promoting quality in Canadian companies.

# Financial Performance Evaluation and Transfer Pricing in Decentralized Companies

## Learning Objectives

After studying Chapter 16, you should be able to:

1. Define responsibility accounting, and describe four types of responsibility centres.

2. Explain why companies decentralize.

3. Compute and interpret return on investment (ROI), residual income (RI), and economic value added (EVA).

4. Discuss the role of transfer pricing in decentralized companies.

# Scenario

Ted Munsen was worried. He had founded Technoco in the mid-1990s to manufacture a scrubbing device for cleaning airborne contaminants from industrial smokestacks. The company's typical customers were large mining companies. Back then, the company consisted of Ted and a few other young engineers who were excited by the potential of the device. They routinely worked 16-hour days, 7 days a week, to see their vision turn into reality. The hard work paid off; the scrubbing device was efficient and effective. Profits at Technoco soared. Through the years, Ted and his associates had purchased several other loosely related companies in the pollution cleanup field; a few years ago they had gone public with the conglom-

erate. Now, as the CEO of an established company, Ted faced new problems. He met with Steve Scully, head of Canadian operations, to discuss them.

Ted: "Steve, look at these projected financial statements. Our net income has increased at a barely noticeable rate. Our return on investment has actually declined from last year. Divisional managers are squabbling over transfer prices when they should be cooperating. What's happening here? I remember when working at this company meant something. We shared a vision. We were working not just for ourselves, but for a better world. It may sound corny, but that vision sure kept me going through some pretty dark days."

Steve (chuckling): "Don't forget the dark nights! Look, Ted—we're older and larger now; it's harder to keep

that culture going when you're a multidivision company. I hardly know some of our newer managers, much less feel sure that we share the same values. What can you do? We just have to accept the inevitable, cut costs, or something. I don't know. What would Bell Canada, GM, or Nortel do?"

Ted: "I don't care what those companies would do—they have enough problems of their own. I also don't want to throw in the towel just yet. Surely we can structure an incentive program to get our managers moving in the same direction again, and have some fun doing it. I want you to do some research on management incentive plans. See what's out there—maybe some other company has faced this problem and solved it. Let's meet again on this matter in two weeks."

*Two weeks later.*

**Steve**: "Ted, I may have a solution to our problems. I spoke to a friend of mine at Thermo Electro. They make high-tech devices, such as very sensitive bomb and drug detectors, and remediation facilities for cleaning gasoline-contaminated soil. They're a lot like us—a great small company that grew like crazy. They had problems keeping their entrepreneurial spirit alive. They handed out stock options to motivate their managers, but it didn't seem to work. The R&D expenditures were crucial to long-term success but were dragging down earnings. Anyway, they experimented with splitting up the company. In 1983, they sold 16 percent of one of their divisions, Thermedics. The managers of Thermedics got 3 percent of the shares, and it really turned them into entrepreneurs. It also raised more than $5 million."[1]

**Ted**: "So far, so good. But what happened to return on investment? And what about the other divisions? Did they resent the special deal Thermedics got?"

**Steve**: "No, the other managers have the same chance. The other Thermo Electro divisions compete to become the new spinoff. Now there are many spinoffs, including Thermo Fibertek (equipment and products for paper-making and recycling industries), Thermo TerraTech (industrial outsourcing and manufacturing support), Thermo Laser (maker of the SoftLight Laser hair removal system), and Thermo Cardiosystems (developer of cardiac support devices). Each one is traded publicly and has its own stock symbol. Possible spinoffs are not considered until the business shows the potential to grow 30 percent per year. Thermo Electro has an average annual ROI of about 20 percent in its spinoffs."

**Ted**: "Sounds good! Let's go through these divisional financial statements and see what we've got. Maybe we can apply some of Thermo Electro's lessons to our own situation."

**Questions to Think About**

1. What problems does Ted face as the CEO of a large, divisionalized company that he did not face as the head of a small company?

2. What values did Steve and Ted share in the company's early days? What values do you suppose the division managers hold now? Are these values the same or different?

3. How do managerial values affect profits? Should they affect profits at all?

4. What is a management incentive plan? Can you think of a plan or plans that would help Ted and Steve move their managers in the directions they want?

## Responsibility Accounting

**Objective 1**

Define responsibility accounting, and describe four types of responsibility centres.

Ideally, the lines of responsibility in an organization should be based on its organizational structure. The traditional organizational chart, with its pyramid shape, illustrates the lines of responsibility flowing from the CEO down through the vice-presidents to middle- and lower-level managers. As the opening scenario indicates, when organizations grow, these lines of responsibility become longer and more numerous and the organizational structure becomes cumbersome. Modern practice is moving toward a flattened hierarchy. Such a structure, which emphasizes teams, is consistent with decentralization. For example, Nelson Thomson Learning (a division of International Thomson Publishing) eliminated much of its previous departmental organization and developed cross-functional teams. One result was that it reduced its levels of hierarchy. GE Capital, as another example, is essentially a group of smaller businesses. The head of each subunit is expected to stay in his or her market area rather than at headquarters. New initiatives are approached as new businesses. When a business grows to $25 million in earnings, it is separated from its creator group.[2]

There ought to be a strong link between an organization's responsibility accounting system and its organizational structure. Ideally, the responsibility accounting system mirrors and supports the organizational structure.

---

1. Jennifer Reese, "How to Grow Big by Staying Small," *Fortune* (December 28, 1992): pp. 50, 54.

2. John Curran, "GE Capital: Jack Welch's Secret Weapon," *Fortune* (November 10, 1997): pp. 116-34.

# Types of Responsibility Centres

**responsibility centre**

A segment of the business whose manager is accountable for specified sets of activities.

**cost centre**

A responsibility centre in which a manager is responsible only for costs.

**revenue centre**

A responsibility centre in which a manager is responsible only for sales.

**profit centre**

A responsibility centre in which a manager is responsible for both revenues and costs.

**investment centre**

A responsibility centre in which a manager is responsible for revenues, costs, and investments.

As a company grows, top management typically creates areas of responsibility, known as **responsibility centres**, and assigns responsibility for each area to a manager. A responsibility centre is a segment of the business whose manager is accountable for a specified set of activities. There are four main types of responsibility centres:

1. **Cost centre**: A responsibility centre in which a manager is financially responsible *only* for *costs*.
2. **Revenue centre**: A responsibility centre in which a manager is financially responsible *only* for *revenues*.
3. **Profit centre**: A responsibility centre in which a manager is financially responsible for *both revenues* and *costs*.
4. **Investment centre**: A responsibility centre in which a manager is financially responsible for *revenues, costs*, and *investments*.

How responsibility centres are established and the types of information available to managers should reflect the company's operations. Exhibit 16–1 displays these centres, along with the types of information they need to manage their operations.

A production department, such as assembly or finishing, is an example of a cost centre. The supervisor of a production department controls manufacturing costs but does not set prices or make marketing decisions. It follows that a production department supervisor is best evaluated based on cost control within his or her cost centre.

The marketing department manager sets prices and projected sales. If overall sales revenues are the responsibility of the marketing manager, the marketing department can be established as a revenue centre and its manager evaluated based on meeting the targeted revenues.

In some companies, plant managers are assigning responsibility for manufacturing *and* marketing their products. Because these managers control both costs and revenues, their plants can be established as profit centres for responsibility accounting purposes. Operating income is an important performance measure for profit centre managers.

Finally, autonomous divisions are often cited as examples of investment centres. Besides having control over costs and pricing decisions, divisional managers have the authority to make investment decisions, such as decisions to build or close a plant and to keep or drop product lines. This means that both operating income and return on investment are important performance measures for investment centre managers.

It is important to realize that although a responsibility centre manager is responsible only for his or her centre's activities, the decisions made by that manager can affect other responsibility centres. Say, for example, that a sales manager begins to offer customers price discounts at the end of each month. Sales increase dramatically, which is good for the marketing department. However, the produc-

EXHIBIT  16-1

Types of Responsibility Centres and Accounting Information Used to Measure Performance

| Accounting Information Used to Measure Performance | | | | |
|---|---|---|---|---|
| | Cost | Sales | Capital Investment | Other |
| Cost centre | X | | | |
| Revenue centre | Direct cost only | X | | |
| Profit centre | X | X | | |
| Investment centre | X | X | X | X |

tion department is forced to institute overtime shifts to meet the increased demand. As a result, total production costs increase, and so do costs per unit. So in practice, managers cannot completely control their operations. Responsibility is often assigned to managers for activities over which they can exercise a reasonable degree of control.

## The Role of Information and Accountability

Information is the key to appropriately holding managers responsible for results. For example, a production department manager can be held responsible for production costs, because he or she knows and understands them. Any differences between actual and expected costs can be best explained at this level. On the other hand, the sales manager can usually be held responsible for sales, because he or she can best explain what is happening regarding sales prices and quantities.

**responsibility accounting**

A system that measures the results of each responsibility centre according to the information managers need in order to operate their centre.

Responsibility should also be linked to *accountability*. Accountability involves measuring performance and holding individuals accountable for differences between actual and expected performance. The system of responsibility, accountability, and performance evaluation is often referred to as responsibility accounting. **Responsibility accounting** involves measuring results against preset criteria, and accounting measures and reports play a key role in providing information to this process.

# Decentralization

## Objective 2

Explain why companies decentralize.

**centralized decision making**

A system in which decisions are made at the top level of an organization and local managers are given the charge to implement them.

**decentralized decision making**

A system in which decisions are made and implemented by lower-level managers.

**decentralization**

The granting of decision-making freedom to lower operating levels.

Companies with multiple responsibility centres usually choose one of two decision-making approaches to organize and manage their diverse and complex activities: *centralized* or *decentralized*. In **centralized decision making**, decisions are made at the very top level, and lower-level managers are charged with implementing those decisions. In contrast, **decentralized decision making** allows managers at lower levels to make and implement key decisions pertaining to their areas of responsibility. **Decentralization** is the practice of delegating decision-making authority to lower levels. Centralized and decentralized decision-making authorities correspond to centralized and decentralized organizational structures, respectively.

Organizational structure can range from highly centralized to highly decentralized. Most organizations fall somewhere in the middle, with the majority of contemporary organizations being closer to decentralized. An appropriate organizational structure depends on the strategy and operating environment of the company and is subject to change as circumstances change.

## Reasons for Decentralization

Several reasons for decentralization exist, including the following:

1. Utilization of local information
2. Strategic focus of central management
3. Training and motivational opportunities for managers
4. Enhanced competition among divisions

### Utilization of Local Information

The quality of decisions is affected by the quality of information available. As a company expands to different markets and regions, central management may not understand local operating conditions. Lower-level managers, who are in contact with immediate operating conditions, such as local competition and the local labour pool, have access to such information. As a result, local managers can often make better decisions. This advantage of decentralization is especially applicable to multinational corporations, whose divisions may be operating in different countries and subject to different legal systems and customs.

A second potential problem is information overload. In an organization that operates in diverse markets with hundreds or thousands of different products, no single individual has the necessary expertise to process, understand, and use all information. Such circumstances call for individuals with specialized skills. Instead of having an individual at headquarters responsible for each specialty area, why not assign direct responsibility to individuals in the field? For example, a manager with an engineering background could head a production plant, while another manager with specialized skills in data analysis could be placed in charge of the information systems centre.

In a centralized setting, it takes time to transmit local information to headquarters and to transmit decisions back to local units. This two-way transmission increases the time required to make decisions and the likelihood that the manager responsible for implementing the decision will misinterpret the instructions. These things in turn decrease the effectiveness of the response. In a decentralized organization, where local managers make and implement decisions, these problems generally do not arise.

### Strategic Focus of Central Management

By decentralizing operating decisions, central management frees itself to engage in strategic planning and decision making. The organization's long-run survival should be a higher-priority issue to central management than its day-to-day operations.

### Training and Motivational Opportunities for Managers

Organizations require well-trained managers to replace senior managers who leave the company. What better way to prepare a future generation of managers than by providing them with the opportunity to make significant decisions? The decentralization of responsibilities also enables top managers to evaluate local managers' capabilities and to promote deserving managers.

Furthermore, greater responsibility can motivate local managers to exert greater effort and increase their job satisfaction. Of course, the extent to which the behavioural benefits can be realized depends on how managers are evaluated and rewarded for their performance.

### Enhanced Competition among Divisions

In a highly centralized company, overall profit margins can mask inefficiencies in different divisions. Large companies are increasingly finding that they cannot afford to keep noncompetitive divisions. It has been suggested that exposing a division more fully to market forces through decentralization is one of the best ways to improve its performance. For example, at Koch Industries, Inc., each unit is expected to act as an autonomous business unit, setting prices both externally and internally. Units that are not competitive will likely disappear.

## The Units of Decentralization

Decentralization is usually achieved by creating units called divisions. One criterion by which divisions can be differentiated is the types of products or services they produce. For example, divisions of PepsiCo include the Snack Ventures Europe division (a joint venture with General Mills), Frito-Lay, Inc., and Tropicana, as well as its flagship soft drink division. These divisions are organized on the basis of product lines. Note that some divisions depend on other divisions. For example, PepsiCo spun off its restaurant divisions to Tricon Global

Restaurant (YUM). As a result, the cola you drink at Pizza Hut, Taco Bell, and KFC will be Pepsi, not Coke.

Divisions can also be created along geographic lines. For example, UAL, Inc.—the parent of United Airlines—has a number of regional divisions: Asia/Pacific, Caribbean, European, Latin American, and North American. When divisions span one or more regions, performance evaluations need to take into account differences in regional environments.

Divisions can also differ by type of responsibility. Investment centres provide the greatest degree of responsibility and accountability, because their managers have the freedom to make the greatest variety of decisions. Profit centres rank second, followed by cost and revenue centres.

Organizational units formed along either product or geographic lines can be established as any of the four types of responsibility centres. The appropriateness of a particular responsibility centre depends on the degree of interdependence among the divisions. For independent autonomous divisions, the investment centre would be appropriate, as it provides the greatest degree of control. At the other end of the spectrum, the cost centre may be the most appropriate responsibility centre for highly interdependent organizational units.

Organizing divisions as responsibility centres allows for greater control of divisions through responsibility accounting. Regardless, a recent Canadian study of 10 "excellent" companies found that decentralization occurred only in selected areas. Even though the companies were highly centralized, there was "talk" about decentralization.[3] The study concluded that although accountability was often decentralized, control essentially remained centralized. It should be noted that such a mismatch between responsibility and accountability can lead to dysfunctional behaviour by divisional managers.

Since performance reports and contribution margin income statements were discussed elsewhere, this chapter focuses on the evaluation of investment centre managers.

# Measuring the Performance of Investment Centres

**Objective 3**

Compute and interpret return on investment (ROI), residual income (RI), and economic value added (EVA).

We must distinguish between the evaluation of investment centres and the evaluation of the managers who run them. The distinction is sometimes subtle, but it is clear that a division can do well or poorly irrespective of the efforts of its manager. For this reason, divisional and managerial evaluations must be separated. This section examines the evaluation of business segments; the evaluation of managers is discussed in Chapter 17. Furthermore, this chapter emphasizes the three popular traditional financial measures: return on investment (ROI), residual income (RI), and economic value added (EVA). Chapter 17 covers other financial and nonfinancial measures.

## Return on Investment

Divisions that are investment centres must prepare an income statement and a balance sheet. So can we simply rank divisions on the basis of net income? Suppose, for example, that a company has two divisions—Alpha and Beta. Alpha's net income is $100,000, and Beta's is $200,000. Did Beta perform better than Alpha? What if Alpha used an investment of $500,000 to produce the contribution of $100,000, whereas Beta used an investment of $2 million to produce the

---

3. Tupper Cawsey, Gene Deszca, and Howard Teall, *Management Control Systems in Excellent Canadian Companies*, Issues Papers, The Society of Management Accountants of Canada (1994): p. 9.

contribution of $200,000? Does your response change? Clearly, relating the reported operating profits to the assets used to produce them is a more meaningful measure of performance.

One way to relate operating profits to assets employed is by computing the profit earned per dollar of investment. **Return on investment (ROI)** is the most common measure of performance for an investment centre. It is defined as follows:

$$\text{ROI} = \text{Operating income} / \text{Average operating assets}$$

Operating income refers to earnings before interest and taxes. **Operating assets** are assets acquired to generate operating income; they include cash, receivables, inventories, land, buildings, and equipment. The average operating assets are computed as follows:

$$\text{Average operating assets} = (\text{Beginning net book value} + \text{Ending net book value})/2$$

Opinions differ regarding how long-term assets such as plant and equipment should be valued. For example, some prefer using gross book value over net book value, and historical cost over current cost. Most companies use historical cost or net book value.[4]

Referring to our example, Alpha's ROI is 20 percent ($100,000/$500,000), whereas Beta's ROI is only 10 percent ($200,000/$2,000,000). The formula for ROI is easy to use. However, additional information can be obtained by decomposing the ROI into margin and turnover.

## Margin and Turnover

A second formula for the ROI is simply margin times turnover. Thus, the ROI can also be expressed as follows:

$$\text{ROI} = \text{Margin} \times \text{Turnover}$$
$$= (\text{Operating income}/\text{Sales}) \times (\text{Sales}/\text{Average operating assets})$$

Suppose, for example, that Alpha had sales of $400,000. Margin would then be 25 percent ($100,000/$400,000), and turnover would be 0.80 ($400,000/$500,000). Alpha's ROI would still be 20 percent ($0.25 \times 0.80$).

**Margin** is simply the ratio of operating income to sales. It expresses the portion of sales that is available for interest, taxes, and profit. **Turnover** is calculated by dividing sales by average operating assets. It shows how productively assets have been used to generate sales.

Although both approaches yield the same ROI, margin and turnover give the manager valuable information. To illustrate this, consider the data in Exhibit 16–2. The Electronics Division improved its ROI from 18 percent in 2004 to 20 percent in 2005. The Medical Supplies Division's ROI, however, dropped from 18 to 15 percent. A better picture of the change in ROIs is gained by computing the margin and turnover ratios for each division. Note that the margins for both divisions dropped between 2004 and 2005. In fact, both divisions experienced a decrease of 16.67 percent. A declining margin could be explained by increased expenses, or decreased selling prices, or both.

In spite of the declining margin, the Electronics Division was able to increase its rate of return. The reason is that the increase in turnover more than compensated for the decline in margin. One explanation for the increased turnover could

**return on investment (ROI)**

The ratio of operating income to average operating assets.

**operating assets**

Assets used to generate operating income, usually consisting of cash, inventories, receivables, property, plant, and equipment.

**margin**

The ratio of net operating income to sales.

**turnover**

The ratio of sales to average operating assets.

---

4. For a discussion of the relative merits of gross book value, see James S. Reese and William R. Cool, "Measuring Investment Centre Performance," *Harvard Business Review* (May–June 1978): pp. 28-46, 174-76.

EXHIBIT  16-2

Comparison of Divisional
Performance

| Comparison of ROI | | |
| --- | --- | --- |
| | **Electronics Division** | **Medical Supplies Division** |
| 2004: | | |
| Sales | $30,000,000 | $117,000,000 |
| Operating income | 1,800,000 | 3,510,000 |
| Average operating assets | 10,000,000 | 19,500,000 |
| ROI[a] | 18% | 18% |
| 2005: | | |
| Sales | $40,000,000 | $117,000,000 |
| Operating income | 2,000,000 | 2,925,000 |
| Average operating assets | 10,000,000 | 19,500,000 |
| ROI[a] | 20% | 15% |

| Margin and Turnover Comparisons | | | | |
| --- | --- | --- | --- | --- |
| | **Electronics Division** | | **Medical Supplies Division** | |
| | **2004** | **2005** | **2004** | **2005** |
| Margin[b] | 6.0% | 5.0% | 3.0% | 2.5% |
| Turnover[c] | x 3.0 | x 4.0 | x 6.0 | x 6.0 |
| ROI | 18.0% | 20.0% | 18.0% | 15.0% |

[a] Operating income divided by average operating assets
[b] Operating income divided by sales
[c] Sales divided by average operating assets

be a reduction in inventories. Note that the average assets employed remained the same for the Electronics Division, even though sales increased by $10 million.

The experience of the Medical Supplies Division was less positive. Because its turnover rate remained unchanged, its ROI dropped. The division could not overcome the decline in margin.

## Advantages of the ROI

At least three positive outcomes can stem from the use of ROI. It encourages managers to focus on the following:

1. Relationships among sales, expenses, and investment.
2. Cost efficiency.
3. Operating asset efficiency.

These advantages are illustrated by the following three scenarios.

### Focus on ROI Relationships

Della Barnes, manager of the Plastics Division, is mulling over a suggestion from her marketing vice-president to increase the advertising budget by $100,000. The marketing vice-president is confident that this increase will boost sales by $200,000 and raise the contribution margin by $110,000. Della realizes that an additional $50,000 of operating assets will be needed to support such a large increase in sales. Currently, the division has sales of $2 million, net operating income of $150,000, and operating assets of $1 million.

If advertising were increased by $100,000 and the contribution margin by $110,000, operating income would increase by $10,000 ($110,000 − $100,000). The ROI without additional advertising is 15 percent ($150,000/$1,000,000). With the additional advertising and $50,000 investment in assets, the ROI would be 15.24

percent ($160,000/$1,050,000). Since ROI would be increased by the proposal, Della decides to authorize the increased advertising.

### Focus on Cost Efficiency

Kyle Chugg, the director of Turner's Battery Division, groans as he reviews the projections for the last half of the current fiscal year. The recession is hurting his division's performance. Adding the projected operating income of $200,000 to the actual operating income of the first half produces expected annual earnings of $425,000. Kyle then divides the expected operating income by the division's average operating assets of $3,500,000 to obtain an expected ROI of 12.14 percent. "This is awful," mutters Kyle. "Last year our ROI was 16 percent. And I'm looking at a couple more bad years before business returns to normal. Something has to be done to improve our performance."

Kyle directs all operating managers to identify and eliminate nonvalue-added activities. They do so, and identify cost reductions of $150,000 for the remainder of the year. This reduction increases the annual operating income from $425,000 to $575,000, which in turn increases ROI from 12.14 percent to 16.43 percent. Interestingly, Kyle finds that some of the reductions can be maintained after business returns to normal.

### Focus on Operating Asset Efficiency

The Electronic Storage Division prospered in its early years. When it developed a new technology for the mass storage of data, sales and ROI were extraordinarily high. However, in the past several years, competitors have developed competing technologies, and as a result the division's ROI has plunged from 30 to 15 percent. Cost cutting helped initially, but further improvements from cost reductions are no longer possible. Moreover, any increase in sales is unlikely—competition is too stiff. The divisional manager searches for ways to increase ROI by at least 3 to 5 percent. The division expects to receive additional capital for R&D only if it can raise ROI to the level achieved by other divisions.

The divisional manager initiates an intensive program to reduce operating assets. Most of the gains are made through inventory reductions. However, one plant is closed due to a long-term reduction in market share. By installing a just-in-time purchasing and manufacturing system, the division succeeds in reducing its assets without threatening its market share. Finally, the reduction in operating assets allows further reductions in operating costs. The end result is a 50 percent increase in the division's ROI, from 15 percent to 22 percent.

## Disadvantages of the ROI

Too much emphasis on the ROI can result in myopic behaviour. More specifically, it can encourage these two negative behaviours:

1. Focus on divisional profitability at the expense of overall company profitability.
2. Focus on the short term at the expense of the long term.

These disadvantages are illustrated by the following two scenarios:

### Narrow Focus on Divisional Profitability

A cleaning products division of a chemical company has an opportunity to invest in two projects for the coming year:

|  | Project I | Project II |
|---|---|---|
| Investment | $10,000,000 | $4,000,000 |
| Operating income | 1,300,000 | 640,000 |
| ROI | 13% | 16% |

The division currently earns an ROI of 15 percent, with operating assets of $50 million and operating income on current investments of $7.5 million. The division has an approval for up to $15 million in new investment capital. The company requires all investments to earn at least 10 percent. This rate represents the corporation's cost of acquiring capital. Any capital not used by a division is invested by headquarters at 10 percent.

The divisional manager has four alternatives: (1) invest in Project I, (2) invest in Project II, (3) invest in both projects, or (4) invest in neither. The divisional ROI has been computed for each alternative as follows:

**Alternatives**

|  | Project I | Project II | Both Projects | Neither Project |
|---|---|---|---|---|
| Operating income | $ 8,800,000 | $ 8,140,000 | $ 9,440,000 | $ 7,500,000 |
| Operating assets | 60,000,000 | 54,000,000 | 64,000,000 | 50,000,000 |
| ROI | 14.67% | 15.07% | 14.75% | 15.00% |

The divisional manager chooses to invest only in Project II, since it will boost the ROI from 15 percent to 15.07 percent.

While the manager's choice has maximized the divisional ROI, it has actually cost the company. If Project I had been selected, the company would have earned $1.3 million. Because it was not, the $10 million in capital was invested at 10 percent, earning only $1 million (0.10 × $10,000,000). The single-minded focus on divisional ROI has cost the company $300,000 in profits ($1,300,000 − $1,000,000).

### Encourages Short-Term Optimization

Ruth Lunsford, the manager of a small tools division, is displeased with her division's performance during the first three quarters. Given the expected income for the fourth quarter, the ROI for the year will be 13 percent—at least two percentage points below what she had hoped. Such an ROI may not be strong enough to bring the promotion she wants. With only three months left, drastic action is needed. Sales are unlikely to increase in the last quarter. Most sales are booked at least two to three months in advance, so emphasizing extra sales activity would benefit next year's performance. Some means to improve this year's performance must be found.

After careful thought, Ruth decides to take the following actions:

1. Lay off five of the highest-paid salespeople.
2. Cut the advertising budget for the fourth quarter by 50 percent.
3. Delay all promotions within the division for three months.
4. Reduce the preventive maintenance budget by 75 percent.
5. Use cheaper raw materials for fourth-quarter production.

In the aggregate, Ruth expects that these steps will reduce expenses, increase income, and raise the ROI to about 15.2 percent.

While Ruth's actions increase the profits and the ROI in the short term, they could have some negative long-term consequences. Laying off the highest-paid (and possibly the best) salespeople may harm the division's future sales-generating capabilities. Future sales could also be hurt by cutting back on advertising and by using cheaper raw materials. Delaying promotions could hurt employee morale, which in turn could lower productivity and future sales. Finally, reducing preventive maintenance would likely increase downtime and decrease the life of the productive equipment.

## Residual Income

To compensate for ROI's tendency to discourage investments that are profitable for the company but that lower a division's ROI, some companies use an alternative performance measure known as residual income. **Residual income (RI)** is the difference between operating income and the minimum dollar return required on a company's operating assets:

Residual income = Operating income – (Minimum rate of return
× Operating assets)

### Advantages of Residual Income

Let's reconsider the case of the cleaning products division. Recall that the divisional manager rejected Project I because it would have reduced the divisional ROI. However, that decision cost the company $300,000 in profits. The use of residual income as the performance measure would have prevented this loss. The residual income for each project is computed next.

**Project I:**

Residual income = Operating income – (Minimum rate of return
× Operating assets)
= $1,300,000 – (0.10 × $10,000,000)
= $1,300,000 – $1,000,000 .
= $300,000

**Project II:**

Residual income = $640,000 – (0.10 × $4,000,000)
= $640,000 – $400,000
= $240,000

Note that both projects have positive residual incomes. For comparative purposes, the divisional residual incomes for the four alternatives are as follows:

| | **Alternatives** | | | |
| --- | --- | --- | --- | --- |
| | **Project I** | **Project II** | **Both Projects** | **Neither Project** |
| Operating assets | $60,000,000 | $54,000,000 | $64,000,000 | 50,000,000 |
| Operating income | $ 8,800,000 | $ 8,140,000 | $ 9,440,000 | $ 7,500,000 |
| Minimum return[a] | 6,000,000 | 5,400,000 | 6,400,000 | 5,000,000 |
| Residual income | $ 2,800,000 | $ 2,740,000 | $ 3,040,000 | $ 2,500,000 |

[a]0.10 × Operating assets.

The table shows that selecting both projects produces the greatest increase in residual income. The use of residual income encourages managers to accept any project that earns above the minimum rate.

### Disadvantages of Residual Income

Residual income, like the ROI, can encourage a short-term orientation. If Ruth Lunsford were being evaluated on the basis of residual income, she might have taken the same actions.

Another problem with residual income is that it is an absolute measure of profitability. Thus, direct comparisons of performance across different investment centres become difficult, since the amount of investment may differ. For example, consider the residual income computations for Division A and Division B, where the minimum required rate of return is 8 percent.

|                            | Division A    | Division B   |
| -------------------------- | ------------- | ------------ |
| Average operating assets   | $15,000,000   | $2,500,000   |
| Operating income           | $ 1,500,000   | $ 300,000    |
| Minimum return[a]          | 1,200,000     | 200,000      |
| Residual income            | $ 300,000     | $ 100,000    |
| Residual return[b]         | 2%            | 4%           |

[a]$0.08 \times$ Operating assets.
[b]Residual income divided by operating assets.

It is tempting to claim that Division A is outperforming Division B, since its residual income is three times higher. Note, however, that Division A used six times the value of assets used by Division B to produce this difference. If anything, Division B is more efficient.

## Economic Value Added

**economic value added (EVA)**

A performance measure calculated by taking the after-tax operating profit minus the total annual cost of capital.

Economic value added, a concept that became popular in the 1990s, is similar to the RI but involves more sophisticated definitions of income and investment. It extends the RI by taking into account the effects of income taxes and debt financing on corporate profitability. **Economic value added (EVA)** is calculated as the after-tax operating income minus the annual cost of capital.[5] If EVA is positive, the company is creating wealth; if it is negative, the company is destroying capital. The underlying premise is that only companies that create wealth can survive in the long term.

Like the RI, the EVA is a dollar figure, not a percentage rate of return. However, it does resemble the ROI, because it links net income to capital employed. The key feature of the EVA is that it emphasizes *after-tax* operating profit and the *actual* cost of capital. The other measures use accounting book values, which may or may not represent the true cost of capital. Investors like the EVA because it relates profits to the amount of resources needed to achieve them.

Several companies have used the EVA. For example, Coca-Cola reported an EVA of $1,562 million for 1999. General Electric, Microsoft, and Merck reported significant increases in wealth for 1999 using the EVA measure.[6] Other companies, such as AT&T, PepsiCo, Hewlett-Packard, America-OnLine, and Sears Roebuck, have experienced decreases in wealth measured by the EVA.

### Calculating EVA

The EVA is after-tax operating income minus the dollar cost of capital employed, calculated as follows:

> EVA = After-tax operating income – (Weighted average cost of capital × Total capital employed)

The computation of the cost of capital employed involves two steps:

1. Determine the weighted average cost of capital.
2. Determine the total dollar amount of capital employed.

To calculate the weighted average cost of capital, the company must identify all sources of invested funds. Typical sources are borrowing and equity (stock issued). The interest on borrowed funds must be adjusted for its tax deductibility.

---

5. EVA is a registered trademark of Stern Stewart and Company (www.eva.com).

6. Geoffrey Colvin, "America's Best and Worst Wealth Creators," *Fortune* (December 18, 2000): pp. 207-16.

For example, if a company has issued 10-year bonds at an annual interest rate of 8 percent and the tax rate is 40 percent, the after-tax cost of the bonds is 4.8 percent [0.08 − (0.4 × 0.08)].

Equity is handled differently. The cost of equity financing is an opportunity cost to investors. Over time, shareholders have received an average return that is 6 percentage points higher than the return on long-term government bonds. If the bond rate is 6 percent, the average cost of equity is 12 percent. Riskier stocks command a higher return, whereas more stable and less risky stocks yield a lower return. Note that the cost of common stock is not tax deductible and thus does not require a tax adjustment. Finally, the proportionate share of each method of financing is multiplied by its proportionate cost and added to yield a weighted average cost of capital.

Suppose a company has two sources of financing: $2 million of long-term bonds paying 9 percent interest and $6 million of common stock, considered to be of average risk. If the company's tax rate is 40 percent and the rate of interest on long-term government bonds is 6 percent, the company's weighted average cost of capital is computed as follows:

|  | Amount | Proportion | x | After-Tax Cost | = | Weighted Average Cost |
|---|---|---|---|---|---|---|
| Bonds | $2,000,000 | 0.25 | | 0.09(1 − 0.4) = 0.054 | | 0.0135 |
| Equity | $6,000,000 | 0.75 | | 0.06 + 0.06 = 0.120 | | 0.0900 |
| Total | $8,000,000 | 1.00 | | | | 0.1035 |

Thus, the company's weighted average cost of capital is 10.35 percent.

The second data point necessary is the amount of capital employed. Clearly, the amount paid for buildings, land, and machinery must be included. However, other expenditures meant to have a long-term payoff, such as R&D, employee training, and so on, should also be included. Even though the latter are classified as expenses by GAAP, they can be considered investments for an internal management accounting measure, such as the EVA.

### EVA Example

Last year, Mahalo, Inc., had an after-tax operating income of $1,700,000. The company used three sources of financing: $2 million of mortgage bonds paying 8 percent interest; $3 million of unsecured bonds paying 10 percent interest; and $10 million in common stock, which was considered to be of average risk. Mahalo pays a marginal tax rate of 40 percent. The after-tax cost of the mortgage bonds is 0.048 [(1 − 0.4) × 0.08]. The after-tax cost of the unsecured bonds is 0.06 [(1 − 0.4) × 0.10]. The cost of common stock is 12 percent, consisting of the long-term treasury bond rate of 6 percent and a premium of 6 percent. The cost of common stock does not require a tax adjustment. The weighted average cost of capital is computed by multiplying the proportion of capital from each source by its cost, as follows:

|  | Amount | Proportion | x | After-Tax Cost | = | Weighted Average Cost |
|---|---|---|---|---|---|---|
| Mortgage bonds | $ 2,000,000 | 0.133 | | 0.048 | | 0.006 |
| Unsecured bonds | $ 3,000,000 | 0.200 | | 0.060 | | 0.012 |
| Common stock | $10,000,000 | 0.667 | | 0.120 | | 0.080 |
| Total | $15,000,000 | 1.000 | | | | |
| Weighted average cost of capital | | | | | | 0.098 |

The dollar cost of capital is obtained by multiplying the weighted average cost of capital by the total capital employed. For Mahalo, the capital employed is $15 million, so the cost of capital is $1,470,000 (0.098 × $15 million).

Mahalo's EVA is calculated as follows:

| | |
|---|---|
| After-tax operating income | $1,700,000 |
| Less: Cost of capital | 1,470,000 |
| EVA | $ 230,000 |

The positive EVA means that Mahalo earned operating profit over and above the cost of capital. It is creating wealth.

Companies such as AT&T and Coca-Cola have experienced a strong correlation between the EVA and stock prices. In fact, it has been found that stock prices are more significantly associated with the EVA than with other accounting measures, such as earnings per share and return on equity.[7]

### *Using the EVA for Individual Projects*

Like the ROI and RI, the EVA can be computed for individual projects. Let's reconsider the case of the cleaning products division. Recall that the divisional manager rejected Project I because it would have reduced the divisional ROI, and that as a result cost the company $300,000 in profits. The use of RI would have prevented this loss, as the RIs for both projects were positive. Thus, the two measures provided a mixed signal. To investigate further, assume that the company's tax rate is 40 percent and the weighted average cost of capital is 10 percent. The EVA for each project is computed as follows:

**Project I:**

$$
\begin{aligned}
\text{EVA} &= \text{After-tax project income} - \text{Cost of capital} \\
&= \$1,300,000 \,(1 - 0.4) - (0.10 \times \$10,000,000) \\
&= \$780,000 - \$1,000,000 \\
&= (\$220,000)
\end{aligned}
$$

**Project II:**

$$
\begin{aligned}
\text{EVA} &= \$640,000 \,(1 - 0.4) - (0.10 \times \$4,000,000) \\
&= \$384,000 - \$400,000 \\
&= (\$16,000)
\end{aligned}
$$

Note that both projects have a negative EVA, indicating that they erode wealth. The three methods produce contradictory results. Instead of accepting Project II (ROI) or both projects (RI), the EVA measure rejects both. Here, because the weighted average cost of capital equals the minimum rate of return, we can attribute the negative results mainly to income taxes. Neither project earns enough after-tax income to contribute to wealth creation. This conclusion is supported by the divisional EVAs for the four alternatives, as shown in the following table:

| | Project I | Project II | Both Projects | Neither Project |
|---|---|---|---|---|
| | | **Alternatives** | | |
| Operating assets | $60,000,000 | $54,000,000 | $64,000,000 | $50,000,000 |
| Operating income | $ 8,800,000 | $ 8,140,000 | $ 9,440,000 | $ 7,500,000 |
| Less: Income taxes | 3,520,000 | 3,256,000 | 3,776,000 | 3,000,000 |
| Net Income | 5,280,000 | 4,884,000 | 5,664,000 | 4,500,000 |
| Cost of capital[a] | 6,000,000 | 5,400,000 | 6,400,000 | 5,000,000 |
| EVA | $ (720,000) | ($ 516,000) | ($ 736,000) | ($ 500,000) |

[a] 0.10 × Operating assets

7. Shawn Tully, "The Real Key to Creating Wealth," *Fortune* (September 20, 1993): pp. 38-50.

### *Behavioural Aspects of EVA*

The use of EVA encourages managers to accept any project that earns greater than the average cost of capital after taxes. It can encourage desired behaviours better than emphasis on operating income alone. The underlying reason is EVA's reliance on the true cost of capital. In many companies, the responsibility for investment decisions rests with corporate management. As a result, the cost of capital is considered a corporate expense. If a division builds inventories and investments, the cost of financing these investments appears only on the corporate income statement—not on the division's income statement. Thus, the investments may falsely appear to be free to the divisional managers, who may abuse them.

Quaker Oats provides a good example of such practices. Before 1991, Quaker Oats evaluated its business segments based on quarterly profits. To keep quarterly earnings on an upward trend, segment managers offered sharp discounts on products at the end of each quarter. This resulted in huge orders from retailers and sharp surges in production at Quaker's plants at the end of each three-month period. This practice is called *trade loading*, because it "loads up the trade" (retail stores) with product. It is costly, however, because it requires large amounts of capital, such as working capital, inventories, and warehouses to store the quarterly spikes in output.

Quaker's plant in Danville produces snack foods and breakfast cereals. Before EVA was implemented, the plant ran well below capacity throughout the early part of the quarter. Purchasing, however, bought huge quantities of boxes, plastic wrappers, granola, and chocolate chips. The raw materials purchases buildup was in anticipation of the production surge in the last six weeks of the quarter. As the products were finished, Quaker packed 15 warehouses with finished goods. All costs associated with inventories were absorbed by corporate headquarters. As a result, the plant managers perceived them as free, and this encouraged them to build ever higher inventories.

The adoption of the EVA and the cancellation of trade loading led to more balanced production throughout the quarter, higher overall production and sales, and lower inventories. Quaker closed one-third of its 15 warehouses, saving $6 million annually in salaries and capital costs, and the Danville plant reduced inventories from $15 million to $9 million.[8]

## Multiple Measures of Performance

ROI, RI, and EVA are important measures of financial performance. However, a temptation may exist for managers to focus only on financial performance measures. The focus on financial measures may not tell the whole story of a company's performance, and managers may be unable to influence net income or investment. This means that nonfinancial performance measures are also important. For example, top management could consider such factors as market share, customer satisfaction, and personnel turnover. By letting lower-level managers know that attention to long-term factors is vital, the company can reduce short-term myopic behaviours and overemphasis on short-term financial results. Nonfinancial performance measures are examined in Chapter 17.

---

8. Ibid.

# Transfer Pricing in Decentralized Companies

**Objective 4**

Discuss the role of transfer pricing in decentralized companies.

**transfer price**

The price charged for goods transferred from one division to another.

An underlying assumption in a typical divisional structure is that divisions are reasonably independent. If the divisions conduct a significant amount of business among themselves, they are not independent, and the establishment of appropriate internal sales prices or transfer prices becomes important. Setting appropriate transfer prices is a complex issue, as divisional managers may not always be motivated to act in the best interest of the company overall.

The **transfer price** in a particular transaction is revenue to the selling division and cost to the buying division. So divisional managers who are evaluated based on income-based measures, such as the ROI, RI, and EVA, may have an incentive to take actions that are contrary to the company's best interests. This section examines the effect of different transfer prices on divisions and on the company as a whole.

## Impact on Performance Measures

Transfer pricing affects both transferring divisions and the company as a whole through its impact on (1) divisional performance measures, (2) companywide profits, and (3) divisional autonomy.

### Impact on Divisional Performance Measures

The price charged for transferred intermediate products affects the costs of the buying division and the revenues of the selling division. Because the profits of both divisions, as well as profit-based performance measures, are affected, transfer pricing can be an emotional issue. Exhibit 16–3 illustrates the effect of the transfer price on two divisions of ABC, Inc. Division A produces a component and sells it to Division C. Since the $30 transfer price is revenue to Division A, it wants the price to be as high as possible. Conversely, since the $30 price is a cost to Division C, just like the cost of any other material, it obviously prefers a lower transfer price.

### Impact on Companywide Profits

Although the actual transfer price cancels out for the company as a whole, transfer pricing can affect the level of profits earned by the company in two ways: by affecting divisional behaviour, and by affecting income taxes. Divisions, if they act independently, may set transfer prices that maximize divisional profits but adversely affect companywide profits. For example, the buying division may decide to purchase a product from an outside party, because the outside price is lower than the transfer price. In reality, the cost of producing the product internally may be lower than the transfer price.

Suppose that Division A in Exhibit 16–3 sets a transfer price of $30 for a component that costs $24 to produce. If Division C can obtain the component from an outside supplier for $28, it will refuse to buy from Division A. Division C will realize savings of $2 per component ($30 internal transfer price – $28 external price). However, assuming that Division A cannot replace the internal sales with external sales, the company as a whole will lose $4 per component ($28 external cost – $24 internal cost). This outcome will increase the total cost to the company.

Transfer pricing can also affect overall corporate income taxes. To gain tax advantage, corporations may set transfer prices to assign more revenues to divisions in low-tax jurisdictions and more costs to divisions in high-tax jurisdictions. Different countries, and even different provinces in Canada, have different tax regulations, which can affect location and transfer pricing decisions by companies.

| ABC, Inc. | |
| --- | --- |
| **Division A** | **Division C** |
| Produces component and transfers it to C for transfer price of $30 per unit | Purchases component from A at transfer price of $30 per unit and uses it in production of final product |
| Transfer price = $30 per unit | Transfer price = $30 per unit |
| Revenue to A | Cost to C |
| Increases net income | Decreases net income |
| Increases ROI | Decreases ROI |

Transfer price revenue = Transfer price cost
Zero net impact on ABC, Inc.

### Impact on Autonomy

Because transfer pricing decisions can affect companywide profitability, top management is often tempted to intervene and dictate desirable transfer prices. If such intervention becomes frequent, however, the organization has effectively abandoned decentralization and its advantages. Organizations decentralize because the benefits are greater than the associated costs. One of these costs is occasional suboptimal behaviour by divisional managers. Intervention by central management to reduce this behaviour may actually be more expensive in the long term than nonintervention.

## The Transfer Pricing Problem

A transfer pricing system should satisfy three objectives:

1. Accurate performance evaluation
2. Goal congruence
3. Preservation of divisional autonomy[9]

*Accurate performance evaluation* means that no divisional manager should benefit at the expense of another. One division should not be made better off while another is made worse off. *Goal congruence* means that divisional managers select actions that maximize companywide benefits. *Autonomy* means that central management should not interfere with the decision-making freedom of divisional managers. The **transfer pricing problem** is concerned with finding a system that simultaneously satisfies all three objectives.

Although direct intervention by central management in setting transfer prices may not be advisable, the development of some general guidelines may be appropriate. One such guideline, called the *opportunity cost approach*, can be used to describe a wide variety of transfer pricing practices. Under the right conditions, this approach is compatible with the objectives of performance evaluation, goal congruence, and autonomy.

**transfer pricing problem**

The problem of finding a transfer pricing system that simultaneously satisfies the three objectives of accurate performance evaluations, goal congruence, and autonomy.

---

9. Joshua Ronen and George McKinney, "Transfer Pricing for Divisional Autonomy," *Journal of Accounting Research* (Spring 1970): pp. 100-1.

**opportunity cost approach**

A transfer pricing system that identifies the minimum price that a selling division would be willing to accept and the maximum price that a buying division would be willing to pay.

**minimum transfer price**

The transfer price that will make the selling division no worse off if an output is sold internally.

**maximum transfer price**

The transfer price that will make the buying division no worse off if an input is acquired internally.

# Opportunity Cost Approach as Guide for Transfer Pricing

In establishing a transfer pricing policy, the views of both the selling division and the buying division must be considered. The **opportunity cost approach** achieves this goal by identifying the minimum price that the selling division would be willing to accept and the maximum price that the buying division would be willing to pay. These minimum and maximum prices correspond to the opportunity costs of transferring internally. They are defined as follows:

1. The **minimum transfer price** is the transfer price that would leave the selling division no worse off than if the transferred input were sold to an external party. This is sometimes referred to as the "floor" of the bargaining range.
2. The **maximum transfer price** is the transfer price that would leave the buying division no worse off than if the transferred input were purchased externally. This is sometimes referred to as the "ceiling" of the bargaining range.

The opportunity cost approach guides divisions in determining when internal transfers should occur. Specifically, the intermediate products should be transferred internally whenever the opportunity cost (minimum price) of the selling division is less than the opportunity cost (maximum price) of the buying division. By its very definition, this approach ensures that neither divisional manager is worse off by transferring internally. The term "no worse off" means that the internal transfer does not decrease divisional profits.

## Market Price

If a perfectly competitive outside market existed for the transferred product, the correct transfer price would be the market price.[10] Divisional managers' actions would optimize divisional profits and companywide profits simultaneously. Furthermore, no division would be able to benefit at the expense of another. Central management would not have to intervene.

The opportunity cost approach also signals that the correct transfer price is the market price. Since the selling division can sell all it produces at the market price, transferring internally at a lower price would make the division worse off. Similarly, the buying division can always acquire the intermediate products at the market price, so it would be unwilling to pay more for an internally transferred product. The only possible transfer price is the market price, since it is the minimum transfer price for the selling division and the maximum price for the buying division. In fact, moving away from the market price would decrease the company's overall profitability. This principle can be used to resolve divisional conflicts that may occur, as the following example illustrates.

Tyson Manufacturers, a large, privately held corporation in Kitchener, Ontario, produces small appliances. The company has adopted a decentralized organizational structure. The Small Parts Division, managed by Ned Kimberly, produces parts that are used by the Small Motor Division, managed by Andrea Ferguson. The parts can also be sold to other manufacturers and wholesalers. For all practical purposes, the market for the parts is perfectly competitive. Andrea has just sent the following memo to Frank Johnston, the vice president:

10. A perfectly competitive market for the intermediate product requires four conditions: (1) the division producing the intermediate product is small relative to the market as a whole and cannot influence the price of the product; (2) the intermediate product is indistinguishable from the same product of other sellers; (3) companies can easily enter and exit the market; and (4) consumers, producers, and resource owners have perfect knowledge of the market.

**MEMORANDUM**

To:              **Frank Johnston, Vice-President**
From:            **Andrea Ferguson**
Subject:         **Transfer Price of Component No. 14**
Date:            **October 15, 2005**

Frank, as you know, our division is operating at 70 percent capacity. Last week we received a request for 100,000 units of Model 1267 at a price of $30. Below are the production costs for the model. Because of the special arrangements, we avoid any distribution costs. The full cost includes the component that we usually buy from Ned's division.

| | |
|---|---|
| Direct materials | $10 |
| Transferred-in component | 8 |
| Direct labour | 2 |
| Variable overhead | 1 |
| Fixed overhead | 10 |
| Total cost | $31 |

As you can see, if we accept the order, we will lose $1 per unit. The purpose of this memo is to register a complaint about the Small Parts Division. I must confess that I am somewhat irritated with Ned. I know that the full cost of the component supplied by his division is $5. I asked for a more favourable transfer price—$6.50 instead of the $8 we normally pay. He absolutely refused and, in fact, seemed somewhat put out by my request. I believe that the concession is needed so that I can accept the order and show a small profit. The benefits of this order are appealing. My capacity utilization would jump to 85 percent, and I would avoid laying off some skilled workers. Avoiding the layoff would save the company at least $50,000 in training costs next year. Also, the special order may open some new markets for the company.

Can't you persuade Ned to make this small concession for the good of the company? In my opinion, more teamwork is needed. After all, I have been a faithful customer of Ned's for several years.

If you were Frank Johnston, how would you react to the memo? Should Frank intervene and dictate a lower transfer price? Is the market price guideline for transfer pricing invalid in this situation? To answer these questions, let's turn to the opportunity cost approach. Since Ned can sell all he produces, the minimum transfer price for his division is the market price of $8. Any lower price would make his division worse off. For Andrea's division, identifying the maximum transfer price that can be paid so that her division is no worse off requires more analysis.

Since the Small Motor Division is operating below capacity, the $10 fixed overhead allocated to Model 1267 is not relevant. The relevant costs are the additional costs that will be incurred only if the order is accepted. These costs, excluding for the moment the cost of the transferred-in component, are as follows:

| | |
|---|---|
| Direct materials | $10 |
| Direct labour | 2 |
| Variable overhead | 1 |
| Total | $13 |

Thus, the contribution to profits before considering the cost of the transferred-in component is $17 ($30 – $13). The division could actually pay $17 for the component and still break even on the special order. However, since the component can always be purchased from an outside supplier for $8, the maximum price that the division should pay internally is $8. If the buying division pays $8, the selling division is no worse off. Furthermore, relative to the status quo, the buying division is better off by $9 ($17 – $8). Thus, the transfer price of $8 should be paid and the special order accepted.

There is no reason for central management to intervene. The market price is the correct transfer price. The vice-president could point out the benefits of the special order to Andrea. The need to do so, however, raises some questions about Andrea's managerial skills and ability to use relevant accounting information.

## Negotiated Transfer Prices

In reality, perfectly competitive markets seldom exist. In many cases, buyers or sellers can influence prices to some degree—for example, through large orders or unique products. When imperfections in the market for the intermediate product exist, market price may no longer be a suitable transfer price. In this situation, negotiated transfer prices may be practical. The opportunity cost approach can be used to define the boundaries for transfer prices.

### Example 1: Avoidable Distribution Costs

To illustrate, assume that a division produces a circuit board that can be sold in the outside market for $22. The division can sell all units produced at $22. Currently, the division sells 1,000 units per day, with variable manufacturing and distribution costs of $12 and $2 per unit respectively. Alternatively, the board can be sold internally to the company's Electronic Games Division. In this situation, the Circuit Board Division avoids the $2 distribution cost.

The Electronic Games Division is also at capacity, producing and selling 350 games per day. Each game is priced at $45 and has a variable manufacturing cost of $32 and variable selling cost of $3 per unit. Sales and production data for each division are summarized in Exhibit 16–4.

Since the Electronic Games Division was acquired very recently, no transfers between the two divisions have taken place yet. Susan Swift, the manager of the Circuit Board Division, requests a meeting with Randy Schrude, manager of the Electronic Games Division, to discuss the possibility of internal transfers. The following is their conversation:

**Susan**: "Randy, I'm excited about the possibility of supplying your division with circuit boards. What is your current demand for the type of board we produce? And how much are you paying for the boards?"

**Randy**: "We would use one in each video game, and our production is about 350 games per day. We pay $22 for each board."

**Susan**: "We can supply that amount simply by displacing external sales. Furthermore, we would be willing to sell them at the same price we charge outside customers. We can at least meet your price. That way, you are no worse off."

**Randy**: "Actually, I was hoping for a better price than $22. The circuit board is by far our most expensive input. By transferring internally, you can avoid some selling, transportation, and collection expenses. I called corporate headquarters, which estimated these costs to be approximately $2 per unit. I'd be willing to pay

EXHIBIT 16-4

Summary of Sales and Production Data

| | Board Division | Games Division |
|---|---|---|
| Units sold: | | |
| Per day | 1,000 | 350 |
| Per year[a] | 260,000 | 91,000 |
| Unit data: | | |
| Selling price | $22 | $45 |
| Variable costs: | | |
| Manufacturing | $12 | $32 |
| Selling | $2 | $3 |
| Annual fixed costs | $1,480,000 | $610,000 |

[a]There are 260 selling days in a year.

$20 each for your units. You'd be no worse off, and, with a less expensive component, I can make about $700 more profit per day. This deal would make the company $182,000 during the coming year."

**Susan**: "Your information about avoiding $2 per unit is accurate. I also understand how the cheaper component can allow you to increase your profits. However, if you were to purchase the board for $22, I could increase my division's profits, and the corporation's for that matter, by $700 per day—just by selling you the 350 units and saving the $2 per unit to sell externally. You would be no worse off, and my division and the corporation would be better off by $182,000 per year. It seems to me that most of the benefits to the corporation come from avoiding the distribution costs incurred when we sell externally. Nonetheless, I'll sweeten the deal. Since we're both members of the same family, I'll let you have the 350 boards for $21.50 each. That price allows you to increase your profits by $175 per day and reflects the fact that most of the savings are generated by my division."

**Randy**: "I don't agree that most of the savings are generated by your division. You can't achieve those savings unless I buy from you. I'm willing to buy internally, but only if there is a fair sharing of the joint benefits. I think a reasonable arrangement is to split the benefits equally. However, I will grant a small concession. I'll buy 350 units at $21.10 each—that will increase your divisional profits by $385 per day and mine by $315 per day. Deal?"

**Susan**: "Sounds reasonable. Let's have a contract drawn up."

This dialogue illustrates how the minimum transfer price ($20) and the maximum transfer price ($22) set the lower and upper limits for transfer prices. The example also demonstrates how negotiation can lead to improved profitability for each division and the company as a whole. Exhibit 16–5 provides income statements for each division before and after the agreement. Note how the company's total profits increase by $182,000—a saving of the $2 shipping charge on 91,000 units—as claimed. Note also how the profit increase is split between the two divisions.

**EXHIBIT  16-5**

Comparative Income
Statements

| Before Negotiation: All Sales External | | | |
|---|---|---|---|
| | **Board Division** | **Games Division** | **Total** |
| Sales | $5,720,000 | $4,095,000 | $9,815,000 |
| Less variable expenses: | | | |
| Cost of goods sold | 3,120,000 | 2,912,000 | 6,032,000 |
| Variable selling | 520,000 | 273,000 | 793,000 |
| Contribution margin | $2,080,000 | $ 910,000 | $2,990,000 |
| Less: Fixed expenses | 1,480,000 | 610,000 | 2,090,000 |
| Net income | $  600,000 | $ 300,000 | $  900,000 |

| After Negotiation: Internal Transfers @ $21.10 | | | |
|---|---|---|---|
| | **Board Division** | **Games Division** | **Total** |
| Sales | $5,638,100 | $4,095,000 | $9,733,100 |
| Less variable expenses: | | | |
| Cost of goods sold | 3,120,000 | 2,830,100 | 5,950,100 |
| Variable selling | 338,000 | 273,000 | 611,000 |
| Contribution margin | $2,180,100 | $ 991,900 | $3,172,000 |
| Less: Fixed expenses | 1,480,000 | 610,000 | 2,090,000 |
| Net income | $  700,100 | $ 381,900 | $1,082,000 |
| Increase in net income | $  100,100 | $  81,900 | $  182,000 |

### Example 2: Excess Capacity

In a perfectly competitive market, the selling division can sell all it wishes at the prevailing market price. In a less ideal setting, it may not be able to sell its entire production, leading to excess capacity.[11]

To illustrate the role of transfer pricing and negotiation in this setting, consider the dialogue between Sharon Bunker, the manager of a plastics division, and Carlos Rivera, the manager of a pharmaceuticals division of Nortex Corporation:

**Carlos**: "Sharon, my division has shown a loss for the past three years. When I took over the division at the beginning of the year, I set a goal with headquarters to break even. At this point, projections show a loss of $5,000—but I think I have a way to reach my goal, if I can get your cooperation."

**Sharon**: "If I can help, I certainly will. What do you have in mind?"

**Carlos**: "I need a special deal on your plastic bottle Model 3. I have the opportunity to place our aspirin with a large retail chain on the west coast—a totally new market for our product. But we have to give them a price break. The chain has offered to pay $0.85 per bottle for an order of 250,000 bottles. My variable cost per unit is $0.60, not including the cost of the plastic bottle. I normally pay $0.40 for your bottle, but if I do that, I'll lose $37,500 on the order. I cannot afford that kind of loss. I know that you have excess capacity. I'll place an order for 250,000 bottles, and I'll pay your variable cost per unit, provided that it's no more than $0.25. Are you interested? Do you have sufficient excess capacity to handle a special order of 250,000 bottles?"

**Sharon**: "I have enough excess capacity to handle the order easily. The variable cost per bottle is $0.15. Transferring at that price would make me no worse off. My fixed costs will be there whether I make the bottles or not. But I'd like to have some contribution from an order like this. I'll tell you what I'll do. I'll let you have the order for $0.20. That way we both make $0.05 contribution per bottle, for a total contribution of $12,500. That'll put you in the black and help me get closer to my budgeted profit goal."

**Carlos**: "Great. This is better than I expected. If this chain provides more orders in the future—as I expect it will—and at better prices, I'll make sure you get our business."

Note the role that the opportunity cost approach played in the negotiation. In this situation, the minimum transfer price is the plastics division's variable cost ($0.15), which represents the incremental outlay if the order is accepted. Since it has excess capacity, only variable costs are relevant to the decision. For the buying division, the maximum transfer price is the purchase price that would allow the division to cover its incremental costs on the special order ($0.25). Adding the $0.25 to the other costs of processing ($0.60), the total incremental costs are $0.85 per unit. Since the selling price is also $0.85 per unit, the division is made no worse off. Both divisions, however, can be better off if the transfer price is between the minimum price of $0.15 and the maximum price of $0.25.

Comparative statements showing the contribution margin earned by each division, and by the company as a whole, are shown in Exhibit 16–6 for each of the four transfer prices discussed. These statements show that the company earns the same profit for all four transfer prices. However, different prices do affect the individual divisions' profits. Because each division is autonomous, however, there is no guarantee that the company will earn the additional profit on the special order. For example, if Sharon had insisted on maintaining the price of $0.40,

---

11. Output can be increased by decreasing selling prices. Of course, decreasing selling prices to increase sales volume may not increase profits—in fact, profits could easily decline. We assume in this example that the divisional manager has chosen the most advantageous selling prices and that the division still has excess capacity.

EXHIBIT 16-6

Comparative Statements

| Transfer Price of $0.40 | Pharmaceuticals | Plastics | Total |
|---|---|---|---|
| Sales | $212,500 | $100,000 | $312,500 |
| Less: Variable expenses | 250,000 | 37,500 | 287,500 |
| Contribution margin | $(37,500) | $ 62,500 | $ 25,000 |
| **Transfer Price of $0.25** | | | |
| Sales | $212,500 | $ 62,500 | $275,000 |
| Less: Variable expenses | 212,500 | 37,500 | 250,000 |
| Contribution margin | $        0 | $ 25,000 | $ 25,000 |
| **Transfer Price of $0.20** | | | |
| Sales | $212,500 | $ 50,000 | $262,500 |
| Less: Variable expenses | 200,000 | 37,500 | 237,500 |
| Contribution margin | $ 12,500 | $ 12,500 | $ 25,000 |
| **Transfer Price of $0.15** | | | |
| Sales | $212,500 | $ 37,500 | $250,000 |
| Less: Variable expenses | 187,500 | 37,500 | 225,000 |
| Contribution margin | $ 25,000 | $        0 | $ 25,000 |

no transfer would have taken place, and the $25,000 increase in profits would have been lost.

### Disadvantages of Negotiated Transfer Prices

The following three disadvantages of negotiated transfer prices are commonly mentioned:

1. A divisional manager with private information may take advantage of other managers.
2. Performance measures may be distorted by the negotiating skills of managers.
3. Negotiation can consume considerable time and resources.

It is interesting that Carlos, the manager of the pharmaceuticals division, did not know the variable cost of producing the plastic bottle. Yet that cost was a key to the negotiation. This lack of knowledge gave Sharon, the plastics division's manager, the opportunity to exploit the situation. For example, she could have claimed that the variable cost was $0.27 and offered to sell for $0.25 per unit as a favour to Carlos, saying that she would be willing to absorb a loss of $5,000 in exchange for a promise of future business. Had she done so, she would have captured the full $25,000 benefit of the transfer. Alternatively, she could have misrepresented the figure and used it to turn down the request, thus preventing Carlos from achieving his budgetary goal. After all, she is in competition with Carlos for promotions, bonuses, salary increases, and so on.

Fortunately, Sharon displayed sound judgment and acted with integrity. For negotiation to work, managers must be willing to share relevant information. How can this requirement be satisfied? The answer lies in the use of good internal control procedures. Perhaps the best internal control procedure is to hire and retain managers who possess integrity. Another possibility would be for top management to provide divisional managers with access to the relevant accounting information of other divisions. This step would reduce the likelihood of exploitive behaviour in situations like the one described.

The second disadvantage of negotiated transfer prices is that divisional profitability may be affected too strongly by the negotiating skills of managers. Although this argument has some merit, it ignores the fact that negotiating skills themselves are desirable managerial skills. Perhaps divisional profitability *should* reflect differences in negotiating skills.

The third criticism of this technique is that negotiating can consume a lot of time. The time that divisional managers spend negotiating with one another is time they could have been spending managing other activities—activities that perhaps have a greater bearing on the success of their divisions. Also, negotiations sometimes reach an impasse, forcing top management to mediate.[12] Although the use of managerial time may be costly, costs could be even higher if this interaction were not allowed. A mutually satisfactory negotiated outcome can result in increased profits for the company, easily exceeding the cost of the managerial time involved. Furthermore, negotiation does not have to be repeated each time for similar transactions.

### Advantages of Negotiated Transfer Prices

Whatever their disadvantages, negotiated transfer prices offer some hope for meeting the three criteria of goal congruence, autonomy, and accurate performance evaluation. Moreover, negotiated transfer prices have been identified as a means by which goal congruence throughout the entire company can be achieved.[13] If negotiation helps ensure goal congruence, there is no need for top management to intervene in divisional affairs. Finally, when the negotiating skills of divisional managers are comparable, or when the company views these skills as important for managers to have, concerns about motivation and accurate performance measures are avoided.

## Cost-Based Transfer Prices

Companies that use cost-based transfer pricing require that all transfers take place at cost. Three forms of cost-based transfer prices are commonly considered:

1. Full cost
2. Full cost plus markup
3. Variable cost plus fixed fee

For all three, standard costs should be used to determine transfer prices in order to avoid passing on inefficiencies from one division to to the next. A more important issue, however, is the appropriateness of cost-based transfer prices. Should they be used? If so, under what circumstances?

### Full-Cost Transfer Pricing

The full cost includes the costs of direct materials, direct labour, variable overhead, and a portion of fixed overhead. This is possibly the least desirable transfer pricing approach; its only real virtue is simplicity. Its disadvantages are considerable. Full-cost transfer pricing can provide perverse incentives and distort per-

---

12. The involvement of top management may be very cursory, however. In the case of a very large oil company that negotiates virtually all transfer prices, two divisional managers could not agree after several weeks and appealed to their superior. His response: "Either come to an agreement within twenty-four hours, or you're both fired." Needless to say, an agreement was reached within the allotted time.

13. For an excellent discussion of the role of negotiated transfer prices in a decentralized organization, see David Watson and John Baumler, "Transfer Pricing: A Behavioural Context," *The Accounting Review* (July 1975): pp. 466-74.

formance measures. As we have seen, the opportunity costs of both the buying and selling divisions are essential for determining proper transfer prices. At the same time, they provide useful reference points for determining a mutually satisfactory transfer price. Only rarely does the full cost provide accurate information about opportunity costs.

In the previous example, the use of full cost as a transfer price would have prevented the transactions from occurring. In the first example, the selling division manager would never have considered transferring internally if the price had to be full cost. Because the transfer took place at selling price less some distribution expenses, both divisions—and the company as a whole—were better off. In the second example, the manager of the pharmaceuticals division would never have accepted the special order from the West Coast chain. Both divisions and the company would have been worse off, in both the short term and the long term.

### Full Cost Plus Markup

Full cost plus markup suffers from the same problems as full cost. It is somewhat less perverse, however, if the markup can be negotiated. Thus, in the first example, a full cost plus markup formula could have been used to represent the negotiated transfer price. In some situations, a full cost plus markup formula may be the outcome of negotiation. If so, it is simply another example of negotiated transfer pricing. At such times, the use of this method is justified. That being said, it is not possible to use full cost plus markup to represent all negotiated prices. For example, it could not have been used in the second example, because the result would not have been beneficial to both divisions. The superior approach in such situations is negotiation.

### Variable Cost Plus Fixed Fee

Like full cost plus markup, variable cost plus fixed fee can be a useful transfer pricing approach, providing that the fixed fee is negotiable. This method has one advantage over full cost plus markup. If the selling division is operating below capacity, variable cost is its relevant cost. Assuming that the fixed fee is negotiable, the variable cost approach can be equivalent to negotiated transfer pricing.

### Appropriateness of Use

In spite of the disadvantages of cost-based transfer prices, companies use these methods, especially full cost and full cost plus markup. There must be some compelling reasons for their use—reasons that outweigh the benefits associated with negotiated transfer prices and the disadvantages of cost-based methods. The cost-based methods do have the virtue of being simple and objective. However, these qualities alone cannot justify their widespread use.

In many situations, transfers between divisions have only a small impact on the profitability of either division. In some cases, it may be cost-beneficial to use an easily identifiable, cost-based formula instead of spending time and resources on negotiation. In other cases, the use of full cost plus markup may simply be the formula agreed upon in negotiations. Once established, this formula can be used until the original conditions change to the point where renegotiation is necessary. In this way, the time and resources of negotiation can be minimized. For example, for custom-made products, managers may not be able to identify an outside market price, and reimbursement of full costs plus a reasonable rate of return may be a good surrogate for the transferring division's opportunity costs.

Many corporations use outsourcing to meet specific production and service needs. This approach reduces the need for internal transfer prices. With outsourcing, the otherwise internally provided intermediate product or service is provided by an external company, and the price is a true market price.

## Special Issues in Multinational Companies

Multinational companies have operations in several countries. Because of geographic, economic, cultural, and other possible differences among countries, international divisions are often established as investment centres for responsibility accounting purposes. Thus, multinational divisionalized companies are special cases of decentralized organizations, with some unique features. Performance evaluation and transfer pricing in multinational companies can be complicated by factors that cannot be controlled.

### Performance Evaluation

With multinational companies, environmental differences make interdivisional comparisons of ROI, RI, and EVA potentially misleading. The ROI measure is used as an example here to demonstrate a potential problem. Suppose a Canadian-based company has three divisions located in the United States, Brazil, and France, with the following information in millions of dollars:

|               | Assets | Revenues | Net Income | Margin | Turnover | ROI |
|---------------|--------|----------|------------|--------|----------|-----|
| Brazil        | $10    | $ 6      | $ 3        | 50%    | 0.60     | 30% |
| United States | 18     | 13       | 10         | 77     | 0.72     | 55  |
| France        | 15     | 10       | 6          | 60     | 0.67     | 40  |

Based on the ROI, it seems that the manager of the American subsidiary performed the best, whereas the manager of the Brazilian subsidiary performed the worst. But is this a fair comparison? France and the United States face very different legal, political, educational, and economic conditions. Inflation has been very high in South America relative to North America. Many South American companies have responded by adjusting reported financial results for inflation. Suppose the American company reports its assets at historical cost and the Brazilian company adjusts its assets for inflation. If inflation during the period in which the assets have been held has averaged 100 percent, the historical cost of the Brazilian assets is $5 million, calculated as follows:

$$x + (100\%)x = \$10$$
$$x + 1.00x = \$10$$
$$2x = \$10$$
$$x = \$5$$

If the Brazilian subsidiary's assets are restated at historical cost, the ROI becomes 60 percent (3/5 = 0.6). If this computation is used, the Brazilian subsidiary seems to be the *most* successful, not the least. Note, however, that accounting for inflationary effects on income and assets is complicated, and that this example is not comprehensive. Even when top management is aware of inflation rates (and it usually is), the lack of consistency in internal reporting may still obscure interdivisional comparisons.

### Transfer Pricing

Differences in income tax rates and regulations in different countries can complicate transfer pricing in multinational companies. If all countries had the same tax structure, transfer pricing issues would be the same as in decentralized companies operating in one country. However, because of tax differences, multinational companies can use transfer pricing to shift costs to high-tax countries, such as Canada, and revenues to low-tax countries, such as the Cayman Islands.

Exhibit 16–7 illustrates this concept using two transfer prices. The first transfer price of $100 is set, as title for the goods passed from the Belgian subsidiary to the reinvoicing centre in Bermuda. Because it is equal to the full cost, profit and taxes payable equal zero. The second transfer price of $200 is set by the reinvoicing centre in Bermuda. The transfer from Bermuda to Canada results in a profit, but no tax is payable, because Bermuda has no corporate income taxes. Finally, the Canadian subsidiary sells the product to an external party for $200. Again, the price equals the cost, with no profit and taxes payable. Without the reinvoicing centre, the goods would have gone directly from Belgium to Canada. If the transfer price were $200, the profit in Belgium would be $100, subject to the tax rate of 42 percent. Alternatively, if the transfer price were $100, no Belgian tax would be paid, but the Canadian subsidiary would realize a profit of $100, subject to the Canadian corporate income tax rate of approximately 46 percent.

It is illegal for companies to *evade* taxes; it is not illegal for companies to *avoid* them. Unfortunately, the difference between avoidance and evasion is often not clear. The situation depicted in Exhibit 16–7 is clearly abusive; other tax-motivated actions may not be. For example, a company may establish an R&D centre in an existing subsidiary located in a high-tax country, since such costs are tax deductible. In fact, many multinational companies have a tax-planning system that minimizes taxes globally.[14]

EXHIBIT   16-7

Use of Transfer Pricing to Affect Taxes Paid

| Action | Tax Impact |
| --- | --- |
| Belgian subsidiary of Parent Company produces a component at a cost of $100 per unit. Title to the component is transferred to a reinvoicing centre in Bermuda at a transfer price of $100 per unit.[a] | 42% tax rate<br>$100 revenue – $100 cost = $0 profit<br>Taxes paid = $0 |
| Reinvoicing centre in Bermuda, also a subsidiary of Parent Company, transfers title of component to Canadian subsidiary of Parent Company at a transfer price of $200 per unit. | 0% tax rate<br>$200 revenue – $100 cost = $100 profit<br>Taxes paid = $0 |
| Canadian subsidiary sells component to external company at $200 per unit. | 46% tax rate<br>$200 revenue – $200 cost = $0 profit<br>Taxes paid = $0 |

[a] Reinvoicing centre takes title to the goods but does not physically receive them. The primary objective of a reinvoicing centre is to shift profits to divisions in low-tax countries.

The Canada Customs and Revenue Agency (CCRA) oversees transfer pricing arrangements for multinational companies. For Canadian-based companies, the CCRA has the authority to reallocate income and deductions among divisions, if it believes that such reallocation will reduce tax evasion.[15] Basically, the transfers should occur at "arm's length," and the transfer prices should be the same as for transfers between unrelated parties.

---

14. It should be noted that differences in income taxes between Canadian provinces may also result in transfer pricing issues and incentives for companies to relocate from one province to another.

15. In Canada, the Income Tax Act (Section 69) and CCRA's Information Circular 87–2 govern transfer pricing arrangements by multinational companies.

# Summary of Learning Objectives

### 1.  Define responsibility accounting, and describe four types of responsibility centres.

A responsibility accounting system is an accounting system that measures the results of responsibility centres and compares the results with expected outcomes. The four types of responsibility centres are cost centres, revenue centres, profit centres, and investment centres.

### 2.  Explain why companies decentralize.

Many companies choose to decentralize in order to increase overall efficiency. The essence of decentralization is decision-making freedom. In a decentralized organization, lower-level managers make and implement decisions; in a centralized organization, lower-level managers are responsible only for implementing decisions. Reasons for decentralization are many. Companies decentralize because local managers can make better decisions using local information. Local managers can also provide more timely responses to changing conditions. Also, cognitive limitations make it necessary for large, diversified companies to decentralize; basically, it is impossible for a central manager to be fully cognizant of all products and markets. Other reasons to decentralize: doing so makes it easier to train and motivate local managers, and frees top management from day-to-day operations so that they can spend time on longer-range strategic activities.

### 3.  Compute and interpret return on investment (ROI), residual income (RI), and economic value added (EVA).

ROI is the ratio of operating income to average operating assets. This ratio can be broken down into two components: margin (the ratio of operating income to sales) and turnover (the ratio of sales to average operating assets). ROI is the most common measure of performance for managers of decentralized units. It encourages managers to focus on improving their divisions' profitability by improving sales, controlling costs, and using assets efficiently. Unfortunately, managers may try to increase ROI by sacrificing long-term gains for short-term benefits. For example, ROI can encourage managers to forgo investments that are profitable for the company but that would lower the divisional ROI.

Residual income (RI) is the difference between operating income and the minimum dollar return on operating assets. It encourages managers to accept any new project that earns more than the minimum rate of return on investment. However, like ROI, it can also encourage a short-term orientation. And since RI is an absolute measure, it is difficult to make comparisons across investment centres.

Economic value added (EVA) is the difference between income and the dollar cost of capital. It is calculated as the after-tax operating income minus the total annual cost of capital. If the EVA is positive, the company is creating wealth. If it is negative, the company is destroying capital. Like RI, EVA is a dollar figure, not a percentage rate of return. The key feature of EVA is that it emphasizes the *after-tax* operating profit and the *actual* cost of capital. Investors like the EVA because it relates profit to the amount of resources needed to achieve it. Like RI, EVA attempts to solve the problems associated with suboptimal behaviours related to ROI but not the problem of short-term orientation. Multiple performance measures are required to encourage long-term focus.

### 4.  Discuss the role of transfer pricing in decentralized companies.

When one division produces a product that is used in production by another division of the same company, a transfer price needs to be set. The transfer price is revenue to the selling division and cost to the buying division. Thus, the price charged for the intermediate products affects the operating income of both divisions. Since both divisions are evaluated based on their profitability, the transfer price charged can be contentious. The transfer pricing problem involves finding a mutually satisfactory transfer price that promotes accurate performance evaluation, and goal congruence, while respecting divisional autonomy.

Three methods are generally used for setting transfer prices: market-based, negotiated, and cost-based. If a perfectly competitive market exists for the intermediate product, market price is the best transfer price. Here, the market price reflects the opportunity costs of both divisions (i.e., buying and selling). If a perfectly competitive market does not exist, a negotiated transfer price is preferred. In this situation, the opportunity costs for the buying and selling divisions form the upper and lower boundaries for the transfer price. The use of cost-based transfer prices is not generally recommended. However, if the transfers have little effect on either division's profitability, such an approach is acceptable. Also, cost-based pricing formulas may be appropriate if they are established through negotiation.

Environmental factors, such as economic, political, and cultural factors, vary among countries. These factors cannot be controlled by managers, yet they affect profits and ROI. So care should be taken when using such measures to evaluate performance. Multinational companies with subsidiaries in both high-tax and low-tax countries may use transfer pricing to shift costs to high-tax countries and revenues to low-tax countries. Extreme care should be taken in following such practices, as the CCRA may interpret them as tax evasion.

## Key Terms

Centralized decision making 747
Cost centre 746
Decentralization 747
Decentralized decision making 747
Economic value added (EVA) 755
Investment centre 746
Margin 750

Maximum transfer price 761
Minimum transfer price 761
Operating assets 750
Opportunity cost approach 761
Profit centre 746
Residual income (RI) 754
Responsibility accounting 747

Responsibility centre 746
Return on investment (ROI) 750
Revenue centre 746
Transfer price 759
Transfer pricing problem 760
Turnover 750

## Review Problems

### I.  TRANSFER PRICING

The Components Division produces a part that is used by the Goods Division. The unit cost of the part is as follows:

| | |
|---|---|
| Direct materials | $10 |
| Direct labour | 2 |
| Variable overhead | 3 |
| Fixed overhead[a] | 5 |
| Total cost | $20 |

[a]Based on a practical volume of 200,000 parts

Other costs incurred by the Components Division are as follows:

| | |
|---|---|
| Fixed selling and administrative | $500,000 |
| Variable selling (per unit) | $1 |

The sales price of the part in the external market is usually between $28 and $30, with a current sales price of $29. The division can produce 200,000 units per year. However, because of a weak economy, only 150,000 parts are expected to be sold next year. The variable selling expenses are avoidable if the part is sold internally.

The Goods Division has been buying the same part from an external supplier for $28. The manager of the Goods Division has offered to buy 50,000 units needed for next year from the Components Division for $18 per unit.

**Required:**

1. Determine the minimum transfer price that the Components Division would accept.
2. Determine the maximum transfer price the Goods Division would pay.
3. Should an internal transfer take place? Why? If you were the manager of the Components Division, would you sell the 50,000 components for $18 each? Explain.
4. Suppose the average operating assets of the Components Division are $10 million. Compute the ROI for the coming year, assuming that the 50,000 units are transferred to the Goods Division for $21 each.

## Solution

1. The minimum transfer price is $15. Because the Components Division has idle capacity, only the incremental or variable manufacturing costs are relevant. Fixed costs are the same whether or not the internal transfer occurs. Only the variable selling expenses are avoidable.
2. The maximum transfer price is $28. The Goods Division would not pay more for the part than it has to pay to an external supplier.
3. Yes, an internal transfer should occur. The opportunity cost of the selling division is less than the opportunity cost of the buying division. The Components Division would earn an additional contribution of $150,000 ([$18-$15] × 50,000). The total joint benefit, however, is $650,000 ([$28-$15] × 50,000). The manager of the Components Division could attempt to negotiate a more favourable outcome for his division.
4. Income statement:

| | |
|---|---:|
| Sales [($29 × 150,000) + ($21 × 50,000)] | $5,400,000 |
| Less: Variable cost of goods sold ($15 × 200,000) | (3,000,000) |
| Less: Variable selling expenses ($1 × 150,000) | (150,000) |
| Contribution margin | $2,250,000 |
| Less: Fixed overhead ($5 × 200,000) | (1,000,000) |
| Less: Fixed selling and administrative | (500,000) |
| Operating income | $750,000 |

$$\text{ROI} = \text{Operating income}/\text{Average operating assets}$$
$$= \$750,000/\$10,000,000$$
$$= 0.075 \text{ or } 7.5\%$$

## II. WEIGHTED AVERAGE COST OF CAPITAL AND EVA

One division of El Sueño, Inc., had after-tax income last year of $600,000. Two sources of financing were used by the company: $2.5 million in mortgage bonds paying 8 percent interest, and $10 million in common stock, which was considered no more or less risky than other stocks. The rate of return on long-term treasury bonds is 6 percent. El Sueño, Inc., pays a marginal tax rate of 40 percent. Total capital employed in the division is $5.3 million.

**Required:**

1. What is the weighted cost of capital for El Sueño?
2. Calculate the EVA for the division.
3. Is the division creating value for its shareholders? Explain.

## Solution

1. After-tax cost of the mortgage bonds: = [(1 − 0.4)(0.08)] = 0.048

   Cost of the common stock = Return on long-term treasury bonds + Average premium
   $$= 6\% + 6\%$$
   $$= 12\%$$

| | Amount | Proportion x | After-Tax Cost = | Weighted Average Cost |
|---|---|---|---|---|
| Common stock | $10,000,000 | 0.80 | 0.120 | 0.0960 |
| Mortgage bonds | 2,500,000 | 0.20 | 0.048 | 0.0096 |
| Total | $12,500,000 | 1.00 | | |
| Weighted average cost of capital | | | | 0.1056 |

2. Cost of capital = $5,300,000 \times 0.1056 = \$559,680$

| After-tax operating income | $600,000 |
|---|---|
| Less: Cost of capital | 559,680 |
| EVA | $ 40,320 |

3. EVA is positive; therefore, the company is creating value.

# Questions for Writing and Discussion

1. Discuss the differences between centralized and decentralized decision making.

2. What is decentralization?

3. Explain why companies choose to decentralize.

4. Explain how access to local information can improve decision making.

5. One division had operating profits of $500,000, and another division had operating profits of $3 million. Which divisional manager did a better job? Explain.

6. Assume that a division earned operating profits of $500,000 on average operating assets of $2 million. What is the division's return on investment? Suppose that another division had operating profits of $3 million and average operating assets of $30 million. Compute this division's ROI. Which division did a better job? Explain.

7. Define margin and turnover. Explain how these concepts can improve the evaluation of an investment centre.

8. What are the three main benefits of the ROI? Explain how each can lead to improved profitability.

9. What are two disadvantages of the ROI? Explain how each can lead to decreased profitability.

10. What is the EVA? Explain how the EVA overcomes one of the ROI's disadvantages.

11. What disadvantage is shared by both the ROI and the EVA? What can be done to overcome this problem?

12. Compare the RI to the ROI and EVA.

13. What problems do owners face in encouraging goal congruence?

14. What is a transfer price?

15. Explain how transfer prices can affect performance measures, companywide profits, and the decision to decentralize decision making.

16. What is the transfer pricing problem?

17. Explain the opportunity cost approach to transfer pricing.

18. If the minimum transfer price of the selling division is less than the maximum transfer price of the buying division, the intermediate product should be transferred internally. Do you agree? Explain why or why not.

19. If a perfectly competitive outside market exists for the intermediate product, what should the transfer price be? Why?

20. Suppose a selling division can sell all it produces for $50 per unit. Of that amount, however, $3 represents avoidable distribution costs (commissions, freight, collections, and so on). What is the minimum internal transfer price? the maximum transfer price?

21. Discuss the advantages of negotiated transfer prices.

22. Discuss the disadvantages of negotiated transfer prices.

23. Identify three cost-based transfer prices. What are the disadvantages of cost-based transfer

prices? When might it be appropriate to use cost-based transfer prices?

24. What environmental factors may affect divisional performance in a multinational company?

25. What behavioural or ethical dilemma may income tax differences among countries create for multinational companies?

---

## Exercises

**16–1**

Types of Responsibility Centres

LO1

Consider each of the following scenarios.

A. Roberto Rossi, plant manager for the laser printer factory of CompuGear, Inc. brushed his hair back and sighed. December had been a bad month; two machines had broken down, and some direct labourers (all on salary) were idle for part of the month. Materials prices and insurance premiums on the plant also increased. He hoped that the marketing vice-president would be able to push through some price increases.

B. Joan Taylor was delighted to see that her ROI figures had increased for the third straight year. She attributed the increase to her campaign to lower costs and to use equipment more efficiently, which enabled her to sell several older machines. In her semiannual performance review, Joan planned to take full credit for the improvements.

C. Gil Phillips, sales manager for Danson Electric, was unhappy with a memo announcing cost increases for toaster ovens. Headquarters suggested raising prices. "Great," thought Gil, "an increase in price will kill sales—and revenues will decrease. Why can't the plant cut costs like other companies in Canada are doing? Why turn this into my problem?"

D. Susan Thomas looked at the quarterly income statement with disgust. Revenues were down, and costs were up—what a combination! If she cut back on equipment maintenance and terminated a product engineer, she reasoned, expenses would decrease—perhaps enough to reverse the trend in income.

E. Anne Winston had just been hired to improve the fortunes of the Eastern Division of ABC, Inc. She met with management to develop a three-year plan to improve the situation. The crux of the plan was to retire obsolete equipment and purchase state-of-the-art computer-assisted machinery. The workers would take some time to learn to use the new equipment, but after that was accomplished, waste would be virtually eliminated.

**Required:**

For each of the above independent scenarios, indicate the type of responsibility centre involved (cost, revenue, profit, or investment) and the accounting numbers on which performance evaluation is likely based.

**16–2**

Margin; Turnover; ROI

LO3

Simmons Company had sales of $100,000, expenses of $83,000, and operating assets of $80,000.

**Required:**

1. Compute the operating income.
2. Compute the margin and turnover ratios.
3. Compute the ROI.

**16–3**

*Margin; Turnover;
ROI; Average
Operating Assets*

LO3

Kaminsky Company provided the following income statement for last year:

| | |
|---|---|
| Sales | $80,000 |
| Less: Variable expenses | 55,000 |
| Contribution margin | $25,000 |
| Less: Fixed expenses | 19,800 |
| Operating income | $ 5,200 |

The company had operating assets of $38,650 at the beginning of last year and operating assets of $41,350 at the end of the year.

**Required:**
1. Compute average operating assets.
2. Compute the margin and turnover ratios.
3. Compute the ROI.

**16–4**

*ROI; RI; Margin;
Turnover*

LO3

Spreadsheet

The following data have been collected for the past two years for the Delta Division of Chancellor Company:

| | 2004 | 2005 |
|---|---|---|
| Sales | $30,000,000 | $30,000,000 |
| Net operating income | 2,400,000 | 2,220,000 |
| Average operating assets | 15,000,000 | 15,000,000 |
| Minimum required rate of return | 15% | 15% |

**Required:**
1. Compute the margin and turnover ratios for each year.
2. Compute the ROI for each year.
3. Explain why the ROI decreased from 2004 to 2005.
4. Compute the RI for each year.
5. Compare the divisional performance using the ROI and RI measures.

**16–5**

*ROI; RI; Margin;
Turnover*

LO3

The following data are for the Theta Division of Chancellor Company:

| | 2004 | 2005 |
|---|---|---|
| Sales | $50,000,000 | $50,000,000 |
| Net operating income | 4,000,000 | 3,700,000 |
| Average operating assets | 25,000,000 | 20,000,000 |
| Minimum required rate of return | 15% | 15% |

**Required:**
1. Compute the margin and turnover ratios for each year.
2. Compute the ROI for each year.
3. Compute the RI for each year.
4. How does the performance of the Theta Division compare with that of the Delta Division (in Exercise 16–4) on the two measures?

**16–6**

*ROI and Investment
Decisions*

LO3

Robin Everest, division manager of Mountain Sports, Inc., was debating the merits of a new product—a two-person tent capable of withstanding winds of up to 160 km. The tent would be a high-end product, designed for climbers of the world's highest peaks, but it was expected to appeal to wealthy weekend climbers as well.

The budgeted income of the division was $3,960,000, with operating assets of $18,000,000. The proposed investment would add income of $450,000 and require an additional investment in equipment of $3,000,000.

**Required:**

1. Compute the ROI for each of the following:
   a. Division if the tent project is not undertaken.
   b. Tent project alone.
   c. Division if the tent project is undertaken.
2. Should the company invest in the new tent? Explain why or why not.

**16–7**

ROI; RI

LO3

Consider the following data for two divisions of the same company:

|  | **Whirlpool Tubs** | **Plumbing Supplies** |
| --- | --- | --- |
| Sales | $3,000,000 | $10,000,000 |
| Average operating assets | 1,000,000 | 3,000,000 |
| Net operating income | 140,000 | 330,000 |
| Minimum required return | 8% | 8% |

**Required:**

1. Compute the residual income for each division. Is it possible to make a useful comparison of divisional performance by comparing RIs?
2. Compute the residual rate of return by dividing the residual income by the average operating assets. Is it possible to say that one division outperformed the other? Explain.
3. Compute the ROI for each division. Can we make meaningful comparisons of divisional performance using the ROI? Explain.
4. Add the residual rate of return computed in Requirement 2 to the required rate of return. Compare these rates with the ROI computed in Requirement 3. Will this relationship always be the same?

**16–8**

Weighted Average Cost of Capital; EVA

LO3

Spreadsheet

Ernhardt, Inc., uses EVA to evaluate its performance. Last year the company had after-tax operating income of $550,000. Two sources of financing were used: $2.5 million in mortgage bonds paying 6 percent interest, and $5 million in common stock, which was considered to be no more or less risky than other stocks. The interest rate on long-term treasury bonds is 5 percent. The company has $4,000,000 in operating assets and pays a marginal tax rate of 40 percent.

**Required:**

1. Calculate the weighted average cost of capital.
2. Calculate the EVA. Is the company creating wealth? Explain.

**16–9**

Weighted Average Cost of Capital; EVA

LO3

Refer to Exercise 16–8. Suppose that Ernhardt, Inc., is considering borrowing $2,000,000 in unsecured bonds at a rate of 8 percent. The money will be used in part to purchase additional operating assets of $1,200,000, making total operating assets $5,200,000. This added investment will enable the company to manufacture products that are budgeted to provide $100,000 in after-tax operating income.

**Required:**

1. Calculate the new weighted average cost of capital.
2. Calculate the EVA, including the new products. Is the new investment a good idea? Explain.

**16–10**

ROI of Two Divisions

LO3

An electronics division has an opportunity to invest in two projects during the coming year: a digital telephone answering machine and a portable video game player. The outlay required for each investment, the dollar returns, and the ROI are as follows:

|              | Answering Machine | Video Game Player |
|--------------|-------------------|-------------------|
| Investment   | $10,000,000       | $4,000,000        |
| Operating income | 1,300,000     | 640,000           |
| ROI          | 13%               | 16%               |

The division is currently earning an ROI of 18 percent, using operating assets of $75 million. Operating income on the current investment is $13.5 million. The division has an approval for $15 million of new investment capital. Corporate headquarters requires that all investments earn at least 12 percent. The weighted average cost of capital for the company is 12 percent.

**Required:**
1. Calculate the ROI for the division under each of the following scenarios:
   a. The company invests in the answering machine.
   b. The company invests in the video game player.
   c. The company invests in both.
   d. The company invests in neither.
2. Which option should the divisional manager choose? Why?

**16–11**

EVA

LO3

Refer to Exercise 16–10.

**Required:**
1. Calculate the EVA for the answering machine.
2. Calculate the EVA for the video game player.
3. Calculate the EVA for the division, if both investments are made.
4. Calculate the EVA for the division, if neither investment is made.
5. If the manager is evaluated based on the EVA, which of the four investment options is he likely to choose? Why?

**16–12**

Transfer Pricing

LO4

Colonnel Home Furnishings, Inc., has two divisions: the Mattress Division and the Furniture Division. The Furniture Division manufactures a line of sofa beds, which use a mattress purchased from an outside supplier for $94. Kel Woodburn, manager of the Mattress Division, has approached Brianna Hessler, manager of the Furniture Division, about selling mattresses to the Furniture Division. Kel has obtained the following costs for the mattress:

| Direct materials          | $20  |
|---------------------------|------|
| Direct labour             | 18   |
| Variable overhead         | 17   |
| Fixed overhead            | 30   |
| Total manufacturing cost  | $85  |

Currently, the Mattress Division has enough capacity to produce 100,000 mattresses but is producing only 50,000. The Furniture Division needs 30,000 mattresses per year.

**Required:**
1. What is the maximum transfer price? The minimum transfer price? Should the transfer occur?
2. Suppose the managers agree on a transfer price of $75. What is the benefit to each division? What is the benefit to the company as a whole?
3. Suppose the Mattress Division is operating at capacity. What should the maximum transfer price be? the minimum transfer price? Should the transfer occur in this situation? Explain why or why not.

**16–13**

Transfer Pricing;
Outside Market with
Full Capacity

LO4

Delbert Company's Container Division produces a variety of containers for the food processing industry, including its own Processing Division. The most frequently used container is a 375-gram can. In the past, the Processing Division has purchased these cans from external suppliers for $0.65 each. The manager of the Processing Division has approached the manager of the Container Division with an offer to buy 200,000 cans a year. The Container Division, which is currently at maximum capacity, produces and sells 300,000 cans of this size to outside customers for $0.65 each.

**Required:**

1. What is the minimum transfer price for the Container Division? What is the maximum transfer price for the Processing Division? Is it important that transfers take place internally? If transfers do take place, what should the transfer price be?

2. Assume that the Container Division incurs selling costs of $0.04 per can that would be avoided if the cans were sold internally. Identify the minimum transfer price for the Container Division and the maximum transfer price for the Processing Division. Should the internal transfer take place? If so, what is the benefit to the company as a whole?

3. You are the manager of the Container Division. You can avoid selling costs of $0.04 per unit if you sell the cans internally. Would you accept an offer of $0.63 from the Processing Division? How much better or worse off would your division be if you accepted this price?

**16–14**

Transfer Pricing; Idle
Capacity

LO4

The Film Division of Malak Photography, Inc., makes 35mm film, which it sells externally, as well as internally to the School Photography Division. Sales and cost data per roll of 35mm film are as follows:

| | |
|---|---|
| Unit selling price | $2.95 |
| Unit variable cost | 1.40 |
| Unit product fixed cost ($600,000/$500,000) | 1.20 |
| Practical capacity | 500,000 units |

In the coming year, the Film Division expects to sell 350,000 rolls of film. The School Photography Division plans to buy 150,000 rolls of film from external suppliers for $2.95 each. The manager of the Film Division has approached the manager of the School Photography Division with an offer to sell 150,000 rolls for $2.94 each. Avoidable selling costs are $0.02 per roll of film, with the savings equally split between the two divisions.

**Required:**

1. What is the minimum transfer price that the Film Division would be willing to accept? What is the maximum transfer price that the School Photography Division would be willing to pay? Should an internal transfer occur? What would the benefit (or loss) to the company be if the internal transfer were to occur?

2. Suppose the Film Division has idle capacity. Do you think that, knowing this, the buying manager would agree to the transfer price of $2.94? Suppose she counters with an offer to pay $2.85? If you were the selling manager, would you be interested in this price? Explain, with supporting calculations.

3. Company policy requires all internal transfers to occur at the full manufacturing cost. What would the transfer price be? Should the transfer take place?

**16–15**

ROI; Margin; Turnover

LO3

Richmond Furrier, Ltd., is facing stiff competition from imported goods. Its operating income has declined steadily for the past several years. The company has been forced to lower prices to maintain its market share. The operating results for the past three years are as follows:

|  | Year 1 | Year 2 | Year 3 |
|---|---|---|---|
| Sales | $10,000,000 | $ 9,500,000 | $ 9,000,000 |
| Net operating income | 1,200,000 | 1,045,000 | 945,000 |
| Average assets | 15,000,000 | 15,000,000 | 15,000,000 |

The president has decided to implement a JIT purchasing and manufacturing system. She estimates that this will reduce inventories by 70 percent in the first year of operation, resulting in a 20 percent reduction in average operating assets. Operating assets would remain unchanged without the JIT system. She also estimates that sales and operating income will be restored to Year 1 levels because of the simultaneous reduction in operating expenses and selling prices. Lower selling prices will allow the company to expand its market share.

**Required:**
1. Compute the ROI, margin, and turnover for Years 1, 2, and 3.
2. Suppose that in Year 4 the sales and operating income were achieved as expected, but inventories remained at the same level as in Year 3. Compute the expected ROI, margin, and turnover. Explain why the ROI increased over the Year 3 level.
3. Suppose that the sales and net operating income for Year 4 remained the same as in Year 3, but inventory reductions were achieved as projected. Compute the ROI, margin, and turnover. Explain why the ROI exceeded the Year 3 level.
4. Assume that all expectations for Year 4 were realized. Compute the expected ROI, margin, and turnover. Explain why the ROI increased over the Year 3 level.

**16–16**

Transfer Pricing and Autonomy

LO4

The Parts Division supplies Part 678 to the Medical Products Division, which uses it in manufacturing a heart monitor. The Medical Products Division is currently operating below capacity by 10,000 units, whereas the Parts Division is operating at full capacity. Part 678 sells externally for $50. The cost of producing the heart monitor is as follows:

| | |
|---|---|
| Part 678 | $ 50 |
| Direct materials | 100 |
| Direct labour | 20 |
| Variable overhead | 30 |
| Fixed overhead | 40 |
| Total unit cost | $240 |

The Medical Products Division has received an order for 1,000 heart monitors from a wholesaler, with an offer price of $230. Since company policy prohibits selling any product below the full cost, the divisional manager requests a price concession from the Parts Division. When that manager refuses the request, the manager of the Medical Products Division files an appeal to the vice-president, arguing that the part should be transferred at full cost to avoid distorting pricing decisions in his division.

**Required:**
1. Assume that the full cost of Part 678 is $30. Will the company as a whole benefit if the part is transferred at $30? Should the vice-president intervene?
2. Is anything wrong with the company policy that a division's selling price cannot be below full cost?

3. Compute the minimum and maximum transfer prices. If a transfer were to take place, what should the transfer price be? Why?

**16–17**

LO4

Canadian Car Company is a decentralized company with several divisions. The Component Division currently sells its product to other manufacturers at a price of $50 per unit. The Assembly Division has been purchasing 500,000 units per year from an external source at a price of $48 per unit. The Component Division has adequate capacity to supply the Assembly Division, and this capacity cannot be used for anything else in the short run. The Component Division would like to supply the Assembly Division, but the Assembly Division is unwilling to pay the $50 price. The Component Division's unit cost is as follows:

| | |
|---|---|
| Direct materials | $18 |
| Direct labour | 14 |
| Variable overhead | 6 |
| Fixed overhead[a] | 4 |
| Total cost | $42 |

[a]Based on a capacity of 4,000,000 units.

### Required:
1. What is the market price of the component?
2. What is the full-cost price of the component?
3. What price range is appropriate for short-run intracompany transfers?
4. From the company's perspective, should the Assembly Division purchase from external sources under current circumstances? Why?
5. What pricing method benefits both divisions in this situation? Why? (CGA Canada adapted)

**16–18**

LO3

Calculate the missing data for each of the four independent companies below.

| | A | B | C | D |
|---|---|---|---|---|
| Revenue | $10,000 | $45,000 | $200,000 | $ — |
| Expenses | 7,800 | — | 188,000 | — |
| Net income | 2,200 | 18,000 | — | — |
| Assets | 20,000 | — | 100,000 | 9,600 |
| Margin | — % | 40% | — % | 6.25% |
| Turnover | — | 0.3125 | — | 2.00 |
| ROI | — | — | — | — |

**16–19**

LO3

Refer to Exercise 16–18. Assume that the weighted average cost of capital is 12 percent for each of the four firms.

### Required:
Compute the EVA for each of the four firms.

**16–20**

LO4

Cartier Industries is a vertically integrated company with several divisions that operate as decentralized profit centres. The company's Systems Division manufactures scientific instruments and uses the products of two other divisions. The Board Division manufactures printed circuit boards. One model is made exclusively for the Systems Division using proprietary designs; less complex models are sold in outside markets. The products of the Transistor Division are sold in a well-developed competitive market. However, one model is also used by the Systems Division. The costs per unit of the products used by the Systems Division are presented below:

|  | Circuit Board | Transistor |
|---|---|---|
| Direct material | $2.50 | $0.80 |
| Direct labour | 4.50 | 1.00 |
| Variable overhead | 2.00 | 0.50 |
| Fixed overhead | 0.80 | 0.75 |
| Total cost | $9.80 | $3.05 |

The Board Division sells its product at full cost plus a 25 percent markup and believes that the board made for the Systems Division would sell for $12.25 per unit on the open market. The market price of the transistors used by the Systems Division is $3.70 per unit.

**Required:**
1. What is the minimum transfer price for the Transistor Division? What is the maximum transfer price of the transistor for the Systems Division?
2. Assume the Systems Division is able to purchase a large quantity of transistors from an outside source at $2.90 per unit. Assume further that the Transistor Division has excess capacity. Can the Transistor Division meet this price?
3. The Board and Systems Divisions have negotiated a transfer price of $11 per printed circuit board. Discuss the impact of this transfer price on each division. (US CMA adapted)

**16–21**

Multiple-Choice
Questions

LO1, LO2

Choose the *best* answer for each of the following multiple-choice questions:

1. Responsibility accounting involves
   a. responsibility, accounting, and budgeting.
   b. responsibility, accountability, and budgeting.
   c. budgeting, planning, and assessing fault.
   d. responsibility, accountability, and performance measurement.
   e. accountability, performance measurement, and centralization.

2. The practice of delegating decision-making authority to lower levels of management is called
   a. centralization.
   b. responsibility accounting.
   c. accountability.
   d. performance measurement.
   e. decentralization.

3. One reason that companies decentralize is to
   a. train and motivate managers.
   b. encourage competition among divisions.
   c. permit upper management to focus on strategies.
   d. take advantage of lower-level managers' knowledge of local issues and conditions.
   e. All of the above.

4. A responsibility centre whose manager is responsible for both revenues and costs is a(n)
   a. cost centre.
   b. revenue centre.
   c. profit centre.
   d. investment centre.
   e. division centre.

## Problems

**16–22**

The manager of a division that produces add-on products for the automobile industry has just been presented with the opportunity to invest in two independent projects. The first is an air conditioner for the back seats of minivans. The second is a turbo charger. Without the investments, the division will have average assets for the coming year of $25.6 million and expected operating income of $3.584 million. The outlay required for each investment and the expected operating incomes are as follows:

|  | Air Conditioner | Turbo Charger |
|---|---|---|
| Capital outlay | $750,000 | $540,000 |
| Operating income | 67,500 | 54,000 |

Corporate headquarters will secure up to $1.3 million in loans for the automotive add-on division for further investments. The company's weighted average cost of capital is 9 percent, and the minimum required rate of return is 10 percent.

**Required:**
1. Compute the ROI for each investment project.
2. Compute the RI for each investment project.
3. Compute the budgeted *divisional* ROI for each of the following four alternatives:
   a. The air conditioner investment is made.
   b. The turbo charger investment is made.
   c. Both investments are made.
   d. Neither additional investment is made.
   Assuming that division managers are evaluated and rewarded based on the ROI, which alternative will they choose?
4. Suppose the investment must be for the entire $1.3 million. Calculate the EVA of the two investments as a package. Ignore income taxes. Based on the EVA, are the investments profitable?
5. Compare the results obtained in Requirements 1 to 4 using the ROI, RI, and EVA methods.

**16–23**

Green Thumb, Ltd., is a nursery with three divisions: the Western Division, the Central Division, and the Eastern Division. All three grow and sell plants for gardens. Recently, the Central Division has acquired a facility that manufactures plastic pots. The pots can be sold both externally and internally. Company policy permits each manager to decide whether to buy or sell internally. Each manager is evaluated based on both ROI and EVA.

The Western Division has been buying its plastic pots in lots of 100 from several vendors. The average price paid is $75 per box of 100 pots. However, the recent acquisition makes the manager of the Western Division wonder whether a more favourable price could be arranged. She approaches the manager of the Central Division with a request to transfer 3,500 boxes at $70 per box.

The cost and revenue of a box of 100 pots is as follows:

| | |
|---|---|
| Direct materials | $35 |
| Direct labour | 8 |
| Variable overhead | 10 |
| Fixed overhead ($200,000/20,000 boxes) | 10 |
| Total unit cost | $63 |
| | |
| Selling price | $75 |
| Production capacity | 20,000 boxes |

**Required:**

1. Suppose the pot facility is producing at capacity and can sell its entire production to outside customers. How should the manager respond to the request for a lower transfer price?
2. Assume that the pot facility is currently selling 16,000 boxes. What are the minimum and maximum transfer prices? Should the manager transfer at $70 per box?
3. Suppose that the company's policy is to make all transfers at full cost plus 20 percent. Should the transfer occur? Explain why or why not.

**16–24**

ROI Calculations with
Varying Assumptions

LO3

Upholstery Products is a division of Domicile Textiles, Inc. During the coming year, it expects to earn a net operating income of $310,000, based on sales of $3.45 million and average net operating assets of $3 million. The division is considering a purchase of new weaving machines. It would require an additional investment of $600,000, and increase sales by $575,000 and net operating income by $57,500. The investment would increase beginning net operating assets by $600,000 and ending net operating assets by $400,000. Assume that the minimum required rate of return is 7 percent.

**Required:**

1. Compute the ROI and RI for the division without the investment.
2. Compute the margin and turnover ratios without the investment. Prove that the product of the margin and turnover ratios equals the ROI computed in Requirement 1.
3. Compute the ROI and RI for the division with the new investment. Do you think the divisional manager will approve the investment? Should he?
4. Compute the margin and turnover ratios for the division with the new investment. Compare them with the old ratios.
5. Assume that a JIT system is installed, reducing average operating assets by $800,000. Compute the ROI with and without the investment under this new scenario. Do you think the division manager will accept the new investment? Should he accept it? Explain.
6. Refer to Requirement 5. Compute the margin and turnover ratios without the investment. Use these ratios to explain why the ROI would increase.

**16–25**

ROI; EVA; Evaluating
Performance

LO3

Northern Resources, Inc., produces tool and die machinery for manufacturers. The company expanded vertically in 1994 by acquiring one of its suppliers of alloy steel plates, Lagoma Steel Company. Lagoma is treated as an investment centre for reporting purposes.

Northern monitors its divisions based on both the unit contribution and the ROI, with investment defined as average operating assets employed. Management bonuses are determined based on the ROI. The average cost of capital is 11 percent of operating investment.

Lagoma's cost of goods sold is entirely variable based on volume; in contrast, administrative expenses do not depend on volume. Selling expenses are mixed costs, with 40 percent attributed to sales volume. Lagoma considered a capital acquisition with an estimated ROI of 11.5 percent. However, divisional management decided against it, believing that it would decrease the overall ROI. The division's operating assets employed were $15,750,000 on November 30, 2005, representing a 5 percent increase over the 2004 year end balance. The income statement for 2005 is as follows:

**Lagoma Steel Division**
**Income Statement**
**For the Year Ended November 30, 2005 (in thousands)**

| | | |
|---|---:|---:|
| Sales revenue | | $25,000 |
| Less expenses: | | |
|    Cost of goods sold | $16,500 | |
|    Administrative expenses | 3,955 | |
|    Selling expenses | 2,700 | 23,155 |
| Income from operations before income taxes | | $ 1,845 |

### Required:

1. Calculate the unit contribution margin, if 1,484,000 units were produced and sold during the year ended November 30, 2005.
2. Calculate the following performance measures for 2005:
   a. Pretax return on average investment in operating assets employed (ROI).
   b. EVA based on average operating assets employed.
3. Explain why the management of Lagoma would have been more likely to accept the capital investment if the EVA instead of the ROI had been used as a performance measure.
4. Identify several items that Lagoma should be able to control for it to be evaluated fairly by either the ROI or EVA measures. (US CMA adapted)

**16–26**

*Setting Transfer Prices—Market Price versus Full Cost*

**LO4**

Videodays, Inc., manufactures stereo receivers, televisions, and VCRs in its four divisions: Receiver, TV, VCR, and Components. The Components Division produces electronic components that can be used by the other three divisions or sold to outside customers. Approximately 70 percent of its output is used internally. The current policy requires that all internal transfers of components occur at full cost.

The new chief executive officer has just decided to review the transfer pricing policy. He is concerned that the current method of pricing internal transfers could result in suboptimal decisions by divisional managers. As part of his inquiry, he gathers information concerning Component 12F, used by the Receiver Division in its production of a clock radio, Model 357K.

The Receiver Division sells 100,000 units of Model 357K each year at $21 per unit. In current market conditions, it is the maximum price for the model. The manufacturing cost of the radio is as follows:

| | |
|---|---:|
| Component 12F | $ 6.50 |
| Direct materials | 5.50 |
| Direct labour | 4.00 |
| Variable overhead | 1.00 |
| Fixed overhead | 2.00 |
| Total unit cost | $19.00 |

The radio is produced efficiently, and no further reduction in manufacturing costs is possible.

The manager of the Components Division has indicated that she could sell 100,000 units of Component 12F (the division's capacity for this part) to outside buyers at $12 per unit. The Receiver Division could also buy the part for $12 from external suppliers. She supplies the following manufacturing costs for the component:

| | |
|---|---:|
| Direct materials | $2.50 |
| Direct labour | 0.50 |
| Variable overhead | 1.50 |
| Fixed overhead | 2.00 |
| Total unit cost | $6.50 |

**Required:**

1. Compute the companywide contribution margins for Component 12F and Model 357K. Compute the contribution margin for each division.
2. Suppose the CEO abolishes the current transfer pricing policy and gives divisions autonomy to set transfer prices. Can you predict what transfer price the manager of the Components Division will set? What should the minimum transfer price be for this part? The maximum?
3. Predict how the new transfer pricing policy will affect the production decision for Model 357K by the Receiver Division manager. How many units of Component 12F will the manager purchase either internally or externally?
4. Given the new transfer price set by the Components Division and your answer to Requirement 3, how many units of Component 12F will be sold externally?
5. Given your answers to Requirements 3 and 4, compute the companywide contribution margin. What happened? Was the decision to grant additional divisional autonomy good or bad?

**16–27**

*Transfer Pricing—Full Cost Plus Policy*

**LO4**

Newden Aluminum manufactures and installs aluminum products for houses, such as siding and eavestroughs. The company is decentralized with two divisions: Manufacturing, and Sales and Installation. Company policy requires that products be manufactured internally and that the transfer price be the full absorption cost plus a markup of 10 percent on cost.

Recently, the Sales Division negotiated a contract with a local builder to supply 40 lots of a particular style of eavestrough, Model 403, at a price of $900 within the next 30 days. The Manufacturing Division, when asked to supply these units, claimed that it would have to produce the units on overtime, because it was already at full capacity. The overtime charges would double the costs of labour and overhead costs as follows:

**Cost and Transfer Price of Model 403 (per unit)**

| | Regular Time | Overtime |
|---|---:|---:|
| Materials | $300 | $300 |
| Direct labour | 100 | 200 |
| Variable overhead[a] | 100 | 200 |
| Fixed overhead[a] | 80 | 160 |
| Total cost | $580 | $860 |
| Plus 10 percent | 58 | 86 |
| Transfer price | $638 | $946 |

[a] Applied based on direct labour dollars.

The Sales Division does not want to pay the additional $308 per unit and has found that it can obtain the same product from another supplier for $825. Sales has asked Manufacturing to match the $825 price. Manufacturing has stood its ground, claiming that it must charge $946 because of company policy. The two divisions appeal to the president to settle the dispute.

**Required:**

1. Should the Sales Division be allowed to purchase Model 403 externally to meet its contract commitments? Provide calculations to support your response, and identify any qualitative factors that should be taken into account in making the decision.
2. Evaluate the effectiveness of decentralization and transfer pricing policies at Newden. (CGA Canada adapted)

**16–28**

*Market Price versus Full Cost Plus Markup*

LO4

Yardcare Manufacturing Corporation produces lawn mowers, snowblowers, and tillers. The company has six divisions; each is set up as an investment centre. Managers of the divisions are evaluated and rewarded based on the ROI and EVA. Company policy requires that parts be purchased internally whenever possible and that the transfer price be the full cost plus 10 percent. Ken Booth, the vice-president of operations, is evaluating the current transfer policy in the light of the following memo from Darlene Davenport, the manager of the Parts Division:

---

**MEMORANDUM**

| | |
|---|---|
| **To:** | **Ken Booth, Vice President of Operations** |
| **From:** | **Darlene Davenport, Manager of Parts Division** |
| **Subject:** | **Transfer Pricing Policy** |

---

Ken, I must register serious concern about our current transfer pricing policy of full cost plus 10 percent. First, I believe that this policy creates a significant understatement of my division's ROI. Second, it creates a disincentive for my division to decrease manufacturing costs.

For example, consider our production of Part 34 (small carburetors). Currently, we can produce 300,000 of these units per year. Of this total, 200,000 are transferred to the Small Motor Division at a price of $16.50 per unit and 100,000 are sold to external customers at $20 each. I know we can sell every carburetor we make to external customers. By being forced to transfer internally, we are losing income and showing a much smaller ROI than we otherwise would.

But the problem is even greater. My engineers have created a new design that will allow us to decrease our fixed manufacturing costs for carburetors by $5 per unit. However, if we implement this design, our transfer price will drop to $11, and the revenues from internal sales will drop significantly. All the savings are transferred to the buying division.

In my opinion, these problems can be resolved by allowing division managers to buy or sell products and set transfer prices, as they see fit.

---

After reading the memo, Ken gathers the following data:

Manufacturing cost of carburetor:

| | |
|---|---|
| Direct materials | $ 6.00 |
| Direct labour | 1.25 |
| Variable overhead | 1.50 |
| Fixed overhead | 6.25 |
| Total cost | $15.00 |

Manufacturing cost of small motor:

| | |
|---|---|
| Carburetor | $16.50 |
| Direct materials | 23.50 |
| Direct labour | 8.75 |
| Variable overhead | 3.25 |
| Fixed overhead | 8.40 |
| Total cost | $60.40 |

Production and sales of small motor:

| | |
|---|---|
| Production | 200,000 |
| Sales | 200,000 |
| Unit price | $75 |

**Required:**

1. Assume that the Parts Division implements the new design change and that the internal demand for carburetors remains constant. Compute the change in profits for the company as a whole from this decision. Compute the change in profits for the Parts Division and the Small Motor Division. Was Darlene's concern valid? Were all benefits of the improved design captured by the Small Motor Division?
2. Refer to Requirement 1. Assume that the reduced cost of the carburetor increases the internal demand from 200,000 to 300,000 units. Evaluate the impact on divisional and companywide profits. If Darlene had anticipated this effect, do you think that she would have implemented the cost-reducing design?
3. Refer to the original data. Assuming that the Small Motor Division would instead buy carburetors of equal quality for $20 from outside suppliers, provide Darlene with a complete assessment of the effect, including the change in companywide and divisional profits. Also, comment on the incentives Darlene would have for implementing the cost-reducing design.

## 16–29

**Full Cost Plus Pricing and Negotiation**

**LO4**

Audiotronics, Inc., has two divisions: Auxiliary Components and Audio Systems. Divisional managers are encouraged to maximize the ROI and EVA. Managers are essentially free to determine transfer prices and whether or not to transfer goods internally. The head office has directed that all internal prices be the full cost plus a markup. The markup is left to the discretion of divisional managers.

Recently, the two divisional managers met to discuss a pricing agreement for a subwoofer that would be sold with a personal computer system. The production of subwoofers is currently at full capacity. Subwoofers can be sold for $31 to outside customers. The Audio Systems Division can also buy the subwoofers from external sources for the same price. However, the manager of this division is hoping to obtain a price concession by buying internally. The full manufacturing cost of subwoofers is $20. If the manager of the Auxiliary Components Division sells the subwoofer internally, $5 of selling and distribution costs will be avoided. The internal purchase volume is expected to be 250,000 units per year, which, although well within the capacity of the producing division, would replace sales to existing customers.

After some discussion, the two managers agree on a transfer pricing scheme, which will be reviewed annually. Any increase in the outside selling price will be added to the transfer price by simply increasing the markup. Any major changes in the factors that led to the agreement could initiate a new round of negotiation. Otherwise, the arrangement would continue into subsequent years.

**Required:**

1. Calculate the minimum and maximum transfer prices.
2. Assume that the two managers have agreed on the transfer price halfway between the minimum and maximum transfer prices. Calculate this transfer price.
3. Refer to Requirement 2. Assume that in the following year, the outside price of subwoofers increases to $32. What is the new transfer price?
4. Assume that two years after the initial agreement, the market for subwoofers softens considerably, causing excess capacity for the Auxiliary Components Division. Would you expect a renegotiation of the transfer pricing arrangement for the coming year? Explain.

**16–30**

Courtland Company is a decentralized organization with a divisional structure. Each divisional manager is evaluated based on the ROI.

The Plastics Division produces a plastic container used by the Chemical Division. Plastics can produce up to 100,000 containers per year. The variable manufacturing costs of the containers are $4.50. The Chemical Division labels the containers and uses them to store a chemical, which is sold to outside customers for $50 per container. The Chemical Division's capacity is 20,000 units. The variable costs of processing the chemical, in addition to the cost of the container, are $26.

**Required:**

1. Assume that all containers produced can be sold to external customers for $12 each. The Chemical Division wants to buy 20,000 containers per year. What should the transfer price be?

2. Refer to Requirement 1. Assume $2 of distribution costs can be avoided by internal transfer. Identify the maximum and minimum transfer prices. Identify the actual transfer price, assuming that the difference is split equally between the two divisions.

3. Assume that the Plastics Division operates at 75 percent of capacity. The Chemical Division currently buys 20,000 containers from an outside supplier for $9.50 each. If, instead, the Plastics Division provides the containers to the Chemical Division, what is the expected transfer price, assuming that any joint benefit will be split evenly between the two divisions? How much will companywide profits increase under this arrangement? How much will the Plastics Division's profits increase, assuming that it sells the extra 20,000 containers internally?

4. Assume that both divisions have excess capacity. Currently, 15,000 containers are transferred between divisions at $8. The Chemical Division has an opportunity to take a special order for 5,000 containers of chemical at $33.75 per container. The manager of the Chemical Division approaches the manager of the Plastics Division and offers to buy an additional 5,000 containers for $5 each. Assuming that the Plastics Division has excess capacity of at least 5,000 units, should the manager take the offer? What is the minimum transfer price? the maximum? Assume that the Plastics Division manager counters with a price of $5.50. Will the Chemical Division manager be interested?

**16–31**

The Industrial Machine Division has requested a specially designed subassembly from the Metal Fabricating Division. No outside market price exists to serve as a reference for establishing an internal transfer price. The Industrial Machine Division will use 10,000 subassemblies per year.

The estimated manufacturing cost of the subassembly is as follows:

| | |
|---|---|
| Direct materials | $100 |
| Direct labour | 25 |
| Variable overhead | 50 |
| Fixed overhead[a] | 30 |
| Total unit cost | $205 |

[a] Represents an allocation of existing fixed overhead. The total fixed overhead is the same whether or not the Metal Fabricating Division produces the subassembly.

**Required:**

1. Assume that producing the special subassembly displaces two other potential jobs. The expected revenues and costs of these jobs are as follows:

| | Job 1 | Job 2 |
|---|---|---|
| Revenues | $2,600,000 | $1,500,000 |
| Variable manufacturing | 1,950,000 | 1,050,000 |
| Fixed overhead | 200,000 | 300,000 |

Compute the minimum price that the Metal Fabricating Division should charge.

2. Assume that the Metal Fabricating Division can produce the subassembly without displacing any work for outside customers. What is the minimum transfer price for the subassembly?

3. Refer to Requirement 2. The manager of the Metal Fabricating Division has offered to supply the subassembly for full cost plus the division's average markup of 35 percent. Compute the offered transfer price. What do you think of this pricing scheme?

4. Refer to Requirement 3. The manager of the Industrial Machine Division refuses to pay the average markup. He indicates that an outside supplier has offered to produce the subassembly for $200 per unit. He offers to pay variable costs plus a lump sum of $125,000 to help cover fixed costs and provide some profit. Do you think the manager of the Metal Fabricating Division should accept this offer? Would she be tempted to do so? Explain.

**16–32**

Transfer Pricing;
Various Computations

LO4

Cornwall Dairy, Ltd., has two divisions: the Milk Division and the Dairy Products Division. Divisional managers are evaluated based on the return on investment. The Milk Division has the capacity to process 1,000,000 litres of milk per year. The Dairy Products Division uses milk to produce ice cream, cheese, and cottage cheese. The following data are available for the Milk Division:

| | |
|---|---|
| Selling price per litre | $1.20 |
| Variable production cost | 0.25 |
| Fixed production cost (Based on 1,000,000 litres of output.) | 0.50 |

The Dairy Products Division uses 600,000 litres of milk per year when it operates at full capacity.

**Required:**

1. Assume that the Milk Division can sell its entire production. The Dairy Products Division operates at 90 percent of capacity. It can buy all milk it needs for $1 per litre from outside suppliers. What are the minimum and maximum transfer prices? What transfer price would you recommend? How many litres of milk will the Dairy Products Division likely buy internally?

2. Refer to Requirement 1. How would your answers differ if the Milk Division can avoid distribution costs of $0.10 per litre by selling milk internally? Explain.

**16–33**

Transfer Pricing

LO4

Pellisar Furnishings, Inc., is a divisionalized furniture manufacturer. The divisions are autonomous segments, with each responsible for its own sales, operating costs, working capital management, and equipment acquisition. Each division serves a different market in the furniture industry. Because the markets and products of the divisions are so different, no transfers between divisions have occurred.

The Commercial Division manufactures equipment and furniture for the restaurant industry. The division plans to introduce a new line of counter and chair units with cushioned seats. John Kline, the divisional manager, has been discussing manufacturing the cushioned seats with Russ Fiegel of the Office Division. Both believe that the cushioned seats currently made by the Office Division for its deluxe office stools could be modified for use on the new counter chairs. John has just asked Russ for a price for 100 units of cushioned seats. The following conversation ensues:

**Russ**: "John, we can make the necessary modifications to cushioned seats easily. The raw materials used in your seats are slightly different and should cost about

10 percent more than those used in our deluxe office stools. But the labour time (0.5 DLH) should be the same, because the fabrication operation is basically the same. I'd price the seats at our regular rate—full cost plus 30 percent markup."

**John:** "That's higher than I expected, Russ. I was thinking that a good price would be your variable manufacturing costs. After all, your capacity costs will be incurred regardless of this job."

**Russ:** "John, I'm at capacity. If I make the cushioned seats for you, I'll have to cut my production of deluxe office stools. Of course, I can increase my production of economy office stools. The labour time freed by not having to fabricate the frames or assemble the deluxe stools can be shifted to the frame fabrication and assembly of the economy office stools. Fortunately, I can switch my labour force between these two models without any loss of efficiency. As you know, overtime is not a feasible alternative. I'd like to sell it to you at variable cost, but I have excess demand for both products. I don't mind changing my product mix to emphasize the economy model if I get a good return on the seats I make for you. Here are my standard costs for the two stools and a schedule of my manufacturing overhead."

**Office Division**
**Standard Costs and Prices**

|  | Deluxe Office Stool | Economy Office Stool |
|---|---|---|
| Raw materials, framing | $ 8.15 | $ 9.76 |
| Cushioned seat, padding | 2.40 | — |
| Vinyl | 4.00 | — |
| Molded seat (purchased) | — | 6.00 |
| Direct labour: |  |  |
| 1.5 DLH @ $7.50 | 11.25 |  |
| 0.8 DLH @ $7.50 |  | 6.00 |
| Manufacturing overhead: |  |  |
| 1.5 DLH @ $12.80 | 19.20 |  |
| 0.8 DLH @ $12.80 |  | 10.24 |
| Total standard cost | $45.00 | $32.00 |
| Selling price (30% markup) | $58.50 | $41.60 |

**Office Division**
**Manufacturing Overhead Budget**

| Overhead Item | Nature | Amount |
|---|---|---|
| Supplies | Variable (at current market prices) | $ 420,000 |
| Indirect labour | Variable | 375,000 |
| Supervision | Nonvariable | 250,000 |
| Power | Use varies with activity; rates are fixed | 180,000 |
| Heat and light | Mixed (light is fixed regardless of production, while heat/air conditioning varies with fuel charges) | 140,000 |
| Property insurance | Nonvariable (any change in amounts/rates is independent of production) | 200,000 |
| Amortization | Fixed dollar total | 1,700,000 |
| Employee benefits | 20% of supervision, direct and indirect labour | 575,000 |
| Total overhead |  | $3,840,000 |
| Capacity in DLH |  | 300,000 |
| Overhead rate/DLH |  | $12.80 |

**John**: "I guess I see your point, Russ, but I don't want to price myself out of the market. Maybe we should talk to the corporate controller to see if he can give us some guidance on this issue."

**Required:**
1. The corporate controller suggests that John and Russ consider using a transfer price based on variable manufacturing costs plus opportunity cost. Calculate a transfer price for the cushioned seats based on this method.
2. Which transfer pricing method—full cost, variable manufacturing cost, or variable manufacturing cost plus opportunity cost—would be the best basis for an intracompany transfer price policy? Explain your answer. (US CMA adapted)

**16–34**

Transfer Pricing in Multinational Companies

LO4

Lanfranoni, Inc., manufactures a broad line of industrial and consumer products. One of its plants is located in Madrid, Spain, and another in Singapore. The Madrid plant is operating at 85 percent of capacity. Softness in the market for its main product, electric motors, has led to predictions of possible further softening of the market, leading perhaps to production at 65 percent of capacity. If that happens, workers will have to be laid off and one wing of the plant will be closed. The Singapore plant manufactures heavy-duty industrial mixers that use the motors manufactured by the Madrid plant as an integral component. Demand for the mixers is strong. Price and cost information for the mixers is as follows:

| | |
|---|---|
| Price | $2,200 |
| Direct materials | 630 |
| Direct labour | 125 |
| Variable overhead | 250 |
| Fixed overhead | 100 |

The annual budgeted fixed overhead costs are $3,500,000, and the budgeted production is 35,000 mixers. The direct material costs include the cost of the motor at $250 (market price).

The Madrid plant's capacity is 20,000 motors per year. Cost data are as follows:

| | |
|---|---|
| Direct materials | $ 75 |
| Direct labour | 60 |
| Variable overhead | 60 |
| Fixed overhead | 100 |

Fixed overhead is based on budgeted fixed overhead of $2,000,000.

**Required:**
1. What is the maximum transfer price that the Singapore plant would accept?
2. What is the minimum transfer price that the Madrid plant would accept?
3. Consider the following environmental factors:

| Madrid Plant | Singapore Plant |
|---|---|
| Full employment is very important. Local government prohibits layoffs without permission, which is rarely granted. | Cheap labour is plentiful. |
| Accounting is legalistic and conservative, designed to ensure compliance with government objectives. | Accounting is based on the British-American model, oriented toward the decision-making needs of creditors and investors. |

How might these environmental factors affect transfer pricing decisions?

## Managerial Decision Cases

**16–35**

ROI and EVA; Ethical
Considerations

LO3

Natural Beauty Products manufactures personal grooming products. The company has six divisions, including the Hair Products Division. Each division is treated as an investment centre. Managers are evaluated and rewarded based on the ROI. Only managers producing the highest ROIs receive bonuses and promotions. Alfonso Berdardi, the manager of the Hair Products Division, has always been one of the top performers. For the past two years, his division has produced the highest ROI. Last year, it earned a net operating income of $2.56 million and employed average operating assets of $16 million. Alfonso was pleased with his division's performance, especially after he was told that if the division did well this year, he would be considered for a promotion.

For the coming year, the Hair Products Division has been promised new capital of $1.5 million. Any of the capital not invested by the division will be invested by the company at 9 percent, which is the company's cost of capital. After some careful investigation, the marketing and engineering staff recommend that the division invest in equipment that can be used to produce a new product: a crimping and waving iron. The cost of equipment is estimated at $1.2 million. The division's marketing manager estimates that the new line will produce an operating income of $156,000 per year.

After reviewing the proposal, Alfonso turns it down. He writes a memo to corporate headquarters, indicating that his division will not be able to employ new capital in any new projects for the next eight to ten months. He notes, however, that he is confident that his marketing and engineering staff will have a project ready by the end of the year, and he would like to have access to the capital at that time.

**Required:**
1. Explain why Alfonso turned down the proposal. Provide computations to support your reasoning.
2. Compute the effect that the new product line would have had on the profitability of the company as a whole. Should the division have produced the product?
3. Suppose the company used the EVA instead of the ROI. Do you think Alfonso's decision might have been different? Explain.
4. Explain why the company might use both the EVA and ROI measures.
5. Did Alfonso display ethical behaviour when he turned down the investment? In discussing this issue, consider why he refused the investment.

**16–36**

Transfer Pricing;
Behavioural
Considerations

LO4

Magna Motors started as a single plant assembling a major subassembly for the auto industry and also producing some parts for that subassembly. It later developed outside markets for some of the parts. As the company grew, it reorganized itself into several divisions. Each division now operates as an autonomous unit. Year-end bonuses are based on divisional performance.

The company's transfer pricing policy permits the divisions to sell to external and internal customers. The price for products transferred between divisions is negotiated between the buying and selling divisions without any interference from top management.

The company's profits have dropped during the current year even though sales have increased. The drop can be traced almost entirely to the Motor Division. The Motor Division purchases switches for its motors from an outside supplier instead of the company's Switch Division. The Switch Division operates at full capacity and refuses to sell its switches to the Motor Division, because it can sell them to outside customers at a price higher than the actual full manufacturing cost that was negotiated in the past with the Motor Division. The Motor Division refuses to pay the market price demanded by the Switch Division. This means that the Motor Division has had to pay an even higher price to an outside supplier!

The chief financial officer is reviewing the transfer pricing policy, because he believes that suboptimization has occurred. The Switch Division has apparently made the correct decision to maximize its profit by not transferring the switches at the actual full manufacturing cost, but this decision is not necessarily in the best interests of the company. The Motor Division is the largest division and has tended to dominate the smaller divisions. The CFO has recently learned that the smaller divisions are now resisting the Motor Division's desire to continue using the actual full manufacturing cost as the negotiated price.

The CFO has asked the accounting department to study alternative transfer pricing methods that promote overall goal congruence, motivate divisional managers, and optimize overall company performance. The following three methods, to be applied uniformly across all divisions if adopted, have been proposed by the accounting department:

a. Standard full manufacturing costs plus markup.
b. Market selling price of the product.
c. Out-of-pocket cost outlay incurred to the point of transfer, plus an opportunity cost per unit.

### Required:

1. Discuss the positive and negative behavioural implications of a negotiated transfer price system. Explain what behavioural problems can arise from using actual full manufacturing costs as a transfer price.
2. Discuss possible behavioural problems arising from the change to a revised corporatewide transfer pricing policy applicable to all divisions.
3. Discuss the likely behaviour of the "buying" and "selling" division managers under each of the three transfer pricing methods. (US CMA adapted)

## Research Assignments

**16–37**

*Research Assignment*

LO4

Use the Internet to research the development of the North American Free Trade Agreement (NAFTA). What are its implications for companies located in Canada? in Mexico? in the United States?

**16–38**

*Cybercase*

LO1, LO4

Go to the Koch Industries website (www.kochind.com) and find information about the philosophy of Charles Koch, the CEO. Relate the concept of "market-based management" to decentralization and to transfer pricing.

# Strategic Performance Evaluation and Management

**After studying Chapter 17, you should be able to:**

1. Discuss environmental factors affecting effective performance management.

2. Compare and contrast functional-based, activity-based, and strategic-based management control systems.

3. Explain the role of process value analysis in strategic performance management.

4. Explain the basic features of and design criteria for effective strategic performance measurement systems in general and for the balanced scorecard framework in particular.

5. Discuss methods of evaluating and rewarding managerial performance.

6. Describe other performance management techniques. (Appendix A)

# Scenario

Rob Martin, president and owner of Telco Systems, was both pleased and concerned. He was pleased because his company, a manufacturer of specialized components for the telecommunications industry, had been able to achieve a significant market share during the first three years of its operations. He was also concerned because his company was facing an increasingly competitive business environment. It had become evident to Rob that he would have to seek better ways of making strategic business decisions and collecting accurate, reliable information to facilitate his decision

making. Moreover, he was convinced that greater efficiency was needed. Operating processes needed to be streamlined, waste needed to be eliminated, and quality and delivery performance needed to be improved.

With the intention of implementing an activity-based management system, he had already initiated an analysis of all business processes. However, he also felt that a new approach was necessary to gain employee support for the revised strategic direction his company had recently implemented. When he expressed these concerns to Paula Pearson, the managing partner of the local office of a national consulting firm, she suggested that he consider

implementing a balanced scorecard to further extend and build on the activity-based management initiative he had started. Wanting to know more, Rob invited Paula for a business lunch. Below are the highlights of their luncheon conversation:

**Rob**: "Paula, I'm anxious to hear what you have to say about the balanced scorecard."

**Paula**: "Rob, one of the most difficult problems in organizations today is the disconnection between performance measures and organizational strategy. Most managers receive a monthly responsibility report that shows their expenses line by line, comparing actual costs to budgeted costs. However, virtually all managers complain that these reports provide very little insight about how to increase efficiency and effectiveness, or what is expected by higher management. At best, these reports provide only historical *feedback* information instead of future-oriented *feedforward* information. As such, they encourage backwards-looking management and reactive decision making instead of more proactive, forward-looking management practices."

**Rob**: "Well, all this may be true, but how can it be corrected? How could the balanced scorecard help?"

**Paula**: "The balanced scorecard is an integrated strategic performance management tool that ties performance objectives and measures to a company's strategy. It recognizes that there has to be a balance between financial and nonfinancial measures, as well as between predictive measures and historical measures—that is, between feedback and feedforward measures."

**Rob**: "It sounds promising. Are you telling me the performance measurement system can be derived from and tied to my own organization's strategy?"

**Paula**: "That's the basic idea."

**Rob**: "And how does activity-based management relate to the balanced scorecard?"

**Paula**: "The balanced scorecard and other similar integrated performance management techniques place a strong emphasis on business processes and their outputs. Since processes are defined by activities, activity management is needed. Activity-based management identifies activities and their costs, outputs, and value to the organization. The outputs of an activity-based management system are critical inputs for an integrated strategic performance measurement and management system, and thus for the balanced scorecard report. Moreover, since activity-based management is all about the economics of an organization, it facilitates and supports the objective of waste reduction. It is fundamental to increasing efficiency and maintaining and improving your competitive position."

**Rob**: "But would my employees readily accept the balanced scorecard approach?"

**Paula**: "Absolutely. A significant advantage of the balanced scorecard is that it links performance measures to a company's strategy, and that it communicates these relationships to employees. This helps employees understand how their actions affect the overall strategy of the organization. More importantly, employee involvement in the development of the balanced scorecard measures, combined with appropriate rewards, can promote employee commitment and further enhance the achievement of strategic goals."

## Questions to Think About

1. Why are financial measures by themselves not sufficient for organizational control and performance management?

2. What is the difference in the information provided by historical (feedback) measures and predictive (feedforward) measures?

3. Why is it important to link performance measures to strategy?

4. Why are processes critically important to performance management?

5. How is activity-based management compatible with the balanced scorecard?

6. What role, if any, do cost reports play in a performance management system?

7. How can an organization achieve an integrated performance management system?

## Strategic Performance Management Environment

**Objective 1**

Discuss environmental factors affecting effective performance management.

The type of environment in which an organization operates can have a significant effect on the type of control and communication system appropriate for that organization. Two examples of companies operating in different environments are provided below. While reading the descriptions, consider which situation more closely resembles the environment faced by Telco Systems in the opening scenario.

The first company produces concrete sewer pipes. The products and production processes are well defined and relatively stable. Functional skills are specialized in order to gain operating efficiencies. Interactions with suppliers and customers are mainly at arm's length. Competition tends to be local or regional, as compared to national or international. A successful company operating in this type of environment tends to emphasize maintaining the status quo: efficient production and the preservation of market share.

The second company produces computers and computer-related products and operates in a rapidly changing environment. Stiff competition is always present, and products and processes need to be constantly redesigned and improved. The competitive environment demands that the company offer customized products and services to diverse customer segments. This company must find cost-effective ways of producing high-variety, low-demand products. This requirement means that more attention needs to be paid to linkages between the company and its key suppliers and customers, with the goal of improving cost control, quality, and response times for all parties. It is obvious that this situation reflects the current operating environment of Telco Systems more accurately than the first example. The environment may have been reasonably stable in the past, but it is obvious from the dialogue between Martin and the consultant that the company is undergoing many changes.

Organizations, such as Telco Systems, that operate in a dynamic environment are finding that change and adaptation are essential to long-term survival. To find ways to improve performance, companies are forced to re-evaluate how they do business. To improve performance, companies must constantly search for ways to eliminate waste—a process known as *continuous improvement*. Waste can appear in the form of excess inventories, unnecessary activities, defective products, too much rework and setup time, and the underutilization of employees' talents and skills. There are various tools for reducing waste; these include JIT purchasing and manufacturing, re-engineering, total quality management, employee empowerment, and computer-aided manufacturing.

## Organizational Control Environment

**organizational environment**

Organizational attributes and circumstances that are largely controllable by the organization in the long term but may be constant in the short term, such as the existing organizational structure, production capacity, and staff levels.

**external environment**

External conditions that are largely uncontrollable by the organization, such as the economy and weather conditions.

As the previous section illustrated, an organization's operations are influenced by its environment. In general, an organization converts inputs, such as materials and labour, into products or services through its processes and activities. Furthermore, the nature of products or services produced can have long-term outcomes for different stakeholders. For example, products that are not "environmentally friendly" can create costly long-term disposal problems and environmental effects for the company, consumers, and society in general. Thus, outcomes are long-term effects, not only on the company that produced the product but also on its wider community. Exhibit 17–1 depicts a general organizational control environment. Environment can be considered to consist of organizational and external elements. **Organizational environment** includes factors that are largely controllable by the organization in the long term but may be constant in the short term, such as existing production capacity and staff levels. **External environment** consists of factors that are largely uncontrollable by the organization, such as economic and weather conditions.

EXHIBIT 17-1

Organizational Control Environment

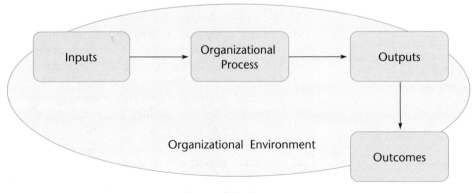

External Environment

Both organizational and external environments have implications for the design of management control systems. An organization's control system should be compatible with its internal and external operating environment. According to this view, which is based on **contingency theory**, there is no single best or universal management control and performance management system. Which system is appropriate depends on various organizational and environmental factors.[1]

### Organizational Factors

Organizations are unique entities that consist of people, physical resources, systems, and structures. Collectively, they provide an organizational context for management controls. Organizational factors that can affect control systems include the following: strategy, structure, size, systems, resources, management philosophy, and staff skills. Strategic planning establishes broad organizational goals. Organizational structure outlines the formal organizational relationships; it also provides a basis for establishing responsibility and accountability relationships. Furthermore, an organization's size, resources, staff skills, and existing systems can influence the types of management controls that are appropriate and possible. Management philosophy and organizational values and norms can also influence individual behaviours and, it follows, reactions to management controls. All these factors can, therefore, either facilitate or hinder the design, implementation, and effective use of management controls.

### External Factors

Beyond the organizational setting, broader technological, economic, cultural, social, regulatory, and political environments also affect organizations and, therefore, have an indirect impact on their management control systems. Modern organizations operate in an increasingly competitive global environment characterized by rapid technological change. They also operate in different political environments and thus are subject to the laws, regulations, and ideologies of governments. Furthermore, organizations must be sensitive to the diverse cultural backgrounds of their customers, employees, and other stakeholders, as well as to current social issues and trends. Besides this, various special interest groups such as environmentalists, as well as the media, may exert strong pressure for certain actions. All these factors can create uncertainty, to which organizations must adapt in order to survive and prosper. However, some control over these factors may be possible in the long run—for example, through strategic renewal and lobbying initiatives. Exhibit 17–2 summarizes organizational and environmental factors.

contingency theory

A theory maintaining that no single best or universal management control and performance management system exists but that the appropriateness of control systems depends on various organizational and environmental factors.

**EXHIBIT 17-2**

Examples of Organizational and Environmental Factors

| Organizational Factors | Environmental Factors |
| --- | --- |
| • Size | • Technology |
| • Strategy | • Competition |
| • Structure | • Economy |
| • Systems | • Culture |
| • Resources | • Social values |
| • Staff skills | • Regulation and legislation |
| • Management philosophy | • Politics |
| • Organizational norms | |

---

1. Classic contingent frameworks are available in the following sources: Lawrence A. Gordon and Danny Miller, "A Contingency Framework for the Design of Accounting Information Systems," *Accounting, Organizations and Society* (1976) 1: pp. 59-69; David C. Hayes, "The Contingency Theory of Managerial Accounting," *The Accounting Review* (1977) 52: pp. 22-39; David T. Otley, "The Contingency Theory of Management Accounting: Achievement and Prognosis," *Accounting, Organizations and Society* (1980) 5: pp. 413-28; John H. Waterhouse and Peter Tiessen, "A Contingency Framework for Management Accounting Systems Research," *Accounting, Organizations and Society* (1978) 3: pp. 65-76.

## Performance Management and Control Systems

Whether the environment is stable or dynamic, an organization needs to exercise control over its operations in order to achieve its objectives. Performance measurement and control systems can have a strong impact on this. "You get what you measure and reward." "If you don't measure it, it won't improve, and if you don't monitor it, it will get worse." These adages are relevant when control systems are being designed. For example, to increase the number of applicants it placed in jobs, an employment agency selected "the number of persons who received an interview" as the key performance measure for rewarding its employees. As a result, the number of interviews increased but even fewer placements occurred! Desired results were obtained when the agency changed the measure to "the number of applicants placed." This example demonstrates that control systems can have a significant impact on outcomes and behaviours.

### Responsibility Accounting

One key role of management accounting systems is to provide information for measuring outcomes and designing rewards. This role of management accounting is referred to as *responsibility accounting*, and it is a fundamental concept in both management control and performance management. The responsibility accounting model has four essential elements:

1. Assigning responsibility
2. Establishing performance measures or benchmarks
3. Evaluating performance
4. Rewarding performance

The objective of responsibility accounting is to influence behaviour in such a way that individual and organizational initiatives are aligned to achieve common goals. Clearly, responsibility accounting systems constitute the foundation of management control systems, which have a broader purpose. **Management control** has traditionally been defined as "the process by which managers assure that resources are obtained and used effectively and efficiently in the accomplishment of the organization's objectives."[2] Efficiency is generally understood to be concerned with achieving given results with minimum resources, and effectiveness with attaining organizational objectives. Management control systems are the prerequisite for performance management. The concept of **performance management** is broader than traditional management control. It is about the effective use of the information provided by management control systems for strategic planning, decision making, and management.

### Management Control Systems

There are three categories of **management control systems**:

1. Functional-based
2. Activity-based
3. Strategic-based

Companies that operate in a stable environment, that produce standardized products using standardized processes, and that face little competition will likely

**management control**

The process by which managers ensure that resources are obtained and used efficiently and effectively in accomplishing an organization's objectives.

**performance management**

Management processes concerned with the effective use of information provided by management control systems for strategic planning, control, and decision making.

**management control systems**

Structures, resources, and processes that facilitate effective management control.

---

2. Robert N. Anthony, *The Management Control Function*, Boston, Mass.: The Harvard Business School Press (1988): p.10. Broader definitions also allow for the recognition of planning, nonfinancial controls, and behavioural factors as integral elements of effective overall management control. For example, see Tony Lowe, "On the Idea of a Management Control System: Integrating Accounting and Management Control," *Journal of Management Studies* (1971): pp.1-12.

find the less complex functional-based responsibility accounting systems to be quite adequate—although they too would benefit from activity-based and strategic-based systems. As organizational complexity increases and the competitive environment becomes more dynamic, the activity-based and strategic-based systems are likely to be more suitable. The functional-based systems are generally oriented toward manufacturing organizations. Service and nonprofit organizations generally require more activity-based or strategic-based systems. The evolution has been from functional-based to activity-based to strategic-based systems. In the following section, we compare the three types of systems in order to provide a clearer basis for systems design choices and for a detailed examination of strategic systems.

## Comparison of Functional-Based, Activity-Based, and Strategic-Based Control Systems

**Objective 2**

Compare and contrast functional-based, activity-based, and strategic-based management control systems.

**functional-based control systems**

Control systems that focus on functional organizational units and measure performance in financial terms.

**activity-based control systems**

Control systems that focus on processes and use both financial and nonfinancial performance measures.

**strategic-based control systems**

Control systems that link an organization's mission and strategy with operational objectives and use multiple financial and nonfinancial measures to measure performance from different stakeholders' perspectives in a balanced manner.

Functional-based, activity-based, and strategic-based control systems use different responsibility accounting foundations and criteria. **Functional-based control systems** assign responsibility to organizational units and express performance measures in financial terms. These systems were developed when most companies were operating in relatively stable environments, primarily in the manufacturing sector. **Activity-based control systems** developed once companies operating in more dynamic, continuous improvement environments began seeking better methods of controlling overhead expenditures. Activity-based systems assign responsibility to processes and use both financial and nonfinancial measures of performance.

Activity-based systems represented a significant change in how responsibility was assigned, measured, and evaluated. Activity-based systems added a process perspective to the financial perspective of functional-based control systems. They also altered the financial perspective by shifting the emphasis from cost control through maintaining the status quo to cost reduction through continuous learning and change. Thus, responsibility accounting changed from a one-dimensional system to a two-dimensional system and from a control system to a learning and cost management system. Adding the process perspective was considered necessary for companies operating in continuous improvement environments. Although these changes were a dramatic step in the right direction, it was soon discovered that the new approach also had some limitations. The most significant shortcoming was that continuous improvement efforts were often fragmented, and that they failed to connect with the organization's overall mission and strategy. Consequently, the expected competitive successes sometimes did not materialize.

More directed continuous improvement was needed. However, a formal guidance system for continuous improvement meant that an organization's managers needed to carefully specify a strategy for their organization and to identify the objectives, performance measures, and initiatives necessary for that strategy. This is why strategic-based control systems were the next step in the evolution of responsibility accounting. **Strategic-based control systems** link an organization's mission and strategy with operational objectives, and they use both financial and nonfinancial measures linked to various stakeholders' objectives. Perhaps the best-known strategic-based system is the balanced scorecard, which has four perspectives: the financial perspective, the customer perspective, the business process perspective, and the learning and growth perspective.[3] Exhibit 17–3 compares the

---

3. Robert S. Kaplan and David P. Norton, *The Balanced Scorecard* (Boston: Harvard Business School Press, 1996).

EXHIBIT 17-3

Comparison of
Functional-Based, Activity-
Based, and Strategic-
Based Control Systems

three types of systems along the four elements of responsibility accounting: assigning responsibility, establishing performance measures, evaluating performance, and rewarding performance. Because of its ubiquity, the balanced scorecard framework is used as an example of strategic-based systems.

| Type of Systems/ Element | Functional-Based Systems | Activity-Based Systems | Strategic-Based Systems |
|---|---|---|---|
| Assigning responsibility | • Organizational unit<br>• Individual in charge<br>• Operating efficiency<br>• Financial outcomes | • Team<br>• Process<br>• Value chain<br>• Financial | • Financial<br>• Customer<br>• Process<br>• Learning and growth |
| Establishing performance measures | • Unit budgets<br>• Standard costs<br>• Static standards<br>• Currently attainable standards | • Optimal<br>• Dynamic<br>• Process oriented<br>• Value added | • Communication of strategy<br>• Balanced measures<br>• Alignment of objectives<br>• Linkage to strategy |
| Evaluating performance | • Financial efficiency<br>• Controllable costs<br>• Actual vs. standard<br>• Financial measures | • Time reductions<br>• Quality improvements<br>• Cost reductions<br>• Trend measures | • Financial measures<br>• Customer measures<br>• Process measures<br>• Learning and growth |
| Rewarding performance | Financial performance:<br>• Promotions<br>• Bonuses<br>• Profit sharing<br>• Salary increases | Multidimensional performance:<br>• Same as for functional-based systems, plus gain sharing and rewards based on team performance | Multidimensional performance:<br>• Same as for activity-based systems, plus rewards based on performance in four responsibility areas above |

## Assigning Responsibility

Functional-based systems focus on functional organizational units and individuals. First, a responsibility centre is identified. This centre is typically an organizational unit such as a department or production line. Responsibility is assigned to the individual in charge of that unit. Responsibility is defined in financial terms—for example, in terms of costs or revenues. In an activity-based system, the focal point changes from units and individuals to processes and teams. However, financial responsibility continues to be vital. The reasons for the change in focus are simple. In a continuous improvement environment, the financial perspective translates into continuously enhancing revenues, reducing costs, and improving resource utilization. To create this continuous growth and improvement, an organization must constantly improve its capabilities for delivering value to customers and shareholders. Processes are chosen as the focus because they are the organization's key to achieving financial objectives. Procurement, product development, customer acquisition, and customer service are examples of processes.

Strategic-based systems maintain the process and financial perspectives of the activity-based approach but typically add customer and learning and growth perspectives. These two additional perspectives consider the interests of customers and employees that were not fully considered by activity-based systems. All four perspectives are generally considered essential for creating a competitive advantage and for allowing managers to articulate, communicate, and evaluate the organization's mission and strategy.

It has been suggested that the four perspectives may not be sufficient and that additional perspectives—for example, environmental and social perspectives—could be useful. However, the basic strategic-based systems framework is flexible and can accommodate additional or modified perspectives. For example, the customer perspective is not directly relevant in public and nonprofit organizations and needs to be replaced or supplemented with the perspectives of other stakeholders. In other words, strategic systems should include the perspectives of all key stakeholders considered critical to the achievement of an organization's strategic goals.

## Establishing Performance Measures

Performance measures must be identified and standards set to serve as benchmarks for performance measurement. Budgeting and standard costing are the cornerstones of functional-based systems. (This, of course, implies that performance measures are objective and financial in nature.) Furthermore, they tend to support the status quo and to remain relatively stable over time. In contrast, performance measures in activity-based systems are concerned with process attributes such as, quality, efficiency, and process time. Performance measurement standards are dynamic and support change. They change to reflect new conditions and goals and to help maintain any progress already realized.

For example, standards can be set to reflect some desired level of process improvement. Once the desired level is achieved, the standard is changed to encourage an additional increment of improvement. Standards should reflect the value added by individual activities and processes, so that value-added and nonvalue-added activities can be identified. Finally, in continuous improvement environments, optimal standards play a vital role in identifying the potential for improvement, although such standards may not practically speaking be attainable.

The strategic-based approach includes the process orientation of activity-based systems. None of the advantages of the activity-based approach are lost. However, the strategic-based approach adds some important further refinements. In strategic-based systems, performance measures must be integrated so that they are mutually consistent and reinforcing, communicate the strategy, and help align individual and organizational goals and initiatives. In fact, an organization's mission, strategy, and objectives should drive its performance measures. Thus, the measures must be balanced and linked to the organization's strategy.

A balanced measurement system requires that a balance be struck between lag measures and lead measures, between objective measures and subjective measures, between financial measures and nonfinancial measures, and between external measures and internal measures. **Lag measures** are outcome measures—that is, measures of results from past efforts (e.g., customer profitability). **Lead measures** are **performance drivers** that drive future performance (e.g., hours of employee training). **Objective measures** are those which can be readily quantified and verified (e.g., market share), whereas **subjective measures** are less quantifiable and more judgment-based (e.g., employee capabilities). **Financial measures** are those expressed in monetary terms (e.g., cost per unit), whereas **nonfinancial measures** use nonmonetary units (e.g., number of dissatisfied customers). **External measures** are those which relate to customers and shareholders (e.g., customer satisfaction and return on investment). **Internal measures** are those which relate to the processes and capabilities that create value for customers and shareholders (e.g., process efficiency and employee satisfaction).

**lag measures**

Outcome measures or measures of results from past efforts.

**lead measures**

Factors that drive future performance.

**performance drivers**

Factors that cause future performance, for example, employee training.

**objective measures**

Measures that can be readily quantified and verified.

**subjective measures**

Measures that are nonquantifiable and whose values are judgmental in nature.

**financial measures**

Measures expressed in dollar terms.

**nonfinancial measures**

Measures expressed in nonmonetary units.

**external measures**

Measures that relate to customer and shareholder objectives.

**internal measures**

Measures that relate to the processes and capabilities that create value for customers and shareholders.

## Evaluating Performance

In a functional-based framework, performance is measured by comparing actual outcomes with budgeted outcomes. Cost performance is strongly emphasized. In a continuous improvement framework, performance is broader than in the functional framework, with both productivity and cost measures being considered important. The objective is to provide low-cost, high-quality products, delivered on a timely basis. Thus, time, quality, and efficiency are also critical dimensions of performance. Measures such as cycle time, defect rates, and on-time delivery can be used as indicators of performance for these dimensions. A fundamental assumption is that improving a process should result in improved financial results. Thus, measures of cost reductions, cost trends, and cost per unit of output can also be useful indicators of process improvement. In principle, progress toward achieving both ultimate and interim standards should be measured.

In a strategic-based system, performance measurement is significantly expanded. Processes are evaluated as before, and so are the financial consequences of executing those processes; but in addition to these, also evaluated are customers and infrastructure factors that enable the organization to learn, change, and execute new and improved processes. Indicators of these dimensions are, for example, customer satisfaction, employee satisfaction, and employee skill levels.

## Rewarding Performance

In all systems, individuals are rewarded or penalized according to the policies and discretion of higher management. Functional-based reward systems are designed to encourage individuals to manage costs and to meet or exceed budgetary standards. In activity-based continuous improvement environments, rewarding individuals is more complicated than in a functional-based setting. Individuals may be accountable for both team and individual performance simultaneously. Since process improvements are achieved mainly through team efforts, group-based rewards are more suitable than individual rewards. For example, an electronics manufacturer has set optimal standards for unit costs, on-time delivery, quality, inventory turnover, scrap, and cycle time. Bonuses are awarded to teams that maintain performance on all measures and that improve performance on at least one measure.[4] Note that this organization is using multidimensional performance criteria.

Strategic-based reward systems use multidimensional performance criteria that relate to all four perspectives. One approach is to distribute the incentive compensation among the four perspectives using a weighting scheme. For example, Pioneer Petroleum assigns 60 percent of its incentive compensation to the financial perspective, 10 percent to the customer perspective, 10 percent to the process perspective, and 20 percent to the learning and growth perspective. Within each category, the bonus is distributed among specific measures. For example, of the 60 percent assigned to the financial perspective, 3 percent is assigned to market growth.[5]

In both activity-based and strategic-based reward systems, gain sharing can also be used. This allows employees to share in gains related to specific improvement projects; it also facilitates the necessary "buy-in" for specific improvement programs.

---

4.  C.J. McNair, "Responsibility Accounting and Controllability Networks," *Handbook of Cost Management* (Boston: Warren Gorham Lamont, 1993): pp. E4-1–E4-33.

5.  Robert S. Kaplan and David P. Norton, *The Balanced Scorecard* (Boston: Harvard Business School Press, 1996): pp. 218-19.

# Process Value Analysis

**Objective 3**

Explain the role of process value analysis in strategic performance management.

Strategic-based control systems must be solidly rooted in process value analysis. The operational focus of activity value analysis provides a basis for internal process improvements. Value chain analysis can be used to evaluative different strategic courses of action and to provide additional value to customers. Moreover, strategic analysis and the management of key relationships with suppliers, customers, and other stakeholders in a supply chain can, through collaboration, improve the competitive position of all members of the supply chain.

## Activity Value Analysis

**activity value analysis**

The process of identifying, describing, and evaluating the activities an organization performs.

**activity inputs**

The resources consumed by an activity in producing its output (the factors that enable the activity to be performed).

**activity output**

The result or product of an activity.

**activity output measure**

The number of times an activity is performed. It is the quantifiable measure of the activity output.

**driver analysis**

The effort expended to identify those factors that are the root causes of activity costs.

**Activity value analysis** is fundamental to activity-based systems; it is also integral to strategic-based systems. Activity analysis is the process of identifying, describing, and evaluating the activities an organization performs. It focuses on accountability for activities rather than costs, and it emphasizes the maximization of systemwide performance rather than individual performance. Activity value analysis requires an understanding of what causes activity costs. Every activity has inputs and outputs. **Activity inputs** are the resources an activity consumes in producing its outputs. **Activity outputs** are the result of performing an activity. An **activity output measure** is the number of times the activity is performed.

### Activity Driver Analysis

The activity output measure is a measure of the demands placed on an activity. It is what has previously been called an *activity driver*. As the demand for an activity changes, the costs of that activity can also change. However, output measures may not correspond to the *root causes* of activity costs; rather, they may be the consequences of the activity performed. Driver analysis can reveal the root causes of activities. Thus, **driver analysis** is the effort expended to identify those factors which are the root causes of activity costs. For example, an analysis may reveal that the root cause of materials moving costs is plant layout. Once the root cause is known, action can be taken to improve the activity. Specifically, reorganizing plant layout can reduce the cost of moving materials.

Activity value analysis should produce four outcomes:

1. Identify the activities to be performed.
2. Identify individuals performing the activities.
3. Identify the time and resources required to perform the activities.
4. Identify the value of the activities to the organization; this includes a recommendation to keep only value-added activities.

Steps 1 to 3 have already been discussed in connection with cost assignment. Step 4—determining the value-added content of activities—is concerned with cost reduction rather than cost assignment. For that reason, it is crucial to activity value analysis. Activities can be classified as value-added or nonvalue-added.[6]

### Value-Added Activities

**value-added activities**

Activities that are necessary to achieve corporate objectives and remain in business.

**Value-added activities** are activities that are necessary to keep the company in business. Some activities, *required activities*, are necessary to comply with legal

---

6. See *Value Chain Analysis for Assessing Competitive Advantage*, Management Accounting Guideline 41, The Society of Management Accountants of Canada (1996).

mandates. The remaining activities are *discretionary*. A discretionary activity is classified as value-added when it simultaneously satisfies three conditions:

1. Activity produces a change of state.
2. Change of state was not achievable by preceding activities.
3. Activity enables other activities to be performed.

For example, consider the production of rods used in hydraulic cylinders. The first activity, cutting rods, cuts long rods into the correct lengths for the cylinders. Next, the cut rods are welded. The rod-cutting activity is value-added because it causes a change of state: uncut rods become cut rods; no prior activity was supposed to create this change of state; and it enables the welding activity to be performed. The value-added properties are easy to see for an operational activity such as cutting rods. Now what about a more general activity, such as supervising production workers? A managerial activity is specifically designed to manage other value-added activities—that is, to ensure that they are performed in an efficient and timely manner. Supervision certainly satisfies the enabling condition. But is there a change in state?

There are two ways of answering in the affirmative. First, supervising can be viewed as an enabling resource that is consumed by the operational activities that do produce a change of state. Thus, supervising is a secondary activity that helps bring about the change of state expected for value-added primary activities. Second, it could be argued that supervision brings order by changing the state from uncoordinated activities to coordinated activities.

Once value-added activities are identified, we can define value-added costs. **Value-added costs** are the costs of performing value-added activities with perfect efficiency.

### Nonvalue-Added Activities

**Nonvalue-added activities** are activities other than those absolutely essential to remain in business. A nonvalue-added activity can be identified by its failure to satisfy any of the three conditions previously listed. Violation of the first two conditions is common for nonvalue-added activities. For example, inspecting cut rods for correct length is a nonvalue-added activity. Inspection is a state-detection activity, not a state-changing activity—that is, it tells us the state of the cut rod (i.e., whether it is the right length or not). Thus, it fails to meet the first condition.

As another example, rework is designed to bring a product from a nonconforming state to a conforming state. Thus, a change of state occurs. Yet the activity is nonvalue-added, because it repeats work. It involves doing something that should have been done by preceding activities, and thus it violates the second condition. **Nonvalue-added costs** are costs that are caused either by nonvalue-added activities or by the inefficient performance of value-added activities. Because of increased competition, many companies are attempting to optimize value-added activities and to eliminate nonvalue-added activities that add unnecessary cost and impede performance. Thus, activity value analysis attempts to identify and eventually eliminate all unnecessary activities, while simultaneously increasing the efficiency of necessary activities.

The main objective of activity analysis is waste elimination. As waste is eliminated, costs are reduced. Note the emphasis on managing the *causes* of the costs rather than the costs themselves. Managing costs may increase an activity's efficiency, but if the activity is unnecessary, it does not matter fundamentally whether it is performed efficiently. An unnecessary activity is wasteful and should be eliminated. For example, moving raw materials and partly finished goods is often cited as a nonvalue-added activity. Installing an automated materials-handling system may increase the efficiency of this activity; however,

**value-added costs**

Costs caused by value-added activities.

**nonvalue-added activities**

All activities other than those that are absolutely essential to remain in business.

**nonvalue-added costs**

Costs that are caused either by nonvalue-added activities or by the inefficient performance of value-added activities.

changing to cellular manufacturing, with on-site, just-in-time delivery of raw materials, could virtually eliminate the activity. It is easy to see which approach is preferable.

Nonvalue-added activities can exist anywhere in the organization. In a manufacturing operation, five major activities are often cited as wasteful and unnecessary:

1. *Scheduling* An activity that uses time and resources to determine when different products have access to processes, when and how many setups must be done, and how much is produced.
2. *Moving* An activity that uses time and resources to move raw materials, work in process, and finished goods from one department to another.
3. *Waiting* An activity in which raw materials or work in process use time and resources by waiting for the next process.
4. *Inspecting* An activity in which time and resources are spent ensuring that the product meets specifications.
5. *Storing* An activity that uses time and resources while a good or raw material is held in inventory.

None of these activities add any value for the customer. The challenge of activity analysis is to find ways to produce the product without using any of these activities.

Analysis of value-added and nonvalue-added activities can reduce costs through activity elimination, selection, reduction, and sharing.[7] **Activity elimination** focuses on nonvalue-added activities. Once activities that fail to add value are identified, measures must be taken to eliminate these activities. **Activity selection** involves choosing among different sets of activities that are caused by competing strategies. Different product design strategies can require significantly different activities with different costs. All other things equal, the lowest-cost design strategy should be chosen. **Activity reduction** decreases the time and resources required by an activity. This approach can be used to improve the efficiency of necessary activities or to implement a short-term strategy for improving nonvalue-added activities until they can be eliminated. **Activity sharing** increases the efficiency of necessary activities by using economies of scale. Specifically, the quantity of the cost driver is increased without increasing the total cost of the activity itself. This lowers the unit cost and the total costs traceable to the products.

## Value Chain Analysis

**Value chain analysis** is a strategic tool that can be used to understand a company's competitive advantage and its relationships with suppliers, customers, and competitors. This understanding is necessary for formulating and evaluating different strategic courses of action and for providing value to customers. Additional value to customers can be achieved by improving product characteristics or by reducing cost—for example, by simplifying distribution, outsourcing parts or processes, and negotiating more favourable terms with suppliers.

The value chain analysis and the activity value analysis described in the previous section are closely related but not synonymous. Value chain analysis is based on activity value analysis, but is a broader concept. The first step in value chain analysis is activity value analysis—that is, the identification of value-added and nonvalue-added activities for the purpose of streamlining activities and

**activity elimination**

The process of eliminating nonvalue-added activities.

**activity selection**

The process of choosing among sets of activities caused by competing strategies.

**activity reduction**

Decreasing the time and resources required by an activity.

**activity sharing**

Increasing the efficiency of necessary activities by using economies of scale.

**value chain analysis**

A strategic tool that can be used to understand an organization's competitive advantage and its relationships with suppliers, customers, and competitors.

---

7.  Peter B.B. Turney, "How Activity-Based Costing Helps Reduce Cost," *Journal of Cost Management* (Winter 1991): pp. 29-35.

reducing costs. However, value chain analysis is concerned with higher-level evaluation of strategic alternatives and their longer-term consequences. For example, the activity value analysis may reveal that eliminating certain activities, and individuals who perform these activities, could reduce costs and deliver immediate savings and value to customers, but that doing so could hinder the company's ability to take advantage of new opportunities in the long term as a result of staff shortages and additional hiring costs. Clearly, value chain analysis is more long-term and strategic than activity value analysis.

The value chain is an interrelated set of activities that increases the usefulness or value of products and services to customers. A typical value chain for a manufacturing company is illustrated in Exhibit 17–4. It has six stages:

1. *R&D*—the generation and development of ideas for new products, services, or processes.
2. *Design*—the determination of detailed engineering specifications for products, services, or processes.
3. *Production*—the acquistion, assembly, and coordination of resources to manufacture products or deliver services.
4. *Marketing*—the means and processes of informing potential customers about products or services and promoting products or services.
5. *Distribution*—the channels and processes by which products or services are delivered to customers.
6. *Customer service*—the after-sale product or service support mechanisms and activities provided to customers.

Administrative functions are not explicit stages in the value chain, as they consist mainly of nonvalue-added activities. Such activities are implicitly included in every step of the value chain, with the understanding that they should be minimized as much as possible. For example, the accounting function provides relevant cost information and analysis for decision making and management at each step of the value chain, but it is not a separate step *per se*. Note

EXHIBIT    17-4

Illustration of Value Chain

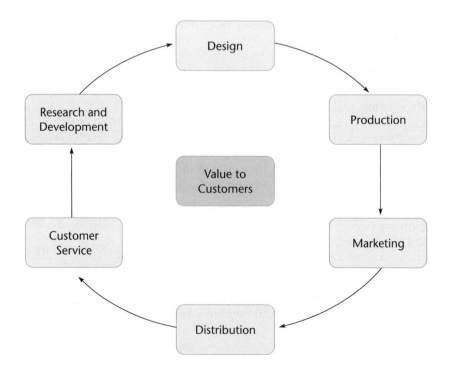

that the knowledge and customer feedback obtained from value chain analysis has R&D implications for future products. Thus, the value chain can be represented as a continuous cyclical process; feedback from the current process has R&D implications for subsequent cycles. Note also the customer focus at the centre of the diagram. Successful businesses never forget the importance of maintaining a customer focus.

All six stages of the value chain may not be equally important to a company. For example, in service organizations the emphasis is naturally on the design, marketing, and distribution stages, since the R&D and the production stages do not directly apply. However, even manufacturing companies may make a strategic decision to develop only certain stages of the value chain. The decision as to which stages of the value chain to develop should be based on strategic comparative analysis. Such analysis reveals the competitive advantage of the company—that is, the areas in which it can provide the most value to customers at the lowest cost.

For example, Dell Computer focuses on the assembly and distribution stages of the value chain. Exhibit 17–5 shows a value chain for Dell computers, with examples of value-added processes and activities at each of the six main steps. The company sees its product design and distribution functions as the most important. The various design options for Dell computers provide value, quality, and choice to customers. Also, the direct-delivery distribution strategy offers lower cost and faster delivery to customers. Of course, the company also performs some functions in the other areas of the value chain.

**EXHIBIT 17-5**

Value Chain for Dell Computers

| Stage | Examples of Value-Added Processes and Activities |
| --- | --- |
| R&D | • Latest technology integrated into products quickly<br>• Process innovation |
| Design | • Flexible systems design features and options<br>• Design options continuously updated<br>• Competitively priced products |
| Production | • Products built to customers' specifications<br>• Order processing and confirmation on Internet and by telephone<br>• Turnover less than ten days |
| Marketing | • Newspapers primarily to individual customers<br>• Dell website to individual and business customers |
| Distribution | • Direct delivery to customers<br>• No intermediaries<br>• Delivery by courier |
| Customer Service | • 24-hour customer service<br>• Personalized product support on line<br>• Customer order tracking on line |

Source: Examples of activities compiled from the Dell website at ausoladcacm.us.dell.com/ostatus/builtorder.asp? language=E and at www.dell.ca/ca/en/gen/corporate/vision_directmodel.htm (as of August 3, 2002)

**supply chain**
All activities that are involved in the efficient and effective movement and transformation of raw materials, through the manufacturing process, into final products to end users.

# Supply Chain Management[8]

A **supply chain** can be defined as all activities that are involved in the efficient and effective movement and transformation of raw materials, through the manufacturing process, into final products and then to end users.[9] The supply chain involves multiple organizations engaged in different activities and processes—for example, sourcing, procurement, production scheduling, manufacturing, order processing, inventory management, warehousing, and customer service. Collectively, these organizations focus on delivering optimal value to end consumers. Exhibit 17–6 illustrates the multiple relationships among different partners in a typical supply chain—for example, suppliers, manufacturers, distributors, and consumers. As illustrated, each organization can participate in multiple supply chains.

EXHIBIT  17-6

Illustration of Supply Chain Relationships

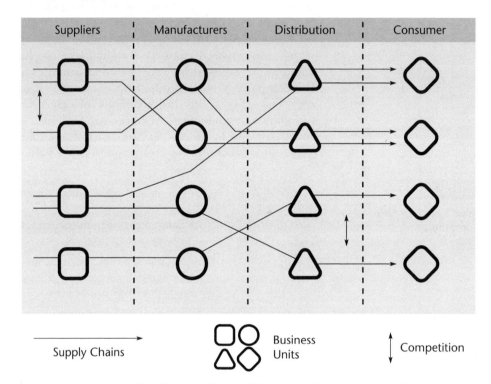

Source: Adapted from Silvio R.I. Pires and Carlos H.M. Aravechia, "Measuring Supply Chain Performance," Proceedings of the Twelfth Annual Conference of the Production and Operations Management Society, POM-2001, Orlando, Florida, March 30-April 2, 2001.

Supply chain management refers to the integrated and process-oriented approach to the design, management, and control of supply chains. Supply chain analysis and management have developed in response to industry demands for more customer-oriented strategies and to the need to deliver value throughout the chain to end customers. The goal of organizations adopting this approach is to meet customer expectations and gain customer loyalty and market share through increased customer satisfaction. Successful integration across the supply chain can improve cycle time, quality, cost, flexibility, and customer service, thus

---

8. The section on supply chain management is based on "Measuring Supply Chain Performance: A Balanced Scorecard Approach," Ph.D. Term Paper (Carleton University, 2001), by Robert Helal, Director, Analytic Applications, Cognos Incorporated.

9. P.C. Brewer and T.W. Speh, "Using the Balanced Scorecard to Measure Supply Chain Performance," *Journal of Business Logistics* (2000) 21: pp. 75-93.

providing value for end customers through the minimization of nonvalue-added activities and their associated costs. Clearly, the objectives are very similar to those of value chain analysis. The difference between the two is that in a supply chain, several companies are involved in a joint initiative, compared to a single organization in the value chain.

Integrated supply chain initiatives require planning, communication, coordination, and evaluation, not only across different functions within a single organization but also across different organizations in the supply chain. Access to shared information among organizations can aid in this process by minimizing uncertainty across partner organizations. Uncertainty can result from diverse planning activities of each organization that are unknown to other organizations. Without shared information across organizations, these uncertainties can lead to suboptimal operations and behaviours across organizations. For example, a study of manufacturers, distributors, and retailers by Andersen Consulting (1997) found that the sharing of information between supply chain partners resulted in improved performance, including improved inventory turnover rates, reduced stockouts, improved fill rates, and reduced costs.[10] Companies that did not share information did not experience the same performance improvements. This example demonstrates that successful integration and collaboration among organizations in the supply chain can improve the competitive position of each of the member organizations.

Performance measurement plays an important role in the successful implementation and management of supply chains. It is important to evaluate the outcomes of such initiatives in order to determine that the benefits outweigh the associated costs, including the loss of confidentiality due to the transparency of operational information. In an effective performance measurement system, all participating organizations gain, resulting in a win–win situation. However, each organization must conduct its own cost–benefit analysis in order to ensure that its participation results in fair outcomes and, in fact, improves its competitive position. The basic principles of performance measurement that apply to a single organization also apply to the supply chain. Unique overall measures can be developed at the system level for the supply chain as a whole. This calls for a coordinating body, consisting of members of each organization, to be responsible for developing, implementing, and evaluating systems level performance measures.

The application of supply chain concepts can be demonstrated well by extending the example of Dell Computers. The company has attributed a significant part of its success in a competitive industry to the effective management of products, information, and cash flows within its supply chain. Products are delivered directly to customers, which saves extra handling costs and provides faster service. Inventory turnover is high, and this minimizes inventory carrying and obsolescence costs. Real-time data are provided to suppliers regarding inventory levels and daily production requirements, which helps key suppliers match their production plans with Dell's needs. Information is also coordinated with contracted customer service providers. Furthermore, by effectively tracking and managing cash flows from customers, Dell is able to collect receivables before it needs to make payments to its suppliers.[11]

---

10. Andersen Consulting (1997) study cited in Stefan Holmberg, "A Systems Perspective on Supply Chain Measurement," *International Journal of Physical Distribution & Logistics Management* (2000) 30: pp. 847-68.

11. The Dell Computer supply chain management process is described in S. Chopra and P. Meindl, *Supply Chain Management: Strategy, Planning and Operations*, Prentice Hall, Upper Saddle River, N.J. (2001): pp. 16-17.

# Strategic Performance Measurement

**Objective** 4

Explain the basic features of and design criteria for effective strategic performance measurement systems in general and for the balanced scorecard framework in particular.

**strategic performance measurement**

The assessment of the achievement of strategic performance objectives of organizations, organizational units, and programs.

**Strategic performance measurement** is a process concerned with assessing the performance of organizations, organizational units, and programs. Its primary function is to monitor the achievement of an organization's strategic objectives; in this way it serves as an important planning, management control, and accountability device. Performance measurement systems provide ongoing feedback on progress toward meeting organizational objectives; in doing so, they make it possible to take timely corrective actions and to capitalize on organizational strengths. In an ideal performance measurement system, well-designed performance measures permit the evaluation of the effects of programs and services on the well-being of all stakeholders. However, because direct measures of well-being do not exist, proxy or surrogate measures of varying degrees of sophistication are useful as crude indicators of the well-being of different stakeholders. Performance measures can thus be viewed as "measuring sticks" of success in achieving an organization's strategies and objectives and, ultimately, of success in assessing an organization's contribution to the well-being of its wider community.

## Nonfinancial Performance Measures

In the past decade, it has been widely recognized that besides conventional financial performance measures, nonfinancial measures are important. Nonfinancial operational measures may be better understood and affected by employees at lower levels of the organization, since they directly relate to the activities and processes these employees are performing. Moreover, nonfinancial measures can be collected and analyzed on a more timely basis than financial measures; financial measures are often available too late to serve as effective warning signals. Poor financial results can often be predicted early by nonfinancial measures related to productivity, quality, customer satisfaction, and so on.

Good performance on nonfinancial measures will typically be reflected in improved financial performance. The evaluation of financial performance—for example, through traditional ratio analysis—is of course still important. However, since such topics are covered well in financial accounting textbooks, the discussion in this section focuses only on nonfinancial measures.

Nonfinancial measures are especially important in nonprofit and government organizations, for which profit-oriented measures may not be available. Management control systems must then, by necessity, rely primarily on nonfinancial measures. For example, Canada Post measures on-time delivery, employee satisfaction, and customer satisfaction in addition to financial data. On-time delivery is measured by "test mail" processed through regular channels; the satisfaction of customers and employees is measured by surveys.[12]

### Level of Responsibility

Performance measures can be developed and used at different organizational levels and across organizational boundaries at the system level. Exhibit 17–7 illustrates such a hierarchical structure of performance measures.

At the base of the pyramid, measures can be developed for individual tasks, activities, and functions. Because of the operational nature and large number of activities at this level, many measures can exist, and these measures tend to be efficiency oriented. Individual frontline employees or work teams are typically

---

12. www.canadapost.ca/common/corporate/about/annual_report/highlights2001-e.asp; and
www.canadapost.ca/corporate/about/annual_report/eng/index.html.

EXHIBIT 17-7

EXHIBIT 17-7

Hierarchy of Performance
Measures

**Number:**
Few

Many

System

Organization

Department or
Program

Function or Task

**Focus:**
Effectiveness

Efficiency

assigned responsibility for these measures, since they can exert significant influence over them. For example, at a Chrysler assembly plant, the measures for assembly line operators may include measures of quality and on-time completion, as these employees can influence performance regarding these dimensions. In a service organization such as the Bay, Tim Horton's, or Royal Bank, frontline employees' primary responsibility is customer service, and performance measures should emphasize this dimension.

As one moves to the departmental and program levels, responsibilities change, and the measures become fewer in number and more effectiveness oriented. Middle managers are usually responsible for coordinating processes and employee development, and their performance measures should reflect these dimensions of their work. For example, if employees at the Bay are not adequately trained or their work schedules are not adequately coordinated, the store manager can usually be held responsible. His or her performance measures should flag a potential problem in these areas.

At the organizational level, top management is responsible for corporate-level performance. Measures at this level focus on effectiveness and on the achievement of strategic objectives. They measure how well an organization is meeting its responsibilities to various stakeholders. For example, organizations are responsible to their shareholders and creditors for their financial performance and to regulatory and government agencies for meeting the requirements of environmental, health and safety, and equity legislation. The chief executive officer typically bears the primary responsibility for performance at this level. The consequences of substandard performance are demonstrated well by the recent failures of large corporations such as Enron and Worldcom. Unfortunately, the performance measurement systems in both companies were not effective enough to flag fundamental problems early enough to prevent major disasters.

System level performance measurement is concerned with measuring aggregated performance across organizations. An example would be measuring performance on some common criteria across companies in a supply chain. Another example would be a regulatory or government agency monitoring performance of individual organizations. For example, Ontario municipalities are required to report selected measures for several programs to the Ontario Ministry of Municipal Affairs and Housing, which summarizes and reports system level measures for municipalities as a whole.[13] Carefully selected generic, system level measures allow for the gauging of system level performance as well as for benchmarking across organizations.

---

13. Ontario, Ministry of Municipal Affairs and Housing (2002). "Municipal Performance Measurement Program," www.mah.gov.on.ca/business/mpmp/mpmp-e.asp.

At each level, a few selected key measures should be used. If the measures are too few, not all critical performance dimensions will be adequately captured. If the measures are too many, they will be difficult to monitor, analyze, and use meaningfully. Note also that each level warrants its own set of measures and that measures unique to individual organizational units cannot be effectively aggregated at higher levels. For example, when the purchasing department measures its efficiency by the number of purchase orders processed, and the marketing department does this by the number of advertisements placed, the performances of the two departments are neither additive nor directly comparable. The measures used cannot reveal the total efficiency of the two departments or which department is more efficient. So another set of unique measures is required at each higher level to assess the performance objectives of that level.[14]

### Criteria for Performance Measures

**measurement criteria**
Standards and benchmarks against which performance can be assessed.

Perfect performance measures do not exist. That being said, effective performance measures exhibit certain key **measurement criteria**: relevance, reliability, accessibility, and simplicity. Relevance means that the measures are meaningfully related to the key strategic goals, decisions, and activities of the organization. Relevance also requires that the measures appropriately balance short- and long-term concerns. Reliability ensures that performance measures are objective, accurate, consistent, complementary, and not subject to manipulation. Accessibility requires that data be collected in a cost-effective manner. Simplicity implies that both managers and employees find the measures easy to understand and use.

Companies have generally found that meeting these technical criteria is simple enough. It seems that the main difficulties encountered with performance measurement systems relate to how the measures are used. Controllability is important for effective use of performance measures: managers should be held accountable for performance only on measures they can reasonably influence. Also, the performance expectations, the measures used, and the results achieved should be communicated clearly and on a timely basis to the employees being evaluated. Participation by employees in setting the measures has been known to increase commitment to and performance on these measures. Finally, for the measures to be taken seriously, they should be used in evaluating and rewarding employees on a regular, timely, and consistent basis.

A recent study identified eighteen factors that significantly contributed to the successful use of performance measurement systems. These factors are listed in Exhibit 17–8. They relate to performance measurement systems' characteristics, controllability, clarity, communication, relevance, responsibility, and usefulness. They are thus consistent with the general and behavioural criteria presented above.

### Performance Measurement Frameworks

**balanced scorecard**
A strategic performance measurement framework that incorporates a balanced mix of financial and nonfinancial measures for internal processes, customer satisfaction, financial performance, and learning and growth.

Nonfinancial performance measurement has been widely advocated in recent years, and several comprehensive performance measurement frameworks have been proposed. Probably the best known and most widely used framework is the "balanced scorecard" developed by Kaplan and Norton. Two other popular initiatives are the "business excellence model" and the "performance prism".

The **balanced scorecard** framework focuses on strategic alignment and consists of a balanced mix of financial and nonfinancial measures for internal

14. Regardless of such general prescriptions, a prominent study found that only measures common to multiple units, and not measures unique to particular units, are used in evaluating units' performance. See Marlys Gascho Lipe and Steven E. Salterio, "The Balanced Scorecard: Judgmental Effects of Common and Unique Performance Measures," *The Accounting Review* (July 2000) 75: pp. 283–98.

| EXHIBIT 17-8 | **Criteria** |
|---|---|
| Criteria for Effective Performance Management Systems | 1. Managers understand the meaning of KPIs.<br>2. Managers have insight into the relationship between business processes and CSFs/KPIs.<br>3. Managers' frames of reference contain similar KPIs.<br>4. Managers agree on changes in the CSF/KPI sets.<br>5. Managers agree on the starting time.<br>6. Managers have earlier (positive) experiences with performance management.<br>7. Managers realize the importance of CSFs/KPIs/BSC to their performance.<br>8. Managers do not experience CSFs/KPIs/BSC as threatening.<br>9. Managers' KPI sets are aligned with their responsibility areas.<br>10. Managers can influence the KPIs assigned to them.<br>11. Managers are involved in making analyses.<br>12. Managers can use their CSFs/KPIs/BSC for managing their employees.<br>13. Managers' results on CSFs/KPIs/BSC are openly communicated.<br>14. Managers are stimulated to improve their performance.<br>15. Managers trust the performance information.<br>16. Managers clearly see the promoter using the performance management system.<br>17. Managers find the performance management system relevant because it has a clear internal control purpose.<br>18. Managers find the performance management system relevant because only those stakeholders' interests that are important to the organization's success are incorporated. |

Source: Adapted from Andre A. de Waal, "The Role of Behavioral Factors in the Successful Implementation and Use of Performance Management Systems," in Andy Neely and Angela Walters (eds.), *Performance Measurement and Management: Research and Action*, Centre for Business Performance, Cranfield University (2002): pp. 157-64. (CSFs are critical success factors, KPIs are key performance indicators, and BSC is a balanced scorecard.)

**business excellence model**
A performance measurement framework that emphasizes total quality management and consists of nine dimensions: leadership, people management, policy and strategy, resources, processes, people satisfaction, customer satisfaction, impact on society, and business results.

**performance prism**
A strategic performance measurement framework that focuses on stakeholders and includes five elements: strategies, processes, capabilities, stakeholder satisfaction, and stakeholder contribution.

processes, customer satisfaction, financial performance, and learning and growth.[15] It provides a more comprehensive approach to performance measurement than traditional financial performance reporting, and it can be used as a basis for performance evaluation and reward systems, as well as for inter- and intra-organizational benchmarking.

The **business excellence model** consists of nine criteria: leadership, people management, policy and strategy, resources, processes, people satisfaction, customer satisfaction, impact on society, and business results. It emphasizes total quality management and can be used by an organization to understand its current position, benchmark against competitors, and pursue continuous improvement. The model has been quite popular in European companies. The European Quality Award is based on the criteria underlying this model.[16]

The **performance prism** is the most recent and comprehensive strategic performance measurement framework. It is a five-faceted model that focuses on stakeholders rather than strategies. The five elements are: strategies, processes, capabilities, stakeholder satisfaction, and stakeholder contribution.[17] It includes

15. Robert S. Kaplan and David P. Norton, "The Balanced Scorecard—Measures that Drive Performance," *Harvard Business Review* (January–February 1992): pp. 71-79.

16. S. Wongrassamee, P.D. Gardiner, and J.E.L. Simmons, "Similar but Not Equal: A Study of the Balanced Scorecard and Business Excellence Model," in Andy Neely and Angela Walters (eds.), *Performance Measurement and Management: Research and Action*, Centre for Business Performance, Cranfield University (2002): pp. 611-18.

17. Andy Neely and Chris Adams, "Perspectives on Performance: The Performance Prism," at www.som.cranfield.ac.uk/som/cbp/prism.htm (as of September 3, 2002). See also Andy Neely (ed.), *Business Performance Measurement: Theory and Practice*, Cambridge University Press (2002).

all four perspectives of the balanced scorecard, but broadens the definition of stakeholders from customers to all stakeholders and recognizes that stakeholders also make contributions to the company. For example, the typical view of customer satisfaction assumes that satisfied customers become loyal and profitable customers. However, increasing customer satisfaction beyond a certain point may result in higher costs than benefits. Customer profitability analysis would reveal profitable and unprofitable customers.

All three approaches to performance measurement allow for benchmarking. **Benchmarking** is a process that uses the best practices of other departments or organizations as standards for evaluating performance. Within an organization, different units performing similar activities can be compared. The performance of the best-performing unit for a given activity serves as the standard for other units. The leading unit can also share information with other units on how it achieved its superior results. Ideally, benchmarking should also involve comparisons with competitors and with other industries, but it is often difficult to obtain the necessary data for external benchmarking. In some situations, however, it may be useful to study the best practices of noncompetitors, since certain activities and processes are common to all organizations. If superior external best practices can be identified, they can be used as standards to motivate internal improvements.[18]

## The Balanced Scorecard

Balanced, comprehensive measurement and reporting tools are central to strategic-based control systems. The balanced scorecard framework developed by Kaplan and Norton is perhaps the most popular and widely adopted strategic performance measurement and reporting framework.[19] Therefore, we use it in this section as a detailed example of a strategic-based control framework. The balanced scorecard *translates* an organization's mission and strategy into operational objectives and performance measures for four different perspectives: the financial perspective, the customer perspective, the internal business perspective, and the learning and growth perspective. The **financial perspective** describes the economic consequences of actions taken in the other three perspectives. The **customer perspective** defines the customer and market segments in which the business unit competes. The **internal business perspective** describes the internal processes required to provide value for customers and owners. Finally, the **learning and growth perspective** defines the capabilities an organization needs in order to create long-term growth and viability. This perspective is concerned with three *enabling factors*: employee capabilities, information system capabilities, and employee attitudes.[20]

**benchmarking**

An approach that uses the best practices as the standard for evaluating activity performance.

**financial perspective**

A balanced scorecard viewpoint that describes the financial consequences of actions taken in the other three perspectives.

**customer perspective**

A balanced scorecard viewpoint that defines the customer and market segments in which the business will compete.

**internal business perspective**

A balanced scorecard viewpoint that describes the internal processes needed to provide value for customers and owners.

**learning and growth perspective**

A balanced scorecard viewpoint that defines the capabilities an organization needs in order to create long-term growth and improvements.

---

18. For more information on benchmarking, see the following publications from the Society of Management Accountants of Canada: *Implementing Benchmarking*, Management Accounting Guideline 16 (1993); *Benchmarking: A Survey of Canadian Practice*, Management Accounting Issues Paper 7 (1994); and *Tools and Techniques for Effective Benchmarking Studies*, Management Accounting Guideline 35 (1995).

19. Kaplan and Norton, "The Balanced Scorecard."

20. In addition, environmental and social perspectives are promoted in Stan Brignall, "The Unbalanced Scorecard: A Social and Environmental Critique," in Andy Neely and Angela Walters (eds.), *Performance Measurement and Management: Research and Action*, Centre for Business Performance, Cranfield University (2002): pp. 85-92. Other perspectives are also considered possible; see Robert S. Kaplan and David P. Norton, *The Strategy-Focused Organization: How Balanced Scorecard Companies Thrive in the New Business Environment*, Harvard Business School Press (2001).

**strategy**

The process of choosing a business's market and customer segments, identifying its critical internal business processes, and selecting the individual and organizational capabilities needed to meet internal, customer, and financial objectives.

### Strategy Translation

**Strategy** in the balanced scorecard framework is defined as follows: "Choosing the market and customer segments the business intends to serve, identifying the critical internal and business processes that the unit must excel at to deliver the value propositions to customers in the targeted market segments, and selecting the individual and organizational capabilities required for the internal, customer, and financial objectives."[21]

Strategy specifies management's desired relationships among the four perspectives. In contrast, *strategy translation* entails specifying objectives, measures, targets, and initiatives for each perspective. Exhibit 17–9 illustrates the strategy translation process. For example, for the financial perspective, a company may specify an *objective*—to increase revenues by introducing new products. The *performance measure* may be the percentage of revenues from the sale of new products. The *target* or *standard* for the measure for the coming year may be 20 percent—in other words, 20 percent of the total revenue for the coming year must be from the sale of new products. The *initiative* describes how this will be accomplished. The "how," of course, involves the other three perspectives. The company must identify the customer segments, internal processes, and individual and organizational capabilities that will permit it to realize its growth objectives. This illustrates the fact that financial objectives are fundamental for the objectives, measures, and initiatives of the three other perspectives.

**EXHIBIT 17-9**

Strategy Translation Process

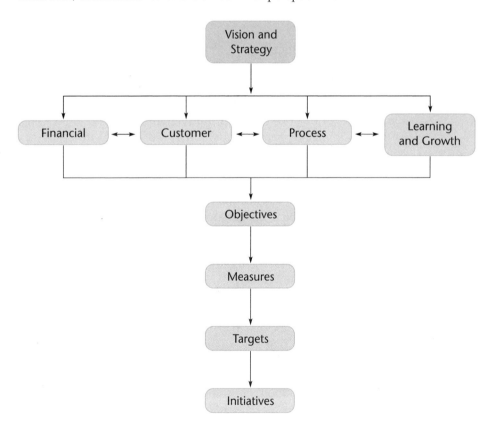

The balanced scorecard is not simply a collection of critical performance measures. The performance measures are derived from the company's vision, strategy, and objectives. These measures must be balanced between outcome measures and lead measures (performance drivers), between objective and sub-

---

21. Kaplan and Norton, *The Balanced Scorecard*: p.37.

jective measures, between external and internal measures, and between financial and nonfinancial measures. Performance measures must also be linked to the company's strategy. Doing so creates significant advantages for an organization. The rapid and widespread adoption of this strategic performance management tool is a strong testimonial for its usefulness.

Balancing outcome measures with performance drivers is essential for linking performance measures with an organization's strategy. Performance drivers are the causes of performance. Consequently, they determine how outcomes are realized. They tend to be unique to a particular strategy. Outcome measures are also important, because they reveal whether the strategy is being implemented successfully (leading to the desired outcomes), and because direct performance drivers are not always available. For example, if the number of defective products is decreased, does this change increase the market share? And does that, in turn, produce more revenues and profits? These questions suggest that the most important principle of linkage is the use of cause-and-effect relationships. In fact, a **testable strategy** can be defined as a set of linked objectives aimed at an overall goal. A strategy's testability is established by restating the strategy as a set of cause-and-effect hypotheses that can be expressed by a sequence of causal statements.[22] For example, consider the following sequence of if–then statements that link quality training with increased profitability:

1. If design engineers receive quality training, then they can redesign products to reduce the number of defective units.
2. If the number of defective units is reduced, then customer satisfaction will increase.
3. If customer satisfaction increases, then market share will increase.
4. If market share increases, then sales will increase.
5. If sales increase, then profits will increase.

The quality improvement strategy, as a sequence of if–then statements, is summarized in Exhibit 17–10. Several interesting points can be noted. First, all four perspectives are present. The learning and growth perspective is represented by the training dimension; the process perspective is represented by the redesign and manufacturing processes; the customer perspective is represented by customer satisfaction and market share; and, finally, revenues and profits represent the financial perspective. All four perspectives are linked through the cause-and-effect relationships hypothesized. Second, the strategy's viability is testable. Strategic feedback allows managers to test the strategy's reasonableness. Hours of training, the number of products redesigned, the number of defective units, customer satisfaction, market share, revenues, and profits are observable measures that can provide such feedback.

If feedback indicates that the expected results have not been achieved, this could be due to an invalid strategy or to implementation problems. First, it is possible that key *performance drivers* such as training and product redesign did not achieve their targeted levels (i.e., fewer hours of training occurred, and/or fewer products were redesigned than had been planned). In this situation, an implementation shortfall would account for the failure to produce the targeted outcomes for defects, customer satisfaction, market share, revenues, and profits. On the other hand, if the targeted levels of performance drivers were achieved and the expected outcomes did not materialize, the problem could well lie with the strategy itself. This is an example of *double-loop feedback*. **Double-loop feedback** occurs whenever managers receive information about both the *effectiveness* of

**testable strategy**

A set of linked objectives aimed at an overall goal that can be restated into a sequence of cause-and-effect hypotheses.

**double-loop feedback**

Information about both the effectiveness of strategy implementation and the validity of assumptions underlying the strategy.

---

22. Kaplan and Norton, *The Balanced Scorecard*: p. 149. Kaplan and Norton describe the sequence of if–then statements only as a strategy.

**EXHIBIT 17-10**

Testable Strategy Illustrated

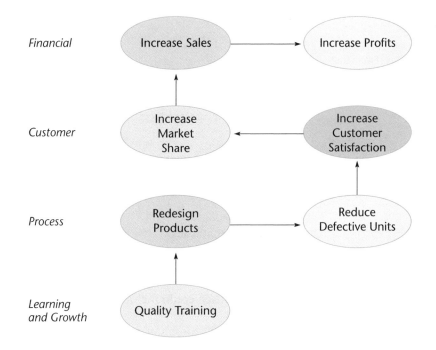

*Financial* — Increase Sales → Increase Profits

*Customer* — Increase Market Share ← Increase Customer Satisfaction

*Process* — Redesign Products → Reduce Defective Units

*Learning and Growth* — Quality Training

**single-loop feedback**
Information about the effectiveness of strategy implementation.

strategy implementation and the *validity* of the assumptions underlying the strategy. In a functional-based control system, typically only *single-loop feedback* is provided. **Single-loop feedback** emphasizes only the effectiveness of implementation. In single-loop feedback, actual results that deviate from planned results are a signal to take corrective action so that the strategy can be executed as intended. Typically, the validity of the assumptions underlying the strategy is not explicitly considered.

An organization's strategy can be developed along the lines of the four perspectives. Furthermore, as the example of the if–then statements illustrates, the four perspectives provide the structure or framework for developing an integrated, cohesive set of performance measures. Once developed, these measures become the means for articulating and communicating the organization's strategy to the managers and employees. The measures also contribute to aligning individual objectives and actions with organizational objectives and initiatives.

### *Financial Perspective*
The financial perspective establishes long- and short-term financial objectives. It is concerned with the global financial consequences of the three other perspectives. The objectives and measures of the other perspectives must be linked to the financial objectives. The financial perspective has three strategic themes: revenue growth, cost reduction, and asset utilization. These themes are the building blocks for developing specific operational objectives and measures. The objectives and typical measures for the financial perspective are summarized in Exhibit 17–11.

For example, *revenue growth* can be accomplished through the following objectives: increase the number of new products, create new applications for existing products, develop new customers and markets, and adopt a new pricing strategy. Once operational objectives are known, performance measures can be designed. For example, possible measures for these objectives are percentage of revenue from new products, percentage of revenue from new applications, percentage of revenue from new customers and market segments, and profitability by product or by customer respectively.

EXHIBIT 17-11

Summary of Objectives
and Measures: Financial
Perspective

| Objectives | Measures |
|---|---|
| **Revenue growth:** | |
| Increase the number of new products | Percentage of revenue from new products |
| Create new applications | Percentage of revenue from new applications |
| Develop new customers and markets | Percentage of revenue from new sources |
| Adopt a new pricing strategy | Product and customer profitability |
| | |
| **Cost reduction:** | |
| Reduce unit product cost | Unit product cost |
| Reduce unit customer cost | Unit customer cost |
| Reduce distribution channel cost | Cost per distribution channel |
| | |
| **Asset utilization:** | |
| Improve asset utilization | Return on investment |
| | Economic value added |

*Cost reduction* could include reducing the cost per unit, customer, or distribution channel. The appropriate measure is obvious: the cost per unit of any cost object. Trends in these measures can reveal whether the costs are being reduced or not. The accuracy of cost assignment is especially important. Activity-based costing can play an essential measurement role in cost reduction, especially for selling and administration costs—costs not usually assigned to cost objects such as customers and distribution channels.

*Asset utilization* is a key objective. Financial measures such as ROI and EVA can be used (see Chapter 16).

### Customer Perspective

The customer perspective is the source of revenue for financial objectives. This perspective outlines the customer and market segments in which the company chooses to compete. Exhibit 17–12 summarizes the objectives and sample measures for the customer perspective.

*Core objectives and measures* are developed after customers and segments have been defined. Core objectives and measures are those which are common to all

EXHIBIT 17-12

Summary of Objectives
and Measures: Customer
Perspective

| Objectives | Measures |
|---|---|
| **Core:** | |
| Increase market share | Market share (percentage of market) |
| Increase customer retention | Percentage growth of business from existing customers |
| | Percentage of repeating customers |
| Increase customer acquisition | Number of new customers |
| Increase customer satisfaction | Ratings from customer surveys |
| Increase customer profitability | Customer profitability |
| | |
| **Customer value:** | |
| Decrease price | Price |
| Decrease postpurchase costs | Postpurchase costs |
| Improve product functionality | Ratings from customer surveys |
| Improve product quality | Percentage of returns |
| Improve delivery reliability | On-time delivery percentage |
| | Ageing schedule |
| Improve product image and reputation | Ratings from customer surveys |

units. Five key core objectives are demonstrated: to increase market share, customer retention, customer acquisition, customer satisfaction, and customer profitability. Possible core measures for those objectives, respectively, are percentage of market, percentage growth of business from existing customers, percentage of repeat customers, number of new customers, customer satisfaction ratings, and individual and segment profitability. Activity-based costing can be a key tool in assessing customer profitability. Note that customer profitability is the only financial measure among the core measures. This measure is critical because it emphasizes the importance of the *right* kind of customers. What good is it to have customers if they are not profitable? The obvious answer spells out the difference between being customer-focused and customer-obsessed.

*Customer value* is the difference between realization and sacrifice. Realization is what the customer receives. Sacrifice is what the customer gives up. Realization includes such things as product features, product quality, reliability of delivery, delivery response time, image, and reputation. Sacrifice includes the product price, time to learn to use the product, and operating, maintenance, and disposal costs. Besides the core objectives and measures, measures (performance drivers) that drive the creation of customer value and core outcomes are needed. For example, providing additional value to customers can increase customer satisfaction, build customer loyalty, and improve customer retention.

The realization and sacrifice value propositions provide the basis for the objectives and measures that will lead to improving the core outcomes. The objectives for the sacrifice value proposition are the simplest: decrease price and decrease *postpurchase costs*. Selling price and postpurchase costs are important measures of value creation. Decreasing these customer costs decreases customer sacrifice, thereby increasing customer value. Increasing customer value should have a favourable impact on most of the core objectives. A similar favourable effect can be obtained by increasing realization. Realization objectives include improving product functionality, product quality, delivery reliability, delivery response time, and product image and reputation. Possible measures for these objectives include customer satisfaction ratings, percentage of returns, on-time delivery percentage, and product recognition rating.

### Internal Business Perspective

Processes are the means for creating customer and shareholder value. Thus, the internal business perspective entails identifying the processes needed to achieve the customer and financial objectives. A process value chain provides the framework needed for this perspective. The process value chain is made up of three processes: the innovation process, the operations process, and the postsales service process. The innovation process anticipates customers' emerging and potential needs and creates new products and services to satisfy those needs. It represents what is called the long-wave of value creation. The operations process produces existing products and services and delivers them to customers. It begins with a customer order and ends with the delivery of the product or service. It is the short-wave of value creation. The **postsales service process** provides critical and responsive services to customers after the product or service has been delivered. The objectives and typical measures for the internal business perspective are presented in Exhibit 17–13.

*The innovation process* objectives include increasing the number of new products and the percentage of revenue from proprietary products, and decreasing the time required to develop new products. Associated measures are the number of actual versus planned new products, the percentage of total revenues from new products, the percentage of revenue from proprietary products, and development cycle time.

*The operations process* objectives often emphasized are: increasing process quality and process efficiency, and decreasing process time. Examples of process

**postsales service process**

A process that provides critical and responsive service to customers after the product or service has been delivered.

**EXHIBIT 17-13**

Summary of Objectives and Measures: Internal Business Perspective

| Objectives | Measures |
|---|---|
| **Innovation:** | |
| Increase the number of new products | Number of new products versus planned |
| Increase proprietary products | Percentage revenue from proprietary products |
| Decrease new product development time | Time to market (from start to finish) |
| | |
| **Operations:** | |
| Increase process quality | Quality costs |
| | Output yields |
| | Percentage of defective units |
| Increase process efficiency | Unit cost trends |
| | Output/input(s) |
| Decrease process time | Cycle time and velocity |
| | MCE |
| | |
| **Postsales Service:** | |
| Increase service quality | First-pass yields |
| Increase service efficiency | Cost trends |
| | Output/input |
| Decrease service time | Cycle time |

**cycle time**

The length of time required to produce one unit of a product.

**velocity**

The number of units that can be produced in a given period of time (e.g., output per hour).

**manufacturing cycle effectiveness (MCE)**

A measure of productive efficiency calculated as follows: processing time/(processing time + move time + inspection time + waiting time).

quality measures are quality costs, output yields (good output/good input), and percentage of defective units (good output/total output). Process efficiency measures are concerned with process costs and process productivity. The measuring and tracking of process costs is facilitated by activity-based costing and process value analysis. Quality costs, quality control, and productivity measurement were discussed in detail in Chapter 15. Common process time measures are cycle time, velocity, and manufacturing cycle effectiveness. **Cycle time** is the length of time it takes to produce a unit of activity output. **Velocity** is the number of units of output that can be produced in a given period of time. **Manufacturing cycle effectiveness (MCE)** is calculated as follows: processing time/(processing time + move time + inspection time + waiting time).

*The postsales service process* objectives include increasing quality and efficiency, and decreasing process time. Service quality, for example, can be measured by first-pass yields, where first-pass yields are defined as the percentage of customer requests resolved with a single service call. Efficiency can be measured by cost trends and productivity measures. Process time can be measured by cycle time, where a cycle's starting point is defined as the receipt of a customer's request, and its finishing point is defined as the time when the customer's problem is solved.

### Learning and Growth Perspective

The learning and growth perspective is the source of the capabilities that allow for the accomplishment of the other three perspectives' objectives. This perspective has three main objectives: increase employee capabilities; increase motivation, empowerment, and alignment; and increase information systems capabilities. Exhibit 17–14 shows the objectives and typical measures for the learning and growth perspective.

*Employee capabilities* can be measured by employee satisfaction ratings, employee turnover percentages, and employee productivity. Examples of lead measures or performance drivers for employee capabilities are hours of training and strategic job coverage ratios. As new processes are created, new skills are often required. Training and hiring are sources of new skills. Furthermore, the percent-

**EXHIBIT 17-14**

Summary of Objectives
and Measures: Learning
and Growth Perspective

| Objectives | Measures |
| --- | --- |
| **Employee Capabilities:** Increase employee capabilities | Employee satisfaction ratings <br> Employee turnover percentages <br> Employee productivity (revenue/employee) <br> Hours of training <br> Strategic job coverage ratio (percentage of critical job requirements filled) <br> Percentage of employees in training programs <br> Percentage of positions filled internally <br> Percentage of employees who received training <br> Percentage of position vacancies filled internally |
| **Employee Motivation, Empowerment, and Goal Alignment:** Increase employee motivation, empowerment, and goal alignment | Suggestions per employee <br> Suggestions implemented per employee <br> Average length of employment by employees <br> Percentage of employees intending to stay with the company |
| **Information system capabilities:** Increase information system capabilities | Percentage of processes with real-time feedback capabilities <br> Percentage of customer-facing employees with on-line access to customer and product information |

age of employees needed in certain key areas with the required skills signals the organization's capacity to meet the objectives of the other three perspectives.

*Employee motivation, empowerment, and alignment* are key indicators of learning and growth potential. Employees must not only have the necessary skills, they must also have the freedom, motivation, commitment, and initiative to use their skills effectively. The number of suggestions per employee and the number of suggestions implemented per employee are possible measures of motivation and empowerment. Suggestions per employee provide a measure of the *degree* of employee involvement, whereas suggestions implemented per employee signals the *quality* of employee participation. This measure also signals to employees whether or not their suggestions are taken seriously. The average length of employment and the intention to leave the company are examples of measures of goal alignment.

*Information systems capabilities* can be demonstrated, for example, by providing accurate and timely information to employees for decision making, planning, and control purposes. Possible measures include percentage of processes with real-time feedback capabilities and percentage of customer-facing employees with on-line access to customer and product information.

# Measuring and Rewarding Managerial Performance

**Objective 5**

Discuss methods of evaluating and rewarding managerial performance.

Some companies consider the performance of the division to be equivalent to the performance of the manager; however, there is a compelling reason to separate the two. The performance of a manager's responsibility centre may be subject to factors beyond the manager's control. It follows that it is important to link a manager's performance evaluation and compensation to factors within that manager's control.

**uncontrollable factors**

Factors that cannot be influenced by a manager during a given time period.

**controllable factors**

Factors that can be influenced by a manager's decisions and actions.

**Uncontrollable factors** cannot be influenced by a manager over a given time period. **Controllable factors** *can* be influenced by a manager's decisions and actions. For example, the performance of a division located in Brazil may be adversely affected by a high inflation rate in that country. The manager in charge of this division should not be held responsible for the effect of inflation on profits when his performance is being compared to that of his Canadian counterparts. However, that effect should be considered when the feasibility of the Brazilian division is being evaluated.

Because they are so close to day-to-day operations, the managers of responsibility centres are often the best people to explain the operating results of their units, although they may not be able to influence some results. In practice, they may be held responsible for those results. For this reason, the term "controllable" is often used loosely to refer to items and events that are affected—although not directly controlled—by a manager's decisions or actions.

## Goal Congruence and Managerial Motivation

Effective performance management systems enhance goal congruence and managerial motivation. Goal congruence exists when individuals and groups in an organization work toward the achievement of the organization's goals. It requires individuals and groups to make decisions that are in the best interests of the organization and also in their own best interests. **Managerial motivation** can be defined as a drive and exertion of effort toward achieving organizational objectives. Because individual goals may differ, and different individuals may be motivated by different factors, incentives are needed to encourage common objectives. For example, some managers value leisure more than work, while others prefer work over leisure, and some are motivated by monetary compensation, while others are driven by nonmonetary factors such as recognition and esteem. Clearly, then, behavioural factors should be a key consideration in the design of performance management systems.

**managerial motivation**

Drive and exertion of effort toward achieving an organization's objectives.

### Goal Setting

**Organizational goals** set specific short- and medium-term performance targets. They can be viewed as specific results that need to be achieved in the near future in order to reach long-term strategic objectives.

**organizational goals**

Short- and medium-term performance targets or interim objectives toward the achievement of long-term strategic objectives.

How difficult to achieve should performance targets be? This question has been studied extensively. Some evidence indicates that employees perform better under specific targets (i.e., as opposed to vague targets) and that targets are at their optimum when they are challenging but also achievable by well-trained and motivated employees.[23] It has been suggested that a 50 percent chance of target achievement promotes optimum motivation. A similar motivational effect can also be obtained using a strategic performance measurement system that sets relatively "loose" standards on some performance dimensions but supplements these with complementary measures on other dimensions. For example, relatively loose budget standards may work well in conjunction with relevant nonfinancial performance standards.[24]

---

23. A good reference on goal setting is E.A. Locke and G.P. Latham, *A Theory of Goal Setting and Task Performance* (Scarborough: Prentice-Hall, 1990).

24. For standard setting in a budgeting context, see, for example, Kenneth A. Merchant, "How Challenging Should Profit Budget Targets Be?" *Management Accounting* (November 1990): pp.46-48; and Kenneth A. Merchant and Jean-Francois Manzoni, "The Achievability of Budget Targets in Profit Centers: A Field Study, *The Accounting Review* (1989) 64: pp. 539-58.

### *Employee Participation in Goal Setting*

**participation**

Employee involvement in decision making.

Since frontline employees are much closer to a company's operations than managers, employee participation in improving organizational performance can be valuable. Competent managers recognize that employees have good ideas for improving their jobs and the operations of the company, and they are not threatened by these ideas. **Participation** can vary from voluntary suggestions to structured goal setting exercises by individuals, work teams, or committees. Participation in goal setting is considered important for at least these three reasons:

1. It can increase employee ownership of the goals, which in turn can increase employee commitment to the organization's goals and promote goal congruence.
2. It utilizes employee skills and knowledge and can motivate employees to develop their skills further and to make even more significant contributions to the organization in the future.
3. It can promote the customer perspective, as employees are in closer contact with customers and their needs than managers.

For effective participation, several conditions must be met. First, employees must possess the necessary information, skills, and aptitude. Information must be freely available to employees if they are to make informed decisions about appropriate standards and goals. All employees are not equally skilled, so training must be available to those who need and desire it. In addition, all employees may not be equally comfortable in a participative environment, so employee contributions in different formats should be valued. Second, employee contributions should be taken seriously. If only superficial attention is paid to employees' opinions and suggestions, the motivational effect may become lost or even be negative. Such superficial participation is called "pseudo-participation." Finally, the measures used to evaluate and reward employees may well determine whether the participative system succeeds in promoting motivation and goal congruence. The measures and rewards must fairly and consistently reflect individuals' contributions to the organization.

## Managerial Incentive Compensation

**incentive compensation**

Monetary or nonmonetary rewards awarded to employees based on their meeting certain performance criteria.

The topics of managerial evaluation and **incentive compensation** would matter little if all managers were equally likely to perform to the best of their abilities and if those abilities were known in advance. In the case of a small company, owned and managed by one individual, there is no problem. The owner puts in as much effort as he or she wishes and receives all of the income from the company. But as that business grows, the owner needs to hire managers to manage day-to-day operations, and delegate decision-making authority to them. For example, the shareholders of a company hire chief executive officers through the board of directors. Then the CEO hires divisional managers to operate divisions on behalf of the shareholders, who must ensure that those managers are providing good service.

There are three possible reasons why managers may not provide good service:

1. They may have low ability.
2. They may prefer to not work hard enough.
3. They may prefer to overuse perquisites.

Avoiding the first problem involves (a) appropriate screening techniques before employees are hired, and (b) appropriate training for existing employees. Pre-employment screening can entail multiple interviews, standardized testing, skills demonstrations, portfolio assessment, peer assessment, and so on. Formal or on-the-job training can be provided to existing employees. As noted earlier, decentralized organizational and responsibility structures are one mechanism for "testing" managers and for training future managers. The prevention of the second and third problems involves monitoring managers' activities and actions with the goal of ensuring that undesirable behaviours do not occur. However, direct monitoring is not often possible or feasible. An alternative solution is to provide managers with incentives that more closely align their goals with those of the organization. Well-structured incentive plans help encourage goal congruence between managers and owners. These plans often include both monetary and nonmonetary incentives tied to performance.

### Monetary Compensation

**monetary compensation**
Salaries, wages, cash bonuses, and other monetary rewards paid to employees.

**Monetary compensation** includes salaries and bonuses. A company can reward good managerial performance by granting periodic raises. However, raises are usually permanent. Bonuses provide a company with more flexibility. Many companies use a combination of salary and bonus to reward performance; that is, they keep salaries fairly stable and allow bonuses to fluctuate with reported income. For example, the bonus can be tied to divisional net income or to targeted increases in net income. Thus, a divisional manager might receive an annual salary of $75,000 and an annual bonus of 5 percent of the increase in reported net income. If net income does not increase, the manager's bonus is zero. This incentive pay scheme makes the increase in net income—which is the company's objective—also important to the manager; in this way it promotes goal congruence.

Of course, income-based compensation can encourage dysfunctional behaviour. Those who structure a reward system need to understand the positive incentives built into the system but also understand the potential for negative behaviours.

### Nonmonetary Compensation

**nonmonetary compensation**
Benefits provided to employees in addition to monetary compensation, for example, prime office space, fancy titles, increased responsibilities and autonomy, the use of a company jet or car, expense accounts, awards, and club memberships.

**perquisites**
A type of fringe benefit over and above salary that is received by managers.

**gain sharing**
Providing cash incentives for a company's entire workforce that relate to quality and productivity gains.

**Nonmonetary compensation** in the form of perquisites can also motivate managers. **Perquisites** are fringe benefits provided in addition to monetary compensation and minimum regulatory benefits. Examples of perquisites are prime office space, prestigious titles, increased responsibilities and autonomy, the use of a company jet or car, expense accounts, awards, and club memberships. Such perquisites signal upper management's approval of lower-level managers' performance and behaviours. Managers may be willing to trade monetary compensation for improved nonmonetary compensation.

Perquisites are an important feature of management compensation. When used wisely, they make managers more efficient. For example, a busy manager may find that the use of a corporate jet allows him or her to more efficiently schedule travel to overseas divisions. However, perquisites can also be abused. For instance, one wonders how the shareholders of RJR Nabisco benefited from the former CEO's use of corporate jets to fly friends around the country.[25]

### Gain Sharing

Providing cash incentives tied to quality and productivity gains to a company's entire workforce is called **gain sharing**. For example, suppose a company has a target of reducing the number of defective units by 10 percent over the next quarter for a particular plant. The company estimates that by achieving that goal, it will save $1,000,000 by avoiding rework and warranty repairs. Gain sharing offers employees a bonus equal to a percentage of these cost savings. For example,

25. Bryan Burrough and John Helyar, *Barbarians at the Gate: The Fall of RJR Nabisco* (New York: Harper and Row, 1990): p. 95.

Palliser, a furniture manufacturer based in Winnipeg, provides a gain-sharing scheme for its workers.

Other companies have instituted gain-sharing programs for their executives. For example, Ford Motor Company may soon be overhauling its compensation program for its top 5,000 executives, by replacing profit-driven bonus structures with performance-based measures such as overall product quality; Sun Microsystems ties bonuses to customer loyalty and customer quality indexes.[26]

## Performance Measures and Behavioural Effects

The behavioural consequences of performance measurement have already been noted, in this chapter and others. Because performance measurement systems work only when employees act and behave appropriately, this topic warrants a separate discussion here. Appropriately used, performance measures promote positive behaviours and goal congruence. In contrast, when they are used to blame or punish employees, they can be perceived as a threat to employees. Employees tend to resist and undermine performance measures when they are used in this way; they are also more likely to engage in dysfunctional behaviours such as data manipulation, suboptimal decision making, and unethical behaviours.[27] These behaviours can become especially prominent if performance measures are used as a base for incentive compensation plans. This section provides some examples of dysfunctional behaviours and possible methods of eliminating them or mitigating their effects.

### Activity Drivers and Behaviour

The objective of reducing nonvalue-added activities should produce a reduction in the demand for these activities and a consequent reduction in their output measures. If a team's performance is affected by its ability to reduce nonvalue-added costs, the selection and use of activity drivers as output measures can affect behaviour. For example, by choosing setup time as the output measure for setup costs, management creates an incentive to reduce setup time. Since the value-added standard for setup costs calls for their complete elimination, the incentive to drive setup time to zero is compatible with the company's objectives, and the induced behaviour is beneficial.

But perhaps the objective is to reduce the number of unique parts a company processes, and thus to reduce the costs of purchasing and inspecting parts. If costs are assigned to products based on the number of parts, the incentive is to reduce the number of parts in a product. This behaviour may be desirable to a point, but it can also have negative consequences. Design teams may actually reduce the product's marketability by eliminating or substituting parts that are necessary for the product's proper functioning. This type of behaviour can be discouraged by the proper use of standards. Functional analysis can be used to identify the **value-added standard** number of parts for each product.[28] The standard can provide a concrete objective and define desirable behaviours.

**value-added standard**

The optimal output level for an activity.

---

26. Both examples come from Melissa Larson, "Betting Your Bonus on Quality" (May 1998), at www.qualitymag.com/articles/may98/0598f3.html.

27. Evidence of dysfunctional behaviours in a budgeting setting has been long established; see, for example, G.H. Hofstede, *The Game of Budget Control* (Tavistock, London, 1968); and Anthony G. Hopwood, "An Empirical Study of the Role of Accounting Data in Performance Evaluation, *Journal of Accounting Research* (Supplement): pp. 156-82. Recent evidence in the performance measurement context is available, for example, in Peter Smith, "Outcome-Related Performance Indicators and Organizational Control in the Public Sector," *British Journal of Management* (1993) 4: pp. 135-51.

28. Functional analysis compares the price customers are willing to pay for a particular product function with the cost of providing that function.

The measurement of delivery reliability can also lead to negative managerial behaviours. On-time delivery is a common measure of delivery reliability. A company can set delivery dates and determine delivery performance by dividing the orders delivered on time by the total number of orders delivered. The goal, of course, is to achieve a ratio of 1. However, this measure may produce unfavourable behavioural consequences.[29] For example, plant managers may give priority to orders that are not late over orders that are already late. This performance measure encourages managers to have one very late shipment rather than several moderately late shipments. A chart showing the age of late deliveries could help mitigate this problem.

### Incentive Compensation and Behaviour

The behavioural effects of performance measurement are stronger when performance measures are used as a basis for incentive compensation plans. Managers may increase short-term measures at the expense of long-term performance by selecting certain accounting policies or by engaging in unethical practices. For example, a manager who receives a bonus based on ROI may decide to increase net income by refusing to invest in newer, more efficient equipment. The result of this decision is a lower amortization expense and higher net income and ROI, but also—possibly— lower productivity and quality. If the bonus is capped at a certain amount—for example, 1 percent of net income but a maximum of $50,000—managers may also be tempted to postpone revenue recognition at the end of a year in which the maximum bonus has already been achieved; they prefer to have that revenue recognized in the following year.

Because changes in accounting methods can affect net income, they can also affect income-based incentive plans. A change in accounting methods (e.g., in amortization methods or inventory valuation methods) changes net income even when sales and costs are steady. New CEOs of troubled companies may change accounting methods in order to take large losses at the beginning of their tenure. This action, referred to as the "big bath," usually results in very low or negative net income for that year. The "books" are  then cleared for a large increase in net income, and a correspondingly large bonus, the following year.

To encourage a long-term orientation, some companies require top executives to purchase and hold company shares as a condition of employment. Eastman Kodak, Xerox, CSX, Gerber Products, Union Carbide, and Hershey Foods have stock ownership guidelines for their top management. A survey of companies in which top executives own relatively large amounts of company shares shows that these companies have higher share prices than companies with low managerial ownership.[30]

### Multiple Measures and Behaviour

The use of single measures for performance evaluation—especially as the basis for incentive compensation plans—encourages negative or dysfunctional behaviours. **Multiple measures**, which balance financial and nonfinancial criteria in the compensation formula, mitigate negative short-term behaviours. The aim should be to balance the measures so that when one criterion is manipulated, other criteria move in the opposite direction; this discourages managers from manipulating measures.

One study examined the use of performance measures in bonus contracts and found that companies pursuing innovation-oriented and quality-focused strategies placed greater emphasis on nonfinancial measures in their bonus contracts.

**multiple measures**
More than one performance measure used to measure the achievement of each performance target.

---

29. Joseph Fisher, "Nonfinancial Performance Measures," *Journal of Cost Management* (Spring 1992): pp. 31-38.

30. Joann S. Lublin, "Buy or Bye," *The Wall Street Journal* (21 April 1993): p. R9.

This supports the idea that companies with different strategic objectives need different types of measures.[31] A Canadian study found that team performance was positively associated with a variety of financial and nonfinancial performance measures; it also found that team performance was enhanced by employee participation in target setting and by a team-oriented approach to compensation.[32]

It is clear from all this that there are definite benefits to establishing a well-balanced and well-designed strategic performance management system. Effective systems can help companies manage and plan better. Regarding this chapter's opening scenario, such a system could help Rob Martin of Telco Systems address his immediate concerns about efficiency and plan for the future using more proactive strategic approaches with increased confidence.

## Appendix: Special Issues in Performance Management and Reporting

**Objective 6**

Describe other performance management techniques.

This appendix deals with the following special issues in performance management and reporting: value-added and nonvalue-added activity cost reporting, kaizen standards, activity capacity management, and life-cycle budgeting.

### Value-Added and Nonvalue-Added Cost Reporting

A company's accounting system should distinguish between value-added costs and nonvalue-added costs, because improving activity performance requires that nonvalue-added activities be eliminated and that value-added activities be optimized. It follows that a company should identify and report the value-added and nonvalue-added costs of each activity. This sort of reporting reveals the magnitude of waste and provides some information about the potential for improvement. This information encourages managers to place more emphasis on controlling nonvalue-added activities. Progress over time can be assessed by preparing trend and cost reduction reports. Trend reports allow managers to assess the effectiveness of activity management programs.

#### Value-Added and Nonvalue-Added Costs

Value-added costs are the only costs an organization should incur. A value-added standard calls for the complete elimination of nonvalue-added activities. For these activities, the optimal output is zero—with zero cost. A value-added standard also calls for the complete elimination of inefficiencies in necessary activities. Thus, value-added activities also have an optimal output level. Identifying the optimal activity output requires that activity output be measured.

By comparing actual activity costs with value-added activity costs, management can assess the level of activity inefficiency and determine the potential for improvement. This requires that output measures be identified for each activity. Once output measures have been identified, value-added standard quantities (*SQ*) for each activity can be defined. Value-added costs can be computed by multiplying the value-added standard quantities by the standard price (*SP*). Nonvalue-added costs can be calculated as the difference between the actual quantity of the activity's output (*AQ*) and the value-added quantity (SQ), multiplied by the unit standard cost (SP). These formulas are presented in Exhibit 17–15.

31. Christopher D. Ittner, David F. Larcker, and Madhav V. Rajan, "The Choice of Performance Measures in Annual Bonus Contracts," *The Accounting Review* (April 1997) 72: pp. 231-55.

32. Thomas W. Scott and P. Tiessen, "Performance Measurement and Managerial Teams," *Accounting, Organizations and Society* (1999) 24: pp. 263-85.

EXHIBIT 17-15

Formulas for Value-Added
and Nonvalue-Added
Costs

Value-added costs = $SQ \times SP$
Nonvalue-added costs = $(AQ - SQ) \times SP$

Where $SQ$ = The value-added output level for an activity
$SP$ = The standard price per unit of activity output measure
$AQ$ = The actual quantity used of flexible resources or practical activity
capacity acquired for committed resources

For flexible resources (i.e., resources acquired as needed), $AQ$ is the actual quantity of activity used. For committed resources (i.e., resources acquired in advance of usage), $AQ$ represents the actual quantity of activity capacity acquired, as measured by the activity's practical capacity. This definition of $AQ$ allows the computation of nonvalue-added costs for both variable and fixed activity costs. For fixed activity costs, $SP$ is budgeted activity costs divided by $AQ$, where $AQ$ is practical activity capacity.

These concepts can be illustrated using four production activities for a JIT company: welding, reworking defective products, setting up equipment, and inspecting purchased components. Of the four activities, two—welding and setups—are viewed as necessary; inspection and rework are unnecessary. The following data pertain to the four activities:

| Activity | Activity Driver | SQ | AQ | SP |
|---|---|---|---|---|
| Welding | Welding hours | 10,000 | 12,000 | $40 |
| Rework | Rework hours | 0 | 10,000 | 9 |
| Setups | Setup hours | 0 | 6,000 | 60 |
| Inspection | Number of inspections | 0 | 4,000 | 15 |

Note that the value-added standards ($SQ$) for rework and inspection call for their elimination. The company should be able to eventually eliminate defective products and the associated rework and inspection costs by improving quality, changing production processes, and so on. Setups are necessary, but in a JIT environment efforts are made to drive setup times to zero.

Exhibit 17–16 classifies the costs for the four activities as value-added or nonvalue-added. For the sake of simplicity, and to show the relationship to actual costs, the actual price per unit of the cost driver is assumed to be equal to the standard price. Here, the value-added cost plus the nonvalue-added cost equals actual cost. Normally, it might be necessary to add a price variance column. This report highlights the nonvalue-added costs and, consequently, emphasizes opportunities for improvement. For example, the company can reduce welding time by redesigning products, rework time by training welders, and inspection time by implementing a supplier evaluation program.

Thus, reporting value-added and nonvalue-added costs can trigger actions to manage activities more effectively. Seeing the amount of waste may induce managers to search for ways to reduce, select, share, and eliminate activities to reduce costs. Reporting these costs may also help managers improve their planning,

EXHIBIT 17-16

Value-Added and
Nonvalue-Added Cost
Report for the Year Ended
December 31, 2005

| Activity | Costs | | |
| | Value-Added | Nonvalue-Added | Actual |
|---|---|---|---|
| Welding | $400,000 | $ 80,000 | $480,000 |
| Rework | 0 | 90,000 | 90,000 |
| Setups | 0 | 360,000 | 360,000 |
| Inspection | 0 | 60,000 | 60,000 |
| Total | $400,000 | $590,000 | $990,000 |

budgeting, and pricing decisions. For example, lowering the selling price to meet a competitor's price may be possible if a reduction in nonvalue-added costs can compensate for the price reduction.

### Trend Report

A trend report can reveal cost reductions resulting from activity improvements over time. Exhibit 17–17 provides a cost report that compares the nonvalue-added costs for 2005 with those for 2004. The 2005 costs are assumed, but would be computed the same way as the costs shown for 2004. *SQ* is assumed to be the same for both years. Comparing nonvalue-added costs for 2005 directly with those for 2004 requires *SQ* to be the same for both years. If *SQ* changes, prior-year nonvalue-added costs are adjusted by simply assuming the same percentage deviation from the standard in the current year as was realized in the prior year.

The trend report shows that cost reductions occurred as expected. More than half of the nonvalue-added costs have been eliminated. There is still ample room for improvement, but activity improvement so far has been successful. Reporting nonvalue-added costs reveals the reduction; it also provides managers with information on the remaining potential for cost reduction. But there is an important qualification. Value-added standards, like other standards, are not cast in stone. New technology, new designs, and other innovations can change the nature of the activities performed. Value-added activities can be converted to nonvalue-added activities, and value-added output levels can change as well. Thus, as new methods of improvement surface, value-added standards can change. Managers should not become complacent; rather, they should constantly seek higher levels of efficiency.

**EXHIBIT** 17-17

Trend Report: Nonvalue-Added Costs

| | Nonvalue-Added Costs | | |
|---|---|---|---|
| **Activity** | **2004** | **2005** | **Change** |
| Welding | $ 80,000 | $ 50,000 | $ 30,000 F |
| Rework | 90,000 | 70,000 | 20,000 F |
| Setups | 360,000 | 200,000 | 160,000 F |
| Inspection | 60,000 | 35,000 | 25,000 F |
| Total | $590,000 | $355,000 | $235,000 F |

## Kaizen Standards

**kaizen costing**

Efforts to reduce the costs of existing products and processes.

**kaizen standard**

An interim standard that reflects the planned improvement for a coming period.

**Kaizen costing** is concerned with reducing the costs of existing products and processes. This translates into reducing nonvalue-added costs. Controlling this cost reduction process is accomplished through the repetitive use of two major subcycles: the kaizen or continuous improvement cycle, and the maintenance cycle. The kaizen subcycle is defined by a Plan–Do–Check–Act sequence, as described below.

When a company emphasizes reducing nonvalue-added costs, the amount of improvement planned for the coming period (month, quarter, year, etc.) can be set (the *Plan* step). A **kaizen standard** reflects the planned improvement for the upcoming period. The planned improvement is assumed to be attainable. Kaizen standards are in this sense a type of currently attainable standard. Actions are taken to implement the planned improvements (the *Do* step). Next, actual results (e.g., costs) are compared with the kaizen standard to provide a measure of the amount of improvement attained (the *Check* step). Setting this new level as the minimum standard for future performance locks in the realized improvements and simultaneously initiates the maintenance cycle and a search for additional improvement opportunities (the *Act* step). The maintenance cycle follows a traditional Standard–Do–Check–Act sequence. A *standard* is set based on prior improvements (locking in these improvements). Next, actions are taken (the *Do* step) and the results are checked to ensure that performance conforms to this new level (the *Check* step). If it does not, corrective actions are taken to restore performance (the *Act* step). The kaizen cost reduction process is summarized in Exhibit 17–18.

**EXHIBIT 17-18**

Kaizen Cost Reduction Process

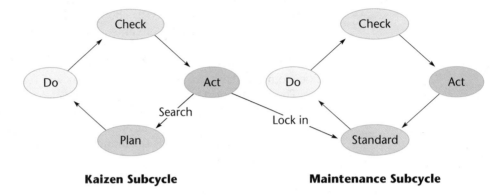

**Kaizen Subcycle**           **Maintenance Subcycle**

## Activity Capacity Management

**activity capacity**

The number of times an activity can be performed.

**Activity capacity** is the number of times an activity can be performed. Activity drivers measure activity capacity. For example, consider inspecting finished products as the activity. A sample of each batch is taken to determine the batch's overall quality. The demand for the inspection activity determines the amount of activity capacity that is required.

For instance, assume that the activity output is measured by the number of batches inspected and that 60 batches are scheduled for production. Thus, the required capacity is 60 batches. Then assume that a single inspector can inspect 20 batches per year. Thus, three inspectors must be hired to provide the necessary capacity. If each inspector is paid $40,000, the budgeted cost of the activity capacity is $120,000. This is the cost of the resources (labour) acquired in advance of usage. The budgeted activity rate is $2,000 per batch ($120,000/60).

What *should* the activity capacity be? The answer to this question provides the ability to measure the amount of improvement that is possible. A second question is: How much of the capacity acquired was actually used? The answer to this question can signal a nonproductive cost and an opportunity for capacity reduction and cost savings.

Exhibit 17–19 shows the calculation of two capacity variances: the *activity volume variance* and the *unused capacity variance*.[33] The **activity volume variance** is the difference between the actual activity level acquired (practical capacity, $AQ$) and the value-added standard quantity of activity that should be used ($SQ$). Assuming that inspection is a nonvalue-added activity, $SQ = 0$ is the value-added standard. The **unused capacity variance**, the difference between activity availability ($AQ$) and activity usage ($AU$), is important because it allows management to take action to reduce the quantity of the activity when capacity exceeds demand significantly.

**activity volume variance**

The difference between the actual activity capacity acquired and the capacity that should be used.

**unused capacity variance**

The difference between acquired capacity (practical capacity) and actual capacity.

33. See Y.T. Mak and Melvin L. Roush, "Flexible Budgeting and Variance Analysis in an ABC Environment," *Accounting Horizons* (June 1994): pp. 93-103; and Robin C. Cooper and Robert Kaplan, "Activity-Based Systems: Measuring the Costs of Resource Usage," *Accounting Horizons* (September 1992): pp. 1-13.

**EXHIBIT 17-19**

Activity Capacity
Variances

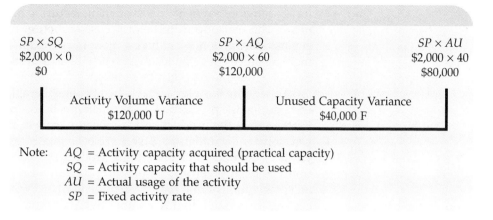

| $SP \times SQ$ | $SP \times AQ$ | $SP \times AU$ |
|---|---|---|
| $\$2,000 \times 0$ | $\$2,000 \times 60$ | $\$2,000 \times 40$ |
| $\$0$ | $\$120,000$ | $\$80,000$ |

| Activity Volume Variance | Unused Capacity Variance |
|---|---|
| $\$120,000$ U | $\$40,000$ F |

Note:  $AQ$ = Activity capacity acquired (practical capacity)
$SQ$ = Activity capacity that should be used
$AU$ = Actual usage of the activity
$SP$ = Fixed activity rate

## Life Cycle Budgeting

The product design stage can have a significant impact on costs. In fact, 90 percent or more of the costs associated with a product are committed during the development stage of the product's life cycle.[34] **Product life cycle** is simply the time a product exists, from conception to abandonment. **Life cycle costs** are all costs associated with the product for its entire life cycle. They include the costs of development (planning, design, and testing), production (conversion activities), and logistics support (advertising, distribution, warranty, and so on).

Because total customer satisfaction has become a vital issue in competitive business settings, whole-life cost has emerged as the central focus of life cycle cost management. **Whole-life product cost** is the life cycle cost of a product plus post-purchase costs that consumers incur, including operation, support, maintenance, and disposal.[35] Since the costs a purchaser incurs after buying a product can be a significant percentage of whole-life costs, and thus an important consideration in the purchase decision, managing activities so that whole-life costs are reduced can provide an important competitive advantage.

Note that cost reduction, not cost control, is the emphasis. Moreover, cost reduction is achieved through judicious analysis and management of activities. Whole-life costing emphasizes managing the entire value chain. Thus, life cycle cost management focuses on managing value chain activities so that a long-term competitive advantage is created. To reach this goal, managers must balance a product's whole-life cost, method of delivery, innovativeness, and various product attributes including performance, features offered, reliability, conformance, durability, aesthetics, and perceived quality.

### Cost Reduction

Because most of a product's costs are committed during the development stage, it makes sense to emphasize management of activities during this phase of a product's existence. Studies have shown that every dollar spent on premanufac-

**product life cycle**

The time a product exists, from conception to abandonment.

**life cycle costs**

All costs that are associated with the product for its entire life cycle.

**whole-life product cost**

The life cycle cost of a product plus costs that consumers incur, including operation, support, maintenance, and disposal.

---

34. The section on life cycle costing is based on the following two sources, with particular emphasis on the first: Callie Berliner and James A. Brimson (eds.), *Cost Management in Today's Advanced Manufacturing* (Boston: Harvard Business School Press, 1988); and John P. Campi, "Corporate Mindset: Strategic Advantage or Fatal Vision," *Journal of Cost Management* (Spring 1991): pp. 53-57.

35. It can be argued that whole-life is an alternative definition of life cycle cost—one that includes the customer's perspective as well as the production perspective. For an excellent treatment of life cycle costing, see Michael D. Schields and S. Mark Young, "Managing Product Life Cycle Costs: An Organizational Model," *Journal of Cost Management* (Fall 1991): pp. 39-52.

turing activities saves $8 to $10 on manufacturing and postmanufacturing activities.[36] The real opportunities for cost reduction occur before manufacturing begins! Managers need to invest more in premanufacturing assets and dedicate more resources to activities in the early phases of the product's life cycle so that overall whole-life costs can be reduced.

Yet despite this observation, the traditional emphasis has been on controlling costs during the production stage, when much less can be done to influence them. Furthermore, the product cost has been narrowly defined as production costs. Development and logistics costs have been treated as period costs and have been virtually ignored when computing product profitability. In addition, little attention has been given to customers' postpurchase costs. This practice may be acceptable for external reporting, but it is not acceptable for managerial product costing. In today's highly competitive environment, world-class competitors need comprehensive product cost information.

### Whole-Life Product Cost

Whole-life product cost consists of four major elements: nonrecurring costs (planning, designing, and testing), manufacturing costs, logistics costs, and the customer's postpurchase costs. Measuring, accumulating, and reporting all whole-life costs for products allow managers to better assess the effectiveness of life cycle planning and build more effective and sophisticated marketing strategies. Life cycle costing also increases their ability to make good pricing decisions and improve the assessment of product profitability.

### Target Costing

Life cycle cost management emphasizes cost reduction, not cost control. Thus, target costing becomes an especially useful tool for establishing cost reduction goals. A **target cost** is the difference between the sales price needed to capture a predetermined market share and the desired profit per unit. The sales price reflects the product specifications or *product functionality*. If the target cost is less than what is currently achievable, management tries to budget cost reductions that move the actual cost toward the target cost. Finding these cost reductions is the principal challenge of target costing.

Three cost reduction methods typically exist: reverse engineering, value analysis, and process improvement. Reverse engineering tears down competitors' products with the objective of discovering design features that create cost reductions. Value analysis attempts to assess the value that customers place on various product functions. If the price customers are willing to pay for a particular function is less than its cost, the function is a candidate for elimination. Both reverse engineering and value analysis focus on product design to reduce costs. The processes used to produce and market a product are also potential sources for cost reductions. Thus, redesigning processes to improve efficiency can also contribute to achieving the needed cost reductions. The target-costing model is summarized in Exhibit 17–20.

Target costs are a type of currently attainable standard; however, they are conceptually different from the value-added standards discussed earlier. What makes them different is the motivating force. The initial definition of cost standards was motivated by the objective of moving toward a value-added standard generated internally by industrial engineers and production managers. In contrast, target costs are externally driven, generated by an analysis of markets and competitors.[37]

**target cost**

The difference between the sales price needed to achieve a projected market share and the desired per-unit profit.

---

36. Mark D. Shields and S. Mark Young, "Managing Product Life Cycle Costs: An Organizational Model"; R.L. Engwall, "Cost Management Systems for Defense Contractors," *Cost Accounting for the 90s, Responding to Technological Change* (Montvale, N.J.: National Association of Accountants, 1988).

37. Also see *Implementing Target Costing*, Management Accounting Guideline 28, The Society of Management Accountants of Canada (1994).

EXHIBIT 17-20

Target-Costing Model

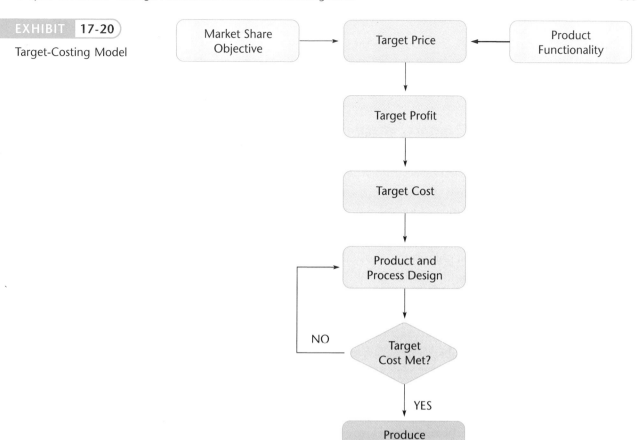

### Short Life Cycles

Although life cycle cost management is important for all manufacturing companies, it is especially important for companies that have products with short life cycles. Products must recover all life cycle costs and provide an acceptable profit. If products have long life cycles, profit performance can be increased by such actions as redesigning products, changing prices, reducing costs, and altering the product mix. In contrast, companies that produce products with short life cycles usually do not have time to react in this way, so their approach must be proactive. For short life cycles, effective life cycle planning is critical, and prices must be set properly in order to recover all life cycle costs and to provide an adequate profit.

# Summary of Learning Objectives

## 1. Discuss environmental factors affecting effective performance management.

For companies operating in dynamic environments, change and adaptation are essential for long-term survival. A company's control system should be compatible with its operating environment. Organizational factors that can affect the appropriateness of control systems include the following: strategy, structure, size, systems, resources, management philosophy, and staff skills. Broader technological, economic, cultural, social, regulatory, and political environments also affect organizations and, therefore, indirectly affect their control systems. Although useful lessons in systems design can be drawn from other companies and industries, no single best control system exists, and organizations must custom tailor their systems to fit their circumstances.

## 2. Compare and contrast functional-based, activity-based, and strategic-based control systems.

Functional-based control systems focus on organizational units such as departments and plants; also, they use financial outcome measures, static standards, and benchmarks to evaluate performance, and emphasize the status quo and organizational stability. In contrast, activity-based systems focus on processes, emphasize and support continuous improvement, and use both financial and nonfinancial performance measures. They consider both financial and process perspectives. Strategic-based systems expand the number of responsibility dimensions from two to four: the customer perspective and the learning and growth perspective are added. Furthermore, performance measures are integrated and linked to the organization's mission and strategy. Functional-based systems work best for organizations that operate in a stable environment, whereas activity-based and strategic-based systems work best for organizations that operate in more dynamic environments.

## 3. Explain the role of process value analysis in strategic performance management.

Activity value analysis provides information about why work is done and how well it is done. It provides a foundation for continuous improvement. Activity analysis identifies and describes activities, assesses their value to the organization, and selects only those which are of value. Emphasis is on identifying and eliminating nonvalue-added activities and costs. Cost reductions can be realized by decreasing, eliminating, selecting, and sharing activities.

In addition, value chain analysis can be used to evaluate different strategic courses of action and to provide additional value to customers. Strategic analysis and management of key relationships with suppliers, customers, and other stakeholders in a supply chain can improve the competitive position of all members of the supply chain through collaboration.

## 4. Explain the basic features of and design criteria for effective strategic performance measurement systems in general and for the balanced scorecard framework in particular.

Strategic performance management requires effective performance measurement. Strategic-based performance measurement is concerned with balancing financial and nonfinancial performance criteria in order to ensure the achievement of short-term and long-term organizational objectives. It can provide early warning signals of impending problems relating to key operational performance dimensions before traditional financial results are available.

Strategic performance measures can be used at any organizational level, but they often cannot be aggregated effectively at higher organizational levels. Unique measures tied to the strategic objectives of each level are needed. The following are the criteria for good performance measures: relevance, reliability, accessibility, and simplicity. Popular performance measurement frameworks include the balanced scorecard, the business excellence model, and the performance prism. The balanced scorecard is the most widely adopted framework.

The balanced scorecard is a strategic management tool that translates an organization's strategy into operational objectives and measures from four perspectives: the financial perspective, the customer perspective, the process perspective, and the learning and growth perspective. The objectives and measures are linked by a series of cause-and-effect hypotheses. This produces a testable strategy that provides strategic feedback to managers. The balanced scorecard is compatible with activity-based responsibility accounting, because it is based on process value analysis and uses activity-based information for many objectives and measures.

## 5. Discuss methods of evaluating and rewarding managerial performance.

Effective performance management systems distinguish between managerial performance and unit performance. Managers should be held responsible only for performance dimensions they can significantly influence. Managerial performance measurement and reward systems should motivate managers to make decisions and take actions that are in the best interest of the organization—that is, they should promote goal congruence.

Participation in goal setting can enhance motivation and goal congruence. However, as individual and organizational goals may conflict, further incentives are needed in order to motivate managers toward optimum goal congruence. Incentives should include a balanced mix of financial and nonfinancial performance criteria, such as profit sharing, gain sharing, and nonfinancial rewards tied to operational performance goals, in order to eliminate or minimize potential dysfunctional behaviours associated with performance-based incentives.

## 6. Describe other performance management techniques. (Appendix A)

This section deals with the following special issues in performance management and reporting: value-added and nonvalue-added activity cost reporting, kaizen standards, activity capacity management, and life-cycle budgeting.

The reporting of value-added and nonvalue-added costs can reveal the magnitude of waste and inefficiency and provide information for eliminating nonvalue-added activities. A trend report reveals whether cost reductions from activity improvements occur over time as expected. Kaizen costing is concerned with reducing the costs of existing products and processes through repetitive continuous improvement and maintenance cycles. Activity capacity management allows for the planning and evaluation of the activity capacity needs and usage. *Activity volume* and *unused capacity* variances can be used as analytical tools in activity capacity management. Life cycle budgeting deals with a product's life cycle costs and revenues over its entire life cycle. Measuring and reporting whole-life costs allows for an assessment of the effectiveness of product life cycle planning, marketing strategies, and pricing decisions.

## Key Terms

| | | |
|---|---|---|
| Activity value analysis 805 | Gain sharing 826 | Participation 825 |
| Activity capacit 832 | Incentive compensation 825 | Performance drivers 803 |
| Activity elimination 807 | Internal business perspective 816 | Performance management 800 |
| Activity inputs 805 | Internal measures 803 | Performance prism 815 |
| Activity outputs 805 | Kaizen costing 831 | Perquisites 826 |
| Activity output measure 805 | Kaizen standard 831 | Postsales service process 821 |
| Activity reduction 807 | Lag measures 803 | Product life cycle 833 |
| Activity selection 807 | Lead measures 803 | Single-loop feedback 819 |
| Activity sharing 807 | Learning and growth perspective 816 | Strategic-based control systems 801 |
| Activity volume variance 832 | Life cycle costs 833 | Strategic performance |
| Activity-based control systems 801 | Management control 800 |   measurement 812 |
| Balanced scorecard 814 | Management control systems 800 | Strategy 817 |
| Benchmarking 816 | Manufacturing cycle effectiveness | Subjective measures 803 |
| Business excellence model 815 |   (MFE) 822 | Supply chain 810 |
| Contingency theory 799 | Managerial motivation 824 | Target cost 834 |
| Controllable factors 824 | Measurement criteria 814 | Testable strategy 818 |
| Customer perspective 816 | Monetary compensation 826 | Uncontrollable factors 824 |
| Cycle time 822 | Multiple measures 828 | Unused capacity variance 832 |
| Double-loop feedback 818 | Nonfinancial measures 803 | Value-added activities 805 |
| Driver analysis 805 | Nonmonetary compensation 826 | Value-added costs 806 |
| External environment 798 | Non-value-added activities 806 | Value-added standard 827 |
| External measures 803 | Non-value-added costs 806 | Value chain analysis 807 |
| Financial measures 803 | Objective measures 803 | Velocity 822 |
| Financial perspective 816 | Organizational goals 824 | Whole-life product cost 833 |
| Functional-based control systems 801 | Organizational environment 798 | |

## Review Problems

### I.  FUNCTIONAL-BASED VERSUS ACTIVITY-BASED CONTROL SYSTEMS

The labour standard for a company is 2 hours per unit produced, which includes setup time. At the beginning of the last quarter, 20,000 units had been produced and 44,000 hours used. The company's production manager was concerned about the prospect of reporting an unfavourable labour efficiency variance at the end of the year. Any unfavourable variance in excess of 9 to 10 percent of the standard usually meant a negative performance rating. Bonuses were adversely affected by negative ratings. Accordingly, for the last quarter, the production manager decided to reduce the number of setups and use longer production runs. He knew that his production workers were usually within 5 percent of the standard. The real problem was with setup times. Reducing the setups would bring the actual hours used within 7 to 8 percent of the standard hours allowed.

**Required:**
1. Explain why the production manager's behaviour is unacceptable for a continuous improvement environment.
2. Explain how activity-based control systems discourage the kind of behaviour described.

**Solution**
1. In a continuous improvement environment, efforts are made to reduce inventories and eliminate nonvalue-added costs. The production manager is focusing on meeting the labour usage standard and is ignoring the impact that longer production runs may have on inventories.
2. Activity-based control systems focus on activities and activity performance. For the setup activity, the value-added standard would be zero setup time and zero setup costs. Thus, avoiding setups would not affect labour time (value-added) and the labour variance.

### II.  ACTIVITY VOLUME VARIANCE; UNUSED ACTIVITY CAPACITY; VALUE-ADDED AND NONVALUE-ADDED COST REPORTS; KAIZEN STANDARDS; BALANCED SCORECARD

Pollard Manufacturing has developed value-added standards for its three activities: using lumber, purchasing, and inspecting. The value-added output levels for each of these activities, their actual levels achieved, and the standard prices are as follows:

| Activity | Activity Driver | SQ | AQ | SP |
|---|---|---|---|---|
| Using lumber | Board feet | 24,000 | 30,000 | $10 |
| Purchasing | Purchase orders | 800 | 1,000 | 50 |
| Inspecting | Inspection hours | 0 | 4,000 | 12 |

Assume that material usage and purchasing costs are flexible resources (acquired as needed) and that inspection uses resources that are acquired in blocks, or steps, of 2,000 hours. The actual prices paid for the inputs equal the standard prices.

**Required:**

1. Assume that continuous improvement efforts reduce the demand for inspection by 30 percent during the year (that is, actual usage drops by 30 percent). Calculate the activity volume and unused capacity variances for the inspection activity. Explain their meaning. Also explain why there is no activity volume or unused capacity variance for the other two activities.
2. Prepare a cost report that details value-added and nonvalue-added costs.
3. Suppose that Pollard wants to reduce nonvalue-added costs by 30 percent in the coming year. Prepare kaizen standards that can be used to evaluate the company's progress toward this goal. How much will this approach save in resource spending?
4. Suppose that Pollard has implemented the balanced scorecard. Explain how nonvalue-added cost reduction, nonvalue-added cost reports, and kaizen standards might fit into the balanced scorecard framework.

## Solution

1.

Actual usage = 4,000 × (1 − 0.3) = 2,800

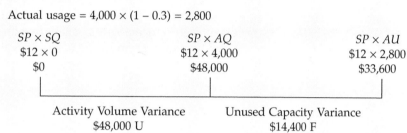

|  | $SP \times SQ$ | $SP \times AQ$ | $SP \times AU$ |
|---|---|---|---|
|  | $12 × 0 | $12 × 4,000 | $12 × 2,800 |
|  | $0 | $48,000 | $33,600 |

Activity Volume Variance $48,000 U          Unused Capacity Variance $14,400 F

The activity volume variance is the nonvalue-added cost. The unused capacity variance measures the cost of the unused activity capacity. The two other activities have no volume variance and no unused capacity variance because they use only flexible resources. There is no activity capacity acquired in advance of usage. Thus, there cannot be an unused capacity variance or an activity volume variance.

2.

| | Costs | | |
|---|---|---|---|
| | **Value-Added** | **Nonvalue-Added** | **Total** |
| Using lumber | $240,000 | $ 60,000 | $300,000 |
| Purchasing | 40,000 | 10,000 | 50,000 |
| Inspection | 0 | 48,000 | 48,000 |
| Total | $280,000 | $118,000 | $398,000 |

3.

| Kaizen Standards | | |
|---|---|---|
| | **Quantity** | **Cost** |
| Using lumber | 28,200 | $282,000 |
| Purchasing | 940 | 47,000 |
| Inspection | 2,800 | 33,600 |

If the standards are met, then the savings are as follows:

| | |
|---|---|
| Using lumber ($10 × 1,800) | $18,000 |
| Purchasing ($50 × 60) | 3,000 |
| Savings | $21,000 |

There is no reduction in resource spending for inspections, because this resource must be purchased in steps of 2,000 hours, and only 1,200 hours were saved—another 800 hours must be reduced before any reduction in resource spending is possible. The unused capacity variance must reach $24,000 (2,000 × $12) before resource spending can be reduced.

4.  The balanced scorecard has four perspectives: financial, customer, internal business, and learning and growth. One of the objectives of the financial perspective is reducing the unit costs of products. Reducing nonvalue-added costs should produce a reduction in the company's product costs. The most direct connection to the balanced scorecard is with the internal business perspective of the balanced scorecard. Value-added and nonvalue-added cost reports relate to internal process efficiency. Similarly, kaizen standards deal with improving internal process efficiency. Activity volume variances and unused capacity measures are also concerned with process efficiency. Finally, the advantage of the balanced scorecard is that it integrates these concepts into the overall strategic framework. The learning and growth perspective provides the enabling factors needed to reduce nonvalue-added costs. As process efficiency increases and costs are reduced, customer value can then be increased by reducing prices. As customer value increases, market share may increase, and this in turn may increase revenues and profits.

## Questions for Writing and Discussion

1.  Describe functional-based control systems.

2.  Describe activity-based control systems. How do they differ from functional-based systems?

3.  Describe strategic-based control systems. How do they differ from activity-based systems?

4.  What is driver analysis? What role does it play in process value analysis?

5.  What is meant by activity inputs? Activity outputs? Activity output measurement?

6.  What is activity analysis? Why is this approach compatible with the goal of continuous improvement?

7.  What are value-added activities? Value-added costs?

8.  What are nonvalue-added activities? Nonvalue-added costs? Give an example of each.

9.  Identify and define four different ways of managing activities so that costs can be reduced.

10. Explain how value-added standards are used to identify value-added and nonvalue-added costs.

11. Explain how trend reports of nonvalue-added costs can be used.

12. What is a kaizen standard? Describe the kaizen and maintenance subcycles.

13. Explain how benchmarking can be used to improve activity performance.

14. Explain how activity output measures (activity drivers) can induce behaviour that is either beneficial or harmful. How can value-added standards be used to reduce the possibility of dysfunctional behaviour?

15. What is the meaning of the activity volume variance? Explain how the unused capacity variance is useful to managers.

16. Describe the benefits of life cycle cost budgeting.

17. What is target costing? Describe how costs are reduced so that the target cost can be met.

18. What is the purpose of a balanced scorecard?

19. Define strategy in the balanced scorecard framework.

20. Explain the differences between lead measures and lag measures.

21. What is a testable strategy?

22. What is meant by double-loop feedback?

23. What are the three strategic themes of the financial perspective?

24. Identify five core objectives of the customer perspective.

25. What is cycle time? Velocity?

26. What is manufacturing cycle efficiency?

27. Identify three objectives of the learning and growth perspective.

28. Identify three objectives of operations in the internal business perspective. Give an example of measures for each objective.

29. How do environmental factors affect management control systems and strategic performance management? Give examples of environmental factors.

30. Explain how management control, responsibility accounting, and performance measurement are related.

31. Explain what is meant by value chain analysis and how it can improve performance management.

32. Explain what is meant by supply chain analysis and how it can improve performance management.

33. Discuss the role of nonfinancial performance measures in effective performance measurement.

34. What criteria must effective performance measures meet?

35. Explain what is meant by goal congruence and why it is important.

36. Why do many companies use both monetary and nonmonetary incentives?

37. Discuss both positive and negative aspects of performance measurement.

38. What is meant by gain sharing?

39. The performance of the divisional manager is equivalent to the performance of a division. Do you agree? Explain.

---

## Exercises

**17–1**

Control Systems;
Strategic Performance
Measurement; Control
Environment

LO1, LO2, LO3, LO4

Choose the *best* answer for each of the following multiple-choice questions:

1. Which of the following elements relate to management control systems?
   a. Assigning responsibility.
   b. Establishing performance benchmarks.
   c. Evaluating performance.
   d. Assigning rewards.
   e. All of the above.

2. A management control system that has both a financial and a process perspective is
   a. a functional-based system.
   b. an activity-based system.
   c. a strategic-based system.
   d. Both b and c.
   e. None of the above.

3. Incremental and constant increases in the efficiency of an existing process are examples of
   a. process innovation.
   b. process improvement.
   c. process creation.
   d. process performance measurement.
   e. all of the above.

4. Strategic-based control systems differ from activity-based systems because they
   a. have three additional perspectives.
   b. have nonfinancial measures.
   c. translate strategy of an organization into operational measures.
   d. assign responsibility to teams.
   e. use process measures.

5. Directed continuous improvement is characteristic of
   a. strategic-based control systems.
   b. functional-based control systems.
   c. activity-based control systems.
   d. both activity-based and strategic-based control systems.
   e. All of the above.

6. Which of the following would *most* likely be a lead measure?
   a. Return on investment.
   b. Number of employee suggestions implemented per employee.
   c. Customer profitability.
   d. Percentage of revenue from new products.
   e. Unit product cost.

7. Which of the following is not an example of process value analysis?
   a. Value chain analysis
   b. Market share analysis
   c. Supply chain analysis
   d. Cost driver analysis
   e. Activity analysis

8. Which of the following is not an example of organizational factors?
   a. Organizational norms.
   b. Strategy.
   c. Leadership skills.
   d. Inflation.
   e. Information systems.

9. Which of the following is a criterion for effective performance measures?
   a. Simplicity.
   b. Reliability.
   c. Accessibility.
   d. Relevance.
   e. All of the above.

10. The achievement of individual and organizational goals simultaneously is called
    a. value-added activity.
    b. strategy alignment.
    c. process improvement.
    d. goal congruence.
    e. None of the above.

**17–2**

Functional-Based
versus Activity-Based
Control Systems

LO2

For each situation below, two scenarios are described, labelled A and B. Identify which scenario describes activity-based control systems and which describes functional-based systems. Comment on the differences between the two systems for each situation, addressing the possible advantages of the activity-based view over the functional-based view.

*Situation 1*

A:  The purchasing manager, receiving manager, and accounts payable manager are given joint responsibility for procurement. The charge given to the group of managers is to reduce costs of acquiring materials, decrease the time required to obtain materials from outside suppliers, and reduce the number of purchasing mistakes (e.g., wrong type of materials or the wrong quantities ordered).

B:  The plant manager commended the manager of the grinding department for increasing his department's machine utilization rates, and doing so without exceeding the department's budget. The plant manager then asked other department managers to make an effort to obtain similar efficiency improvements.

*Situation 2*

A:  Delivery mistakes had been reduced by 70 percent, saving over $40,000 per year. Furthermore, delivery time to customers had been cut by two days. According to company policy, the team responsible for the savings was given a bonus equal to 25 percent of the savings attributable to improving delivery quality. Company policy also provided a salary increase of 1 percent for every day saved in delivery time.

B:  Bill Johnson, manager of the product development department, was pleased with his department's performance on the previous quarter's projects. It had managed to complete all projects under budget, virtually assuring Bill a large bonus, just in time to help with his Christmas purchases.

*Situation 3*

A:  "Harvey, don't worry about the fact that your department is producing at only 70 percent capacity. Increasing your output would simply pile up inventory in front of the next production department. That would be costly for the organization as a whole. Sometimes one department must reduce its performance so that the performance of the entire organization can improve."

B:  "Susan, I am concerned about the fact that your department's performance measures have really dropped over the past quarter. Labour usage variances are unfavourable, and I also see that your machine utilization rates are down. Now, I know that your department is not a bottleneck department, but I get a lot of flak when my managers' efficiency ratings drop."

*Situation 4*

A:  Colby was muttering to himself. He had just received last quarter's budgetary performance report. Once again, he had managed to spend more than budgeted for both materials and labour. The real question now was how to improve his performance for the next quarter.

B:  Great! Cycle time had been reduced, and at the same time, the number of defective products had been cut by 35 percent. Cutting the number of defects reduced production costs by more than planned. Trends were favourable for all three performance measures.

*Situation 5*

A:  Cambry was furious. An across-the-board budget cut! "How can they expect me to provide the computer services required on less money? Management is convinced that costs are out of control, but I would like to know where—at least in my department!"

B:  After a careful study of the accounts payable department, it was discovered that 80 percent of an accounts payable clerk's time was spent resolving discrepancies between the purchase order, the receiving document, and the supplier's invoice. Other activities, such as recording and preparing cheques, consumed only 20 percent of a clerk's time. A redesign of the procurement process eliminated virtually all discrepancies and produced significant cost savings.

*Situation 6*

A: Five years ago, the management of Breeann Products commissioned an engineering consulting firm to conduct a time-and-motion study so that labour efficiency standards could be developed and used in production. These labour efficiency standards are still in use today and are viewed by management as an important indicator of productivity.

B: Janet was quite satisfied with this quarter's labour performance. When compared with the same quarter of last year, labour productivity had increased by 23 percent. Most of the increase was due to a new assembly approach suggested by production line workers. She was also pleased to see that materials productivity had increased. The increase in materials productivity was attributed to reducing scrap because of improved quality.

*Situation 7*

A: "The system converts materials into products, not the people at work stations. Therefore, process efficiency is more important than labour efficiency—but we also must pay particular attention to those who use the products we produce, whether inside or outside the firm."

B: "I was quite happy to see a revenue increase of 15 percent over last year, especially when the budget called for a 10 percent increase. However, after reading the recent copy of our trade journal, I now wonder whether we are doing so well. I found out that the market expanded by 30 percent, and our leading competitor increased its sales by 40 percent."

**17–3**

*Activity Based versus Strategic-Based Control Systems*

**LO2**

Cameron Roy, president of Party Novelties, was considering a memo sent to her by Shelly Sundsrom, the vice-president of operations. The memo argued that the company needed to change its control system from an activity-based approach to a strategic-based approach. Shelly was convinced that the change would enhance the company's overall competitiveness. She had requested a meeting to explain the similarities and differences between the two approaches. Cameron agreed to the meeting, but asked Shelly to prepare a memo in advance listing the most important similarities and differences between the activity-based and strategic-based approaches.

**Required:**
Prepare the memo requested by Cameron.

**17–4**

*Functional-Based, Activity-Based, and Strategic-Based Control Systems; Ethical Issues; Incentives*

**LO2, LO4, LO5**

David Christensen, plant manager, was in charge of producing 120,000 bolts used in the manufacture of small twin-engine aircraft. Directed by his divisional manager to give the bolt production priority over other jobs, he had two weeks to produce the units. Meeting the delivery date was crucial for renewal of a major contract with a large airplane manufacturer. Each bolt requires 20 minutes of direct labour and 150 grams of metal. After the production of a batch of bolts, each bolt is subjected to a stress test. Those that pass are placed in a carton, which is stamped "Inspected by Inspector No. _____" (the inspector's identification number is inserted). Defective units are discarded, having no salvage value. Because of the nature of the process, rework is not possible.

At the end of the first week, the plant had produced 60,000 acceptable units and used 24,000 direct labour hours, 4,000 hours more than the standard allowed. Furthermore, a total of 65,000 bolts had been produced and 5,000 had been rejected, creating an unfavourable materials usage variance of 750 kilograms. David knew that a performance report would be prepared when the 120,000 bolts were completed. This report would compare the labour and materials usage with that allowed. Any variance in excess of 5 percent of standard would be investigated. David expected the same or worse performance for the coming week and was worried about a poor performance rating for himself.

At the beginning of the second week, David moved his inspectors to the production line (all inspectors had production experience). However, for reporting purposes the production hours provided by inspectors would not be counted as part of direct labour. They would still appear as a separate budget item on the performance report. Additionally, David instructed the inspectors to pack the completed bolts in the cartons and stamp them as inspected. One inspector objected; David reassigned the inspector temporarily to material handling and gave an inspection stamp with a fabricated identification number to a line worker who was willing to stamp the cartons of bolts as inspected.

**Required:**

1. Explain why David stopped inspections on the bolts and reassigned inspectors to production and material handling. Discuss the ethical implications of this decision.

2. What features in the functional-based control system provided the incentives(s) for David to take the actions described? Would an activity-based or strategic-based system have provided incentives that discourage this kind of behaviour? Explain.

3. What likely effect would David's actions have on the quality of the bolts? Was the decision justified by the need to obtain renewal of the contract, particularly if the plant returns to a normal inspection routine after the rush order is completed? Do you have any suggestions about the quality approach taken by this company? Explain why activity-based or strategic-based systems might play a useful role in this setting.

|  |  |
|---|---|
| **17–5** | Six independent situations are presented below: |
| Calculation of Nonvalue-Added Costs | A. It takes 45 minutes and 6 kilograms of material to produce a product using a traditional manufacturing process. A process reengineering study provided a new manufacturing process design (using existing technology) that would take 15 minutes and 4 kilograms of material. The cost per labour hour is $12, and the cost per kilogram of materials is $8. |
| LO2, LO3 | |

B. With its original design, a product requires 15 hours of setup time. Redesigning the product could reduce the setup time to an absolute minimum of 30 minutes. The cost per hour of setup time is $200.

C. A product currently requires eight moves. By redesigning the manufacturing layout, the firm can reduce the number of moves from eight to zero. The cost per move is $10.

D. Inspection time for a plant is 8,000 hours per year. The cost of inspection consists of the salaries of four inspectors, totalling $120,000. Inspection also uses supplies costing $2 per inspection hour. A supplier evaluation program, product redesign, and process redesign reduced the need for inspection by creating a zero-defect environment.

E. Each unit of a product requires 5 components. The average number of components used is actually 5.3 due to component failure that requires rework and extra components. By developing relationships with the right suppliers and increasing the quality of the purchased component, the firm can reduce the average number of components used to 5 components per unit. The cost per component is $600.

F. A plant produces 100 different electronic products. Each product requires an average of eight components, which are purchased externally. The components are different for each part. Redesigning the products will make it possible to produce the 100 products so that they have four components in common. This change will reduce the demand for purchasing, receiving, and paying bills. Estimated savings from the reduced demand are $900,000 per year.

**Required:**
Provide the following information for each of the six situations presented above:
1. An estimate of the nonvalue-added cost caused by each activity.
2. The root causes of the activity cost (such as plant layout, process design, and product design).
3. The cost reduction measure: activity elimination, activity reduction, activity sharing, or activity selection.

**17–6**

Calculation of Value-Added and Nonvalue-Added Costs; Activity Volume and Unused Capacity Variances

LO2, LO3, LO6

Spreadsheet

Toyworld, Inc. produces a variety of plastic toys. Because of competitive pressures, the company has been making an effort to reduce costs. As part of this effort, management has implemented an activity-based management system and has begun focusing its attention on processes and activities. Purchasing is one of the processes that has been carefully studied. The study revealed that the number of purchase orders is a good cost driver for purchasing costs. During the last year, the company incurred fixed purchasing costs of $140,000 (the combined salaries of four employees). The fixed costs provide a capacity of processing 16,000 orders (4,000 per employee at practical capacity). Management has decided that the value-added standard number of purchase orders is 8,000. The actual orders processed in the most recent period were 14,000.

**Required:**
1. Calculate the activity volume and unused capacity variances for the purchasing activity. Explain what each variance means.
2. Prepare a report that presents value-added, nonvalue-added, and actual costs. Explain why highlighting the nonvalue-added costs is important.
3. Explain why purchasing would be viewed as a value-added activity. List all possible reasons. Also list some possible reasons that explain why the demand for purchasing is more than the value-added standard.
4. Assume that management is able to improve the purchasing activity and reduce the demand for purchasing from 14,000 orders to 12,000 orders. What actions should be taken regarding activity capacity management?

**17–7**

Cost Report; Value-Added and Nonvalue-Added Costs

LO3, LO6

Timberlake Company has developed value-added standards for four activities: purchasing parts, assembling parts, administering parts, and inspecting parts. The activities, the activity drivers, the standard and actual quantities, and the price standards for 2005 are as follows:

| Activities | Activity Driver | SQ | AQ | SP |
|---|---|---|---|---|
| Purchasing parts | Orders | 500 | 700 | $300 |
| Assembling parts | Labour hours | 60,000 | 66,500 | 12 |
| Administering parts | Number of parts | 6,000 | 8,600 | 110 |
| Inspecting parts | Inspection hours | 0 | 25,000 | 15 |

The actual prices paid per unit of each activity driver were equal to the standard prices.

**Required:**
1. Prepare a cost report that lists the value-added costs, nonvalue-added costs, and actual costs for each activity.
2. Which activities are nonvalue-added? Explain why. Explain why value-added activities can have nonvalue-added costs.

**17–8**

Refer to Exercise 17–7. Suppose that Timberlake Company used an activity analysis program during 2006 in an effort to reduce nonvalue-added costs. The value-added standards, actual quantities, and prices for 2006 are as follows:

| Activity | Activity Driver | SQ | AQ | SP |
|---|---|---|---|---|
| Purchasing parts | Orders | 500 | 600 | $300 |
| Assembling parts | Labour hours | 60,000 | 62,000 | 12 |
| Administering parts | Number of parts | 6,000 | 8,000 | 110 |
| Inspecting parts | Inspection hours | 0 | 15,000 | 15 |

**Required:**

1. Prepare a trend report that compares the nonvalue-added costs for 2005 and 2006.
2. Comment on the value of the trend report.

**17–9**

Kenzie Sorensen, controller of Randell Company, has been helping an outside consulting group install an activity-based control system. The new system is designed to support the company's efforts to become more competitive. For the past two weeks, Kenzie has been identifying activities, associating workers with activities, and assessing the time and resources consumed by individual activities. Now she and the consulting group have entered into the fourth phase of activity analysis: assessing value content.

At this stage, Kenzie and the consultants plan to identify drivers for assigning costs to cost objects. Furthermore, as a preliminary step to improving activity efficiency, they have decided to identify the potential root causes of activity costs. Kenzie's assignment is to assess the value content of five activities, choose a suitable activity driver for each, and identify the possible root causes of the activities. Following are the five activities she is investigating, along with possible activity drivers:

| Activity | Possible Activity Drivers |
|---|---|
| Setting up equipment | Setup time, number of setups |
| Creating scrap[a] | Kilograms of scrap, number of defective units |
| Welding subassemblies | Welding hours, subassemblies welded |
| Handling materials | Number of moves, distance moved |
| Inspecting parts | Hours of inspection, number of defective parts |

[a] Scrap is defined as a bad product or subassembly that cannot be reworked and must therefore be discarded.

Kenzie runs a regression analysis for each potential activity driver, using the method of least squares to estimate the variable- and fixed-cost components. In all five cases, costs are highly correlated with the potential drivers. Thus, all drivers appear to be good candidates for assigning costs to products. The company plans to reward production managers for reducing product costs.

**Required:**

1. For each activity, assess the value content and classify each activity as value-added or nonvalue-added, justifying the classification. Identify some possible root causes of each activity, and describe how this knowledge can be used to improve activity management. Assume that the value-added activities are not performed with perfect efficiency.
2. Describe behaviours that each activity driver encourages and evaluate their effect on creating a sustainable competitive advantage.

**17–10**

*Kaizen Costing*

**LO6**

Olve Motors Division has been given the charge to reduce the delivery time of its tractor motors from three days to one day. To help achieve this goal, engineering and production workers have made a commitment to reduce setup times. Current setup times are 12 hours. Setup cost is $50 per setup hour. For the first quarter, engineering develops a new process design that it believes will reduce setup time from 12 hours to 8 hours. After the design is implemented, the actual setup time dropped from 12 to 7 hours—an hour more than expected. In the second quarter, production workers suggest a new setup procedure. Engineering's evaluation of the suggestion is positive, and it projects that the new approach will save an additional hour of setup time. Workers are trained to perform new setup procedures. The actual reduction in setup time based on the suggested changes is 1.5 hours.

**Required:**

1. What is the kaizen setup standard that would be used at the beginning of each quarter?
2. Describe the kaizen subcycle using the data for the two quarters.
3. Describe the maintenance subcycle using the data for the two quarters.
4. What is the amount of nonvalue-added costs that have been eliminated by the end of the two quarters?
5. How does kaizen costing differ from standard costing?

**17–11**

*Life Cycle Costing;
Target Costing*

**LO6**

The product development department at Metcalf Electronics is in the process of developing a new model for its cellular phone line. The product life cycle is estimated to be 27 months. Estimated sales over its life cycle are 200,000 units. For the current design, the development, production, and logistics costs for the life cycle are estimated to be $12,000,000. The product specifications and the targeted market share call for a price of $90 per unit. The target profit per unit is $40. Postpurchase costs for the current design are estimated to be $5 per unit.

**Required:**

1. What is the amount of total life cycle profit desired for the new model?
2. What is the amount of projected life cycle profit for the new model?
3. What is the amount of target cost? By how much must costs be reduced per unit and in total for this target to be met? Describe three approaches available for reducing costs so that the target cost is met.
4. Should postpurchase costs be included in life cycle costing? In target costing? Explain.

**17–12**

*Balanced Scorecard;
Strategy Translation;
Single- and Double-
Loop Feedback*

**LO4**

NBH Company, a small electronics firm, buys circuit boards and manually inserts various electronic devices into the printed circuit board. NBH sells its products to original equipment manufacturers. Profits for the last two years have been less than expected. Natalie Henson, the owner, is convinced that the company needs to adopt a revenue growth strategy to increase overall profits. To help build a viable strategy, she hires a consultant. After a careful review, the consultant tells Natalie that the high (5 percent) defect rate is the main obstacle for increasing revenues. By decreasing the defect rate, the company could increase revenues and market share. The consultant made the following suggestions to help ensure the success of the revenue growth strategy:

- Improve the soldering capabilities by sending employees to a training course.
- Redesign the insertion process to eliminate some common mistakes.
- Improve the procurement process by selecting suppliers that provide higher-quality circuit boards.

**Required:**
1. State the revenue growth strategy using a series of cause-and-effect relationships expressed as if–then statements. It is possible to have a compound if–then statement (more than one cause for one effect).
2. Illustrate the strategy using a flow diagram.
3. Explain how the revenue growth strategy can be tested. In your explanation, discuss the role of lead and lag measures, targets, and double-loop feedback.

**17–13**

Balanced Scorecard;
Classification of
Performance Measures

LO4

Listed below are a number of scorecard measures. Classify each performance measure according to the following: Perspective (for example, customer or learning and growth), Financial or Nonfinancial, Subjective or Objective, External or Internal, and Lead or Lag.
a. Number of new customers
b. Percentage of customer complaints resolved with one contact
c. Unit product cost
d. Cost per distribution channel
e. Suggestions per employee
f. Quality costs
g. Product functionality ratings (from surveys)
h. Cycle time for solving a customer's problem
i. Strategic job coverage ratio
j. On-time delivery percentage
k. Percentage of revenues from new products

**17–14**

Internal Process
Perspective; Cycle
Time and Velocity;
MCE

LO3, LO4

Spreadsheet

A manufacturing cell has the theoretical capability to produce 30,000 stereo speakers per quarter. The conversion cost per quarter is $60,000. There are 5,000 production hours available within the cell per quarter.

**Required:**
1. Compute the theoretical velocity (per hour) and the theoretical cycle time (minutes per unit produced).
2. Compute the ideal amount of conversion costs that will be assigned per speaker.
3. Speaker production uses two minutes of move time, one minute of waiting time, and two minutes of inspection time. Compute the amount of conversion costs actually assigned to each speaker. Calculate the MCE ratio.
4. Based on your analysis in Requirements 2 and 3, how much nonvalue-added time is used? How much is it costing per speaker?

# Problems

**17–15**

Continuous
Improvement;
Balanced Scorecard;
Performance
Measurement

LO3, LO4

At the beginning of 2005, Westboro Company implemented a low-cost strategy to improve its competitive position. Its objective was to become the lowest-cost producer in its industry. To lower costs, Westboro undertook a number of improvement activities, such as JIT production, total quality management, and activity-based management. Now, after two years of operating under this new system, the president wants an assessment of the system's achievements. To help provide this assessment, the following information on one product has been gathered:

|  | 2005 | 2006 |
|---|---|---|
| Theoretical annual capacity (units)[a] | 96,000 | 96,000 |
| Actual production (units)[b] | 76,000 | 88,000 |
| Production hours available (20 workers) | 40,000 | 40,000 |
| Postpurchase costs per unit | $20 | $10 |
| Scrap (kilograms) | 10,000 | 8,000 |
| Materials used (kilograms) | 100,000 | 100,000 |
| Actual cost per unit | $125 | $100 |
| Days of inventory | 6 | 3 |
| Number of defective units | 4,500 | 2,000 |
| Suggestions per employee | 2 | 6 |
| Hours of training | 100 | 400 |
| Selling price per unit | $150 | $140 |
| Number of new customers | 2,000 | 8,000 |

[a] Amount that could be produced given the available production hours.
[b] Amount that was produced given the available production hours.

**Required:**
1. Compute the following measures for 2005 and 2006:
   a. Theoretical velocity and cycle time
   b. Actual velocity and cycle time
   c. Percentage change in postpurchase costs (for 2006 only)
   d. Labour productivity (output/hours)
   e. Scrap as a percentage of total material issued
   f. Percentage change in actual product cost (for 2006 only)
   g. Percentage change in days of inventory (for 2006 only)
   h. Defective units as a percentage of total units produced
   i. New customers
   j. Hours of training
   k. Selling price per unit (as given)
   l. Total employee suggestions
2. For the measures listed in Requirement 1, list likely strategic objectives, classified according to the balanced scorecard perspectives. Next classify each measure as a lead or lag measure. Finally, evaluate the strategy's success. Would you like any additional information to carry out the evaluation? Explain.
3. Based on the results in Requirement 2, express the company's strategy as a series of if–then statements. What does this tell you about balanced scorecard measures?

**17–16**

Activity-Based
Management;
Nonvalue-Added
Costs; Target Costs

LO1, LO3, LO6

Donna Martens, president of Mays Electronic, was concerned about the end-of-the-year marketing report that she had just received. According to Larry Polowsky, marketing manager, a price decrease for the coming year was again needed to maintain the company's annual sales volume of integrated circuit boards (CBs). This would make a bad situation worse. The current selling price of $18 per unit was producing a $2-per-unit profit—half the customary $4-per-unit profit. Foreign competitors kept reducing their prices. To match the latest reduction would reduce the price from $18 to $14, below the cost of producing and selling each unit. How could Mays's competitors sell for such a low price? In order to determine whether there were problems with the company's operations, Donna hired a consultant. The consultant identified the following activities and costs:

| | |
|---|---:|
| Batch-level activities: | |
| Setting up equipment | $ 125,000 |
| Material handling | 180,000 |
| Inspecting products | 122,000 |
| Product-sustaining activities: | |
| Engineering support | 120,000 |
| Handling customer complaints | 100,000 |
| Filling warranties | 170,000 |
| Storing goods | 80,000 |
| Expediting goods | 75,000 |
| Unit-level activities: | |
| Using materials | 500,000 |
| Using power | 48,000 |
| Manual insertion labour[a] | 250,000 |
| Other direct labour | 150,000 |
| Total costs[b] | $1,920,000 |

[a] Diodes, resistors, and integrated circuits are inserted manually into the circuit board.
[b] This total cost produces a unit cost of $16 for last year's sales volume.

The consultant reported that the unit cost can be reduced by at least $7. The marketing manager indicated that the market share (sales volume) for the boards could be increased by 50 percent if the price were reduced to $12.

**Required:**
1. What is activity-based management? What phases of activity analysis did the consultant provide? What else remains to be done?
2. Identify as many nonvalue-added costs as possible. Compute the cost savings per unit that would be realized if these costs were eliminated. Was the consultant correct in his cost reduction assessment? Discuss actions that the company can take to reduce or eliminate the nonvalue-added activities.
3. Compute the target cost required to maintain the current market share while earning a profit of $4 per unit. Compute the target cost required to expand sales by 50 percent. How much cost reduction would be required to achieve each target?
4. Assume that further activity analysis revealed the following: switching to automated insertion would save $60,000 of engineering support and $90,000 of direct labour costs. What is the total potential cost reduction per unit available from activity analysis? With these additional reductions, can Mays achieve the target cost to maintain current sales? to increase them by 50 percent? What type of activity management is this: reduction, sharing, elimination, or selection?
5. Calculate income based on current sales, prices, and costs. Calculate the income using a $14 price and a $12 price, assuming that the maximum cost reduction possible is achieved, including the reduction in Requirement 4. What price should be selected?

**17–17**

Value-Added and
Kaizen Standards;
Nonvalue-Added
Costs; Volume
Variance; Unused
Capacity

LO3, LO6

Clement Mallet, vice president of Suegros, has been supervising the implementation of an activity-based cost management system. One of Clement's objectives is to improve process efficiency by improving the activities that define the processes. To illustrate the new system's potential to the company's president, Clement decided to focus on two processes: production and customer service.

Within each process, one activity will be selected for improvement: materials usage for production, and sustaining engineering for customer service. Sustaining engineers are responsible for redesigning products based on customer needs and feedback. Value-added standards are identified for each activity. For materials usage, the value-added standard calls for 6 kilograms per unit of output.

Although the products differ in shape and function, their size, as measured by weight, is uniform. The value-added standard is based on the elimination of all waste due to defective moulds. The standard price of materials is $5 per kilogram. For sustaining engineering, the standard is 58 percent of current practical activity capacity. This standard is based on the fact that about 42 percent of the complaints relate to design features. Such complaints could have been avoided or anticipated by the company.

Current practical capacity (at the end of 2005) is defined by the following requirements: 6,000 engineering hours for each product group that has been on the market or in development for five years or less, and 2,400 hours per product group of more than five years. Four product groups have less than five years' experience, and ten product groups have more. There are 24 engineers, each paid a salary of $60,000. Each engineer can provide 2,000 hours of service per year. There are no other significant costs for the engineering activity.

Actual materials usage for 2005 was 25 percent above the level called for by the value-added standard; engineering usage was 46,000 hours. There were 80,000 units of output produced. Clement and the company's operational managers have selected some improvement measures that promise to reduce nonvalue-added activity usage by 40 percent in 2006. Selected annual results achieved for 2006 are as follows:

| | |
|---|---|
| Units produced | 80,000 |
| Materials used | 584,800 |
| Engineering hours | 35,400 |

The actual prices paid for materials and engineering hours are identical to the standard or budgeted prices.

**Required:**
1. Calculate the nonvalue-added usage and costs for material usage and sustaining engineering for 2005. Also, calculate the cost of unused capacity for the engineering activity.
2. Using the targeted reduction, establish kaizen standards for materials and engineering for 2006.
3. Using the kaizen standards prepared in Requirement 2, compute the 2006 usage variances, expressed in both physical and financial measures for materials and engineering. For engineering, compare actual resource usage with the kaizen standard. Comment on the company's ability to achieve its targeted reductions. In particular, discuss what measures the company must take to capture any realized reductions in resource usage.

**17–18**

Homedec Products has two plants that manufacture a line of recliners. One plant is located in Edmonton and the other in Calgary. Each plant is set up as a profit centre. During the past year, both plants sold the regular model for $450. Sales volume averages 20,000 units per year in each plant. Recently, the Calgary plant reduced the price of the regular model to $400. Discussion with the Calgary manager revealed that the price reduction was possible because the plant had reduced its manufacturing and selling costs by reducing what was called "nonvalue-added costs." The Calgary plant's manufacturing and selling costs for the regular chair were $350 per unit.

The Calgary manager offered to loan the Edmonton plant his cost accounting manager to help them achieve similar results. The Edmonton plant's manager readily agreed, knowing that his plant must keep pace, not only with the Calgary plant but also with the company's competitors. A local competitor had also reduced its price on a similar model, and the Edmonton plant's marketing manager had indicated that the price must be matched or sales would drop dramatically. In fact, the marketing manager suggested that if the price were dropped to $390 by the end of the year, the plant could expand its share of the market by 20 percent. The plant manager agreed, but insisted that the current profit per unit must be maintained and now wants to know if the plant can at least match the Calgary plant's cost of $350 per unit. He also wants to know if the plant can achieve the cost reduction using the Calgary plant's approach.

The Edmonton plant's controller and the Calgary plant's cost accounting manager have assembled the following data from the Edmonton plant for the most recent year. Assume that the actual prices of activity units equal the standard prices. The actual cost of inputs, the value-added (ideal) quantity levels, and the actual quantity levels are as follows for the production of 20,000 units:

| | SQ | AQ | Actual Cost |
|---|---|---|---|
| Materials (kilograms) | 237,500 | 250,000 | $5,250,000 |
| Labour (hours) | 57,000 | 60,000 | 750,000 |
| Setups (hours) | — | 4,000 | 300,000 |
| Material handling (moves) | — | 10,000 | 700,000 |
| Warranties (number repaired) | — | 10,000 | 1,000,000 |
| Total | | | $8,000,000 |

**Required:**

1. Calculate the target cost for expanding the Edmonton market share by 20 percent, assuming that the per-unit profitability is maintained as requested by the plant manager.
2. Calculate the nonvalue-added cost per unit. Assuming that nonvalue-added costs can be reduced to zero, do you think the Edmonton plant can match the Calgary plant's unit cost? Can the target cost for expanding market share be achieved? What actions would you take if you were the Edmonton plant's manager?
3. Describe the role that benchmarking played in the Edmonton plant's effort to protect and improve its competitive position.

**17–19**

Manley Manufacturing Company makes products with average life cycles of three years. The first year involves product development, and the remaining two years emphasize production and sales. Expected sales for two proposed products are 200,000 units each. The price has been set to yield a 50 percent gross margin ratio. A budgeted life cycle income statement is as follows.

|                              | Product A   | Product B   | Total       |
|------------------------------|-------------|-------------|-------------|
| Sales                        | $4,000,000  | $5,000,000  | $9,000,000  |
| Cost of goods sold           | 2,000,000   | 2,500,000   | 4,500,000   |
| Gross margin                 | $2,000,000  | $2,500,000  | $4,500,000  |
| Period expenses:             |             |             |             |
| Research and development     |             |             | 2,000,000   |
| Marketing                    |             |             | 1,150,000   |
| Life cycle income            |             |             | $1,350,000  |

Upon seeing the budget, Rick Moss, the president met with LeeAnn Gordon, the marketing manager, and Art Cummings, the design engineer.

**Rick**: "These two products are earning only a 15 percent return on sales. We need 20 percent to earn an acceptable return on our investment. Can't we raise prices?"

**LeeAnn**: "I doubt that the market would bear any increase in prices. However, I will do some additional research and see what's possible. The gross profit ratio is already high. The problem appears to be with R & D. Those expenses seem higher than normal."

**Art**: "These products are more complex than usual, and we need the extra resources—at least if you want to have a product that functions as we are claiming it will. Also, we are charting some new waters with the features these products offer. Specifically, our design is intended to reduce postpurchase costs, including operation, support, maintenance, and disposal. LeeAnn, you mentioned a year ago that our competitors were providing products that had lower postpurchase costs. This new design was intended to make us market leaders in this area. In the future, we can probably get by on less—after we gain some experience. But it wouldn't be much less—perhaps $50,000."

**Rick**: "That would still allow us to earn only about 15.6 percent—even after you get more proficient. Maybe we ought to stay with our more standard features."

**LeeAnn**: "Before we abandon these new lines, perhaps we ought to look at each product individually. Maybe one could be retained. These new features will give us an edge in the market. Also, I'll bet that if Art knew what was driving those costs, he could redesign the product so that production costs could be lowered. I'm concerned that our competitors will exploit their postpurchase cost advantage. We really need to be leaders in this area—our reputation is at stake. If we're not careful, we'll lose market share."

**Required:**
1. Suggest improvements to the company's life cycle cost management system.
2. Assume that the "period" expenses are traceable to each product. Product A is responsible for 60 percent of research and development costs and 50 percent of marketing costs. Prepare a revised income statement for each product. Based on this analysis, do you think that either product should be produced?
3. Based on the revised income statements from Requirement 2, by how much should production costs be reduced to make each product acceptable? Discuss how activity analysis can help achieve this outcome. Explain why this analysis should occur now, not after the products are in production.
4. According to Art, the motivation for the new design was to reduce the postpurchase costs of the new products. Explain why whole-life cost should be the focus of life cycle cost management.

**17–20**

Internal Business
Perspective; Cycle
Time; MCE

LO4, LO5

A manufacturing cell has the theoretical capability to produce 60,000 space heaters per quarter. The conversion cost per quarter is $600,000. There are 20,000 production hours available within the cell per quarter.

**Required:**

1. Compute the theoretical velocity (per hour) and the theoretical cycle time (minutes per unit produced).
2. Compute the ideal amount of conversion cost that will be assigned per heater.
3. Suppose that the actual time required to produce a heater is 30 minutes. Compute the amount of conversion cost actually assigned to each heater. Discuss how this approach to assigning conversion costs can improve delivery time.
4. Calculate the MCE ratio. How much nonvalue-added time is being used? How much is it costing per heater?
5. Cycle time, velocity, MCE, conversion cost per unit (theoretical conversion rate X actual conversion time), and nonvalue-added costs are measures of process efficiency. Discuss the incentives provided by these measures.

**17–21**

MCE

LO3, LO4

Anderson Company makes a product that involves the following activities:

| | Hours |
|---|---|
| Processing (two departments) | 30 |
| Inspecting | 2 |
| Rework | 5 |
| Moving (three moves) | 8 |
| Waiting (for the second process) | 24 |
| Storage (before delivery to customer) | 31 |

**Required:**

1. Compute the MCE ratio for this product.
2. Discuss how process value analysis can help improve this efficiency measure.
3. Is this a lead measure or a lag measure? If it is a lag measure, what would be some lead measures that would affect this measure?

**17–22**

Functional-Based,
Activity-Based, and
Strategic-Based
Systems and Measures

LO2, LO4

Continuous improvement is the governing principle of an activity-based control system. The following list provides several performance measures, which are associated with functional-based or activity-based control systems.

a. Materials price variances
b. Cycle time
c. Comparison of actual product costs with target costs
d. Materials quantity or efficiency variances
e. Comparison of actual product costs over time (trend reports)
f. Comparison of actual overhead costs, item by item, with the corresponding budgeted costs
g. Comparison of product costs with competitors' product costs
h. Percentage of on-time deliveries
i. Quality reports
j. Reports of value-added and nonvalue-added costs
k. Labour efficiency variances
l. Machine utilization rates
m. Days of inventory
n. Downtime
o. Manufacturing cycle efficiency (MCE)

    p. Unused capacity variance

    q. Labour rate variance

    r. Using a sister plant's best practices as a performance standard

**Required:**

1. Classify each measure as functional-based or activity-based. If functional-based, discuss the measure's limitations for an activity-based environment. If activity-based, describe how the measure supports the objectives of an activity-based environment.
2. Classify the measures into operational (nonfinancial) and financial categories. Explain why operational measures are better for control of production activities than financial measures. Should any financial measures be used at the operational level?
3. Discuss how strategic-based control systems differ from activity-based systems. Provide examples of measures that would be added to the above list if a strategic-based system were used.

**17–23**

Cycle Time; Velocity;
Product Costing

LO3

Whitestone Company has a JIT system. Each manufacturing cell is dedicated to the production of a single product or major subassembly. One cell, dedicated to the production of paint guns, performs four operations: machining, finishing, assembly, and testing. The machining process is automated, whereby the paint gun's body, cup, and nozzle are machined using computers. The three parts of the paint gun are then assembled. Finishing involves sandblasting, buffing, and anodizing. Finally, each paint gun is tested using 20 millilitres of paint.

    The paint gun cell had the following budgeted costs and cell times (both at theoretical capacity) for the next year:

| | |
|---|---|
| Budgeted conversion costs | $2,500,000 |
| Budgeted raw materials | $3,000,000 |
| Cell time | 4,000 hours |
| Theoretical output | 30,000 paint guns |

The following actual results were obtained during the year:

| | |
|---|---|
| Actual conversion costs | $2,500,000 |
| Actual materials | $2,600,000 |
| Actual cell time | 4,000 hours |
| Actual output | 25,000 paint guns |

**Required:**

1. Compute the velocity (number of paint guns per hour) that the cell can theoretically achieve. Compute the theoretical cycle time (number of hours or minutes per paint gun) that it takes to produce one paint gun.
2. Compute the actual velocity and the actual cycle time.
3. Compute the MCE ratio. Comment on the efficiency of the operations.
4. Compute the budgeted conversion cost per minute. Using this rate, compute the conversion cost per paint gun if theoretical output is achieved. Using this measure, compute the conversion cost per paint gun for actual output. Does this product-costing approach provide an incentive for the cell manager to reduce cycle time? Explain.

**17–24**

Balanced Scorecard

LO4

Following its strategy of product differentiation, Hightech, Inc. makes calculators and markets them through major electronics and office supply chain stores. It is also considering whether to start marketing them through the Internet. The following comparative information is available for 2004 and 2005:

|                                              | 2004      | 2005      |
| -------------------------------------------- | --------- | --------- |
| Number of units produced and sold            | 50,000    | 52,500    |
| Selling price per unit                        | $40       | $44       |
| Total direct materials costs                  | $200,000  | $231,000  |
| Manufacturing capacity in units               | 62,500    | 62,500    |
| Total conversion costs                        | $250,000  | $277,500  |
| Total selling and customer service costs      | $180,000  | $181,250  |
| Number of customers                           | 30        | 29        |

A unique compact product design and high quality are key factors that allow the company to differentiate its product and charge a premium price. Direct material costs depend on the number of units produced, conversion costs on production capacity in units, and selling and customer service costs on the number of customers. The industry market size for calculators increased 10 percent from 2004 to 2005, mostly in the low-price end of the market.

### Required:

Recommend a performance measure that you consider the most important for each of the four perspectives: internal process, financial, customer, and learning and growth. Briefly explain why each measure is important for Hightech in light of its current situation.

**17–25**

*Comprehensive Problem; Balanced Scorecard; Nonvalue-Added Activities; Kaizen Costing; Incentive Compensation*

LO1, LO2, LO3, LO4, LO5, LO6

At the beginning of the last quarter of 2005, Microcom, Inc., a large consumer products firm, hired Leming Imai to take over one of its divisions. The division manufactured small home appliances and was struggling to survive in a very competitive market. Leming immediately requested a projected income statement for 2005. In response, the controller provided the following statement:

| Sales                | $25,000,000   |
| -------------------- | ------------- |
| Variable expenses    | 20,000,000    |
| Contribution margin  | $ 5,000,000   |
| Fixed expenses       | 6,000,000     |
| Projected loss       | $(1,000,000)  |

After some investigation, Leming realized that the products had a serious quality problem. He requested the controller's office to supply a report on the level of quality costs. Leming received the following report from the controller:

| Inspection costs, finished product | $ 400,000   |
| ---------------------------------- | ----------- |
| Rework costs                        | 2,000,000   |
| Scrapped units                      | 600,000     |
| Warranty costs                      | 3,000,000   |
| Sales returns (quality-related)     | 1,000,000   |
| Customer complaint department       | 500,000     |
| Total estimated quality costs       | $7,500,000  |

Leming was surprised by the high level of quality costs—30 percent of sales. He knew that to survive, the division had to produce high-quality products. The number of defective units produced needed to be reduced dramatically. Thus, Leming decided to pursue a quality-driven turnaround strategy. Revenue growth and cost reduction could be achieved if quality could be improved. By increasing revenues and decreasing costs, the company could increase profitability.

After Leming met with the managers of production, marketing, purchasing, and human resources, the following decisions were made, effective immediately (end of November 2005):

1. More will be invested in employee training. Workers will be trained to detect quality problems and empowered to make improvements. Workers will be allowed a bonus of 10 percent of any cost savings produced by their suggested improvements.
2. Two design engineers will be hired immediately, with expectations of hiring one or two more within a year. These engineers will be in charge of redesigning processes and products with the objective of improving quality. They will also be given the responsibility of working with selected suppliers to help improve the quality of their products and processes. Design engineers were considered a strategic necessity.
3. A new process, the evaluation and selection of suppliers, will be implemented, with the objective of selecting a group of suppliers that are willing and able to provide nondefective components.
4. Effective immediately, the division will begin inspecting purchased components. According to production, many of the quality problems are caused by defective components purchased from outside suppliers. Incoming inspection was viewed as a transitional activity. Once the division has developed a group of suppliers capable of delivering nondefective components, this activity will be eliminated.
5. Within three years, the goal is to produce products with a defect rate of less than 0.1 percent. Marketing is confident that reducing the defect rate to this level will increase market share by at least 50 percent and also increase customer satisfaction. Products with better quality will help establish an improved product image and reputation, allowing the division to capture new customers and increase market share.
6. Accounting will be made responsible for implementing a quality information reporting system. Daily reports on operational quality data, for example, percentage of defective units; weekly updates of trend graphs, posted throughout the division; and quarterly cost reports are the types of information required.
7. To help direct the improvements in quality activities, kaizen costing will also be implemented. For example, for the year 2006, for rework costs, a kaizen standard of 6 percent of the selling price per unit was set, a 25 percent reduction from the current actual cost.

To ensure that the quality improvements were directed and translated into concrete financial outcomes, Leming also began to implement a balanced scorecard for the division. By the end of 2006, progress was being made. Sales had increased to $26,000,000, and the kaizen improvements were meeting or exceeding expectations. For example, rework costs had dropped to $1,500,000.

At the end of 2007, two years after the turnaround quality strategy was implemented, Leming received the following quality cost report:

| | |
|---|---:|
| Quality training | $ 500,000 |
| Supplier evaluation | 230,000 |
| Incoming inspection costs | 400,000 |
| Inspection costs, finished product | 300,000 |
| Rework costs | 1,000,000 |
| Scrapped units | 200,000 |
| Warranty costs | 750,000 |
| Sales returns (quality-related) | 435,000 |
| Customer complaint department | 325,000 |
| Total estimated quality costs | $4,140,000 |

Leming also received an income statement for 2007:

| Sales | $30,000,000 |
| Variable expenses | 22,000,000 |
| Contribution margin | $ 8,000,000 |
| Fixed expenses | 5,800,000 |
| Income | $ 2,200,000 |

Leming was pleased with the outcomes. Revenues had grown, and costs had been reduced by at least as much as he had projected for the two-year period. He believed that the next year's growth would be even greater, because he was beginning to observe a favourable effect from the higher-quality products. Also, further quality cost reductions should materialize, because incoming inspections were showing much higher-quality purchased components.

**Required:**

1. Identify the strategic objectives, classified by balanced scorecard perspectives. Next, suggest measures for each objective. Classify the measures as lead and lag measures.
2. Using the results from Requirement 1, describe Leming's strategy using a series of if–then statements. Prepare a visual diagram of the strategy.
3. Explain how you would evaluate the success of the quality-driven turnaround strategy. What additional information would you like to have for this evaluation?
4. Explain why Leming felt that the balanced scorecard would increase the likelihood that the turnaround strategy would actually produce good financial outcomes.
5. The kaizen standard for rework was 6 percent of sales for 2006. Was the standard met? What would be the maintenance standard at the end of 2006? Describe the role for kaizen costing in Leming's strategy.
6. Of the quality activities listed in the 2007 report, which ones are nonvalue-added? By eliminating all nonvalue-added activities, how much further cost reduction is possible?

**17–26**

Managerial
Performance
Evaluation

**LO4, LO5**

Greg Heron has recently been appointed the vice president of operations for Webster Corporation. Greg was previously the operations manager of one of Webster's divisions. The business segments of Webster include the manufacture of heavy equipment, food processing, and financial services.

In a recent conversation with Magdalena Hansen, the chief financial officer, Greg suggested that segment managers be evaluated based on segment data appearing in the annual financial report. This report presents revenues, earnings, identifiable assets, and amortization for each segment for a five-year period. Greg believes that evaluating segment managers by criteria similar to those used to evaluate top management would be appropriate. Magdalena expressed some reservations about using segment information from the annual financial report for this purpose and suggested that Greg consider other ways of evaluating the performance of segment managers.

**Required:**

1. Explain why the segment information prepared for public reporting purposes may not be appropriate for the evaluation of segment manager performance.
2. Describe the possible behavioural impact on segment managers if their performance is evaluated based on the information in the annual financial report.
3. Identify and describe several types of financial information that would be more appropriate for Greg to review when evaluating the performance of segment managers. (US CMA adapted)

**17–27**

Transpo, Inc., a truck manufacturing conglomerate, has recently purchased two divisions, Meyers Service Company and Wellington Products, Inc. Meyers provides maintenance services on large truck cabs for 12-wheeler trucks, and Wellington produces air brakes for the trucks.

The employees at Meyers take pride in their work, and Meyers is proclaimed to offer the best maintenance service in the trucking industry. The management of Meyers, as a group, has received additional compensation from a 10 percent bonus pool based on income before taxes and bonus. The company plans to continue to compensate the Meyers management team on this basis, since it is the same incentive plan used for all other divisions.

Wellington offers a high-quality product to the trucking industry, which is the premium choice even when compared to foreign competition. The management team at Wellington strives for zero defects and minimal scrap costs. Current scrap levels are at 2 percent. The incentive compensation plan for Wellington management has been a 1 percent bonus based on gross profit margin. The company plans to continue to compensate the Wellington management team on this basis.

Following are the condensed income statements for both divisions for the fiscal year ended May 31, 2005.

**Transpo, Inc.**
**Divisional Income Statements**
**For the Year Ended May 31, 2005**

|  | Meyers Service Company | Wellington Products, Inc. |
|---|---|---|
| Revenues | $4,000,000 | $10,000,000 |
| Cost of product | $ 75,000 | $ 4,950,000 |
| Salaries[a] | 2,200,000 | 2,150,000 |
| Fixed selling expenses | 1,000,000 | 2,500,000 |
| Interest expense | 30,000 | 65,000 |
| Other operating expenses | 278,000 | 134,000 |
| Total expenses | $3,583,000 | $ 9,799,000 |
| Income before taxes and bonus | $ 417,000 | $ 201,000 |

[a] Each division has $1,000,000 of management salary expense that is eligible for the bonus pool.

The company invited managers from all divisions to an off-site management workshop in July, where the bonus cheques will be presented. It is concerned that the different bonus plans at the two divisions may cause some heated discussion.

**Required:**
1. Determine the 2005 bonus pool available for the management team at
   a. Meyers Service Company
   b. Wellington Products, Inc.
2. Identify at least two advantages and at least two disadvantages to the company of the bonus pool incentive plan at
   a. Meyers Service Company
   b. Wellington Products, Inc.
3. Having two different types of incentive plans for two operating divisions of the same corporation can create problems.
   a. Discuss behavioural problems that could arise within management for the divisions as a result of having different types of incentive plans.
   b. Present arguments that the company can give to managers of both divisions to justify having two different incentive plans.

**17–28**

Management
Compensation

LO5

Morecam Enterprises is contemplating the idea of establishing an incentive scheme for its divisional executive group. It is a large public company whose shares trade on the Toronto Stock Exchange. The company is organized into several divisions, each headed by a divisional vice-president. Head office is overseen by the president and five senior vice-presidents. Currently, the head office executives are compensated, in part, by a stock option plan based on annual company earnings. For the divisional group, the board of directors has recommended a performance bonus based on the achievement of annual divisional return on investment. The bonus pool will be defined as a percentage, for example, 6 percent, of the company's net income after taxes. Divisional income is currently defined as net income after all head office charges and taxes, and investment is defined as total assets.

**Required:**

Evaluate the proposal to establish an incentive plan for the divisions. Include in your answer an assessment of the strengths and weaknesses of the performance evaluation scheme and a discussion of ways in which these weaknesses can be corrected. Briefly comment on the stock option plan already in place. (CGA Canada adapted)

## Managerial Decision Cases

**17–29**

Managerial Evaluation
and Rewards; Ethical
Considerations;
Control Environment

**LO1, LO4, LO5**

Tim Ireland, controller of Roberts Electronics Division, was having lunch with Jimmy Jones, the division's chief design engineer. Tim and Jimmy were good friends, having belonged to the same fraternity during their university days. The luncheon, however, was more business than pleasure.

**Jimmy**: "Well, Tim, you indicated this morning that you have something important to tell me. I hope this isn't too serious. I don't want my weekend ruined."

**Tim**: "Well, the matter is important. You know that at the beginning of this year, I was given the charge to estimate postpurchase costs for new products. This is not an easy task."

**Jimmy**: "Yeah, I know. That's why I had our department supply you with engineering specs on the new products—stuff like expected component life."

**Tim**: "This new product you've been developing has a problem. According to your reports, there are two components that will wear out within about fourteen months. According to your test runs, the product starts producing subpar performance during the thirteenth month."

**Jimmy**: "Long enough to get us past the twelve-month warranty. So why worry? There are no warranty costs for us to deal with."

**Tim**: "Yes, but the customer must then incur substantial repair costs. And the product will have to be repaired once again before its useful life is ended. The estimated repair costs, when added to the normal life cycle costs, put the whole-life cost above the target cost. According to the new guidelines, we are going to have to scrap this new product—at least using its current design. Perhaps you can find a new design that avoids the use of these two components—or find ways that they won't be so stressed so that they last much longer."

**Jimmy**: "Listen, Tim, I don't have the time or the budget to redesign this product. I have to come in under budget, and I have to meet the targeted production date—otherwise, I'll have the divisional manager down my throat. Besides, you know that I'm up for the engineering management position at headquarters. If this project goes well, then it'll give me what I need to edge out Thompson

Division's chief engineer. If I do the redesign, my opportunity for the job is gone. Help me out on this. You know how much this opportunity means to me."

**Tim**: "I don't know what I can do. I have to file the whole-life cost report, and I'm required to supply supporting documentation from marketing and engineering."

**Jimmy**: "Well, that's easy to solve. Linda, the engineer who ran the tests on this product, owes me a favour. I'll get her to redo the tests so that the data produce a twenty-four-month reliability period for the components. That should cut your estimated repair costs in half. Would that be enough to meet the targeted whole-life costs?"

**Tim**: "Yes, but …"

**Jimmy**: "Hey, don't worry. If I tell Linda that I'll push her for chief divisional engineer, she'll cooperate. No sweat. This is a one-time thing. How about it? Are you a player?"

### Required:

1. What pressures does Tim have to comply with Jimmy's requests? Do you think he should comply? Would you, if you were Tim? If not, how would you handle the situation?
2. Assume that Tim cooperates with Jimmy and covers up the design deficiency. What standards of ethical conduct for management accountants are violated?
3. Suppose that Tim refuses to cooperate. Jimmy then gets Linda to rerun the tests anyway, with the new, more optimistic results. He then approaches Tim with the tests and indicates that he is sending a copy of the latest results to the divisional manager. Jimmy indicates that he will challenge any redesign recommendations that Tim makes. What should Tim do?

## Research Assignments

**17–30**

Research Assignment

LO4

You are a newly employed strategic analyst working for a medium-sized manufacturing company. This company is facing intense competition from foreign and domestic companies. Your supervisor, Kathy Winslow, has asked you to research the use of nonfinancial performance measures. Use library's resources, paying particular attention to articles appearing in the following journals: *Management Accounting, Journal of Cost Management*, and *Harvard Business Review*. Once you have collected what you can on the topic, write a two-page memo to Kathy that addresses the following issues:

1. What factors have resulted in the rise of nonfinancial measures?
2. What are the deficiencies of the traditional accounting performance measures?
3. What nonfinancial measures should be used and why?
4. How can control be achieved through the use of nonfinancial measures?
5. What problems or limitations are associated with nonfinancial measures?
6. What is your recommendation concerning the use of nonfinancial measures?

You may address any other substantive issues that you discover in your research. List the sources for your views in your memo.

**17–31**

Cybercase

LO1, LO4

Using Internet resources, conduct research on performance measurement systems of three organizations. Find examples of how these organizations use strategic performance measurement systems such as the balanced scorecard. For each organization, list its performance objectives and at least one performance measure used for each objective. Identify the most important environmental factors facing each organization and explain how they can influence the objectives and measures of each organization.

# Glossary

## A

**absorption costing** A product-costing method that assigns all manufacturing costs to a product: direct materials, direct labour, variable overhead, and fixed overhead.

**acceptable quality level (AQL)** An approach to quality control that permits or allows defects to occur provided that they do not exceed a predetermined level.

**accounting rate of return** The rate of return obtained by dividing the average accounting net income by the original investment (or by average investment).

**Accounting Standards Board** Establishes financial accounting standards, including the nature of inputs and the rules and conventions governing financial accounting processes.

**activity attributes** Nonfinancial and financial information items that describe individual activities.

**activity-based budgeting system** In activity-based budgeting, the workload (demand) for each activity is estimated and the resources required to sustain this workload are established.

**activity-based control systems** Control systems that focus on processes and use both financial and nonfinancial performance measures.

**activity-based costing (ABC)** A cost assignment approach that first uses direct and driver tracing to assign costs to activities and then uses drivers to assign costs to cost objects.

**activity-based costing (ABC) system** A cost system that first traces costs to activities and then traces costs from activities to products.

**activity-based cost management information system** An improved management accounting information system based on the principles of activity-based management and activity-based costing.

**activity-based management** A systemwide, integrated approach that focuses management's attention on activities with the objective of improving customer value and the profit achieved by providing this value. It includes driver analysis, activity analysis, and performance evaluation, and draws on activity-based costing as a major source of information.

**activity-based management (ABM) accounting system** An accounting system that emphasizes the use of activities for assigning and managing costs.

**activity capacity** The number of times an activity can be performed.

**activity dictionary** A list of activities described by specific attributes, such as name, definition, classification as primary or secondary, and activity driver.

**activity drivers** Factors that measure the consumption of activities by products and other cost objects.

**activity elimination** The process of eliminating non-value-added activities.

**activity flexible budgeting** The prediction of what activity costs will be as activity usage changes.

**activity inputs** The resources consumed by an activity in producing its output (the factors that enable the activity to be performed).

**activity output** The result or product of an activity.

**activity output measure** The number of times an activity is performed. It is the quantifiable measure of the activity output.

**activity reduction** Decreasing the time and resources required by an activity.

**activity selection** The process of choosing among sets of activities caused by competing strategies.

**activity sharing** Increasing the efficiency of necessary activities by using economies of scale.

**activity value analysis** The process of identifying, describing, and evaluating the activities an organization performs.

**activity volume variance** The difference between the actual activity capacity acquired and the capacity that should be used.

**actual costing** An approach that assigns actual costs for direct materials, direct labour, and overhead to products.

**adjusted cost of goods sold** The cost of goods sold after all adjustments for overhead variance are made.

**administrative costs** All costs associated with the general administration of the organization that cannot be reasonably assigned to either marketing or production.

**aesthetics** A quality attribute that is concerned with the appearance of tangible products (e.g., style and beauty) as well as the appearance of the facilities, equipment, personnel, and communications materials associated with services.

**allocation** Assignment of indirect costs to cost objects.

**annuity** A series of future cash flows.

**applied overhead** Overhead assigned to production using predetermined rates.

**appraisal costs** Costs incurred to determine whether products and services are conforming to requirements.

## B

**balanced scorecard** A strategic performance measurement framework that incorporates a balanced mix of financial and nonfinancial measures for internal processes, customer satisfaction, financial performance, and learning and growth.

**base period** A prior period used to set the benchmark for measuring productivity changes.

**batch-level activities** Activities that are performed each time a batch is produced.

**benchmarking** An approach that uses the best practices as the standard for evaluating activity performance.

**best-fitting line** The line that fits a set of data points the best, in the sense that the sum of the squared deviations of the data points from the line is the smallest.

**binding constraints** Constraints whose resources are fully utilized.

**bottom-up budgeting** A participative budgeting process that allows managers considerable input into the budget levels and processes.

**breakeven point** The point where total sales revenue equals total costs; the point of zero profits.

**budget committee** A committee responsible for setting budgetary policies and goals, reviewing and approving the budget, and resolving any differences that may arise in the budgetary process.

**budget director** The individual responsible for coordinating and directing the overall budgeting process.

**budgetary slack** The process of padding the budget by overestimating costs and underestimating revenues.

**budgets** Plans of action expressed in financial terms.

**business excellence model** A performance measurement framework that emphasizes total quality management and consists of nine dimensions: leadership, people management, policy and strategy, resources, processes, people satisfaction, customer satisfaction, impact on society, and business results.

## C

**capital budgeting** The process of making capital investment decisions.

**capital cost allowances (CCAs)** Deduction for Canadian income tax purposes related to the capital cost of fixed assets.

**capital investment decisions** The process of planning, setting goals and priorities, arranging financing, and identifying criteria for making long-term investments.

**carrying costs** The costs of holding inventory.

**cash budget** A detailed plan that outlines all sources and uses of cash.

**causal factors** Activities or variables that invoke service costs. Generally, it is desirable to use causal factors as the basis for allocating service costs.

**centralized decision making** A system in which decisions are made at the top level of an organization and local managers are given the charge to implement them.

**Certified General Accountant (CGA)** An accountant who holds the CGA designation after satisfying the examination and practice requirements. CGAs are found both in public practice and in private- and public-sector organizations.

**Certified Management Accountant (CMA)** An accountant who holds the CMA designation after satisfying the entrance examination, the professional program, and experience requirements. CMAs are found primarily in private- and public-sector organizations.

**Chartered Accountant (CA)** An accountant who holds the CA designation after satisfying the examination and public practice requirements. CAs are found in both public practice and private and public sector organizations.

**coefficient of correlation** The square root of the coefficient of determination, which is used to express not only the degree of correlation between two variables but also the direction of the relationship.

**coefficient of determination** The percentage of total variability in a dependent variable (e.g., cost) that is explained by an independent variable (e.g., activity level). It assumes a value between 0 and 1.

**committed fixed costs** Costs incurred for the acquisition of long-term activity capacity, usually as the result of strategic planning.

**committed resources** Resources that are purchased in advance of usage. These resources may or may not have unused (excess) capacity.

**common costs** The costs of resources used in the output of two or more services or products.

**common fixed expenses** Fixed expenses that cannot be directly traced to individual segments and that are unaffected by the elimination of any one segment.

**compounding of interest** Paying interest on interest.

**constraint set** The collection of all constraints that pertain to a particular optimization problem.

**constraints** Mathematical expressions that express resource limitations.

**consumption ratio** The proportion of an overhead activity consumed by a product.

**contingency theory** A theory maintaining that no single best or universal management control and performance management system exists but that the appropriateness of control systems depends on various organizational and environmental factors.

**continuous budget** A moving 12-month budget with a future month added as the current month expires.

**continuous improvement** The process of searching for ways to increase the overall efficiency and productivity of activities by reducing waste, increasing quality, and reducing costs.

**continuous replenishment** A system where a manufacturer assumes the inventory management function for the retailer.

**contribution margin** Sales revenue minus total variable cost or price minus unit variable cost.

**contribution margin ratio** Contribution margin divided by sales revenue. It is the proportion of each sales dollar available to cover fixed costs and provide for profit.

**control** The process of setting standards, receiving feedback on actual performance, and taking corrective action whenever actual performance has deviated significantly from planned performance.

**control activities** Activities performed by an organization to prevent or detect poor quality (because poor quality may exist).

**control costs** Costs incurred from performing control activities.

**control limits** The maximum allowable deviation from a standard.

**controllable costs** Costs that managers have the power to influence.

**controllable factors** Factors that can be influenced by a manager's decisions and actions.

**controller** The chief accounting officer, who supervises all accounting departments and activities.

**conversion cost** The sum of direct labour cost and overhead cost.

**cost** The cash or cash equivalent value sacrificed for goods and services that are expected to bring a current or future benefit to the organization.

**cost assignment** The process of associating the costs, once measured, with the units produced.

**cost behaviour** The way in which a cost changes in relation to changes in activity usage.

**cost centre** A responsibility centre in which a manager is responsible only for costs.

**cost formula** The linear function $Y = F + VX$, where $Y =$ Total mixed cost, $F =$ Fixed cost, $V =$ Variable cost per unit of activity, and $X =$ Activity level.

**cost measurement** The act of determining the dollar amounts of direct materials, direct labour, and overhead used in production.

**cost object** Any item, such as products, departments, projects, activities, and so on, for which costs are measured and assigned.

**cost of goods manufactured** The total cost of goods completed during the current period.

**cost of goods sold** The cost of direct materials, direct labour, and overhead attached to the units sold.

**cost of goods sold budget** The estimated costs for the units sold.

**cost reconciliation** The final section of the production report and the section that compares the costs to account for with the costs accounted for to ensure that they are equal.

**costs of quality** Costs incurred because poor quality may exist or because poor quality does exist.

**cost–volume–profit graph** A graph that depicts the relationships among costs, volume, and profits. It consists of a total revenue line and a total cost line.

**currently attainable standards** Standards that reflect an efficient operating state; they are rigorous but attainable.

**customer perspective** A balanced scorecard viewpoint that defines the customer and market segments in which the business will compete.

**customer value** The difference between what a customer receives (customer realization) and what the customer gives up (customer sacrifice).

**cycle time** The length of time required to produce one unit of a product.

## D

**decentralization** The granting of decision-making freedom to lower operating levels.

**decentralized decision making** A system in which decisions are made and implemented by lower-level managers.

**decision making** The process of choosing among competing alternatives.

**decision model** A specific set of procedures that, when followed, produces a decision.

**defective product** A product or service that does not conform to specifications.

**degree of operating leverage (DOL)** A measure of the sensitivity of profit change to changes in sales volume. It measures the percentage change in profits resulting from a percentage change in sales.

**dependent variable** A variable whose value depends on the value of another variable. For example, $Y$ in the cost formula $Y = F + VX$ depends on the value of $X$.

**direct costs** Costs that can be easily and accurately traced to a cost object.

**direct fixed expenses** Fixed costs that are directly traceable to a given segment and, consequently, disappear if the segment is eliminated.

**direct labour** Labour that is traceable to the goods or services being produced.

**direct labour budget**  A budget showing the total direct labour hours needed and the associated cost for the number of units in the production budget.

**direct materials**  Materials that are traceable to the goods or services being produced.

**direct materials purchases budget**  A budget that outlines the expected usage of materials for production and purchases of the direct materials required.

**direct method**  A method that allocates service costs directly to producing departments. This method ignores any interactions that may exist among support departments.

**direct tracing**  The process of identifying costs that are specifically or physically associated with a cost object.

**discount rate**  The rate of return used to compute the present value of future cash flows.

**discounting models**  Capital investment models that explicitly consider the time value of money in identifying criteria for accepting or rejecting proposed projects.

**discretionary fixed costs**  Costs incurred for the acquisition of short-term capacity or services, usually as the result of yearly planning.

**double-loop feedback**  Information about both the effectiveness of strategy implementation and the validity of assumptions underlying the strategy.

**driver analysis**  The effort expended to identify those factors that are the root causes of activity costs.

**driver tracing**  The use of drivers to assign costs to cost objects.

**drivers**  Factors that cause changes in resource usage, activity usage, costs, and revenues.

**drum–buffer–rope (DBR) system**  The TOC (theory of constraints) inventory management system that relies on the drum beat of the major constrained resources, time buffers, and ropes to determine inventory levels.

**drummer**  The major binding contraint in an organization.

**durability**  The length of time a product functions.

**dysfunctional behaviour**  Individual behaviour that conflicts with the goals of the organization.

## E

**economic order quantity (EOQ)**  The amount that should be ordered (or produced) to minimize the total ordering (or setup) and carrying costs.

**economic value added (EVA)**  A performance measure calculated by taking the after-tax operating profit minus the total annual cost of capital.

**electronic business (e-business)**  Business transactions and information exchanges executed using information and communication technology.

**electronic commerce (e-commerce)**  Buying and selling products using information and communication technology.

**electronic data interchange (EDI)**  An inventory management method that allows suppliers access to a buyer's on-line database.

**employee empowerment**  The authorization of operational personnel to plan, control, and make decisions without explicit authorization from middle and higher-level management.

**ending finished goods inventory budget**  A budget that describes planned ending inventory of finished goods in units and dollars.

**equivalent units of output**  Complete units that could have been produced given the total amount of manufacturing effort expended during the period.

**ethical behaviour**  Choosing actions that are "right" and "proper" and "just." Our behaviour can be right or wrong, it can be proper or improper, and the decisions we make can be fair or unfair.

**expected activity capacity**  Expected activity output for the coming year.

**expenses**  Expired costs.

**external constraints**  Limiting factors imposed on the firm from external sources (such as market demand).

**external environment**  External conditions that are largely uncontrollable by the organization, such as the economy and weather conditions.

**external failure costs**  Costs incurred because products fail to conform to requirements after being sold to outside parties.

**external linkages**  The relationship of a firm's activities within its segment of the value chain with those activities of its suppliers and customers.

**external measures**  Measures that relate to customer and shareholder objectives.

## F

**facility-level activities**  Activities that sustain a facility's general manufacturing process.

**failure activities**  Activities performed by an organization or its customers in response to poor quality (poor quality *does* exist).

**failure costs**  The costs incurred by an organization because failure activities are performed.

**favourable (F) variances**  Variances produced whenever the actual amounts are less than the budgeted or standard allowances.

**feasible set of solutions**  The collection of all feasible solutions.

**feasible solution**  A product mix that satisfies all constraints.

**features (quality of design)** Characteristics of a product that differentiate functionally similar products.

**feedback** Information that can be used to evaluate or correct the steps being taken to implement a plan.

**feedback control** Control processes and mechanism focused on explaining past performance.

**feedforward control** Control processes and mechanism focused on planning for future performance.

**FIFO costing method** A process-costing method that separates units in beginning inventory from those produced during the current period. Unit costs include only current-period costs and production.

**financial accounting information system** An accounting information subsystem which is concerned mainly with producing outputs for external users and which uses well-specified economic events as inputs and processes that meet certain rules and conventions.

**financial budgets** The portions of the master budget that include the cash budget, the budgeted balance sheet, the budgeted statement of cash flows, and the capital budget.

**financial measures** Measures expressed in dollar terms.

**financial perspective** A balanced scorecard viewpoint that describes the financial consequences of actions taken in the other three perspectives.

**financial productivity measure** A productivity measure in which inputs and outputs are expressed in dollars.

**fitness of use** The suitability of a product for carrying out its advertised functions.

**fixed activity rate** The fixed activity cost divided by the total capacity of the activity driver.

**fixed cost** Costs that, *in total*, are constant within the relevant range as the activity output varies.

**fixed overhead denominator variance** The difference between budgeted fixed overhead and applied fixed overhead.

**fixed overhead spending variance** The difference between actual fixed overhead and applied fixed overhead.

**flexible budget** A budget that can specify costs for a range of activity.

**flexible budget variance** The sum of price variances and efficiency variances in a performance report comparing actual costs to expected costs predicted by a flexible budget.

**flexible resources** Resources that are acquired as used and needed. There is no unused or excess capacity for these resources.

**functional-based control systems** Control systems that focus on functional organizational units and measure performance in financial terms.

**functional-based costing (FBC)** An approach for assigning costs of shared resources to products and other cost objects using only production or unit-level drivers.

**functional-based management (FBM) accounting system** An accounting information system that emphasizes the use of functional organizational units to assign and manage costs.

**future value** The value that will accumulate by the end of an investment's life if the investment earns a specified compounded return.

## G

**gain sharing** Providing cash incentives for a company's entire workforce that relate to quality and productivity gains.

**goal congruence** The alignment of a manager's personal goals with those of the organization.

**goodness of fit** The degree of association between $Y$ and $X$ (cost and activity). It is measured by how much of the total variability in $Y$ is explained by $X$.

## H

**heterogeneity** One of the four qualities that distinguish services from products—the fact that there is a greater chance of variation in the performance of services than in the production of products.

**hidden quality costs** Opportunity costs resulting from poor quality.

**high–low method** A method for fitting a line to a set of data points using the high and low points in the data set. For a cost formula, the high and low points represent the high and low activity levels. This method is used to break out the fixed and variable components of a mixed cost.

**homogeneous cost pool** A collection of overhead costs associated with activities that have the same process and the same level, and that can use the same activity driver to assign costs to products.

## I

**ideal standards** Standards that reflect perfect operating conditions.

**incentive compensation** Monetary or nonmonetary rewards awarded to employees based on their meeting certain performance criteria.

**incentives** The positive or negative measures taken by an organization to induce a manager to exert effort toward achieving the organization's goals.

**independent projects** Projects that, if accepted or rejected, will not affect the cash flows of another project.

**independent variable** A variable whose value does not depend on the value of another variable. For example, in the cost formula $Y = F + VX$, the variable $X$ is an independent variable.

**indirect costs** Costs that cannot be traced to a cost object.

**industrial value chain** The linked set of value-creating activities, from basic raw materials to end-use customers.

**industry volume variance** A difference in profit due to the difference between budgeted sales volume based on expected industry sales volume and budgeted sales volume based on actual industry sales volume.

**input tradeoff efficiency** The least-cost, technically efficient mix of outputs.

**inseparability** One of the four qualities that distinguish services from products—the fact that producers of services and buyers of services must usually be in direct contact for an exchange to take place.

**intangibility** One of the four qualities that distinguish services from products—the fact that buyers of services cannot see, feel, hear, or taste a service before it is bought.

**intercept parameter** The fixed cost, representing the point where the cost formula intercepts the vertical axis. In the cost formula $Y = F + VX$, $F$ is the intercept parameter.

**internal business perspective** A balanced scorecard viewpoint that describes the internal processes needed to provide value for customers and owners.

**internal constraints** Limiting factors found within the firm (such as machine time availability).

**internal failure costs** Costs incurred because products and services fail to conform to requirements, where lack of conformity is discovered prior to external sale.

**internal linkages** Relationships among activities within a firm's value chain.

**internal measures** Measures that relate to the processes and capabilities that create value for customers and shareholders.

**internal rate of return (IRR)** The rate of return that equates the present value of a project's cash inflows with the present value of its cash outflows (i.e., it sets the net present value equal to zero). Also, the rate of return being earned on funds that remain internally invested in a project.

**internal value chain** The set of activities required to design, develop, produce, market, distribute, and service a product (the product could be a service).

**inventory** The money an organization spends in turning raw materials into throughput.

**investment centre** A responsibility centre in which a manager is responsible for revenues, costs, and investments.

### J

**job-order costing system** A costing system in which costs are collected and assigned to units of production for each individual job.

**joint products** Products that are inseparable prior to a split-off point. All manufacturing costs up to the split-off point are joint costs.

### K

**kaizen costing** Efforts to reduce the costs of existing products and processes.

**kaizen standard** An interim standard that reflects the planned improvement for a coming period.

**Kanban system** An information system that controls production on a demand-pull basis through the use of cards or markers.

**keep-or-drop decisions** Relevant cost analyses that focus on keeping or dropping a segment of business.

### L

**labour efficiency variance** The difference between the actual direct labour hours used and the standard direct labour hours allowed multiplied by the standard hourly wage rate.

**labour rate variance** The difference between the actual hourly rate paid and the standard hourly rate multiplied by the actual hours worked.

**lag measures** Outcome measures or measures of results from past efforts.

**lead measures** Factors that drive future performance.
**lead time** For purchasing, the time to receive an order after it is placed. For manufacturing, the time to produce a product from start to finish.

**learning and growth (infrastructure) perspective** A balanced scorecard viewpoint that defines the capabilities an organization needs in order to create long-term growth and improvements.

**life cycle costs** All costs that are associated with the product for its entire life cycle.

**line positions** Positions that have direct responsibility for the basic objectives of an organization.

**linear programming** A method that searches among possible solutions until it finds the optimal solution.

**long run** A period of time in which all costs are variable.

**loose constraints** Constraints whose limited resources are not fully used by a product mix.

### M

**make-or-buy decisions** Relevant cost analyses that focus on whether a component should be made internally or purchased externally.

**Management Accounting Guidelines** A document published by CMA Canada to help management accountants fulfil their responsibilities; however, management accountants are under no obligation to follow any set of standards except as they relate to external reporting.

**management accounting information system** An information system that produces outputs using inputs as well as the processes needed to satisfy specific management objectives.

**management control** The process by which managers ensure that resources are obtained and used efficiently and effectively in accomplishing an organization's objectives.

**management control systems** Structures, resources, and processes that facilitate effective management control.

**managerial motivation** Drive and exertion of effort toward achieving an organization's objectives.

**manufacturing cycle effectiveness (MCE)** A measure of productive efficiency calculated as follows: processing time/(processing time + move time + inspection time + waiting time).

**margin** The ratio of net operating income to sales.

**margin of safety** The units sold or expected to be sold or sales revenue earned or expected to be earned above the breakeven volume.

**market share variance** A difference in profit due to the difference between the budgeted market share and the actual market share.

**marketing (selling) costs** The costs necessary to market and distribute a product or service.

**markup** The percentage applied to a base cost; it includes desired profit and any costs not included in the base cost.

**master budget** The collection of all area and activity budgets representing a firm's comprehensive plan of action.

**materials purchase price variance** The materials price variance based on materials purchased.

**materials usage variance** The difference between the direct materials actually used and the direct materials allowed for the actual output multiplied by the standard price.

**maximum transfer price** The transfer price that will make the buying division no worse off if an input is acquired internally.

**measurement criteria** Standards and benchmarks against which performance can be assessed.

**method of least squares** A statistical method to find a line that best fits a set of data. This method is used to break out the fixed and variable components of a mixed cost.

**minimum transfer price** The transfer price that will make the selling division no worse off if an output is sold internally.

**mixed cost** A cost that has both a fixed and a variable component.

**monetary compensation** Salaries, wages, cash bonuses, and other monetary rewards paid to employees.

**monetary incentives** Economic rewards used to motivate managers.

**multiple measures** More than one performance measure used to measure the achievement of each performance target.

**multiple-period quality trend report** A graph that plots quality costs (as a percentage of sales) against time.

**multiple regression** The use of the least-squares method to determine the parameters in a linear equation involving two or more explanatory variables.

**mutually exclusive projects** Projects that, if accepted, preclude the acceptance of competing projects.

**myopic behaviour** Managerial actions that improve budgetary performance in the short run at the expense of the long-run welfare of the program.

## N

**net income** Operating income less income taxes.

**net present value (NPV)** The difference between the present value of a project's cash inflows and the present value of its cash outflows.

**nondiscounting models** Capital investment models that identify criteria for accepting or rejecting projects without considering the time value of money.

**nonfinancial measures** Measures expressed in nonmonetary units.

**noninventoriable (period) costs** Costs that are expensed in the period in which they are incurred.

**nonmonetary compensation** Benefits provided to employees in addition to monetary compensation, for example, prime office space, fancy titles, increased responsibilities and autonomy, the use of a company jet or car, expense accounts, awards, and club memberships.

**nonmonetary incentives** Psychological and social rewards used to motivate managers.

**nonproduction costs** Costs associated with the functions of selling and administration.

**nonunit-level activity drivers** Factors that measure the consumption of nonunit-level activities by products and other cost objects.

**Nonunit-level drivers** Factors, other than the number of units produced, that measure the consumption of activities by cost objects.

**Nonvalue-added activities** All activities other than those that are absolutely essential to remain in business.

**Nonvalue-added costs** Costs that are caused either by nonvalue-added activities or by the inefficient performance of value-added activities.

**normal activity capacity** The average activity output for a given period.

**normal cost of goods sold** The cost of goods sold before adjustment for any overhead variance.

**normal costing** An approach that assigns the actual costs for direct materials and direct labour to products but uses a predetermined rate to assign overhead costs.

## O

**objective function** The function to be optimized, usually a profit function; thus, optimization usually means maximizing profits.

**objective measures** Measures that can be readily quantified and verified.

**observable quality costs** Quality costs that are available from an organization's accounting records.

**one-half rule** The rule that restricts the amount of CCA that can be claimed in the year of acquisition to one-half of the CCA rate for the class.

**operating assets** Assets used to generate operating income, usually consisting of cash, inventories, receivables, property, plant, and equipment.

**operating budgets** Budgets associated with the income-producing activities of an organization.

**operating expenses** The money an organization spends in turning inventories into throughput.

**operating income** Revenues minus expenses from the firm's normal operations. Income taxes are excluded.

**operating leverage** The use of fixed costs to extract higher percentage changes in profits as sales activity changes. Leverage is achieved by increasing fixed costs while lowering variable costs.

**operation costing** A hybrid costing method that assigns material costs to a product using a job-order approach and assigns conversion costs using a process approach.

**operational productivity measure** A measure that is expressed in physical terms.

**opportunity cost** The benefit sacrificed or forgone when one alternative is chosen over another.

**opportunity cost approach** A transfer pricing system that identifies the minimum price that a selling division would be willing to accept and the maximum price that a buying division would be willing to pay.

**optimal solution** The feasible solution that produces the best value for the objective function (the largest value if seeking to maximize the objective function; the minimum otherwise).

**ordering costs** The costs of placing and receiving an order.

**organizational environment** Organizational attributes and circumstances that are largely controllable by the organization in the long term but may be constant in the short term, such as the existing organizational structure, production capacity, and staff levels.

**organizational goals** Short- and medium-term performance targets or interim objectives toward the achievement of long-term strategic objectives.

**overapplied overhead** The amount by which applied overhead exceeds actual overhead.

**overhead** All production costs other than direct materials and direct labour.

**overhead budget** A budget that reveals the planned expenditures for all indirect manufacturing items.

**overhead variance** The difference between actual overhead and applied overhead.

## P

**parallel processing** A processing pattern in which two or more sequential processes are required in order to produce a finished good.

**partial productivity measurement** A ratio that measures productive efficiency for one input.

**participative budgeting** An approach to budgeting that allows managers who will be held accountable for budgetary performance to participate in the budget's development.

**payback period** The time required for a project to return its investment.

**performance** The measure of how consistent and well a product functions.

**performance drivers** Factors that cause future performance, for example, employee training.

**performance management** Management processes concerned with the effective use of information provided by management control systems for strategic planning, control, and decision making.

**performance prism** A strategic performance measurement framework that focuses on stakeholders and includes five elements: strategies, processes, capabilities, stakeholder satisfaction, and stakeholder contribution.

**performance reports** Reports that compare the actual data with planned data.

**perishability** One of the four qualities that distinguish services from products—the fact that services cannot be stored for future use by the consumer.

**perquisites** A type of fringe benefit over and above salary that is received by managers.

**physical flow schedule** A schedule that reconciles units to account for with units accounted for. The physical units are not adjusted for percent of completion.

**planning** Setting objectives and identifying methods of achieving those objectives.

**postpurchase costs** The costs of using, maintaining, and disposing of a product.

**postsales service process** A process that provides critical and responsive service to customers after the product or service has been delivered.

**practical activity capacity** The activity output produced when the activity is performed efficiently.

**practical capacity** The efficient level of activity performance.

**predatory pricing** The practice of setting prices below cost for the purpose of injuring competitors and eliminating competition.

**predetermined overhead rate** An overhead rate computed using estimated data.

**present value (PV)** The current value of a future cash flow. It represents the amount that must be invested now if the future cash flow is to be received, assuming compounding at a given rate of interest.

**prevention costs** Costs incurred to prevent defects in products or services being produced.

**price gouging** A subjective term referring to the practice of setting an "excessively" high price.

**price (rate) variance** The difference between the standard price and the actual price multiplied by the actual quantity of inputs used.

**price-recovery component** The difference between the total profit change and the profit-linked productivity change.

**price standard** The price that should be paid per unit of input.

**primary activity** An activity that is consumed by products or customers.

**prime cost** The sum of direct materials cost and direct labour cost.

**process** A series of activities (operations) that are linked to perform a specific objective.

**process-costing system** A costing system that accumulates production costs by process or by department for a given period of time.

**producing departments** Units within an organization that are responsible for producing the products or services that are sold to customers.

**product cost** A cost assignment method that satisfies a well-specified managerial objective.

**product diversity** The situation present when products consume overhead in different proportions.

**product-level (sustaining) activities** Activities that are performed to enable the production of each different type of product.

**product life cycle** The time a product exists, from conception to abandonment.

**production budget** A budget that shows how many units must be produced to meet sales needs and satisfy ending inventory requirements.

**production costs** Costs associated with the manufacture of goods or the provision of services.

**production drivers** Drivers that are highly correlated with production output (volume).

**production Kanban** A card or marker that specifies the quantity that the Kanban system should produce.

**production report** A document that summarizes the manufacturing activity that takes place in a process department for a given period of time.

**productivity** The efficient production of output, using the least quantity of inputs possible.

**productivity measurement** The assessment of productivity changes.

**profile measurement** A series or vector of separate and distinct partial operational measures.

**profit centre** A responsibility centre in which a manager is responsible for both revenues and costs.

**profit-linked productivity measurement** The assessment of the amount of profit change (from the base period to the current period) attributable to productivity changes.

**profit–volume graph** A graph that depicts the relationship between profits and sales volume.

**profit volume variance (gross)** Consists of a profit volume variance (net) and a sales mix variance.

**profit volume variance (net)** Measures the effect on profit of the difference in total sales volume between the budget and the actual volume, with other factors—including sales mix and contribution margin per unit—remaining constant.

**pseudoparticipation** A budgetary system in which top management solicits inputs from lower-level managers and then ignores those inputs. Thus, in reality, budgets are dictated from above.

## Q

**quality of conformance** Conforming to the design requirements of the product.

**quality product or service** A product that meets or exceeds customer expectations.

**quantity standard** The quantity of input allowed per unit of output.

## R

**reciprocal method** A method that simultaneously allocates service costs to all user departments. It gives full consideration to interactions among support departments.

**relevant costs** Future costs that change across alternatives.

**relevant range** The range over which an assumed cost relationship is valid for the normal operations of a firm.

**reliability** The probability that the product or service will perform its intended function for a specified length of time.

**reorder point** The point in time at which a new order (or setup) should be initiated.

**residual income (RI)** The difference between operating income and the minimum dollar return required on a company's operating assets.

**resource drivers** Factors that measure the consumption of resources by activities.

**responsibility accounting** A system that measures the results of each responsibility centre according to the information managers need in order to operate their centre.

**responsibility centre** A segment of the business whose manager is accountable for specified sets of activities.

**return on investment (ROI)** The ratio of operating income to average operating assets.

**revenue centre** A responsibility centre in which a manager is responsible only for sales.

**ropes** Actions taken to tie the rate at which raw material is released into the plant (at the first operation) to the production rate of the constrained resource.

## S

**safety stock** Extra inventory carried to serve as insurance against fluctuations in demand.

**sales budget** A budget that describes expected sales in units and dollars for the coming period.

**sales mix** The relative combination of products (or services) being sold by an organization.

**sales mix variance** Measures the effect of the change from the budgeted sales mix.

**sales price variance** Measures the direct effect of the change in selling prices on profit.

**scattergraph** A plot of (X, Y) data points. For cost analysis, X is activity usage and Y is the associated cost at that activity level.

**scatterplot method** A method of fitting a line to a set of data using two points that are selected by judgment. It is used to break out the fixed and variable components of a mixed cost.

**secondary activity** An activity that is consumed by primary activities and/or other secondary activities.

**segment** A subunit of a company that is sufficiently important to warrant the production of performance reports.

**segment margin** The contribution a segment makes to cover common fixed costs and variable costs and provide for profit after direct fixed costs and variable costs are deducted from the segment's sales revenue.

**segmented reporting** The preparation of financial performance reports for each segment of importance within a firm.

**sell-or-process further decision** Relevant cost analysis that focuses on whether a product should be processed beyond the split-off point.

**selling and administrative expenses budget** A budget that outlines planned expenditures for nonmanufacturing activities.

**sensitivity analysis** The "what-if" process of altering certain key variables to assess the effect on the original outcome.

**sequential (or step) method** A method that allocates service costs to user departments in a sequential manner. It gives partial consideration to interactions among support departments.

**sequential processing** A processing pattern in which units pass from one process to another in a set order.

**serviceability** The ease of maintaining and/or repairing a product.

**services** Tasks or activities performed for a customer using an organization's products or facilities.

**setup costs** The cost of preparing equipment and facilities so that they can be used for production.

**short run** A period of time in which at least one cost is fixed.

**simplex method** An algorithm that identifies the optimal solution for a linear programming problem.

**single-loop feedback** Information about the effectiveness of strategy implementation.

**slope parameter** The variable cost per unit of activity usage, represented by $V$ in the cost formula $Y = F + VX$.

**special-order decisions** Relevant cost analyses that focus on whether a specially priced order should be accepted or rejected.

**split-off point** The point at which products become distinguishable after passing through a common process.

**staff positions** Positions that are supportive in nature and have only indirect responsibility for an organization's basic objectives.

**standard cost per unit** The per-unit cost that should be achieved given materials, labour, and overhead standards.

**standard cost sheet** A listing of the standard costs and standard quantities of direct materials, direct labour, and overhead that should apply to a single product.

**standard hours allowed** The direct labour hours that should have been used to produce the actual output (Unit labour standard x Actual output).

**standard quantity of materials allowed** The quantity of materials that should have been used to produce the actual output (Unit materials standard x Actual output).

**static budget** A budget for a particular level of activity.

**step cost** A cost function in which cost is defined for ranges of activity use rather than point values. The function has the property of displaying constant cost over a range of activity use and then changing to a different cost level as a new range of activity use is undertaken.

**stock-out costs** The costs of insufficient inventory.

**strategic-based control systems** Control systems that link an organization's mission and strategy with operational objectives and use multiple financial and nonfinancial measures to measure performance from different stakeholders' perspectives in a balanced manner.

**strategic cost management** The use of cost data to develop and identify superior strategies that will produce a competitive advantage.

**strategic decision making** Choosing among alternative strategies with the goal of selecting the strategy or strategies that provide a company with reasonable assurance for long-term growth and survival.

**strategic performance measurement** The assessment of the achievement of strategic performance objectives of organizations, organizational units, and programs.

**strategic plan** The long-term plan for future activities and operations, usually involving at least five years.

**strategy** The process of choosing a business's market and customer segments, identifying its critical internal business processes, and selecting the individual and organizational capabilities needed to meet internal, customer, and financial objectives.

**subjective measures** Measures that are nonquantifiable and whose values are judgmental in nature.

**sunk cost** A cost for which the outlay has already been made and that cannot be affected by a future decision.

**supplies** Those materials necessary for production that do not become part of the finished product or that are not used in providing a service.

**supply chain** All activities that are involved in the efficient and effective movement and transformation of raw materials, through the manufacturing process, into final products to end users.

**supply chain management** The management of material flows beginning with suppliers and their upstream suppliers, moving through the transformation of materials into finished goods, to customers and their downstream customers.

**support departments** Units within an organization that provide essential support services for producing departments.

## T

**tactical decision making** Choosing among alternatives with an immediate or limited end in view.

**Taguchi loss function** A function that assumes that any variation from the target value of a quality characteristic causes hidden quality costs.

**tangible products** Goods that are produced by converting raw materials through the use of labour and capital inputs such as plant, land, and machinery.

**target cost** The difference between the sales price needed to achieve a projected market share and the desired per-unit profit.

**target costing** A method of determining the cost of a product or service based on the price (target price) that customers are willing to pay.

**technical efficiency** The point at which, for any mix of inputs that will produce a given output, no more of any one input is used than is absolutely necessary.

**testable strategy** A set of linked objectives aimed at an overall goal that can be restated into a sequence of cause-and-effect hypotheses.

**throughput** The rate at which an organization generates money through sales.

**time buffer** The inventory needed to keep the constrained resource busy for a specified time interval.

**time ticket** A source document by which direct labour costs are assigned to individual jobs.

**top-down budgeting** A budgeting process in which budgets are set unilaterally by top management.

**total preventive maintenance** A program of preventive maintenance that has zero machine failures as its standard.

**total product** The complete range of tangible and intangible benefits that a customer receives from a purchased product.

**total productive efficiency** The point at which technical and price efficiency are achieved.

**total productivity measurement** The assessment of productive efficiency for all inputs combined.

**total profit variance** The difference between actual and budgeted profit.

**total quality management** An approach to quality in which manufacturers strive to create an environment that will enable workers to manufacture perfect (zero-defect) products.

**traceability** The ability to assign a cost directly to a cost object in an economically feasible way using a causal relationship.

**tracing** Assigning costs to a cost object using an observable measure of the cost object's resource consumption.

**transfer price** The price charged for goods transferred from one division to another.

**transfer pricing problem** The problem of finding a transfer pricing system that simultaneously satisfies the three objectives of accurate performance evaluations, goal congruence, and autonomy.

**transferred-in costs** Costs transferred from a prior process to a subsequent process.

**treasurer** The person responsible for the finance function. Specifically, the treasurer raises capital and manages cash and investments.

**turnover** The ratio of sales to average operating assets.

## U

**uncontrollable factors** Factors that cannot be influenced by a manager during a given time period.

**underapplied overhead** The amount by which actual overhead exceeds applied overhead.

**unfavourable (U) variances** Variances produced whenever the actual input amounts are greater than the budgeted or standard allowances.

**unit cost** The total costs assigned to a product divided by the number of units produced of that product.

**unit-level activities** Activities that are performed each time a unit is produced.

**unit-level activity drivers** Factors that measure the consumption of unit-level activities by products and other cost objects.

**unit-level drivers** *See* production drivers.

**unused capacity variance** The difference between acquired capacity (practical capacity) and actual capacity.

**usage (efficiency) variance** The difference between standard quantities and actual quantities multiplied by standard price.

## V

**value-added activities** Activities that are necessary to achieve corporate objectives and remain in business.

**value-added costs** Costs caused by value-added activities.

**value-added standard** The optimal output level for an activity.

**value chain** The set of activities required to design, develop, produce, market, and deliver products and services to customers; *or,* an interrelated set of activities that increases the usefulness or value of products or services to customers.

**value chain analysis** A strategic tool that can be used to understand an organization's competitive advantage and its relationships with suppliers, customers, and competitors.

**variable activity rate** The total variable activity cost divided by the amount of activity driver used.

**variable budgets** *See* flexible budget.

**variable cost** Costs that, in total, vary in direct proportion to changes in a cost driver.

**variable costing** A product-costing method that assigns only variable manufacturing costs—direct materials, direct labour, and variable overhead—to production. Fixed overhead is treated as a period cost.

**variable-cost ratio** Variable costs divided by sales revenues. It is the proportion of each sales dollar needed to cover variable costs.

**variable overhead efficiency variance** Assuming that direct labour hours are used to apply overhead costs, the difference between the actual direct labour hours used and the standard hours allowed multiplied by the standard variable overhead rate.

**variable overhead spending variance** The difference between the actual variable overhead and the budgeted variable overhead based on the actual hours used to produce the actual output.

**velocity** The number of units that can be produced in a given period of time (e.g., output per hour).

**vendor Kanbans** Cards or markers that signal to a supplier the quantity of materials that need to be delivered and the time of delivery.

## W

**weighted average costing method** A process-costing method that combines beginning inventory costs with current-period costs to compute unit costs. Costs and output from the current period and the previous period are averaged to compute unit costs.

**what-if analysis** A method to deal with uncertainty where the assumptions on which the analysis is based are changed and their effect assessed (see **sensitivity analysis**).

**whole life product cost** The life-cycle cost of a product plus costs that consumers incur, including operation, support, maintenance, and disposal.

**withdrawal Kanban** A marker or card that specifies the quantity that a subsequent process should withdraw from a preceding process.

**work in process** All partly completed units found in production at a given point in time.

**work-in-process file** A file that is the collection of all job-order cost sheets.

## Z

**zero defects** A quality performance standard that requires all products and services to be produced and delivered according to specifications.

# Name Index

# Company/Organization Index

# Subject Index